EDICIONES EL VISO

DRAWINGS ALAN GLASS PARIS

1954-1962

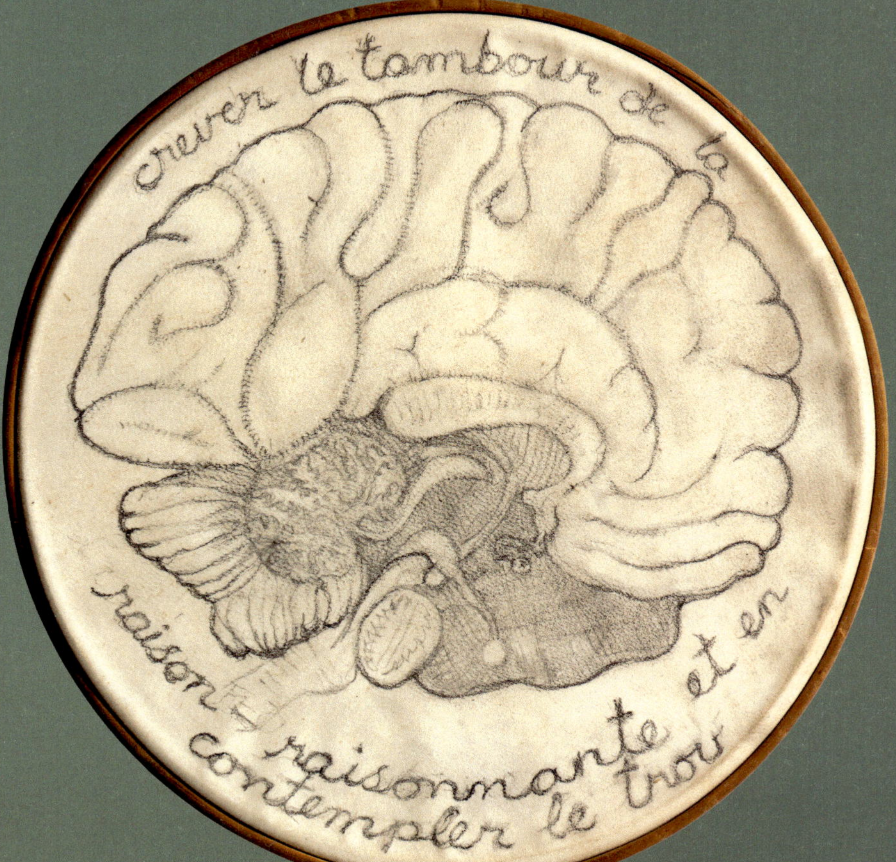

The phrase in the drawing was taken from "Du surréalisme en ses œuvres vives," André Breton (1953).

MUSEO
DEL PALACIO DE
BELLAS ARTES

Canadä

DRAWINGS
ALAN GLASS
PARIS
1954-1962

TEXTS

CARLOS DE LABORDE-NOGUEZ
PIERRE DE LIGNY BOUDREAU
ALEJANDRO JODOROWSKY
KRISTOFFER NOHEDEN
NADINE M. ORENSTEIN
ABIGAIL SUSIK

Acknowledgments:

TEOPAN
Francisco Luis de Yturbe
Carlos de Laborde-Noguez
and
Jean-Paul Paré, *who recovered the drawings of Alan Glass*
Carolina Escalante

Editorial Coordination
Carlos de Laborde-Noguez

Photography
Archivo fotográfico de Alan Glass

Publication Graphic Design
Ricardo Salas & Frontespizio
Eleazar Cruz

English Translation
Magdalena Menocal and Quentin Pope

French Translation
Neige Sinno and Divina Cabo

Copy-editing
Lilian Luna Segura, Bruni Mayor, Alfred Hyatt Mayor and Valentina Gatti

Additional Photography
Francisco Kochen
Daniel de Laborde-Noguez (*cover*)

Ediciones El Viso
Gonzalo Saavedra
Lorena Ahuactzin

Untitled
(Galerie Le Terrain Vague period)
ca. 1954-1962
Monochrome blue ballpoint pen drawing, on paper.
25.6 x 17 cm
Artist's collection
Cover and p. 287

ISBN 978-84-128466-2-1
DL M-8192-2024

Printed in Spain

INDEX

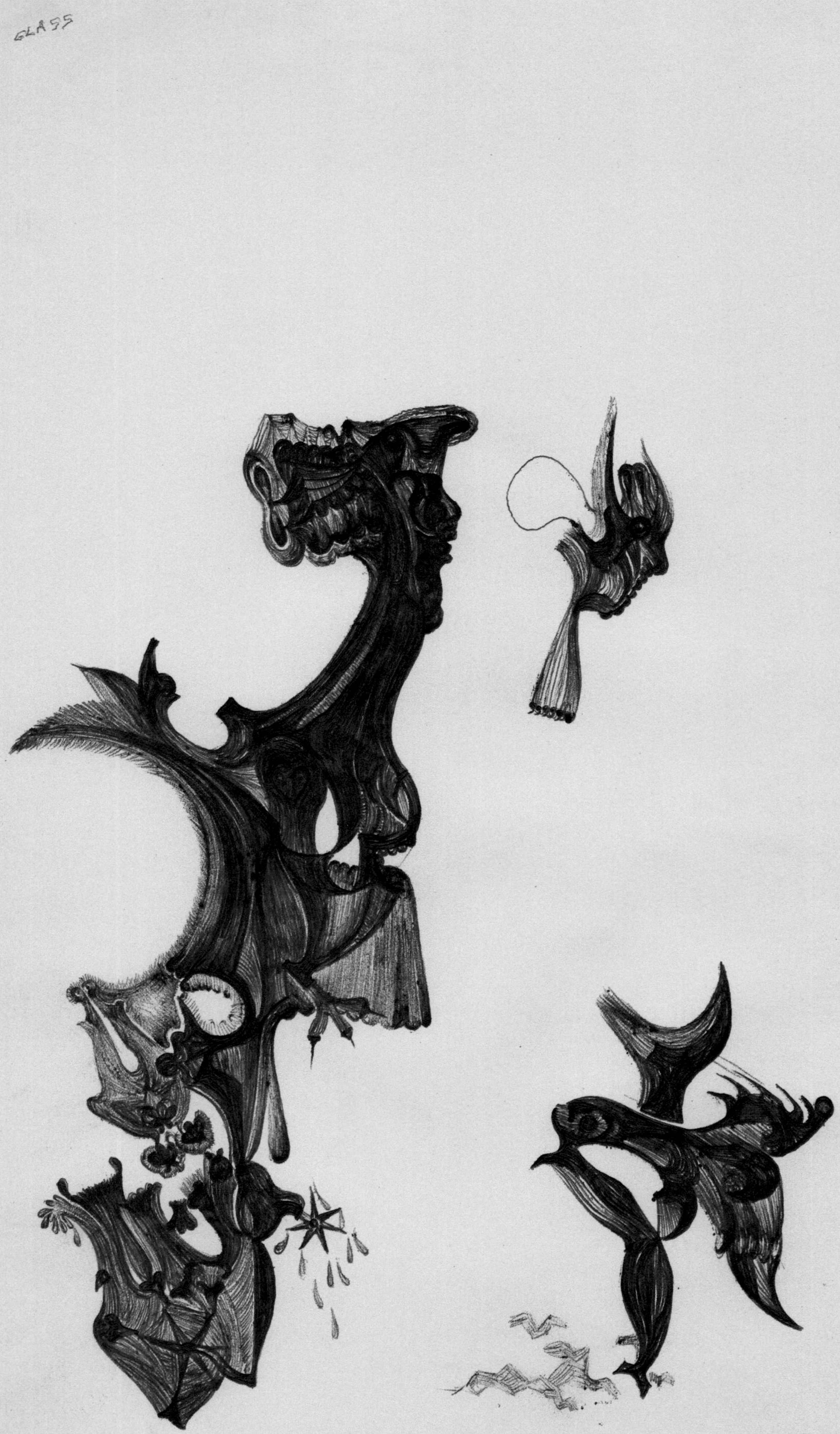
GLASS

A thank you to the following people for their unconditional support.

PIERRE DE LIGNY BOUDREAU
AUBE ELLÉOUËT
BRIDGET TICHENOR
ALEJANDRO JODOROWSKY
CARLOS DE LABORDE-NOGUEZ

Untitled
(Rue Manuel period)
ca. 1954-1962
Monochrome blue ballpoint pen drawing, on paper.
30 x 21 cm
Artist's collection
Previous page

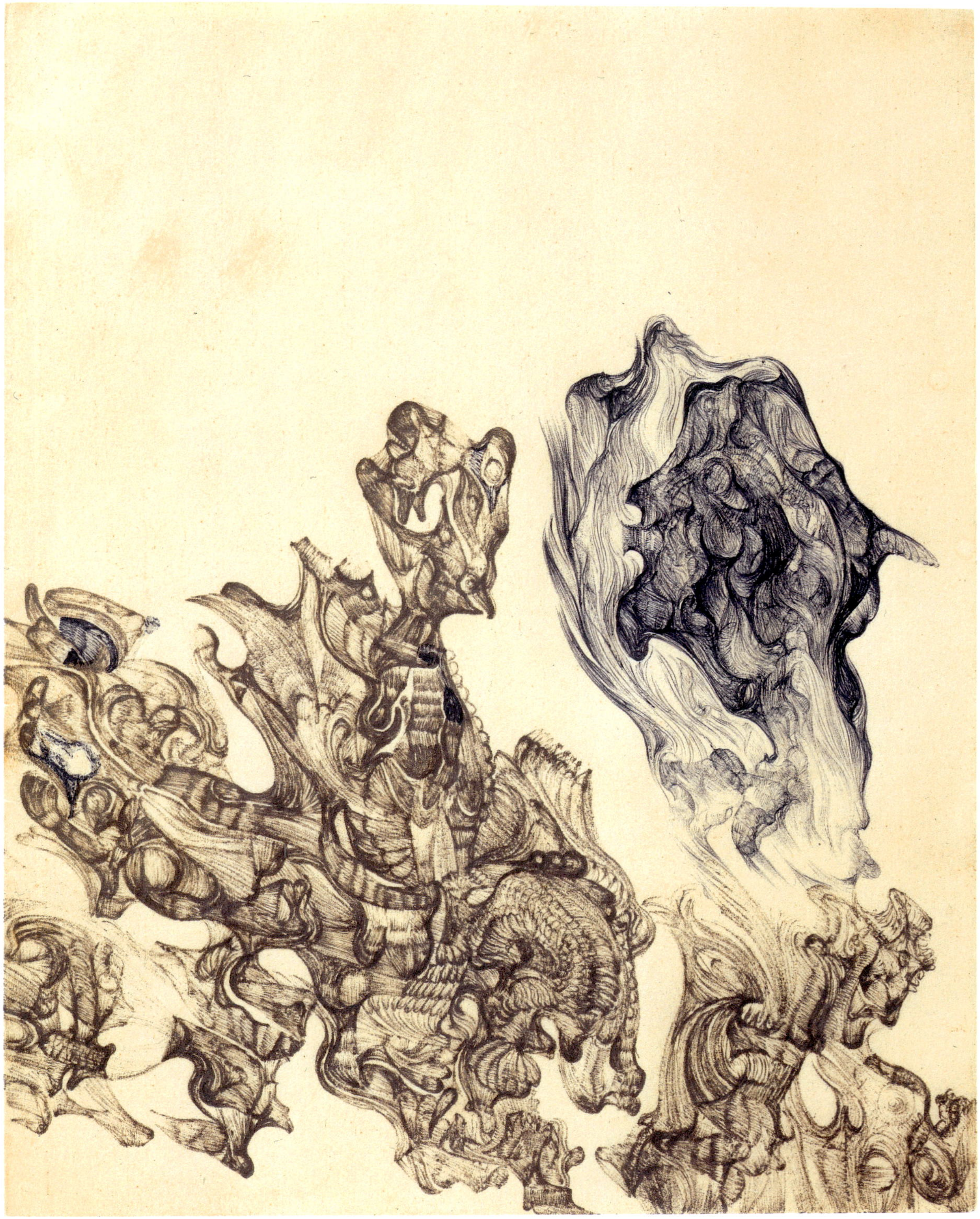

THE STORY OF HOW WE FOUND ALAN GLASS'S DRAWINGS FROM HIS PARIS PERIOD[1]

Carlos de Laborde-Noguez

Yesterday evening, June 30, 2021, Carolina and I went to have dinner with Alan to celebrate his 89th birthday.

He was waiting for us at the door at the appointed time and announced he was leaving behind the 8 in his age. This is certainly true for the tens, but there's still a chance as regards the single numbers. Throughout the day, he'd received many phone calls, presents, and kind messages.[2]

Alan is a very popular person who has always known how to stay very much in touch with his friends.

AN OBJECTIVE CHANCE

That very day, Alan had found a photocopy of Matthias Grünewald's *Resurrection of Christ* in Colmar as reinterpreted by him.

He also found under his front door a letter from Jean Paul Paré (one of Micheline Beauchemin's good friends) informing him that he had found, inside a pair of boxes, the binders containing his lost drawings, the famous drawings he had made in Paris between 1954 and 1962 that were the subject matter of that painful and unsuccessful suit he had had to file against his friend Micheline.

Also that evening, Alejandro González Iñárritu sent a message asking if he could pass by Tabasco 35 with his wife María Eladia to have another look at his works and buy one. Regarding his birthday, the text of the message read as follows:

"*Abrazo a todos y un abrazo especial de felicitación a Alan que a sus 89 es más niño y luminoso que todos*" [Warmest regards to everyone and a special congratulatory hug to Alan who at 89 is more childlike and luminous than all of us]

It was an extraordinary day for many of us, and also for Alan who was able to see and link together fabulous stories.

Untitled
(Galerie Terrain Vague period)
1956
Black and navy blue two-tone ballpoint pen drawing, on paper.
21.3 x 17 cm
Private collection
Previous page

[1] Diary kept during the trip from September 29 to October 4, 2021.

[2] We gave him an old hand mirror and a wooden cutout of a swallow covered with an illustration we'd found in Haïtze just before returning to Mexico City.

Before taking his leave that evening, Alan confided that the news regarding a possible lead on the binders with his Paris works was a "resurrection" of him.

I began preparing the trip. Travel to Canada was very complicated because of the closed borders due to Covid 19, and it would apparently be impossible before fall.

THE JOURNEY

SEPTEMBER 30

We were finally able to leave. We had all the permits from the Canadian authorities as well as the medical requirements. A veritable tour de force. Alan, Carolina, and I are travelling together. For Alan, the idea of recovering his drawings is singularly motivating, very exciting and heartwarming for us.

OCTOBER 1
MONTREAL-GRONDINES

Yesterday was a long, intense day.

Good omens along the road: the maples and staghorn sumacs displayed their most beautiful fall colors, ranging from variations of fading greens to the most intense yellows and reds.

Grondines is halfway between Montreal and Quebec, where carriage horses used to be changed out for fresh ones. On the Route du Roy, bordering the Saint Lawrence River, is the former house of Micheline Beauchemin, acquired in 1966 and now inherited by Jean Paul Paré. The house was built in 1679 precisely as a coaching inn. In the main building, under the roof, Micheline had set up the large studio where she worked, creating a great number of tapestries in all sorts of colors and materials, from natural warm wools to raffias and bright industrial materials that gave her work its originality.

Jean Paul gave us a tour of the house. The sitting room is on the ground floor, as are the dining area and two bedrooms, including the one Alan would be staying in, the same one he used during his sojourns with MB. The wood floors were painted orange, and the furniture, most of it from MB's time, consists of beautiful old Canadian items in whitewood; in the back is the kitchen with its old bread oven.

On the dining room table, Jean Paul had arranged the bundles containing the drawings in their original wrapping, never having been opened. There was also the double watercolor and a painted egg they had bought during the exhibition at the Gilles Corbeil gallery. JP also wished to part with these objects.

Lunch at Jean Paul's neighbors, Cung Nguyen and Isabelle, just across the road on the banks of the Saint Lawrence. They live year-round in an old schoolhouse they've restored on the land that reaches all the way to the banks of the river, landscaped into a beautiful garden. We enjoyed pre-lunch aperitifs under the shade of a tree, looking out over the river on which barges carrying huge cargos travelled effortlessly, noiselessly. Here, the river is two kilometers wide, a force of nature that dictates life in the area.

The layout of the house is simple: on the ground floor there's a very large space housing the dining room and a large kitchen where Cung, like the finest chef, cooked a fish caught in the river. We drank a 1984 Sauternes with foie gras as a starter, with coconut sorbet prepared by Isabelle between courses.

It was during lunch that Alan raised his glass in a toast to Micheline in recognition of their long friendship and erasing all the bad experiences.

Back to the coaching inn. Jean Paul invited Carolina and me up to the attic to see the fabulous studio under century-old beams. The loom was quiet. Several works were suspended from the beams, and Jean Paul showed them off with admiration. Micheline had worked hard and with great intensity; she wasn't constrained by the technique. She was inspired by the reflection of the skylights on the river. The tapestries ranged in size from a few square centimeters to enormous ones to cover the walls of office building lobbies or be used for theater curtains.

As for Jean Paul, he's doing a great job cataloguing MB's works.

We packed the drawings in two binders that Alan will only open in Mexico City, with the watercolor and egg each enveloped in bubble wrap.

SATURDAY, OCTOBER 2

Grondines-Almaville en Bas to Shawinigan-Montreal.

After breakfast at the inn in Grondines where we spent the night, we went back to Jean Paul's to pick up Alan and get on the road back to Montreal. Before placing the binders in the car, JP invited us to take a look at the farmhouse out back where the drawings were found, in a loft, a place accessible only by leaning a ladder against the wall and where MB's trainees had put away the binders. Fortunately, this hidden corner was never exposed to humidity or bad weather of any kind. We'd be on our way also taking with us two small works by Micheline.[3]

VISIT TO THE CHURCH IN ALMAVILLE EN BAS

Ozias Leduc's last work for a church was for the one in Shawinigan;[4] it took 15 years. He died in the thirteenth year after working in his studio using Mexican burlap canvases, which were then rolled up and mounted directly on the church walls. Except for one of the large paintings on the ceiling executed by his colleague Gabrielle Messier, and the altarpieces of the Stations of the Cross, they were all by the same hand. The painted scenes along the sides reference ordinary Canadian work life at the time, the extremely sober colors producing a feeling of profound collectedness and calm.

Arrival in Montreal at a modern-trendy and very comfortable hotel on Peel Street in a district that is being redeveloped and whose point of reference will always be the Farine Five Roses sign atop a former flour mill.

ALAN IS GLADLY WELCOMED

Dinner that same evening at Patrice Leroux's—a nephew of Odette and of Solange Legendre—at his delightful house in the Town of Mount Royal district. On the walls hung paintings by Canadian artists and several portraits by Solange including those of Xavière and Hélène. A very generous and friendly act of kindness.

OCTOBER 3

Lunch yesterday with Julienne Faubert[5] and her daughter Hélène Vannier[6] at the St. Hubert, just roast chicken and then on to visit places that were part of Alan's childhood. It was a charming reunion. They spoke movingly of

[3] A model of a tapestry planned for the reception hall of the Hudson's Bay Company (65/67) and the model for the hooked rug with a fringe of a thousand threads she exhibited at the Galerie Denyse Delrue in 1959.

[4] Ozias Leduc was a very pious man and began his last work at the age of 77.

[5] Julienne Faubert is a childhood friend of Alan's. They often played and went to school together. She later married the engineer Vannier, living a different life and remaining permanently in the region.

[6] Hélène had just retired after transforming the Old Presbytery of St. Bruno-de-Montarville into an exhibition center and naming a large exhibition hall after Alan Glass. During lunch, Hélène offered to try to organize an exhibition of Alan's drawings for which she would write a text, to be scheduled for Fall 2022.

their childhood memories with exceptional recall of details and of their adventures.

We took a short drive to the Mount Bruno Country Club where to the right of the clubhouse Alan pointed out the pro shop his father had run for so many years. There's a story behind this club: designed by his uncle Willie Park, Jr. in the forties, to this day it gathers the élite of Montreal society. We then went on with our tour until we arrived in front of Alan's former house. So many emotions and memories...

In the evening we went to dinner at Louise Deschâtelets's with Guy and Marise Fournier. Louise, an actress, is still very active on television and plans to go on tour as soon as the pandemic is over. The conversation was filled with humor and laughter. Alan has so many good friends who never stop showing their appreciation and celebrating him.

[5] Julienne Faubert is one of Alan's childhood friends: they often played and went to school together. She later married the engineer Vanier, and led a different kind of life, always remaining in the region.

[6] Helène had just retired from the Vieux Presbytère de St Bruno de Montarville which she had transformed into an art center. She named one of the main galleries after Alan Glass. During that meal, Helène suggested organizing an exhibition of Alan's drawings. She would write the texts and schedule the event for the fall of 2022.

SUNDAY, OCTOBER 3

Yesterday a meeting with Pierre Larocque at his gallery at 6341 Blvd. Saint Laurent to see his works on display, covering the period from 1983 to the present. Jean-Pierre works in charcoal using a technique whereby he uncovers whites and grays by erasing—very different from the varied colors of his early works. He also makes high-temperature ceramics. After lunch, we strolled to Saint-Louis Square where another great friend of Alan's lived, Pauline Julien. A few steps further on, Alan wanted to see if his other friend was at home: Anne Pritchard. As luck would have it, she was in fact sitting at her window, as if waiting for him. Anne previously worked with Louis Malle.

Back to the hotel. While Alan had a rest, Carolina and I took a walk to the Museum of Fine Arts, stopping by Emmanuel Cazeault's gallery.

Dinner at Guy and Marise Fournier's, who live in a magnificent apartment along the banks of the majestic river, overlooking Montreal. Also there were Maurice Ferron, and Claude and Marie José Fournier. Claude is Guy's twin brother. He was in the film industry and told us he was editing a short film about Alan in Mexico City...

There was talk of exhibiting the recovered drawings at the Musée de Québec, a dream we hope will become a reality.

MONDAY, OCTOBER 4

On this last day, we went to Mont Saint Hilaire to meet Thérèse Chabot. Also an artist, she works in ceramics and lives near her brother who for several years has been running a large plant nursery with a group of Mexicans from Zacatecas who come back each year.

That evening we boarded the flight back to Mexico City, binders on the plane!

This experience with Alan was a very emotional one, going back to his home ground during which we lost track of time and were never overcome by fatigue. The recovery of these drawings undoubtedly closes a gap in Alan Glass's oeuvre, and is of great importance in order to appreciate and understand his surrealist vein and the strong and boundless friendship of all his friends.

Mexico City, January 2022.

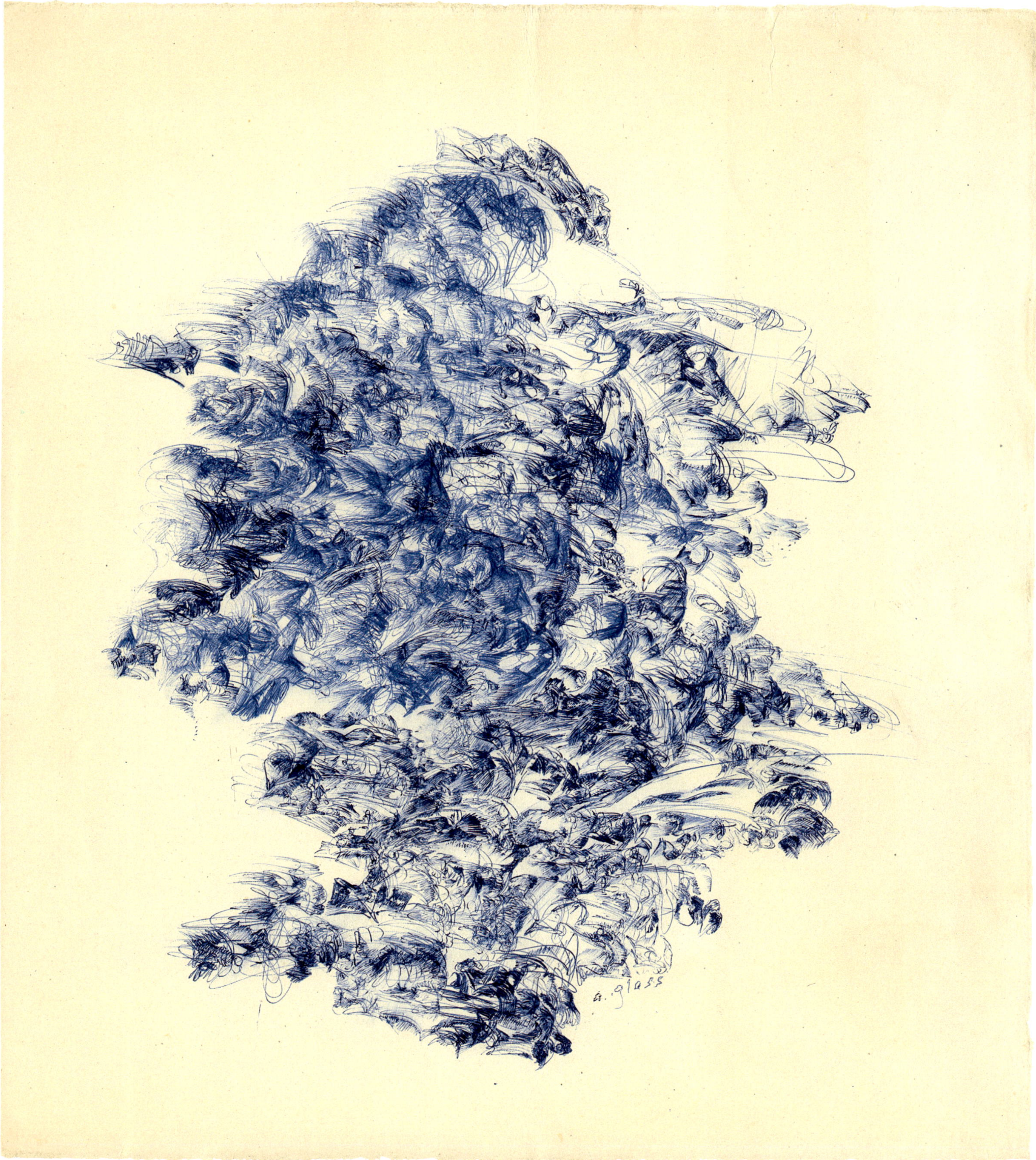

Untitled
(Club Saint-Germain period)
ca. 1954-1962
Blue/navy blue ballpoint
pen drawing, on paper.
27.5 x 25 cm
Artist's collection

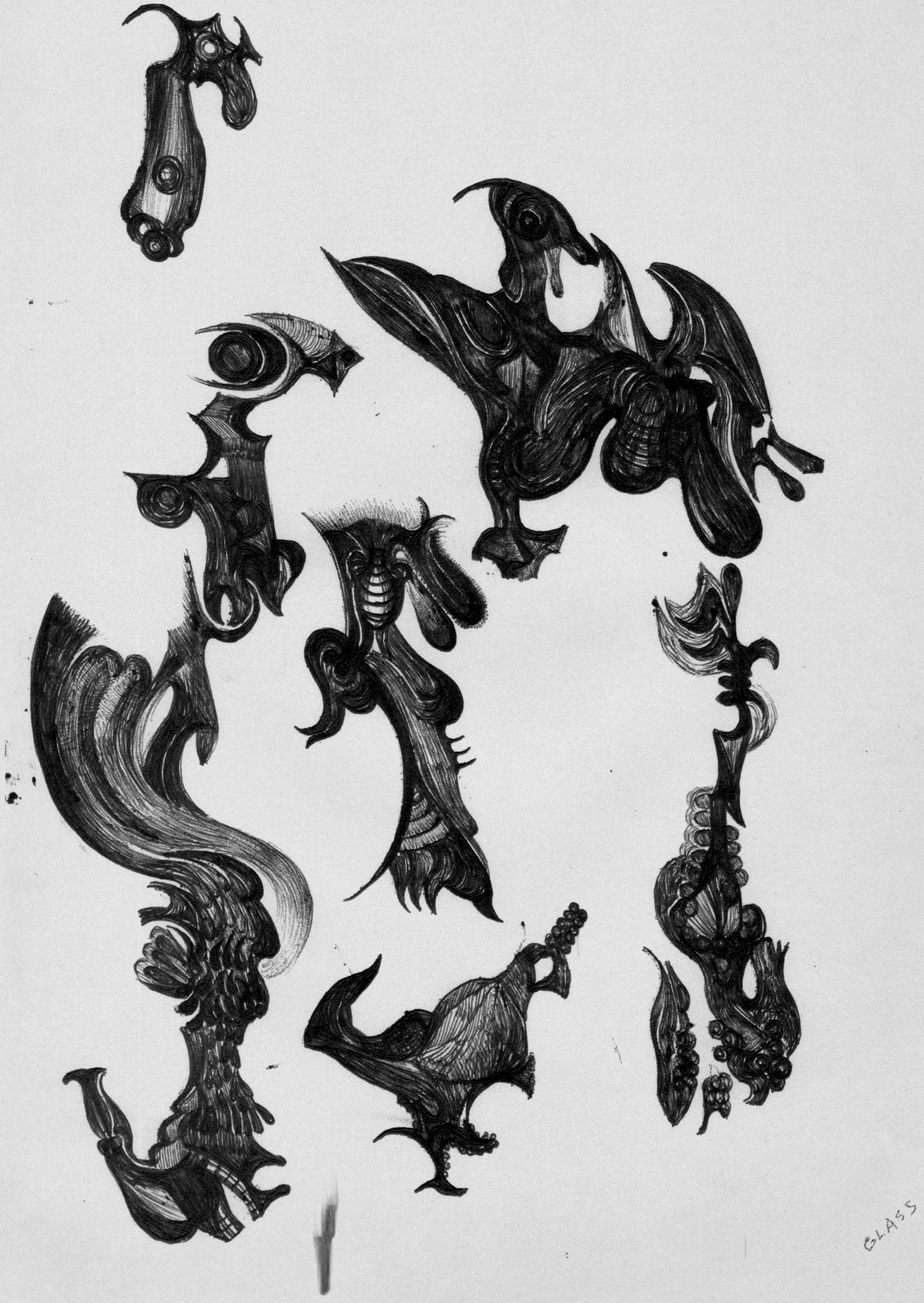
GLASS

INTRODUCTION

Nadine M. Orenstein
Drue Heinz Curator in Charge,
Department of Drawings and Prints,
The Metropolitan Museum of Art
New York

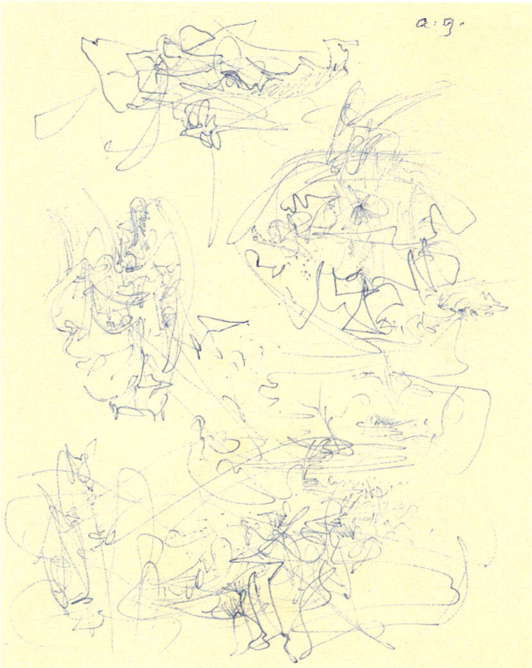

Untitled
(Club Saint-Germain period)
ca. 1954-1962
Monochrome blue ballpoint
pen drawing,
on paper.
13.5 x 10.5 cm
Artist's collection

Untitled
(Rue Manuel period)
ca. 1954-1962
Monochrome blue ballpoint
pen drawing, on paper.
30 x 21 cm
Artist's collection
Previous page

Like the spectral evocations of a parallel world, Alan Glass's graphic works bring to the surface of paper a marvelous, densely inhabited realm that seems to materialize from another dimension. In these drawings, an alternate universe emerges as if glimpsed through the sinuous strands of a momentarily posed cigarette. Glass's imagery conjures the eternal and the fleeting. It includes both the familiar—faces, animals, plants, and everyday objects can be discerned among the intertwined forms—and the extraordinary—do ancient deities populate his large drawings? They seem Aztec, Indian, or even alien in origin. Is he putting forth a futuristic vision of an over-crowded, organically developing world or is he rendering a parallel universe? We must stand close, dive in, to see these places and their inhabitants more clearly.

Glass's graphic work is entirely different in nature from the three-dimensional works for which he is better known. Not every artist is equally able to craft distinct visual vocabularies and visions as they express themselves in alternate media. While in his boxes and sculptures Glass pieces together marvelous, surreal visions from everyday objects that hold vivid associations for him, each work unique in character from responds to the found objects incorporated. In drawing, print, and painting, he allows us to see his skilled artistic hand at work and he uses the two-dimensional techniques to create an ethereal environment that seems to continue throughout the works from drawings to paintings, to prints.

In early drawings from the 1950s and early 60s, Glass created abstract forms with blue and black ballpoint pens. The images resemble fast moving clouds. Yet he used the ballpoint, a precise, viscous, long lasting medium, to render

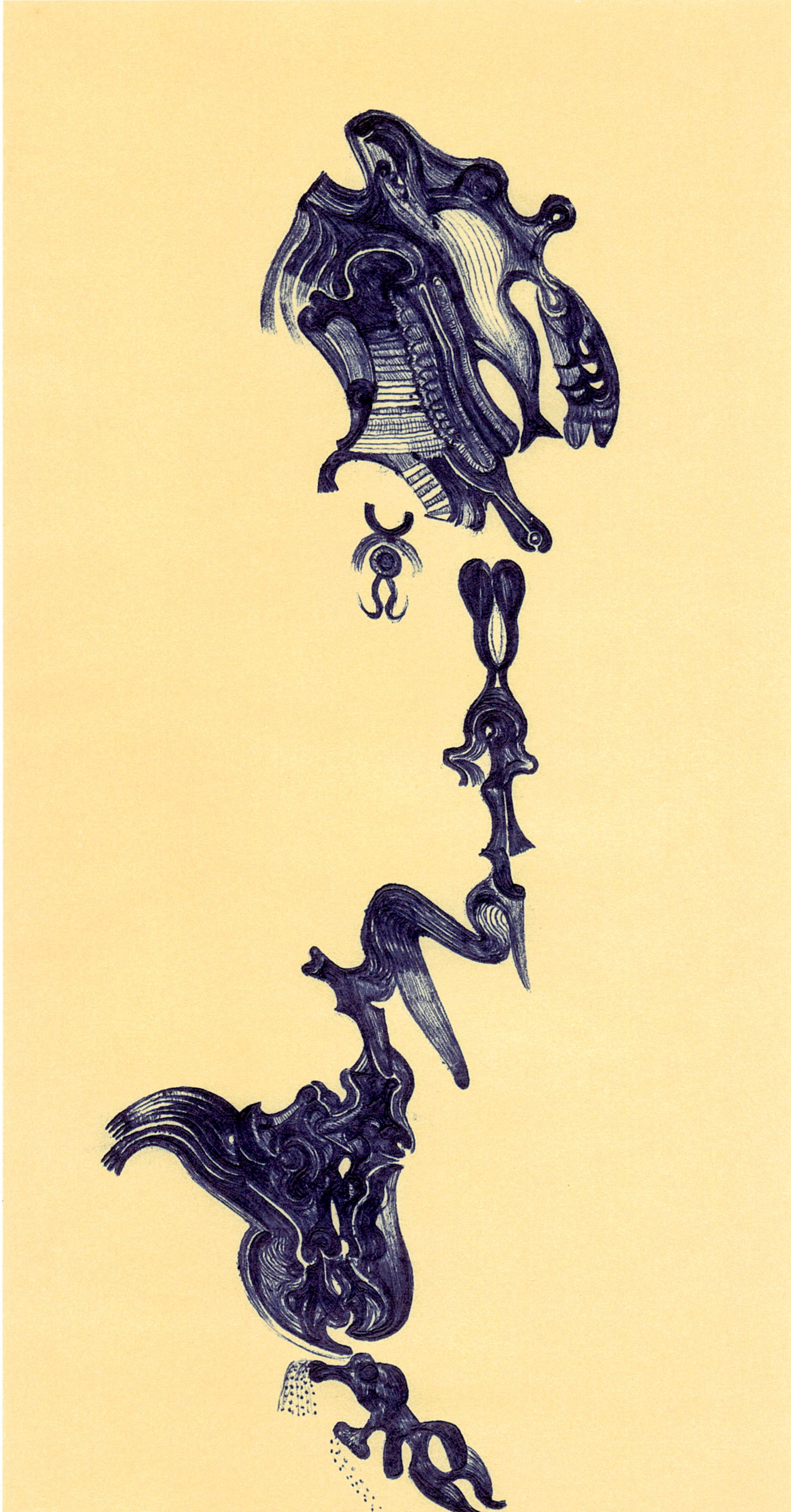

Untitled
(Rue Manuel period)
ca. 1954-1962
Monochrome blue ballpoint
pen drawing, on paper.
30 x 15 cm
Artist's collection

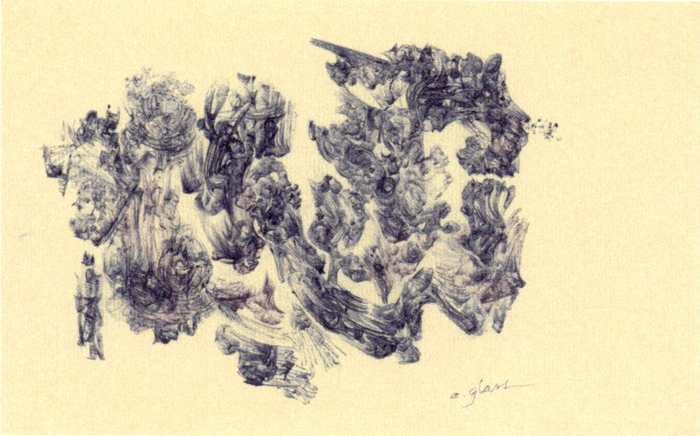

something that appears weightless and unfixed. His strokes of the pen combine into gestures that evoke the energetic ink-laden brushwork of Chinese calligraphy.

For all of his fantastic, otherworldly, automatic drawing, Glass's graphic work is also grounded in the knowledge of earlier art. The *horror vacui* of his flowered spaces recall the mille-fleur tapestries of the Middle Ages. The glowing aura in the untitled tempera from 1964, reminds us of Matthias Grunewald's *Resurrection of Christ* from his famous altarpiece in Colmar. Glass is a devoted disciple of Rodolphe Bresdin (Le-Fresne-sur-Loire 1822-1885 Sèvres), the nineteenth-century French etcher and lithographer. He seems to channel this graphic predecessor, particularly in his small prints whose formats and treatment of light and dark even echo Bresdin's small etchings. Bresdin's compositions, spiky, writhing forests that are home to figures, animals, and even skulls that appear from the darkest recesses find their echo in Glass's densely intertwined twisting linear hives of figures. Is it mere coincidence that Bresdin was one of the few nineteenth-century French artists who also lived for a time in Canada? Indeed he spent four years teaching printmaking in Montreal between 1873 and 1877 before returning to France. This Canadian-French experience reverberates in Glass's own cross-Atlantic biography.

Glass's boxes can be viewed in a certain sense as windows to another moment; however, his drawings open up for us a view into another dimension, one that may be just beyond our detection. These works bring us into a different reality, a world of fantastic landscapes, symmetry and reversals, and of the recognizable intermingling with the surreal. The Renaissance gave us the concept of the painting's picture plane as a window to the reality that lies beyond. Glass's graphic work opens a window to another world that engulfs the everyday within a flowing puzzle.

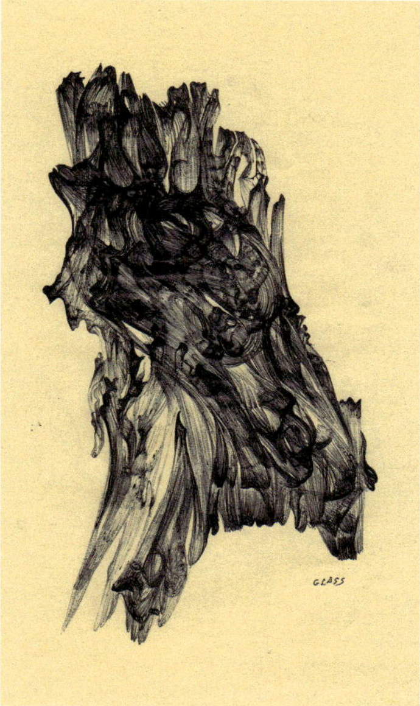

Untitled
(Club Saint-Germain period)
ca. 1954-1962
Monochrome blue ballpoint pen drawing with a touch of violet pencil, on paper.
16 x 24 cm
Artist's collection

Untitled
(Club Saint-Germain period)
ca. 1954-1962
Monochrome black ballpoint pen drawing,
on paper.
28 x 22.5 cm
Artist's collection

5

E MANU
PARIS

IXE

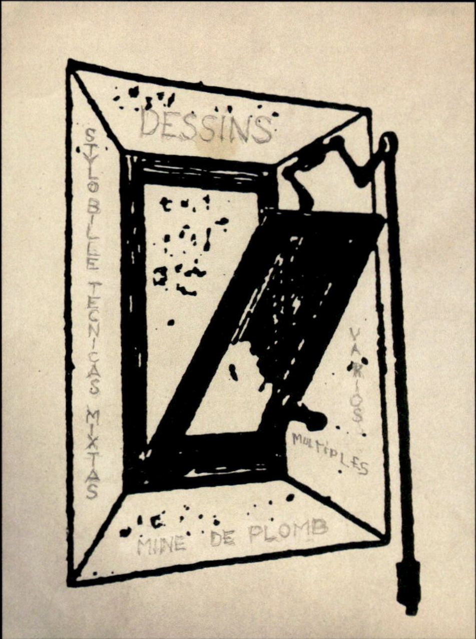

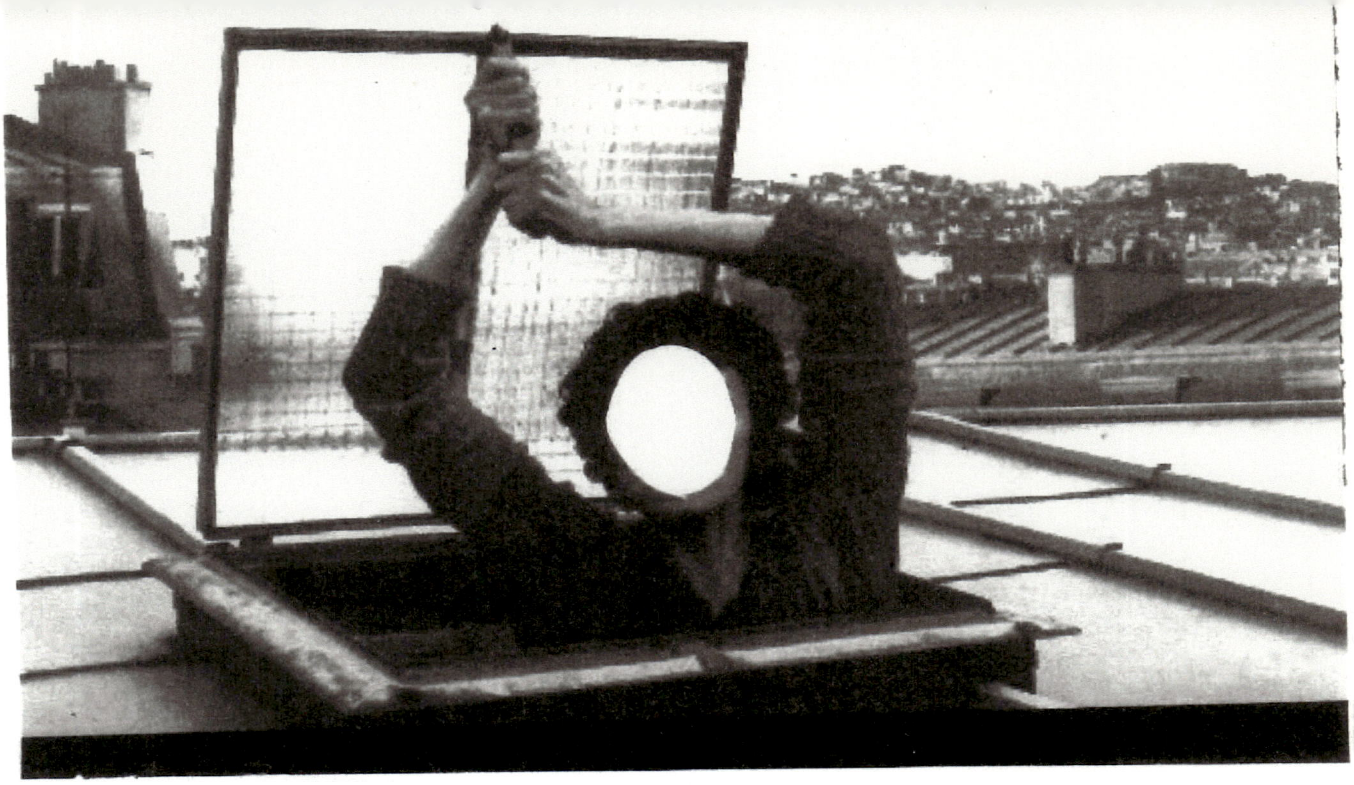

5
RUE
MANUEL

PARIS
IXe

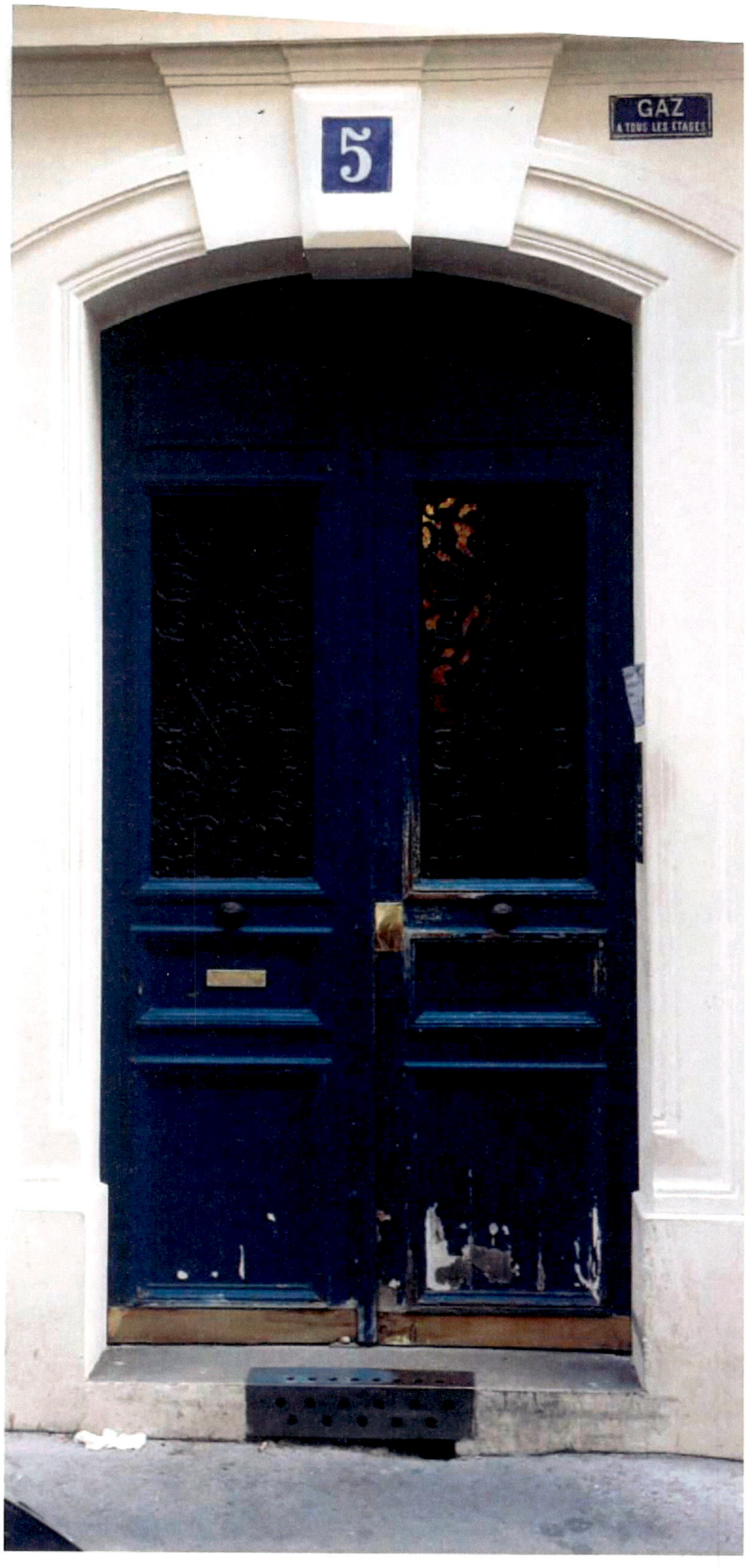

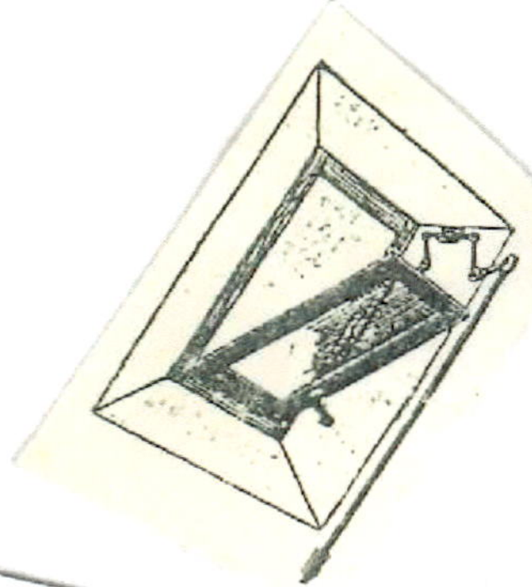

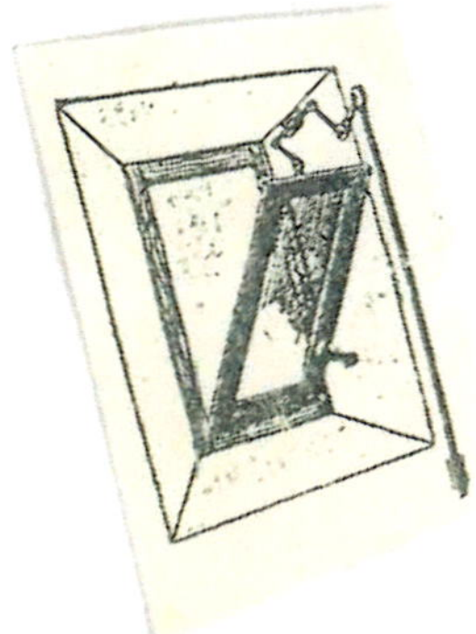

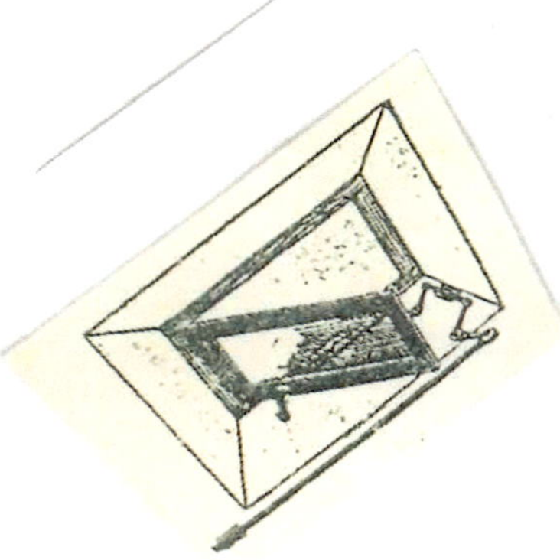

(l'ex livre)

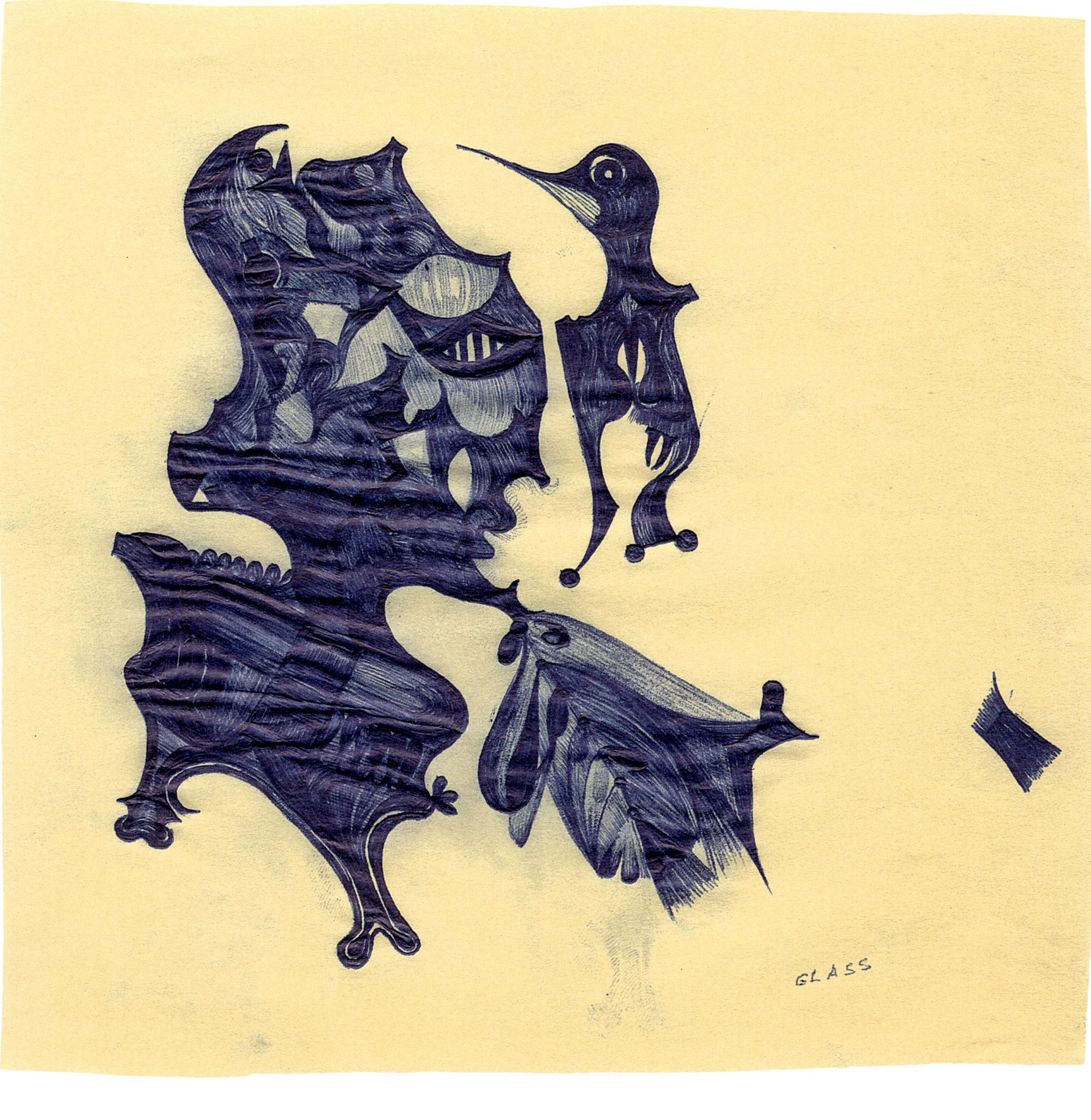

Untitled
(Rue Manuel period)
ca. 1954-1962
Monochrome blue ballpoint pen drawing, on paper.
18.6 x 18.4 cm
Artist's collection

GLASS

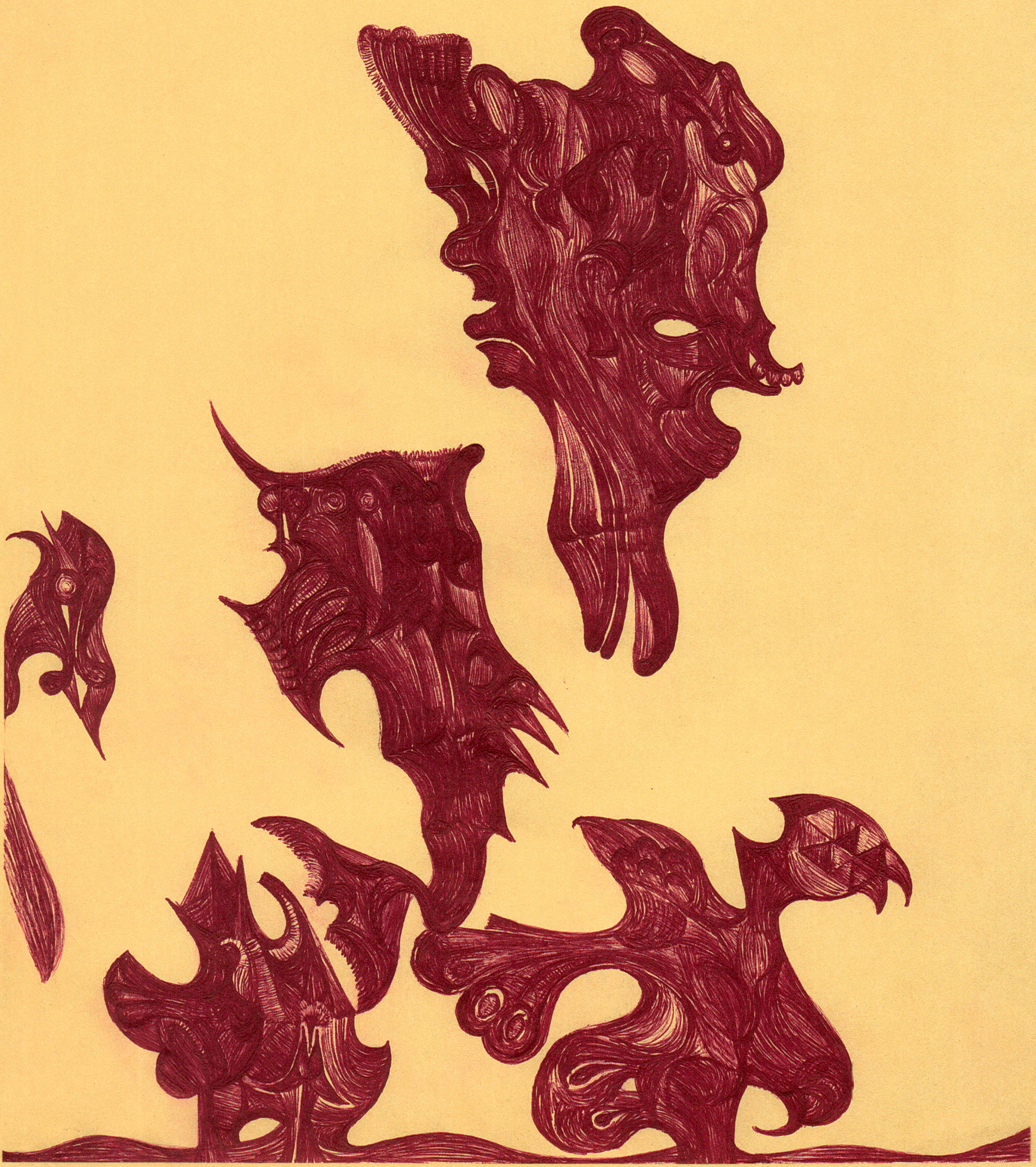

BAROQUE PORTRAIT ALAN GLASS

(EXTRACT)

Pierre de Ligny Boudreau
Vie des Arts No 84
Fall 1976

Wanting to be on time for my appointment, I sped through a deserted Paris; the month was August and barely seven o'clock in the morning. Boulevard Raspail, Rue du Bac, Boulevard Saint-Germain…in a car that was far too noisy for the time of day, I was overcome by the feeling of being a bizarre insect trespassing on places signed Magritte or Giorgio De Chirico. The empty streets also brought back memories of the post-war period, which led to memories of when I was in my twenties, in the nineteen-fifties. Rues des Saints-Pères, Rue Saint-Benoît…So, I was going to see Alan. Diffidently, I took a quick look as if hoping to come across the past, which, as everyone knows, roams about at night…in Saint-Germain-des-Prés.

Back then, Alan Glass was the sensitive, friendly doorman of what at the time was the most celebrated nightclub: the Club Saint-Germain. He used to tell me that in order to deal with the eccentrics, he would stop at every café on his way to work and drink a calvados. Once at his post, sitting on a stool behind a small end table, the club's not-very-busy waiters would ply him with it all night, and not in small bistro tumblers, but in so-called tasting glasses. One day, the proprietress, on checking the wine cellar, was astonished to discover that the entire reserve of calvados had been drunk. This seemed very odd, the fashion being whisky for dandies and brandy and water for latecomers. An investigation was conducted: it was Alan who, little by little and cool as you please, had drunk it all. It became necessary to take action: the "kid" was put on a diet of one *calva* per day. Nevertheless, although shrouded in the mists of Normandy, every night, to amuse himself, he would sketch very beautiful drawings in ballpoint pen. Lunar-like

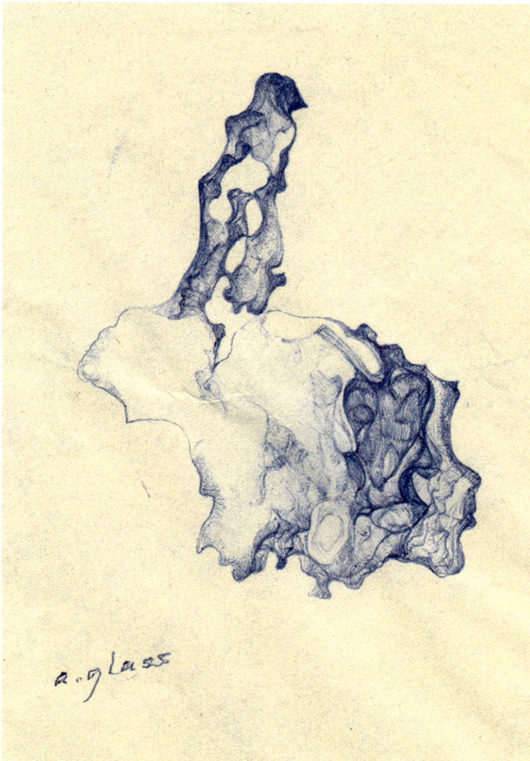

Untitled
(Rue Manuel period)
ca. 1954-1962
Monochrome blue pen drawing, on a paper envelope.
14.5 x 11.5 cm
Private collection

Untitled
(Rue Manuel period)
ca. 1954-1962
Monochrome red ballpoint pen drawing, on paper.
27 x 21 cm
Artist's collection
Previous page

landscapes of a sort, composed of an entire iconography of shaded hatchings and symbols forming large shapes, sometimes with a play on planes and distant fade-outs. In fact, Matta introduced him to a gallery that organized an exhibit of those drawings. The gallery was fittingly located on the Rue du Cherche-Midi, a beautiful name perfectly suited to Alan! He subsequently found the *midi* in Mexico. Canadians often long for southern climes. Who can blame them?

A steadfast gathering of night owls would haunt the *quartier*. They all knew him: Jeanne Moreau would come sit on the stairs to listen to the jazz; Boris Vian, on the lookout for friends, would poke his head in; Alexandre would stop by to borrow a thousand francs; Solange...Nights would often continue on to Les Halles, then the climbing up to Montmartre under the pale dawn sky... Oh! wasn't Saint-Germain wonderful then... And to be twenty and living in Paris... It was our university. We took childlike pride in knowing it well: the streets, the nightclubs, the theaters, the restaurants, the bakeries, the cafés where the wine was better than anywhere else, the lovely overlooked spots. This knowledge gave us the delicious feeling of being Parisian, of being at home in this fabulous Paris... absolutely delightful, let me tell you! "Whoa, not so fast! Take it easy! No speeding! It's already daylight!", and we are, I think, in 1975. Enough of this posturing; all that is in the past. You, my memories and your gloating glances, begone! Don't let me catch you again! That's how car accidents happen...begone! And nostalgia under double-lock and key! I'll be late and he'll be all hot and bothered waiting for me on the sidewalk. I turn onto Rue La Fayette, then left on Rue Notre-Dame-de-Lorette and up the Rue des Martyrs. On the first floor of a grey turn-of-the-century building, a child peeks out from behind a lace curtain. It's little Léautaud waiting for his mother who has lingered at the Paris-Madrid or at Tortoni's... the lonely *Petit*, The Little Thing, as he'd coyly say. Paris and its celebrities...every street has at least one! On mine, it was Barbey d'Aurevilly, Gauguin. Arriving at a square whose name I've forgotten, I make two right turns, one left, and I'm there. Oof! Almost on time, but not quite since I see Alan Glass on the doorstep of number 5 nervously searching the horizon surrounded by his things, a veritable private flea market. In an attempt to explain my tardiness and by way of an apology, I mumble *Le Petit chose*, Vian, Jeanne... Thinking that my morning coffee has gone to my head, he looks at me in bewilderment, but, tolerant, says not a word. He asks for five minutes to say goodbye to La Barrera, his faithful landlady, and disappears. Keeping watch, I chat with the neighbor across the street, the concierge of a hotel so modest it's not even classified. "Ah! were it not for La Barrera, the Rue Manuel wouldn't be the same," she says with admiration and respect. The neighbor, a tiny mouse in carpet slippers with a threadbare shawl around the shoulders, has a keen eye and sharp tongue even though she's but a countrywoman; La Barrera, meanwhile, is a star, the boss, the street's bigwig. A former dressmaker, she dressed the Duchess of Sutherland and

Untitled
(Rue Manuel period)
ca. 1954-1962
Monochrome blue ballpoint pen drawing, on paper.
28 x 22.5 cm
Artist's collection

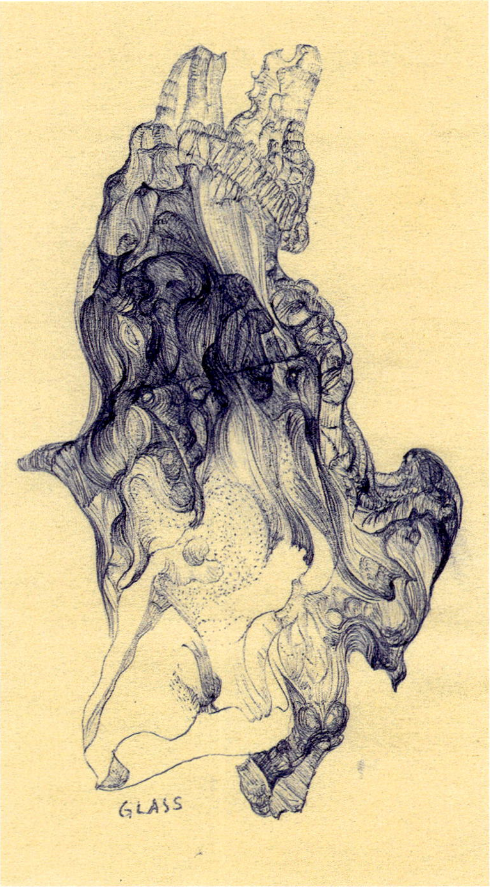

the élite of Buenos Aires, so you can imagine! From her second-floor window, she manages her property, keeps an eye on the comings and goings, knows all the area's residents, and is aware of everything that goes on. Sociable but rarely familiar, she has never forgotten her fashionable clientele, and when she pulls aside the curtain and extends her hand in greeting, she's the spitting image of the Queen Mother. Wearing heavy makeup in the old-fashioned way and coiffed in a beehive, her dark hair gleams like a policeman's cocked hat. Does she speak Spanish? *Claro*! Of course! Like a state-of-the-art machine gun. However, although a long-time Parisian, she still mangles the French language. She washes her face only with rosewater, and every day at precisely five o'clock she takes tea in the company of the Duchess, visible atop the chimney chatting with Daisy de la Roche-Guyon, *née* Guiness, at the Longchamp paddock; with the vanity of an elderly lady, the Duchess always seems to be about to sit down with La Barrera, yet never makes up her mind to do so. Even now, it is with this notable past—despite the years, the wounds, the dust and the moths—that La Barrera adorns herself. As for Alan Glass, he calls her Mamita, avowing an almost filial gratitude towards her, which homage she proudly accepts. From what planet did the benevolent genie who arranged the meeting between these two come from?

Glass is a creature of the Moon. A prototypical Cancer, ergo very vulnerable, from a very young age he had to learn to protect his sensibilities, to keep the prosaic and the coarse at a distance. He does so in civilized fashion by standing on the sidelines, thus avoiding disagreeable ideas, people and places. Mindful of others' sensibilities, he does so without making a fuss or causing hurt, in the Scottish way, you might say, he being of Scottish descent. It is almost impossible to dissociate him from his works; to talk about him is to talk about them.

Today he's returning to Mexico, and the reason I'm here is to drive him to Orly. Arriving in France two months ago with one suitcase, he's leaving with six, a great number of bags, rollers, an entire and extraordinary collection of stuff: a treasure trove. Ever at work, he's disguised his departure and belongings as if he were moving house, in such a way as no taxi driver would ever agree to transport them. We have a final drink at the local café: "Ladies! Gentlemen!" It's the trusty street sweeper, already a bit tipsy, ceremoniously greeting us. Fitting the luggage into the car required the know-how of an architect, and once accomplished, left us breathless and with just enough room to be able to sit. Off we go. The sleepy street, slowly, unhurriedly, stirs, stretches and shakes itself awake. The river, carrying along remnants of the night, sparkles in the sun. Paris is beautiful in the morning. Why leave? Were I to ask him, he'll answer that his cat is pining away; that Rose, his concierge, is getting bored; that the plants in a bathtub on his balcony are in trouble; that his walls are concerned; that it's imperative that he return. Therefore, I say nothing. Nevertheless, I suspect that, once the delight in being home has

Untitled
(Rue Manuel period)
ca. 1954-1962
Monochrome blue ballpoint pen drawing, on paper.
29.5 x 21 cm
Artist's collection

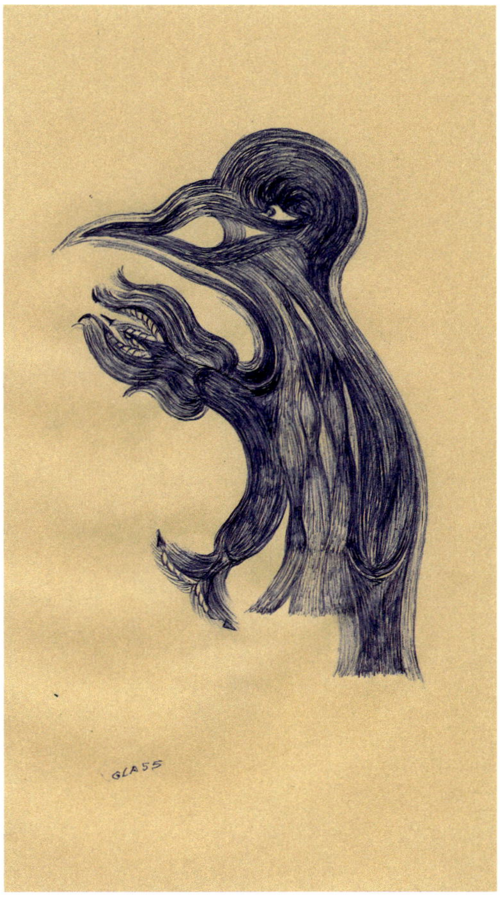

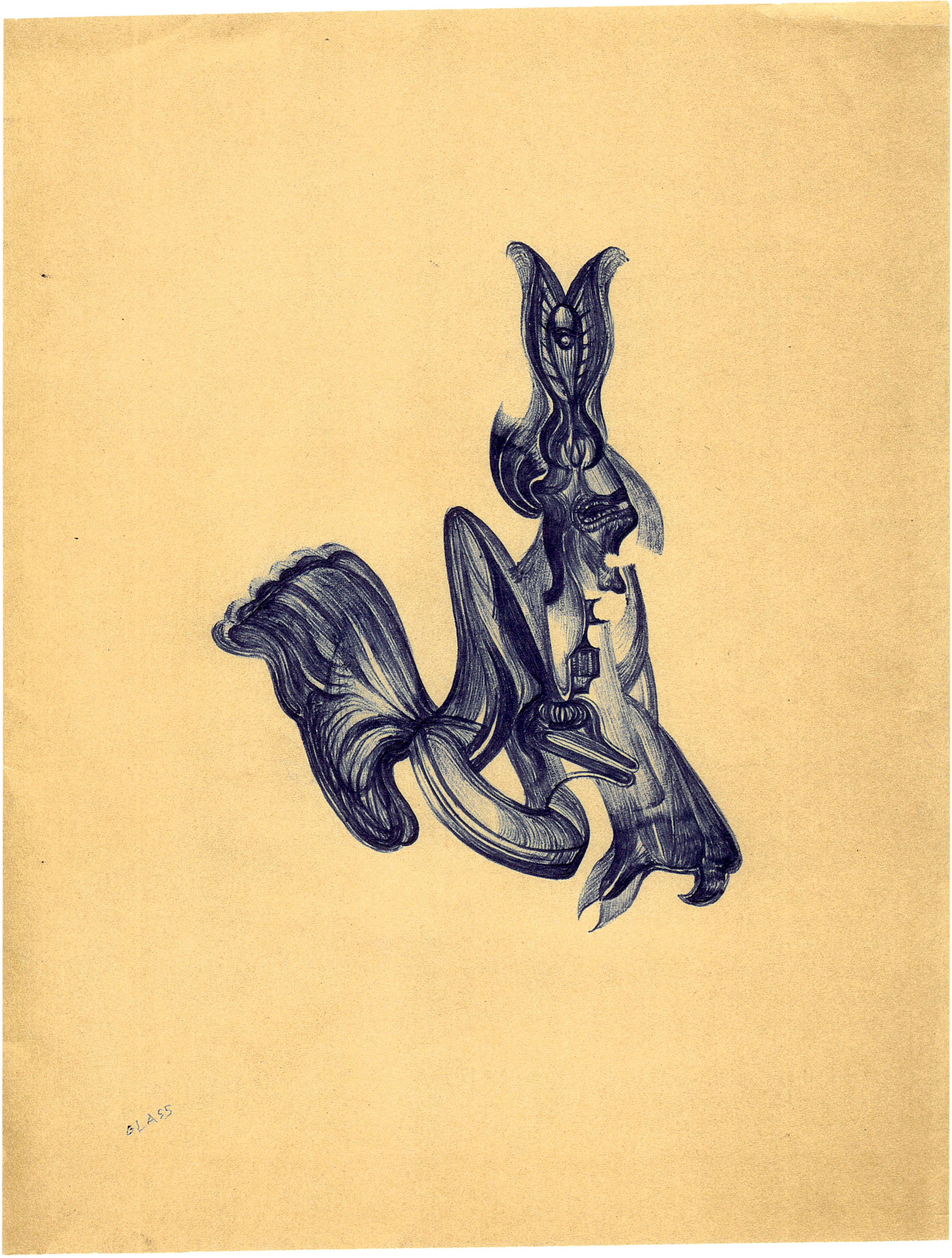
GLASS

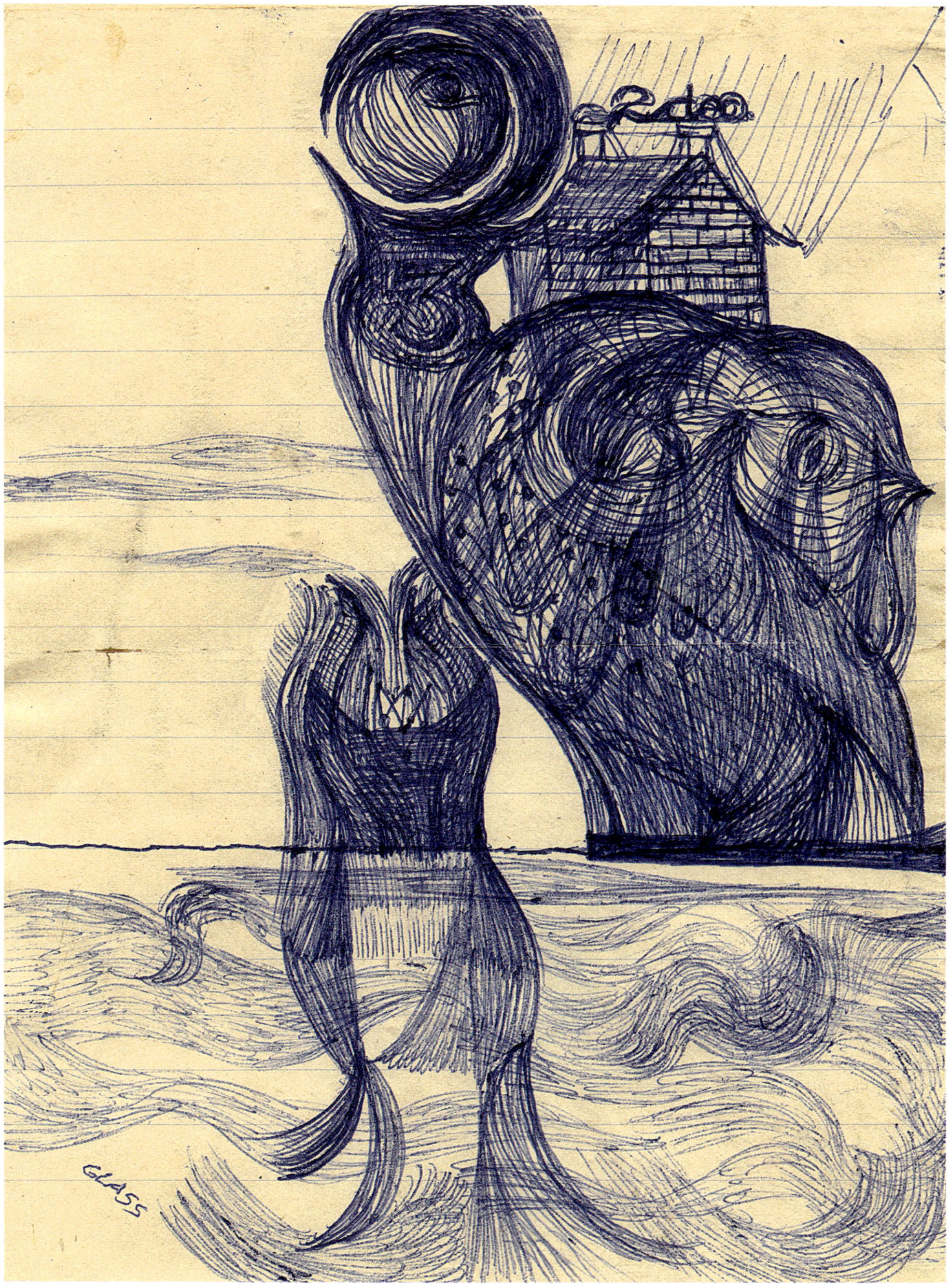

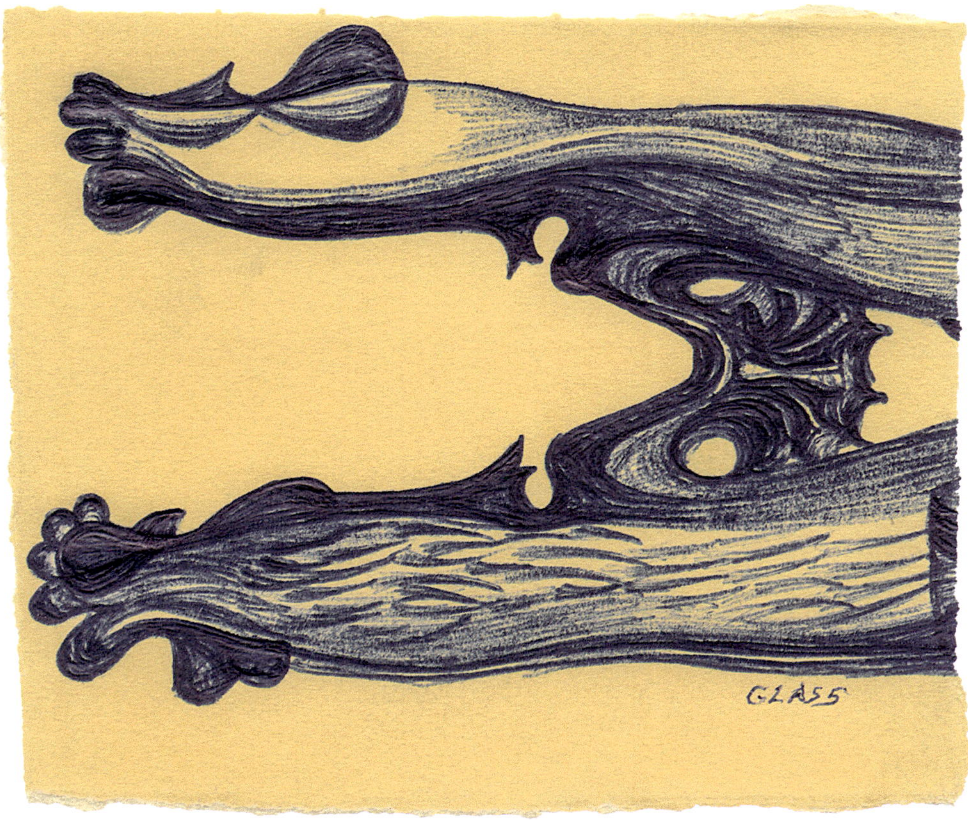

Untitled
(Rue Manuel period)
ca. 1954-1962
Monochrome blue ballpoint pen drawing, on paper.
28 x 22 cm
Artist's collection
Previous page

Untitled
(Rue Manuel period)
ca. 1954-1962
Monochrome blue ballpoint pen drawing, on paper.
18.5 x 13.5 cm
Artist's collection

Untitled
(Rue Manuel period)
ca. 1954-1962
Monochrome blue ballpoint pen drawing, on paper.
10.5 x 8.5 cm
Artist's collection

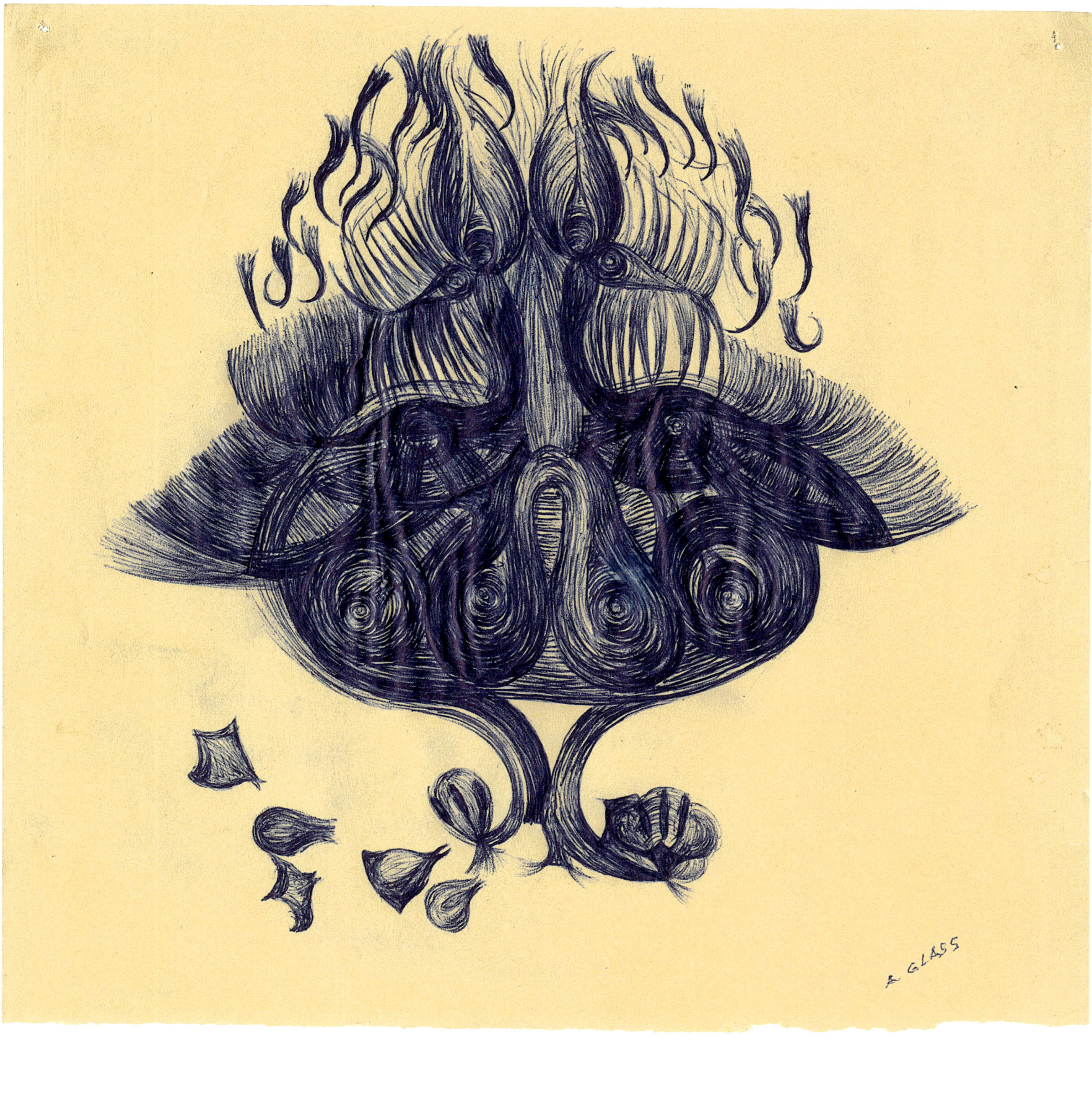

Untitled
(Rue Manuel period)
ca. 1954-1962
Monochrome blue ballpoint pen drawing, on paper.
19.5 x 21 cm
Artist's collection

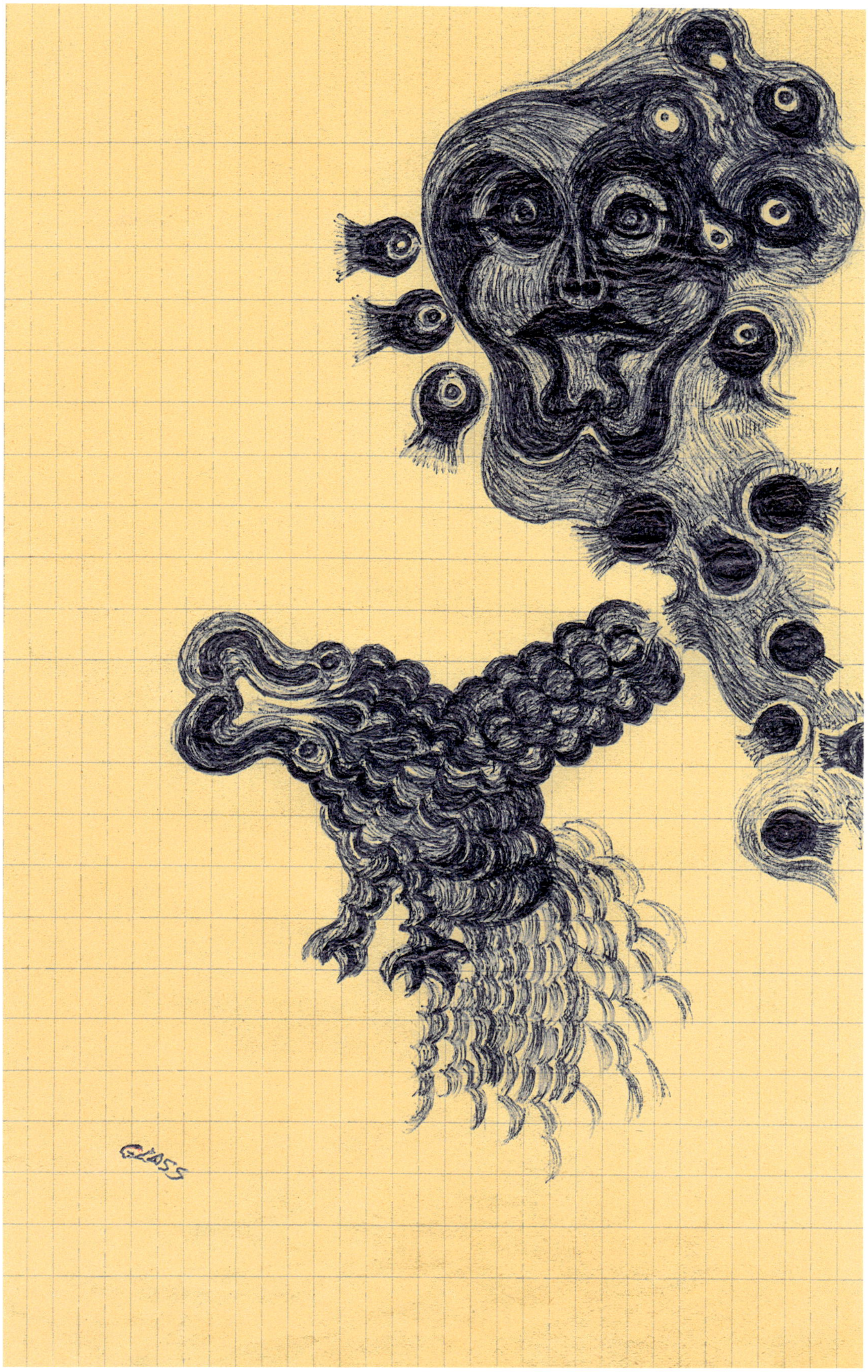

Untitled
(Rue Manuel period)
ca. 1954-1962
Monochrome blue ballpoint
pen drawing, on paper.
21 x 13.5 cm
Artist's collection

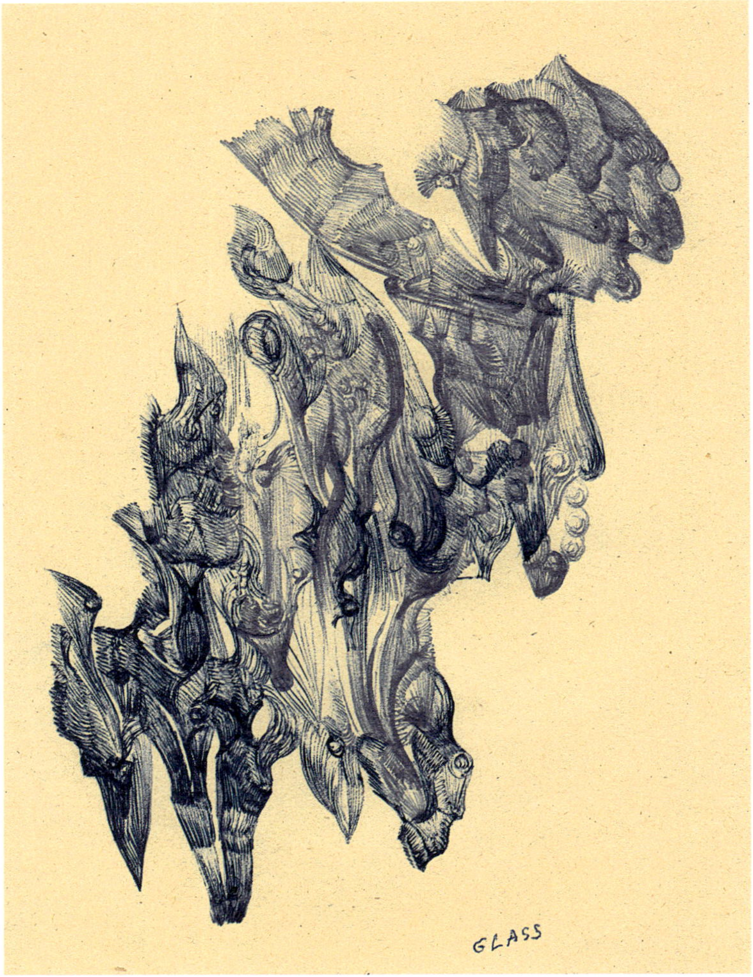

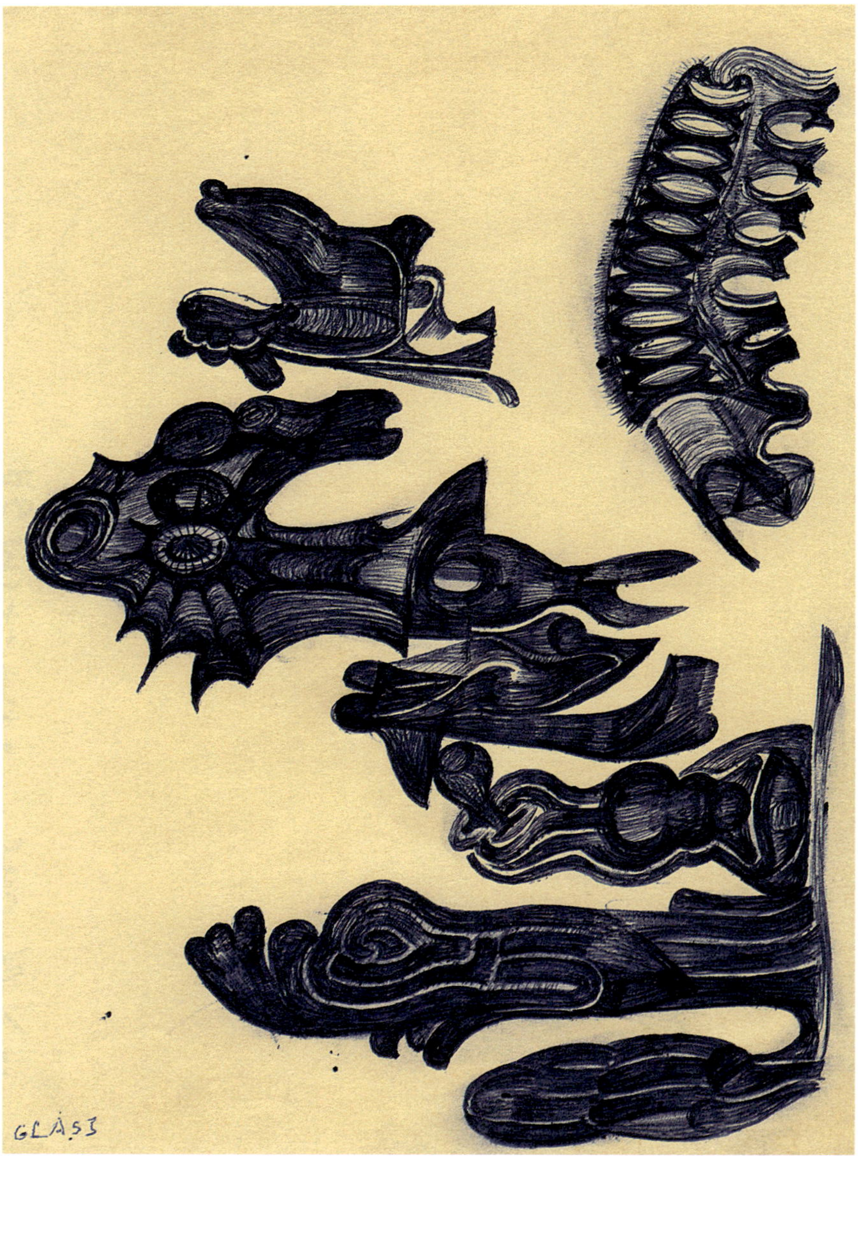

Untitled
(Rue Manuel period)
ca. 1954-1962
Monochrome blue ballpoint
pen drawing, on paper.
27 x 21 cm
Artist's collection

Untitled
(Rue Manuel period)
ca. 1954-1962
Monochrome blue ballpoint
pen drawing, on paper.
13 x 17 cm
Artist's collection

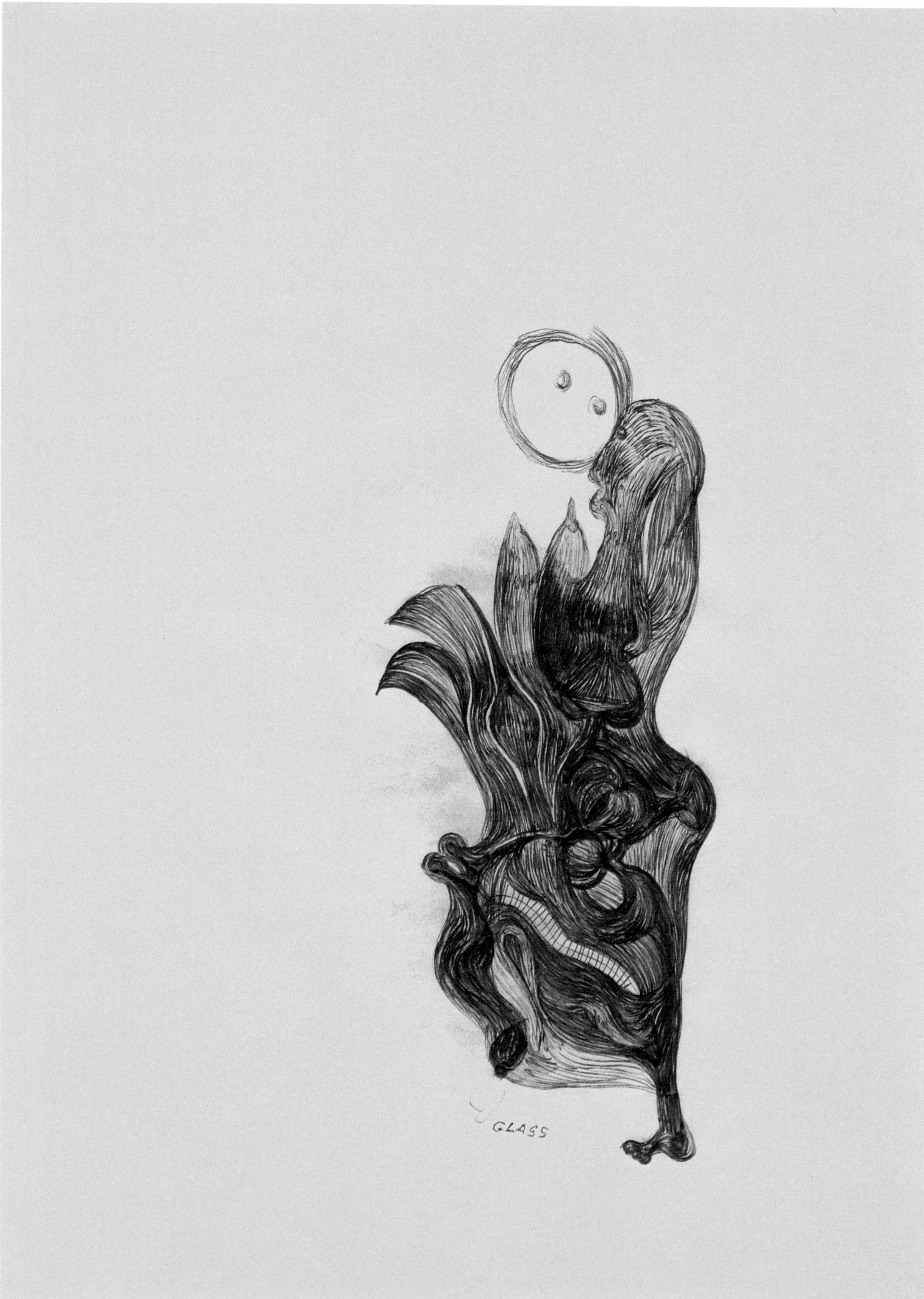

Untitled
(Rue Manuel period)
ca. 1954-1962
Monochrome blue ballpoint pen drawing, on paper.
29.5 x 21 cm
Artist's collection

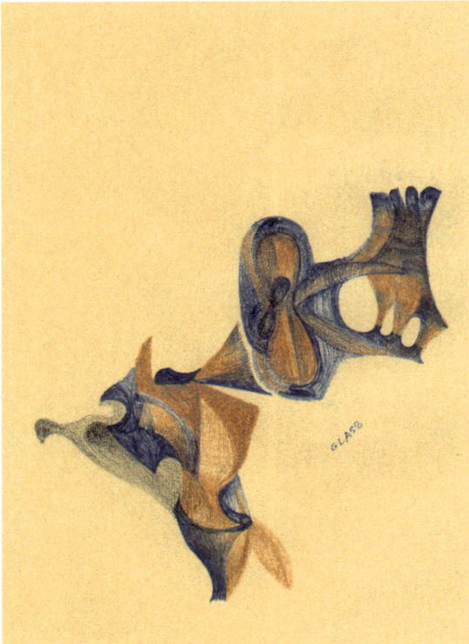

Untitled
(Rue Manuel period)
ca. 1954-1962
Blue pen drawing, with graphite and brown color, on paper.
27 x 21 cm
Artist's collection

passed, he'll go through a painful time, and it will take weeks to pack away the memories of the Paris he loves so much and before he is able to get back to work.

[...] On the way, Alan has to hold back a suitcase made of "Samar aluminum" that's as elegant as a Vuitton, but might just knock me out. His personal effects are those of a gypsy, of those "nomadic itinerants." The customs gentlemen, I am sure, will not remain indifferent to all his paraphernalia; are they familiar with magicians? I remind him that French customs officers are tolerant, Americans are very wary, and as for Mexican customs...He quickly reassures me he has nothing to fear since in Mexico he'll be welcomed by no less a person than the daughter of an undersecretary of state.

[...] Mexico. Why did he choose to live there rather than elsewhere? Just because and somewhat by chance, I think—because the weather is nice, because the living is easy and fairly trouble-free, because the artisanal and handicrafts sector is very dynamic.

[...] Just like his Celtic ancestors, he set off one day for India, continuing on as far as Nepal, where he spent a year. It was, he said, too long and too short. For a more profound experience, more time would have been necessary; merely as a sightseeing trip, it was too long. Nonetheless, he knows how to travel: he looks, assimilates, accepts feeling like a fish out of water, opens doors and windows, opens himself up. The journey left its mark: a surfeit of emotions, impressions and discoveries, too much exoticism all at once, and he's returning to Mexico fed up, reeling, slightly dazed, like an alpine butterfly intoxicated by the scent of wild strawberries.

From then on, echoes of Asian art appear in his work: a plethora of fantastic beings, profusions of ornaments, objects, shapes, interlocking movements, chimeras, fantasies whose rich sensuality sometimes verges on the erotic. However, any excess, should it exist, is quickly corrected, tempered by the prevailing and incomparable gentleness, by the inordinate musicality of the melody. Shrouded in dreams, in ethereality, these wonderlands shimmer like precious brocades or certain Byzantine mosaics. Contemplating them, we sometimes also get a sense of the Tuscan countryside seen in *quattrocento* portraits: *Là tout n'est qu'ordre et beauté, luxe, calme, et volupté.*[1] And Venice is not far, with its rose-colored palaces furrowed by the lagoon that strews them to the horizon, generating along the way the sumptuous iridescent reflections of Saint Mark, visible until nightfall, when the shadows descend upon the street, face hidden behind a domino; nor those faraway lands where the sirocco blows across cities bathed in all the white shades of the spectrum, a delight and an oasis for our eyes sometimes weary of so many electric blues, yellows and reds. He paints with absolute and uncommon mastery: the glitters and sparkles of a dizzying mannerism deriving from an extraterrestrial world; and if one looks more closely, sfumato gives way to strict, vigorous organization. Admittedly, such an imaginative motif endows the whole, the subject, with surrealist-like resonance, but light, because of its ubiquity, is consistent with other pictorial concerns; Mark Tobey in particular comes to mind, as well as older works by Sam Francis, even those of Riopelle when in some of his works he flirts with a magical wonderland, which Glass embraced.

Oh! And don't forget, he says, *to send me that paper from Lefèvre-Foinet*. It's because he wants to begin drawing in silverpoint like François Clouet in the 16th century that he needs a special paper that can only be found here, and on which he will relish using a technique so difficult as to preclude any corrections.

Paralyzed by his impending departure, and already too late to have a conversation, we chat half-heartedly. Alan looks serious, nervous; he's already somewhere else. Partings are always difficult, especially if one is leaving Paris. Paris, his small homeland, where he was able to find again the extraordinary world that as a child, in Saint-Hilaire, he came across in picture books. After a few years of study at the Montreal School of Fine Arts, he left for France. Discovering Paris is what shaped and fulfilled him. Encountering such artistic abundance, he quickly learned to choose, focusing only on what could heighten his imagination and nourish his spirit. Surrounded by the extended family of painters he loved, he worked on the sidelines, guided only by his hypersensibility.

Not everyone can go to Corinth, says a Greek proverb. It's understood: few are chosen; but Glass did go. The Spaniards, who are very good at aphorisms, have a saying: Beware of those returning from Granada. Alas! Artists, however, have the advantage of being able to prolong the illusion; or at least they can try, day after day, to do so. They can confine themselves to an inner life that protects them from life's contingencies and from the vulgar. They possess many compartments they can open at will, in which they amass a treasure trove of immaterial wealth. They know how to experience the magic of an echo: Granada, even if one has left it, is always there.

Passengers on Air France flight 007 bound for Mexico City, please proceed to…

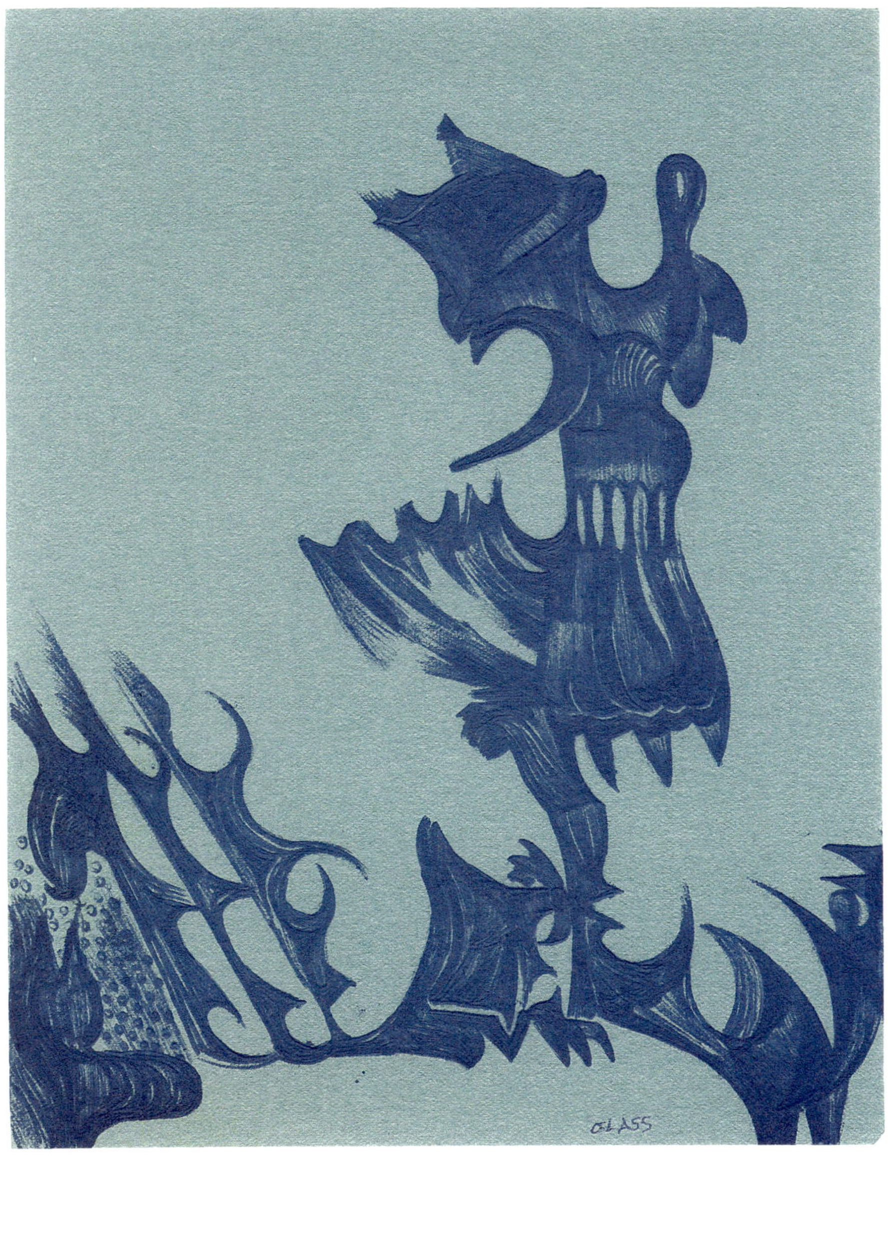

Untitled
(Rue Manuel period)
ca. 1954-1962
Monochrome blue ballpoint pen drawing, on blue paper.
21 x 16 cm
Artist's collection

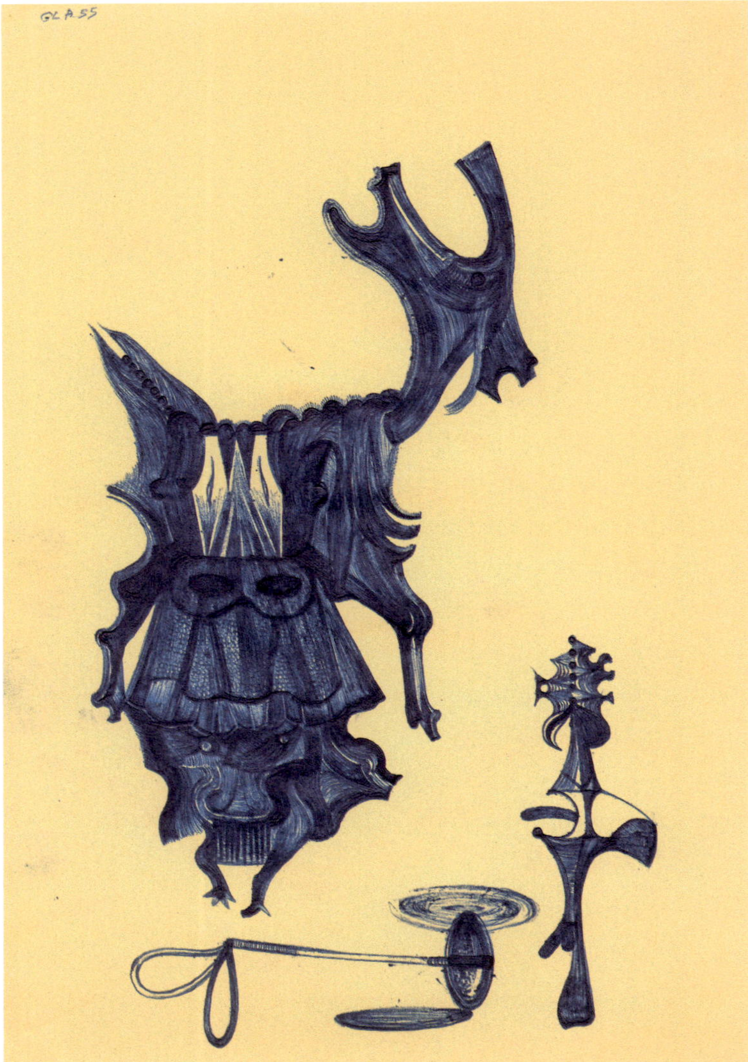

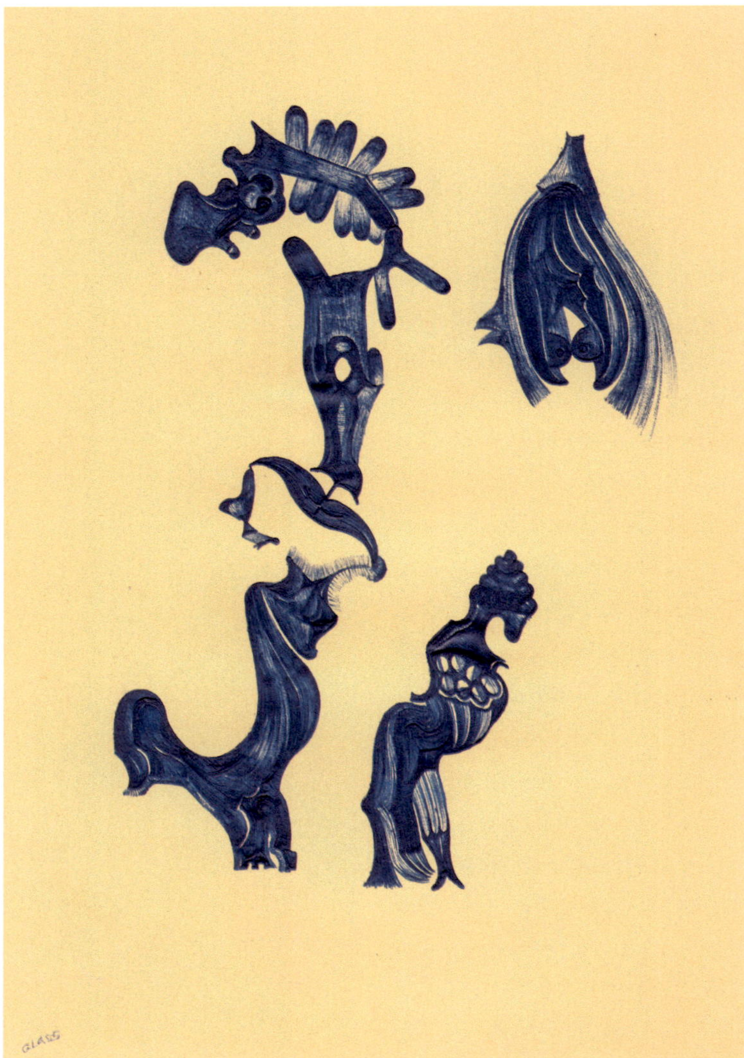

Untitled
(Rue Manuel period)
ca. 1954-1962
Monochrome blue ballpoint
pen drawing, on paper.
30 x 21 cm
Artist's collection

Untitled
(Rue Manuel period)
ca. 1954-1962
Monochrome blue ballpoint
pen drawing, on paper.
30 x 21 cm
Artist's collection

Untitled
(Rue Manuel period)
ca. 1954-1962
Monochrome blue ballpoint
pen drawing, on paper.
30 x 21 cm
Artist's collection
Following page

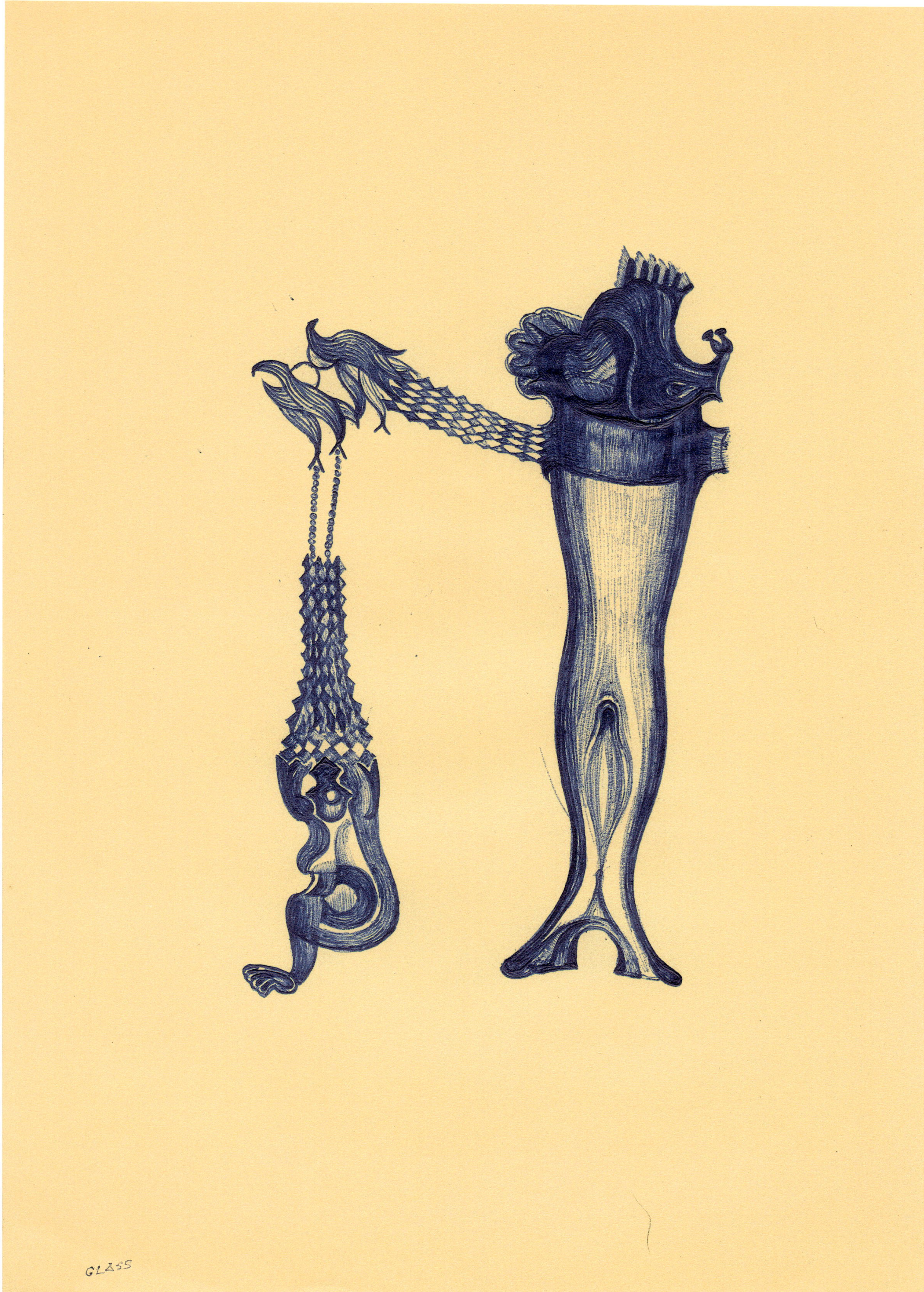
GLASS

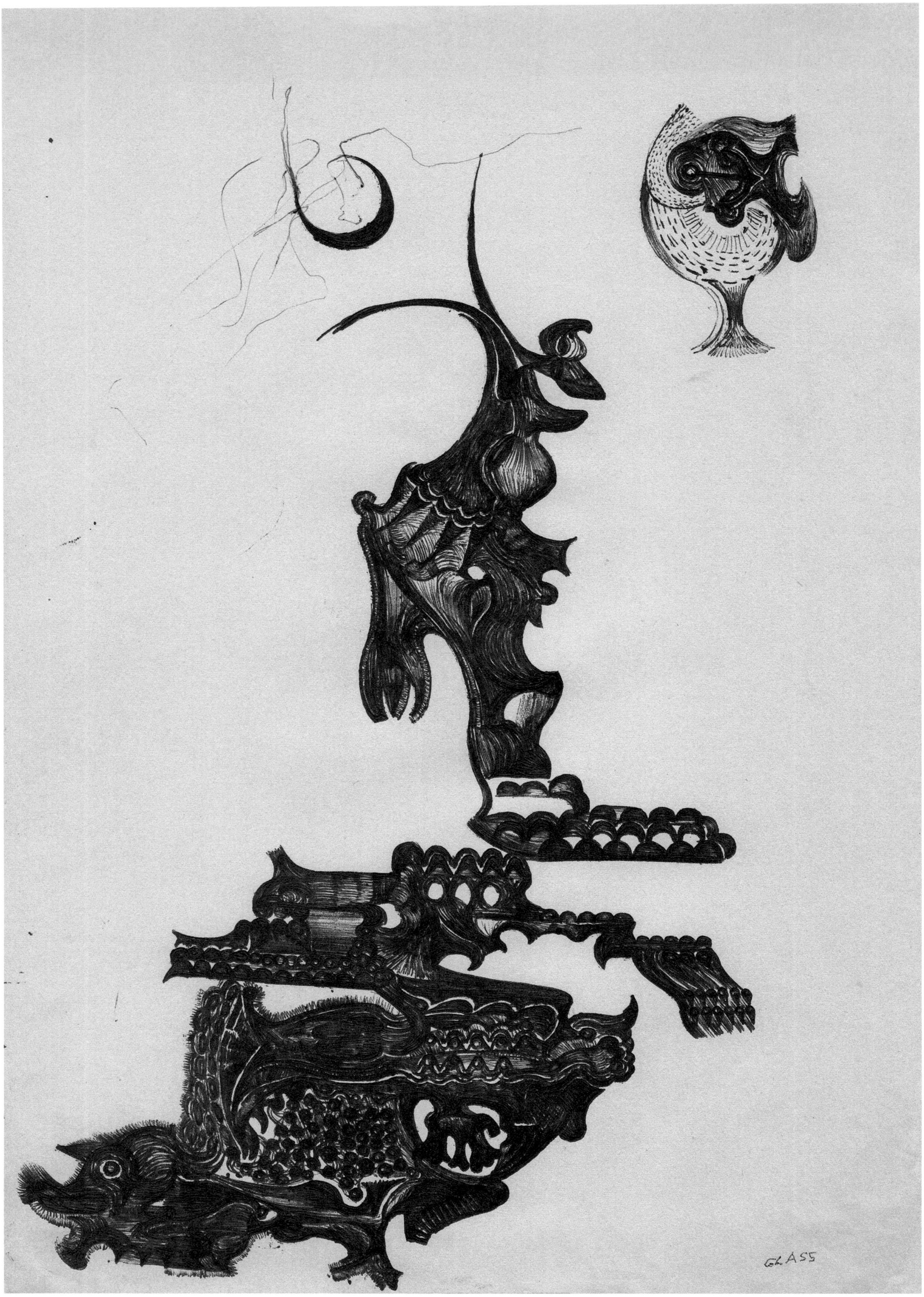

Untitled
(Rue Manuel period)
ca. 1954-1962
Monochrome blue ballpoint
pen drawing, on paper.
30 x 21 cm
Artist's collection

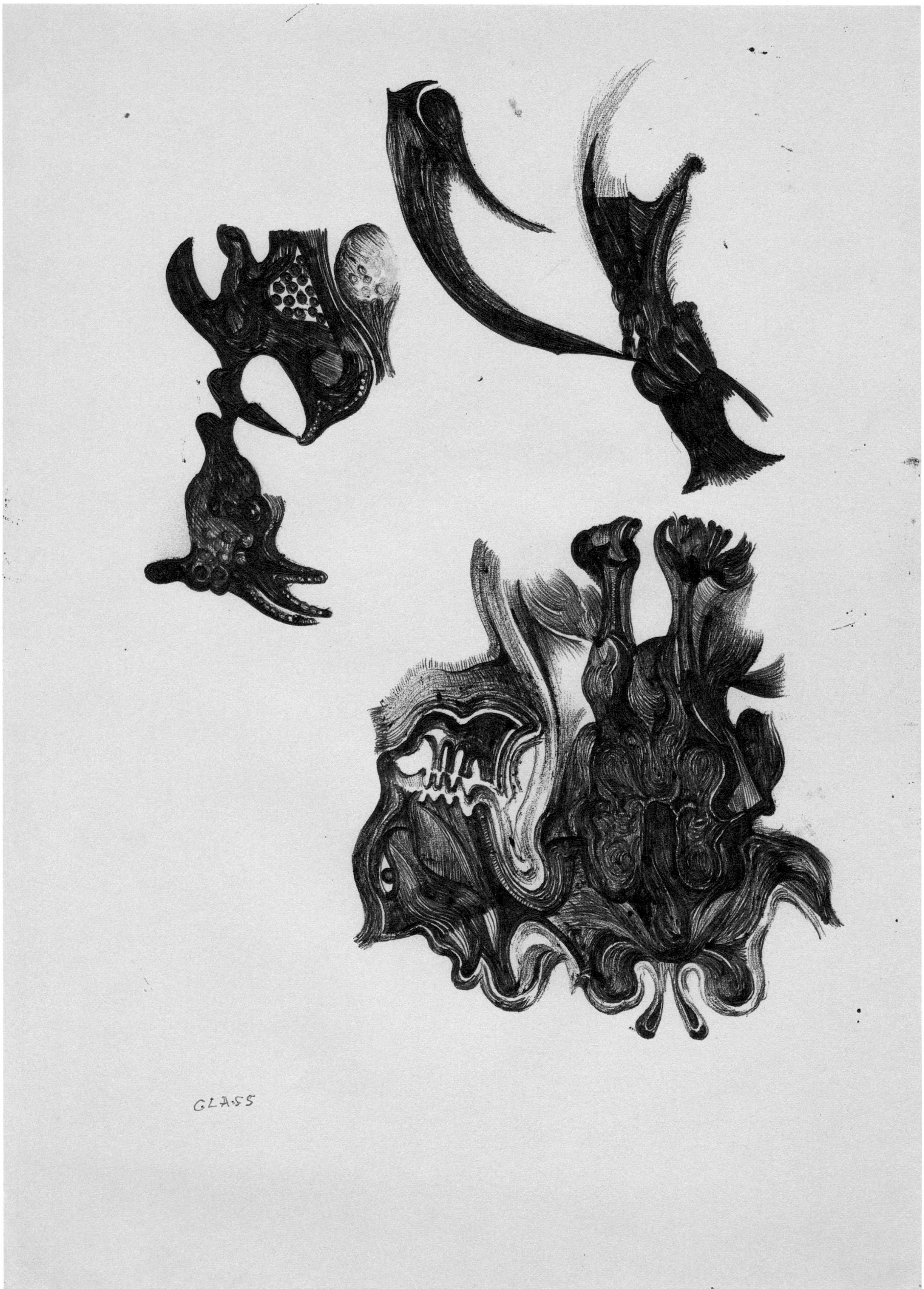

Untitled
(Rue Manuel period)
ca. 1954-1962
Monochrome blue ballpoint pen drawing, on paper.
30 x 21 cm
Artist's collection

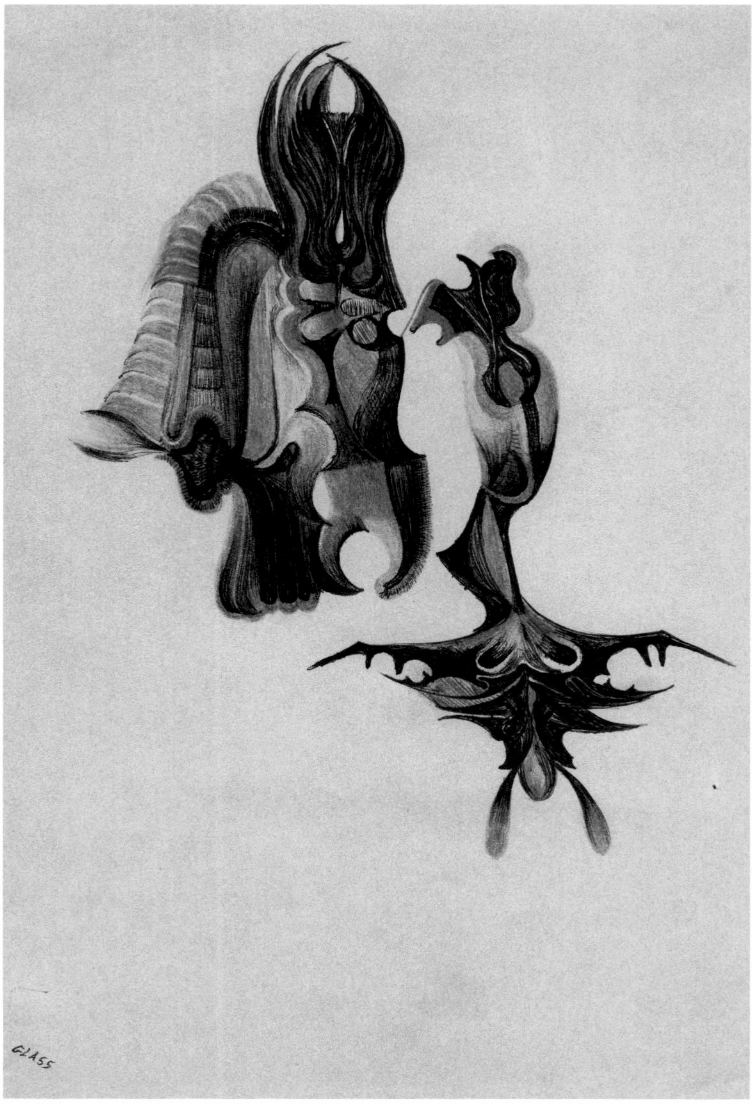

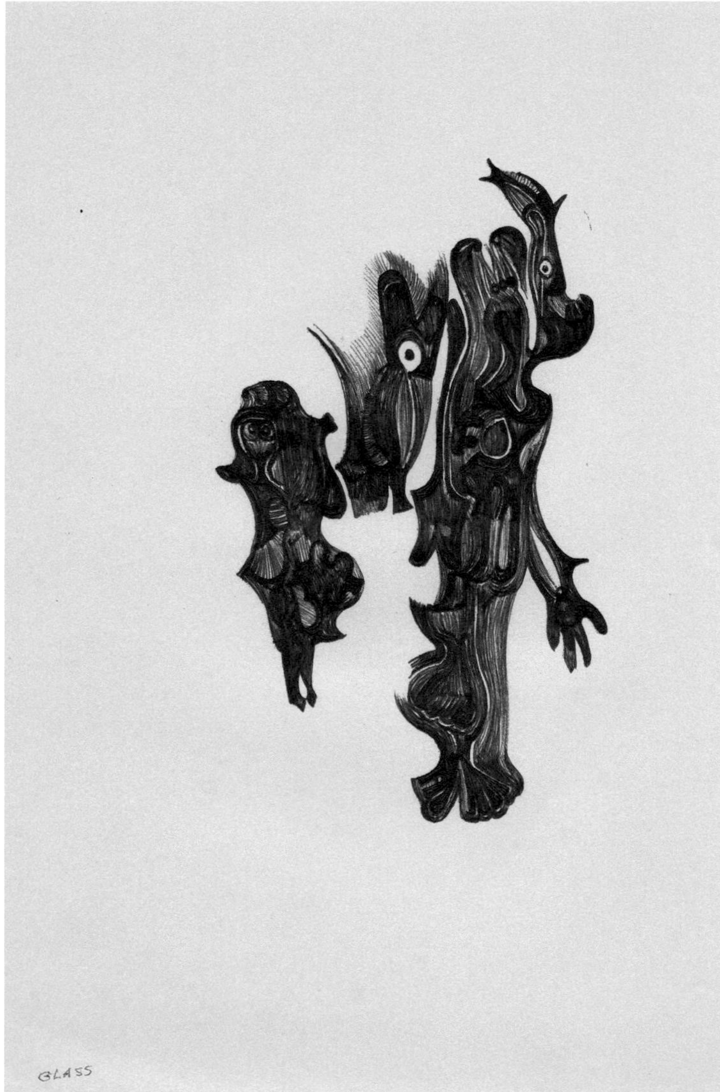

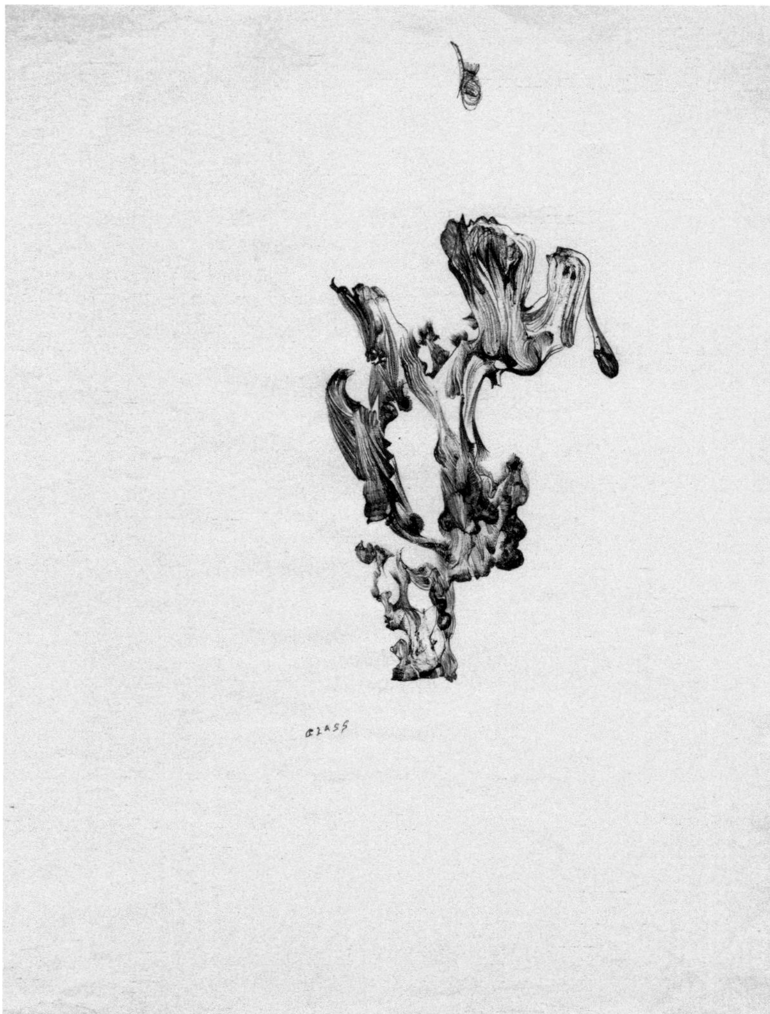

Untitled
(Rue Manuel period)
ca. 1954-1962
Bicolor blue and black
ballpoint pen drawing, on paper.
27 x 19 cm
Artist's collection

Untitled
(Rue Manuel period)
ca. 1954-1962
Monochrome blue ballpoint
pen drawing, on paper.
30 x 21 cm
Artist's collection

Untitled
(Rue Manuel period)
ca. 1954-1962
Monochrome black ballpoint
pen drawing, on paper.
28 x 22.5 cm
Artist's collection

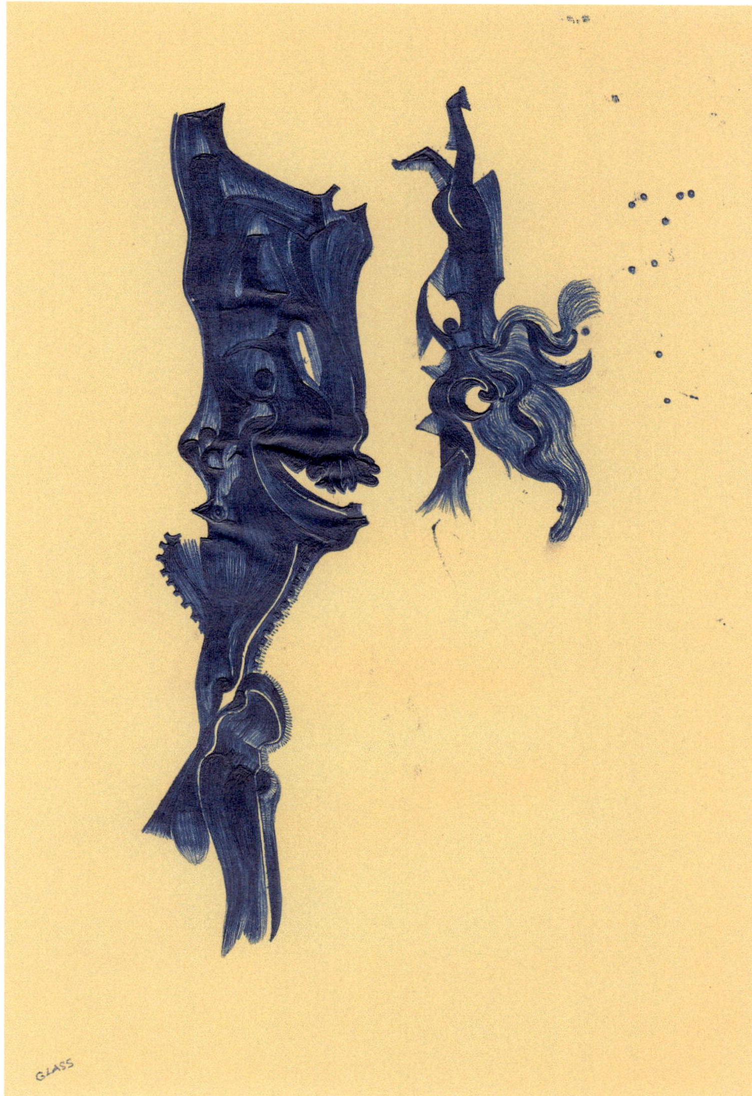

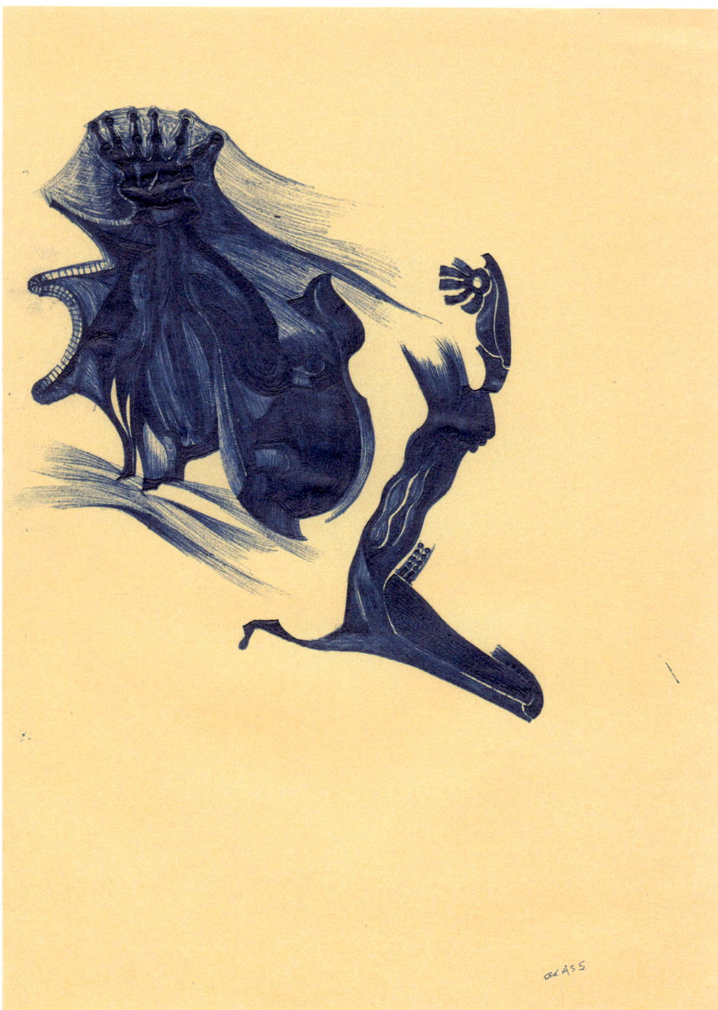

Untitled
(Rue Manuel period)
ca. 1954-1962
Monochrome blue ballpoint pen drawing, on paper.
30 x 21 cm
Artist's collection

Untitled
(Rue Manuel period)
ca. 1954-1962
Monochrome blue ballpoint pen drawing, on paper.
30 x 21 cm
Artist's collection

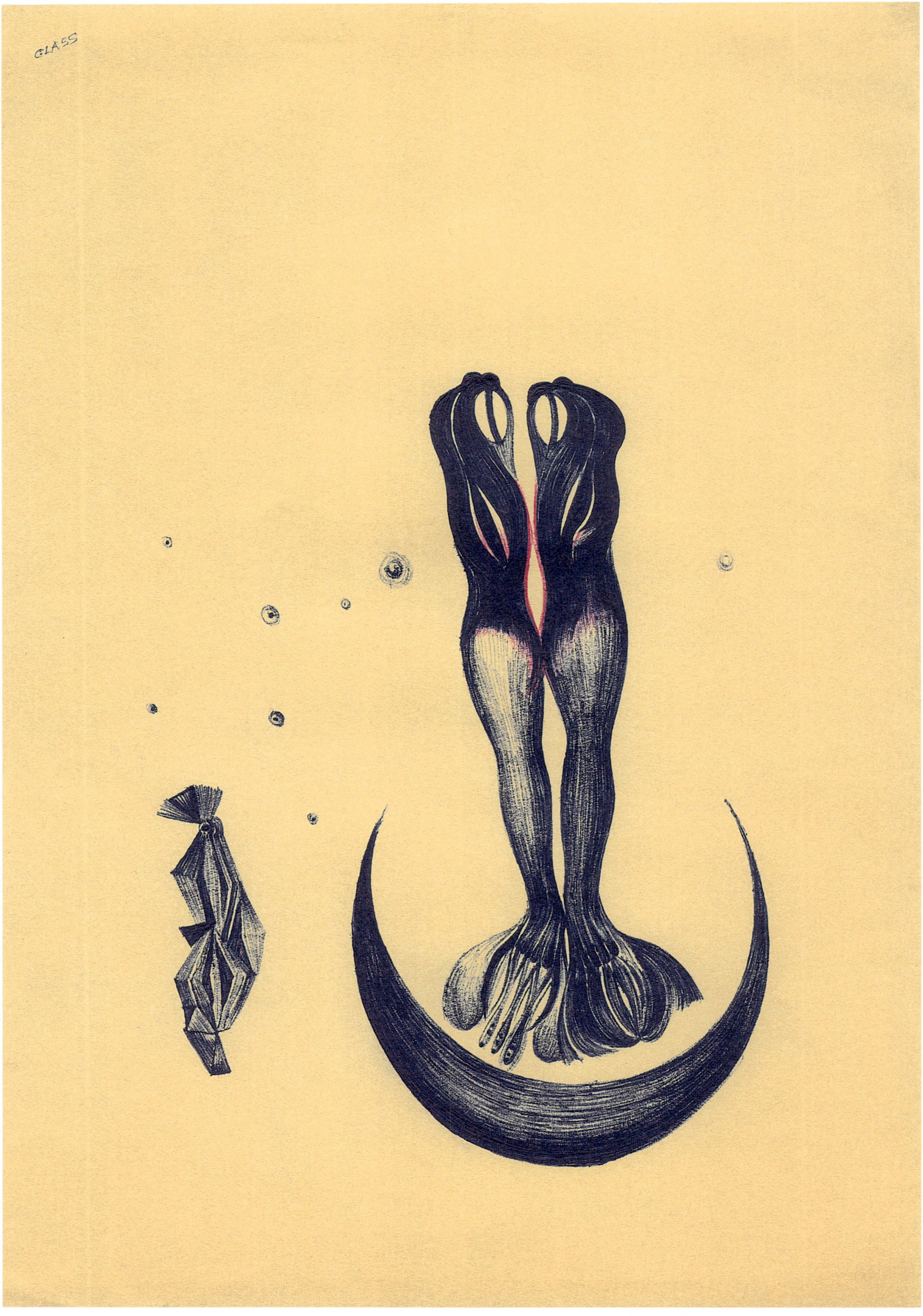

Untitled
(Rue Manuel period)
ca. 1954-1962
Bicolor blue and red ballpoint
pen drawing, on paper.
30 x 21 cm
Artist's collection

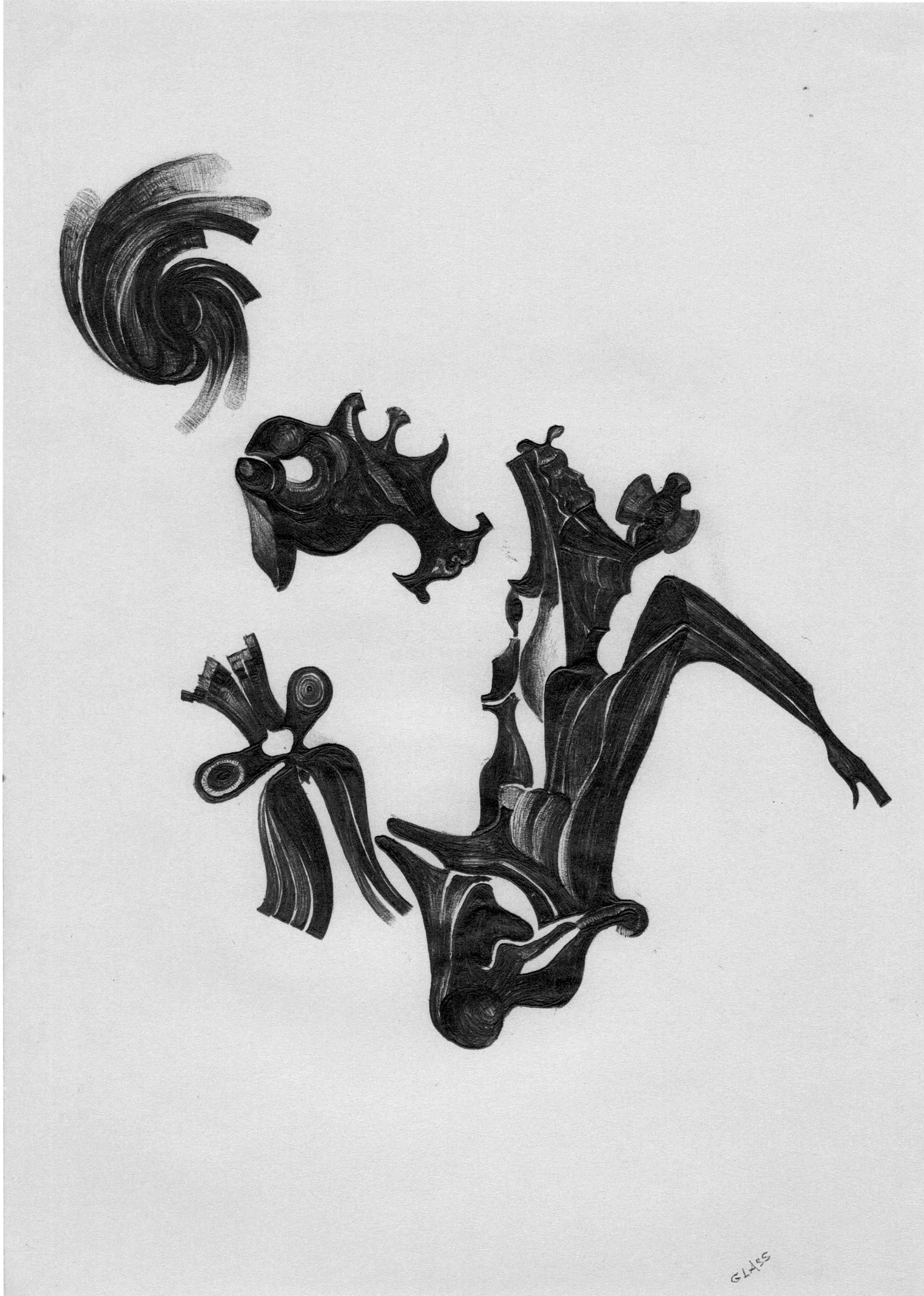

Untitled
(Rue Manuel period)
ca. 1954-1962
Monochrome blue ballpoint
pen drawing, on paper.
30 x 21 cm
Artist's collection

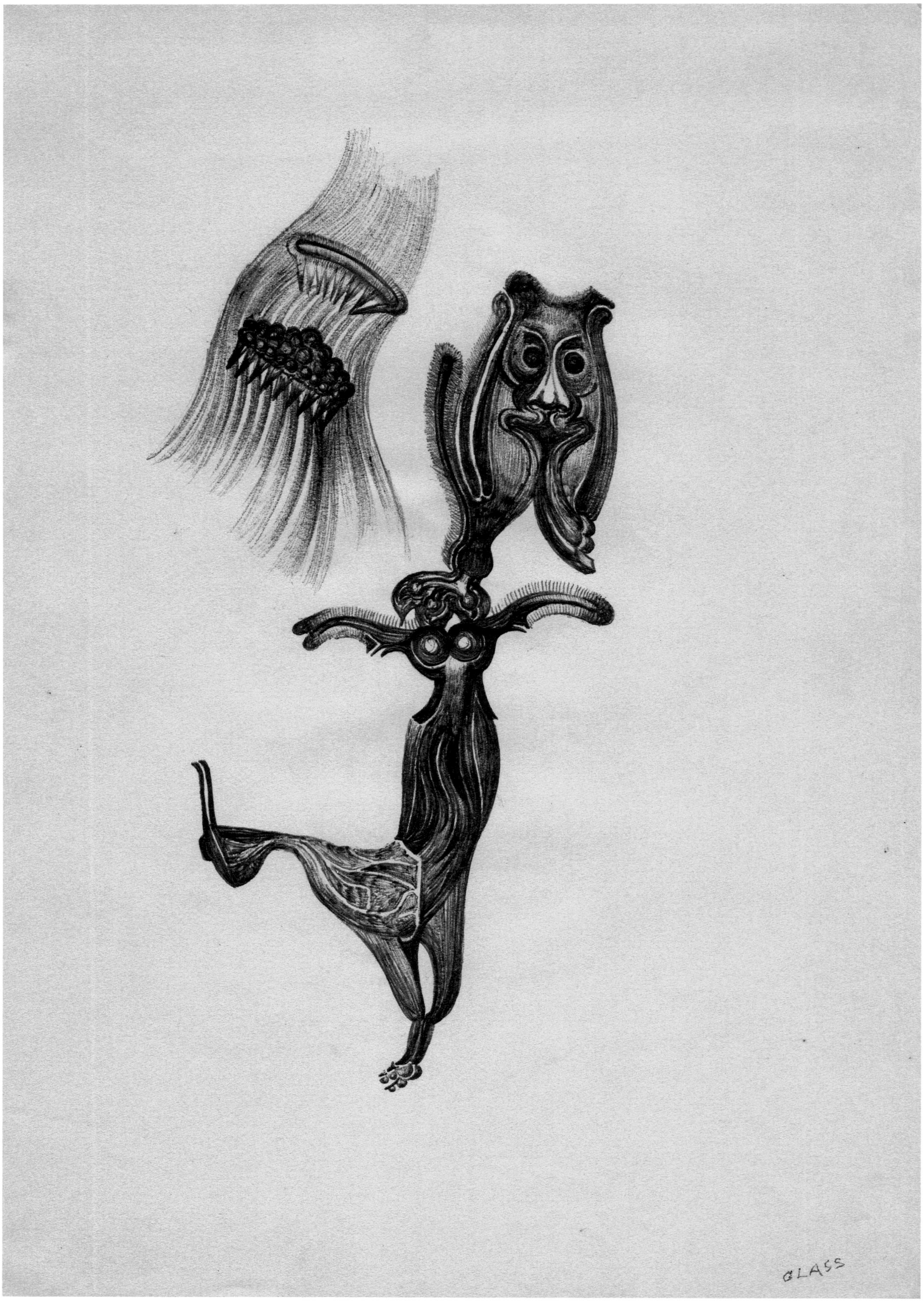

Untitled
(Rue Manuel period)
ca. 1954-1962
Monochrome blue ballpoint
pen drawing on paper.
30 x 21 cm
Artist's collection

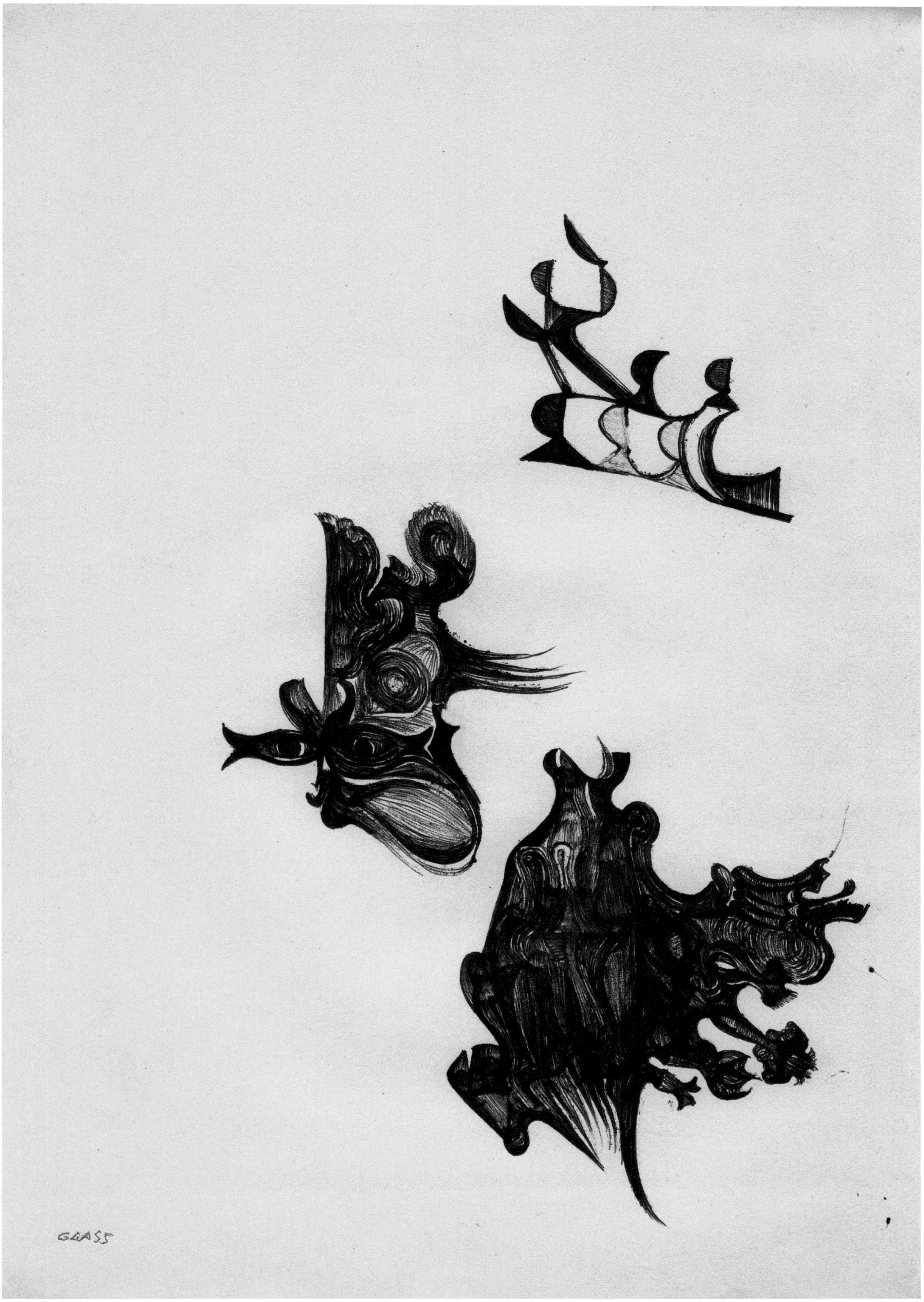

Untitled
(Rue Manuel period)
ca. 1954-1962
Monochrome blue ballpoint pen drawing, on paper.
30 x 21 cm
Artist's collection

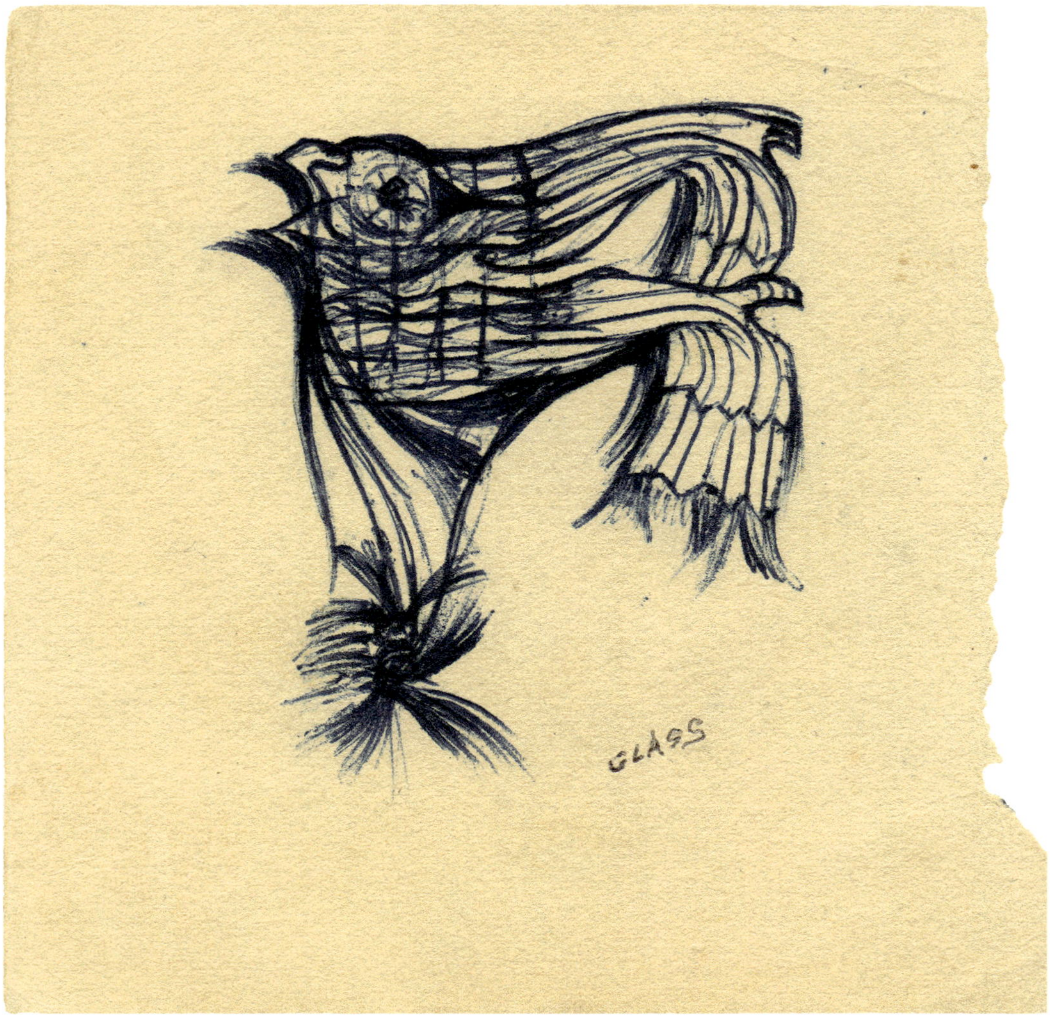

Untitled
(Rue Manuel period)
ca. 1954-1962
Monochrome blue
ballpoint pen drawing,
on advertising paper.
12.5 x 12 cm
Artist's collection

Untitled
(Rue Manuel period)
ca. 1954-1962
Monochrome black ballpoint
pen drawing on paper.
28 x 22.5 cm
Artist's collection
Following page

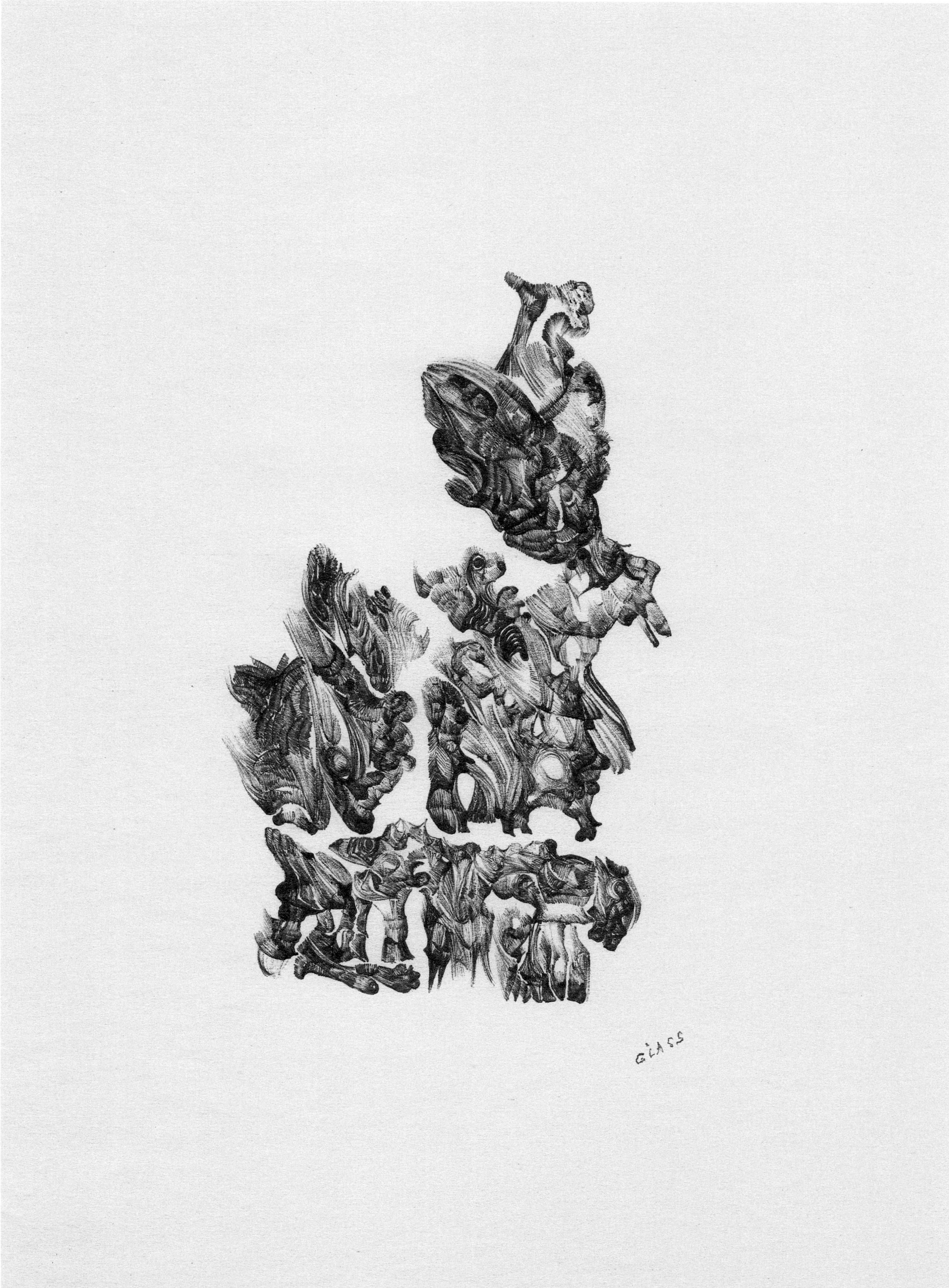
GLASS

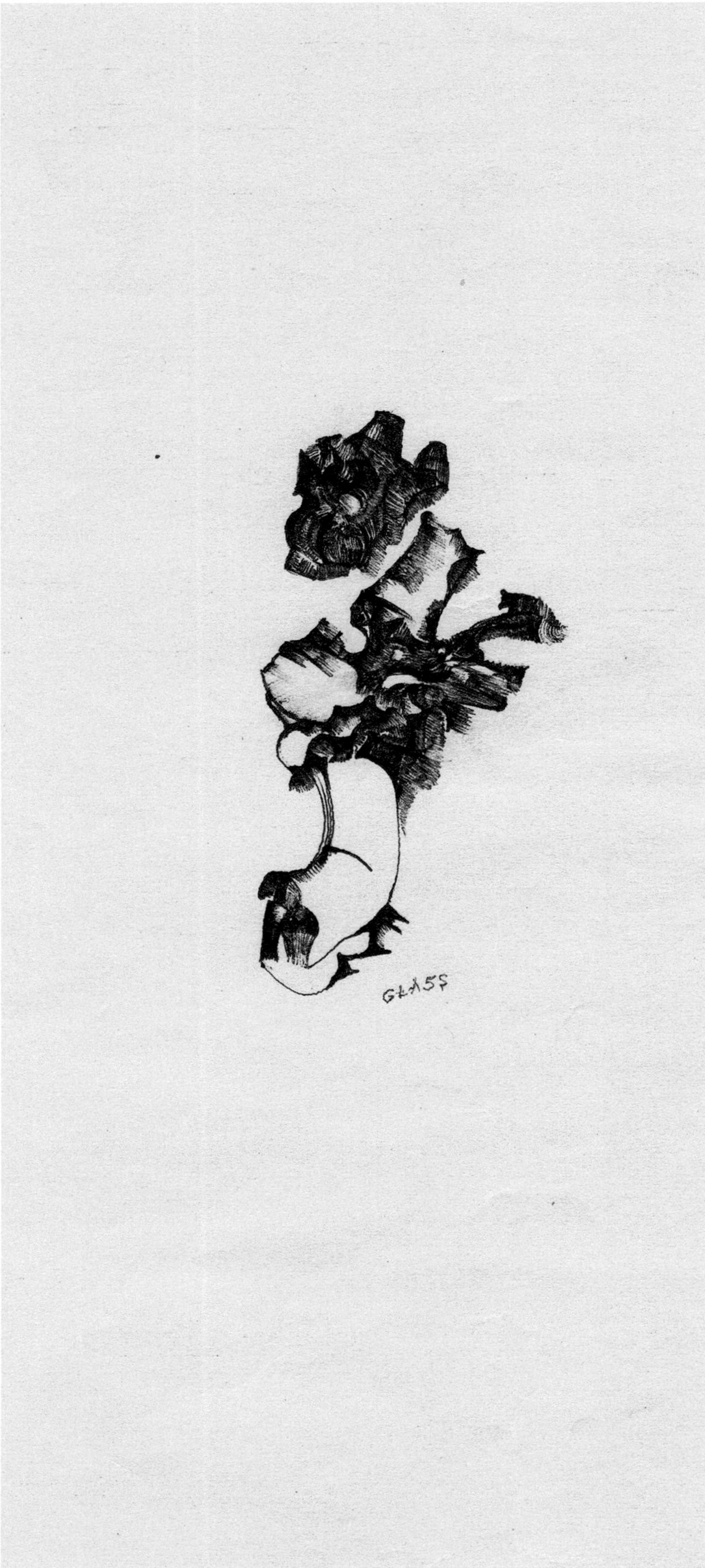

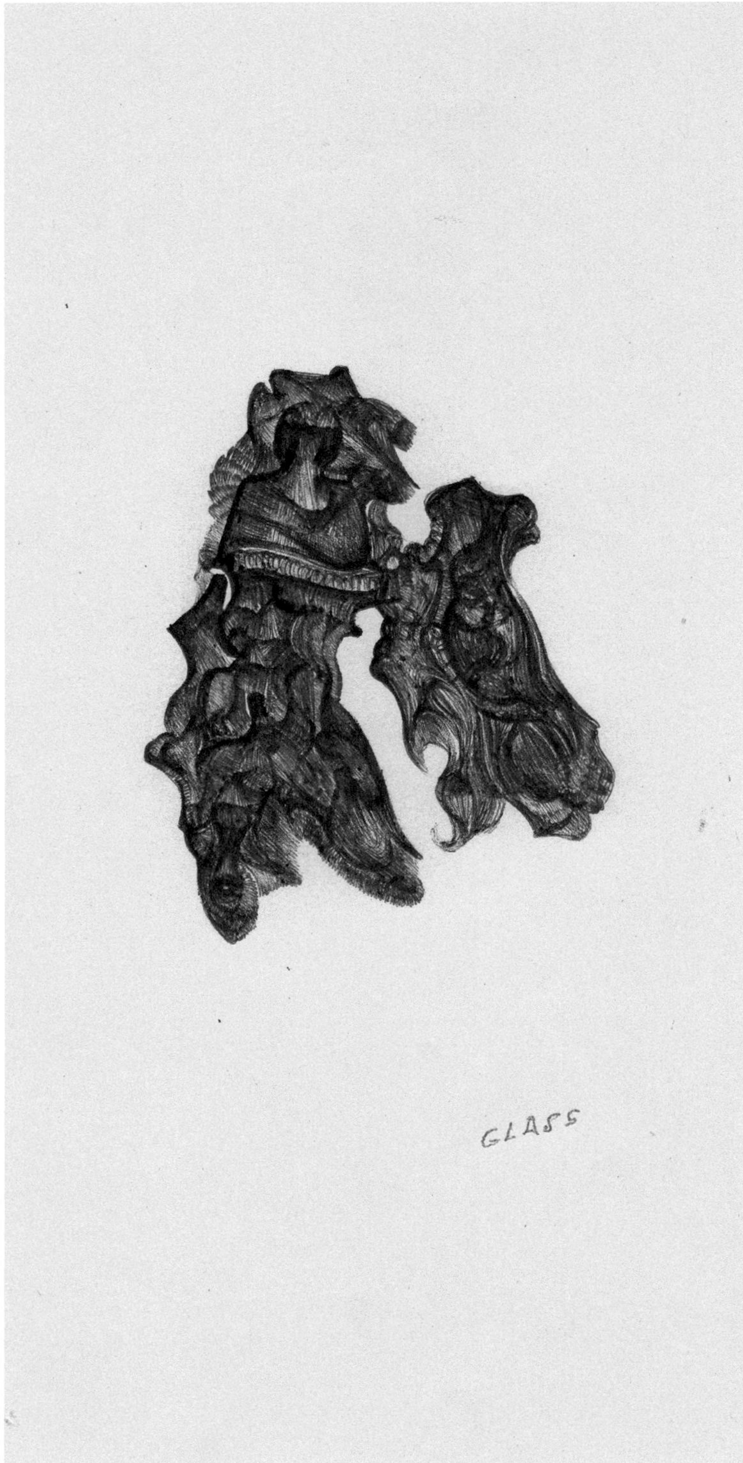

Untitled
(Rue Manuel period)
ca. 1954-1962
Monochrome black ballpoint
pen drawing, on paper.
28 x 22.5 cm
Artist's collection

Untitled
(Rue Manuel period)
ca. 1954-1962
Monochrome blue ballpoint
pen drawing, on paper.
22 x 13.5 cm
Artist's collection

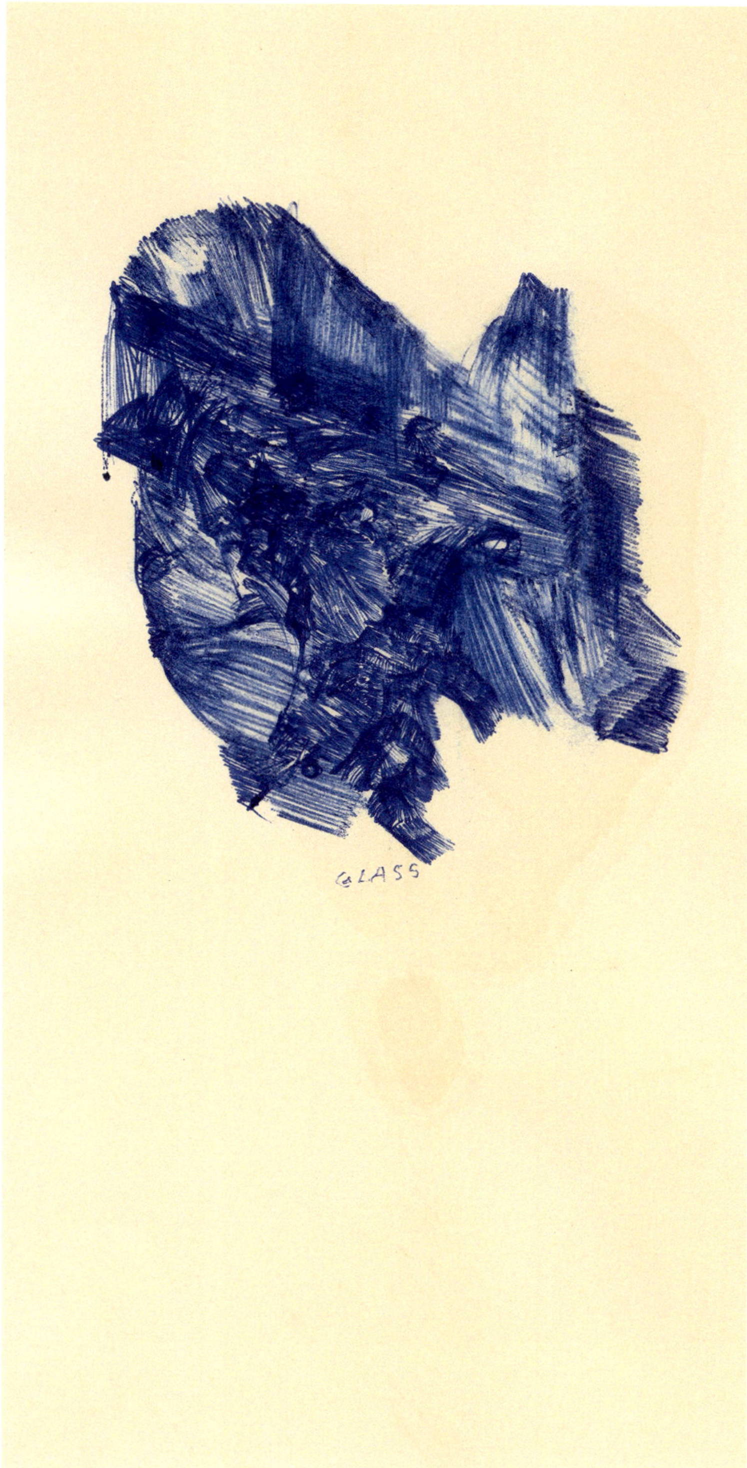

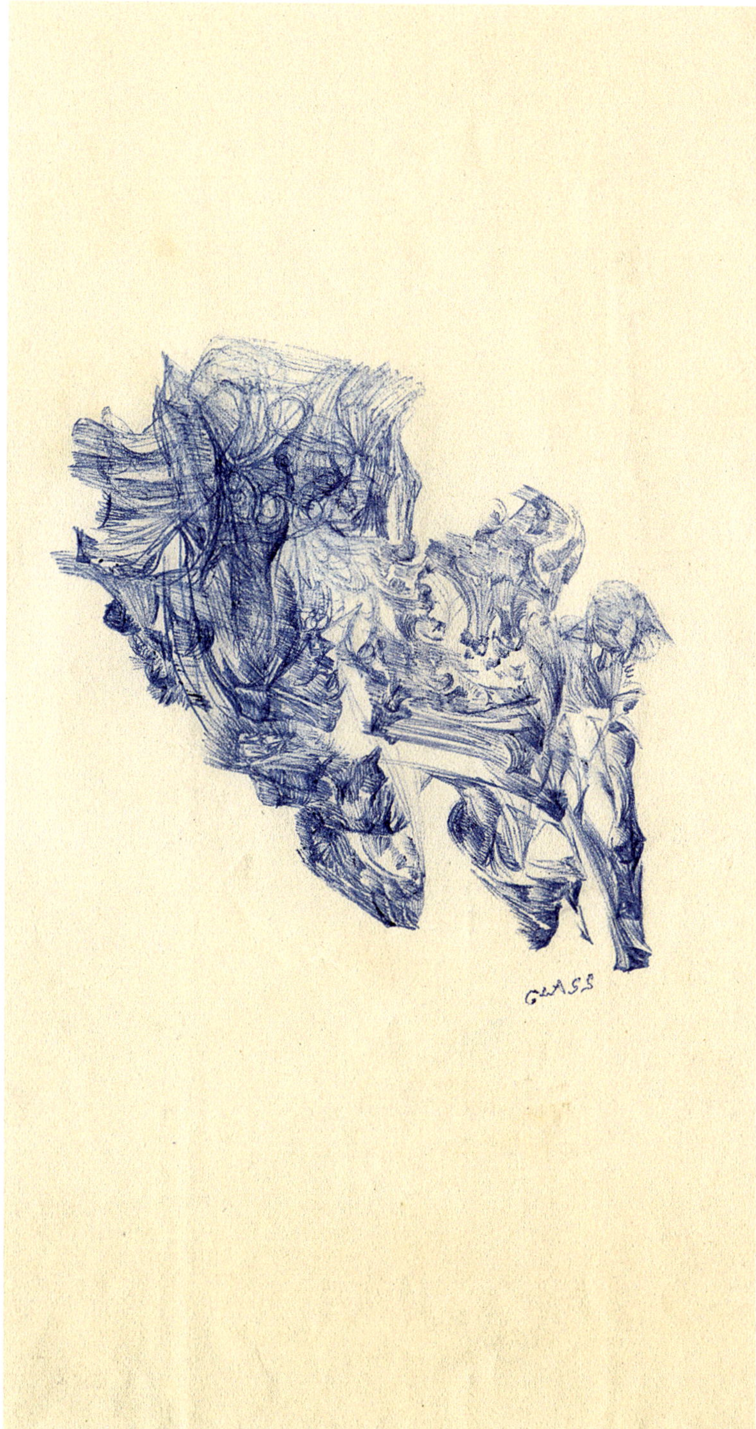

Untitled
(Rue Manuel period)
ca. 1954-1962
Monochrome blue ballpoint pen drawing, on paper.
32 x 25 cm
Artist's collection

Untitled
(Rue Manuel period)
ca. 1954-1962
Monochrome blue ballpoint pen drawing, on paper.
21 x 27 cm
Artist's collection

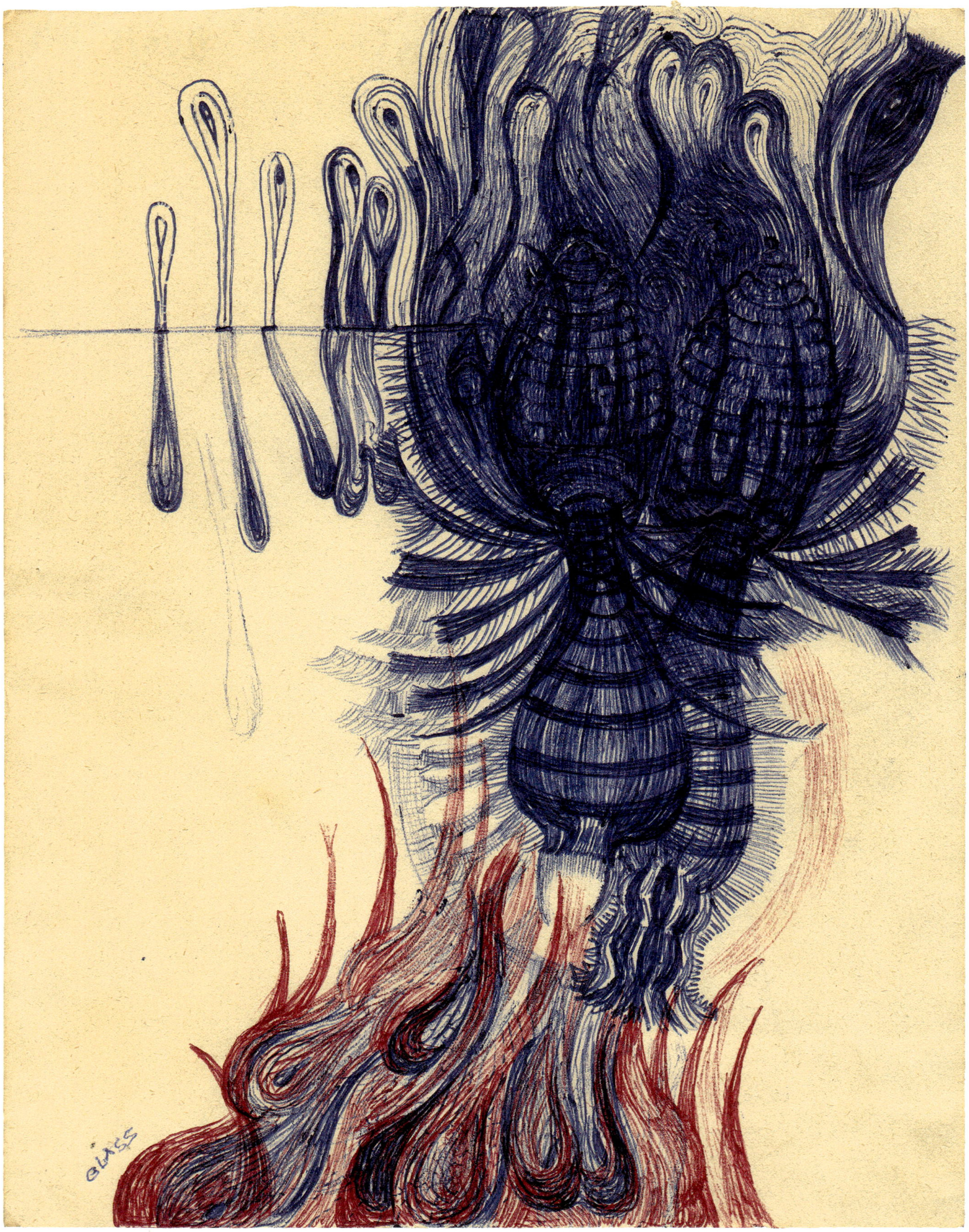

Untitled
(Rue Manuel period)
ca. 1954-1962
Bicolor blue and red ballpoint
pen drawing on paper.
21.5 x 17 cm
Artist's collection

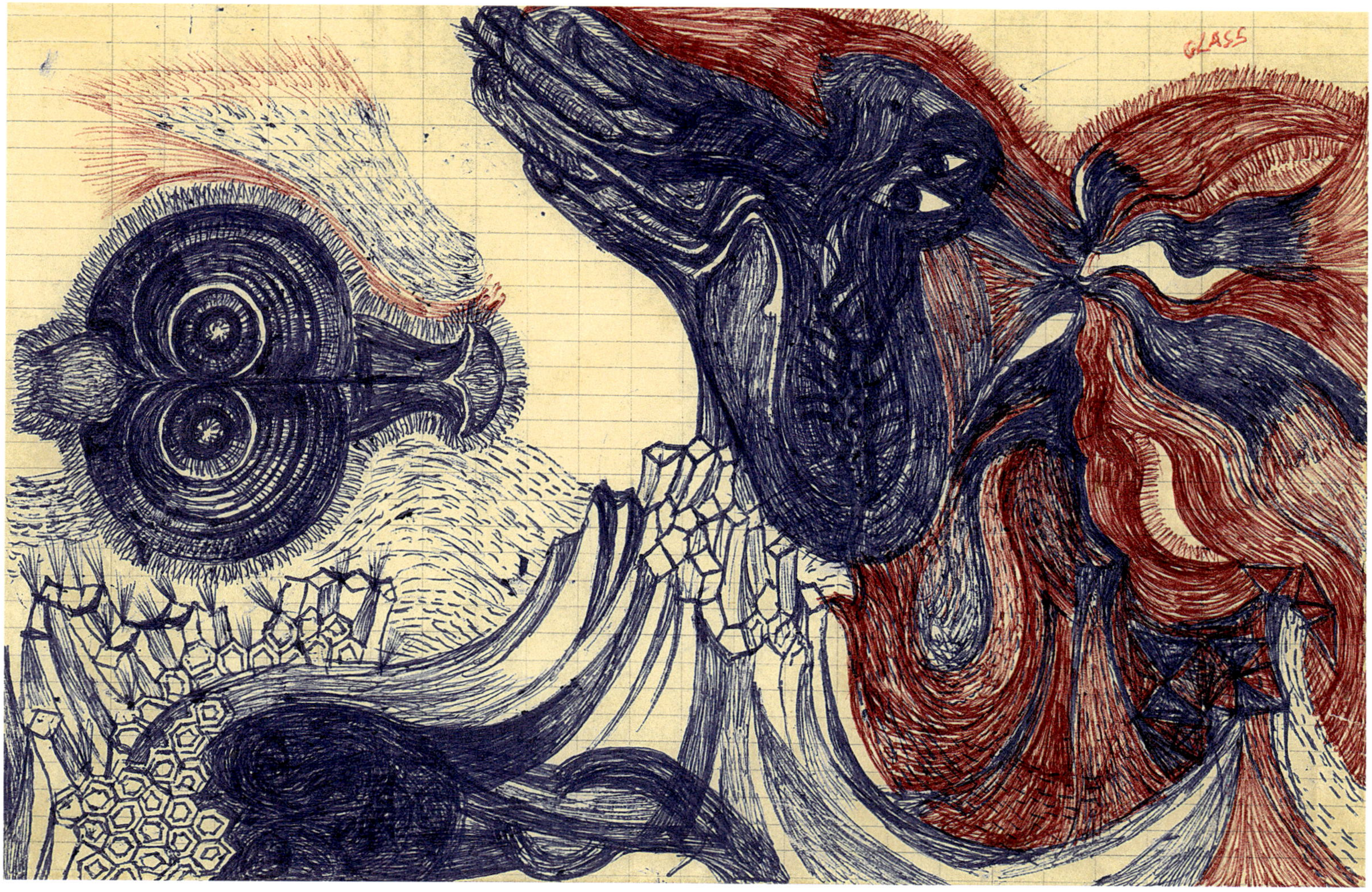

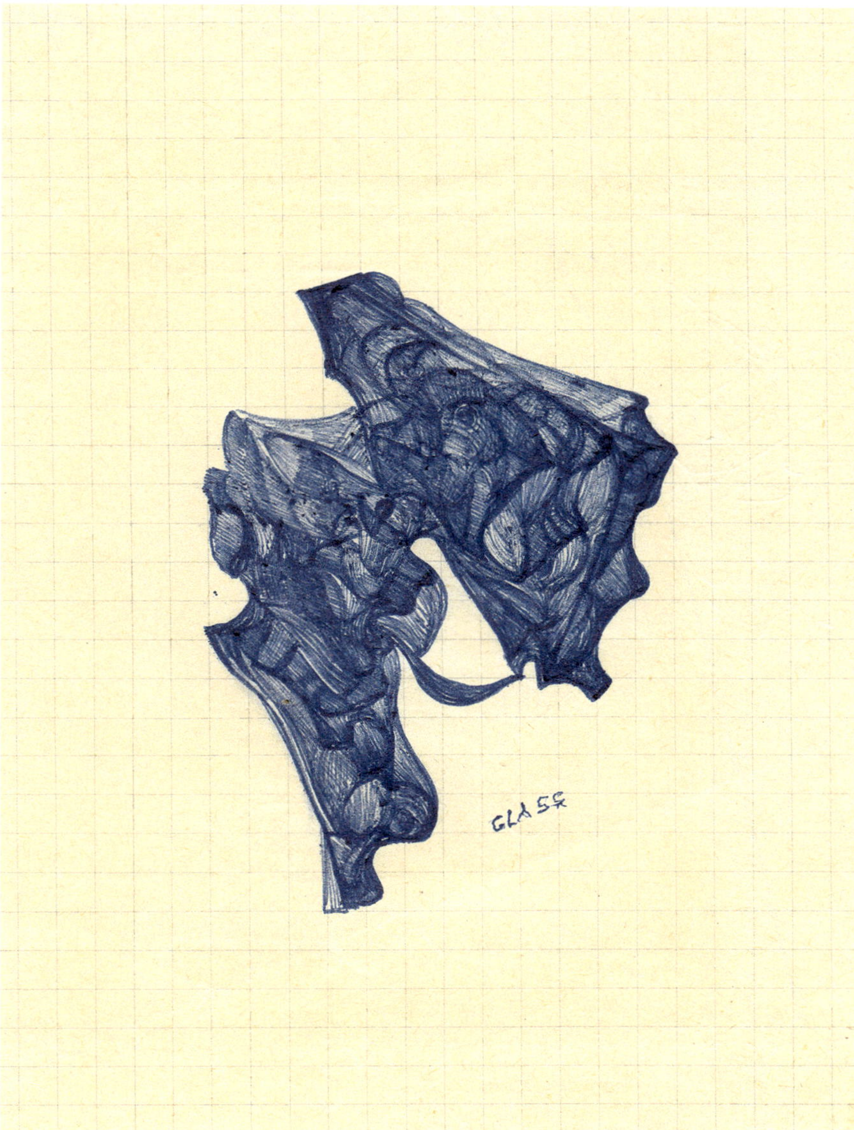

Untitled
(Rue Manuel period)
ca. 1954-1962
Bicolor blue and red ballpoint pen drawing on paper.
13.5 x 20.5 cm
Artist's collection

Untitled
(Rue Manuel period)
ca. 1954-1962
Monochrome blue ballpoint pen drawing, on paper.
19 x 13 cm
Artist's collection

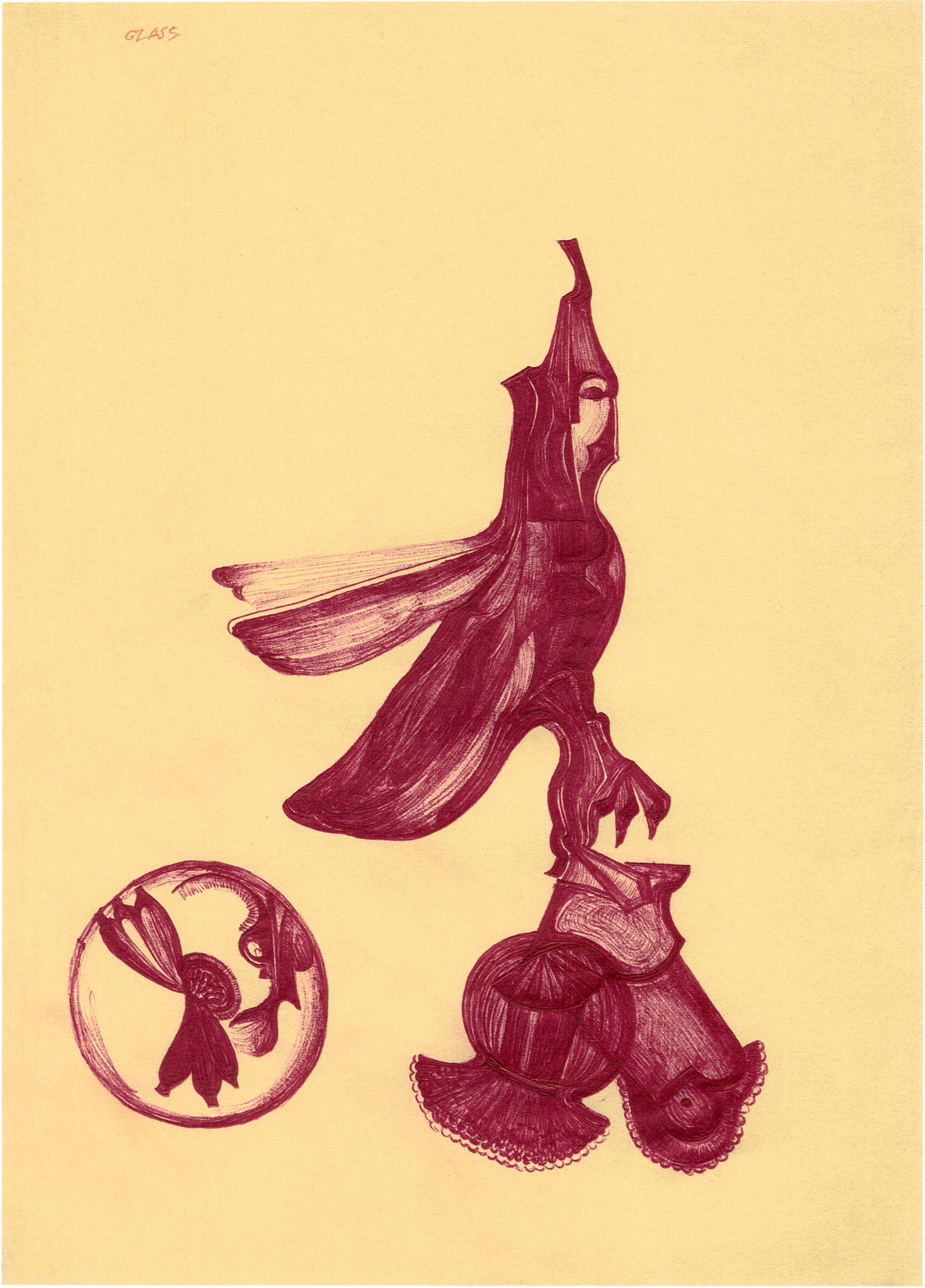

Untitled
(Rue Manuel period)
ca. 1954-1962
Monochrome red ballpoint pen
drawing, on paper.
30 x 21 cm
Artist's collection

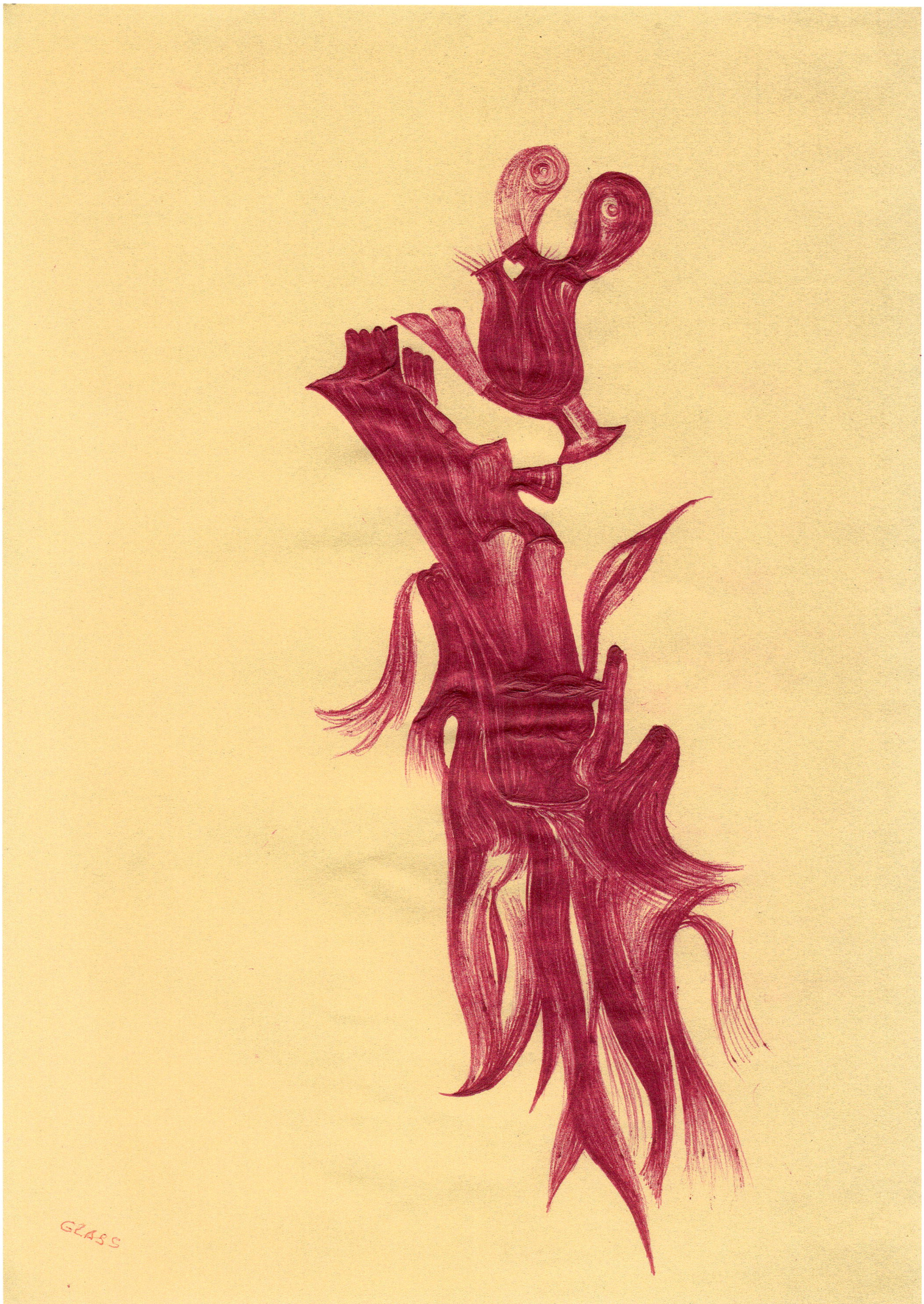

Untitled
(Rue Manuel period)
ca. 1954-1962
Monochrome red ballpoint pen drawing, on paper.
30 x 21 cm
Artist's collection

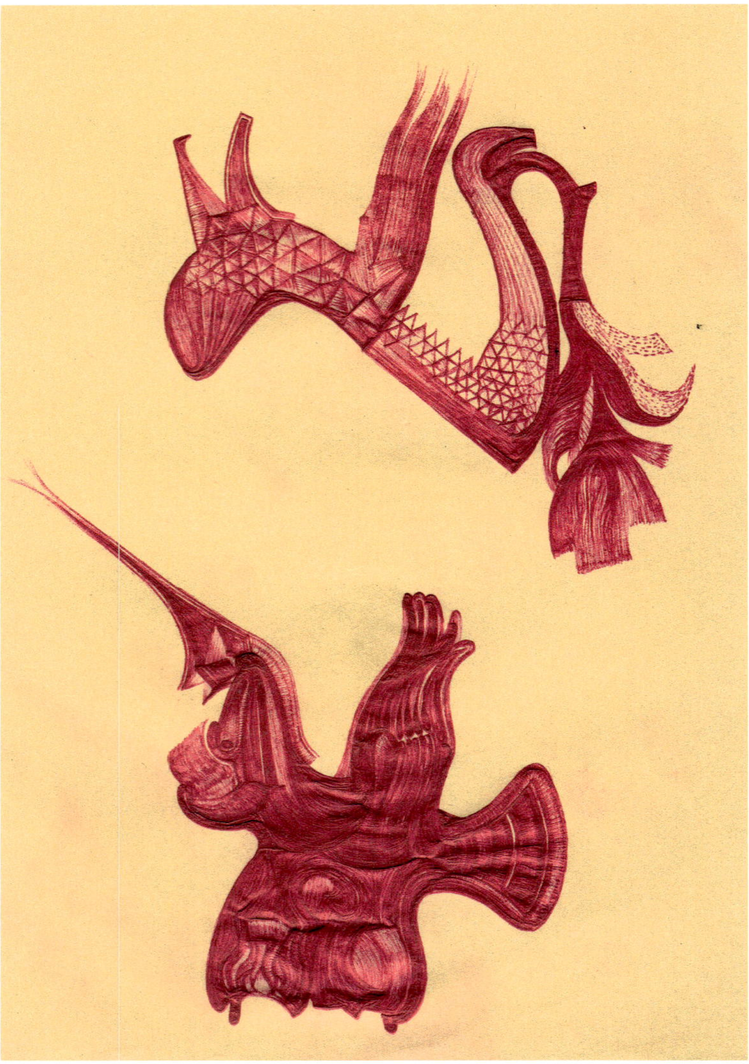

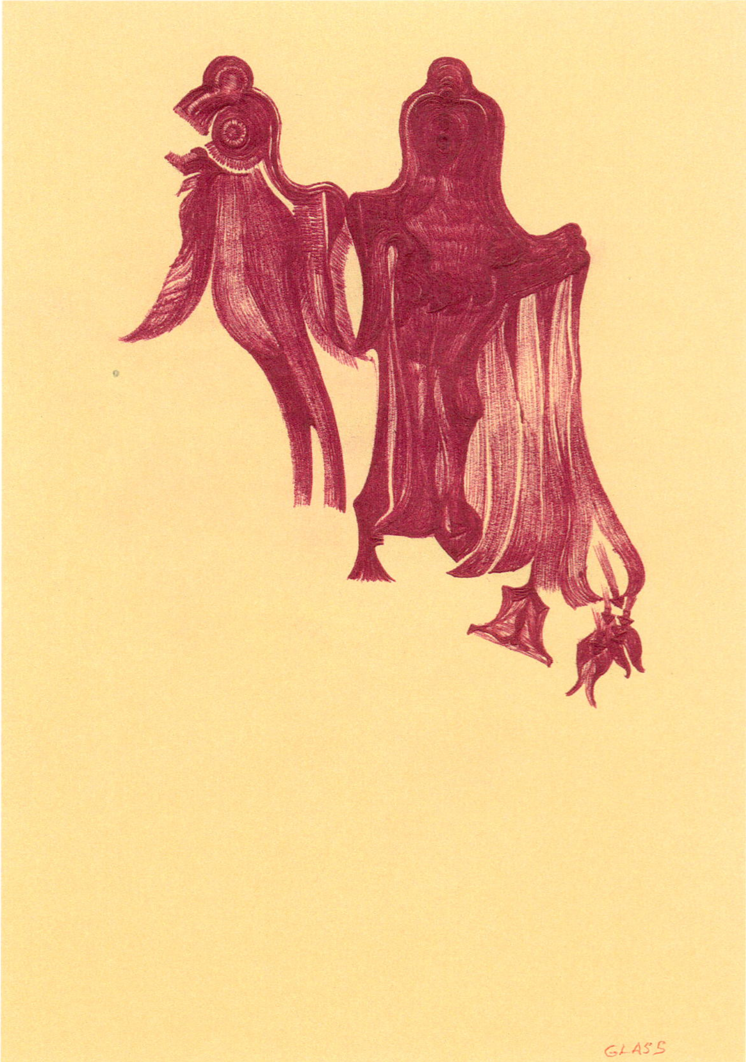

Untitled
(Rue Manuel period)
ca. 1954-1962
Monochrome red ballpoint
pen drawing, on paper.
30 x 21 cm
Artist's collection

Untitled
(Rue Manuel period)
ca. 1954-1962
Monochrome red ballpoint
pen drawing, on paper.
30 x 21 cm
Artist's collection

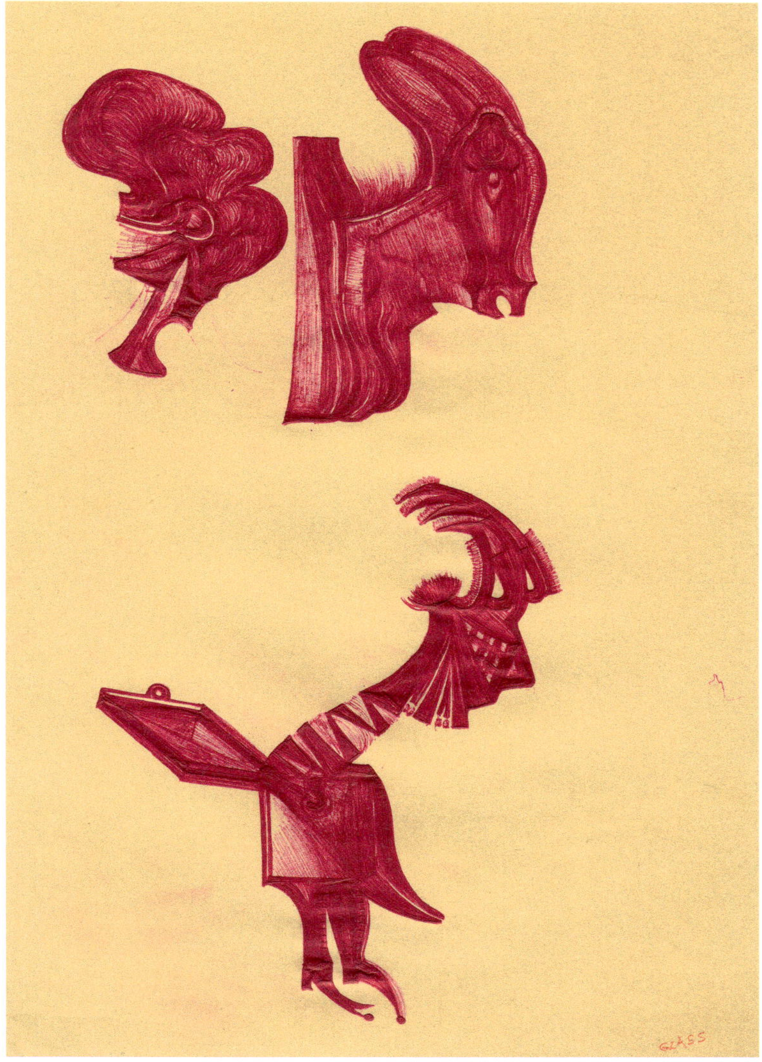

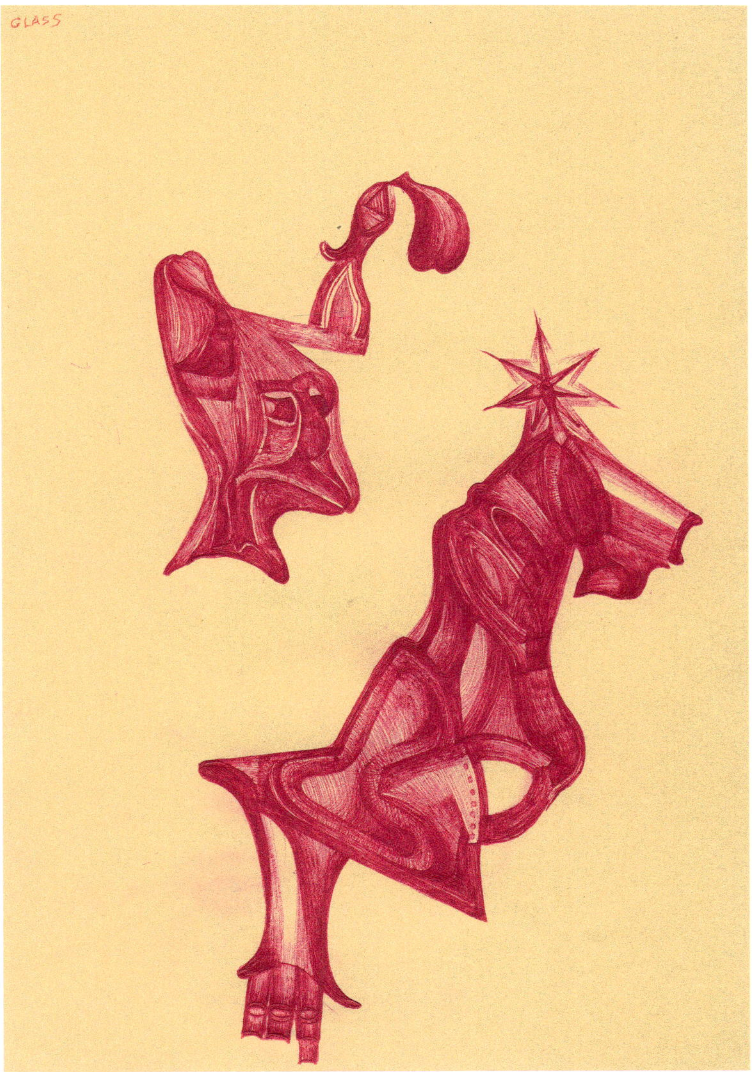

Untitled
(Rue Manuel period)
ca. 1954-1962
Monochrome red ballpoint pen drawing, on paper.
30 x 21 cm
Artist's collection

Untitled
(Rue Manuel period)
ca. 1954-1962
Monochrome red ballpoint pen drawing, on paper.
30 x 21 cm
Artist's collection

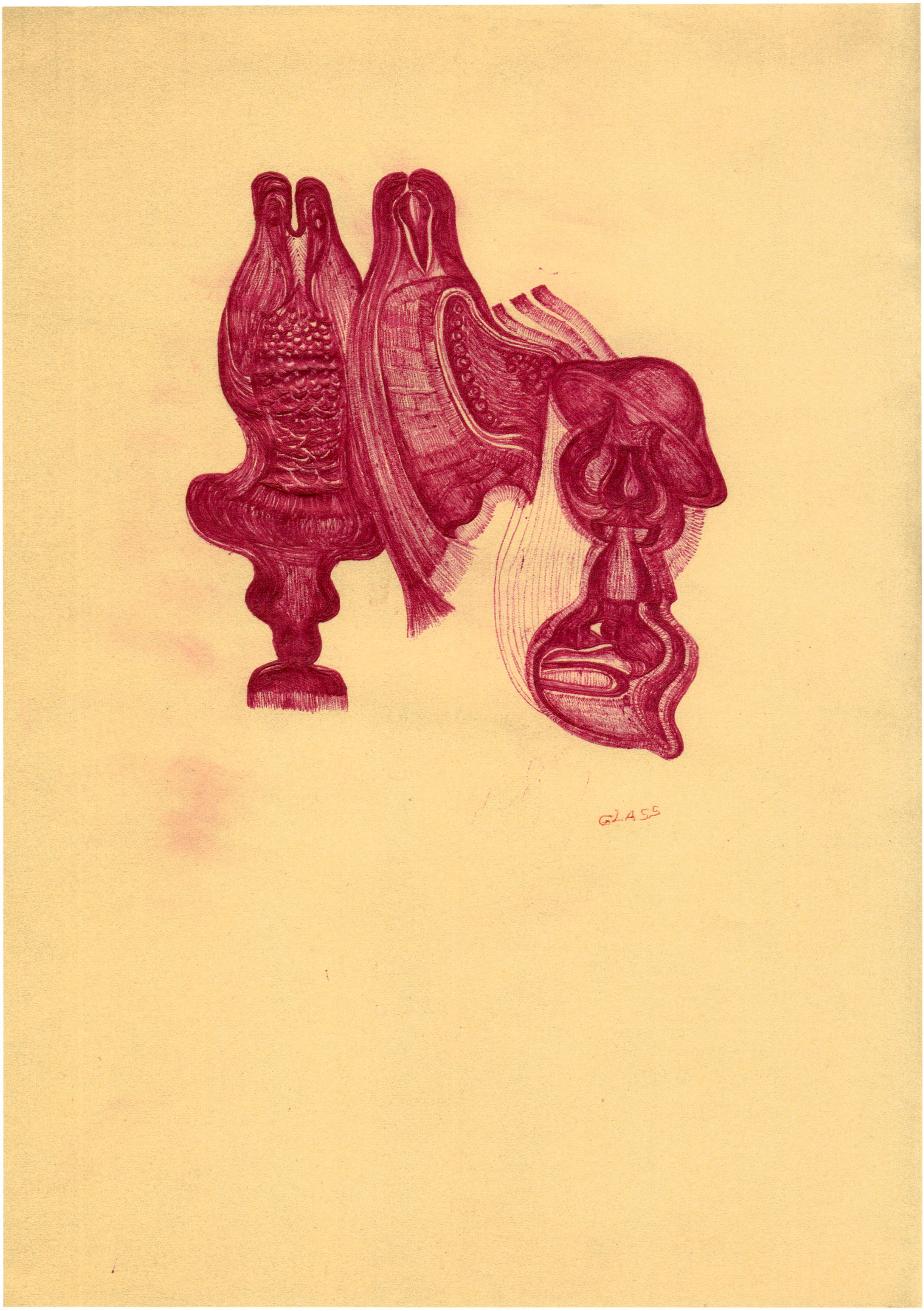

Untitled
(Rue Manuel period)
ca. 1954-1962
Monochrome red ballpoint pen
drawing, on paper.
30 x 21 cm
Artist's collection

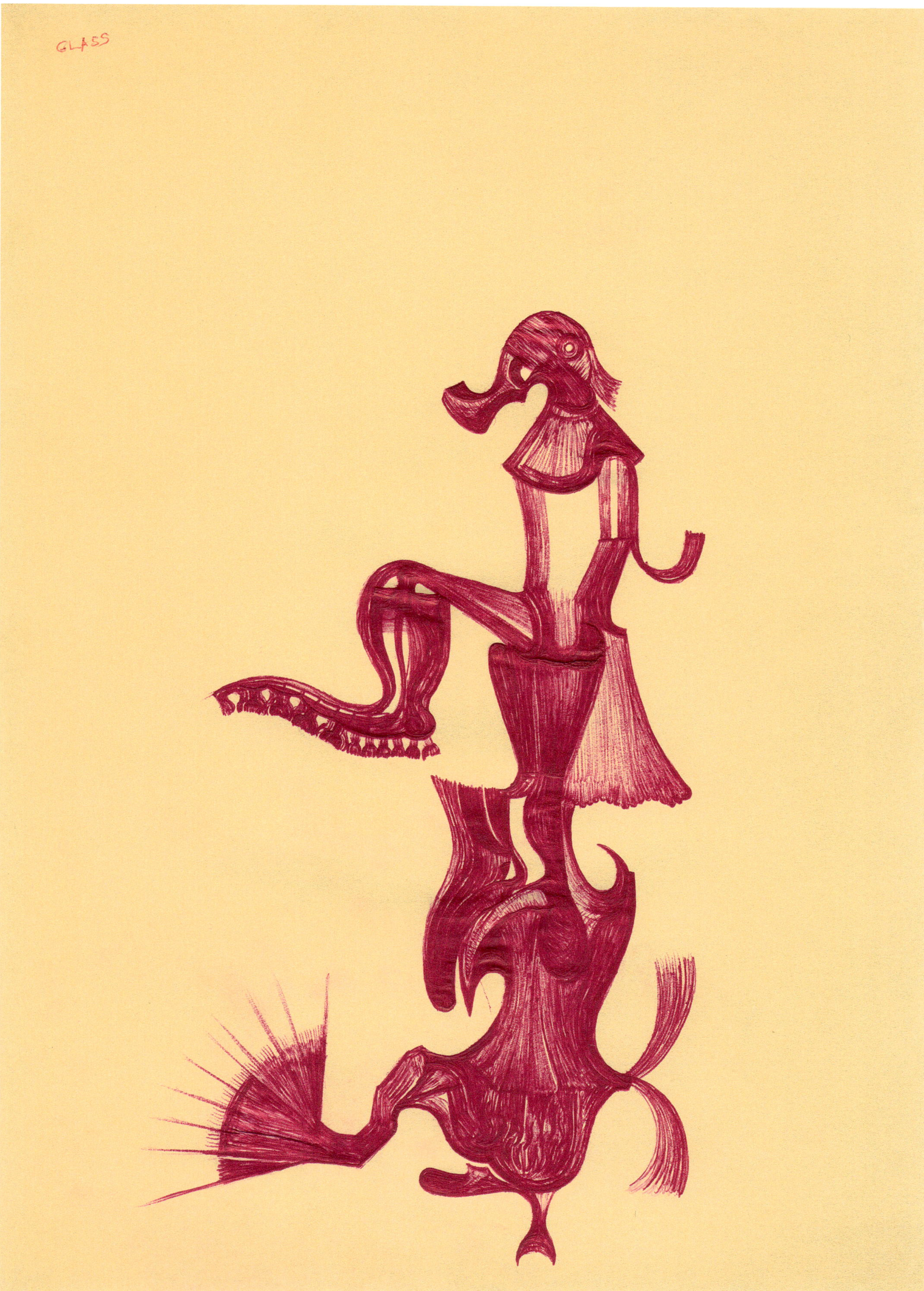

Untitled
(Rue Manuel period)
ca. 1954-1962
Monochrome red ballpoint pen drawing, on paper.
30 x 21 cm
Artist's collection

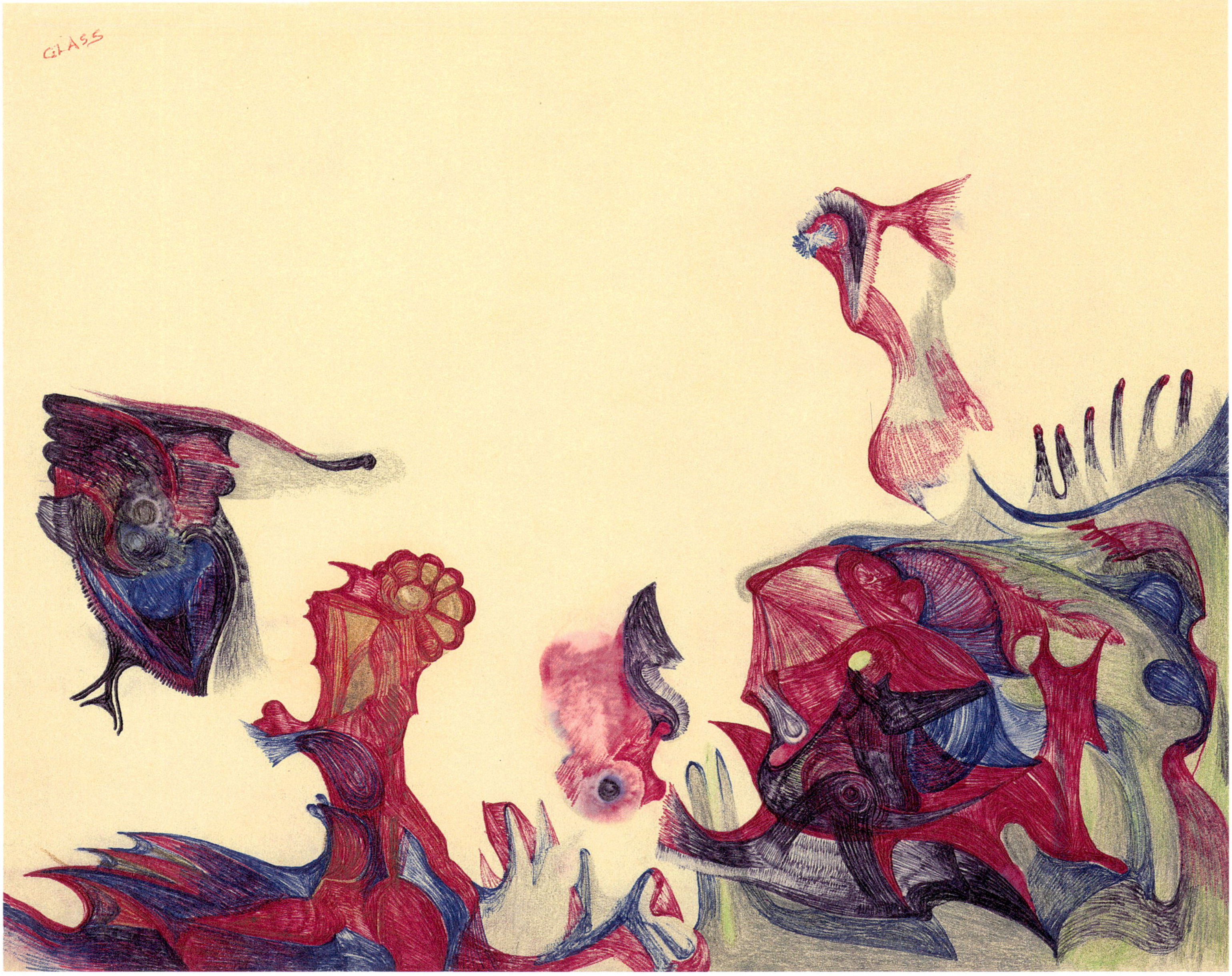

Untitled
(Rue Manuel period)
ca. 1954-1962
Blue pen drawing, graphite,
green and brown colors,
on paper.
21 x 27 cm
Artist's collection

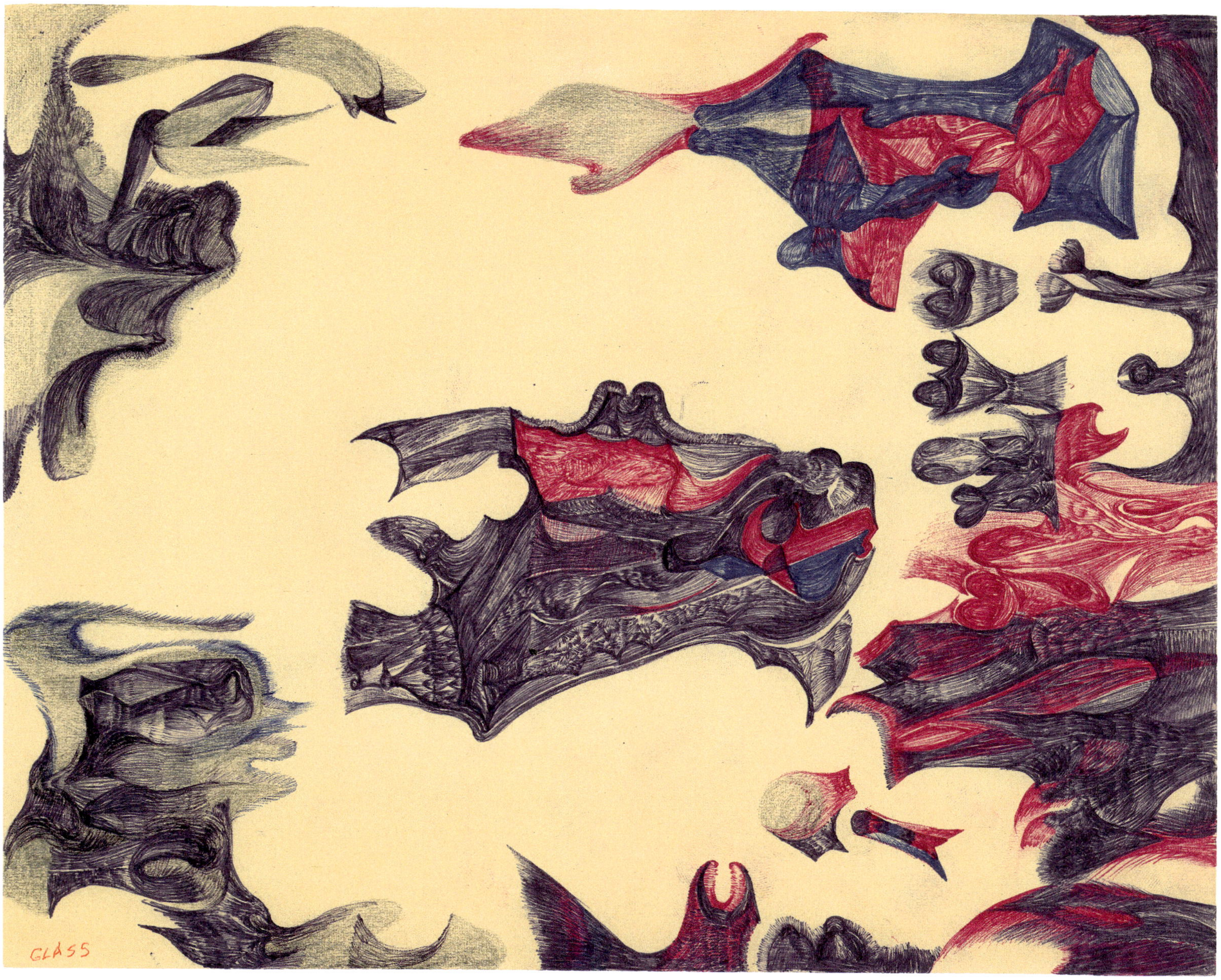

Untitled
(Rue Manuel period)
ca. 1954-1962
Blue, navy blue, and red pen
drawing with graphite,
on paper.
21 x 27 cm
Artist's collection

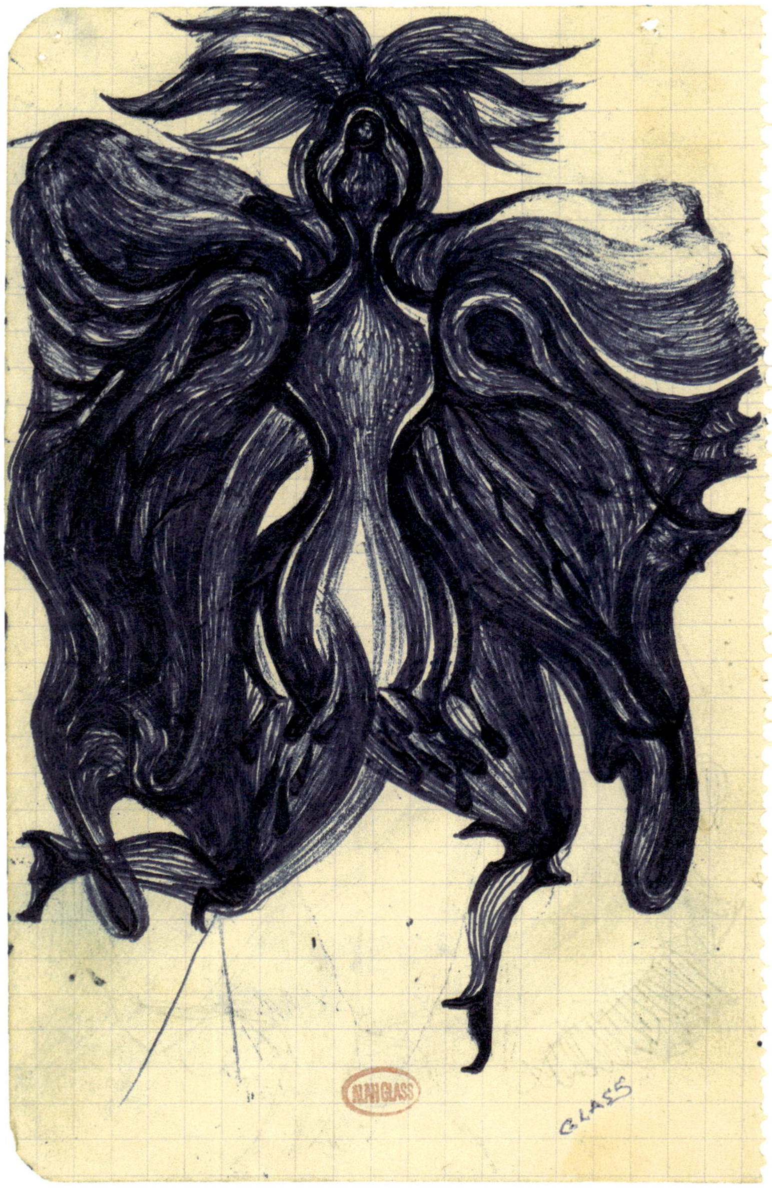

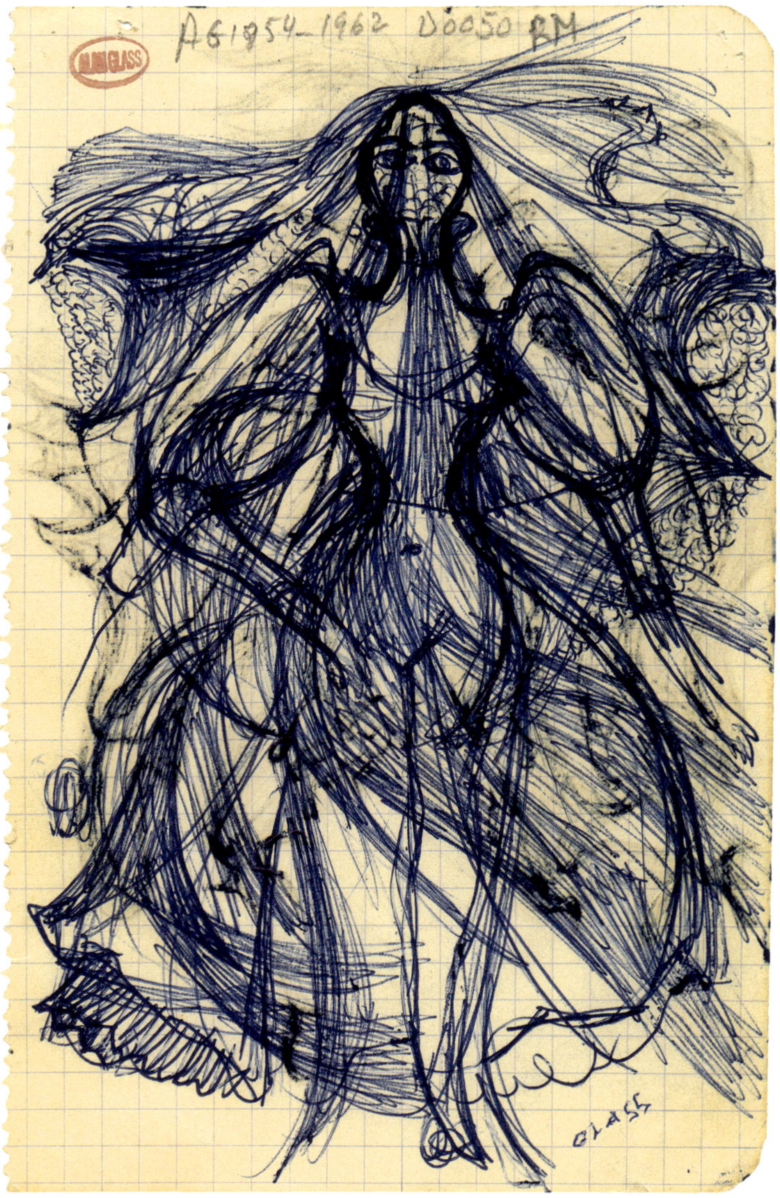

Untitled
(Rue Manuel period)
ca. 1954-1962
Monochrome blue ballpoint
pen drawing, on both sides,
on squared paper.
17 x 10.5 cm
Artist's collection

Untitled
(Rue Manuel period)
ca. 1954-1962
Monochrome blue ballpoint
pen drawing, on squared paper.
17 x 10.5 cm
Artist's collection

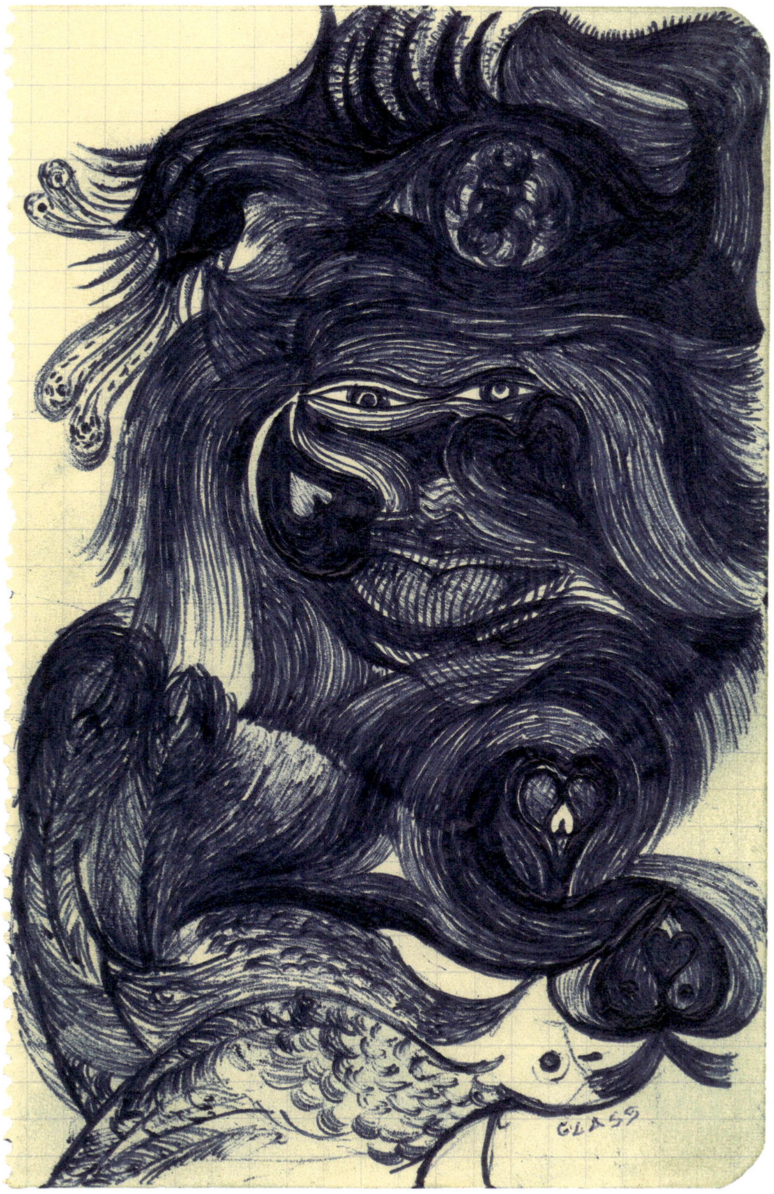

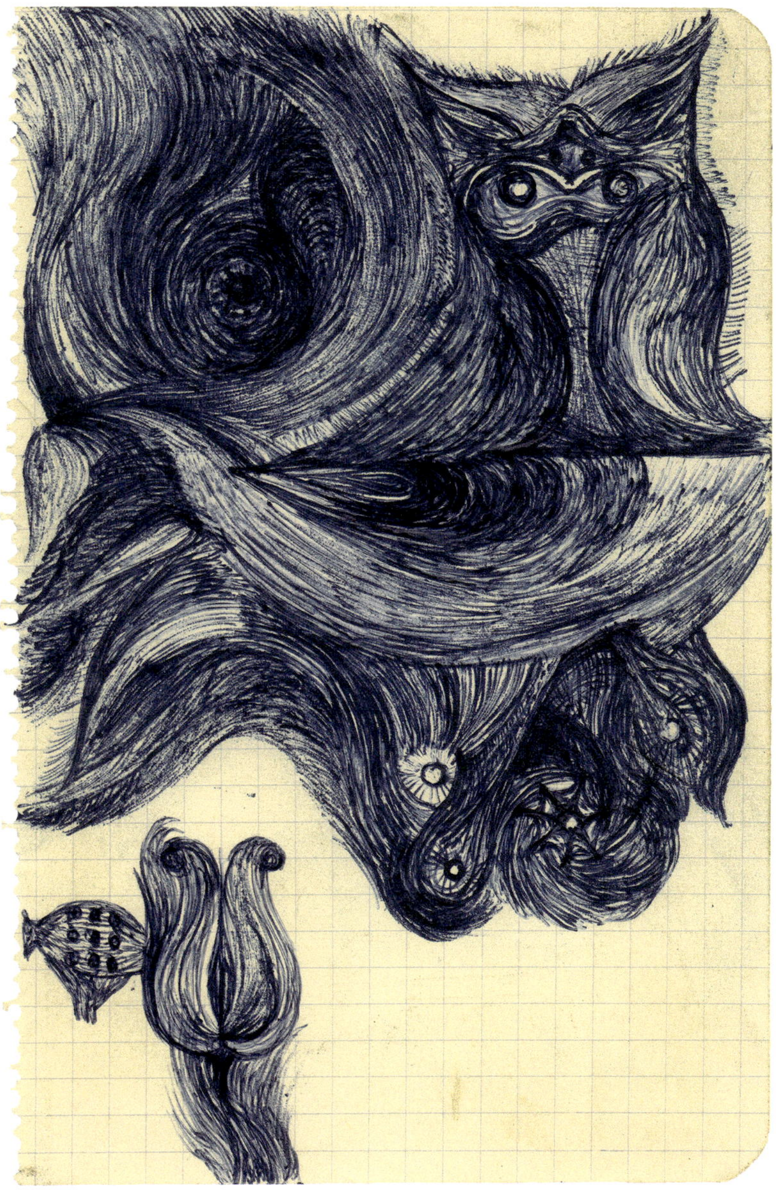

Untitled
(Rue Manuel period)
ca. 1954-1962
Monochrome blue ballpoint pen drawing, on squared paper.
17 x 10.5 cm
Artist's collection

Untitled
(Rue Manuel period)
ca. 1954-1962
Monochrome blue ballpoint pen drawing, on both sides, on squared paper.
17 x 10.5 cm
Artist's collection

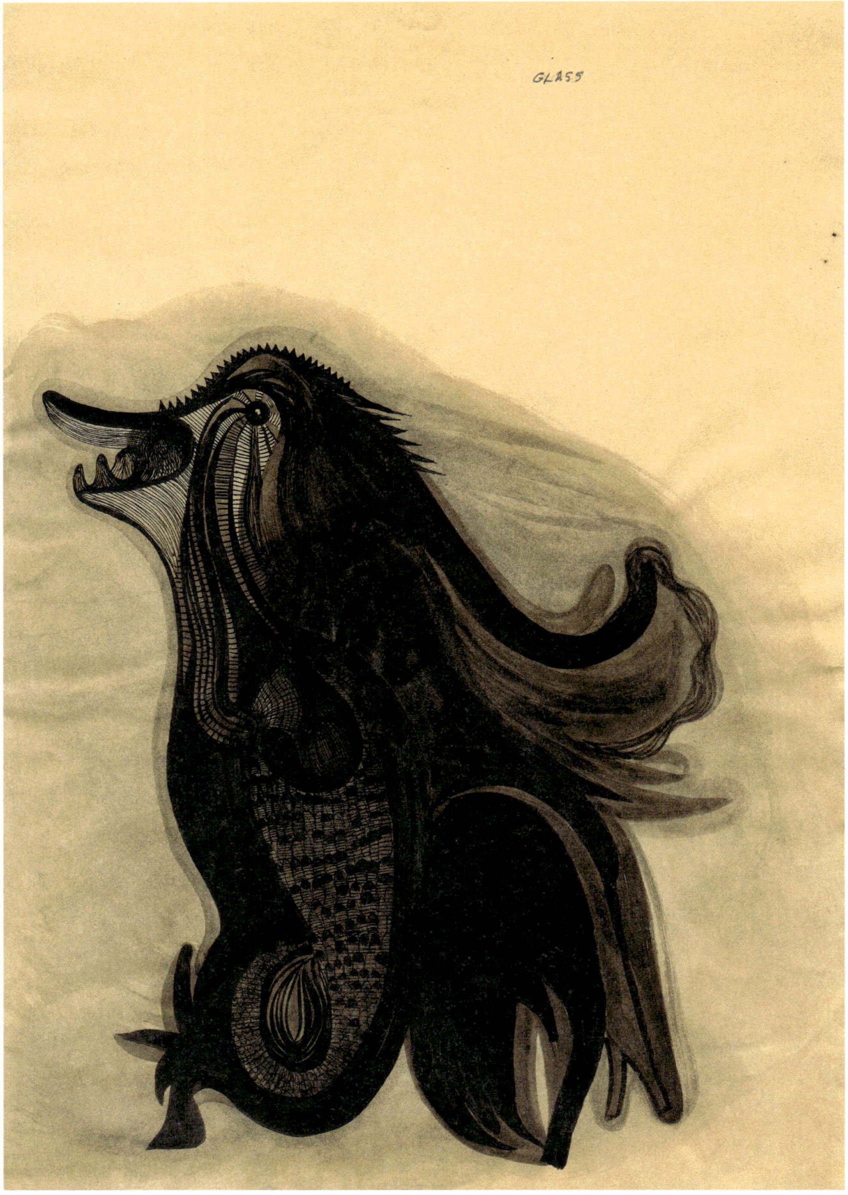

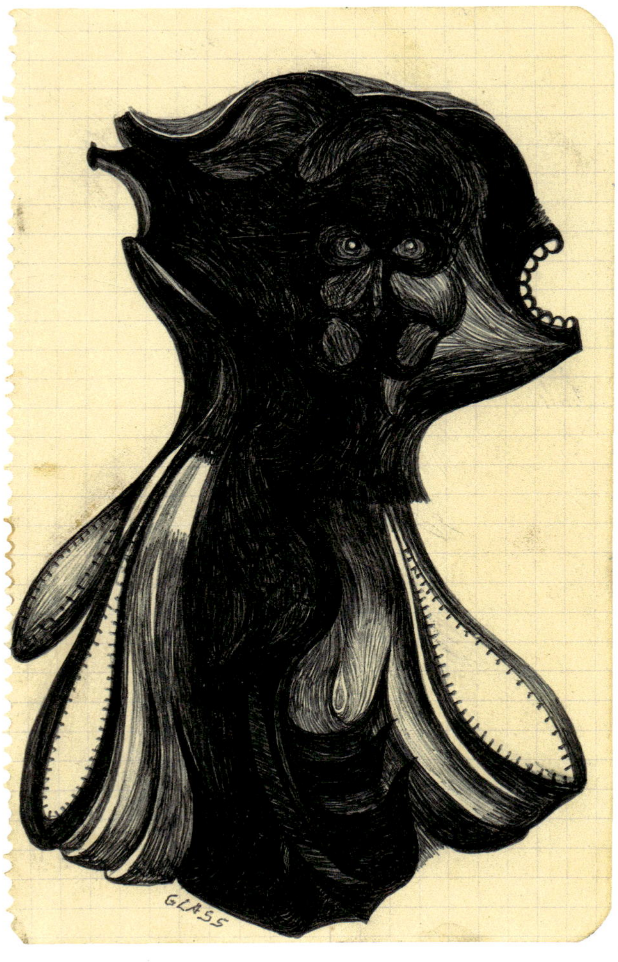

Untitled
(Rue Manuel period)
ca. 1954-1962
Monochrome black pen
drawing and India ink,
on paper.
29.5 x 21 cm
Artist's collection

Untitled
(Rue Manuel period)
ca. 1954-1962
Monochrome black ballpoint
pen drawing, on squared paper.
17 x 10.5 cm
Artist's collection

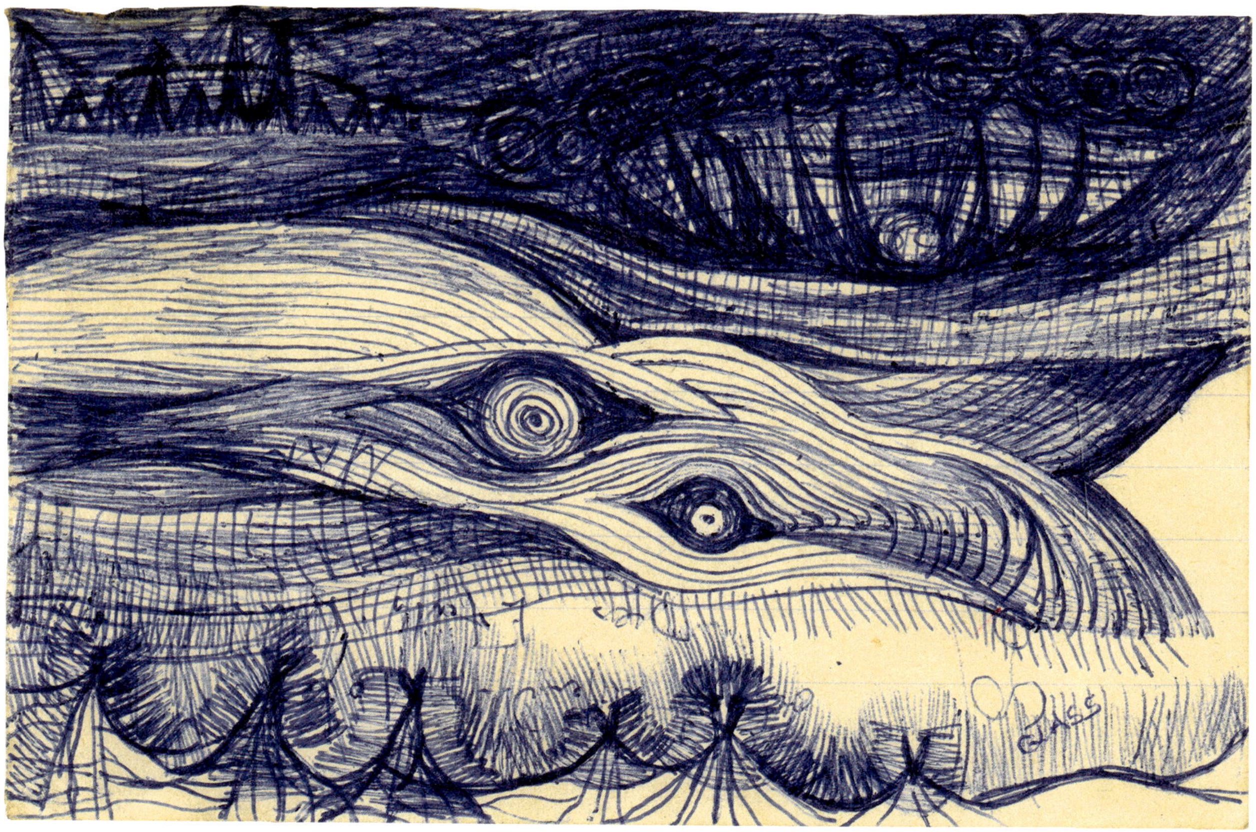

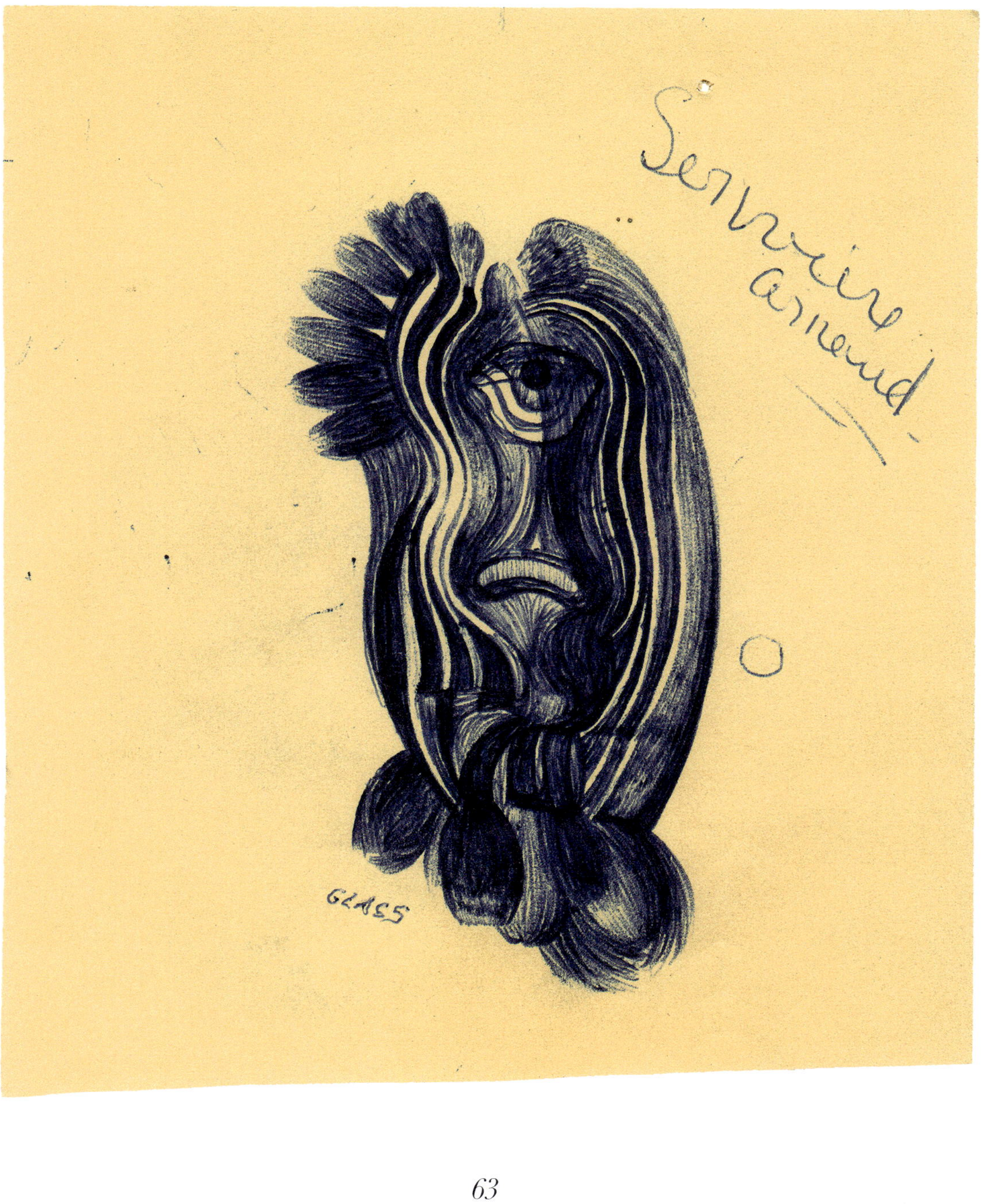

Untitled
(Rue Manuel period)
ca. 1954-1962
Monochrome blue ballpoint pen drawing, on lined notebook paper.
9 x 14 cm
Artist's collection

Untitled
(Rue Manuel period)
ca. 1954-1962
Monochrome blue ballpoint pen drawing, on paper.
14 x 12.5 cm
Artist's collection

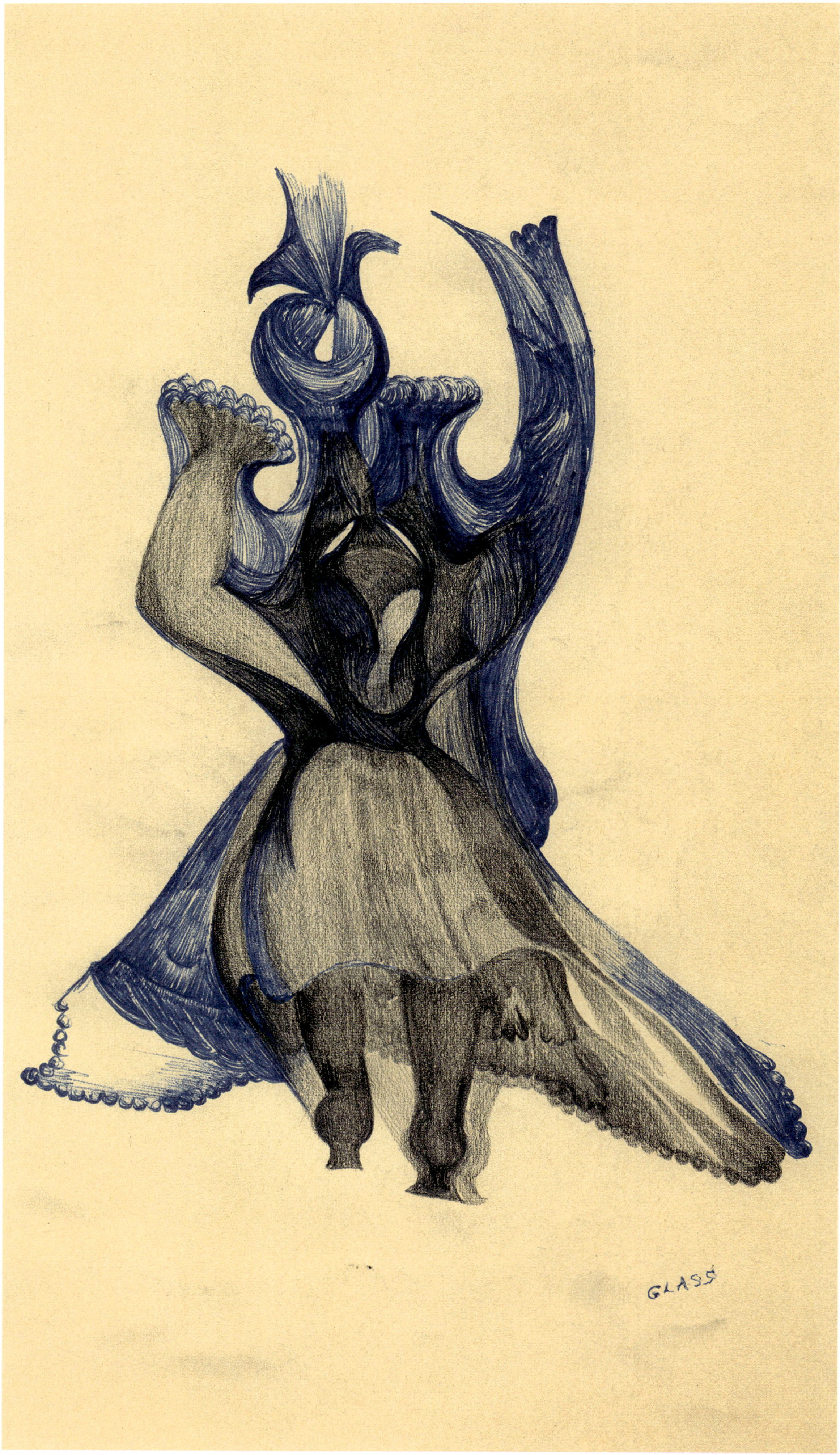

Untitled
(Rue Manuel period)
ca. 1954-1962
Drawing in blue pen and graphite, on paper.
27 x 21 cm
Artist's collection

Untitled
(Rue Manuel period)
ca. 1954-1962
Drawing in blue pen, graphite and green, brown, and yellow colors, on paper.
27 x 20.5 cm
Aube Elléouët Breton collection
Following page

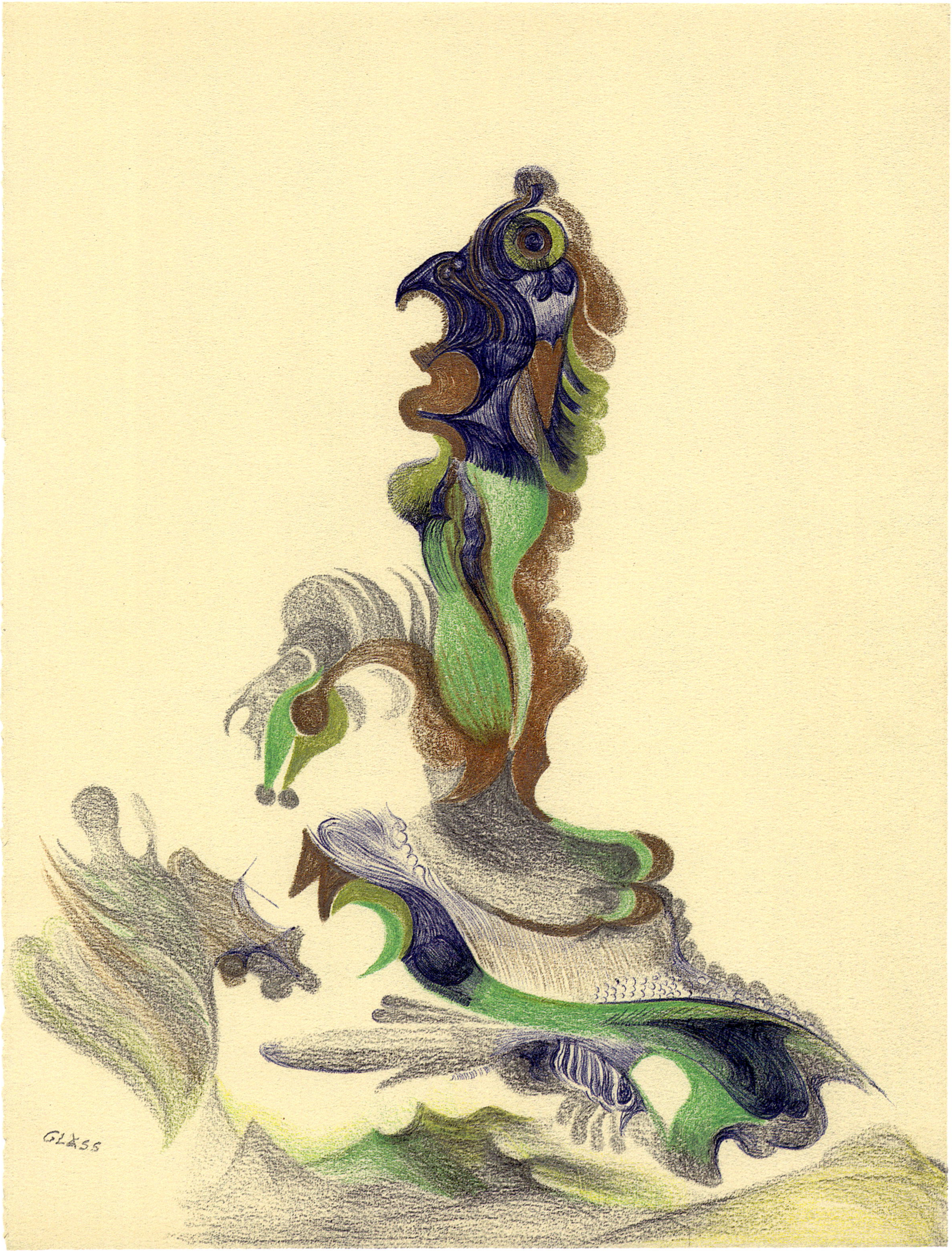
GLASS

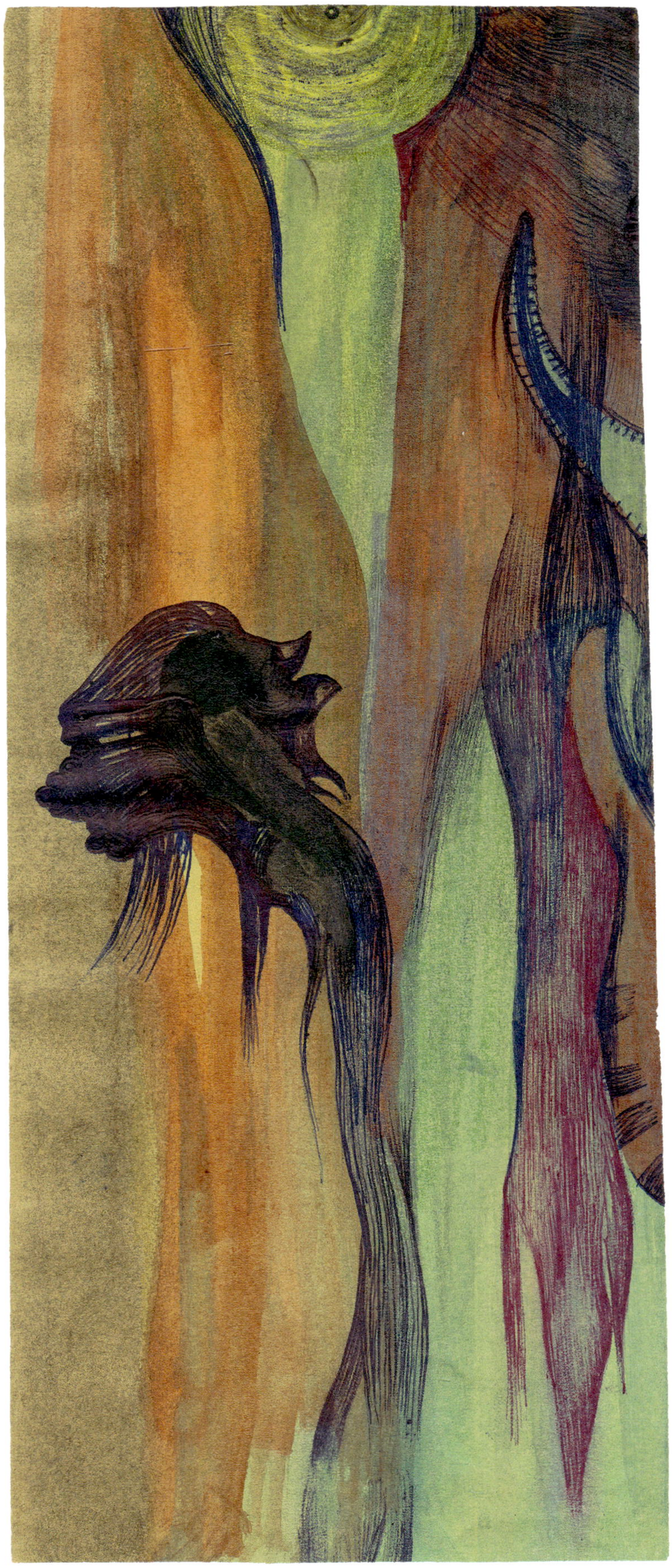

Untitled
(Rue Manuel period)
ca. 1954-1962
Blue, black and red pen drawing with green, yellow, orange, and violet colors, on paper.
23.5 x 10 cm
Artist's collection

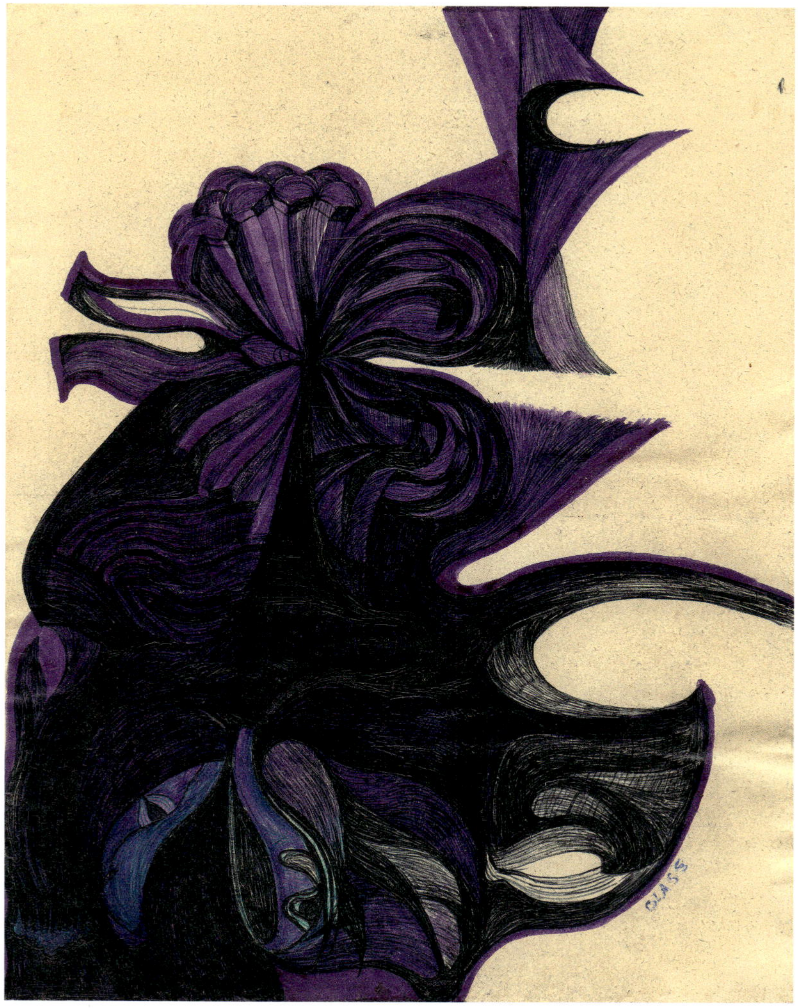

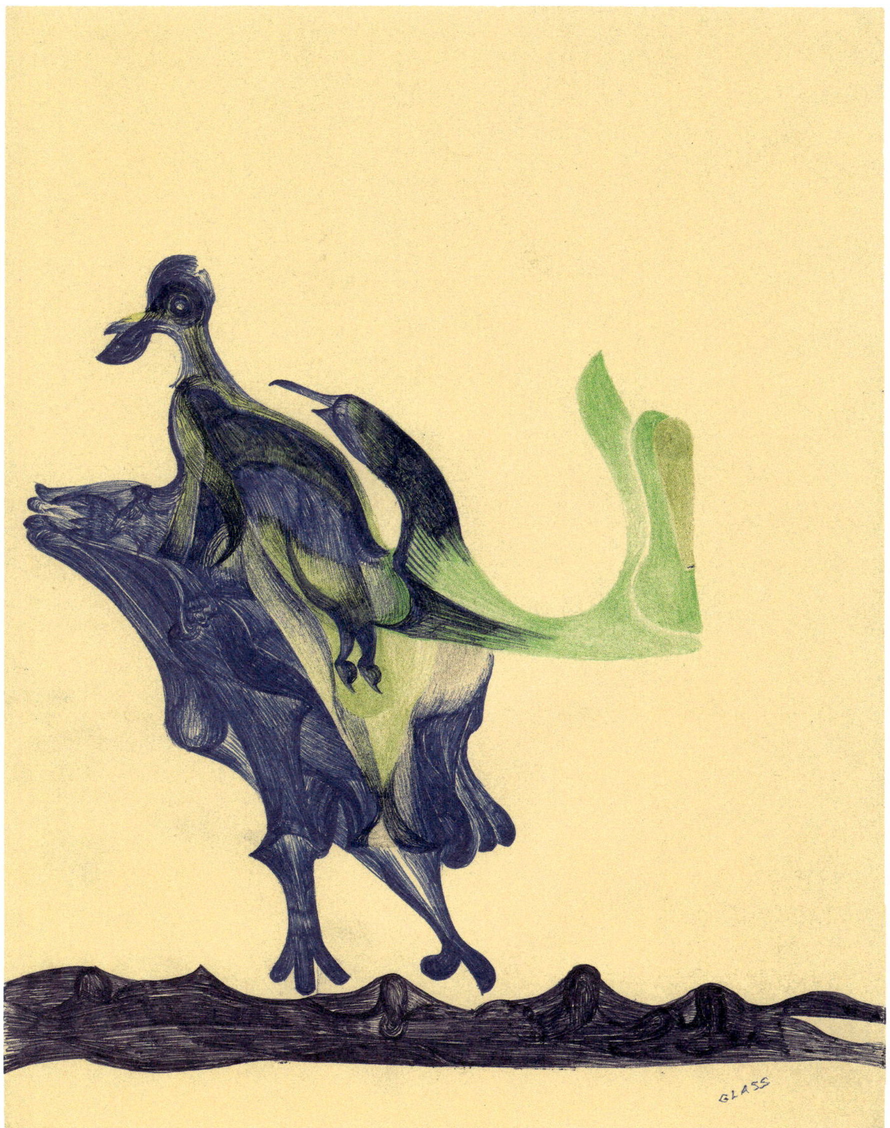

Untitled
(Rue Manuel period)
ca. 1954-1962
Drawing in blue, black, and purple ballpoint pen, with a touch of aquamarine, on paper.
21.5 x 17 cm
Artist's collection

Untitled
(Rue Manuel period)
ca. 1954-1962
Blue pen drawing with green color, on paper.
27 x 21 cm
Artist's collection

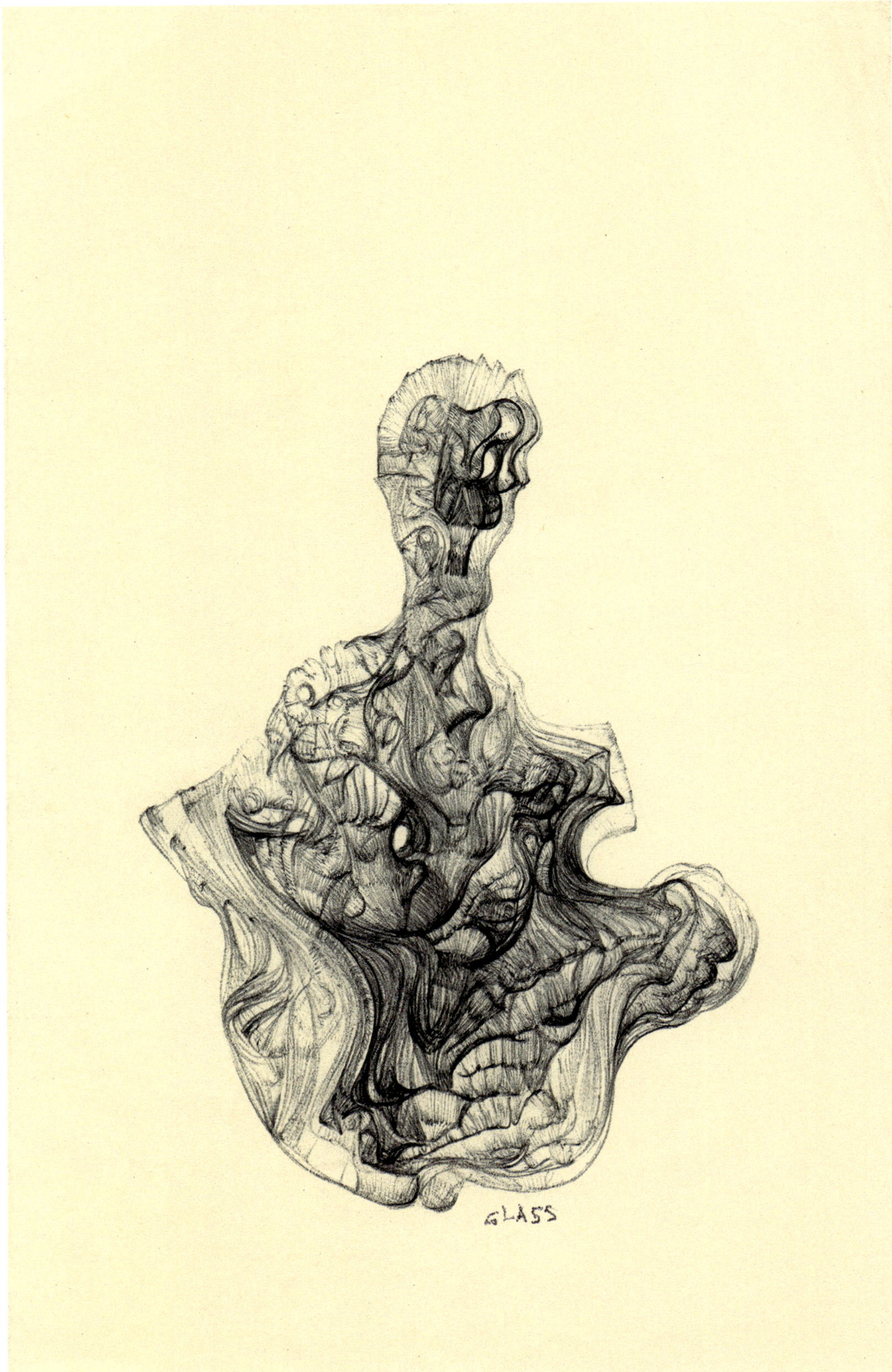

Untitled
(Rue Manuel period)
ca. 1954-1962
Monochrome black ballpoint pen drawing, on paper.
21 x 13.5 cm
Artist's collection

Untitled
(Rue Manuel period)
ca. 1954-1962
Drawing in blue and black pen, with blue, orange, and green colors, on paper.
28 x 22.5 cm
Artist's collection
Following page

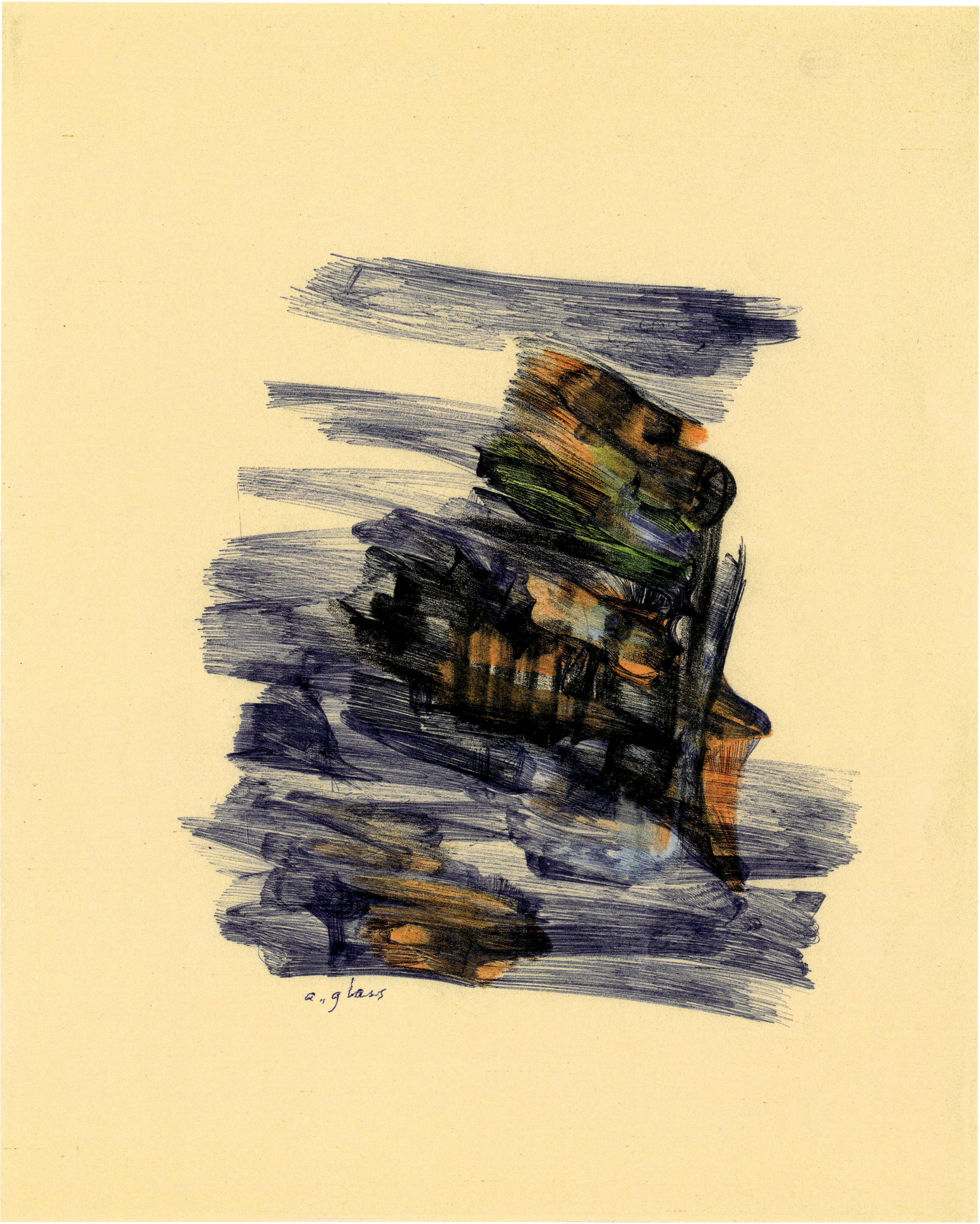

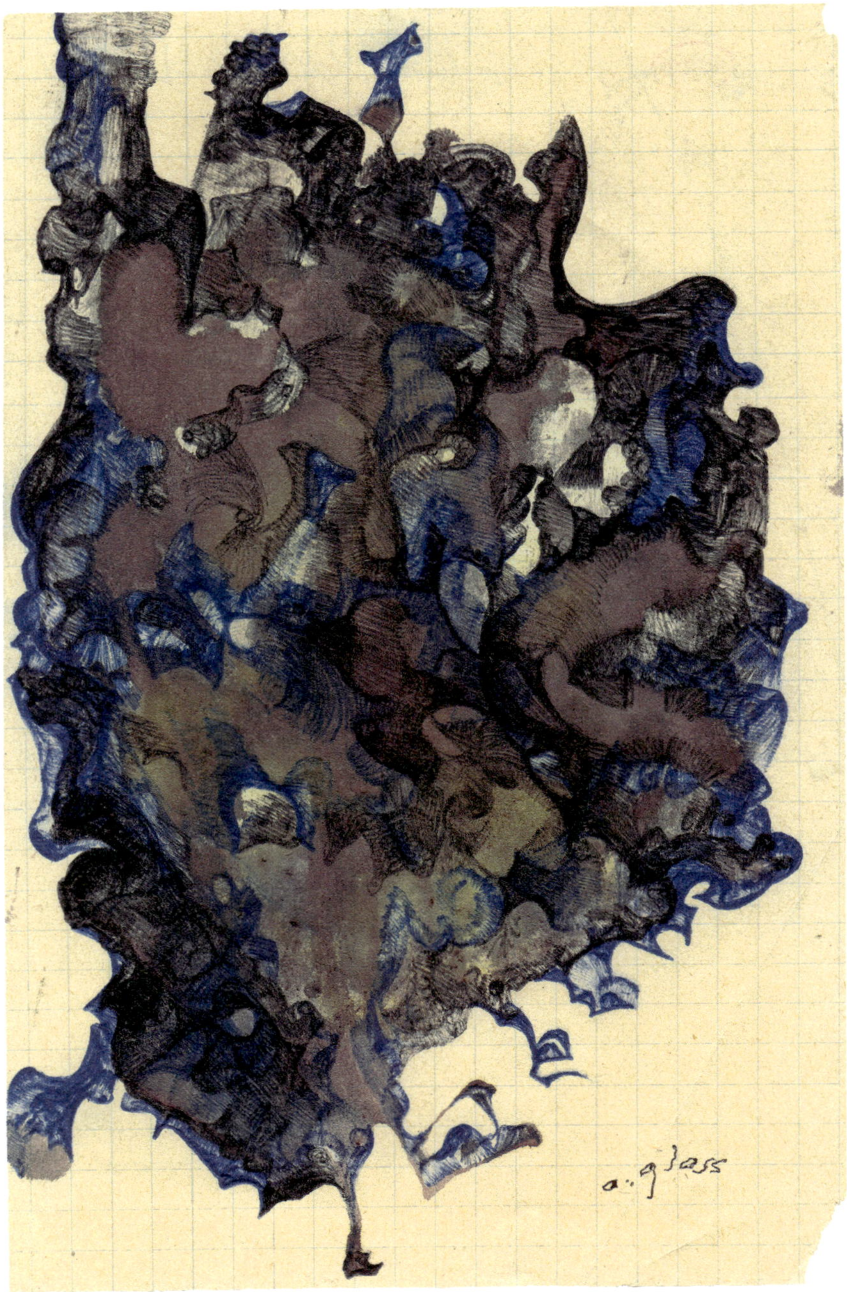

Untitled
(Rue Manuel period)
ca. 1954-1962
Drawing in bicolor blue and black ballpoint pen with wine color, on squared paper.
17 x 10.5 cm
Artist's collection

Untitled
(Rue Manuel period)
ca. 1954-1962
Blue pen drawing with red, yellow, and orange watercolor, on paper.
28 x 22.5 cm
Artist's collection
Following page

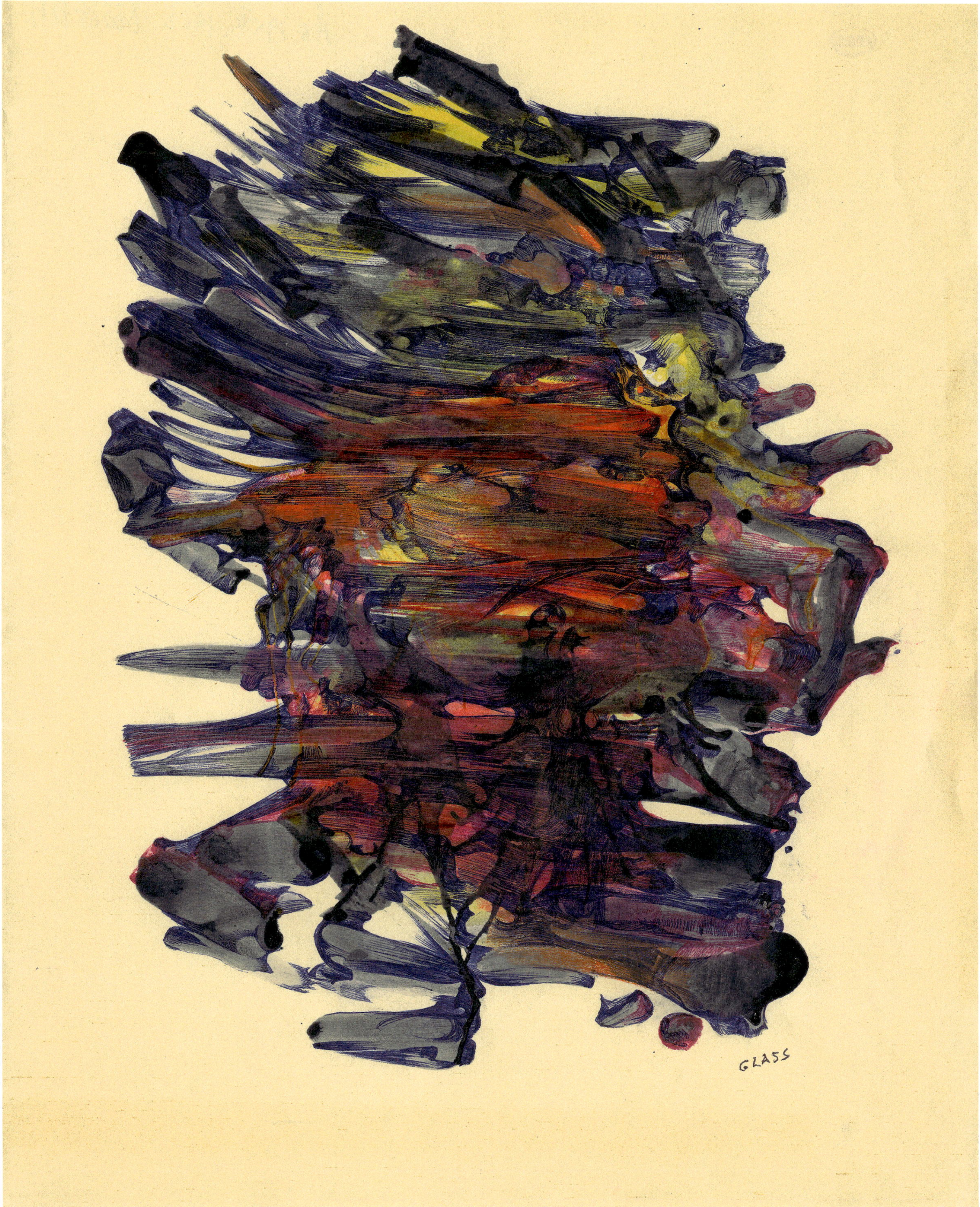
GLASS

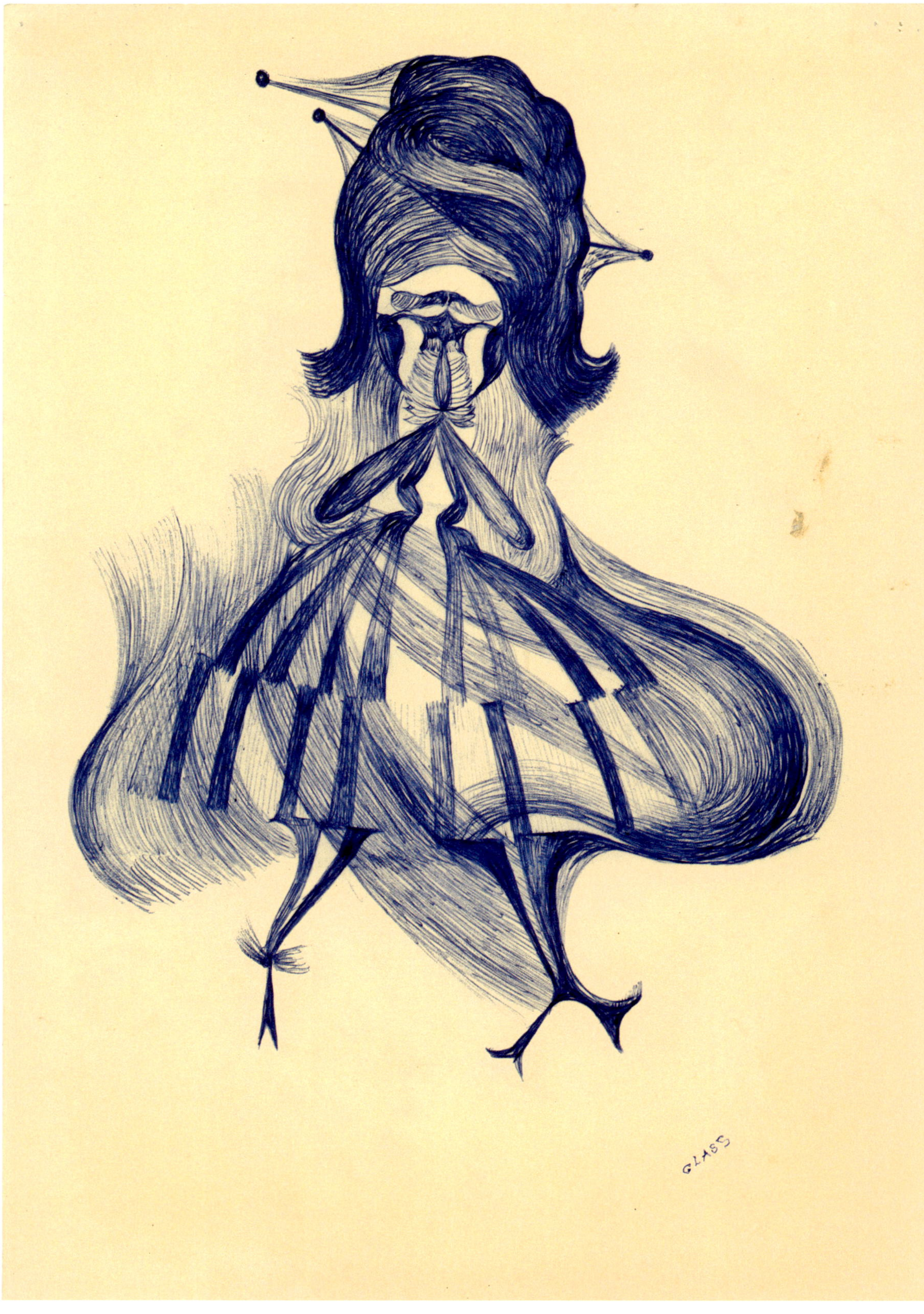

Untitled
(Rue Manuel period)
ca. 1954-1962
Drawing in blue monocolor
ballpoint pen, on paper.
29.8 x 21.1 cm
Artist's collection

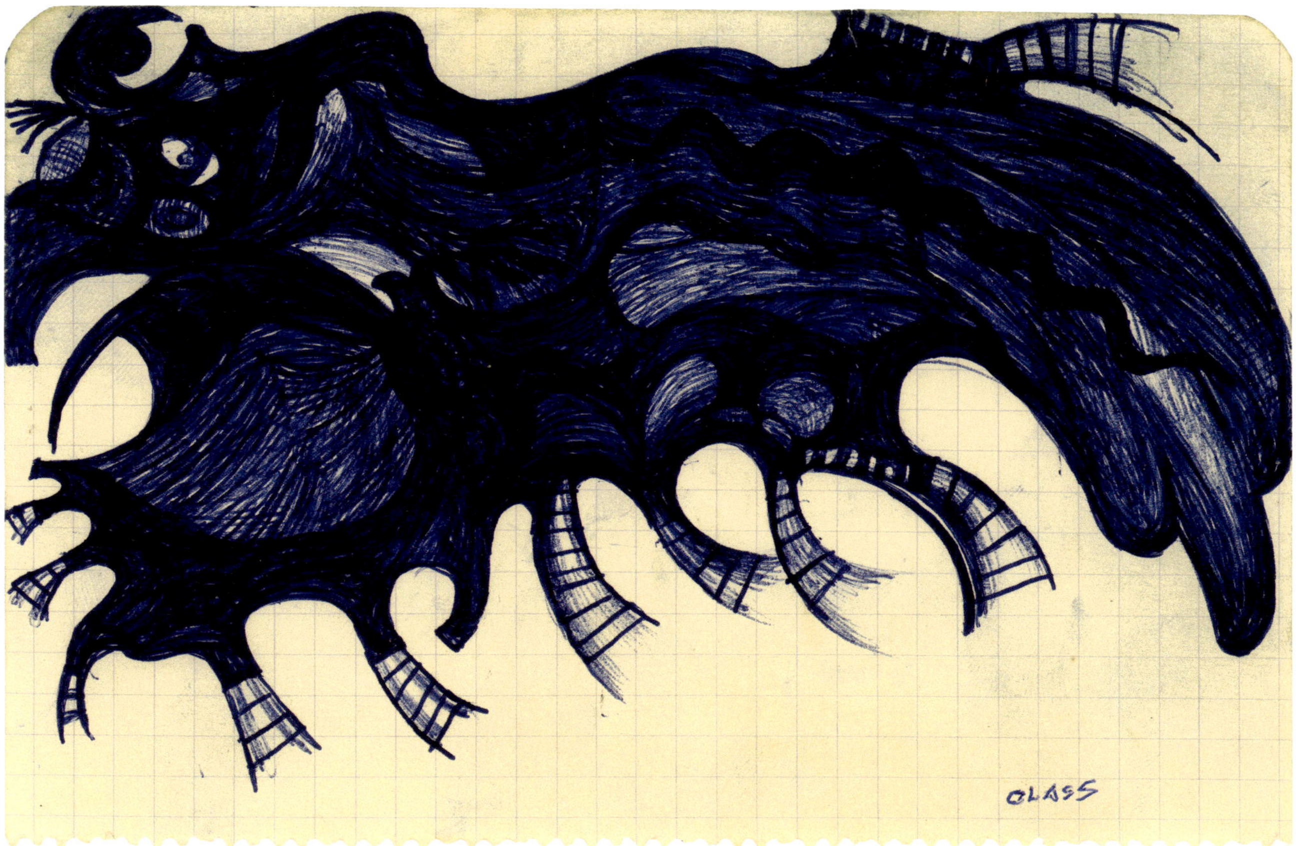

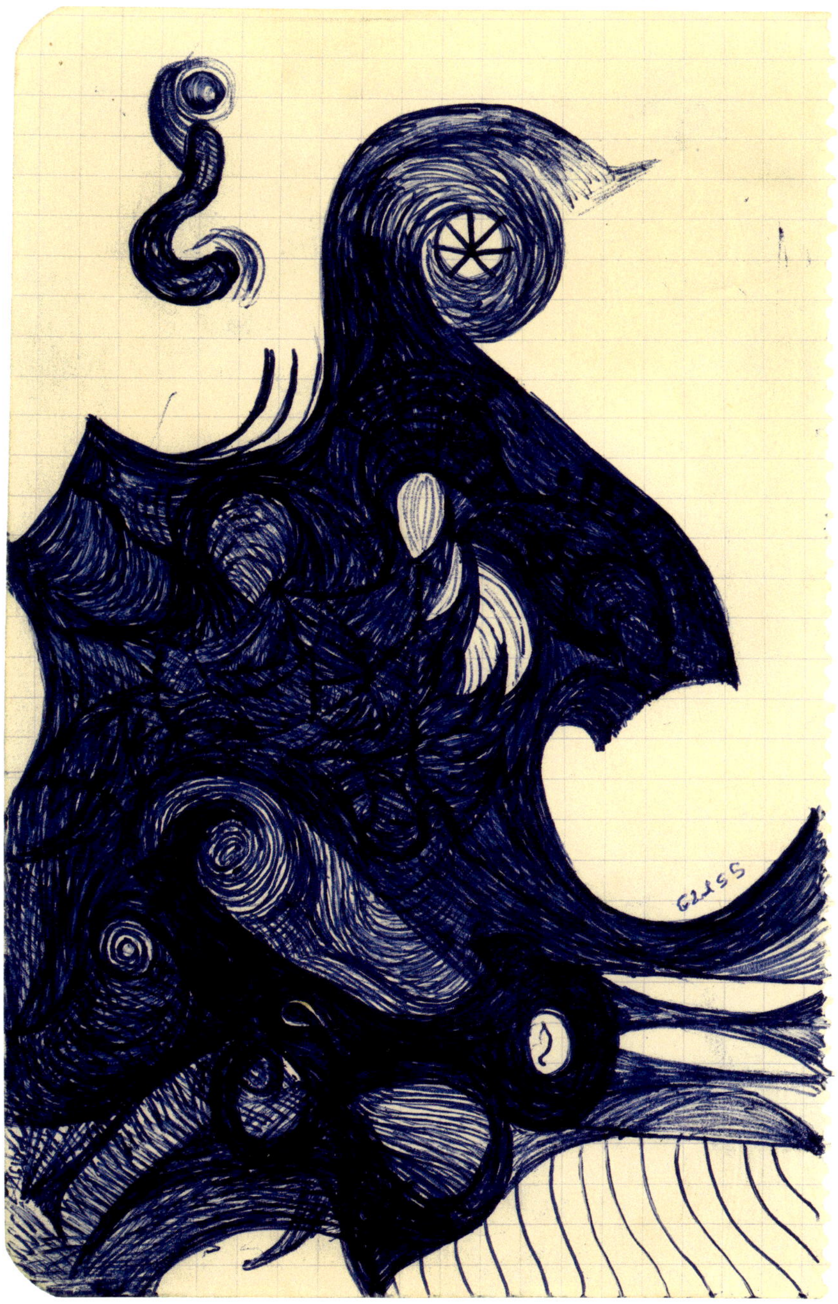

Untitled
(Rue Manuel period)
ca. 1954-1962
Drawing in blue monocolor ballpoint pen, on squared paper.
10.3 x 16 cm
Artist's collection

Untitled
(Rue Manuel period)
ca. 1954-1962
Drawing in blue monocolor ballpoint pen, on squared paper.
16 x 10.3 cm
Artist's collection

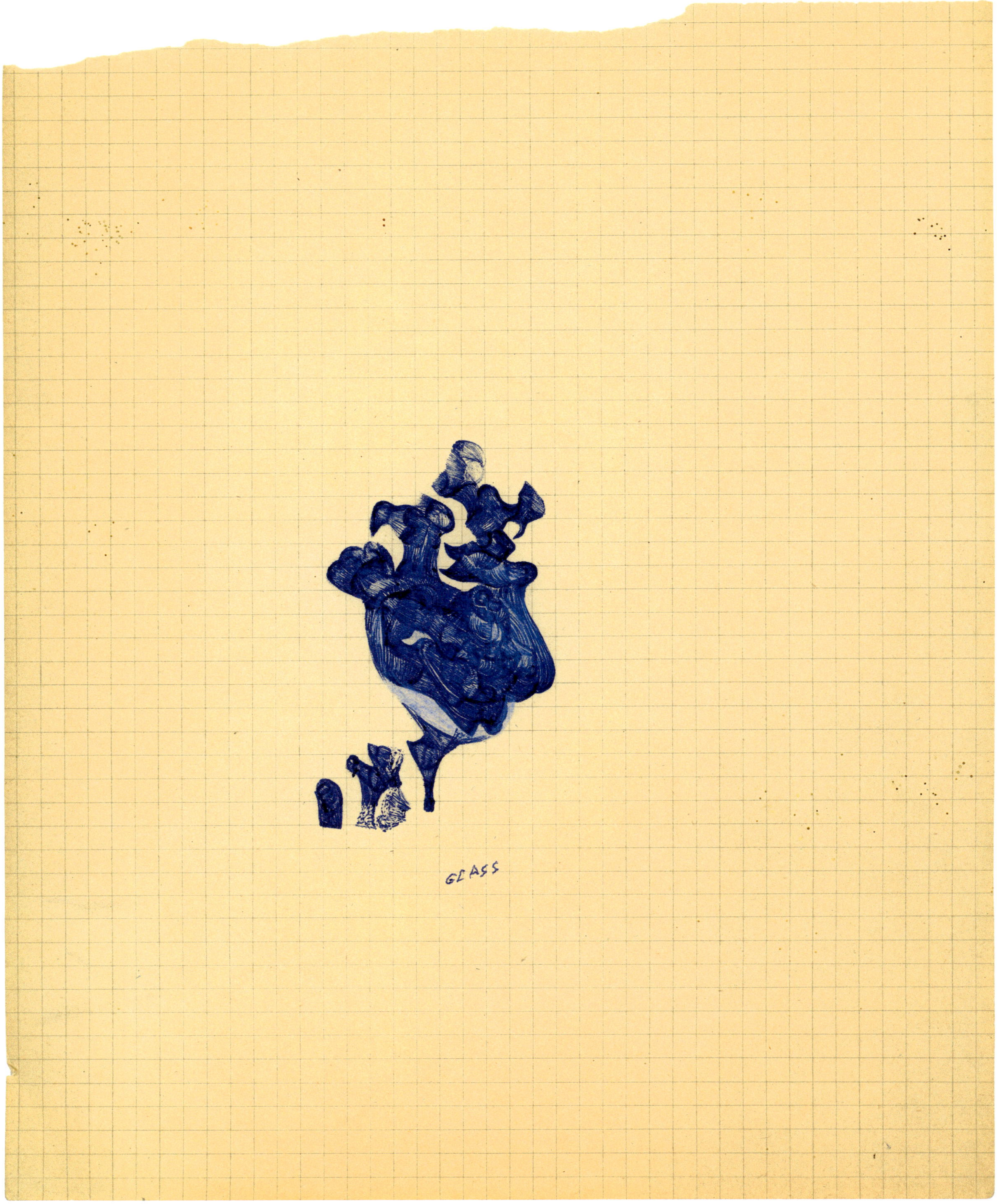

Untitled
(Rue Manuel period)
ca. 1954-1962
Monochrome blue ballpoint pen drawing, with a touch of sky blue pencil, on squared paper.
25.4 x 21.1 cm
Artist's collection

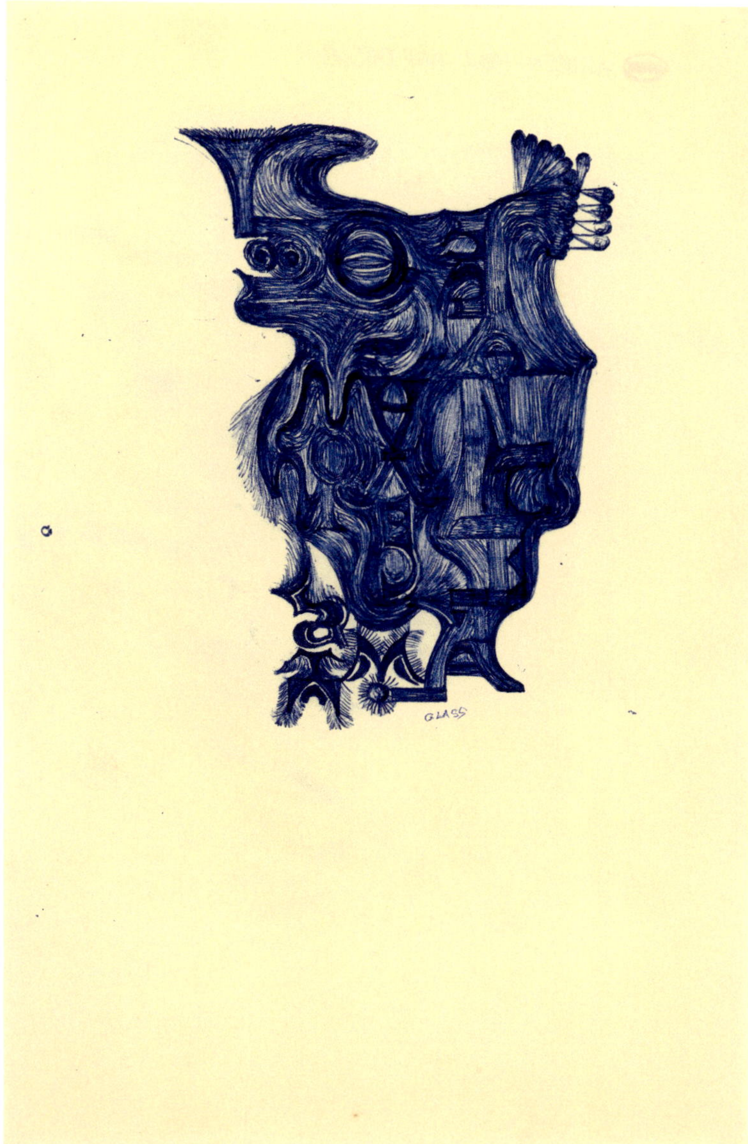

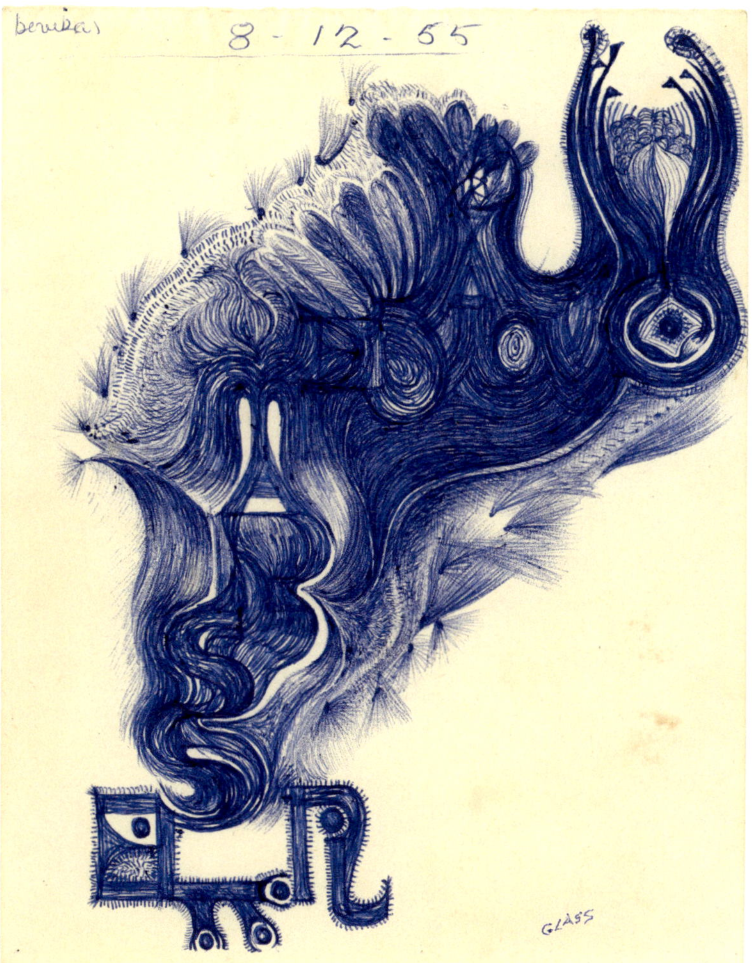

Untitled
(Rue Manuel period)
ca. 1954-1962
Monochrome blue ballpoint pen drawing, on paper.
27.2 x 17.9 cm
Artist's collection

Untitled
(Rue Manuel period)
1955
Drawing in blue monocolor ballpoint pen, on paper.
21.9 x 17 cm
Artist's collection

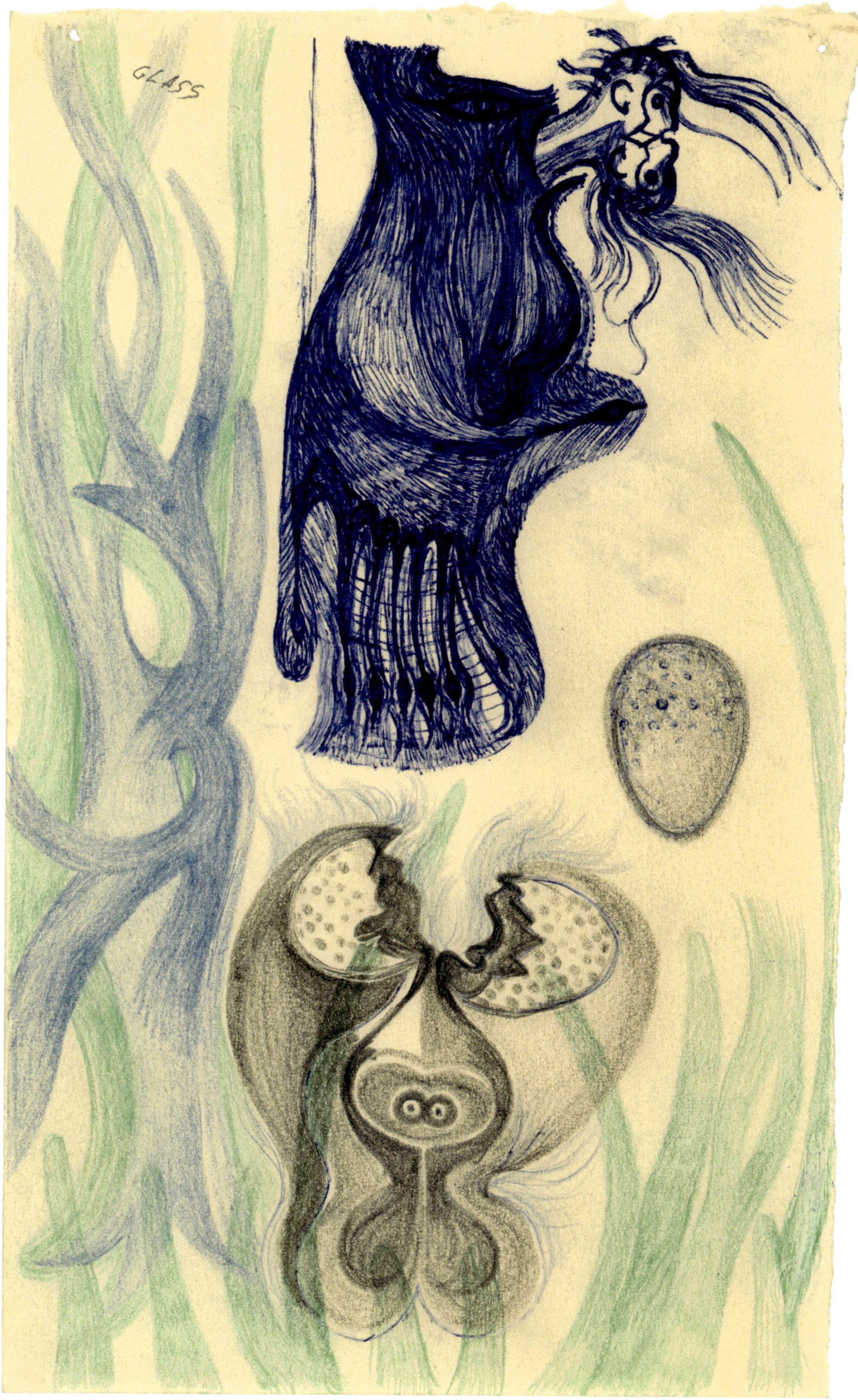

Untitled
(Rue Manuel period)
ca. 1954-1962
Drawing in blue monocolor ballpoint pen with graphite, green, and blue pencil, on paper.
22.2 x 13.4 cm
Artist's collection

Untitled
(Rue Manuel period)
ca. 1954-1962
Drawing in blue monocolor ballpoint pen, on squared paper.
16 x 10.3 cm
Artist's collection
Next page

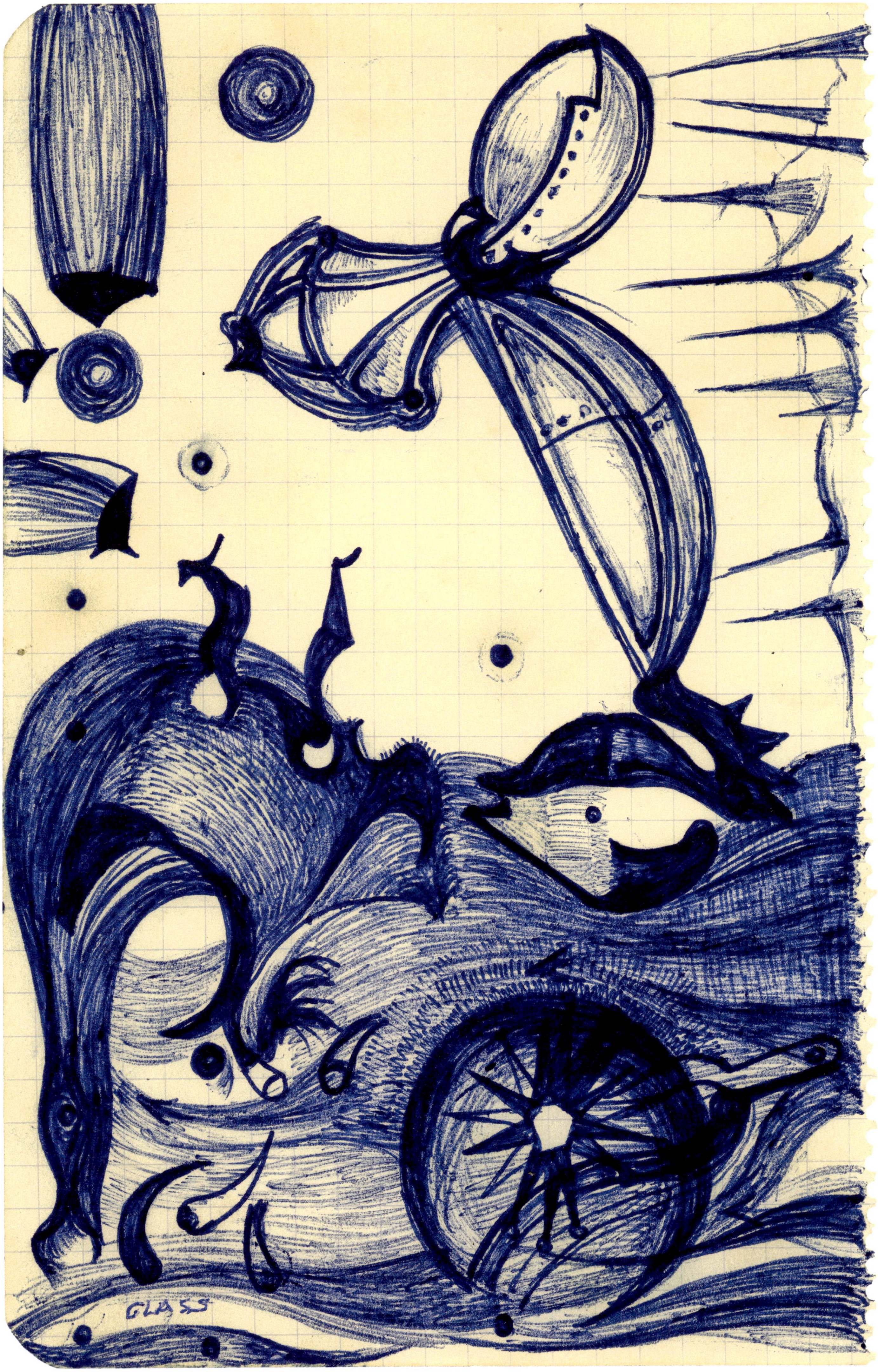
GLASS

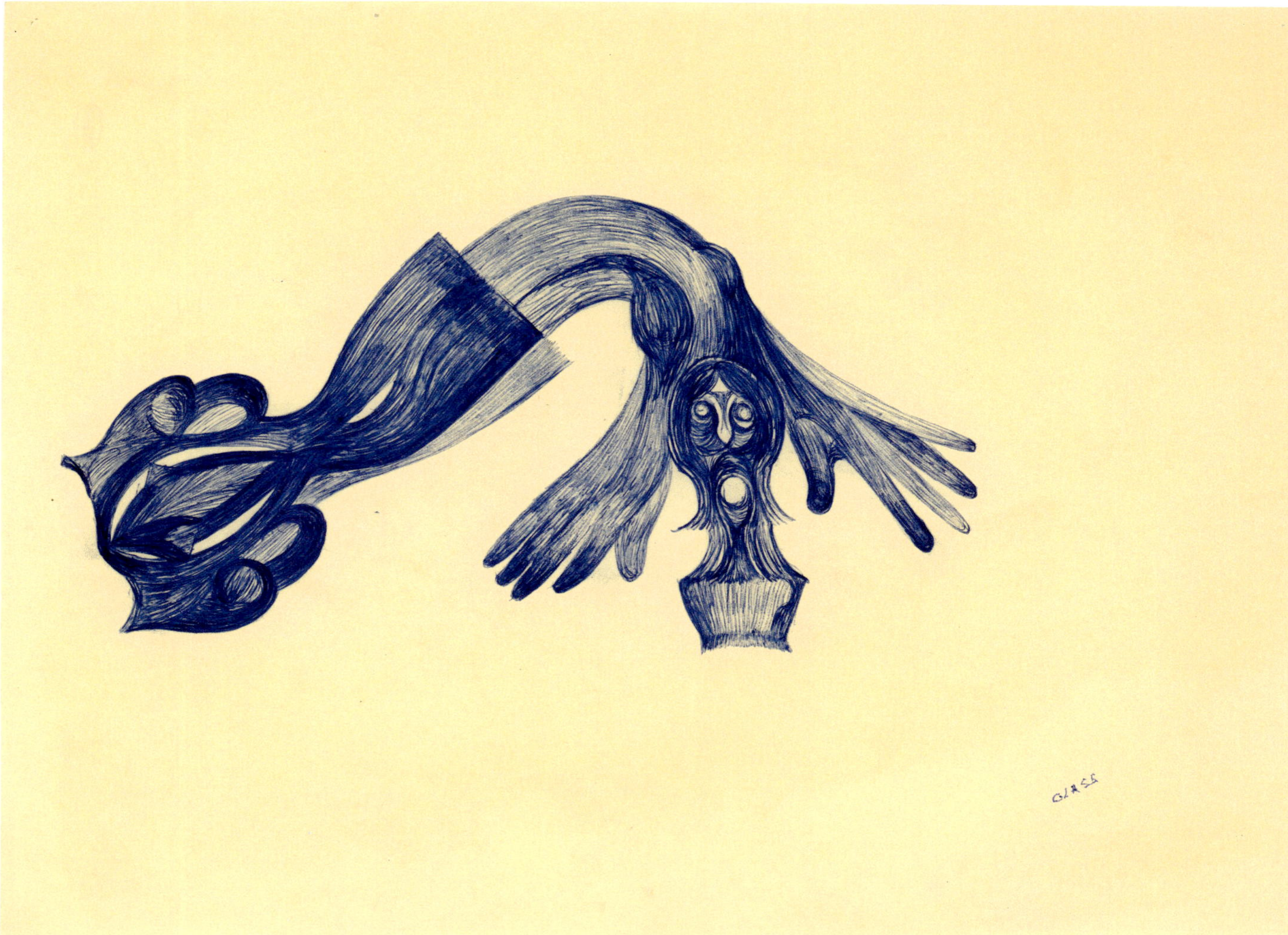

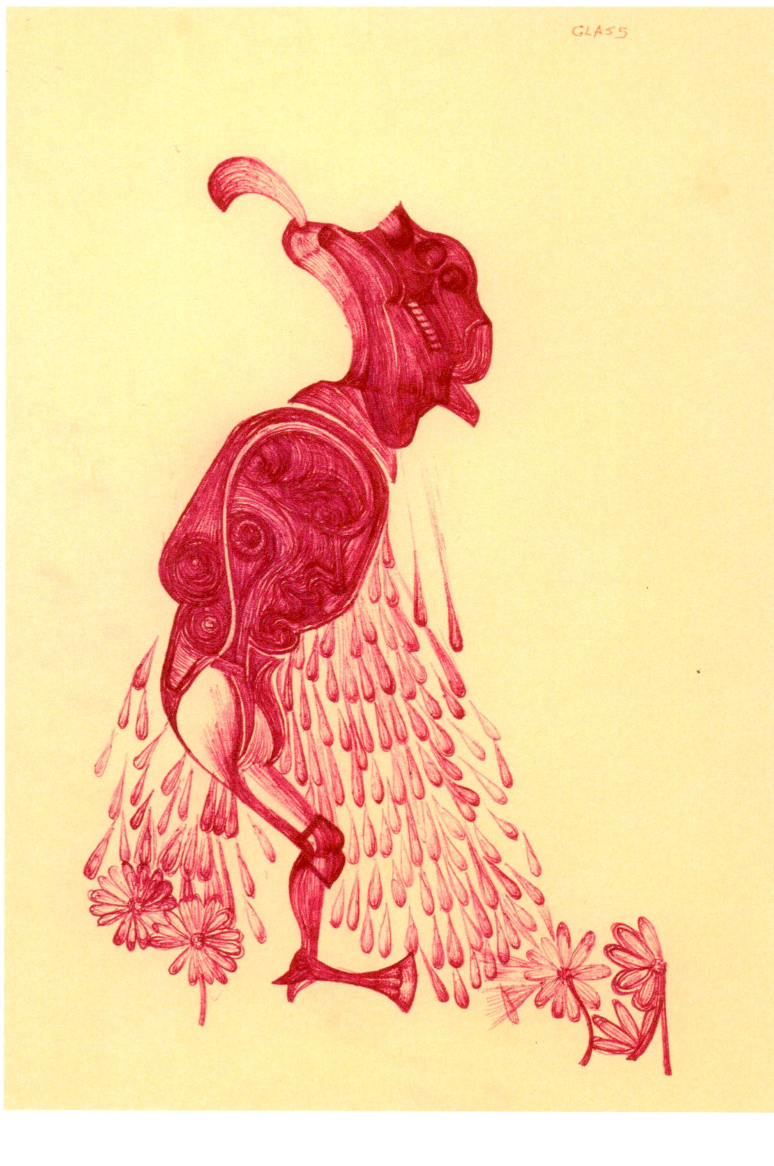

Untitled
(Rue Manuel period)
ca. 1954-1962
Drawing in blue monocolor ballpoint pen, on paper.
21 x 29.7 cm
Artist's collection

Untitled
(Rue Manuel period)
ca. 1954-1962
Drawing in red monocolor ballpoint pen, on paper.
29.8 x 21.1 cm
Artist's collection

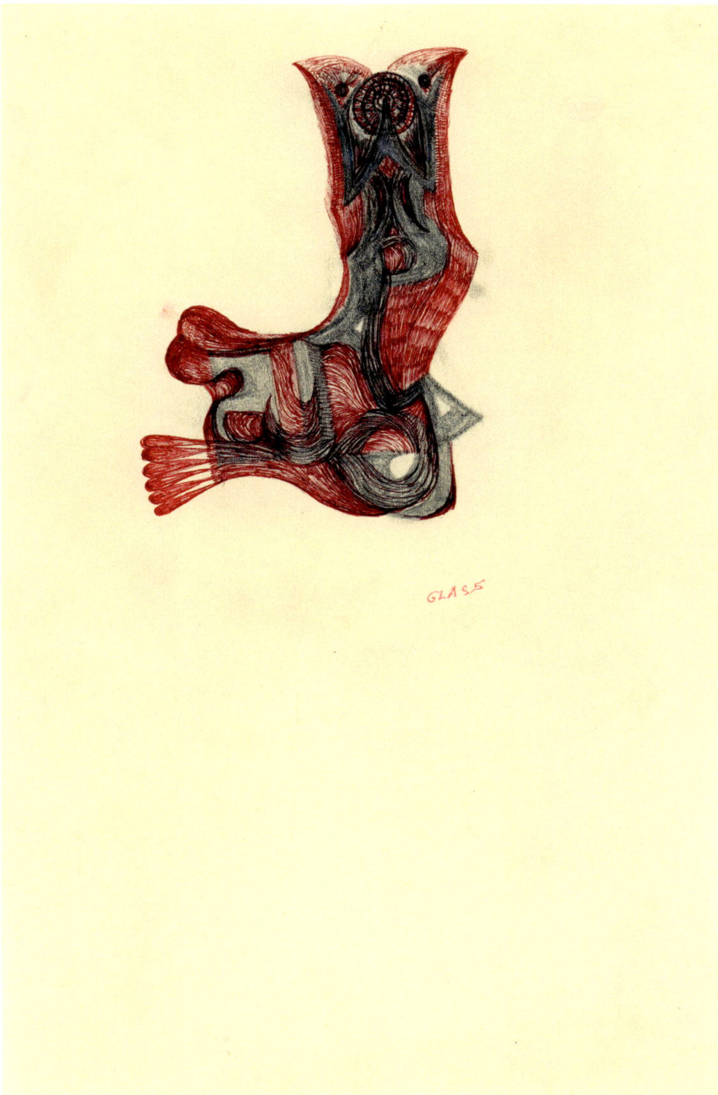

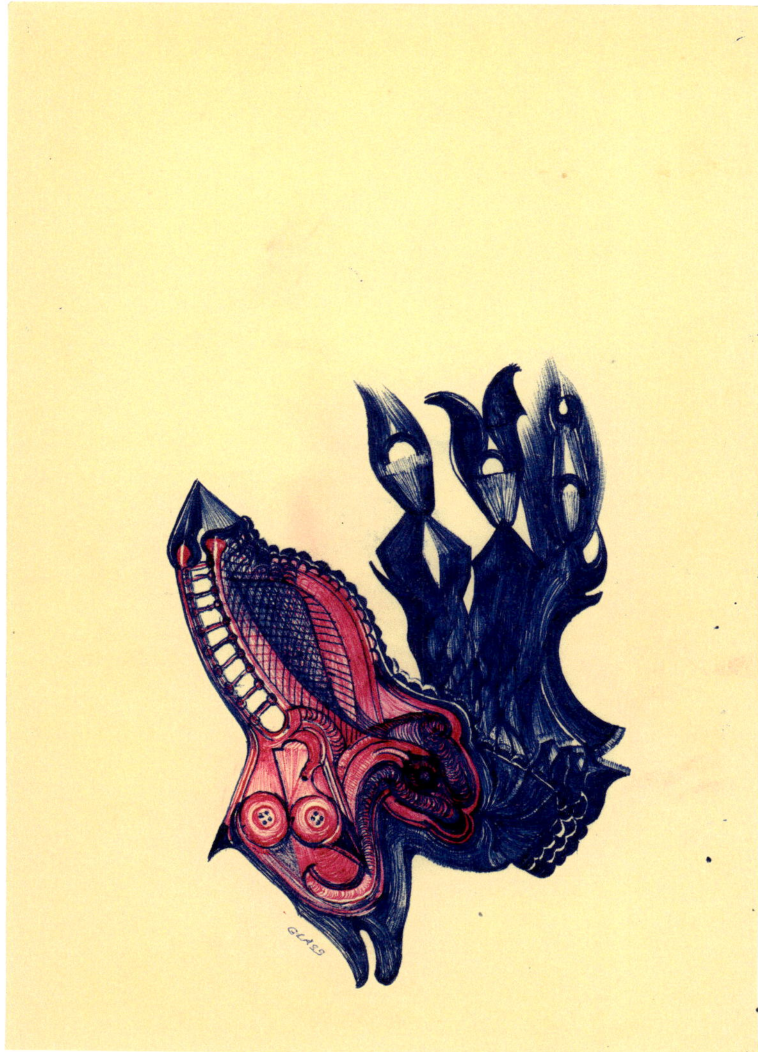

Untitled
(Rue Manuel period)
ca. 1954-1962
Drawing in red monocolor pen with graphite, on paper.
27.2 x 17.9 cm
Artist's collection

Untitled
(Rue Manuel period)
ca. 1954-1962
Drawing in blue and red bicolor ballpoint pen, on paper.
29.8 x 21.1 cm
Artist's collection

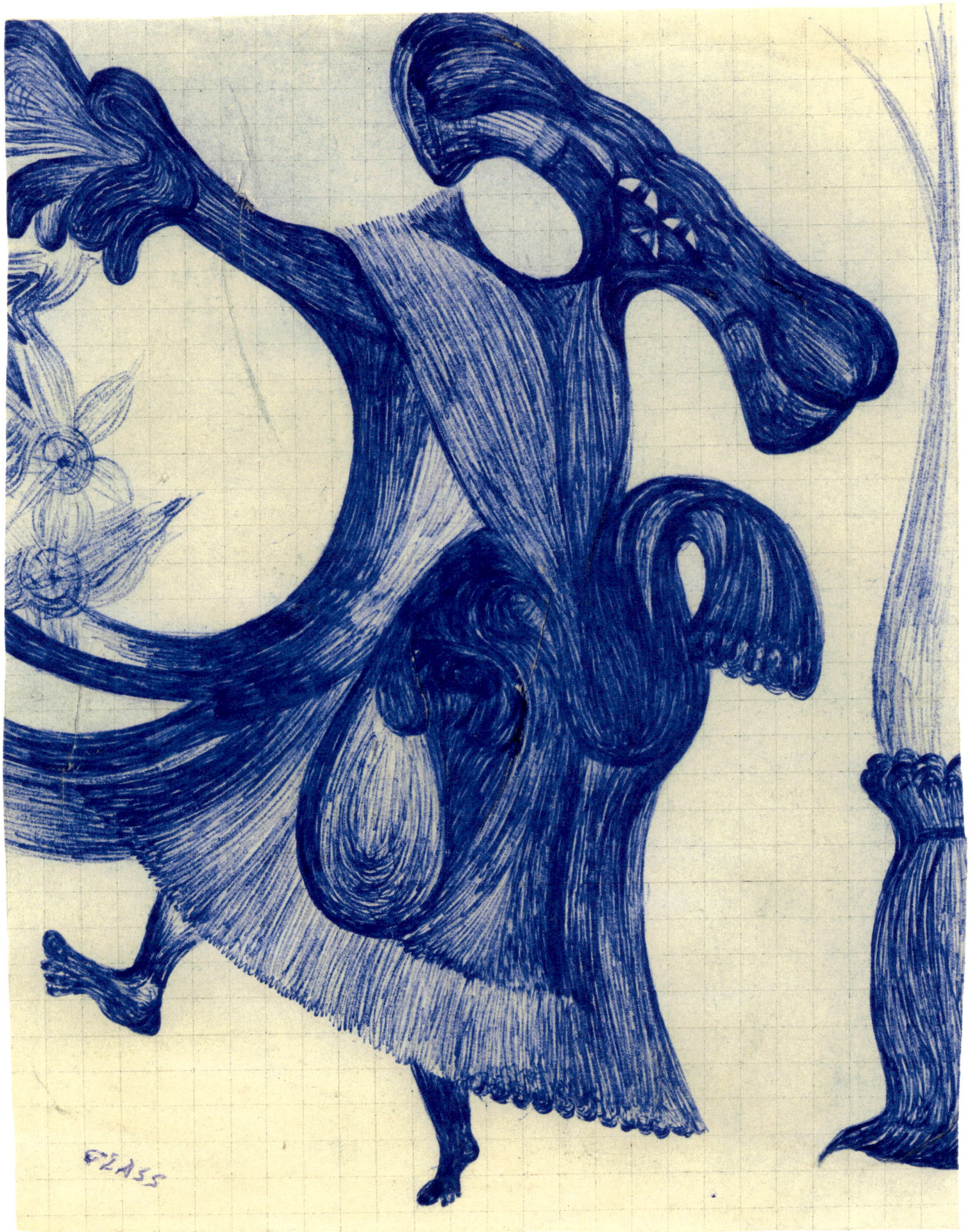

Untitled
(Rue Manuel period)
ca. 1954-1962
Monochrome blue ballpoint pen drawing, blurred with a sky blue pencil, on squared paper.
16.8 x 13.1 cm
Artist's collection

Untitled
(Rue Manuel period)
ca. 1954-1962
Drawing in blue monocolor ballpoint pen, on squared paper.
19.5 x 13.1 cm
Artist's collection
Next page

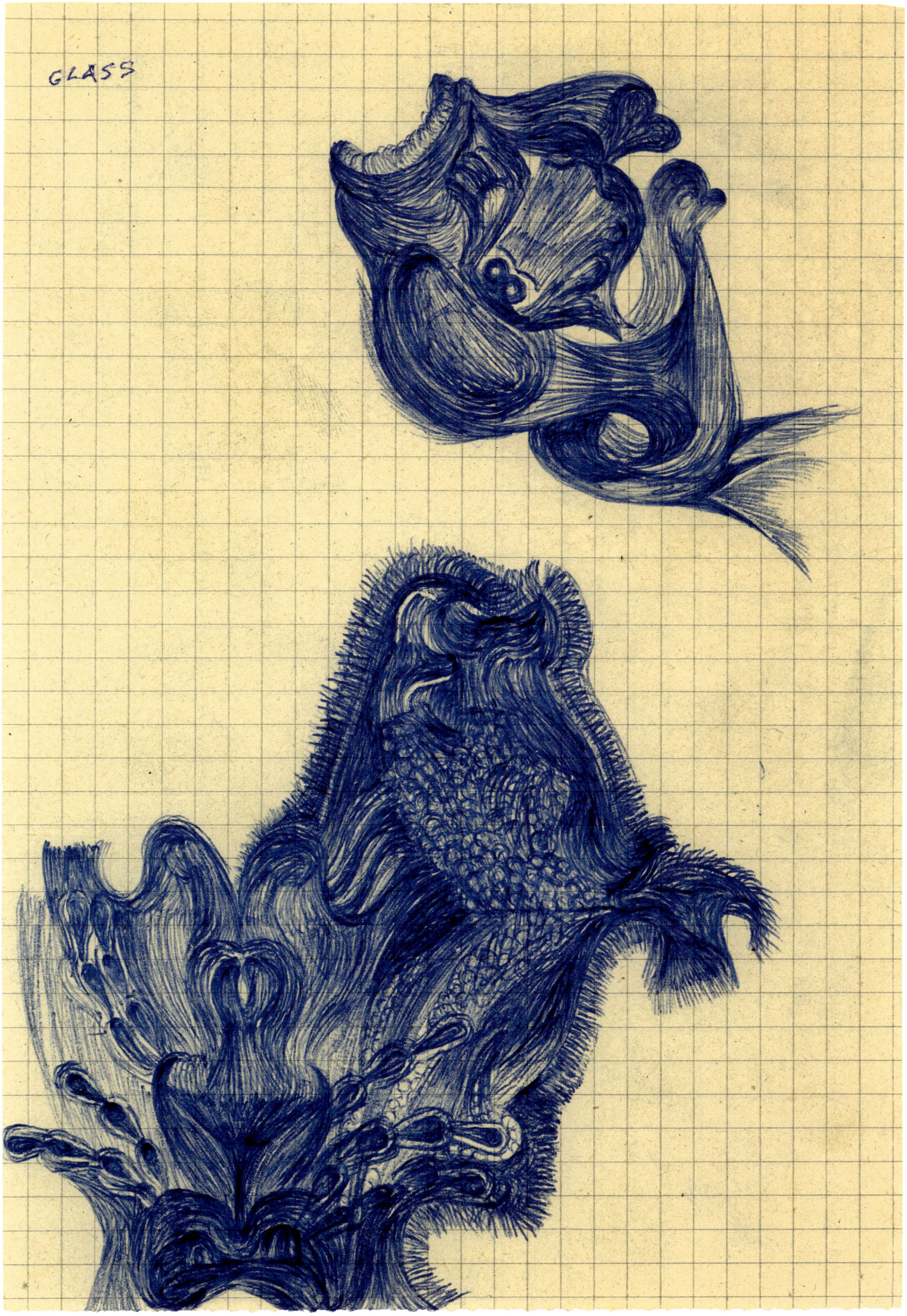
GLASS

CHAPTER II

CLUB St GERMAIN -DES- PRÉS PARIS VIe

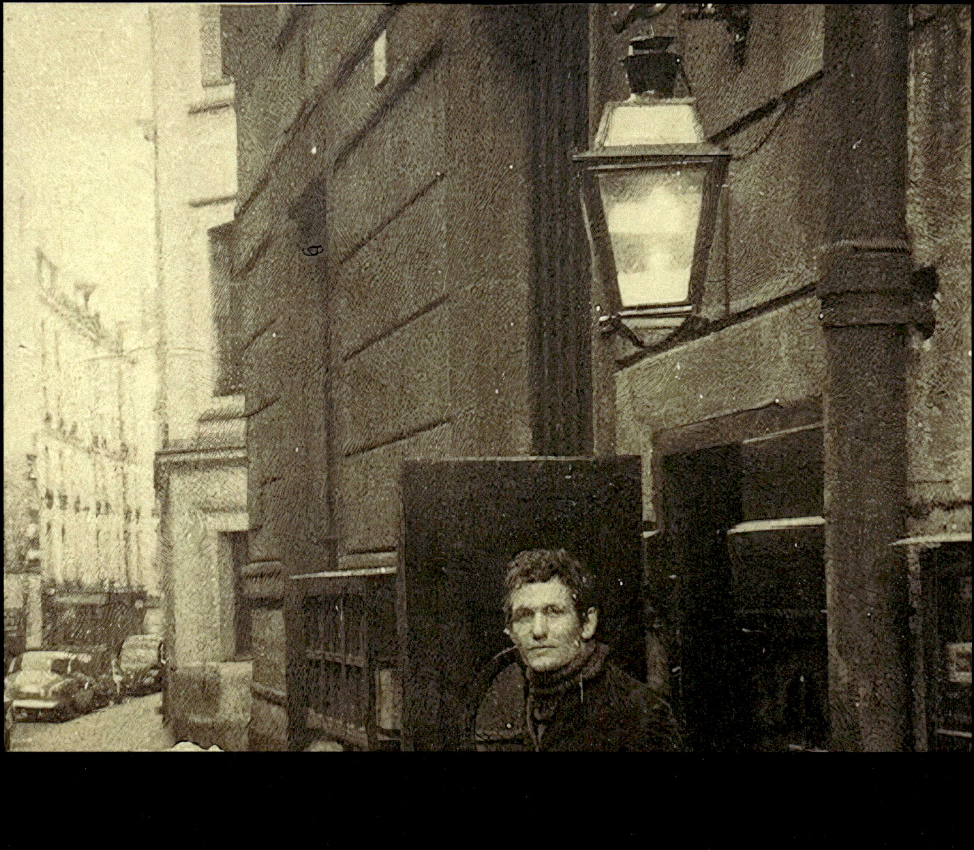

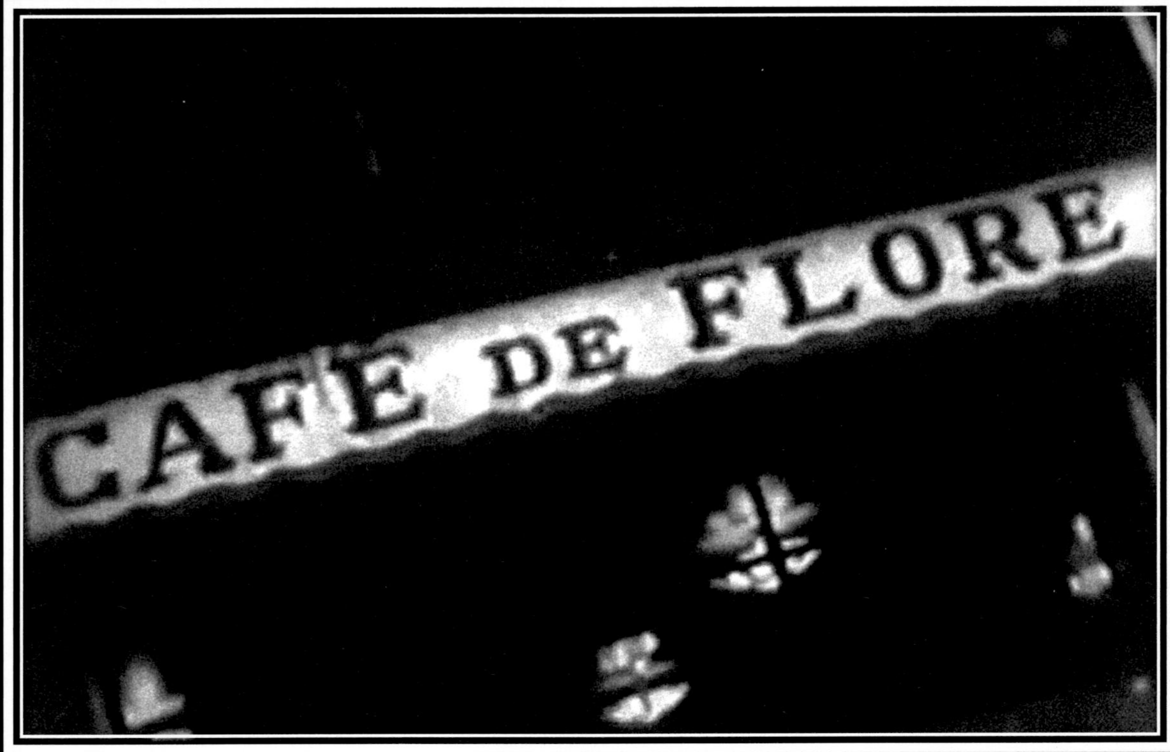
CAFE DE FLORE

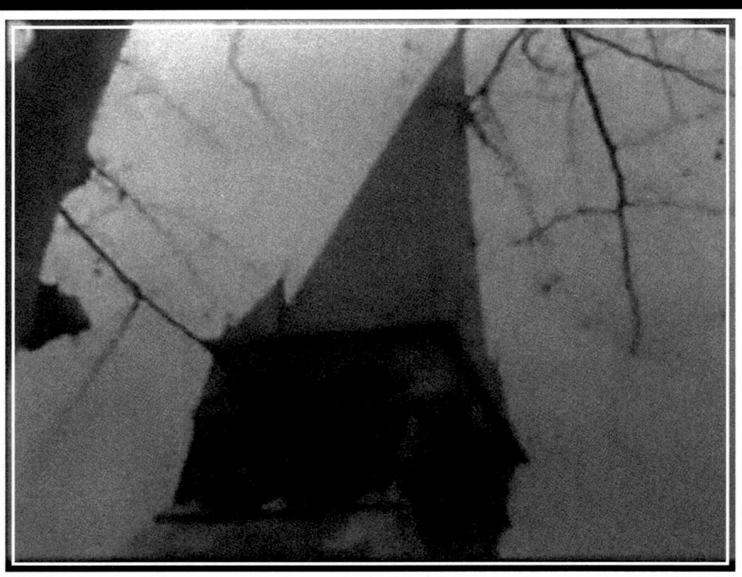

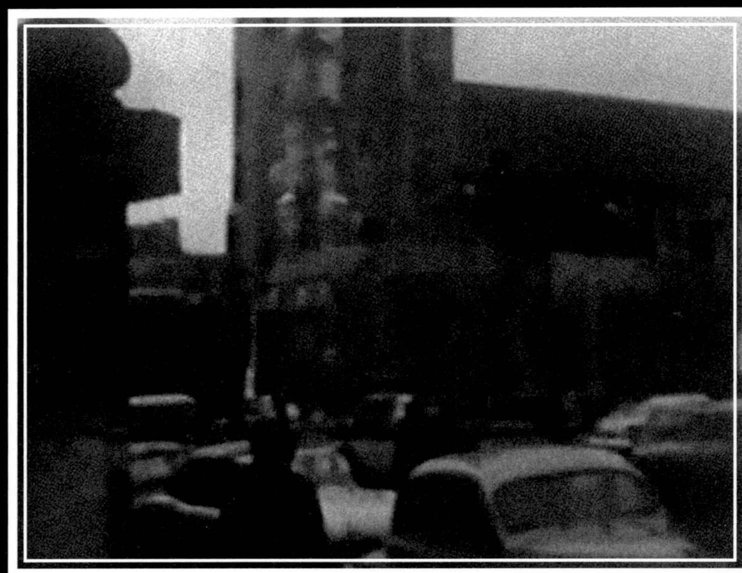

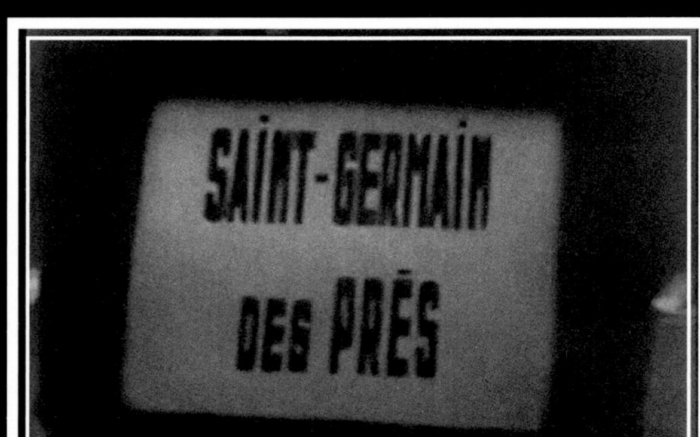
SAINT-GERMAIN
DES PRÉS

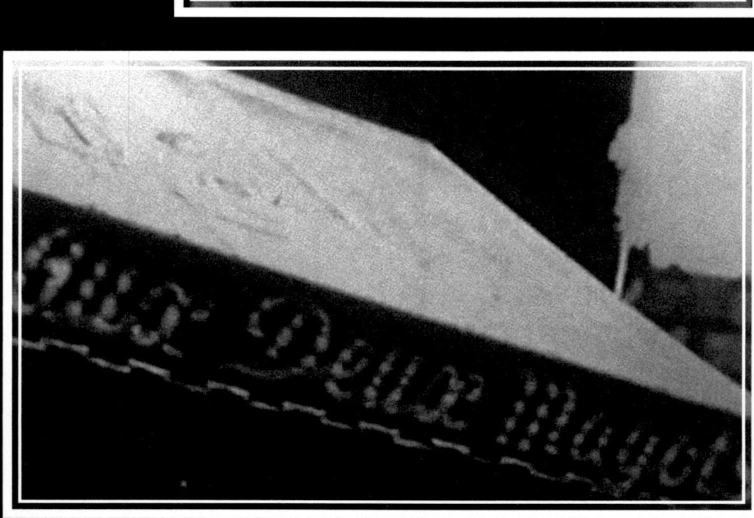
Deux Magot

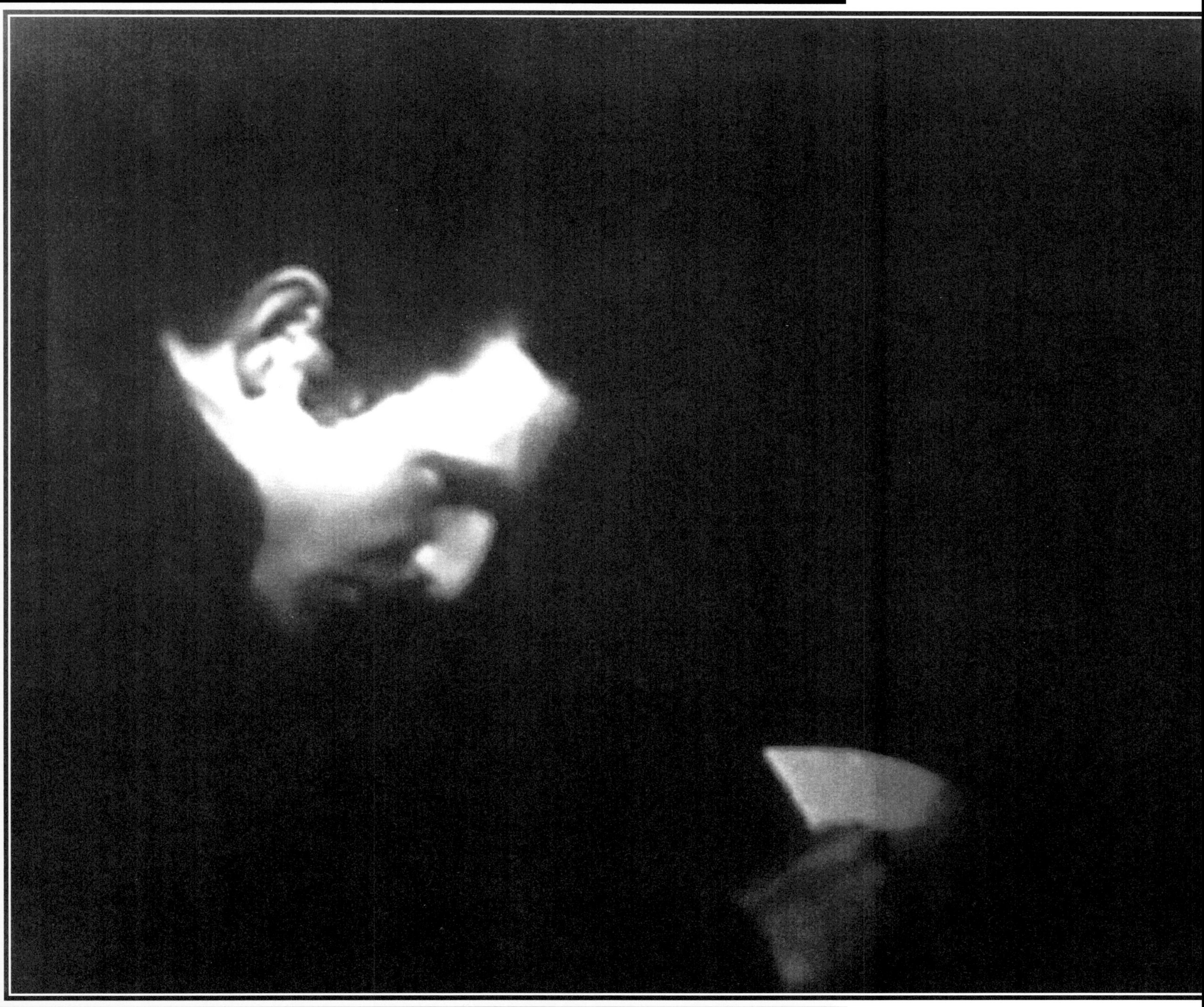

Images taken from the video made by Radio Canada, *ca.* 1950.
Duration 3'.

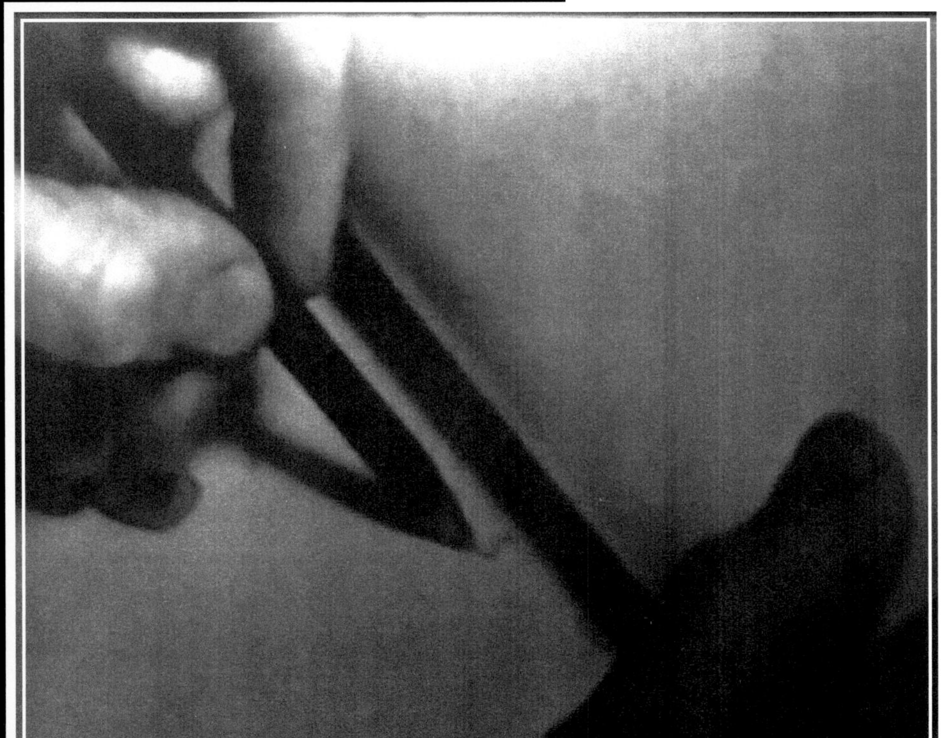

CLUB St GERMAIN-DES-PRÉS
13, RUE SAINT-BENOIT
PARIS-VIe LIT. 81-84

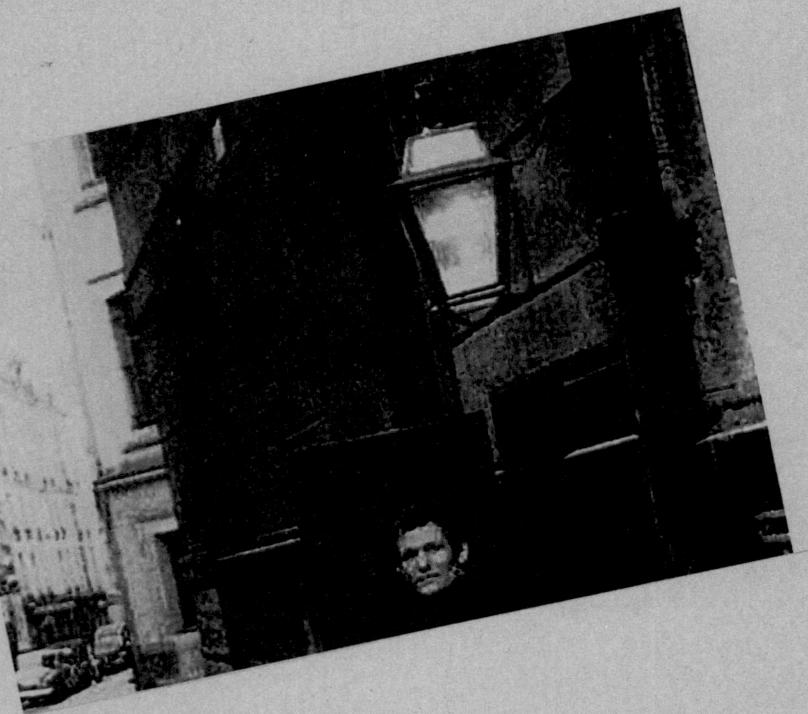

CLUB St GERMAIN-DES-PRÉS
13, RUE SAINT-BENOIT
PARIS-VIe LIT. 81-84

FONDÉ PAR BORIS VIAN-1945-49
(verificar)

Acceulant depuis lors les plus ménoromes mu… du milieu du Jazz d'amerique et de France.
Boris Vian
Sidney Bechet
Stephan Grapelli
Django Reinehart
Miles Davis
Modern Jazz Quartet
Art Blakey's - jazz messengers
Bud Powell
Barney Whilen
Sasha Distel
Reñé Urtreger
Marcial Solal

Con apariciones breves de Billy Holiday y Juliette Greco

CLUB St GERMAIN-DES-PRÉS
13, RUE SAINT-BENOIT
PARIS-VIe LIT. 81-84

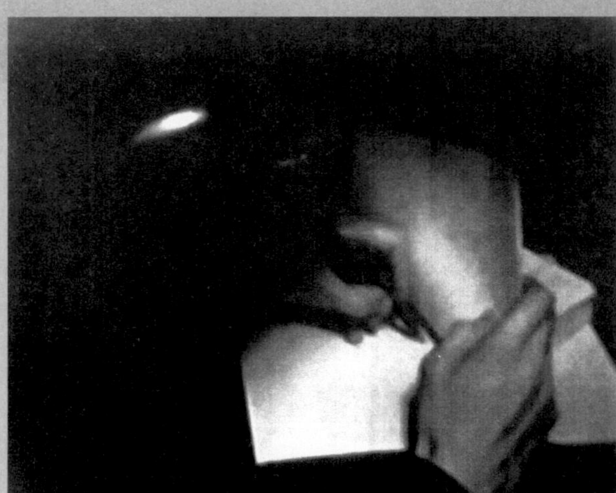

CLUB DE St GERMAIN-DES-PRÉS
LIBRAIRIE GALERIE D'ART
13, RUE SAINT-BENOIT (VIe)
R. C. 348.084 LIT. 81-84

PARIS le 17 Mars 1958

Je soussignée Madame MICHEL, Présidente de la SOCIETE D'EXPLOITATION DU CLUB DE SAINT-GERMAIN DES-PRES 13 Rue Saint-Benoit PARIS (6°),

certifie employer en qualité de Portier dans mon Etablissement, Monsieur Alain GLASS demeurant 5 Rue Manuel Paris (9°), de nationalité Canadienne.

Cet employé est entré à mon service le 1er Août 1956 au Salaire Net actuel de 29.030 Frs.

Fait à PARIS le 17 Mars 1958

La Présidente,

CLUB St-GERMAIN-DES-PRÉS - PARIS-6e - 13, Rue St-Benoit

Madame MICHEL Michèle

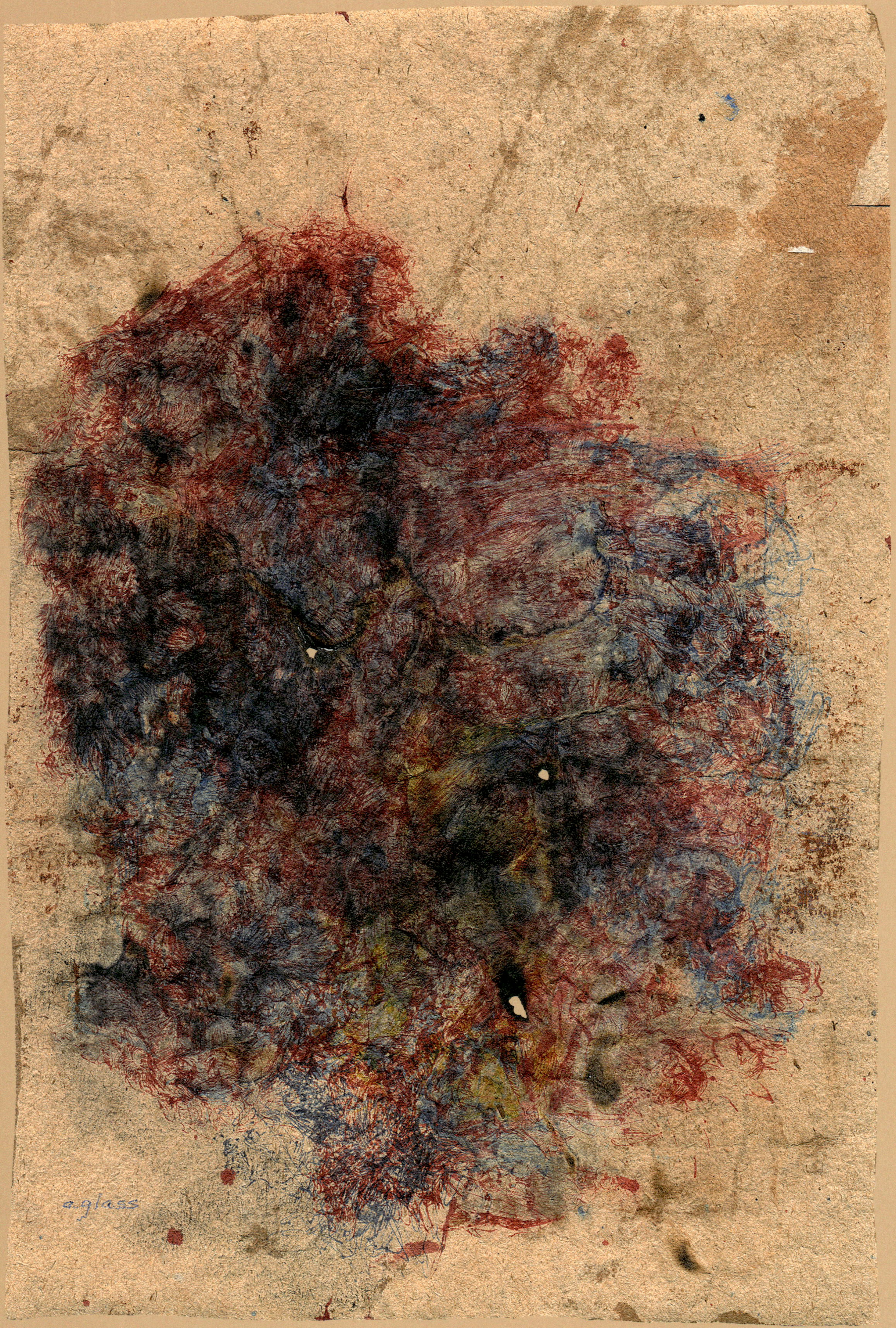
a.glass

ALAN GLASS'S NIGHT SHIFT AUTOMATISM: BALLPOINT PENS, BEBOP JAZZ, AND THE CLUB SAINT-GERMAIN DRAWINGS

Abigail Susik

This is the most beautiful night of all, the lightning-filled night: day, compared to it, is night.
[C'est la plus belle des nuits, la nuit des éclairs: le jour, auprès d'elle, est la nuit.]

André Breton,
Manifeste du surréalisme, 1924.

I
IMAGINING A NIGHT IN THE LIFE OF A JAZZ CLUB DOORMAN: SUNDAY, DECEMBER 21, 1958

It is 9 PM on a weekday evening in late December, and the young Canadian artist Alan Glass has just arrived for his night shift as the doorman for the Club Saint-Germain-des-Prés, the renowned *cave* or cellar jazz club in on the Left Bank of Paris, not far from the Jardin du Luxembourg.[1] He has walked clear across the breadth of central Paris, as he does every workday, from the Right Bank area of Pigalle/Montmartre in the 9me arrondissement to the 6me arrondissement on the Left Bank. This ambulatory, chilly commute takes him about forty minutes each way if he keeps up his pace, but after two years already on the job, he has long since become accustomed to this peripatetic routine. Our doorman starts out from his tiny top-floor *chambre de bonne* [attic] room, rented *sans* plumbing, at 5 rue Manuel, not far from the venerable Musée national Gustave Moreau. He then passes nearby the decayed shopping arcades, such as the Passage des Panoramas, as well as the Bibliothèque nationale at Richelieu and the Louvre, before crossing the river and arriving in the Saint-Germain-des-Prés quarter, located a few blocks from the banks of the River Seine.[2]

Evenings like this one in late 1958, on the verge of the winter *fêtes*, find the Saint-Germain-des-Prés neighborhood bustling and lively with revelry. On the corner of Boulevard Saint-Germain, the celebrated establishments of Café de Flore and Les Deux Magots vie for customers. These opulent 19th-century cafes had benefitted from renewed cachet following World War II and the fall of the French Third Republic, particularly with the *rive gauche* intellectual set who attended the nearby universities and frequented the quarter's many bookstores and publishing houses. Such late-night cafes also catered to the crowds that frequented

Untitled
(Club Saint-Germain period)
ca. 1954-1962
Bicolor blue and red ballpoint pen drawing, with touches of allumettage, on amate paper.
29.4 x 19.9 cm
Artist's collection

[1] I would like to thank Alan Glass, Carlos de Laborde, Marcel Fleiss, and Andrew Wilk for their assistance with research and images for this essay.

[2] Interview with Alan Glass, Mexico City, May 2022. Gérard Lhéritier, *Le Saint-Germain-des-Prés: l'écume des années Vian* (Paris: Le Musée des lettres et manuscrits, 2009), p. 24.

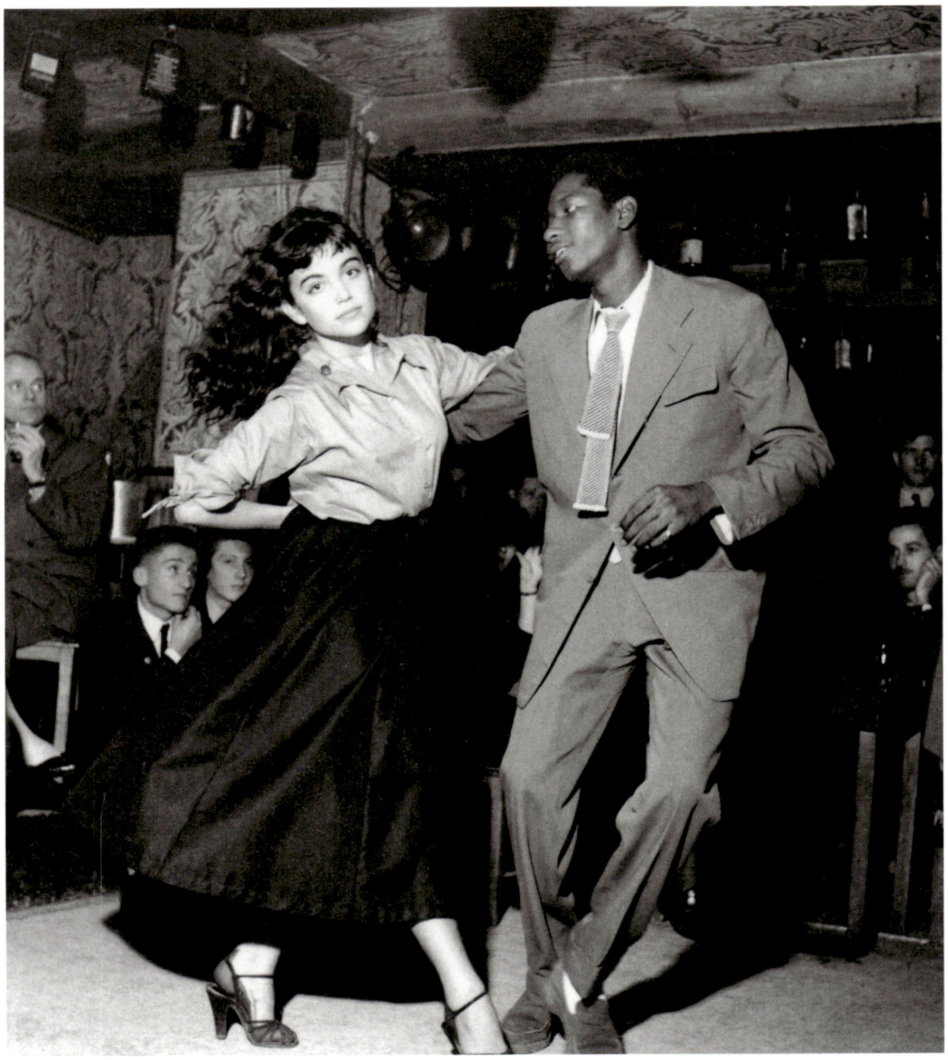

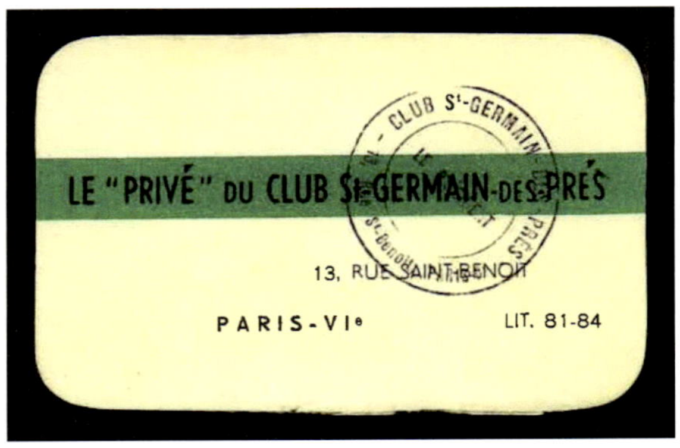

Figure 1.
Robert Doisneau. *Be-Bop in a Cellar*, *ca.* 1951. Paris, James Campbell and Claude Mocquery at the Club Saint-Germain, Saint-Germain-Des-Pres (Photo by Robert Doisneau/Gamma-Rapho/Getty Images).

Figure 2.
Member Card of Club Saint-Germain-des-Prés, *ca.* 1950. Royalty free.

the jazz clubs founded in the area following the war, such as the renowned Le Tabou jazz club, which, like Club Saint-Germain-des-Prés at a certain point during its tenure, required a membership card worth at least a month's worth of payment, *une carte d'abonnement*, to get inside (Figures 1 and 2).

Famous writers, artists, film directors, and musicians, such as Simone de Beauvoir, Jean-Paul Sartre, Juliette Gréco, and Jean Cocteau, increasingly became regulars in the neighborhood as France's post-war reconstruction marched steadfastly into the morass of the Algerian War.[3] This social scene had been already fictionalized by artist and director Jean Cocteau in his haunting, melancholy film, *Orphée* (1950). Cocteau's cinematic depiction of the fictional Café des poètes, the classic caricature of early beatnik bohemianism, featured the actress and chanteuse Juliette Gréco and many of the youthful, black-clad habitués from the *quartier* Saint-Germain-des-Prés cellar demimonde.[4] Gréco was a luminous and beloved fixture at the local clubs, and her renditions of classic *chansons* were a Francophile complement to the jazz sets offered by the mostly American musicians who headlined the shows.

The Club Saint-Germain, as members and regulars called it, sits on a narrow stretch of street at 13 rue Saint-Benoît, tucked between Boulevard Saint-Germain and rue de l'Abbaye. When Alan Glass arrives for his night shift, he settles into the compressed space of the unmarked door to the club, located on the street level, just adjacent to the stairs that lead down to the grotto. This ticket zone is connected to the main stage area of the club only by a small, locked door with an oval porthole window divided by crosswise panes. He sits down on the wooden stool, in front of the little table provided him, and removes a couple of Bic Cristal *stylos*, the plastic ballpoint pens that had only lately been introduced to France in the years following the war. As jazz lovers and night owls of all kinds begin to drop in and pay their way to enter the cellar club for the show that night, Glass takes their money or glances at their stamped membership cards.

Between customers, he quietly begins to draw with his cheap pens constructed of clear plastic and topped with brightly colored caps. He deploys random sheets of paper or sometimes found scraps and announcements from the clubs and *boîtes* nearby. He is not exactly neglecting his doorman work at the club, since the abstract drawings are made in a state of relaxed distraction or trance, rather than through the traditional observation techniques of still life sketching— but neither is he fully alert

[3] Rosemary Wakeman, *The Heroic City: Paris, 1945-1958* (Chicago: The University of Chicago Press, 2009) 246–8. Also see, Herbert R. Lottman, *The Left Bank: Writers, Artists, and Politics from the Popular Front to the Cold War* (Boston: Houghton Mifflin, 1982), 238–40.

[4] Boris Vian, *Manual of Saint-Germain-des-Prés* (1950), trans. Paul Knobloch (New York: Rizzoli, 2005), 115, 126.

"on the job." As the meandering lines of the roller ball pen slowly fill the page, he likewise occupies the numerous minutes in which he is ensconced in the compressed space of the *guichet*, or ticket area. His night shift is about six hours long, lasting until 3 AM, and he is making the most of the measure of time that, in turn, earns him his much-needed pay.[5]

II
Ballpoint Bebop

The post-war market success of the ballpoint pen had rendered the fountain pen outmoded, although of course not everyone was enamored of these new-fangled writing devices. The novelty of the recently-invented ballpoint design, based on wartime advancements in engineering, chemical plastics, and mass production technology, aided and sustained Glass in his aimless drawing pursuit. Plus, their low price could not be beaten. Glass favored the blue and black Bic *stylo-billes*, but sometimes the red and green options had their appeal. There were just five color choices with these mass-manufactured roller ball pens—Glass did not have a predilection for the available violet color— but he made the most of this limited spectrum by gradating the tonality through the density of the web of lines and the thickness of the layered strokes.[6] Sometimes, he combined two or three colors in one drawing.

Much like the club's jazz saxophonists who could play their instruments continually thanks to an energetic and disciplined form of circular breathing, Glass need never lift the self-inking pen from the surface of the page. His drawing activity poured across the page. The lines unraveled endlessly until the ink ran out and the disposable pen could be thrown away. Enabled by this new type of writing tool, his non-mimetic drawings arose without preconception or artistic control, in the precise manner that surrealism's recipe for automatism, first strategized in the mid-1920s, would dictate. Indeed, that is what Glass thought of these abstract and sometimes biomorphic drawings: they were automatic emissions from *elsewhere*. Over the course of his tenure at the club, his drawings had become freer, looser, and more abstract; the automatist trance state had increasingly taken hold of him. He was never aware of what he was doing until the night shift was over and the drawing reached this time-based "completion" or ending. The free-flowing ink of the *stylo-bille* roller balls facilitated a continuous and vibrant type of unhinged contour that allowed one drawn form to mutate into the next without effort or pause.

Much like Alan Glass's Parisian existence as a Canadian expatriate working for a club that hosted traveling American musicians, the story of the Bic Cristal ballpoint pen also arose directly out of the context of wartime diaspora and expatriate ventures. Glass's particular species of automatism, therefore, is an explicit product of the post-war milieu. While the fountain pen first became commercially viable in New York during the mid-1880s, the ballpoint mechanism did not find success on the market until after the Second World War, despite the fact that one early version of its apparatus was first patented in the late 1880s.[7] It was a Hungarian entrepreneur by the name of László Bíró who launched the first successful ballpoint pen in 1942, in Argentina.

[5] Telephone interview with Alan Glass, March 7, 2022.

[6] James Ward, *The Perfection of the Paper Clip: Curious Tales of Invention, Accidental Genius, and Stationery Obsession* (New York: Touchstone, 2015), 26.

[7] Ward, *The Perfection of the Paper Clip*, 32. Susan Lambert, "Bic Cristal Pen, France," *Iconic Designs: 50 Stories about 50 Things*, ed. Grace Lees-Maffei(New York: Bloomsbury, 2014), 127.

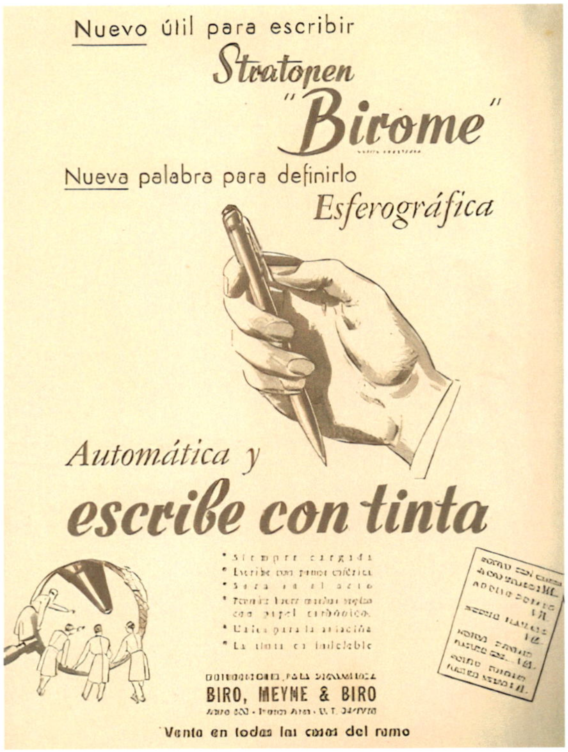

Figure 3.
Anonymous. Advertisement for the "automática" Birome ballpoint pen. Revista Leoplán, 1945. Fair use.

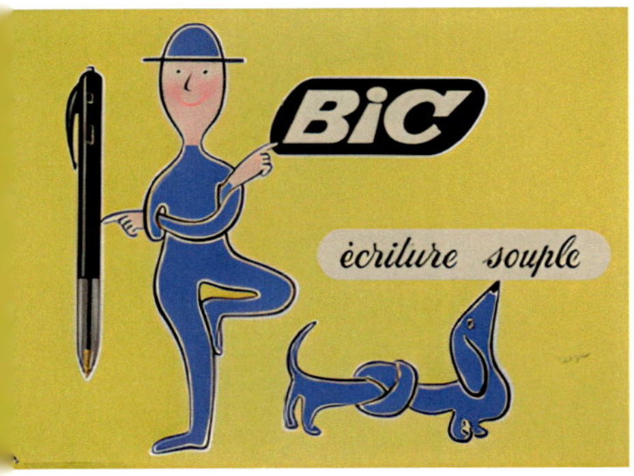

Figure 4.
Raymond Savignac. *Écriture souple*. Advertisement for Bic Cristal, 1956. Author's collection.

Bíró was a Hungarian Jew who was forced to flee to South America due to antisemitic religious persecution. Following his emigration from Europe, his first product on the Argentinian market was the "Eterpen," a name signaling the power of limitless or eternal script.[8]. By 1945 he was calling his pen the "Birome" and advertising it in Buenos Aires as "automática" because of its unprecedented fluid utility (Figure 3).

Many companies around the world jumped on the ballpoint bandwagon after hearing about Bíró's novel South American product, but in France, it was Marcel Bich, another émigré who had moved to France from Italy during the 1930s, who led the pack. His company's Bic Cristal bolted onto the French postwar market at the end of 1950, and by 1951 the sales already numbered in the millions.[9] The disposable Bic Cristal that Alan Glass preferred cost anywhere from 50-80 francs during the 1950s (about $2.50 today), but there were also more expensive refillable and luxury versions available.[10] However, these refined models remained well beyond Glass's budget.

In 1952, French designer Raymond Savignac launched a strikingly cheerful promotional campaign for the Bic Cristal pen, and by 1956, he unveiled the "écriture souple" [supple script] advertisement, depicting a cartoonish contortionist in a blue bodysuit and a pretzel-tied blue dachshund on a bright yellow ground (Figure 4). The idea behind the Bic campaign was clear: their *stylo-bille* was flexible and fun, and it could outpace the fusty fountainpen any day. Glass's jazz club drawings were indeed roping the contour line of the beaux arts draughtsman into the most labyrinthine of automatist knots. The key idea with the ballpoint pen is that the writer never had to stop writing, which made it an ideal tool for postwar automatist practice, at least in the hands of Alan Glass. Since as early as 1924, French surrealists had been seeking a perfect fluidity of speed in automatic writing.[11]

III

The Night Shift as Jazz Nocturne

Our doorman-artist was in the habit of making one drawing per night shift. The drawing commenced when he sat down at the stool next to the club entrance and ended when the last customers were heading up the stairs to go home and the musicians were packing up their gear. In this way, each drawing represented one night of work, just as each night shift earned Glass barely enough to pay his way for an extremely modest lifestyle in the capital city.[12]

No one seemed to mind his workplace doodling activities, including his boss, Michelle Michel (whose sister, Maria Mauban, was a well-known actress at the time). He had gotten hooked up with the job during the summer of 1956, about four years after he moved to Paris from Canada, having rapidly completed his first years of the obligatory formal classes at l'École des Beaux-

[8] Lees-Maffei, *Iconic Designs*, 127.

[9] Ward, *The Perfection of the Paper Clip*, 26–7.

[10] Ward, *The Perfection of the Paper Clip*, 27.

[11] See for example, Francis Gérard, "L'État d'un surréaliste," *La Révolution surréaliste* 1 (December 1, 1924): 30. Also see my discussion of the writing technologies associated with 1920s surrealism in chapter 2 of my book: Abigail Susik, *Surrealist Sabotage and the War on Work* (Manchester: Manchester University Press, 2021), 50–109.

arts in Montreal to the astonishment of all (he completed a four-year degree in just two). Subsequently, he had the privilege of being admitted to the Alfred Pellan atelier for painting, and this was how Glass eventually received a fellowship from the French government to study art in Paris. Pellan, who had been living in Paris since the late 1920s, in the avant-garde métier of arts, returned to Canada at the outbreak of the Second World War. His arrival was a revelation to the Canadian art scene of the time, an explosion of color and imagination never seen before in those grey-colorless years during the war.[13]

Glass's automatic drawing practice was already well underway by the time he became a doorman (paintings were a rarity in his oeuvre after he departed from Canada), and there was no reason for him to stop this activity despite his new employment. As a Canadian ex-pat, he needed the money so that he could afford to live after his French government fellowship to study art had run out. Even though postwar Paris was still cheap, and although his characteristic austerity meant that he could survive on next to nothing, it was a struggle to get by. Knowing that he needed money, one of Glass's friends had slipped a note under his room door informing him of the job opening.[14]

The night shift allowed him to devote part of his day to making artworks in the limited space available in his cramped attic *chambre*, and the nature of this doorman gig also meant that he could wield the rolling ballpoint pen however he liked during his nocturnal session. The Saint-Germain-des-Prés drawings, therefore, encompassed a different kind of *art-work*. This was automatism produced on the boss's clock. Drawings resulted from the soft sabotage tactic of stealing time while on the job.[15] It was also a strategy of killing boredom during the largely passive hours of surveying the club door. The required work hours filled with the repetitive actions of taking money, giving tickets, stamping membership cards—and above all waiting, waiting for the next customer, waiting for the night to end—morphed into a state of prolonged distraction. The boundaries of the work of art were determined by this artificially imposed waged time.

As night shift artworks, Glass's drawings resulted in a transmogrified and industrialized version of the aesthetic category of the *nocturne*. In the late 19th century, American painter James Abbott McNeill Whistler adopted "nocturne" from the world of classical music and granted it fresh aesthetic applications related to his fine art practice.[16] For the 19th-century European musicians who adopted the "nocturne" framework from their Enlightenment-era predecessors, this category either referred to compositions devoted to the subject of the nighttime, or those that were meant to be played late at night, such as a moonlit serenade performed at midnight.[17] In Whistler's appropriation of this notion of art made in the absence of the sun's rays, from within the foggy realm of sleep and dreams, a painterly nocturne was not so much a denotative or figurative depiction of the night as it was an aesthetic meditation on a contemplative state of mind or mood, often rendered on the canvas as a near-abstract arrangement of forms in harmony.[18] As expressed by author Hélène Valance in her study *Nocturne: Night in American Art, 1890-1917* (2018): "The nocturne, in moving inward toward an art

[12] Telephone interview with Alan Glass, March 17, 2022.

[13] Alan Glass, email to author, July 25, 2022.

[14] Telephone interview with Alan Glass, March 25, 2022.

[15] For a discussion of sabotage tactics in relation to interwar surrealism, see, Susik, *Surrealist Sabotage and the War on Work*, 1–21.

[16] Hélène Valance, *Nocturne: Night in American Art, 1890-1917*, trans. Jane Marie Todd (New Haven: Yale University Press, 2018), 17–32.

[17] John Michael Cooper, *Historical Dictionary of Romantic Music* (Lanham, MD: Scarecrow Press, 2013), 408–09.

[18] Valance, *Nocturne*, 19–21.

where less is seen, and even, strictly speaking, where there is almost nothing to see, imposed a new form of perceiving, consuming, and interpreting the image."[19] For Valance, late-19th century visual art nocturnes were "vague and inward-looking" explorations of an unknown space, "antivisions" that placed themselves "outside the field of the visible."[20]

Since its inception in the early 1920s, surrealism had been preoccupied with the substance of the dream and the possibility of artificially conjuring oneirism outside the confines of nighttime sleep, through trance states, collective seances, waking dreams, and a range of other techniques meant to loosen the grip of conscious rationality. This was because, as stated by André Breton in his 1924 *Manifesto of Surrealism*, in everyday life, "the dream finds itself reduced to a mere parenthesis, as is the night. And, like the night, dreams generally contribute little to furthering our understanding."[21] The activity of dreaming in sleep was corralled into a sequestered portion of experience and consciousness, and so remained largely inaccessible for aesthetic or investigative purposes. The collective and individual practice of surrealist psychic automatism was not necessarily tied to a literal sleep state as such, nor was it inherently connected to those hours of obscurity after sundown and before dawn. In Breton's *Manifesto*, automatic writing (*l'écriture automatique*) is described simply as the "actual functioning of thought," and moreover, automatism is "dictated by thought in the absence of any control exercised by reason."[22]

Nevertheless, the nighttime did occupy something of a privileged role in the movement. For Breton, surrealist automatism itself could be likened to the experience of a gorgeous nighttime thunderstorm in which bolts of lightning repeatedly shatter the enveloping darkness. These figurative lightning strikes were the surrealist sparks of light created by the clash of discontinuous associations, for the images obtained through the practice of psychic automatism possessed electricity, a restless and self-emanating light, according to Breton. In the *Manifesto* he writes:

> And just as the length of the spark increases to the extent that it occurs in rarefied gases, the Surrealist atmosphere created by automatic writing, which I have wanted to put within the reach of everyone, is especially conducive to the production of the most beautiful images. One can even go so far as to say that in this dizzying race the images appear like the only guideposts of the mind. By slow degrees the mind becomes convinced of the supreme reality of these images. At first limiting itself to submitting to them, it soon realizes that they flatter its reason, and increase its knowledge accordingly. The mind becomes aware of the limitless expanses wherein its desires are made manifest, where the pros and cons are constantly consumed, where its obscurity does not betray it. It goes forward, borne by these images which enrapture it, which scarcely leave it any time to blow upon the fire in its fingers. This is the most beautiful night of all, the *lightning-filled night:* day, compared to it, is night.[23]

Alan Glass's night shift automatism can be provocatively conceptualized in relation to Breton's musings on the subjects of the

[19] Valance, *Nocturne*, 17.

[20] Valance, *Nocturne*, 17.

[21] André Breton, "Manifesto of Surrealism," in *Manifestoes of Surrealism*, trans. Richard Seaver and Helen R. Lane (Ann Arbor: University of Michigan Press, 1972), 11.

[22] Breton, "Manifesto of Surrealism," 26.

[23] Breton, "Manifesto of Surrealism," 37–9.

dream, sleep, and the night. What did it mean for our doorman, a Canadian expatriate in Paris, to undertake a nightly work shift practice of automatic drawing in the post-World War II period? How can we understand the immense significance of his time-based, nocturnal automatism as a type of gateway to the unconscious states that might be enabled through the descent into a cellar and the immersion of the self in an aural world of improvisational jazz? Interwar surrealism had provided the framework for a subversion of the wage labor imperative through the active sabotage of its constraints on human life and consciousness, but there was no concrete theory of a music-based stratagem of psychic automatism. Glass's reconfiguration of the sequestered activity of sleep and dreams into the confines of waged nighttime work at a jazz club converts the nocturnal realm into an overarching tool for the extraction of surrealist images and the induction of sparks fomenting from the deepest reaches of the mind.

Writing about the life of Marcel Fleiss, a contemporary of Alan Glass, the French artist Jean-Jacques Lebel has described the 1950s jazz world of New York and Paris as a "nocturnal counter-society."[24] Born in Paris and raised in Brazil during the World War II years, Fleiss was sent by his parents to New York in the early 1950s for professional training as a furrier. While in New York, Fleiss became enamored of the city's jazz scene and began taking photographs of the musicians and the clubs. When he returned to Paris in the mid-1950s, he continued exploring jazz and became a regular at Club Saint-Germain in the years just before Glass started working there. In the early 1970s, Fleiss co-founded the Quatre Mouvements Gallery in Paris, which showed works by artists of the dada and surrealist movements, among other avant-garde selections. According to Lebel, the jazz milieu allowed Marcel Fleiss to "come into contact with his own impulses," because it was in essence a "nocturnal counter-society" that was "governed by laws and autonomous criteria waiting beyond or beneath the system of capitalism."[25] In the act of pursuing jazz by night, following his professional training during the day, Fleiss was able to "free himself somewhat from the laws of the labor market and social conventions."[26]

To what extent was Alan Glass able to comparably "free himself" from the constraints of his necessary paid labor as the doorman of Club Saint-Germain through his automatic drawing practice, fueled in no small part by the spontaneous structures of evening jazz sessions? By transforming his night shift work into the double-production of art-making, Glass actively subverts the confinements of waged employment and its circumscribed hours. By merging the workaday world with the less regulated arenas of night, sleep, play, and pleasure, Glass's night shift automatism conflates the repetitive actions and habits of the worker with the meandering thoughts, fulminating images, and uncontrolled movements and convulsions of the dreamer.

IV
TELEVISION PERSONALITIES

Club Saint-Germain had already enjoyed a long life in the Left Bank artistic milieu. It was founded in 1948 by a group of investors including the writer, musician, and performer Boris Vian. During

[24] Jean-Jacques Lebel, "Flash-back sur un passion," in *Now's the Time*, by Marcel Fleiss et al. (Bleu Outre Mers: Toulon, 2005), 13. My translation.

[25] Lebel, "Flash-back," 13. My translation.

[26] Lebel, "Flash-back," 13. My translation.

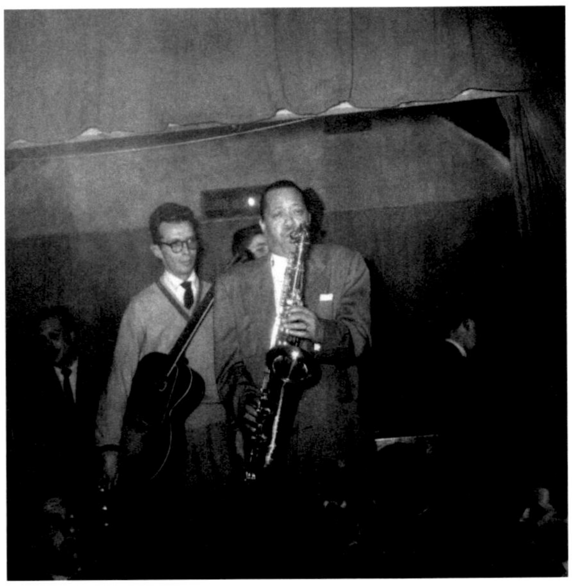

Figure 5.
Marcel Fleiss. *Lester Young y Jimmy Gourley, Club Saint-Germain*, 1954.
Courtesy of Marcel Fleiss.

the immediate postwar years it played host to the major players of the French jazz world, such as Django Reinhardt and Stéphane Grappelli.[27] In those years, Grappelli did not yet enjoy what would soon become his future world fame, although he was already well known by audiences thanks to his previous work with Reinhardt. Grappelli played his violin every night at Club Saint-Germain, and Glass had the pleasure of becoming well acquainted with him.[28]

By the time Glass landed his job at Club Saint-Germain, American jazz musicians were dominating the calendar, especially performers such as Charlie Parker, Stan Getz, Art Blakey, Sidney Bechet, Lester Young ("Pres"), and Miles Davis (Figure 5). The atmospheric American cool jazz scene that kicked off in the late-1940s had given way to the strident rhythms and catchy riffs of bebop and then the syncopations of hard bop by the mid-to-late '50s. Forward-looking artists such as Miles Davis were already beginning to experiment with the more gently gradated modal tunes that would soon infiltrate jazz by the end of the 1950s, with records such as Davis's 1959 *Kind of Blue*.

As the doorman for one of the most prestigious jazz clubs in Paris, Glass had the chance to become casually acquainted with most of the performers, and he was also privy to limited interactions with the movie stars and celebrities who passed by his ticket window. From the start, Club Saint-Germain had established its reputation as an elegant and exclusive *cave*. Gaining admission was difficult since there was not much space in the decrepit cellar downstairs, and especially because there were frequently pairs of dancers swinging wildly in front of the stage.[29] Charlie Chaplin, Brigitte Bardot, and the Prince of Monaco were all attendees, but Glass was never particularly excited by this, nor was he adept at spotting these luminaries and granting them the VIP access they expected. The trance state induced by the automatic night shift drawings perhaps contributed to this obliviousness, which ultimately cost him the job. After working at Club Saint-Germain for years, Glass was eventually dismissed because, to the bewilderment and frustration of the waitstaff and his boss, he kindheartedly permitted penniless nobodies into the club while turning away the elites by mistake.[30]

Club Saint-Germain was extremely popular with American jazz musicians, and nearly all of them sought out a jam session there.[31] The dapper Miles Davis was a particular favorite for the doorman. Davis had become friendly with co-owner, Boris Vian, soon after the club had opened a decade earlier, in the late 1940s, and Vian did everything he could to introduce Paris to the trumpeter's incomparable talent.[32] Davis's band played a range of gigs at Club

[27] Elizabeth Vihlen McGregor, *Jazz and Postwar French Identity: Improvising the Nation* (Lanham, MD: The Rowman & Littlefield Publishing Group, 2016), 31–2.
[28] Alan Glass, email to author, July 25, 2022.
[29] Marcel Fleiss, email to author, July 13, 2022.
[30] Telephone interview with Alan Glass, March 17, 2022.
[31] Marcel Fleiss, email to author, July 13, 2022.
[32] John F. Szwed, *So What: The Life of Miles Davis* (New York: Simon & Schuster, 2002), 82–4, 155–56.

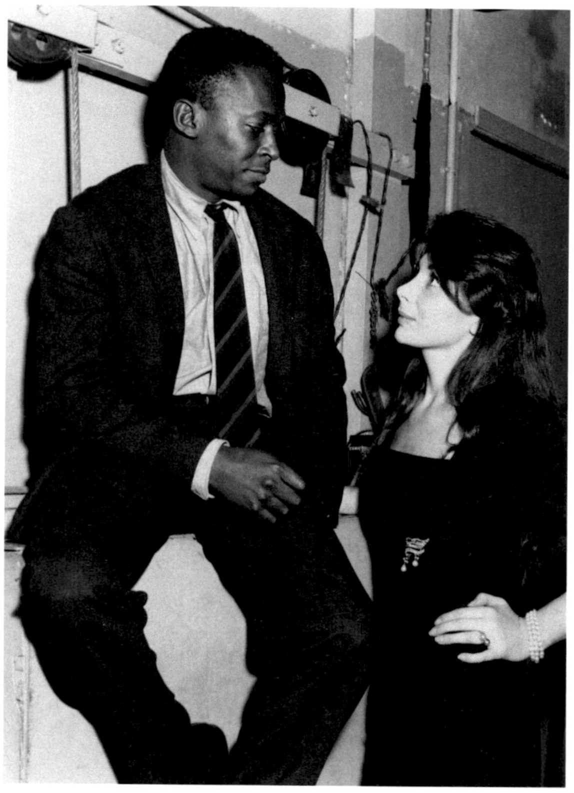

Figure 6.
Juliette Gréco and and Miles Davis in Paris, France. (Photo by Andre SAS/Gamma-Rapho via Getty Images). Club Saint-Germain-des-Prés, *ca*. 1950s.

Saint-Germain in 1957 during the era of albums such as *Birth of the Cool* and *'Round About Midnight*, and he had spent some happy evenings at Club Saint-Germain a year later in 1958 with his girlfriend at the time, Juliette Gréco (Figure 6).[33]

Occasionally, people who passed by the entrance of the Club Saint-Germain noticed the doorman quietly making drawings. On one recent night, for instance, Glass realized that someone was watching him over his shoulder as he drew, and he turned around to see an extravagantly mustachioed man peering through the porthole window in the door. His voyeur was the renowned French Lyrical Abstraction painter Georges Mathieu, famous for his dynamic live painting performances and his outrageous self-presentation. Matthieu was a pioneer of what would later come to be called the "happening." Starting in 1954, he had begun to organize media spectacles around his action painting sessions with oversize canvases, a unique take on the abstract expressionist vogue trumpeted by so many artworld savants from the United States. By 1956, he gave a painting performance with a massive twelve by four-meter canvas and 800 tubes of paint for around 2,000 people at the Théâtre de la Ville-Sarah-Bernhardt. In 1959, he performed for a Paris television network while jazz drummer Kenny Clarke soloed next to the canvas (Figure 7).[34]

Once Glass spied the mustachioed man peering through the door, Mathieu approached and asked if he could see the drawings. "I don't look at my drawings until they are finished," Glass told him, explaining that he wasn't conscious of what he was doing as he worked on the page. "Come back after the show and we will see if it's done." Mathieu left, and toward the end of the night returned to see if Glass was finally ready to share his drawing. Taken aback, Glass politely but firmly declined. The band's set was still blasting up the stairs and he remained gripped by the temporality of his automatic session. The annoyed Mathieu skulked away. "Vous avez tort!" [you're mistaken] Mathieu cried, assuming that Glass did not know who he was.

Yet, the truth was that Glass had already seen plenty of famous people and television personalities come through the door, and he didn't feel he needed to share his drawings with anyone.[35] Indeed, Glass's interest in invisibility and hermeticism only became more entrenched once the artist moved to Mexico during the first years of the 1960s. By the end of that decade, he enjoyed making drawings so miniature and so fine, they required a magnifying glass for viewing.

If the free-flowing improvisation of bebop jazz was certainly an influence for Mathieu, his take on the total abandon of control

[33] McGregor, *Jazz and Postwar French Identity*, 42.

[34] Jill Carrick, *Nouveau réalisme, 1960s France and the Neo-avant-garde: Topographies of Chance and Return* (Burlington, VT: Ashgate, 2010), 56–7.

[35] Interview with Alan Glass, Mexico City, May 2022.

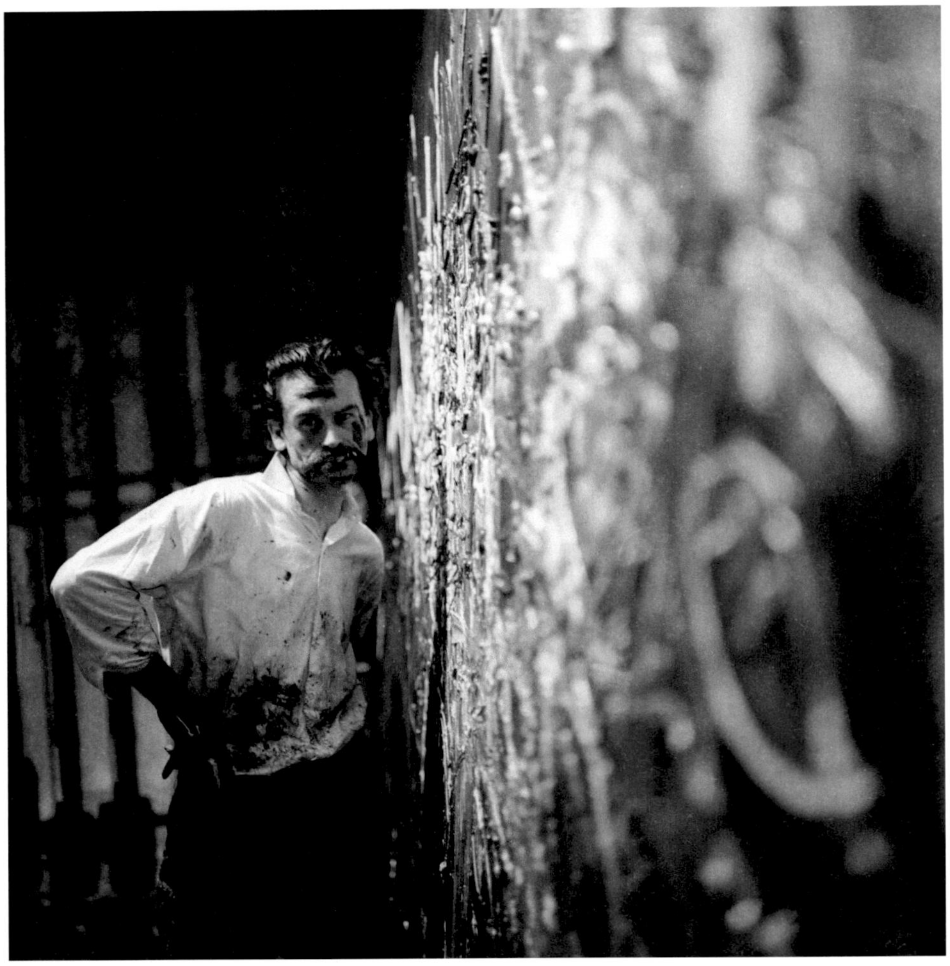

Figure 7. Anonymous, *French Painter Georges Mathieu during one of his special paint performances*, 1959. (Photo by Imagno/Getty Images).

in surrealist automatism was stubbornly vague. Abstract expressionism's rapport with surrealist automatism was tense to say the least. One wonders what Mathieu's opinion of Glass's drawings would have been had the doorman relented. Even when Glass's drawings assumed an all-over composition of tactile scratch marks and hatchings, somewhat akin to Ab Ex stylings, the scriptural nature of his 'inscribed' drawings, if you will—their 'written' quality— always aligned them closer to a surrealist genealogy than any sweeping action painting gesture.

The ironic fact was that Glass had himself already been featured in a television sequence earlier that year. A Canadian TV crew filmed him during his doorman shift at the club as part of a short feature devoted to the occasion of Glass's first solo gallery show at Eric Losfeld's Galerie Le Terrain Vague in Paris at the beginning of 1958, an exhibition that surrealists André Breton and Benjamin Péret had been instrumental in organizing. The after-hours footage lingered briefly on the glitzy electric signage of Saint-Germain-des-Prés and played up the contrast of this luminosity with the black saturation of the darkness outside. Glass appears in the footage not unlike a Toulouse-Lautrec of the 20th century, a denizen of the night who observes everything from his aloof perch. Amidst all of this attention, Bic pen corporation caught wind of Glass's show at Galerie Le Terrain Vague, and a representative from the firm purchased one of Glass's automatic drawings for the company's art collection.

V
ART BLAKEY AND THE JAZZ MESSENGERS ON RECORD AT CLUB SAINT-GERMAIN

Back at the Club-Saint Germain, on a Sunday evening in late December at the end of 1958, just before Christmas, Glass is selling tickets, checking dog-eared membership cards, and applying his ballpoint pen to the sheets of paper he brought with him. Meanwhile, the jazz drummer and bandleader from Pittsburgh, Art Blakey, is coordinating with his Jazz Messengers to get ready for their first set of the night. There are two shows offered today, as the club's advertisement card states—a matinee, and a soiree. If customers don't have a membership card, they can pay 1,000 francs to sit at the bar, 1,000 for the matinee, or 1,500 for the main *salle* (Figure 8).

The band had been in residence at the club for five days that winter of 1958, between December 16 and 20, and they liked the place so much they decided to record the final day's performance for a series of three vinyl pressings that would eventually be released and later celebrated as some of the band's all-time top recordings. Lee Morgan is there, on trumpet, as is Benny Golson on tenor, Bobby Timmons on piano, and Jimmie (Jymie) Merritt on bass. Percussionists Kenny Clarke (drums) and someone else on bongos or congas (possibly Gana M'Bow, but no one remembers for sure now) also jump in at certain points during the sets, adding more impact to Blakey's innovations with the drum kit. Raymond Treillet was present to manage the mono recordings for the RCA pressings, which were eventually released exclusively in France.[36] A second series of recordings was made by the band at the larger Olympia concert hall, but record collectors later came to covet the rarer Club Saint-Germain vinyl.

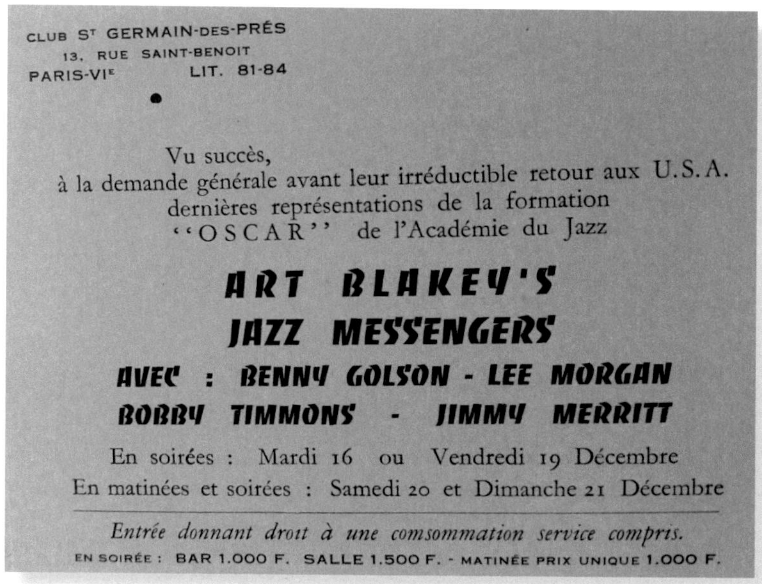

Figure 8.
Advertisement card,
Club Saint-Germain-des-Prés,
December 21, 1958.
Collection of Alan Glass.

Once the evening gig starts, Glass can easily hear the music from where he is seated on his stool. He can't see the players on stage, nor can he surmise the mood of the crowd, packed as they are into the tight space below. But he keeps his eye on the door, since that's his job, after all, and he can get a feel for the composition of the audience as customers queue up to enter. The house is full to the gills, so Glass is not able to get into a groove with his automatic drawing practice until well after 10 PM. As he sits at the little table near the door, he can see reflections of the glowing lights of the Saint-Germain-des-Prés *quartier* and hear voices of people strolling by, talking and enjoying the brisk Parisian evening. But for the most part, Glass can't help but be enveloped by the music of Blakey and the Messengers, who are already launching into their first set. His graphic activity on the page creates a conversation of sorts—a non-verbal exchange betwixt sounds, lines, and shapes—echoes of the flourishes embellished by the jazz musicians are inevitably shaped by his individual perception of the music.

The power of Benny Golson's tenor sax blows up the stairs, and the timbre of Lee Morgan's horn is powerfully clear. The band bounds forward with the swinging rhythm and blues tune "Politely," written not long before by American trumpeter Bill Hardman, which stretches out for over fifteen minutes once all the musicians get a chance to solo. The crowd and the players are quickly drawn into the energy of the song, and Glass can hear excited cries that punctuate the crescendos of the drums and the synchronized phrasing of the two brass instruments (Figure 9).

Under the lamp of the ticket booth, Glass's blue Bic pen glides across the expanse of cream-colored paper (Figure 10). As he pushes the roller ball of the pen into the fibrous texture of the paper, dense areas of saturation begin to emerge. A flock of sinuous, organic-seeming forms are gradually aggregated on the page, vaguely

[36] Andrew Wilk, "Art Blakey: Au Club St Germain Vol 3 (1958) RCA," *LondonJazzCollector* (August 27, 2011), https://londonjazzcollector.wordpress.com/2011/08/27/art-blakeys-messengers-club-st-germain-vol-3-1958-france-only-mono/.

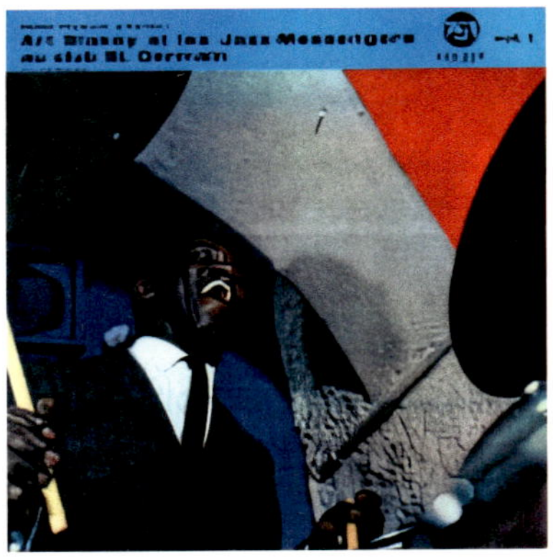

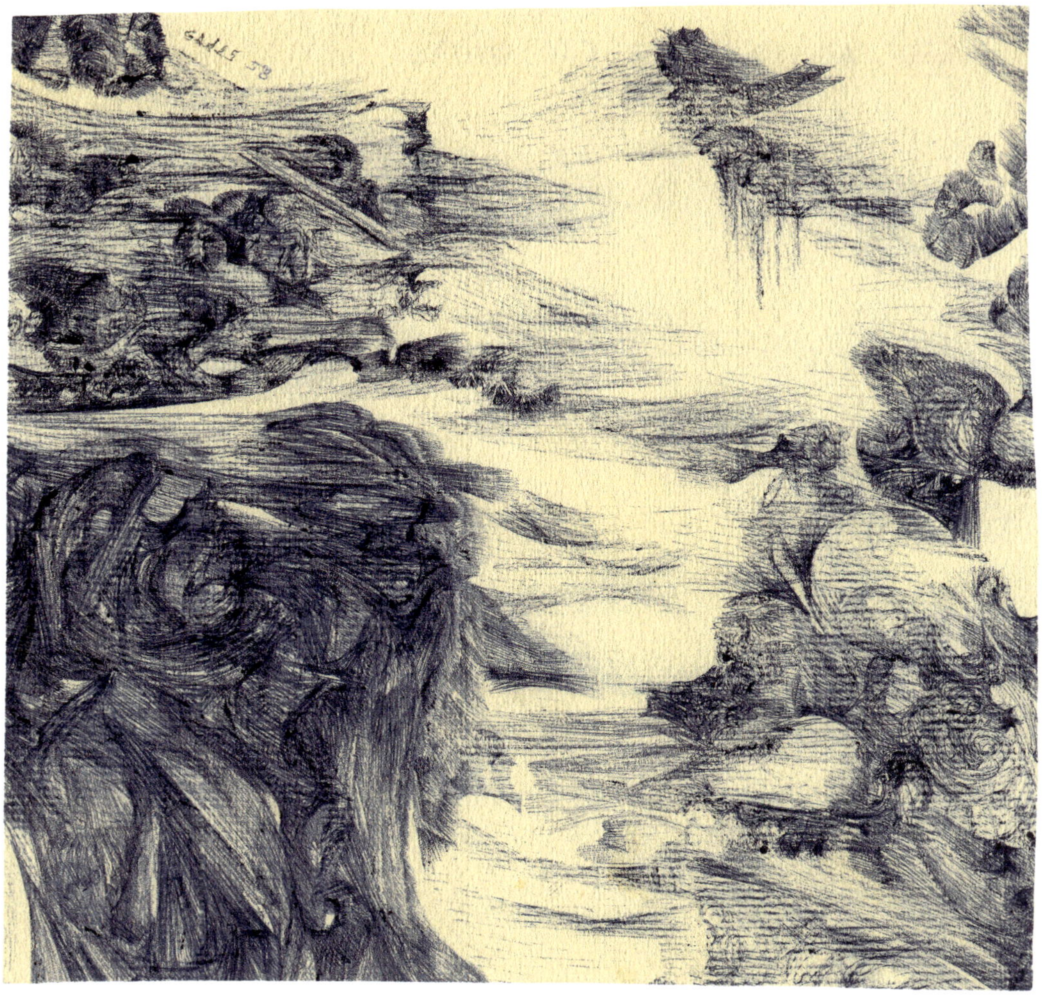

Figure 9.
Art Blakey et Les Jazz-Messengers plus Kenny Clarke au club St. Germain, 1958, volume 1 of 3. RCA Records France.

Figure 10
Untitled
(Club Saint Germain period)
1958
Monochrome blue ballpoint pen drawing, on corrugated paper.
18 x 19.4 cm
Artist's collection

resembling ligaments or the modeling of human musculature. Yet, although the disorienting scale evoked by these abstract forms conjures the mountainous crevices of a moonscape here, or the magnified image of unidentified body parts there, no mimetic image ever coalesces. Lavish detail is granted to the most amorphous of shapes, and a dynamic tide of lines engulfs the paper surface, achieving a dispersed and "all-over" composition.

As pianist Bobby Timmons pushes into a driving and staccato piano solo that drives the crowd into a frenzy of vocalizations, and the band members burst into a chant of "ALL NIGHT LONG!," Glass's pen erupts in a new formation at the bottom right of the page. A compact globular entity with a series of appendages appears adjacent to the serpentine construction opposite. The compositional void at the center of the page only increases the tension between the interplaying forms drawn there. Timmons reaches the end of his solo and someone in the audience shouts, "GOD DAMN!" The dancers in the center of the room pulsate to the beat, unbeknownst to the removed doorman as he sits placidly at his stool above, stopping to smoke a cigarette from time to time.

It isn't until Blakey cues the band to wrap up the next song, a cover of the more relaxed composition "Whisper Not," written by American tenor saxophonist Benny Golson two years earlier, in 1956, that Glass's blue Bic Cristal pen pauses for a few moments. Rather than making just a single drawing per night, tonight's session is unusual. It will accommodate a second "set" of automatic markings, just as Blakey's band was recording multiple sets that day. He lays the blue Bic aside and takes a new sheet, contemplating the allure of the ruby-hued "red" *stylo-bille* he brought with him (Figure 10). The fluid movement of the prior automatic drawing remains, but the new drawing is more contained on the page, hovering over the white ground of the paper. Forms composed of finely nested lines congeal into a larger, snaking shape that winds across the surface. This second automatic drawing comes alive over the course

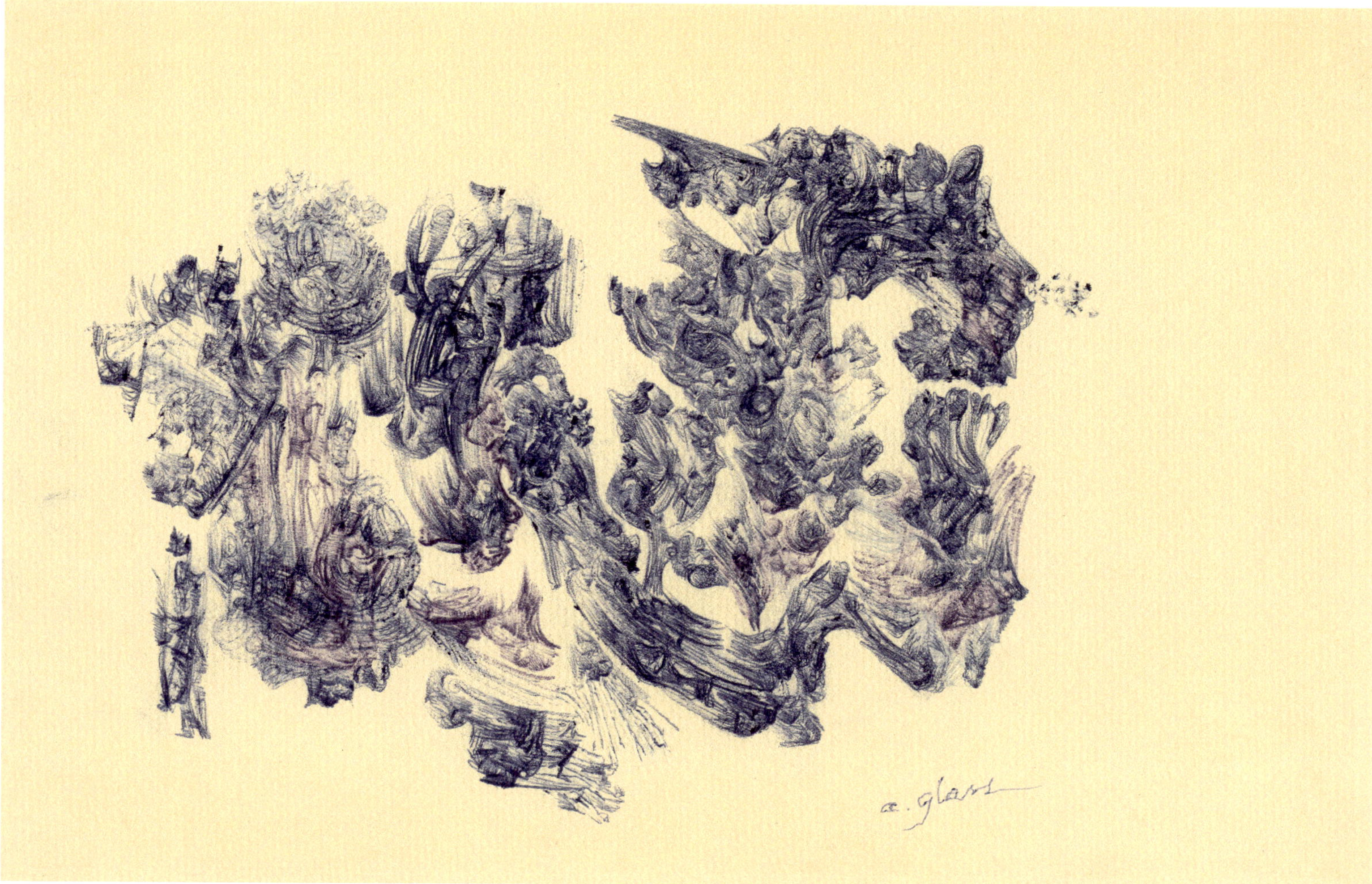

of the set, reaching completion only when Blakey opens the band's cover of "(Evidence) We Named it Justice," by Thelonious Monk, with a powerful drum solo. Blakey's intro is immediately followed by a piercing, brilliant salvo that spills out from Morgan's trumpet. The doorman's Bic pen swerves across the paper. The red ink blends gently into the dominant areas of blue.

EXPATRIATE AUTOMATISM AND TRANSATLANTIC POSTWAR CULTURE

These night shift work sessions exert dramatic effects on Glass's art production. Although the doorman of Club Saint-Germain is not a particularly avid fan of any type of modern music, his night shift "work" produces a unique strain of surrealist automatism—one infused with the playful energy of jazz improvisation and the lively energy of post-Vichy Paris. There is a hallucinatory quality to his passive alertness at the ticket table. Unconscious emissions arise from Glass's job as a threshold "watchman." He is not a jazz enthusiast, but the music surrounds him as he engages the page. Now and then, when he has a break, he descends the stairs of the club so that he can watch the performance.

However, other figures associated with surrealism are enthusiastic jazz fans, such as the sculptor Alberto Giacometti, the poet-filmmaker-artist Georges Hugnet, and the poet-critic Georges Goldfayn, who frequently takes in shows in the Saint-Germain-des-Prés neighborhood.[37] Goldfayn likes to visit Club Saint-Germain, as does the Chilean painter Roberto Matta (who bought one of Alan's drawings earlier that year at the Galerie Le Terrain Vague exhibition), who drops in sometimes.[38]

At about 3.30 AM, when the audience has largely dispersed, and Blakey and the Messengers have nearly finished packing up their gear in preparation for the conclusion of their extended residency at Club Saint-Germain, Glass gathers his pens and drawings and prepares to head home. His Chilean friend, the mime and actor Alejandro Jodorowsky, has stopped by the club to join Glass for the long and bracing

Figure 11.
Untitled
(Club Saint-Germain period)
ca. 1954-1962
Monochrome blue ballpoint pen drawing, with hints of violet, on paper.
16 x 24 cm
Artist's collection

[37] Vian, *Manual of Saint-Germain-des-Prés*, 126, 129–130. Also see, Michael Richardson, "Georges Goldfayn," in *The International Encyclopedia of Surrealism*, ed. Michael Richardson et al. (London: Bloomsbury Press, 2019), 331. Elsewhere, Richardson has traced surrealism's profound affinity with jazz through the tenet of spontaneity. Richardson also discusses the importance of jazz for other surrealists and surrealist associates over the course of the 20th and 21st centuries, such as Victor Brauner, Jayne Cortez, Robert Goffin, Ted Joans,

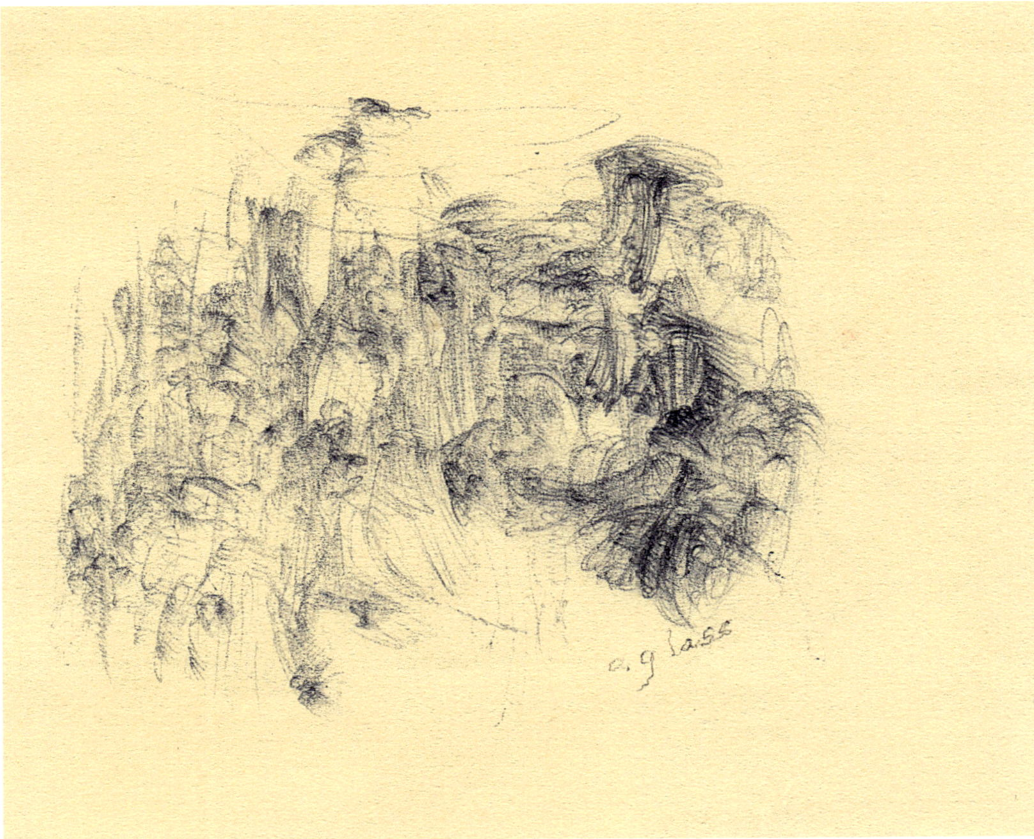

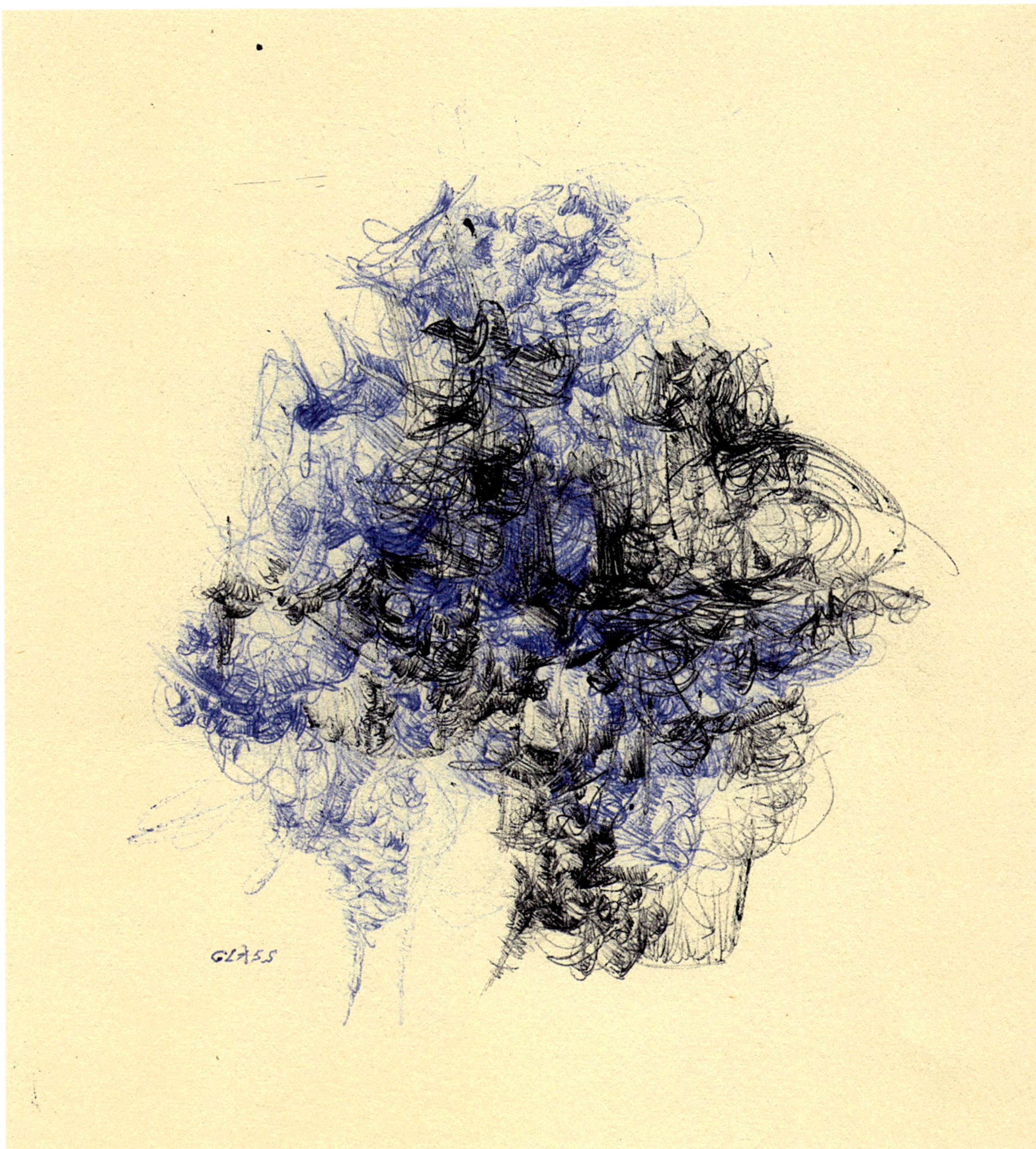

Untitled
(Club Saint-Germain period)
ca. 1954-1962
Monochrome blue ballpoint pen drawing, on paper.
32 x 25 cm
Artist's collection

Untitled
(Club Saint-Germain period)
ca. 1954-1962
Blue and navy blue two-tone ballpoint pen drawing, on paper.
31 x 28 cm
Artist's collection

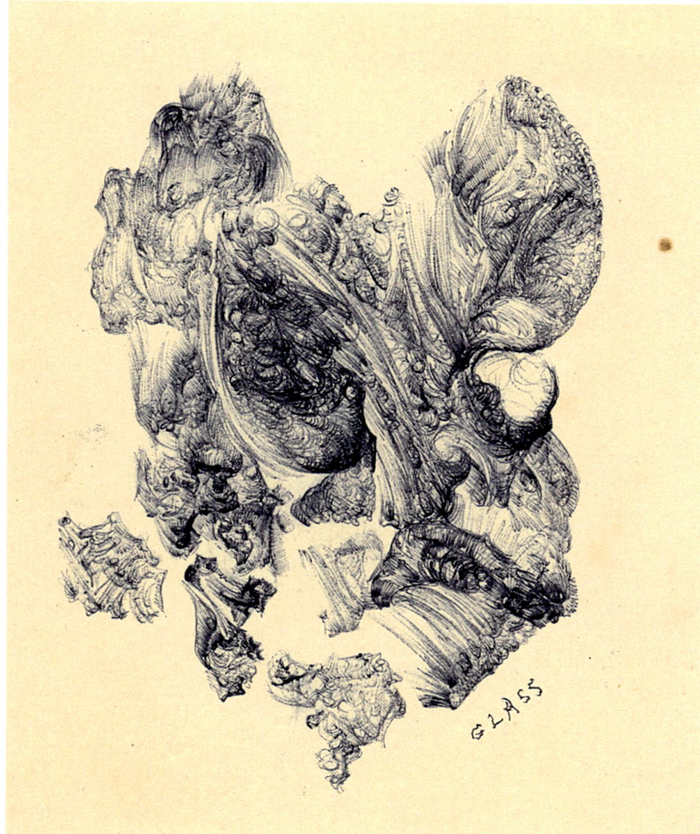

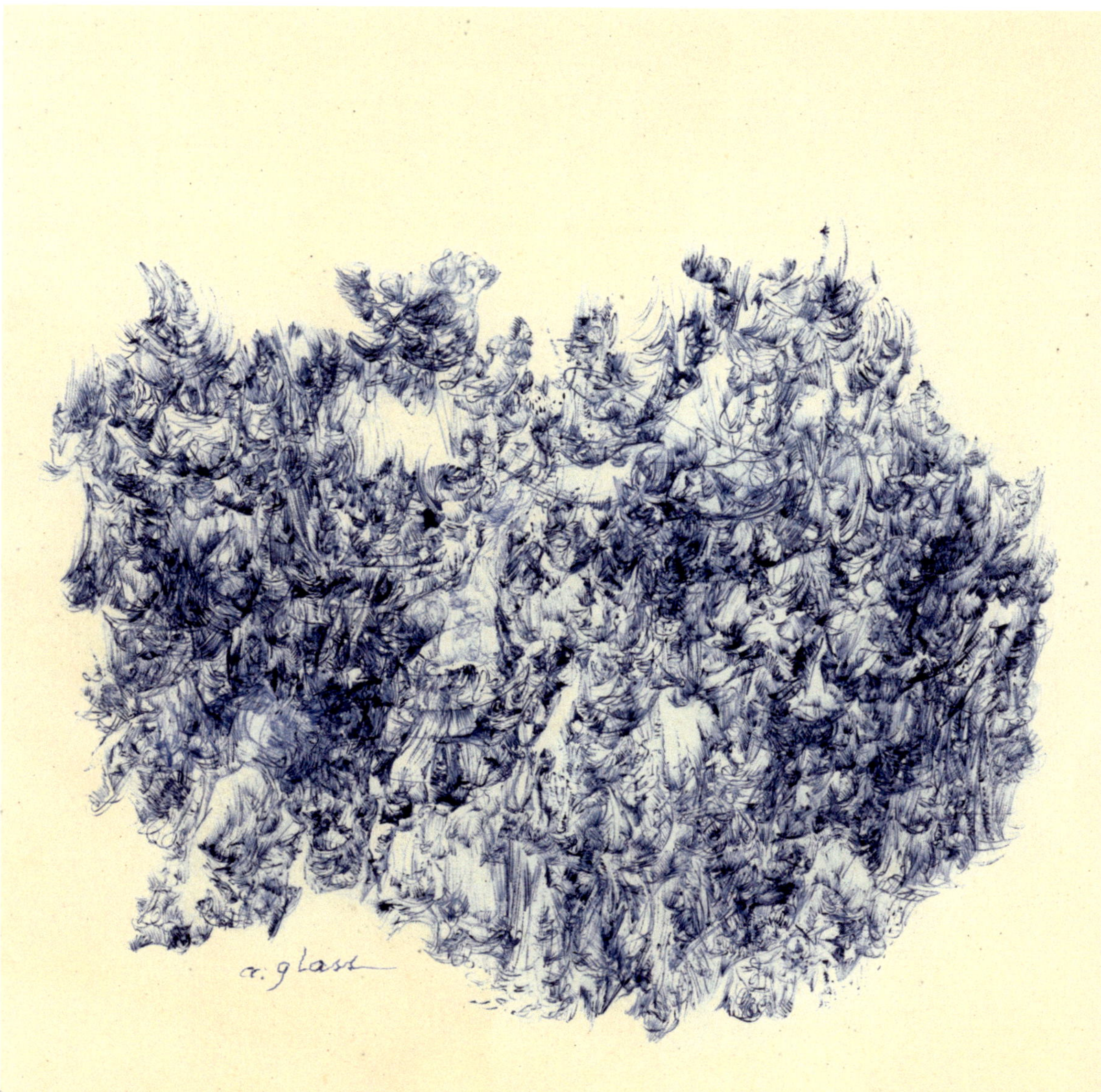

Untitled
(Club Saint-Germain period)
ca. 1954-1962
Monochrome blue ballpoint pen drawing, on paper.
13.5 x 10.5 cm
Artist's collection

Untitled
(Club Saint-Germain period)
ca. 1954-1962
Monochrome blue ballpoint pen drawing, on paper.
25 x 32.5 cm
Artist's collection

walk back toward Montmartre. Jodorowsky lives in a hotel near the Place de Clichy, about fifteen minutes northwest of Glass's place on the rue Manuel, so it is convenient for them to accompany one another. Just two years earlier, Jodorowsky had finished making his first film, the short farce, *Les Têtes interverties* [The Transposed Heads; or, The Severed Heads] (1956), also known as *La Cravate*, which he had written, directed, and starred in. As two expatriates from the north and south antipodes of the Americas, Glass and Jodorowsky had formed a special bond, and their frequently late-night treks across Paris only drew them closer together.

Jodorowsky knew that Glass's experiences at Club Saint-Germain, saturated as they were in the bravado language of jazz, and in particular the boisterous melodies of American bebop, were inseparable from the kind of linear abandon that Glass's nightshift automatic drawings achieved. Less than a year prior, in January of 1958, Jodorowsky had published a short essay for the exhibition pamphlet of Glass's Galerie Le Terrain Vague show. Jodorowsky's text drives the point home: "The ballpoint pen is the implement which opposes the fewest obstacles between impulse and action. It's a question of going faster than consciousness. The ballpoint pen ... comparable to jazz, improvisation, trance, auto-hypnosis. Explosion."[39]

As usual, Glass and Jodorowsky wander through the Les Halles market district on their way home from the Left Bank, stopping to buy a snack of *pommes de terre frites* from the lady who always sells hot French fries outside the Claire de Lune café on the street in the middle of the night. For a few francs they each get a pile of sizzling potatoes wrapped in a cone of newspaper, what Jodorowsky calls a *cucurucho*, while the generous sales lady, seeing that the two men are thin and famished, smiles from ear to ear and heaps on an additional handful for the hungry men. Alejandro cries in response to this magnanimity, "all we want in life is a second handful of fries!"[40]

When Glass and Jodorowsky arrive on the corner of rue Manuel, they notice that the restaurant next door, Gabby and Haynes, located at number 7, is open late to accommodate some of the visiting American jazz musicians who wanted a meal after their sets. Through the illuminated glass windows, they can see the air filled with smoke as people relax at the end of the night. Although Glass could never afford to eat at the restaurant, he was intrigued to observe that some of the very same jazzmen and women who appeared at the Club Saint-Germain eventually ended up at Gabby and Haynes, mixing with the local Black ex-pat community of GI soldiers, writers, and artists, who chose a new life in Paris in the face of Jim Crow segregation laws and rampant racism in the United States.[41]

As an African American man from Kentucky, restaurant co-founder Leroy Haynes saw all the advantages to remaining in Europe after his Army service in Germany had concluded. He moved to Paris and married a Frenchwoman named Gabrielle Lecarbonnier, and in 1949 the couple opened their restaurant, which specialized in Black soul food, such as spareribs, red beans and rice, and collard greens. Within a decade, Gabby and Haynes restaurant became a famous and beloved spot for African Americans in

Michel Leiris, Roberto Matta, Franklin Rosemont, and others. Michael Richardson, "Jazz," in *The International Encyclopedia of Surrealism*, ed. Michael Richardson et al. (London: Bloomsbury Press, 2019), 369–72. Alan Glass's Club Saint-Germain drawings are a crucial but previously overlooked component of this history of the surrealist engagement with jazz and Black arts. Richardson's discussion of the first essay comparing surrealism and jazz, written by Robert Goffin in 1944 is particularly relevant in relation to Glass's 1950s Saint-Germain-des-Prés drawings, although I will not discuss it here. Jean-Jacques Lebel states that Elisa Breton (a concert pianist), Gérard Legrand, and Claude Tarnaud, among other surrealist associates of the Paris group at mid-20th century, should also be counted as jazz enthusiasts. Lebel also cites the importance of Victor Brauner's 1948 painted portrait of Thelonious Monk, and Maurice Henry's 1954 drawn portrait of Monk. Lebel, "Flash-back," 19, 24, 31.

38 Interview with Alan Glass, Mexico City, May 2022.

39 Jodorowsky, untitled text in *Alain* [*sic*] *Glass*, n.p. My translation. On the subject of Glass's 1958 exhibition at Le Terrain Vague, also see: Abigail Susik, "The Alchemy

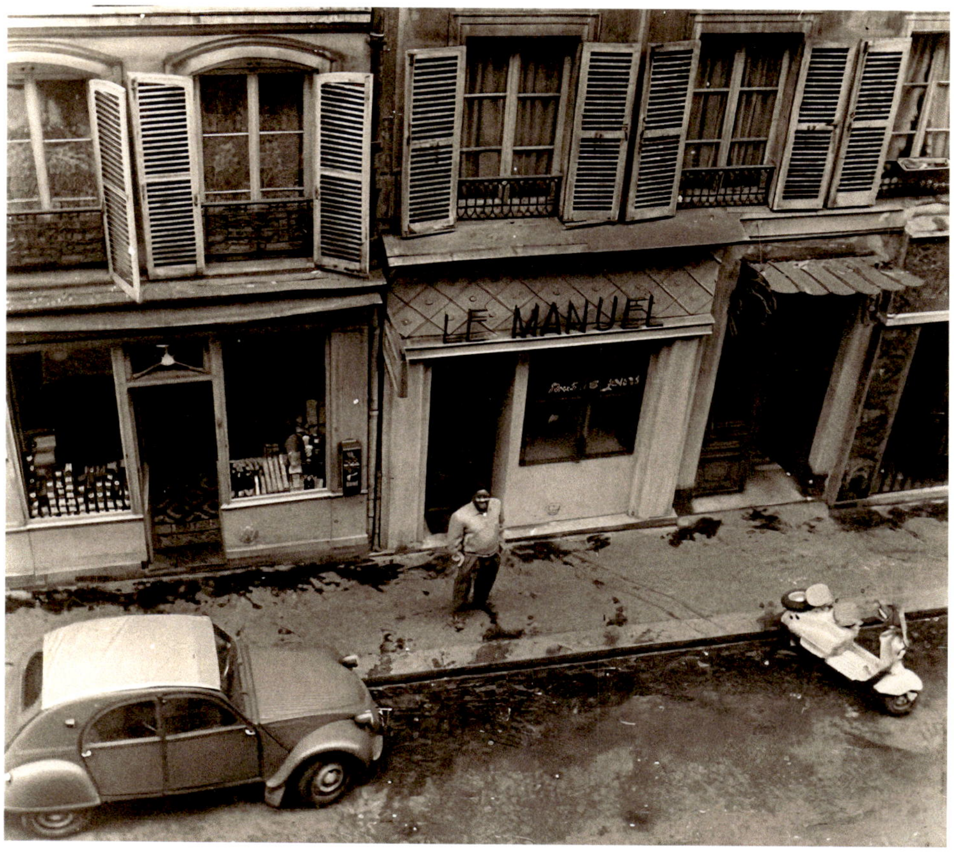

Figure 12.
Anonymous. *Leroy Haynes in front of his restaurant at 7 rue Manuel*, Paris, *ca*. 1950s. Fair use.

Paris. Writers such as Chester Himes, Richard Wright, and James Baldwin, and music stars like Cab Calloway and Louis Armstrong, all became dear friends of the owners (Figure 12).[42]

Alan Glass's workday, therefore, both began and ended near some of the spots that formed the very heart of the Parisian jazz scene and the city's post-war Black expatriate community. As a North American himself, Glass's night shift automatism was inescapably impacted by his interactions with and observations of this community, just as the bulk of his close friendships in this era were developed through his own ex-pat circle of French Canadians. Even while Glass was frequenting surrealist galleries and meetings during his decade in Paris, he was also spending a great deal of energy deepening relationships with fellow Canadian artists such as his surrealist friends Mimi Parent, and Jean Benoît, as well as Leon Bellefleur, Micheline Beauchemin, Solange Legenare, and the poet-painter Roland Giguere. Glass also socialized with the painter and sculptor Pierre de Ligny Boudreau, who became the director of the Pierre Matisse Gallery in New York City a few years later.[43] Finally, Glass occasionally reconnected with Paris-based members of the *Québécois* group, Les Automatistes, with whom he had become acquainted while still in Montreal, such as Paul-Émile Borduas (author of the manifesto, *Refus Global*, 1947-48), Jean-Paul Riopelle, and Marcelle Ferron Hamelin.[44] These gatherings were always organized by a common friend of the Automatistes and Glass.

In many ways, Glass's night shift automatism was borne of this transnational constellation of experiences and interactions, which interwove his exposure to the Paris surrealist group, the American bebop scene, the Black ex-pat community of Paris, and the Canadian ex-pat artist community with his unique plastic sensibilities and tendencies. Perhaps this is why, according to Glass, Paris emblematized his idea of liberty.[45] The post-war diaspora created an environment rich with a diversity of socio-cultural possibilities for interaction, and these conditions transformed the nature of a nocturnal, night shift automatism practiced by a Canadian doorman immersed in jazz. If there was ever a palpable connection between surrealism and the jazz tradition, the Club Saint-Germain drawings of Alan Glass, neglected heretofore as they have been in art history and the annals of surrealism, represent one of the most vibrant, pivotal, and provocative links.

At 4.15 AM, Glass finally climbs the seven flights of stairs to his 1.5 x 3-meter room.[46] He adds the two new nightshift drawings to the stack on the narrow wooden bar and removes the Bic pens from his pocket. He lights the little alcohol stove on the table to make a cup of tea before going to bed and ignites a couple of coals so

of Surrealist Presence in Alejandro Jodorowsky's *The Holy Mountain*," in Kristoffer Noheden and Abigail Susik (eds.), *Surrealism and Film after 1945: Absolutely Modern Mysteries* (Manchester: Manchester University Press, 2021), 187–206; Abigail Susik and Kristoffer Noheden, "*Sorprendente hallazgo* ("Chance Find"): Alan Glass and Contemporary Surrealism in Mexico," *Burlington Contemporary* 4 (June 2021).

[40] Interview with Alan Glass, Mexico City, May 2022.

[41] For a recent overview of the culture of African American music in Paris during the postwar period, see Celeste Day Moore, *Soundscapes of*

that the room will warm slightly. He sparks a final cigarette. If he is careful to conserve his fuel, he can heat a little water the next day so that he can bathe with a basin of warm suds. He might also spare a few *allumettes* [matches] for the morning so that he can make additions to some of the drawings he started in the room earlier that week. These indirect strokes of burn marks are created by lightly caressing and searing the paper with an open flame, a technique he calls *allumettage*, in homage to the smoke-based *fumage* surrealist technique developed by the artist Wolfgang Paalen in the 1930s.[47]

But for now, he puts out his cigarette butt and takes his warm tea, crawling under the sheets and clutching the cup in his hands as he tries to shake off the cold. Echoes of Blakey's Jazz Messengers spiral and loop in his mind. At 8 PM the next day, he must be ready to head back to the club and start another drawing.

Liberation: African American Music in Postwar France (Durham: Duke University Press, 2021).

[42] Thomas Chatterton Williams, "In Another Country," in *The Best American Travel Writing*, ed. Bill Bryson (Boston: Houghton Mifflin Harcourt, 2016), 267–9.

[43] Telephone interview with Alan Glass, March 17, 2022.

[44] Telephone interview with Alan Glass, March 17, 2022.

[45] Telephone interview with Alan Glass, March 17, 2022.

[46] Alejandro Jodorowsky, untitled essay, in *Alan Glass: Surrealism's Secret*, exhibition catalog, ed. Abigail Susik and Kristoffer Noheden (forthcoming).

[47] Telephone interview with Alan Glass, March 25, 2022.

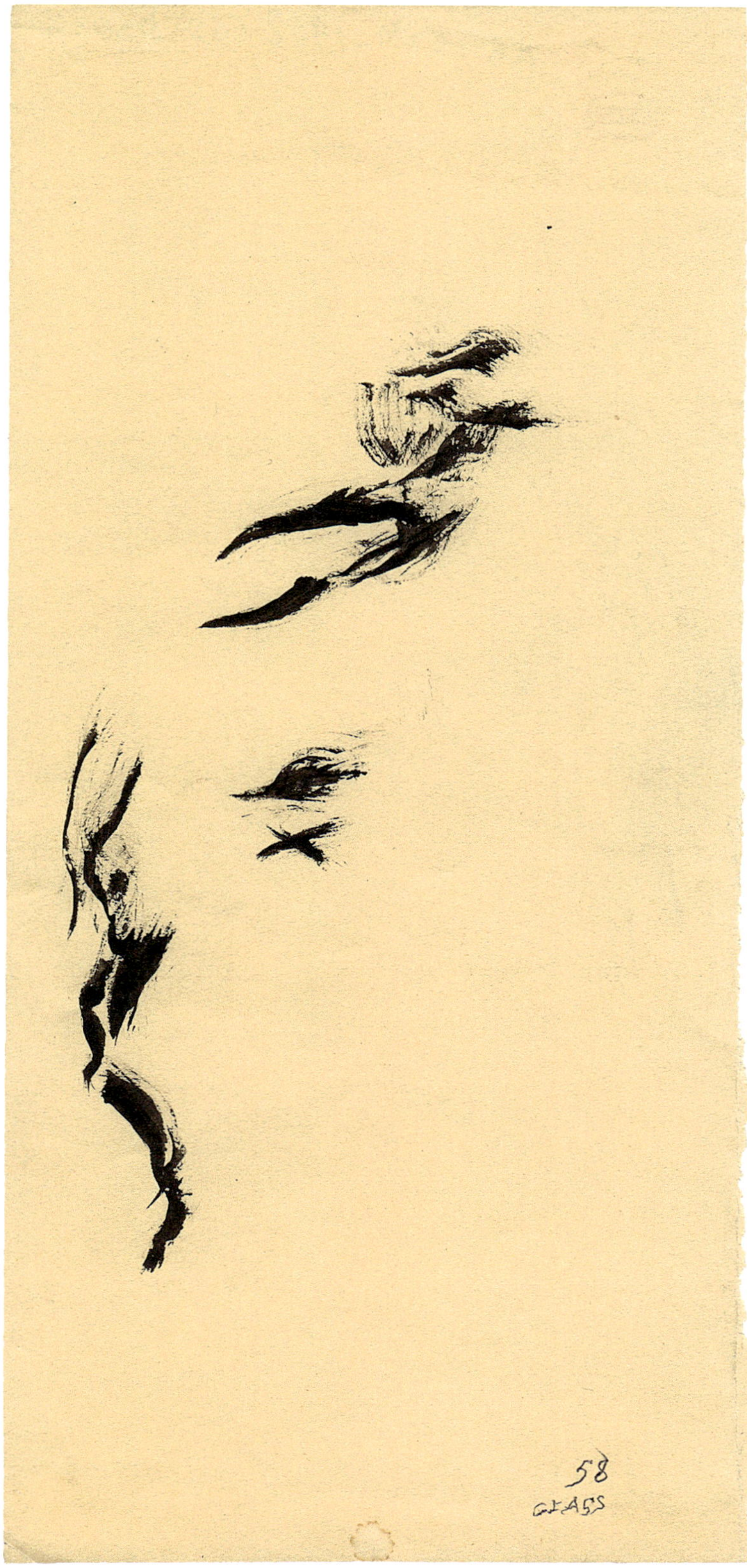

Untitled
(Club Saint-Germain period)
1958
India ink strokes, on paper.
21.2 x 14 cm
Artist's collection

ABIGAIL SUSIK
is Associate Professor of Art History at Willamette University and author of *Surrealist Sabotage and the War on Work* (Manchester University Press, 2021). She is co-editor of *Surrealism and Film after 1945: Absolutely Modern Mysteries* (Manchester University Press, 2021) and *Radical Dreams: Surrealism, Counterculture, Resistance* (Penn State University Press, 2022). She has contributed essays to many publications on surrealism and the avant-garde, including *Surrealism Beyond Borders* (Metropolitan Museum of Art; Tate Modern, 2021). Susik is a founding board member of the International Study for the Society of Surrealism and co-organizer of its annual conferences.

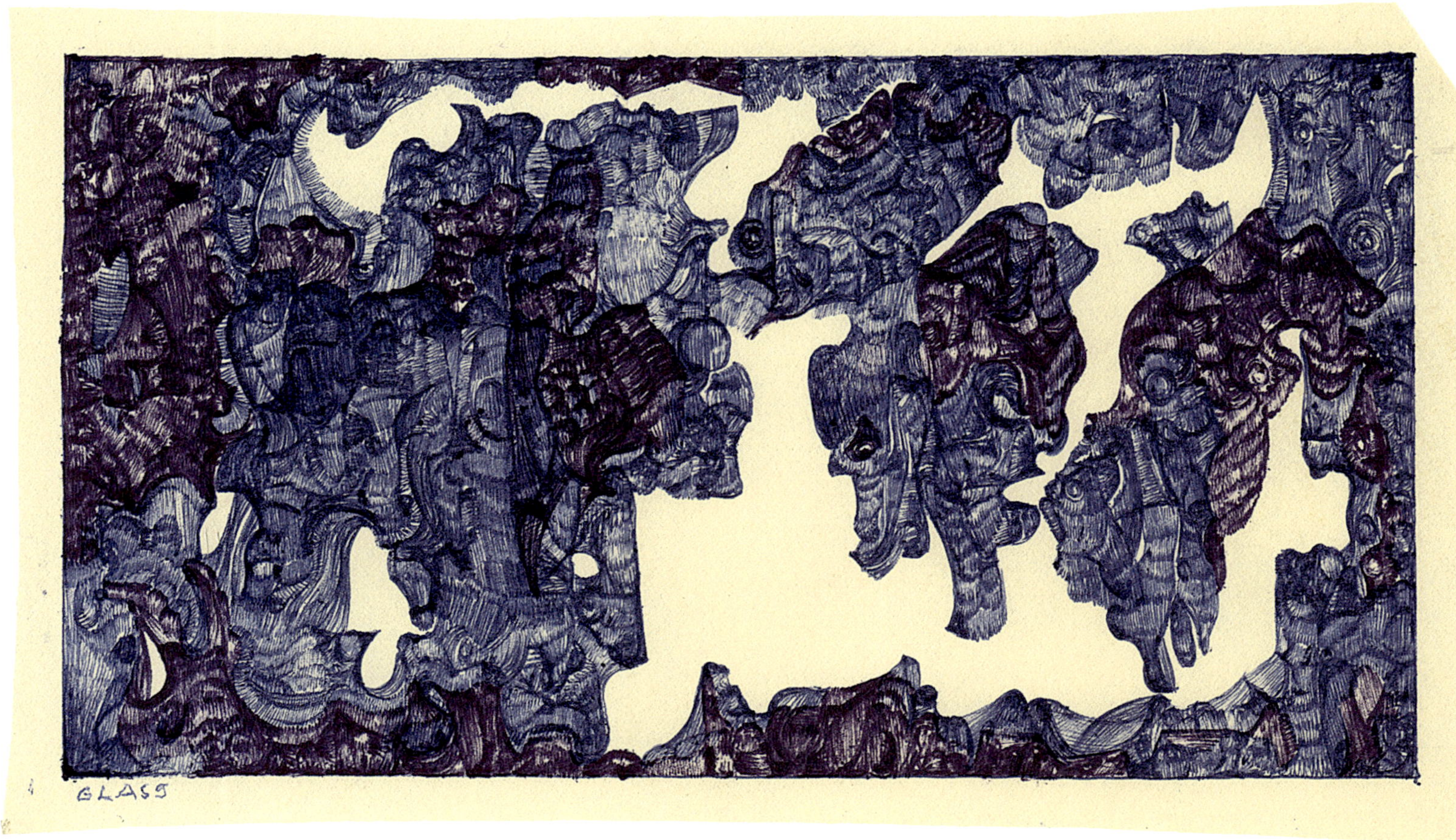

Untitled
(Club Saint-Germain period)
ca. 1954-1962
Blue and navy blue two-tone
ballpoint pen drawing,
on paper.
9.5 x 17.5 cm
Artist's collection

Untitled
(Club Saint-Germain period)
ca. 1954-1962
Monochrome blue ballpoint
pen drawing, on paper.
28 x 22.5 cm
Artist's collection

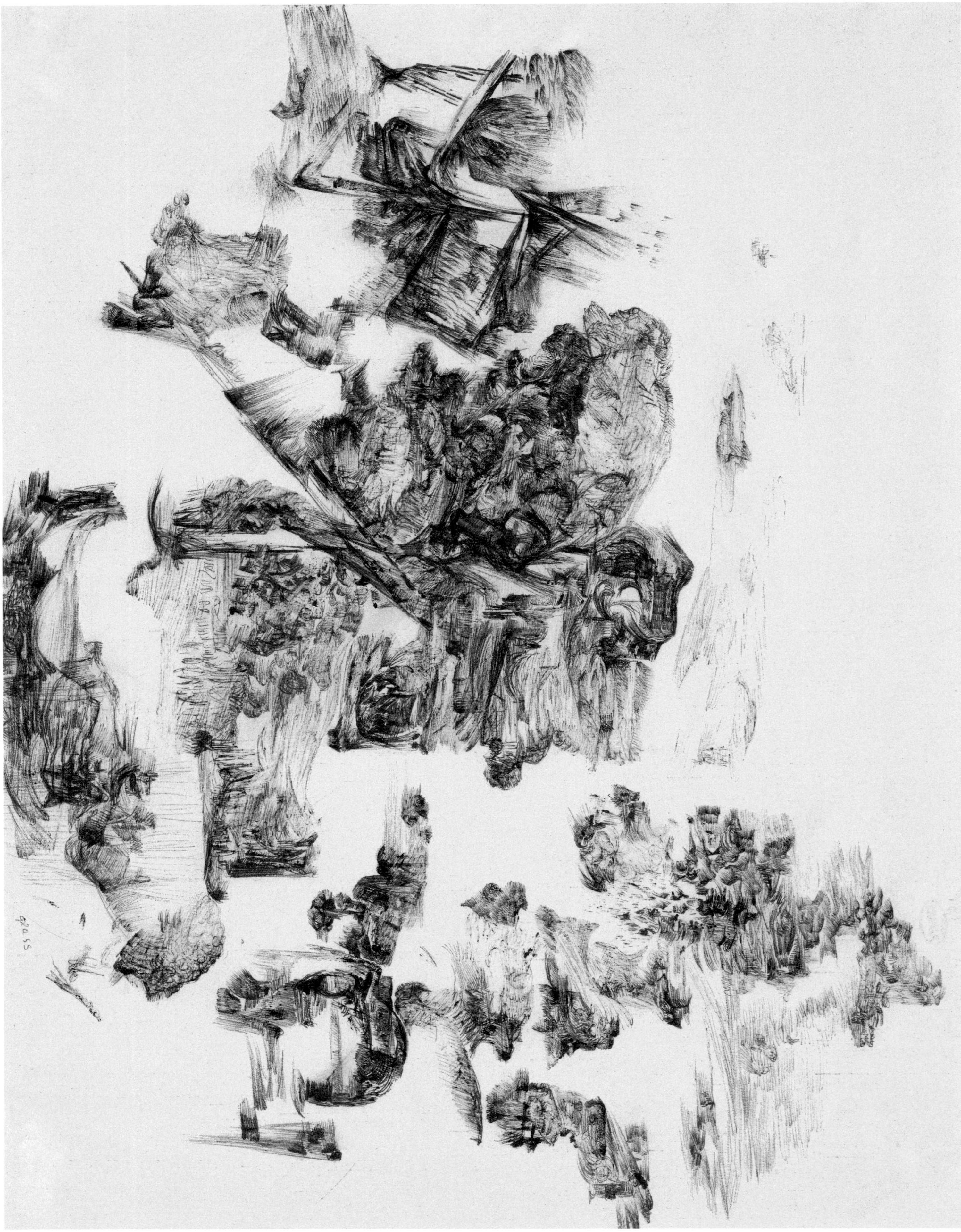

Untitled
(Club Saint-Germain period)
ca. 1954-1962
Monochrome black ballpoint
pen drawing, on paper.
28 x 22 cm
Artist's collection

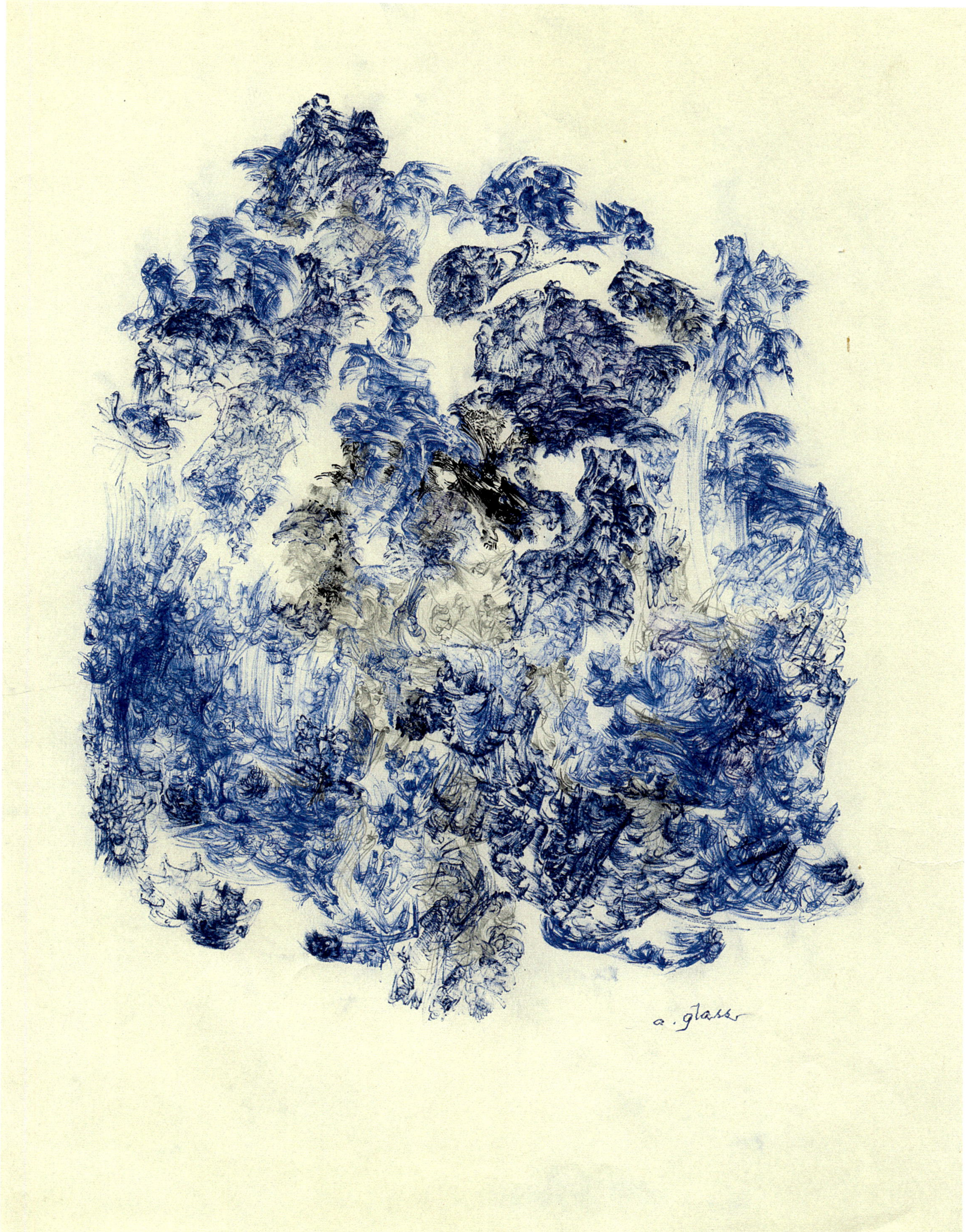

Untitled
(Club Saint-Germain period)
ca. 1954-1962
Blue, black and violet tricolor ballpoint pen drawing, on paper.
27 x 21 cm
Artist's collection

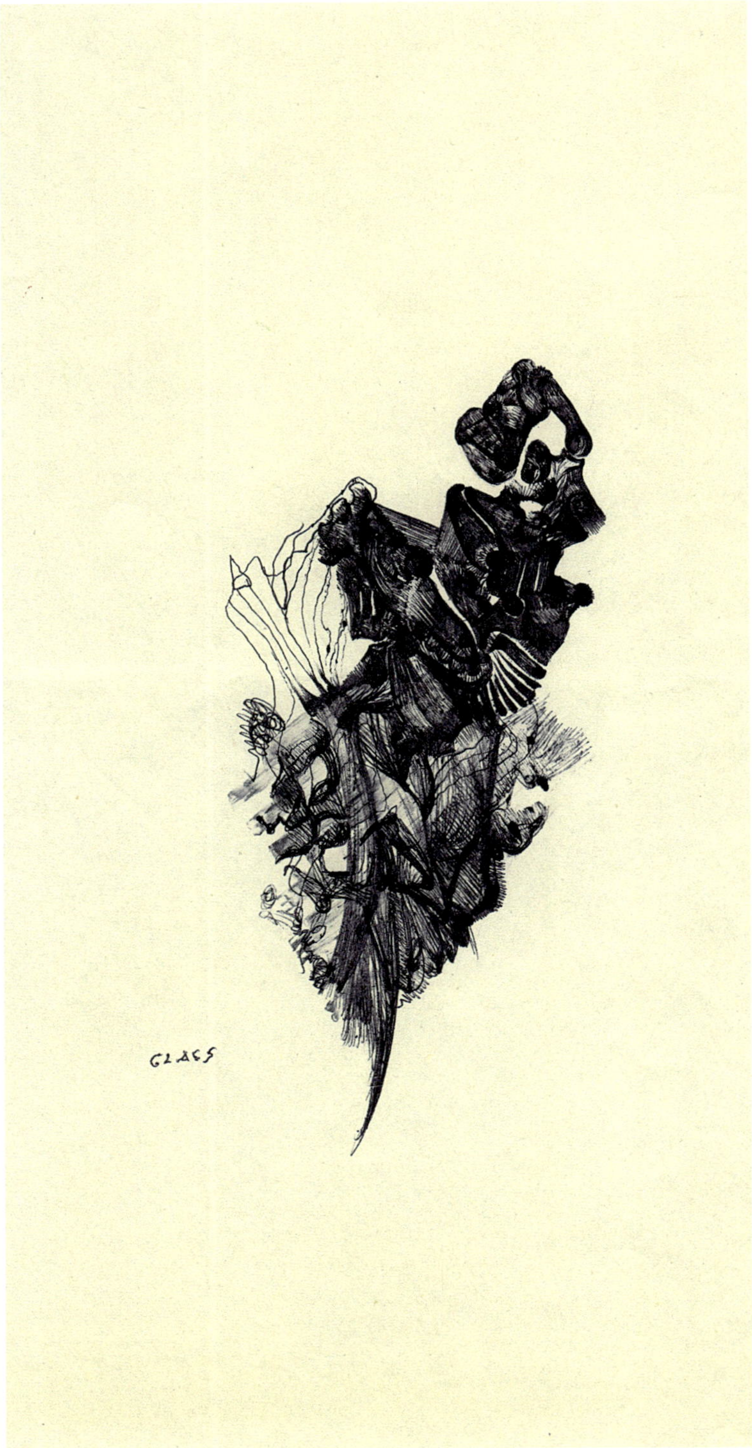

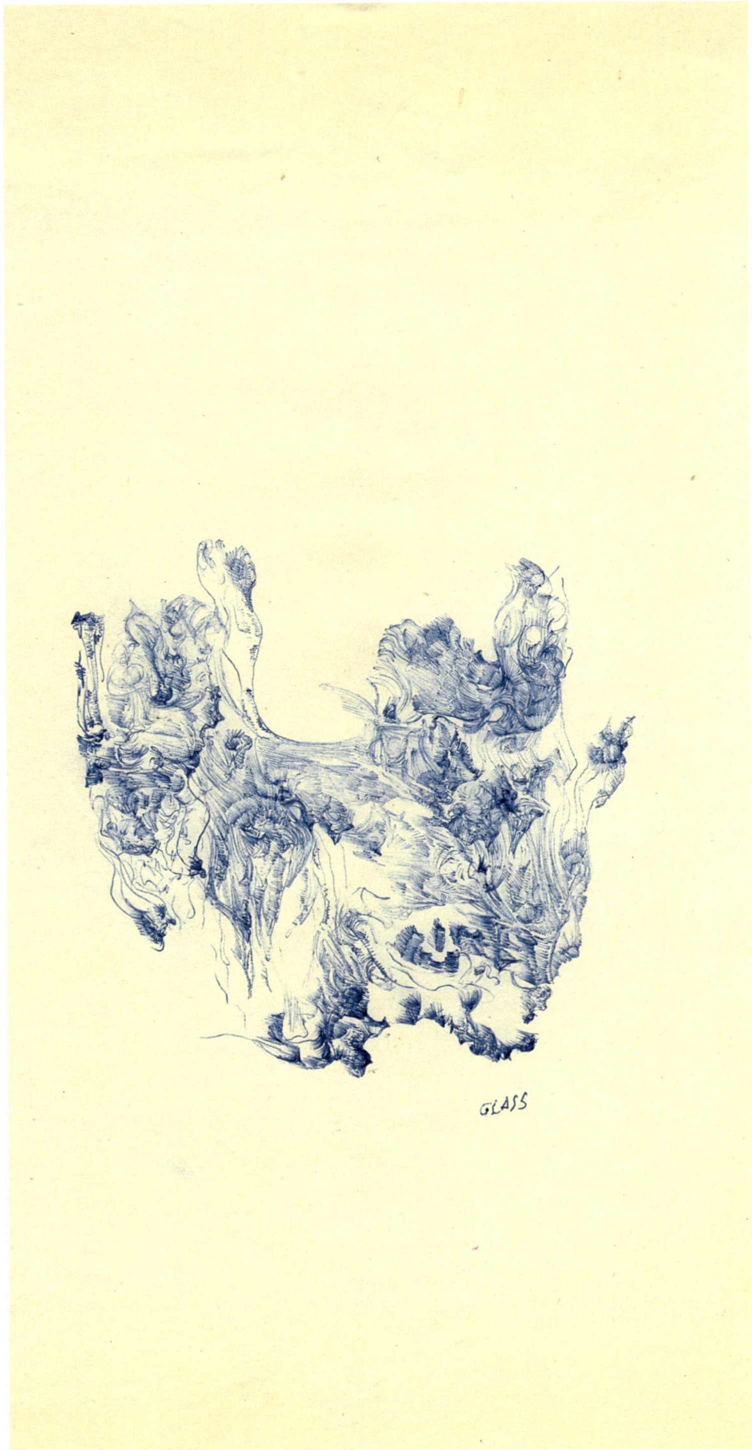

Untitled
(Club Saint-Germain period)
ca. 1954-1962
Monochrome black ballpoint pen drawing, on paper.
27.1 x 21.2 cm
Artist's collection

Untitled
(Club Saint-Germain period)
ca. 1954-1962
Monochrome blue ballpoint pen drawing, on paper.
27 x 21 cm
Artist's collection

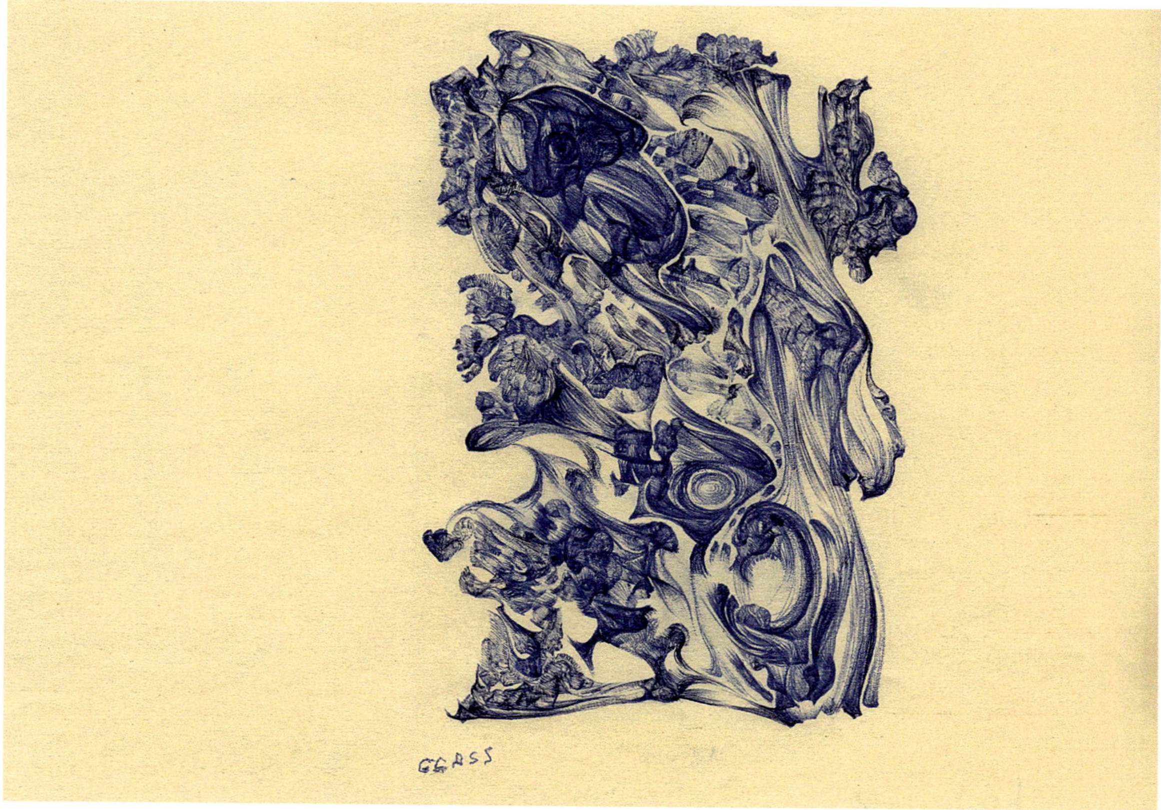

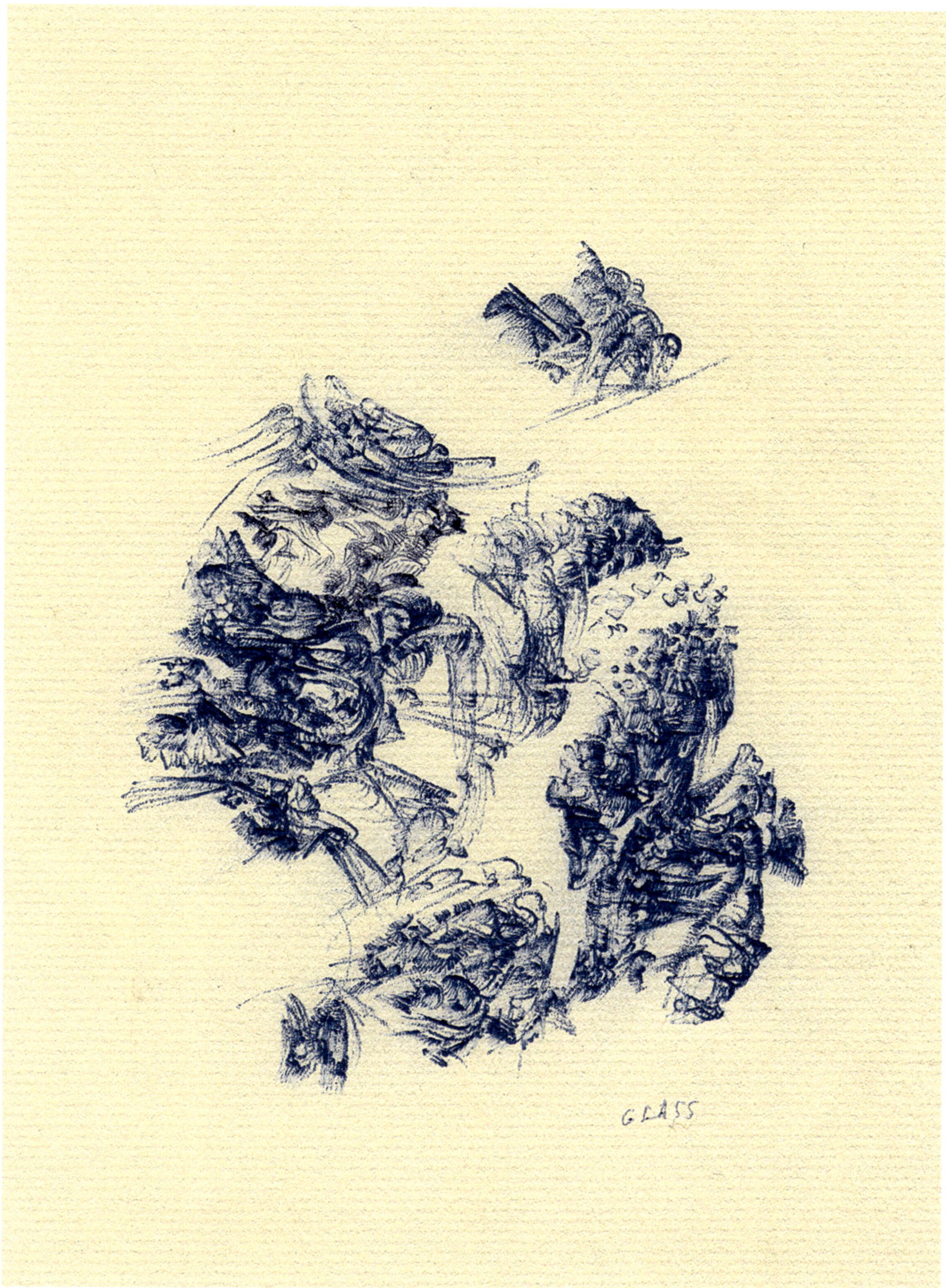

Untitled
(Club Saint-Germain period)
ca. 1954-1962
Monochrome blue ballpoint pen drawing, on paper.
28 x 22.5 cm
Artist's collection

Untitled
(Club Saint-Germain period)
ca. 1954-1962
Monochrome blue ballpoint pen drawing, on paper.
24 x 16 cm
Artist's collection

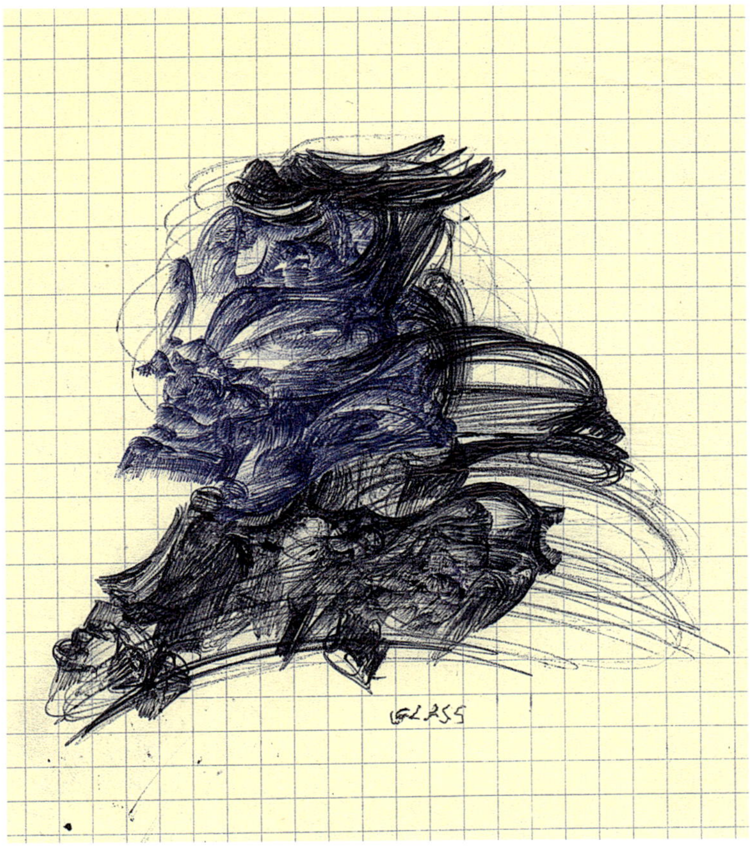

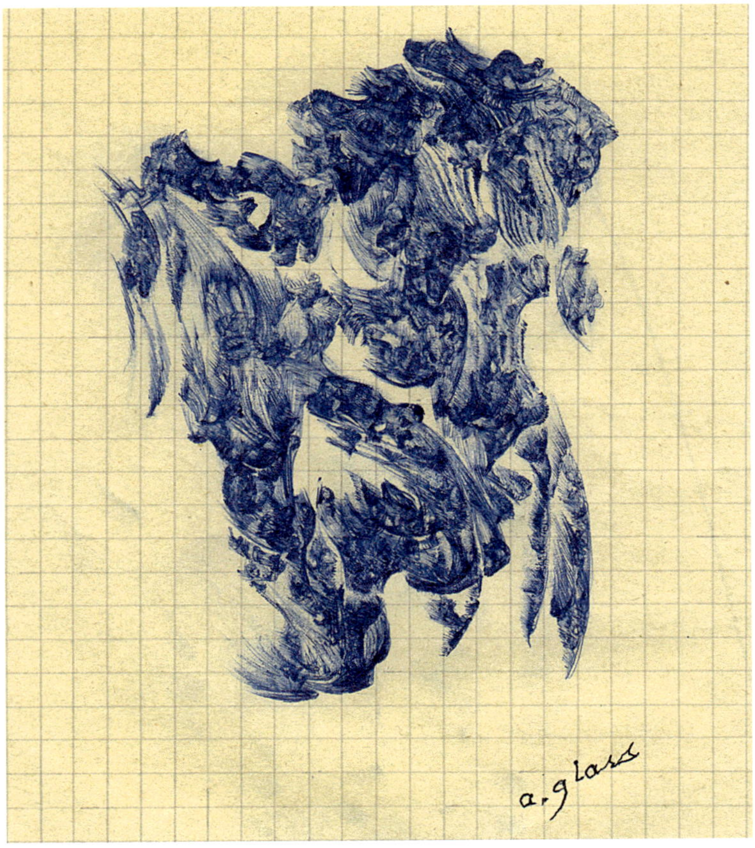

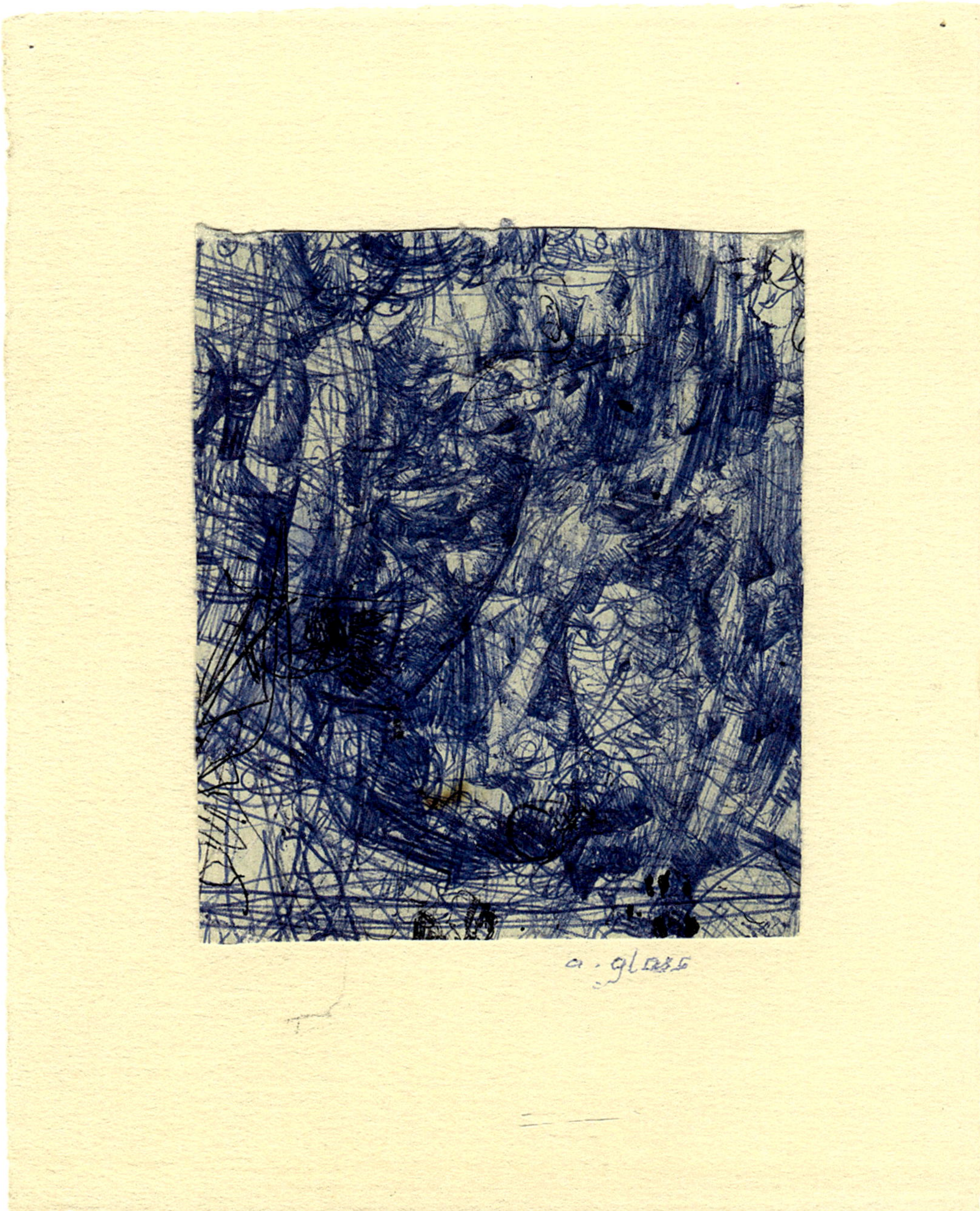

Untitled
(Club Saint-Germain period)
ca. 1954-1962
Bicolor blue and black ballpoint pen drawing, on squared paper.
21.5 x 16.5 cm
Artist's collection

Untitled
(Club Saint-Germain period)
ca. 1954-1962
Monochrome blue ballpoint pen drawing, on squared paper.
25.5 x 21 cm
Artist's collection

Untitled
(Club Saint-Germain period)
ca. 1954-1962
Monochrome blue ballpoint pen drawing with alumettage detail, on paper.
16.5 x 13.2 cm
Artist's collection

Untitled
(Club Saint-Germain period)
ca. 1954-1962
Monochrome black ballpoint pen drawing, on red paper.
20.5 x 15.5 cm
Artist's collection

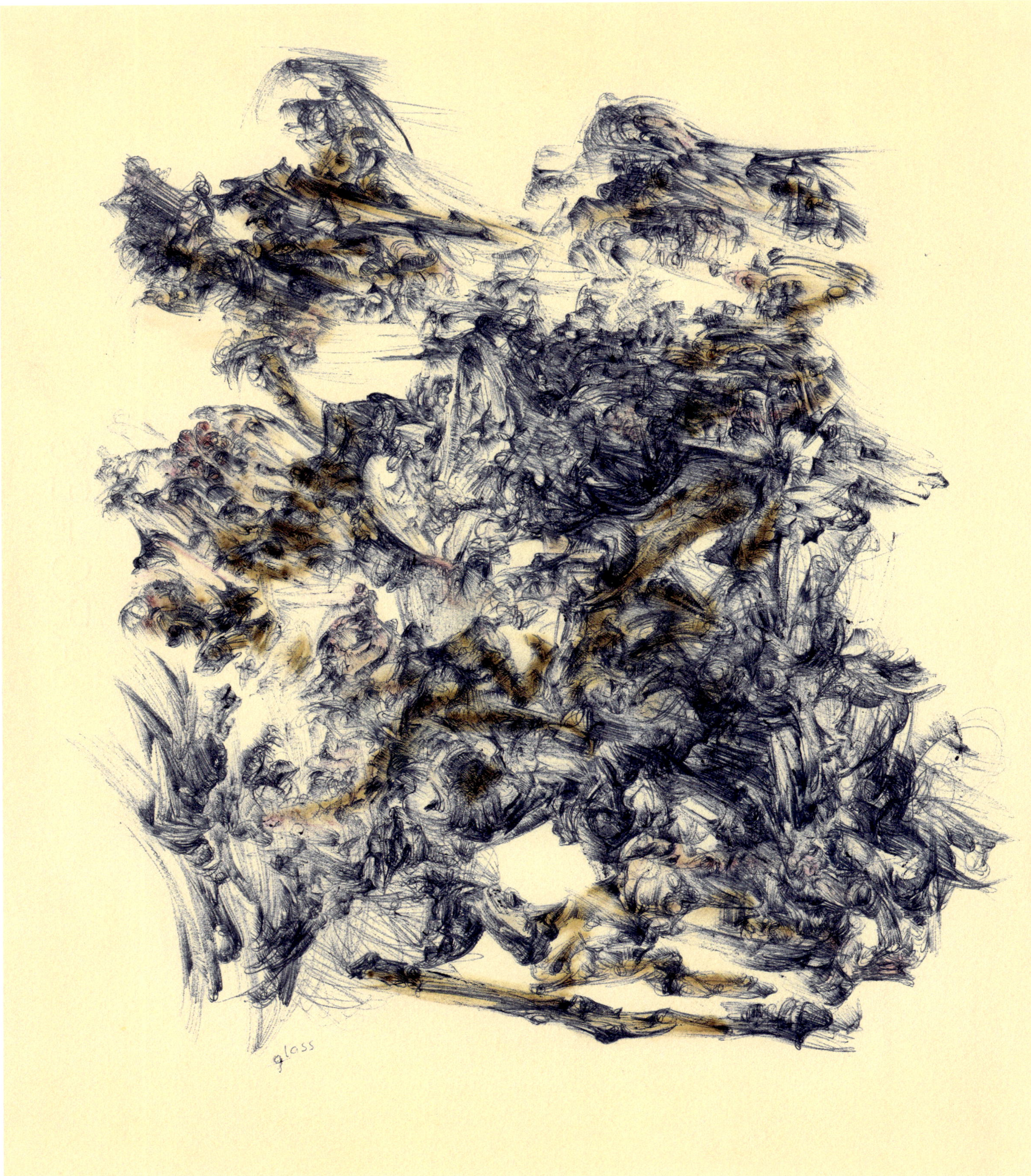

Untitled
(Club Saint-Germain period)
ca. 1954-1962
Monochrome blue ballpoint pen drawing with touches of allumettage, on paper.
28.2 x 25.2 cm
Artist's collection

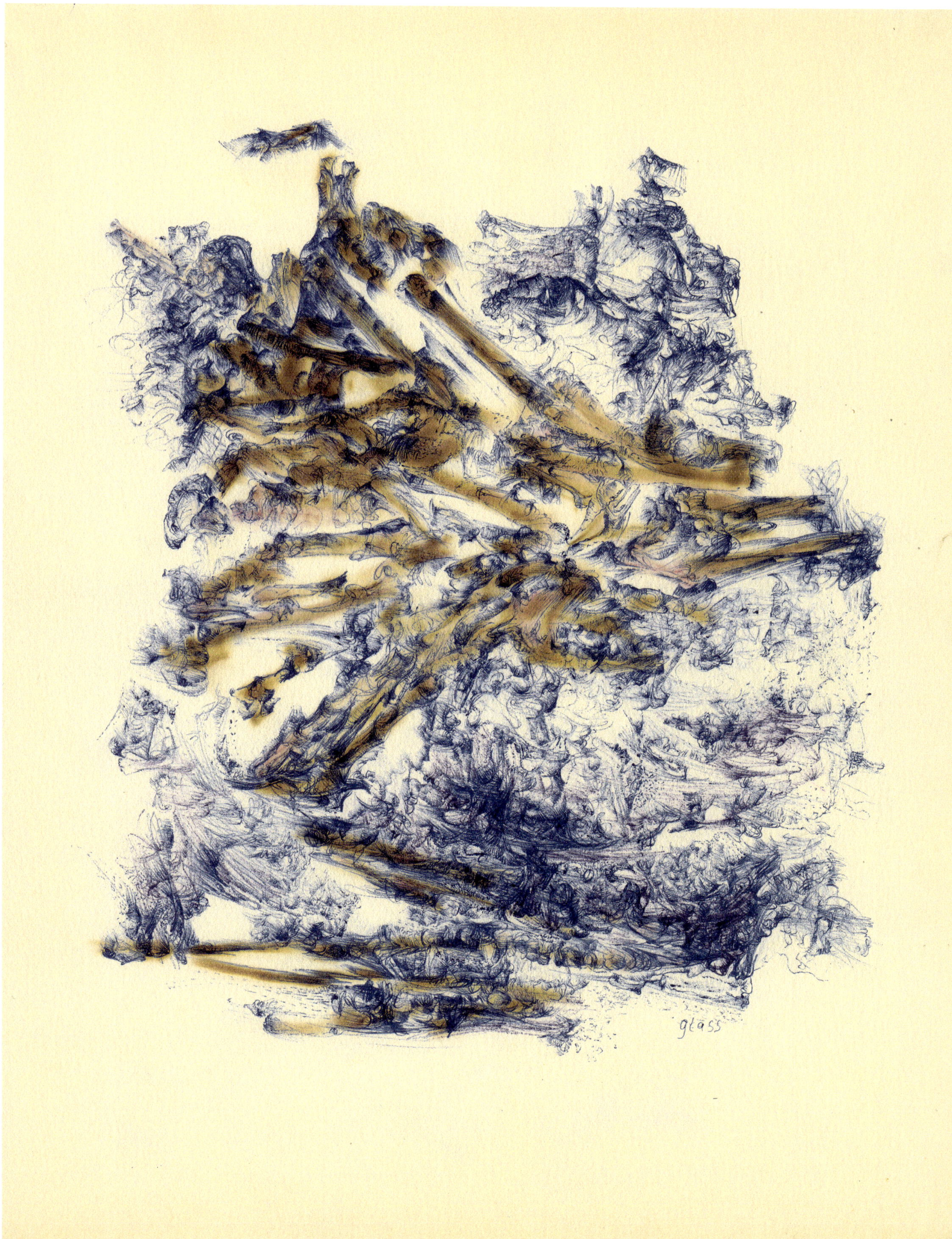

Untitled
(Club Saint-Germain period)
ca. 1954-1962
Monochrome blue ballpoint pen drawing with touches of allumettage, on paper.
31.4 x 24.4 cm
Artist's collection

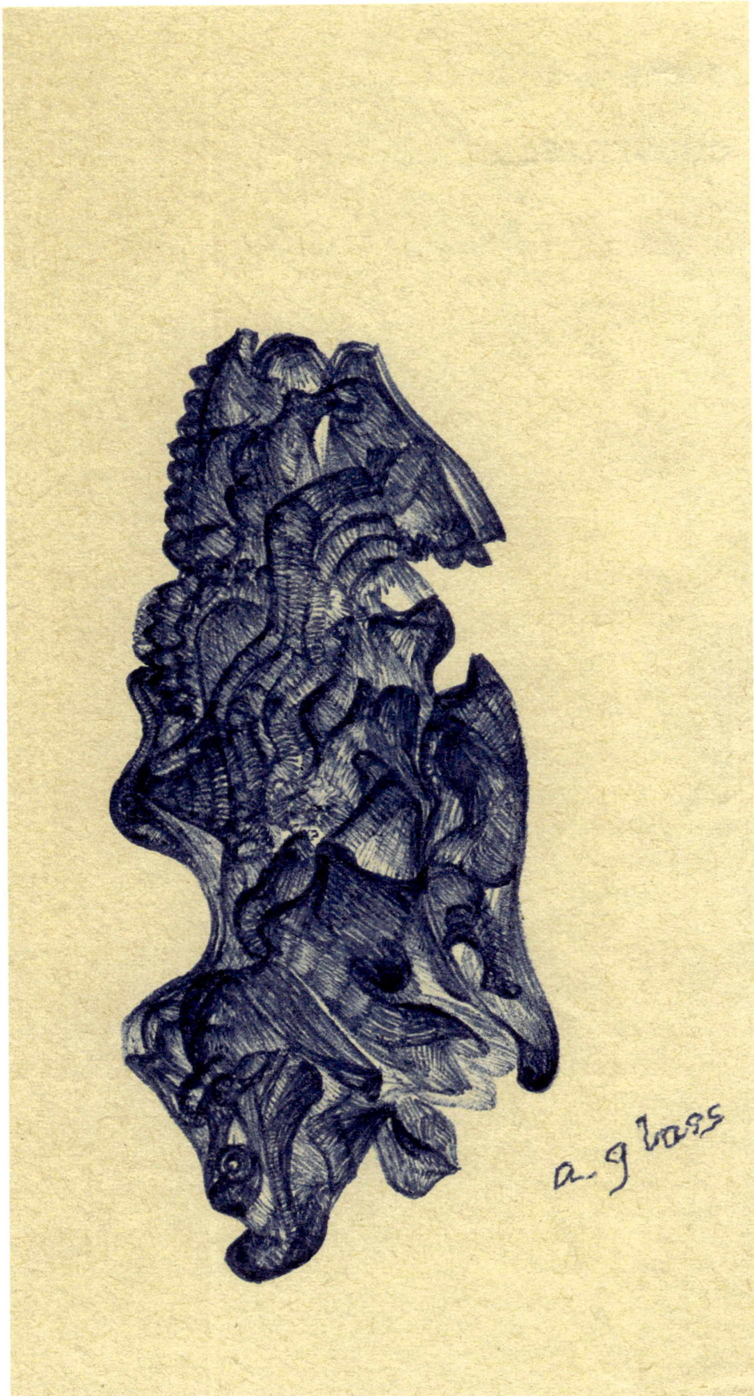

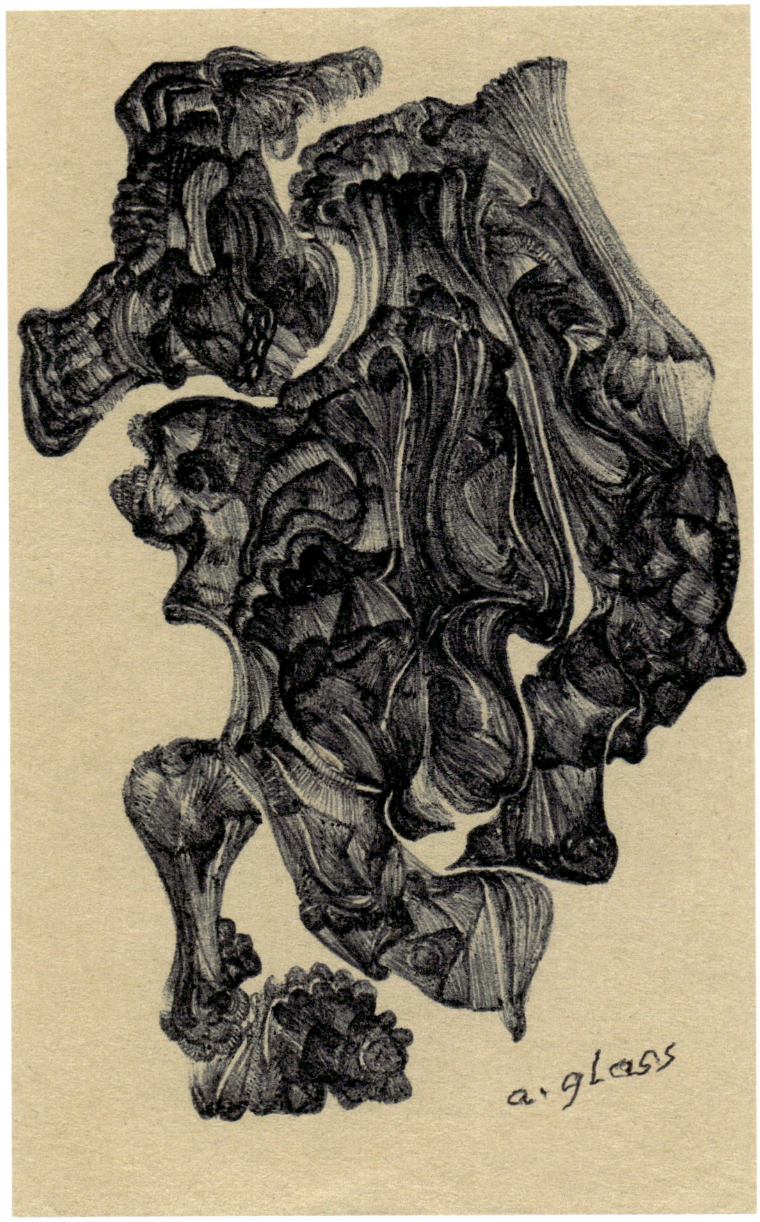

Untitled
(Club Saint-Germain period)
ca. 1954-1962
Monochrome blue ballpoint pen drawing, on the order of Club Saint-Germain.
12.6 x 7.6 cm
Artist's collection

Untitled
(Club Saint-Germain period)
ca. 1954-1962
Monochrome black ballpoint pen drawing, on the order of Club Saint-Germain.
13.2 x 8 cm
Artist's collection

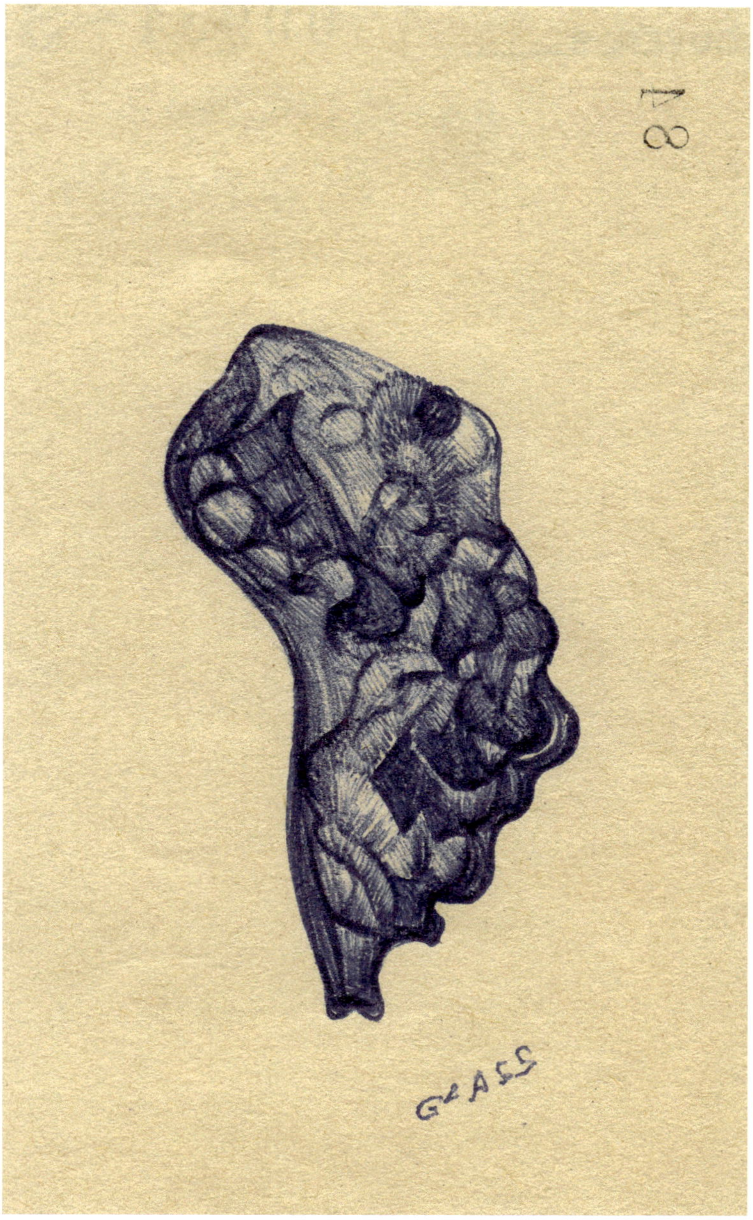

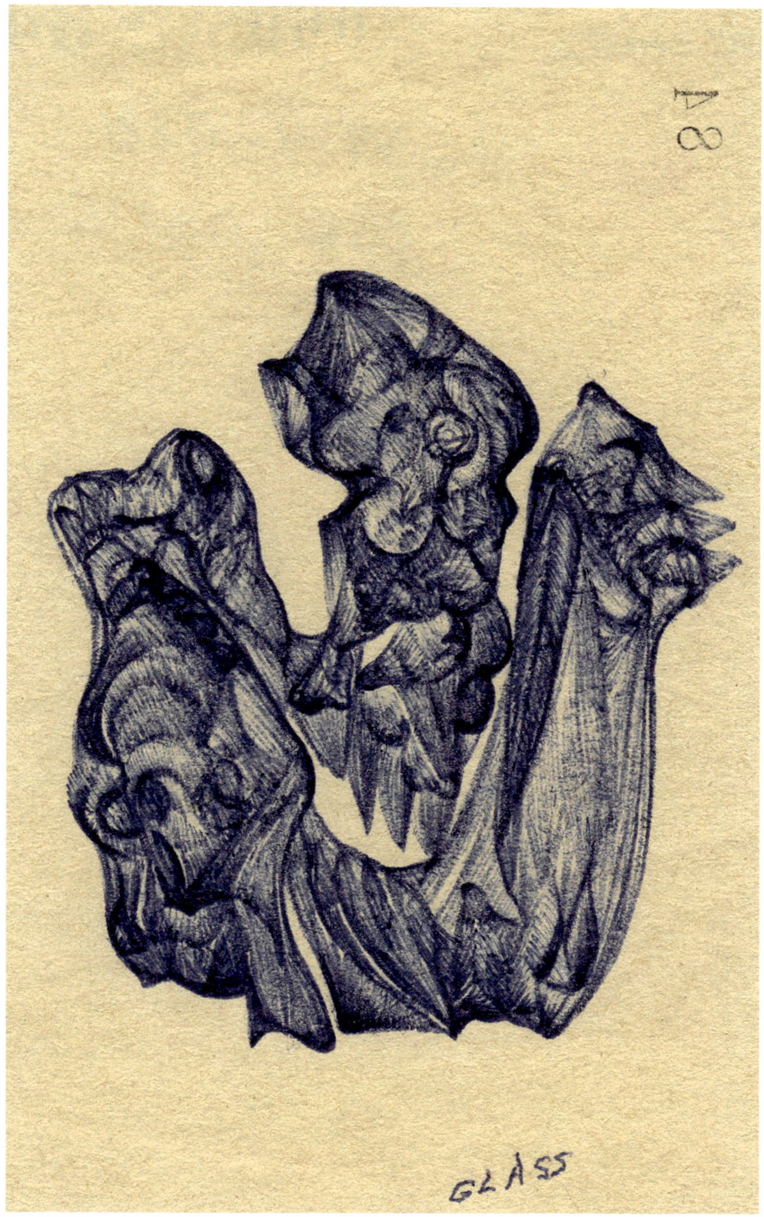

Untitled
(Club Saint-Germain period)
ca. 1954-1962
Monochrome blue ballpoint pen drawing, on the order of Club Saint-Germain.
13.1 x 8 cm
Artist's collection

Untitled
(Club Saint-Germain period)
ca. 1954-1962
Monochrome blue ballpoint pen drawing, on the order of Club Saint-Germain.
13.1 x 8 cm
Artist's collection

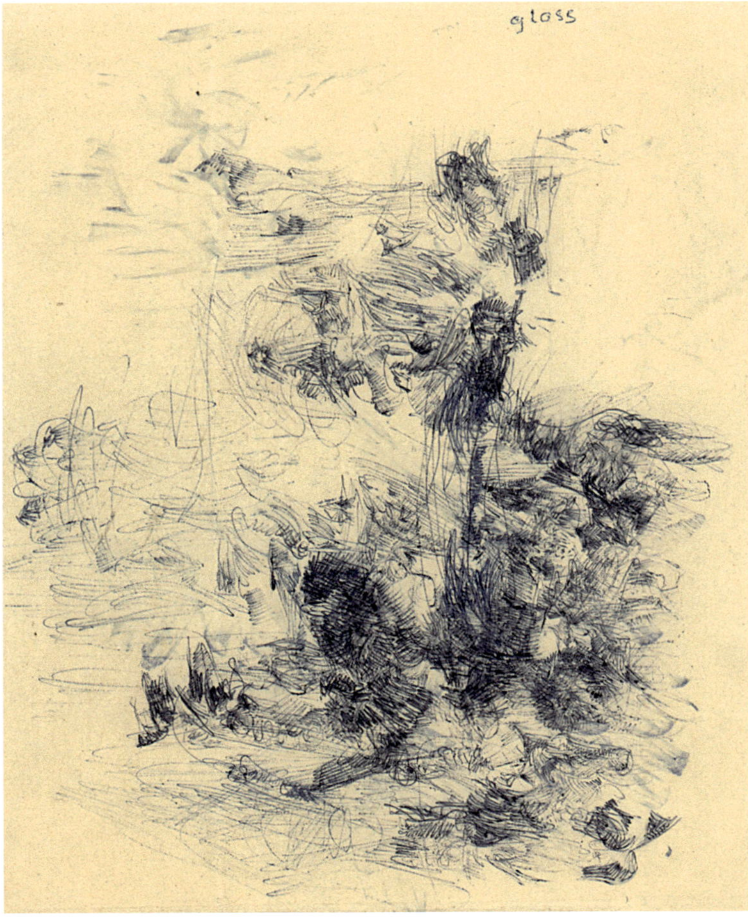

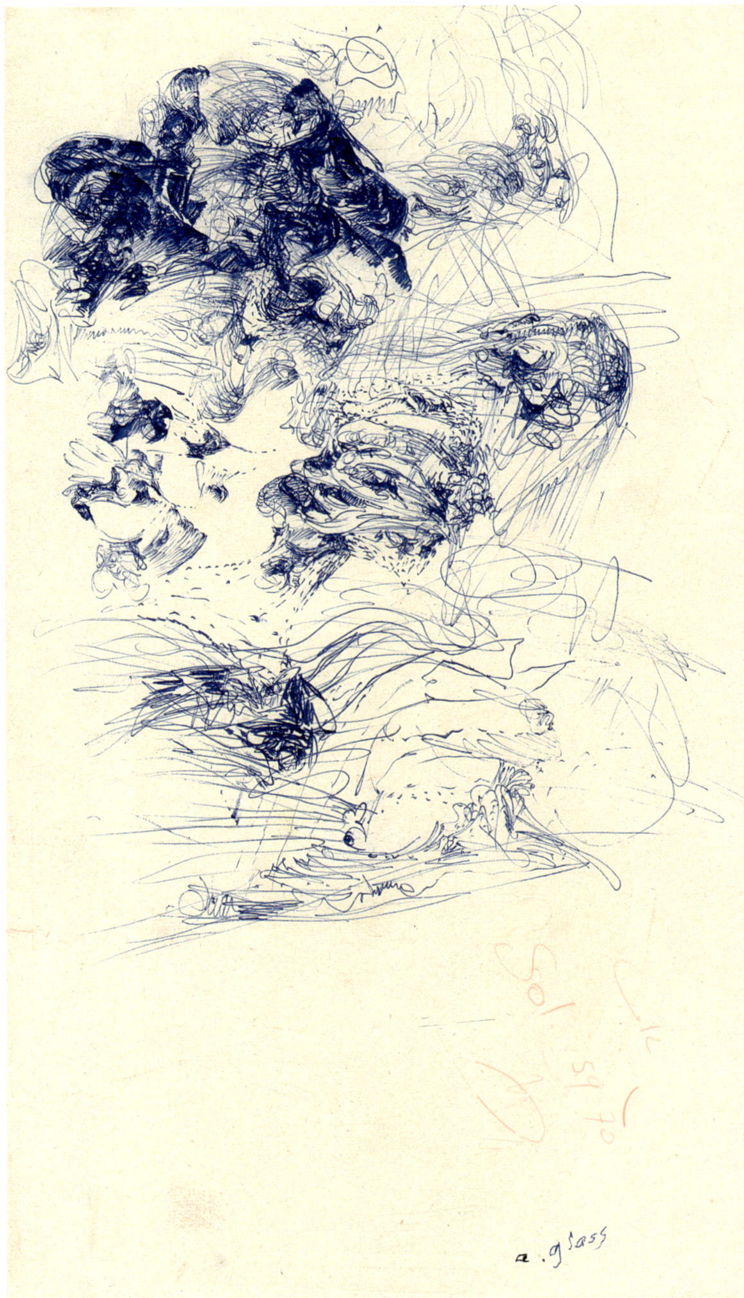

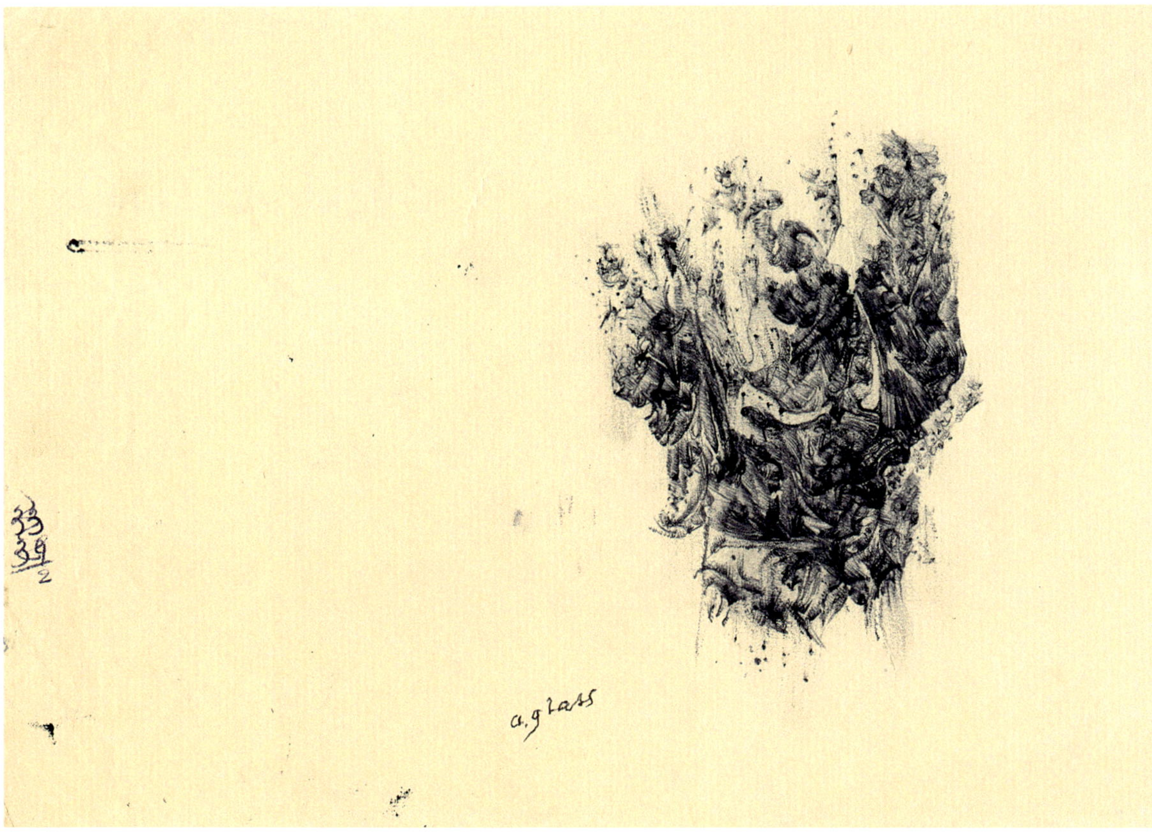

Untitled
(Club Saint-Germain period)
ca. 1954-1962
Monochrome navy blue ballpoint pen drawing, on paper.
12 x 10 cm
Artist's collection

Untitled
(Club Saint-Germain period)
ca. 1954-1962
Monochrome blue ballpoint pen drawing, on paper.
23.5 x 13.5 cm
Artist's collection

Untitled
(Club Saint-Germain period)
ca. 1954-1962
Monochrome navy blue ballpoint pen drawing, on paper.
16.5 x 25.2 cm
Artist's collection

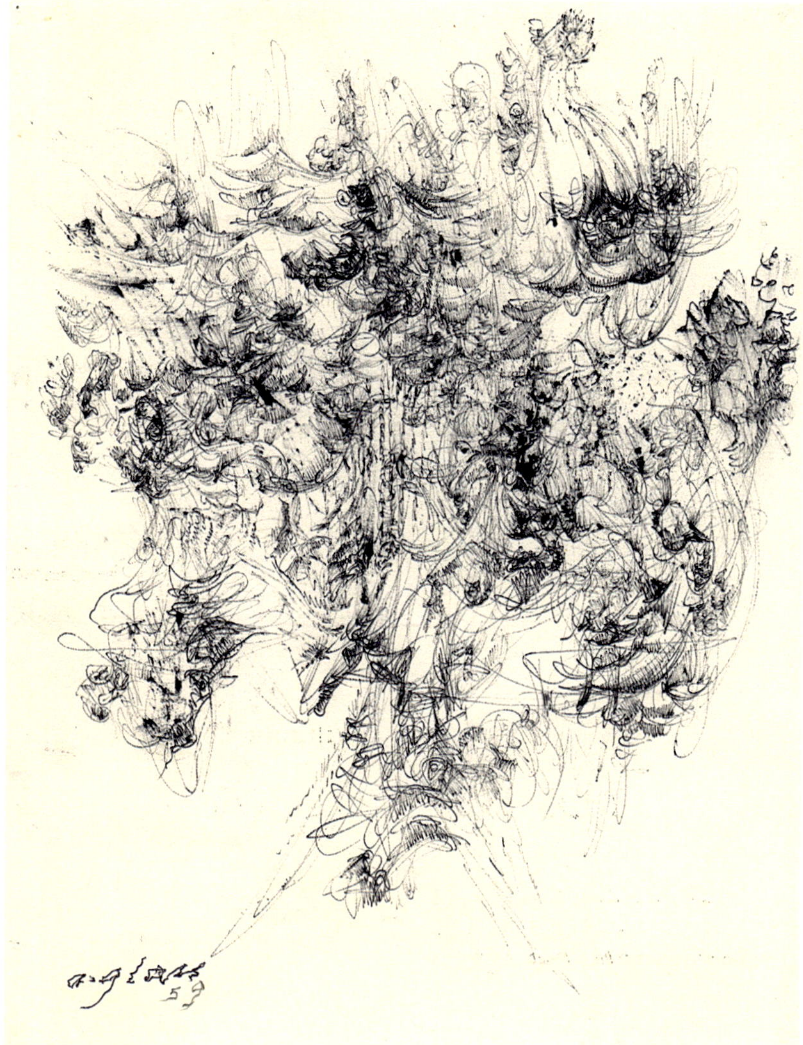

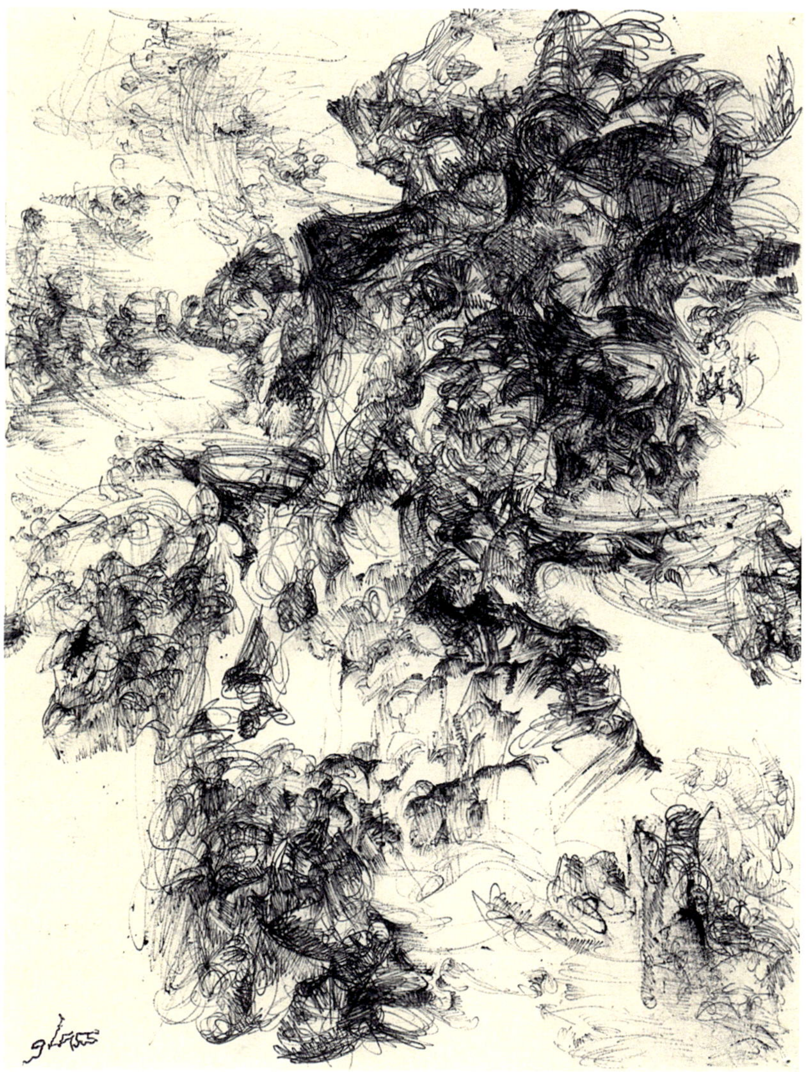

Untitled
(Club Saint-Germain period)
1959
Monochrome black ballpoint pen drawing, on Club Saint-Germain invitation card.
14 x 10.5 cm
Artist's collection

Untitled
(Club Saint-Germain period)
ca. 1954-1962
Monochrome black ballpoint pen drawing, on Club Saint-Germain invitation card.
14 x 10.5 cm
Artist's collection

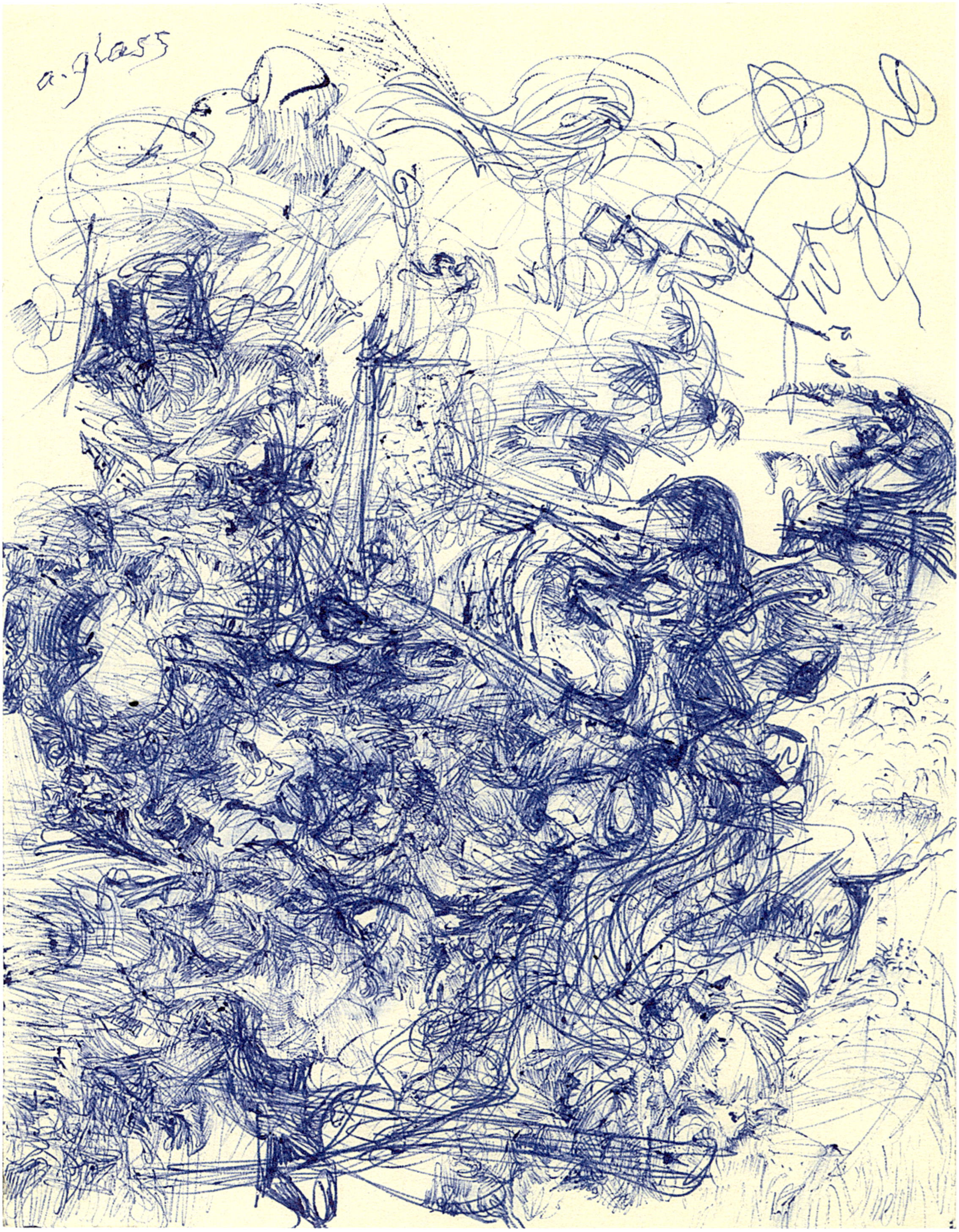

Untitled
(Club Saint-Germain period)
ca. 1954-1962
Monochrome blue ballpoint pen drawing, on Club Saint-Germain invitation card.
13.5 x 10.5 cm
Artist's collection

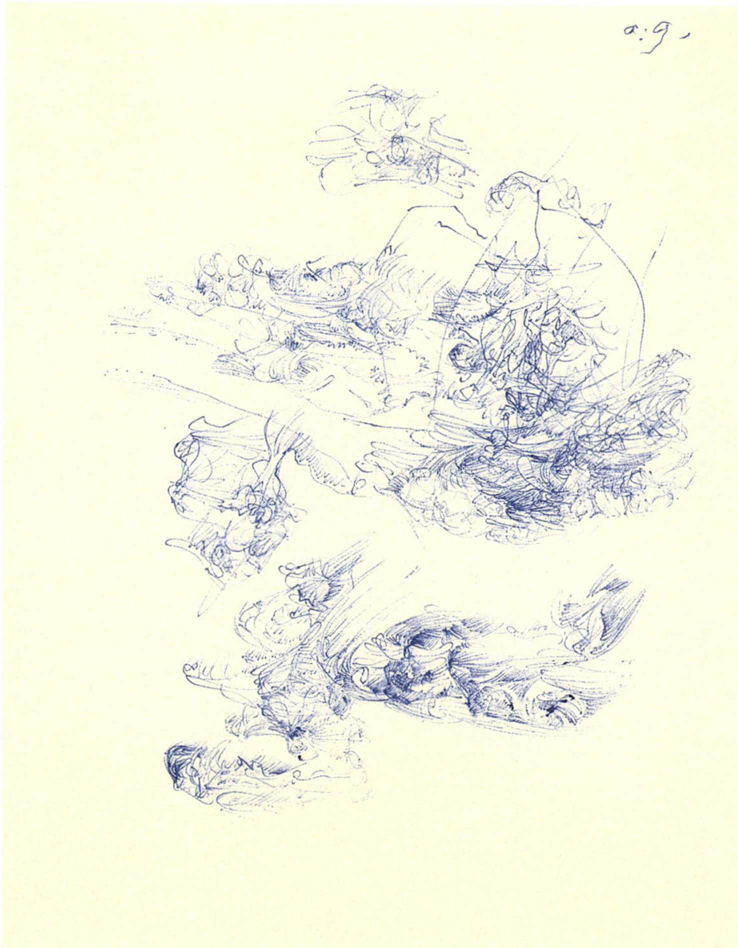

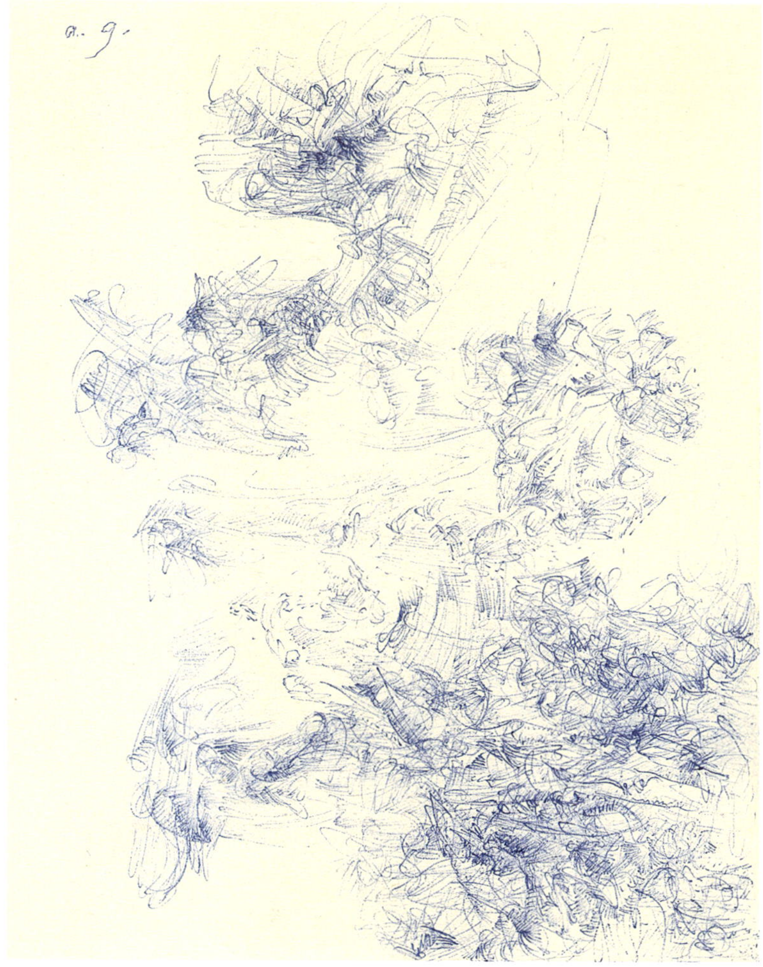

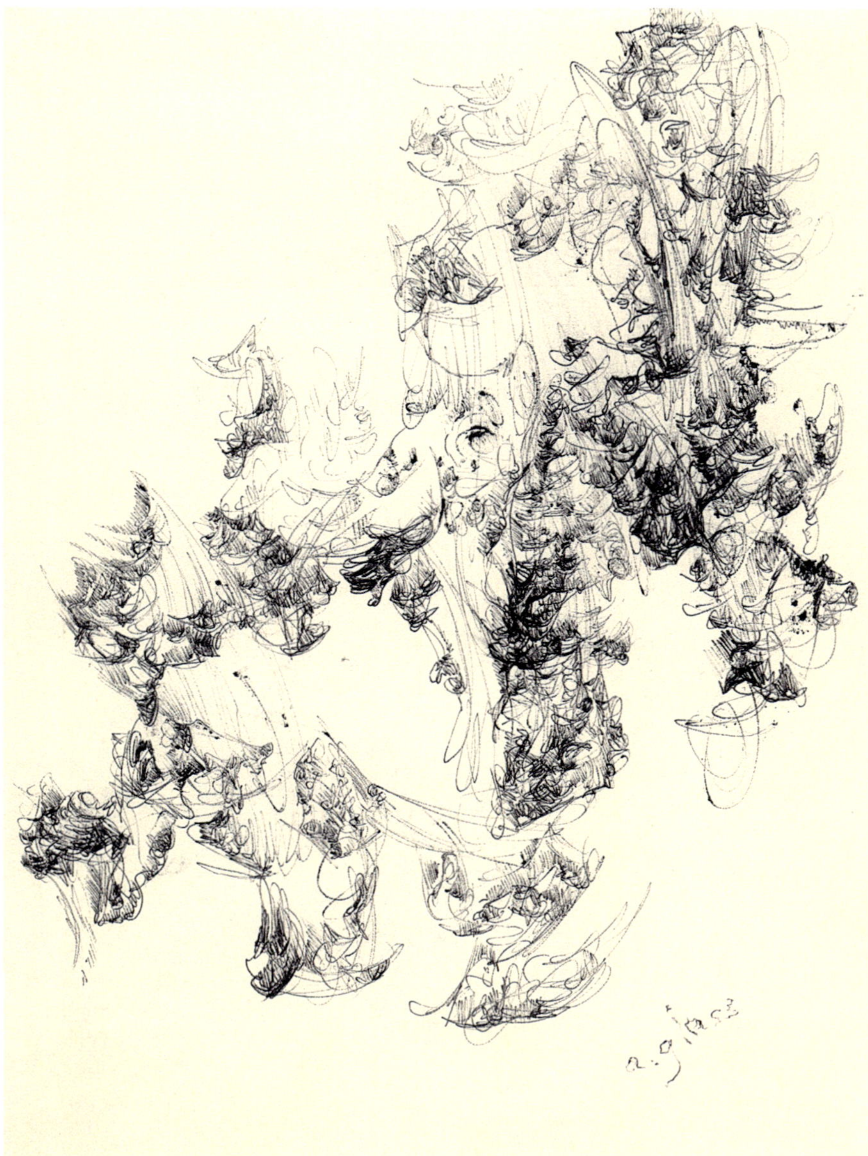

Untitled
(Club Saint-Germain period)
ca. 1954-1962
Monochrome blue ballpoint pen drawing, on Club Saint-Germain invitation card.
13.5 x 10.5 cm
Artist's collection

Untitled
(Club Saint-Germain period)
ca. 1954-1962
Monochrome blue ballpoint pen drawing, on Club Saint-Germain invitation card.
13.5 x 10.5 cm
Artist's collection

Untitled
(Club Saint-Germain period)
ca. 1954-1962
Monochrome black ballpoint pen drawing, on Club Saint-Germain invitation card.
14 x 10.5 cm
Artist's collection

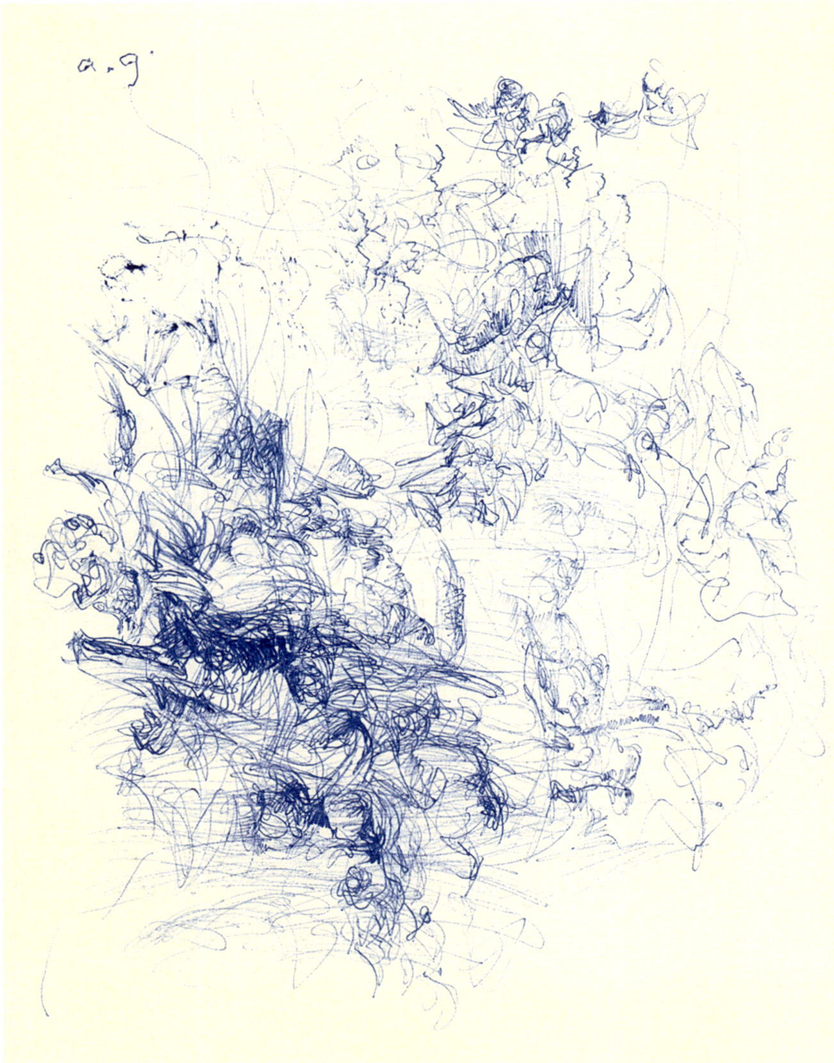

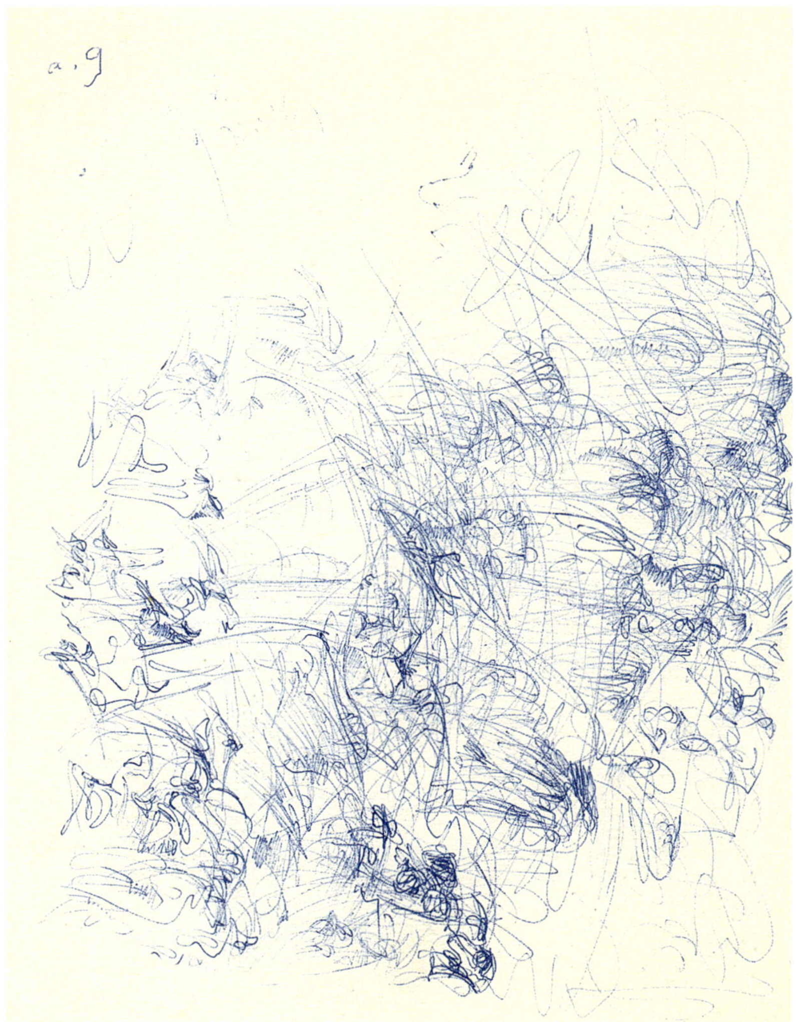

Untitled
(Club Saint-Germain period)
ca. 1954-1962
Monochrome blue ballpoint pen drawing, on Club Saint-Germain invitation card.
13.5 x 10.5 cm
Artist's collection

Untitled
(Club Saint-Germain period)
ca. 1954-1962
Monochrome blue ballpoint pen drawing, on Club Saint-Germain invitation card.
13.5 x 10.5 cm
Artist's collection

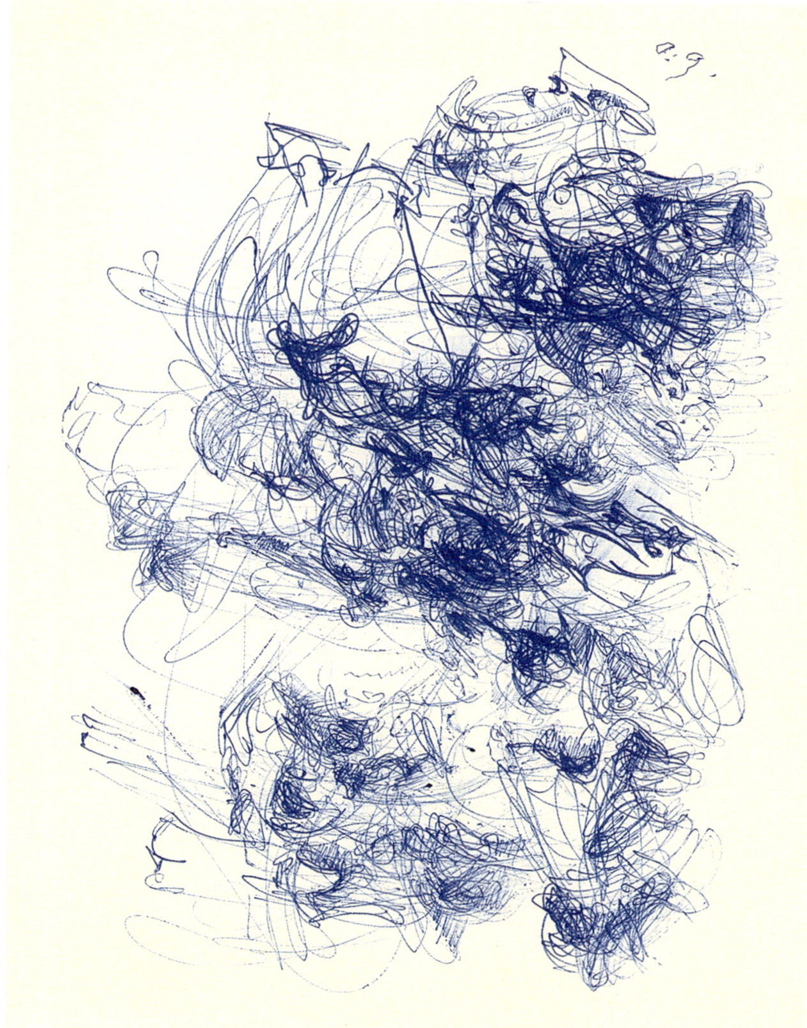

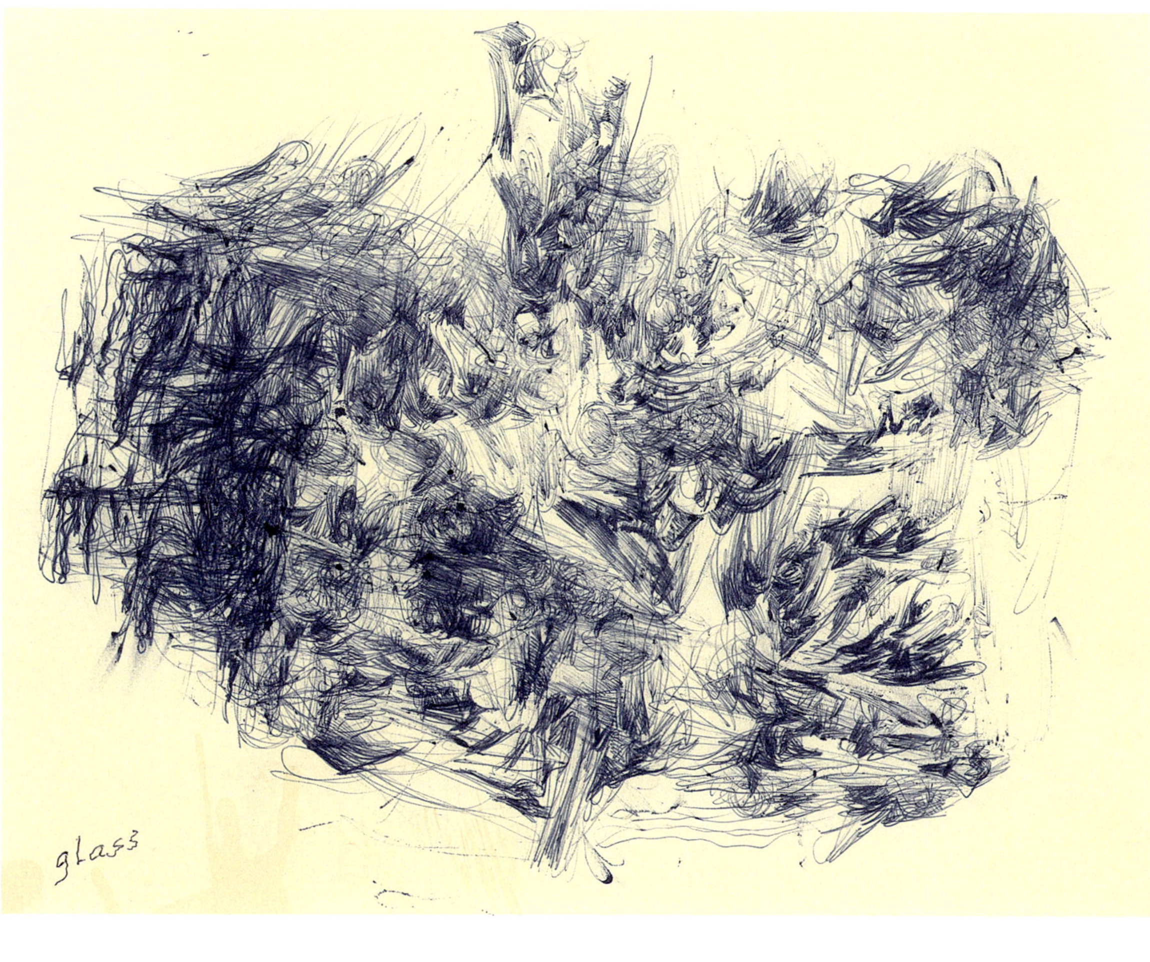

Untitled
(Club Saint-Germain period)
ca. 1954-1962
Monochrome blue ballpoint pen drawing, on Club Saint-Germain invitation card.
13.5 x 10.5 cm
Artist's collection

Untitled
(Club Saint-Germain period)
ca. 1954-1962
Monochrome navy blue ballpoint pen drawing, on paper.
14.5 x 18.5 cm
Artist's collection

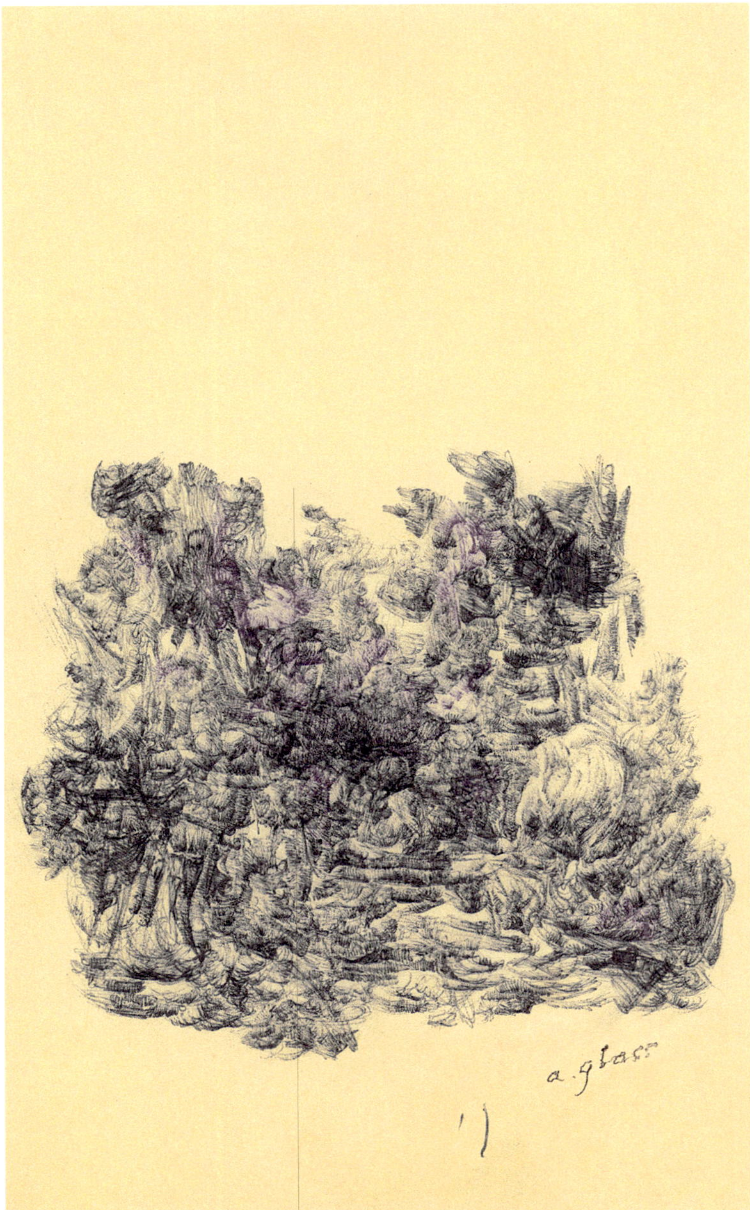

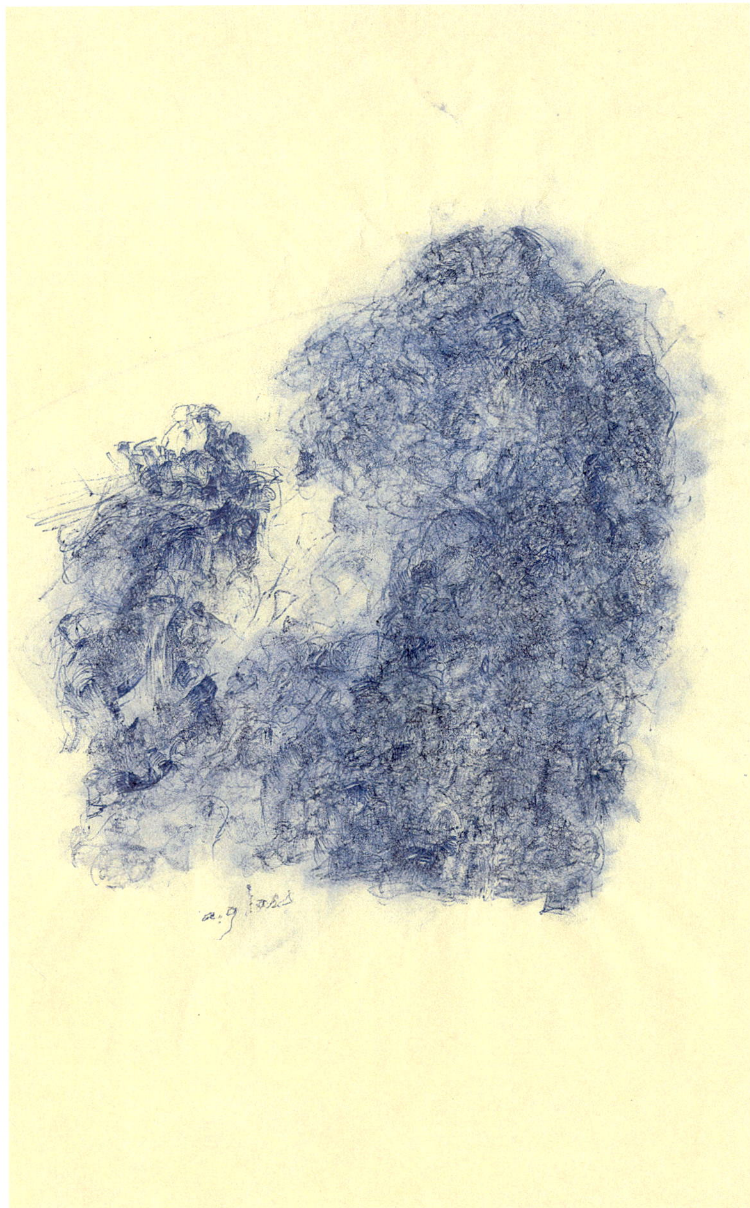

Untitled
(Club Saint-Germain period)
ca. 1954-1962
Bicolor blue and violet pen drawing, on paper.
22 x 13.7 cm
Artist's collection

Untitled
(Club Saint-Germain period)
ca. 1954-1962
Monochrome blue ballpoint pen drawing with a touch of watercolor, on paper.
20.6 x 24.6 cm
Artist's collection

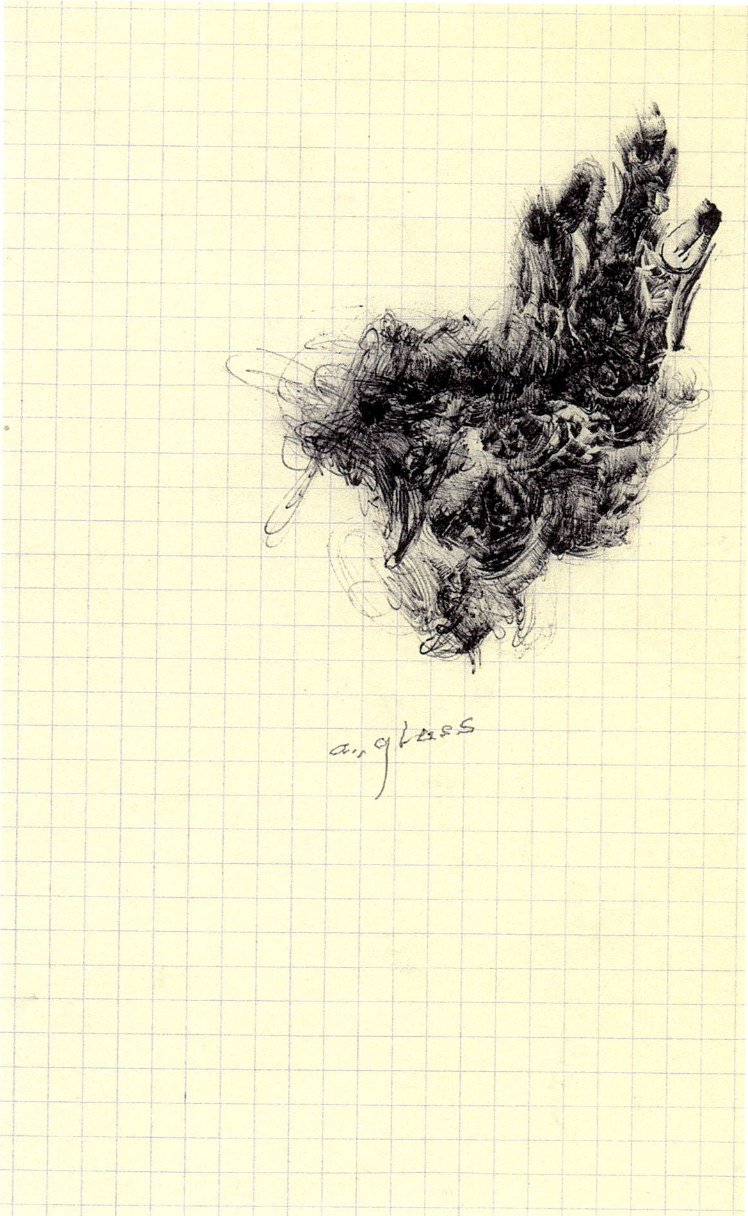

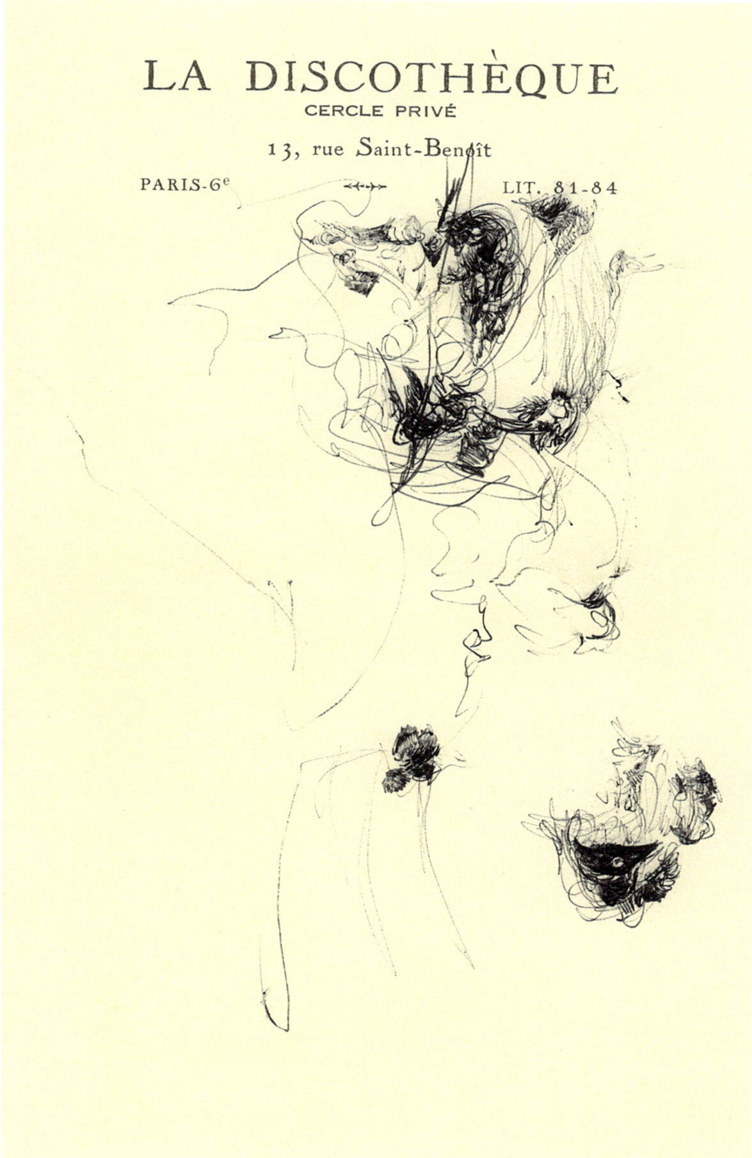

Untitled
(Club Saint-Germain period)
ca. 1954-1962
Monochrome black ballpoint pen drawing, on squared paper.
21.8 x 17 cm
Artist's collection

Untitled
(Club Saint-Germain period)
ca. 1954-1962
Monochrome black ballpoint pen drawing, on invitation from La Discothèque.
17.9 x 11.5 cm
Artist's collection

Untitled
(Club Saint-Germain period)
ca. 1954-1962
Graphite pencil drawing,
on paper.
21 x 27 cm
Artist's collection

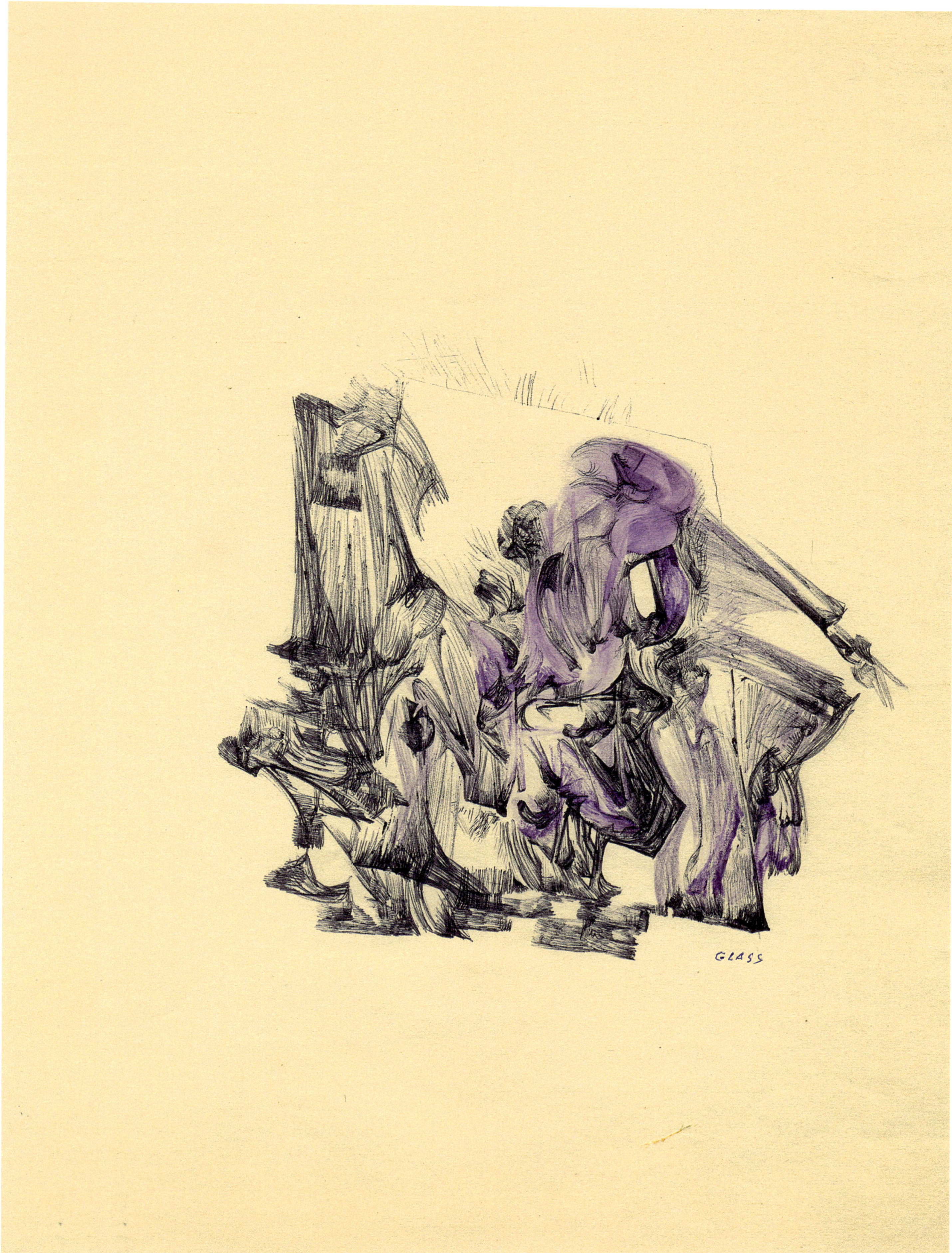

Untitled
(Club Saint-Germain period)
ca. 1954-1962
Monochrome pen drawing
in navy blue and violet
watercolor, on paper.
28 x 22.5 cm
Artist's collection

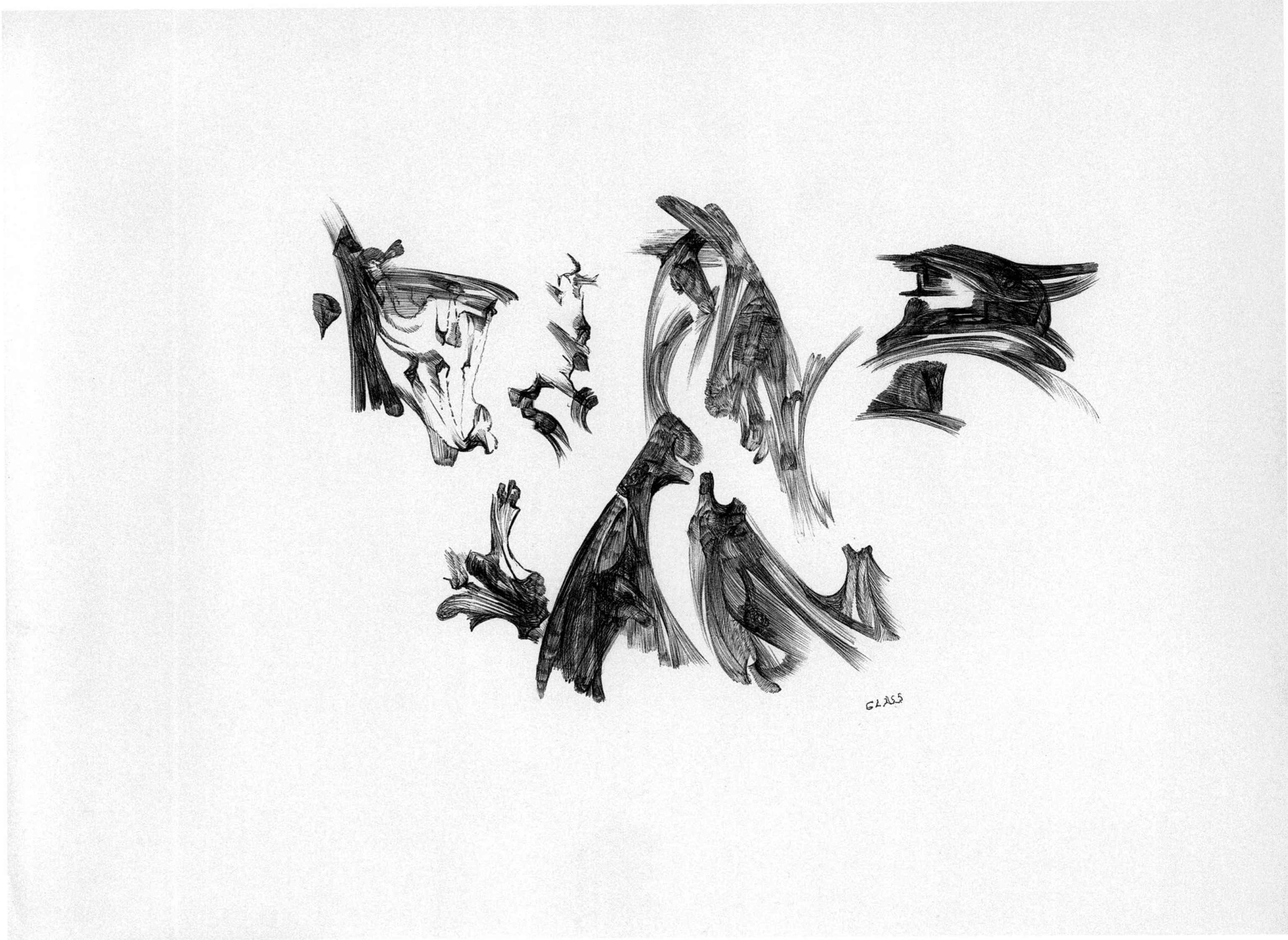

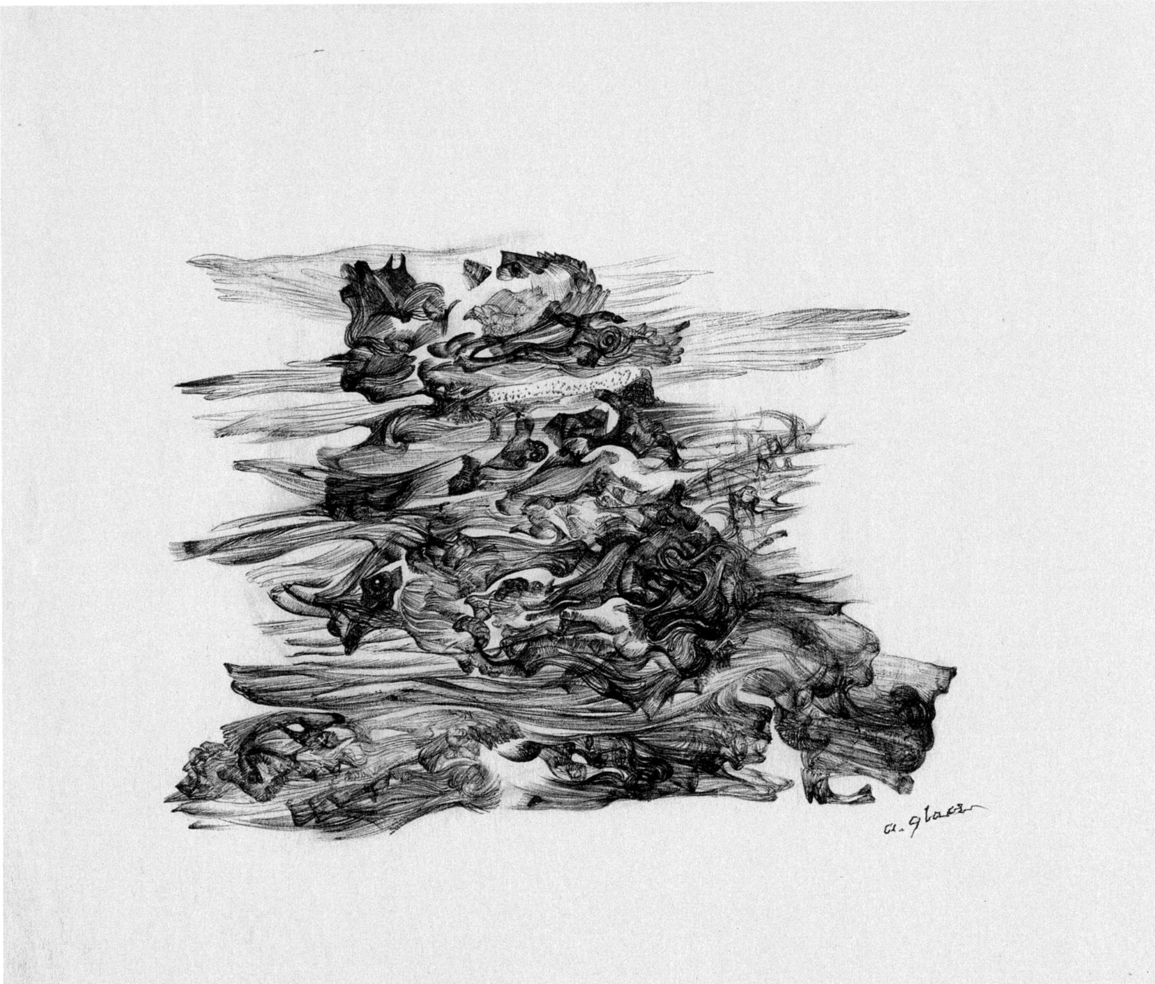

Untitled
(Club Saint-Germain period)
ca. 1954-1962
Monochrome navy blue
ballpoint pen drawing,
on paper.
25 x 32.5 cm
Artist's collection

Untitled
(Club Saint-Germain period)
ca. 1954-1962
Monochrome navy blue
ballpoint pen drawing,
on paper.
22.5 x 28 cm
Artist's collection

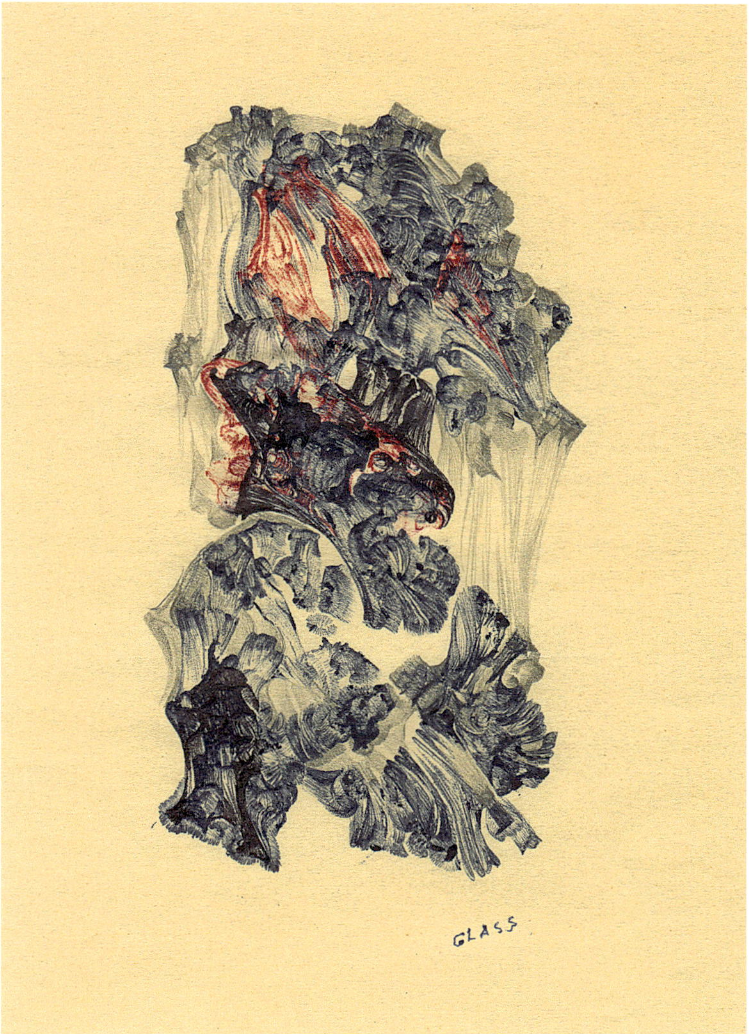

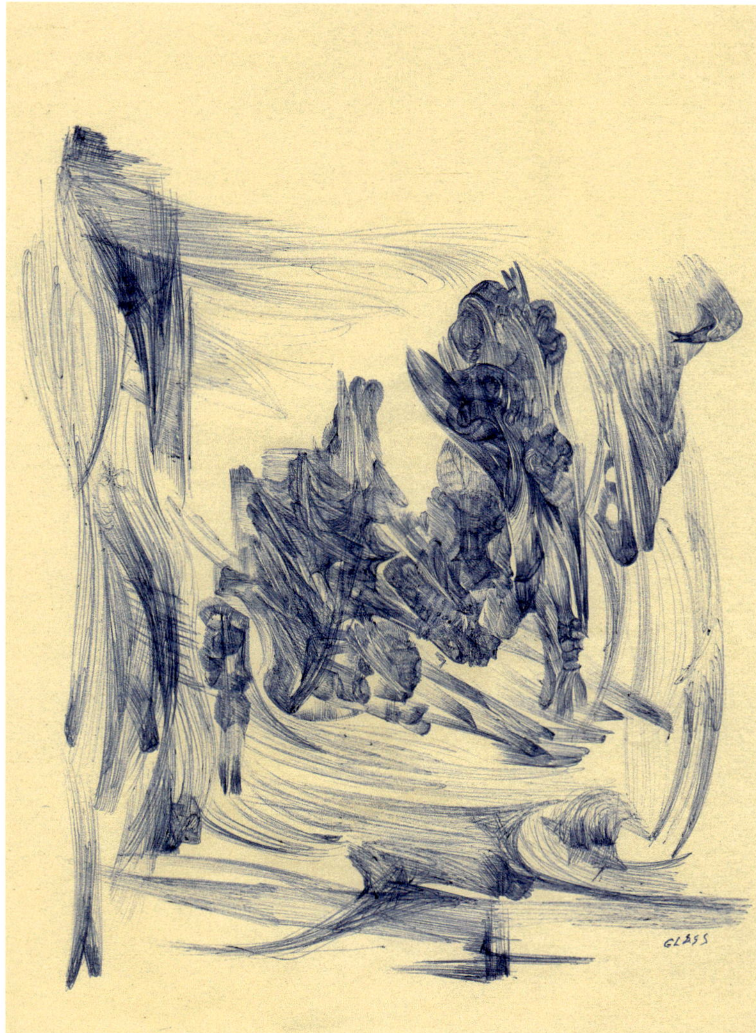

Untitled
(Club Saint-Germain period)
ca. 1954-1962
Monochrome blue ballpoint pen drawing, on paper.
28 x 22.5 cm
Artist's collection

Untitled
(Club Saint-Germain period)
ca. 1954-1962
Monochrome pen drawing in navy blue and red, on paper.
28 x 22.5 cm
Artist's collection

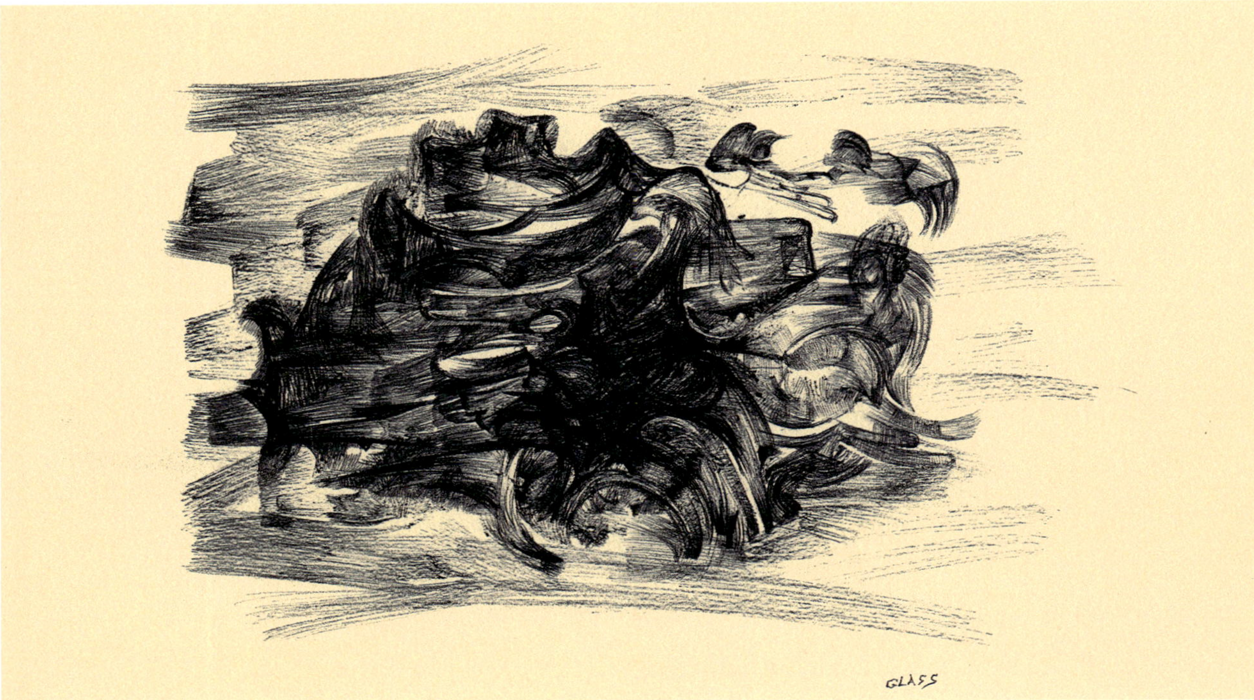

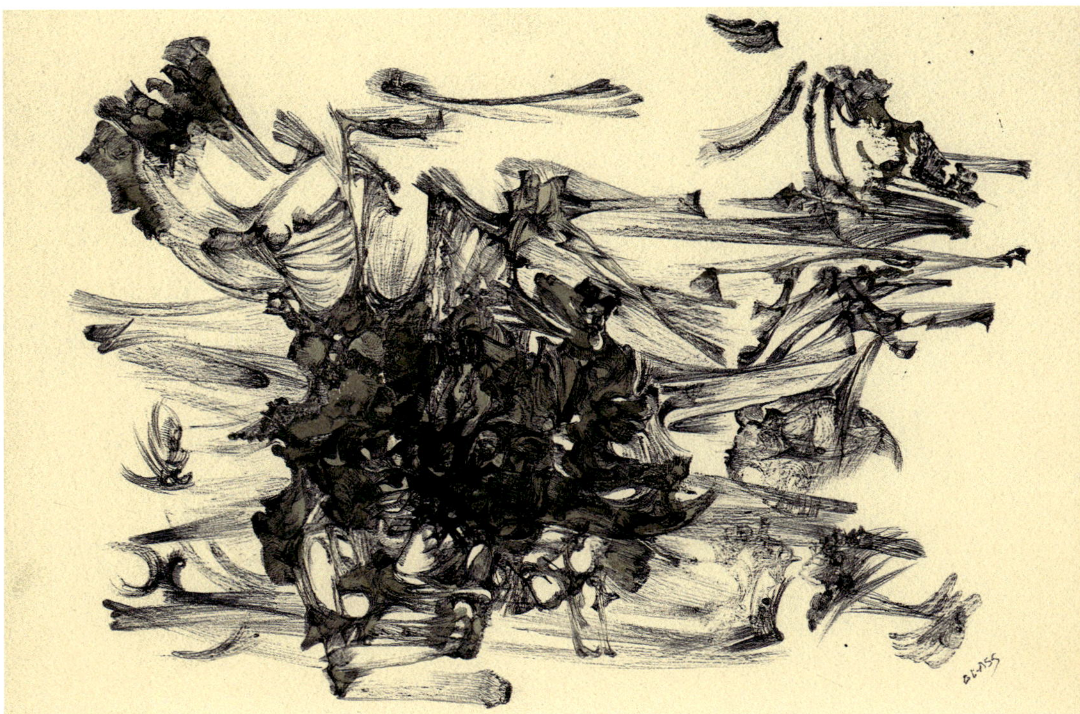

Untitled
(Club Saint-Germain period)
ca. 1954-1962
Navy blue monocolor ballpoint pen drawing, on cardboard paper.
18 x 26 cm
Artist's collection

Untitled
(Club Saint-Germain period)
ca. 1954-1962
Monochrome black pen drawing and Indian ink, on cardboard paper.
18 x 26 cm
Artist's collection

Untitled
(Club Saint-Germain period)
ca. 1954-1962
Monochrome black pen drawing and Indian ink, on cardboard paper.
18 x 26 cm
Artist's collection

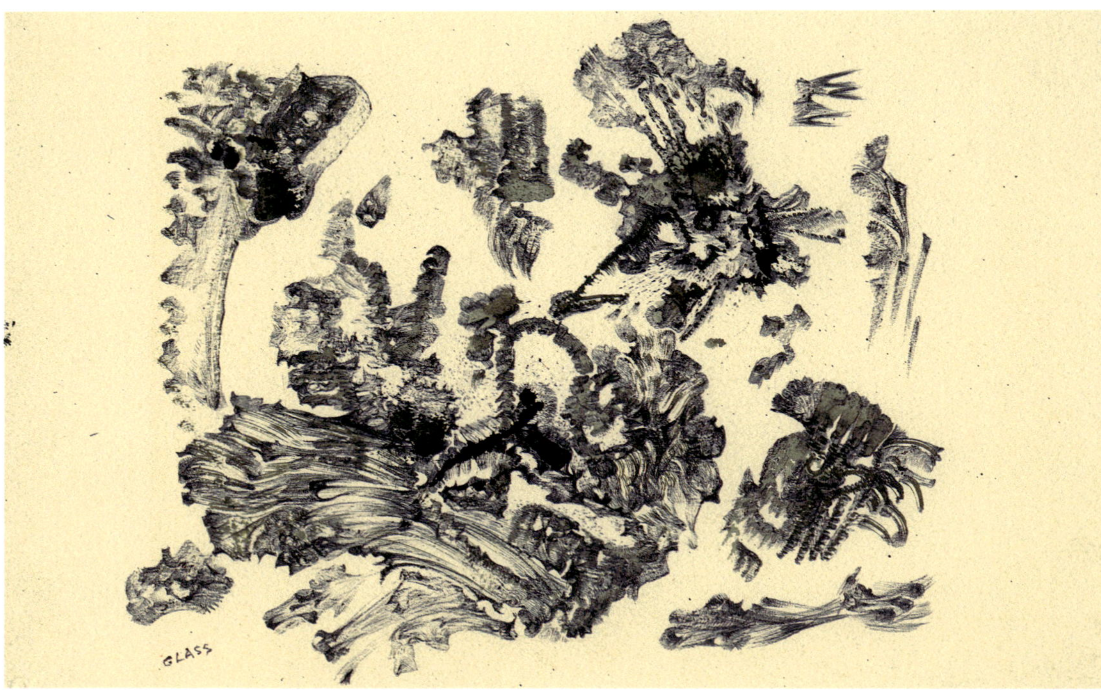

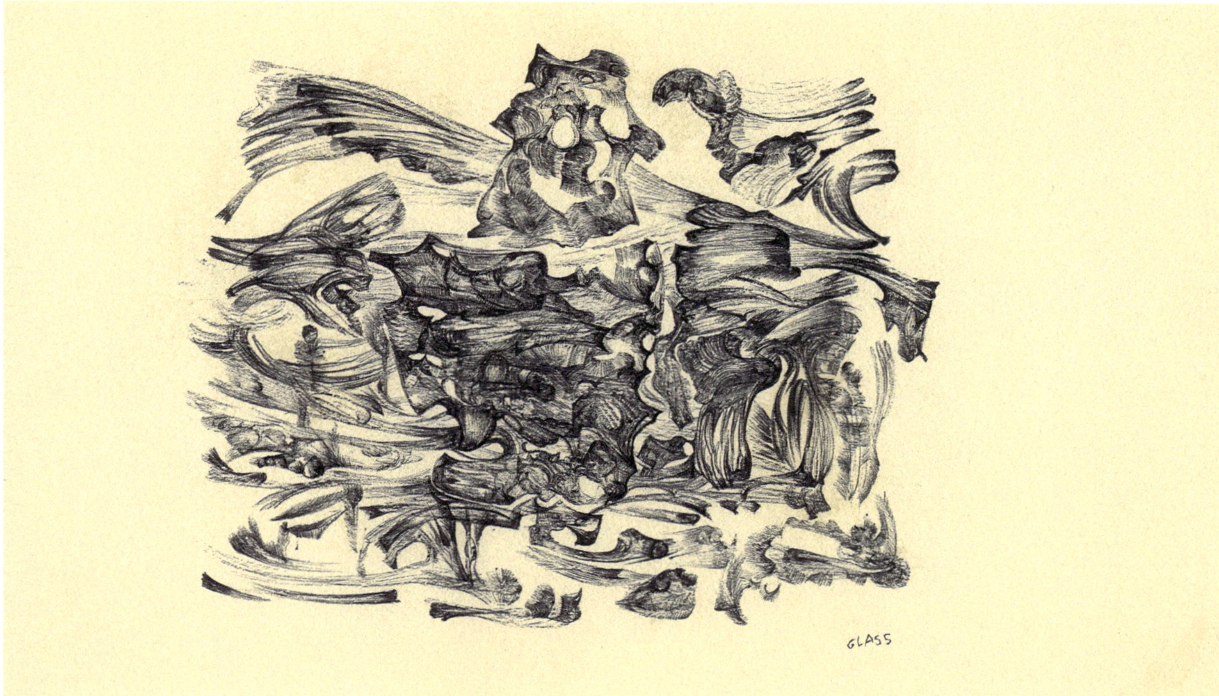

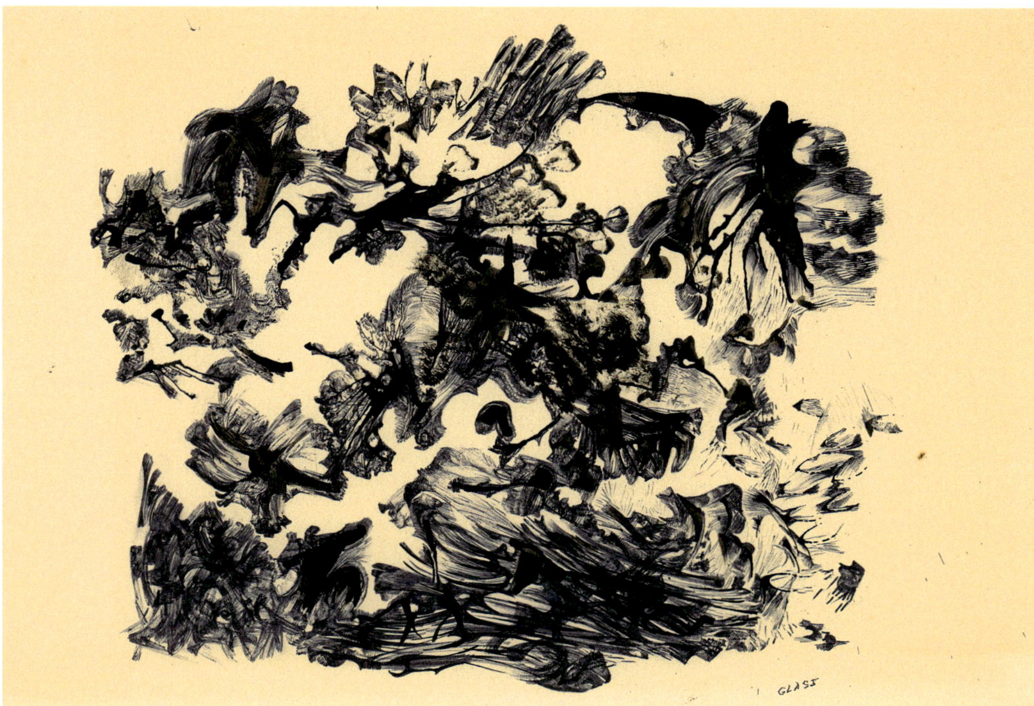

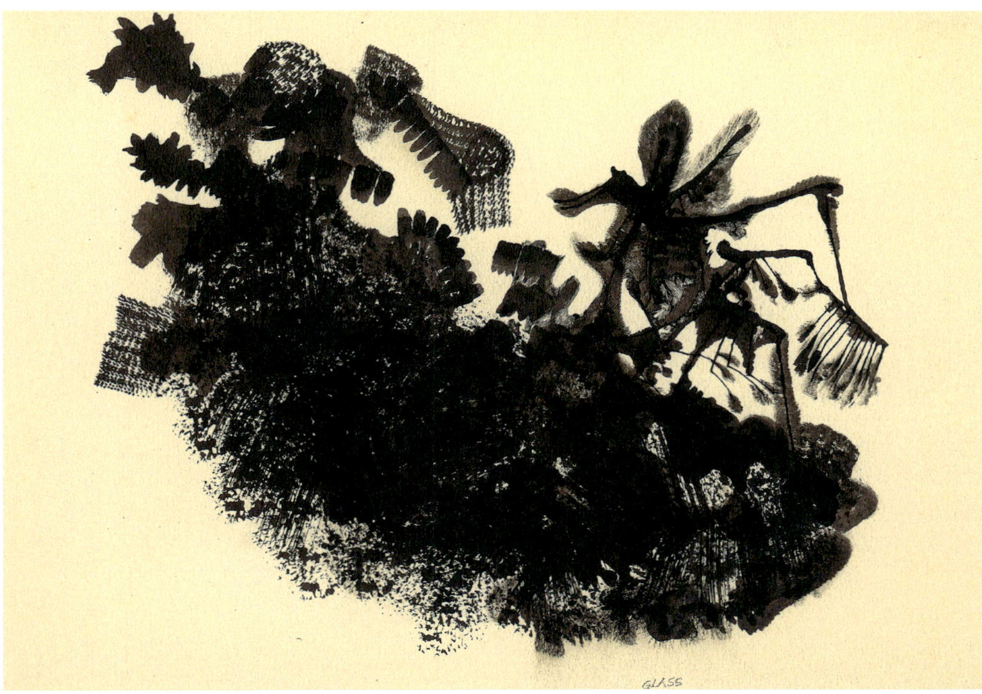

Untitled
(Club Saint-Germain period)
ca. 1954-1962
Monochrome black pen
drawing and Indian ink,
on cardboard paper.
18.5 x 25.7 cm
Artist's collection

Untitled
(Club Saint-Germain period)
ca. 1954-1962
Monochrome black pen
drawing and Indian ink,
on paper.
21.5 x 26 cm
Artist's collection

Untitled
(Club Saint-Germain period)
ca. 1954-1962
Monochrome black pen
drawing and Indian ink,
on cardboard paper.
26 x 37.5 cm
Artist's collection

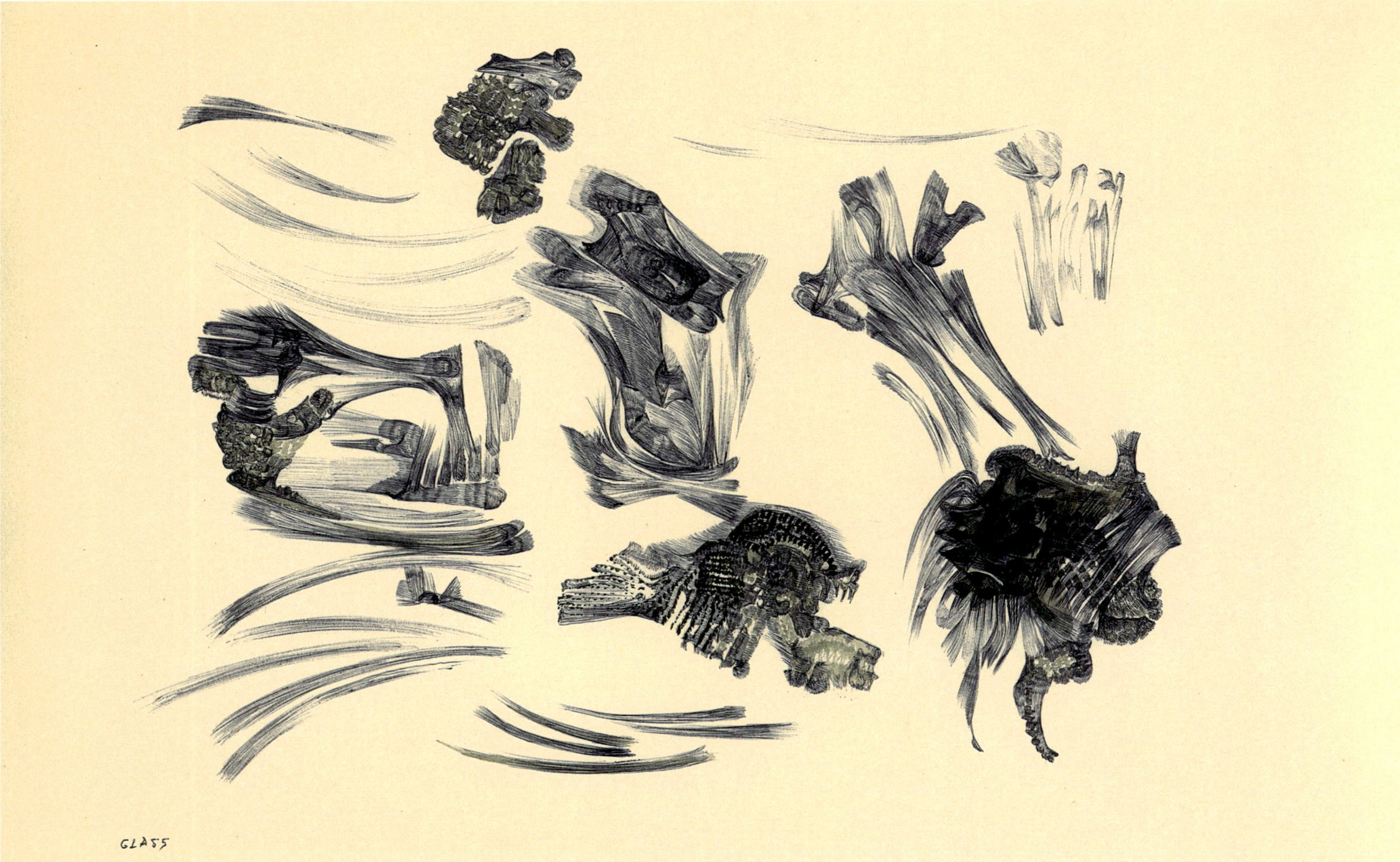

Untitled
(Club Saint-Germain period)
ca. 1954-1962
Monochrome black
pen drawing, on paper.
25 x 32.5 cm
Artist's collection

Untitled
(Club Saint-Germain period)
1958
Monochrome black
pen drawing, on paper.
28.5 x 21.5 cm
Artist's collection

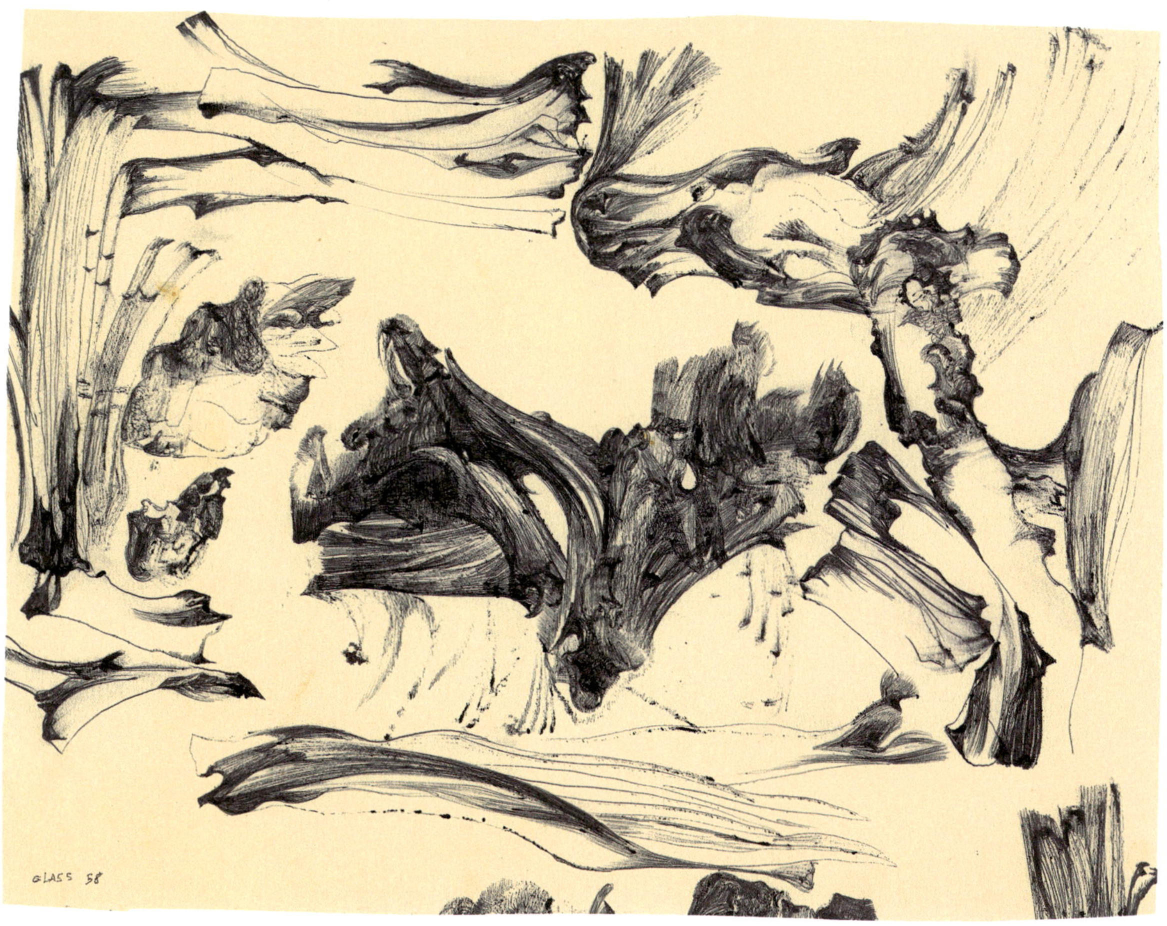

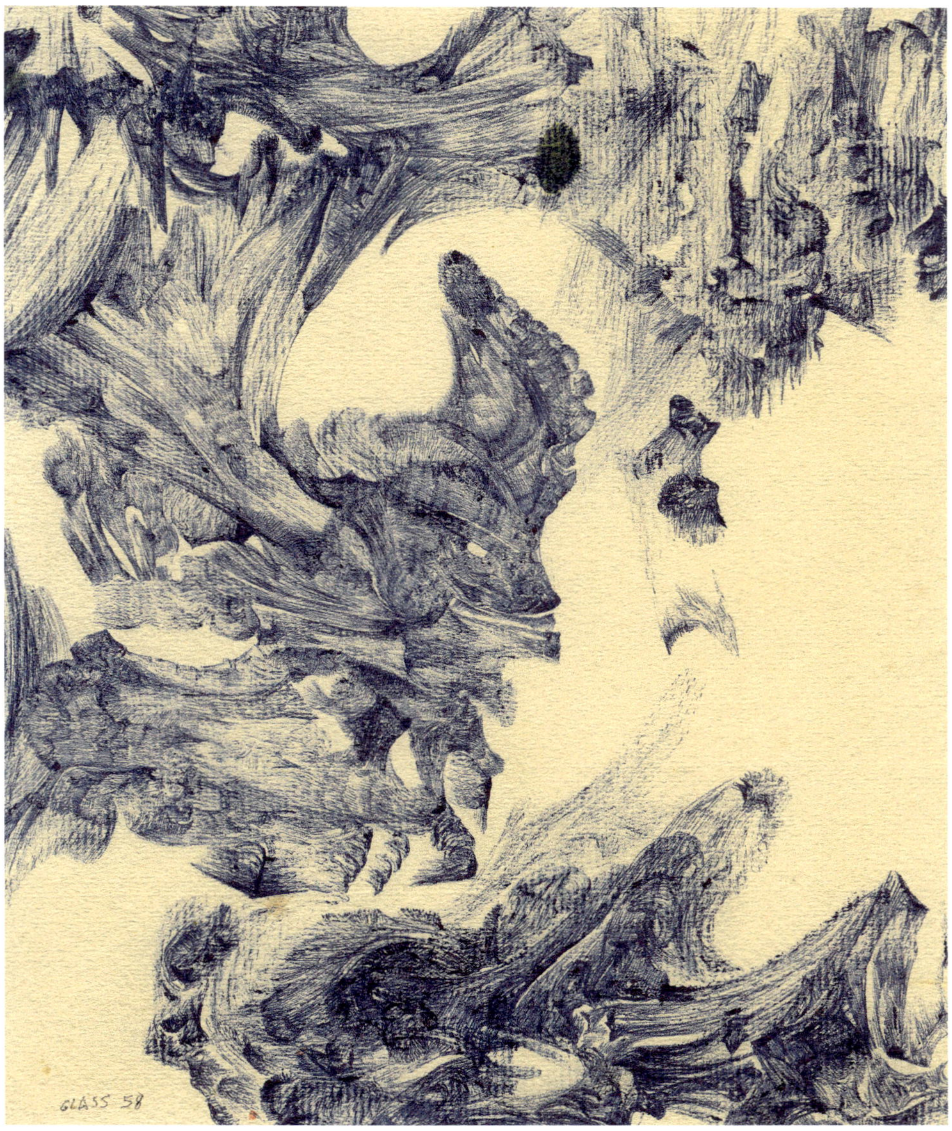

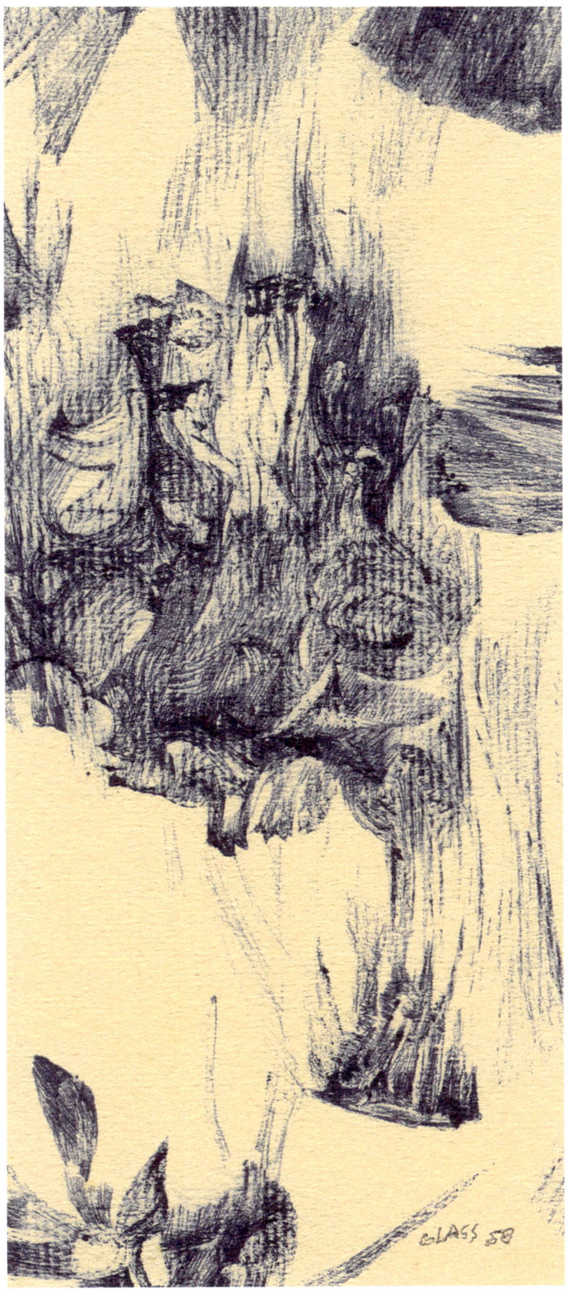

Untitled
(Club Saint-Germain period)
1958
Monochrome blue ballpoint pen drawing, on corrugated paper.
22.3 x 18.8 cm
Artist's collection

Untitled
(Club Saint-Germain period)
1958
Monochrome blue ballpoint pen drawing, on corrugated paper.
19.2 x 8.5 cm
Artist's collection

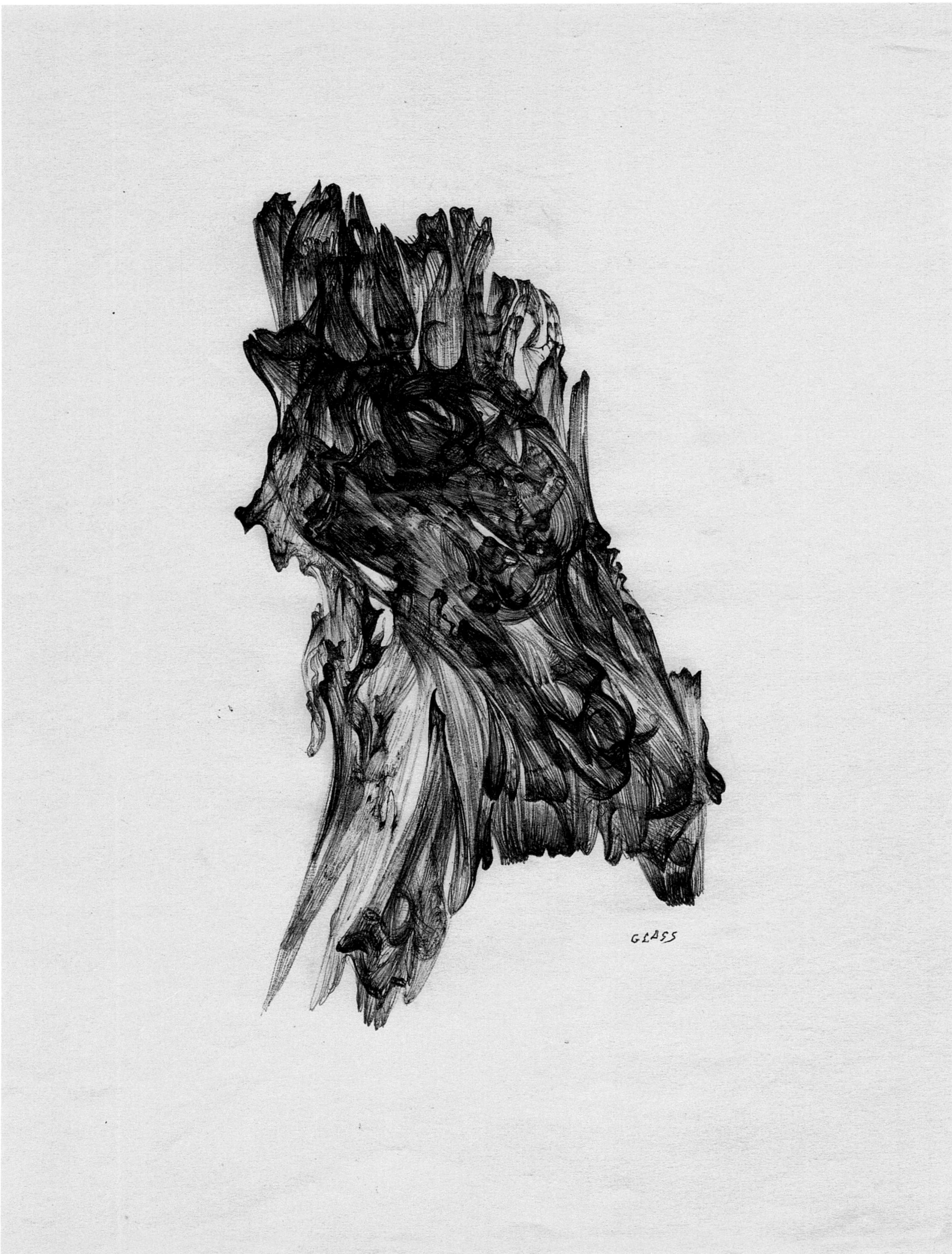

Untitled
(Club Saint-Germain period)
ca. 1954-1962
Monochrome black pen
drawing, on paper.
28 x 22.5 cm
Artist's collection

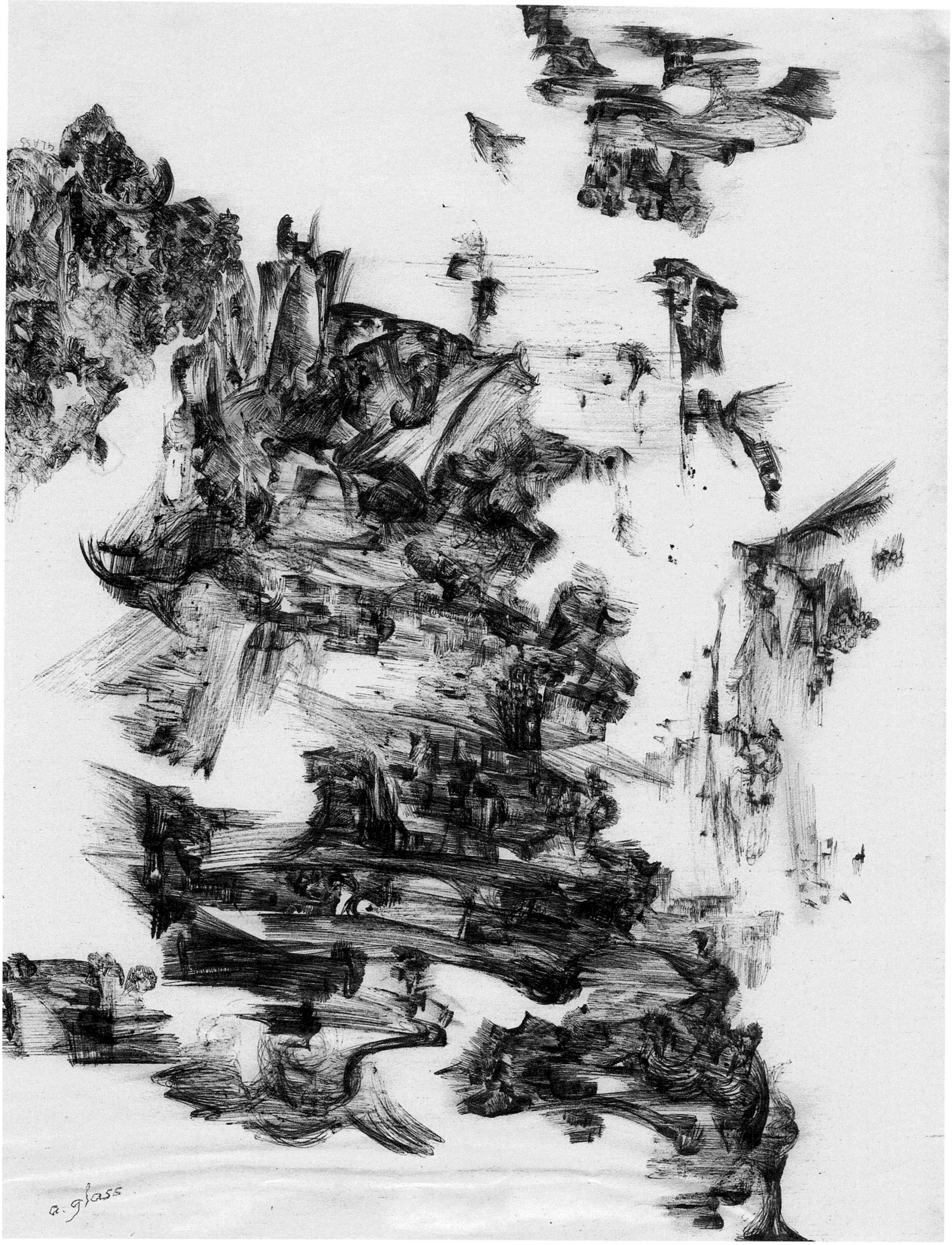

Untitled
(Club Saint-Germain period)
ca. 1954-1962
Monochrome black pen
drawing, on paper.
28 x 22 cm
Artist's collection

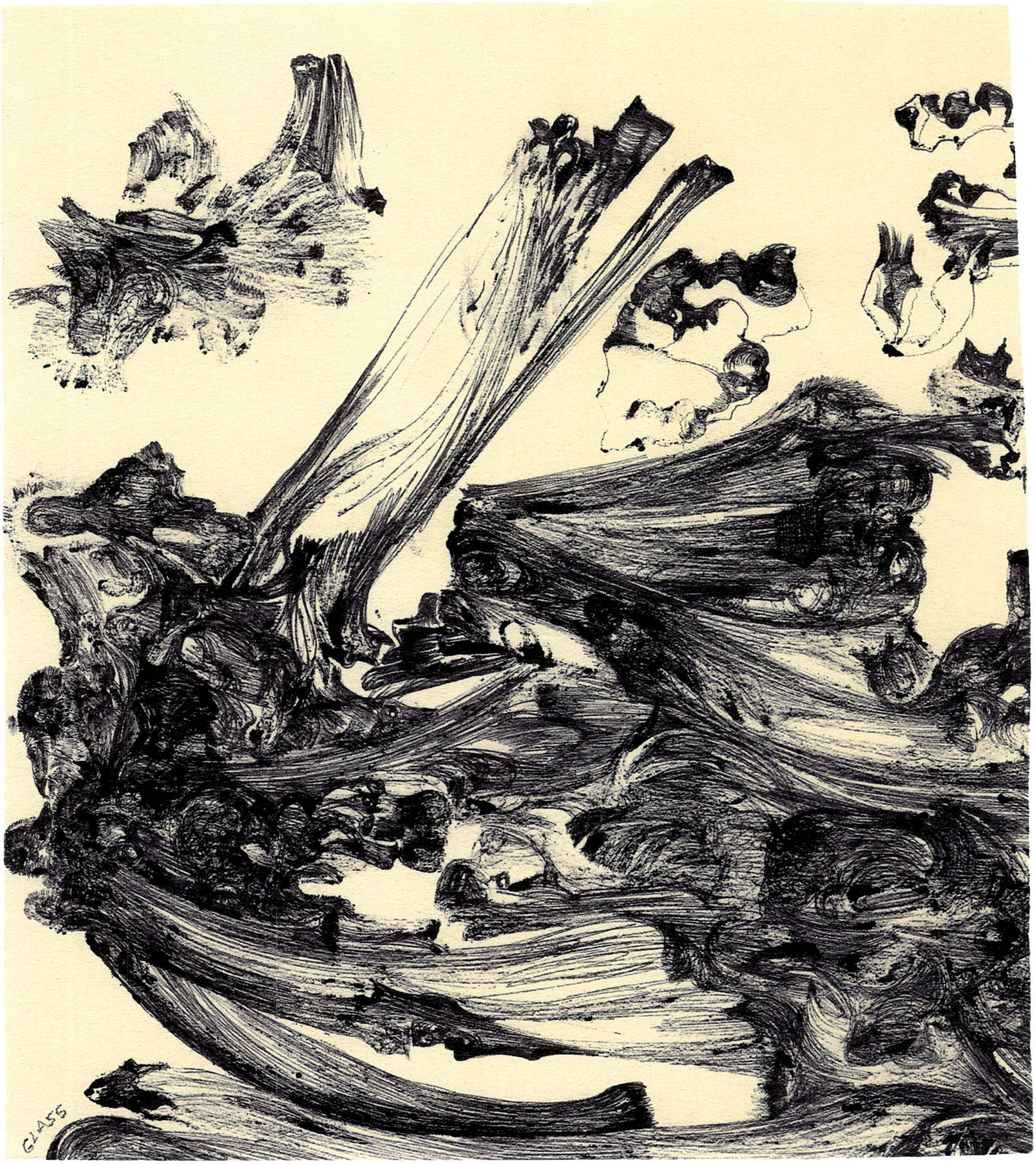

Untitled
(Club Saint-Germain period)
ca. 1954-1962
Monochrome black pen
drawing, on paper.
19.5 x 17 cm
Artist's collection

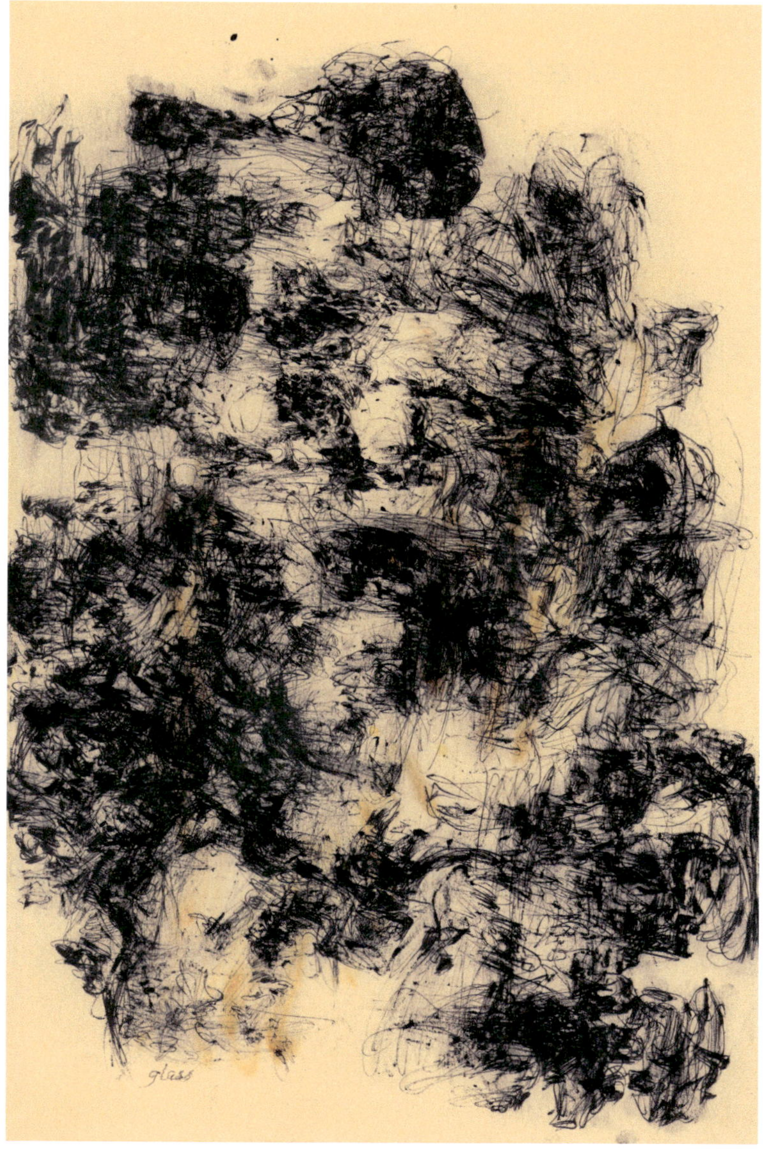

Untitled
(Club Saint-Germain period)
ca. 1954-1962
Monochrome black ballpoint pen drawing, on paper.
26 x 17 cm
Artist's collection

Untitled
(Club Saint-Germain period)
ca. 1954-1962
Monochrome black ballpoint pen drawing with touch of alumettage, on paper.
26 x 17 cm
Artist's collection

Untitled
(Club Saint-Germain period)
1959
Blue and navy blue two-tone ballpoint pen drawing, on paper.
28 x 22.5 cm
Artist's collection

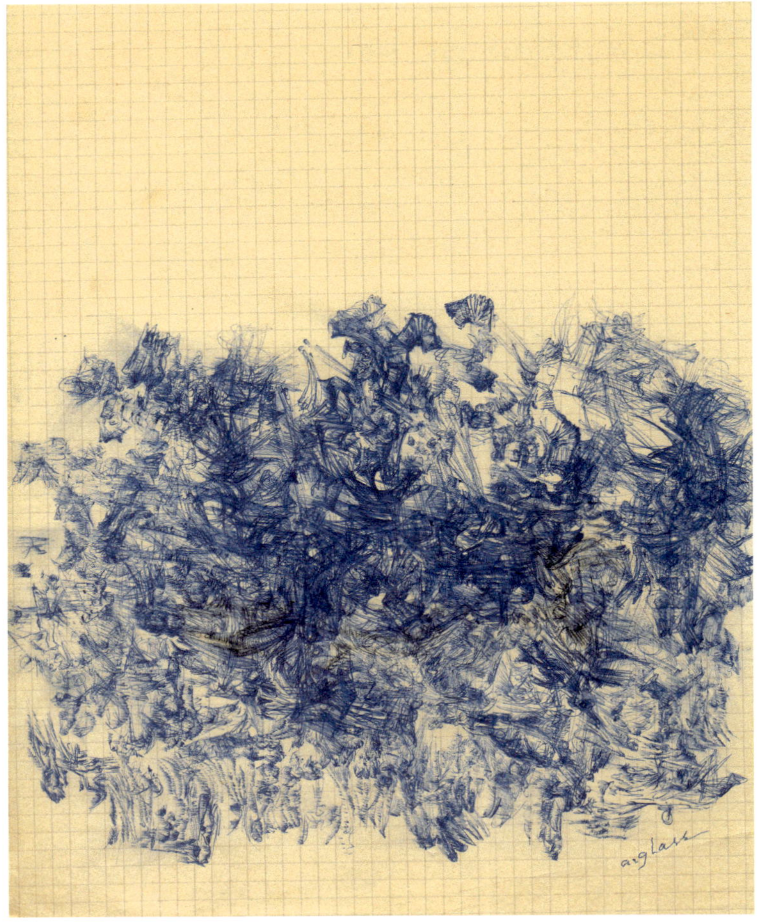

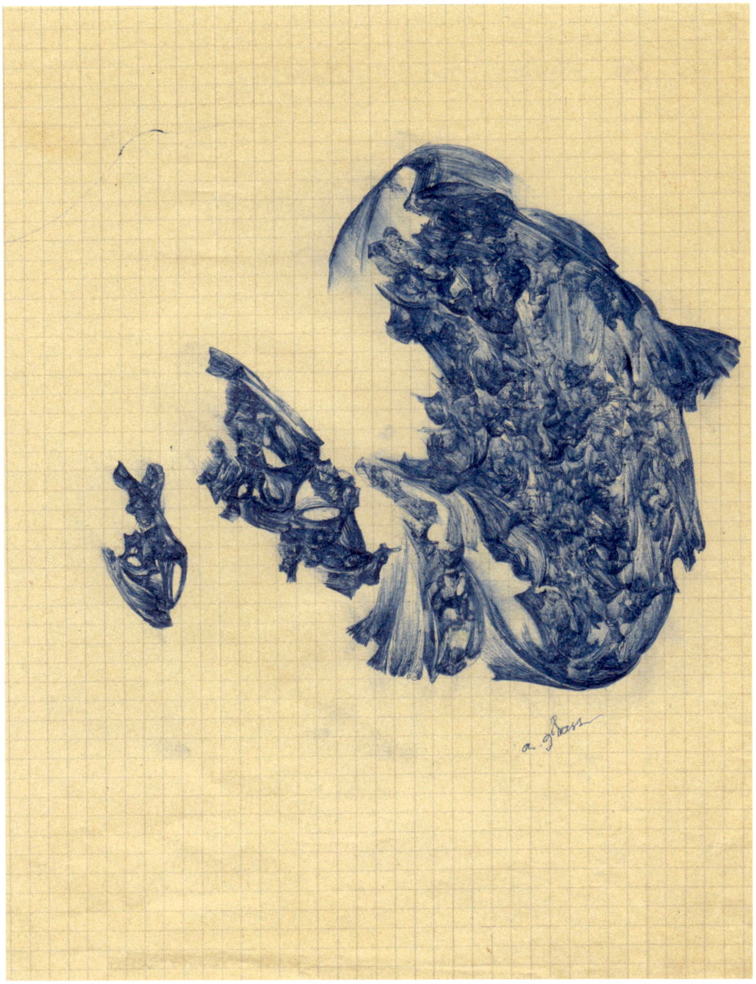

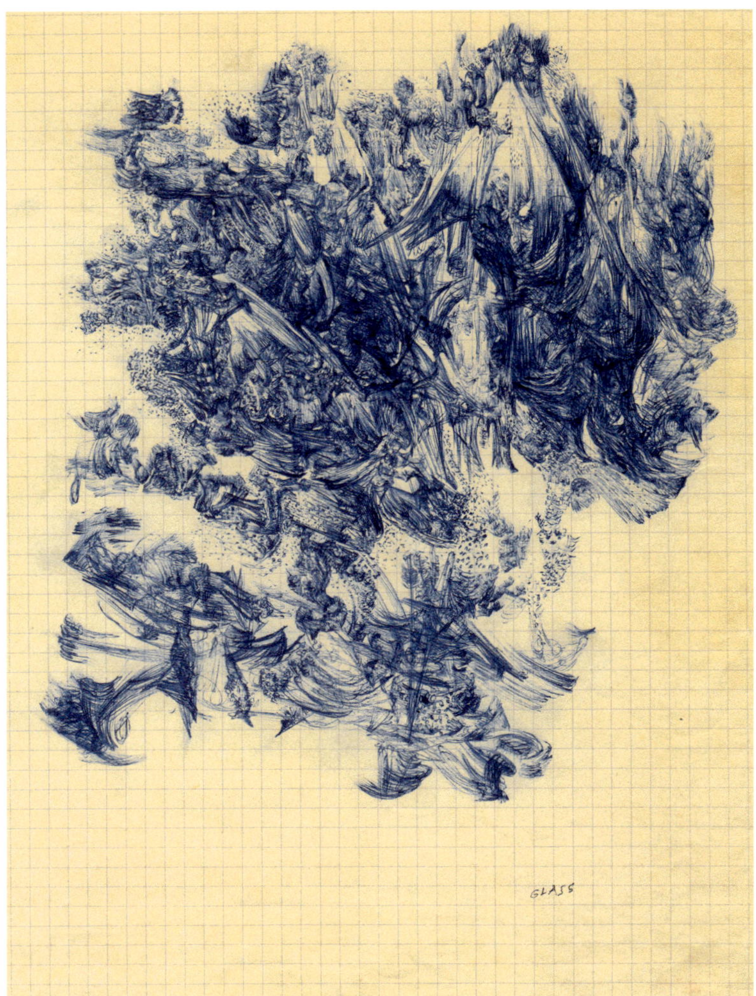

Untitled
(Club Saint-Germain period)
ca. 1954-1962
Monochrome blue ballpoint
pen drawing, on squared paper.
25.4 x 21 cm
Artist's collection

Untitled
(Club Saint-Germain period)
ca. 1954-1962
Monochrome blue ballpoint
pen drawing, on squared paper
25.4 x 21 cm
Artist's collection

Untitled
(Club Saint-Germain period)
ca. 1954-1962
Monochrome blue ballpoint
pen drawing on squared paper.
27 x 21 cm
Artist's collection

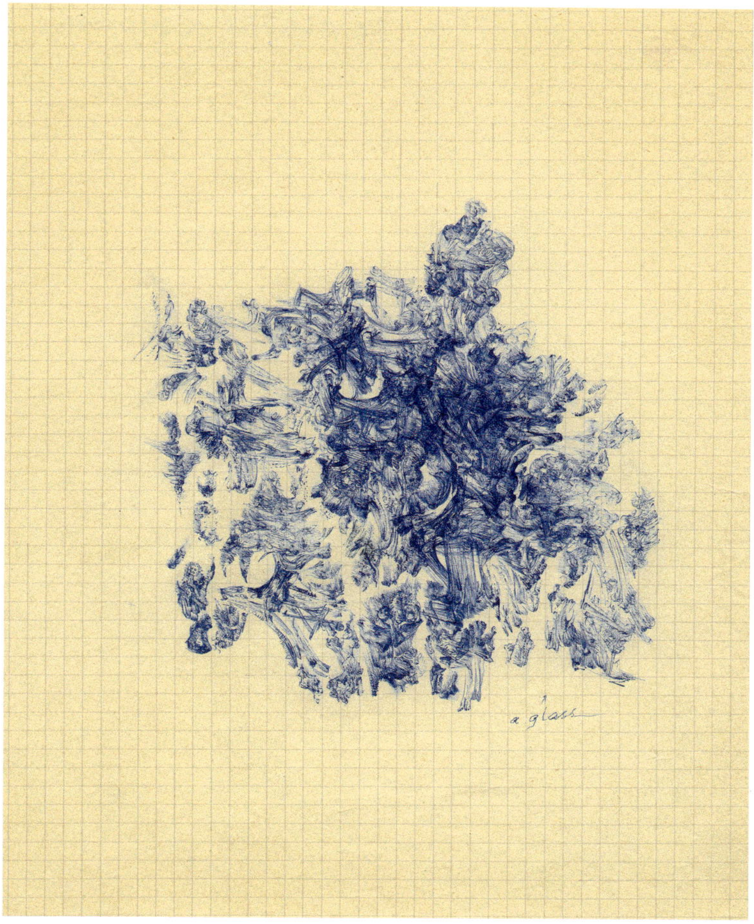

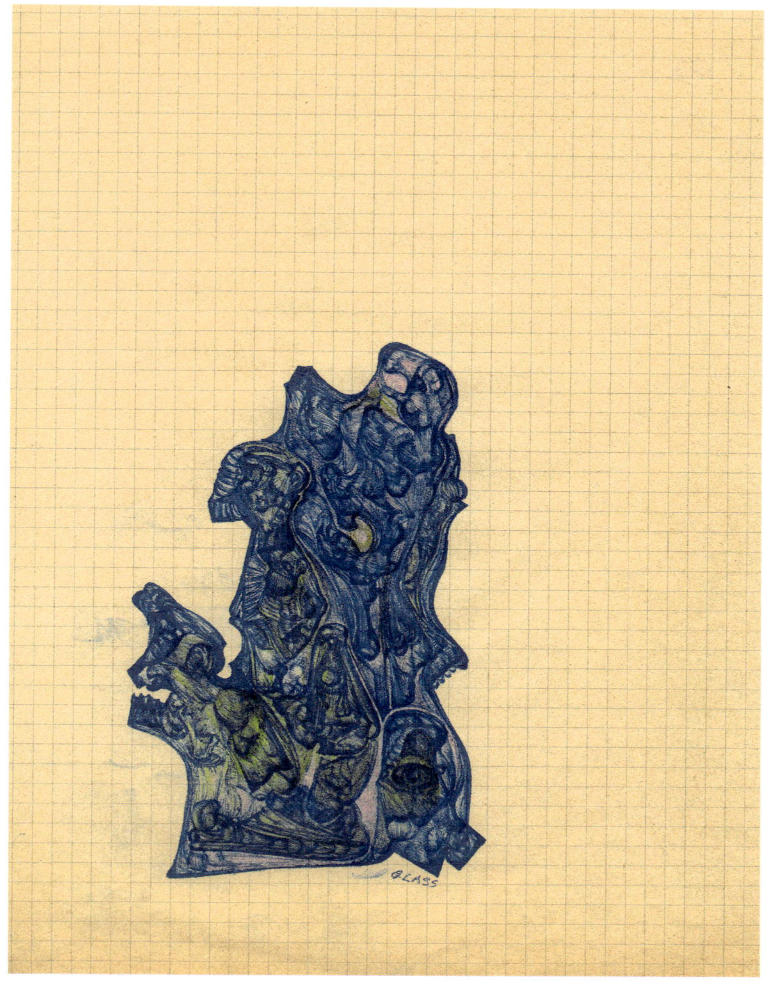

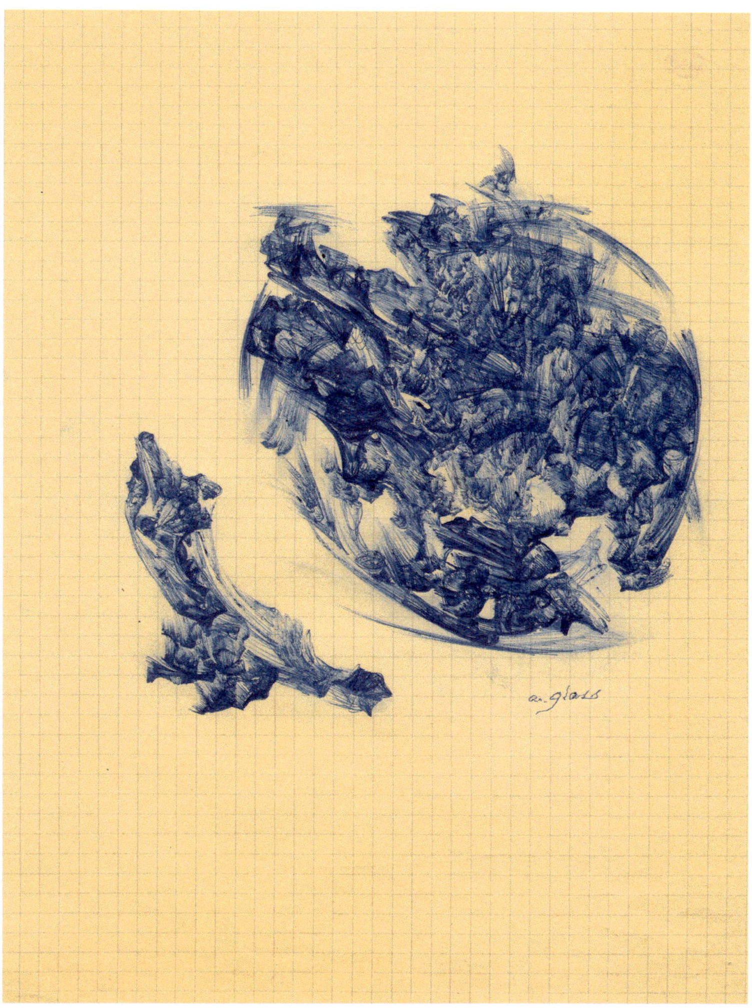

Untitled
(Club Saint-Germain period)
ca. 1954-1962
Monochrome blue ballpoint
pen drawing on squared paper.
25.5 x 21 cm
Artist's collection

Untitled
(Club Saint-Germain period)
ca. 1954-1962
Bicolor blue and green
ballpoint pen drawing,
on squared paper.
25.5 x 21 cm
Artist's collection

Untitled
(Club Saint-Germain period)
ca. 1954-1962
Monochrome blue ballpoint
pen drawing on squared paper.
25.5 x 21 cm
Artist's collection

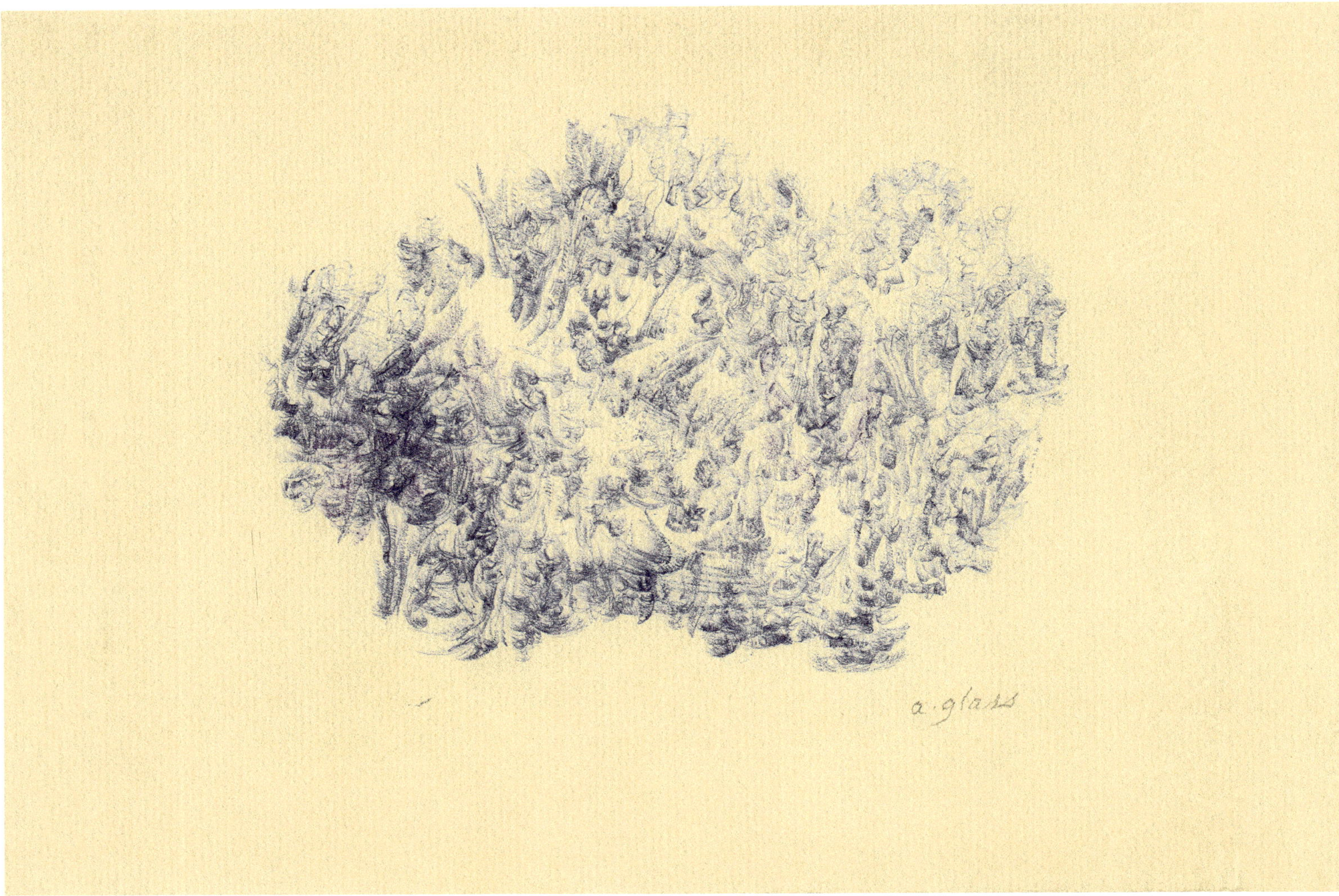

Untitled
(Club Saint-Germain period)
ca. 1954-1962
Bicolor blue and violet pen drawing on paper.
15.5 x 24 cm
Artist's collection

Untitled
(Club Saint-Germain period)
ca. 1954-1962
Monochrome navy blue ballpoint pen drawing, on paper.
28 x 22.5 cm
Artist's collection
Following page

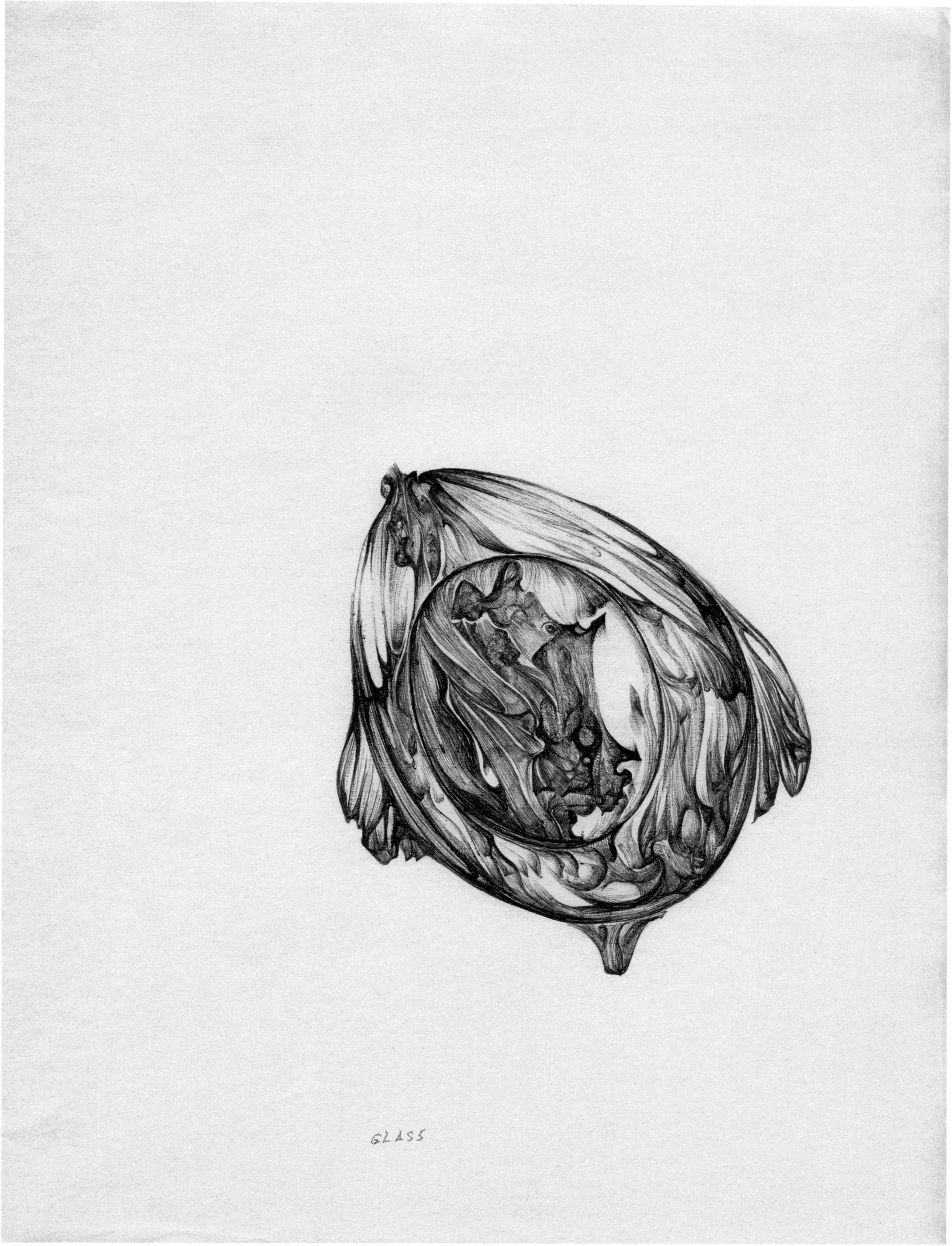
GLASS

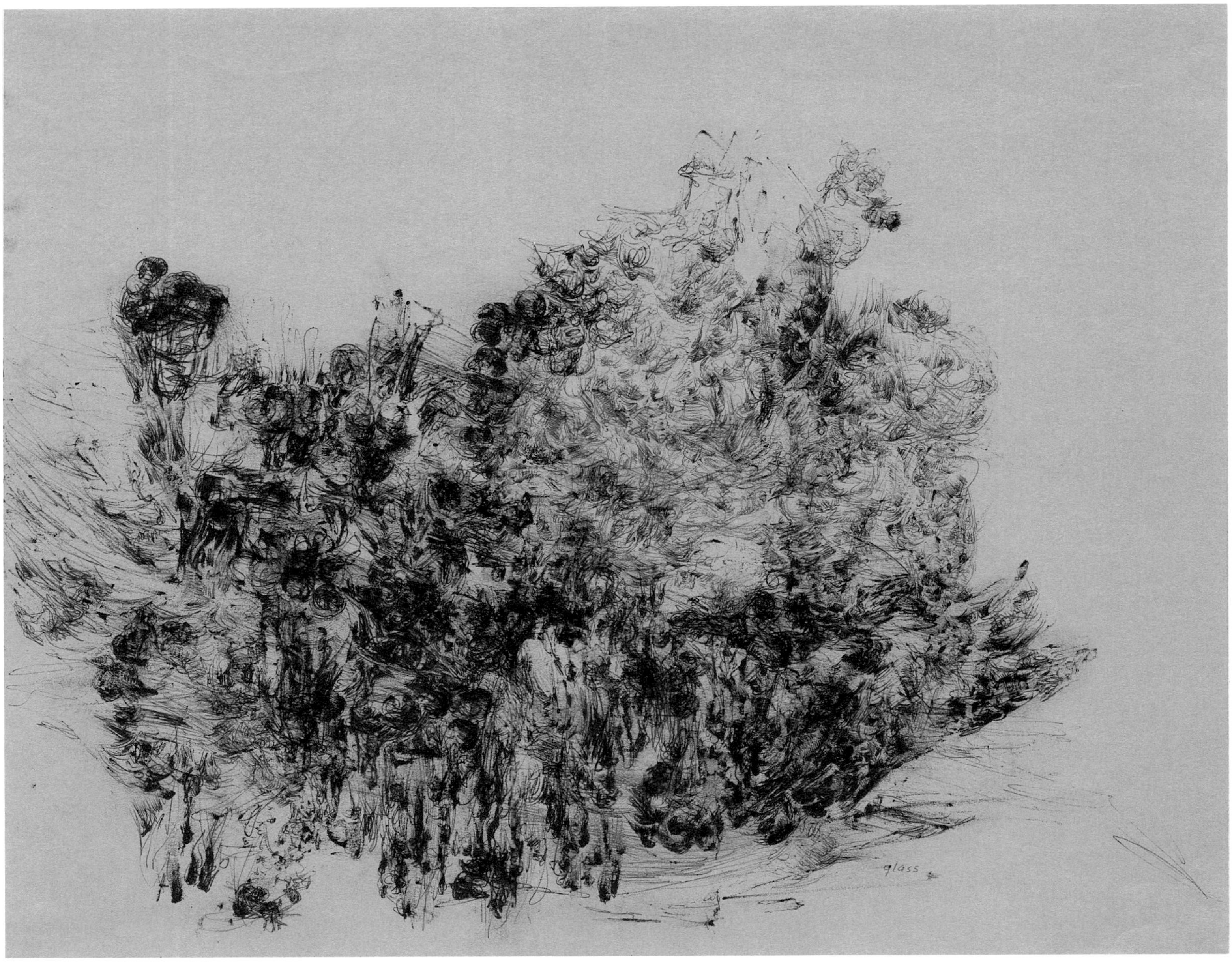

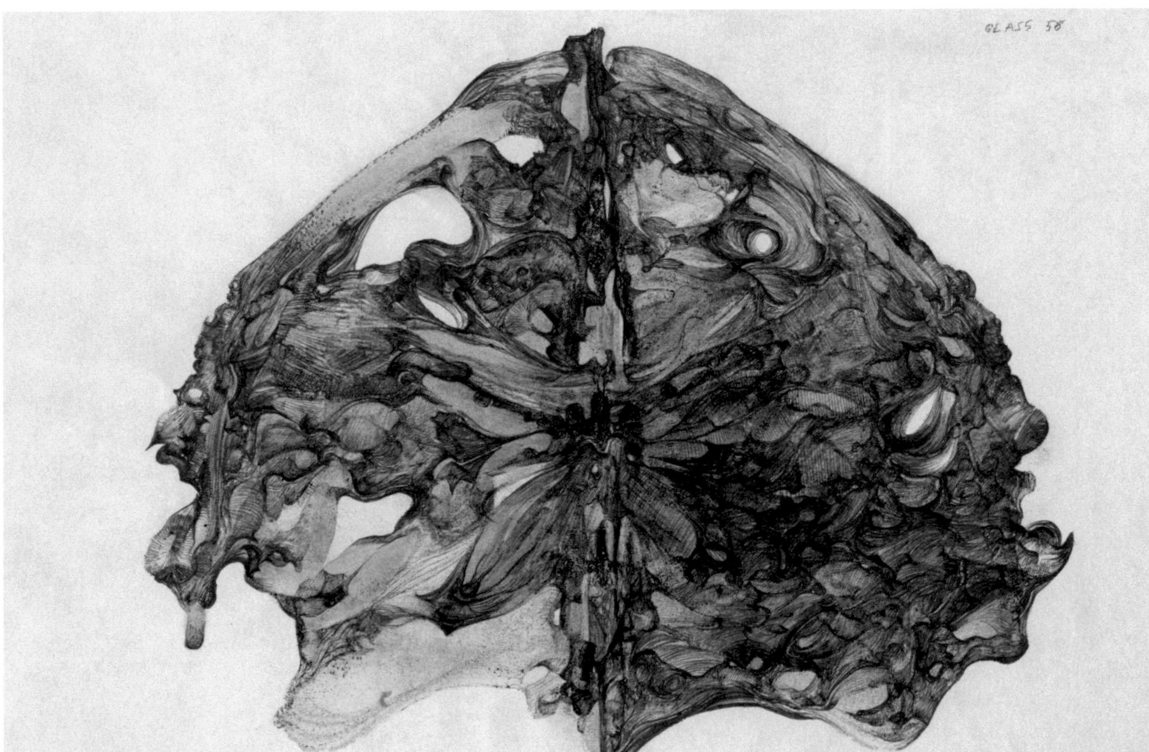

Untitled
(Club Saint-Germain period)
ca. 1954-1962
Monochrome black ballpoint pen drawing, on paper.
21.7 x 28 cm
Artist's collection

Untitled
(Club Saint-Germain period)
1958
Bicolor blue and black ballpoint pen drawing, with violet color and graphite, on paper.
18 x 26.5 cm
Artist's collection

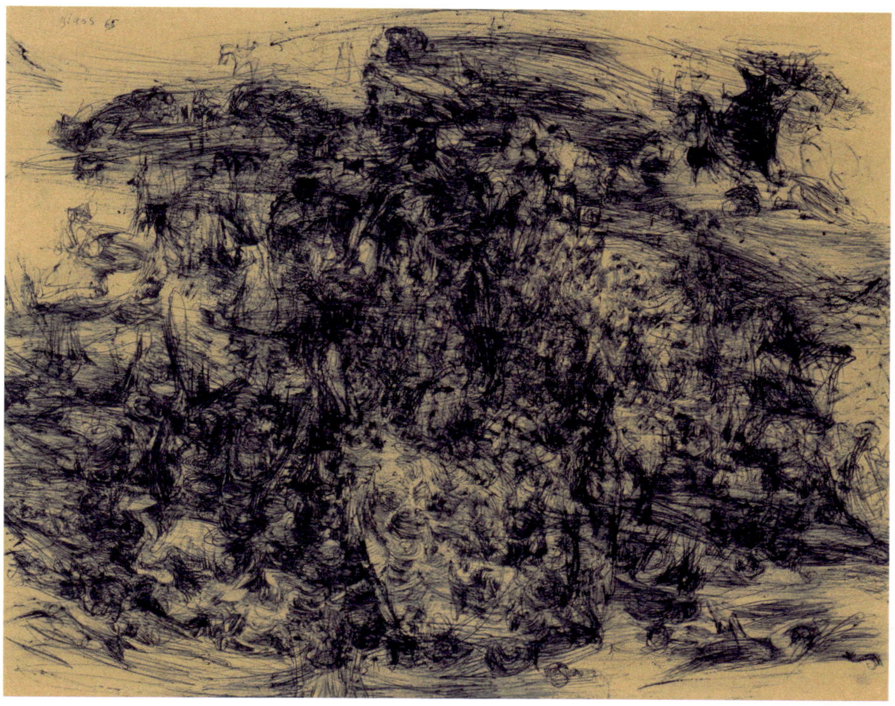

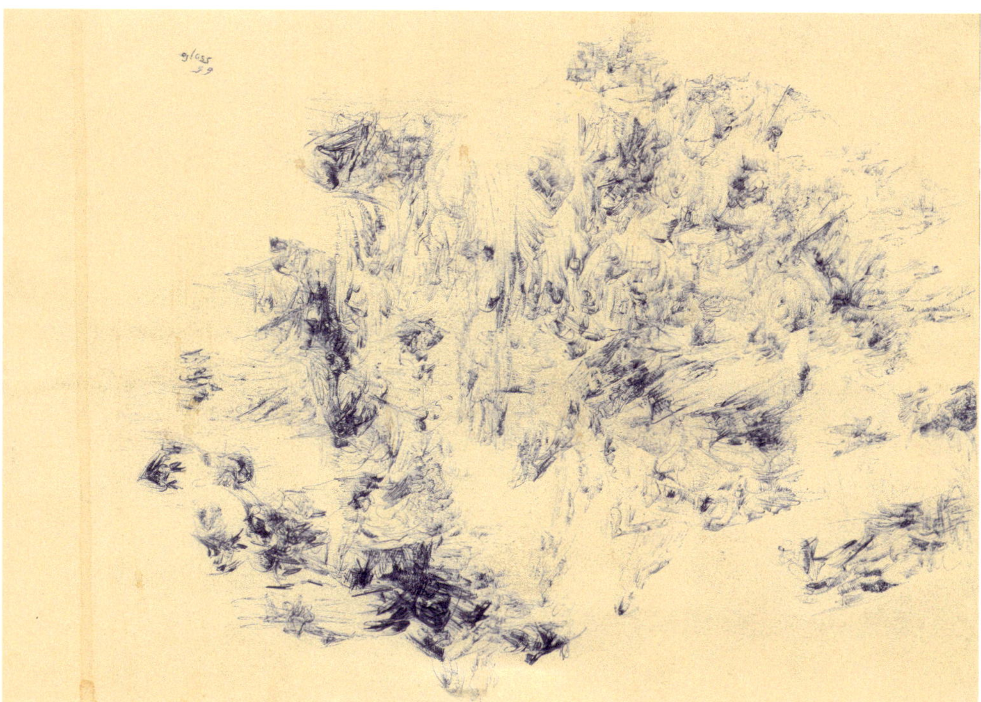

Untitled
(Club Saint-Germain period)
1959
Monochrome blue ballpoint pen drawing, on paper.
21.9 x 28 cm
Artist's collection

Untitled
(Club Saint-Germain period)
1959
Monochrome navy blue ballpoint pen drawing, on paper.
22 x 28 cm
Artist's collection

Untitled
(Club Saint-Germain period)
1959
Monochrome blue ballpoint pen drawing, on paper.
24.5 x 32.5 cm
Artist's collection

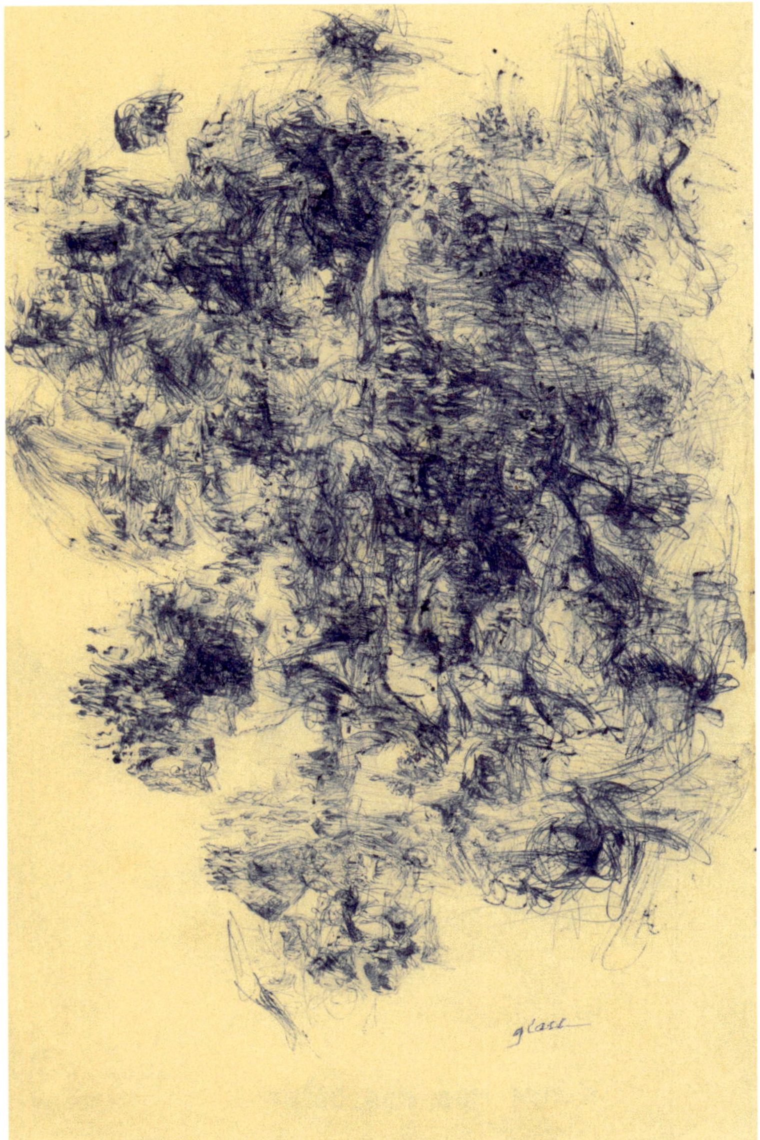

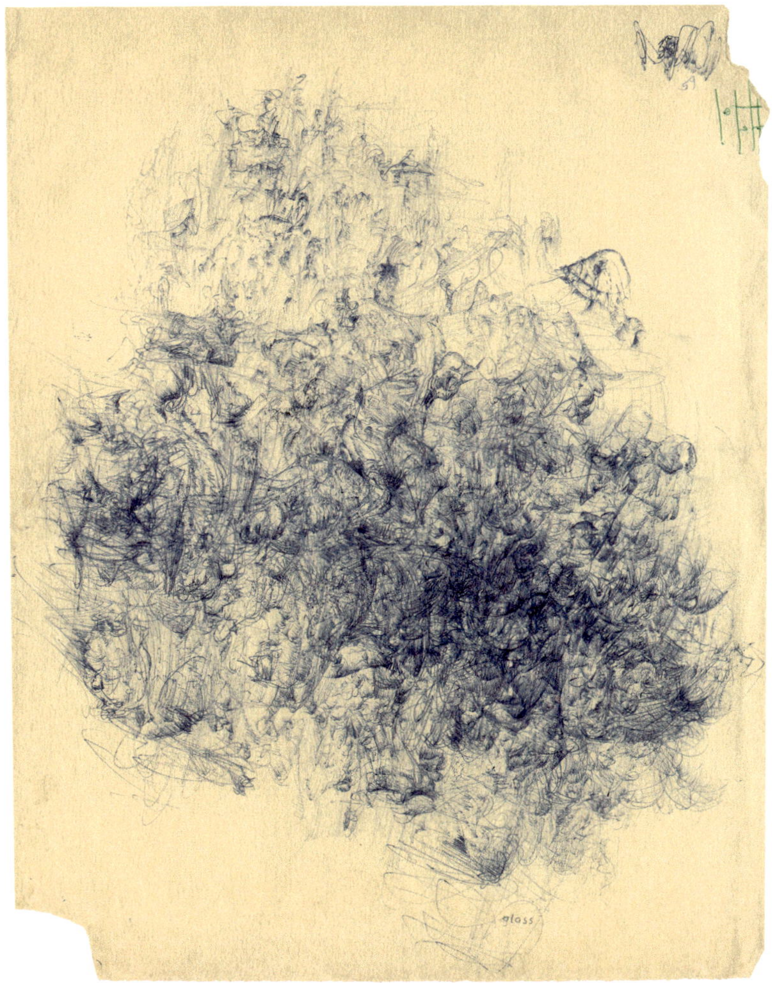

Untitled
(Club Saint-Germain period)
ca. 1954-1962
Monochrome blue ballpoint pen drawing, on paper.
26 x 17 cm
Artist's collection

Untitled
(Club Saint-Germain period)
ca. 1954-1962
Monochrome blue ballpoint pen drawing, on paper.
28 x 24 cm
Artist's collection

Untitled
(Club Saint-Germain period)
1959
Monochrome navy blue ballpoint pen drawing, on paper.
32 x 25.5 cm
Artist's collection

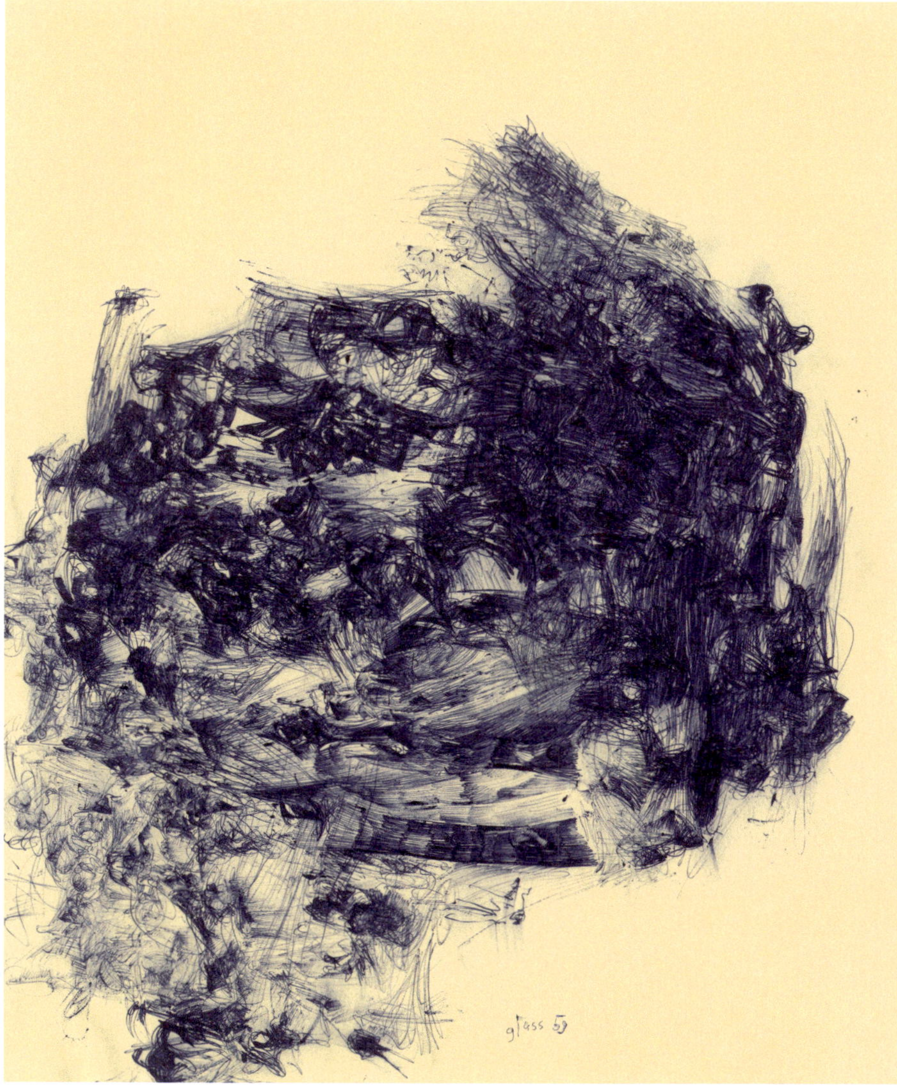

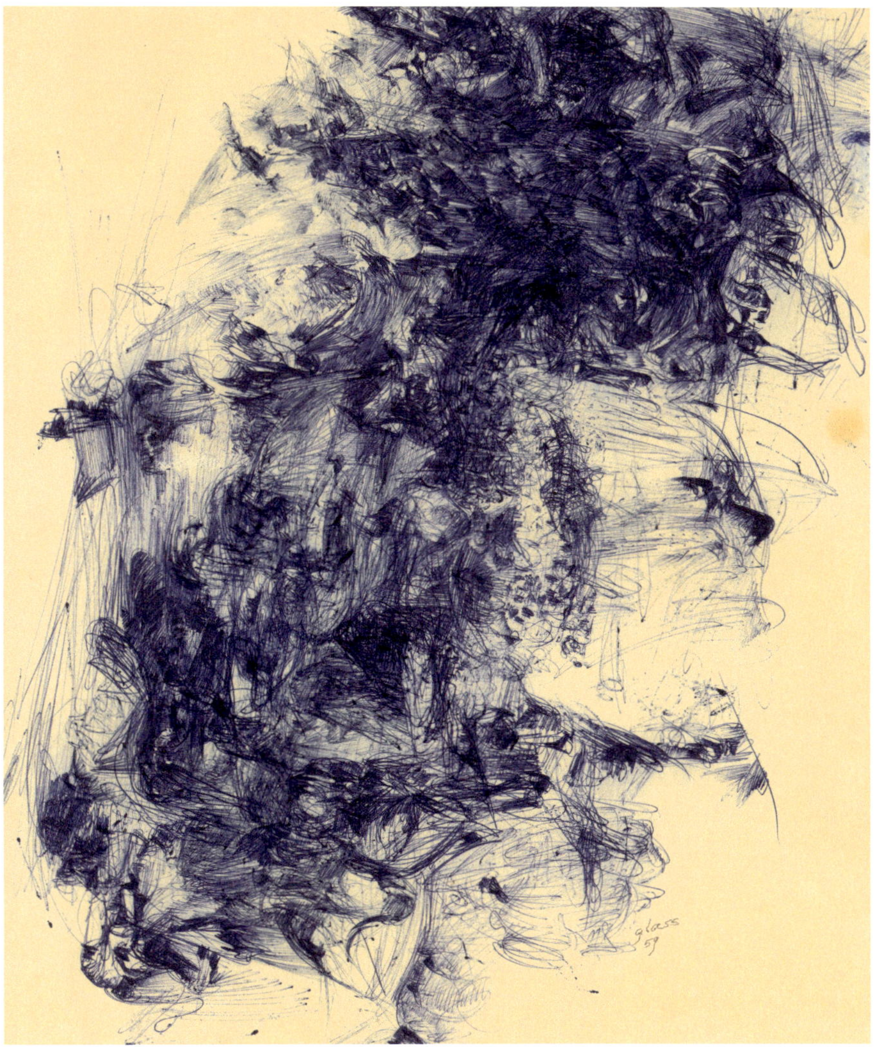

Untitled
(Club Saint-Germain period)
1959
Monochrome blue ballpoint pen drawing, on paper.
32 x 24.5 cm
Artist's collection

Untitled
(Club Saint-Germain period)
1959
Monochrome blue ballpoint pen drawing, on paper.
26.5 x 22.5 cm
Artist's collection

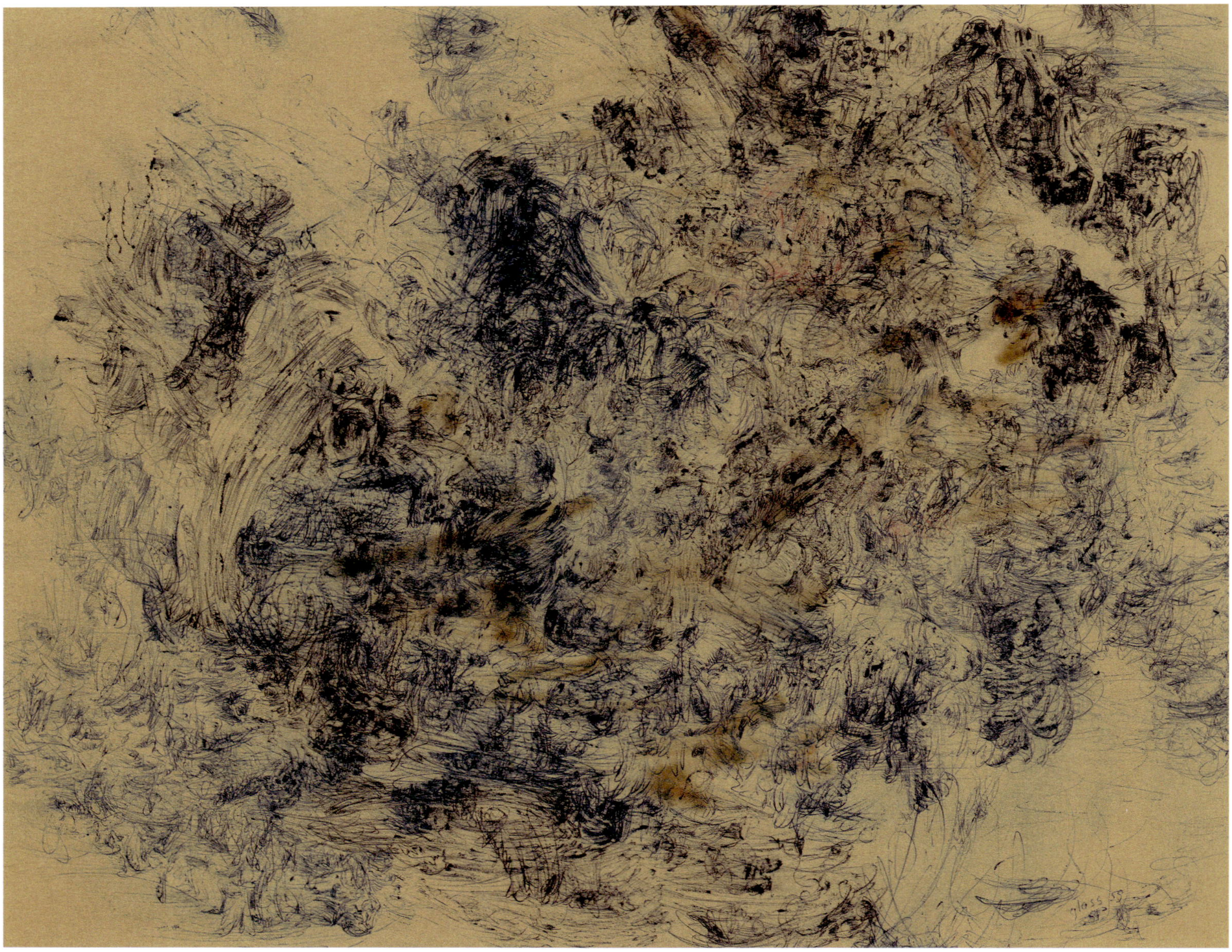

Untitled
(Club Saint-Germain period)
ca. 1954-1962
Monochrome navy blue
ballpoint pen drawing with
touches of allumettage.
21.5 x 28 cm
Artist's collection

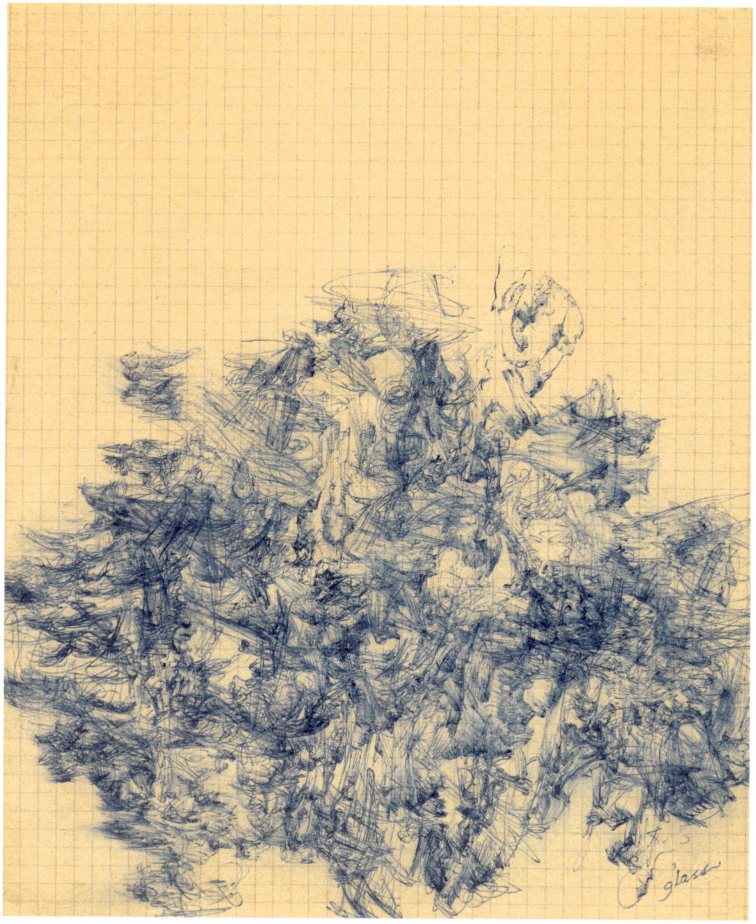

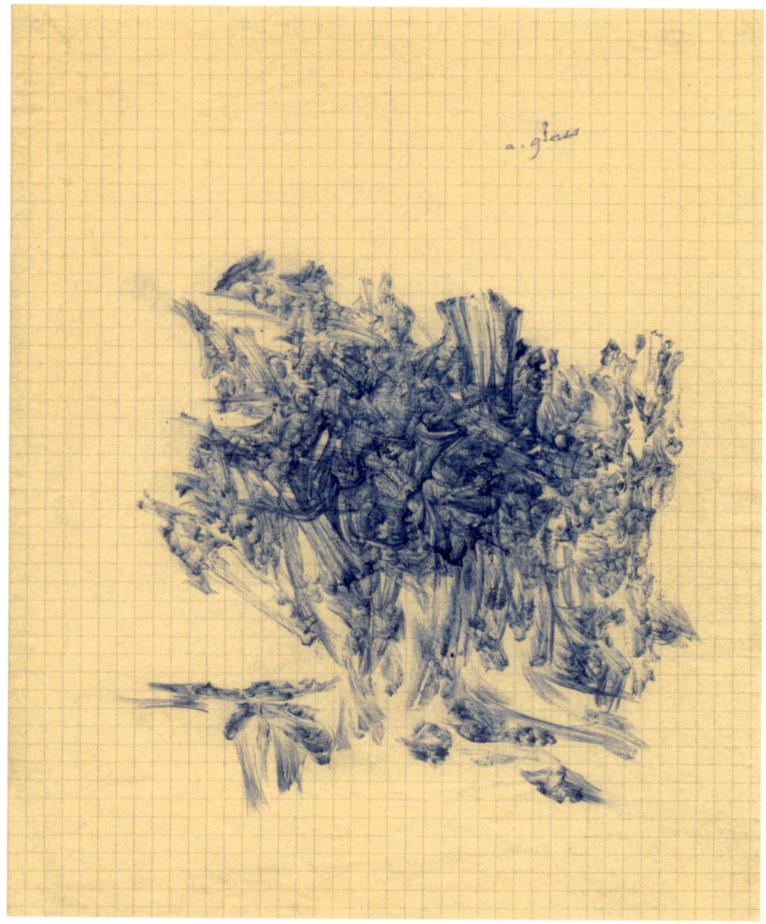

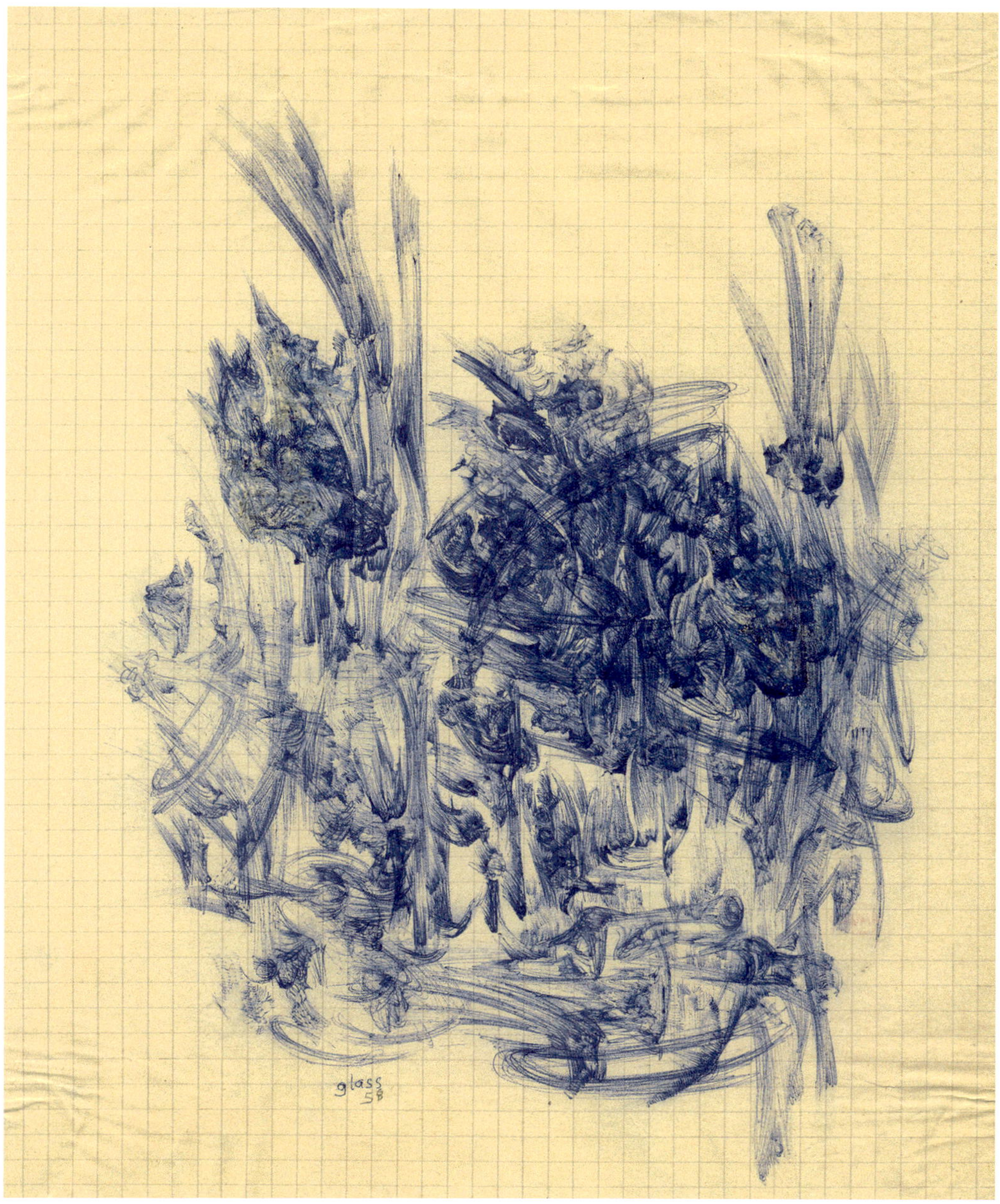

Untitled
(Club Saint-Germain period)
ca. 1954-1962
Monochrome blue ballpoint pen drawing on squared paper.
25.5 x 21 cm
Artist's collection

Untitled
(Club Saint-Germain period)
ca. 1954-1962
Monochrome blue ballpoint pen drawing on squared paper.
25.5 x 21 cm
Artist's collection

Untitled
(Club Saint-Germain period)
1958
Monochrome blue ballpoint pen drawing on squared paper.
27.9 x 23.9 cm
Artist's collection

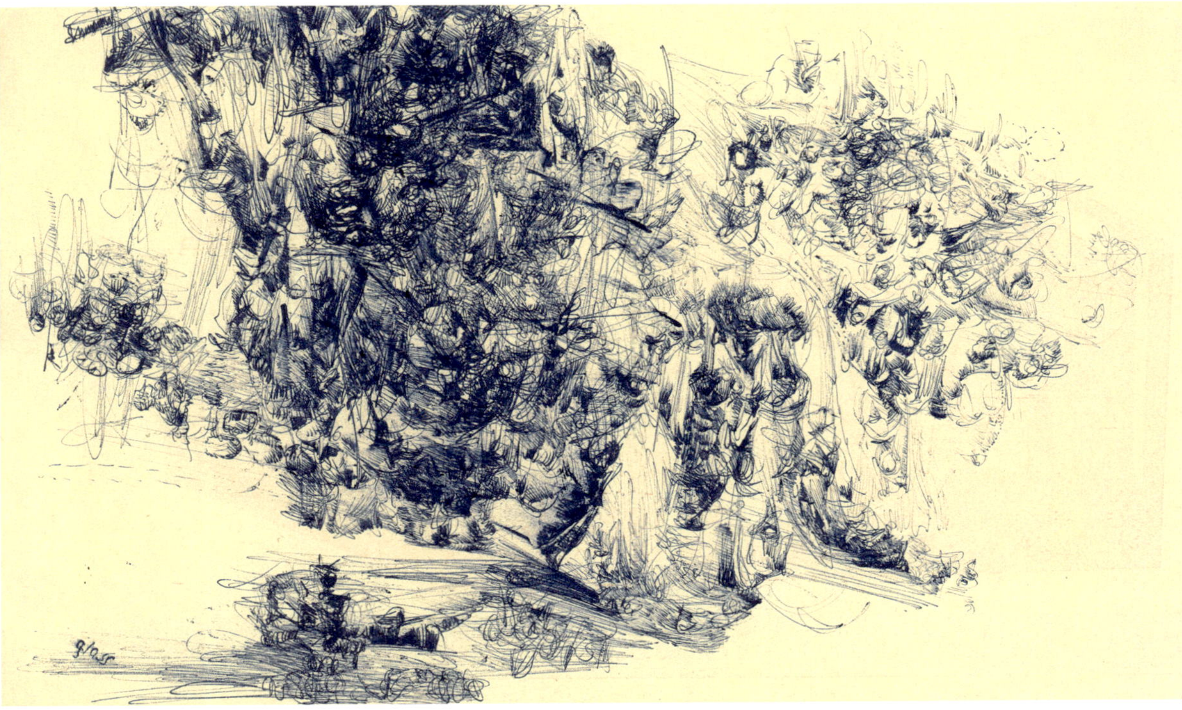

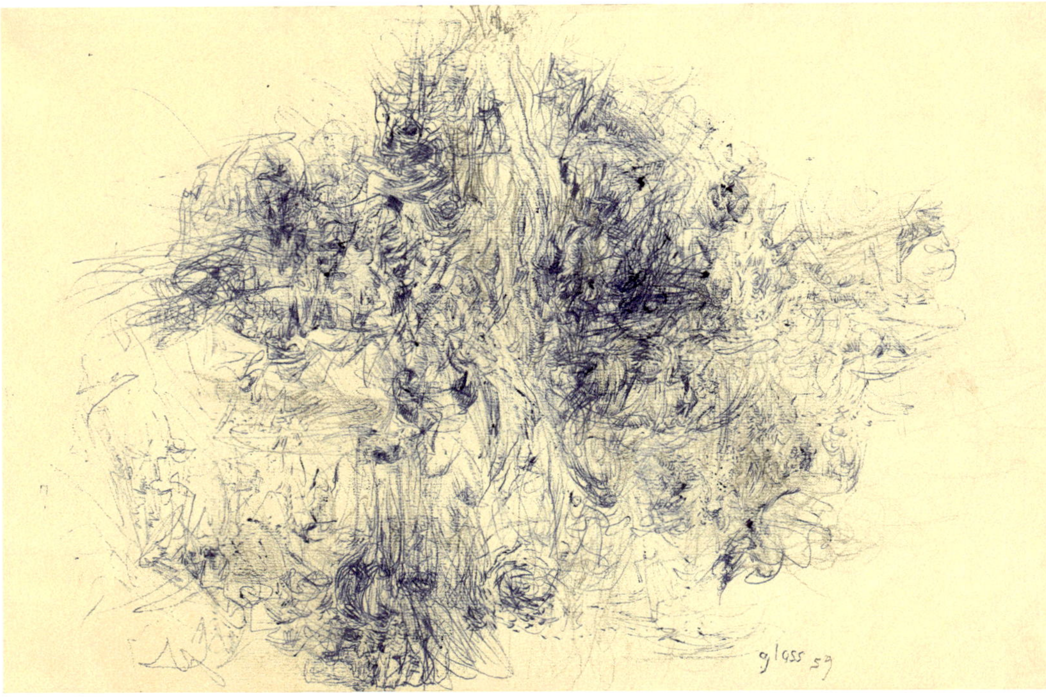

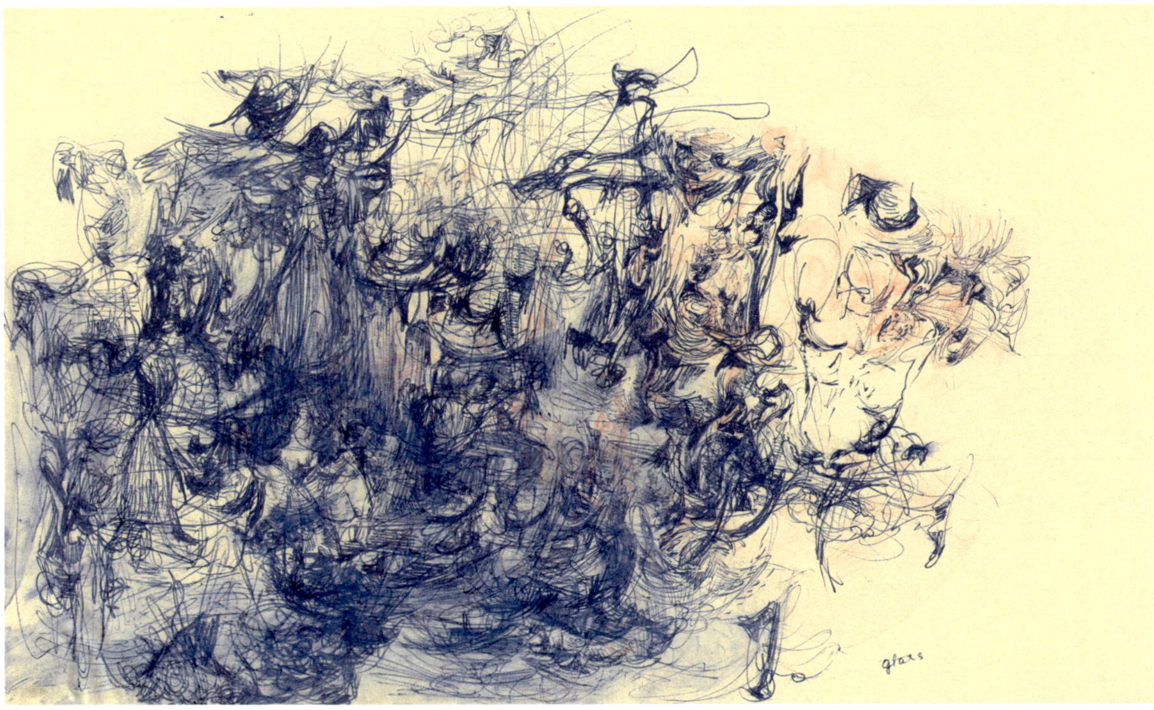

Untitled
(Club Saint-Germain period)
ca. 1954-1962
Monochrome navy blue ballpoint pen drawing, on Club Saint-Germain invitation.
13.5 x 23.5 cm
Artist's collection

Untitled
(Club Saint-Germain period)
1959
Monochrome navy blue ballpoint pen drawing, on paper.
15.5 x 24 cm
Artist's collection

Untitled
(Club Saint-Germain period)
ca. 1954-1962
Monochrome blue ballpoint pen drawing with red markings, on Club Saint-Germain invitation.
13.5 x 23.5 cm
Artist's collection

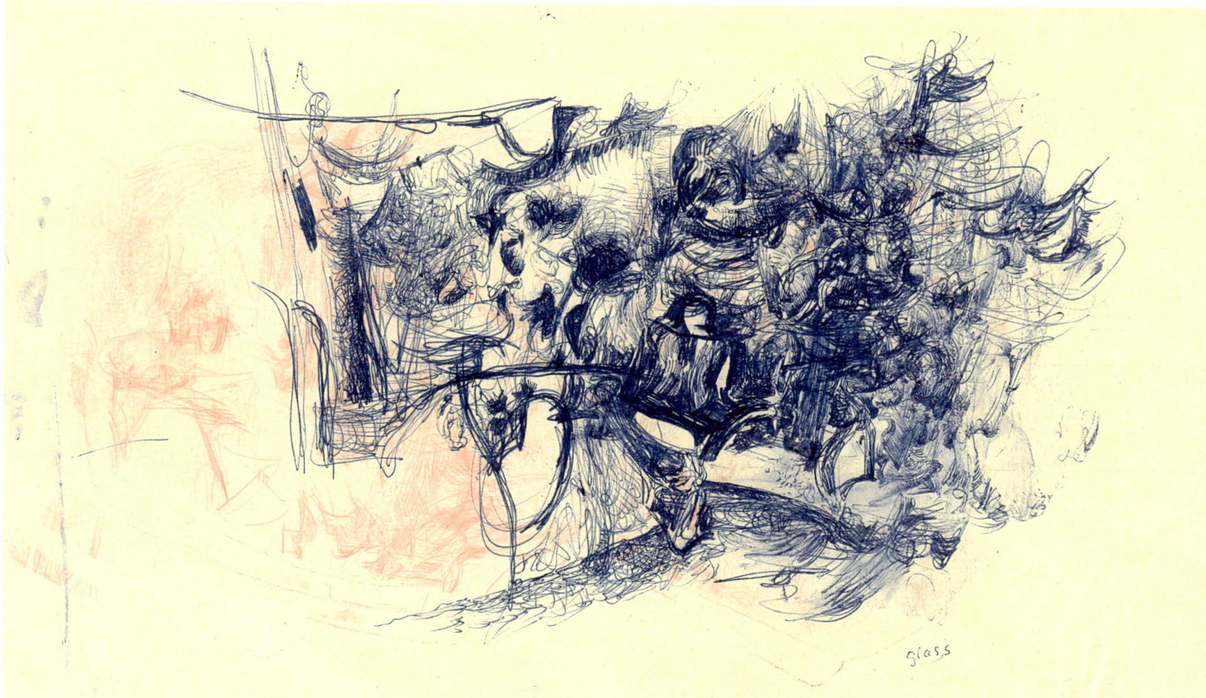

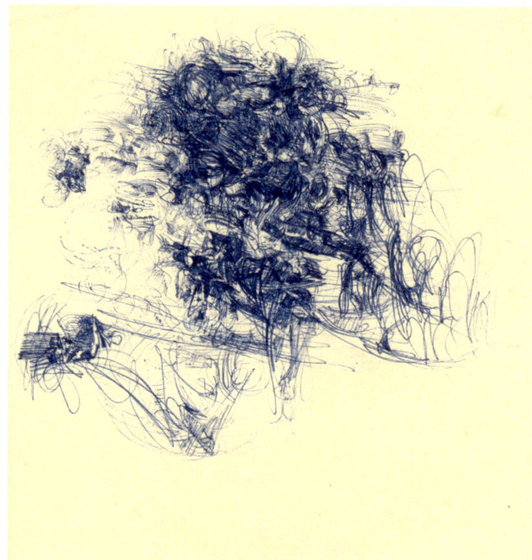

Untitled
(Club Saint-Germain period)
ca. 1954-1962
Monochrome blue ballpoint pen drawing with red markings, on Club Saint-Germain invitation.
13.5 x 23.5 cm
Artist's collection

Untitled
(Club Saint-Germain period)
ca. 1954-1962
Monochrome blue ballpoint pen drawing, on Club Saint-Germain invitation.
13.5 x 23.5 cm
Artist's collection

Untitled
(Club Saint-Germain period)
ca. 1954-1962
Monochrome blue ballpoint pen drawing, on paper.
19 x 17.5 cm
Artist's collection

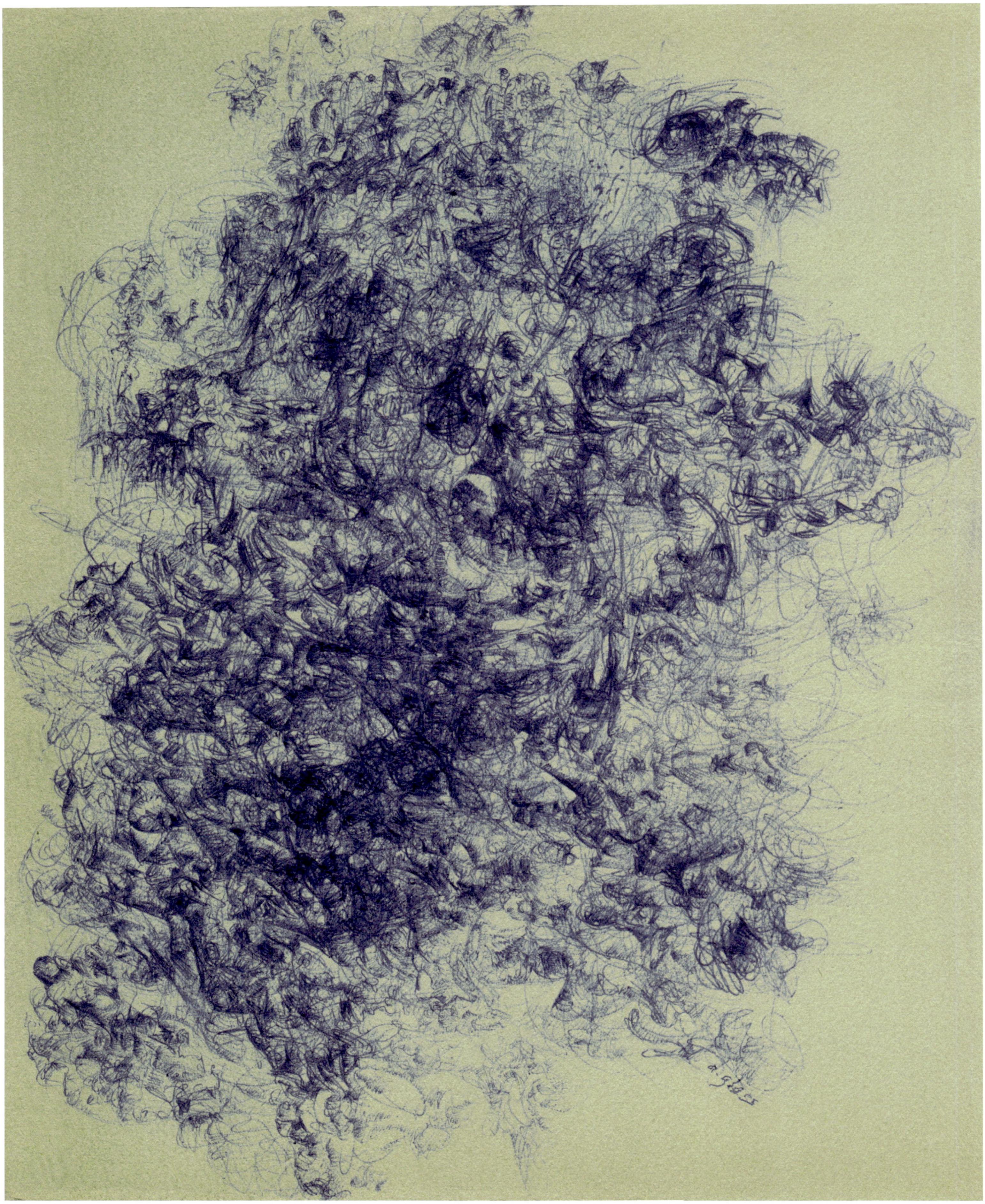

Untitled
(Club Saint-Germain period)
ca. 1954-1962
Monochrome blue ballpoint
pen drawing, on green
corrugated paper.
21 x 25.5 cm
Artist's collection

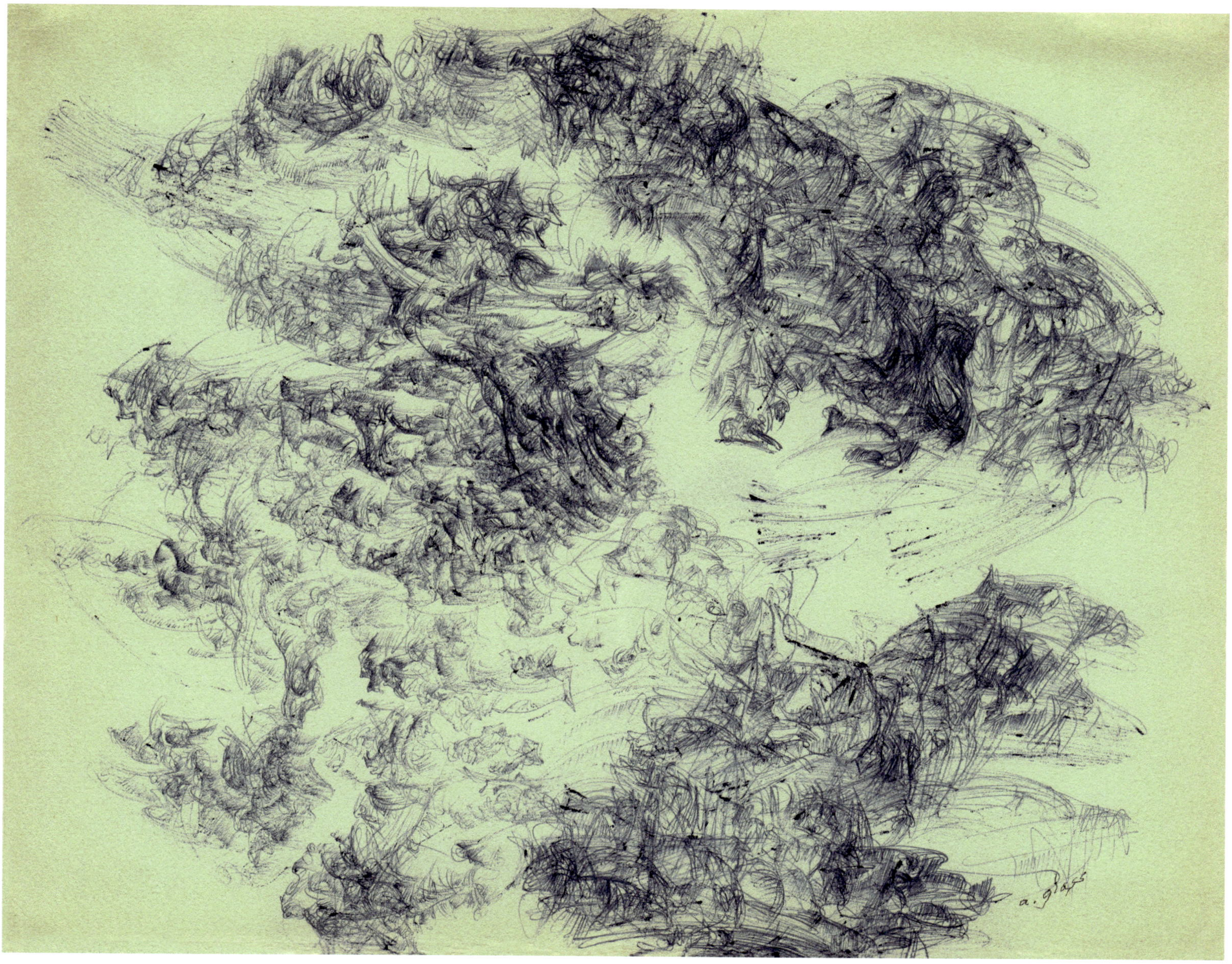

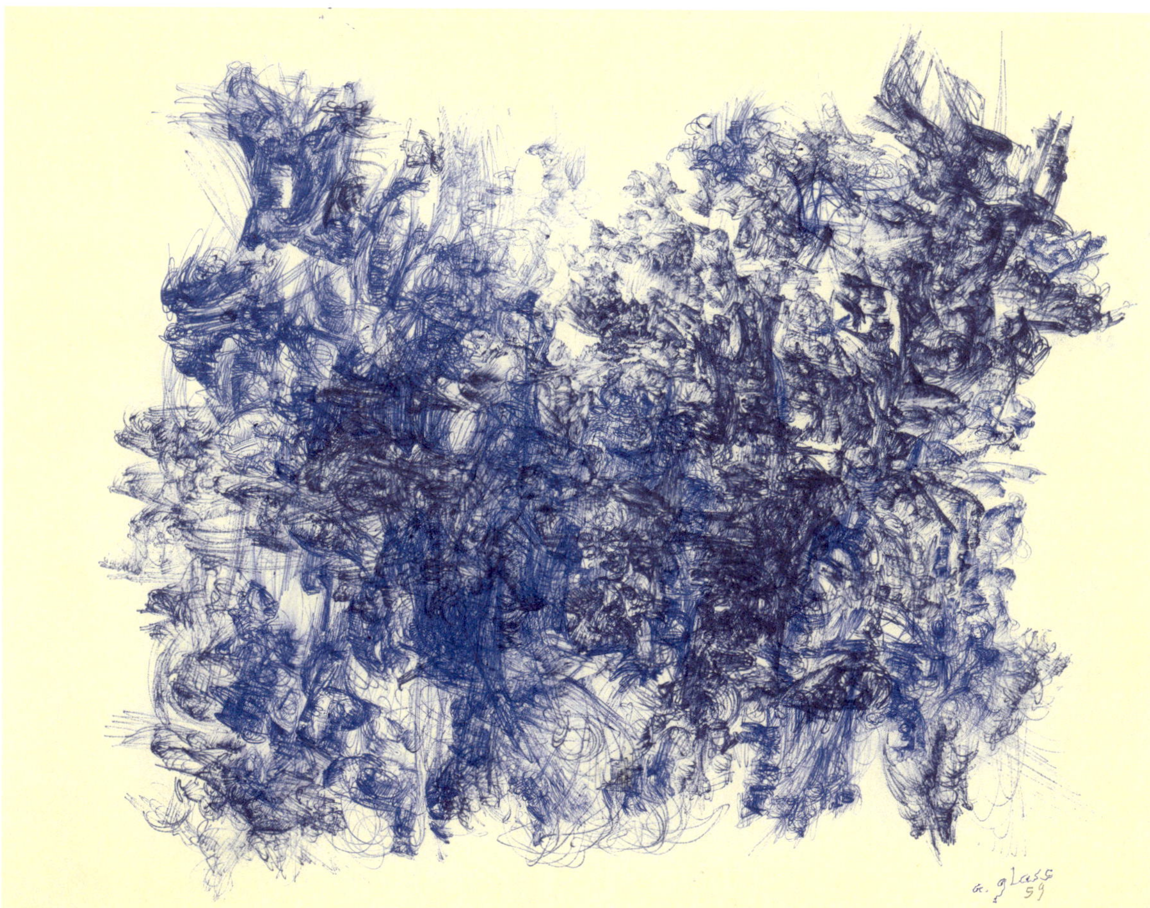

Untitled
(Club Saint-Germain period)
ca. 1954-1962
Monochrome blue ballpoint pen drawing, on green corrugated paper.
25.5 x 32.5 cm
Artist's collection

Untitled
(Club Saint-Germain period)
1959
Monochrome blue ballpoint pen drawing on paper.
21 x 27 cm
Artist's collection

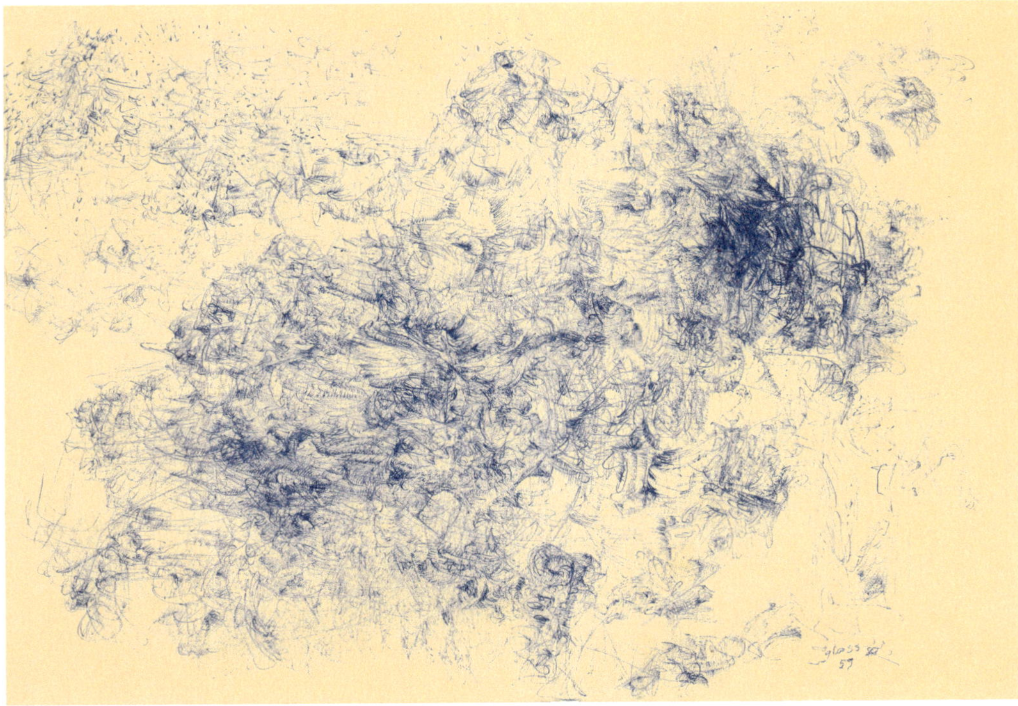

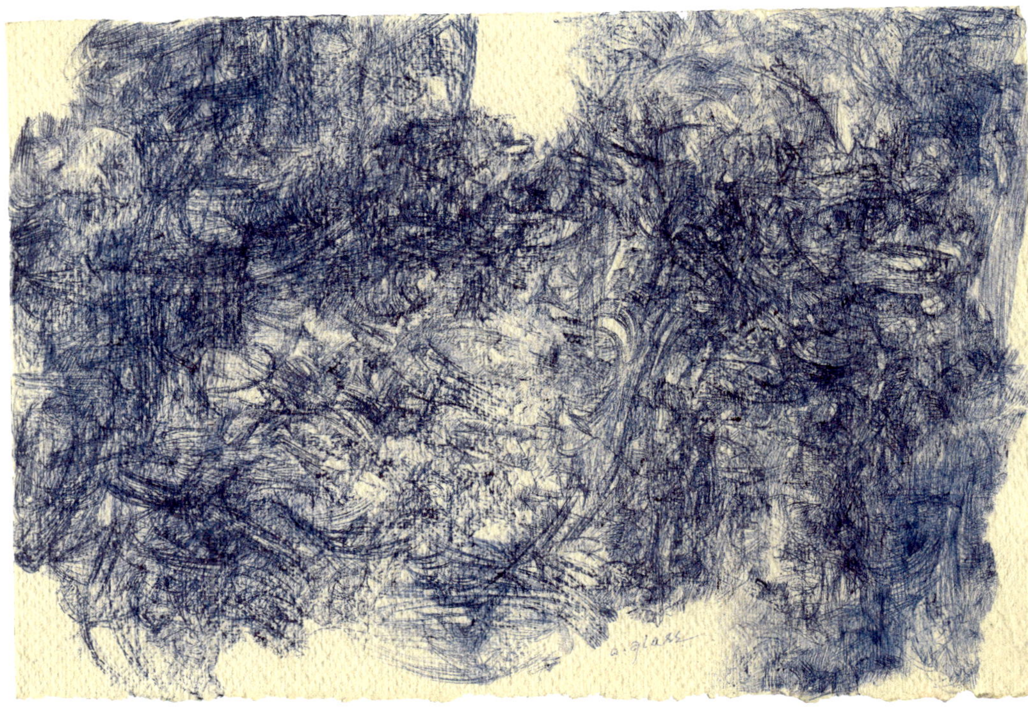

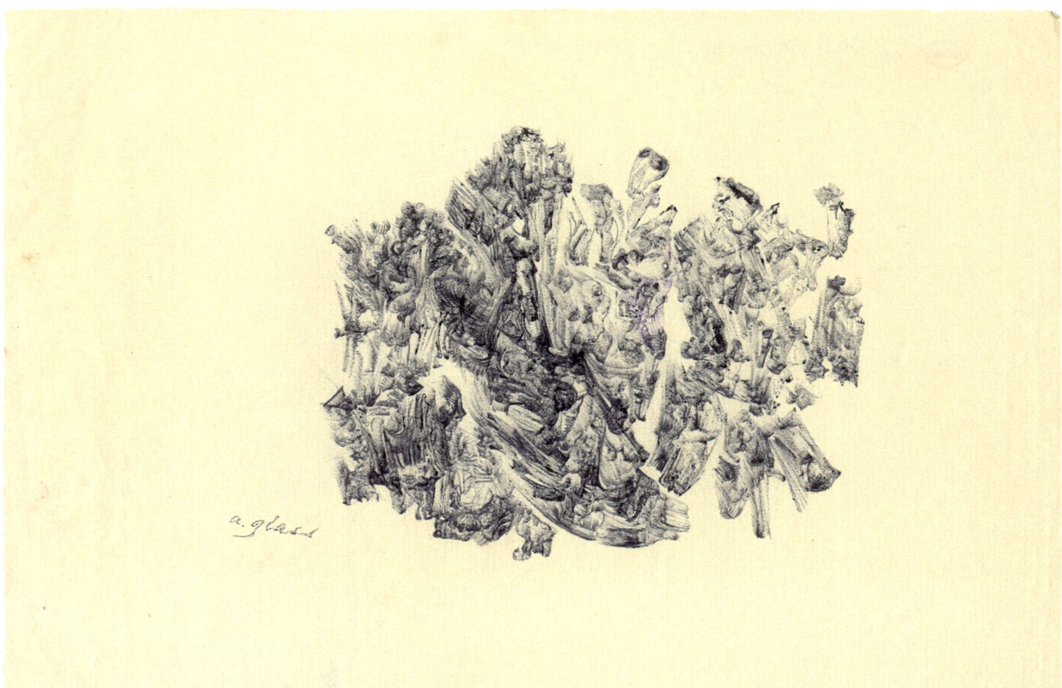

Untitled
(Club Saint-Germain period)
1959
Monochrome blue ballpoint
pen drawing, on paper.
19 x 28 cm
Artist's collection

Untitled
(Club Saint-Germain period)
ca. 1954-1962
Monochrome blue
ballpoint pen drawing,
on corrugated paper.
19 x 28 cm
Artist's collection

Untitled
(Club Saint-Germain period)
ca. 1954-1962
Monochrome navy blue
ballpoint pen drawing,
on paper.
16.5 x 25 cm
Artist's collection

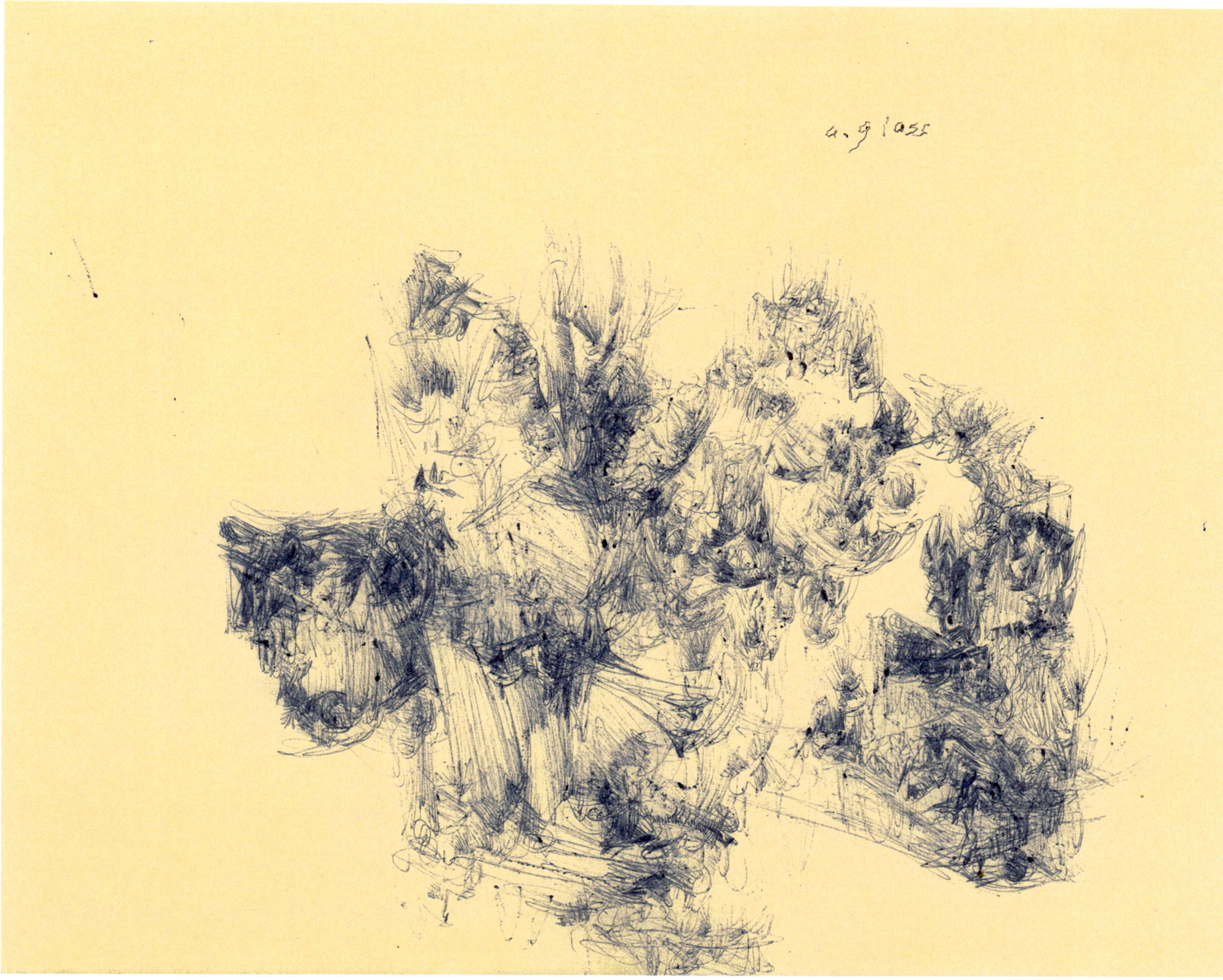

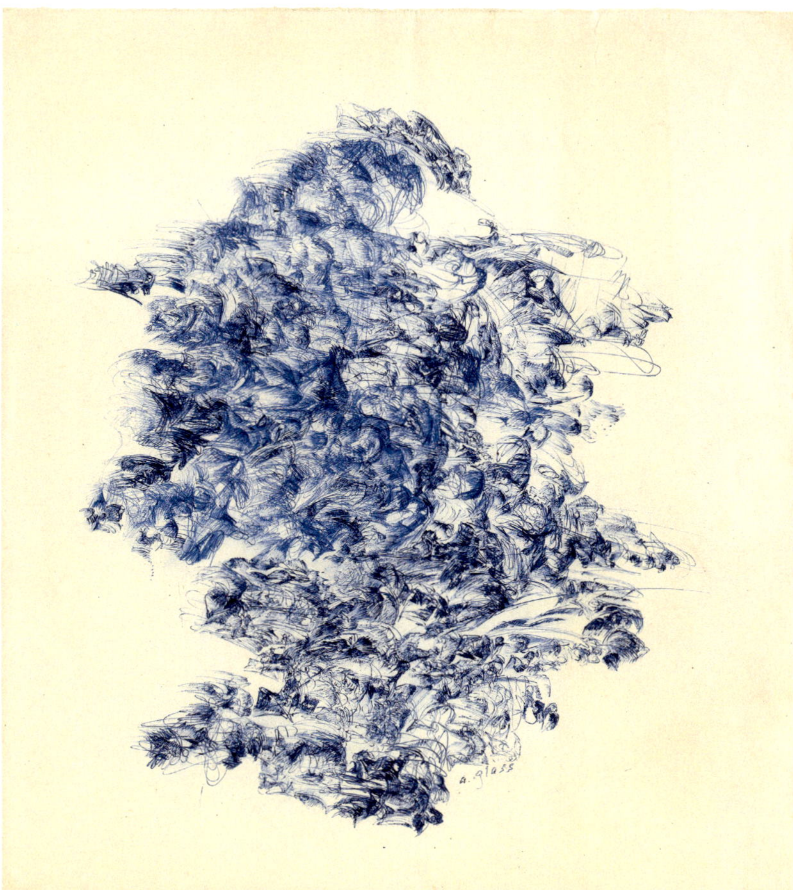

Untitled
(Club Saint-Germain period)
ca. 1954-1962
Monochrome navy blue
ballpoint pen drawing,
on paper.
17 x 26 cm
Artist's collection

Untitled
(Club Saint-Germain period)
ca. 1954-1962
Blue and navy blue two-tone
ballpoint pen drawing,
on paper.
27.5 x 25 cm
Artist's collection

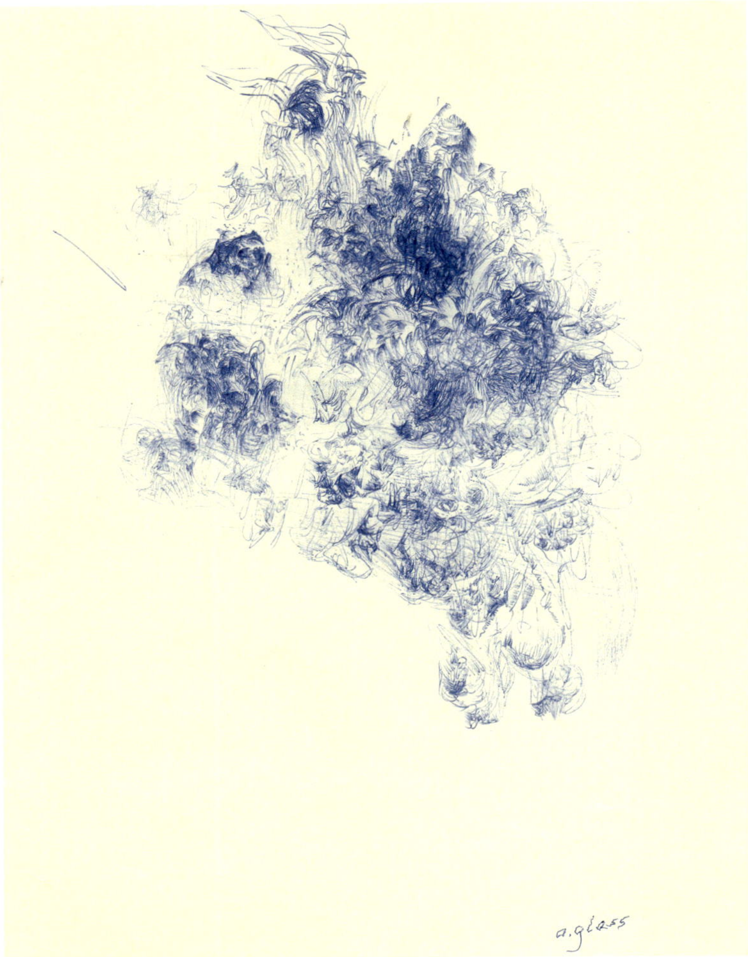

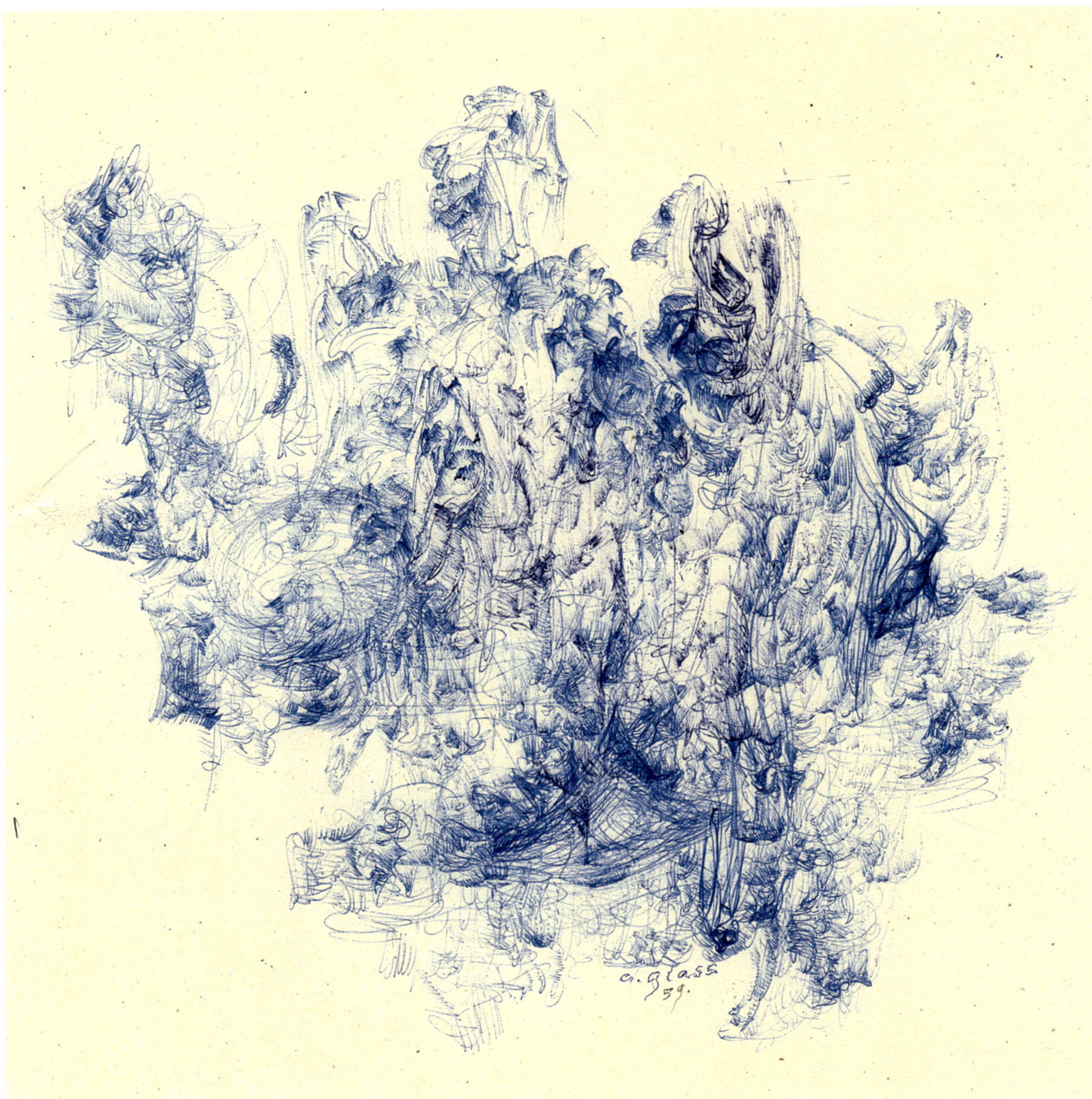

Untitled
(Club Saint-Germain period)
ca. 1954-1962
Monochrome blue ballpoint pen drawing, on paper.
27 x 21 cm
Artist's collection

Untitled
(Club Saint-Germain period)
1959
Blue and navy blue two-tone ballpoint pen drawing, on paper.
32 x 25 cm
Artist's collection

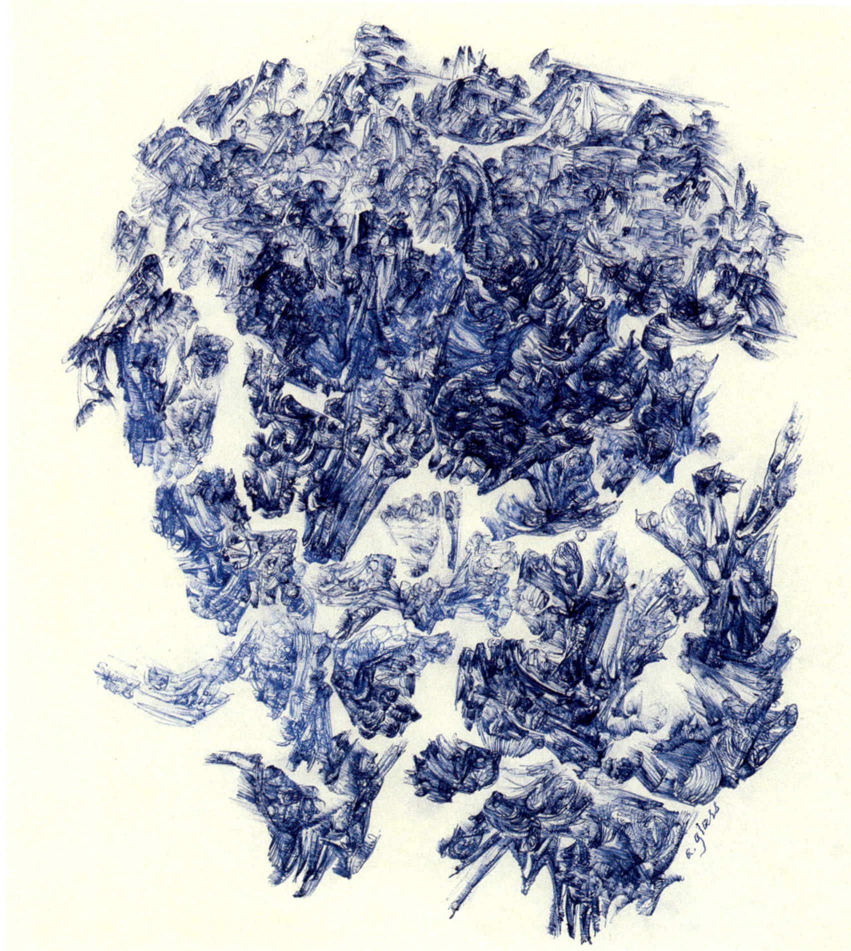

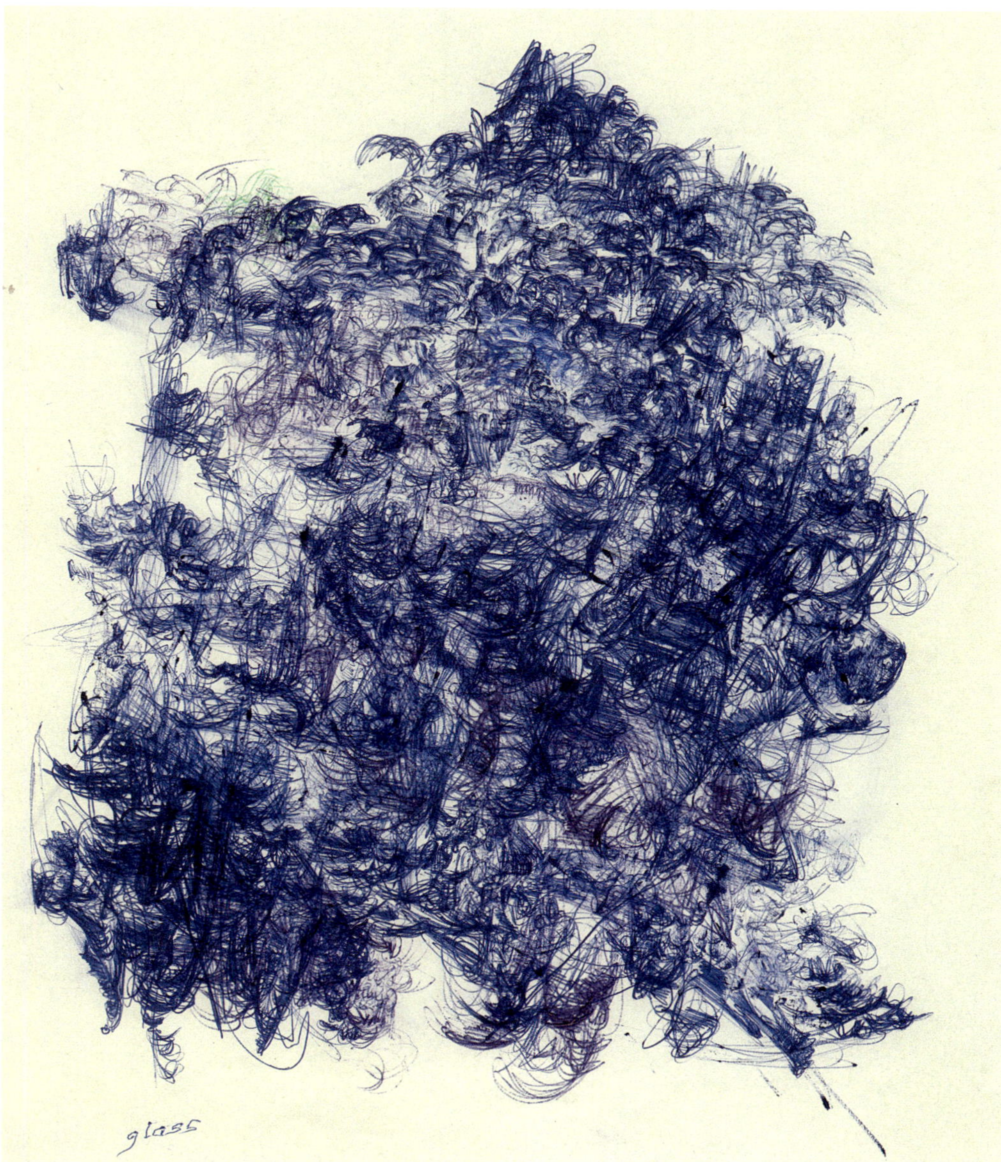

Untitled
(Club Saint-Germain period)
ca. 1954-1962
Monochrome blue ballpoint pen drawing, on paper.
27 x 21 cm
Artist's collection

Untitled
(Club Saint-Germain period)
ca. 1954-1962
Bicolor blue and violet pen drawing, on paper.
27 x 21 cm
Artist's collection

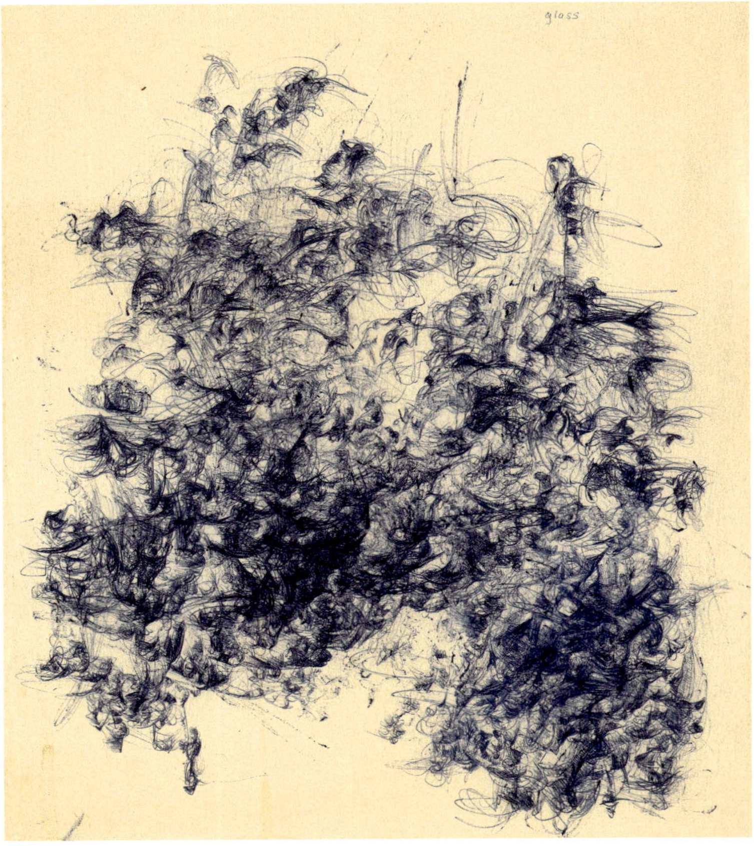

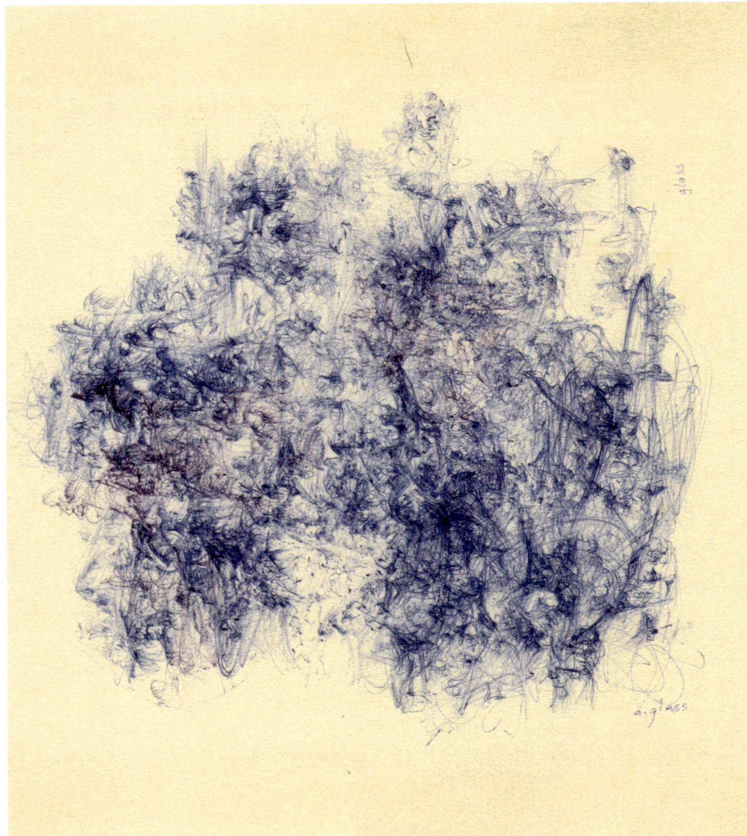

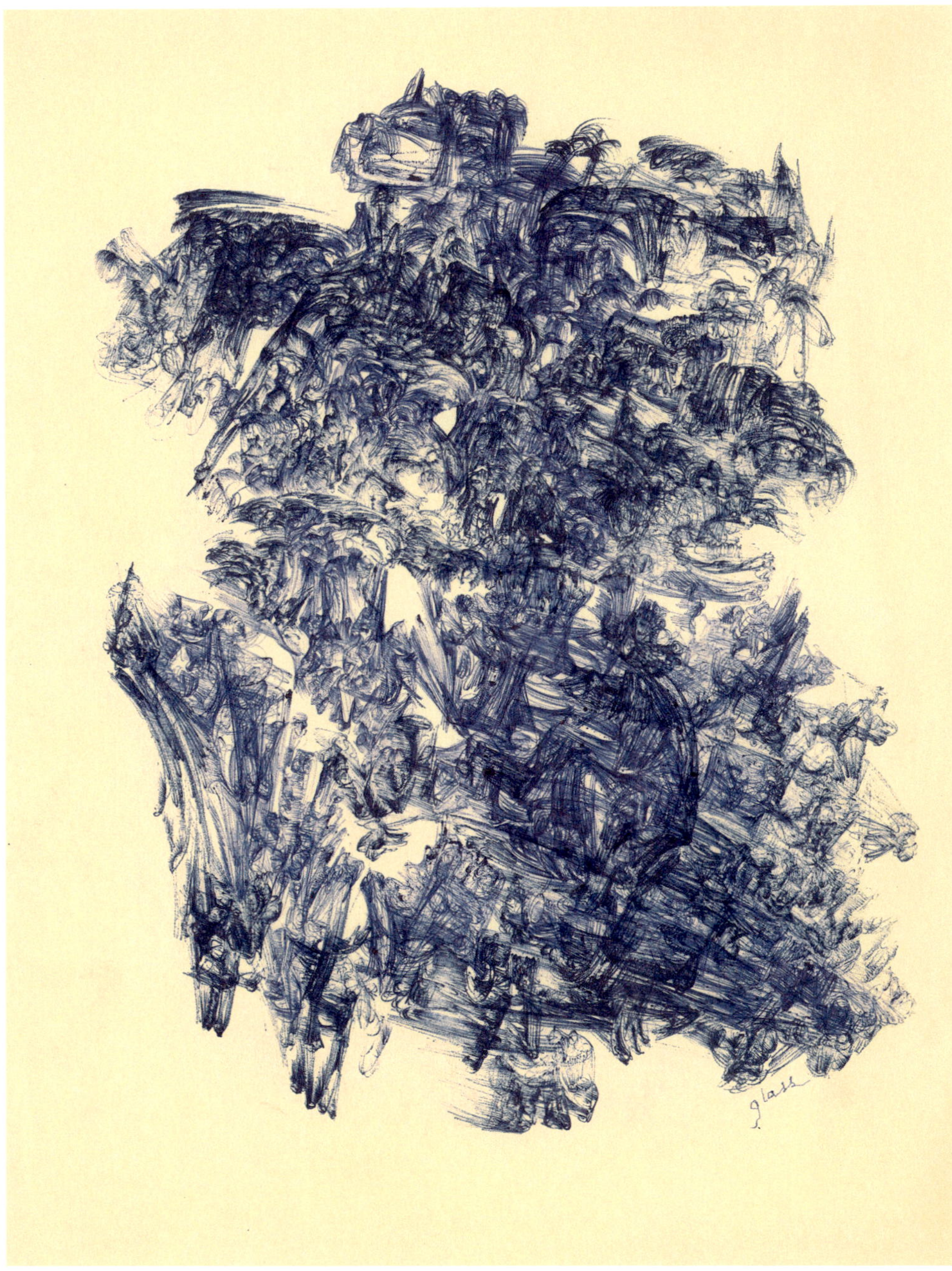

Untitled
(Club Saint-Germain period)
ca. 1954-1962
Monochrome navy blue
ballpoint pen drawing,
on paper.
30.5 x 28 cm
Artist's collection

Untitled
(Club Saint-Germain period)
ca. 1954-1962
Bicolor blue and violet
ballpoint pen drawing,
on paper.
28 x 32 cm
Artist's collection

Untitled
(Club Saint-Germain period)
ca. 1954-1962
Blue and navy blue two-tone
ballpoint pen drawing,
on paper.
32 x 24 cm
Artist's collection

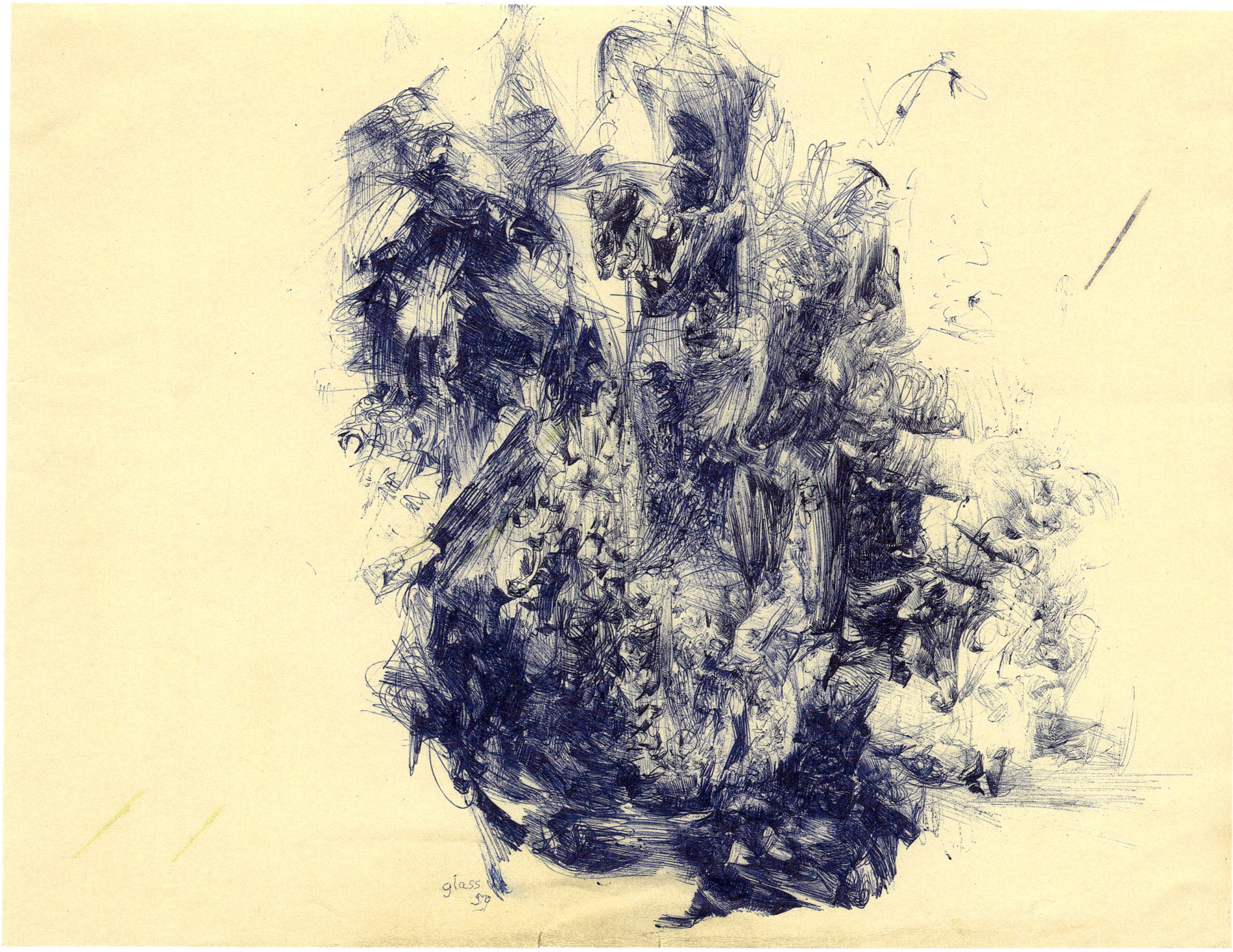

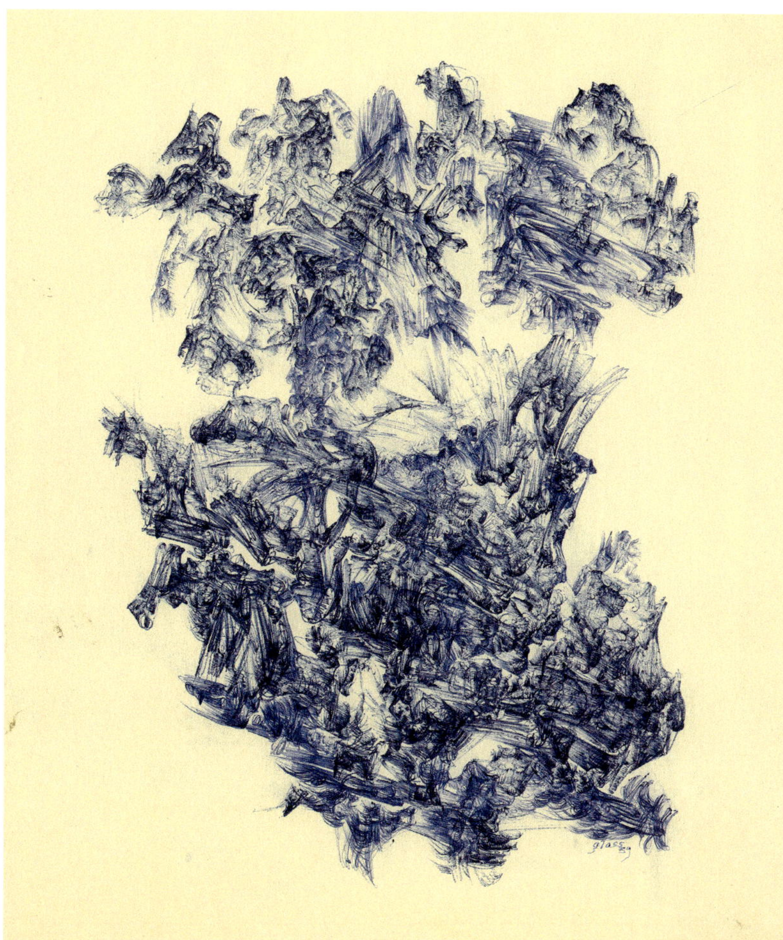

Untitled
(Club Saint-Germain period)
1959
Monochrome navy blue
ballpoint pen drawing,
on paper.
24 x 32 cm
Artist's collectionn

Untitled
(Club Saint-Germain period)
1959
Blue and navy blue two-tone
ballpoint pen drawing,
on paper.
32 x 24 cm
Artist's collectionn

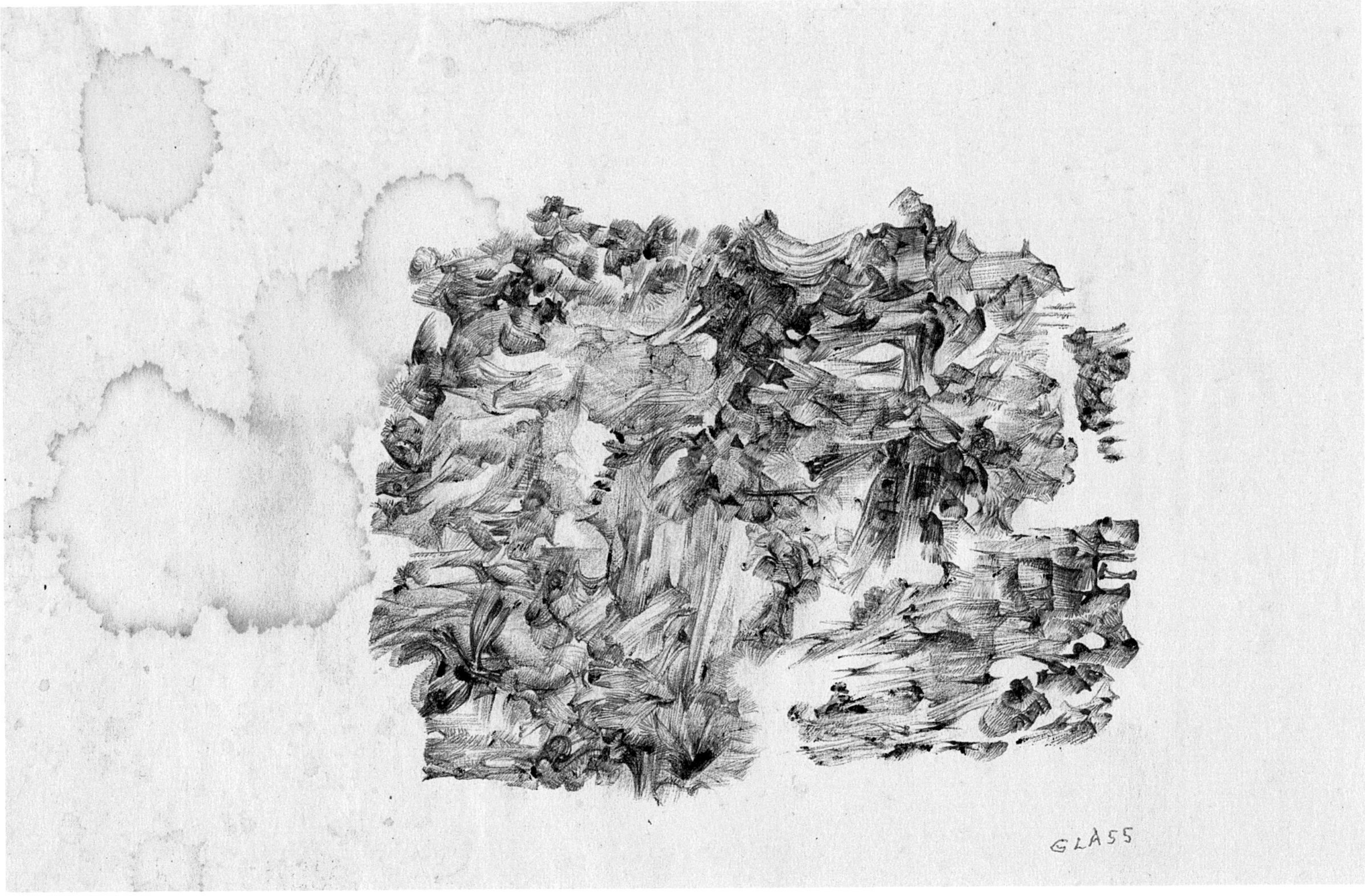

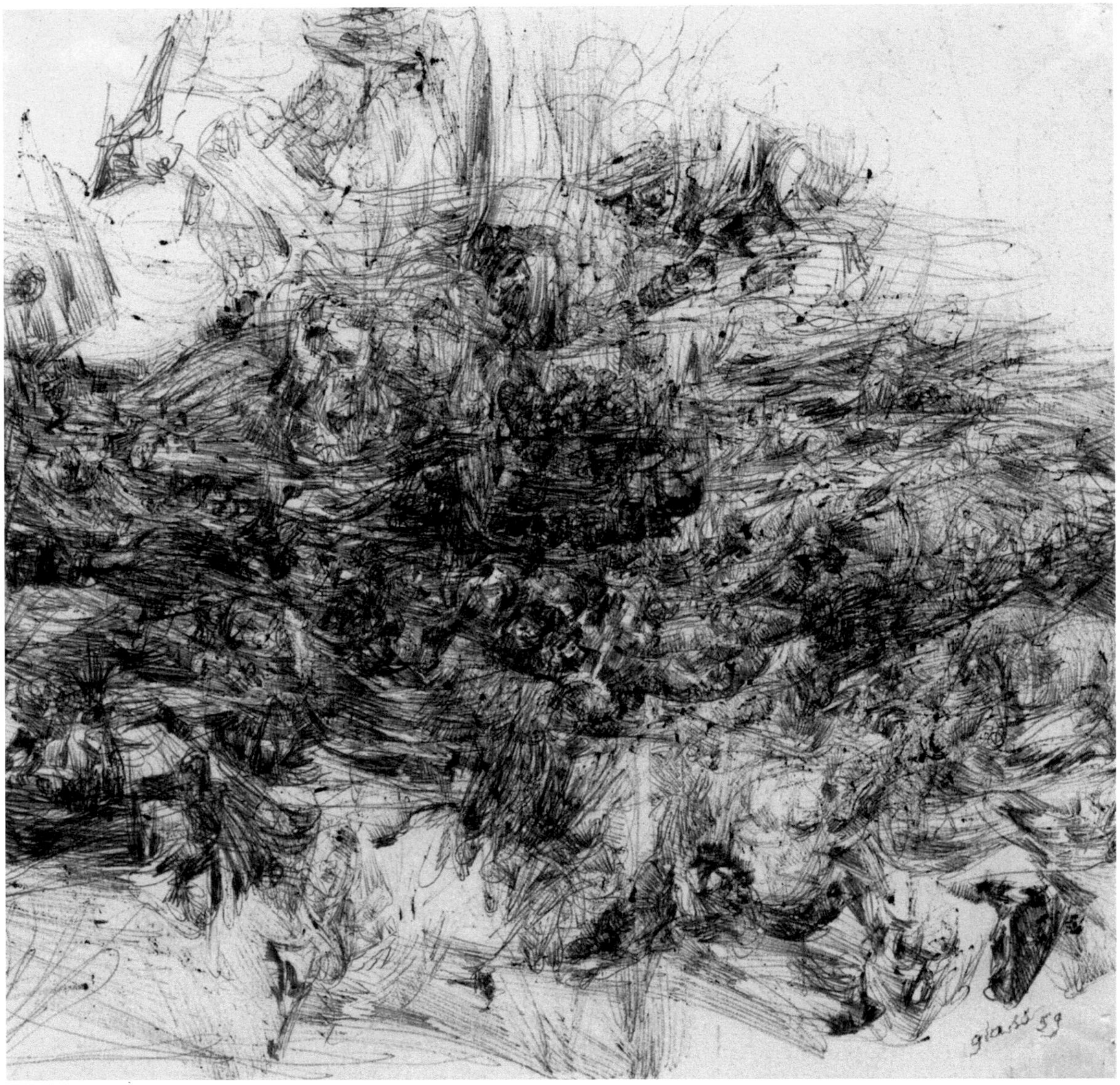

Untitled
(Club Saint-Germain period)
ca. 1954-1962
Monochrome blue ballpoint pen and graphite drawing, on paper.
22.5 x 28 cm
Artist's collection

Untitled
(Club Saint-Germain period)
1959
Monochrome navy blue ballpoint pen drawing, on paper.
14.5 x 15 cm
Artist's collection

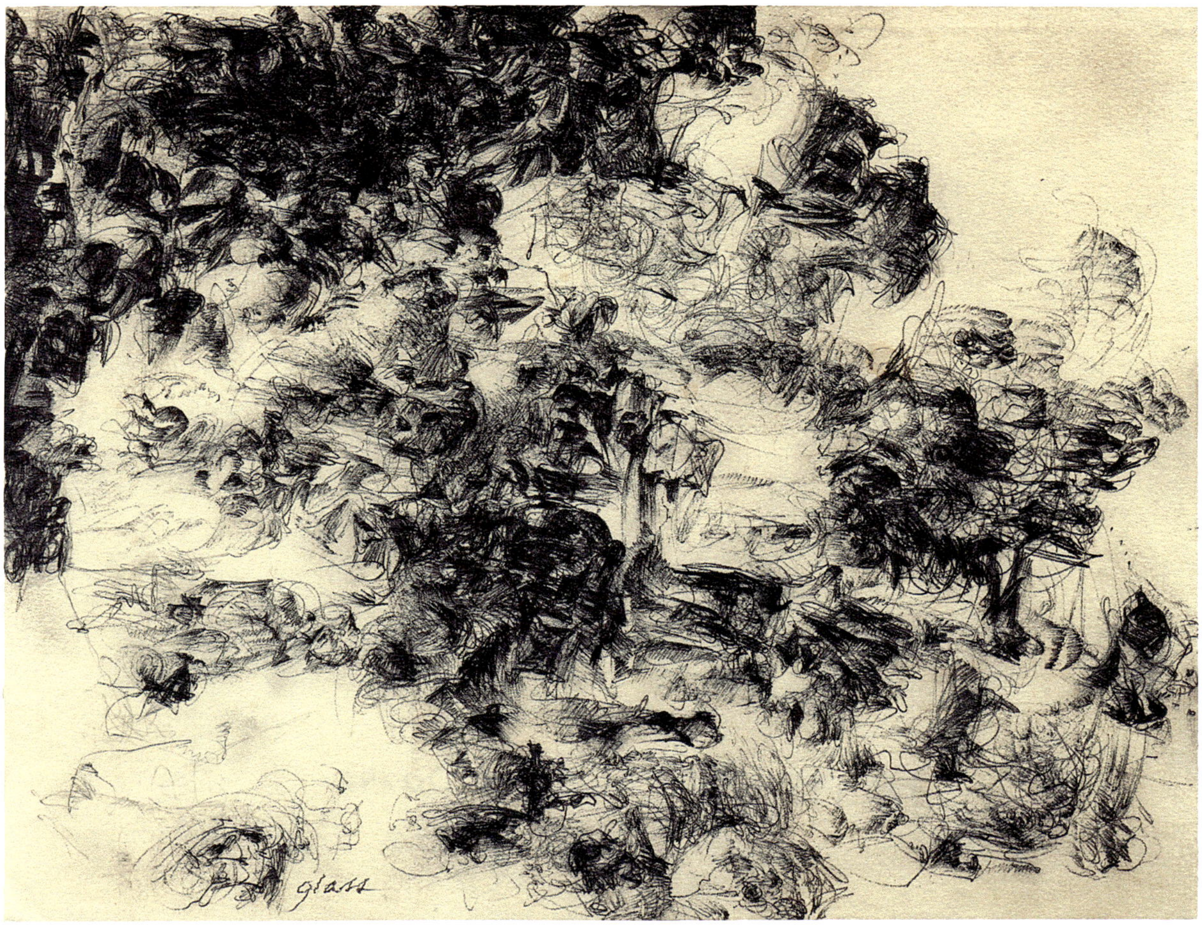

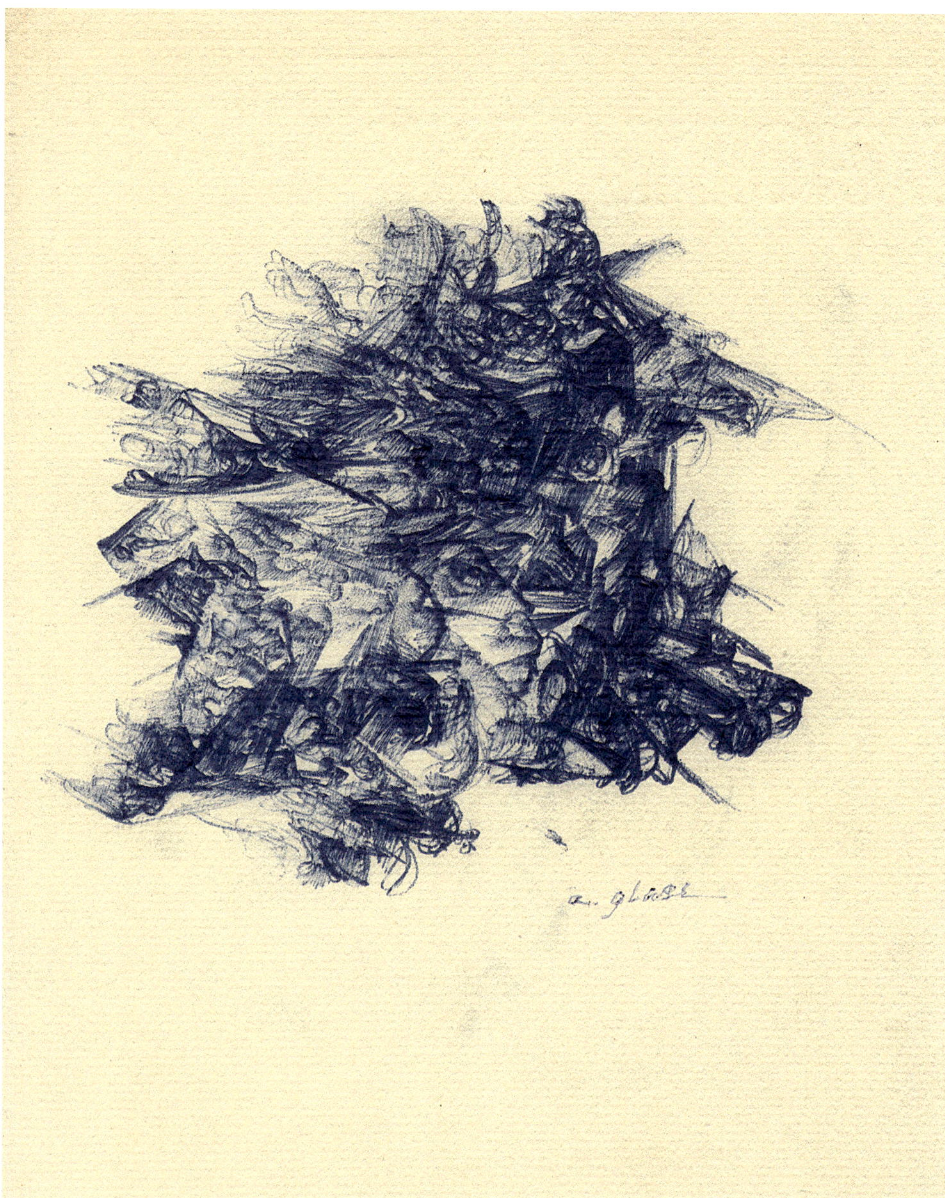

Untitled
(Club Saint-Germain period)
ca. 1954-1962
Monochrome black ballpoint pen drawing, on paper.
13.5 x 17.5 cm
Artist's collection

Untitled
(Club Saint-Germain period)
ca. 1954-1962
Monochrome blue ballpoint pen drawing, on paper.
24 x 16 cm
Artist's collection

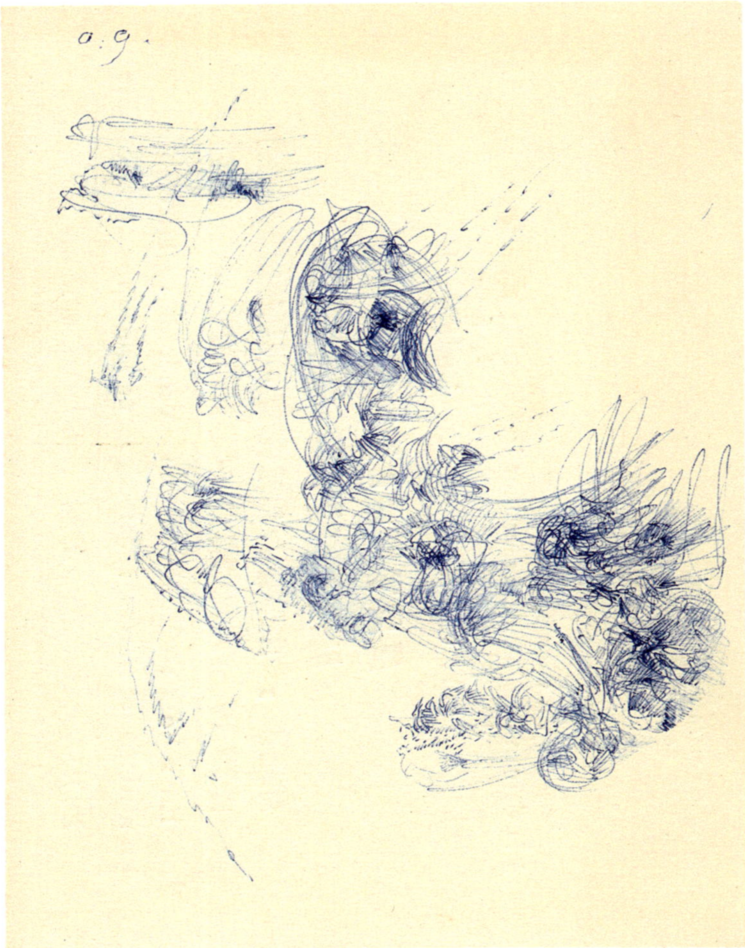

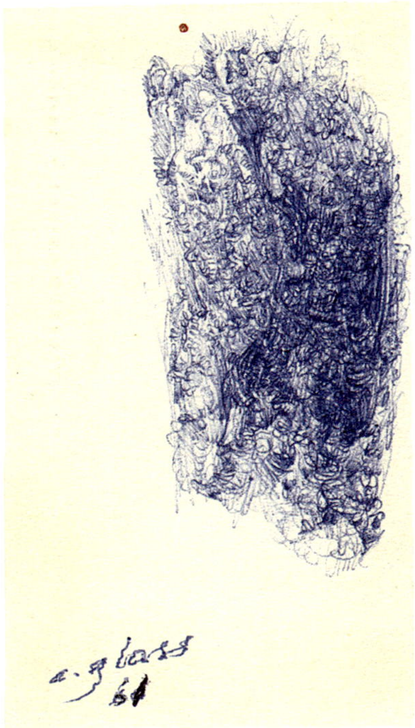

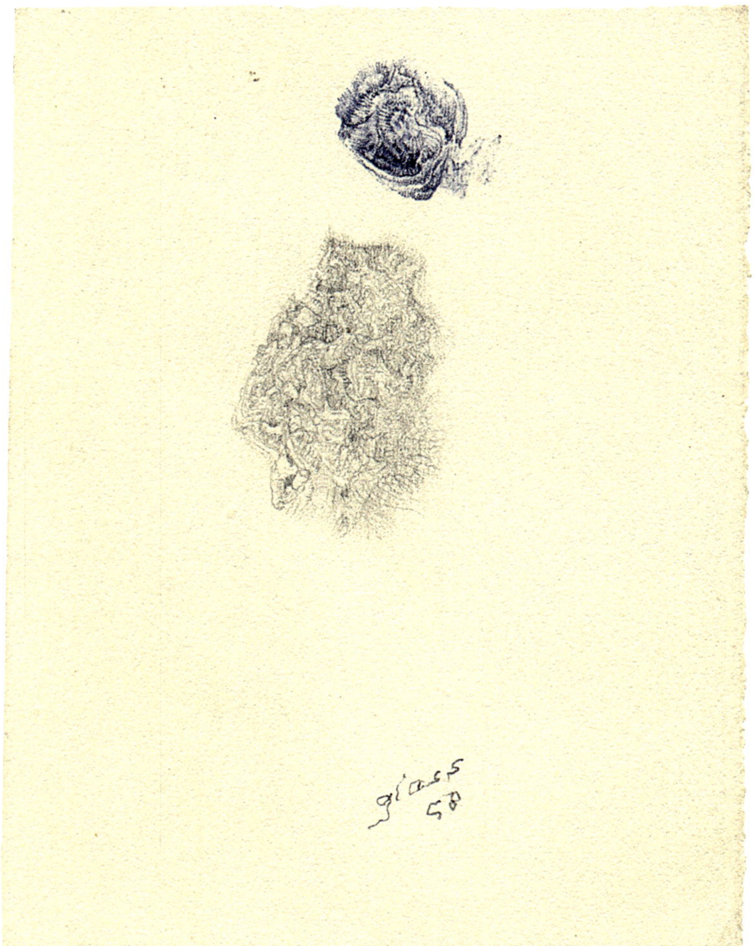

Untitled
(Club Saint-Germain period)
ca. 1954-1962
Monochrome blue ballpoint pen drawing, on Club Saint Germain invitation card.
13.5 x 10.5 cm
Artist's collection

Untitled
(Club Saint-Germain period)
1961
Monochrome blue ballpoint pen drawing, on business card.
9 x 5 cm
Artist's collection

Untitled
(Club Saint-Germain period)
1958
Monochrome blue ballpoint pen drawing and graphite, on paper.
11.7 x 9.2 cm
Artist's collection

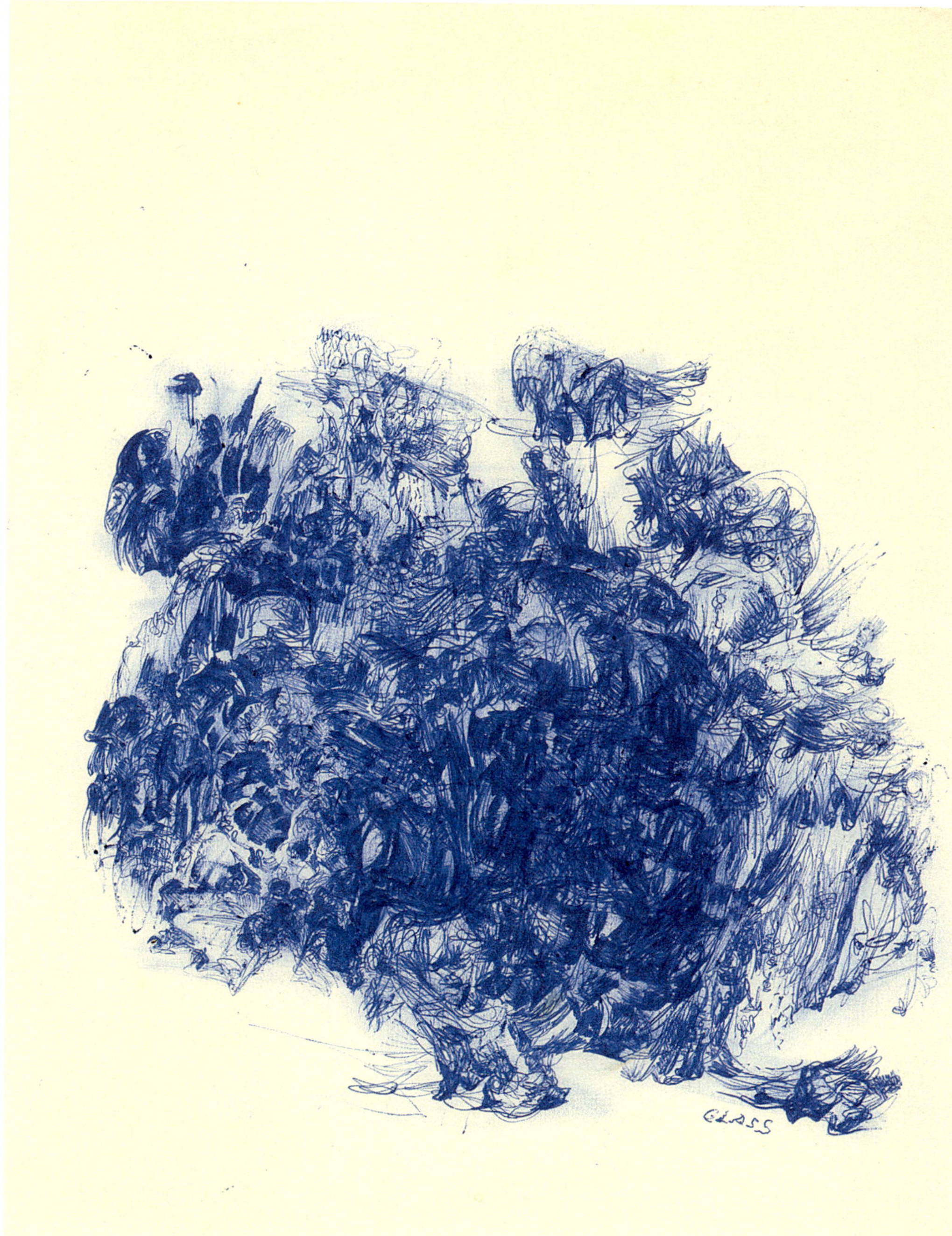

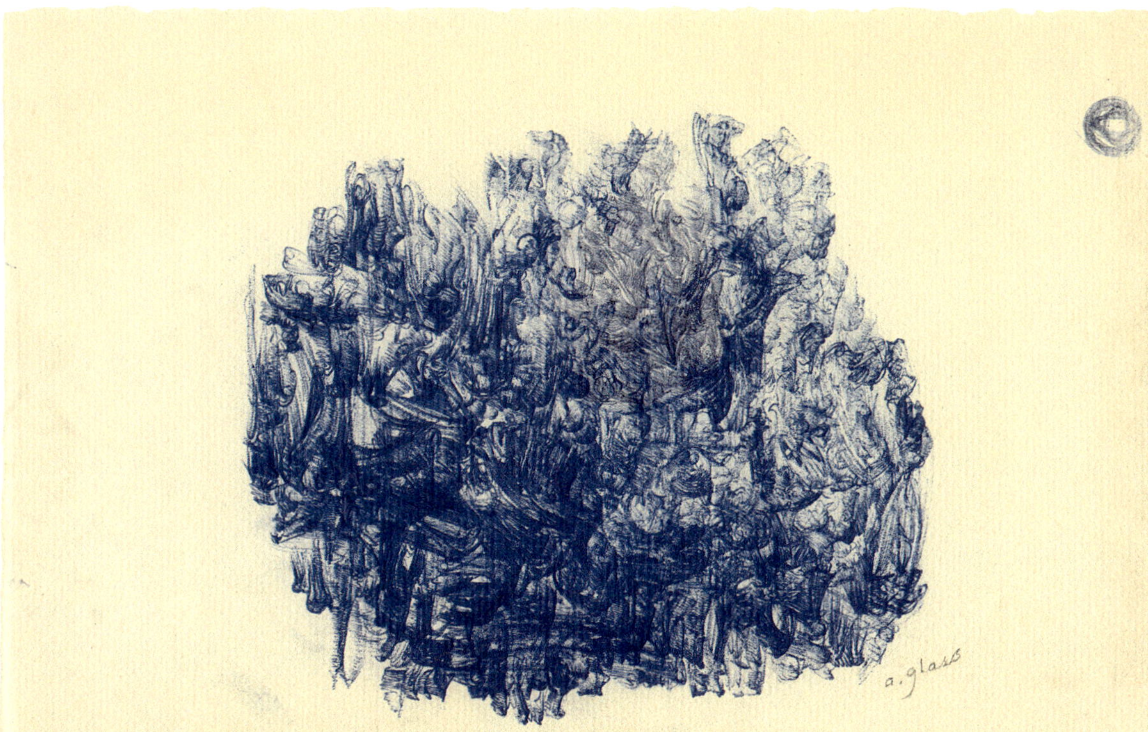

Untitled
(Club Saint-Germain period)
ca. 1954-1962
Monochrome blue ballpoint pen drawing, on paper.
22 x 16 cm
Artist's collection

Untitled
(Club Saint-Germain period)
ca. 1954-1962
Blue and navy blue two-tone ballpoint pen drawing, on paper.
16 x 24 cm
Artist's collection

Untitled
(Club Saint-Germain period)
ca. 1954-1962
Monochrome blue ballpoint
pen drawing, on paper.
29 x 25 cm
Artist's collection

Untitled
(Club Saint-Germain period)
ca. 1954-1962
Bicolor blue and black
ballpoint pen drawing,
on paper.
19 x 28 cm
Artist's collection

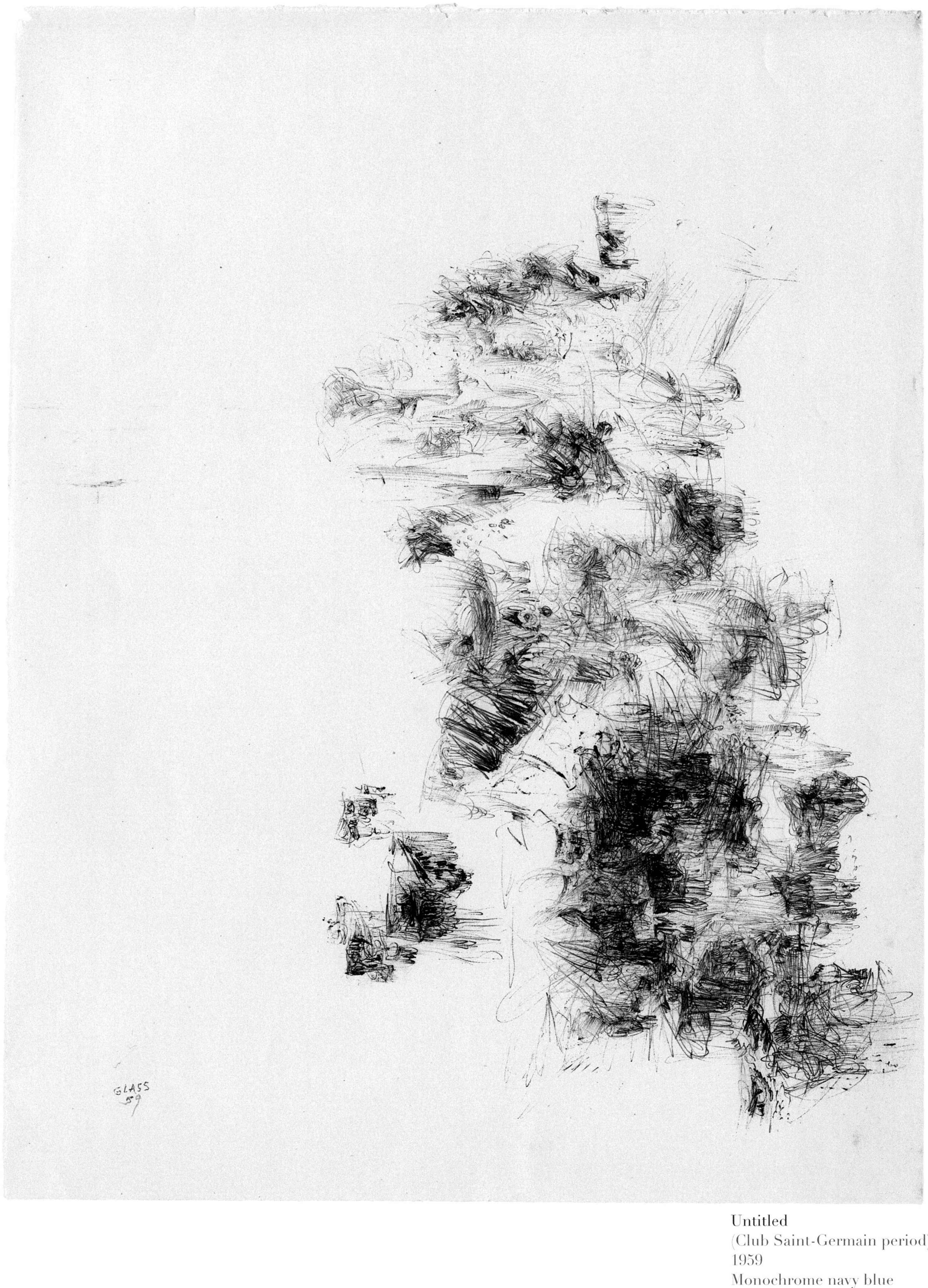

Untitled
(Club Saint-Germain period)
1959
Monochrome navy blue ballpoint pen drawing, on paper.
32 x 25 cm
Artist's collection

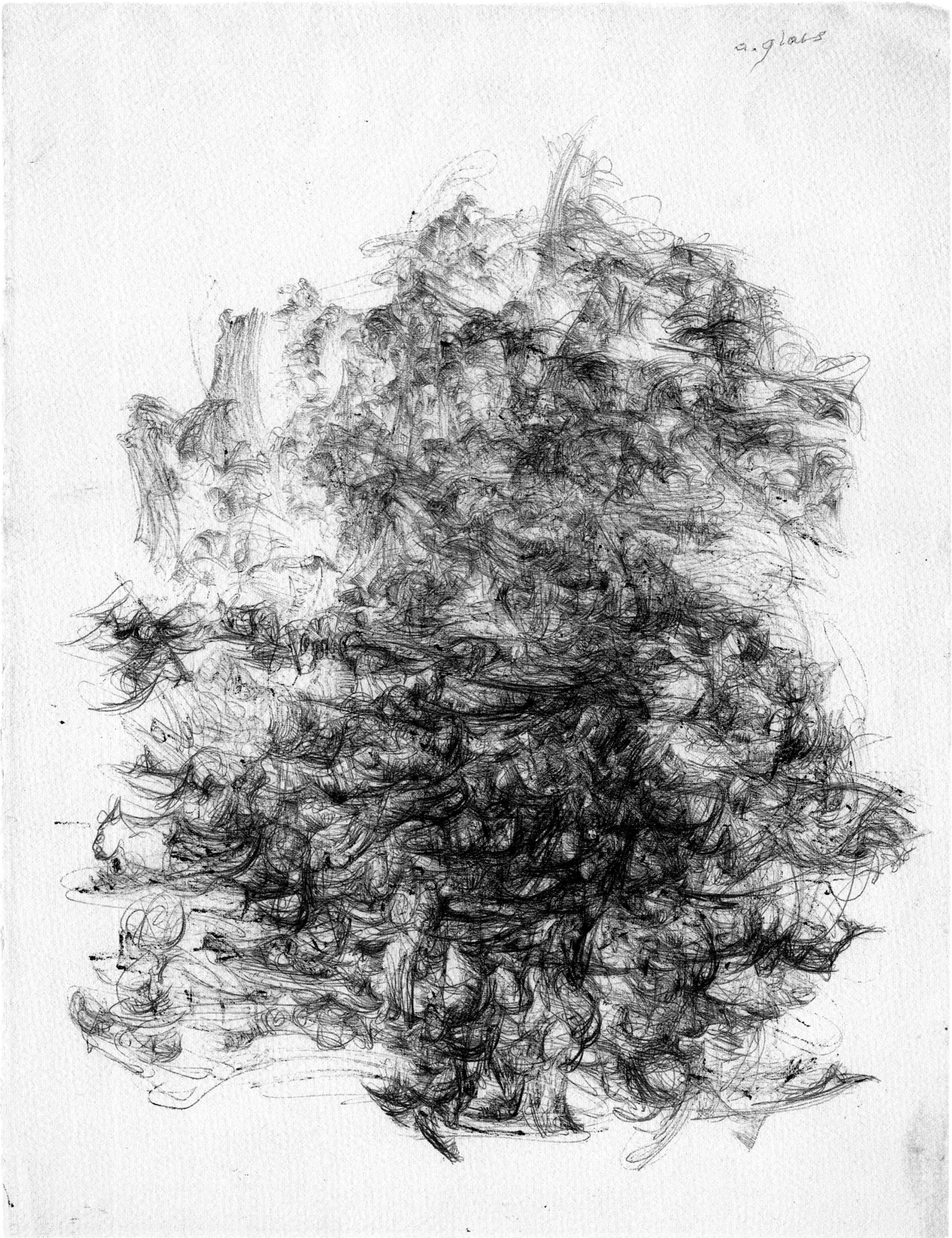

Untitled
(Club Saint-Germain period)
ca. 1954-1962
Monochrome blue ballpoint
pen drawing, on paper.
32 x 25 cm
Artist's collection

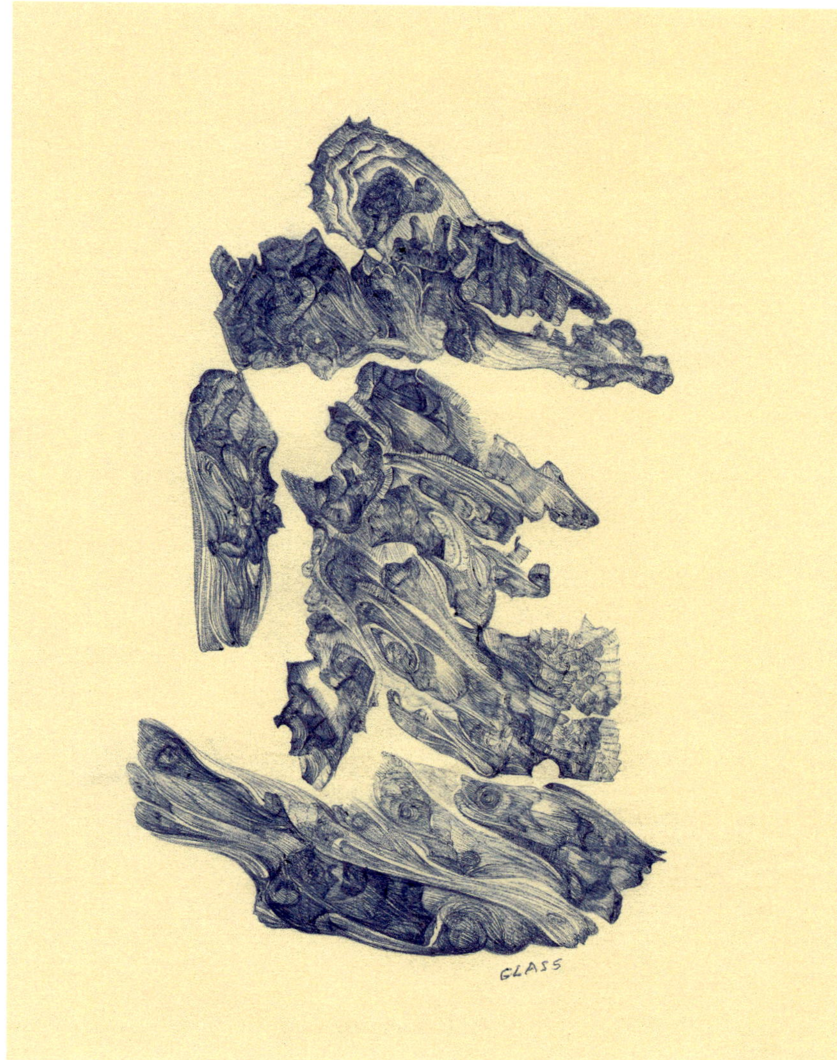

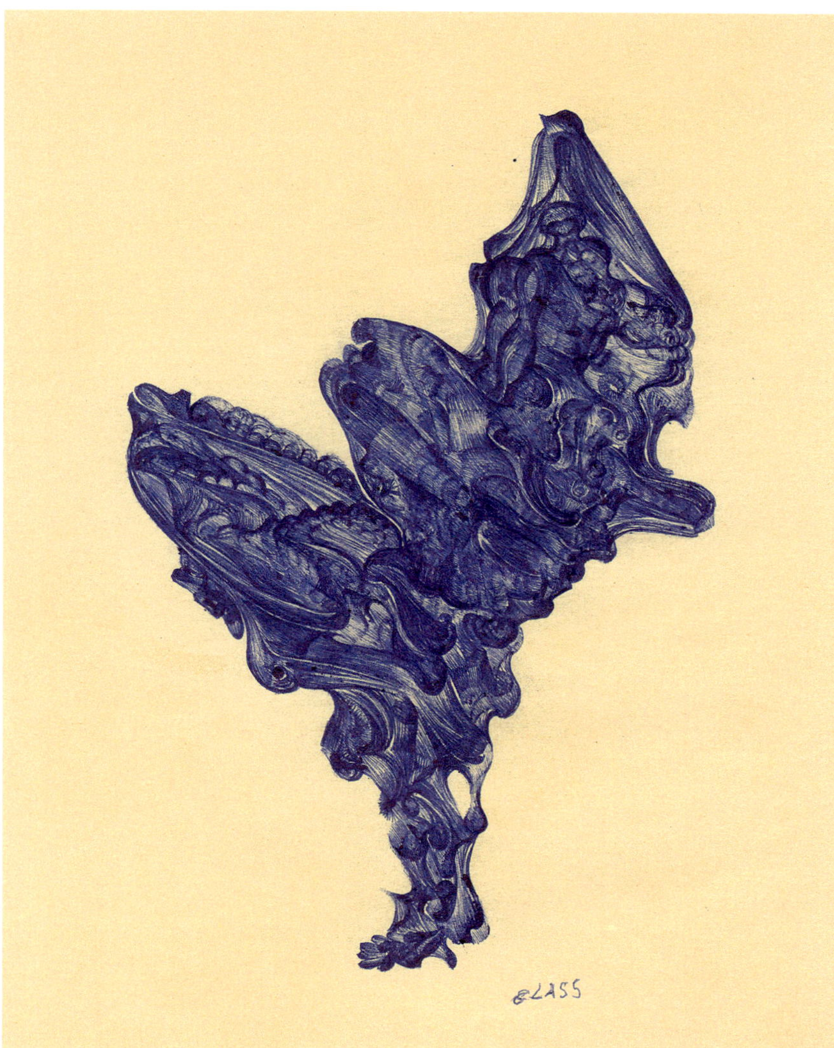

Untitled
(Club Saint-Germain period)
ca. 1954-1962
Monochrome blue ballpoint pen drawing, on paper.
28 x 22.5 cm
Artist's collection

Untitled
(Club Saint-Germain period)
ca. 1954-1962
Monochrome blue ballpoint pen drawing, on paper.
27 x 22 cm
Artist's collection

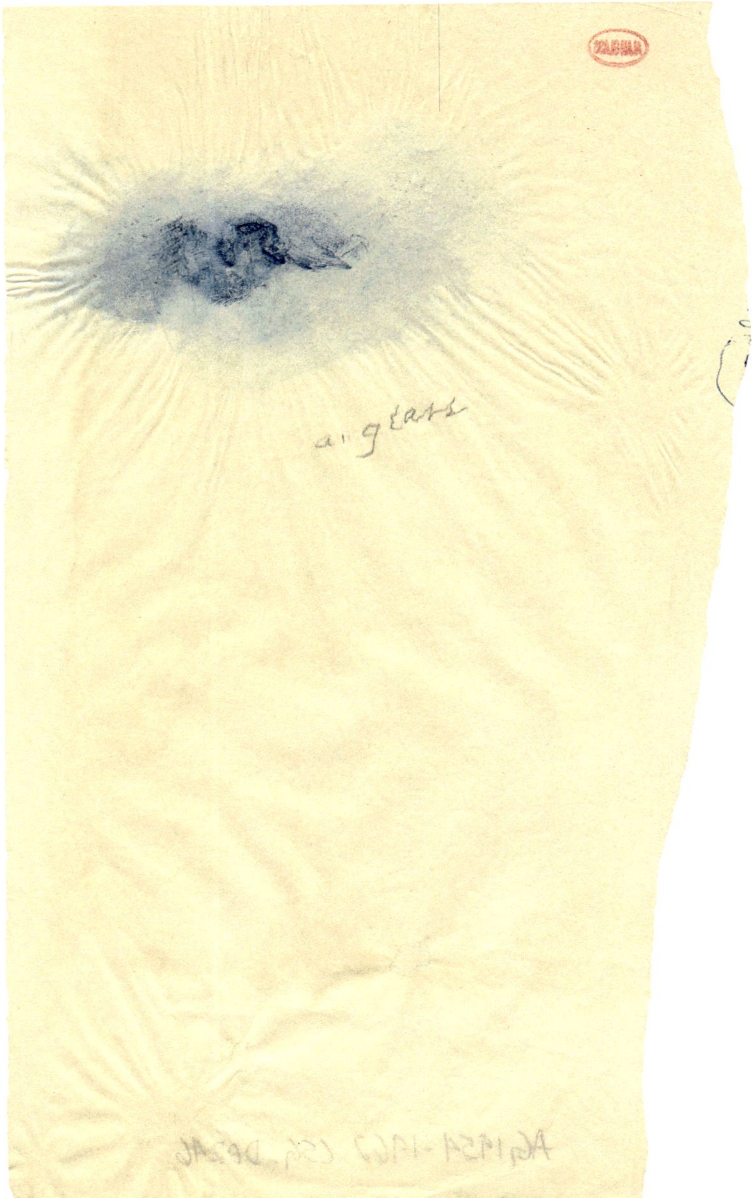

Untitled
(Club Saint-Germain period)
ca. 1954-1962
Monochrome blue ballpoint pen drawing with blue watercolor, on paper.
21 x 13 cm
Artist's collection

Untitled
(Club Saint-Germain period)
ca. 1954-1962
Graphite drawing, on paper.
9.2 x 5 cm
Artist's collection

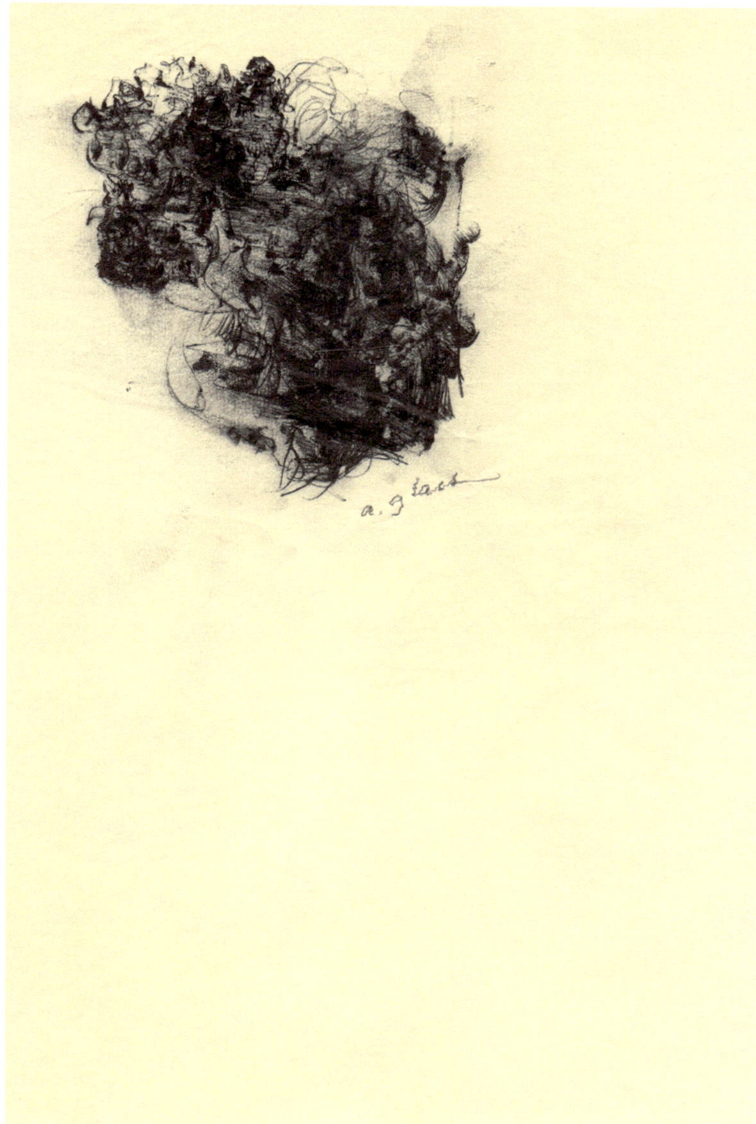

Untitled
(Club Saint-Germain period)
ca. 1954-1962
Monochrome navy blue
ballpoint pen drawing,
on paper.
32 x 25 cm
Artist's collection

Untitled
(Club Saint-Germain period)
ca. 1954-1962
Monochrome black ballpoint
pen drawing, on paper.
21 x 13.5cm
Artist's collection

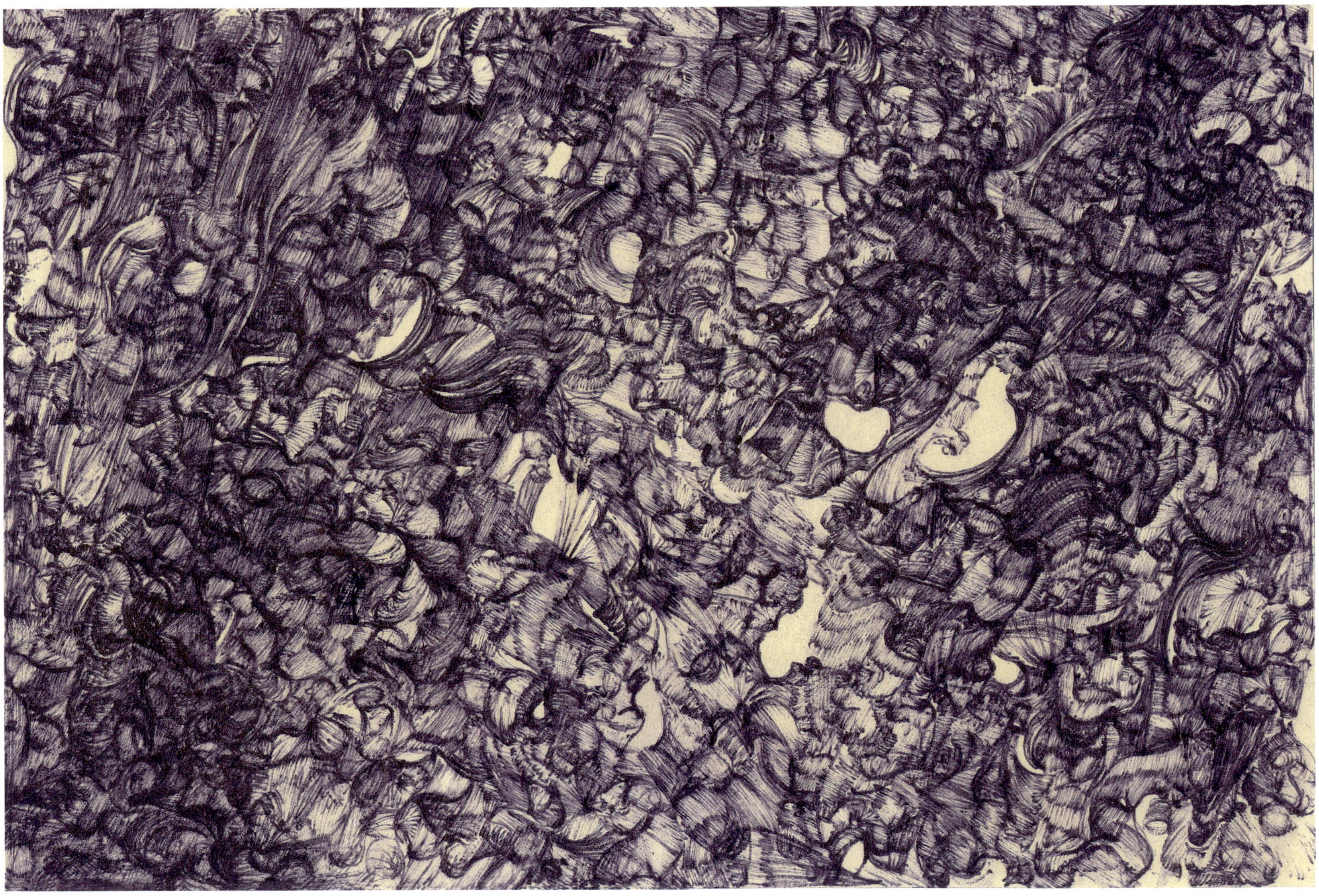

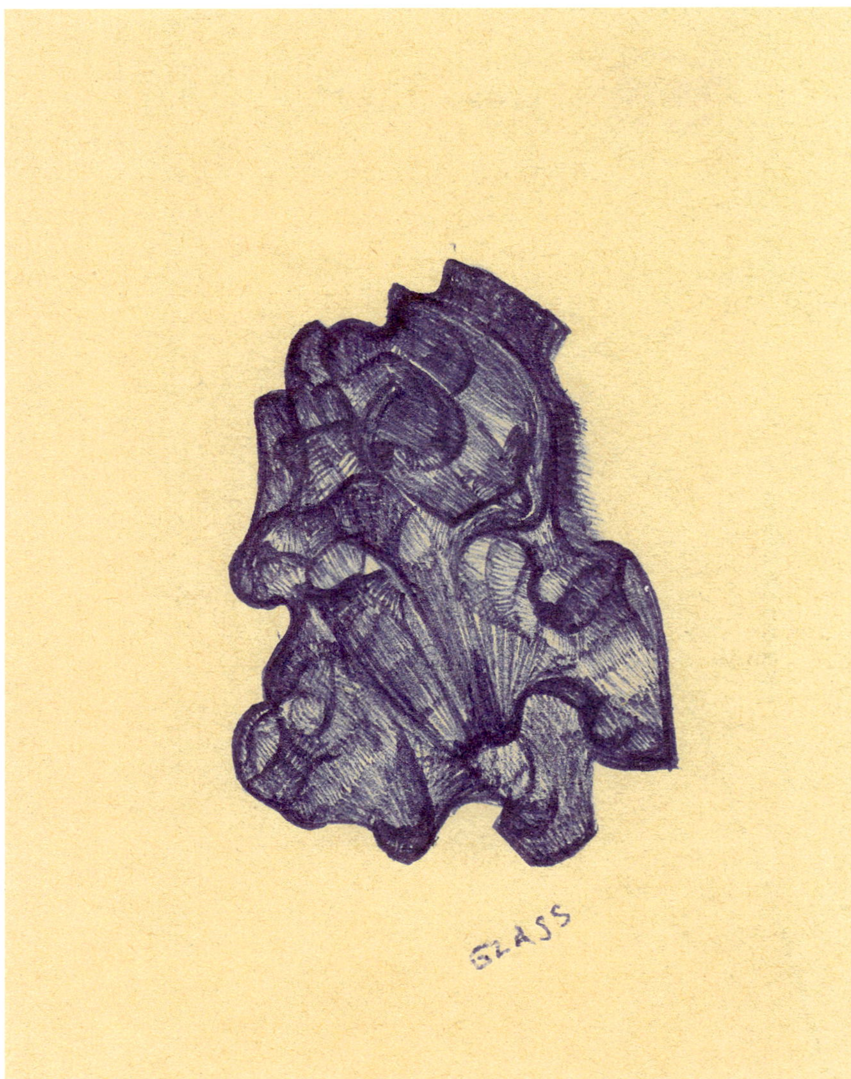

Untitled
(Club Saint-Germain period)
ca. 1954-1962
Drawing in violet monochrome
ballpoint pen, on paper.
15 x 21 cm
Artist's collection

Untitled
(Club Saint-Germain period)
ca. 1954-1962
Monochrome blue ballpoint
pen drawing, on the order of
Club Saint Germain.
12.6 x 7.6 cm
Artist's collection

Untitled
(Club Saint-Germain period)
ca. 1954-1962
Monochrome blue ballpoint
pen drawing, on paper.
28 x 22.5 cm
Artist's collection
Following page

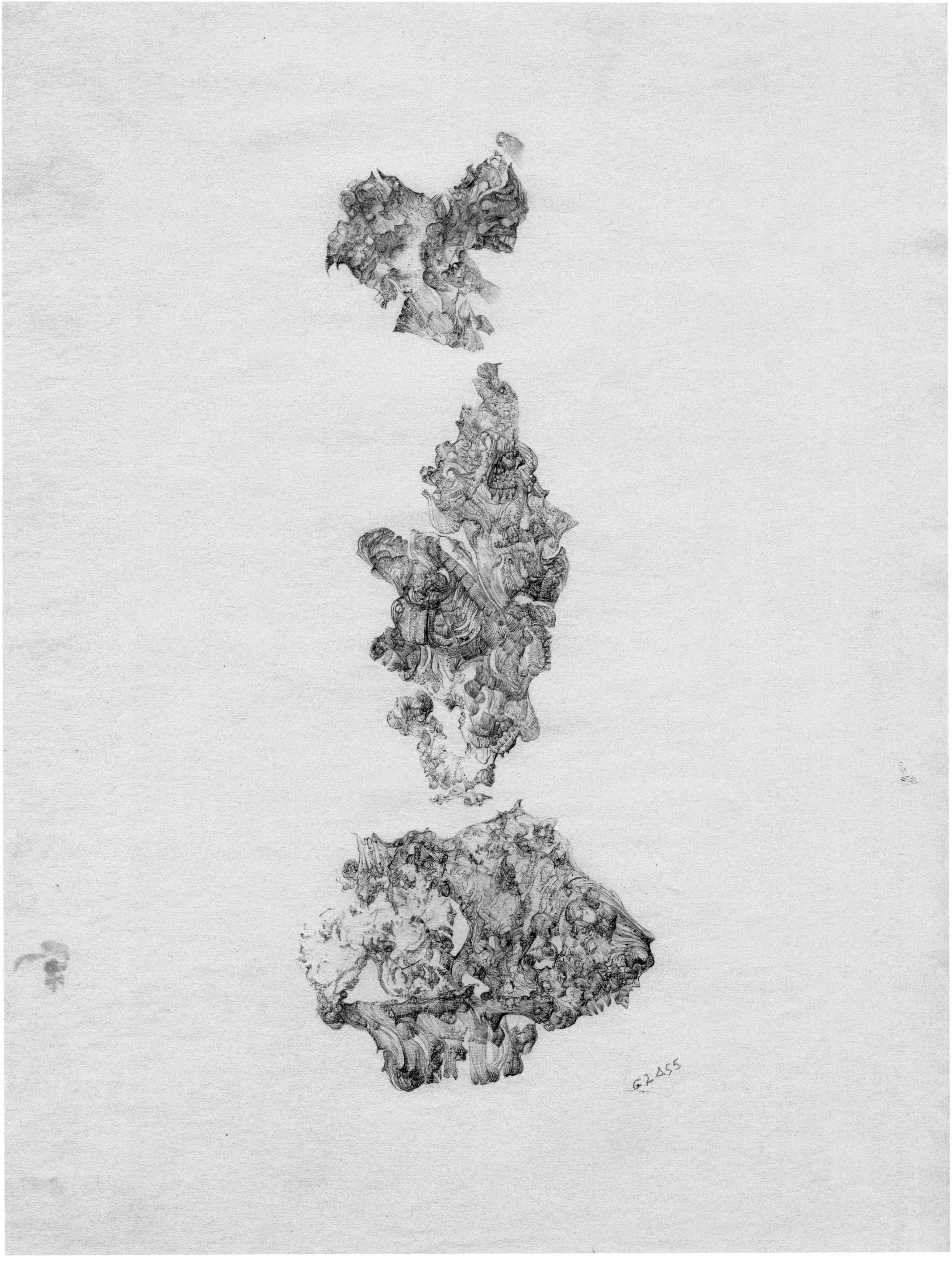
GLASS

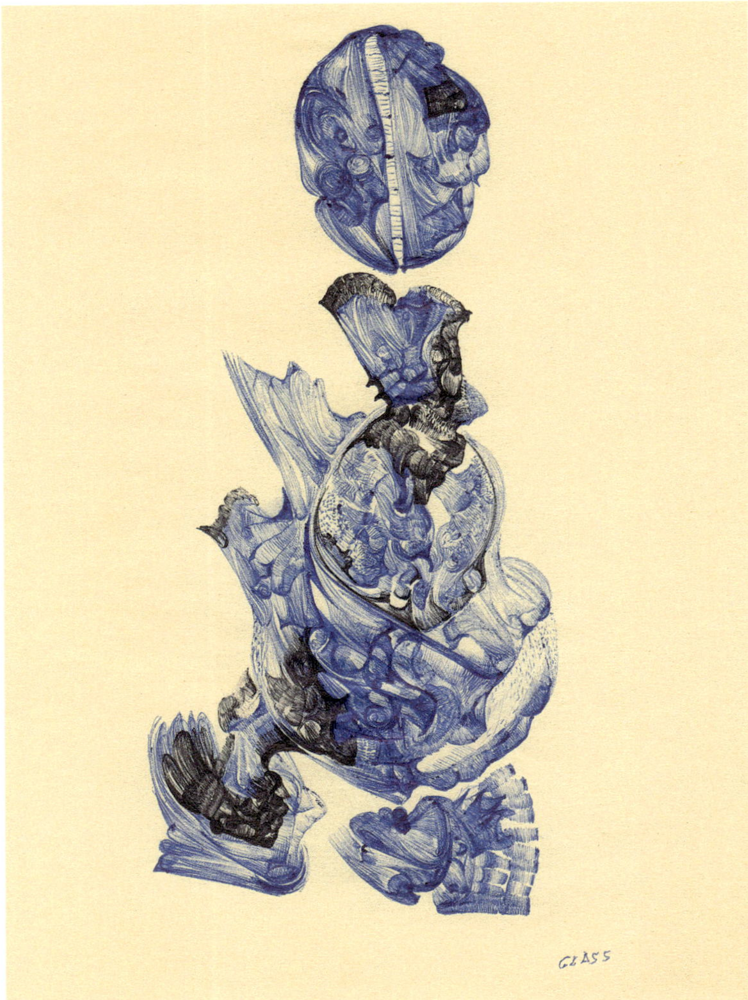

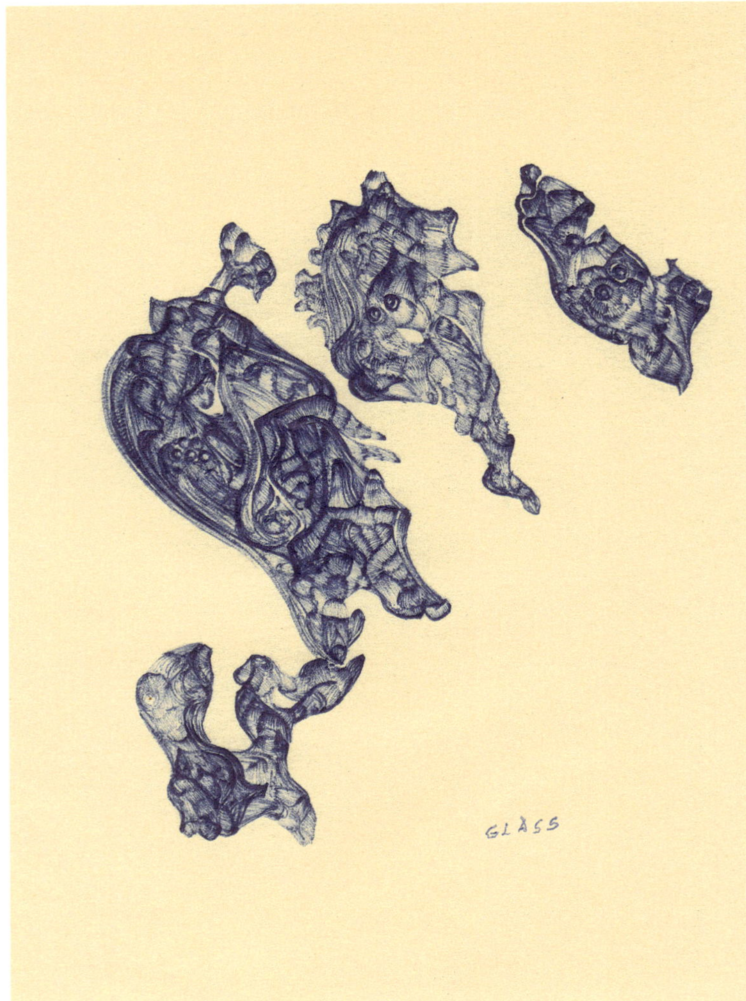

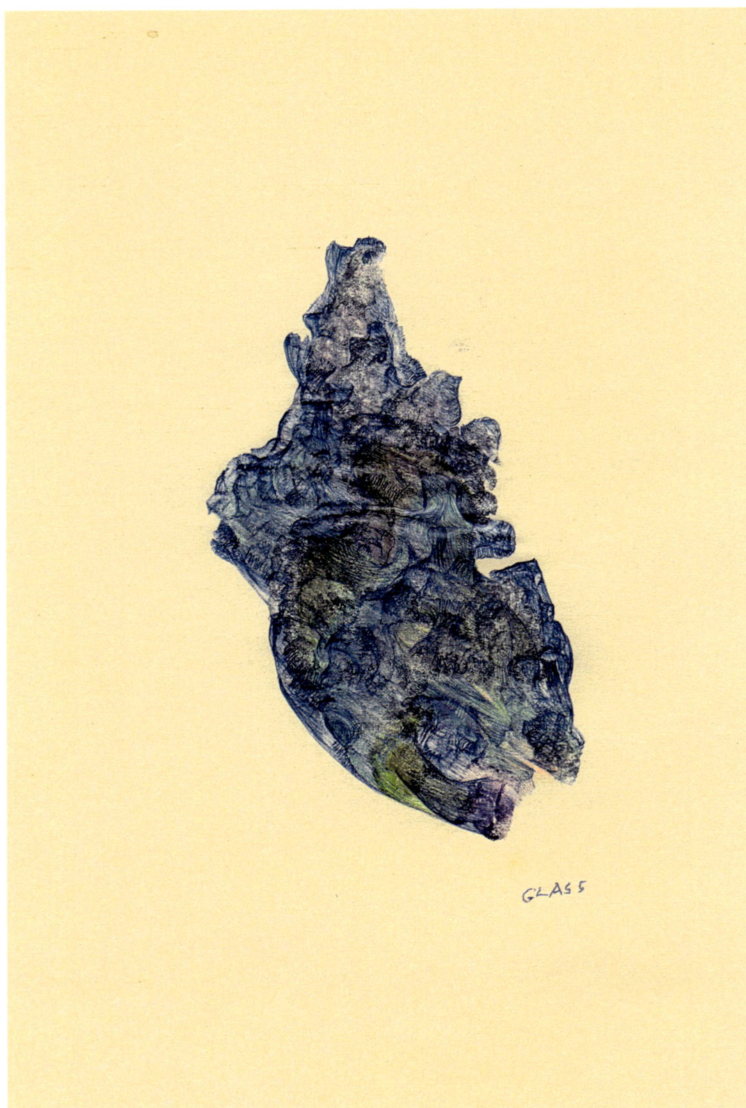

Untitled
(Club Saint-Germain period)
ca. 1954-1962
Bicolor blue and black ballpoint pen drawing, on paper.
28 x 22.6 cm
Artist's collection

Untitled
(Club Saint-Germain period)
ca. 1954-1962
Monochrome blue ballpoint pen drawing, on paper.
27 x 22.3 cm
Artist's collection

Untitled
(Club Saint-Germain period)
ca. 1954-1962
Blue, green and violet tricolor ballpoint pen drawing, on paper.
28 x 22.5 cm
Artist's collection

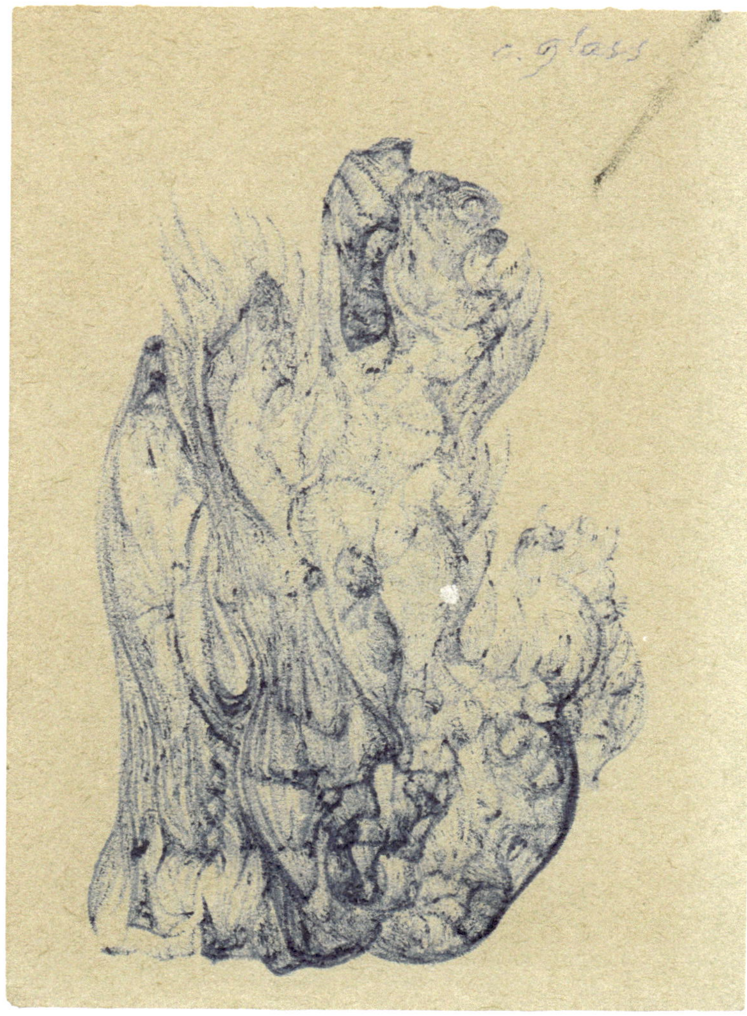

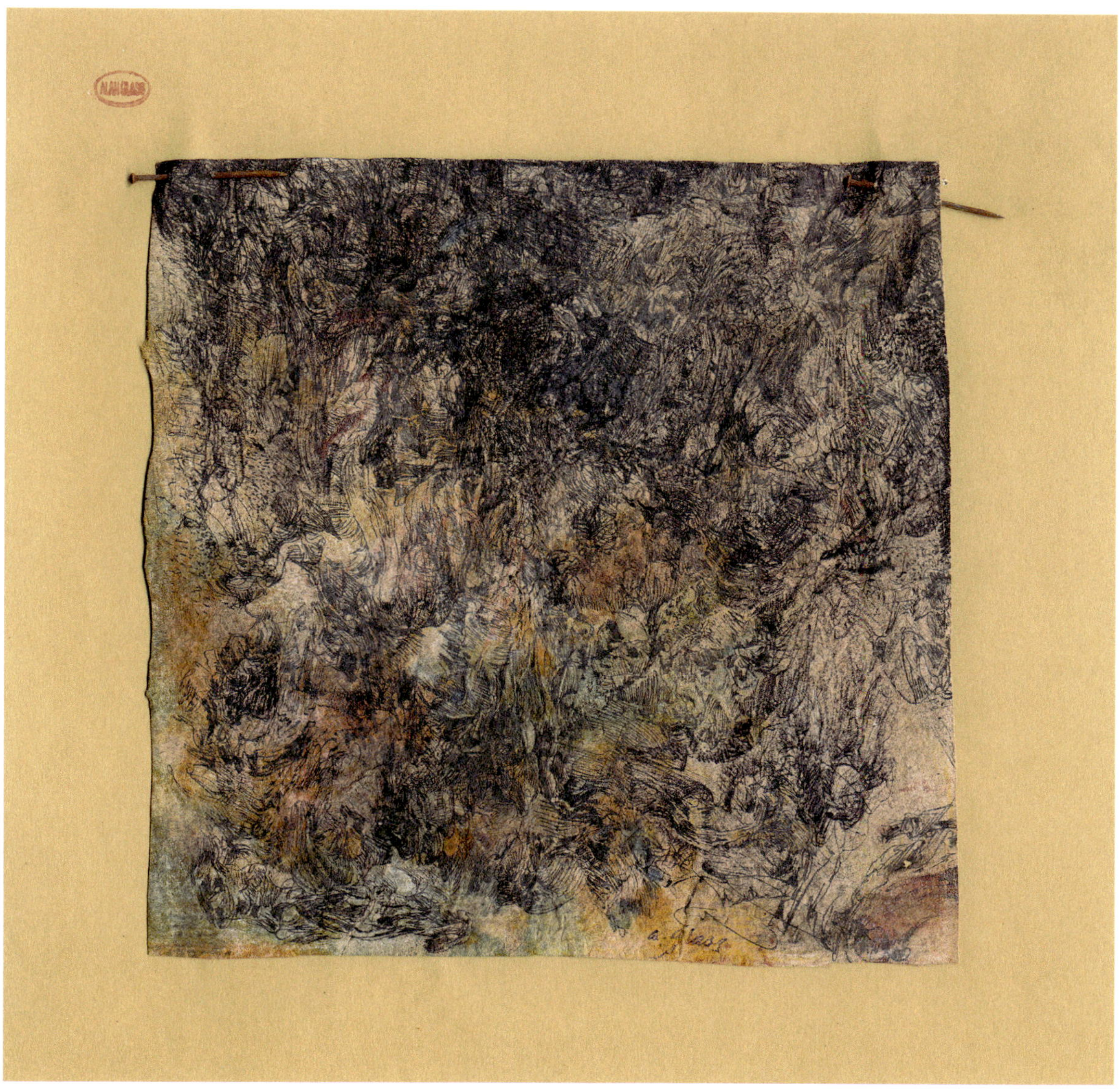

Untitled
(Club Saint-Germain period)
ca. 1954-1962
Monochrome blue ballpoint pen drawing, on olive paper.
10.7 x 7.9 cm
Artist's collection

Untitled
(Club Saint-Germain period)
ca. 1954-1962
Monochrome black ballpoint pen drawing, with green and brown pencil, with a touch of allumettage, on paper.
14.7 x 15 cm
Artist's collection

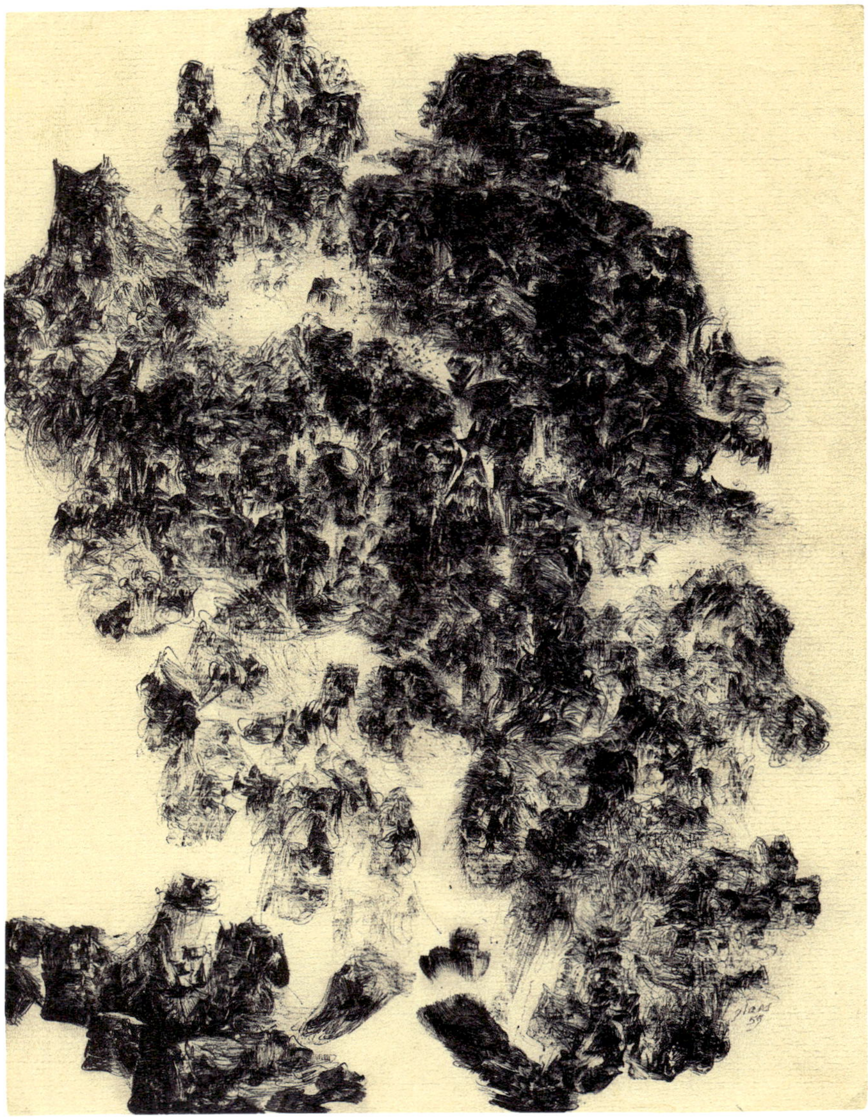

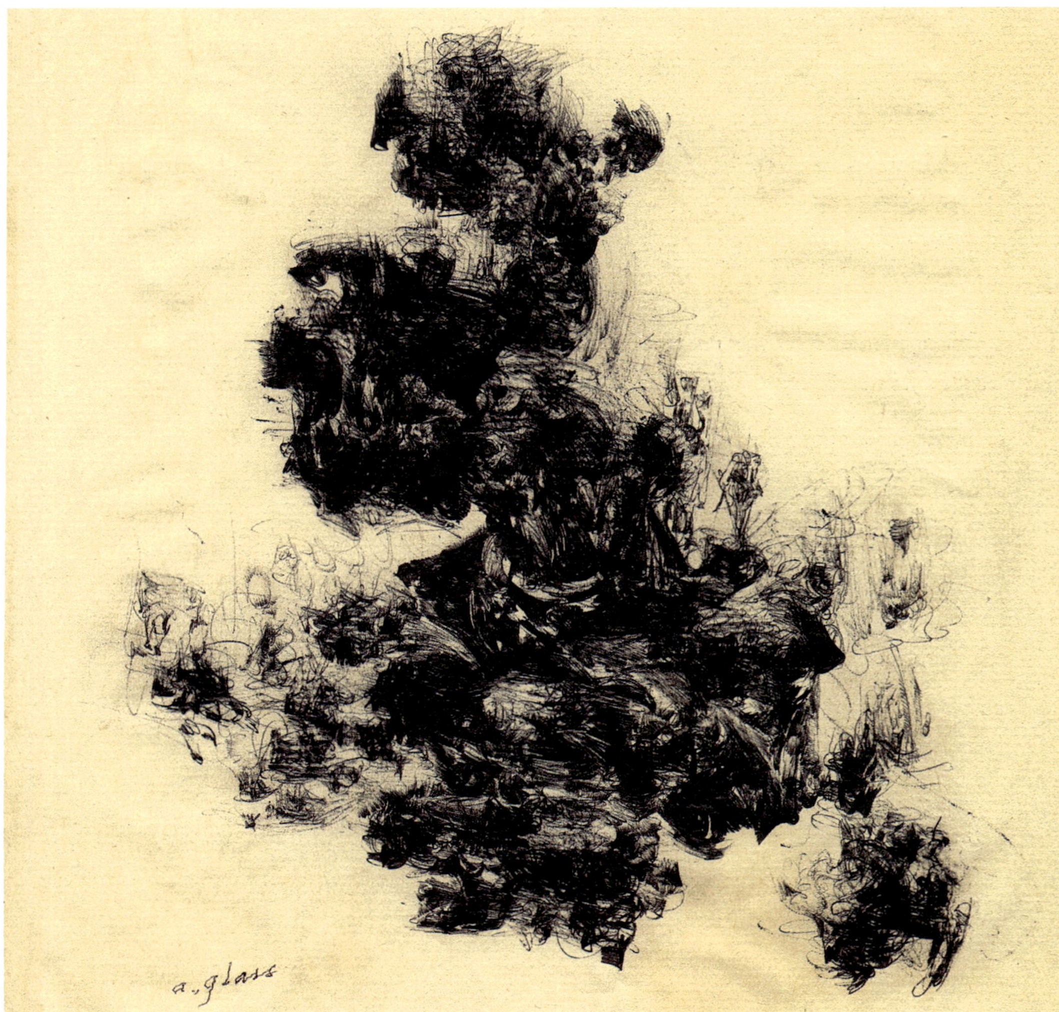

Untitled
(Club Saint-Germain period)
1959
Monochrome black pen
drawing and India ink,
on paper.
26.9 x 20.9 cm
Artist's collection

Untitled
(Club Saint-Germain period)
ca. 1954-1962
Monochrome black pen
drawing and India ink,
on paper.
27 x 20.5 cm
Artist's collection

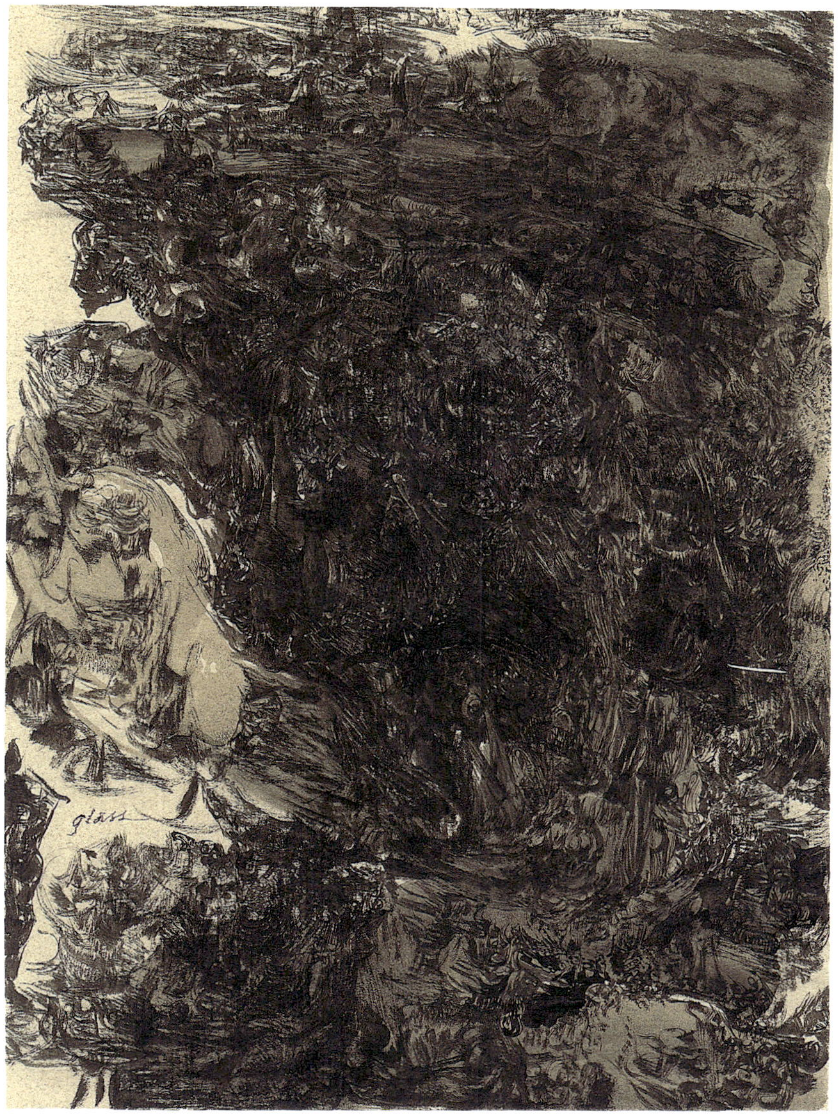

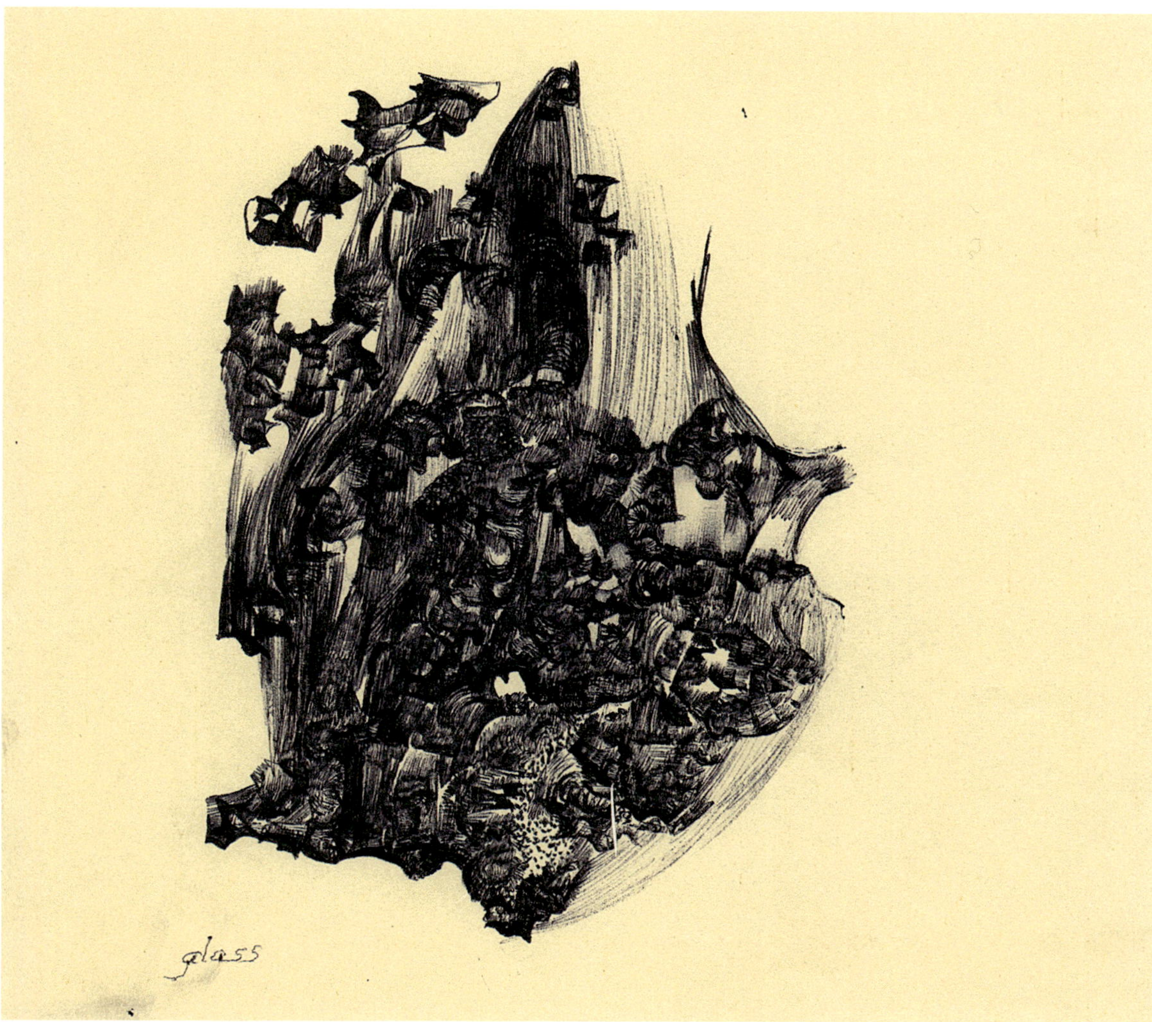

Untitled
(Club Saint-Germain period)
ca. 1954-1962
Monochrome black pen
drawing and India ink,
on paper.
19.5 x 14.5 cm
Artist's collection

Untitled
(Club Saint-Germain period)
ca. 1954-1962
Monochrome black ballpoint
pen drawing, on paper.
22.5 x 20.5 cm
Artist's collection

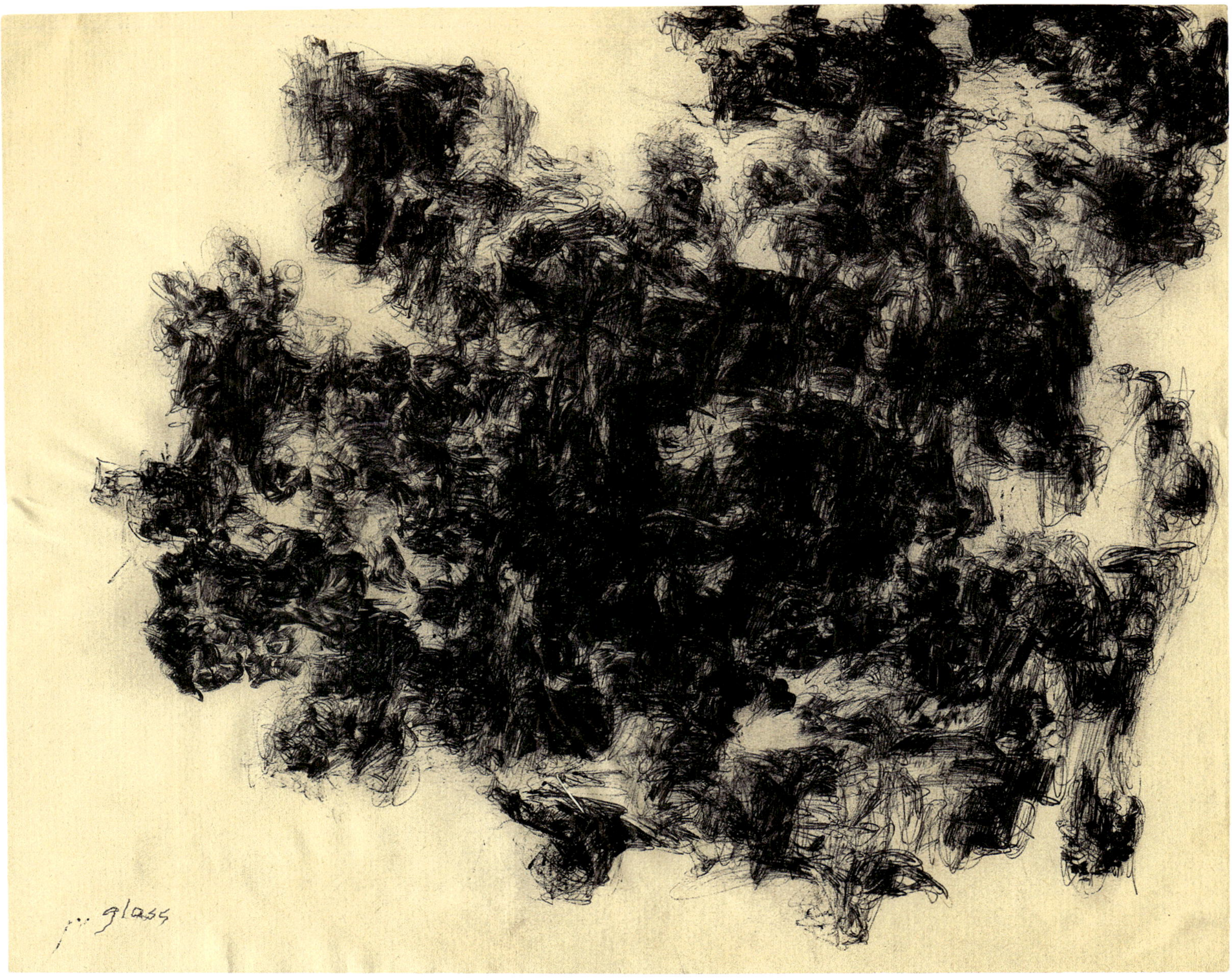

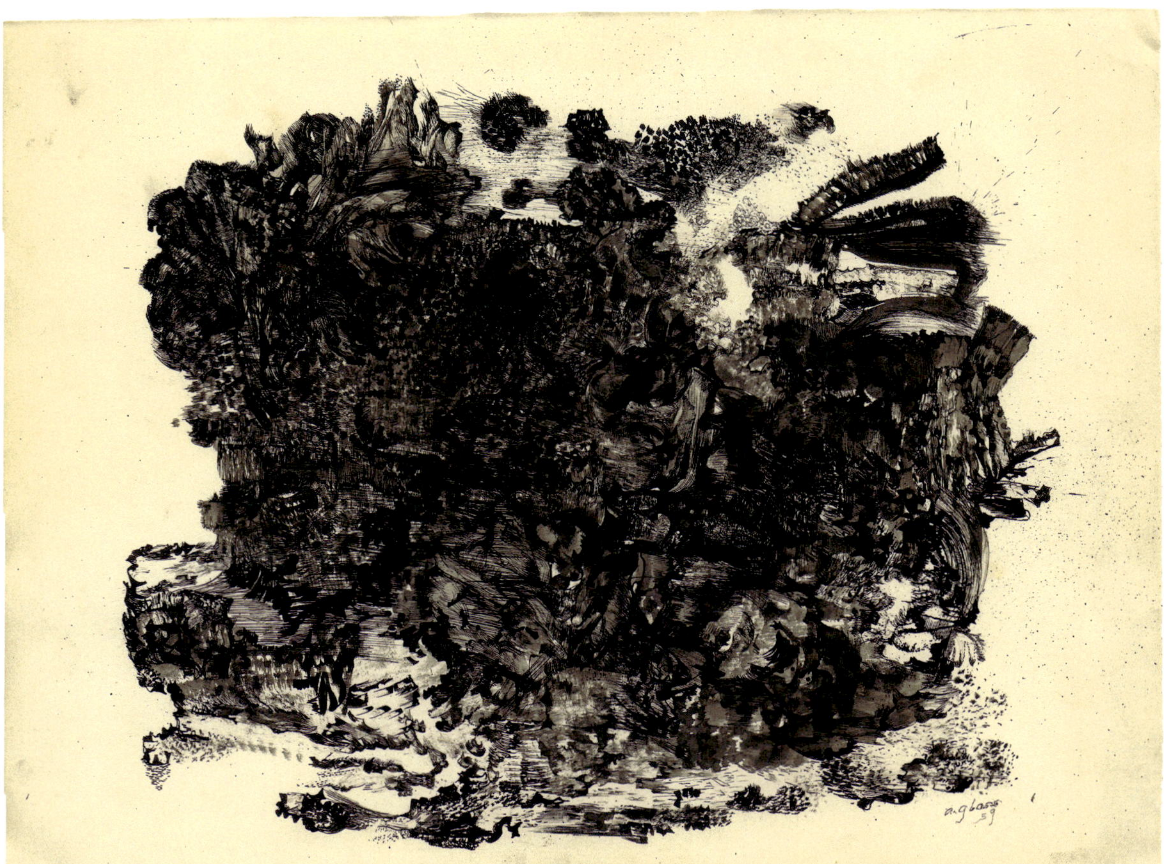

Untitled
(Club Saint-Germain period)
ca. 1954-1962
Black fountain pen drawing
and Indian ink, on paper.
21 x 27 cm
Artist's collection

Untitled
(Club Saint-Germain period)
1959
Black fountain pen drawing
and Indian ink, on paper.
28 x 37.5 cm
Artist's collection

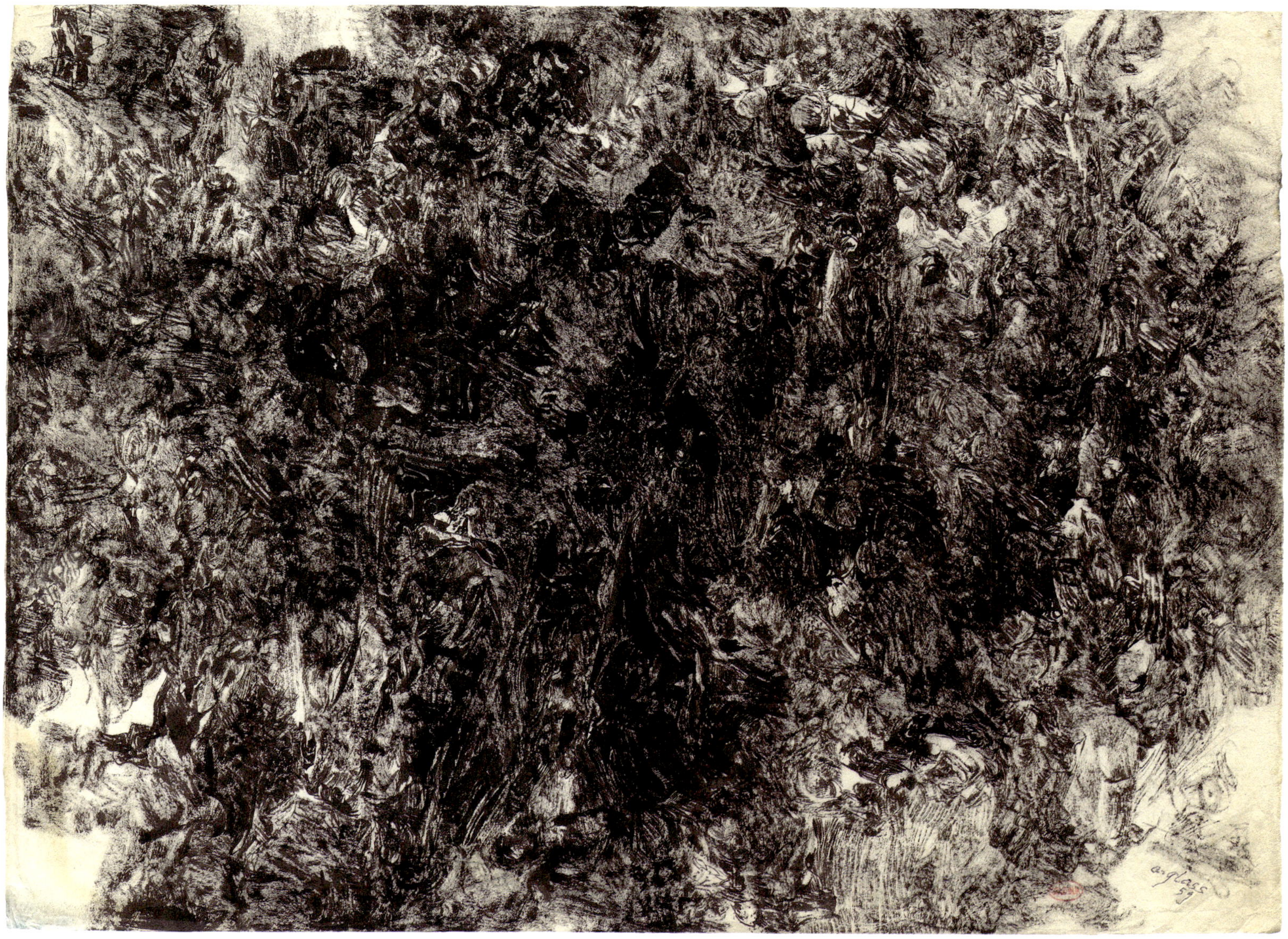

Untitled
(Club Saint-Germain period)
1959
Black fountain pen drawing and Indian ink, on Japanese paper.
27.5 x 38.5 cm
Artist's collection

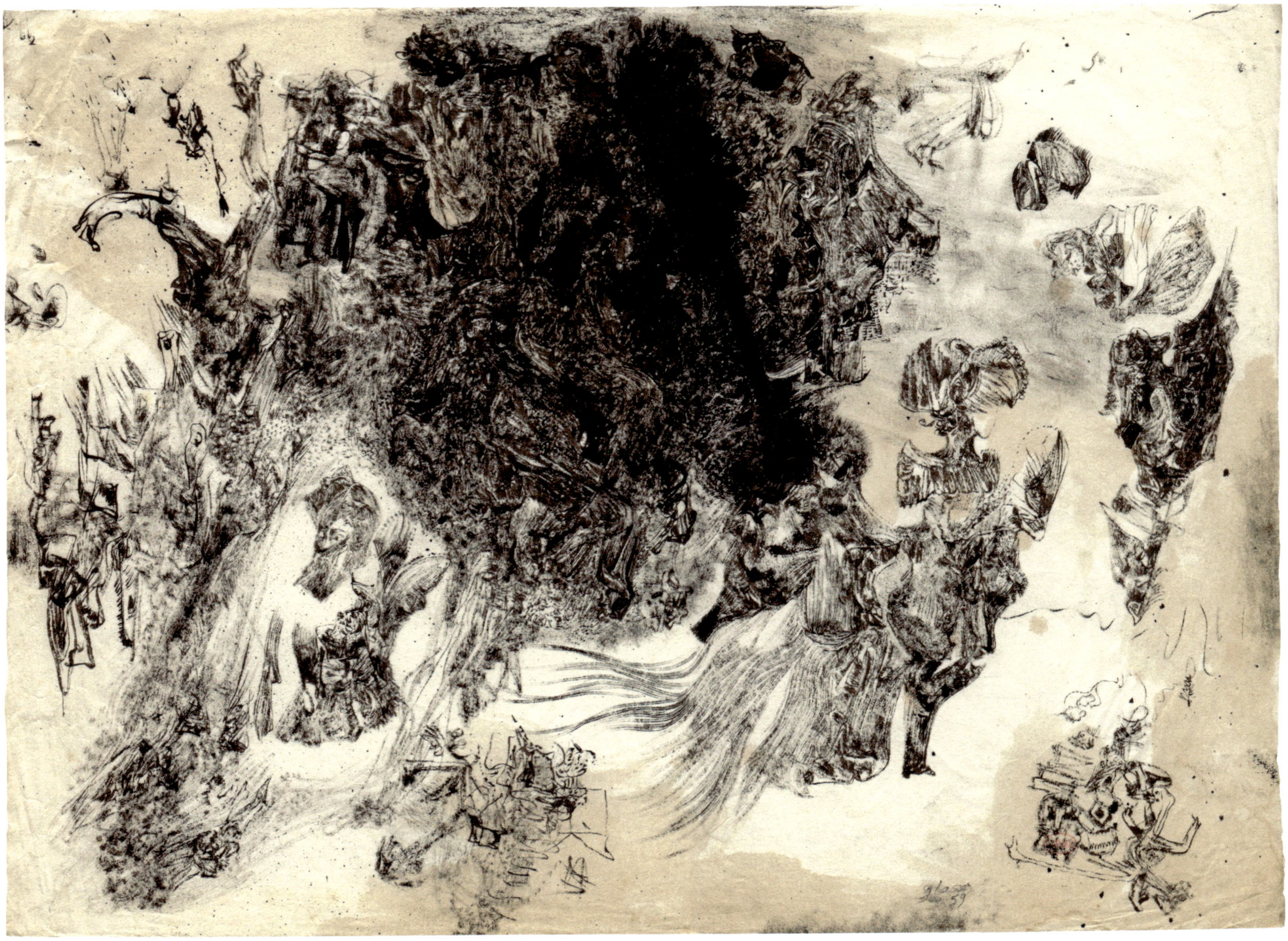

Untitled
(Club Saint-Germain period)
1959
Black fountain pen drawing and Indian ink, on Japanese paper.
27.5 x 38.5 cm
Artist's collection

Untitled
(Club Saint-Germain period)
1959
Navy blue and violet two-tone ballpoint pen drawing, on paper.
32 x 28 cm
Artist's collection

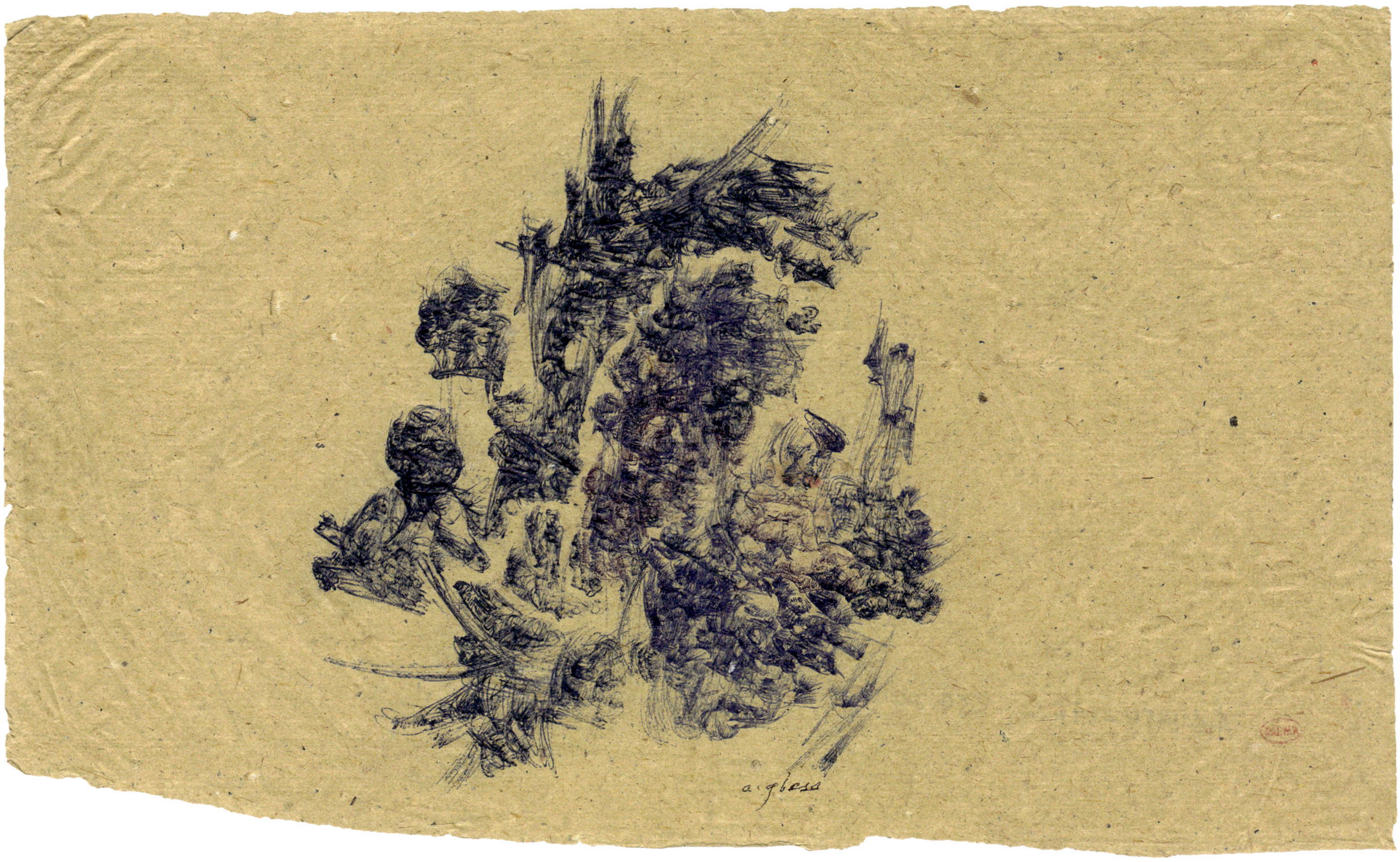

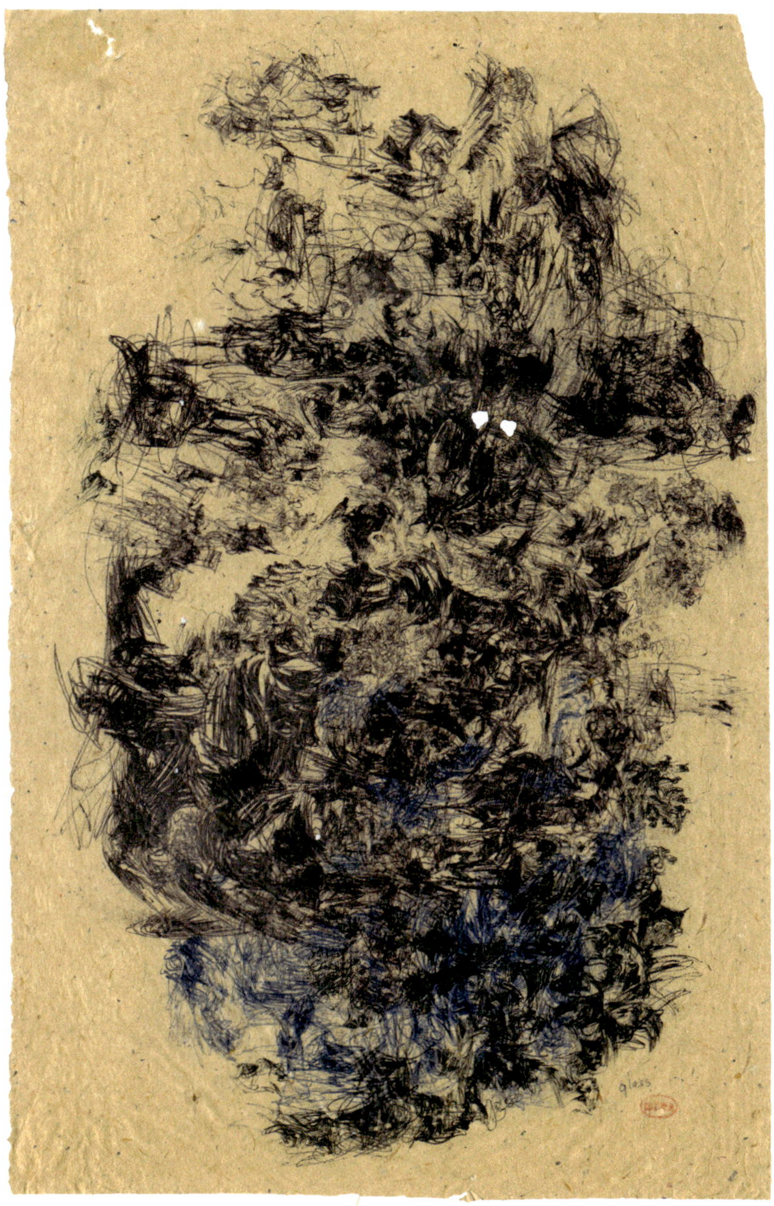

Untitled
(Club Saint-Germain period)
ca. 1954-1962
Blue and violet two-tone ballpoint pen drawing on composite paper.
20 x 34.5 cm
Artist's collection

Untitled
(Club Saint-Germain period)
ca. 1954-1962
Blue and black two-tone ballpoint pen drawing on composite paper.
32.5 x 21 cm
Artist's collection

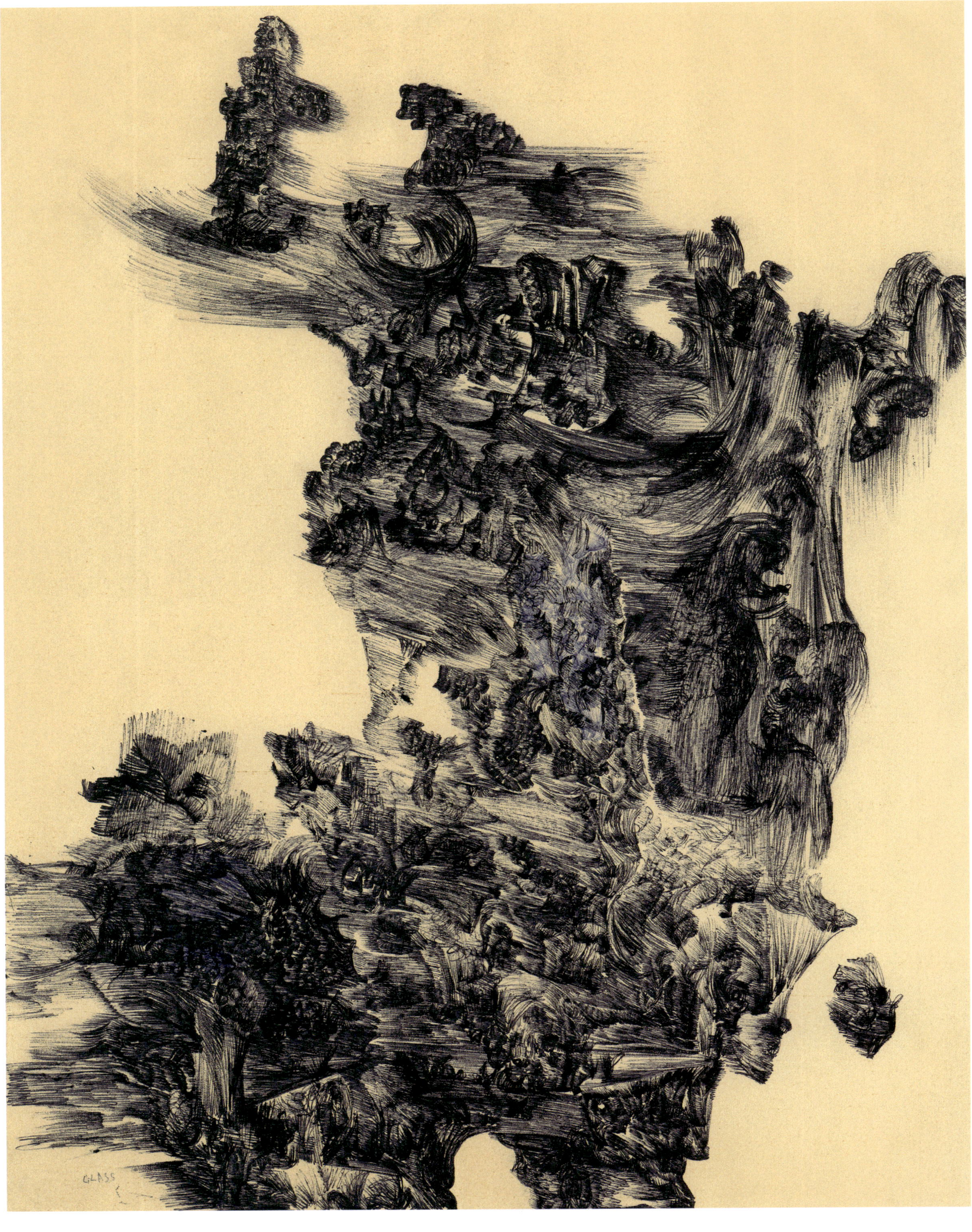
GLASS

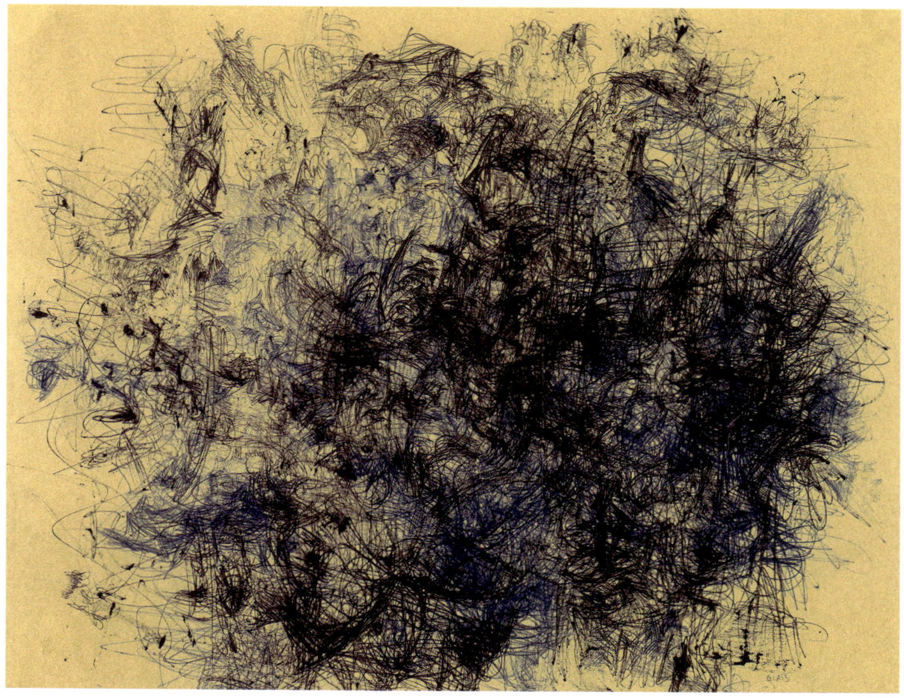

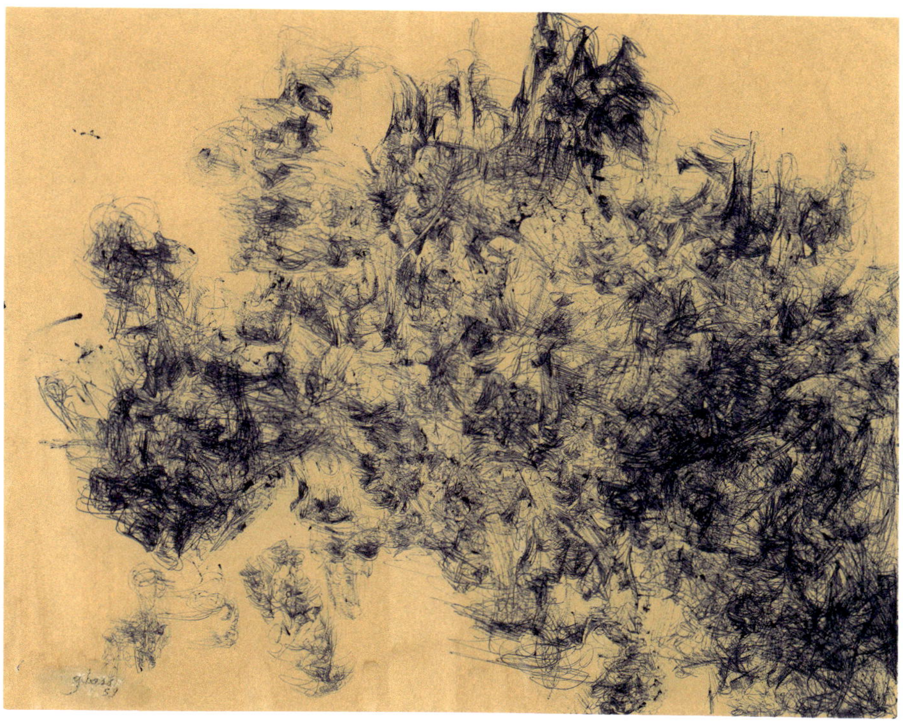

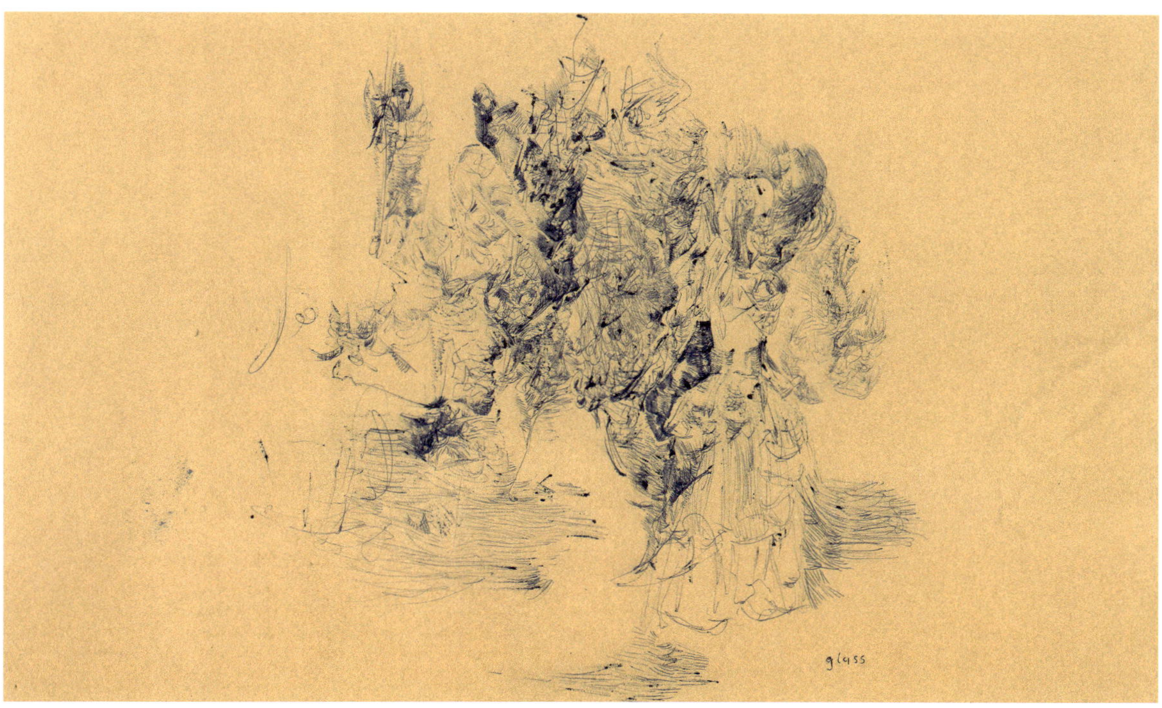

Untitled
(Club Saint-Germain period)
ca. 1954-1962
Monochrome black ballpoint pen drawing, on paper.
28 x 22 cm
Artist's collection

Untitled
(Club Saint-Germain period)
ca. 1954-1962
Bicolor blue and black ballpoint pen drawing, on paper.
22 x 28 cm
Artist's collection

Untitled
(Club Saint-Germain period)
1959
Monochrome blue ballpoint pen drawing, on paper.
21.5 x 28 cm
Artist's collection

Untitled
(Club Saint-Germain period)
ca. 1954-1962
Monochrome blue ballpoint pen drawing, on paper.
21 x 28 cm
Artist's collection

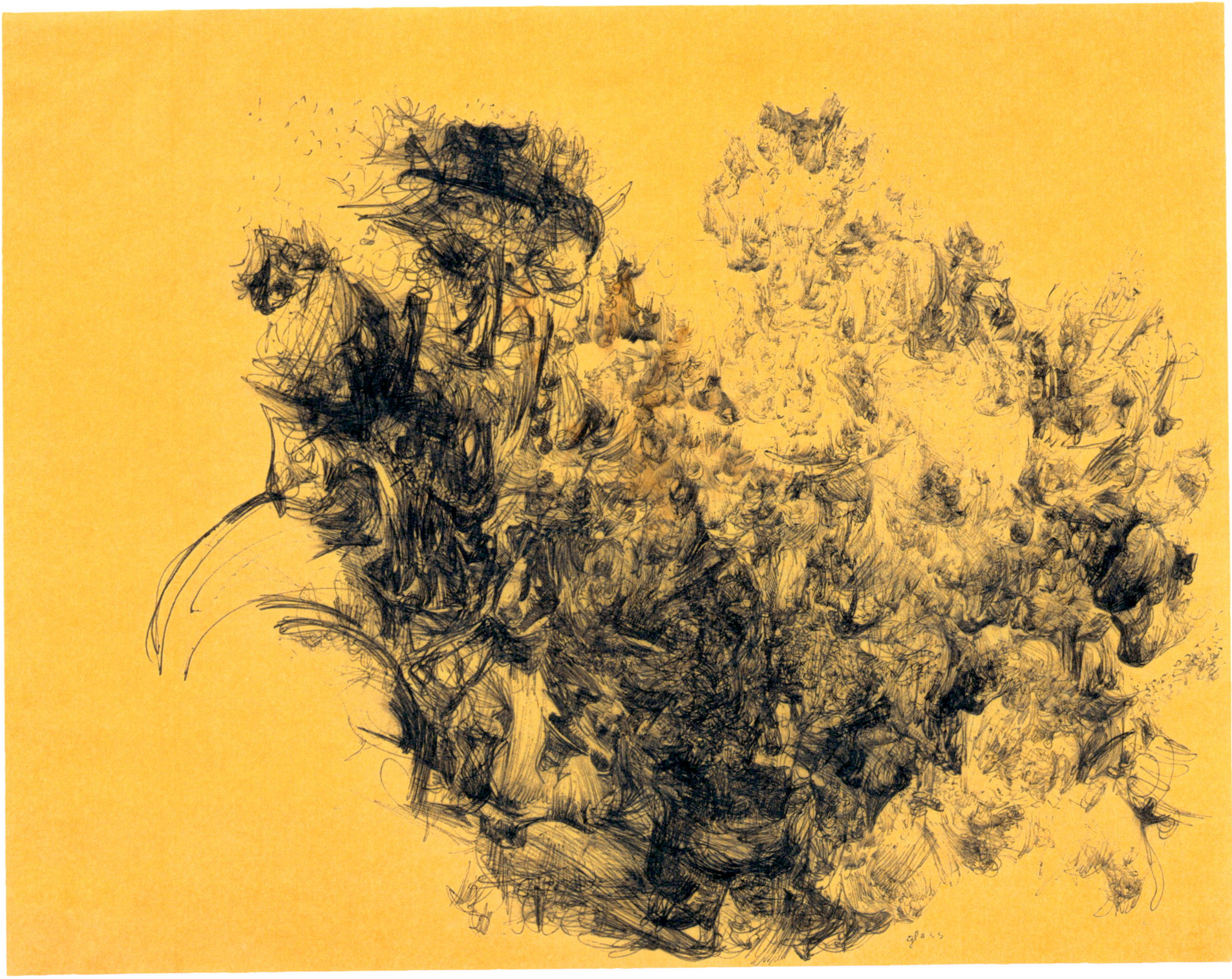

Untitled
(Club Saint-Germain period)
ca. 1954-1962
Monochrome blue ballpoint
pen drawing with a touch of
allumettage, on yellow paper.
22.8 x 28.8 cm
Artist's collection

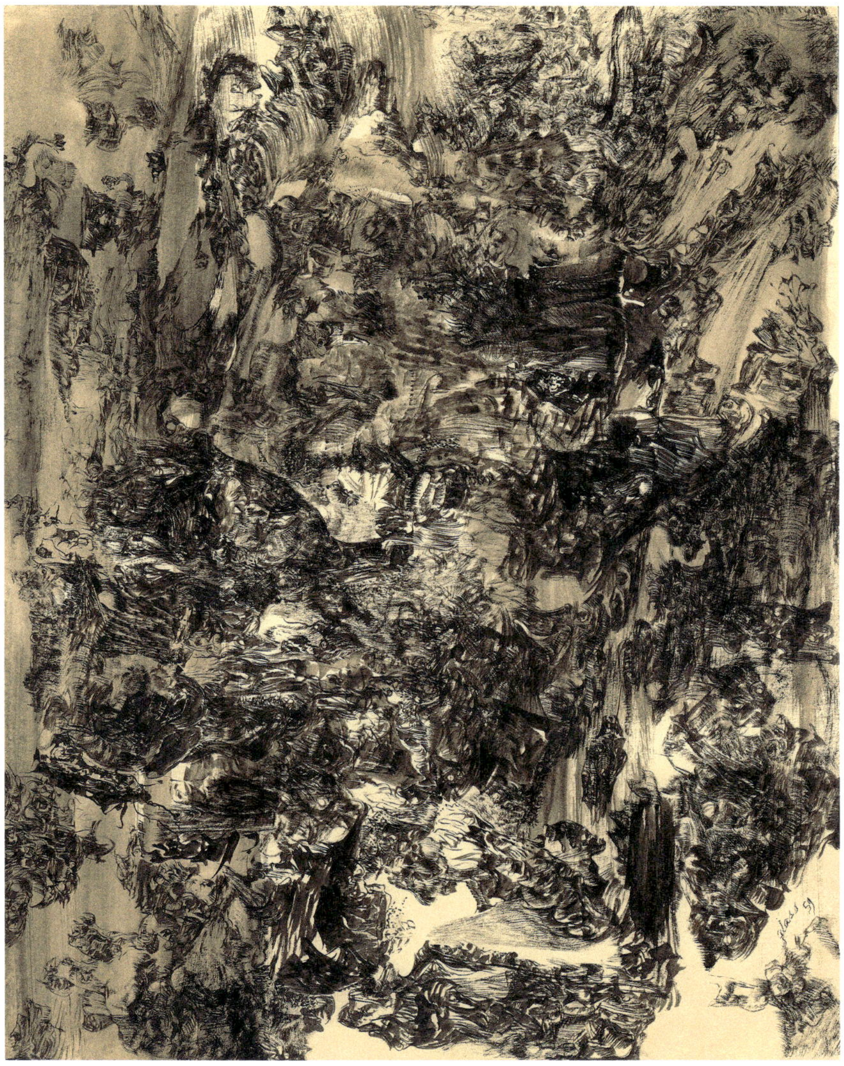

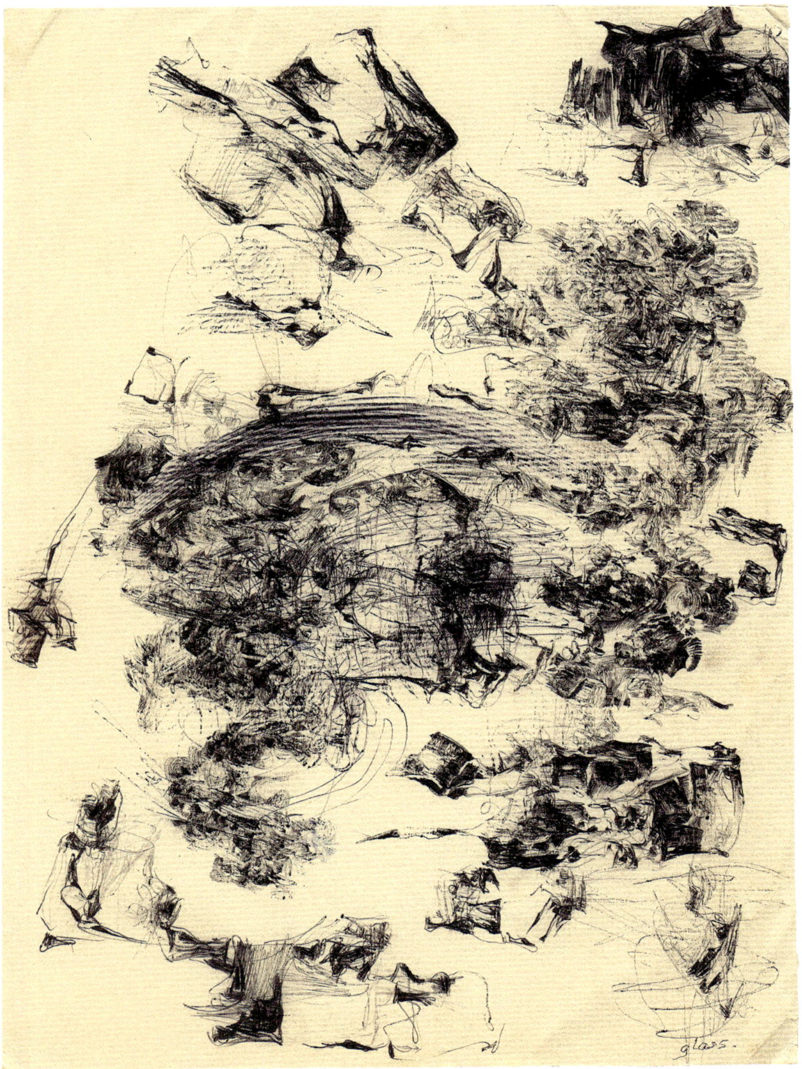

Untitled
(Club Saint-Germain period)
1959
Drawing with Indian ink and black watercolor, on paper.
28 x 22.6 cm
Artist's collection

Untitled
(Club Saint-Germain period)
ca. 1954-1962
Monochrome black ballpoint pen drawing, on paper.
28 x 21 cm
Artist's collection

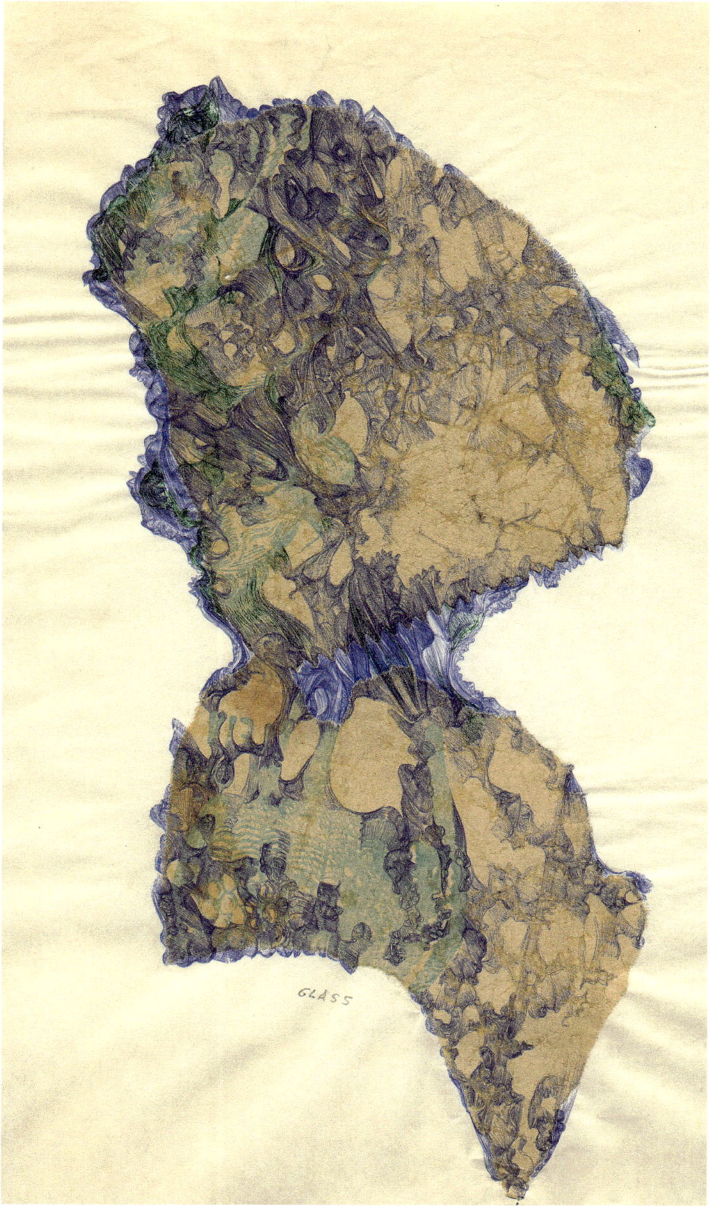

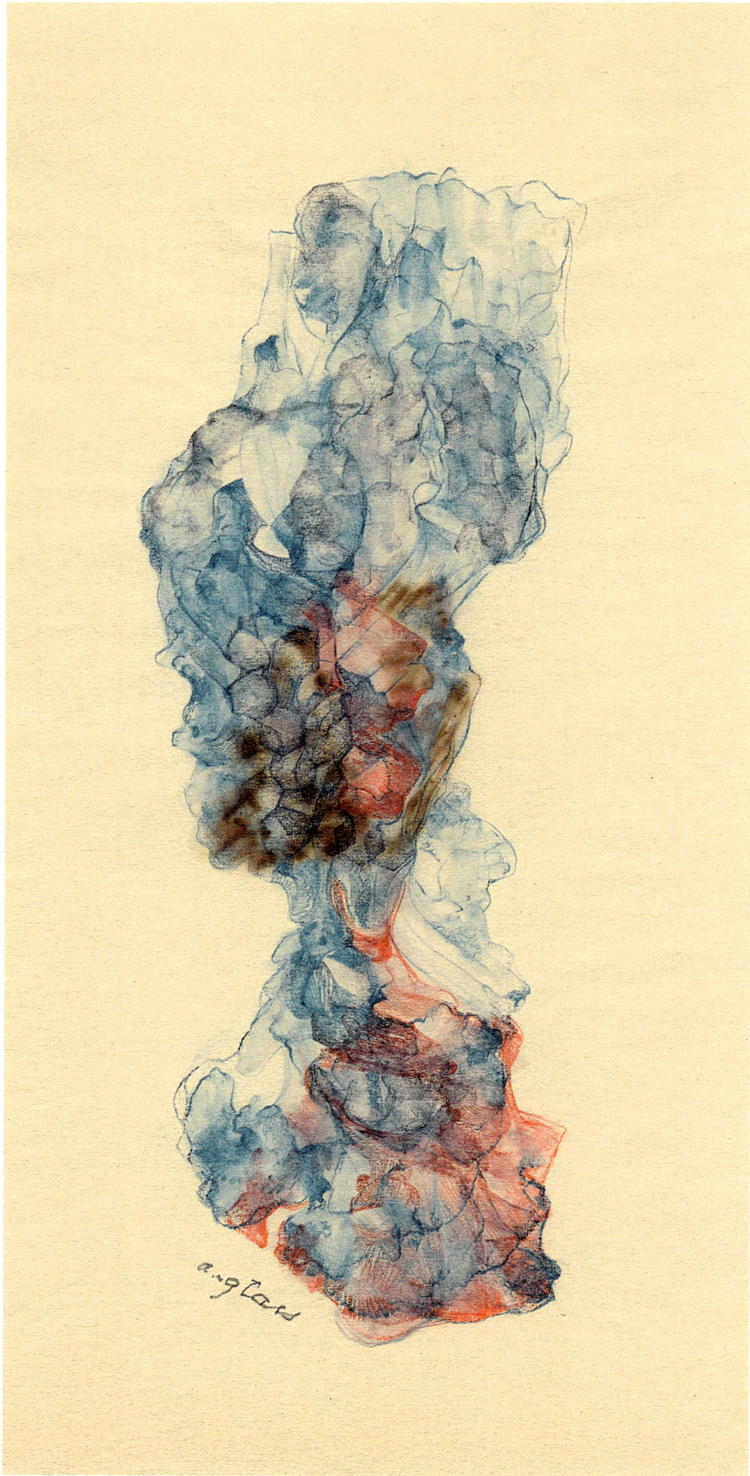

Untitled
(Club Saint-Germain period)
ca. 1954-1962
Blue, navy blue and green tricolor pen drawing, beige watercolor, collage applications, on paper.
35 x 21 cm
Artist's collection

Untitled
(Club Saint-Germain period)
ca. 1954-1962
Red and blue colored pencil drawing, watercolored and with a touch of alumettage, on paper.
28 x 22.5 cm
Artist's collection

Untitled
(Club Saint-Germain period)
ca. 1954-1962
Bicolor blue and navy blue ballpoint pen drawing, with green, blue, and red watercolor, with a touch of graphite, on paper.
28 x 22.5 cm
Artist's collection
Following page

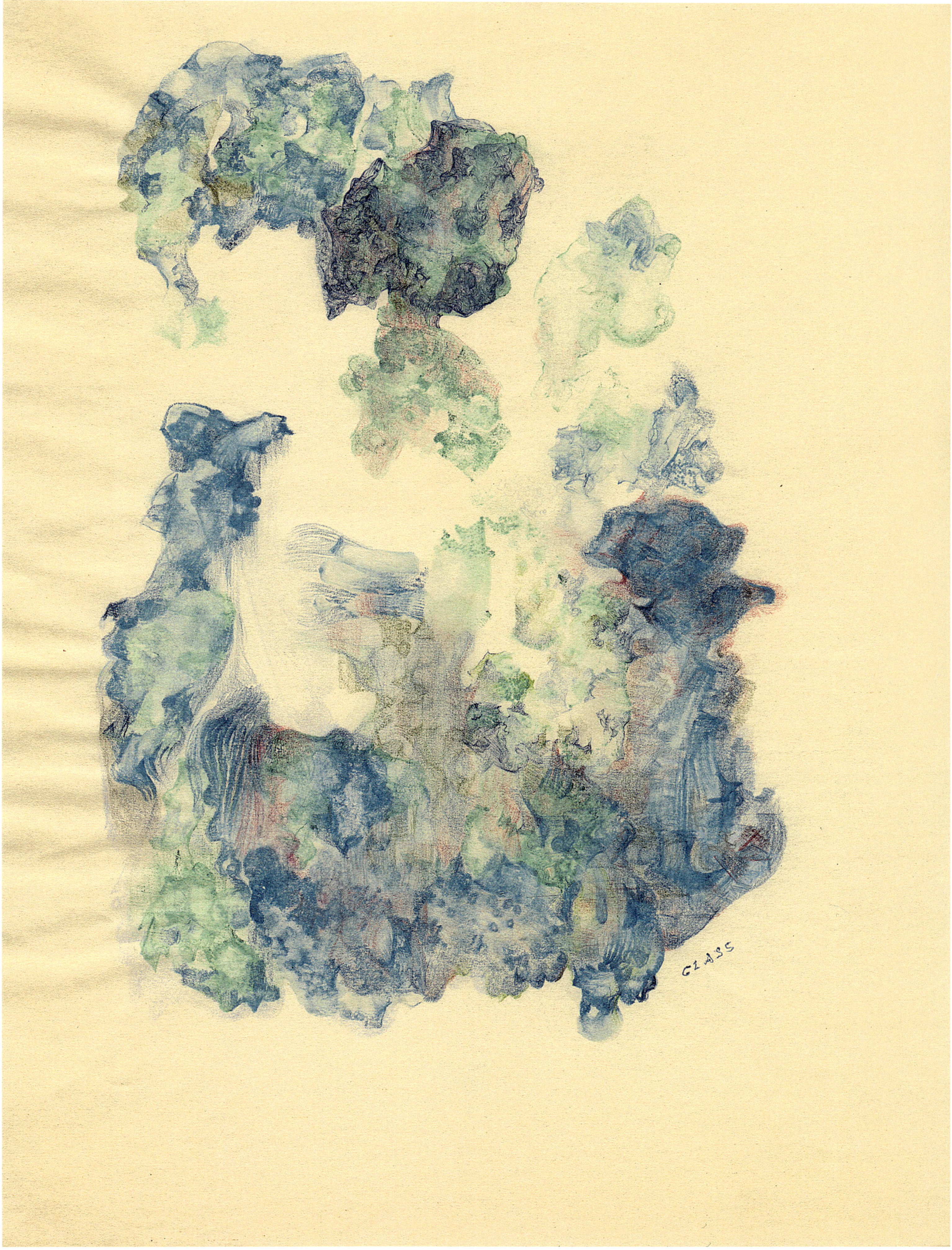
GLASS

Untitled
(Club Saint-Germain period)
1959
Bicolor blue and violet
ballpoint pen drawing, with
touches of allumettage,
on paper.
30 x 28.5 cm
Artist's collection

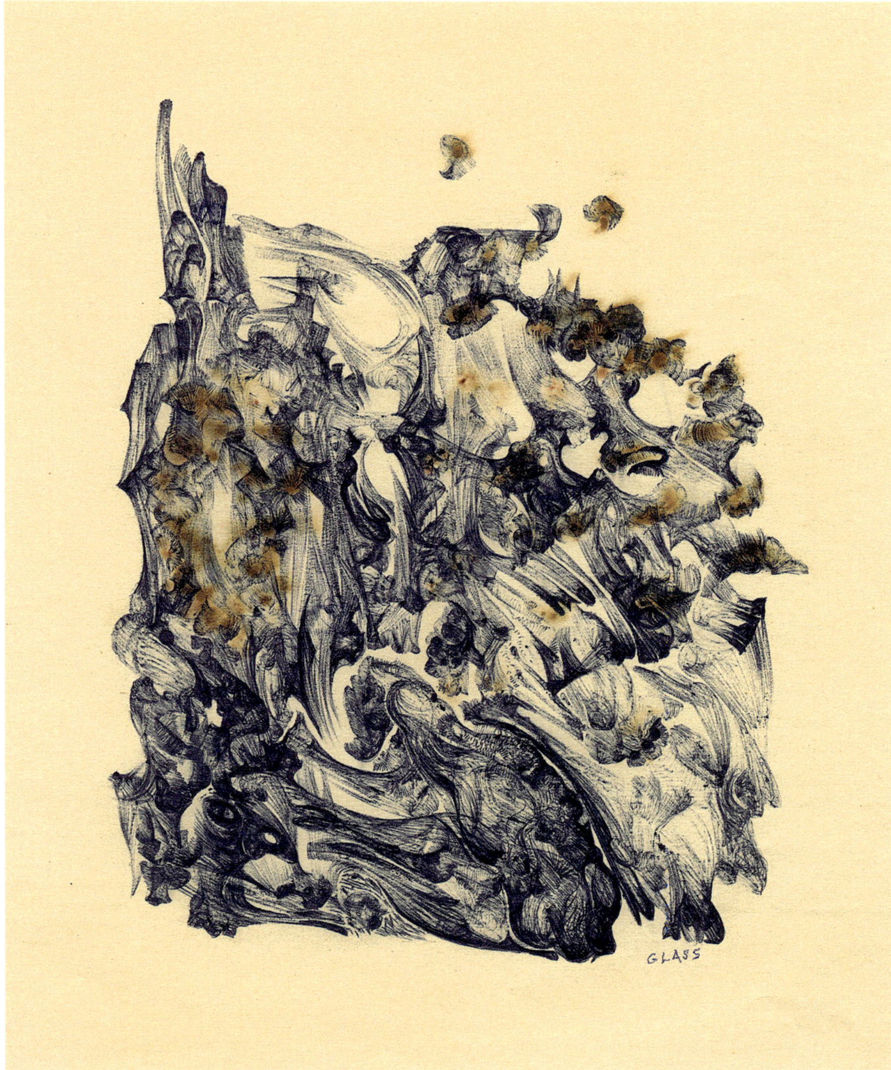

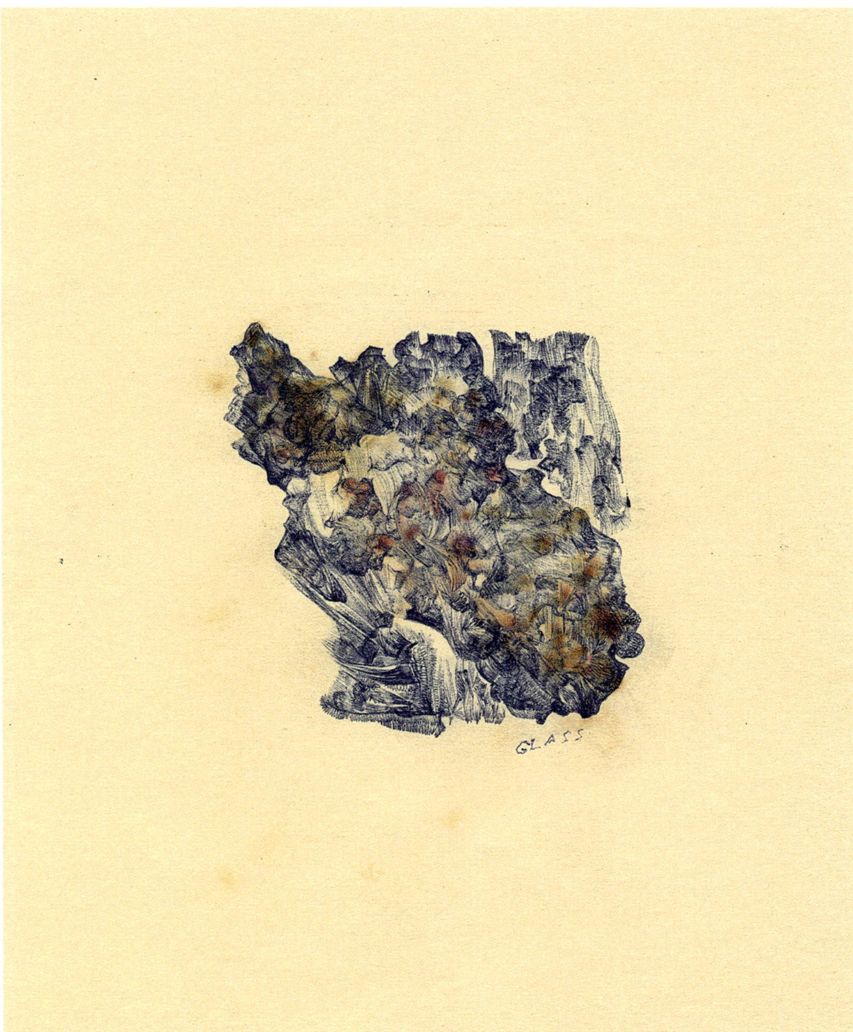

Untitled
(Club Saint-Germain period)
ca. 1954-1962
Monochrome blue ballpoint pen drawing with touches of allumettage, on paper.
28 x 22.5 cm
Artist's collection

Untitled
(Club Saint-Germain period)
ca. 1954-1962
Monochrome blue ballpoint pen drawing with touches of allumettage, on paper.
28 x 22.5 cm
Artist's collection

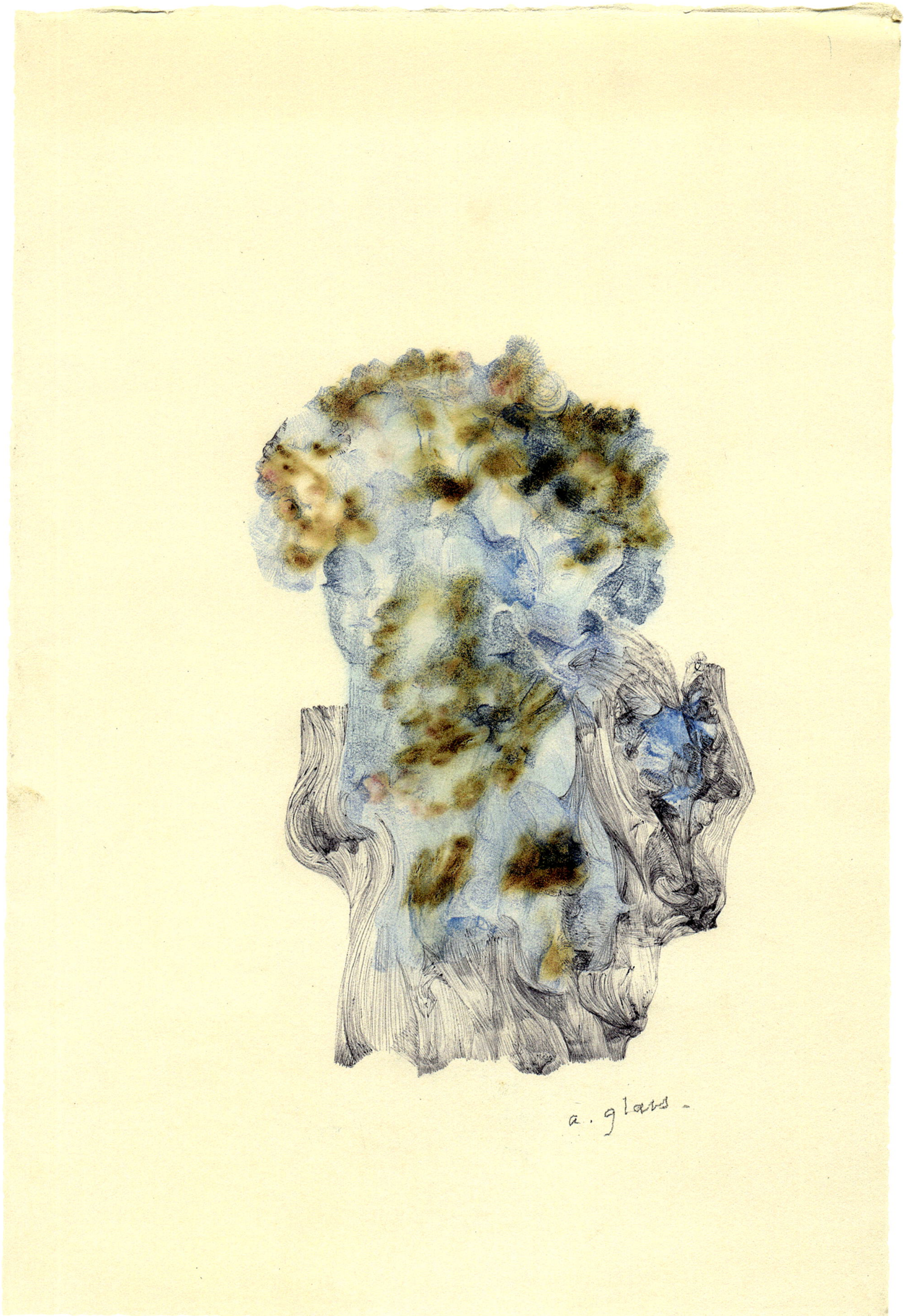

Untitled
(Club Saint-Germain period)
ca. 1954-1962
Monochrome navy blue ballpoint pen drawing and sky blue pencil, with touches of allumettage, on paper.
28 x 18.8 cm
Artist's collection

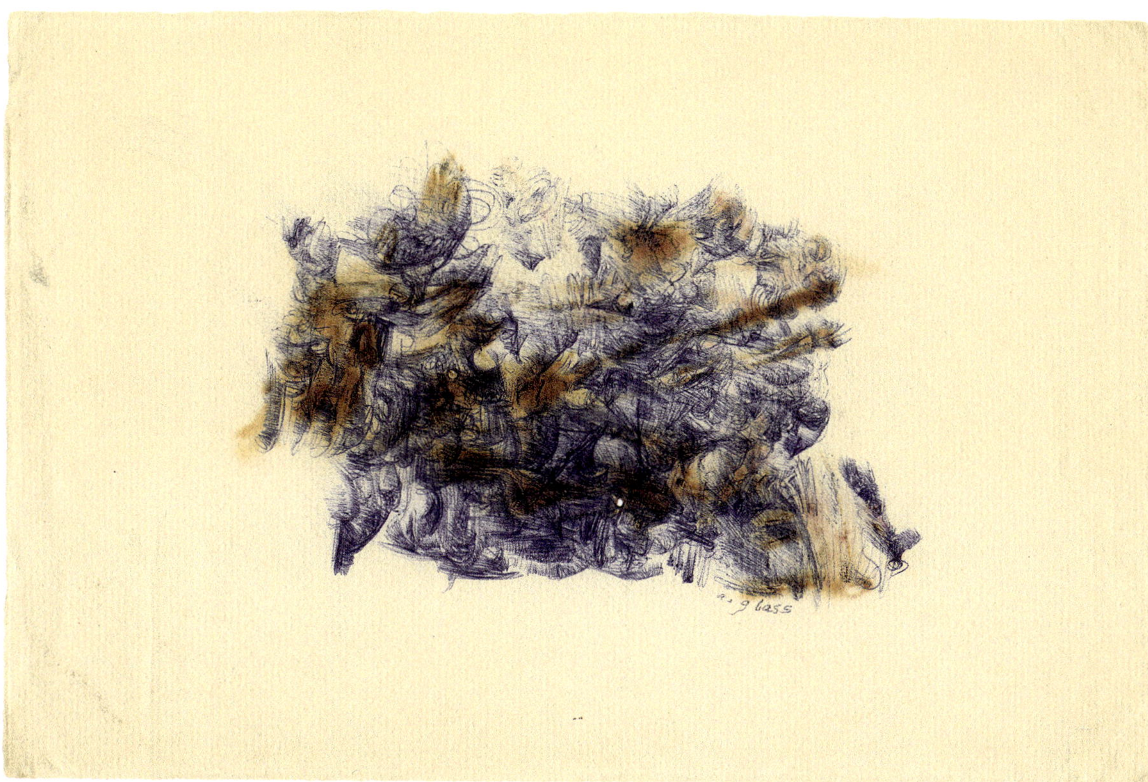

Untitled
(Club Saint-Germain period)
ca. 1954-1962
Touches of allumettage,
on paper.
24.5 x 15.8 cm
Artist's collection

Untitled
(Club Saint-Germain period)
ca. 1954-1962
Monochrome blue ballpoint
pen drawing with touches of
allumettage, on paper.
15.9 x 24.4 cm
Artist's collection

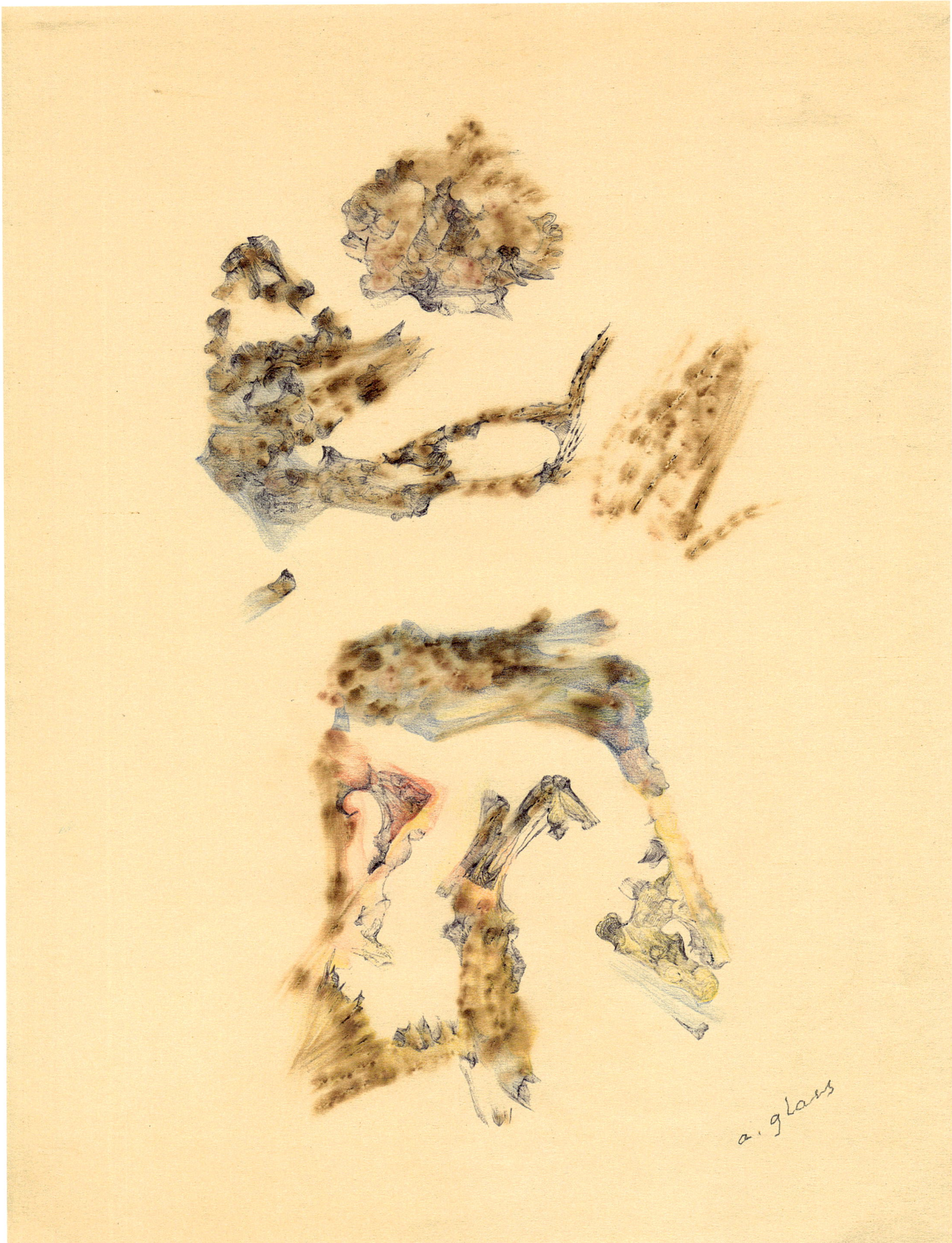

Untitled
(Club Saint-Germain period)
ca. 1954-1962
Drawing in blue monocolor ballpoint pen and blue and red colored pencil, with touches of allumettage, on paper.
28 x 22.5 cm
Artist's collection

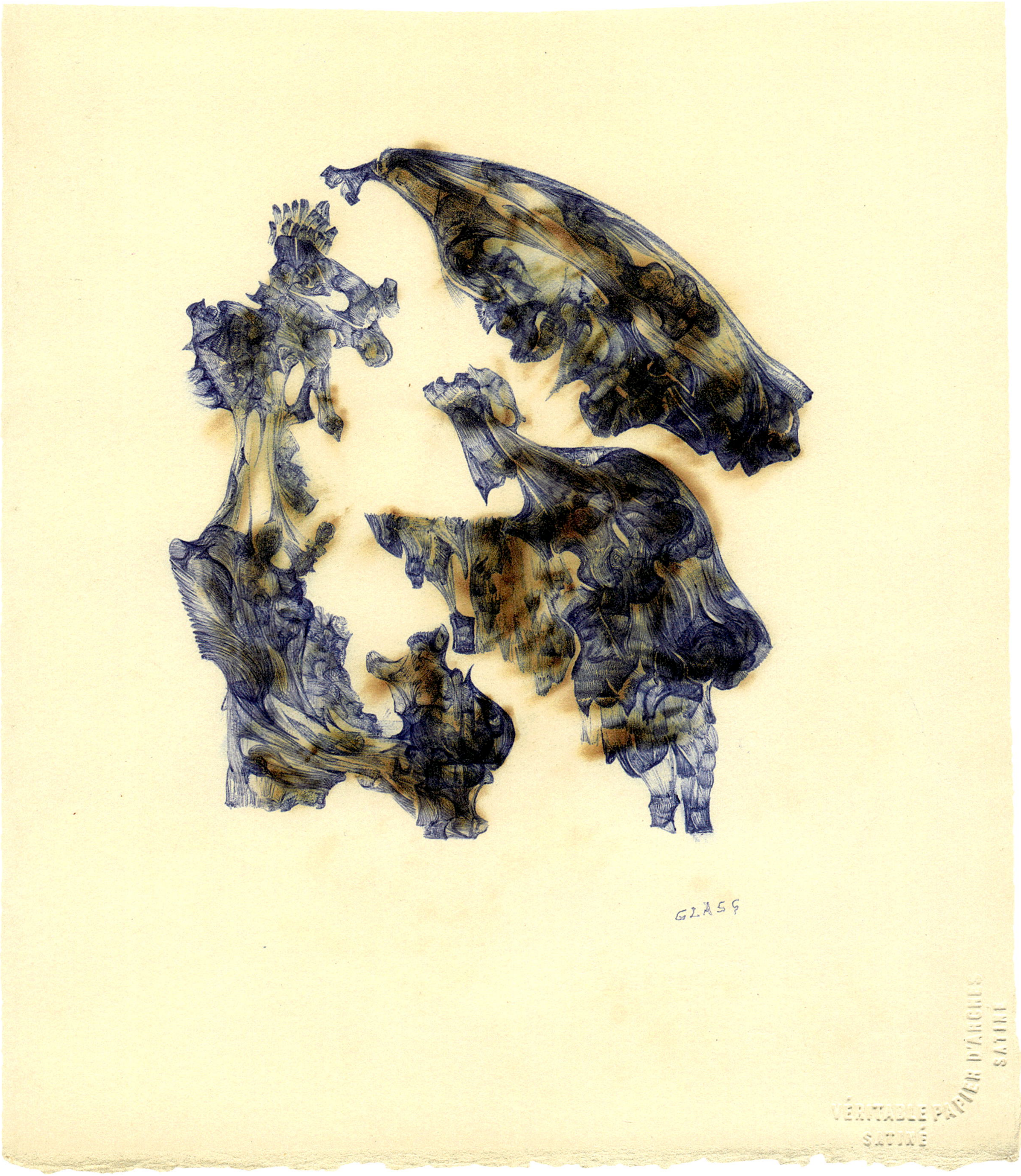

Untitled
(Club Saint-Germain period)
ca. 1954-1962
Monochrome blue ballpoint pen drawing with touches of allumettage, on paper.
21.7 x 19 cm
Artist's collection

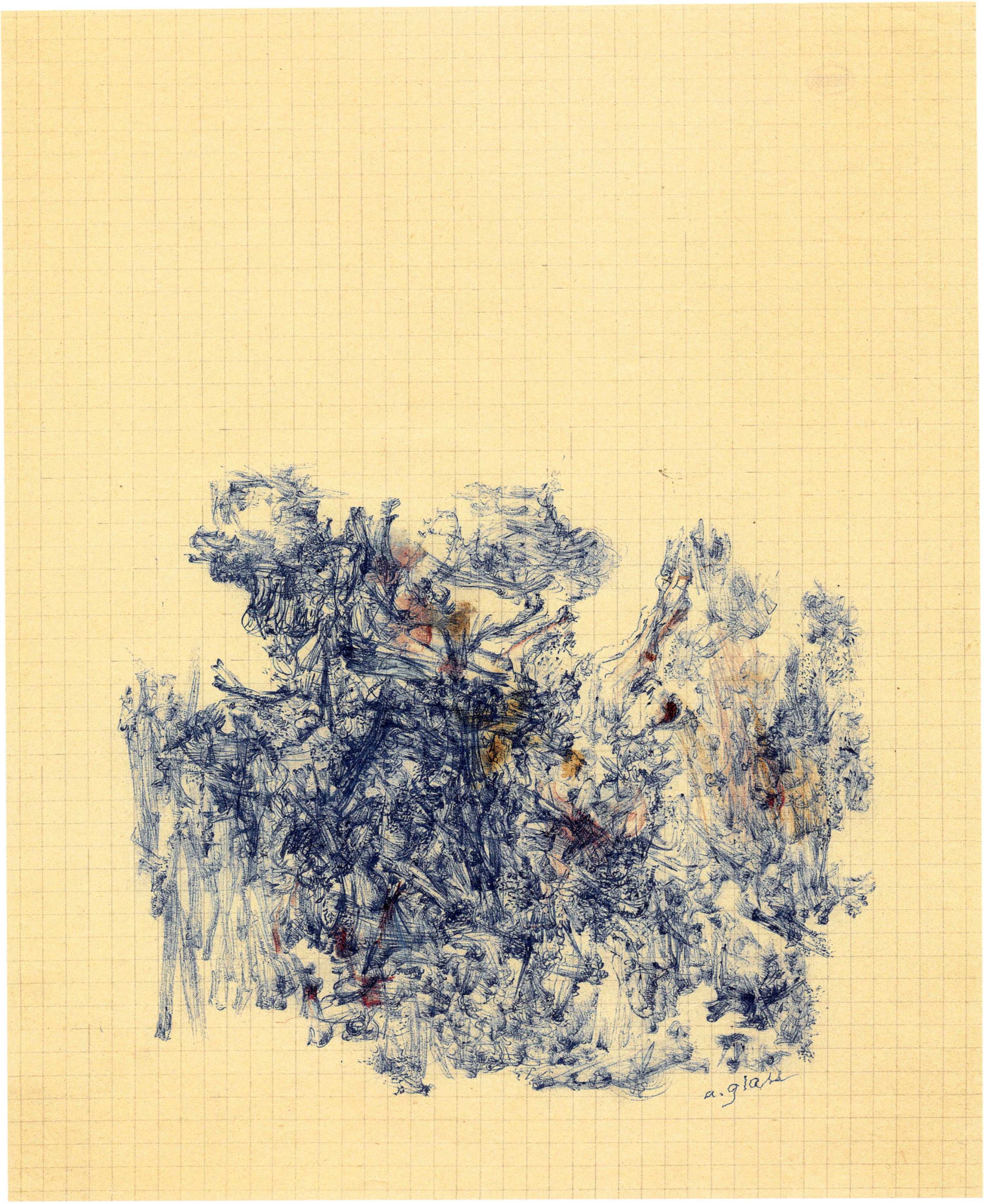

Untitled
(Club Saint-Germain period)
ca. 1954-1962
Monochrome blue ballpoint
pen drawing, with red
watercolor and a touch of
alumettage, on squared paper.
25.5 x 21 cm
Artist's collection

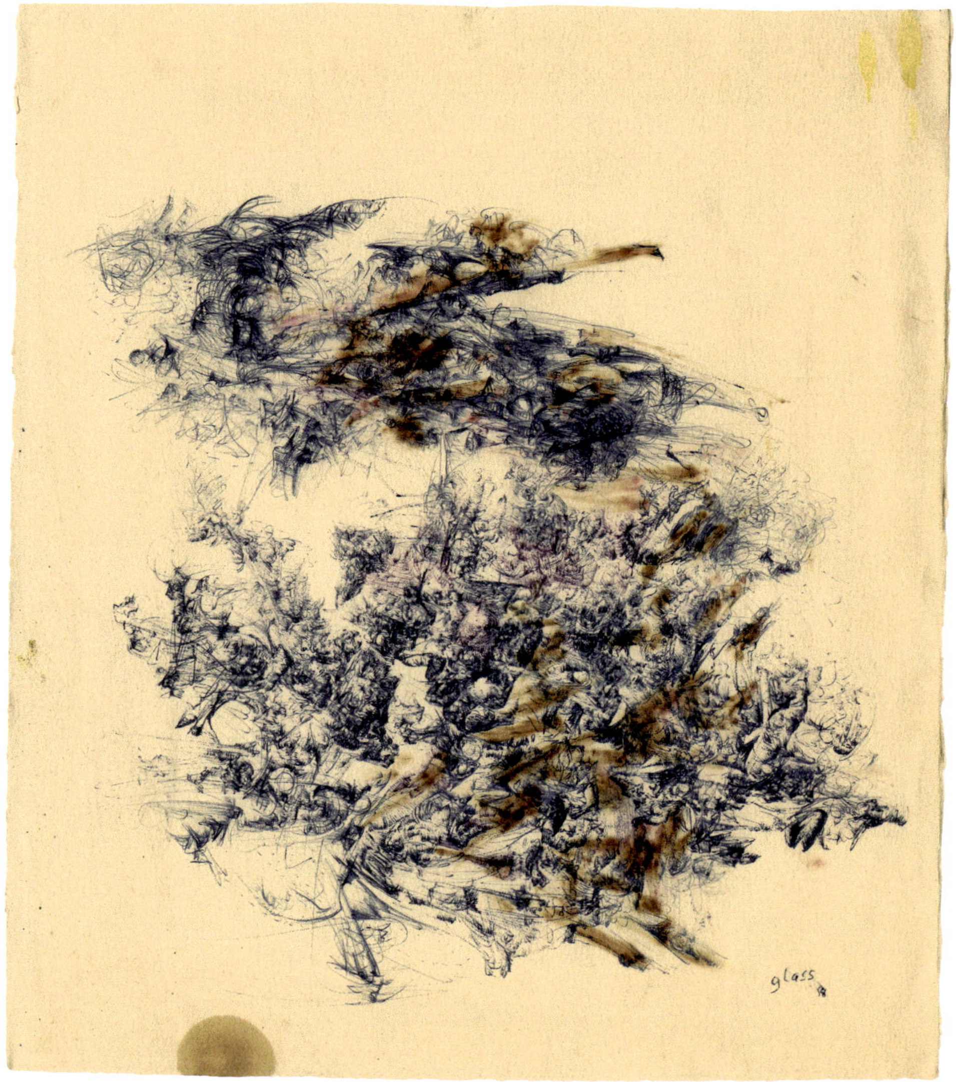

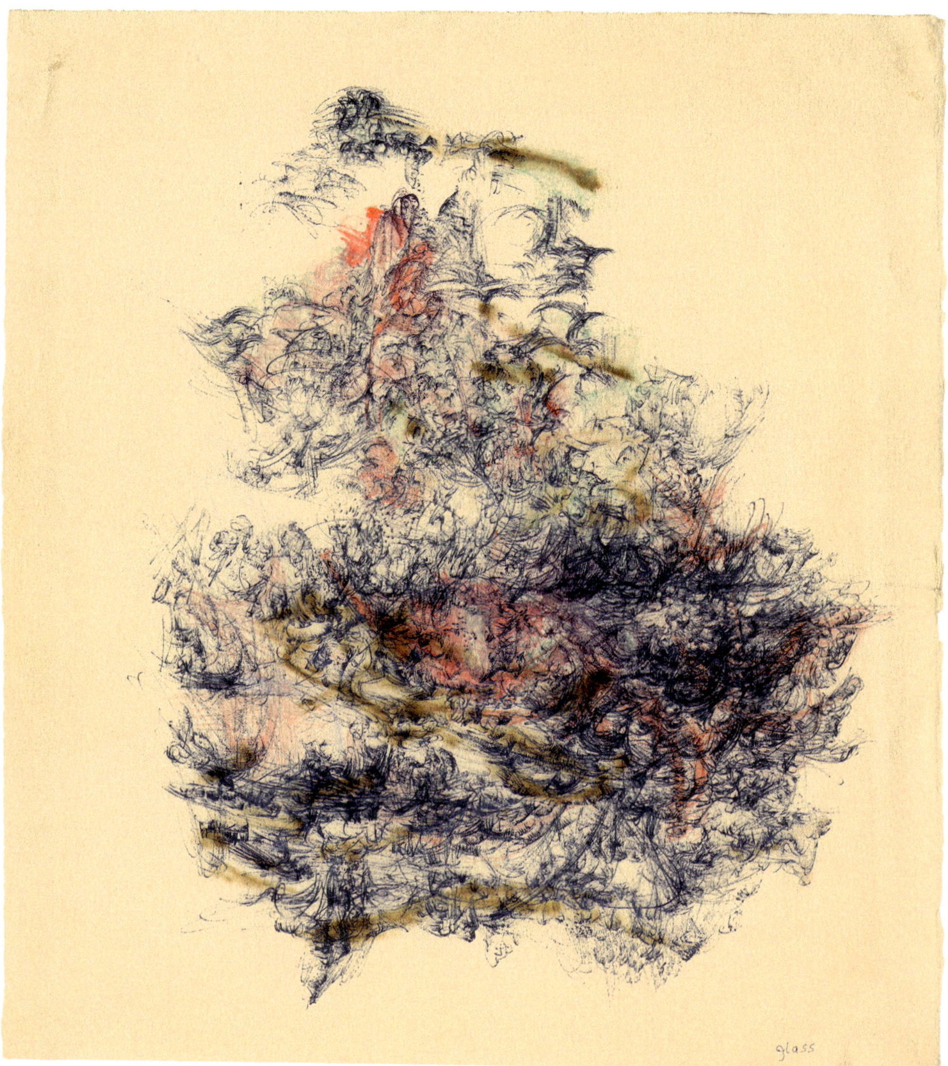

Untitled
(Club Saint-Germain period)
1958
Bicolor blue and purple ballpoint pen drawing with touches of allumettage, on paper.
31.6 x 28.3 cm
Artist's collection

Untitled
(Club Saint-Germain period)
ca. 1954-1962
Monochrome blue ballpoint pen drawing and orange and aqua pencil, with touches of allumettage, on paper.
31 x 28.3 cm
Artist's collection

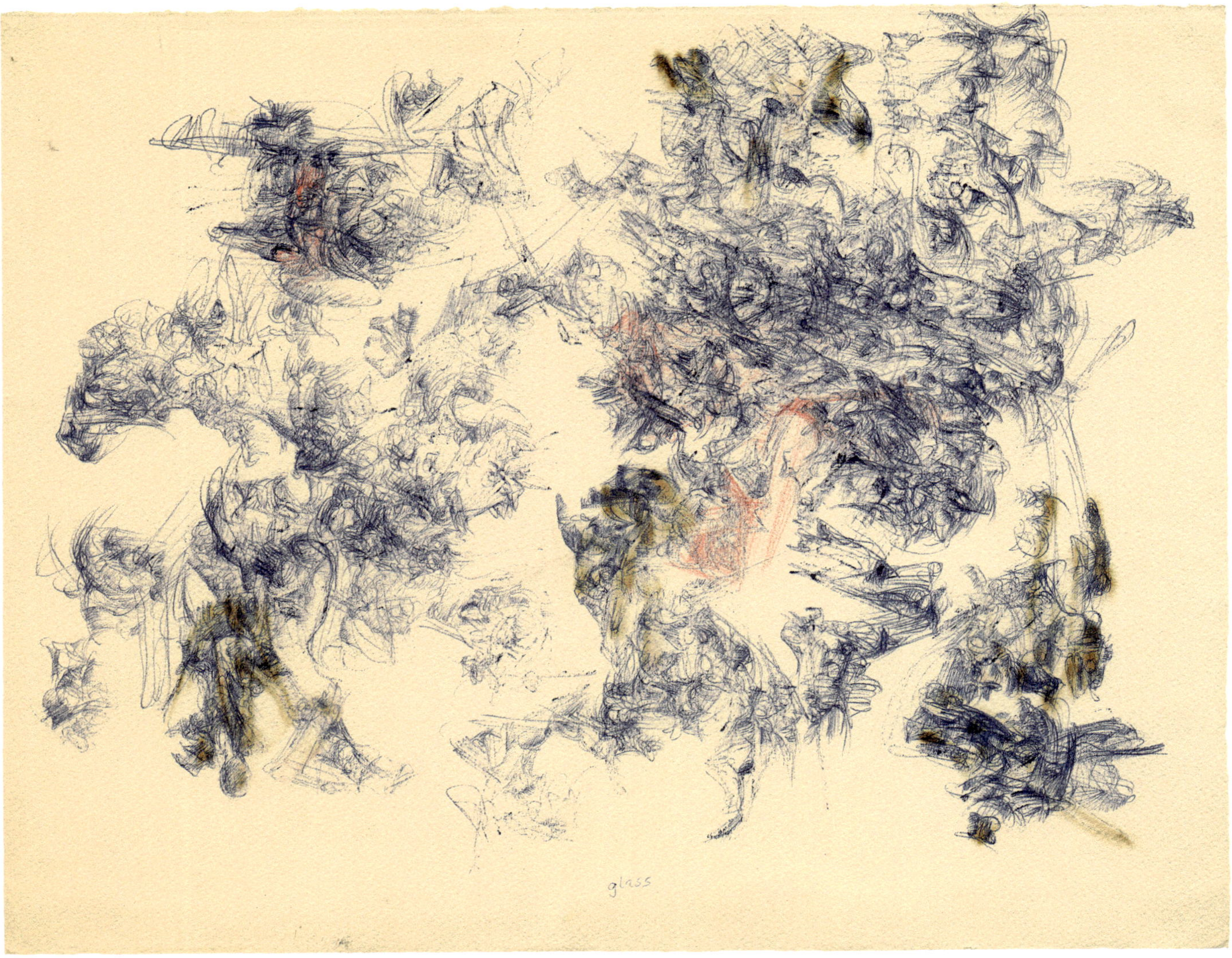

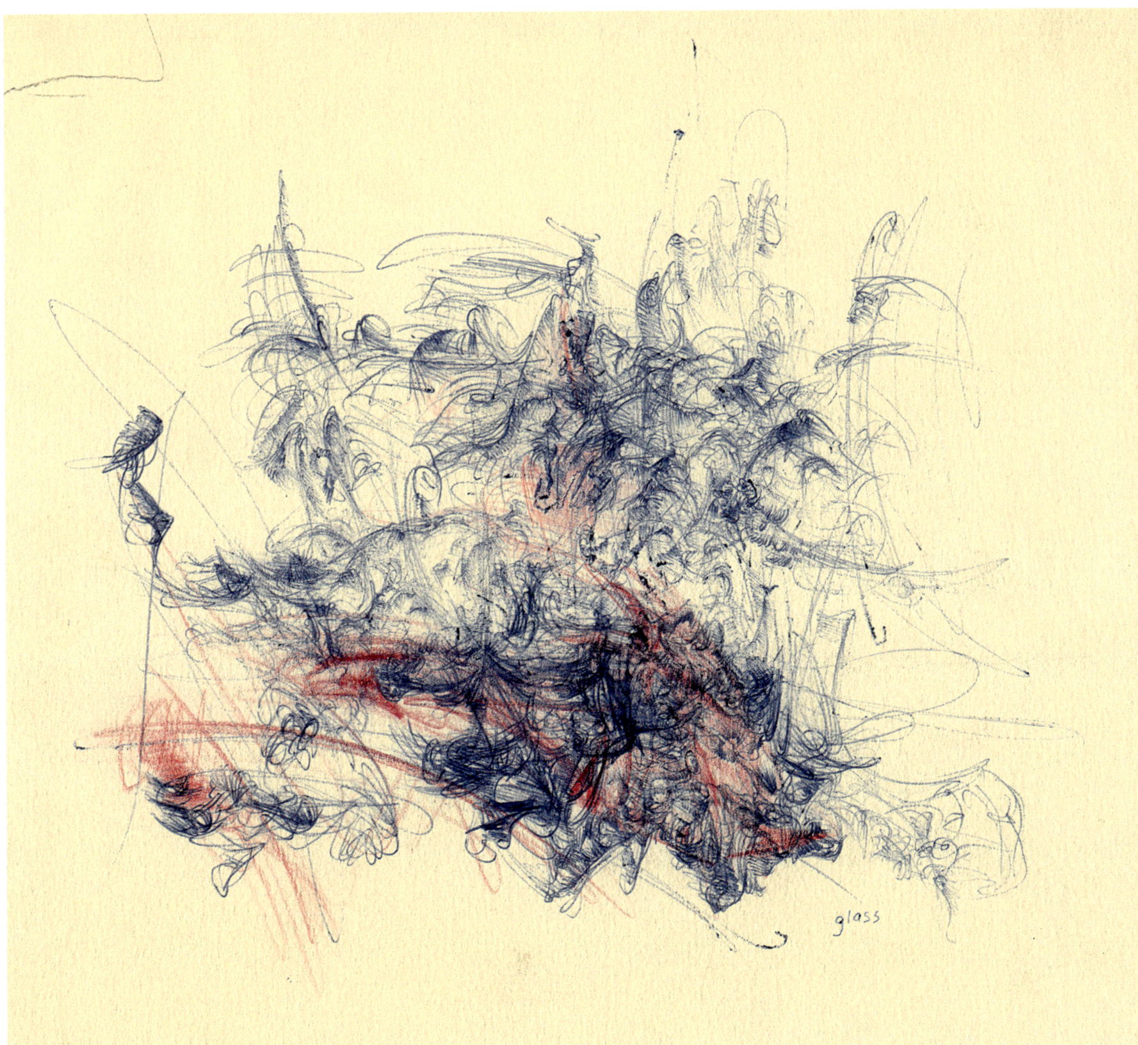

Untitled
(Club Saint-Germain period)
ca. 1954-1962
Monochrome blue ballpoint pen and orange pencil drawing, with touches of allumettage, on paper.
25 x 32.5 cm
Artist's collection

Untitled
(Club Saint-Germain period)
ca. 1954-1962
Monochrome blue ballpoint pen and red pencil drawing, on paper.
21 x 23.4 cm
Artist's collection

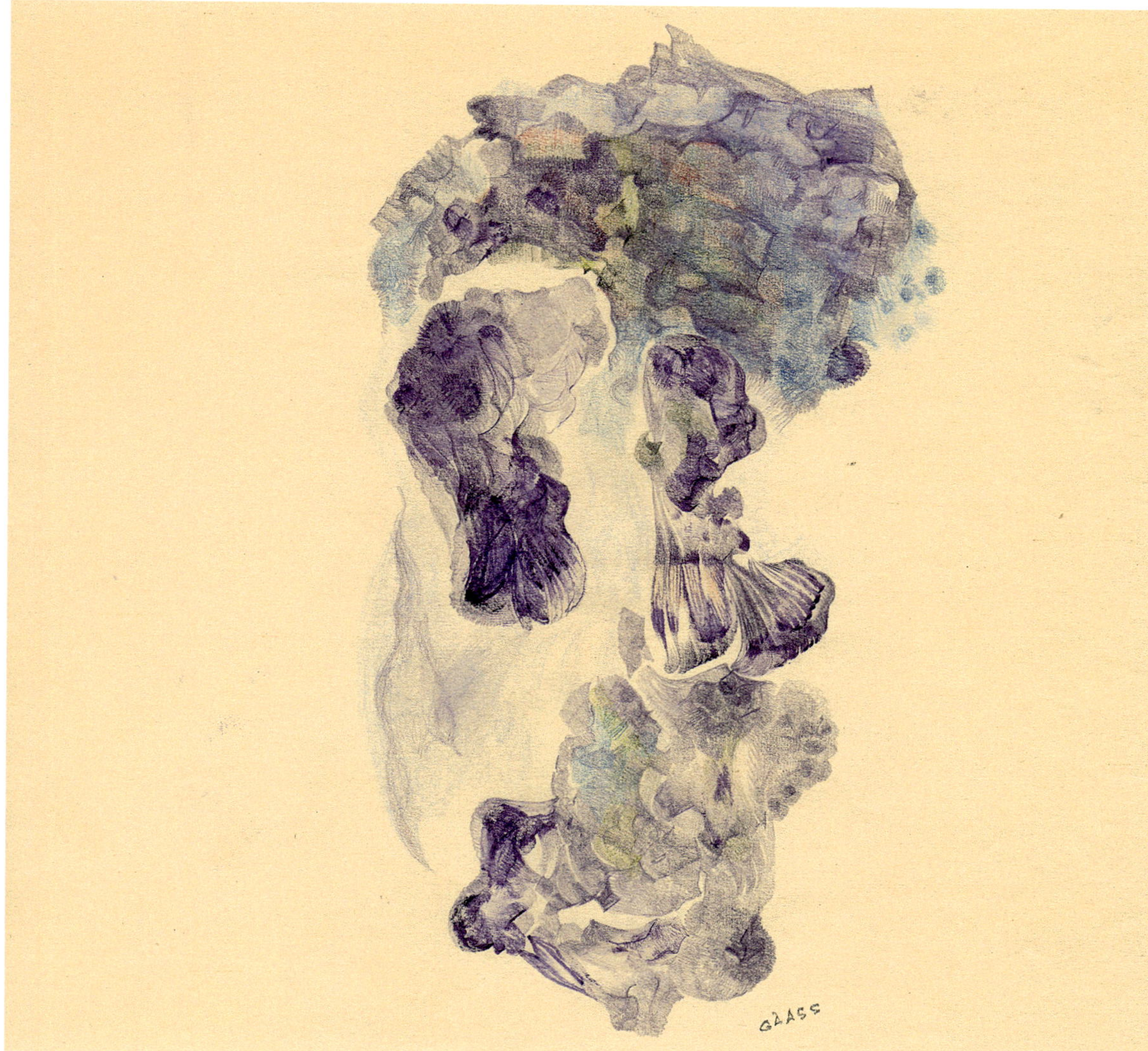

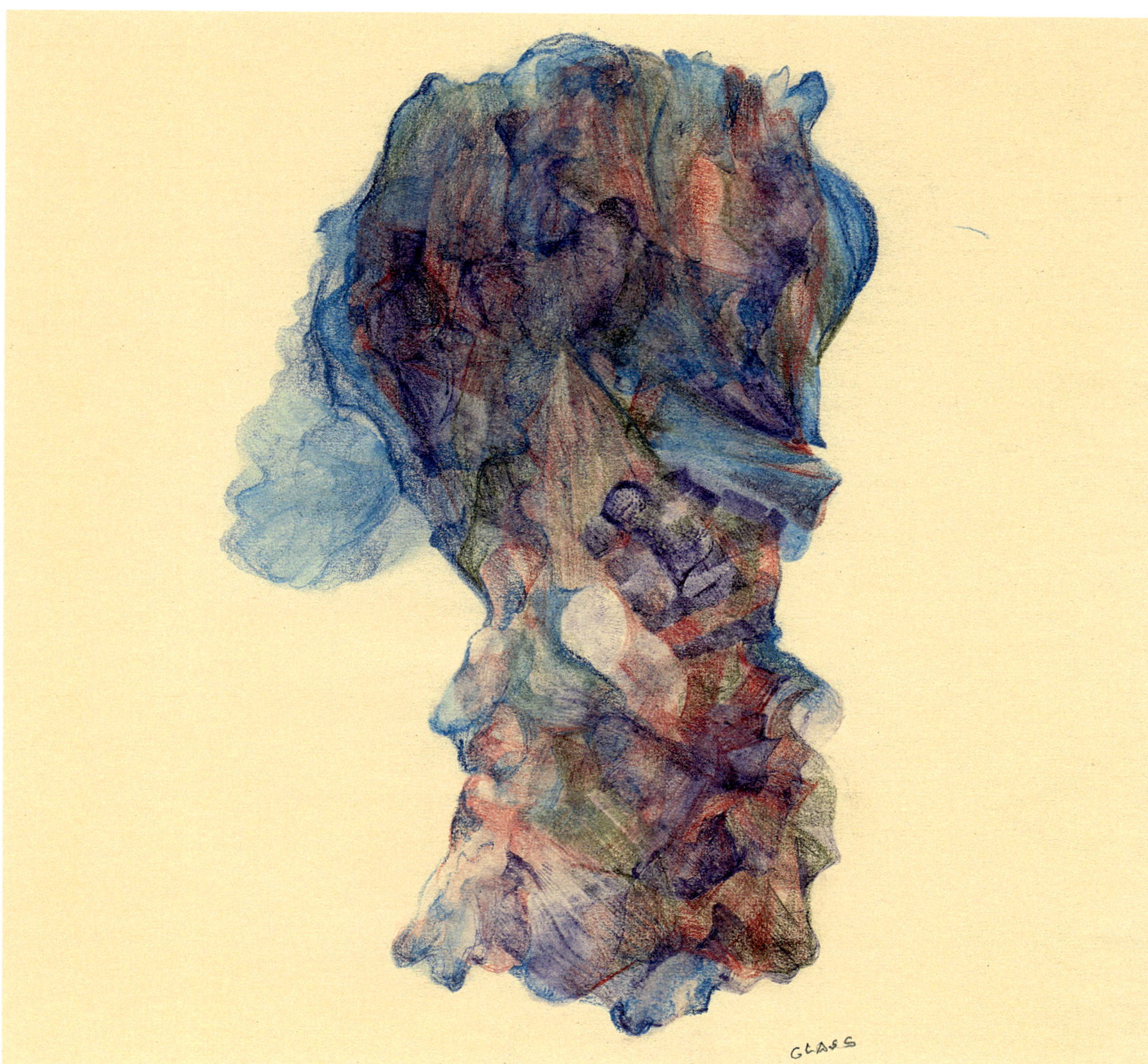

Untitled
(Club Saint-Germain period)
ca. 1954-1962
Monochrome purple ballpoint pen drawing with red, blue and green colored pencil, on paper.
28 x 22.6 cm
Artist's collection

Untitled
(Club Saint-Germain period)
ca. 1954-1962
Monochrome purple ballpoint pen drawing with blue, green, red and purple colored pencil, on paper.
28 x 22.8 cm
Artist's collection

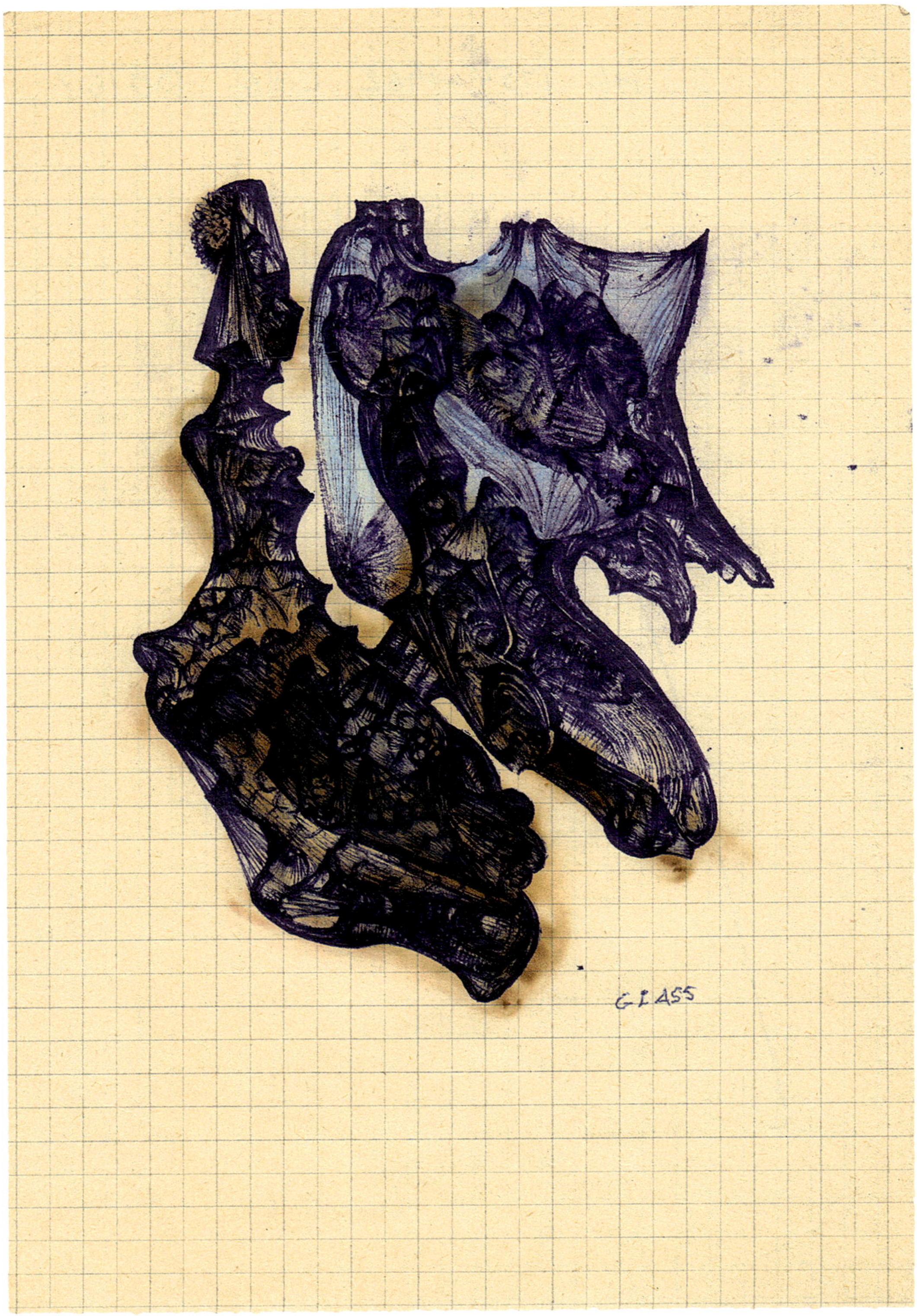

Untitled
(Club Saint-Germain period)
ca. 1954-1962
Bicolor blue and purple
ballpoint pen drawing with
touches of allumettage, on
squared paper.
19.5 x 13.5 cm
Artist's collection

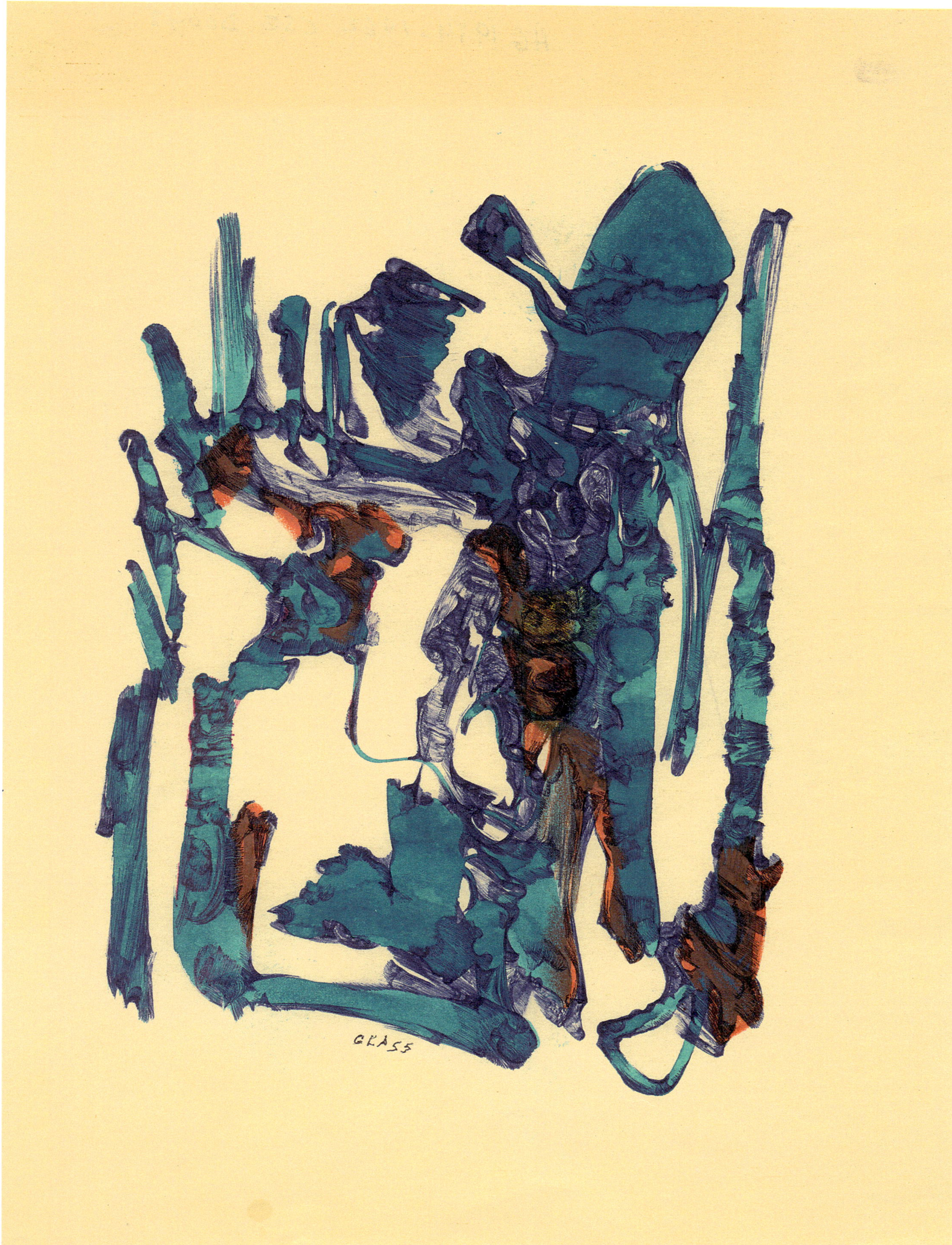

Untitled
(Club Saint-Germain period)
ca. 1954-1962
Blue pen drawing with blue and orange watercolor, on paper.
28 x 22.5 cm
Artist's collection

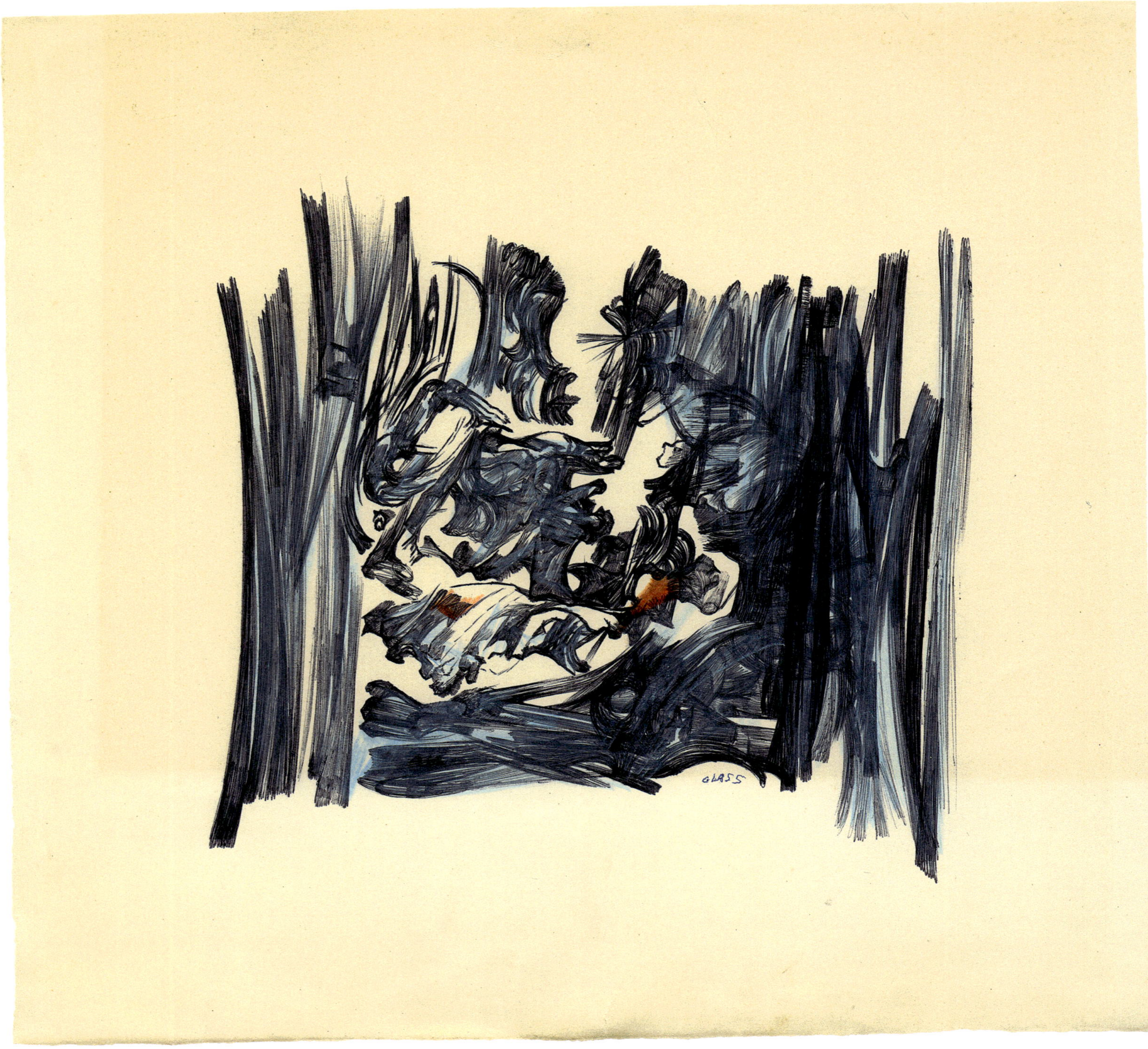

Untitled
(Club Saint-Germain period)
ca. 1954-1962
Monochrome black ballpoint pen drawing with orange and sky blue pencil, on paper.
25 x 27.6 cm
Artist's collection

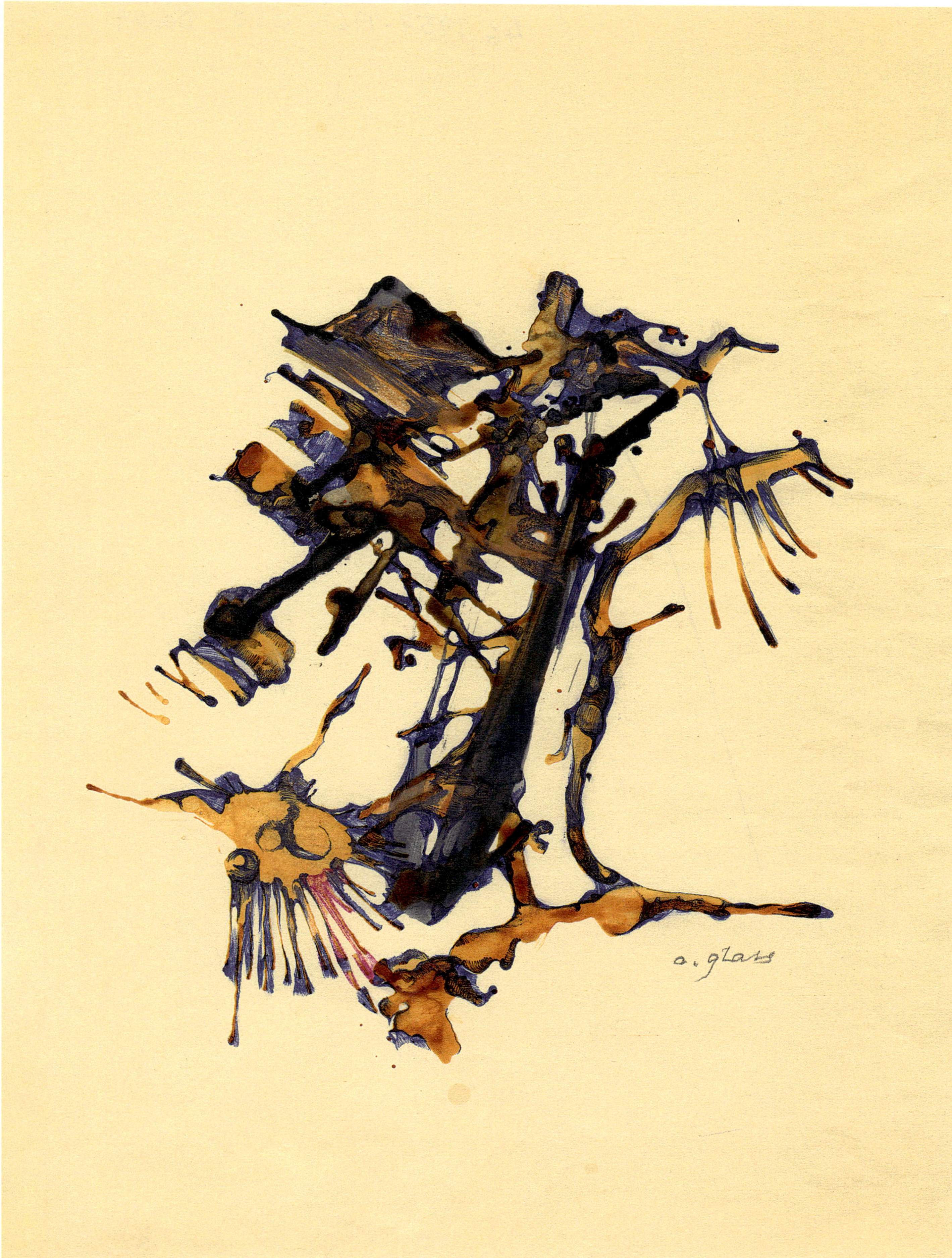

Untitled
(Club Saint-Germain period)
ca. 1954-1962
Bicolor blue and red ballpoint pen drawing, with black and brown watercolor, on paper.
28 x 22.5 cm
Artist's collection

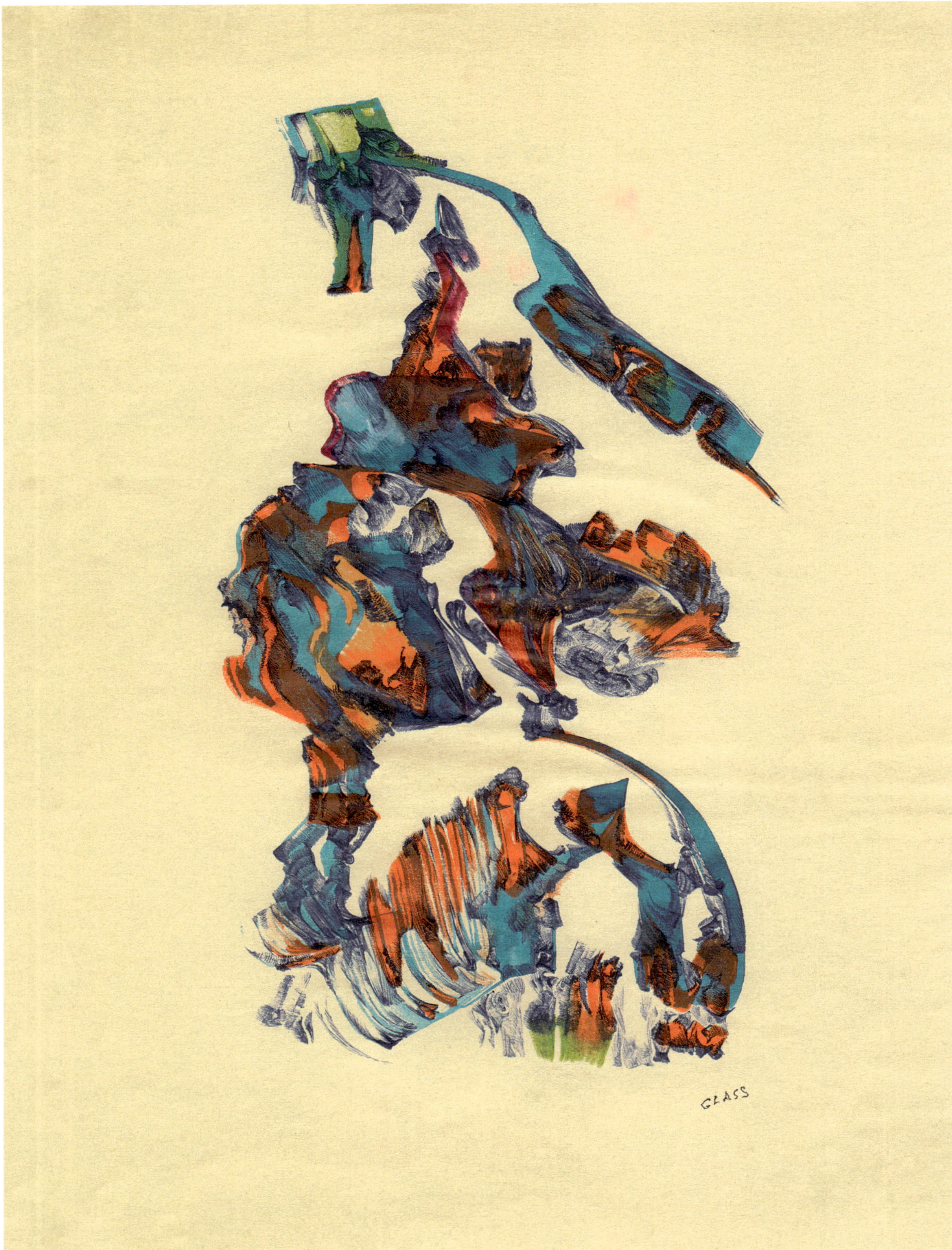

Untitled
(Club Saint-Germain period)
ca. 1954-1962
Drawing in blue pen, with red and green watercolor, on paper.
28 x 22.5 cm
Artist's collection

Untitled
(Club Saint-Germain period)
ca. 1954-1962
Drawing in ballpoint blue pen with green and red watercolor, on paper.
28 x 22.5 cm
Artist's collection
Following page

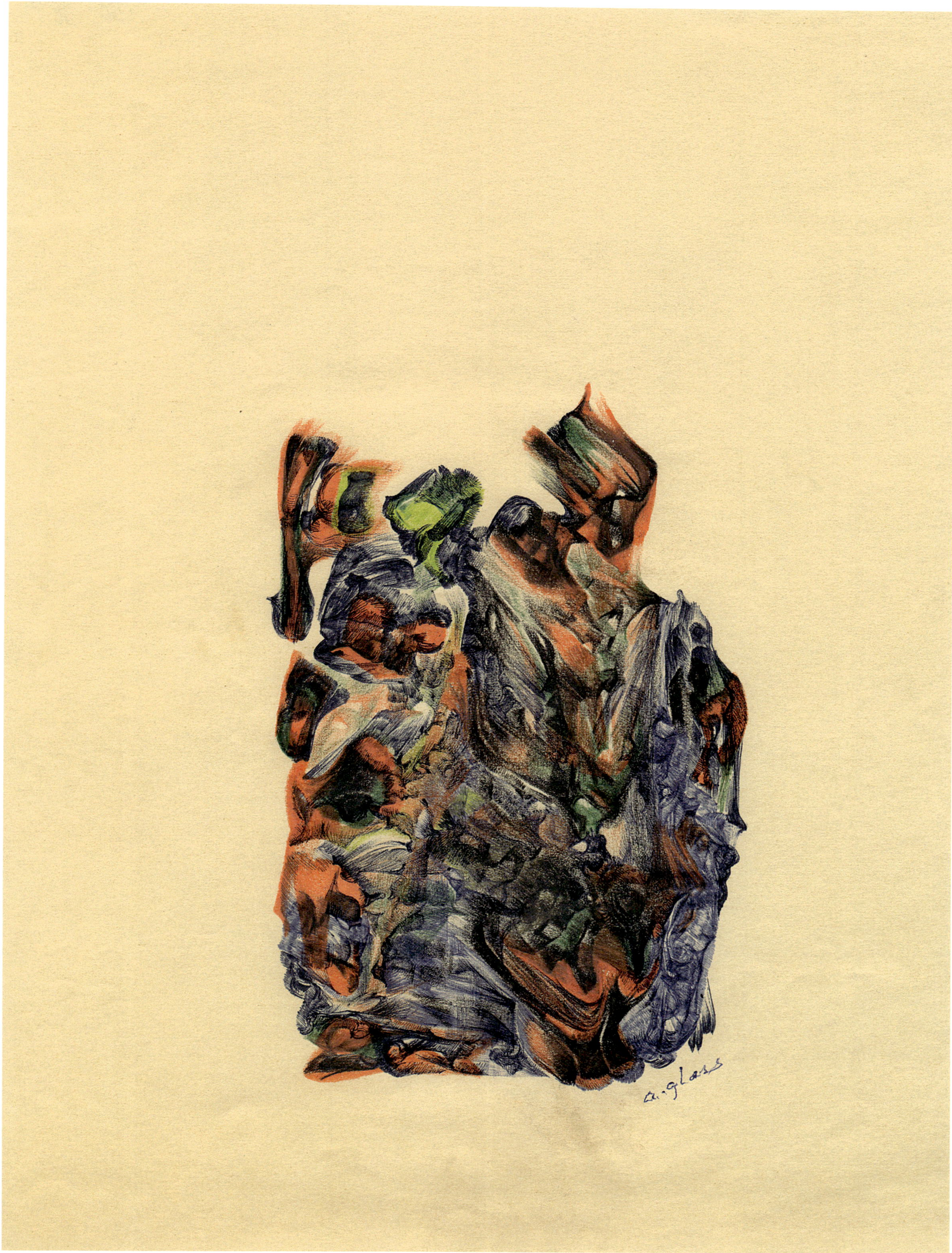
a. glass

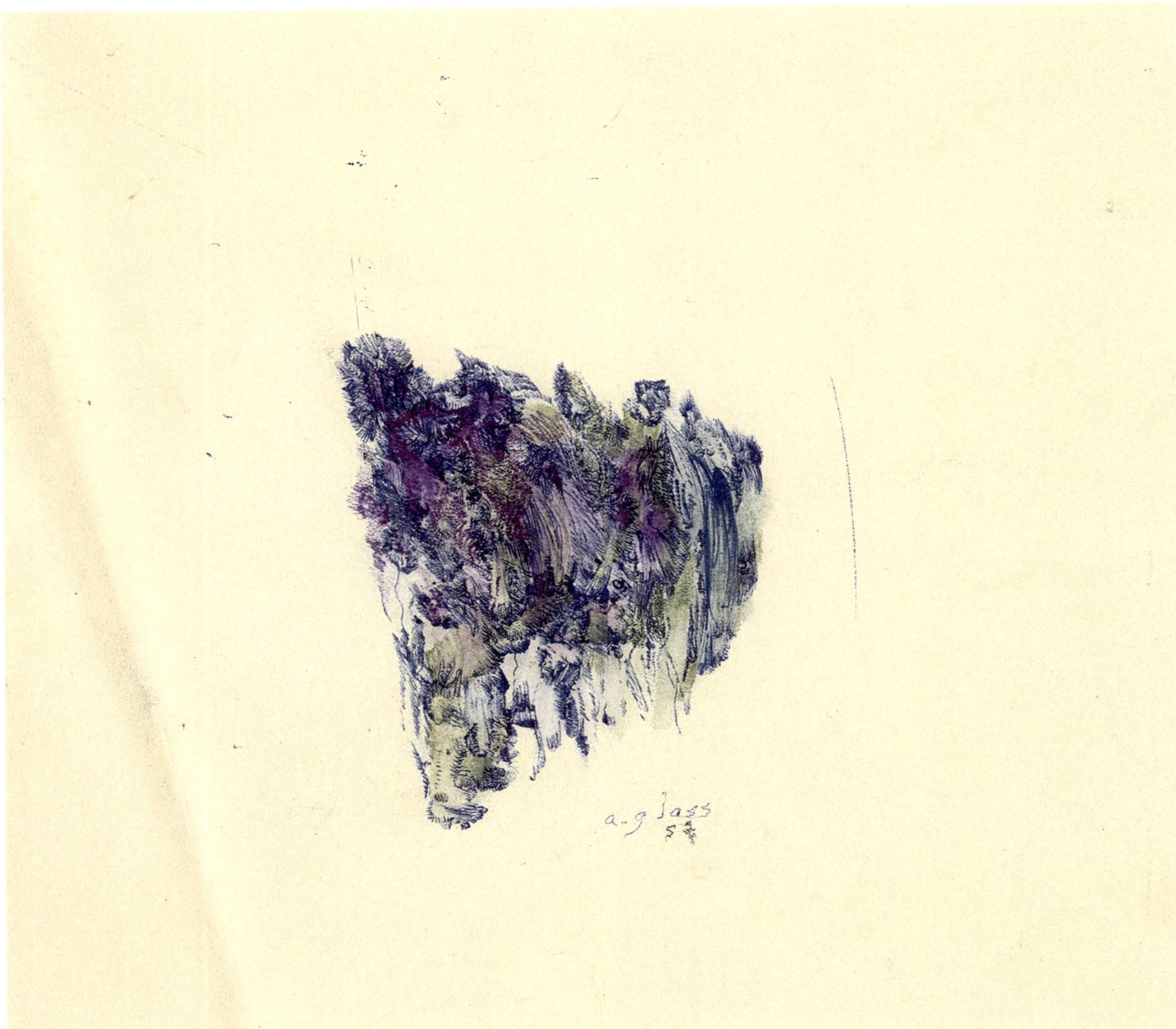

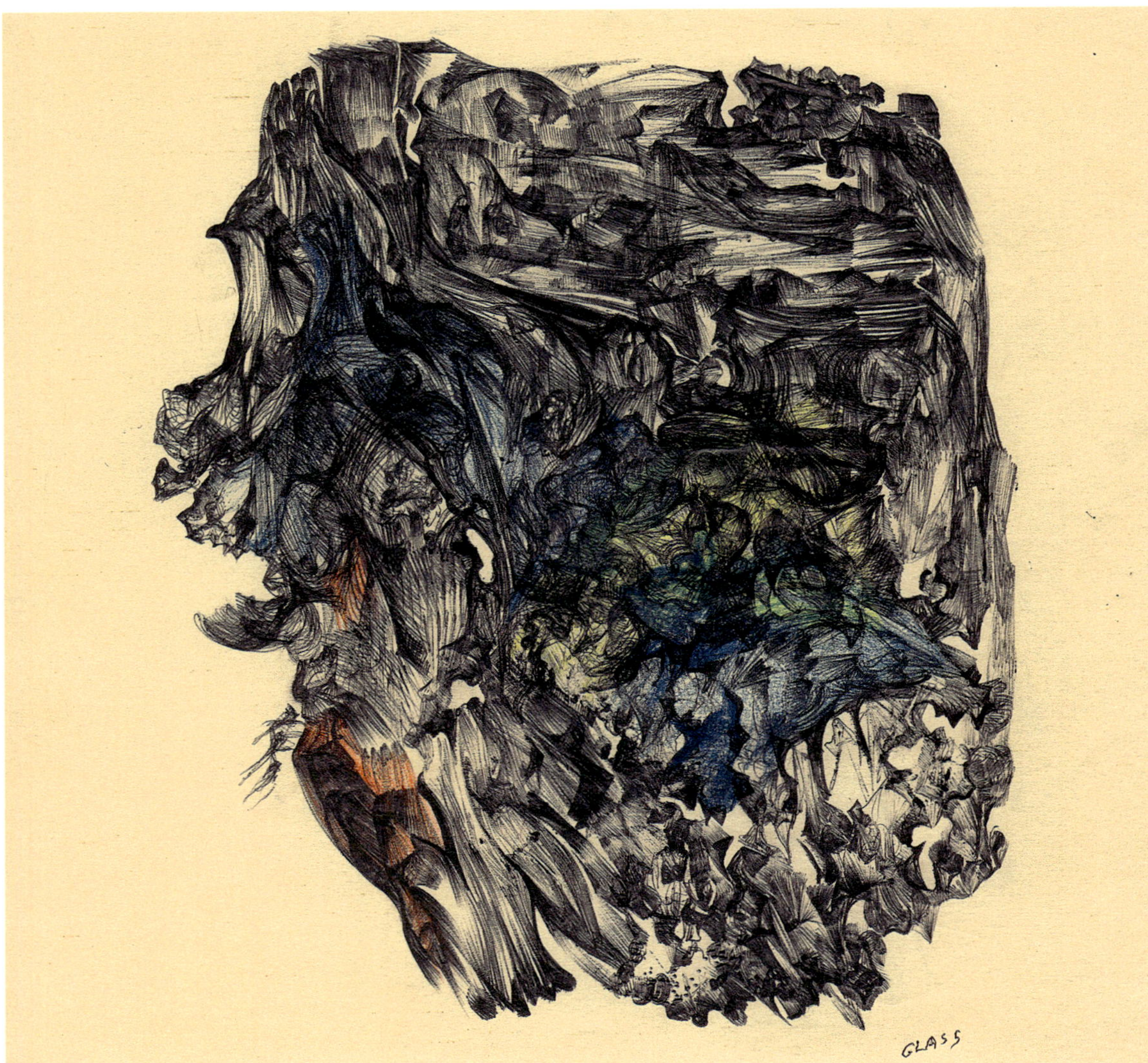

Untitled
(Club Saint-Germain period)
1959
Monochrome blue ballpoint pen drawing with purple, green and blue pencil, on paper.
28.6 x 25 cm
Artist's collection

Untitled
(Club Saint-Germain period)
ca. 1954-1962
Monochrome black ballpoint pen drawing with orange, blue and green pencil, on paper.
28 x 22.8 cm
Artist's collection

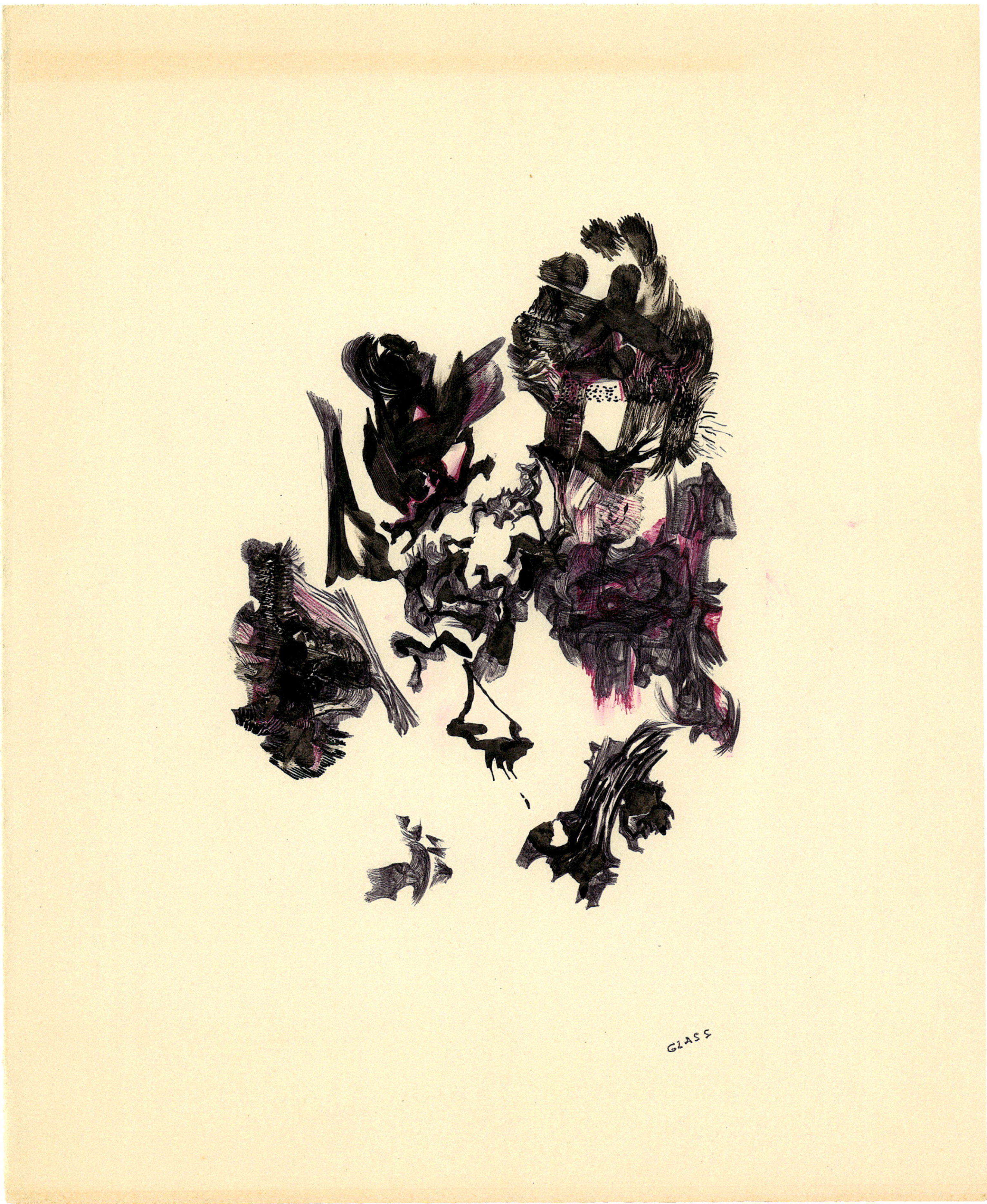

Untitled
(Club Saint-Germain period)
ca. 1954-1962
Bicolor black and pink
ballpoint pen drawing with
touches of Indian ink,
on paper.
29.8 x 25 cm
Artist's collection

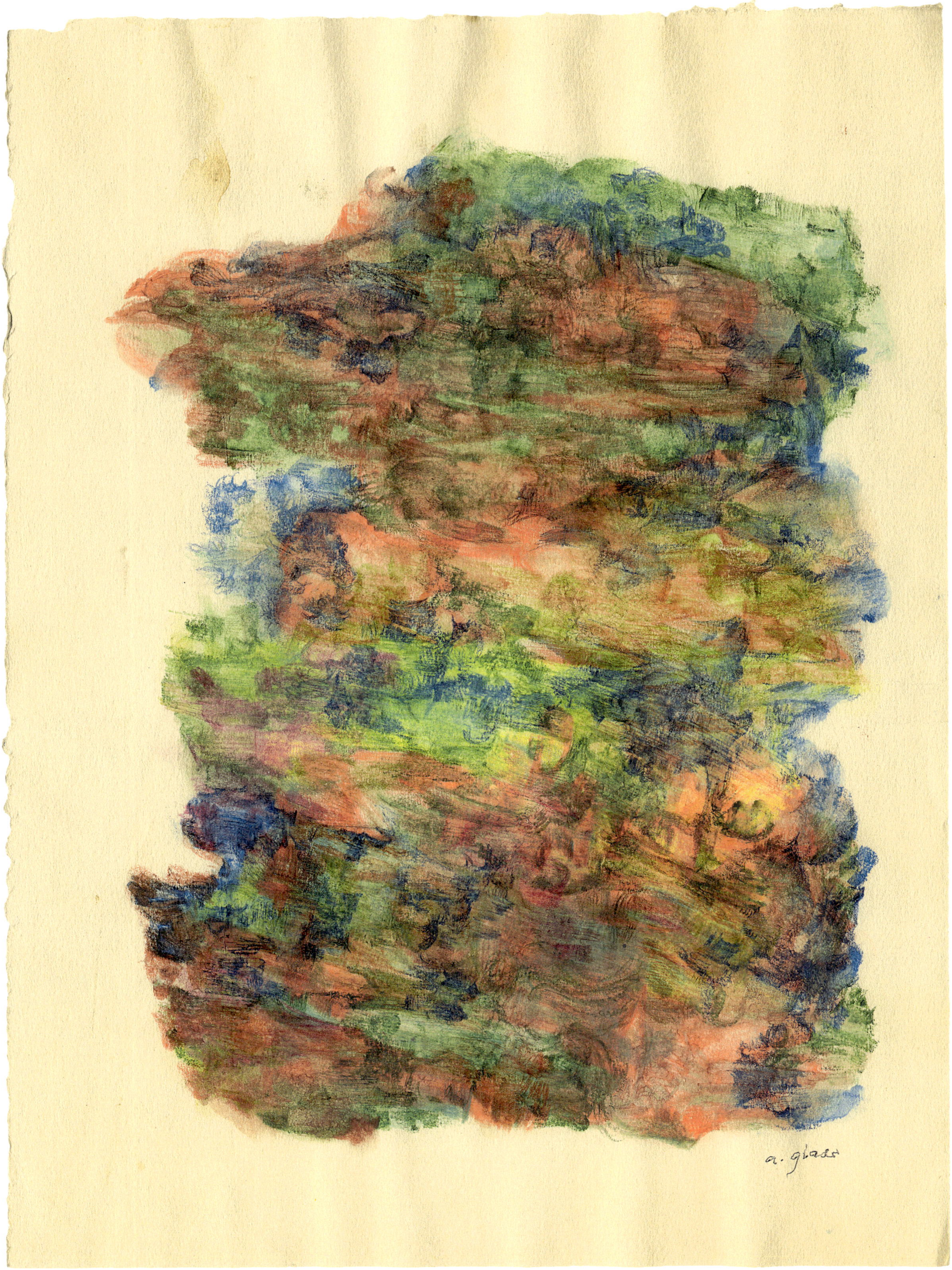
a. glass

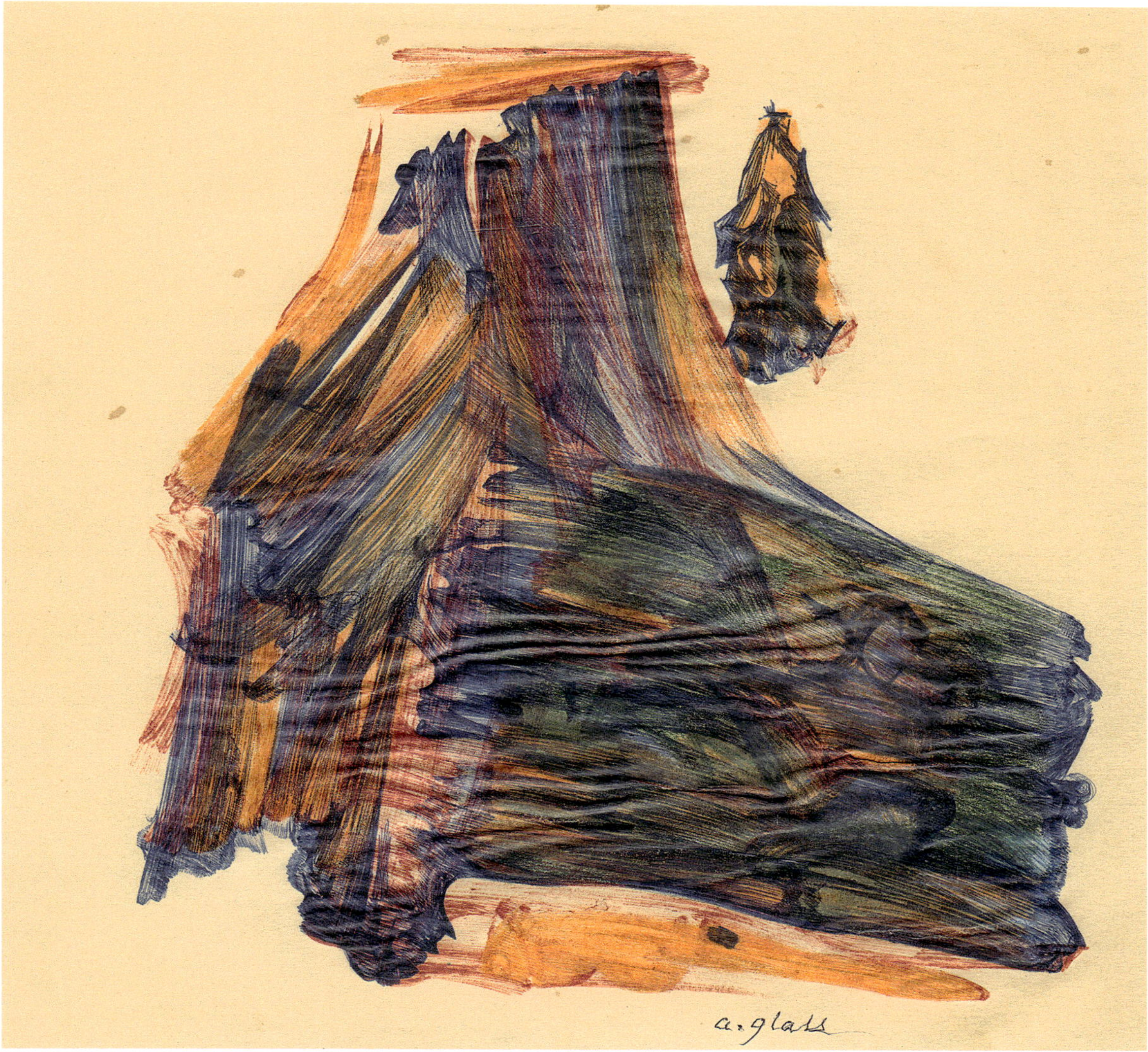

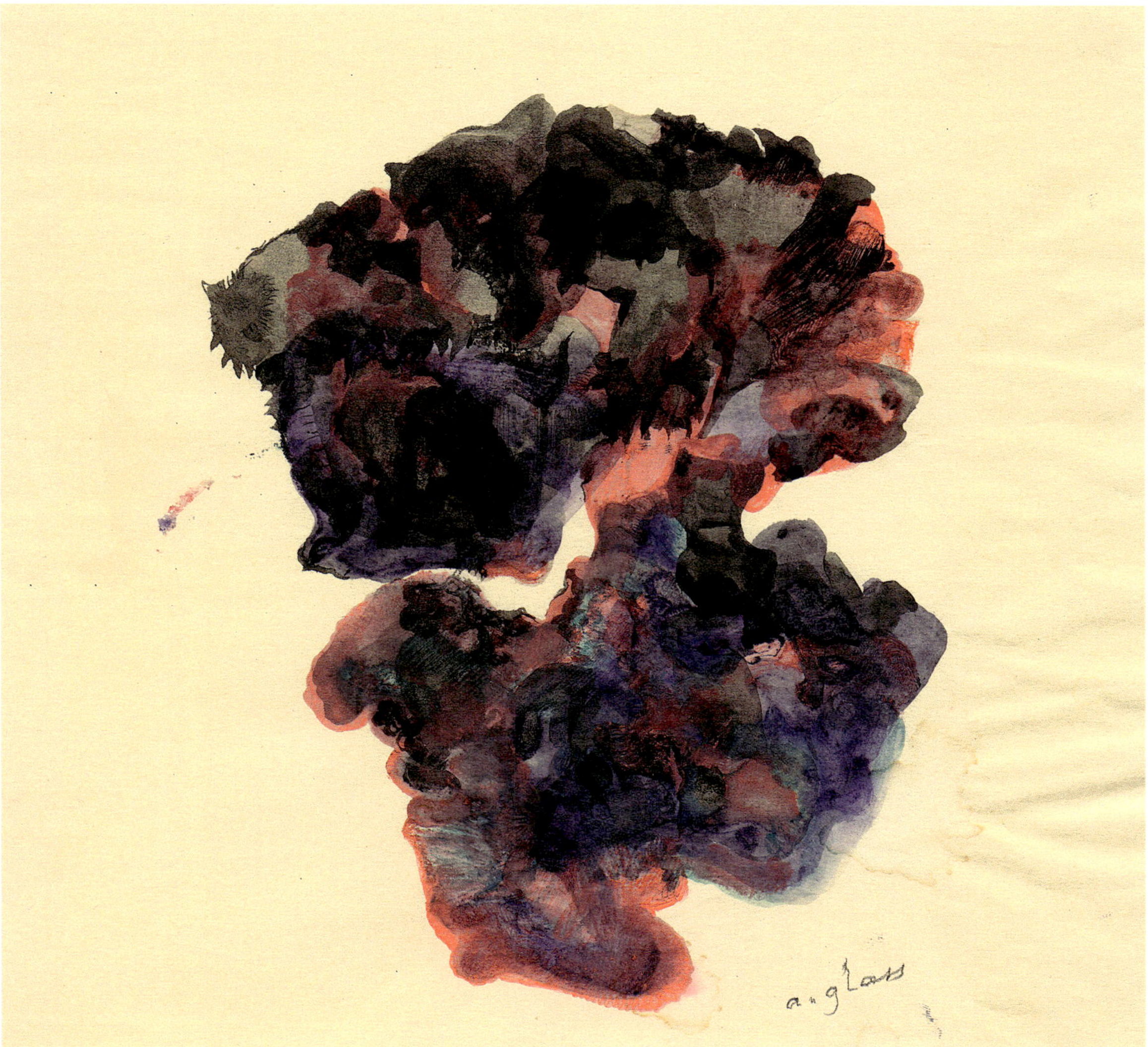

Untitled
(Club Saint-Germain period)
ca. 1954-1962
Blue, orange, green and yellow watercolor drawing, on paper.
32.8 x 25 cm
Artist's collection
Previous page

Untitled
(Club Saint-Germain period)
ca. 1954-1962
Bicolor blue and red ballpoint pen drawing, with orange, green and blue colored pencil, on paper.
28 x 22.6 cm
Artist's collection

Untitled
(Club Saint-Germain period)
ca. 1954-1962
Black, orange, purple and aqua watercolor drawing on paper.
28 x 25.6 cm
Artist's collection

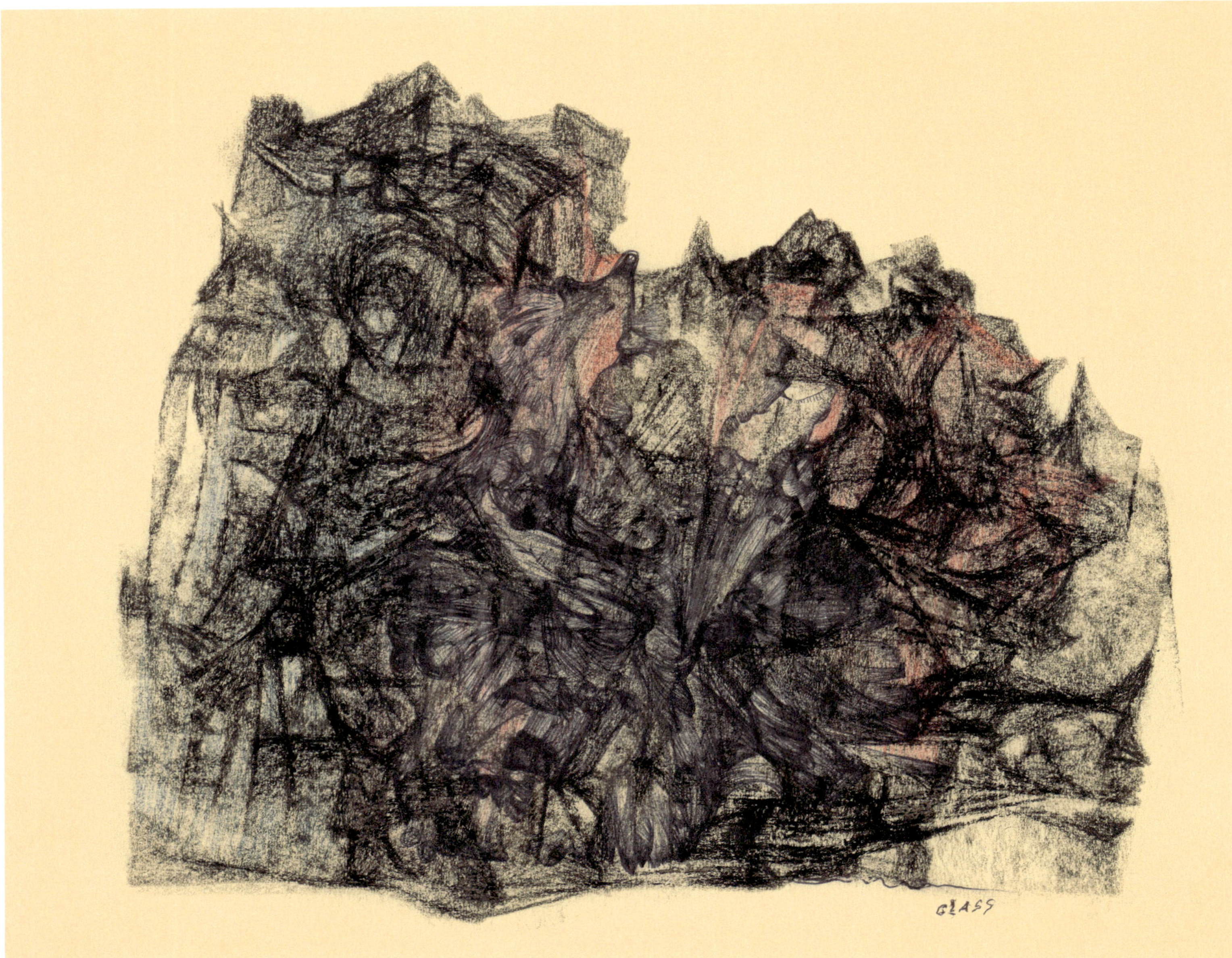

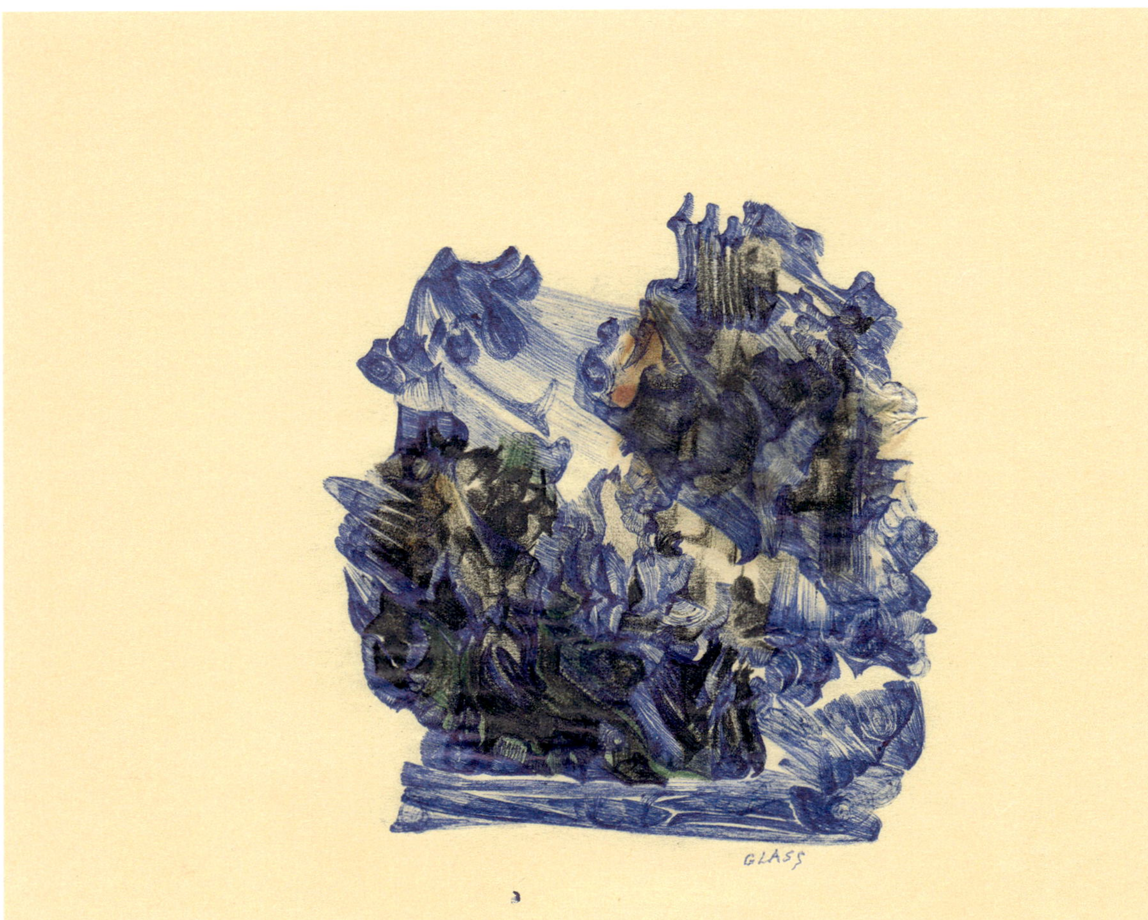

Untitled
(Club Saint-Germain period)
ca. 1954-1962
Monochrome black ballpoint pen drawing with red, blue and black pencil, on paper.
22.5 x 28 cm
Artist's collection

Untitled
(Club Saint-Germain period)
ca. 1954-1962
Monochrome blue ballpoint pen drawing with olive green and grass green pencil, with a touch of allumettage, on paper.
28 x 25 cm
Artist's collection

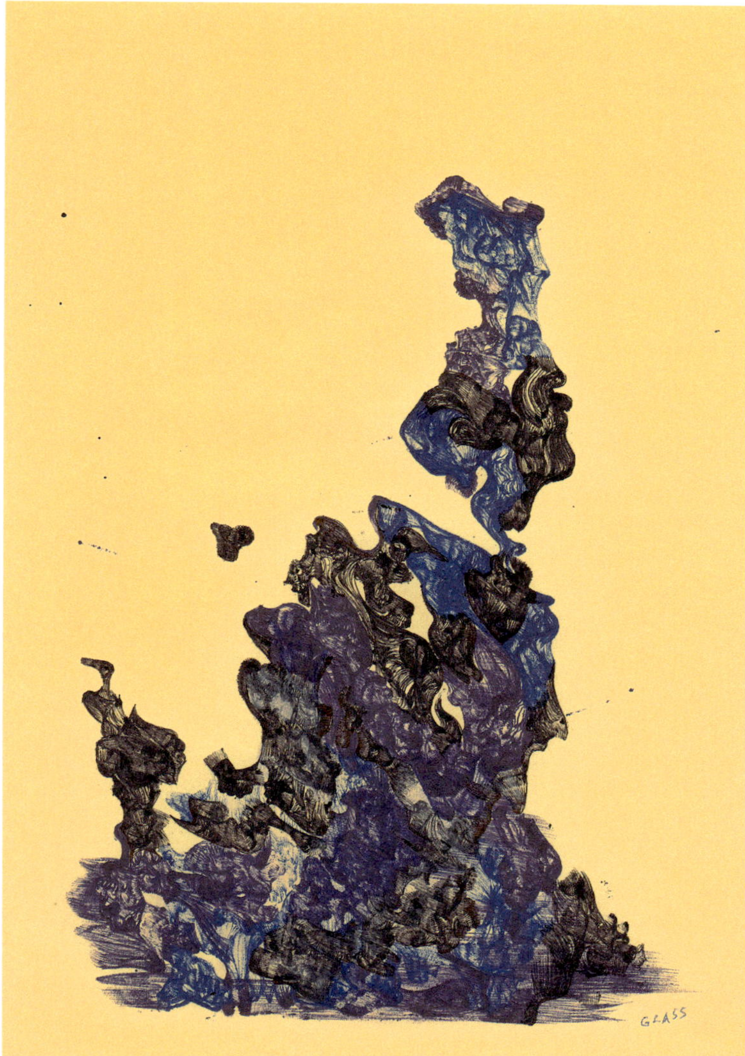

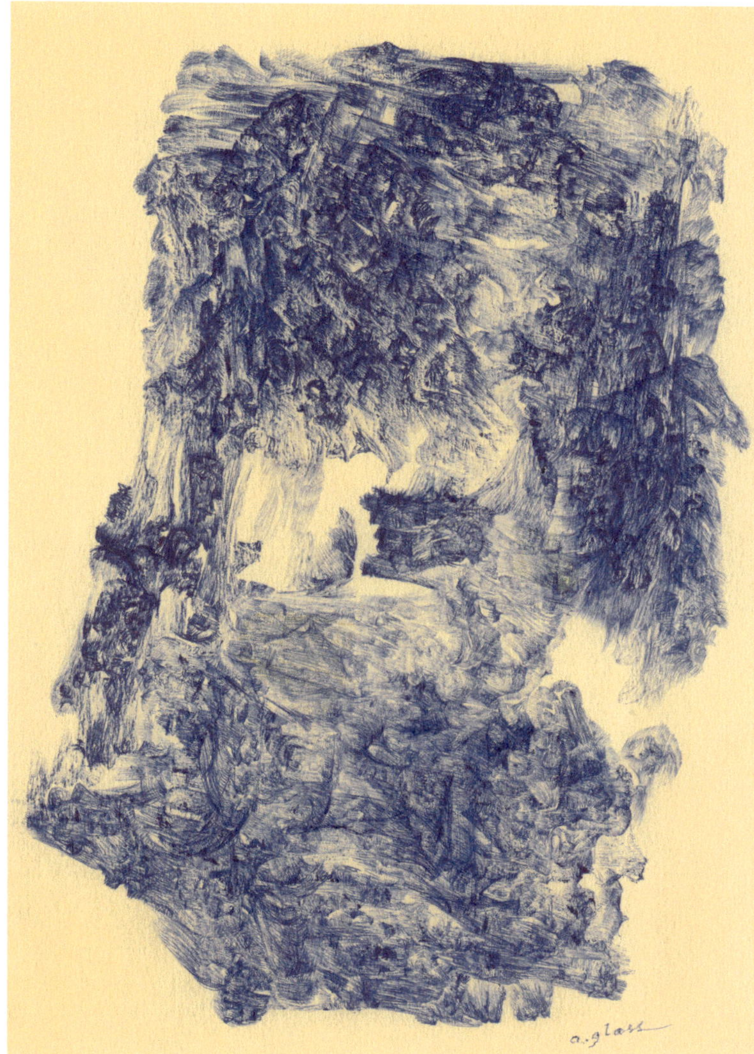

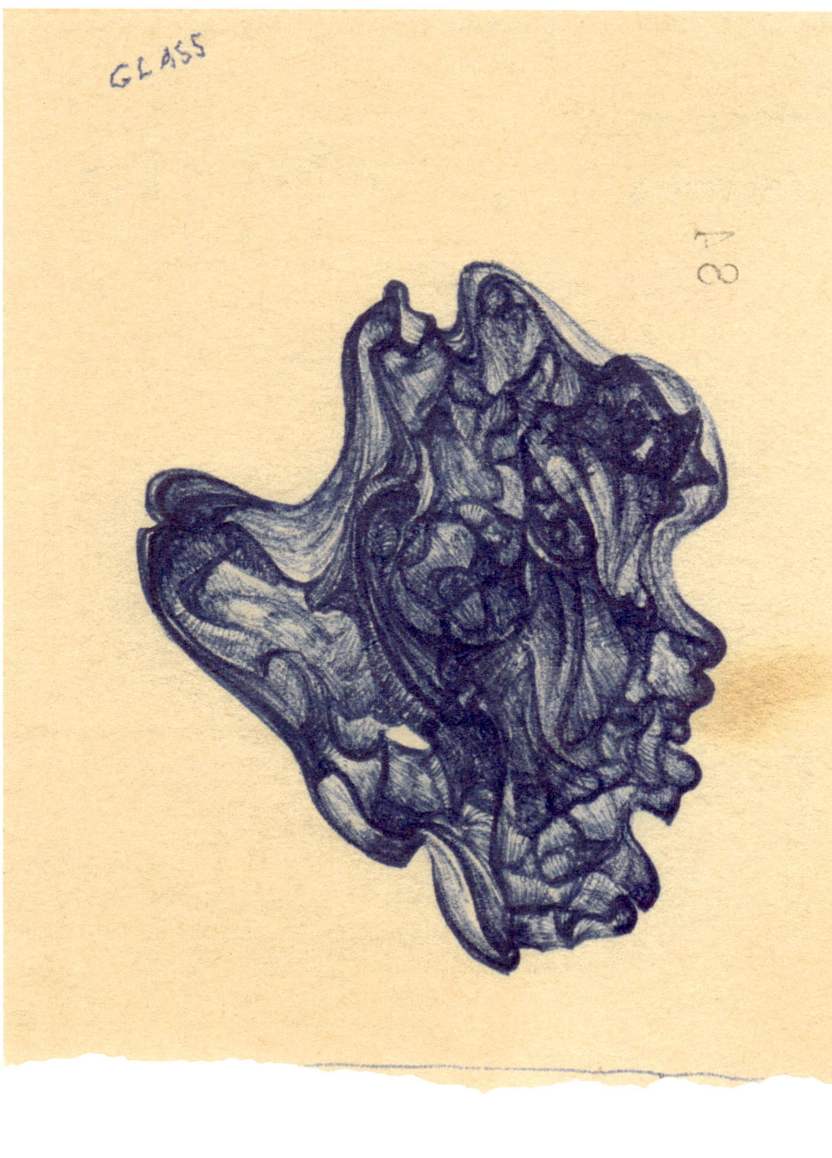

Untitled
(Club Saint-Germain period)
ca. 1954-1962
Blue, black, and purple tricolor ballpoint pen drawing.on paper.
27 x 21.1 cm
Artist's collection

Untitled
(Club Saint-Germain period)
ca. 1954-1962
Monochrome blue ballpoint pen drawing, on paper.
32.8 x 25 cm
Artist's collection

Untitled
(Club Saint-Germain period)
ca. 1954-1962
Monochrome blue ballpoint pen drawing, on the order of Club Saint Germain.
10.8 x 7.6 cm
Artist's collection

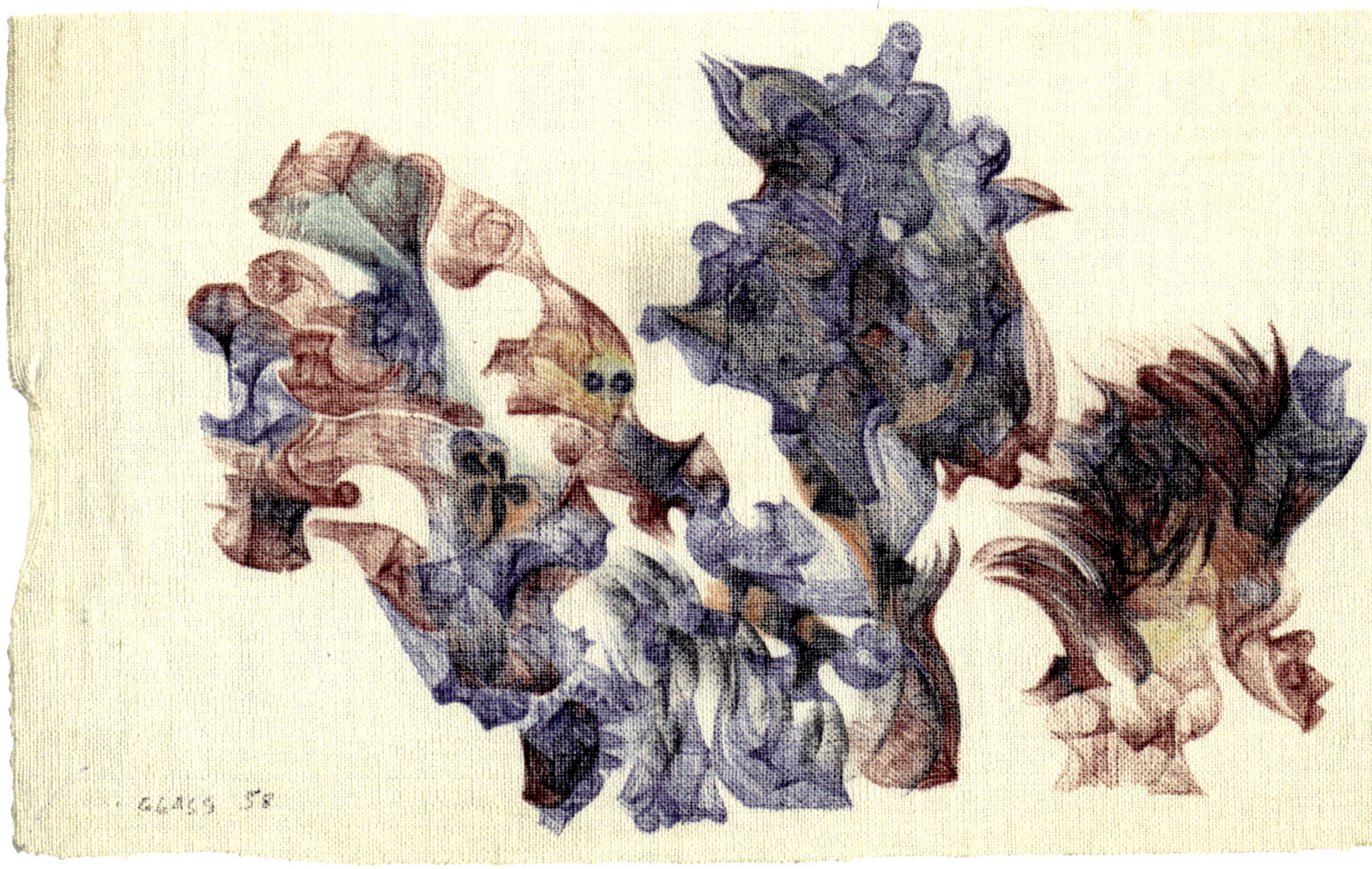

Untitled
(Club Saint-Germain period)
1958
Blue, red, and black tricolor
pen drawing, with turquoise
and brown pencil, on canvas.
13.3 x 22.5 cm
Artist's collection

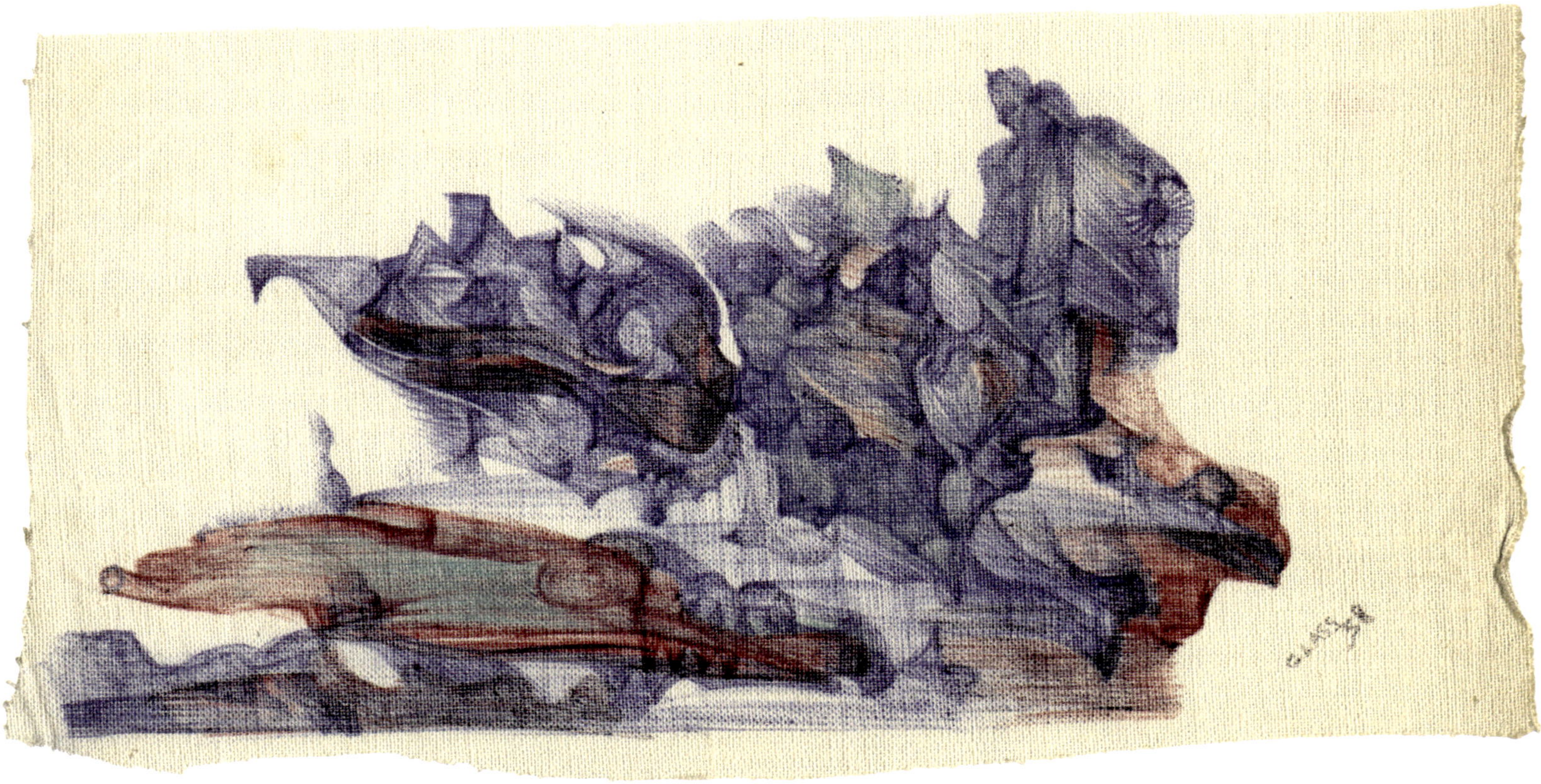

Untitled
(Club Saint-Germain period)
1958
Blue, red, and black tricolor pen drawing, with turquoise and brown pencil, on canvas.
11.5 x 23.3 cm
Artist's collection

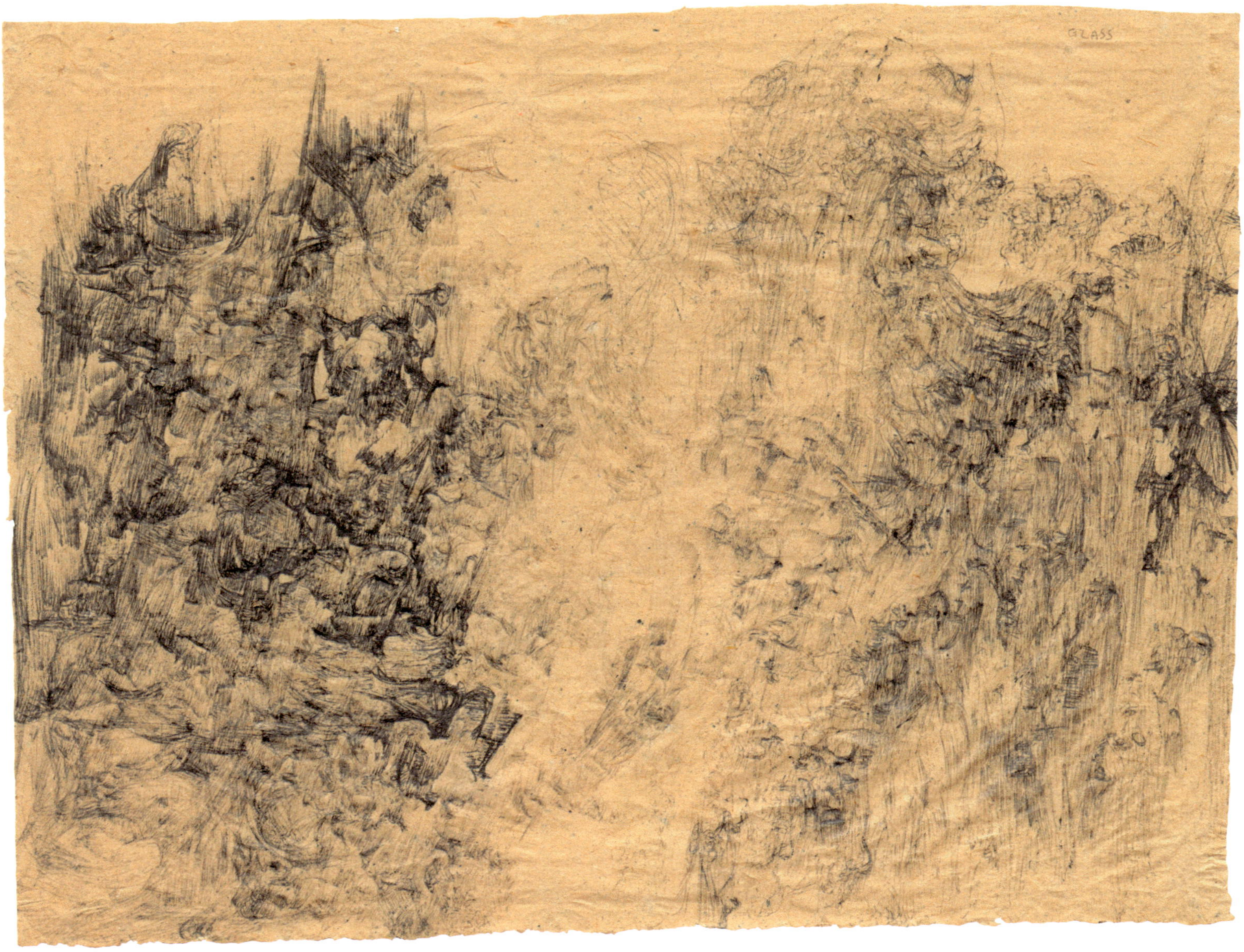

Untitled
(Club Saint-Germain period)
ca. 1954-1962
Monochrome black ballpoint
pen drawing, on paper.
22 x 29 cm
Artist's collection

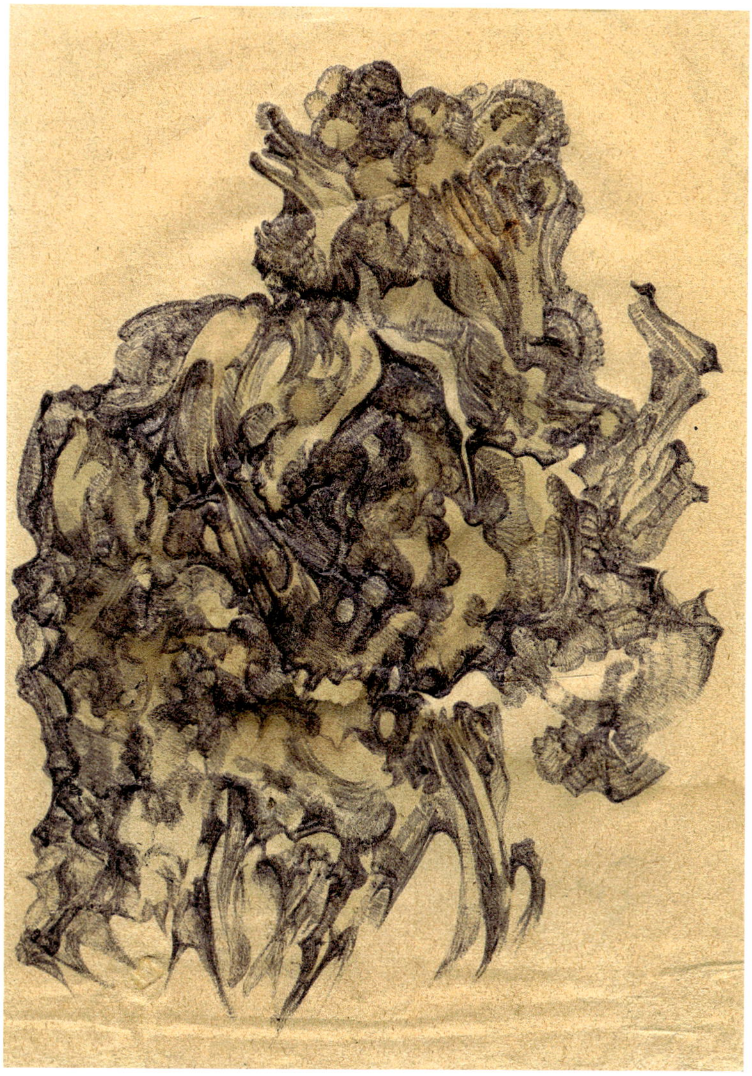

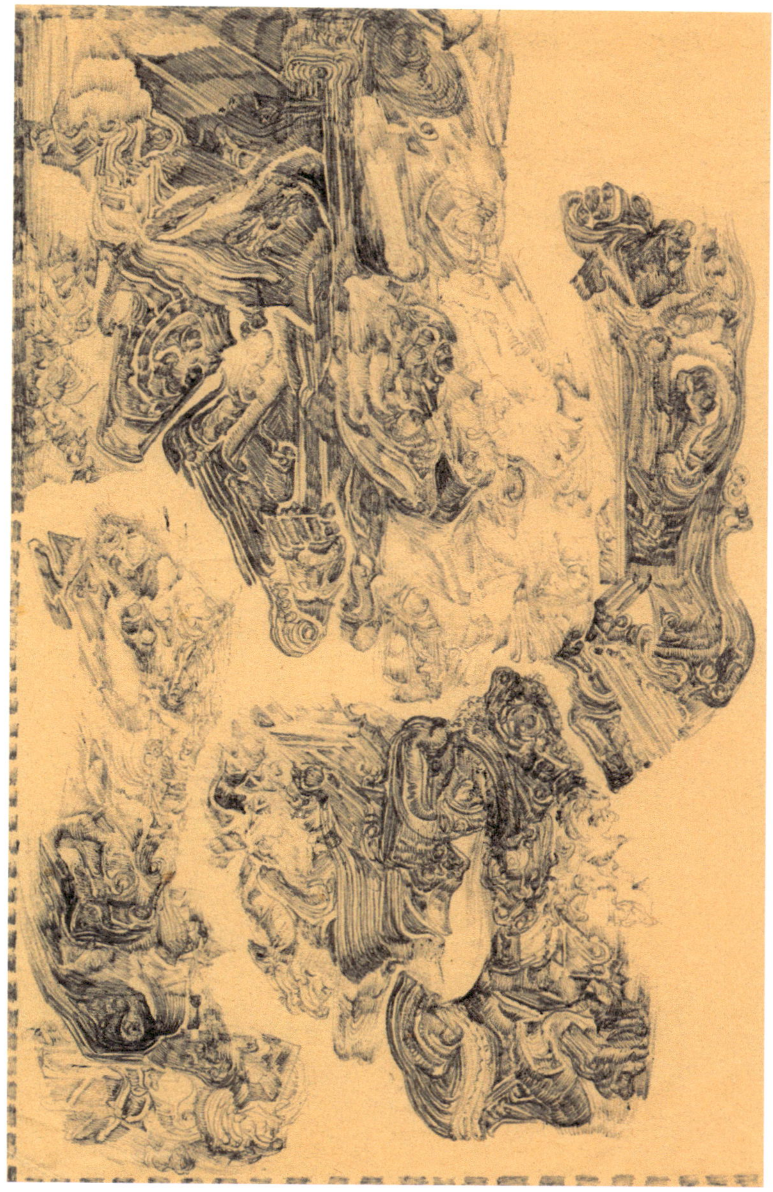

Untitled
(Club Saint-Germain period)
ca. 1954-1962
Monochrome black ballpoint pen drawing, with a touch of allumettage, on paper.
14.9 x 10.4 cm
Artist's collection

Untitled
(Club Saint-Germain period)
ca. 1954-1962
Monochrome black ballpoint pen drawing, on paper.
21.5 x 13.8 cm
Artist's collection

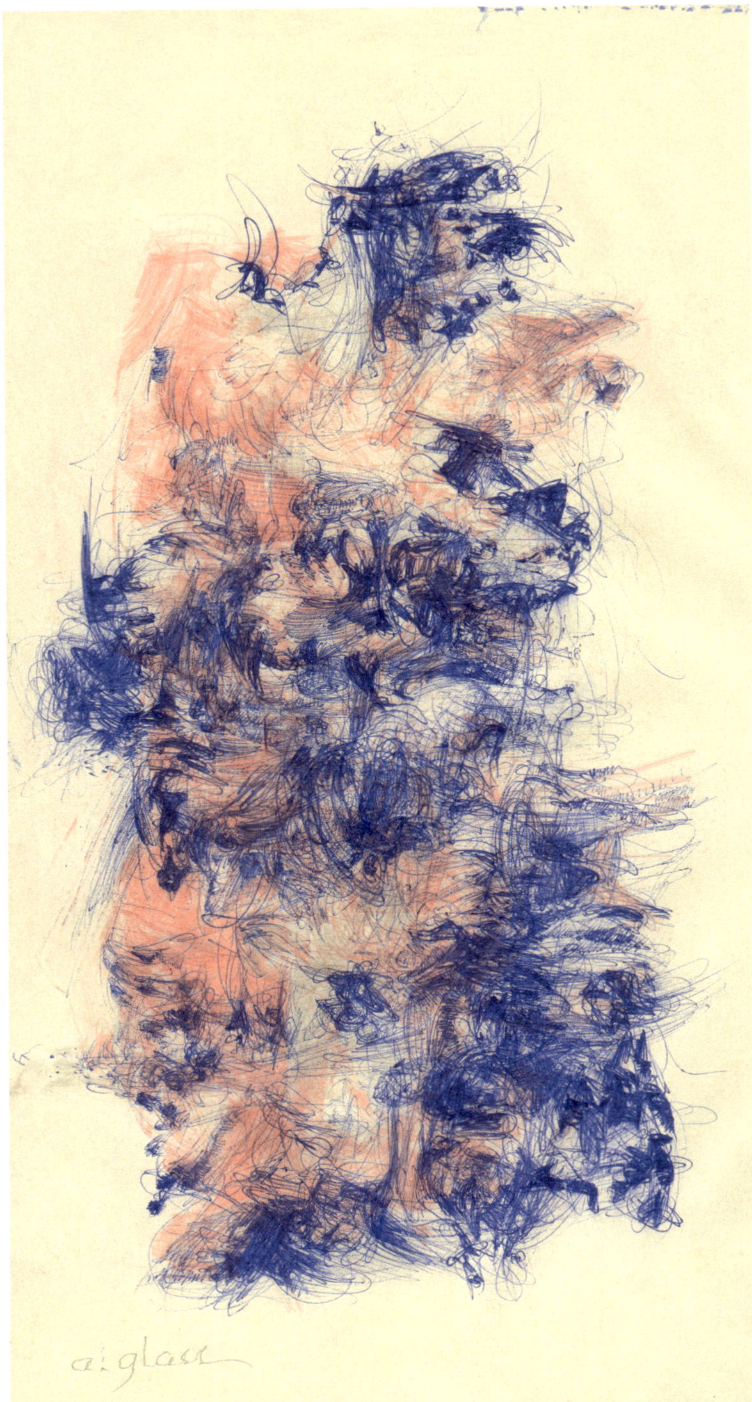

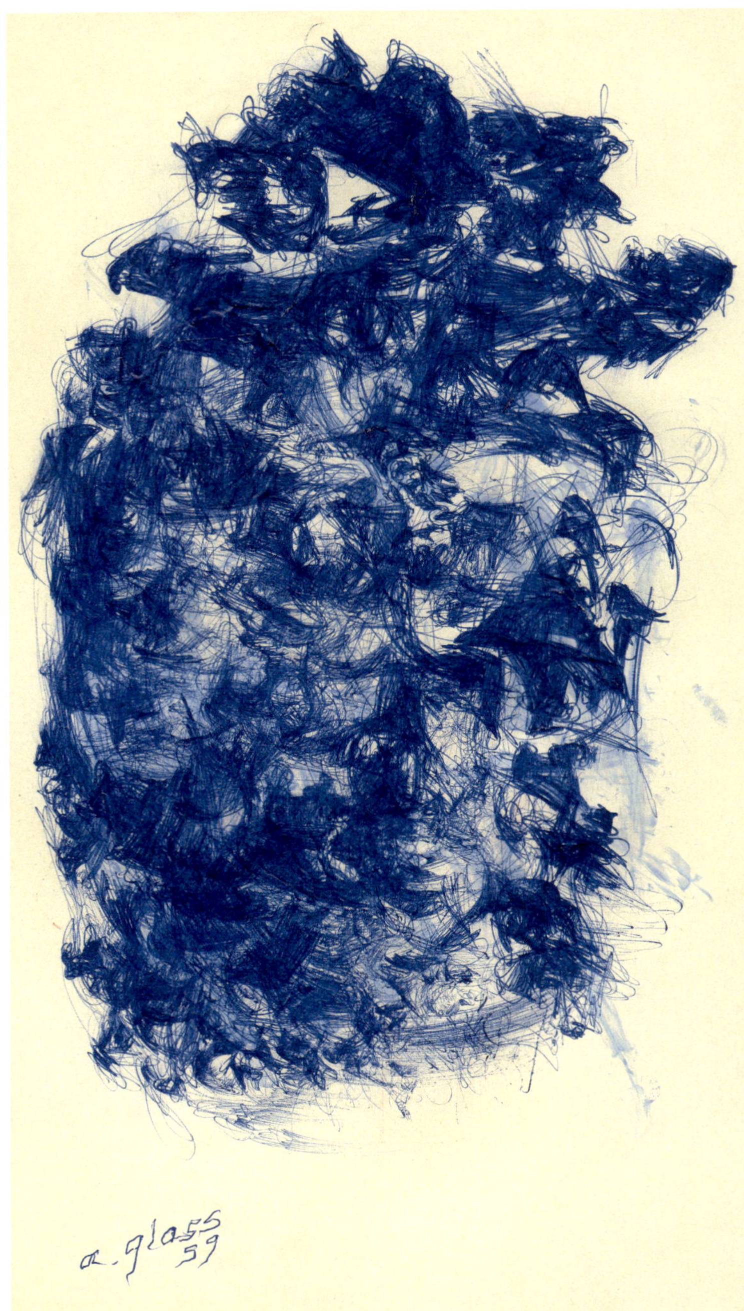

Untitled
(Club Saint-Germain period)
ca. 1954-1962
Bicolor blue and red ballpoint pen drawing, on Club Saint-Germain invitation.
23.5 x 13.6 cm
Artist's collection

Untitled
(Club Saint-Germain period)
1959
Bicolor blue and red ballpoint pen drawing, on Club Saint-Germain invitation.
23.5 x 13.6 cm
Artist's collection

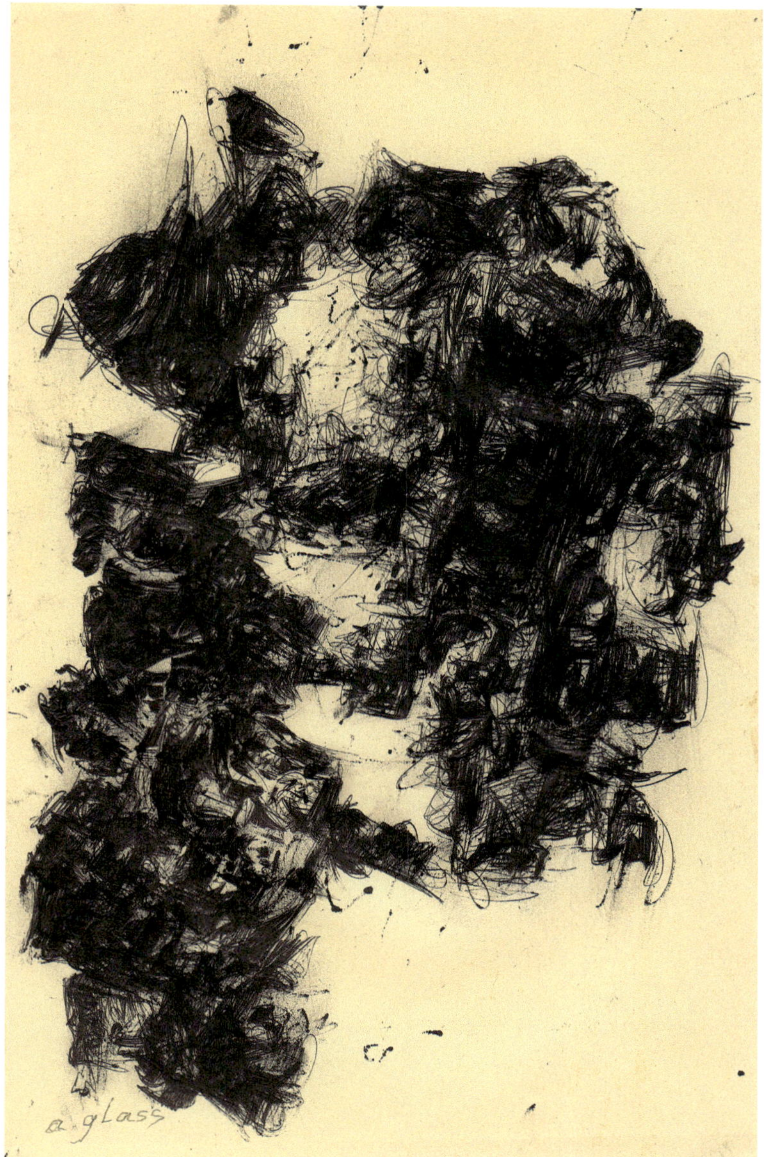

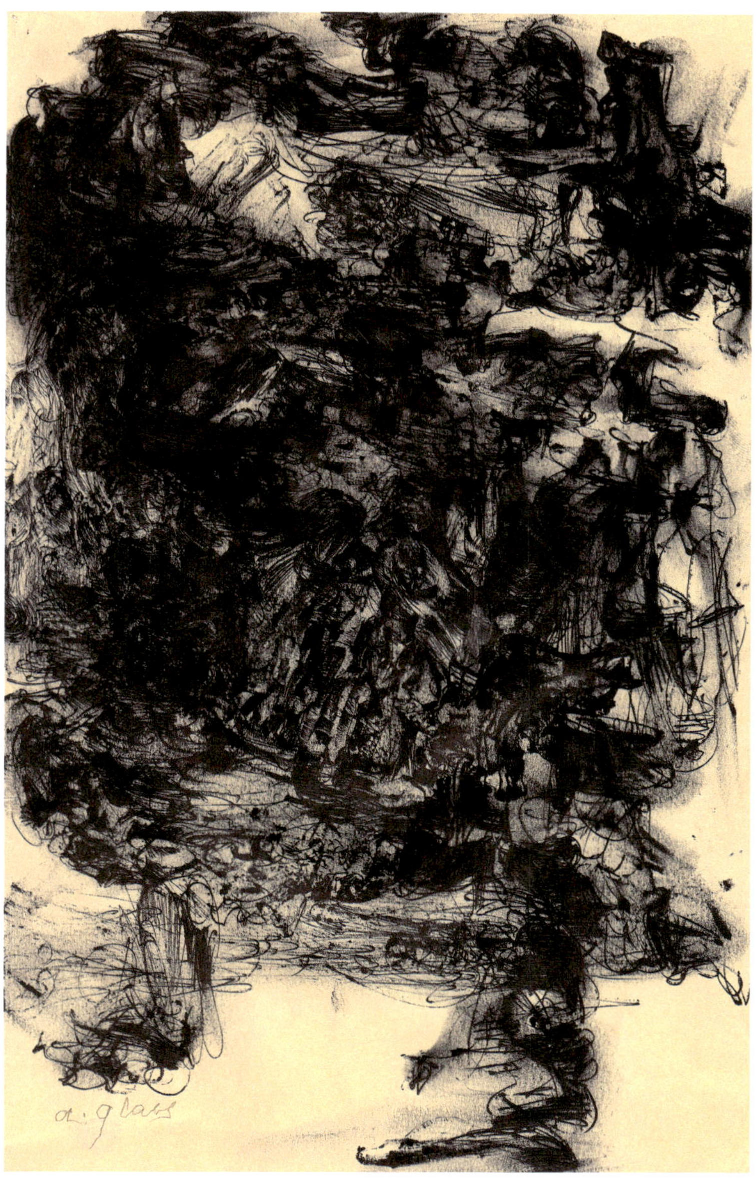

Untitled
(Club Saint-Germain period)
ca. 1954-1962
Monochrome black ballpoint pen drawing, on paper.
26 x 17 cm
Artist's collection

Untitled
(Club Saint-Germain period)
ca. 1954-1962
Monochrome black ballpoint pen drawing, on paper.
26 x 17 cm
Artist's collection

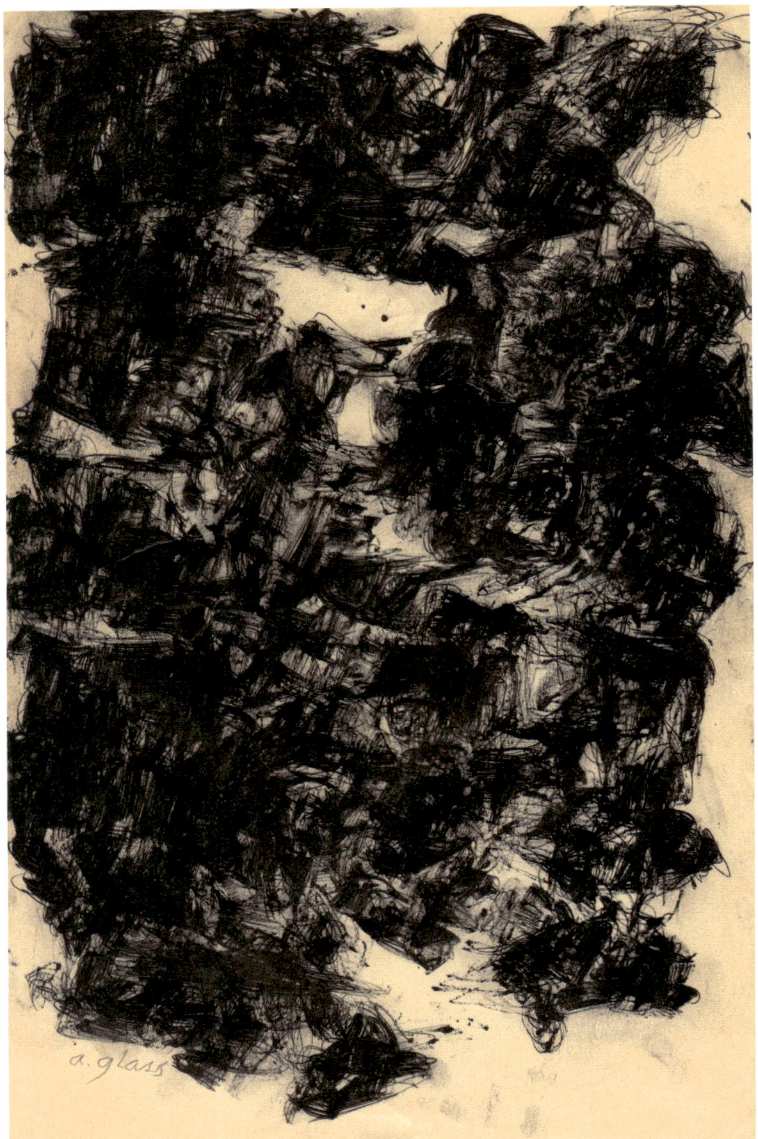

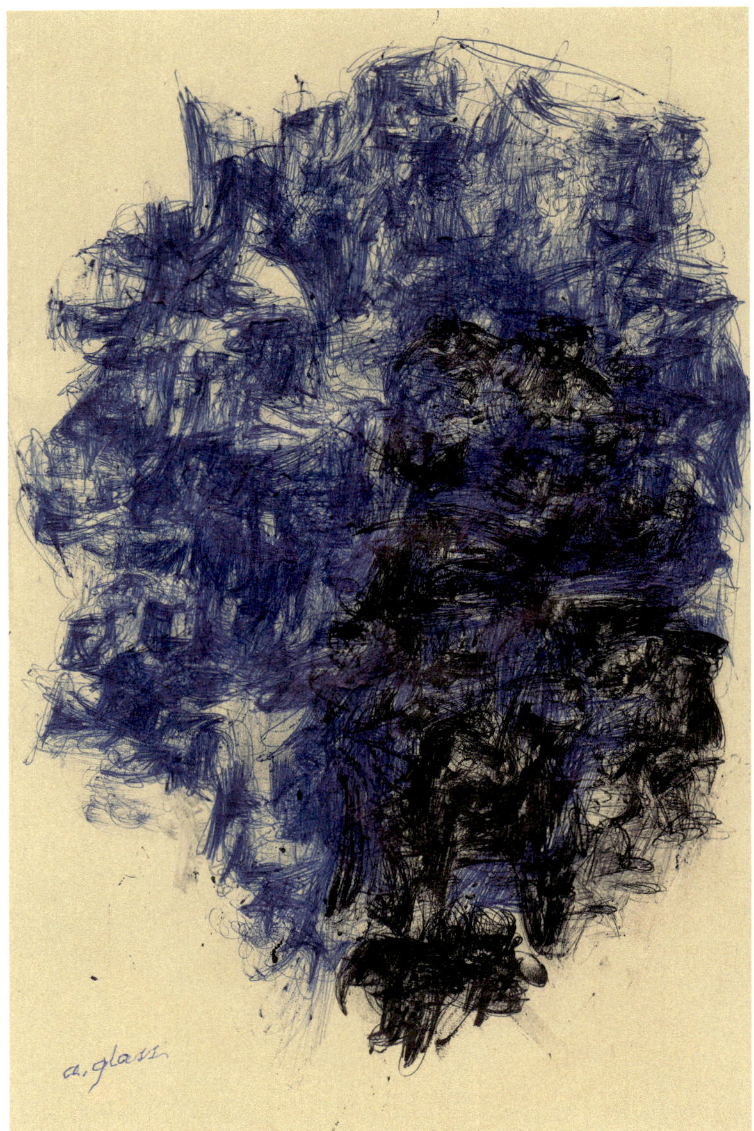

Untitled
(Club Saint-Germain period)
ca. 1954-1962
Monochrome black ballpoint pen drawing, on paper.
26 x 17.3 cm
Artist's collection

Untitled
(Club Saint-Germain period)
ca. 1954-1962
Bicolor blue and black ballpoint pen drawing, on paper.
26 x 17 cm
Artist's collection

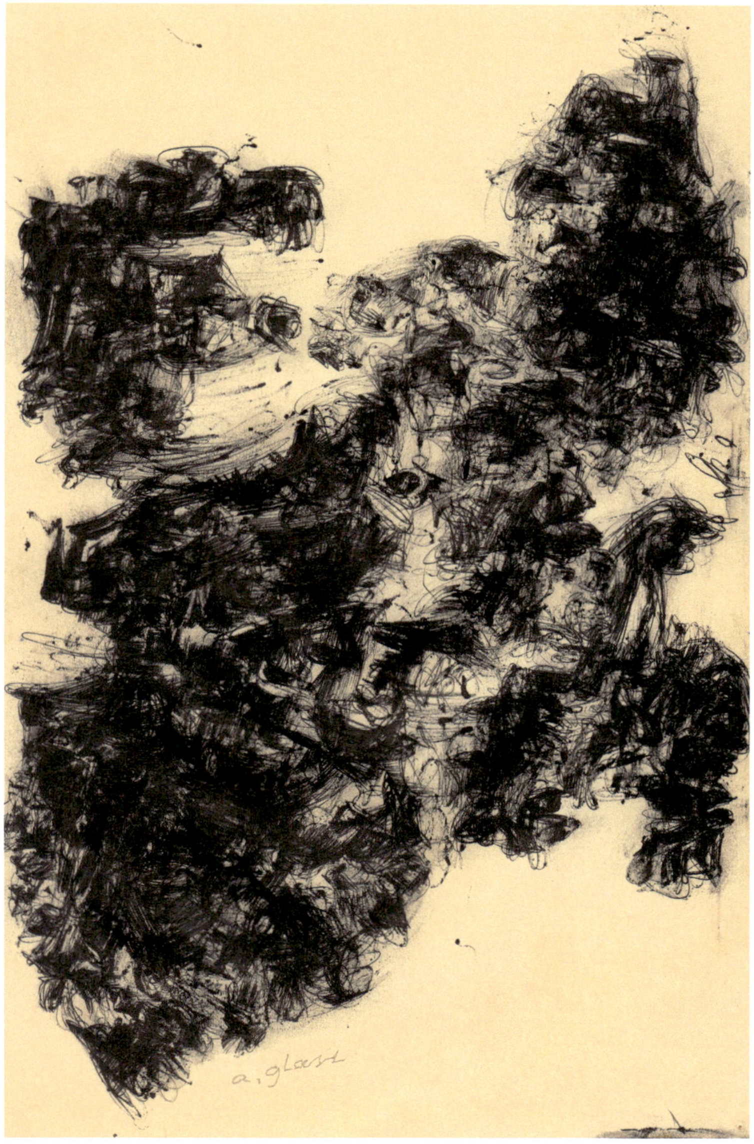

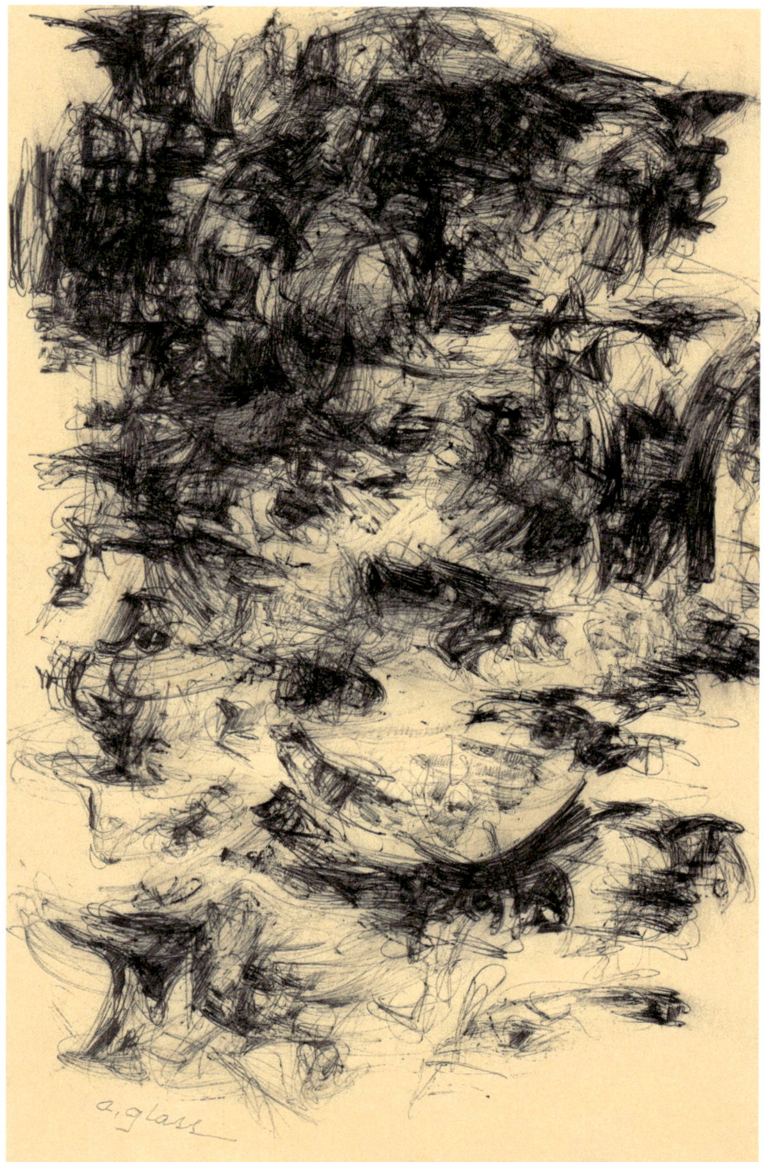

Untitled
(Club Saint-Germain period)
ca. 1954-1962
Monochrome black ballpoint pen drawing, on paper.
26 x 17 cm
Artist's collection

Untitled
(Club Saint-Germain period)
ca. 1954-1962
Monochrome black ballpoint pen drawing, on paper.
26 x 17 cm
Artist's collection

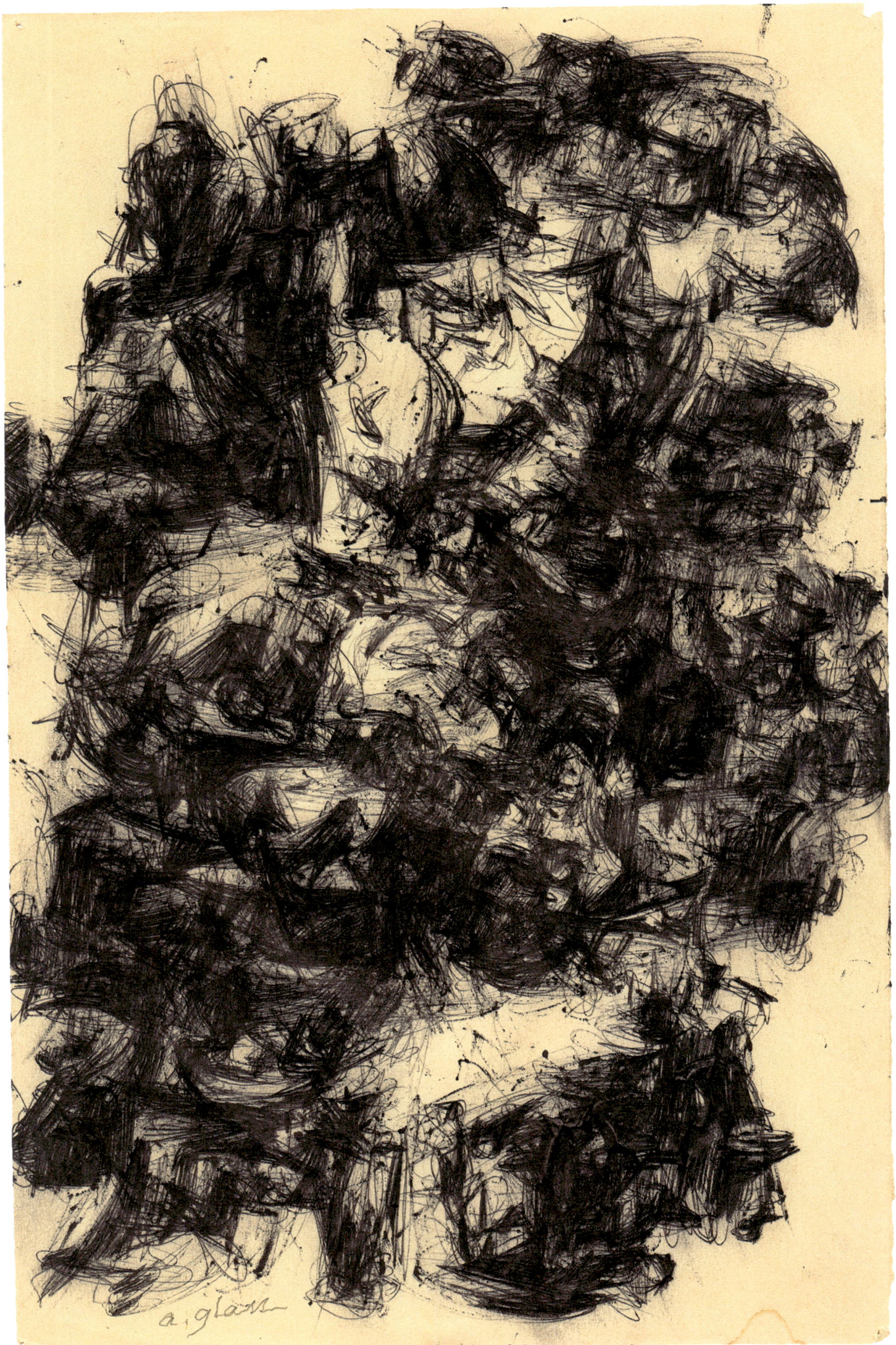

Untitled
(Club Saint-Germain period)
ca. 1954-1962
Monochrome black ballpoint pen drawing, on paper.
26 x 17.3 cm
Artist's collection

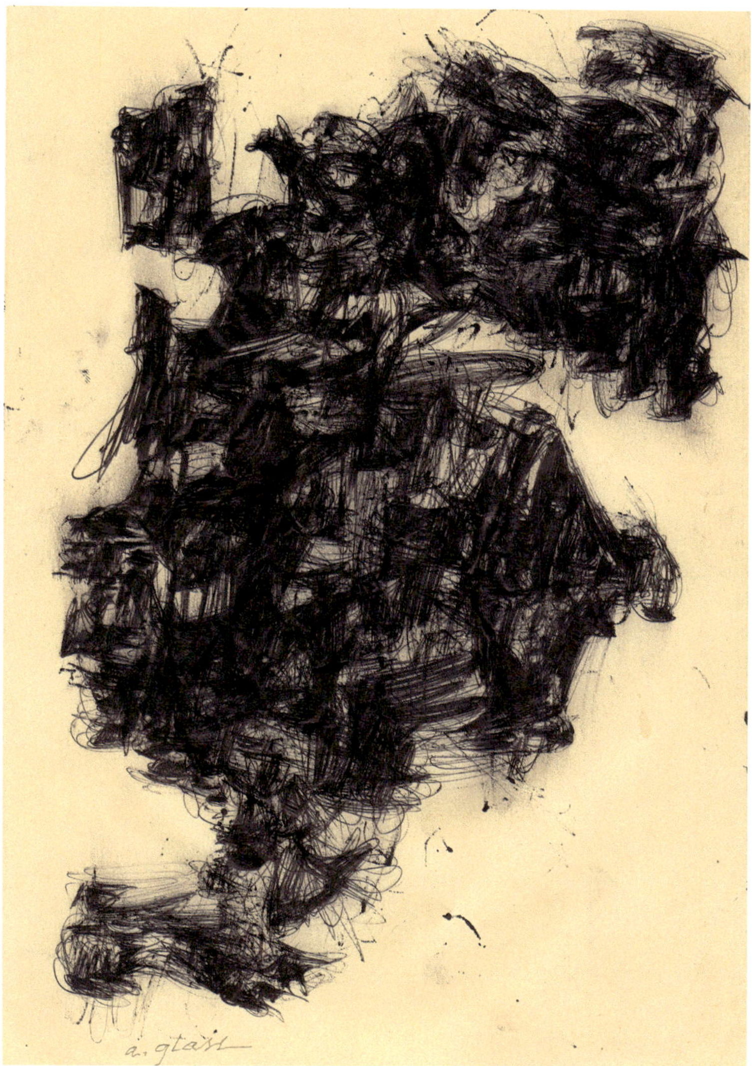

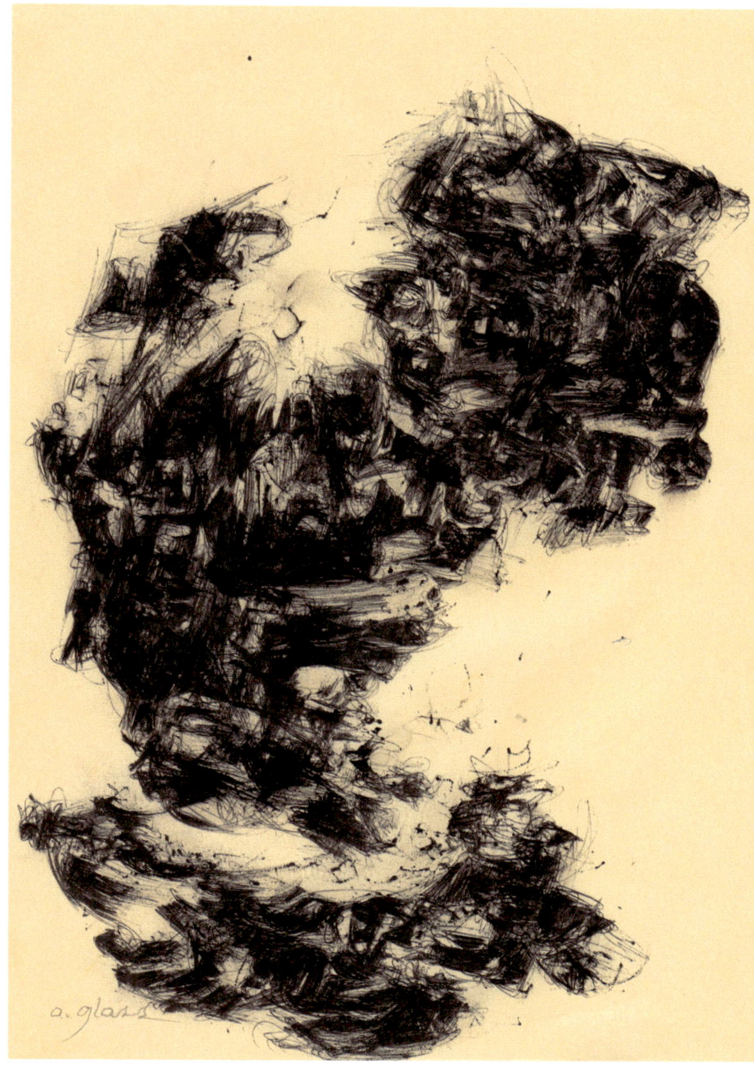

Untitled
(Club Saint-Germain period)
ca. 1954-1962
Monochrome black ballpoint
pen drawing, on paper.
26 x 17 cm
Artist's collection

Untitled
(Club Saint-Germain period)
ca. 1954-1962
Monochrome black ballpoint
pen drawing, on paper.
26 x 17 cm
Artist's collection

Untitled
(Club Saint-Germain period)
ca. 1954-1962
Monochrome blue ballpoint
pen drawing, on paper.
26 x 17.3 cm
Artist's collection

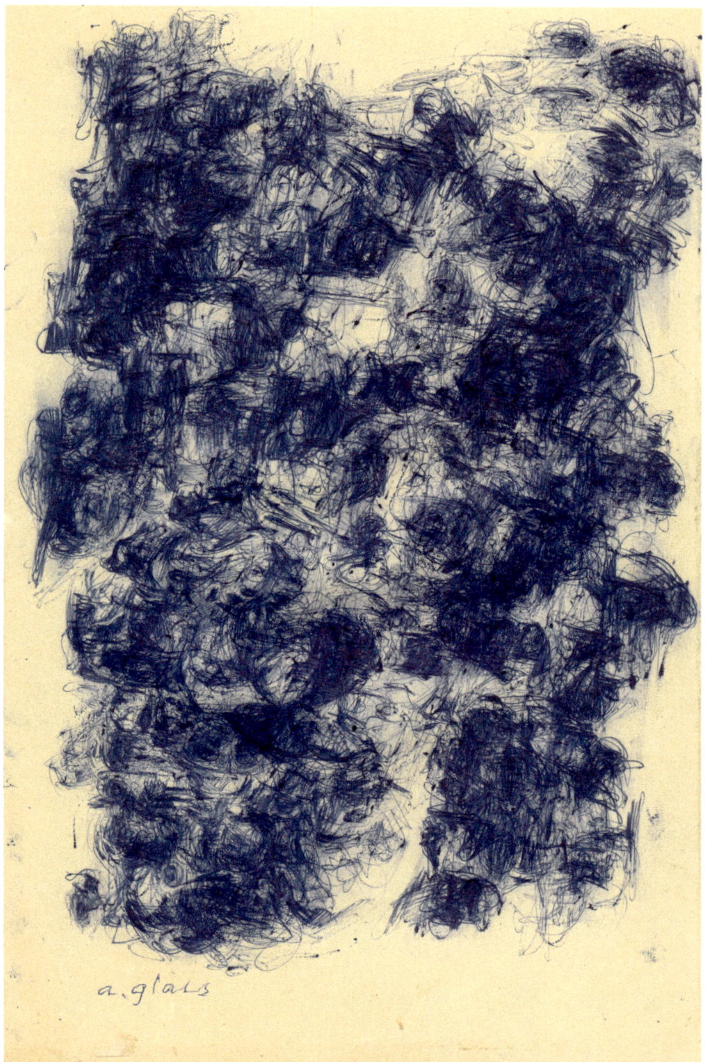

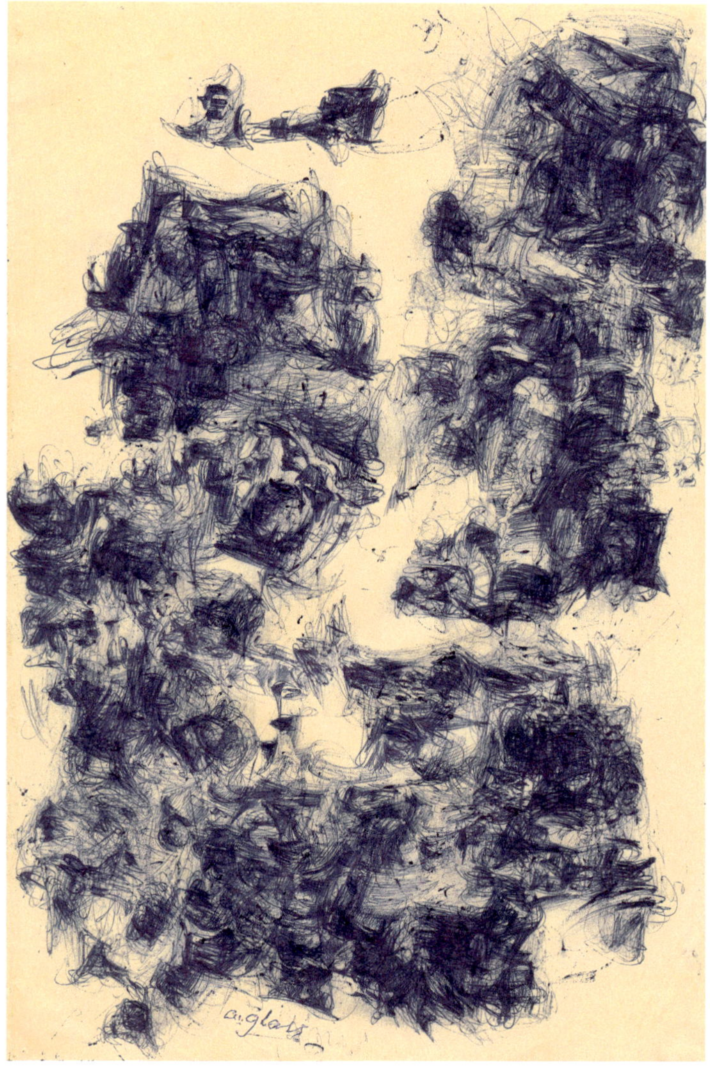

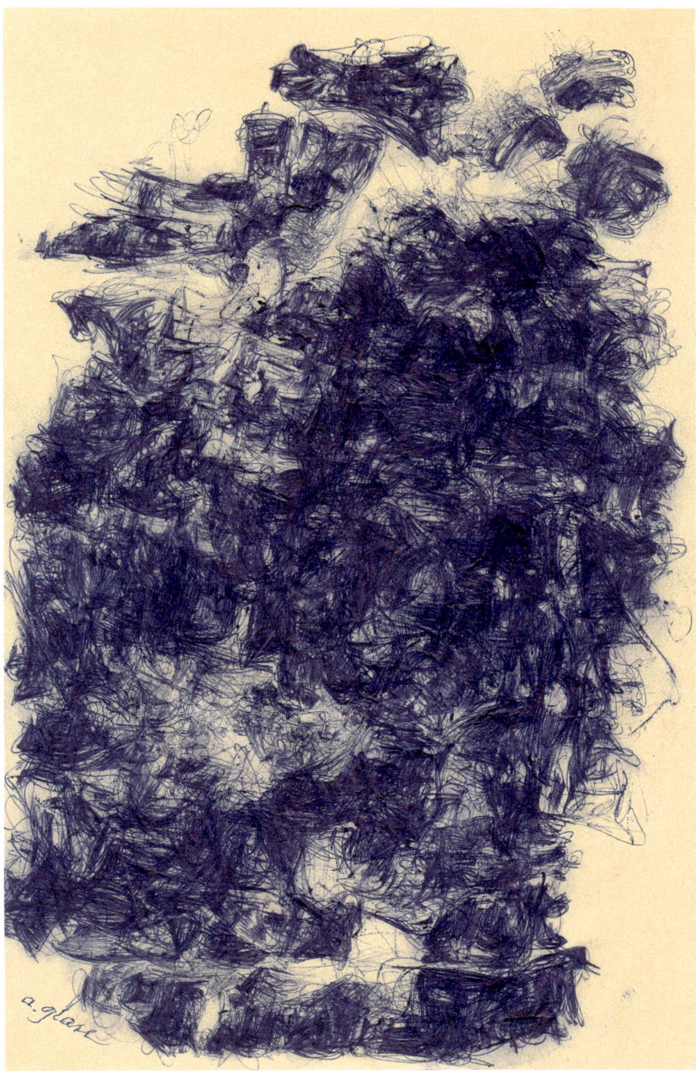

Untitled
(Club Saint-Germain period)
ca. 1954-1962
Monochrome blue ballpoint pen drawing, on paper.
26 x 17.1 cm
Artist's collection

Untitled
(Club Saint-Germain period)
ca. 1954-1962
Monochrome blue ballpoint pen drawing, on paper.
26 x 17.3 cm
Artist's collection

Untitled
(Club Saint-Germain period)
ca. 1954-1962
Monochrome blue ballpoint pen drawing, on paper.
26 x 17.1 cm
Artist's collection

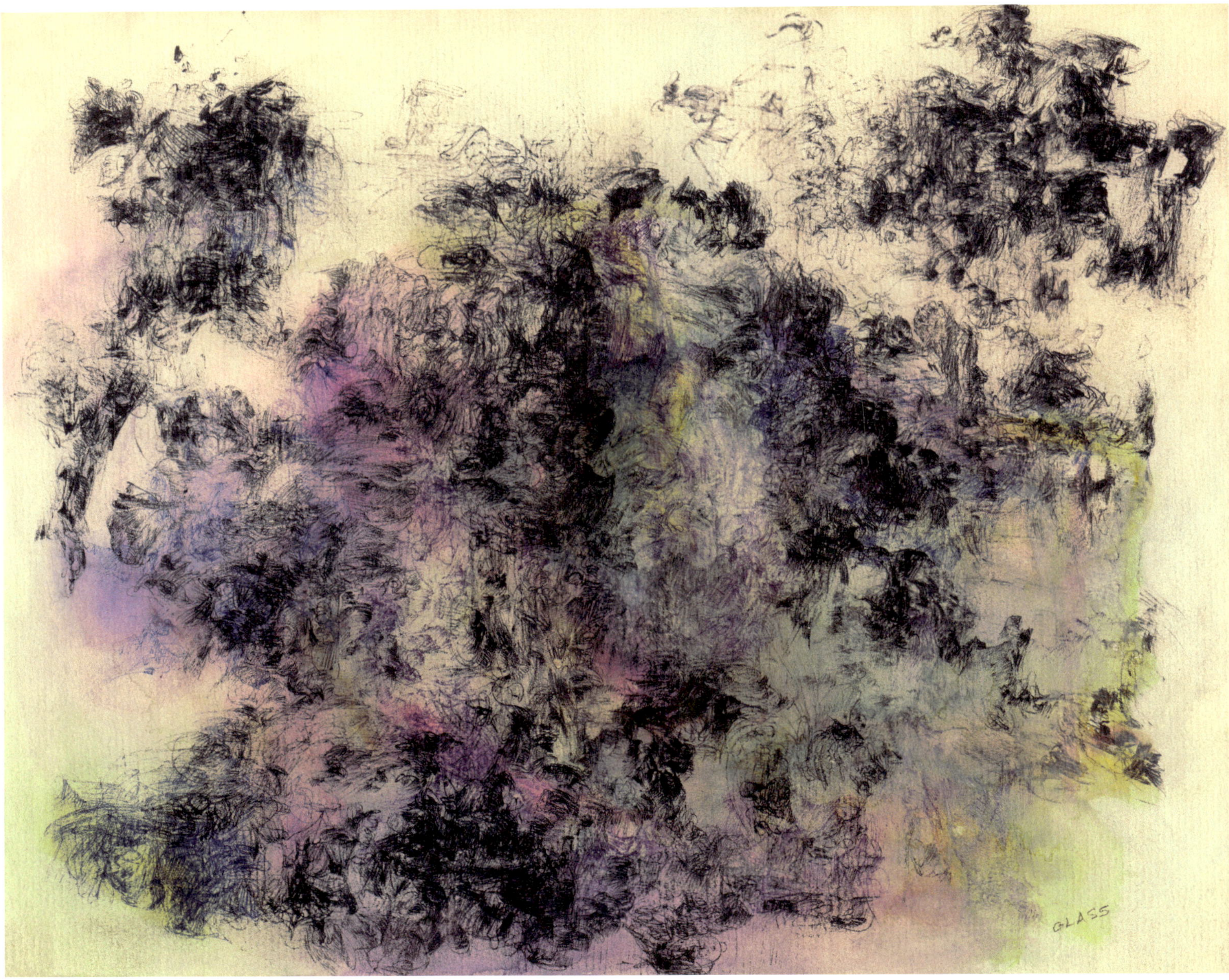

Untitled
(Club Saint-Germain period)
ca. 1954-1962
Monochrome black ballpoint pen drawing, with yellow, green, aqua, orange, pink and lilac watercolor, on paper.
20.9 x 26.8 cm
Artist's collection

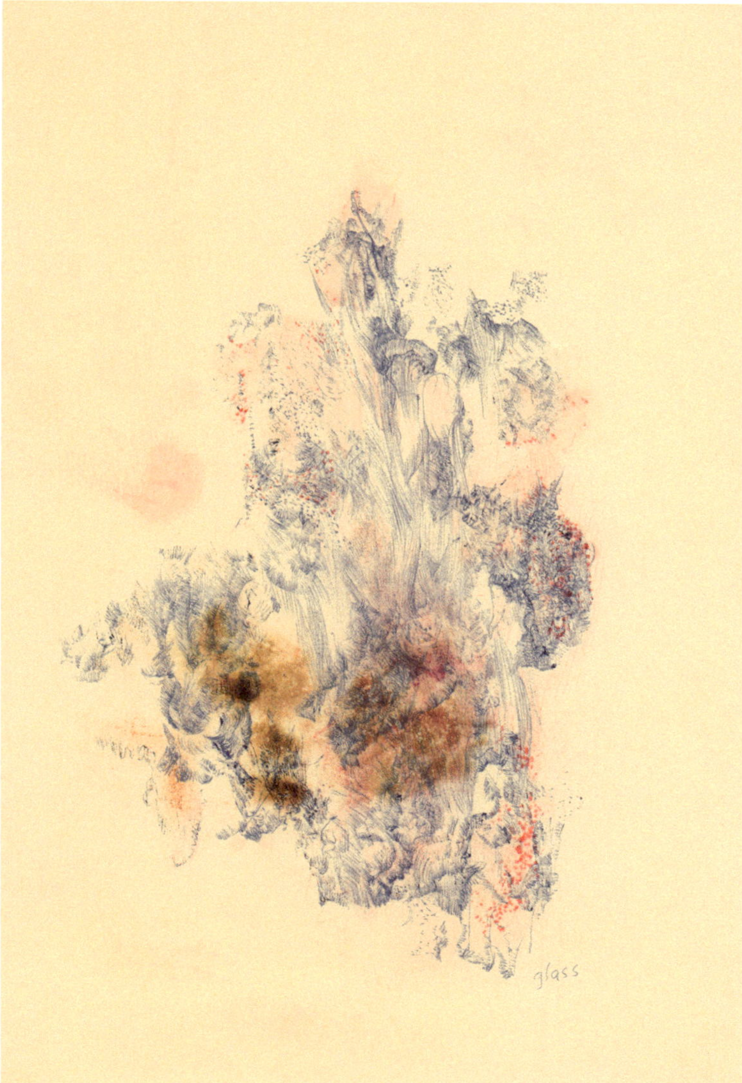

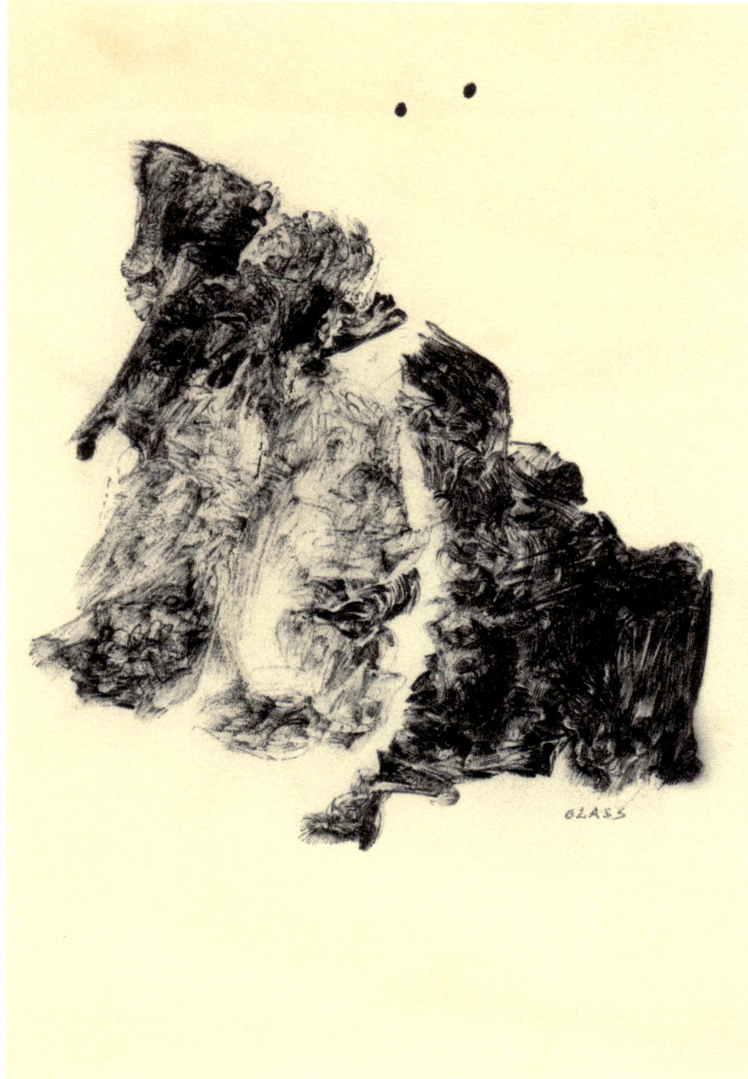

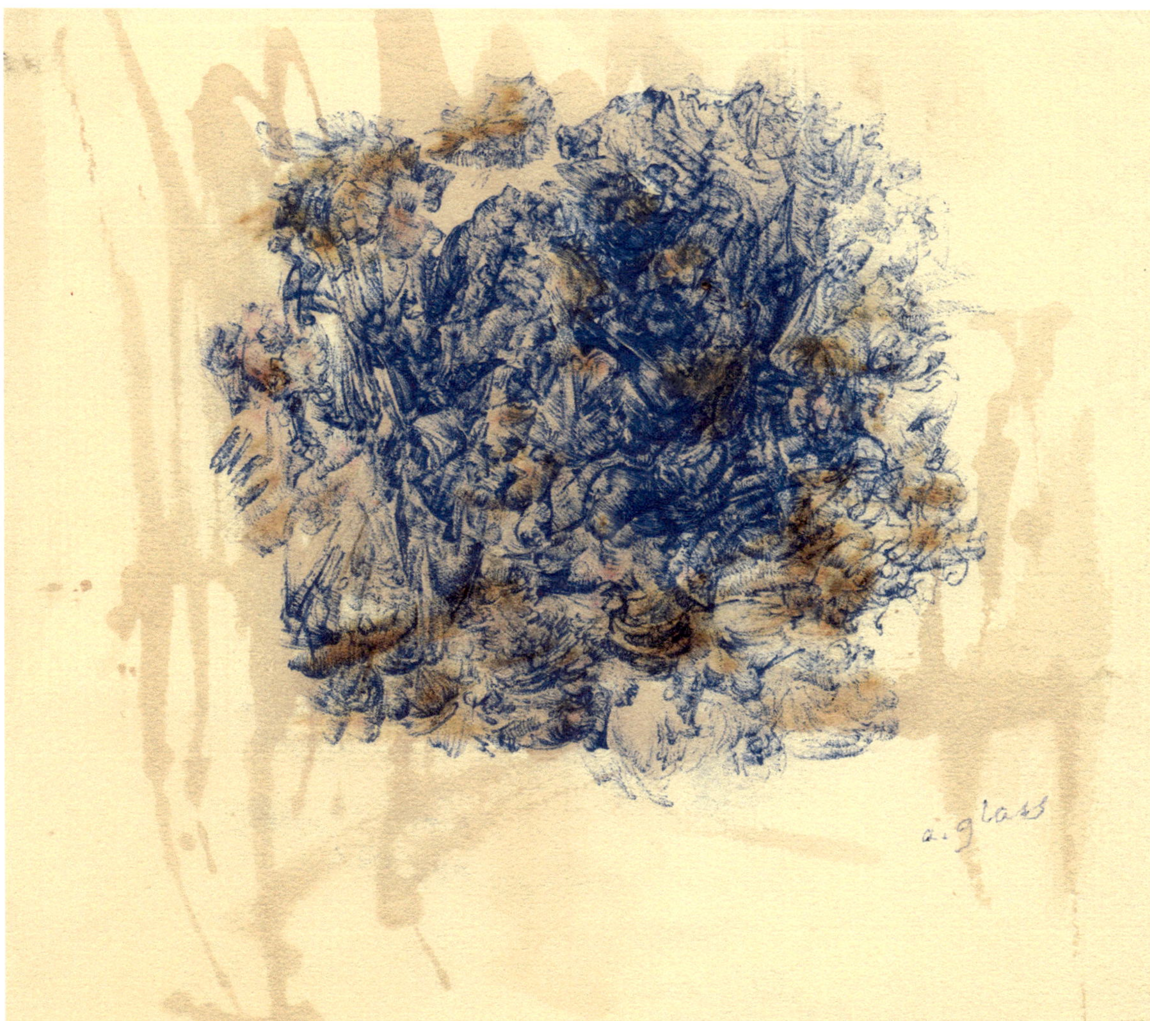

Untitled
(Club Saint-Germain period)
ca. 1954-1962
Bicolor blue and red ballpoint pen drawing, with a touch of allumettage, on paper.
17.7 x 12 cm
Artist's collection

Untitled
(Club Saint-Germain period)
ca. 1954-1962
Monochrome black ballpoint pen drawing, on paper.
20 x 20 cm
Artist's collection

Untitled
(Club Saint-Germain period)
ca. 1954-1962
Monochrome blue ballpoint pen drawing with watercolor and touch of allumettage, on paper.
15.7 x 19.9 cm
Artist's collection

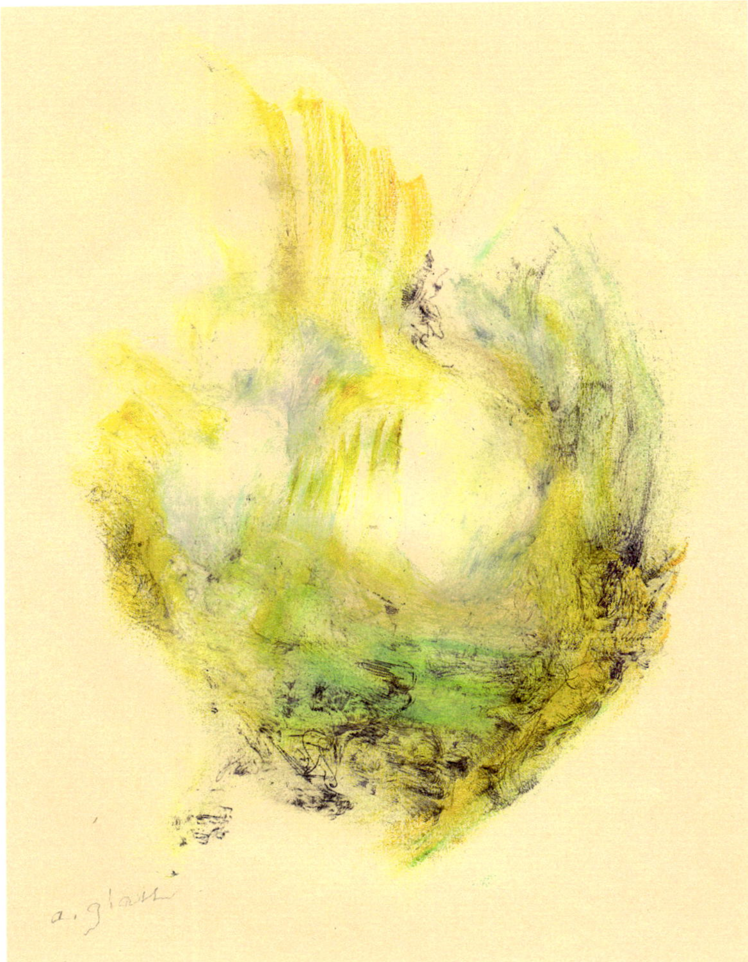

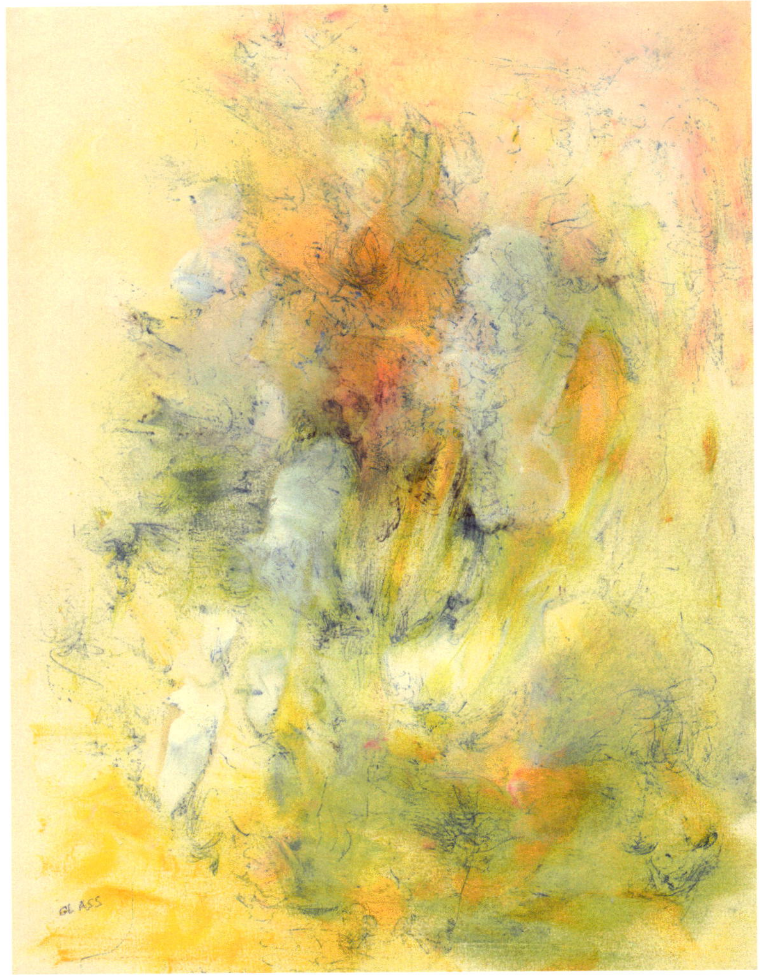

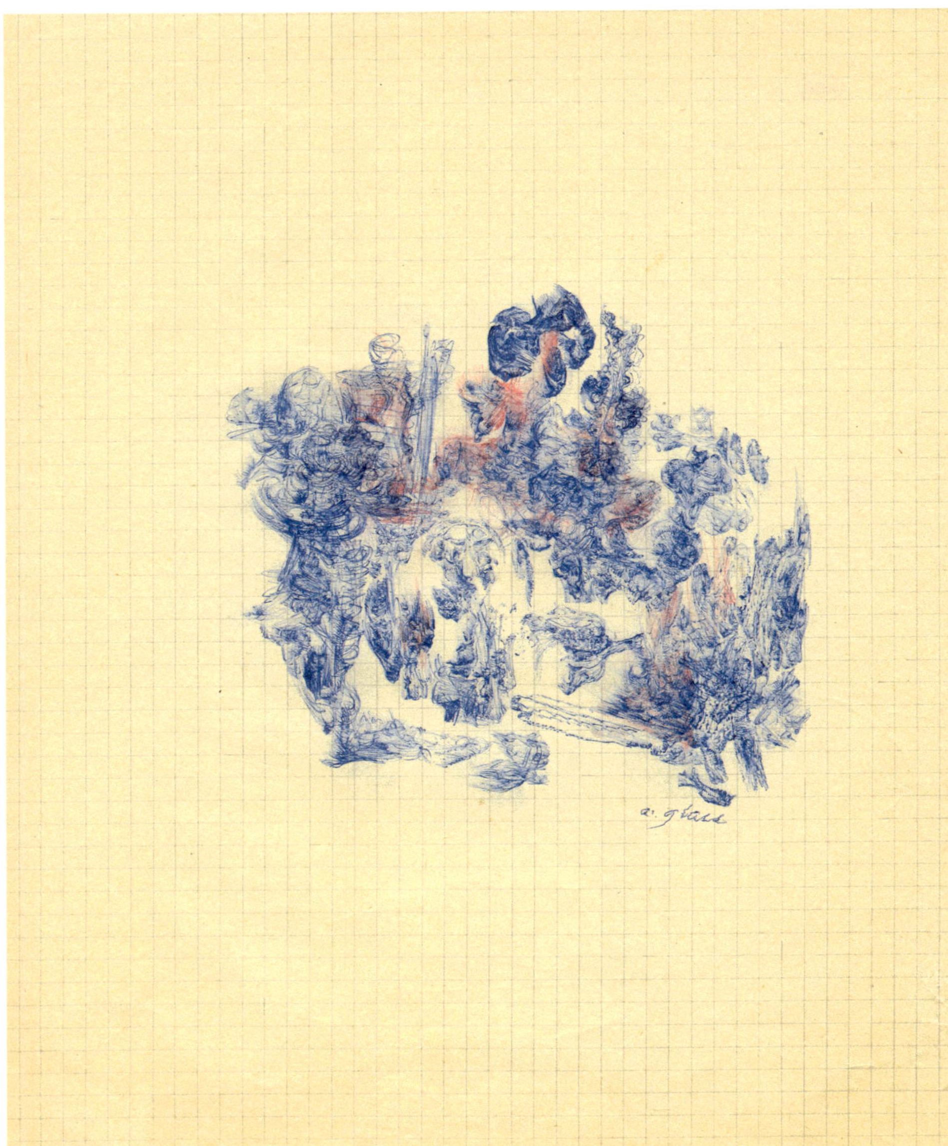

Untitled
(Club Saint-Germain period)
ca. 1954-1962
Monochrome black ballpoint pen drawing with yellow, green, and aqua watercolor, on paper.
27 x 21 cm
Artist's collection

Untitled
(Club Saint-Germain period)
ca. 1954-1962
Monochrome blue ballpoint pen drawing with yellow, green, aqua, and orange watercolor, on paper.
27 x 21 cm
Artist's collection

Untitled
(Club Saint-Germain period)
ca. 1954-1962
Monochrome blue ballpoint pen drawing with orange pencil, on squared paper.
25.5 x 21 cm
Artist's collection

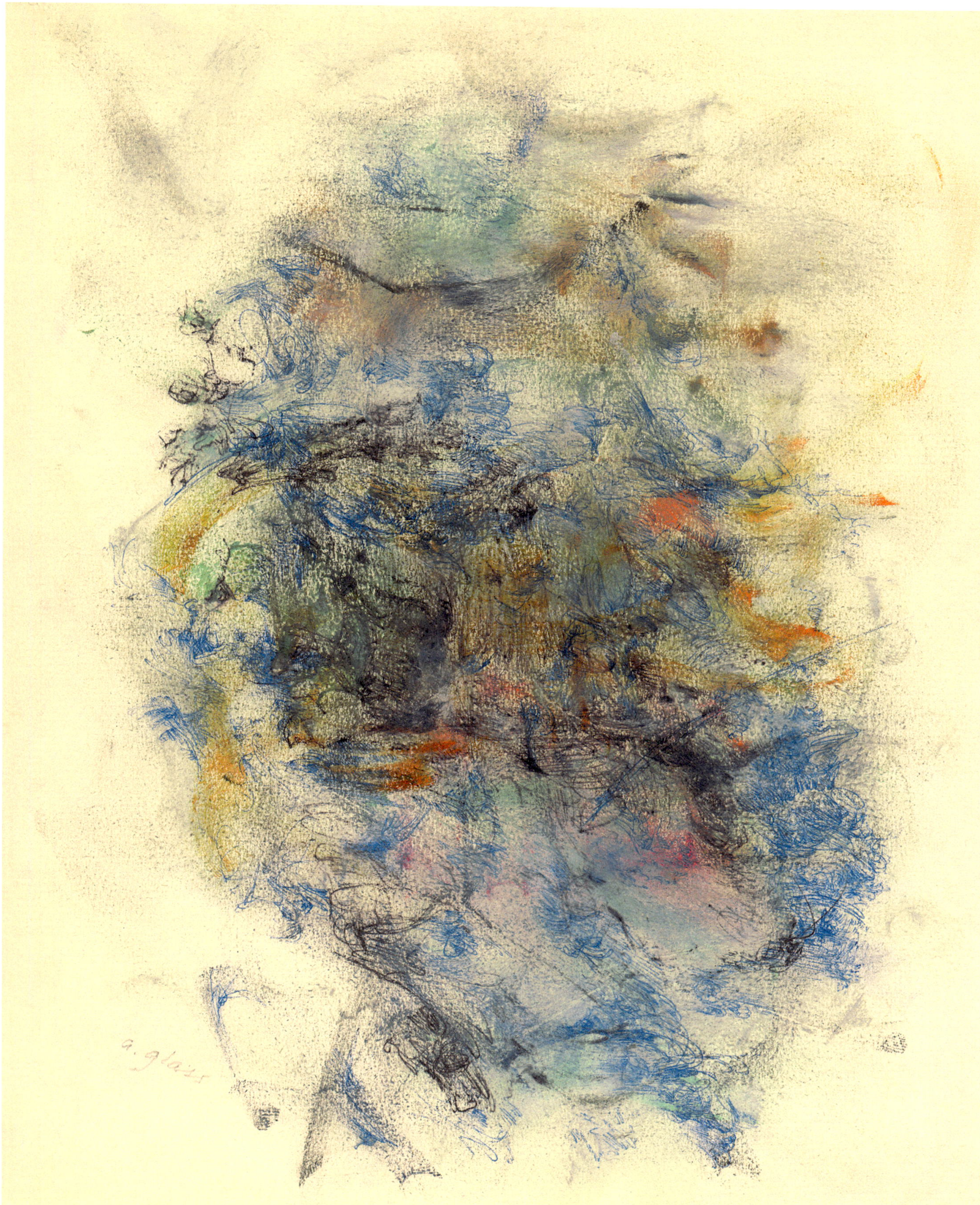

Untitled
(Club Saint-Germain period)
ca. 1954-1962
Bicolor blue and black ballpoint pen drawing, with yellow, green, aqua, orange, pink, and blue watercolor, on paper.
27 x 21 cm
Artist's collection

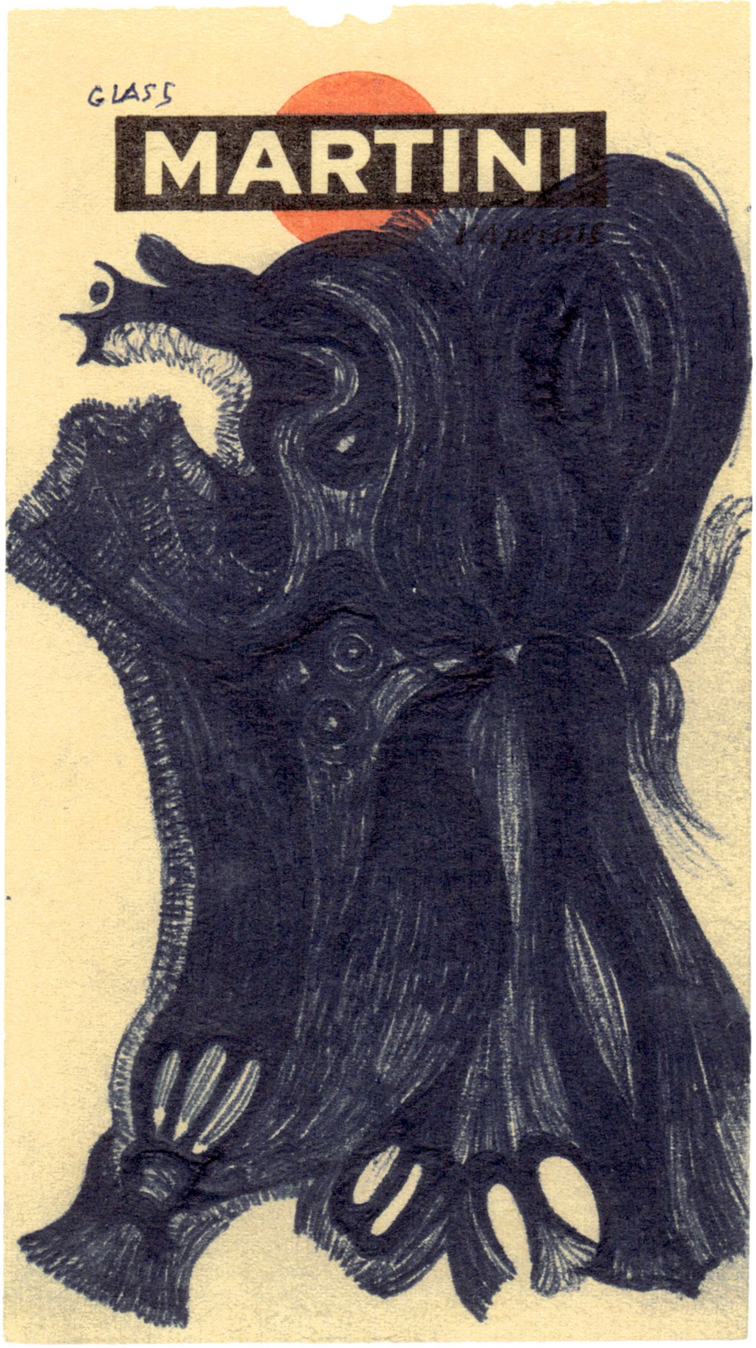

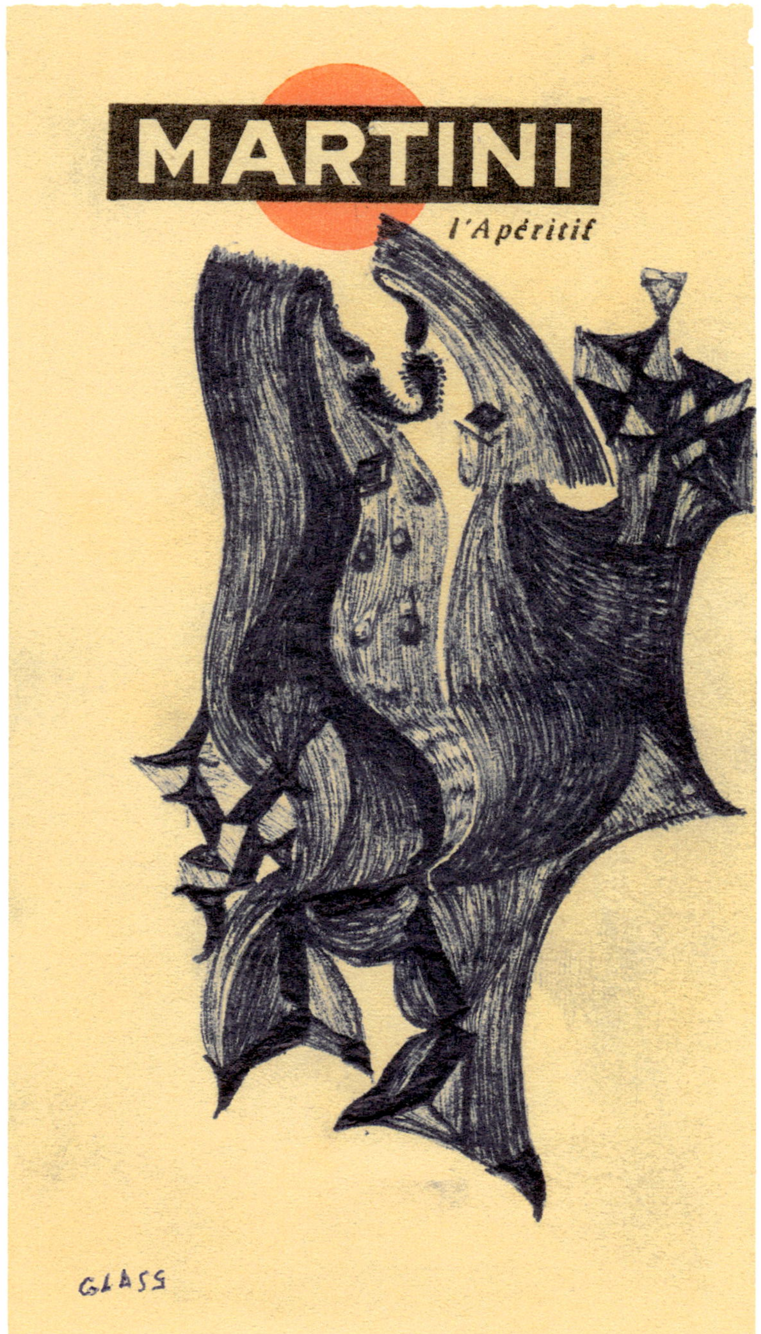

Untitled
(Club Saint-Germain period)
ca. 1954-1962
Monochrome blue ballpoint pen drawing, on the order slip of Club Saint-Germain.
15 x 8.4 cm
Artist's collection

Untitled
(Club Saint-Germain period)
ca. 1954-1962
Monochrome blue ballpoint pen drawing, on the order slip of Club Saint-Germain.
15 x 8.4 cm
Artist's collection

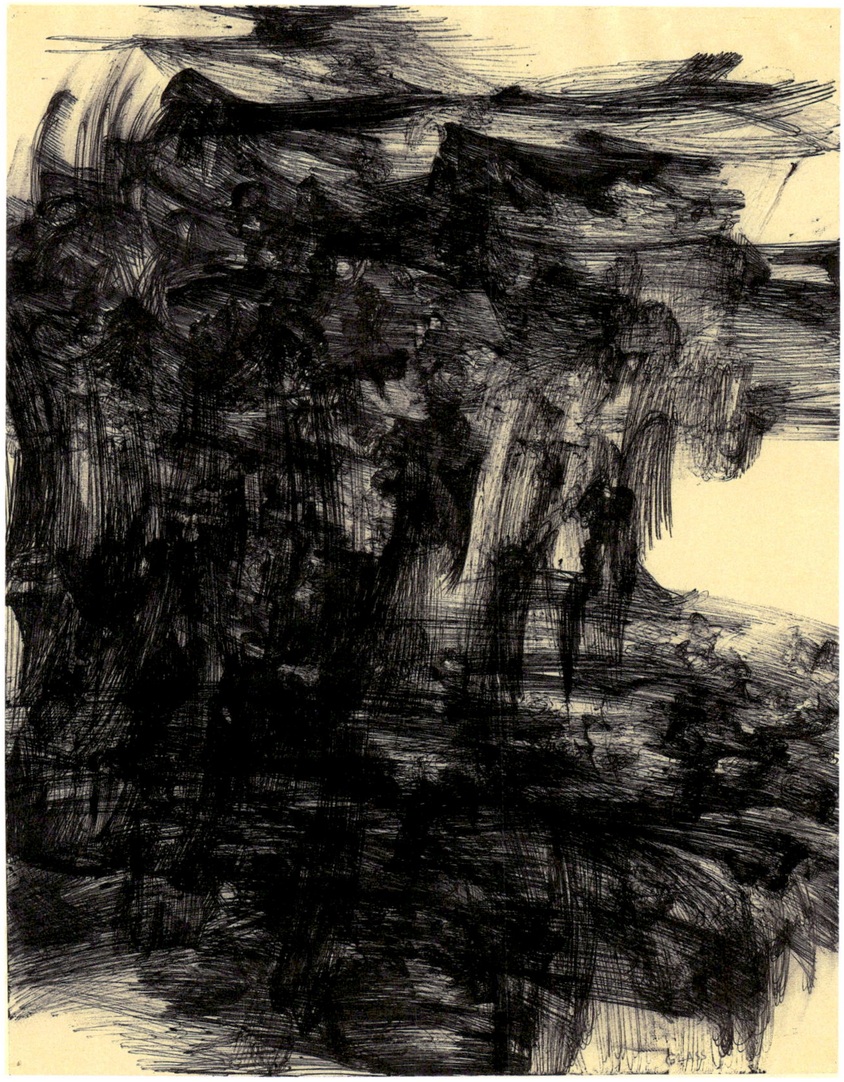

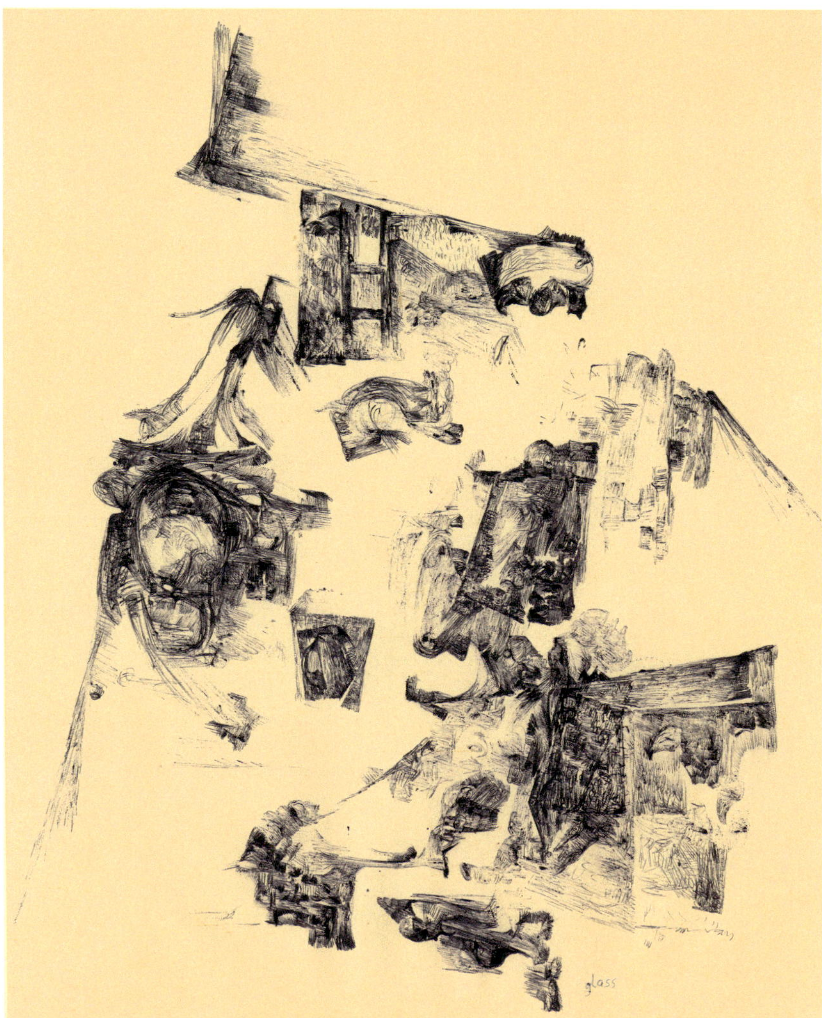

Untitled
(Club Saint-Germain period)
ca. 1954-1962
Monochrome black ballpoint pen drawing, on paper.
28.2 x 22.4 cm
Artist's collection

Untitled
(Club Saint-Germain period)
ca. 1954-1962
Monochrome black ballpoint pen drawing, on paper.
28 x 22.3 cm
Artist's collection

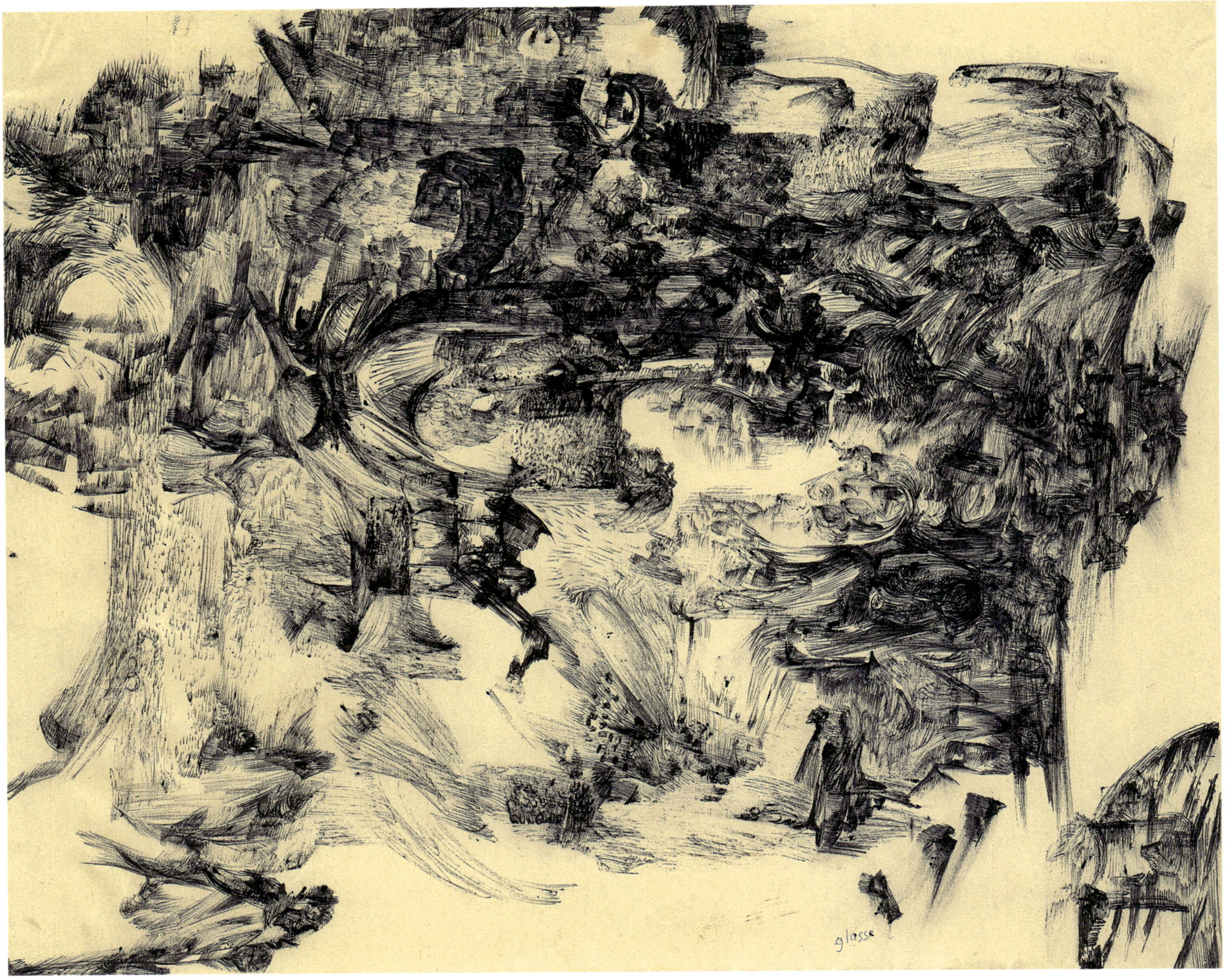

Untitled
(Club Saint-Germain period)
ca. 1954-1962
Monochrome black ballpoint
pen drawing, on paper.
22.4 x 28.1 cm
Artist's collection

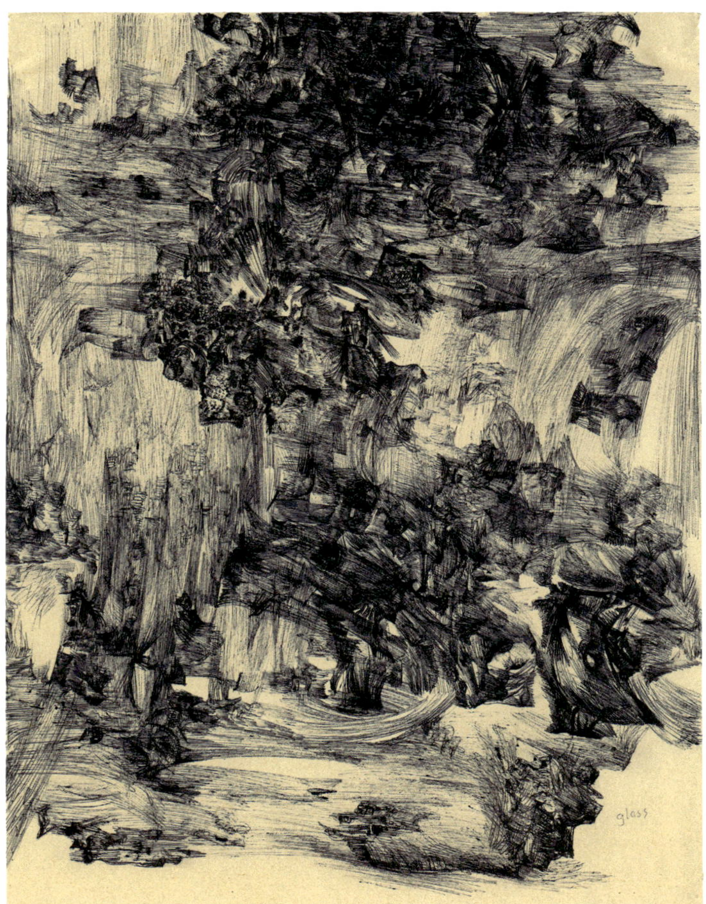

Untitled
(Club Saint-Germain period)
ca. 1954-1962
Monochrome black ballpoint
pen drawing, on paper.
28.1 x 22.3 cm
Artist's collection

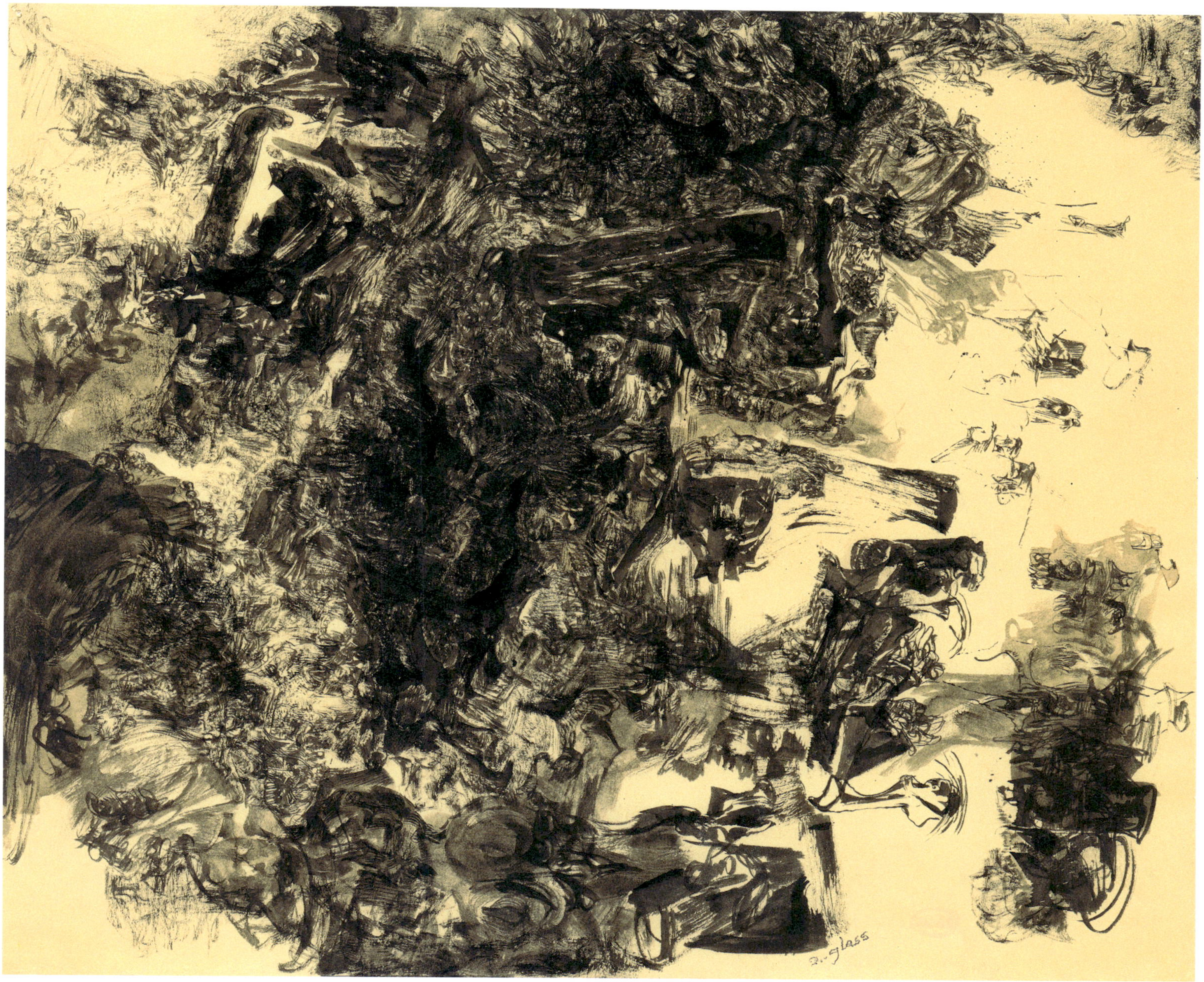

Untitled
(Club Saint-Germain period)
ca. 1954-1962
Drawing with Chinese ink and black watercolor, on paper.
22 x 27 cm
Artist's collection

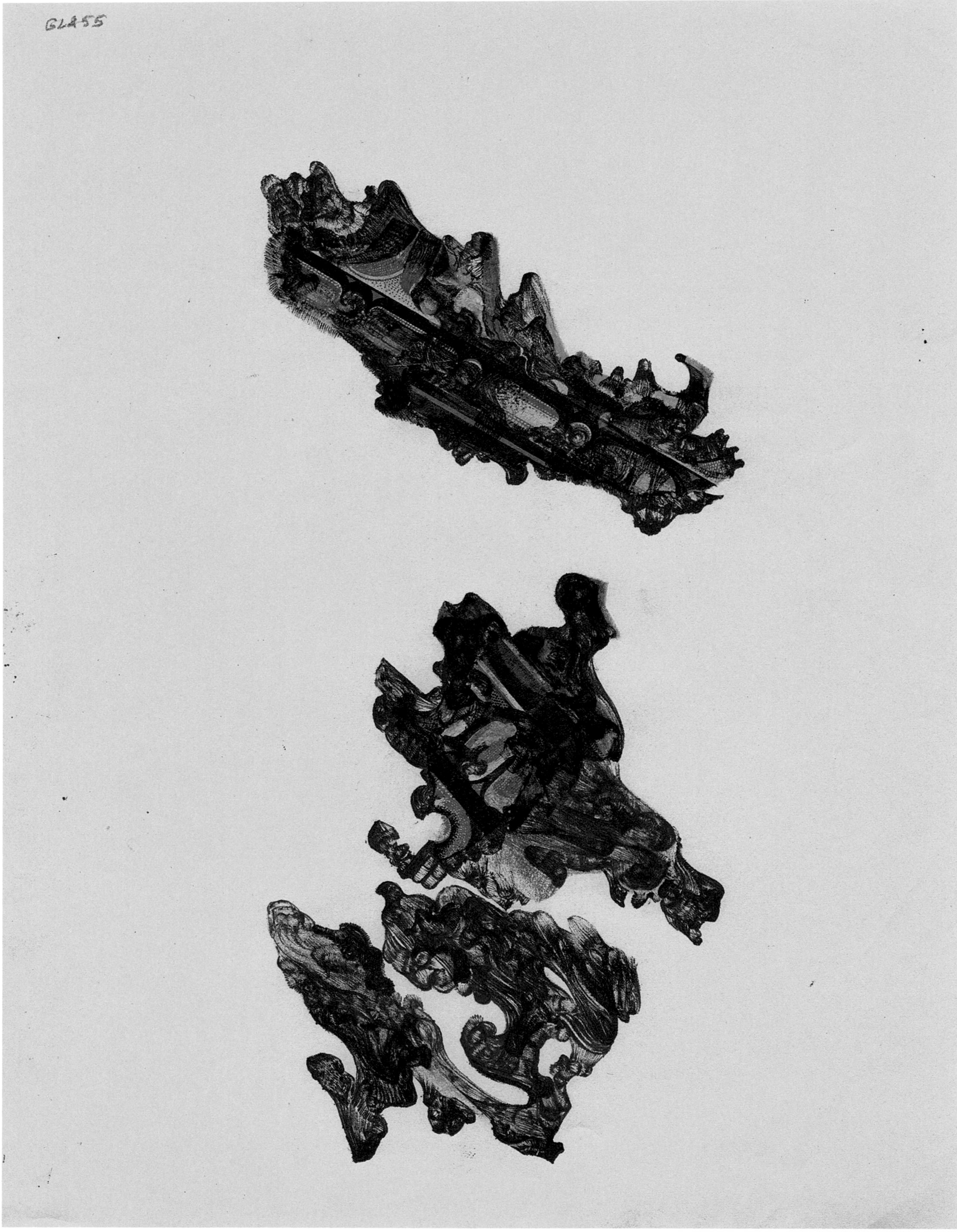

Untitled
(Club Saint-Germain period)
ca. 1954-1962
Bicolor blue and purple
ballpoint pen drawing,
with green and orange
colored pencil, with collage
application, on paper.
27 x 21 cm
Artist's collection

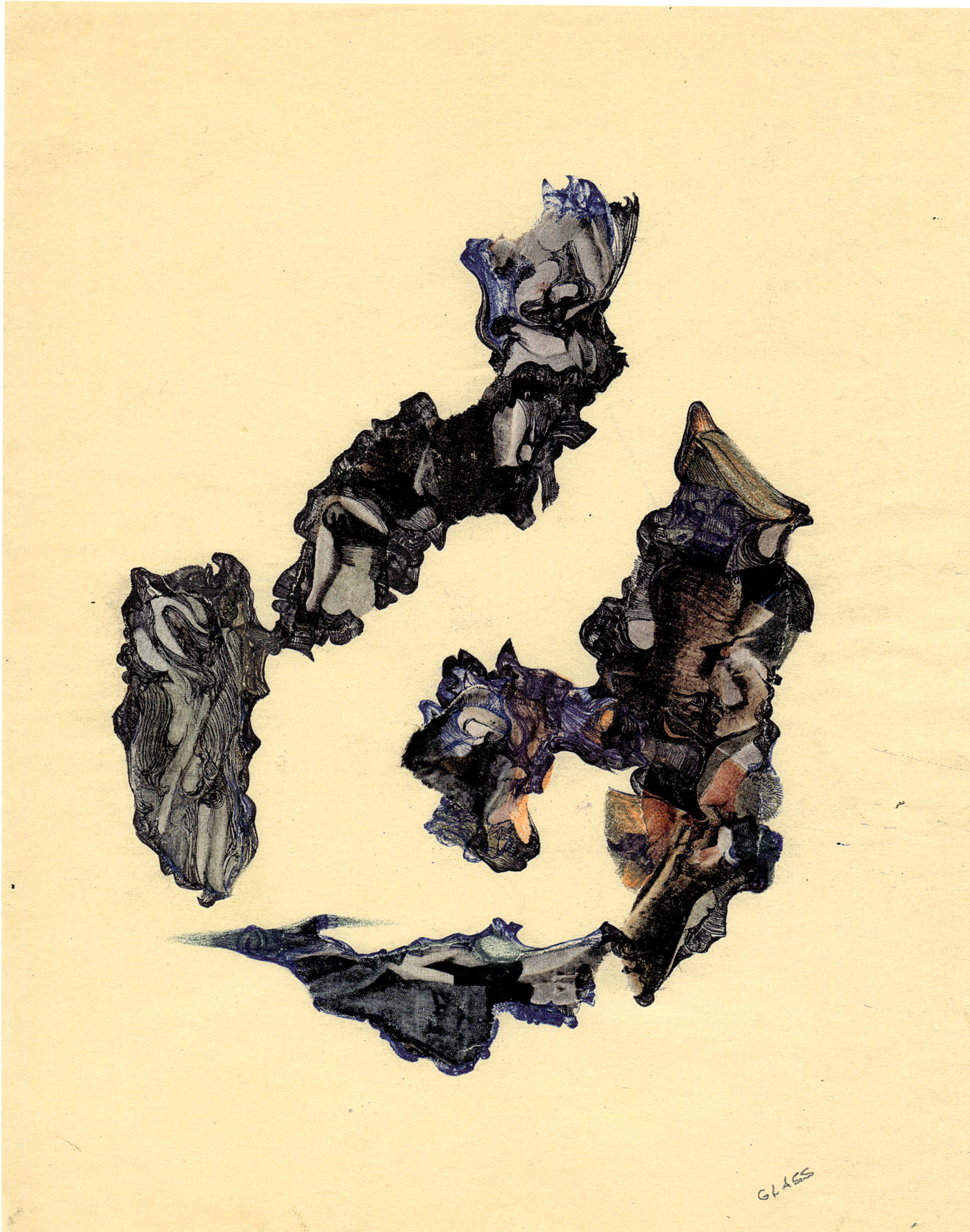

Untitled
(Club Saint-Germain period)
ca. 1954-1962
Drawing in blue, purple, and black tricolor ballpoint pen, with orange and green colored pencil, with collage application, on paper.
27 x 21.7 cm
Artist's collection

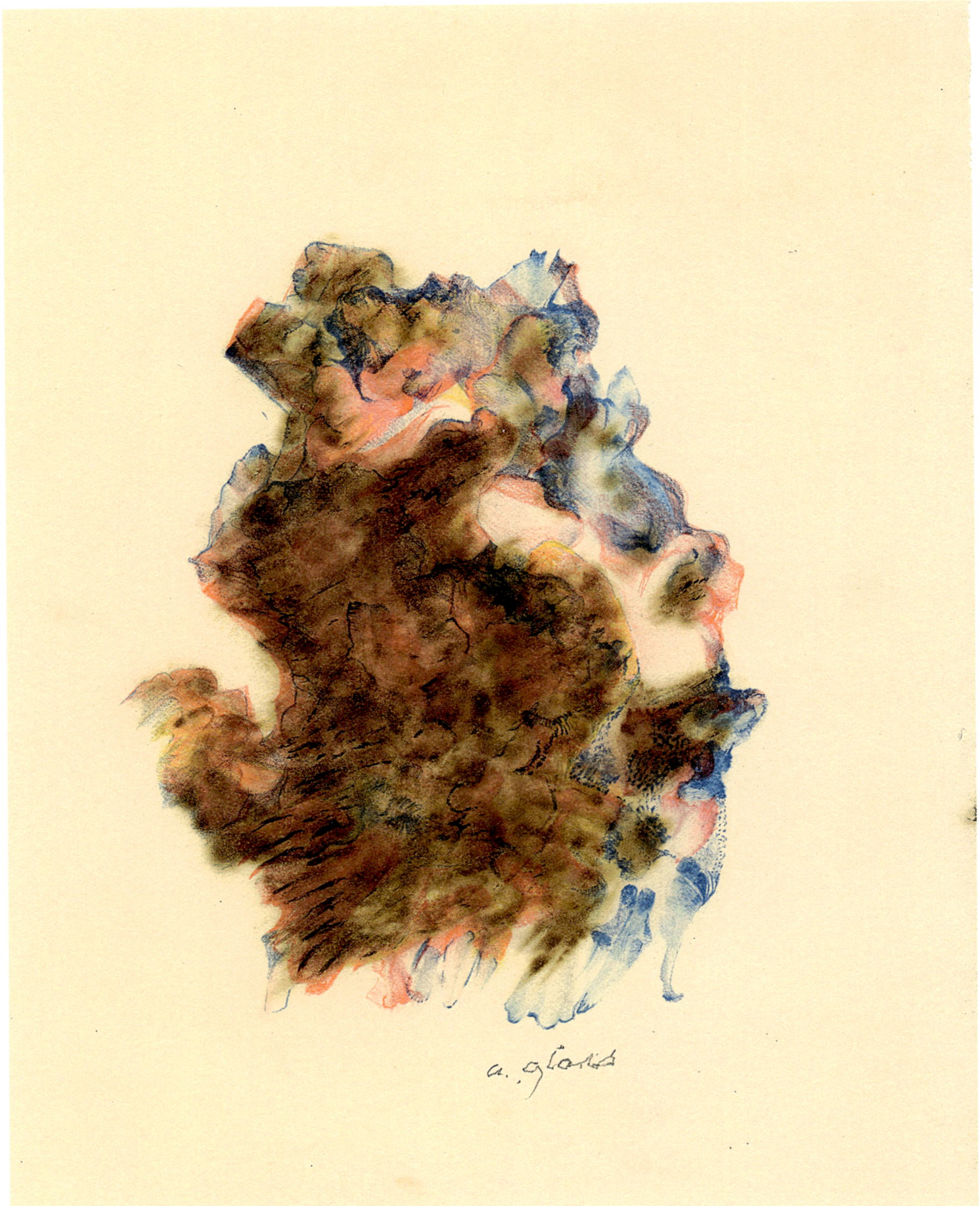

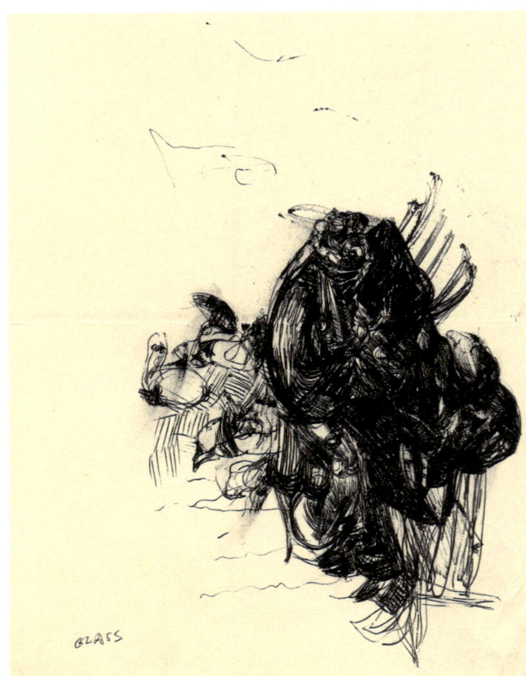

Untitled
(Club Saint-Germain period)
ca. 1954-1962
Monochrome blue ballpoint pen drawing with orange pencil and touches of allumettage, on paper.
28 x 19 cm
Artist's collection

Untitled
(Club Saint-Germain period)
ca. 1954-1962
Monochrome black ballpoint pen drawing, on paper.
17.7 x 13.5 cm
Artist's collection

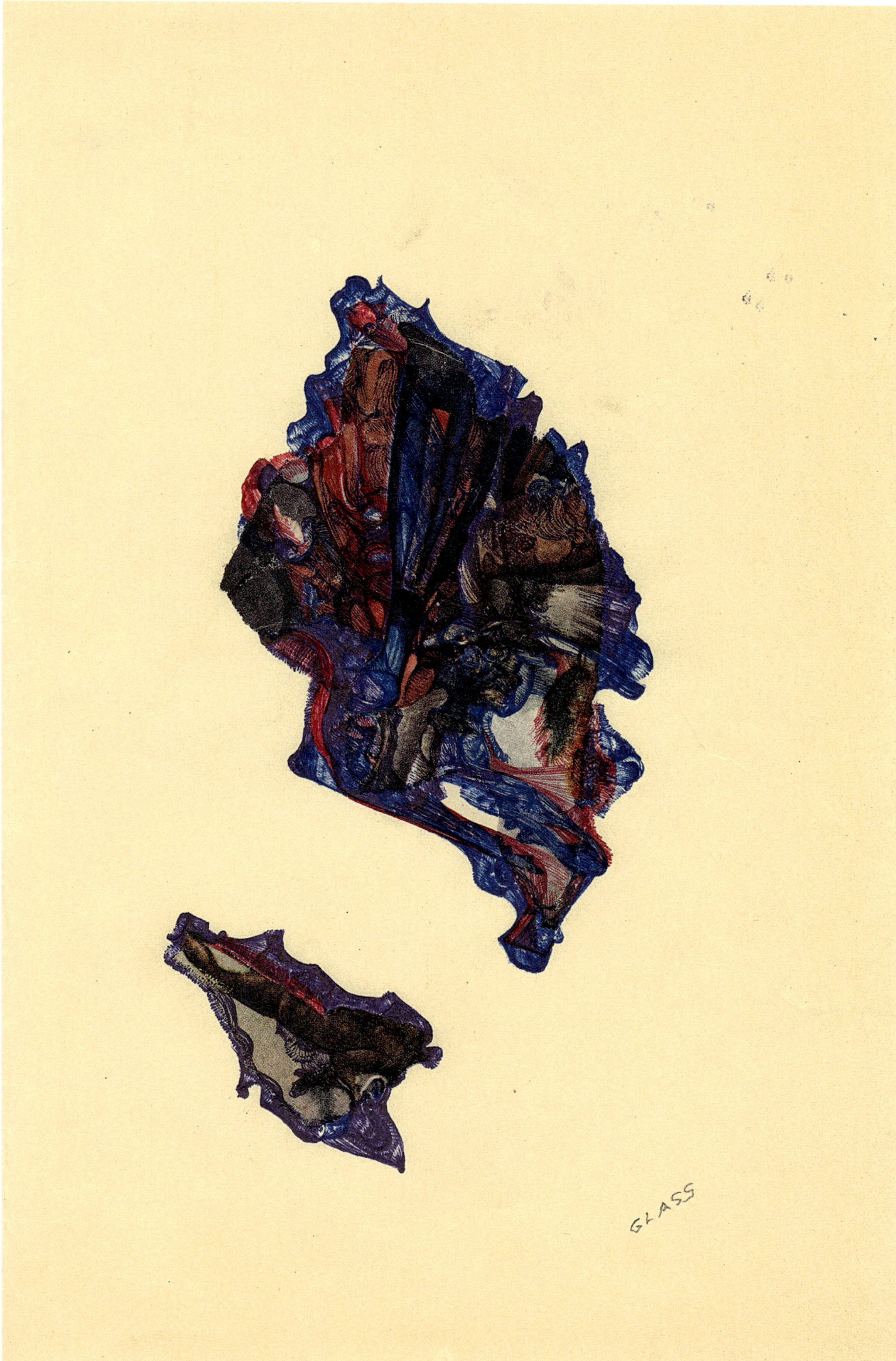

Untitled
(Club Saint-Germain period)
ca. 1954-1962
Blue, purple, and red tricolor pen drawing, with collage application, on paper.
26 x 17 cm
Artist's collection

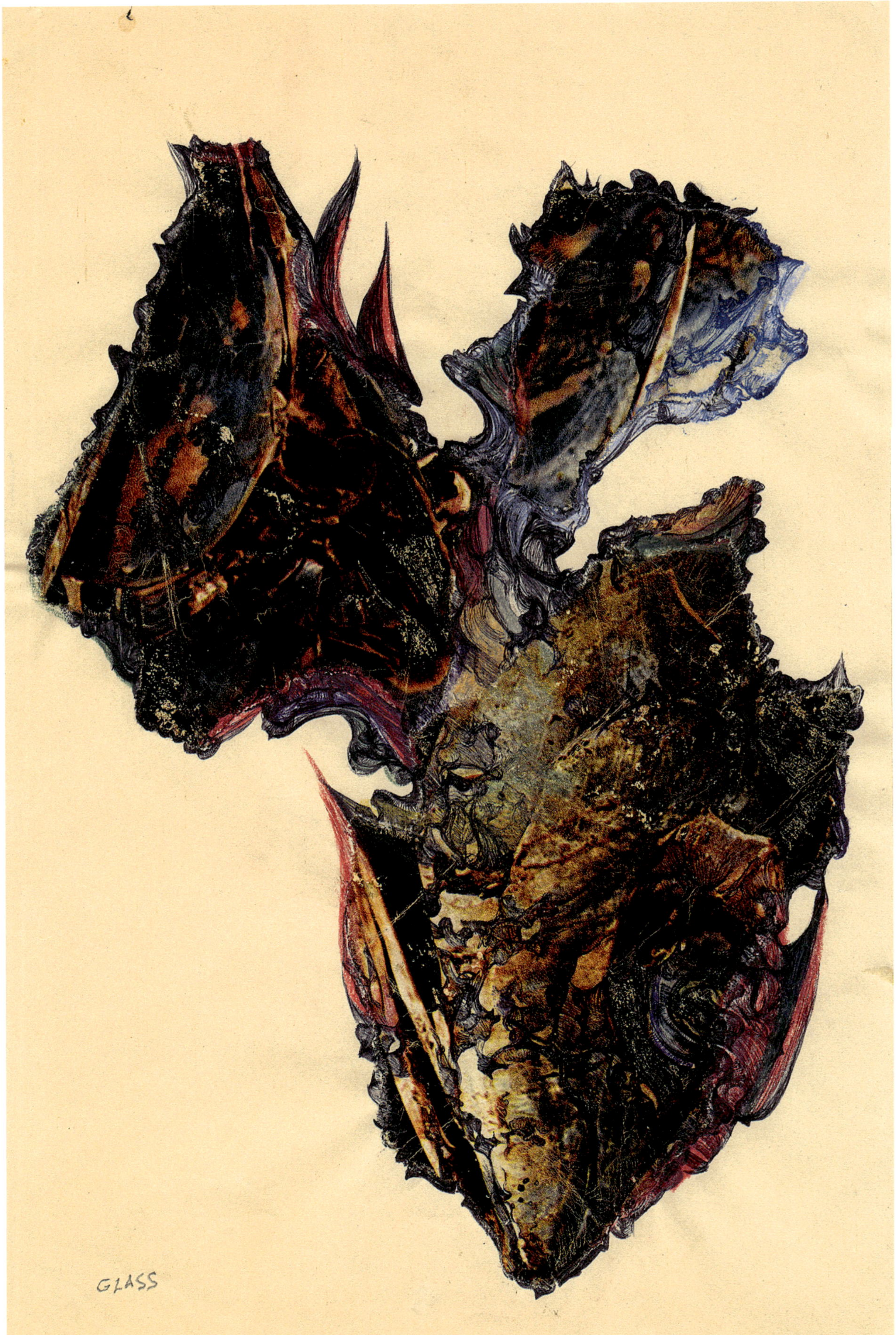

Untitled
(Club Saint-Germain period)
ca. 1954-1962
Drawing in black and blue bicolor ballpoint pen, with green, orange, and red colored pencil, with collage application, on paper.
27.1 x 17.9 cm
Artist's collection

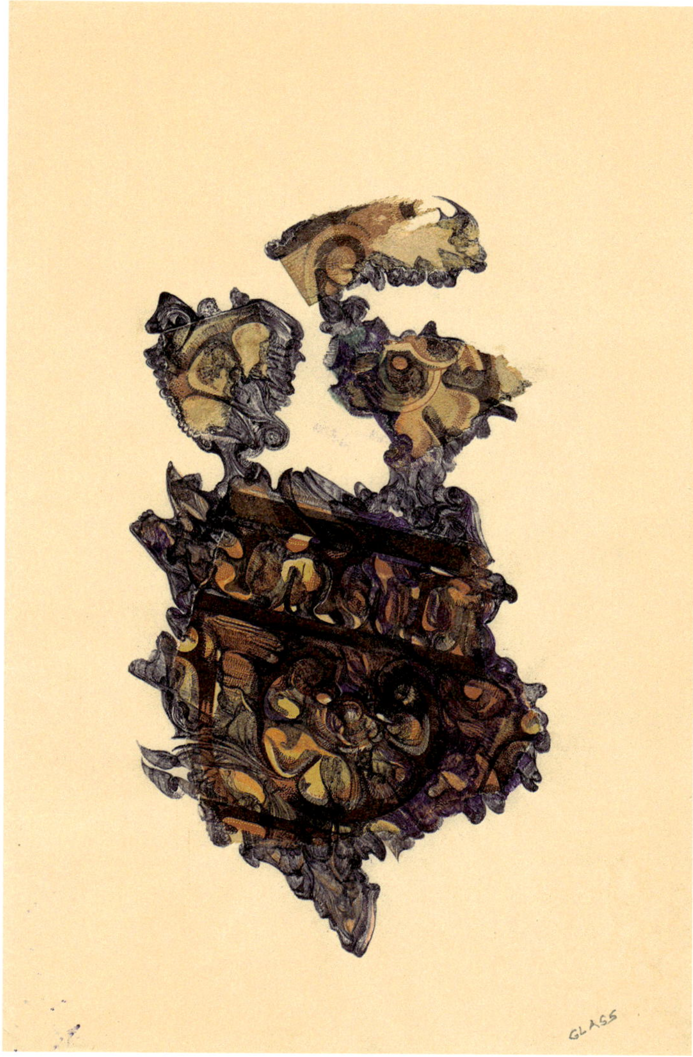

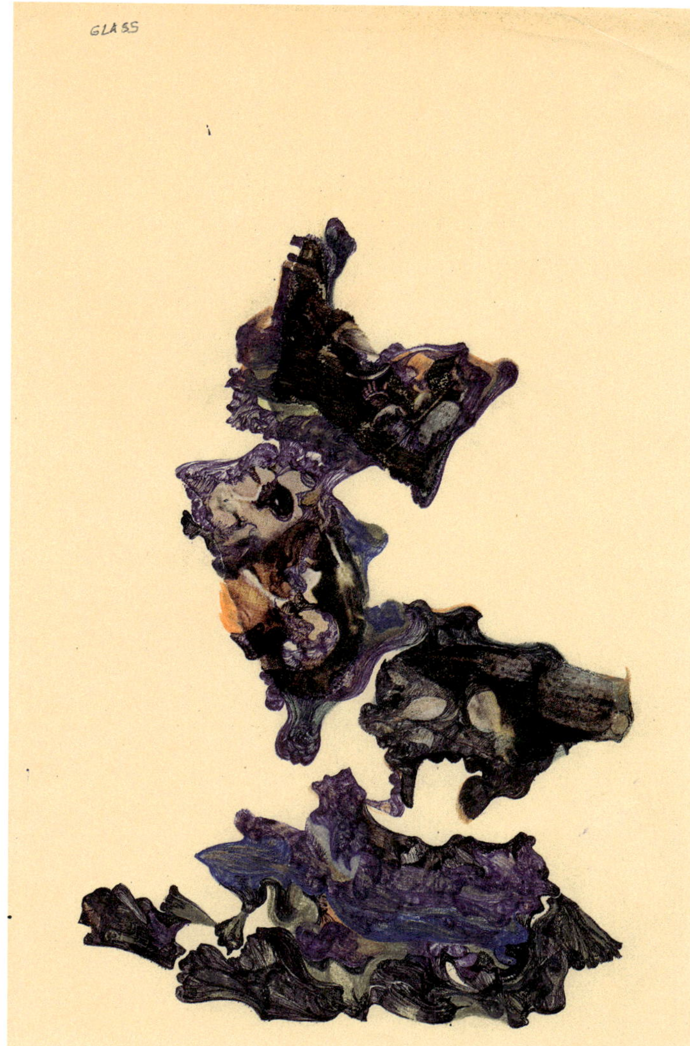

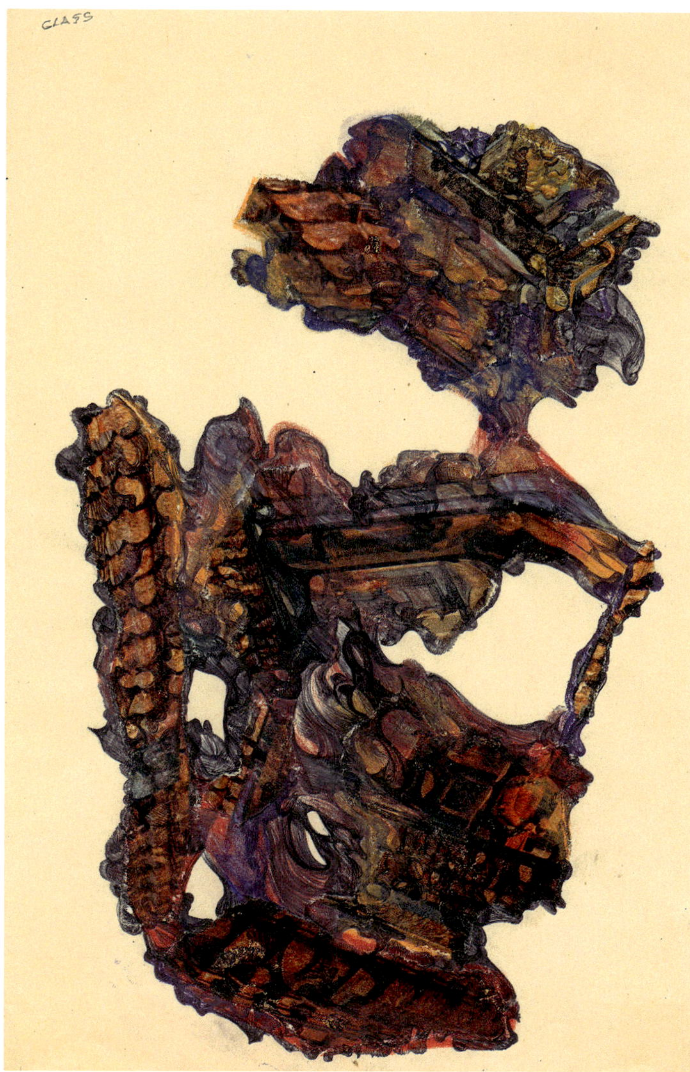

Untitled
(Club Saint-Germain period)
ca. 1954-1962
Drawing in black and purple bicolor ballpoint pen, with green and orange pencil, with collage application, on paper.
26 x 17 cm
Artist's collection

Untitled
(Club Saint-Germain period)
ca. 1954-1962
Bicolor black and purple ballpoint pen drawing, with green and orange colored pencil, with collage application, on paper.
26 x 17 cm
Artist's collection

Untitled
(Club Saint-Germain period)
ca. 1954-1962
Drawing in black and purple bicolor ballpoint pen, with green, orange and red colored pencil, with collage application, on paper.
26 x 17 cm
Artist's collection

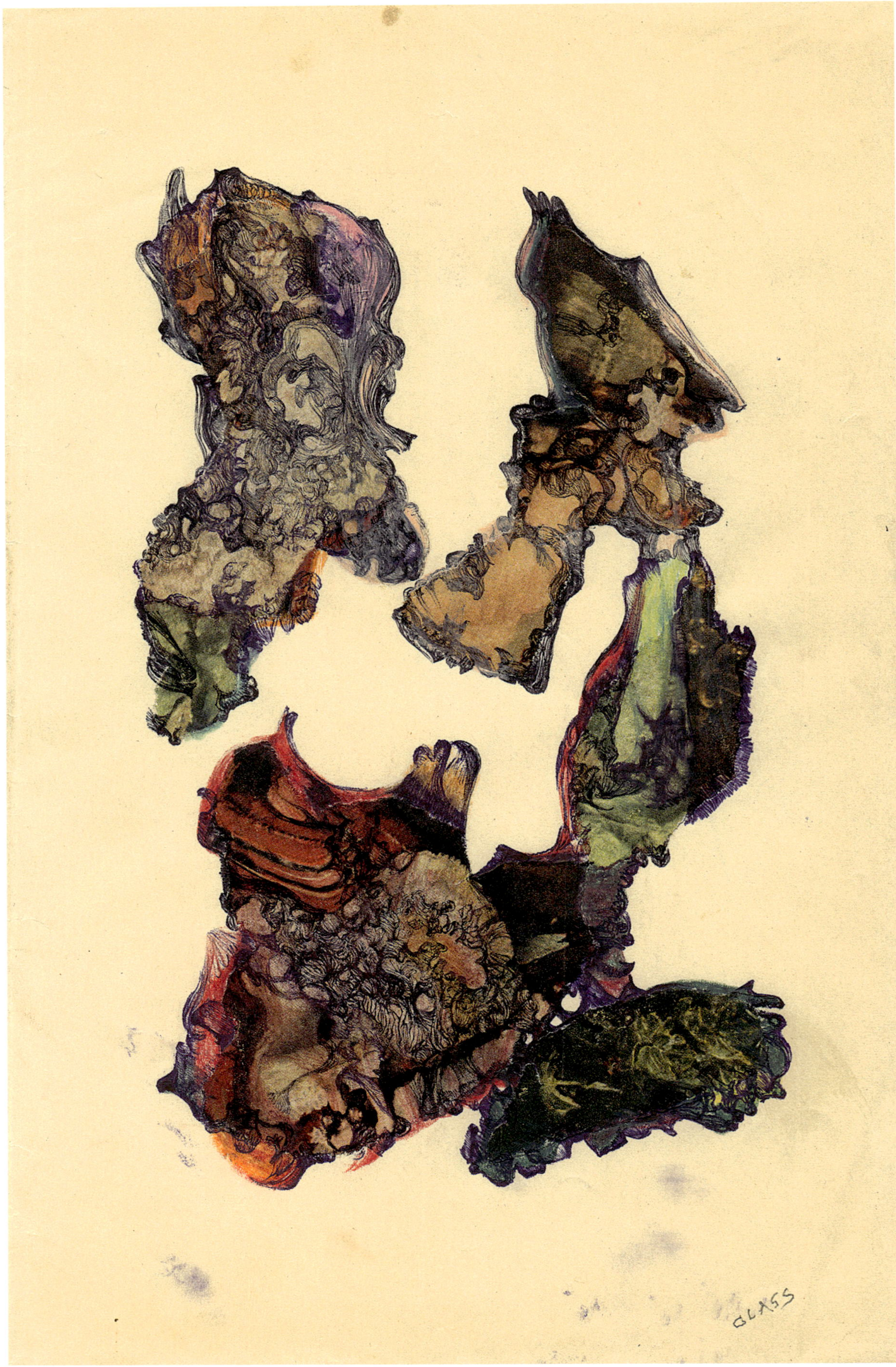

Untitled
(Club Saint-Germain period)
ca. 1954-1962
Drawing in black and blue bicolor ballpoint pen, with green, orange, and red colored pencil, with collage application, on paper.
26 x 17 cm
Artist's collection

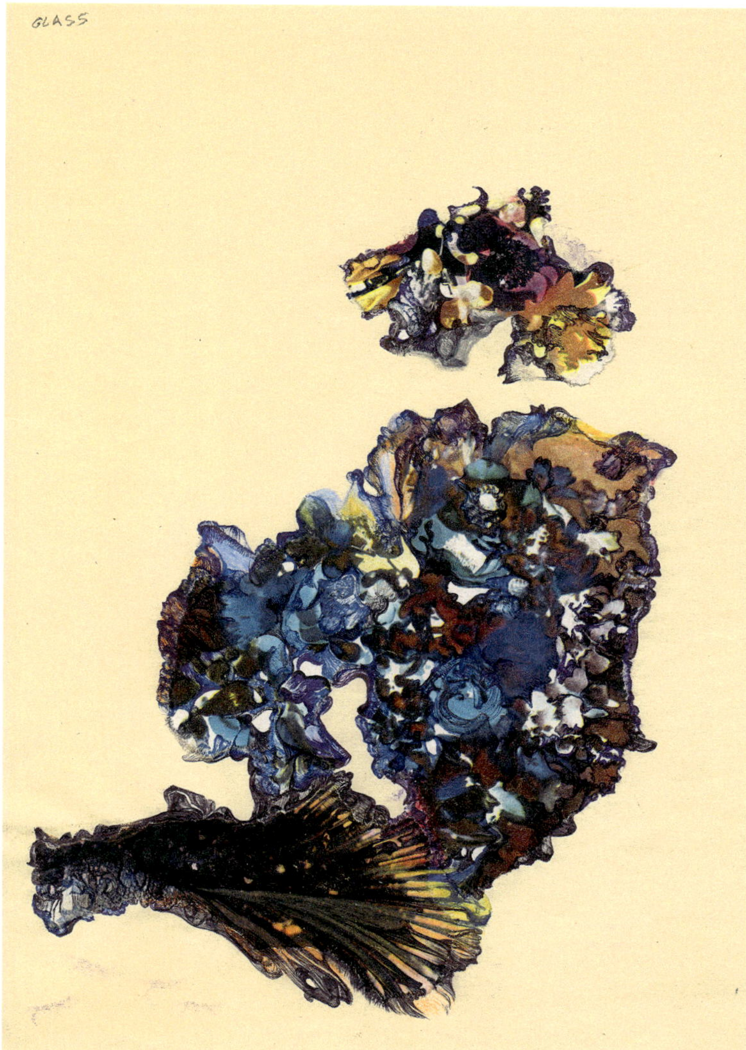

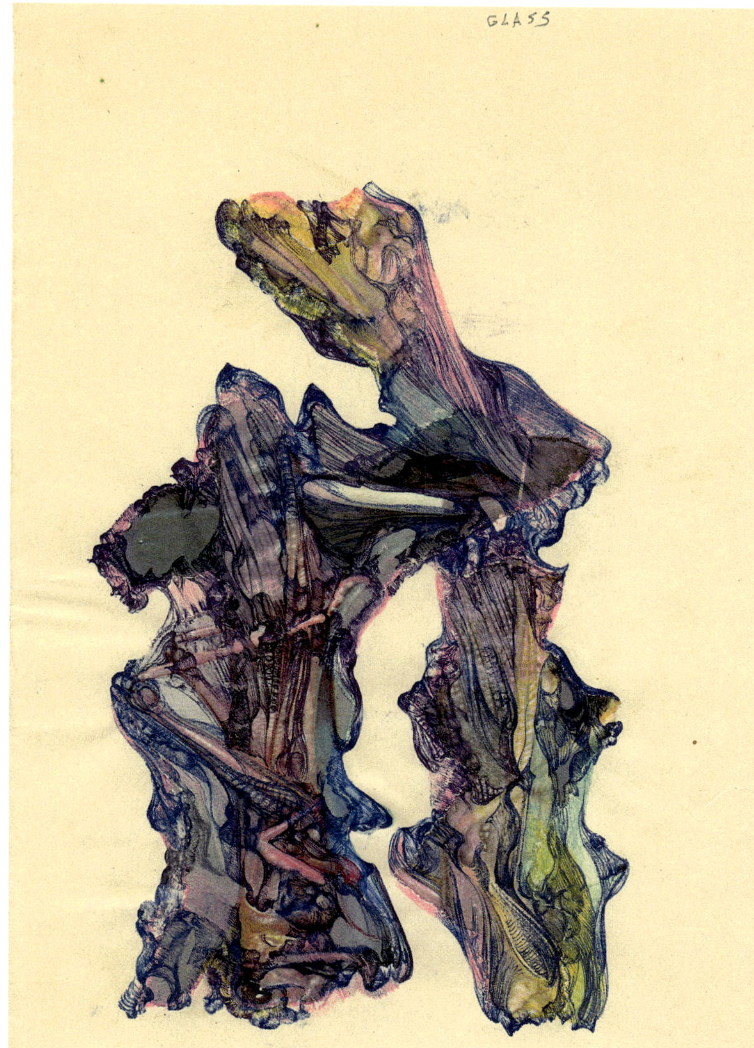

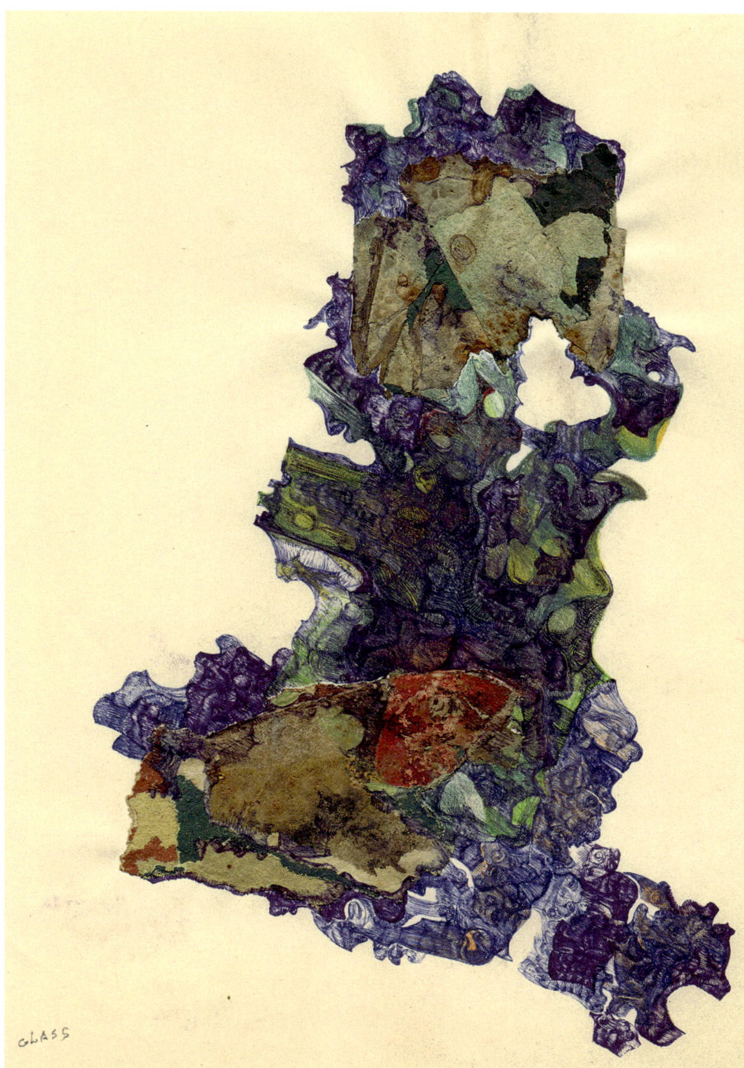

Untitled
(Club Saint-Germain period)
ca. 1954-1962
Drawing in blue, purple, and black tricolor ballpoint pen, with orange and yellow colored pencil, with collage application, on paper.
27 x 21.7 cm
Artist's collection

Untitled
(Club Saint-Germain period)
ca. 1954-1962
Bicolor blue and purple ballpoint pen drawing, with green, yellow, and pink colored pencil, with collage application, on paper.
26 x 17 cm
Artist's collection

Untitled
(Club Saint-Germain period)
ca. 1954-1962
Bicolor blue and purple ballpoint pen drawing, with green and orange colored pencil, with collage application, on paper.
27 x 21 cm
Artist's collection

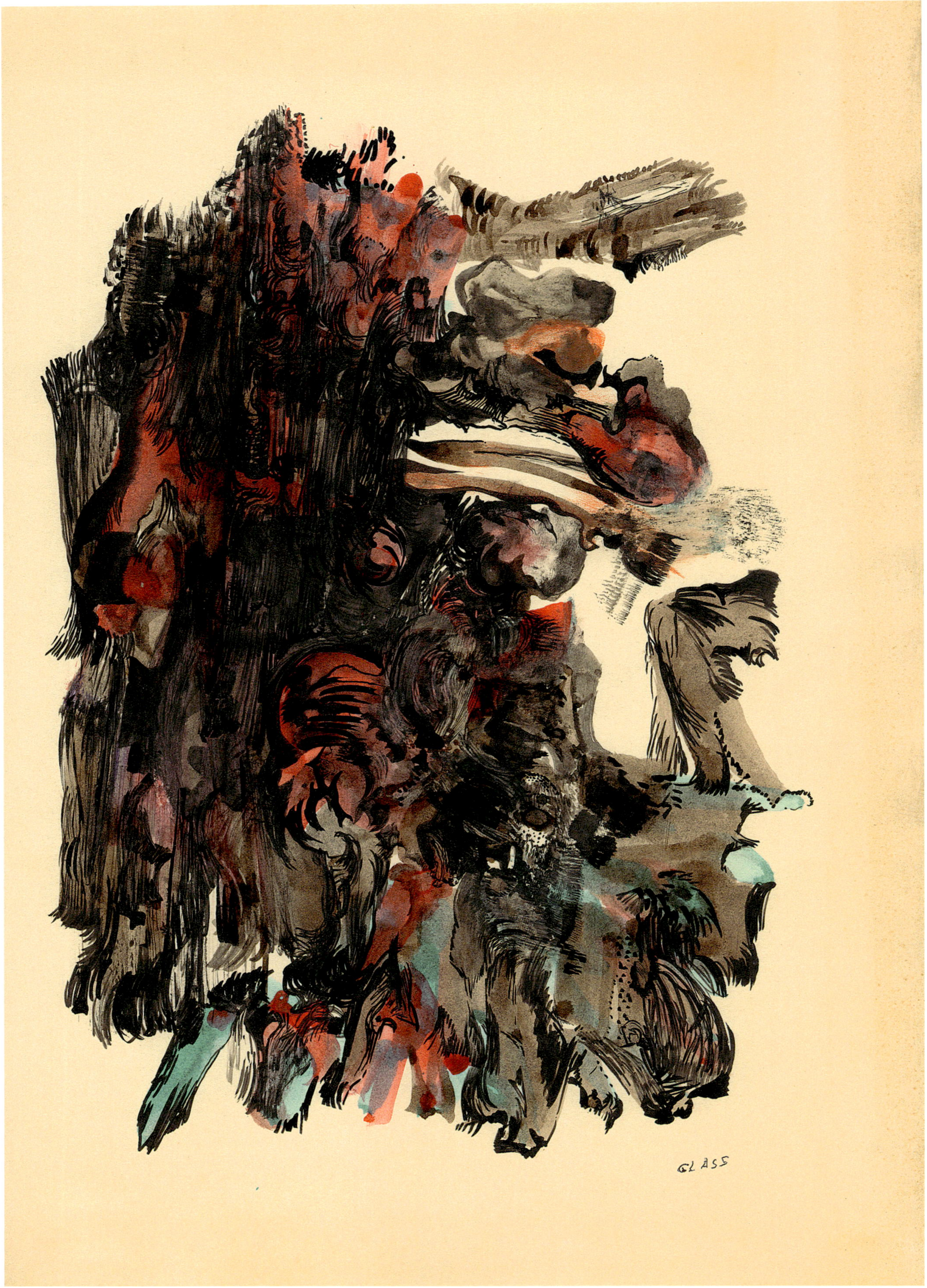

Untitled
(Club Saint-Germain period)
ca. 1954-1962
Indian ink drawing,
blue and red watercolor,
on paper.
30 x 24.5 cm
Artist's collection

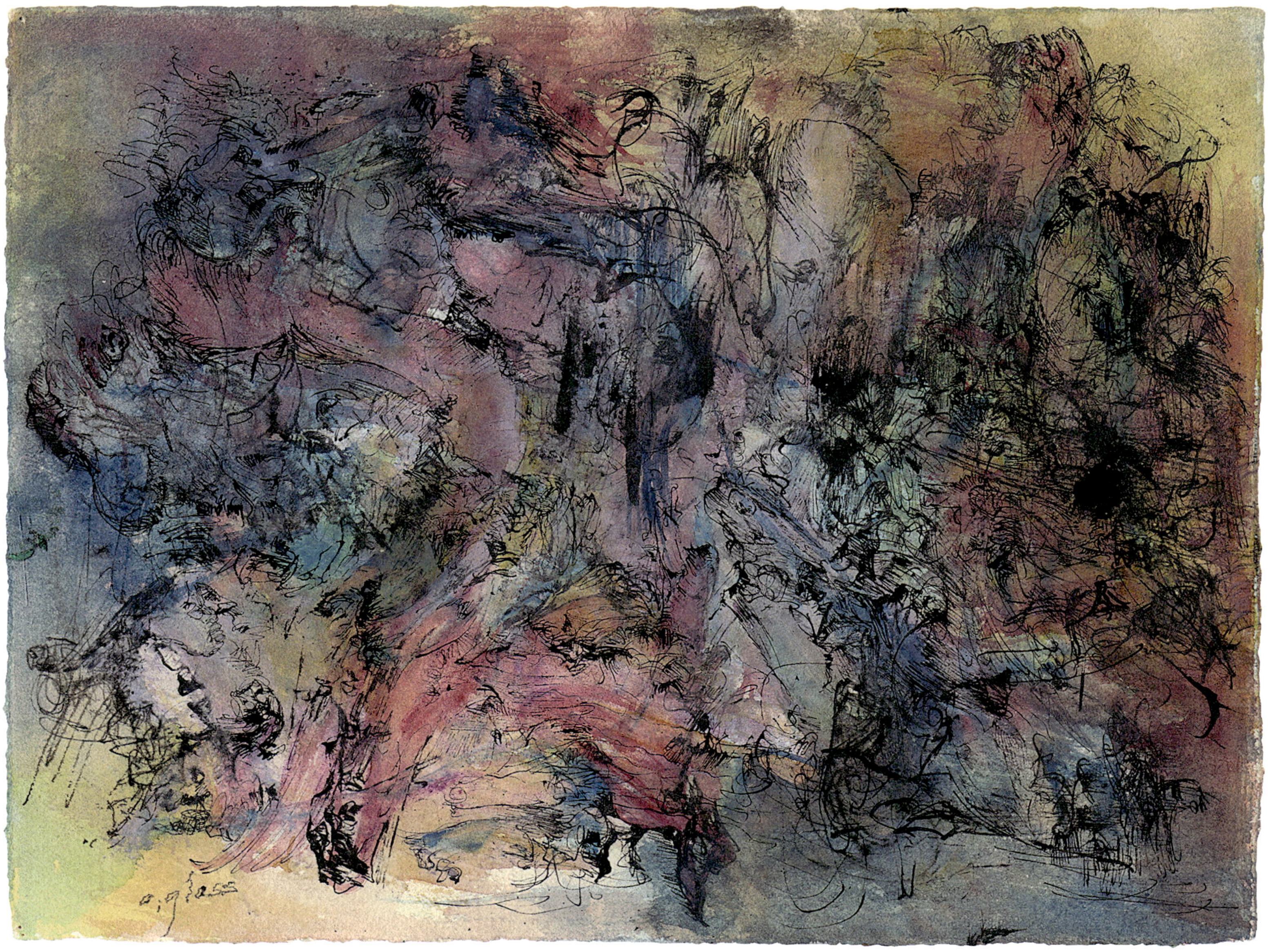

Untitled
(Club Saint-Germain period)
ca. 1954-1962
Black pen drawing, Indian ink, with brown, aqua blue, pink, and yellow watercolor, on paper.
14 x 19.1 cm
Artist's collection

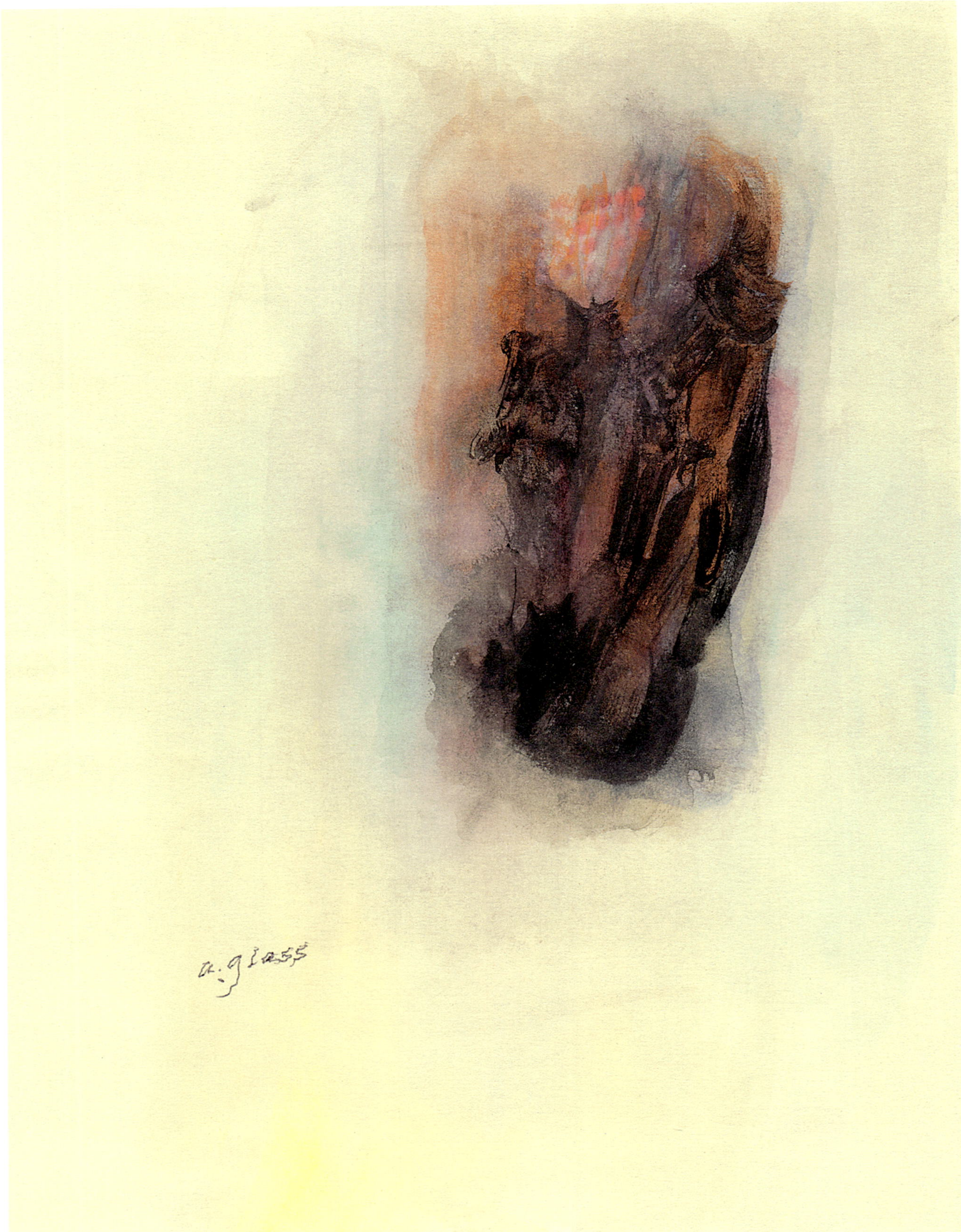

Untitled
(Club Saint-Germain period)
ca. 1954-1962
Black pen drawing, Indian ink, with brown, aqua blue, and pink watercolor, on paper.
19.8 x 12.2 cm
Artist's collection

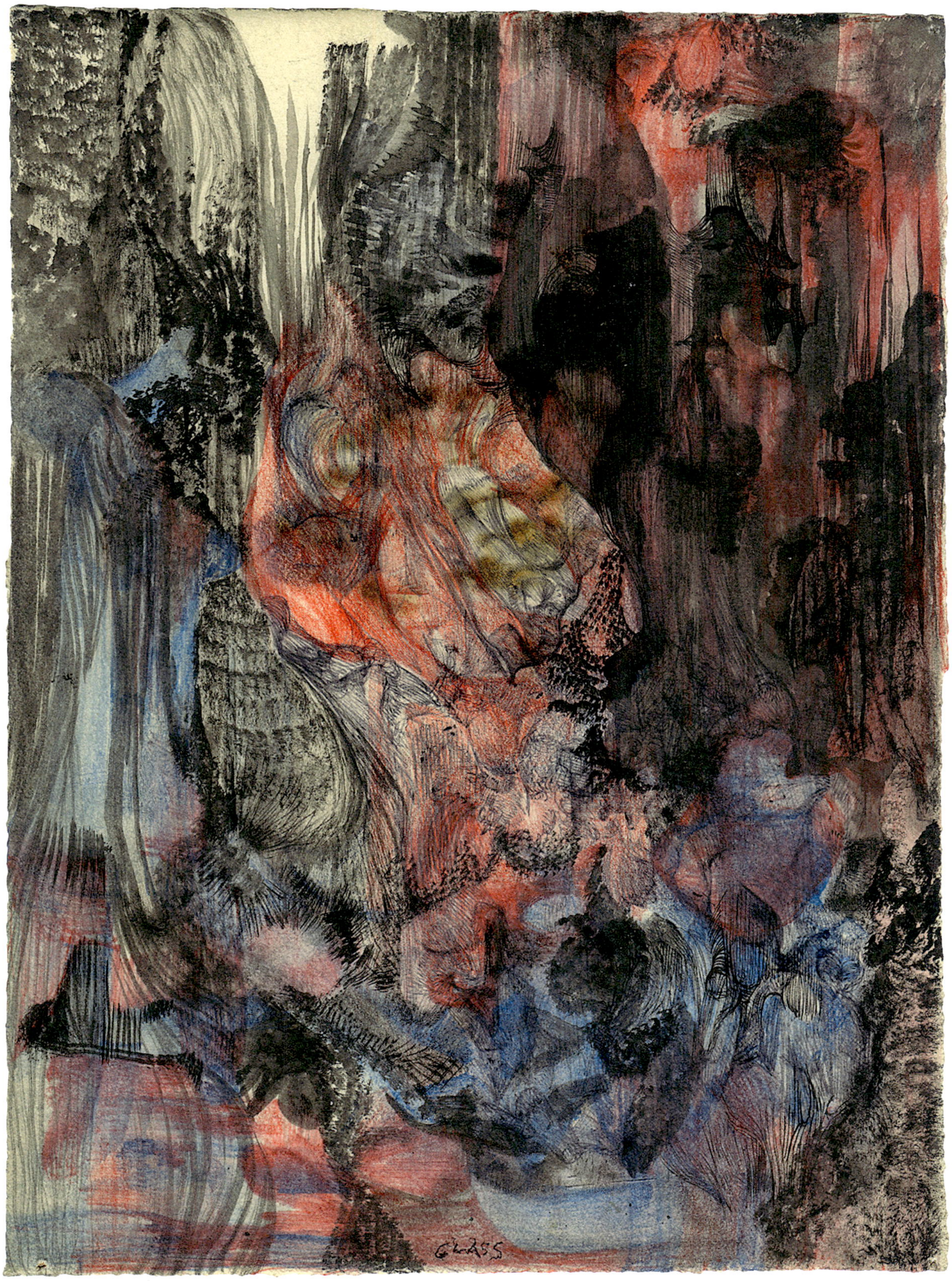

Untitled
(Club Saint-Germain period)
ca. 1954-1962
Blue pen drawing, India ink, blue and red color, on paper.
19 x 14 cm
Artist's collection

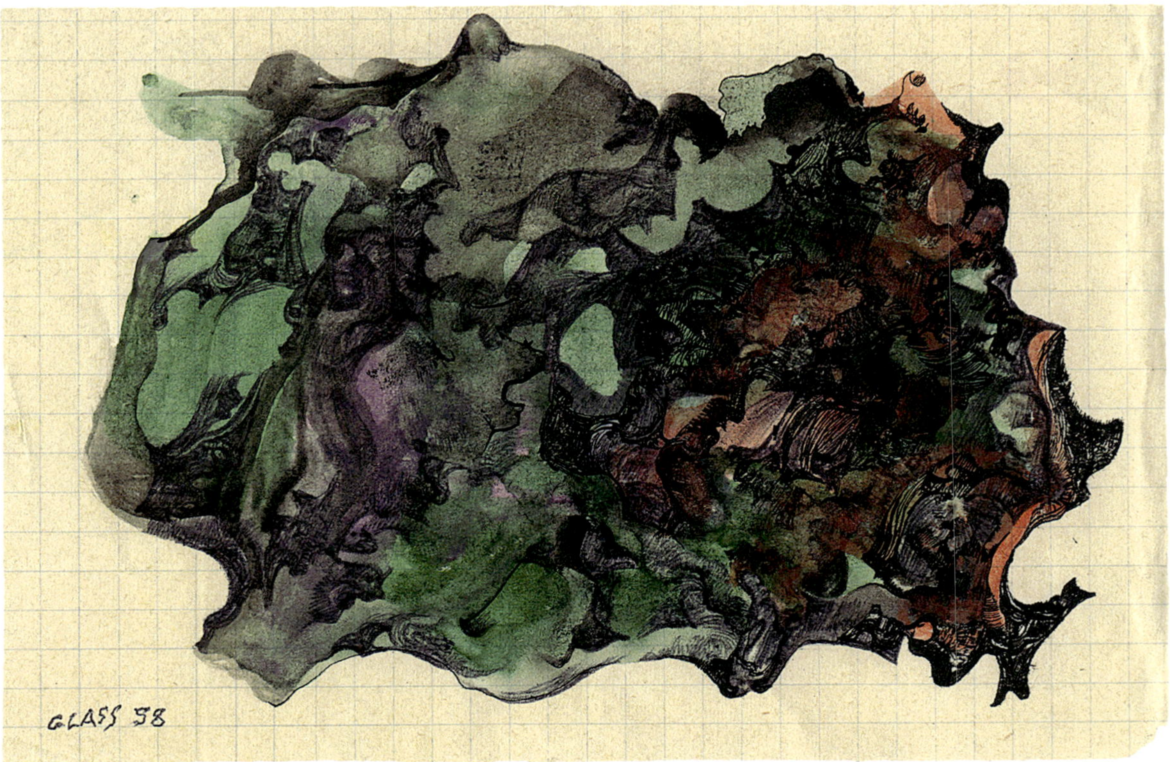

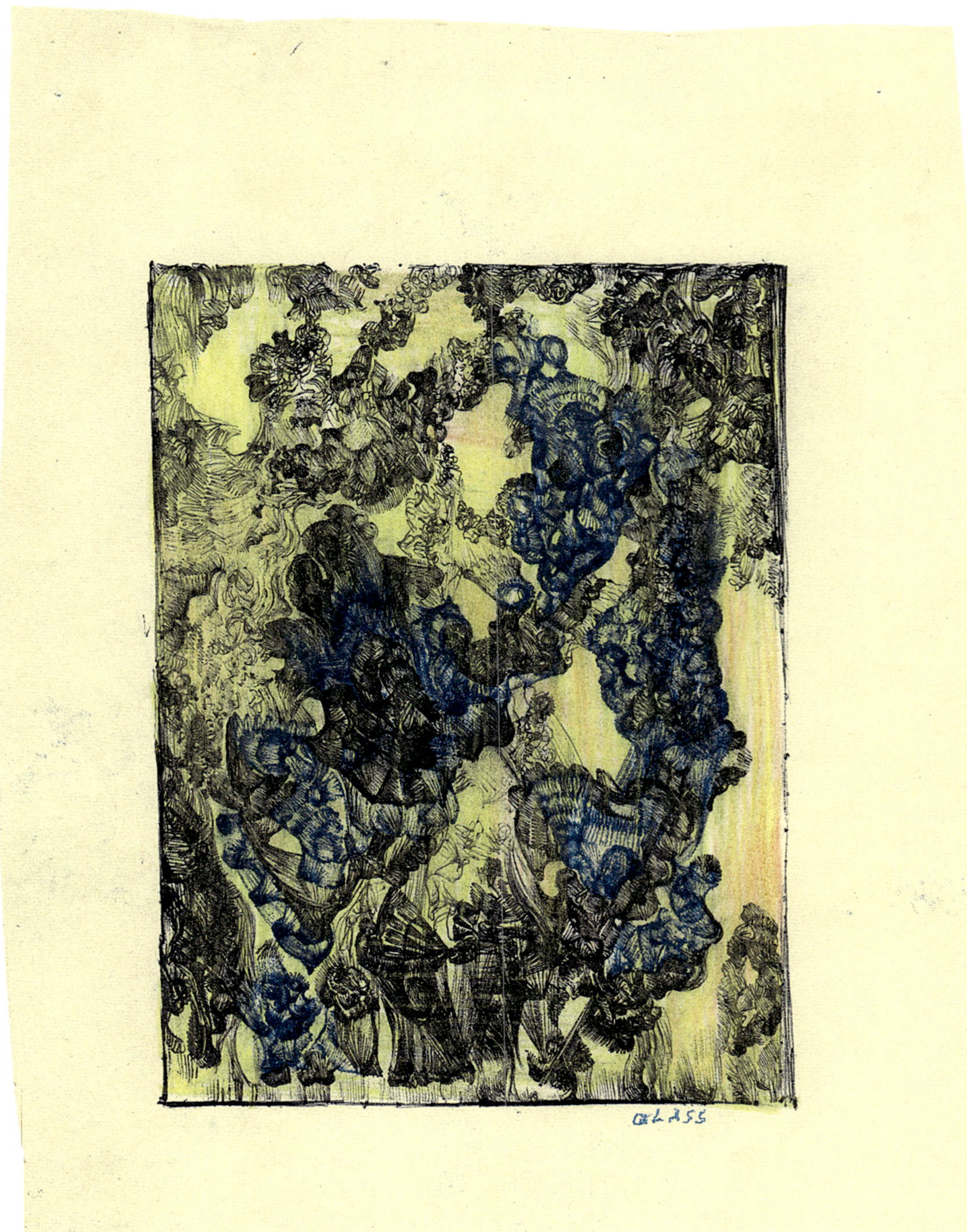

Untitled
(Club Saint-Germain period)
1958
Black pen drawing, India ink, with green, violet, and orange watercolor, on squared paper.
9.5 x 15.1 cm
Artist's collection

Untitled
(Club Saint-Germain period)
ca. 1954-1962
Blue, purple, orange, yellow, and black watercolor, on paper.
21.5 x 14 cm
Artist's collection

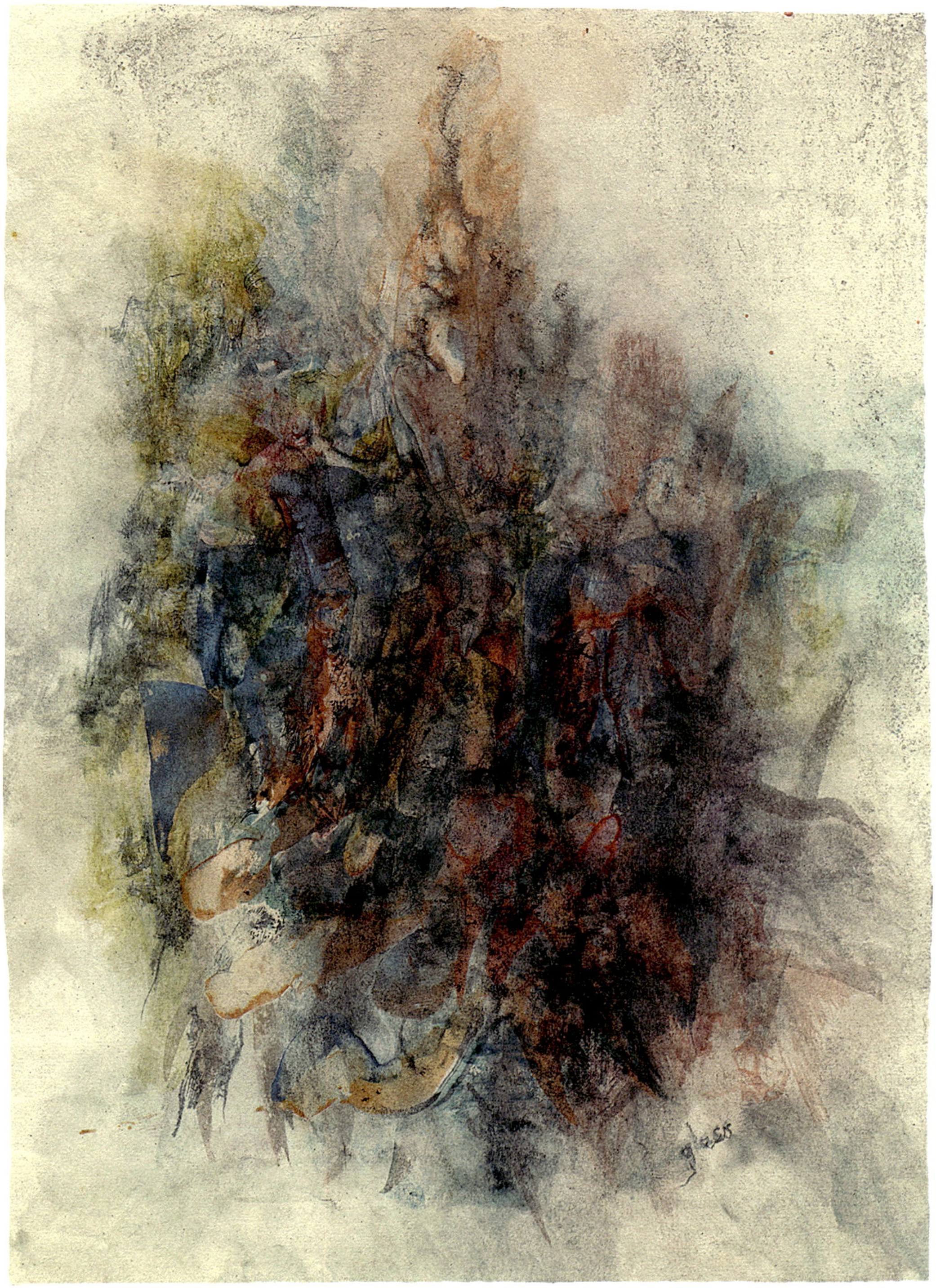

Untitled
(Club Saint-Germain period)
ca. 1954-1962
Blue, purple, orange, yellow,
and black watercolor,
on paper.
17.3 x 12.5 cm
Artist's collection

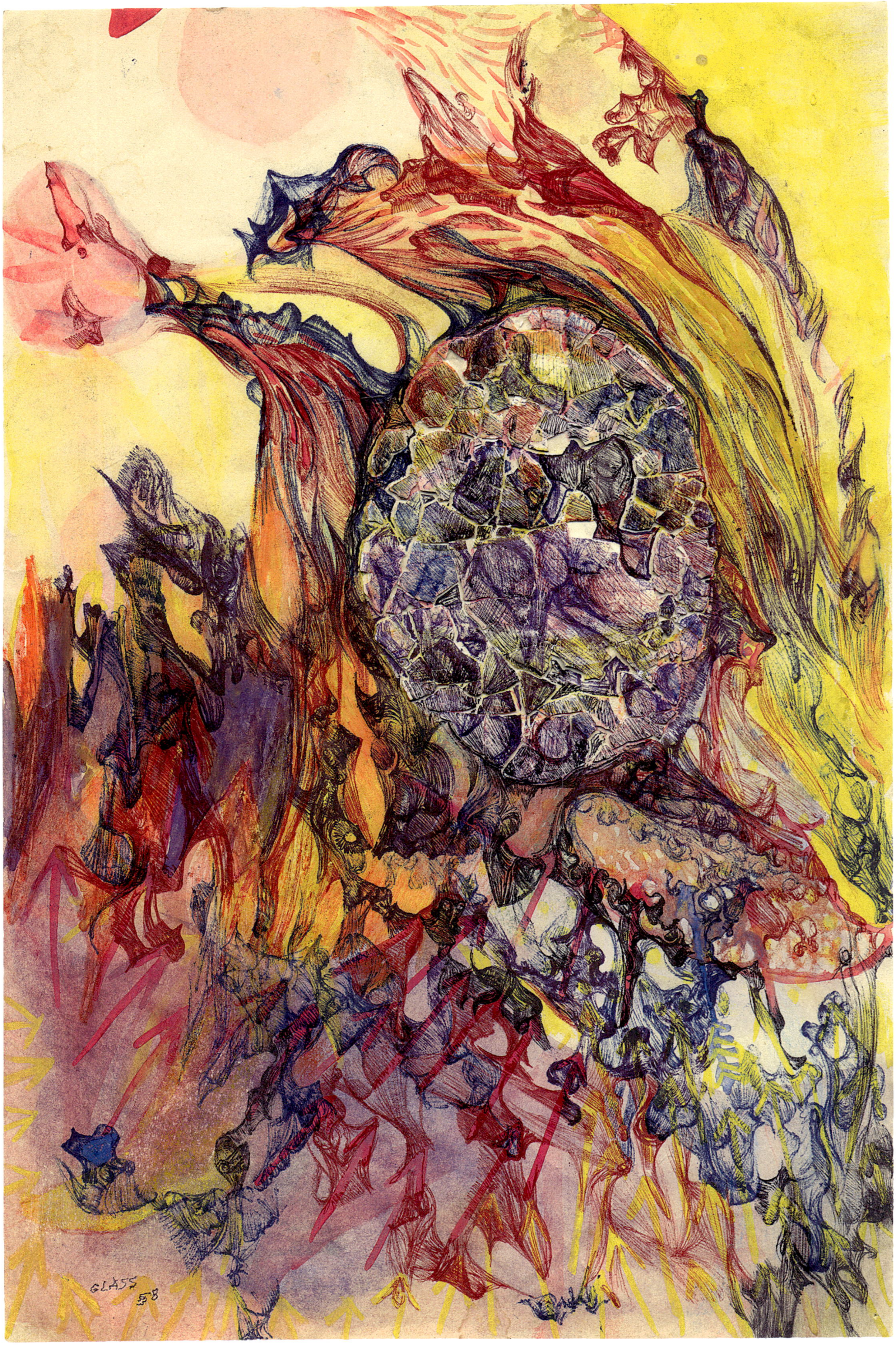
GLASS
58

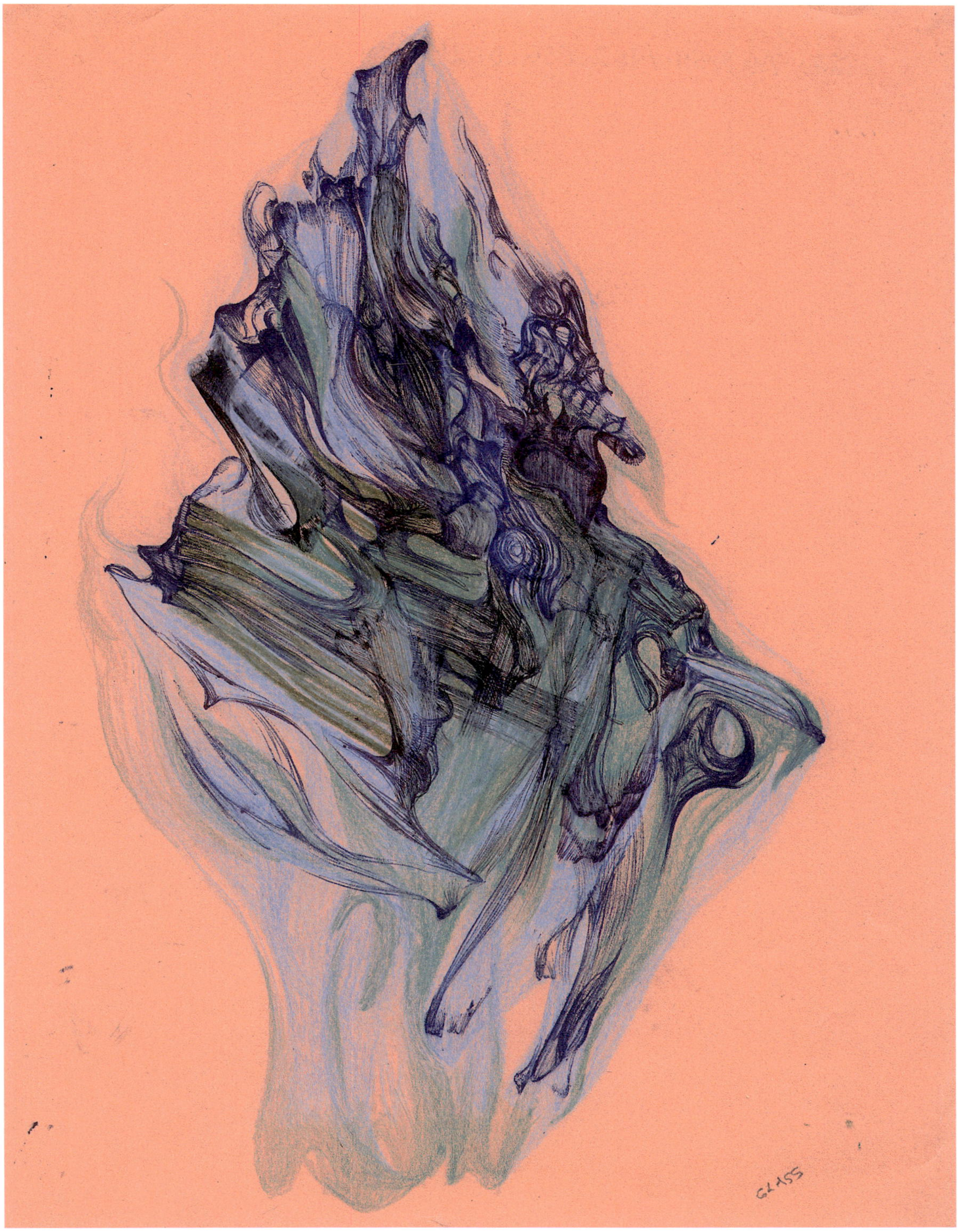

Untitled
(Club Saint-Germain period)
1958
Blue, purple, red, and black quadricolor pen drawing, with orange, yellow and lilac watercolor pencil with eggshell application, on paper.
27 x 18 cm
Artist's collection
Previous page

Untitled
(Club Saint-Germain period)
ca. 1954-1962
Blue, purple and black tricolor pen drawing, with sky blue, turquoise and olive green pencil, on pink paper.
27 x 21.1 cm
Artist's collection

LE
RAIN
AGUE
PARIS
VIE

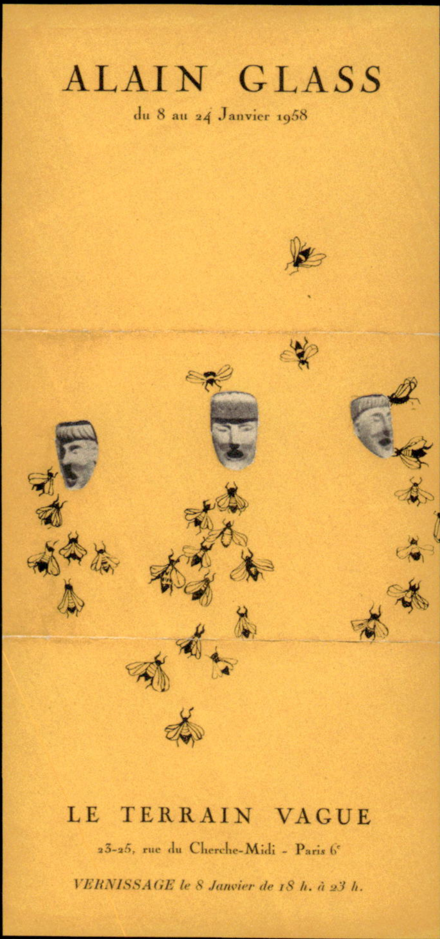

ALAIN GLASS

du 8 au 24 Janvier 1958

LE TERRAIN VAGUE

23-25, rue du Cherche-Midi - Paris 6e

VERNISSAGE le 8 Janvier de 18 h. à 23 h.

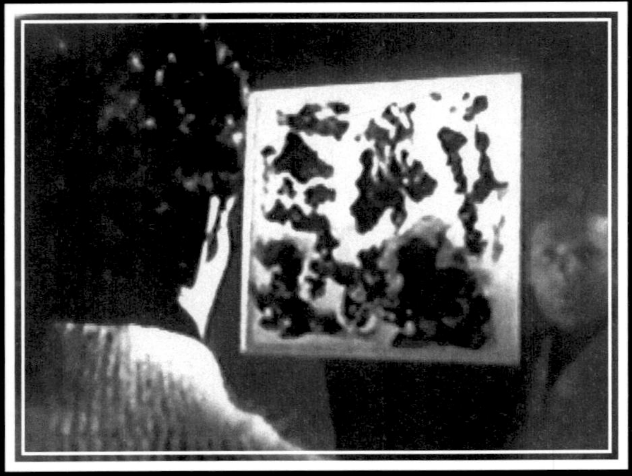
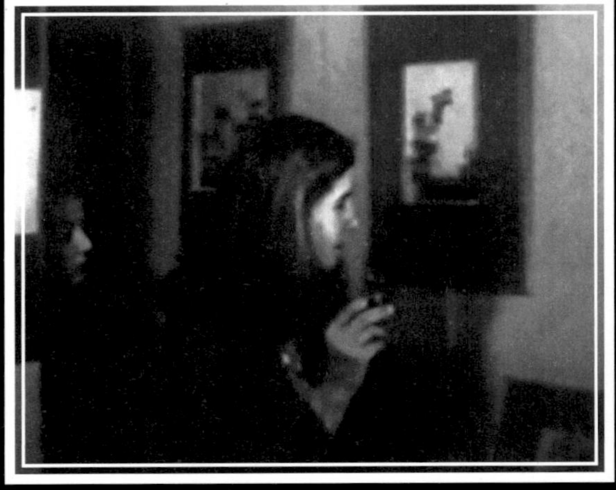
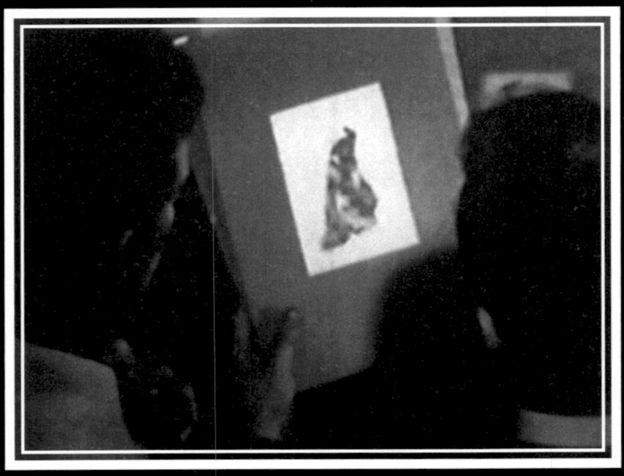
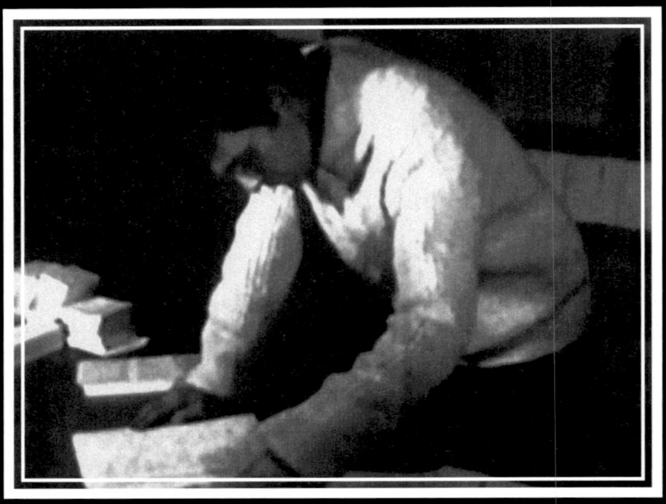
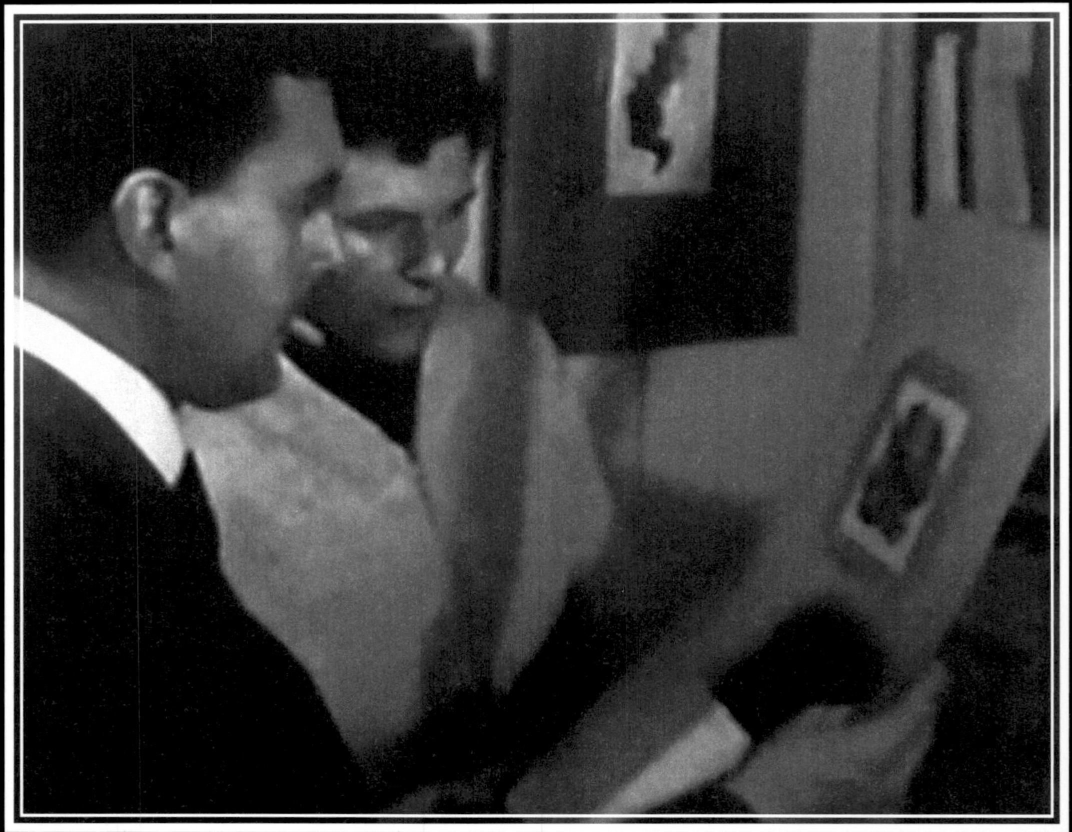

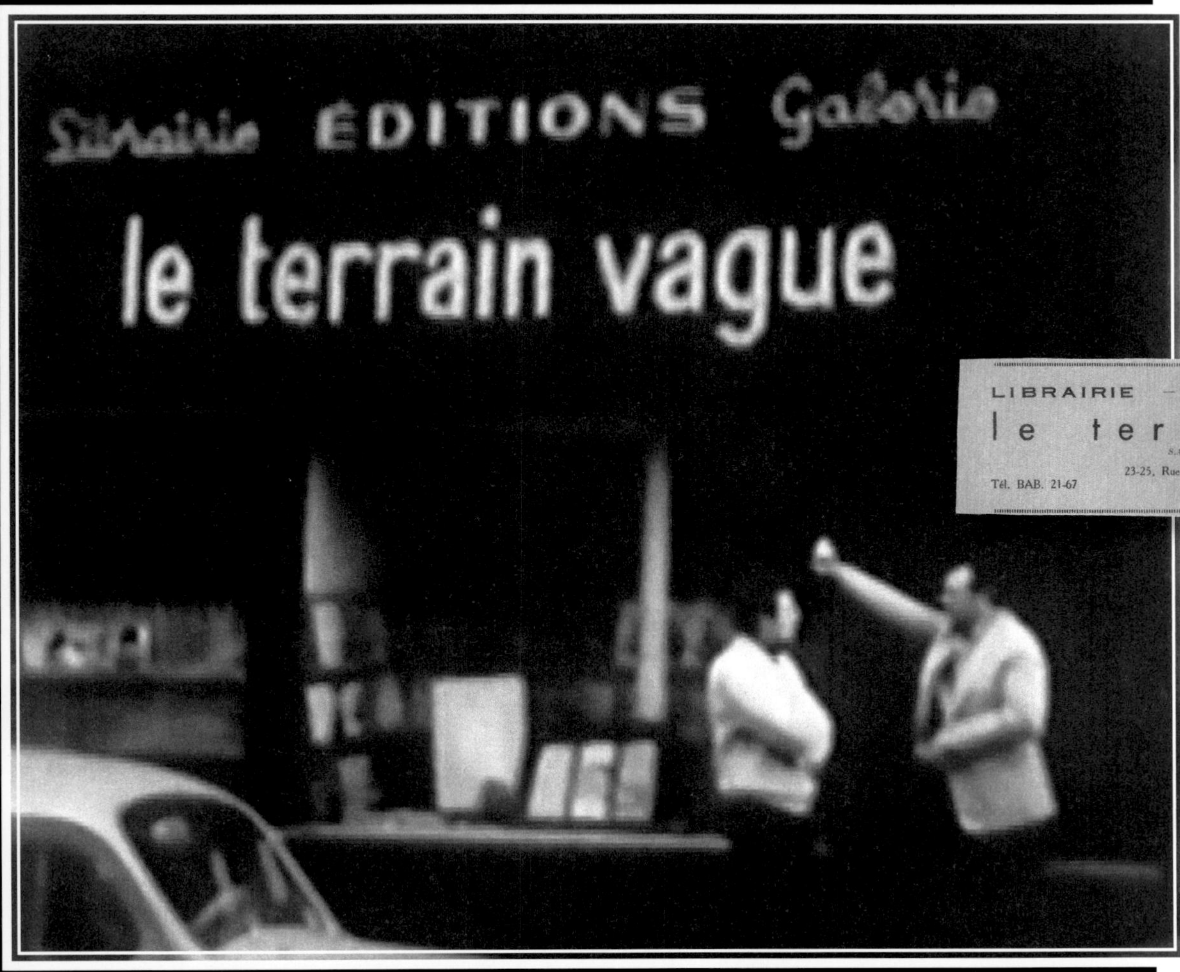

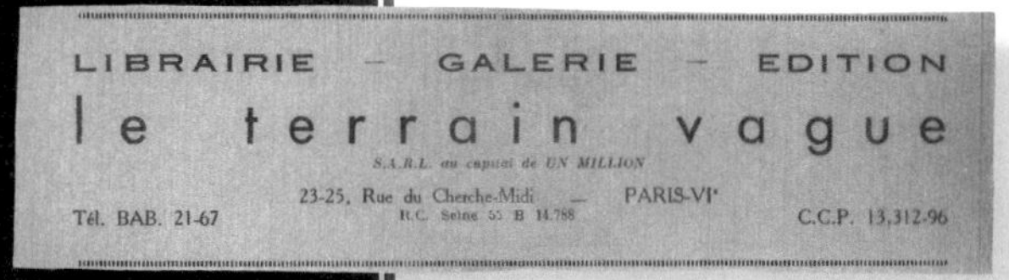

Images taken from the video made by Radio Canada, *ca*. 1950.
Duration 3'.

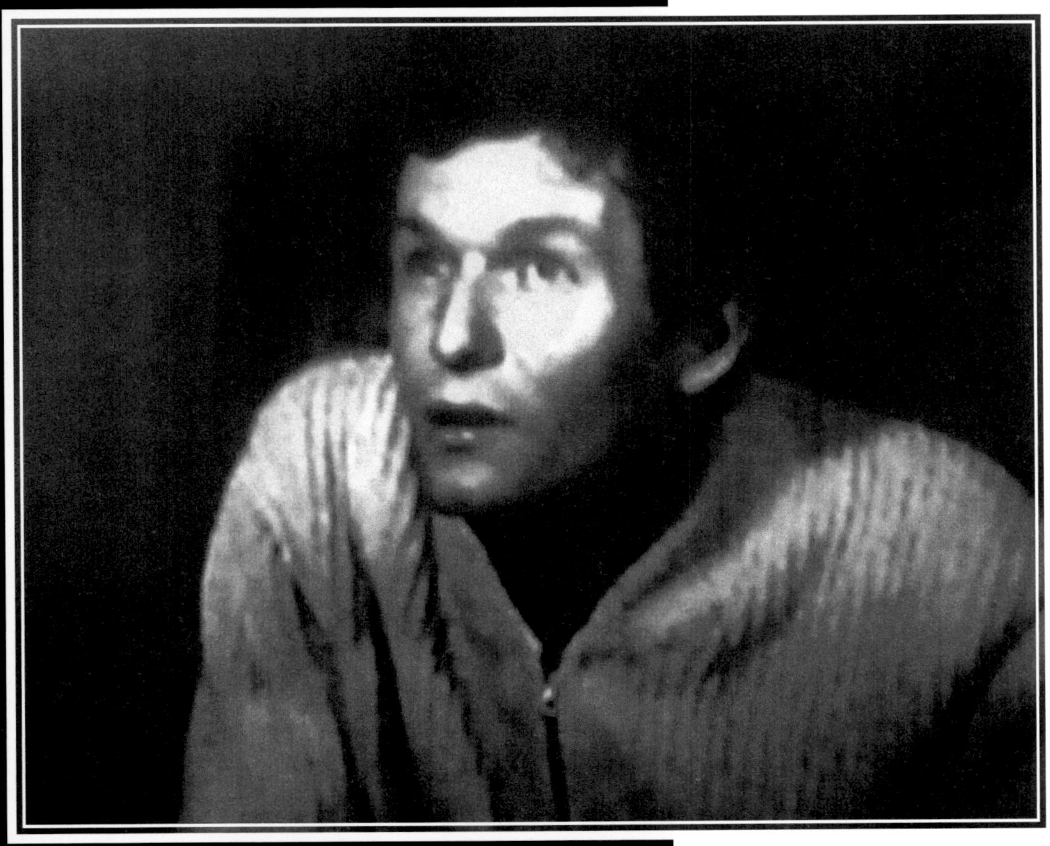

ALAIN GLASS

du 8 au 24 Janvier 1958

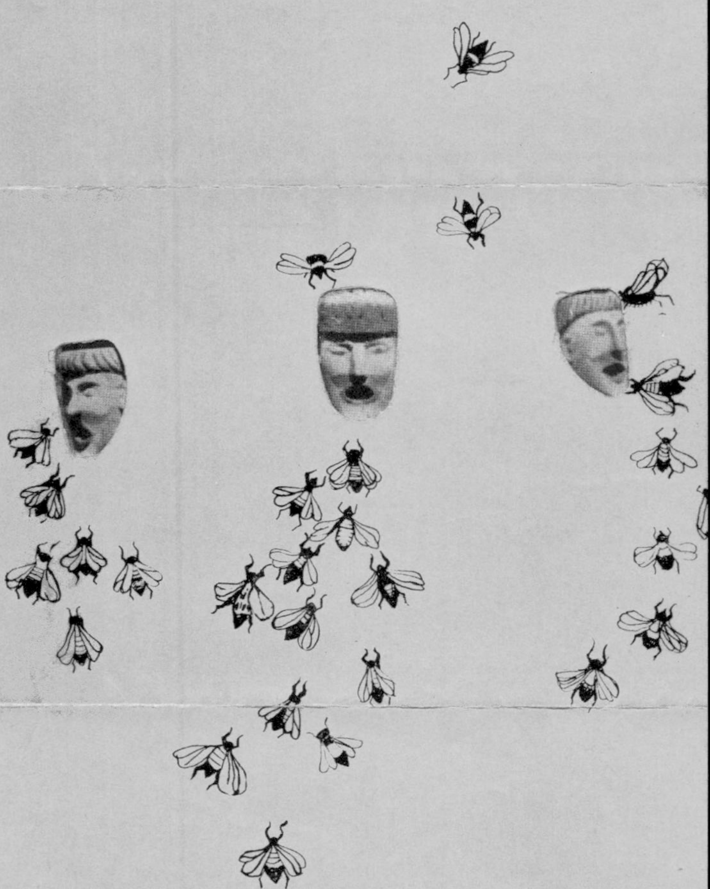

LE TERRAIN VAGUE

23-25, rue du Cherche-Midi - Paris 6e

VERNISSAGE le 8 Janvier de 18 h. à 23 h.

Le paysage terrestre étouffe. Au-delà de la gravité. Tout flotte. Ne pas flotter est antihumain. Univers en expansion. La loi et la philosophie de l'époque : "le coup de bombe". Le dessin part d'un point sans idée préconçue de "ligne" ou de "trajet" — (le mouvement, ce n'est pas "se diriger vers un point" mais "s'éloigner d'un point") — et s'étend pour finir quand les doigts s'arrêtent d'épuisement ou de dégoût. Le dégoût : sentiment qui appartient seulement à la conscience. Si cette conscience n'intervenait pas, l'homme continuerait à dessiner sur sa table, sur les rues, sur les villes comme une explosion atomique en chaine. Le désir de destruction totale pour arriver au changement définitif. Pour renouveler, il faut des moyens neufs. Le crayon à bille est l'élément qui oppose le moins d'obstacles entre l'impulsion et l'action. Il s'agit d'aller plus vite que la conscience. Le crayon à bille produit instantanément des différences d'intensité et de tonalité. Il est plus "musical". Comparable au Jazz. Improvisation. Transe, auto-hypnotisme. Explosion. Les doigts tâtonnent dans le vide, "l'abstrait", pour retrouver soudain un objet, "le figuratif", dramaticuement réel dans sa qualité de matière explosive, dans sa menace de désintégration. Conscience aigüe du périssable. Le mépris du matériel. L'acte de dessiner devient irrationnel, une décharge d'énergie comme un coup de pistolet. Le dessin se forme à mesure qu'on dessine, à mesure qu'on "existe". Acte comparable à la ligne d'un sismographe : il faut savoir lire en elle la force du tremblement de terre. Sans morale. Non artiste. Vital. Vrai. Sans employer d'une manière scolaire la symbolique freudienne, d'une façon congelée ; mais vécue, en assumant le subsconsient mais sans l'exploiter commercialement. En regardant ces dessins on rentre comme dans une fusée directement aux couches les plus profondes du cerveau. Le beau intégré au terrible. Organique. Bonsoir.

ALEJANDRO JODOROWSKY

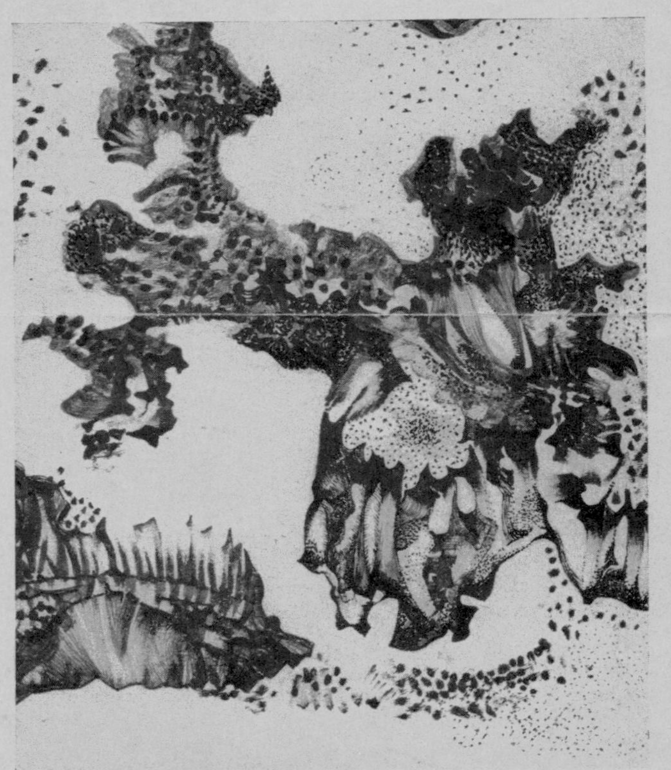

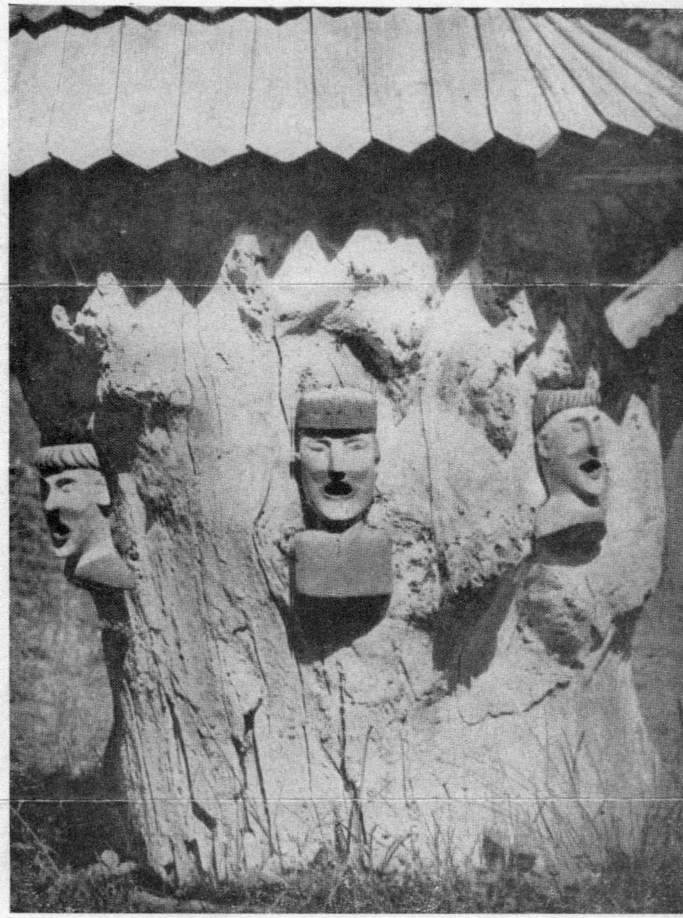

Le problème de la composition dans un "espace donné", le problème de "se révolter" contre un "espace donné" sont de faux problèmes. Il n'y a pas un espace à remplir. L'Objet est créé à mesure qu'on le dessine. C'est l'objet qui crée l'espace. Ni commencement ni fin : chaque dessin est la continuation de quelque chose. On peut unir tous les dessins dans un casse-tête géant. Abstrait et figuratif à la fois. Ces deux contraires réduits à une seule dimension. Alain Glass trouve de nouvelles formes parce qu'il n'est pas parti à leur recherche. Forme et contenu réduits à une seule dimension. Le dessin vient d'un monde extérieur à la surface ou l'abandonne pour l'invisible. La limite du "carré" n'existe plus. Ses dessins se donnent dans une surface infinie. Chaque forme n'a de relation qu'avec elle-même. Intégration au cosmique.

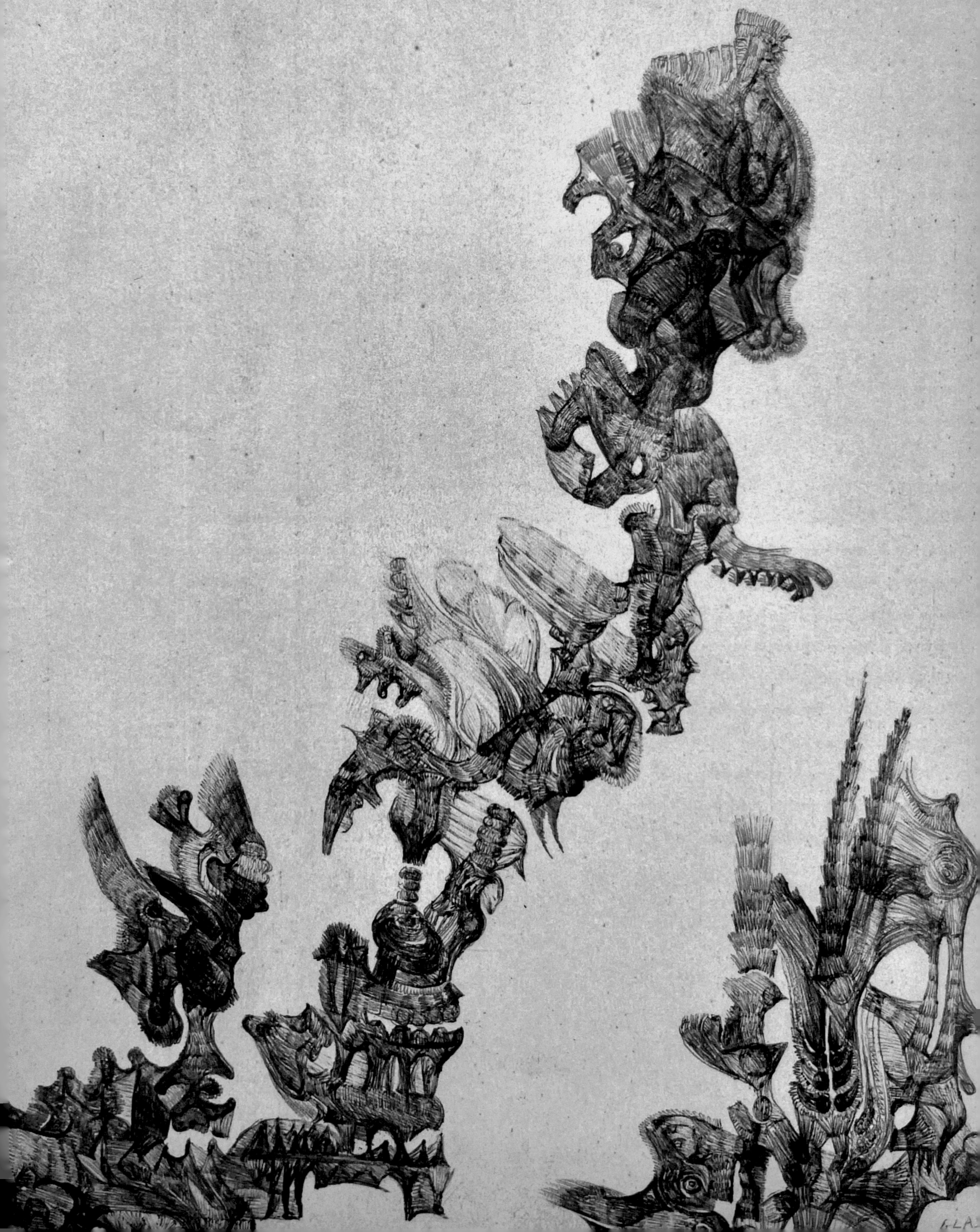

ALAIN GLASS
LE TERRAIN VAGUE

Alejandro Jodorowsky

Alan Glass
January 8 to 24, 1958
LE TERRAIN VAGUE
23-25, rue du Cherche-Midi – Paris 6e
Private view
January 8, 6 to 11 p.m.

THE PROBLEM WITH COMPOSITION WITHIN A "GIVEN SPACE," THE PROBLEM WITH "rebelling" against a "given space" are not true problems. There is no space to be filled. The object is created as it is being drawn. It is the object that creates the space. No beginning or end: each drawing is the continuation of something. All drawings can be joined together in a gigantic puzzle. Simultaneously abstract and figurative. These two opposites reduced to a single dimension. Alan Glass finds new forms because he did not go looking for them. Form and content pared down to a single dimension. The draftsmanship comes from a world other than the surface or abandons it for the invisible. The boundaries of the "square" no longer exist. His drawings take shape within an infinite surface. Each shape is unrelated to anything other than itself. Integration with the cosmic.

Terrestrial landscapes stifle. Beyond gravity. Everything floats. Not to float is anti-human. The expanding universe. The law and philosophy of the times: "detonation of a bomb." The drawing's starting point has no preconceived idea as to "line" or "trajectory"—the movement is not "to head towards a point," but "to move away from a point"—and continues until the fingers stop from exhaustion or in distaste. Distaste: a sentiment belonging only to awareness. Were this awareness not to come into play, man would continue drawing on tables, on streets, on cities as in an explosive atomic chain-reaction. The desire for total

Untitled
(Galerie Le Terrain Vague period)
ca. 1950
Blue Bic pen, on paper.
21.5 x 14 cm
Philippe Scrive collection,
France
Previous page

destruction in order to arrive at permanent change. Renewal requires new methods. A ballpoint pen instantly produces differences in intensity and tonality. It is more "musical." Comparable to jazz. Improvisation. Trance, self-hypnosis. Explosion. Fingers grope in the void, "the abstract," to suddenly find an object, "the figurative," dramatically real in its capacity as explosive matter, in its threat of disintegration. Acute awareness of the perishable. Disdain for the material. The act of drawing becomes irrational, a burst of energy like a gunshot. The drawing takes shape as one draws, as one "exists." An act comparable to a seismographic line: one has to know how to read in it the strength of the earthquake. Without a moral. Non-artist. Vital. True. Without the didactic use of Freudian symbolism, in a petrified way, but rather experientially, accepting the subconscious but without exploiting it commercially. Looking at these drawings one penetrates, as if on a rocket, directly into the deepest layers of the mind. The beautiful integrated into the dreadful. Organic.

Goodnight.

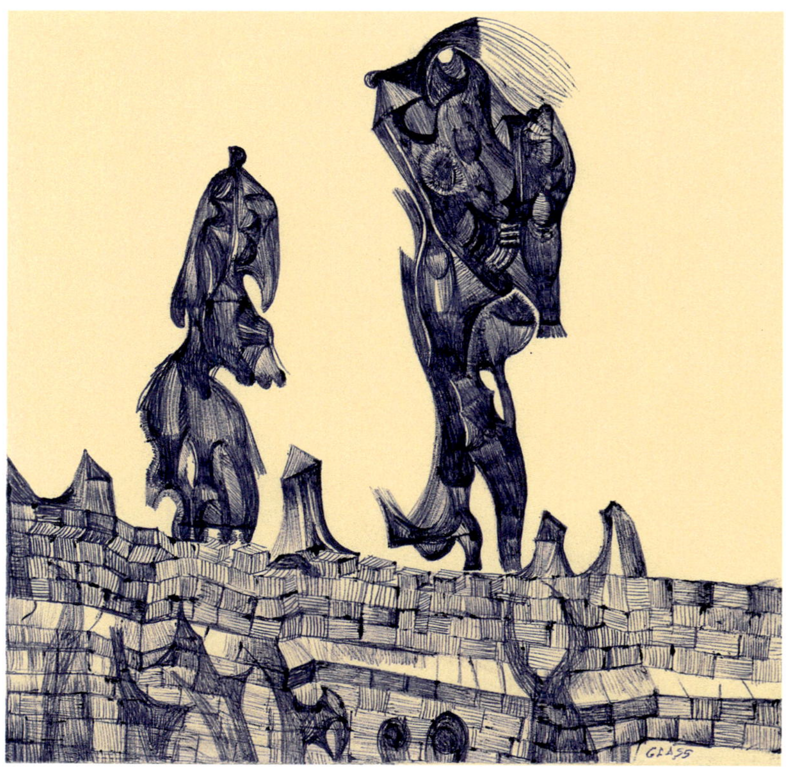

Untitled
(Galerie Le Terrain Vague period)
ca. 1954-1962
Monochrome blue ballpoint pen drawing, on paper.
15.2 x 15.8 cm
Artist's collection

Untitled
(Galerie Le Terrain Vague period)
ca. 1954-1962
Drawing in blue and purple bicolor pen with yellow, olive green, and lemon green pencil, on paper.
26 x 17 cm
Artist's collection
Previous page

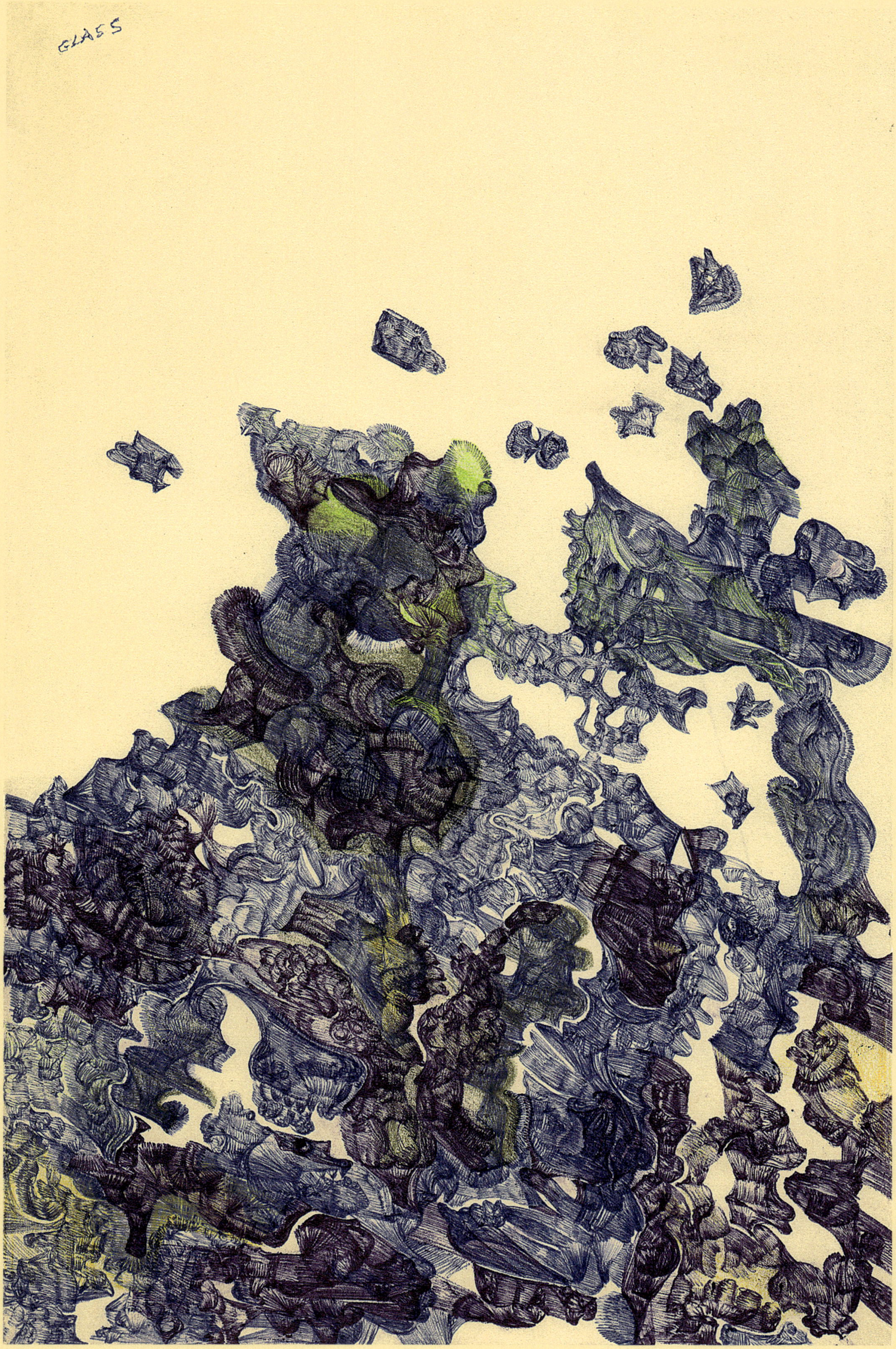
GLASS

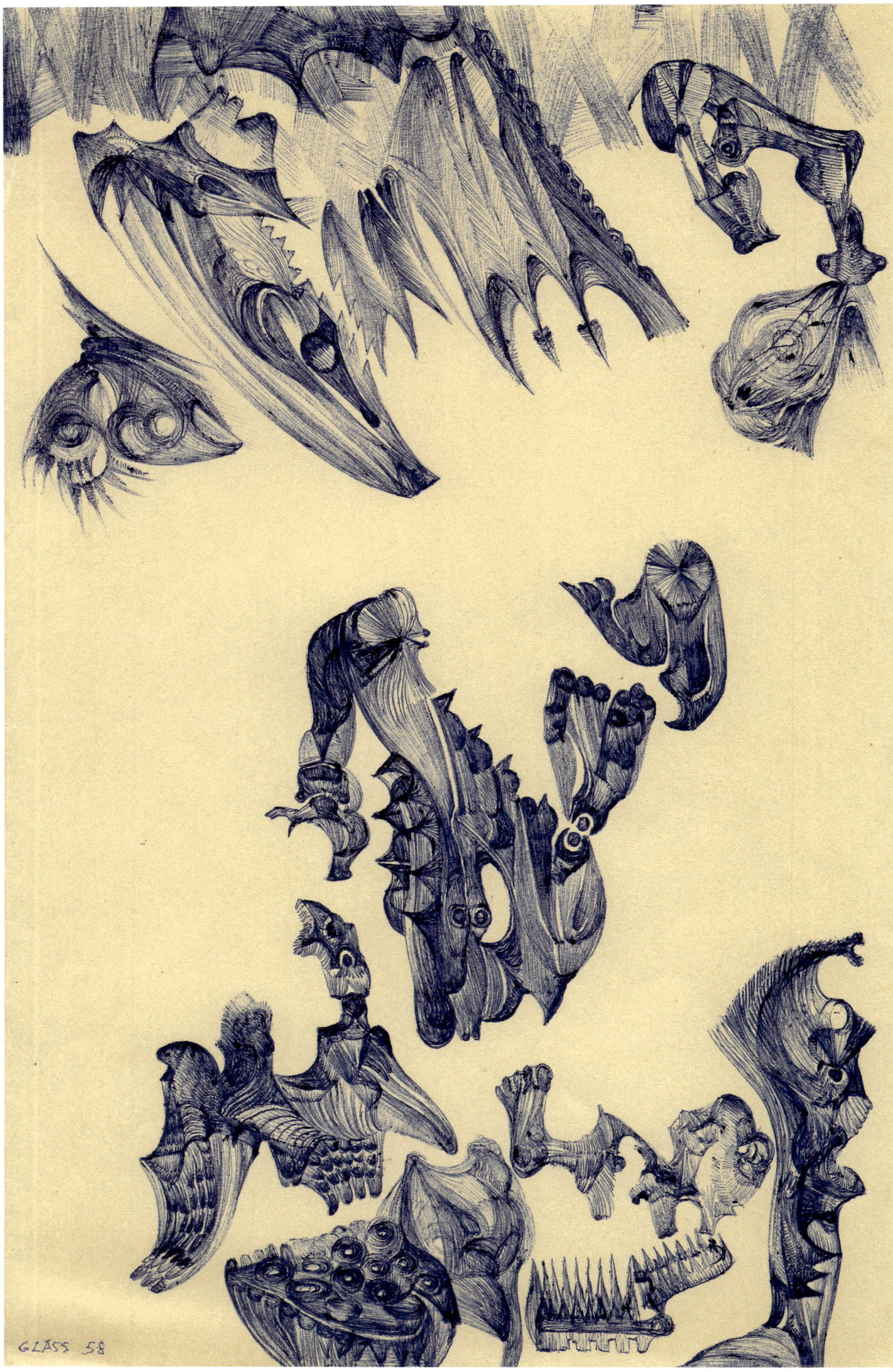

Untitled
(Galerie Le Terrain Vague period)
1958
Monochrome blue ballpoint
pen drawing, on paper.
26 x 17 cm
Artist's collection

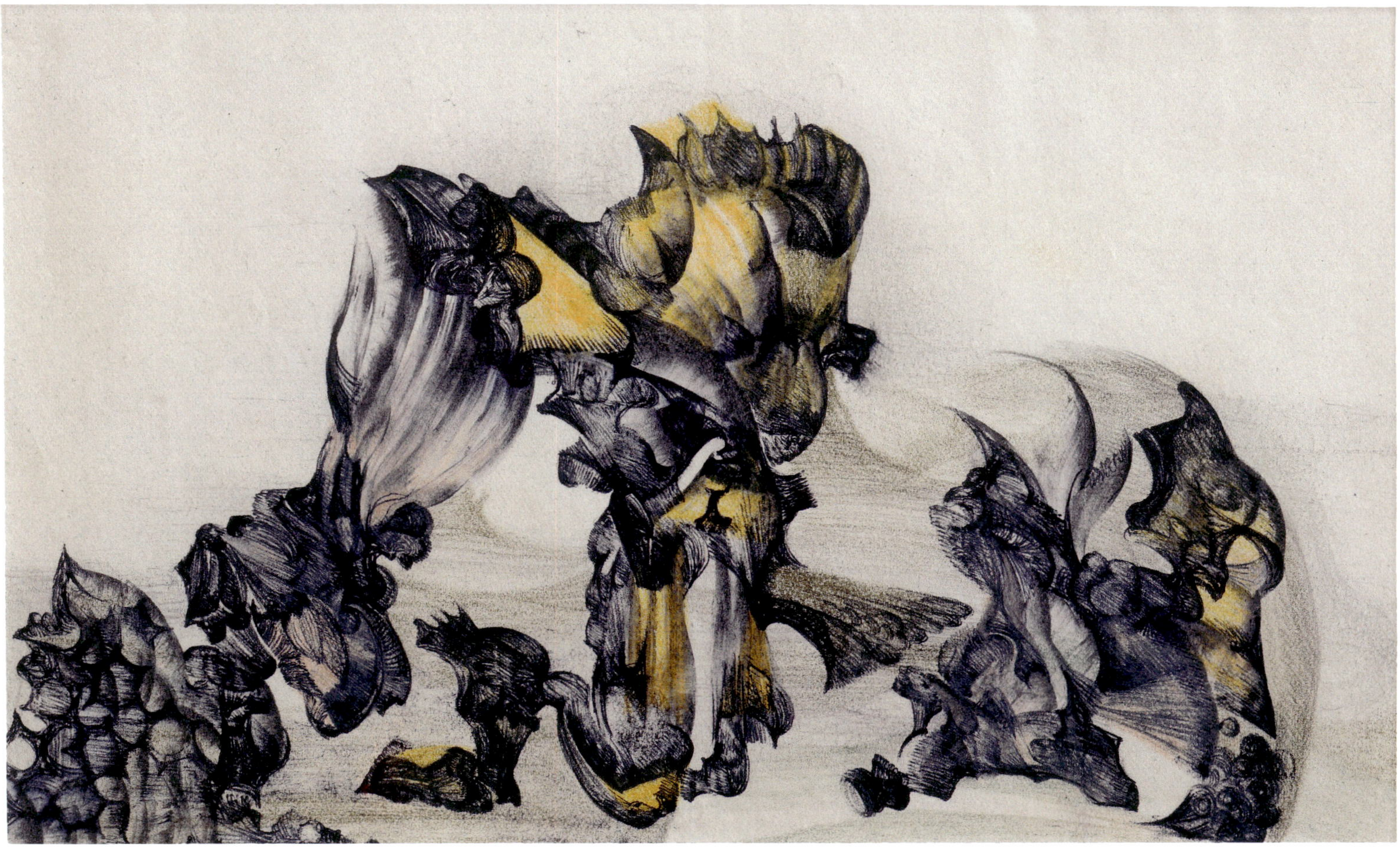

Untitled
(Galerie Le Terrain Vague period)
ca. 1950
Blue Bic pen, on paper.
14 x 25 cm
Louise Deschetelet collection,
Canada

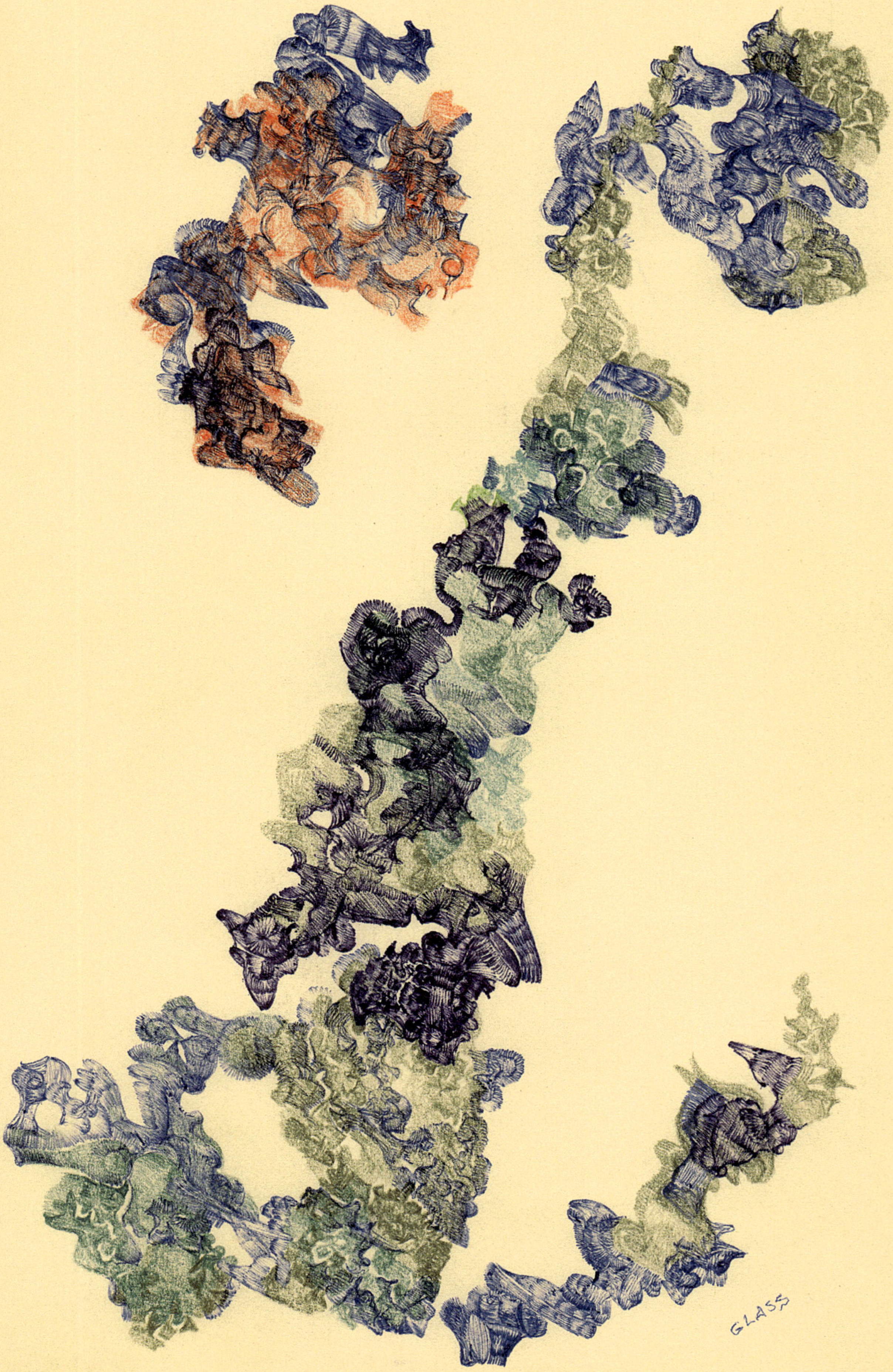
GLASS

THE GENIUS OF THE HAND: ALAN GLASS'S VISIONARY ART

Kristoffer Noheden

INTRODUCTION

ALAN GLASS'S DRAWINGS FROM THE 1950S ARE LIKE SWIRLS OF SMOKE ON THE verge of assuming solid shape, like rock coming alive and metamorphosing, like plants and animals commingling, their branches and limbs, their eyes and tendrils seeking new paths. Utilizing the newly invented ballpoint pen from 1954 to 1962, Glass used this modest instrument to create remarkably intricate and detailed drawings, using variations in pressure and density to conjure forth alternately lush and thick, light and crowded shapes with the appearance of inert matter coming alive. Among the several hundred drawings that Glass produced, there are some in which he used such an abundance of ink that the drawings almost take on the texture of paintings. Here, the flimsy paper is saturated to the degree of appearing soaked in the intense blues that have been a frequently recurring element of Glass's art for almost 70 years. It was the ballpoint-pen drawings that led to Glass's first solo exhibition, organized at Galerie Le Terrain Vague by André Breton and Benjamin Péret in January 1958.

Glass's drawings may appear to be drastically different from his more well-known assemblages, created from the early 1960s and up until the present. At first glance, the small format of the drawings, their often seemingly evanescent appearance, and their frequent monochromatism imbue them with a kind of aesthetic modesty far removed from Glass's large-format assemblages. Yet, closer examination reveals similarities in terms of both technique and motifs, not to mention a consistent, visionary approach to reality and that which can be gleaned of the invisible beyond its veil. Glass's drawings often contain mutable shapes that tend towards the biomorphic or the lithomorphic, with

Untitled
(Galerie Le Terrain Vague period)
ca. 1954-1962
Drawing in blue and purple bicolor pen with orange, olive green, grass green, and turquoise pencil, on paper.
26 x 17 cm
Artist's collection
Previous page

striking parallels with the use of mushrooms, plants, feathers, and stones in many of his assemblages.

Max Ernst said that he was constantly in search of his identity, but that he would be doomed if he actually found it. Glass's work during this period seems to be a restless search for artistic identity, but it is also as though his identity was firmly in place almost from the beginning. Ernst asserted, alluding to the concluding sentence in Breton's *Nadja* (1928), that identity should be convulsive or not be at all.[1] Glass's artistic identity appears, more precisely, to be fixed-explosive, as Breton described convulsive beauty it in *Mad Love* (1937).[2] It shifts between recurring themes and the sudden jolt of new discoveries, between contemplative stasis and the rush of organic growth. A man of great simplicity and great sophistication, openness and secrecy, Glass's art is characterized by transparency and mystery, restraint and excess, the visible and the invisible; it is easy to picture him drawing with the ballpoint pen, fixed in concentration, the images growing on the paper like soft explosions of pollen.

Glass's art is also kin to the way in which Breton lauds crystals and corals as examples of aesthetic perfection, both in the way in which it appears to grow organically from its creator's pen, paintbrush, or collection of found objects, and in the way in which it incorporates elements or patterns from the natural world.[3] A drawing from 1958 is dominated by a flattened mushroom-like shape, which parallels the incorporation 50 years later, in the vitrine-encased assemblage *Madera de Vida—Baño de Diana* (2010), of a dried giant mushroom painted with watercolours so translucent that the motif takes on the appearance of spectral figures emerging from the fungal depths. The presence of what looks like hieratic women figures in some of the early drawings anticipates Glass's preoccupation with the sacred feminine in numerous later works, such as the inclusion in *Madera de Vida—Baño de Diana* of the Roman goddess Diana in the form of a small replica of the 2nd-century Roman sculpture known as *Diana of Versailles*, which is placed next to the mentioned mushroom. Intimations of lacework in some of the drawings also connect this body of work with the use of lace in boxes ranging from *Reina Isabela con escarabajos* (1966) to *El purgatorio dulceria* (2021). Finally, most of Glass's drawings appear to depict a peek behind the veil of phenomenal appearances, and into a protean reality where spirit and matter intermingle and where nature is animated by creative forces; Glass continued such explorations in his paintings, but also in the creative detection of correspondences between objects, and between objects and words, throughout his assemblages, including *Sorprendente hallazgo* (1996), based on chance finds relating to Breton's autobiographical essay *Nadja*. That particular object is also one of many examples of the way in which Glass's works have tended to circle back to his years in Paris in the 1950s and 60s.

ARRIVING IN PARIS

"This is paradise!", Solange Legendre exclaimed when Alan Glass arrived in Paris in June 1952, just a few weeks shy of his twentieth birthday. The two friends had both been students of Alfred Pellan's at l'École des Beaux-arts in Montreal, and they had travelled to Paris to continue their

[1] Max Ernst, *Beyond Painting: And Other Writings by the Artist and His Friends*, trad. Dorothea Tanning (New York: Wittenborn, Schultz, 1948), 19.

[2] André Breton, *Mad Love*, trans. Mary Ann Caws (Lincoln: University of Nebraska Press, 1987), 19.

[3] Breton, *Mad Love*, 11–15.

artistic paths. Glass had recived a scholarship from the French government to study art, and he signed up for courses at l'École des Beaux-Arts and the Musée de l'homme, as well as to work with lithography at Maurice Jaudon's studio.

Glass's first encounter with Paris suggests that he was predestined to meet the surrealists in the city. Arriving on a boat from Montreal, he found accommodation at Le Sphinx hotel in Montparnasse. Recently converted into a home to students and artists, the building, which is featured in Breton's *Nadja*, used to be a brothel. Le Sphinx was located on the Boulevard Edgar Quinet, at the corner of the rue du Départ, and next to Gare Montparnasse. The view of the train station was familiar to Glass from Giorgio de Chirico's 1916 painting *The Melancholy of Departure*. He relishes the fact that he arrived in Paris on the street of departure, and the place's resonances with Breton and Chirico made it become a significant element in Glass's evolving personal mythology. Glass's next abode was a small maid's room at the top floor of 5 rue Manuel in the 9th arrondisement, where he would remain until he left Paris in 1962.

In Paris, Glass developed many friendships; in some cases they would be lifelong. He became close friends with the Chilean-born Alejandro Jodorowsky and his Canadian wife Denise Brosseau. Glass was also reunited with several Canadian friends, including the mentioned Solange Legendre, the poet and engraver Roland Giguère, the artist Micheline Beauchemin, and the married artist couple Jean Benoït and Mimi Parent. Jodorowsky used to comment that Parent, who was eight years older than Glass, was "like a mother" to him.[4] Surrounded by friends in this mid-century "paradise," Glass decided to stay on in Paris when his scholarship expired, and he supported himself through a variety of menial jobs. Sometimes he sought out these temporary employments in the company of Alejandro Jodorowsky; one time they ended up packing antibiotics in pile upon pile of cardboard boxes.

The importance of Glass's time at 5 rue Manuel can be gleaned from a 2019 assemblage, in which the address is written with prominent letters, alongside a piece of stationery from La Barrera, a haute couture store located at the address and run by Glass's landlady. The box also features a large metal parrot, referencing the landlady's parrot-like demeanour.[5] The artist's later assemblages frequently treat personal memory and history in similar ways, by incorporating the names of key places or persons together with images that evoke layers of Glass's personal mythology. The different elements come together in constellations where stings of nostalgia are complemented with a perpetual freshness. Refracted through the artist's poetic sensibility, the past is made present through a unique spell that combines images and objects into multi-layered, living symbols. As René Alleau states, "A symbol does not signify; it evokes and focuses, assembles and concentrates, in an analogically versatile manner, a multiplicity of meanings that cannot be reduced to one or many single meanings."[6] A symbol, thus defined, is not easily decoded; rather than having a predetermined meaning, a symbol, for Alleau, is a concatenation of images and associations.[7] Much as Glass expertly locates in natural

[4] Interview with Alan Glass, Mexico City, February 2022.
[5] Alan Glass, *Scrapbook* (Mexico City: Teopan, 2011), pictures 113–116; interview with Alan Glass, Mexico City, February 2022.
[6] René Alleau, *The Primal Force in Symbol: Understanding the Language of Higher Consciousness*, trans. Ariel Godwin (Rochester, VT: Inner Traditions, 2009), 3.
[7] Alleau, *The Primal Force in Symbol*, 47.

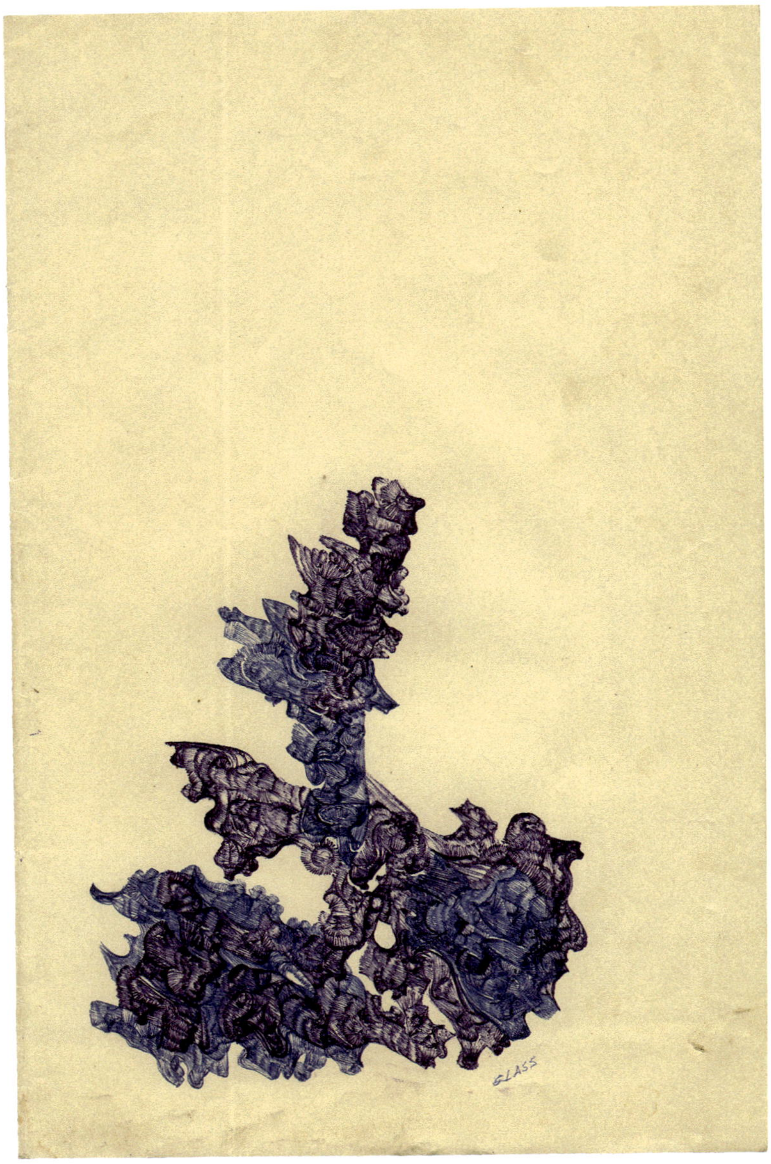

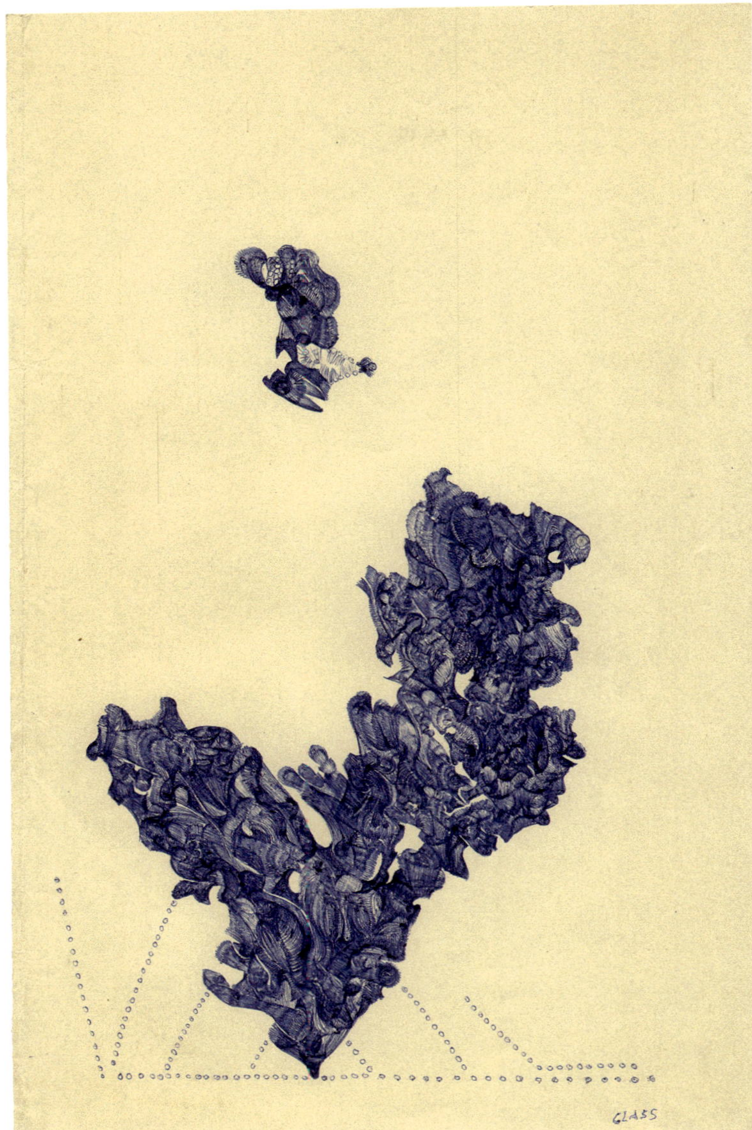

Untitled
(Galerie Le Terrain Vague period)
ca. 1954-1962
Drawing in bicolor blue and violet ballpoint pen, on paper.
26 x 17 cm
Artist's collection

Untitled
(Galerie Le Terrain Vague period)
ca. 1954-1962
Monochrome blue ballpoint pen drawing, on paper.
26 x 17 cm
Artist's collection

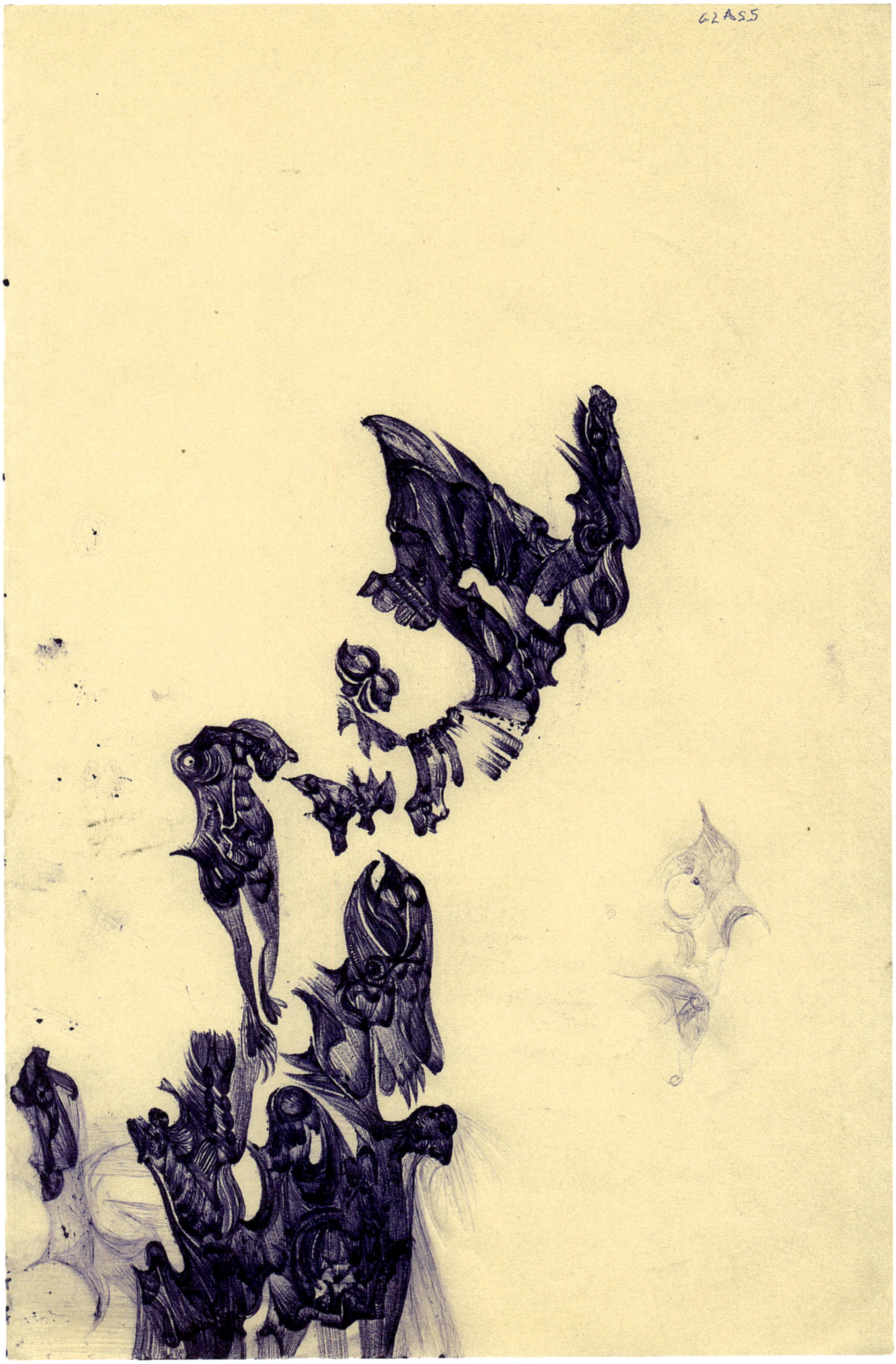

Untitled
(Galerie Le Terrain Vague period)
ca. 1954-1962
Monochrome blue ballpoint
pen drawing, on paper.
26 x 17 cm
Artist's collection

imagery, as used in drawings as well as in boxes, the analogies between the visible and the invisible, the mental and the material, so his mnemosymbolic boxes create a rich and vibrant communication across time and place.

"IT RUNS"

Glass tried out a variety of artistic techniques during his studies and subsequent time in Paris. A few examples from the summer of 1952 are included in the *Scrapbook* that Glass published in 2011. Among them are drawings of nudes, but also two drawings, reminiscent of Paul Klee and André Masson, of elongated human figures amidst abundant vegetation with prominently featured beehives, a motif that recurs throughout his oeuvre. A few years later, in 1955, he drew striking charcoal portraits of Benoît and Parent.[8]

Leaving art school seems to have had a liberating effect on Glass. It was in 1954 in his maid's room on 5 rue Manuel that he first started drawing with the newly invented ballpoint pen. In Paris, the ballpoint had been introduced in 1950 when the Bic Cristal hit the market. An early advertising campaign said of the pen, "elle court, elle court,"—"it runs, it runs." The smoothly rolling ballpoint and the fast-drying ink made it possible to write or draw with a prodigal speed that had not been possible with the fountain pen. Earlier in the 20th century, Dadaists, surrealists, and other radical artists started approaching drawing as an art form in its own right, rather than merely as a medium for studies. Jean Arp was "disgusted with oil painting" and made dada works with torn strips of paper. The writer Louis Aragon considered collage to be a brusque "challenge to painting."[9] Oil painting was deemed "luxurious," while drawing and collage were "poor," and so possibly capable of rescuing art from being trapped by the market.[10] Come the 1950s and the ballpoint pen created new possibilities to bring forth the marvellous with meager means. The Bic was eminently affordable, and since it could be used on virtually any kind of paper it also liberated drawing further from economic constraints. In the hundreds of ballpoint drawings he made between 1954 and 1962, Glass took full advantage of these new liberties, of speed as well as the possibility of drawing on any kind of paper in virtually any place.

Looking back, Glass says that the ballpoint pen was a natural fit with his hand.[11] He barely needed to accustom himself to the way the pen moved effortlessly over the paper. As soon as he started using the Bic, images of a characteristic simplicity-complexity—the fixed-explosive, again—came forth. Few of the drawings from the Paris years are made on art paper; most of them are executed on whatever pieces or slips of paper was at hand. Glass's earliest ballpoint drawings, made there in the maid's room on the top floor, are characterized by their intense blues, often forming human- or animal-like figures, which blend into one another and into more vegetal or mineral surroundings. Or, rather, there is little difference between figure and ground, main motif and surroundings; instead, the drawings congeal into tight yet dynamic fields of blue, surrounded by the otherwise untouched surface of the paper.

In some of the drawings mask-like faces take shape. These motifs may have been inspired by Glass's time as a student at the

[8] Glass, *Scrapbook*, pictures 133, 138.
[9] Leslie Jones, "Tracing Dreams: Surrealist Drawing 1915–1950," in Leslie Jones with Isabelle Dervaux and Susan Laxton, *Drawing Surrealism* (Los Angeles: Los Angeles County Museum of Art, 2012), 13.
[10] Jones, "Tracing Dreams," 13.
[11] Interview with Alan Glass, Mexico City, February 2022.

ethnographic museum, Musée de l'homme, when he first arrived in Paris, where he would have seen masks from many different cultures. Concealing the wearer's face, masks reveal the presence of gods, spirits, or natural forces, so pointing to the coexistence of different layers of reality, much like Glass's art does. When birds' heads look like they emerge from tree trunks in one drawing, they are redolent of the way in which animals come forth from wood in Max Ernst's series of frottages, *Histoire naturelle* (1926). Ernst created his visions of an alternative natural history by rubbing a lead pencil over paper pressed against textured surfaces, coaxing forth animals, vegetation, and celestial bodies from the patterns transferred. In Glass's drawings, in contrast, nature erupts simply through the quick movements of the biro across the paper.

It was also on 5 rue Manuel that Glass stuck his head out of the *vasistas* to gaze out over the rooftops of Paris. Examining his drawings now, I wonder if the view allowed him to see some of the gargoyles jutting out from so many roofs in Paris; gargoyle-like forms appear in many of these early drawings.

Glass's swift lines of blue ink cohere into patterns that alternately resemble the swift transformations of organic growth and the deep time of crystallization and eroding rocks. The resulting shapes are frequently protean, with the seeming potential to turn into a myriad different forms. Sometimes they are more fixed, as when an iron cauldron dominates one drawing or a brick wall forms a firm ground level. In these early ballpoint drawings, he uses such tight parallel lines that the shapes tend to appear dense and solid. While Glass took quickly to the ballpoint pen, in these early works he has not yet developed the exquisite variations in pressure and intensity that would soon lend such a delicate vividness to his drawings. More compact and with more pronounced figurative tendencies, some of these early drawings feature sacred women figures, teeming eyes, and tadpole-like clusters that indicate that many of Glass's long-term obsessions were already firmly in place. In some drawings, Glass combines different-coloured Bic pens. A small oblong drawing uses blue and purple pens to great effect. The motif looks like the inside of a mountain, but the rock, the stalactites, and the stalagmites have an organic appearance, like fantasy fish and imaginary fossils on the brink of coming back to life.

The intimations in Glass's drawings of natural shapes that have not yet been fully formed, like seeds about to explode in growth and with the potential for radical transformation, make these works appear to be attempts at seeing what the world is like behind surface appearances. In the words of Breton, this is a kind of art "that reject[s] what is merely cortical in favour of returning to the source, the living sap."[12] Another way of putting it is that Glass, like many seers and philosophers before him, from antiquity to Romanticism, is attempting to lift the Veil of Isis, a prominent symbol of the way in which nature keeps her secrets, in order to convey something of that which is invisible to ordinary vision.

Glass was, Jodorowsky remarks, "a surrealist without knowing it" at the time.[13] Yet, he was certainly aware of surrealism, from the circulation of surrealist books and periodicals

[12] André Breton, *Surrealism and Painting*, trans. Simon Watson Taylor (Boston: MFA Publications, 2002), 341. Italics removed.

[13] Alejandro Jodorowsky, untitled essay, in *Alan Glass: Surrealism's Secret*, exhibition catalog, ed. Kristoffer Noheden and Abigail Susik (forthcoming).

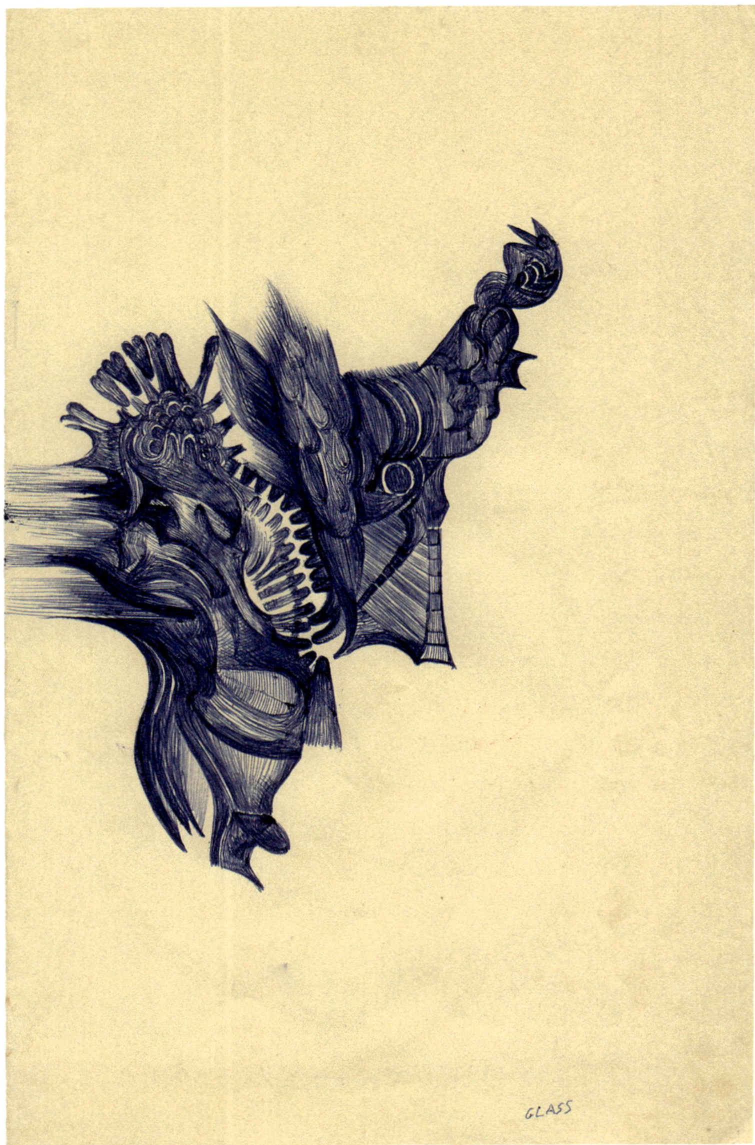

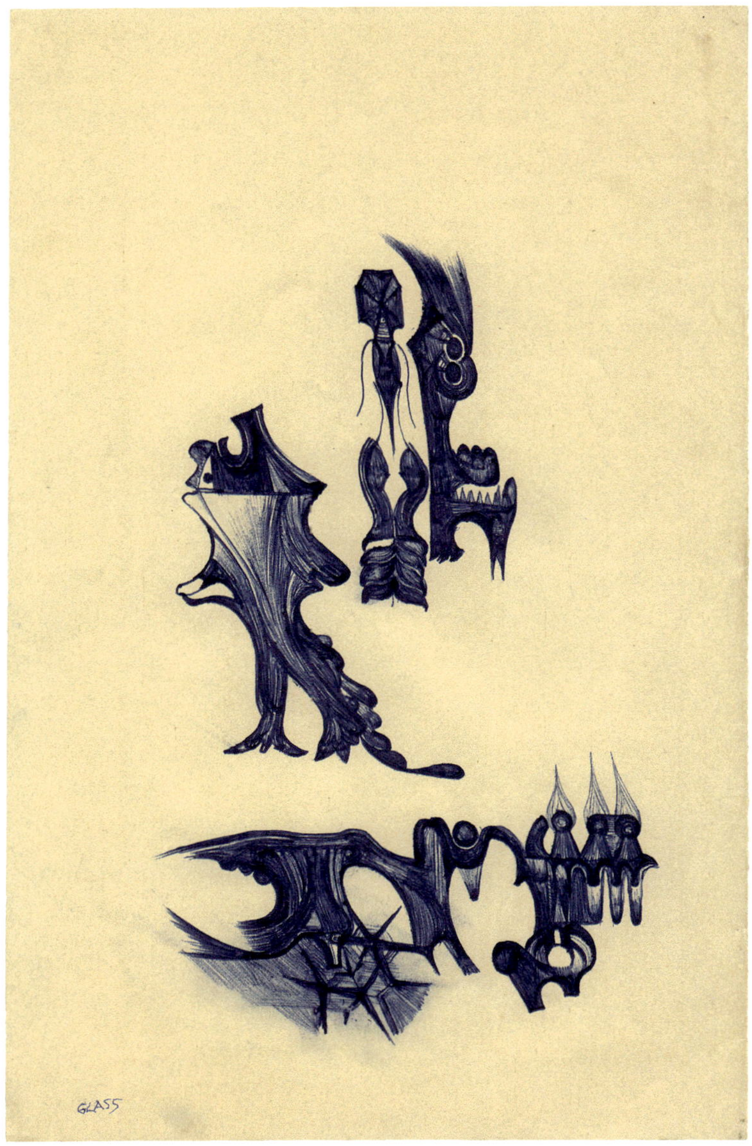

Untitled
(Galerie Le Terrain Vague period)
ca. 1954-1962
Monochrome blue ballpoint pen drawing, on paper.
26 x 17 cm
Artist's collection

Untitled
(Galerie Le Terrain Vague period)
ca. 1954-1962
Monochrome blue ballpoint pen drawing, on paper.
26 x 17 cm
Artist's collection

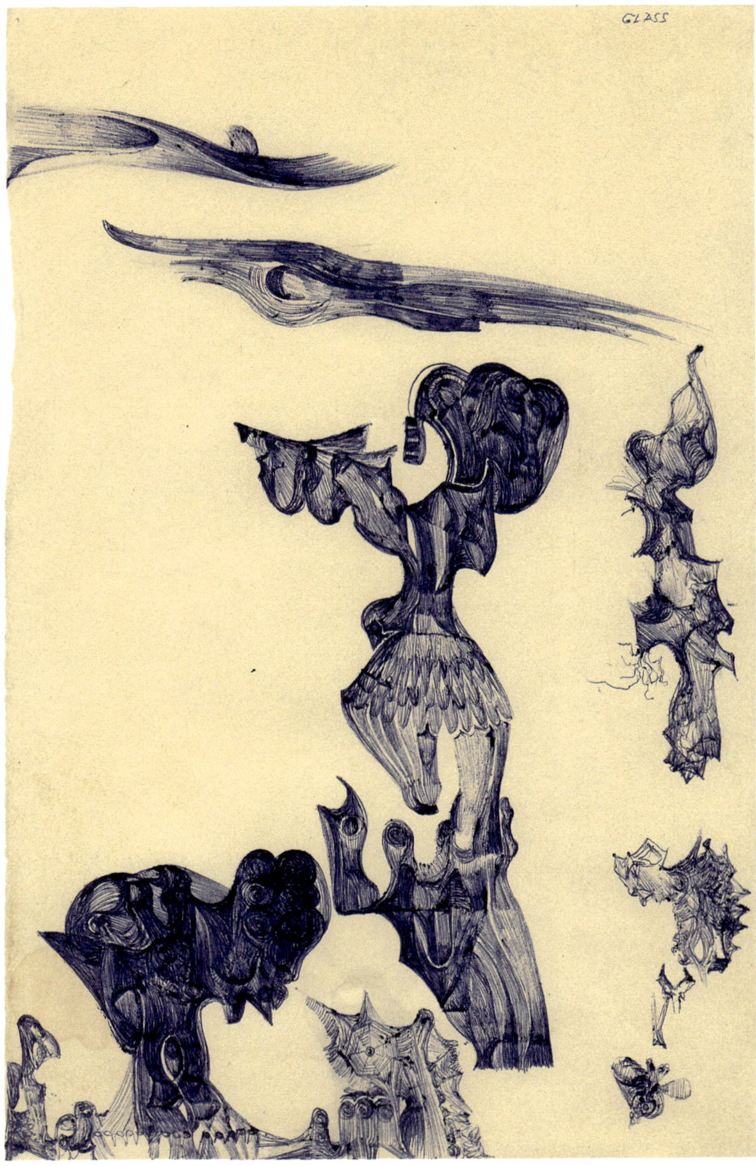

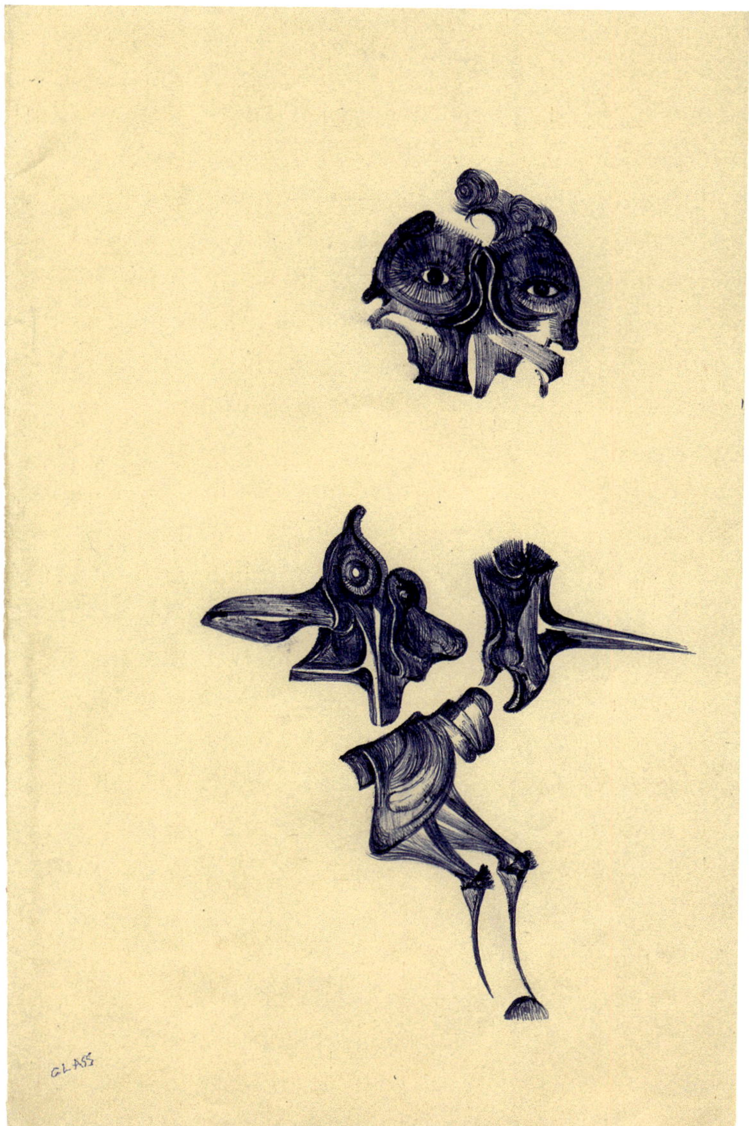

Untitled
(Galerie Le Terrain Vague period)
ca. 1954-1962
Monochrome blue ballpoint pen drawing, on paper.
26 x 17 cm
Artist's collection

Untitled
(Galerie Le Terrain Vague period)
ca. 1954-1962
Monochrome blue ballpoint pen drawing, on paper.
26 x 17 cm
Artist's collection

in French-speaking Canada, to the prominent position of the Quebec automatists, drawing on surrealist methods and ideas, in Canada in the late 1940s, and on to his teacher Alfred Pellan's proximity to surrealism. In Paris, Glass became more closely acquainted with new surrealist art. One of the exhibitions that made a great impression on him was by the Swedish painter Max Walter Svanberg at Breton's gallery A l'Étoile Scellée in March and April 1955. While his attempts to look behind the surface of everyday reality is a central indication of why his art would eventually be welcomed with such enthusiasm by the surrealists, Glass's sensibility ultimately cannot be entirely subsumed under schools, movements, or labels. His capacity to gaze into the hidden recesses of things both natural and man-made, to locate the both playful and fearsome spirit within matter, stems from formative visionary experiences, but also relate to his evolving attraction to various esoteric teachings from tantric Buddhism, to Gnosticism, to Henry Corbin's luminous writings on Iranian Sufism.

SAINT-GERMAIN-DES-PRÉS

In August 1956, Glass started working as a doorman at the jazz club Saint-Germain-des-Prés, located on 13 rue Saint-Benoît in Paris's 6th arrondisement. Club Saint-Germain-des-Prés was founded in 1949 by the prolific writer and jazz musician Boris Vian, and it quickly attracted a diverse crowd of surrealists, existentialists, and celebrities eager to hear the latest French and American jazz in the cellar.[14] Among the artists who performed at Saint-Germain-des-Prés were Miles Davis, Coleman Hawkins, Django Reinhardt, Art Blakey's Jazz Messengers, Sacha Distel, and Vian himself.

Glass's six-year stint at the club had a significant and direct effect on his art, as he drew ensconced behind his *portier* desk to the rhythmic sound of the jazz music played in the *cave* downstairs. An article on Glass in the French-Canadian newspaper *La Presse* speaks with palpable fascination about this surrealist artist who makes a living as a doorman. The reporter relates that Glass would constantly draw while at work, and describes how, when he had to get up and escort the guests to the cellar, he would carefully tuck away his works-in-progress under a sheet of paper.[15] Under the influence of the sounds and atmosphere of Saint-Germain-des-Prés, Glass's drawings evolved in different ways. Initially, they took on greater complexity and nuance in tandem with his explorations of the possibilities of the ballpoint pen, which he now used to create a stronger sense of depth and fragility. Glass continued to take a seemingly unpremeditated approach to his drawings, using whatever paper was at hand. Some of the drawings are executed on checkered notepad paper. Two small drawings, at once dense and delicate, are made on flimsy pieces of paper branded with the Martini logo on top. A series of abstract drawings are made on the back of cards made with thicker paper stock announcing a gig by Art Blakey's Jazz Messengers. In the later stage of his time at Saint-Germain-des-Prés, his drawings became more frenzied and crowded, leaving less blank space untouched; here, the quiet sense of organic growth in the earlier drawings is largely replaced by a

[14] Interview with Alan Glass, Mexico City, February 2022. See also Boris Vian, *Manual of Saint-Germain-des-Prés*, trans. Paul Knobloch (New York: Rizzoli, 2005).

[15] Jean Gachon, "Alain Glass, portier pour vivre, expose des dessins surréalistes," *La Presse*, Friday, January 10, 1958, 18.

claustrophobic atmosphere, the undulating lines giving way to more sharp, spiky, and seemingly aggressive movements. Glass describes the process behind these later drawings as more directly automatic and influenced by the jazz music reaching him from the cellar.[16]

Glass also welcomed chance events into his drawings. In one of them, what looks like a splash of red wine forms a biomorphic pattern on the textured paper. On top of and around these chance marks, Glass has drawn with the ballpoint pen. The wine accident likely happened at 5 rue Manuel, since, he is careful to point out, he only drank calvados at the club, and he would have brought the paper with him from home. Other drawings, as well as a few paintings, from the time are marked by Glass's habit of chain-smoking. He made the brown streaks and spots in these images by moving a lit match across the paper. Much like Max Ernst with his frottages or Wolfgang Paalen with his fumages, Glass incorporated these patterns into his work, allowing them to form part of the motifs or elaborating on the shapes they suggested with ballpoint pen or watercolour. In one drawing, the matchstick has created three elongated shapes that look like trees, around which Glass has drawn further organic shapes, conjuring up a haunted fairytale forest.

When we looked at these works together in February 2022, Glass playfully dubbed the technique "allumettage," after "allumette," French for matchstick, and in line with Paalen's notion of fumage. Glass's use of allumettage arose from his nervous habit of constantly smoking, and so it creates one more connection between the environment, the artist's body, and the ballpoint-pen drawings; jazz syncopes, the lighting of matches, the crackle of the cigarette glow, and Glass's swiftly moving hands came together to engender these delicately sprawling shapes that grow organically on the paper.

WITH THE SURREALISTS AT LE TERRAIN VAGUE

In 1958, a Canadian television team visited Glass at Saint-Germain-des-Prés to make a short feature about the artist who was making art while working as a doorman. The occasion was Glass's first solo show. Glass had left his address in the guest book at A l'Étoile Scellée when he visited the Svanberg exhibition in the spring of 1955, and a few weeks later the young surrealist poet Jacques Sénelier paid him a visit at home on 5 rue Manuel. Seeing the drawings pinned to the walls, Sénelier suggested that Glass meet Breton. Glass brought along a selection of drawings to 42 rue Fontaine and showed them to Breton and his third wife, Elisa. Together with his longtime close friend, the poet Benjamin Péret, Breton organized Glass's first exhibition.

At this point, A l'Étoile Scellée had ceased operations, and the surrealists were once again without a gallery of their own. Instead, Glass's exhibition was held at Galerie Le Terrain Vague in the bookstore Libraire Le Terrain Vague at rue du Cherche-Midi, just a few blocks away from Saint-Germain-des-Prés. Earlier shows at Galerie Le Terrain Vague included Marcel Jean and Henri Pastoreau in 1956 and Jacques Le Maréchal in 1957.[17] Le Terrain Vague was a publishing

[16] Interview with Alan Glass, Mexico City, February 2022.
[17] Losfeld, *Endetté comme une mule, ou la Passion d'éditer* (Paris: Belfond, 1979), 80.

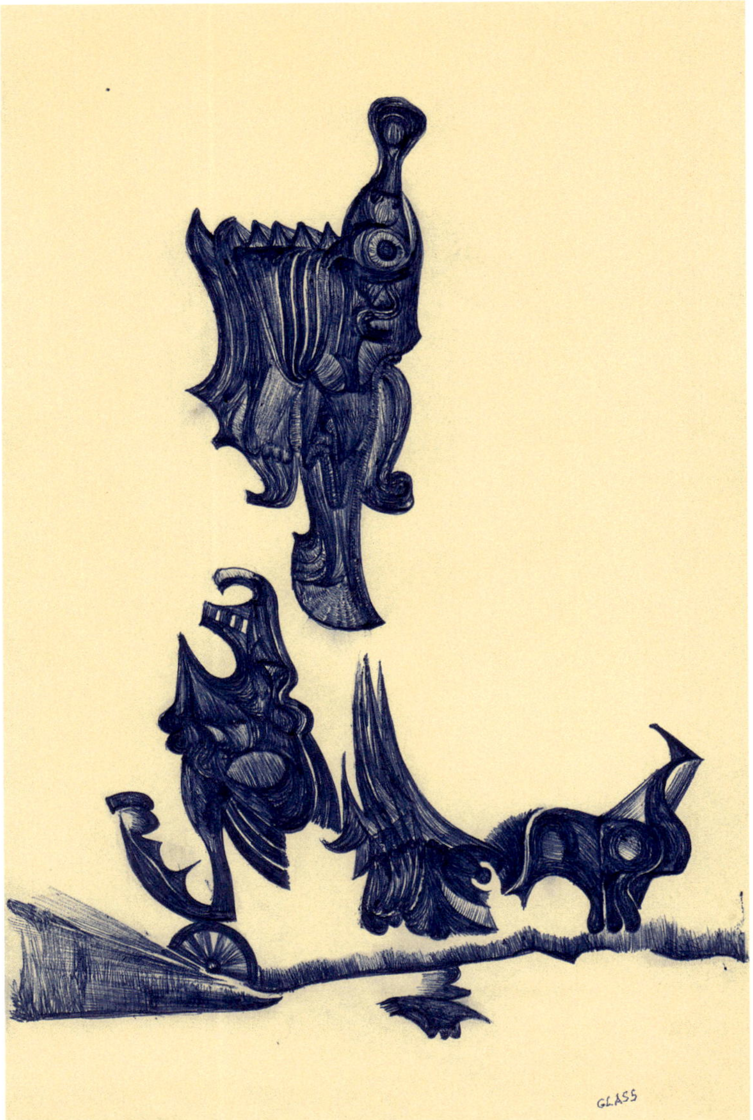

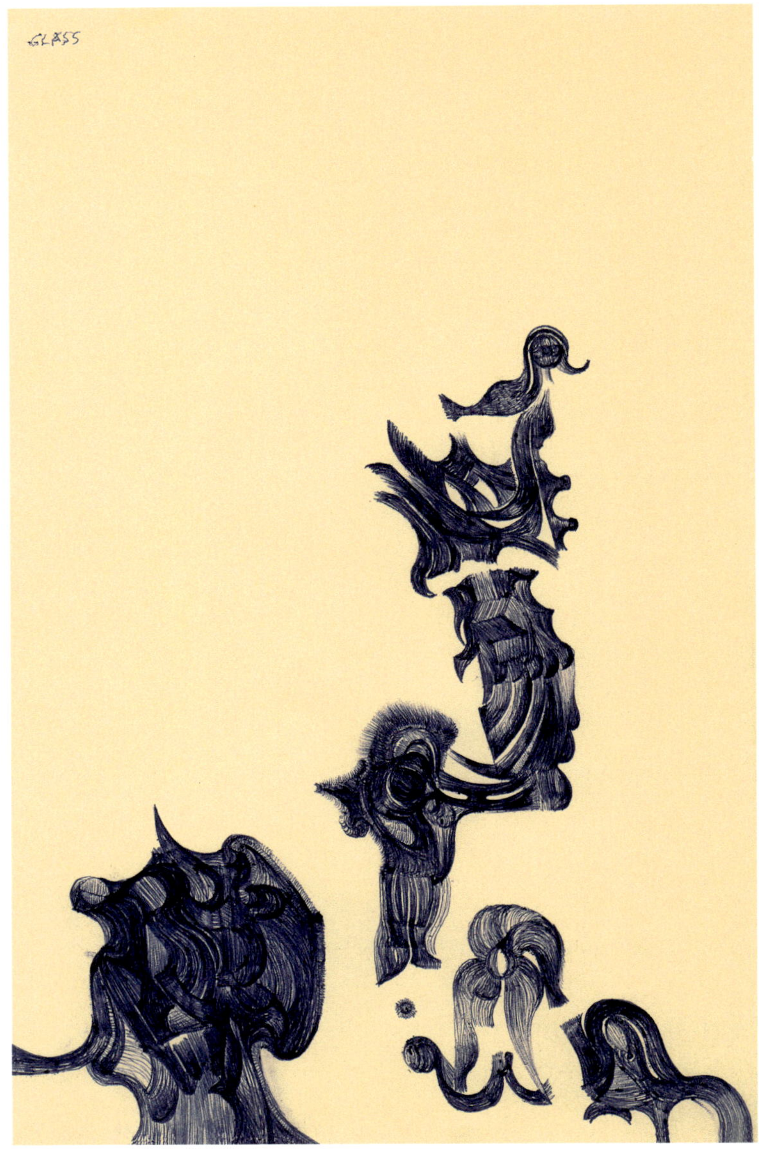

Untitled
(Galerie Le Terrain Vague period)
ca. 1954-1962
Monochrome blue ballpoint
pen drawing, on paper.
26 x 17 cm
Artist's collection

Untitled
(Galerie Le Terrain Vague period)
ca. 1954-1962
Monochrome blue ballpoint
pen drawing, on paper.
26 x 17 cm
Artist's collection

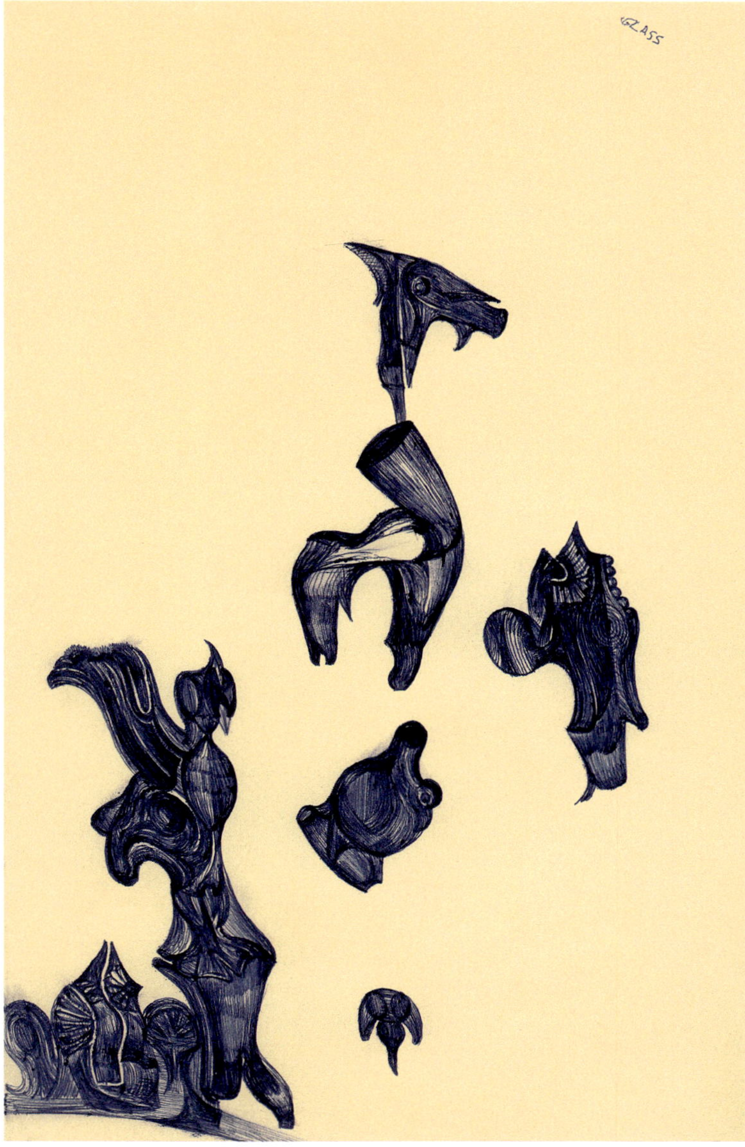

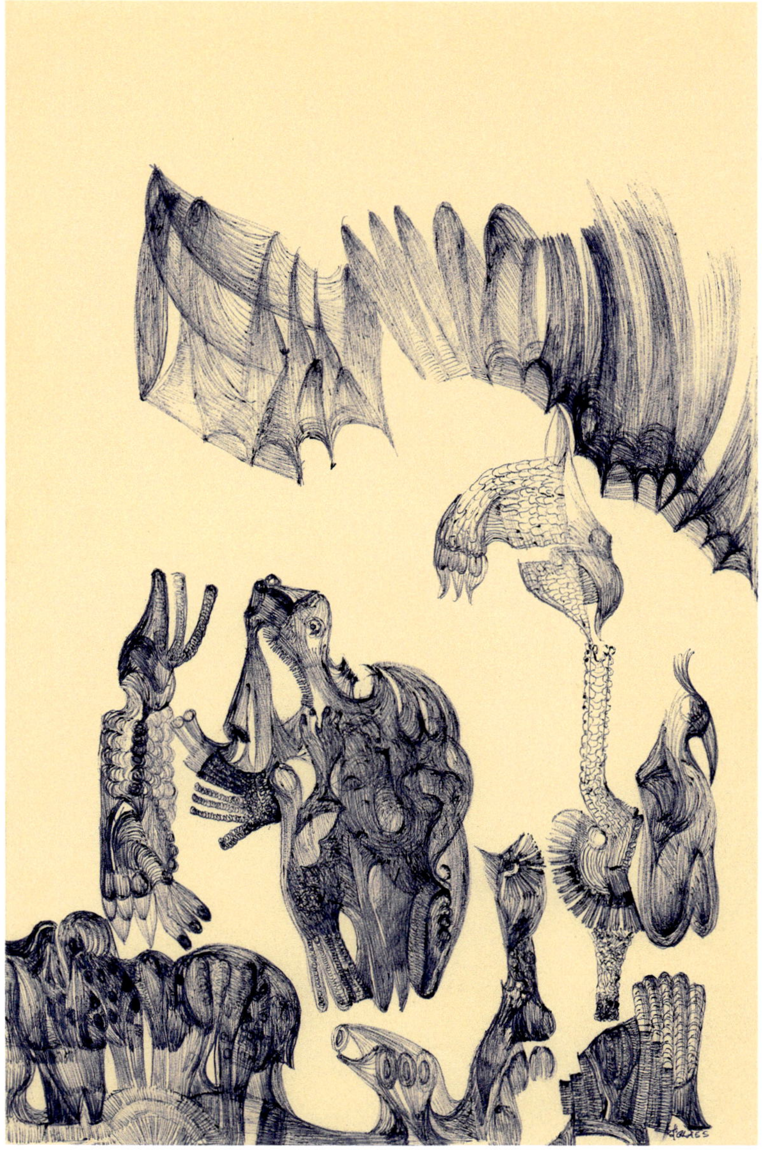

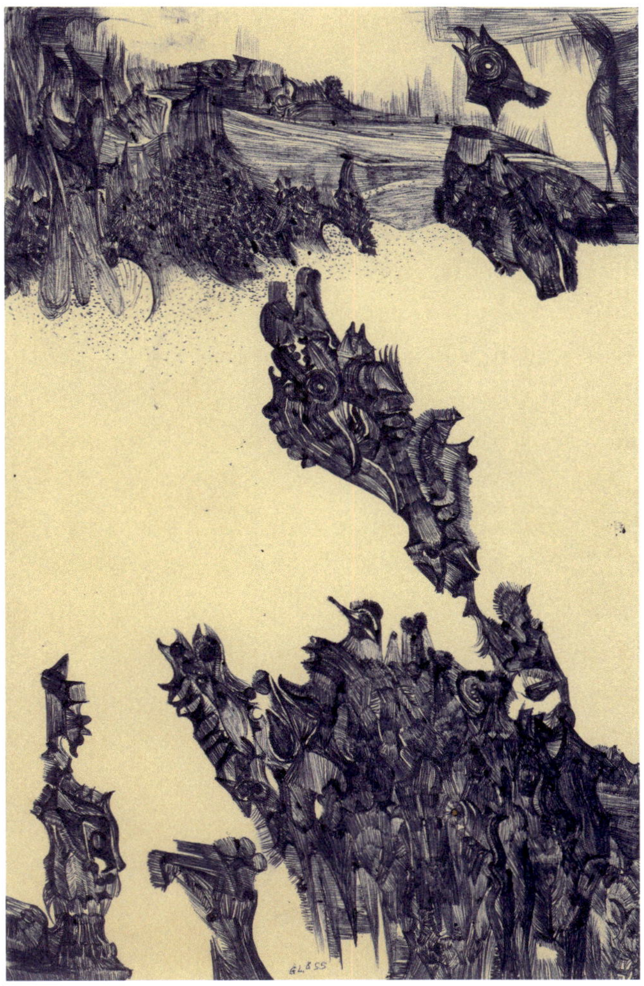

Untitled
(Galerie Le Terrain Vague period)
ca. 1954-1962
Monochrome blue ballpoint
pen drawing, on paper.
26 x 17 cm
Artist's collection

Untitled
(Galerie Le Terrain Vague period)
ca. 1954-1962
Monochrome blue ballpoint
pen drawing, on paper.
26 x 17 cm
Artist's collection

Untitled
(Galerie Le Terrain Vague period)
ca. 1954-1962
Monochrome blue ballpoint
pen drawing, on paper.
26 x 17 cm
Artist's collection

house and bookstore owned by Eric Losfeld, who by the 1950s had "become the surrealist publisher par excellence."[18] Under the imprint of Le Terrain Vague, founded in 1955, Losfeld published the surrealist journals *Médium: Communication surréaliste*, *Bief: Jonction surréaliste*, and *La Brêche: Action surréaliste*, as well as books by surrealists including Péret, Nelly Kaplan, Ado Kyrou, and Hans Bellmer. Losfeld funded his ventures through a daring publishing programme of erotic literature, including Emmanuelle Arsan's first *Emmanuelle* novel. In his autobiography, Losfeld says that it was André Breton who suggested that his imprint be called Terrain Vague, without realizing that Losfeld is Flemish for "terrain vague," or "wasteland." This instance of objective chance made Losfeld predict that his new activities would be affected by a particular, beneficial type of magic.[19] Glass's exhibition may have been one such magical outcome.

The catalog for Alan Glass's exhibition at Le Terrain Vague is modest, but it is charged with the artist's particular brand of poetry. The handmade pamphlet has a yellow cover featuring a drawing of swarms of bees, which approach three die-cut holes, through which can be seen three male wooden faces. Inside the pamphlet, it is revealed that these faces are part of a photograph of a French wooden beehive; the busts are carved directly into a sturdy tree trunk, and the bees enter through their mouths. The pamphlet also features an essay by Jodorowsky alongside a reproduction of one of the drawings from the exhibition. According to Jodorowsky, Glass was offered "a selection of famous surrealist names" to write the catalog essay, but "as if by magic," he asked Jodorowsky, "an unknown artist at the time ... thus provoking a negative reaction on the part of Breton's colleagues and disciples."[20] In his essay, Jodorowsky characterizes Glass's drawings as "Abstract and figurative at the same time. ... Form and content reduced to a single dimension. The drawing comes from a world on the other side of the surface or abandons it for the invisible. ... Integration into the cosmic. ... Beyond gravity. Everything flows."[21]

Jodorowsky's staccato prose positions Glass's art as at once finely attuned to the present with all its horrors—"the law and philosophy of the time: an exploding bomb"; "like the line of a seismograph"— and the result of a sensibility that evades the surface of both appearances and the mind—"trance, auto-hypnosis."[22] On the one hand, the drawings are marked by the bustling surrounding world, and on the other by a search for cosmic unity. Jodorowsky's evocation of the ancient Greek philosopher Heraclitus's dictum "Panta rhei," everything flows, suggests that he detects in Glass's drawings an intuitive natural philosophy predicated on an insight in the incessant transformations pulsating beyond the surface of reality.

At this point, some of Glass's drawings had taken on a near-sculptural character, whereas others are smoke-like and evanescent; sometimes, these two tendencies combine. A blue and purple ballpoint drawing features a line of what looks like truncated beehives beneath swirling forms redolent of insect wings, leafs, and pods rising like smoke. A blue ballpoint drawing depicts a host of organic forms blending into each other and seemingly petrified in the midst of motion; an eye and a moth

[18] Gérard Durozoi, *History of the Surrealist Movement*, trans. Alison Frank (Chicago: University of Chicago Press, 2002), 525.

[19] See Losfeld, *Endetté comme une mule*, 81.

[20] Jodorowsky, untitled essay 2020.

[21] Jodorowsky, untitled essay 1958, in *Alain Glass: du 8 au 24 Janvier 1958* (Paris: Le Terrain Vague, 1958), n.p.

[22] Jodorowsky, untitled essay 1958, n.p.

open in the living rock, suggesting the face of a fantastic animal. Once again, the fixed and the explosive co-exist in a state of tension that brings forth a vision of a mobile and dynamic world.

The opening of Glass's exhibition at Le Terrain Vague on the evening of January 8 drew a large crowd. Glass sold three drawings: to the Chilean surrealist artist Roberto Matta, to a representative from Bic, the ballpoint pen manufacturers, and to [ask Alan]. The French-Canadian daily newspaper *La Presse* covered the exhibition twice. On January 10, they published a text about the exhibition by Jean Gachon, remarking upon Glass's inventive use of the ballpoint pen as his means of expression. "With this simple and monochromatic instrument, Alan Glass manages to create purely surrealist compositions, with a stunning variety in nuance of the two sole colours, blue and red." The article ends with a wish that Glass will find the time needed to develop his "sympathetic method."[23] On January 25, the day after the exhibition closed, *La Presse* ran a more extensive feature on the surrealist doorman, by the Canadian journalist Jean V. Dufresne, ordinarily an art critic at *La Patrie*. Drawing on Jodorowsky's catalog text, Dufresne seeks to formulate an aesthetics based on Glass's enigmatic drawings. He describes Glass as a free person and a poet, who is not so much an avantgardist as someone who creates out of natural necessity. Dufresne also perceives a link between Glass's drawings and nature, and perceptively states that "this free man takes the liberty to love bees. His drawings are a little bit like the flight of a bee."[24] As indicated by the bees and beehives on the catalog cover, Glass has a lifelong predilection for these insects. A few years after his exhibition at Le Terrain Vague, he made a striking boxed assemblage, *Nouvelle rosée, nouveau miel* (1963), which features a honeycomb and real bees and connects them with his attraction to the eternal feminine, by way of an incorporated reproduction of Queen Elizabeth. The queen bee becomes a symbol of a sacred matriarchy, exuding golden nourishment in the form of honey.

Around the time of Glass's exhibition at Le Terrain Vague, he attended meetings by the surrealist group at their regular café. As a newcomer, he was seated right next to Breton. Always uncomfortable with being the center of attention, Glass soon elected to sit off-center, with Toyen and Elisa Breton. As much as he was drawn to surrealism, and for all his lasting admiration for Breton, he was also wary of having his work judged by the group and subsumed under the aims of a movement. Therefore, he did not participate in *EROS*, the international surrealist exhibition at Galerie Daniel Cordier in 1959–60, although he did attend the private inauguration of the exhibition at Joyce Mansour's apartment. There, Glass stood next to Breton when Jean Benoît executed his infamous performance, the Execution of the Testament of the Marquis de Sade, which culminated with Benoît branding himself with a red-hot iron in the shape of the letters SADE; captivated by the moment, Matta rushed up and branded himself with the iron, too, exclaiming: "Ouch!"[25]

At *EROS*, Glass saw Robert Rauschenberg's combine *Bed* (1955), Max Walter Svanberg's pearl mosaic *Portrait of a Star III* (1957–58), and a fetish crypt installation by Mimi Parent, featuring objects by Meret Oppenheim, Adrien Dax, and Parent herself.

[23] Gachon, "Alain Glass."
[24] Jean V. Dufresne, "Un jeune artiste canadien à Paris," *La Presse*, January 25, 1958, 42.
[25] Interview with Alan Glass, Mexico City, February 2022.

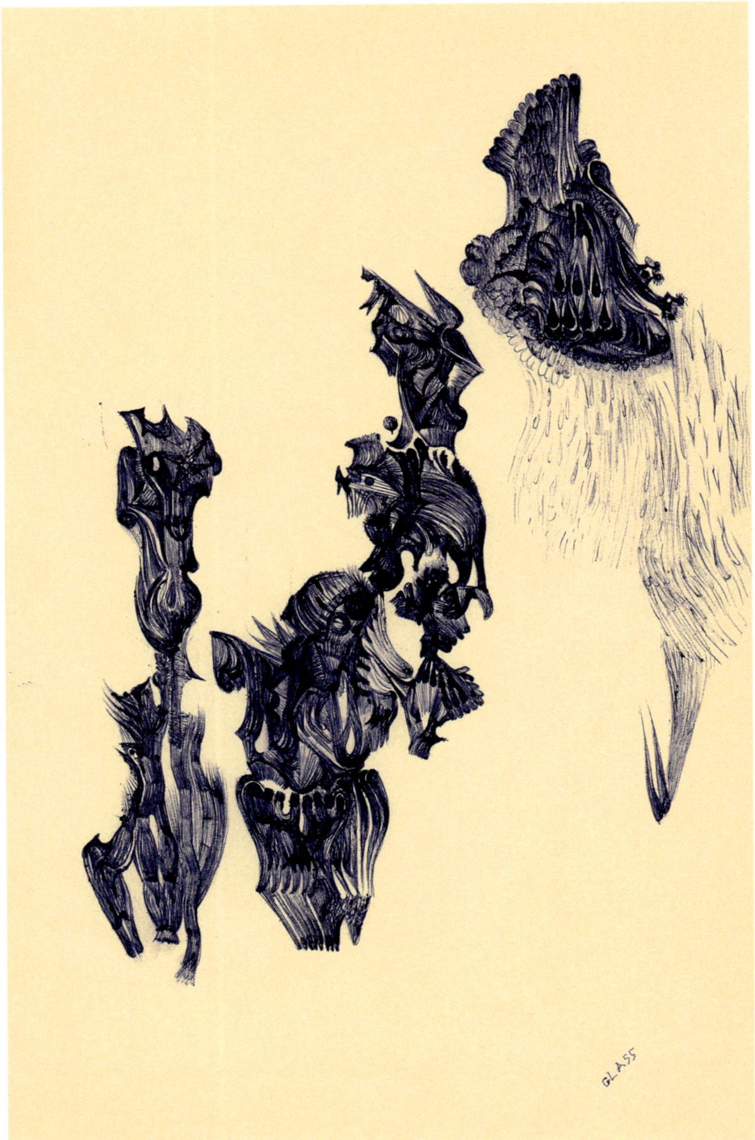

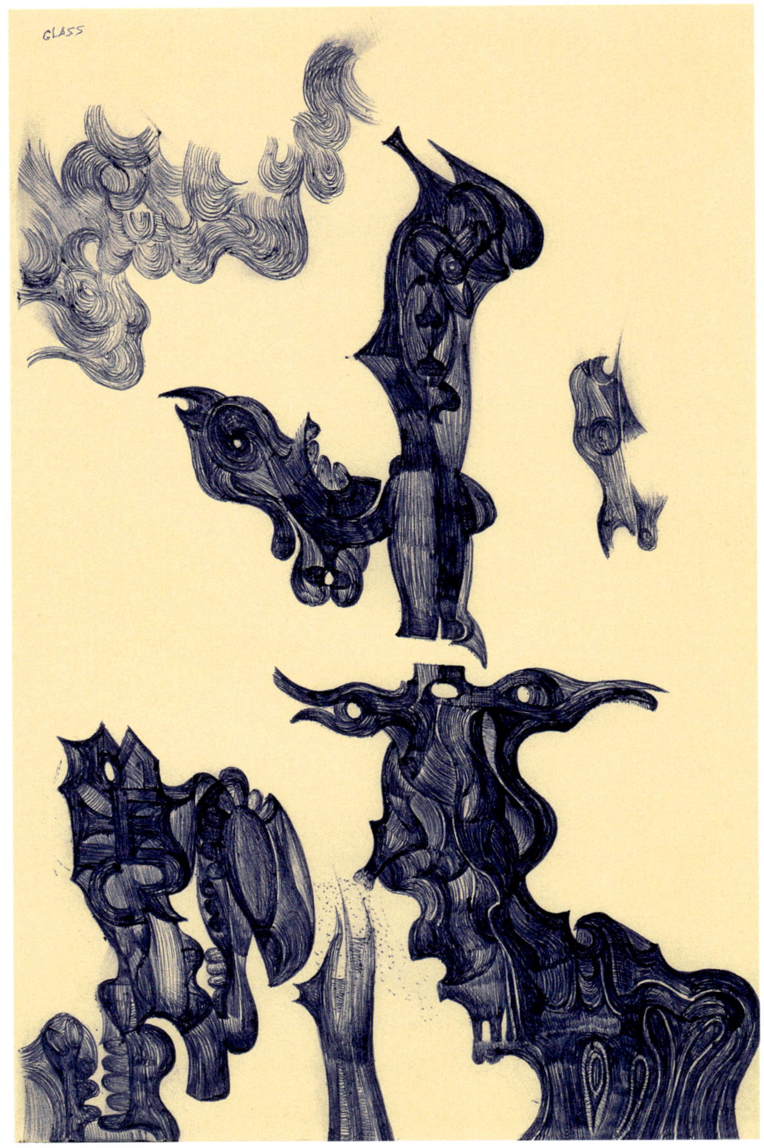

Untitled
(Galerie Le Terrain Vague period)
ca. 1954-1962
Monochrome blue ballpoint
pen drawing, on paper.
26 x 17 cm
Artist's collection

Untitled
(Galerie LeTerrain Vague period)
ca. 1954-1962
Monochrome blue ballpoint
pen drawing, on paper.
26 x 17 cm
Artist's collection

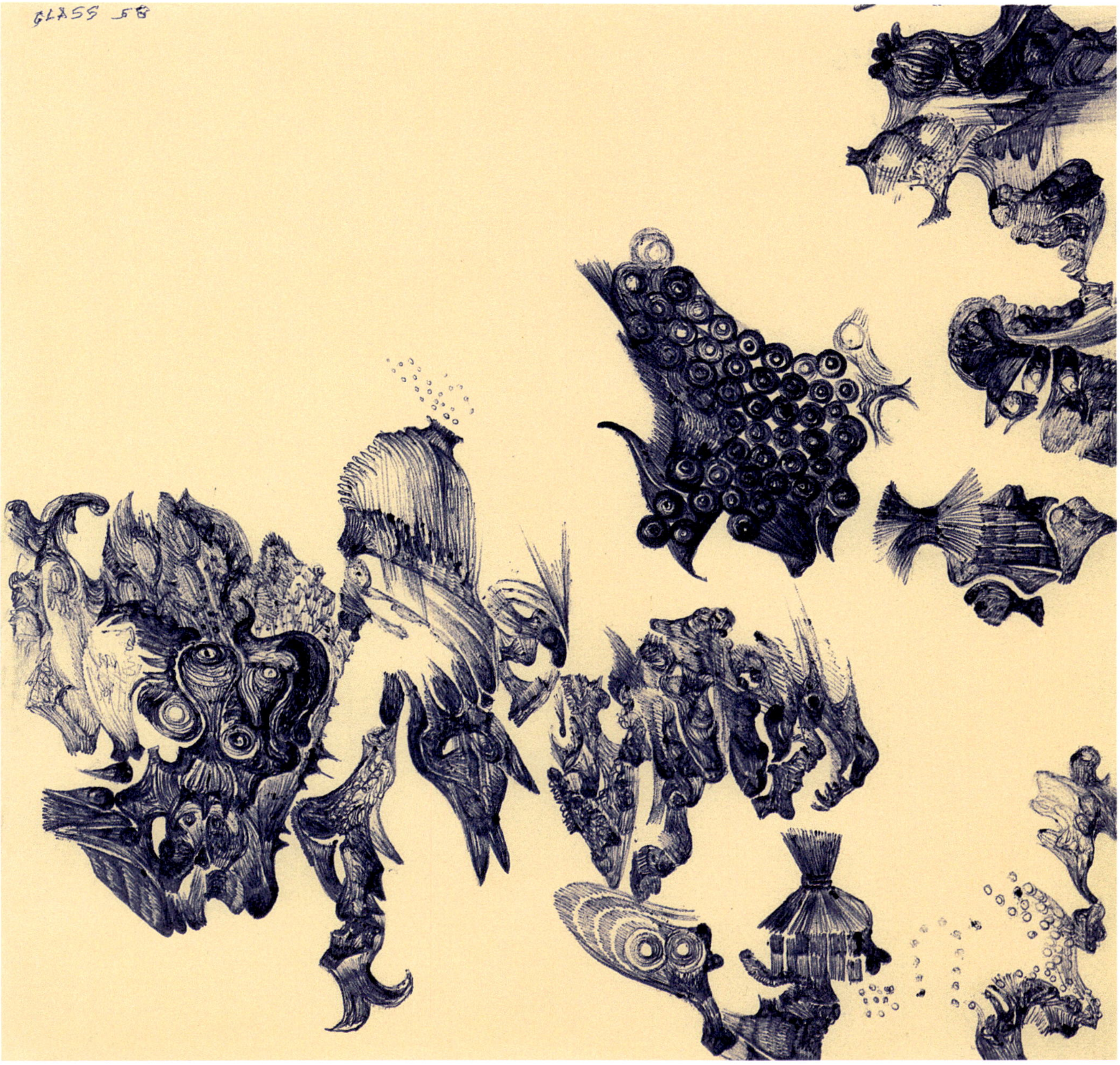

Untitled
(Galerie Le Terrain Vague period)
1958
Monochrome blue ballpoint
pen drawing, on paper.
16.4 x 17.1 cm
Artist's collection

These examples of an ever-evolving surrealist assemblage art may have inspired his own decision to start making objects in the early 1960s. While he never joined the surrealist group, Glass has kept in contact with many surrealists, both in France and Mexico, and he has reflected upon his affinity with surrealism in numerous boxes that allude to surrealist art, the surrealist tradition, and, not least, Breton himself. One striking example of the latter is *Vers l'ôr du temps (Tribute to André Breton)* (2002), in which a golden metal ship is placed in an old-fashioned bird cage; on the floor of the cage below the ship lies a golden helm and fine, golden metal wire is threaded across the object. So Glass evokes the phrase "je cherche l'ôr du temps," "I seek the gold of time," inscribed on Breton's tombstone, but also demonstrating, through the sheer poetic power of the object, that this search is an ongoing quest.

Glass has pursued the search for poetry through drawing, painting, and assemblage, always with an innate surrealist receptivity to the hieroglyphic messages received from the unconscious or nature, from found things or the tip of the ballpoint pen.

GNOSIS OF THE HAND

When I visited Alan Glass in February 2022, the first thing I saw at the desk with stacks of envelopes and folders containing his Parisian oeuvre was a handwritten sentence on a Manila folder: "The hand rivals and surpasses the mind." The quote, from the symbolist poet Paul Valéry, seems to encapsulate the spirit that animates Glass's early drawings. The speed with which he drew them must have facilitated a bypassing of the conscious mind. As much as Glass's stunning *métier* can be seen in the way in which he coaxes such intricate motifs from the simple Bic Cristal, the images took form without any preconceived intentions; it was this kind of automatic approach that drew the surrealists to these early works. But the idea that "the hand rivals and surpasses the mind" is also telling for Glass's consistent disavowal of insight into the meaning of his complex images and boxes; their motifs and arrangements arise from places beyond the conscious mind. Valéry's phrase resonates in particular with the recurring connections made between hands and visionary poetry in later works by Glass. The two hands in the diptych *Juégos pirotechnicos* (2002) spark and crackle with gnostic knowledge coaxed, by the artist's own sensitive hands, from objects found and made: palmistry notes are placed around the hand, bee-shaped firecrackers are attached to the fingers, and a plastic beehive is lodged in the palm. An untitled box from 2005 features a charro glove equipped with eye-like appendages that suggest that the *voyant* may see through his hands, the fingertips bristling with a tactile vision attuned to the most intimate secrets of matter.

Glass's drawings, and the technique behind them, also relate to some of the central tendencies in surrealist art and art criticism in the 1950s, in particular the intersection of automatism and abstraction. The surrealists first explored automatism through writing. In May and June 1919, Breton and Philippe Soupault famously sat down and wrote the collaborative automatic texts that would be published as *Les Champs magnétiques* (1920). In the years to follow, Breton and other surrealists drew inspiration from spiritualist mediums as much as from Sigmund Freud's use of free association as they turned automatism into the central method of early surrealism.[26] Automatic writing was predicated on a disregard for "aesthetic and moral concerns" and the bypassing of the ego in order to let the unconscious stream forth in jagged displays of "the real functioning of thought."[27] The poet's pen took down the "magic dictation" from what Victor Hugo called "the mouth of shadows."[28] But whereas the first surrealist manifesto equates surrealism with "psychic automatism in its pure state," by 1933 a somewhat disillusioned Breton wrote that "the history of automatic writing in surrealism [...] is one of continual misfortune."[29] Closer to the time of Glass's participation in surrealism, Breton revisited the perceived gap between the promise of automatism and its sometimes disappointing results. In his 1955 essay "On Surrealism in Its Living Works," he wrote that even though "the *practice* of automatic writing was abandoned so quickly," the surrealists believed that they had discovered "the 'prime matter' (in the alchemical sense) of language. After that, we knew *where* to get it, and it goes without saying that we had no interest in reproducing it to the point of satiety."[30] Automatism was a treasure that, once found, did not need to be replicated time and again; its very discovery prompted a transmutation of language, creativity, and being. If that discovery constituted a moment of contact with the Philosopher's Stone, this, it seems to me, is a Stone that Glass, too, has touched with a radically transformative result.

If automatic writing waned in importance for many surrealists, automatism had a more lasting place in the visual art and art-theoretical writings by surrealists. In the movement's early years, Jean Arp, Max Ernst, and André Masson explored visual automatism through chance operations and the invention of frottage, and by drawing without any preconceived content. Arp's and Ernst's automatic techniques rest on the incorporation of more or less readymade materials or imagery: strips of paper strewn across the canvas for Arp, and the transfer of images through rubbing for Ernst. In contrast, Masson made fragments of figurative motifs appear in the midst of swirls of Matisse-like, undulating lines: a torso, a fish, a plant.[31] In the mid-1930s, Oscar Dominguez made a decisive contribution to the repertoire of automatic methods, as well as to the surrealist visual lexicon, when he adopted decalcomania, originally a technique for transferring patterns onto glass, for the purposes of surrealist image-making. In decalcomania,

[26] See André Breton, *The Lost Steps*, trans. Mark Polizzotti (Lincoln: University of Nebraska Press, 1996), 92–95.
[27] André Breton, *Manifestoes of Surrealism*, trans. Richard Seaver and Helen R. Lane (Ann Arbor: University of Michigan Press, 1972), 26.
[28] Breton, *The Lost Steps*, 91.
[29] Breton, *Break of Day*, 130.
[30] Breton, *Manifestoes of Surrealism*, 299.
[31] See Clark V. Poling, *André Masson and the Surrealist Self* (New Haven: Yale University Press, 2008), 47–48.

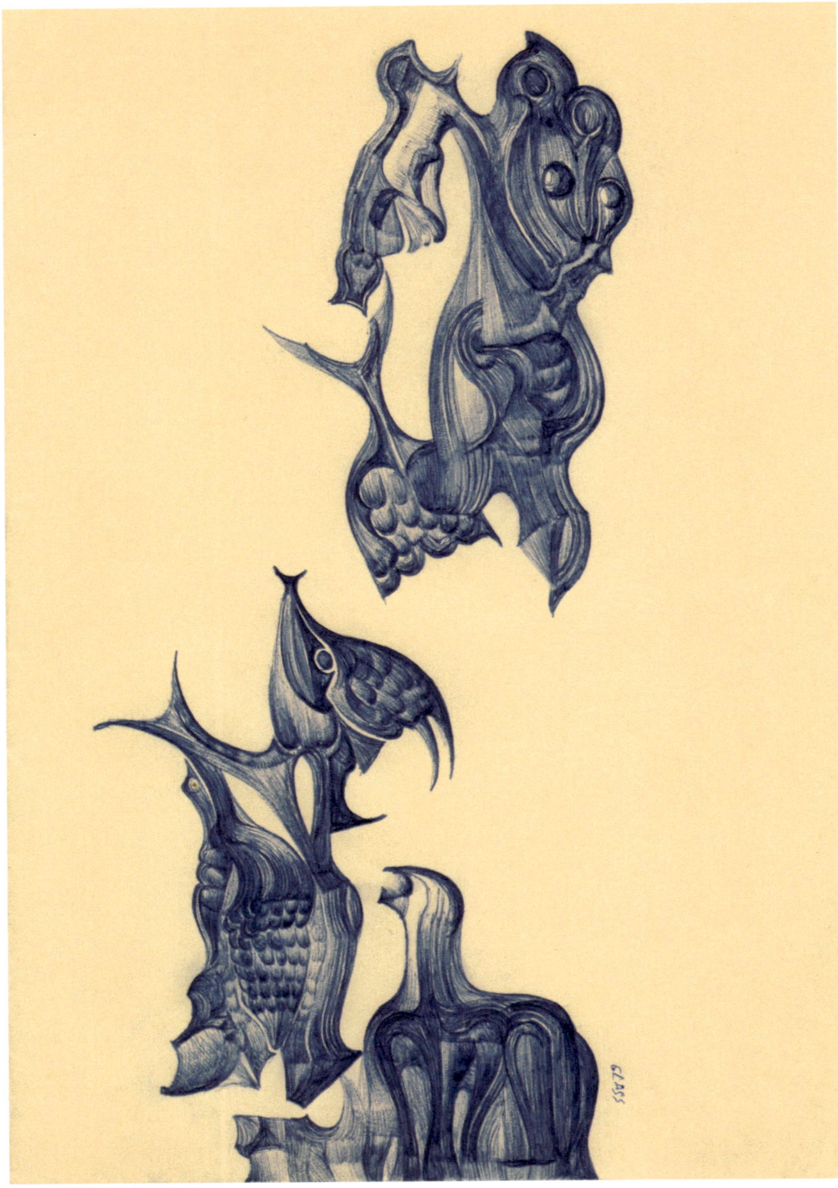

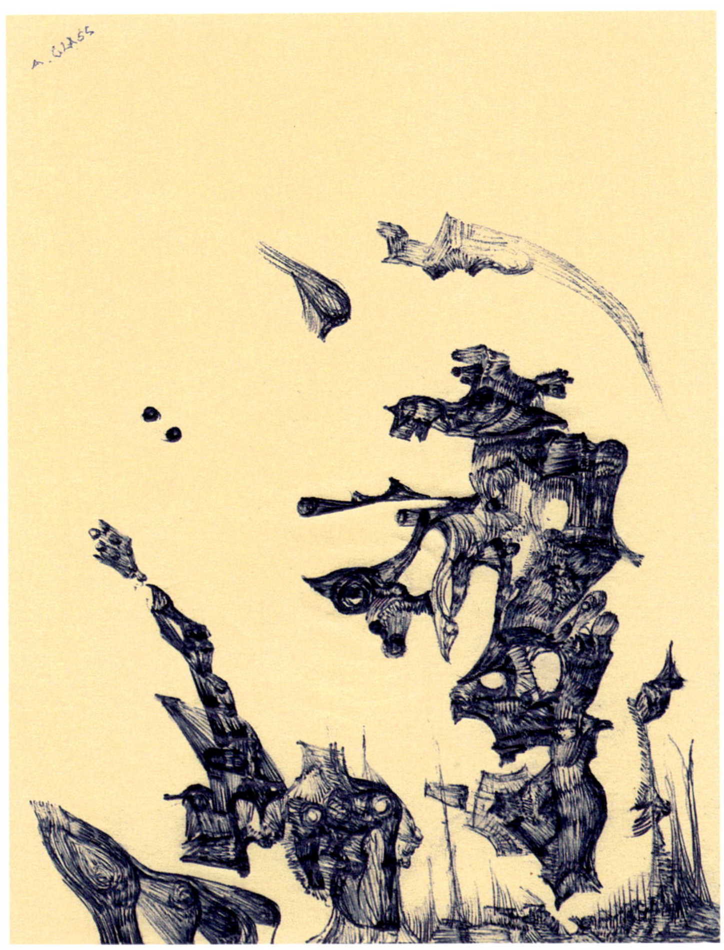

Untitled
(Galerie Le Terrain Vague period)
ca. 1954-1962
Monochrome blue ballpoint
pen drawing, on paper.
26 x 17 cm
Artist's collection

Untitled
(Galerie Le Terrain Vague period)
ca. 1954-1962
Monochrome blue ballpoint
pen drawing, on paper.
17.1 x 13 cm
Artist's collection

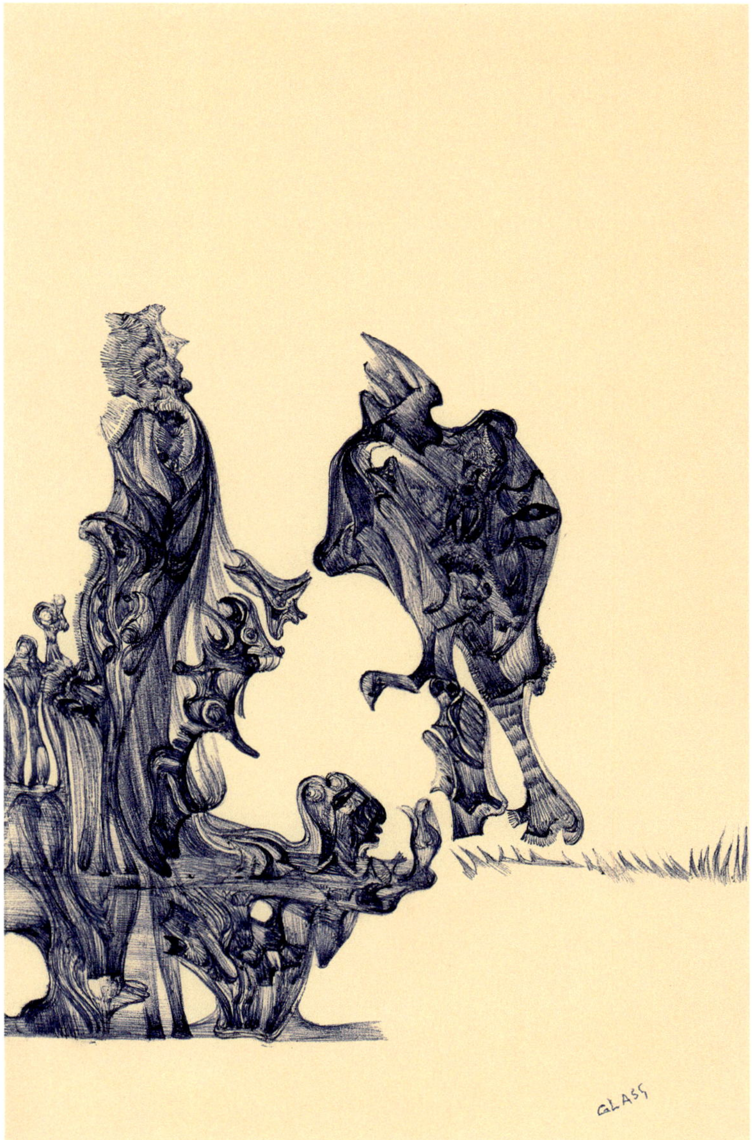

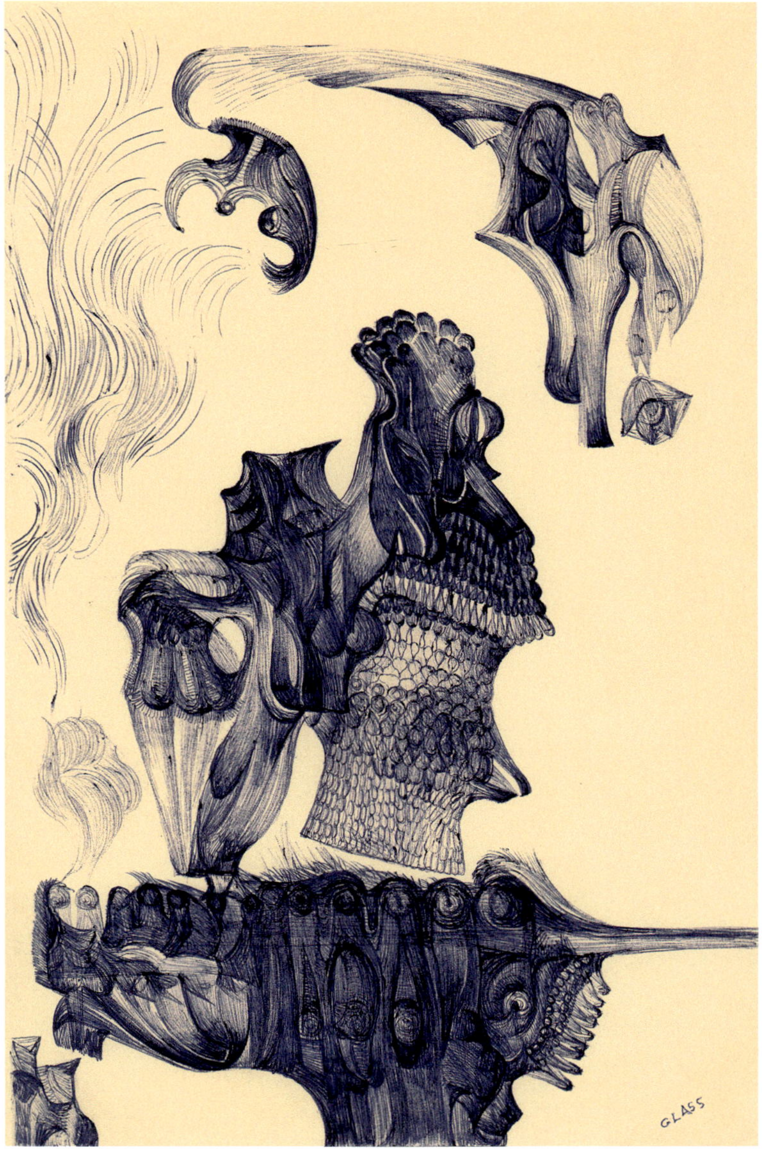

Untitled
(Galerie Le Terrain Vague period)
ca. 1954-1962
Monochrome blue ballpoint
pen drawing, on paper.
26 x 17 cm
Artist's collection

Untitled
(Galerie Le Terrain Vague period)
ca. 1954-1962
Monochrome blue ballpoint
pen drawing, on paper.
26 x 17 cm
Artist's collection

many surrealist artists found a way of swiftly creating marvellous landscapes—like the interior of rocks, underwater caverns, or rolling hillsides—to be incorporated into paintings or as raw material to be elaborated on with pen or paintbrush. Soon thereafter, Wolfgang Paalen invented fumage. By passing the flame of a candle across the canvas, he created spectral patterns, which he then elaborated upon with oil paint.

These automatic techniques responded to the challenges of untethering consciousness and intention from the generation of images. In a 1950 essay, the surrealist painter Adrien Dax writes that the "mechanical" techniques of visual automatism, including fumage and frottage, "have the incontestable advantage of reducing the conscious participation of the artist, who is thereby reliant upon a kind of chance."[32] These chance methods, Dax reminds us, have often resulted in imagery with a striking resemblance to natural objects and processes. Organic growth, the formation of stalactites, and the interior of agates can be discerned in decalcomania, grattage, and frottage. But for all the creative possibilities enabled by visual automatism, it, too, "reveals, alongside some successes, a long string of failures," which nevertheless, even if they fail as art, have considerable merit as "irritants" of the spirit.[33]

Glass's approach to drawing largely evades the "mechanical" means discussed by Dax. The one exception is his mentioned use of allumettage, moving lighted matches across the paper or canvas to create dark spots and streaks that are sometimes suggestive of natural forms. In other ways, Glass's drawing technique appears to have been closer in spirit to automatic writing. His labour-intensive drawing routine depended on a relaxation of the conscious mind and a disregard for intention. Nevertheless, his use of the ballpoint pen to create these intricate images was not so much a way of adhering to automatism in a programmatic manner, as it was a novel contribution to the existing trove of automatic methods. The organic and mineral forms that take shape in his drawings differ from Masson's incorporation in his automatic drawings of recognizable animal, human, and vegetable elements. Glass's drawings are closer to natural processes in themselves, conjuring up the way in which *phusis* in ancient Greece signified nature as, above all, growth and generation.[34] Or, as Arp would have it, they are not illusionistic copies of nature, but new additions to the world, similar to the way in which a fruit grows on a tree.[35]

That is not to say that resemblances between Glass's art and other surrealists are lacking. Sometimes the formations he draws are eerily similar to the landscapes created through decalcomania, even as they are made with a ballpoint pen rather than with mechanical means. At other times, the way in which birds and trees can be made out in the drawings recall Ernst's depiction of animals and plants in his frottages. Still other drawings evoke the crystalline structures

[32] Dax, "Automatic Perspective," in *The Surrealism Reader*, 302.
[33] Dax, "Automatic Perspective," 308–309.
[34] See Pierre Hadot, *The Veil of Isis: An Essay on the History of the Idea of Nature*, trans. Michael Chase (Cambridge, MA: Belknap, 2006).
[35] Jean Arp, *On My Way*.

explored by Jacques Hérold or Paalen. One work made with jittery ballpoint lines combined with yellow, green, and light blue watercolour, forming what looks like a heart or vibrant plumage, is strongly reminiscent of Dax's work at the time.

During Glass's years as a doorman at Saint-Germain-des-Prés, his drawings also became increasingly abstract, in a way that dovetailed with the reception of abstraction in surrealism. During World War II, surrealism was a decisive influence on the emergence of abstract expressionism in the United States.[36] In exile in, or near, New York, surrealists including Breton, Ernst, and Masson contributed to the adoption of automatic methods by several painters, including Jackson Pollock, whose use of the drip technique was lifted from Ernst's *The Bewildered Planet* (1942). Writing in 1947 and staking out new boundaries for the movement, Breton defined surrealism in opposition to pure abstraction as much as to realism.[37] But in the 1950s, partly under the influence of art critic Charles Estienne, surrealism and abstraction once again drew closer.[38] Painters working in abstraction, whether as their main focus or incidentally, including Riopelle, Jean Degottex, Marcelle Loubchansky, and Judit Reigl had, sometimes short-lived, associations with surrealism. Alan Glass can be added to this cohort. His use of modest means—the cheap ballpoint pen and disposable paper—along with the small format of the drawings appear to be a rebuttal to Pollock's glaringly monumental canvases. In an essay on Degottex, Breton writes that it is the great merit of modern poetry and art "to have attacked the world of appearances increasingly vigorously and effectively" in order to cross the threshold to "the real world, not the world that is foisted upon us as real."[39] Like Degottex, in Breton's lyrical description, Glass's drawings allow us to "enter this blossoming universe."[40]

When Jodorowsky writes that "everything floats" in his essay for the Terrain Vague pamphlet, so evoking Heraclitus's "Panta rhei," he suggests that Alan Glass's drawings are visionary insights in the constitution of reality beyond appearances. In her book on Glass, Masayo Nonaka remarks that, "throughout his life Glass has been able to decode the analogies between the physical and the metaphysical."[41] "Nature loves to hide," Heraclitus also stated with characteristic cryptic fervour. It has been the task of poets, artists, and natural philosophers from antiquity to Romanticism and on to surrealism to discover what nature may hide behind the veil of appearances. As the French philosopher Pierre Hadot puts it, "Since earliest antiquity, the poet has been thought to be the true interpreter of nature, who knew its secrets precisely insofar as it was imagined that nature acts like a poet, and that what nature produces is a poem."[42] Realist and representational art lingers at the surface. Visionary art, including surrealism and work produced by

[36] See Martica Sawin, *Surrealism in Exile and the Beginning of the New York School* (Cambridge, MA: MIT Press, 1995).

[37] André Breton, *Free Rein*, trans. Michel Parmentier and Jacqueline d'Amboise (Lincoln: University of Nebraska Press, 1995), 92.

[38] Durozoi, *History of the Surrealist Movement*, 549–550.

[39] Breton, *Surrealism and Painting*, 341.

[40] Breton, *Surrealism and Painting*, 341.

[41] Nonaka, *Alan Glass*.

[42] Hadot, *The Veil of Isis*, 201.

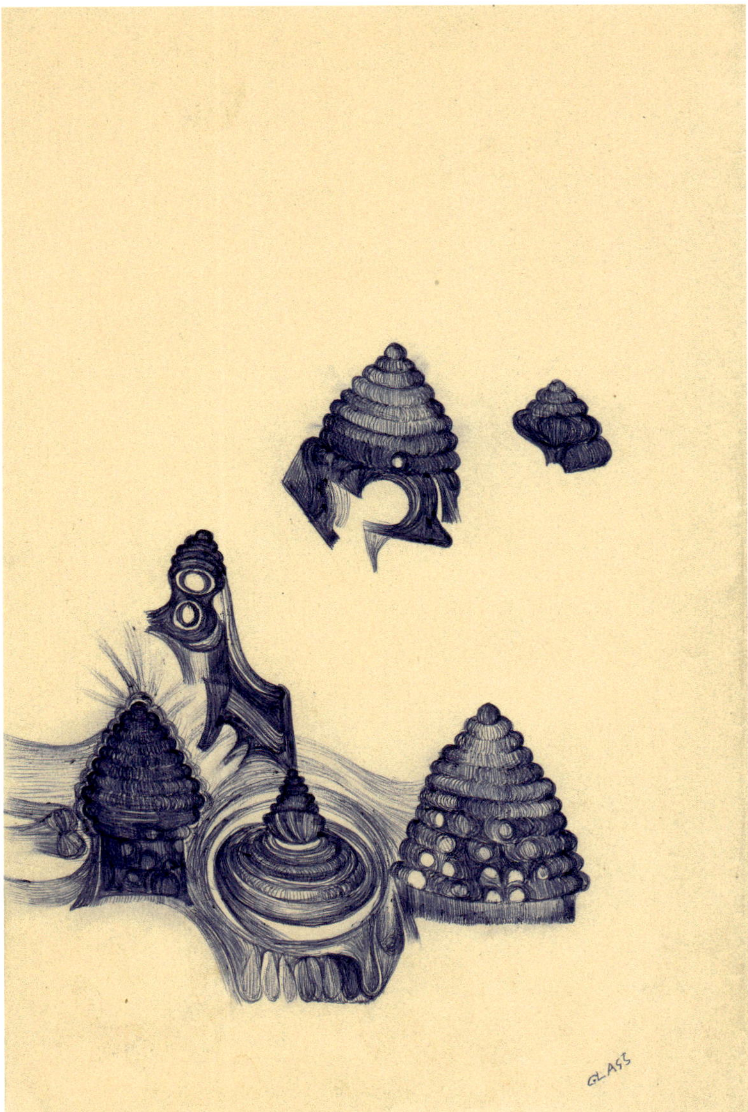

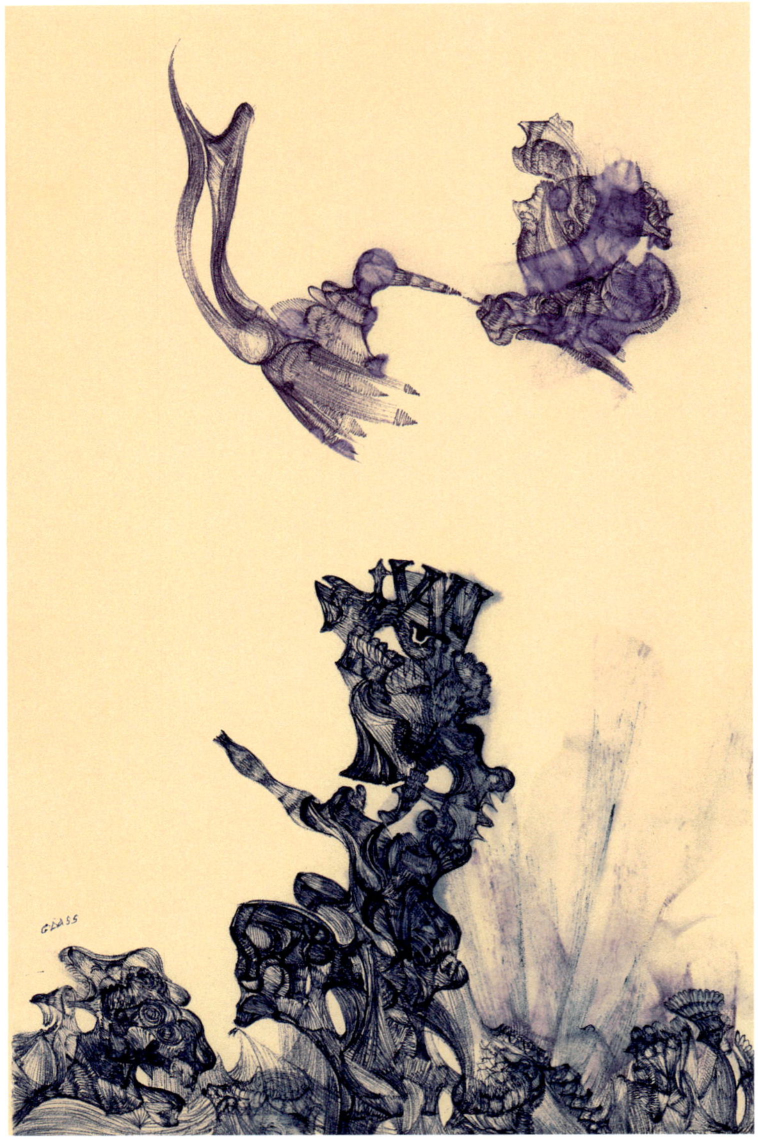

Untitled
(Galerie Le Terrain Vague period)
ca. 1954-1962
Monochrome blue ballpoint
pen drawing, on paper.
26 x 17 cm
Artist's collection

Untitled
(Galerie Le Terrain Vague period)
ca. 1954-1962
Drawing in blue and violet
bicolor pen, on paper.
26 x 17 cm
Artist's collection

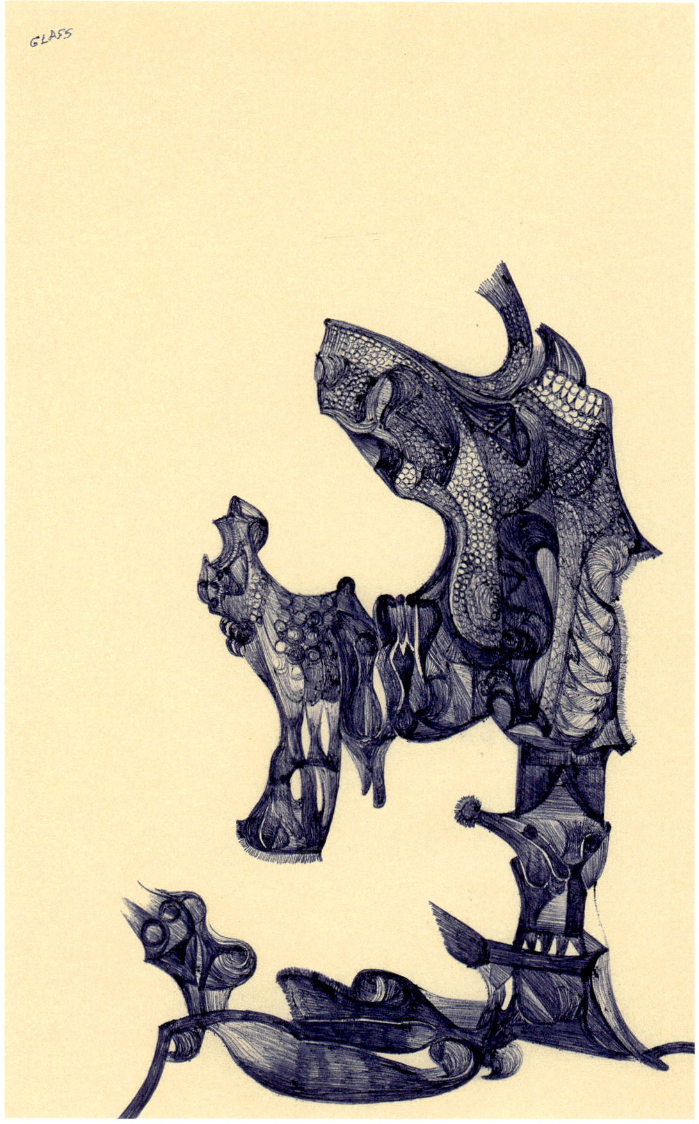

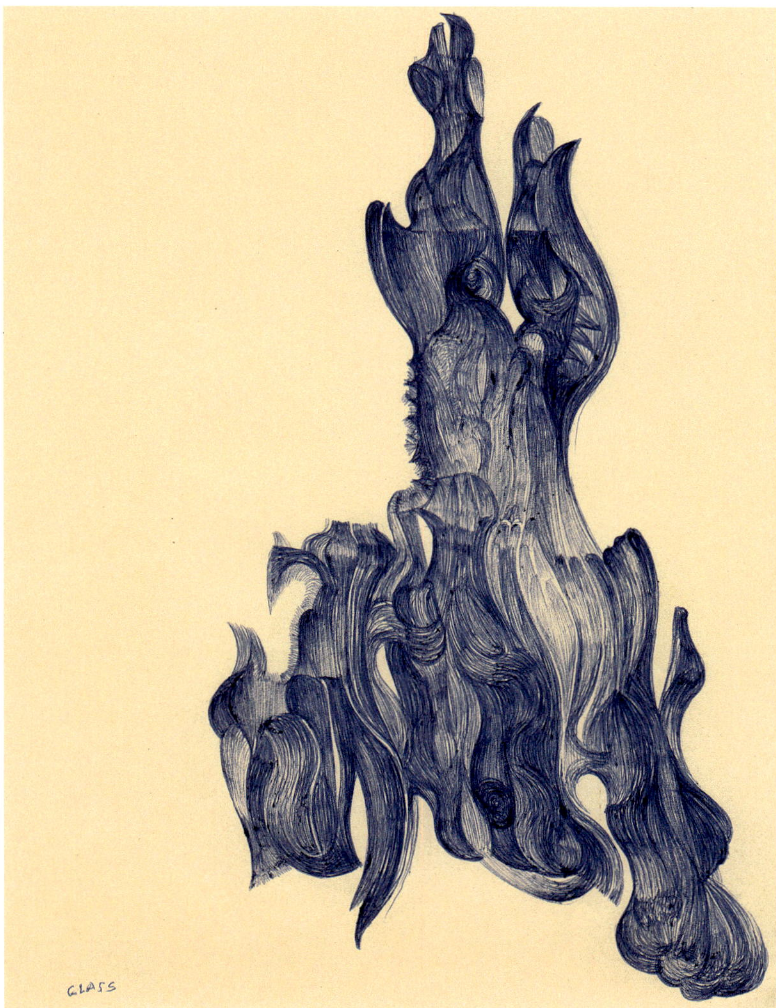

Untitled
(Galerie Le Terrain Vague period)
ca. 1954-1962
Monochrome blue ballpoint
pen drawing, on paper.
26 x 17 cm
Artist's collection

Untitled
(Galerie Le Terrain Vague period)
ca. 1954-1962
Monochrome blue ballpoint
pen drawing, on paper.
26 x 17 cm
Artist's collection

mediums, shares with Heraclitus a drive to look beyond the bark at the living sap, the flowing nucleus of the world. It is in itself a species of organic growth, an extension of nature. Through the movements of the hand, liberated from stifling conscious intention, Glass turns the ballpoint pen into an instrument of gnosis, a revelatory, experiential, immediate kind of insight that surpasses restrictive logic and mechanical rationality.

The German romantic poet Novalis opens his unfinished *The Novices of Saïs* in the following way:

> Various are the roads of man. He who follows and compares them will see strange figures emerge, figures which seem to belong to that great cipher which we discern written everywhere, in wings, eggshells, clouds and snow, in crystals and in stone formations, on ice-covered waters, on the inside and outside of mountains, of plants, beasts, and men, in the lights of heaven, on scored disks of pitch or glass or iron filings round a magnet, and in strange conjunctures of chance.[43]

Novalis, a *Naturphilosoph* intent on deciphering the links between the human mind and nature, here evokes an age-old idea that the world is inscribed with a language that can be detected in the marvellous beauty of nature. The natural objects he enumerates are of a kind that can often be discerned in Glass's drawings; wings, eggshells, stones, and plants are frequently incorporated into the artist's boxed assemblages. For Novalis, the meaning of this natural language is evasive in a time that has lost the sacred key to nature. Understanding the magic grammar of nature hinges on lifting the veil of a statue of Isis: "if according to the inscription, no mortal can lift the veil, we must seek to become immortal; he does not seek to lift it, is no true novice of Saïs."[44] Glass consistently explores the particular kind of beauty found in natural patterns by those who believe that there may still be an opening key to the world.

There are also drawings that appear to betray the kind of anxieties alluded to in Jodorowsky's essay. Sometimes, Glass's drawings evince a similar kinetic energy as Matta's non-Euclidean imagery. At other times, his abstract tendencies appear to be attempts at capturing the essence of smoke. A heavy smoker, he may have been transfixed by the movements of the smoke emanating from his cigarette, and, possibly unwittingly, channeled its swirling through the movement of his hand. Perhaps his drawings are a species of capnomacy, or the use of smoke for divination purposes. A similar smoke-like quality can be detected in many of Glass's later paintings, in which parades of ghostly apparitions emerge and vanish. Like the ballpoint drawings, his paintings are often dominated by shades of blue. For Glass, the intense blue of lapis lazuli, as used, finely ground, in Winsor & Newton's discontinued Ultramarine Ash

[43] Novalis, *The Novices of Saïs*, 3.

[44] Novalis, *The Novices of Saïs*, 17.

Blue, is "associated with the memory of his childhood home and the landscape at Mt. Bruno. Gloria Feman Orenstein has described this blue as 'an ether, an elixir, and a vibratory incantation ... The energy-surrounds of his paintings, like astral essences, project a spirit-matter that suddenly makes the invisible manifest.'"[45] Blue evokes the ocean and the sky, and the particular intense blue specked with gold of lapis lazuli looks like the starlit night sky. The precious stone ground into pigment speaks to the incessant transformations that take place in Glass's two-dimensional works.

There is something truly alchemical in Glass's way of making the cheap blue ink of the Bic pen take on the sacred hues of lapis lazuli, but also in his very use of the mass-produced and modest pen to coax forth his marvellous manual visions. As different as the results appear to be at first sight, this approach is also similar to the way in which his later assemblages transform the detritus of consumer culture—old toys, food packaging, perfume bottles—into poetic condensations and cosmic evocations. Mass-produced prime matter and cheap pens are transformed into complex works. Altogether, Glass's drawings display a genius of the freely roving hand. Breton concludes "On Surrealism in Its Living Works," by lauding poetic intuition, which "seeks not only to assimilate all known forms but also boldly to create new forms—that is to say, to be in a position to embrace all the structures of the world, manifested or not. It alone provides the thread that can put us back on the road of gnosis as knowledge of suprasensible Reality, 'invisibly visible in an eternal mystery.'"[46] For Glass, the gnosis of the hand pulls back the veil of appearances only to allow us to detect hints of further depths through curtains of smoke.

ENGRAVINGS AND PAINTINGS

While the drawings constitute the main part of the corpus of works that Alan Glass created in Paris, he also worked with engraving and painting during these years.

When he first came to Paris, Glass tried out working with lithography. A couple of years later he continued to pursue graphic work: he came across a few copper plates and started experimenting with them in his maid's room at 5 rue Manuel. His Parisian engravings parallel the development of his drawings. The earliest dated engravings from 1956 are characterized by fluid shapes redolent of animals and vegetation, with shading suggesting depth. The later engravings resemble his drawings from the last few years at Saint-Germain-des-Prés, with hectic lines forming crowded thickets. These graphic works are made in very small editions, from one to three. Glass's early engravings are the first steps towards developing a practice that has been an important part of his artistic oeuvre. Throughout the years, he has also worked with drypoint and silver point. His later engravings tend to be as delicate as his drawings and paintings. The

[45] Nonaka, *Alan Glass*, 258.

[46] Breton, *Manifestoes of Surrealism*, 304.

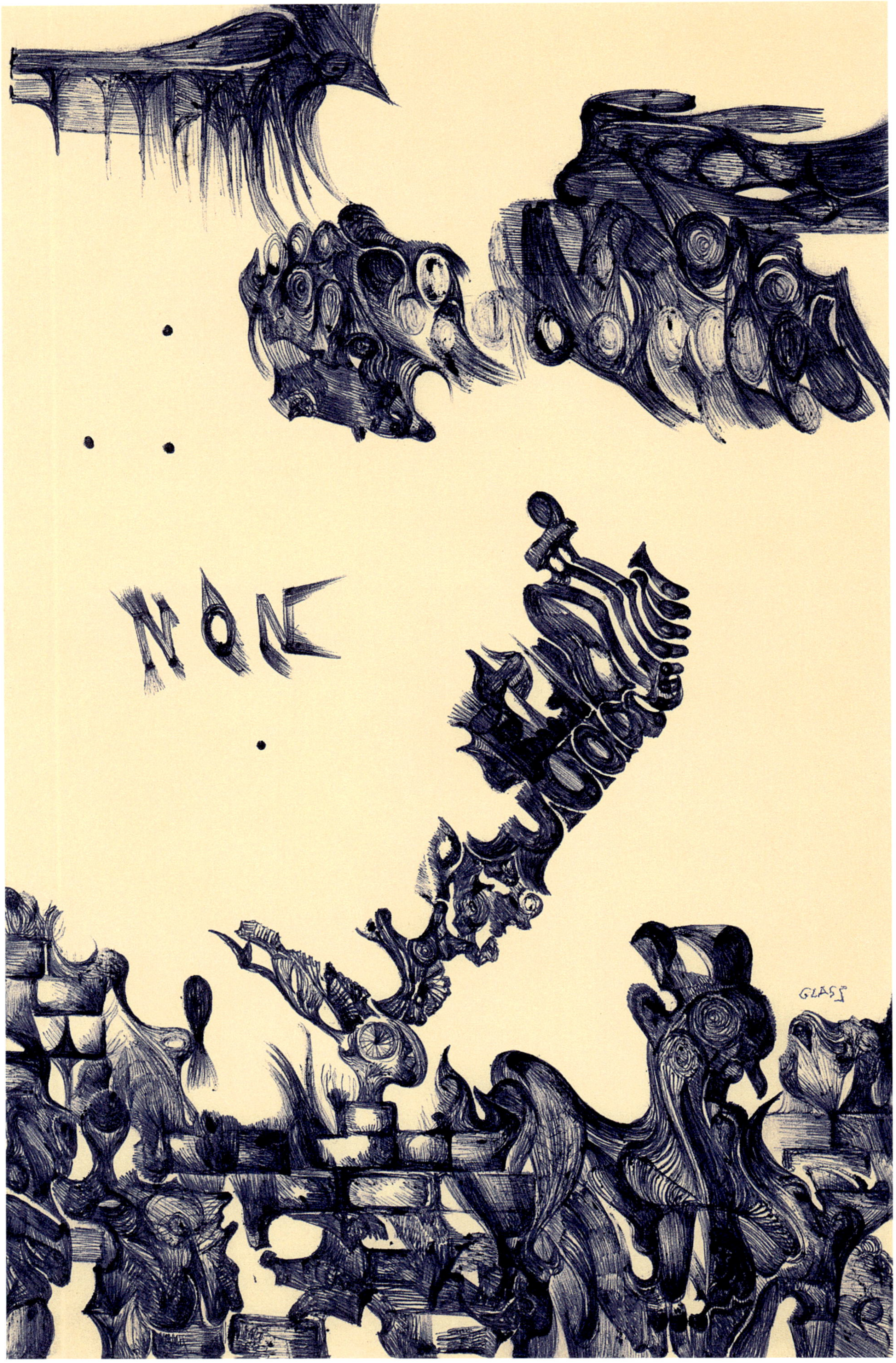

Untitled
(Galerie Le Terrain Vague period)
ca. 1954-1962
Monochrome blue ballpoint
pen drawing, on paper.
26 x 17 cm
Artist's collection

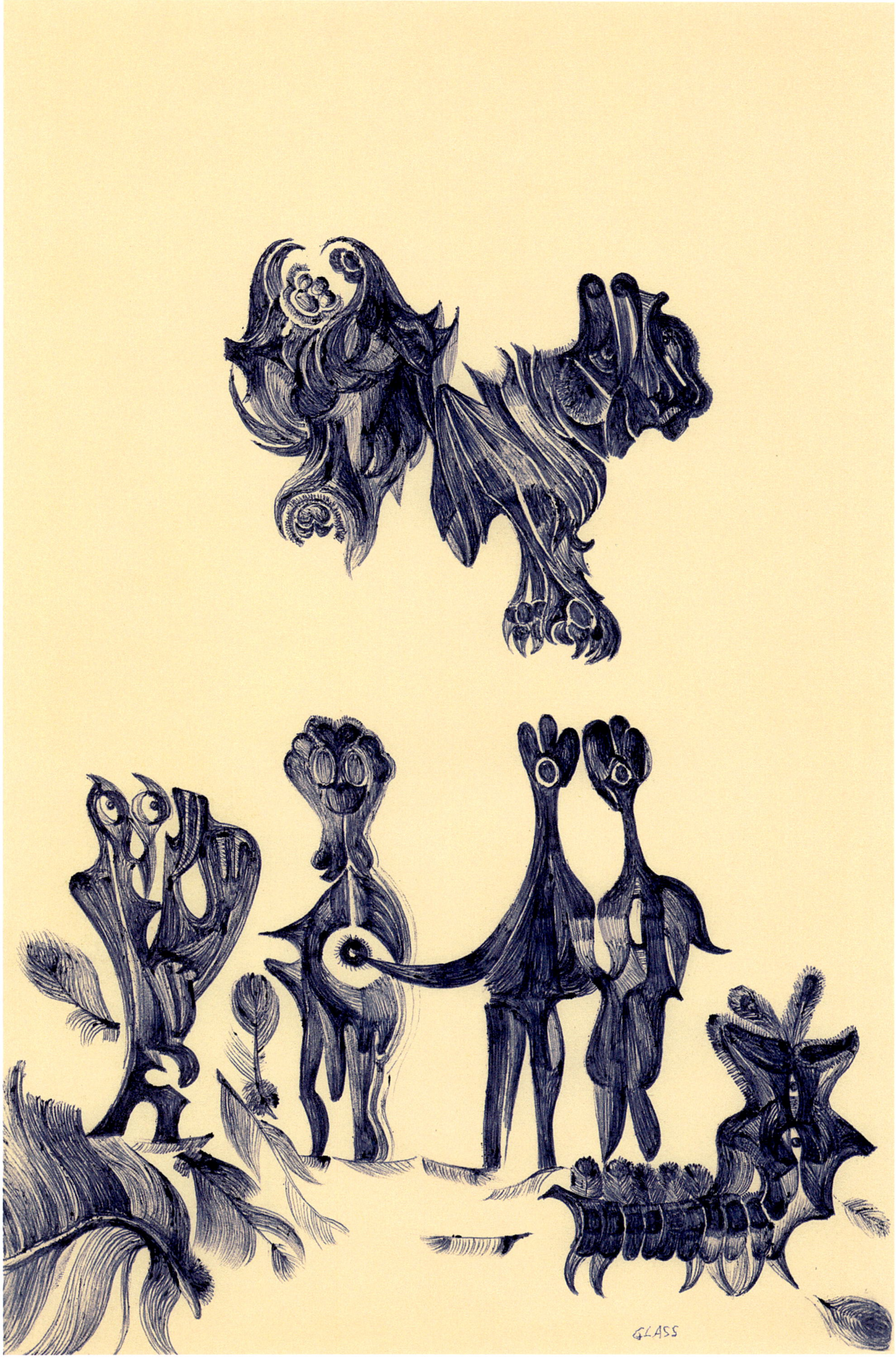

Untitled
(Galerie Le Terrain Vague period)
ca. 1954-1962
Monochrome blue ballpoint
pen drawing, on paper.
25.8 x 17 cm
Artist's collection

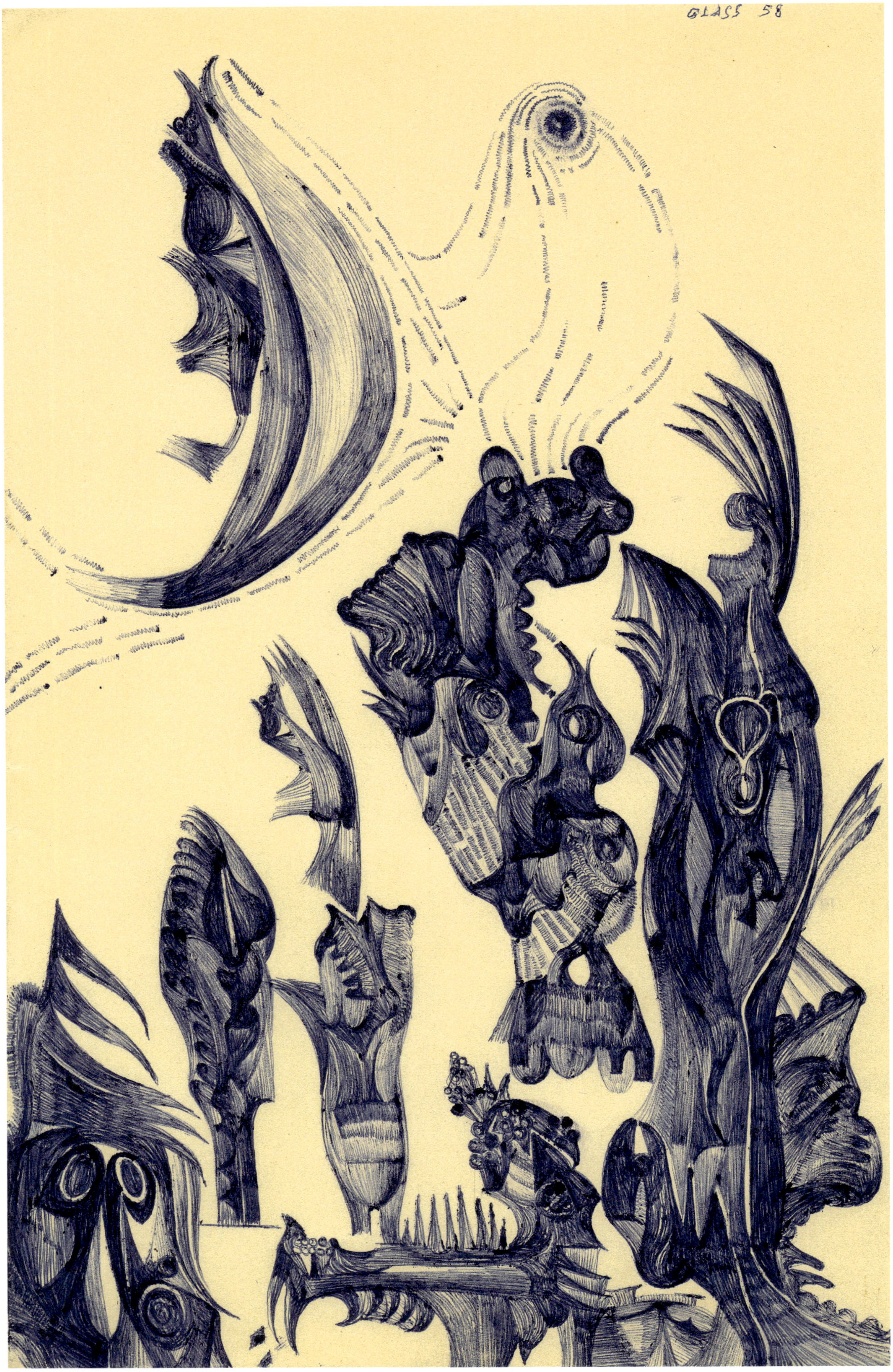

Untitled
(Galerie Le Terrain Vague period)
1958
Monochrome blue ballpoint
pen drawing, on paper.
26 x 17 cm
Artist's collection

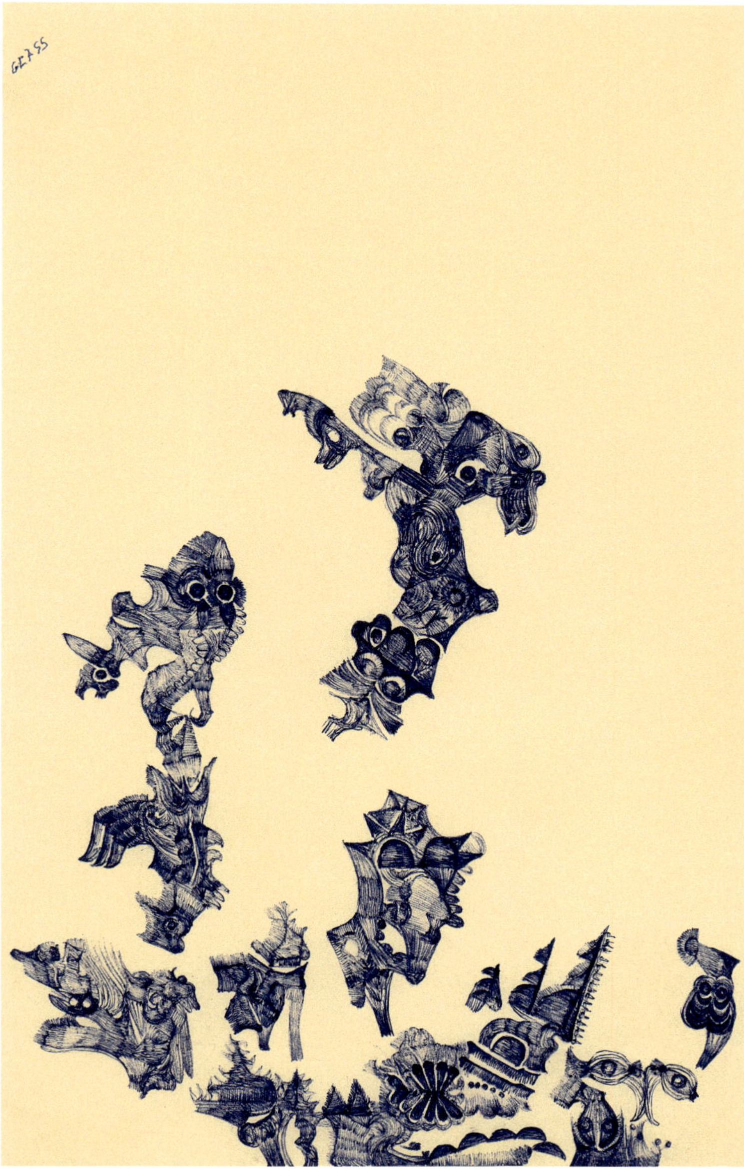

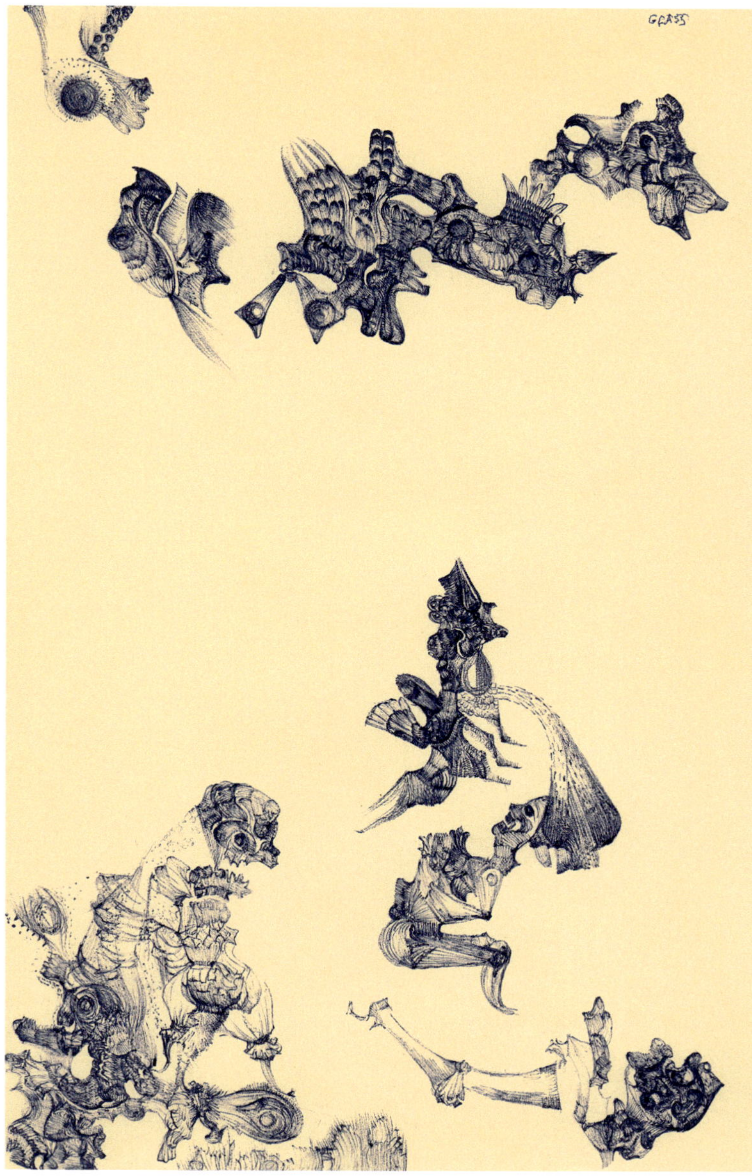

Untitled
(Galerie Le Terrain Vague period)
ca. 1954-1962
Monochrome blue ballpoint
pen drawing, on paper.
25.6 x 17 cm
Artist's collection

Untitled
(Galerie Le Terrain Vague period)
ca. 1954-1962
Monochrome blue ballpoint
pen drawing, on paper.
26 x 17 cm
Artist's collection

fine lines often form spectral shapes that morph like smoke rising from a cigarette, or like dripping ectoplasm, as is suggested by the seeming allusions to mediumism in many of them. Other engravings are more directly figurative, including one that depicts a fantasticated version of Glass's house in Roma Norte. The editions have mostly been small, in part because the delicacy of the engravings means that the plates wear out quickly. Most notably, Glass has collected his drypoints in two portfolios, e *La unidad del multiple* (2003–5) and *Le Maréchal* (2016), which are accompanied with poems by his friends Leonora Carrington and Alejandra Pizarnik, respectively. *La unidad del multiple* is placed together with a collage in a handmade box decorated with a small painting, so bridging the many media in which he works.

During his time as a student of Alfred Pellan's at l'École des beaux arts in Montreal, Glass focused mainly on painting.[47] Before leaving for Paris, he destroyed all of his artworks but for one single painting that he brought with him. However, alongside his ballpoint-pen drawings, Glass also started painting again in Paris. Many of the paintings evince a similar approach as the drawings. In some works, he even combines the techniques. In one drawing, the blue ballpoint pen is combined with splashes of intense yellow watercolour, which look like puddles of liquid sunlight. An intricate drawing of equine creatures seemingly undergoing metamorphoses is made against a background of soft pink and turquoise watercolour. One image combines delicate shapes made with blue and black ballpoint pens with a background in yellow watercolour. There are fossils and rock formations here, too, but also figures that resemble Kachina dolls.

Other works that combine these techniques are more sinister. A 1959 piece made with black ballpoint pen and watercolour seems to be animated by energies going in all directions. Figurative shapes emerge here and there, as intimations of the swirling faces and bodies populating Glass's later paintings. The overall effect, however, is that of a landscape tormented by demonic forces.

Still other works add elements of collage, but these are often overpainted to the extent that they meld together with the rest of the image in terms of motifs, and rather take on the appearance of tactile relief additions. One work combines watercolour, ballpoint pen, and collage to form an egg-like shape decorated with such fervent colours that it looks bejewelled. Other works are made solely with watercolour. One of these is dominated by blue, purple, and orange hues, with shapes resembling butterfly wings and flowers, possibly wild pansy, in bloom. Glass's love of various shades of blue comes through in these works, as he uses turquoise watercolour to create what looks like a rock formation or living diamond; in another painting, the main motif looks like living matter suspended in fluid, placed against

[47] See Nonaka, *Alan Glass*.

a turquoise background. Overall, Glass's watercolours are further evidence of his tendency to approach the organic growth of nature, and in particular its processes of growth, transformation, and engendering of new life.

Glass also explored very different painting techniques. He spent the summer of 1958 in Greece together with friends including Jean Benoît and Mimi Parent, and was particularly enamoured of the islands of Greece. His love of the place had a very direct effect on his art, as he started diluting his paint and ink with seawater. A series of paintings on thick, textured paper feature flowing black sections that look almost like decalcomania. Their overall appearance is highly organic, with shapes that are reminiscent of fungus, clouds, and vegetation, amidst swirls of smoke and soft explosions suggested by splashes of ink. Another painting combines a light blue watercolour foundation with powerful biomorphic shapes and mineral formations made with black ink. A very different series of paintings are made on large sheets of rag paper. Here, the black ink forms soft, hazy clouds or tufts of smoke, which sometimes congeal into more sinister abstract patterns.

The latter paintings include a series of watercolours from June 1960 to 1962 that look like exercises in the art of invisibility. A folder labelled Mexico contains very soft watercolours, some of which are so delicate that the colour is close to imperceptible. These images are almost entirely non-figurative, with the exception of a pale yellow watercolour that features two eyes peering out, but these can only barely be distinguished. These paintings contrast markedly against the frenzied lines and claustrophobic atmosphere in the drawings Glass made at the same time and anticipate his later attempts at painting the invisible.

REMEMBERING ARRIVALS PAST

In 1961, Glass had to leave his job as a doorman at Saint-Germain-des-Prés. The owner found his lack of physiognomic skills, as Glass puts it, to be untenable. Always sensitive to hierarchical injustices, the artist-*portier* would allow the riff-raff to come in from the streets, but would not recognize celebrities such as Charles Chaplin or the Prince of Monaco, whom he refused entry three nights in a row. Not long thereafter, Glass would be prompted by the poetic jolt effected by the sight of Mexican sugar skulls to leave Paris for a one-year stay in Mexico, which eventually turned into a permanent relocation.

Judging by his art, the formative Paris years seem to be ever-present for Glass. Visual and textual allusions to Paris are everywhere in his art. In 2016, he completed a series of four boxes that reflect back on his arrival in Paris. In these assemblages, he incorporates elements taken from reproductions of Giorgio de Chirico's 1914 painting *Gare Montparnasse (The Melancholy of Departure)* (1914), which depicts the train station close to Glass's

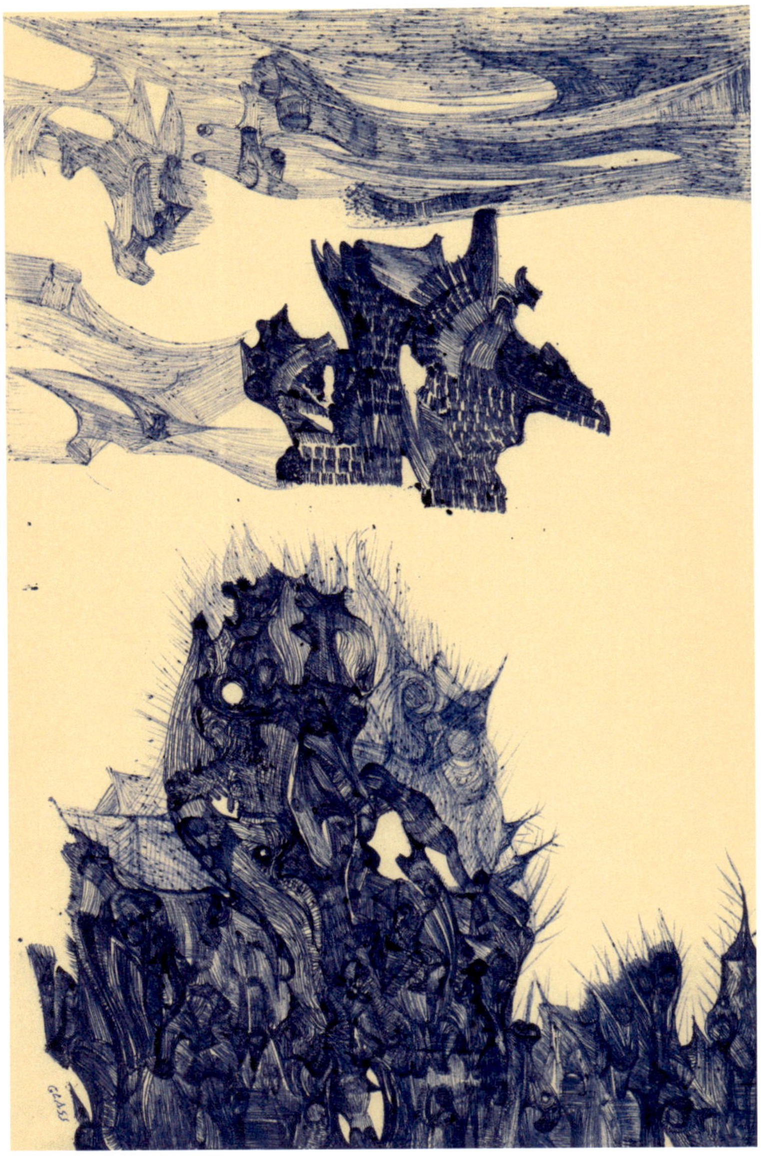

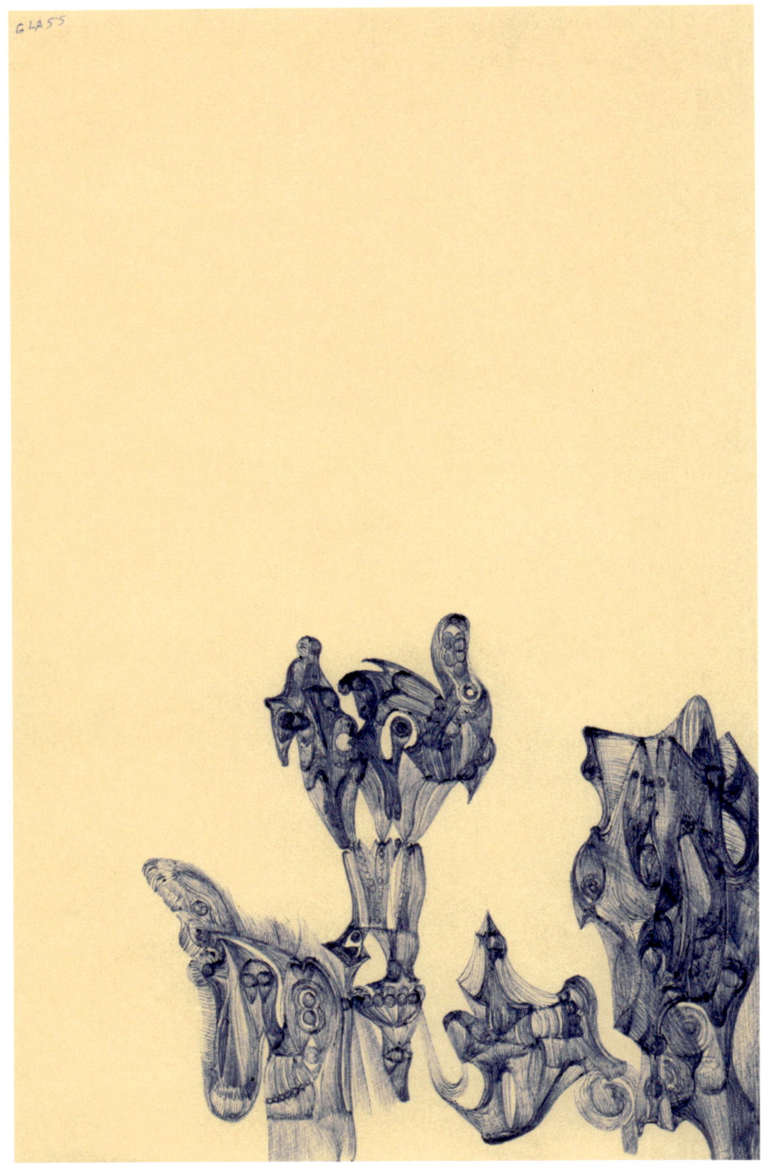

Untitled
(Galerie Le Terrain Vague period)
ca. 1954-1962
Monochrome blue ballpoint
pen drawing, on paper.
26 x 17 cm
Artist's collection

Untitled
(Galerie Le Terrain Vague period)
ca. 1954-1962
Monochrome blue ballpoint
pen drawing, on paper.
26 x 17 cm
Artist's collection

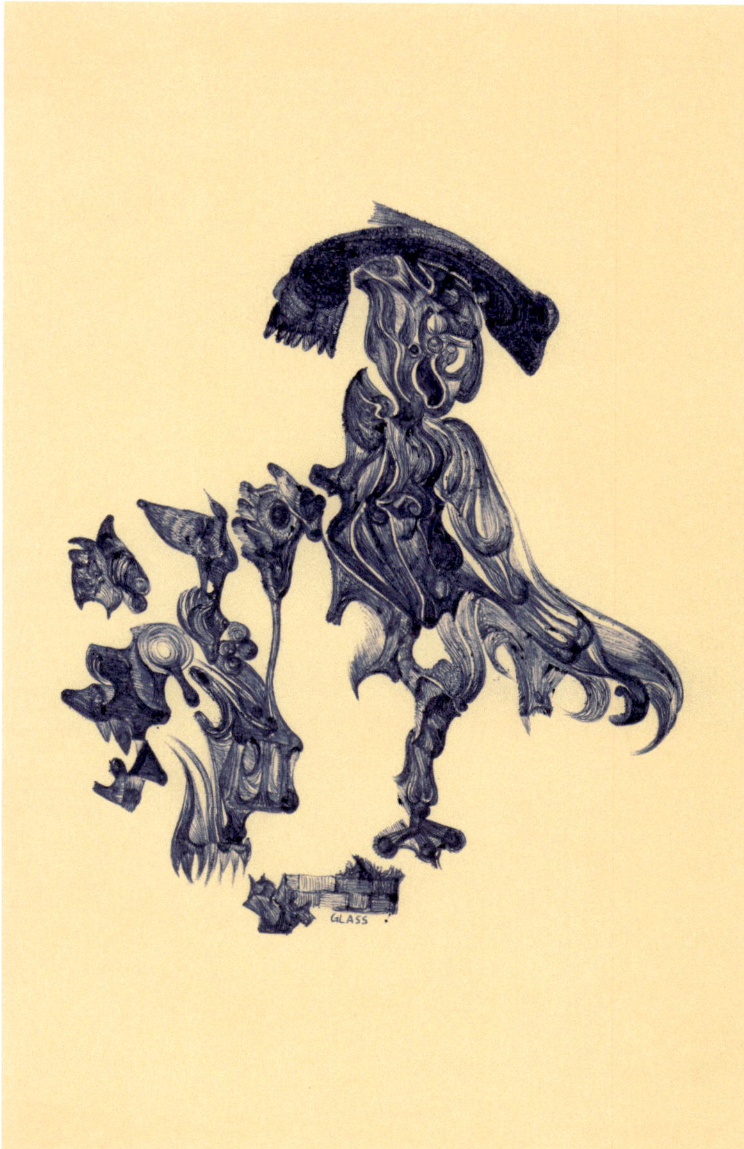

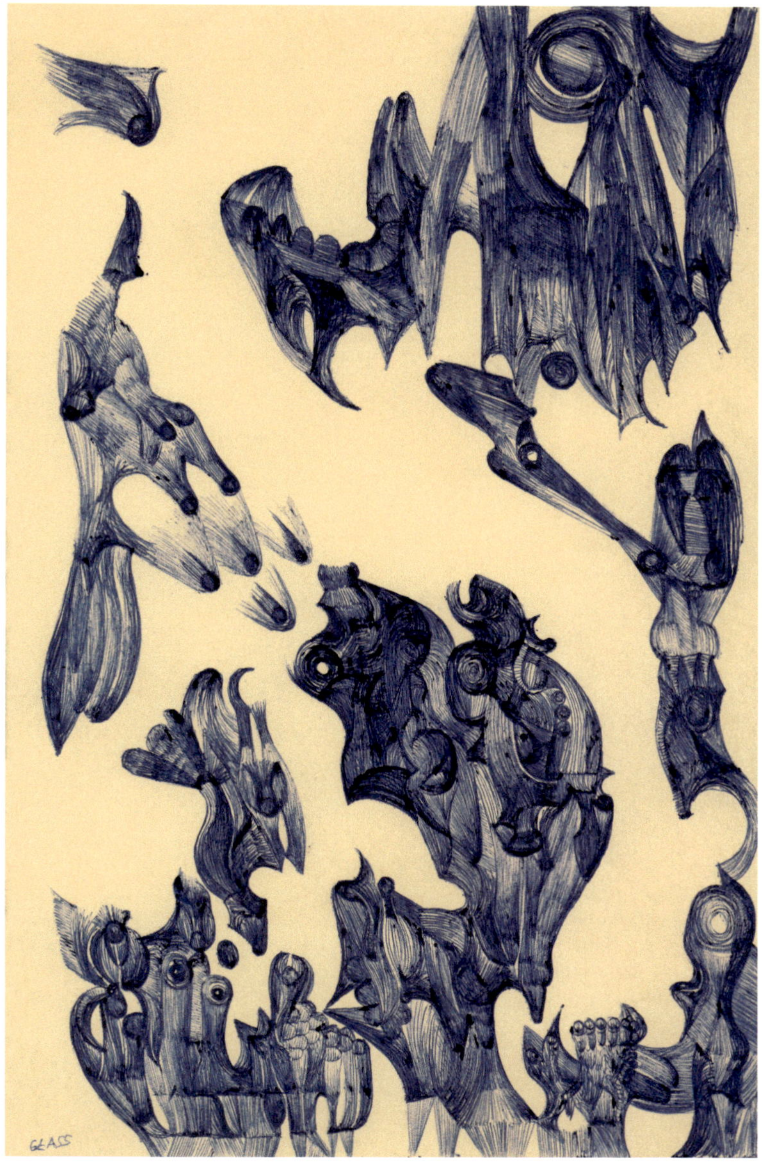

Untitled
(Galerie Le Terrain Vague period)
ca. 1954-1962
Monochrome blue ballpoint pen drawing, on paper.
26 x 17 cm
Artist's collection

Untitled
(Galerie Le Terrain Vague period)
ca. 1954-1962
Monochrome blue ballpoint pen drawing, on paper.
26 x 17 cm
Artist's collection

first Paris abode Le Sphinx. To these he adds imagery from Chirico's related works *Mystery and Melancholy of a Street* (1914) and *The Melancholy of Departure* (1916). Alternately shrinking and magnifying details of de Chirico's paintings, Glass places them in contact with each other as well as with found objects in order to sound out and crystallise his memories of migration, where excitement and expectation, melancholy and displacement, appear to have been equally strong. The suite of boxes is an enigmatic treatment of the double feeling of departing at arrival. In another, box dated 2000–2021, Glass has affixed a miniature sign saying rue du Cherche-Midi, the address of Le Terrain Vague, on the side a box containing a black-and-white photograph of Paris, in turn placed within a box inside the main frame. Emerging from a drawing of a flower collaged onto the photograph, a drawing of woman in 19th-century dress has her face obscured by a dark oval, so that only her eyes peer out. Surrounded by miniature cobblestones, the boxes within a box are evocative of the poetic possibilities and promises of those years in Paris that led to Glass's first exhibition and encounter with the surrealists.

In closing, let us return to René Alleau on the power of symbols: "For those of vision, the symbol restores the spectacle of a universe in the nascent state – that universe which has become crystallized, solidified, opaque, and closed or off-limits to those of thought."[48] For Glass, vision is a matter of the liberated movements of the hand, turned into an instrument of gnosis. Whether through the use of a ballpoint pen, watercolour, or the deft organization of found objects in glasses and vitrines, he renders the universe less opaque as he reveals its hidden layers as glimpsed through tufts of smoke.

[48] Alleau, *The Primal Force in Symbol*, 32.

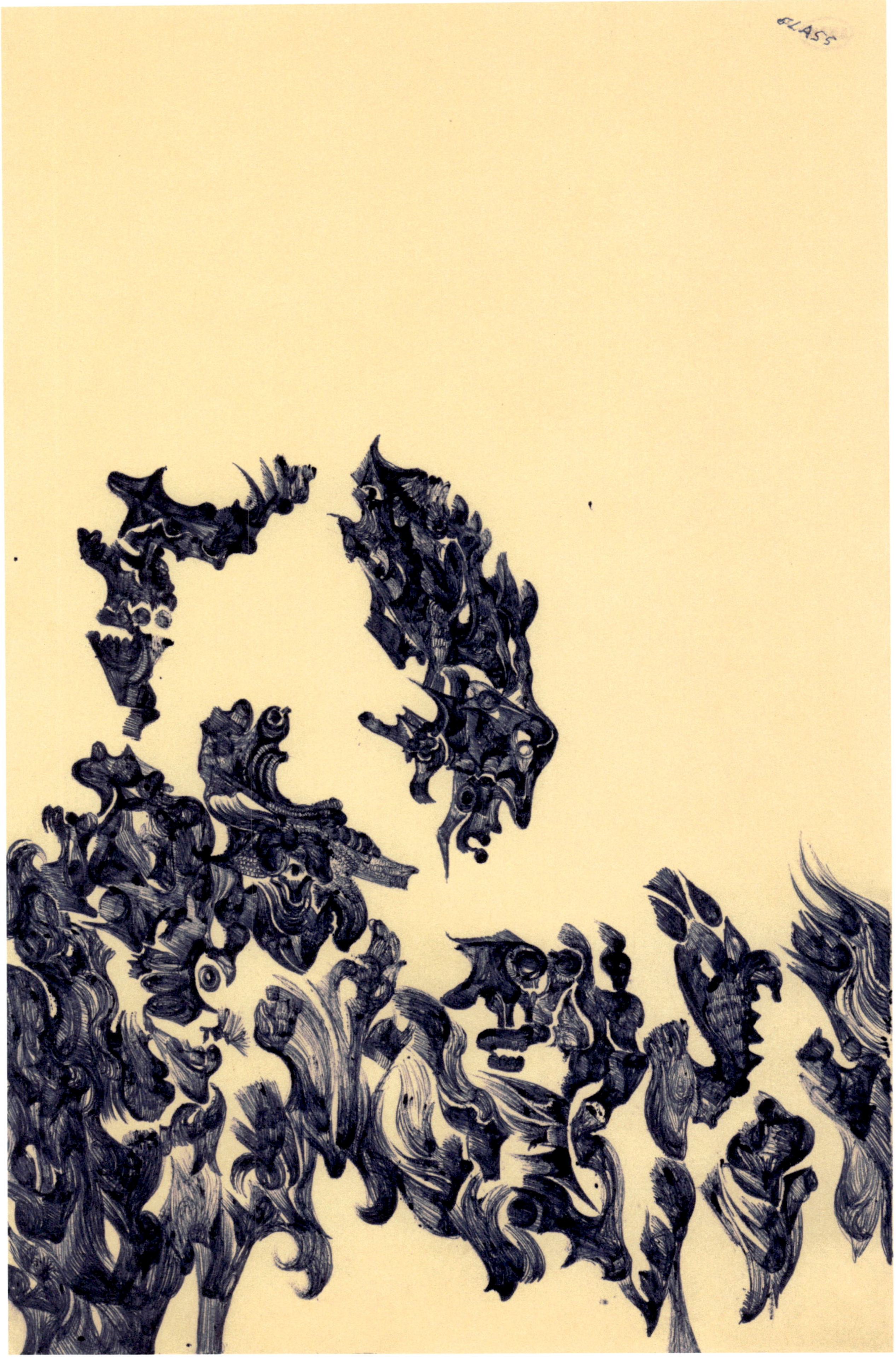

Untitled
(Galerie Le Terrain Vague period)
ca. 1954-1962
Monochrome blue ballpoint
pen drawing, on paper.
26 x 17 cm
Artist's collection

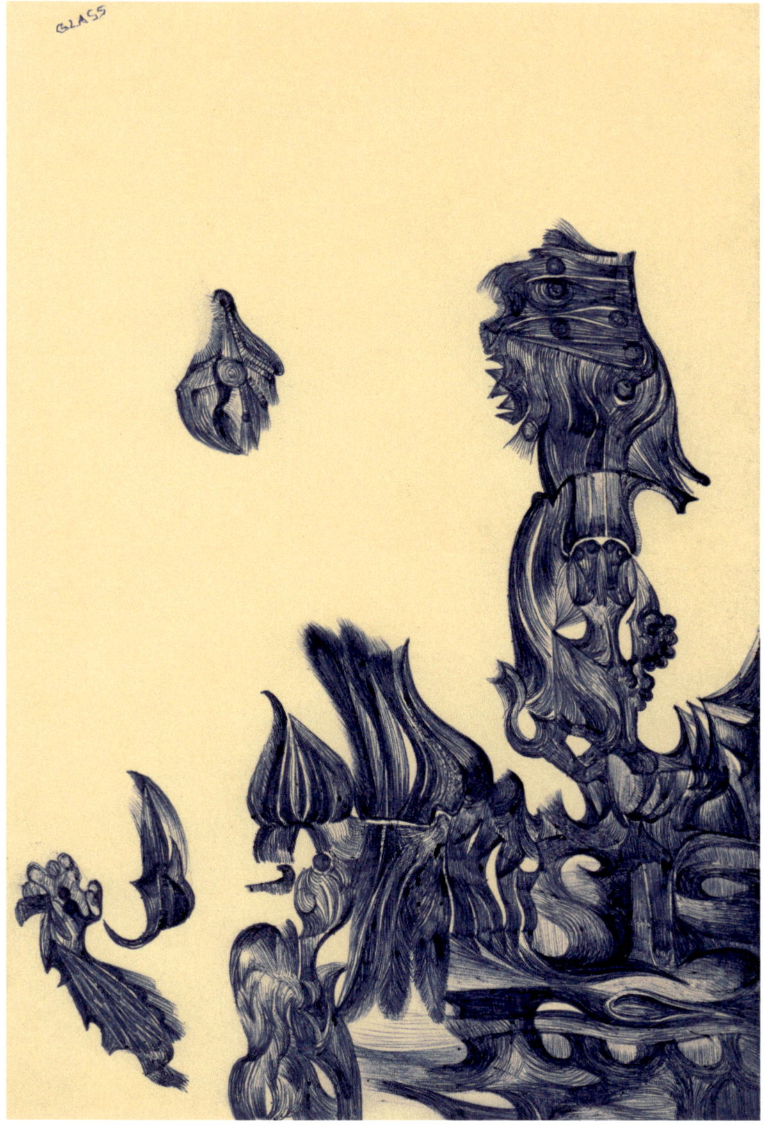

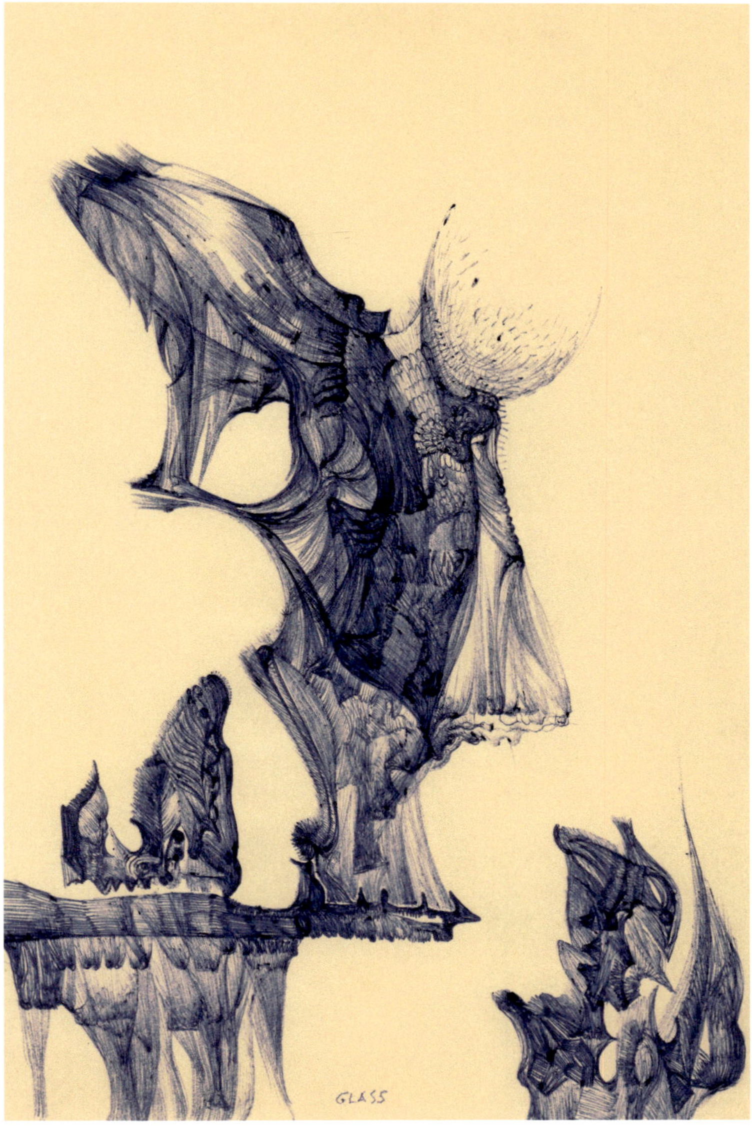

Untitled
(Galerie Le Terrain Vague period)
ca. 1954-1962
Monochrome blue ballpoint
pen drawing, on paper.
26 x 17.2 cm
Artist's collection

Untitled
(Galerie Le Terrain Vague period)
ca. 1954-1962
Monochrome blue ballpoint
pen drawing, on paper.
26 x 17 cm
Artist's collection

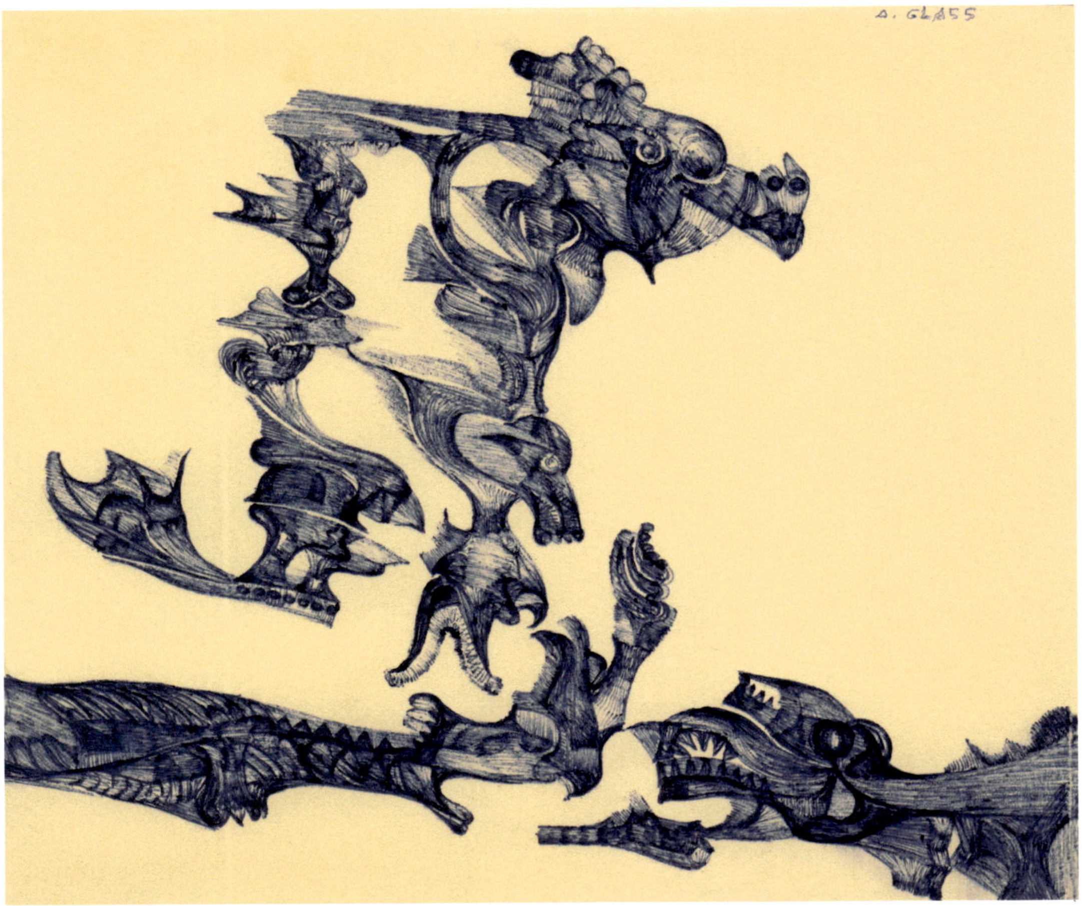

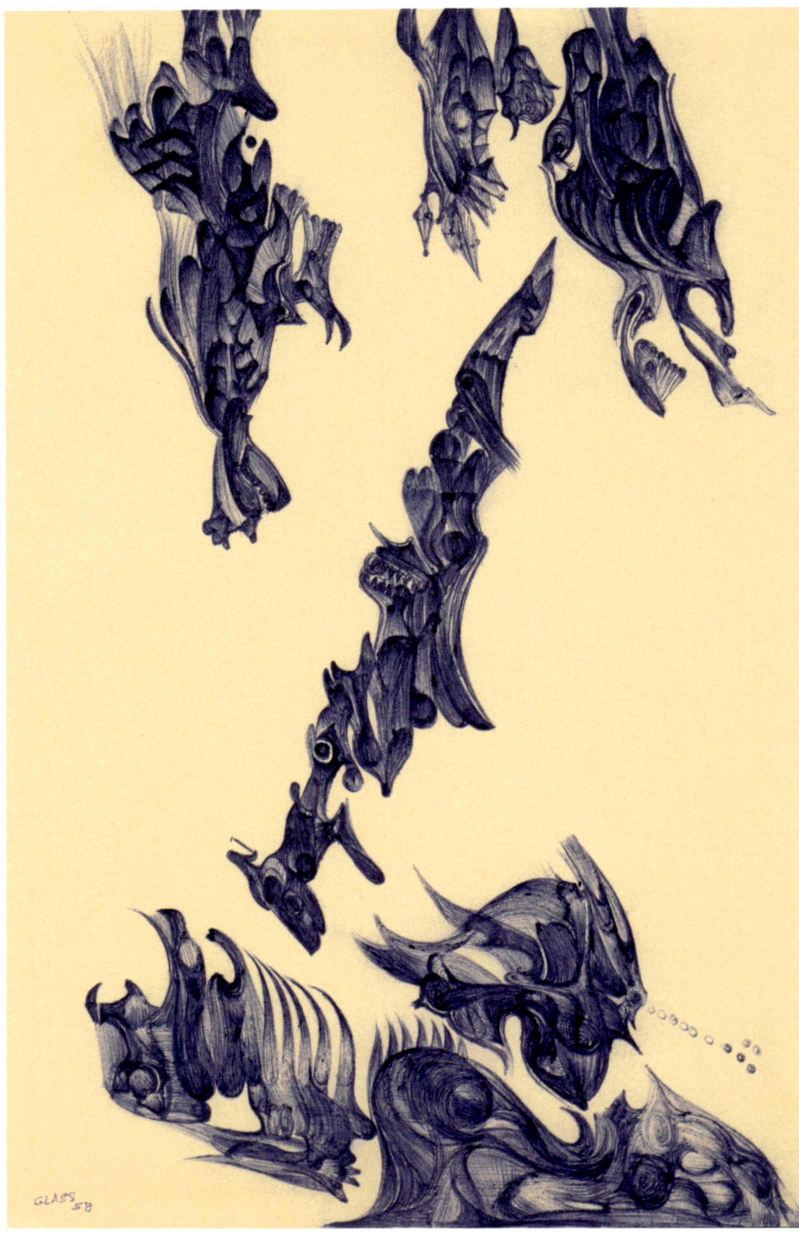

Untitled
(Galerie Le Terrain Vague period)
ca. 1954-1962
Monochrome blue ballpoint
pen drawing, on paper.
14.3 x 17 cm
Artist's collection

Untitled
(Galerie Le Terrain Vague period)
1958
Monochrome blue ballpoint
pen drawing, on paper.
26 x 17 cm
Artist's collection

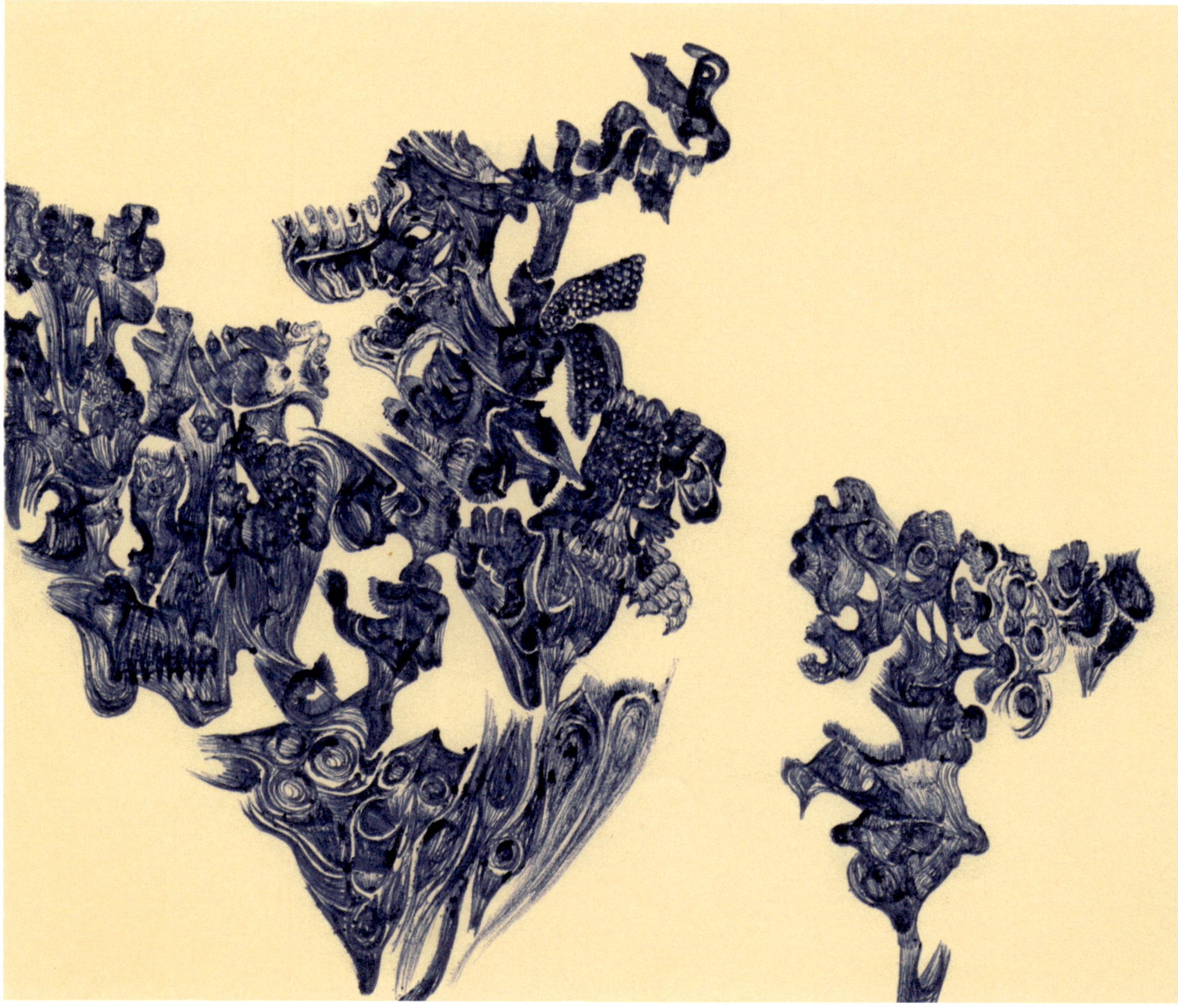

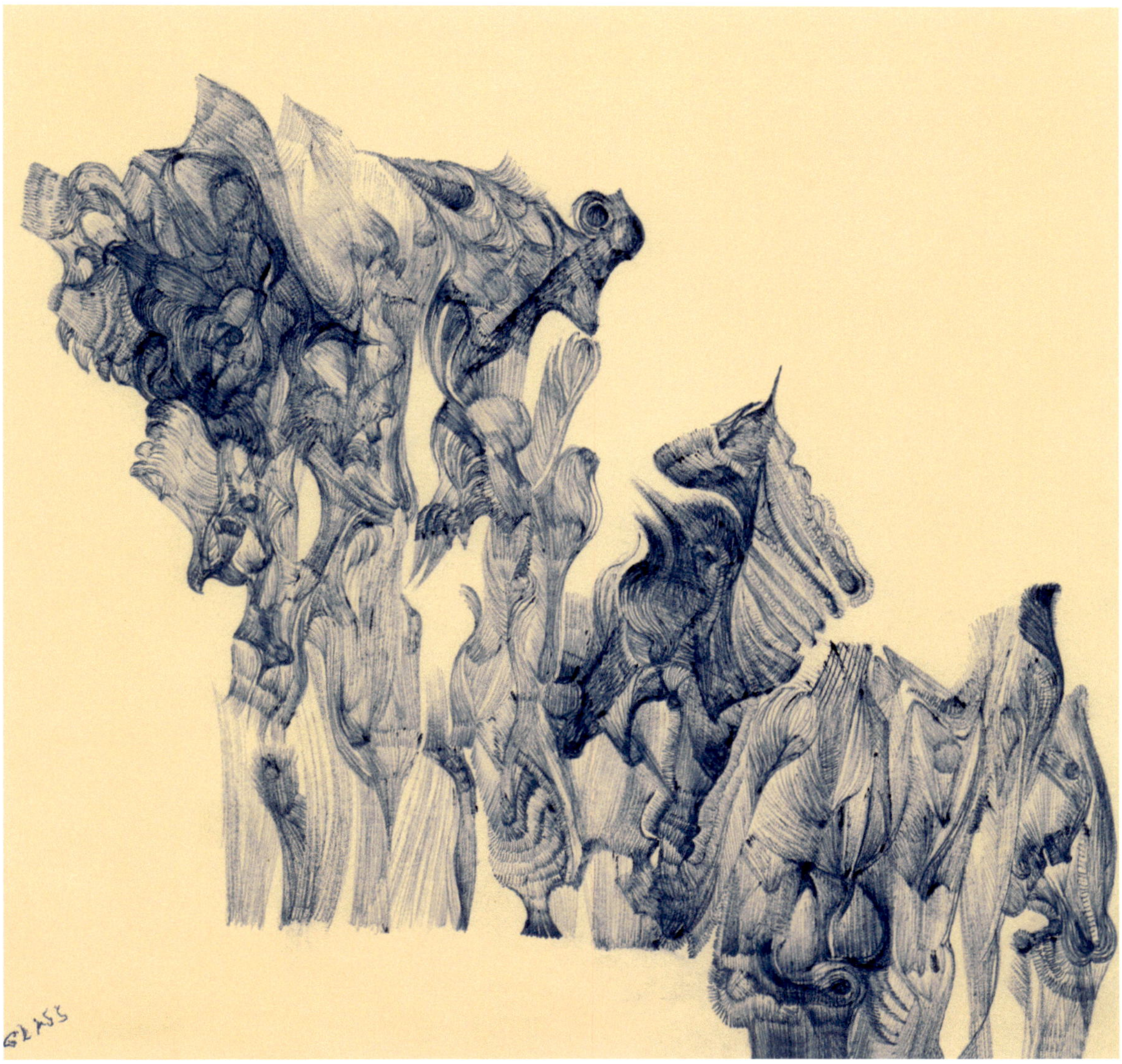

Untitled
(Galerie Le Terrain Vague period)
ca. 1954-1962
Monochrome blue ballpoint pen drawing, on paper.
14.5 x 17 cm
Artist's collection

Untitled
(Galerie Terrain Vague period)
ca. 1954-1962
Monochrome blue ballpoint pen drawing, on paper.
15.5 x 17 cm
Artist's collection

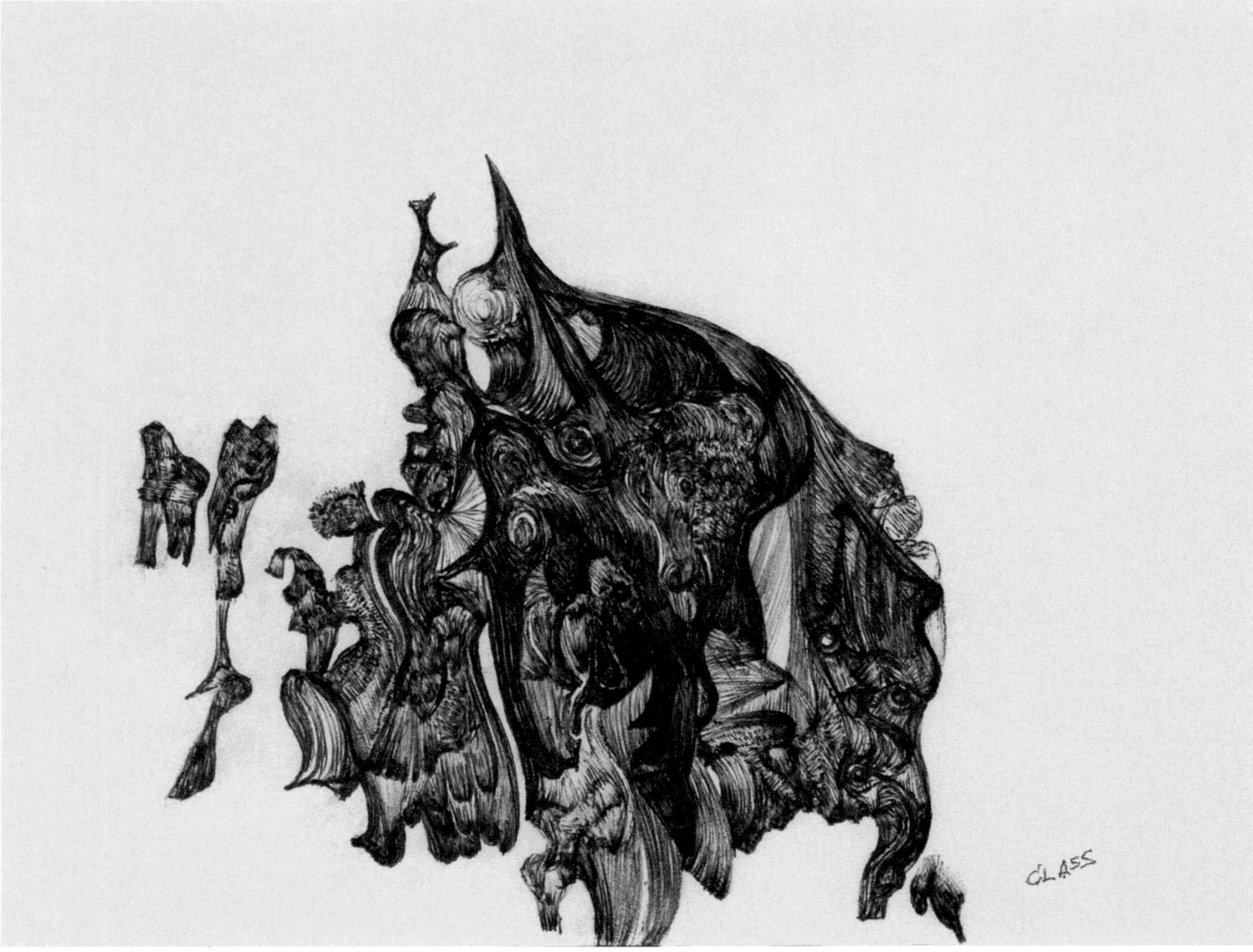
GLASS

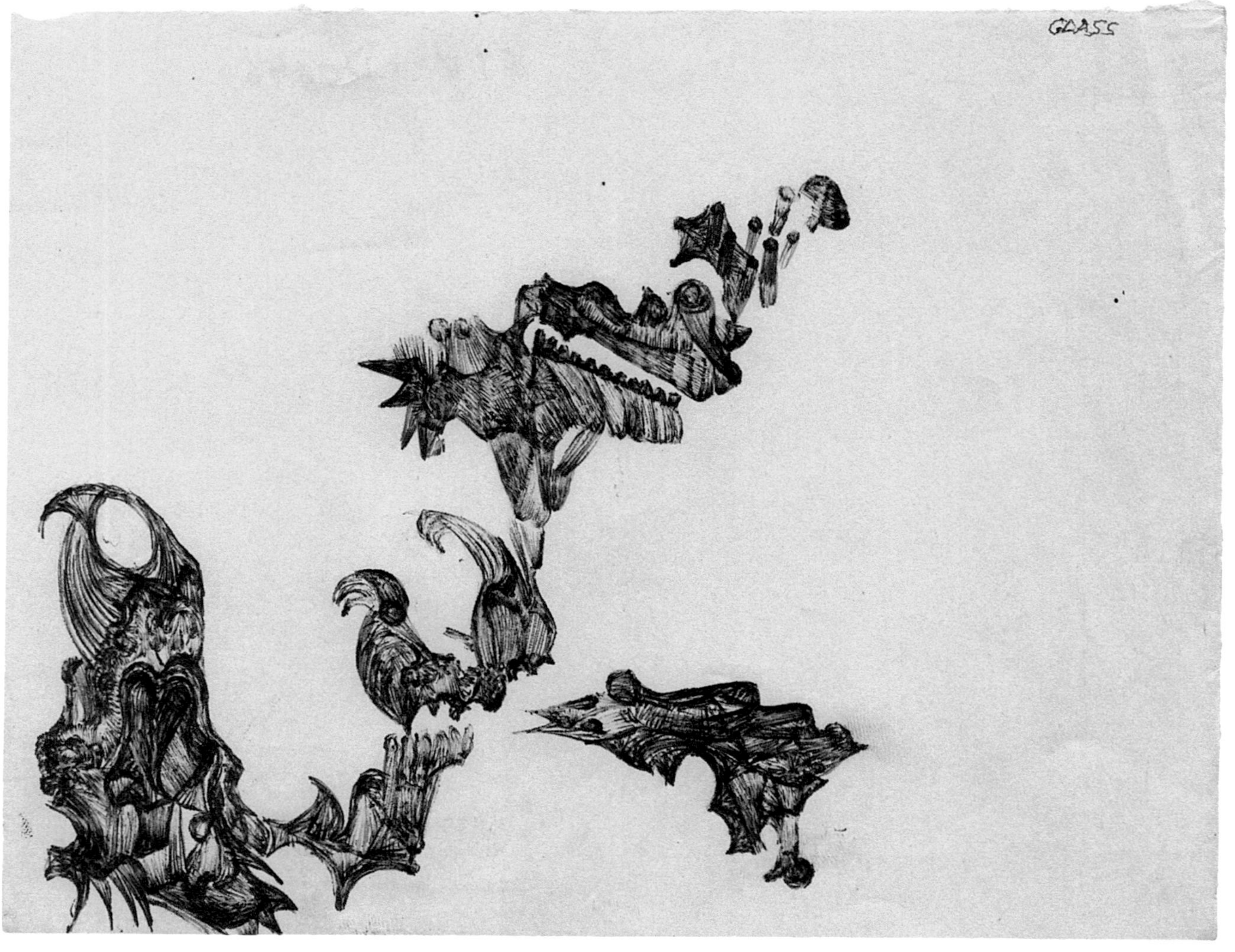
GLASS

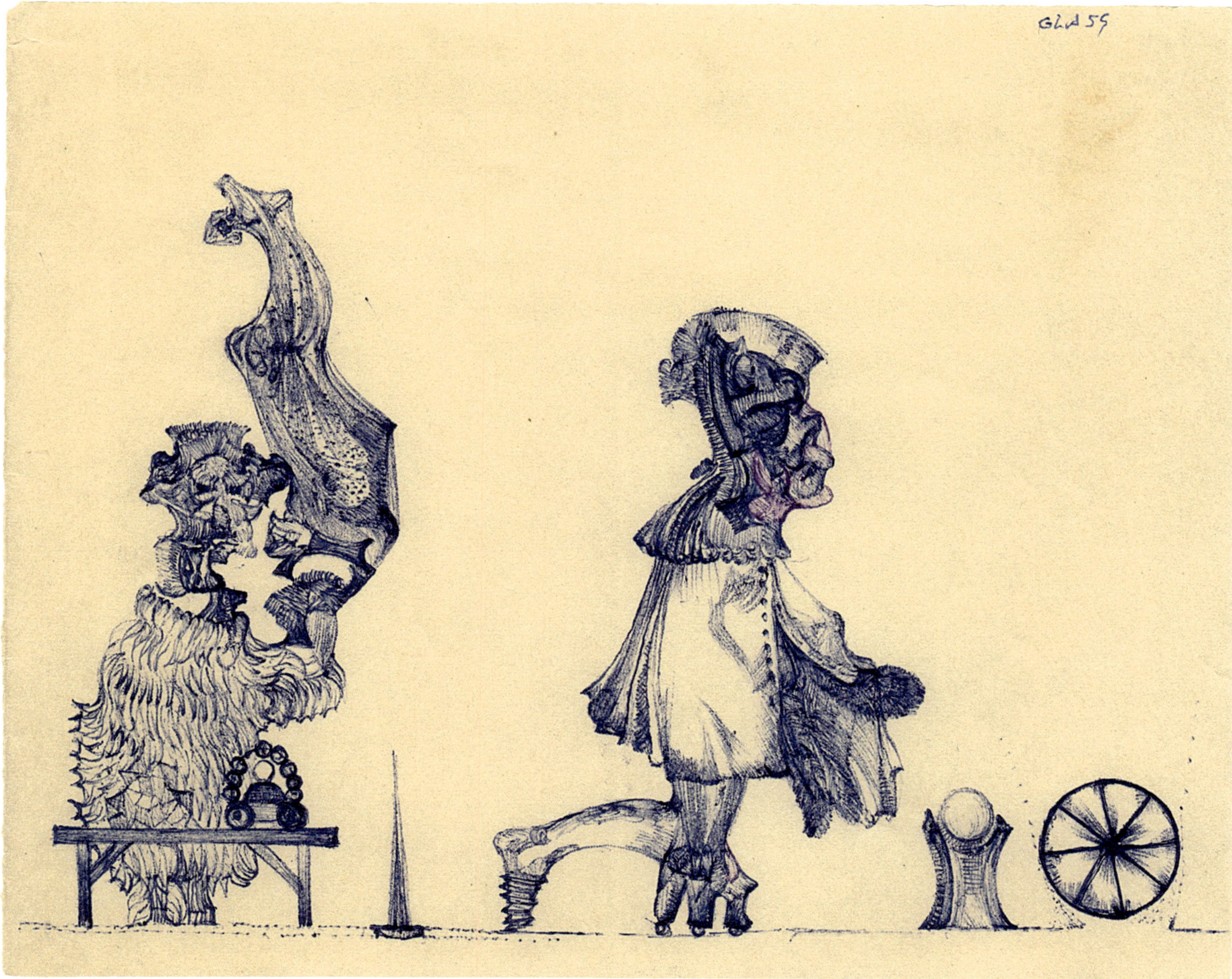

Untitled
(Galerie Le Terrain Vague period)
ca. 1954-1962
Monochrome blue ballpoint
pen drawing, on paper.
13 x 17 cm
Artist's collection
Previous page up

Untitled
(Galerie Le Terrain Vague period)
ca. 1954-1962
Monochrome blue ballpoint
pen drawing, on paper.
13 x 17 cm
Artist's collection
Previous page down

Untitled
(Galerie Le Terrain Vague period)
1959
Drawing in blue and purple
bicolor pen, on paper.
13.6 x 17 cm
Artist's collection

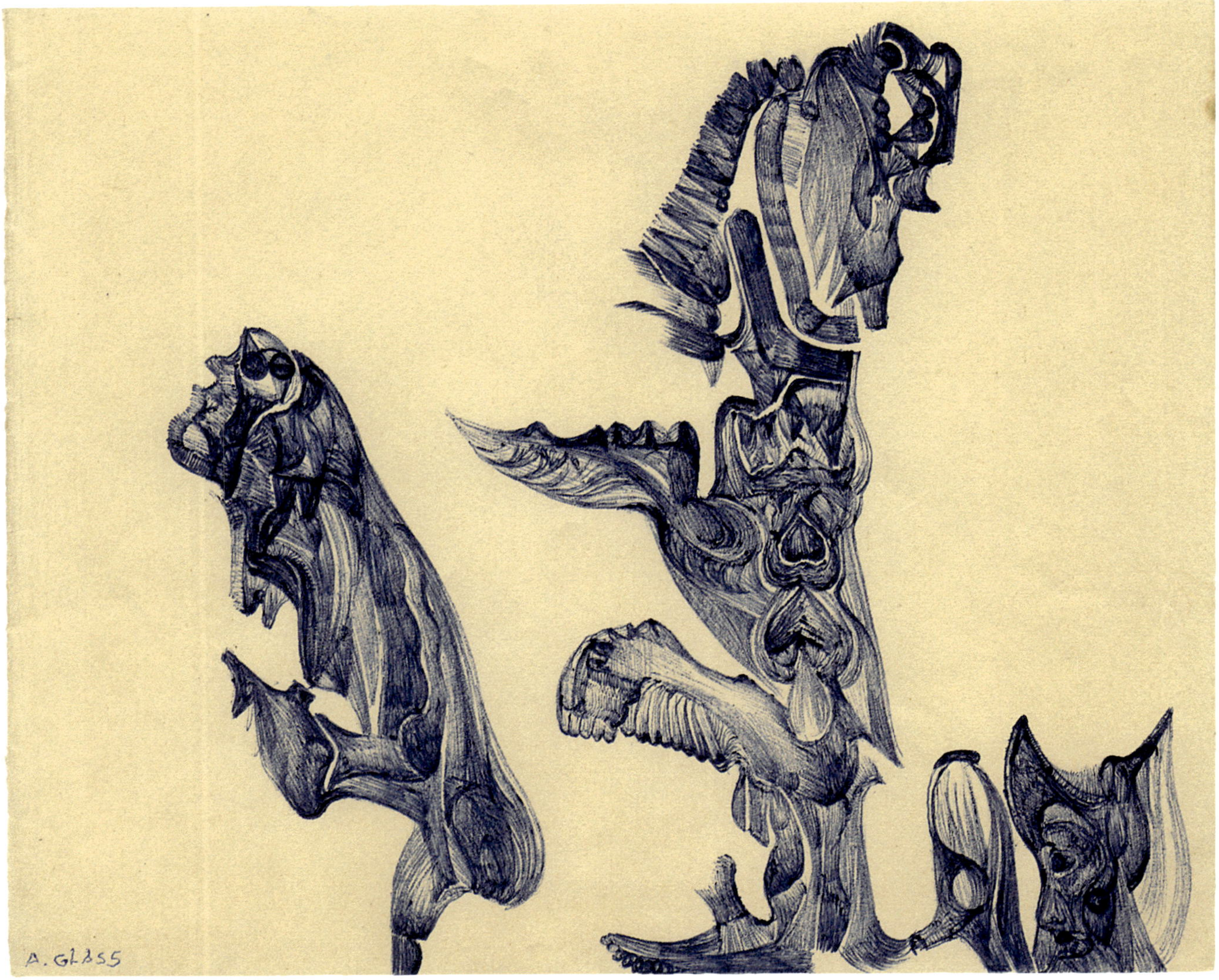

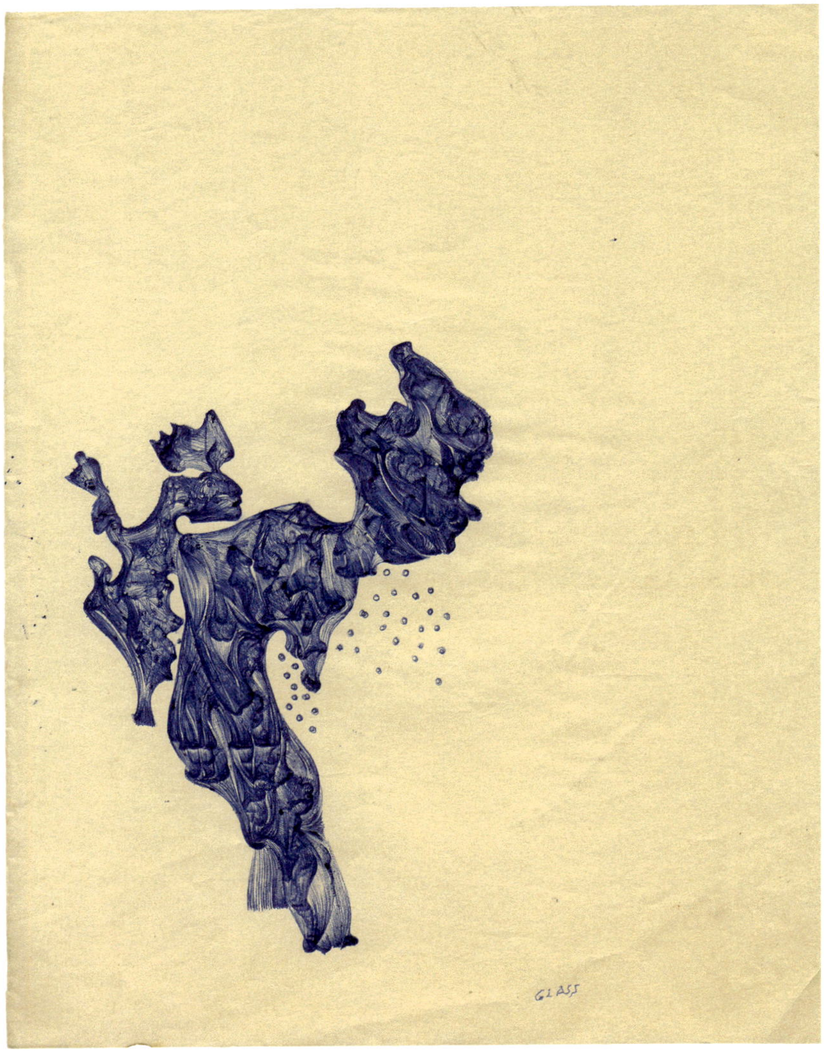

Untitle
(Galerie Le Terrain Vague period)
ca. 1954-1962
Monochrome blue ballpoint
pen drawing, on paper.
13.7 x 17 cm
Artist's collection

Untitled
(Galerie Le Terrain Vague period)
ca. 1954-1962
Monochrome blue ballpoint
pen drawing, on paper.
27 x 21.5 cm
Artist's collection

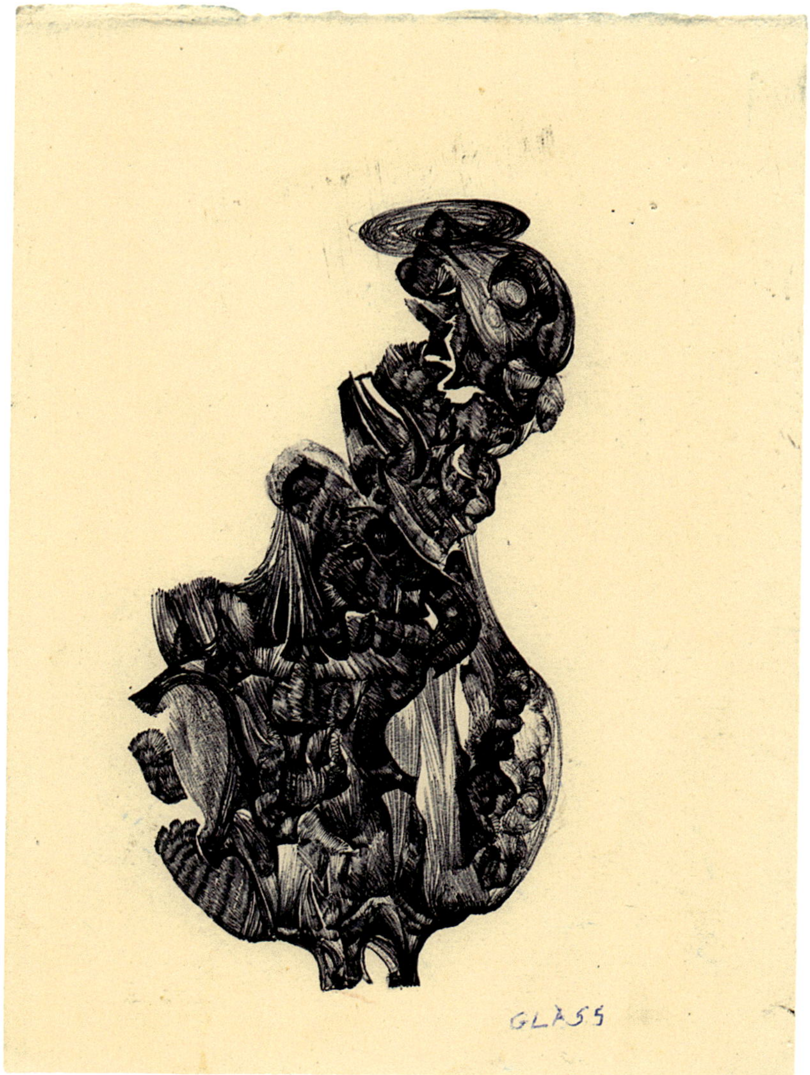

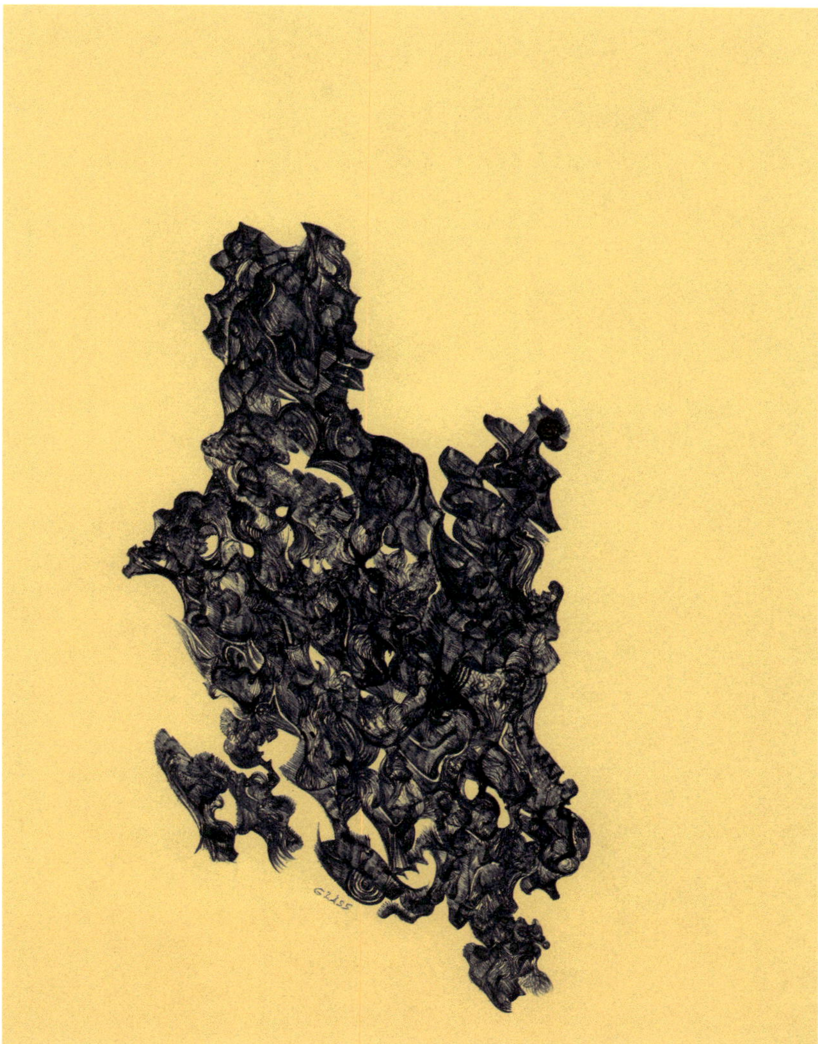

Untitled
(Galerie Le Terrain Vague period)
ca. 1954-1962
Drawing in black monocolor ballpoint pen, on invitation to the 6th anniversary of the Discothèque de Jean-Claude Merle.
14 x 10.4 cm
Artist's collection

Untitled
(Galerie Le Terrain Vague period)
ca. 1954-1962
Monochrome blue ballpoint pen drawing, on paper.
27 x 21 cm
Artist's collection

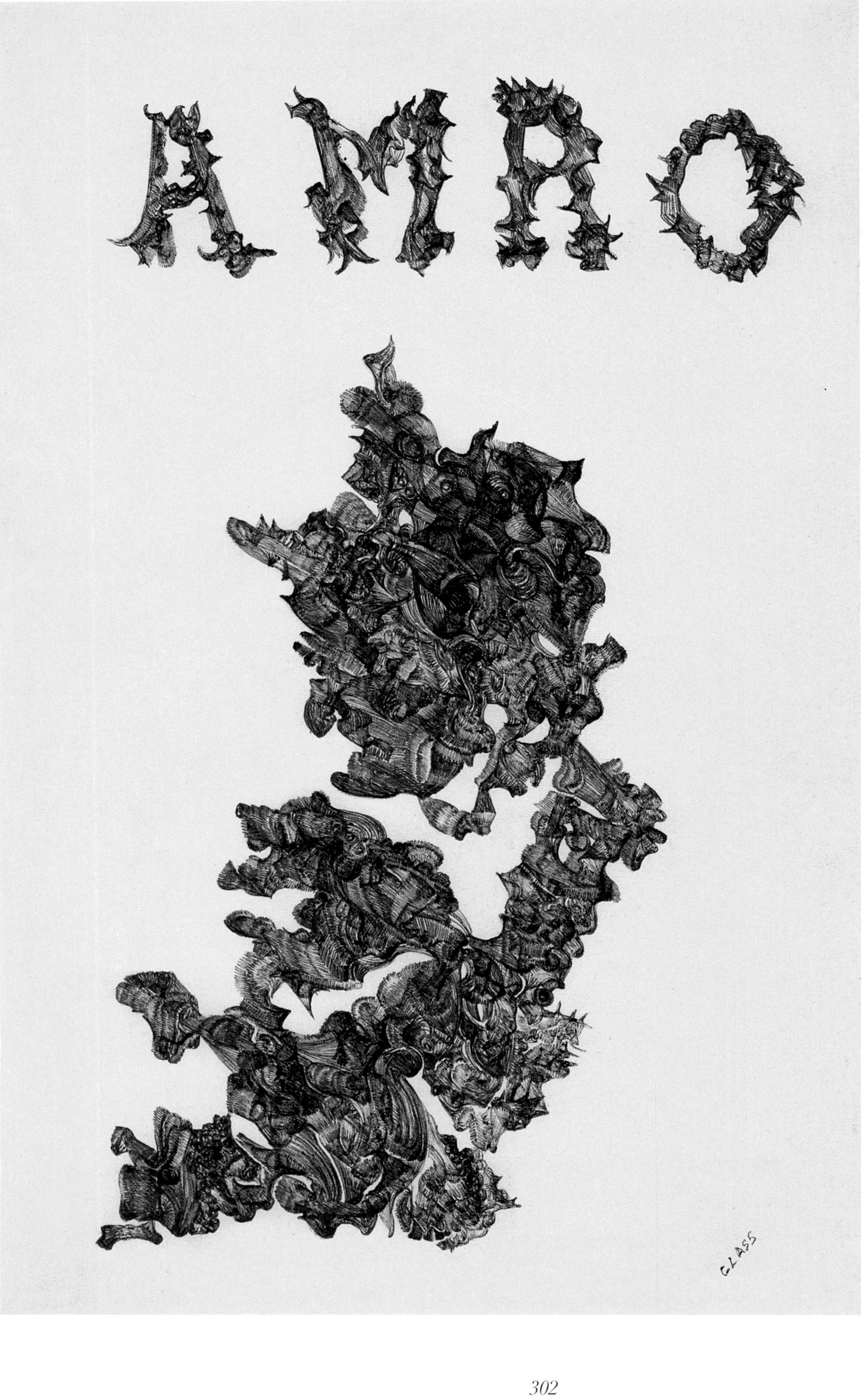
AMRO
GLASS

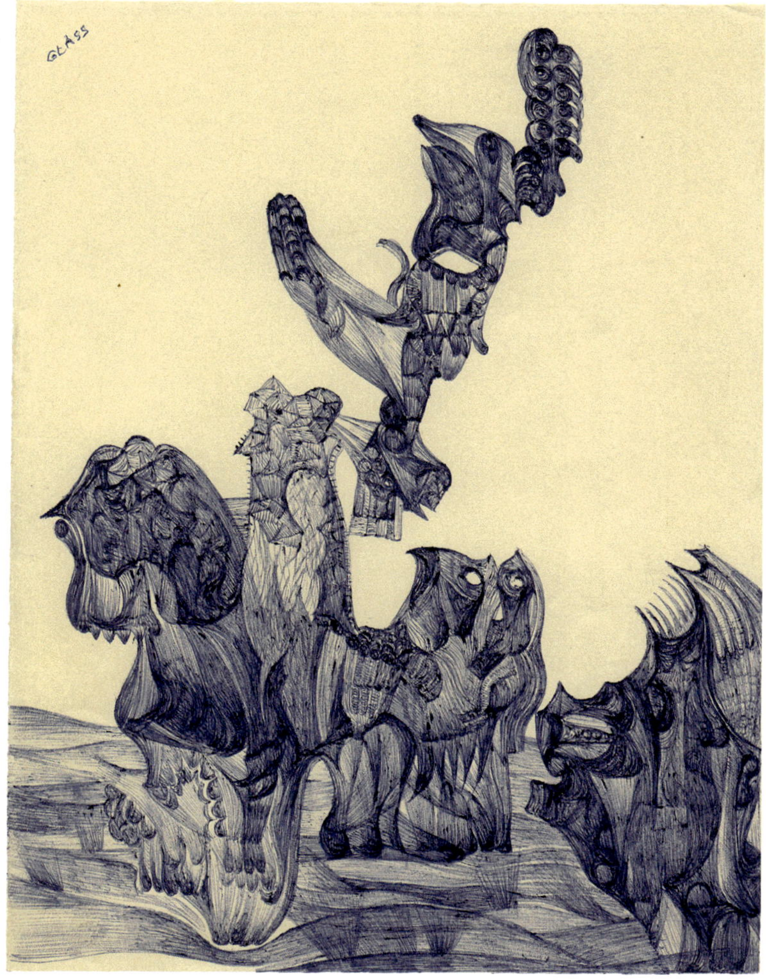

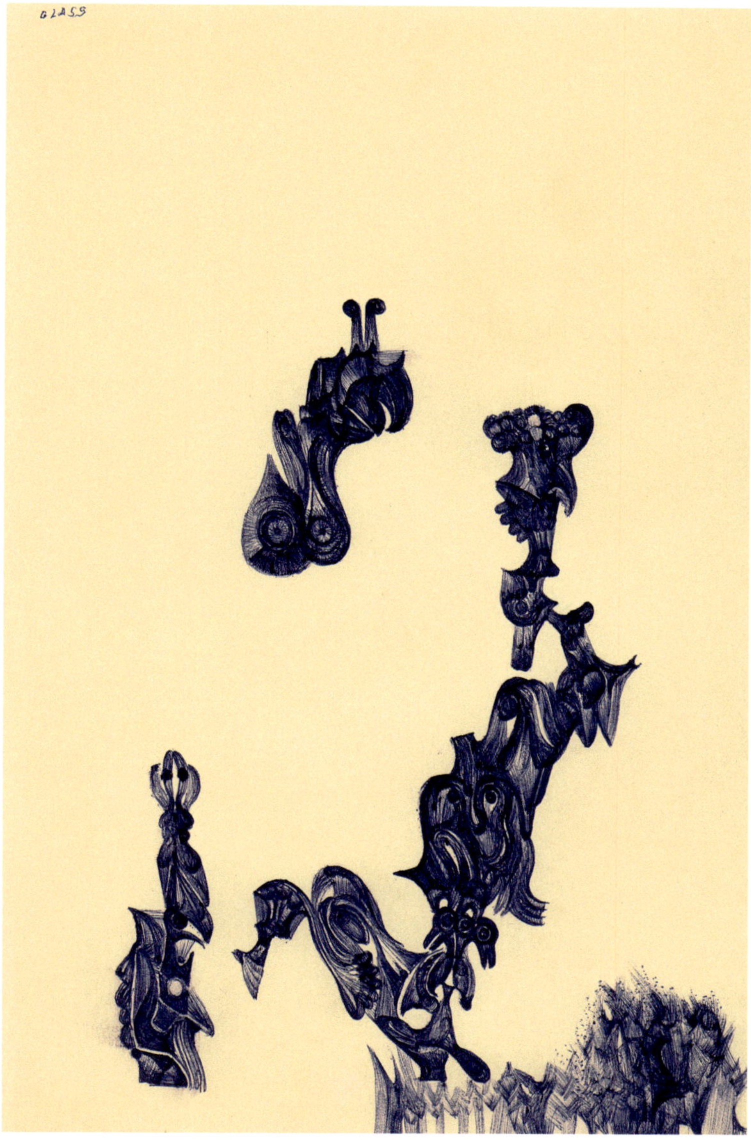

Untitled
(Galerie Le Terrain Vague period)
ca. 1954-1962
Drawing in blue monocolor ballpoint pen with a touch of olive green pencil, on paper.
26 x 17 cm
Artist's collection
Previous page

Untitled
(Galerie Le Terrain Vague period)
ca. 1954-1962
Monochrome blue ballpoint pen drawing, on paper.
26 x 17.1 cm
Artist's collection

Untitled
(Galerie Le Terrain Vague period)
ca. 1954-1962
Monochrome blue ballpoint pen drawing, on paper.
22.1 x 17 cm
Artist's collection

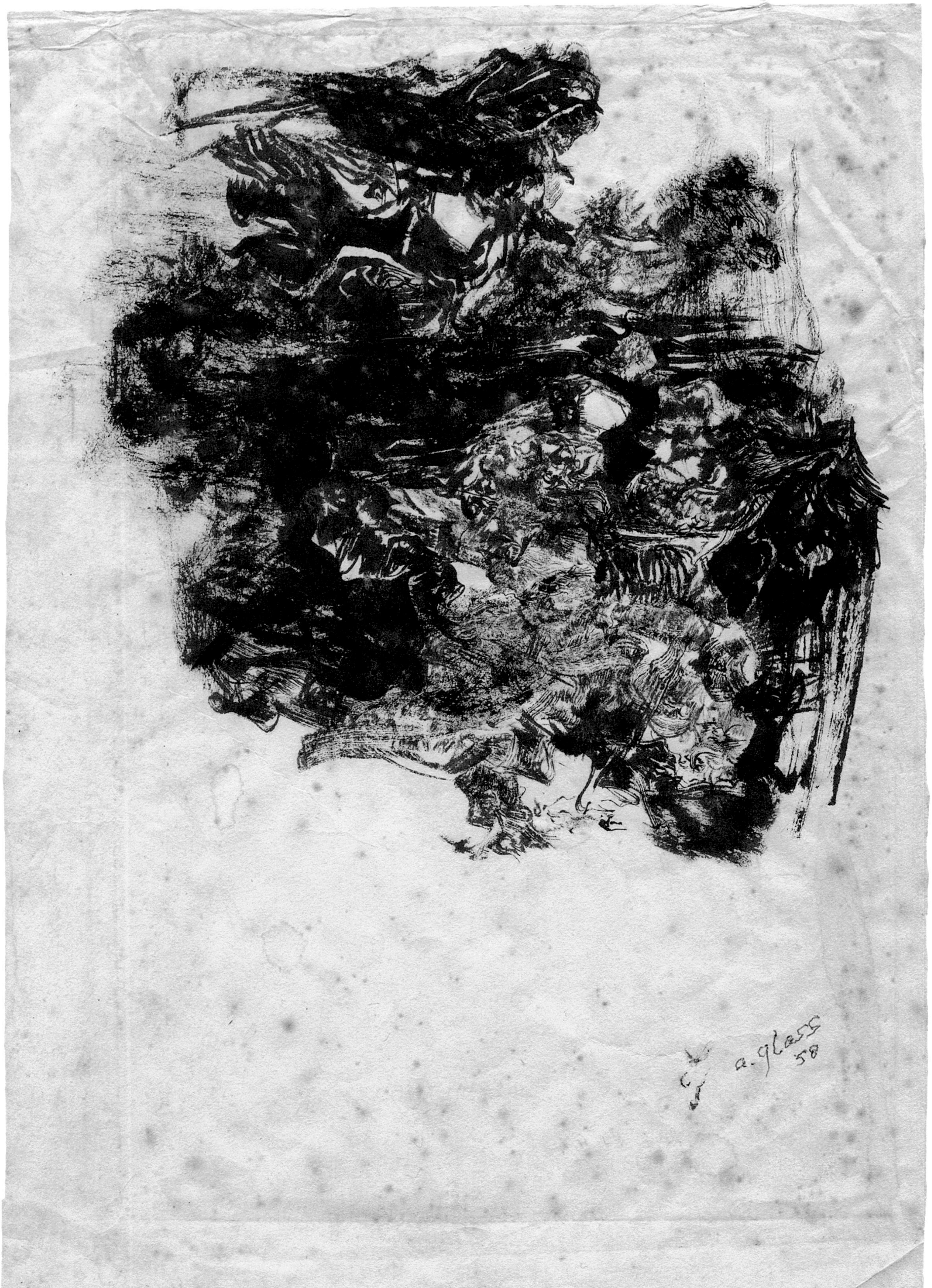
a. glass
58

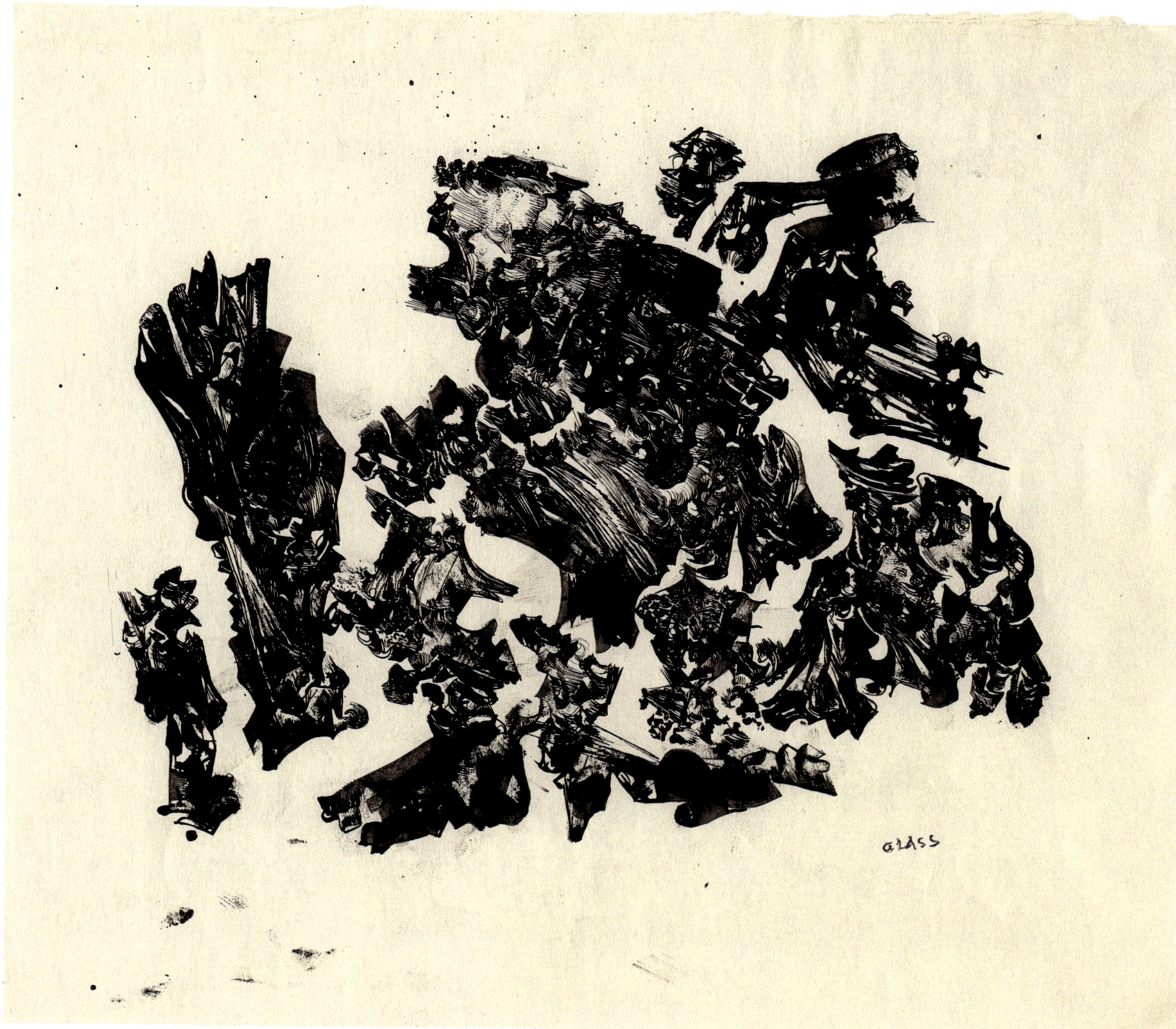

Untitled
(Galerie Le Terrain Vague period)
1958
Drawing in black monocolor ballpoint pen with Chinese ink, on butter paper.
27.8 x 19.5 cm
Artist's collection
Previous page

Untitled
(Galerie Le Terrain Vague period)
ca. 1954-1962
Drawing with fountain pen and Chinese ink, on paper.
18.3 x 21.1 cm
Artist's collection

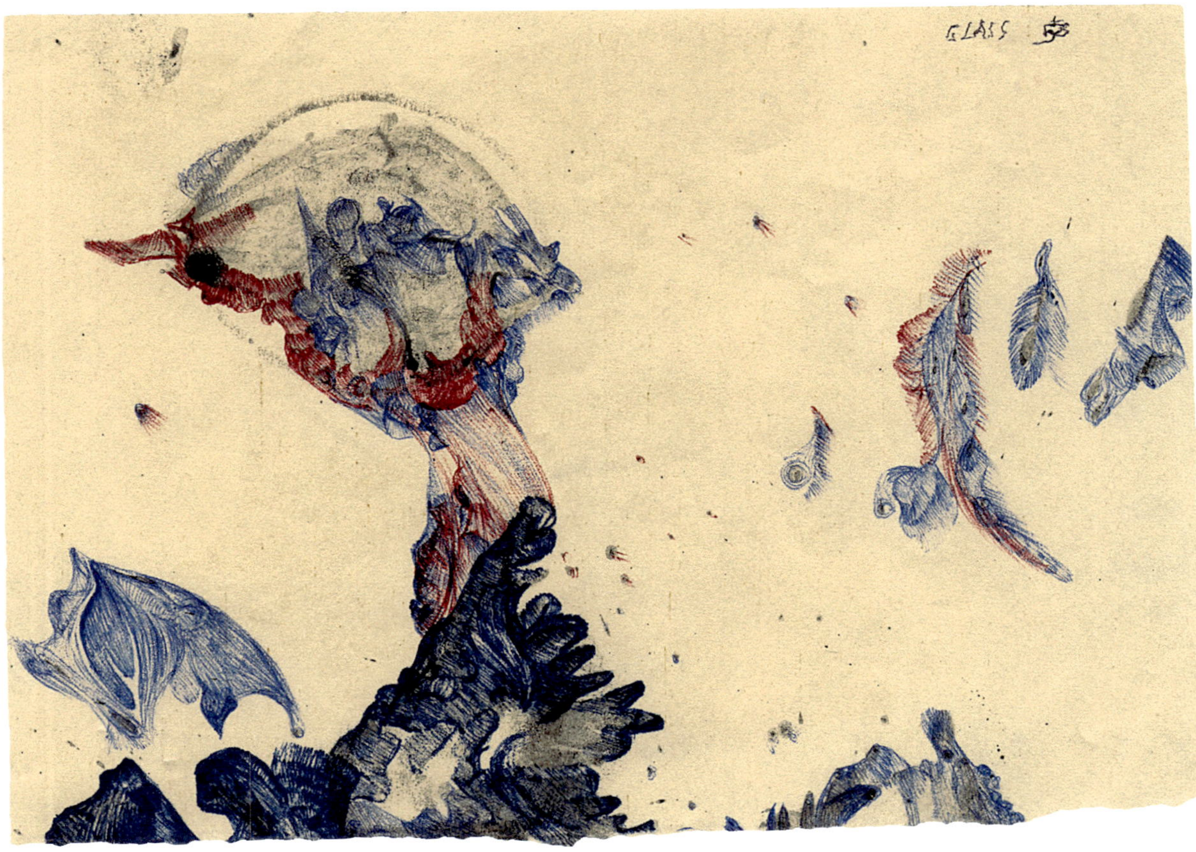

Untitled
(Galerie Le Terrain Vague period)
1958
Drawing in blue and red
bicolor pen with graphite,
on paper.
10.2 x 14.9 cm
Artist's collection

Untitled
(Galerie Le Terrain Vague period)
ca. 1954-1962
Drawing in blue and black
bicolor pen with orange and
green pencil, on paper.
28.1 x 21.5 cm
Artist's collection
Following page

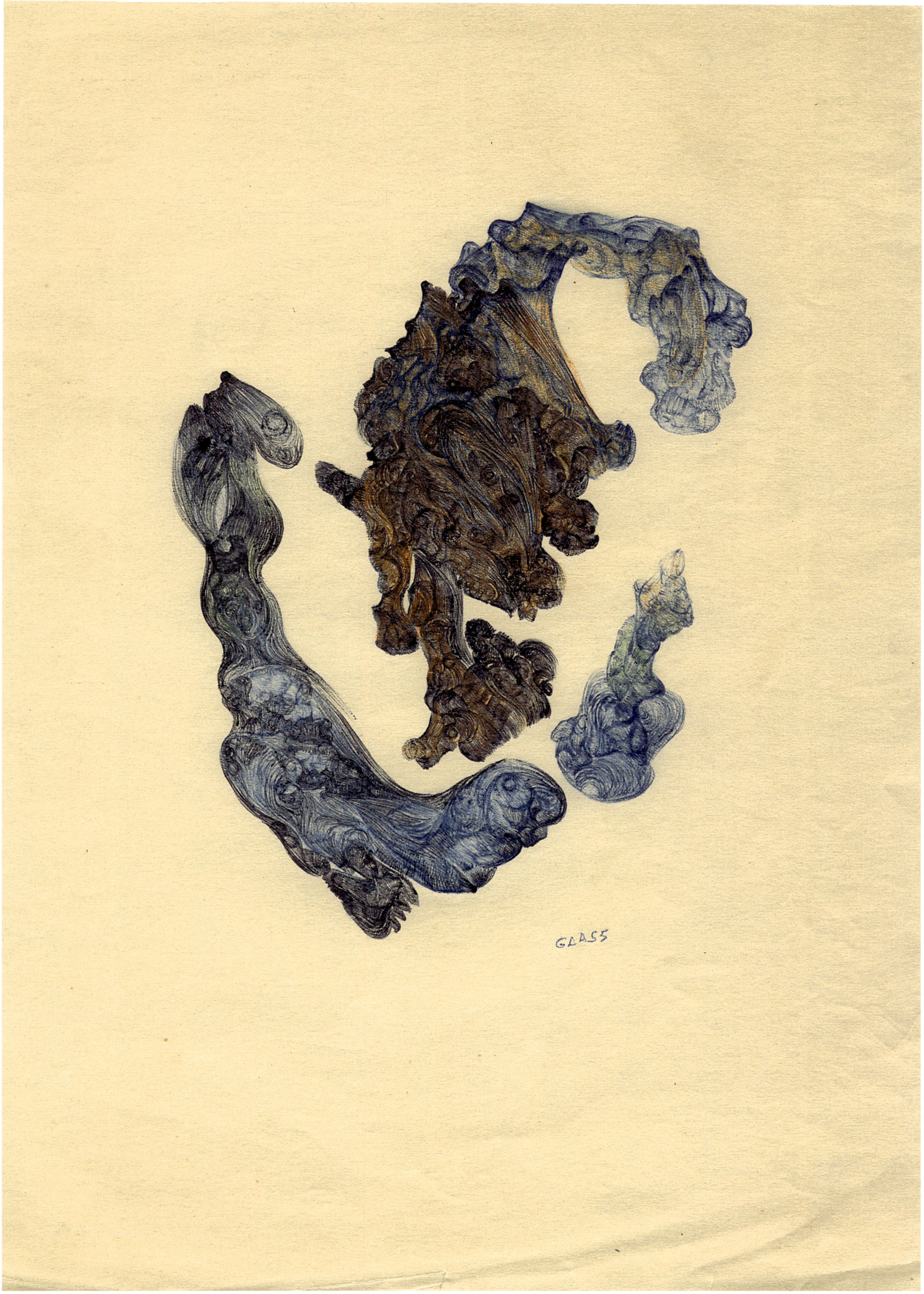
GLASS

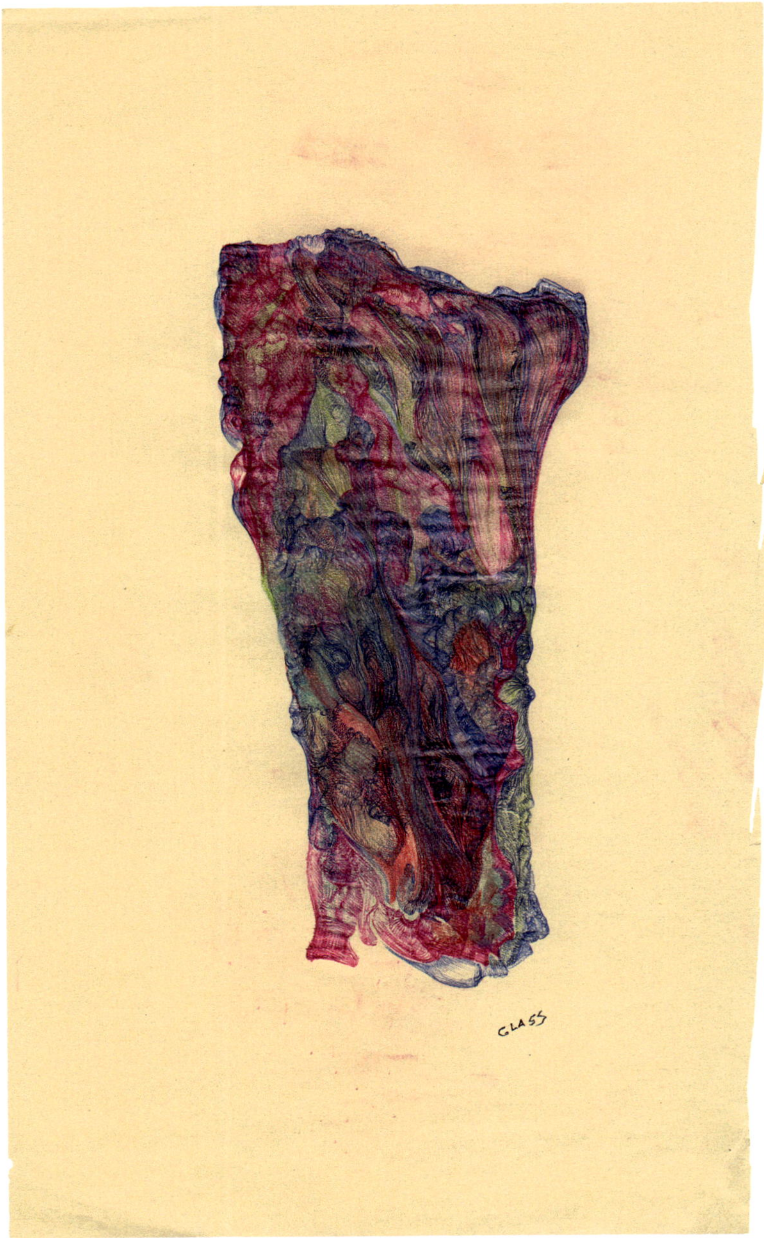

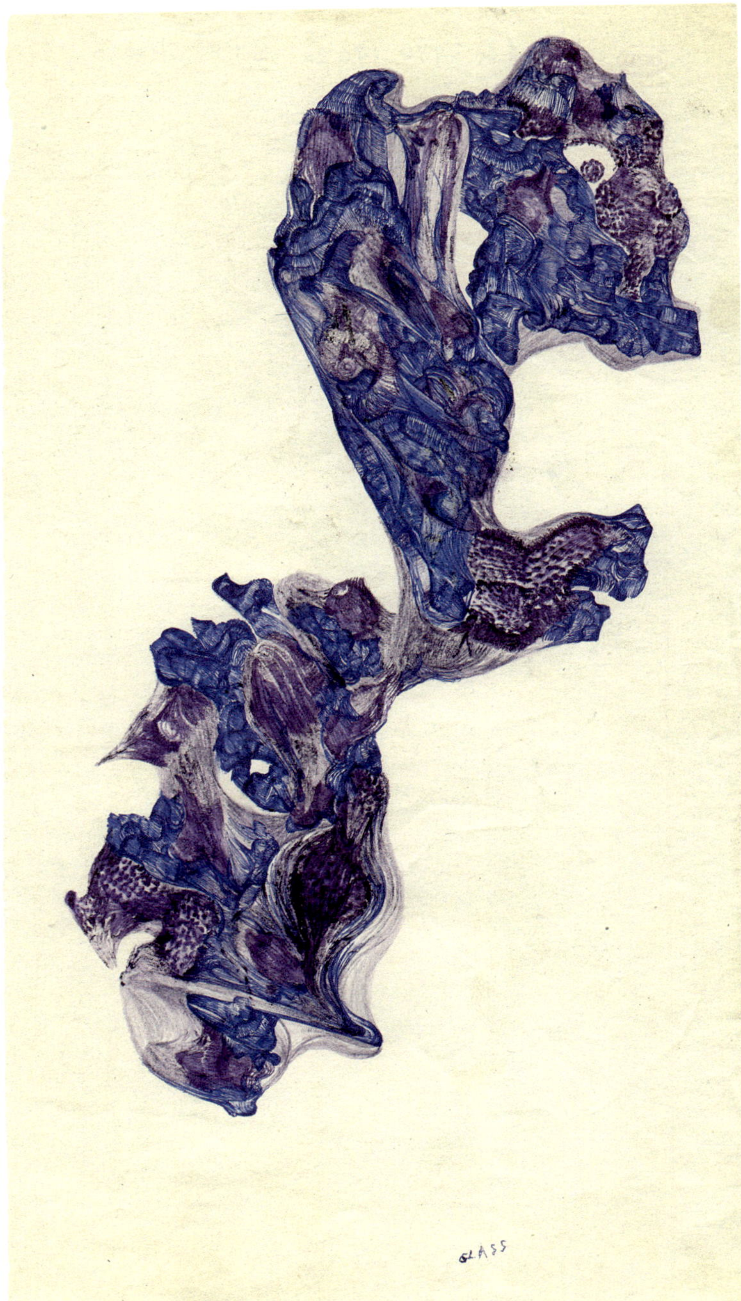

Untitled
(Galerie Le Terrain Vague period)
ca. 1954-1962
Drawing in blue and pink bicolor pen with orange, lemon green, olive green, and pink pencil, on paper.
28.1 x 17.3 cm
Artist's collection

Untitled
(Galerie Le Terrain Vague period)
ca. 1954-1962
Drawing in blue and purple bicolor ballpoint pen, on paper.
27.1 x 15.5 cm
Artist's collection

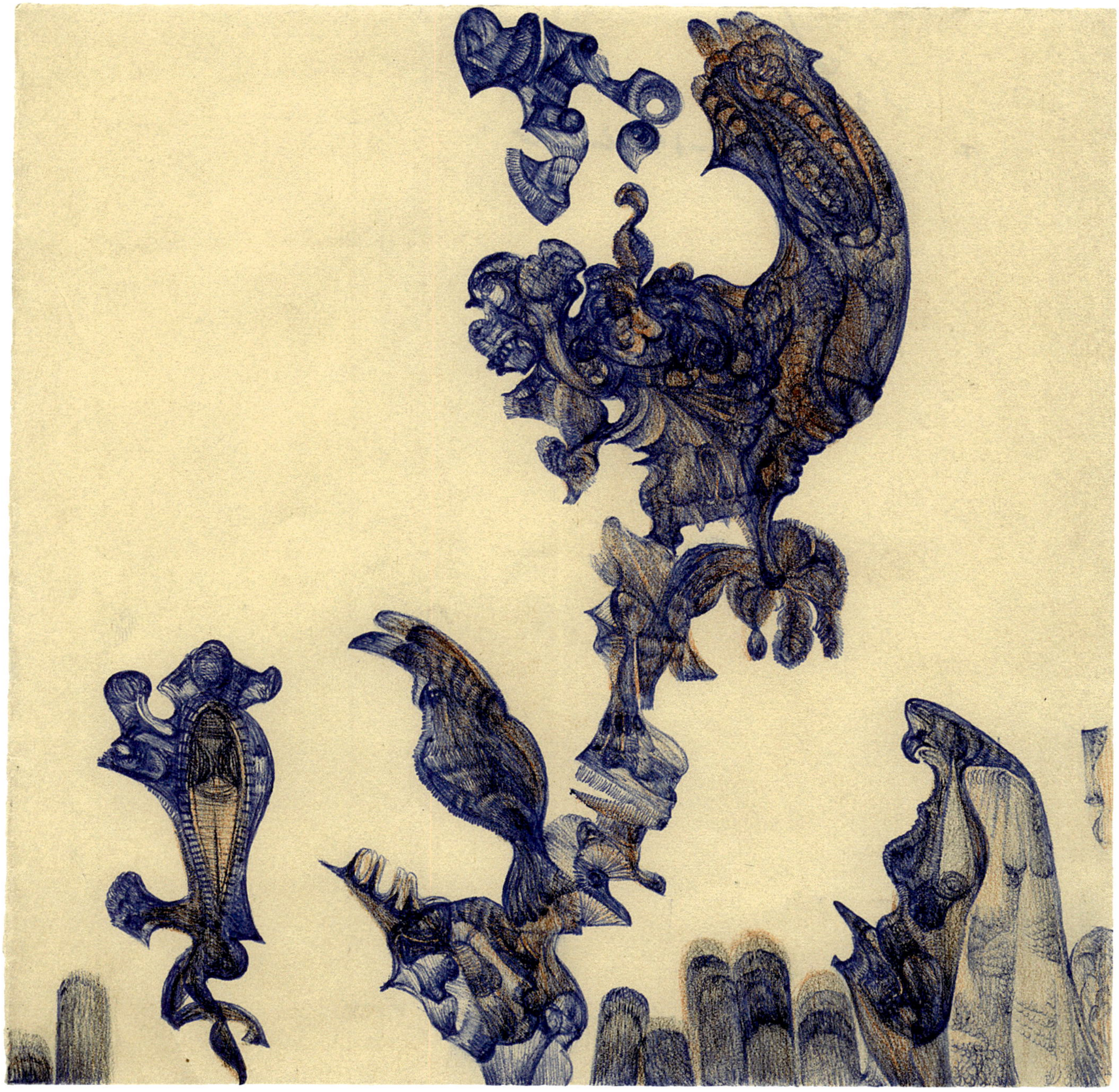

Untitled
(Galerie Le Terrain Vague period)
ca. 1954-1962
Drawing in blue monocolor
pen with orange pencil,
on paper.
16.7 x 17.1 cm
Artist's collection

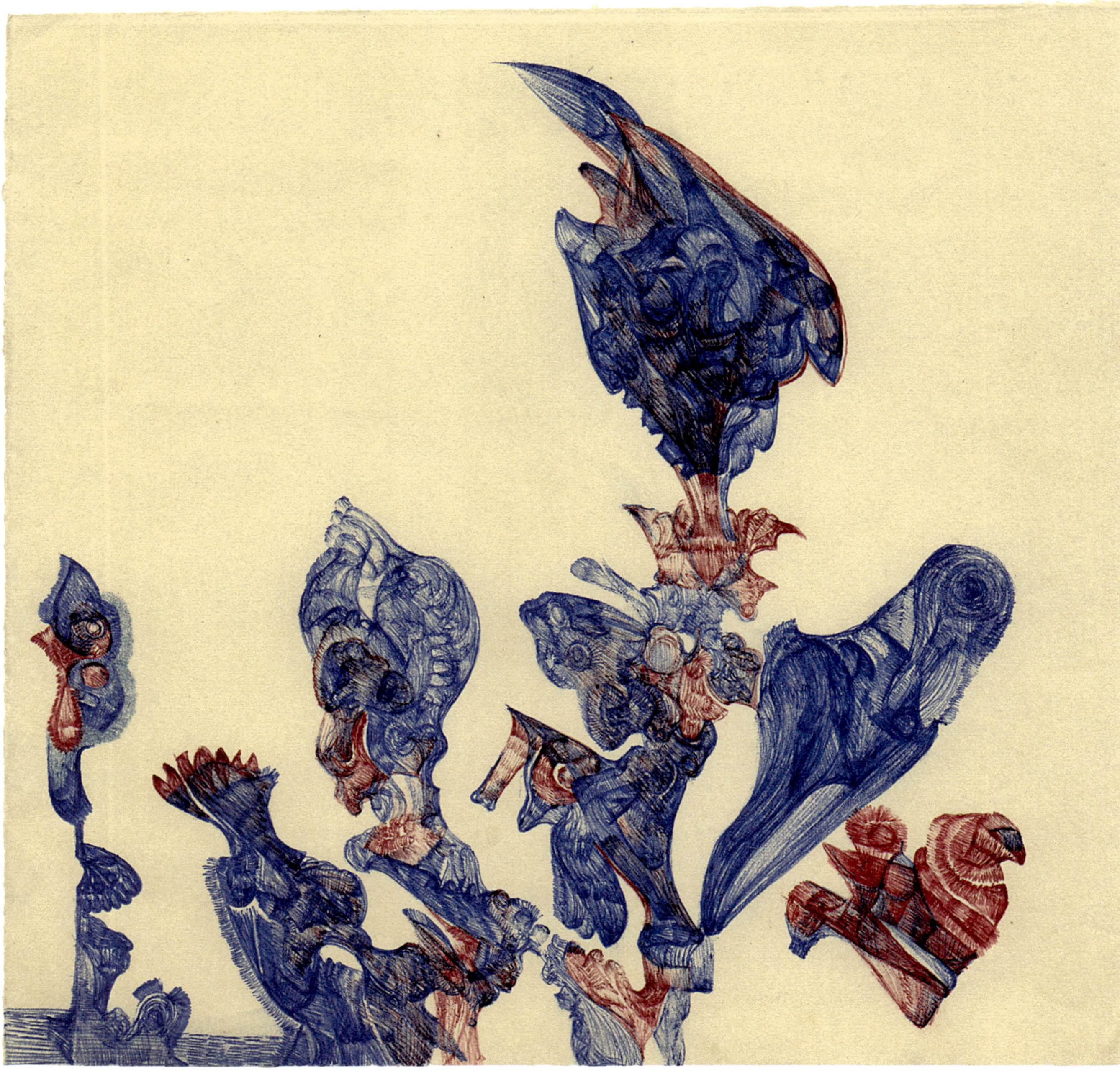

Untitled
(Galerie Le Terrain Vague period)
ca. 1954-1962
Drawing in blue and red
bicolor ballpoint pen,
on paper.
16.3 x 17.1 cm
Artist's collection

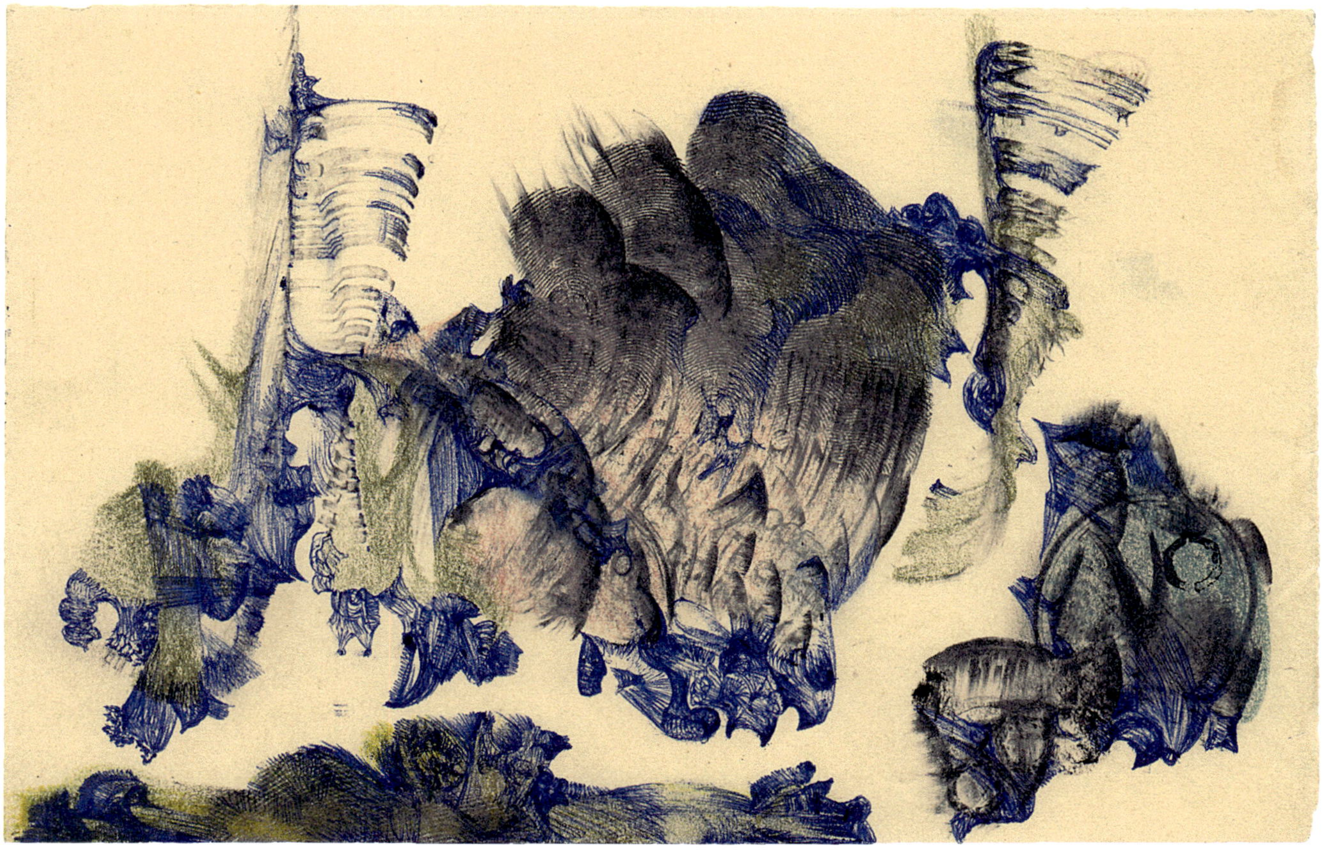

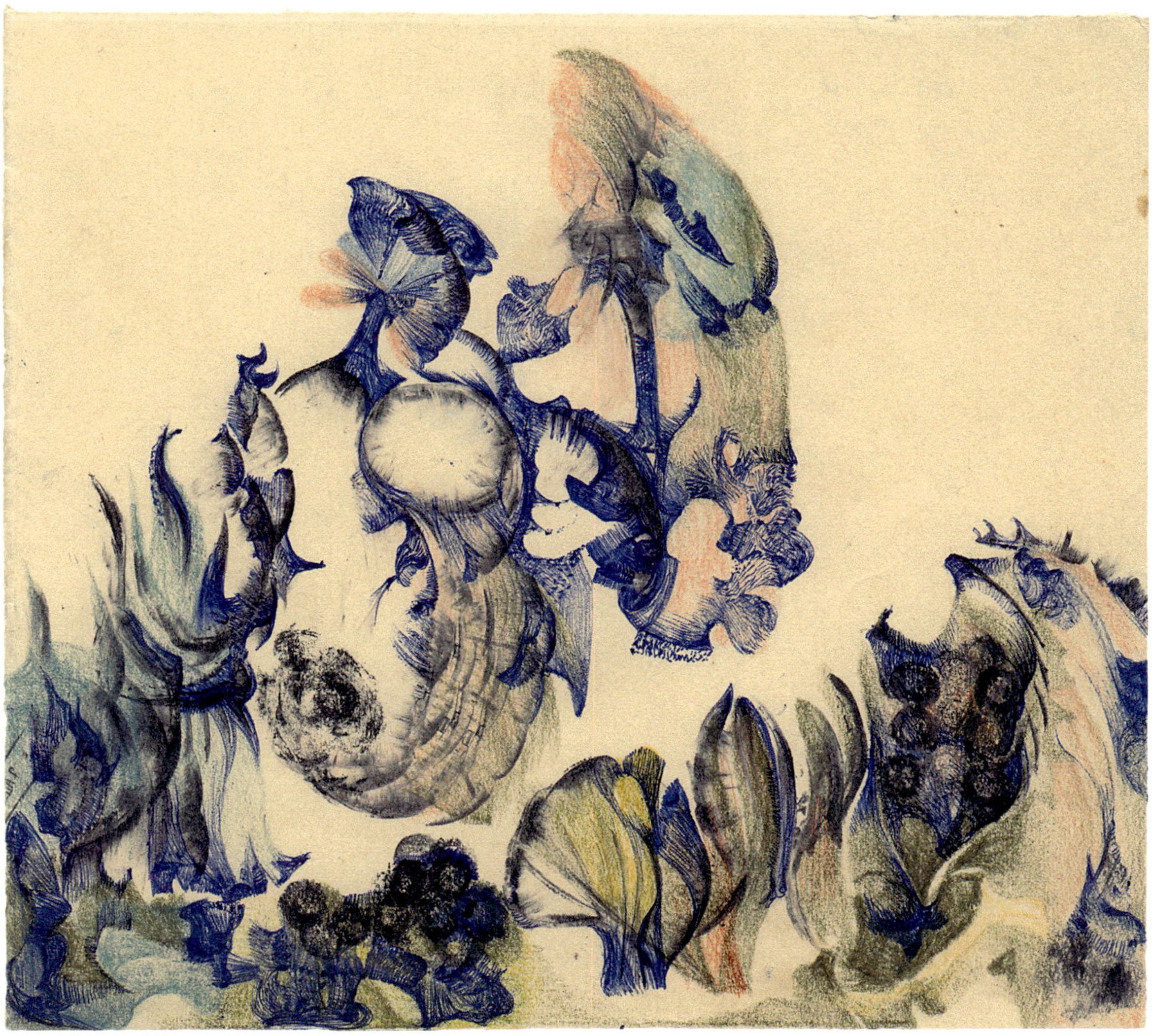

Untitled
(Galerie Le Terrain Vague period)
ca. 1954-1962
Drawing in a monocolor blue ballpoint pen with turquoise, olive green, and yellow pencils. Fingerprints with black seal ink, on paper.
10.9 x 17.1 cm
Artist's collection

Untitled
(Galerie Le Terrain Vague period)
ca. 1954-1962
Drawing in blue monocolor ballpoint pen with beige, turquoise, olive green, and yellow pencil, on paper.
15.1 x 17 cm
Artist's collection

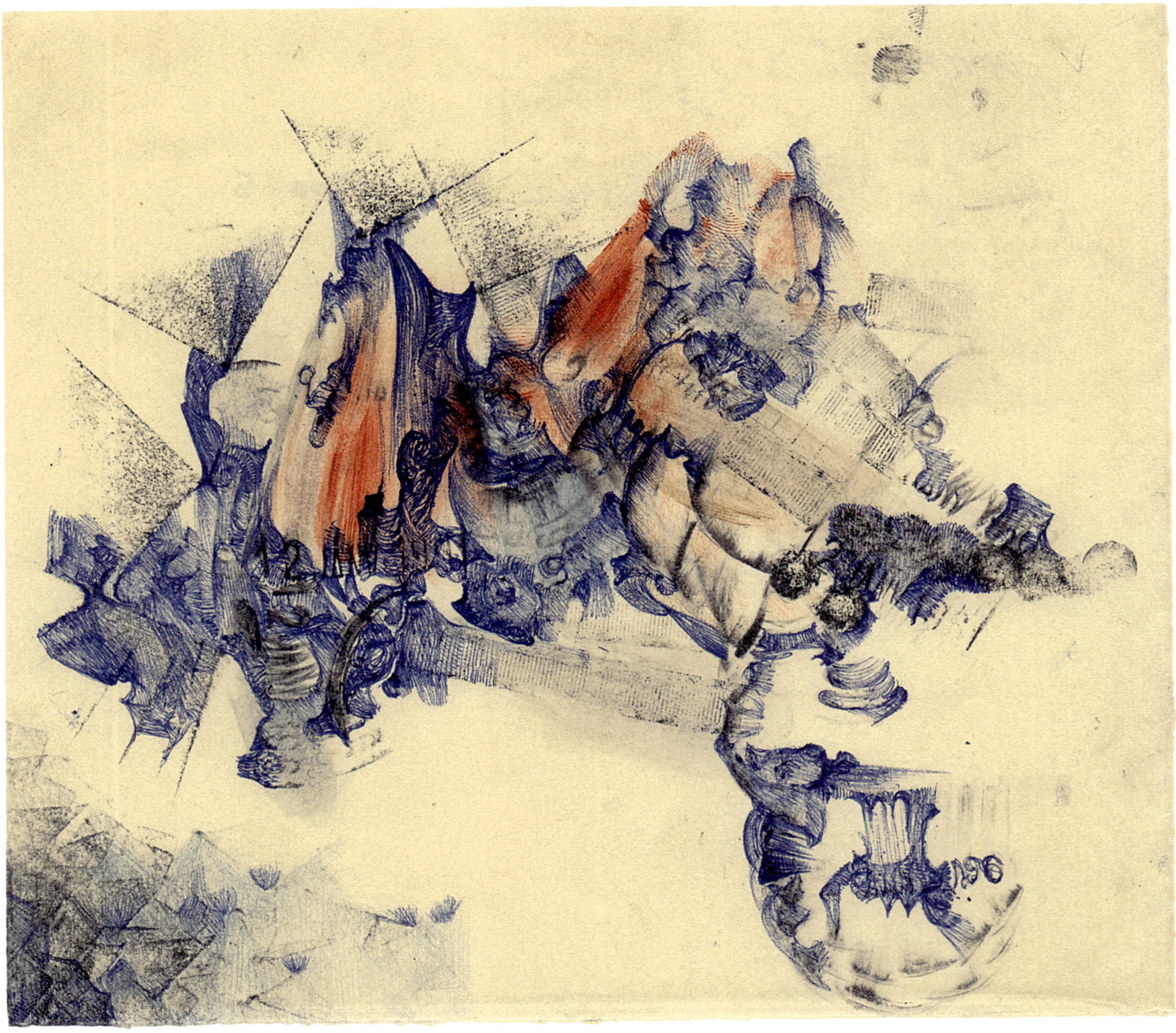

Untitled
(Galerie Le Terrain Vague period)
ca. 1954-1962
Drawing in blue monocolor
ballpoint pen with orange, sky
blue, and black stamp ink,
on paper.
19.4 x 17.1 cm
Artist's collection

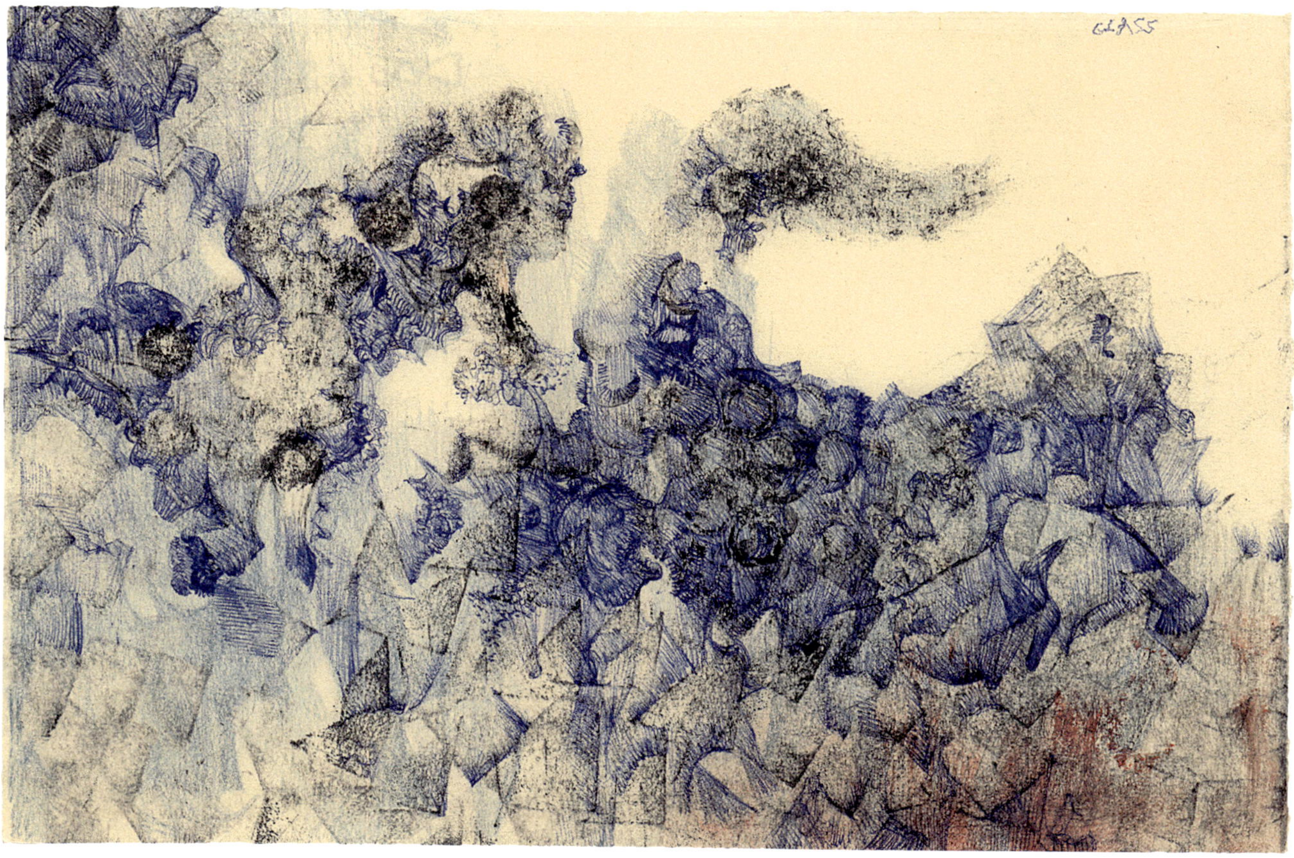

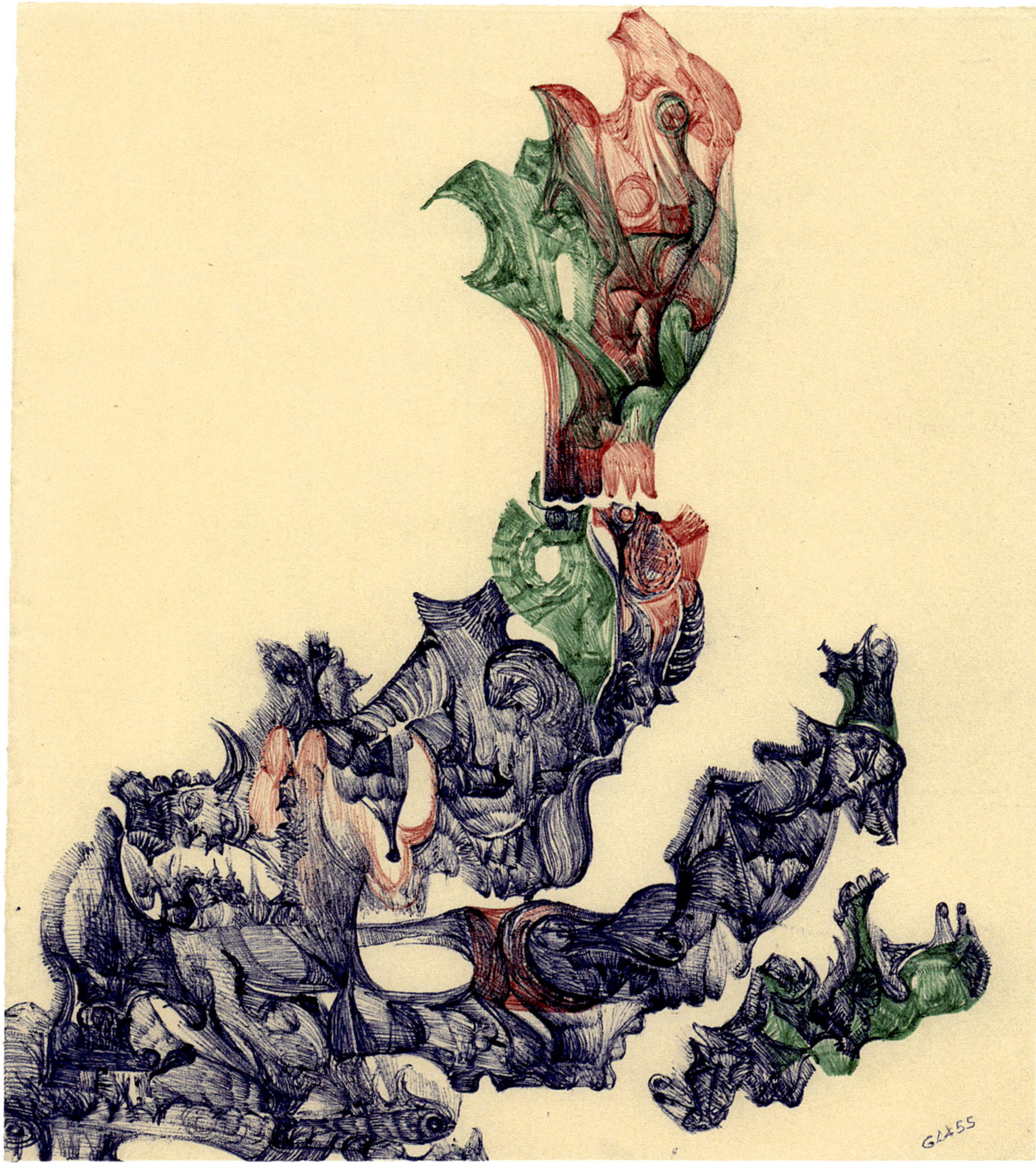

Untitled
(Galerie Le Terrain Vague period)
ca. 1954-1962
Drawing in monocolor blue pen with brown, sky blue, black pencil, and black seal ink, on paper.
11.1 x 17.1 cm
Artist's collection

Untitled
(Galerie Le Terrain Vague period)
ca. 1954-1962
Drawing in blue, green, and red tricolor ballpoint pen, on paper.
19.4 x 17.1 cm
Artist's collection

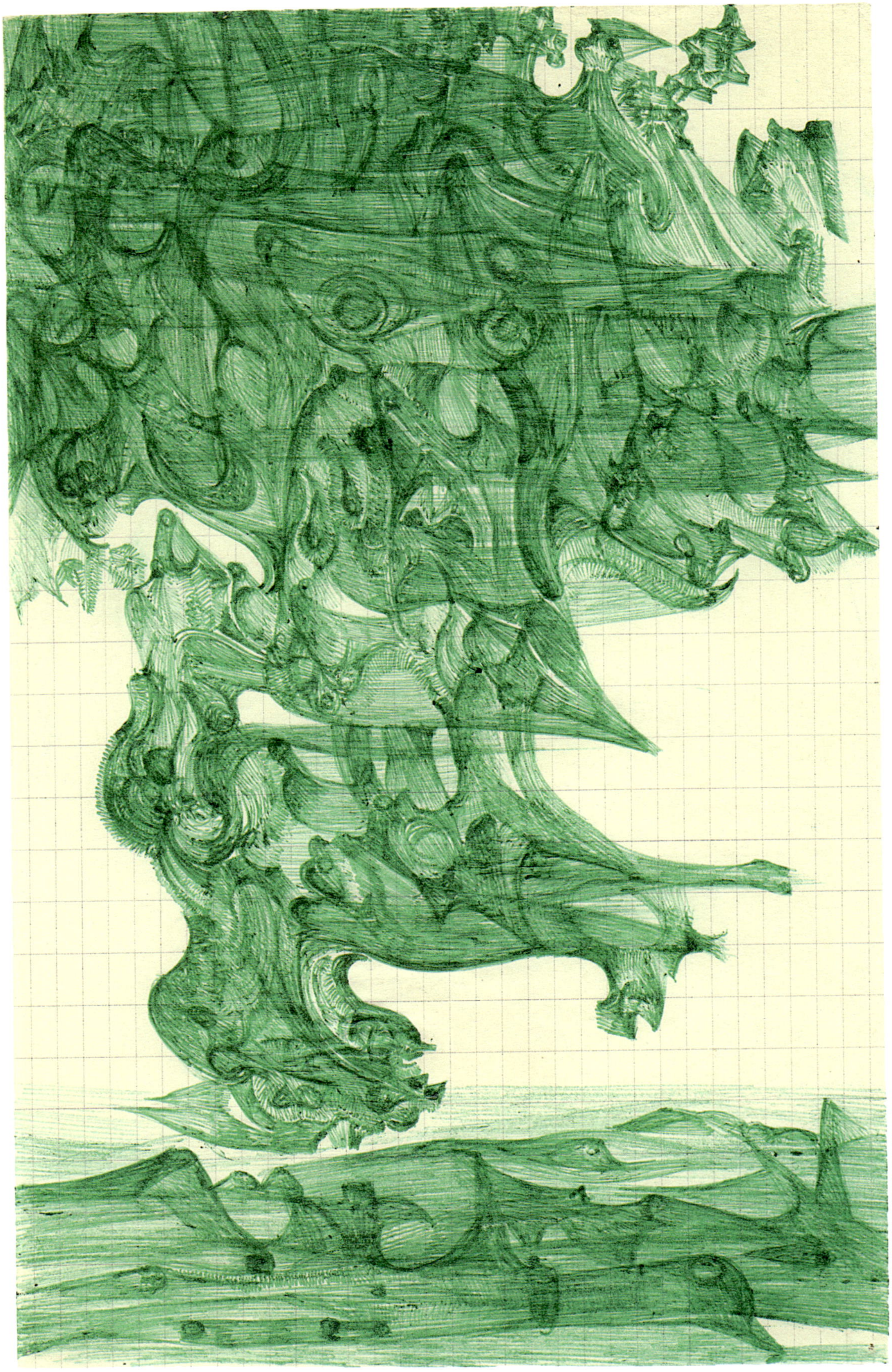

Untitled
(Galerie Le Terrain Vague period)
ca. 1954-1962
Drawing in green monocolor
ballpoint pen,
on squared paper.
21 x 13.4 cm
Artist's collection

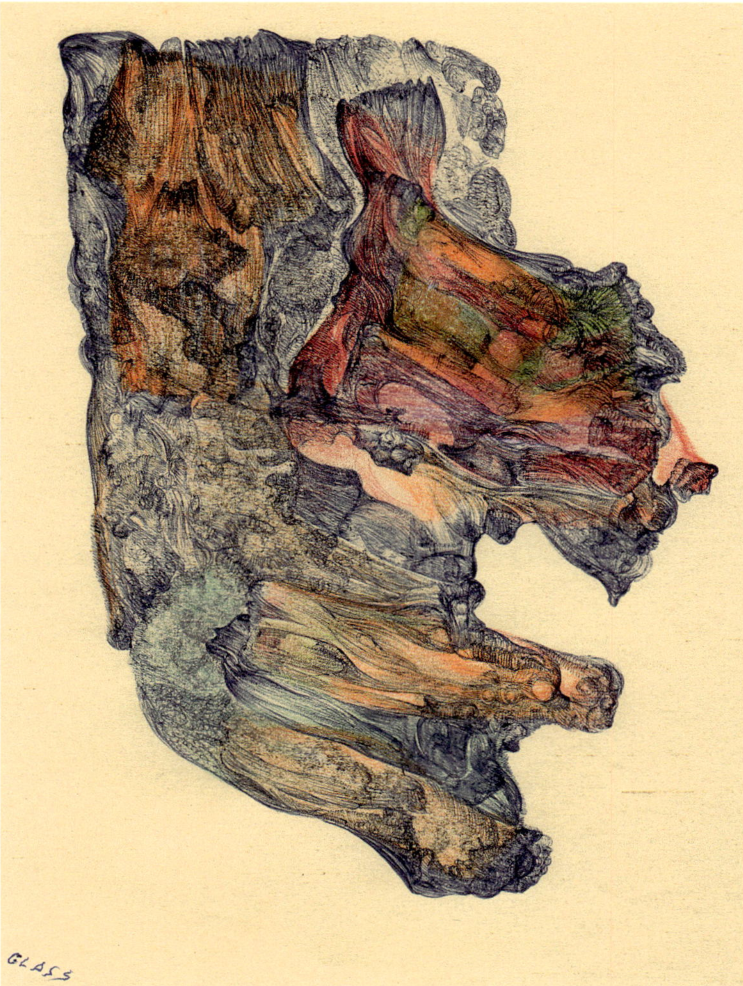

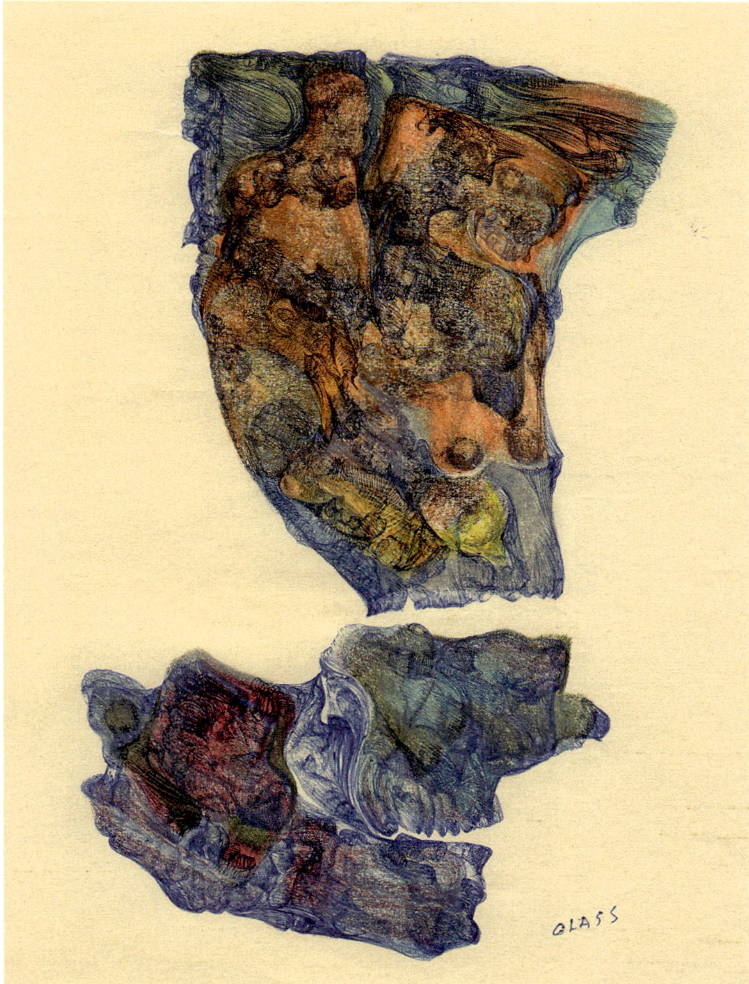

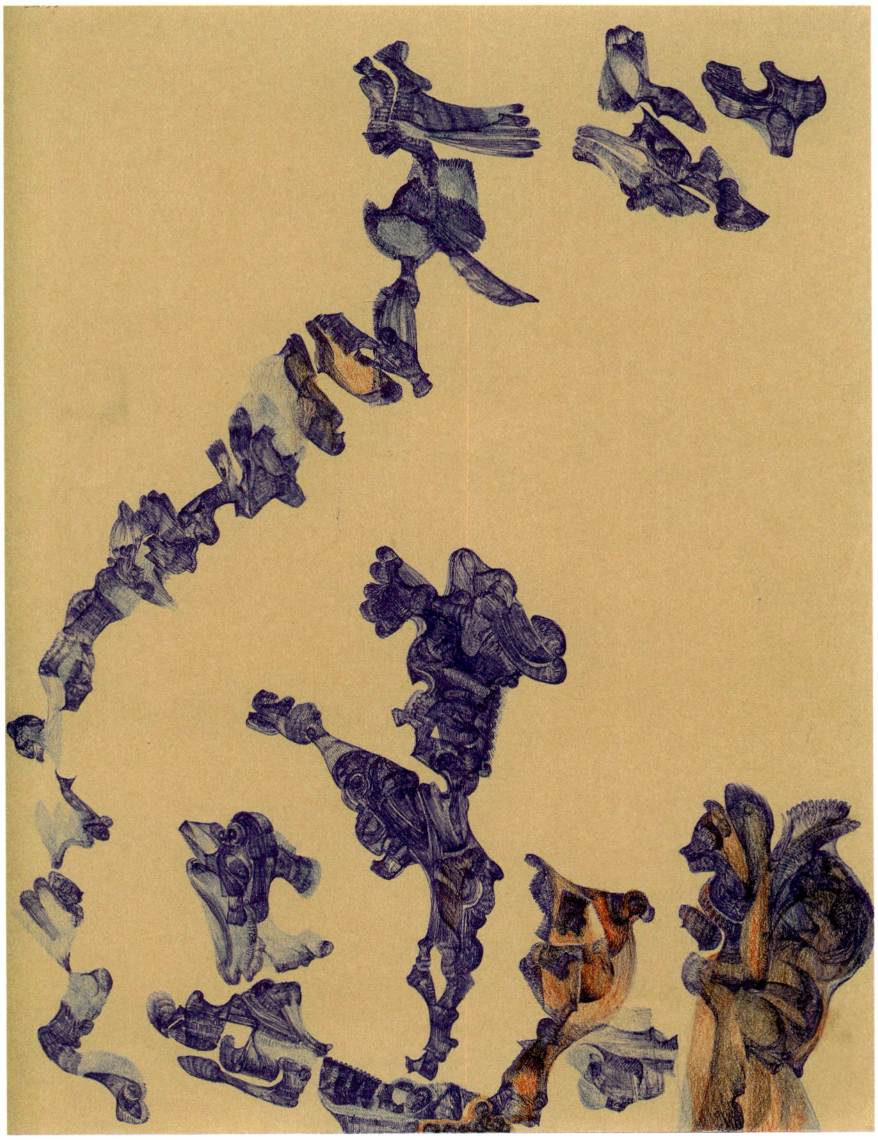

Untitled
(Galerie Le Terrain Vague period)
ca. 1954-1962
Drawing in blue monocolor ballpoint pen with turquoise, orange, grass green, and pink pencil, on paper.
28 x 21.7 cm
Artist's collection

Untitled
(Galerie Le Terrain Vague period)
ca. 1954-1962
Drawing in blue monocolor ballpoint pen with turquoise, orange, olive green, yellow, and red pencil, on paper.
28 x 21.7 cm
Artist's collection

Untitled
(Galerie Le Terrain Vague period)
ca. 1954-1962
Drawing in blue monocolor pen ballpoint with orange and blue pencil, on paper.
28 x 22 cm
Artist's collection

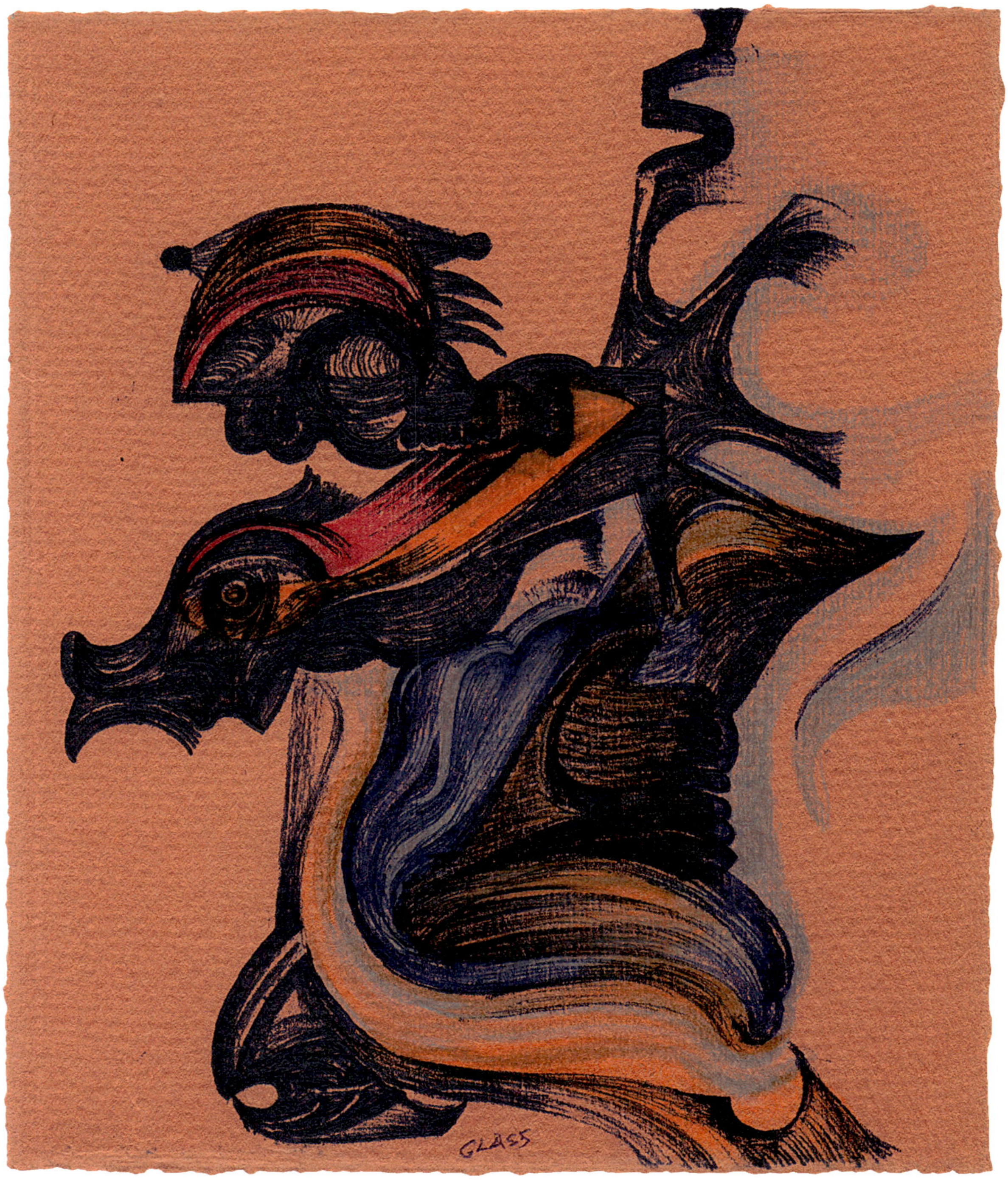

Untitled
(Galerie Le Terrain Vague period)
ca. 1954-1962
Drawing in blue monocolor ballpoint pen with orange, sky blue, olive green, and pink pencil, on red corrugated paper.
16.5 x 14 cm
Artist's collection

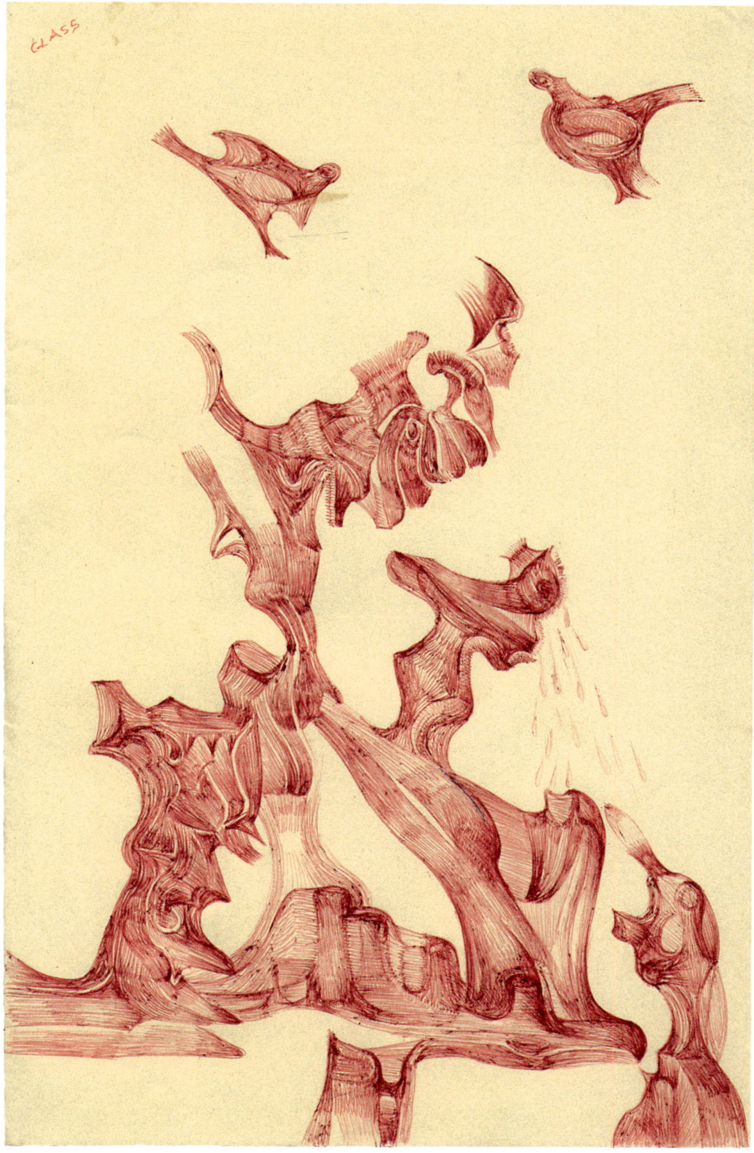

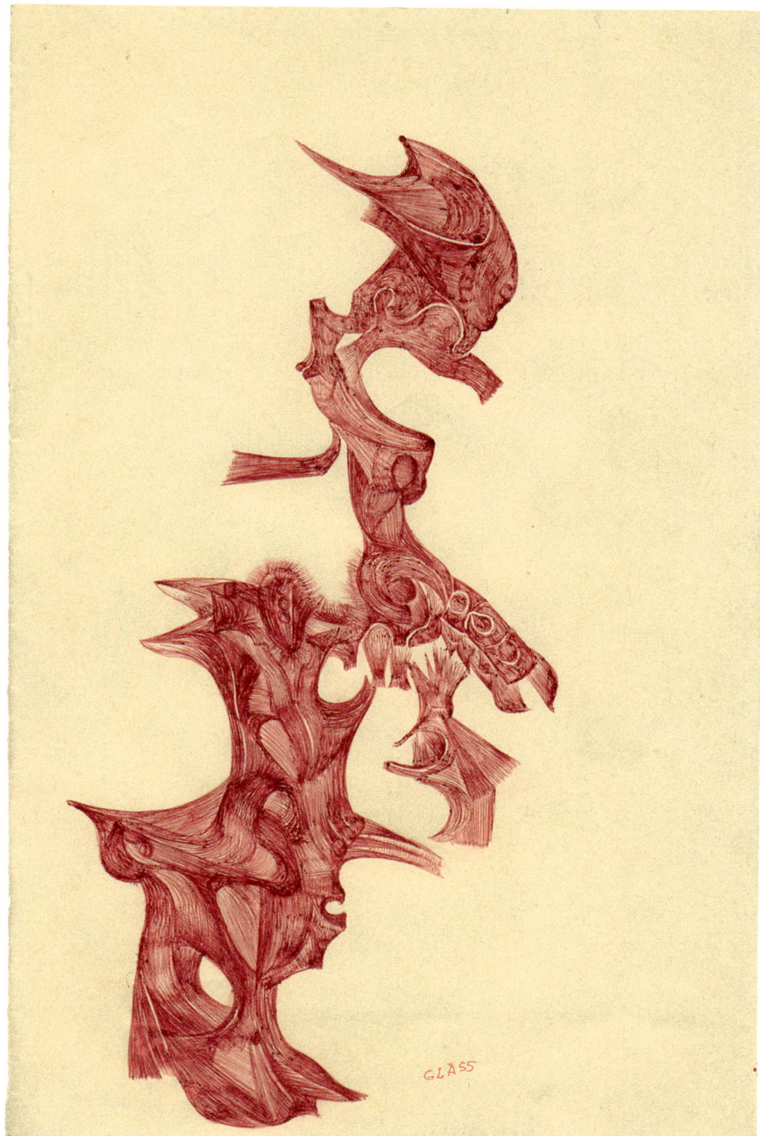

Untitled
(Galerie Le Terrain Vague period)
ca. 1954-1962
Drawing in red monocolor ballpoint pen, on paper.
26 x 17 cm
Artist's collection

Untitled
(Galerie Le Terrain Vague period)
ca. 1954-1962
Drawing in red monocolor ballpoint pen, on paper.
26 x 17.1 cm
Artist's collection

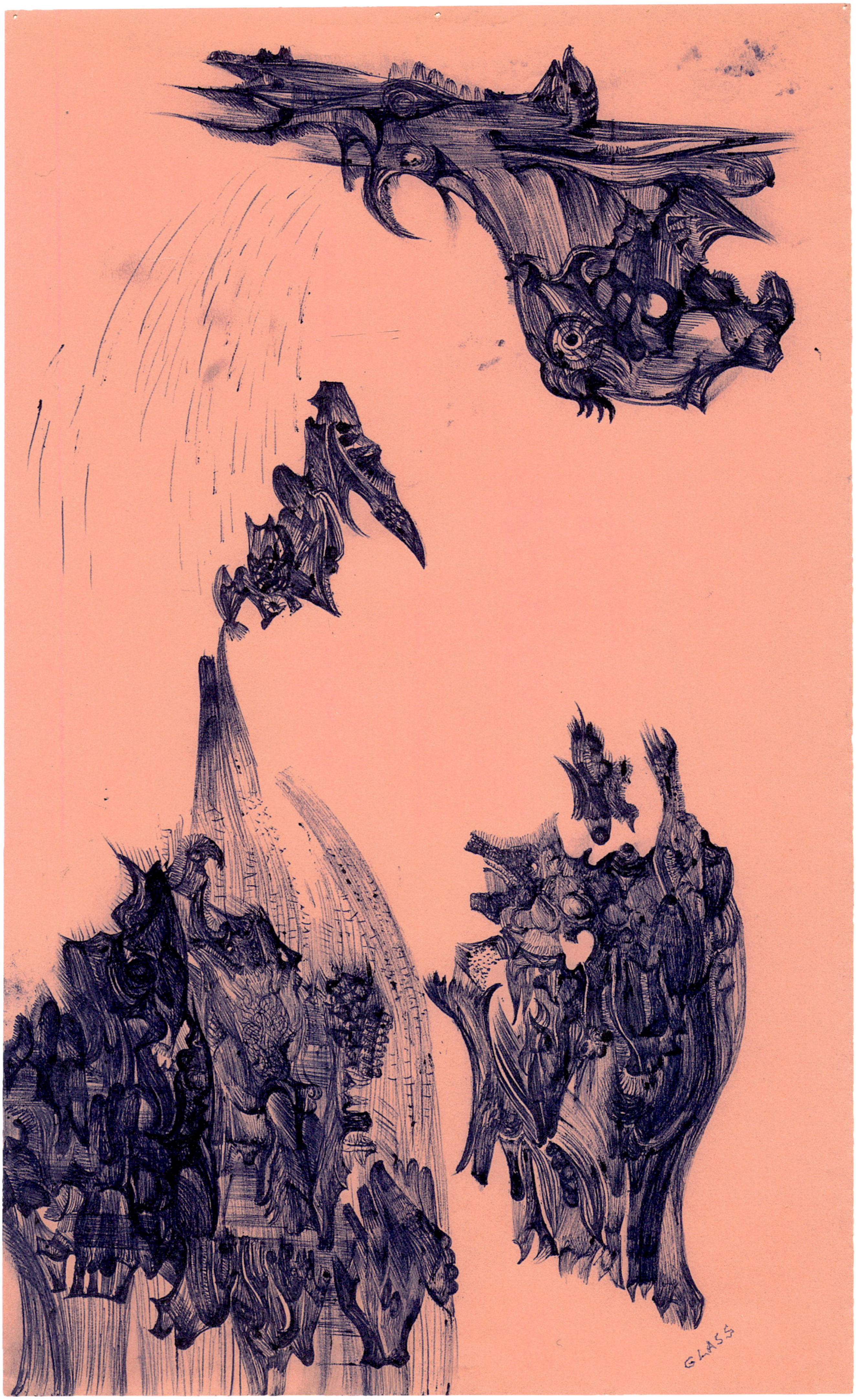
GLASS

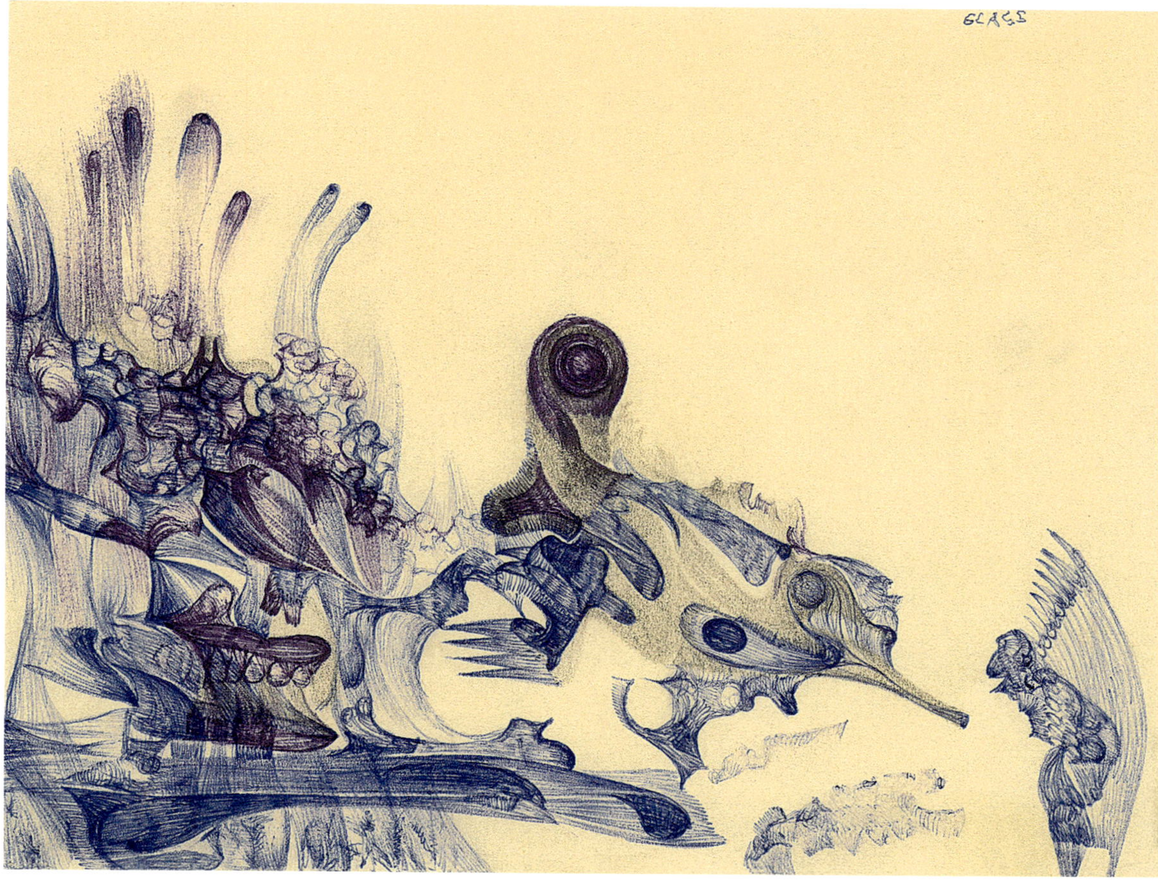

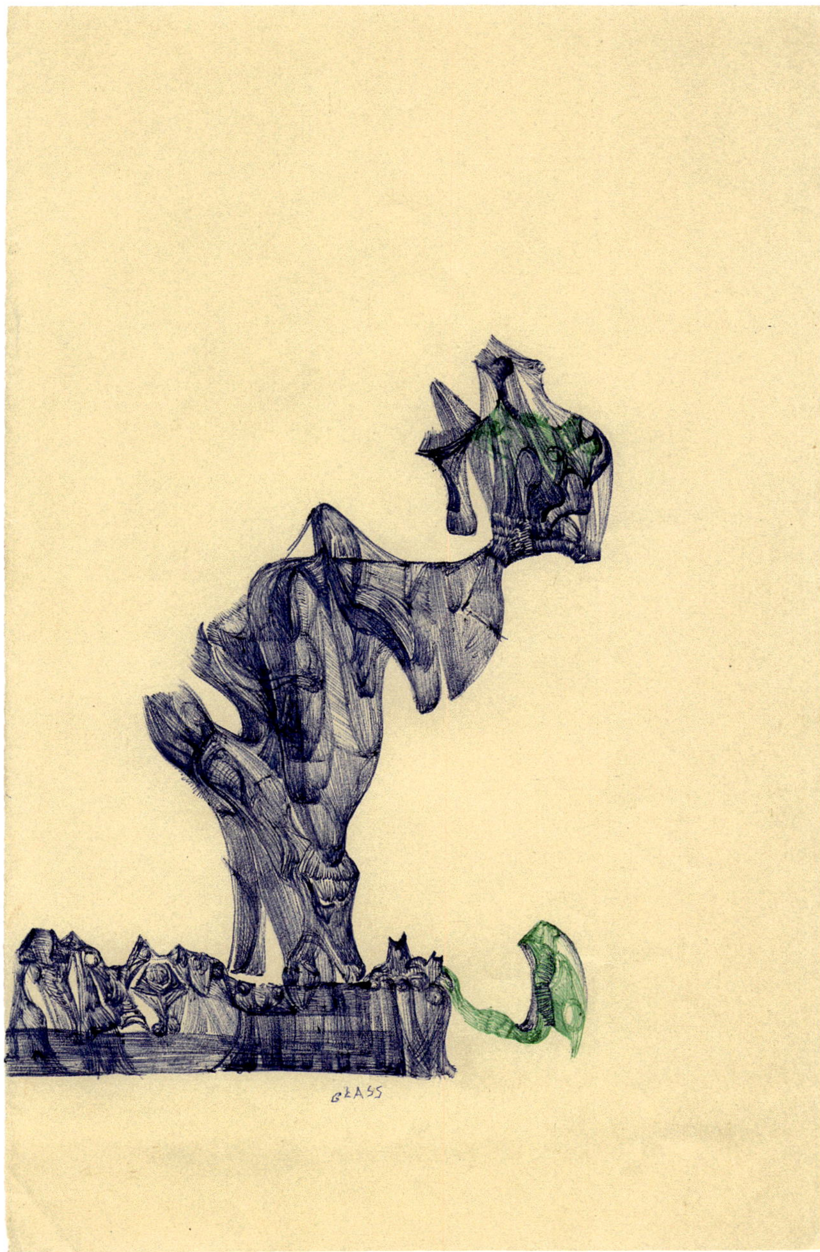

Untitled
(Galerie Le Terrain Vague period)
ca. 1954-1962
Drawing in blue monocolor
ballpoint pen, on pink paper.
27 x 16.5 cm
Artist's collection
Previous page

Untitled
(Galerie Le Terrain Vague period)
ca. 1954-1962
Drawing in blue and purple
bicolor pen with black pencil,
on paper.
12.8 x 17 cm
Artist's collection

Untitled
(Galerie Le Terrain Vague period)
ca. 1954-1962
Drawing in blue and green
bicolor pen, on paper.
26 x 17.1 cm
Artist's collection

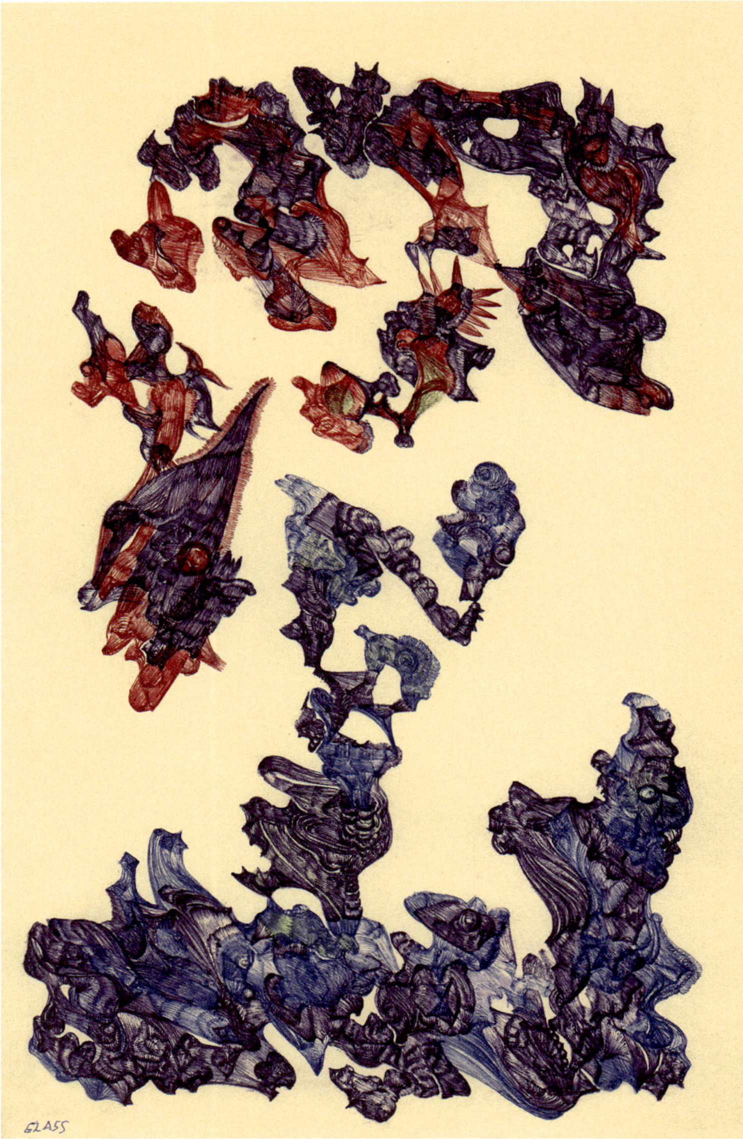

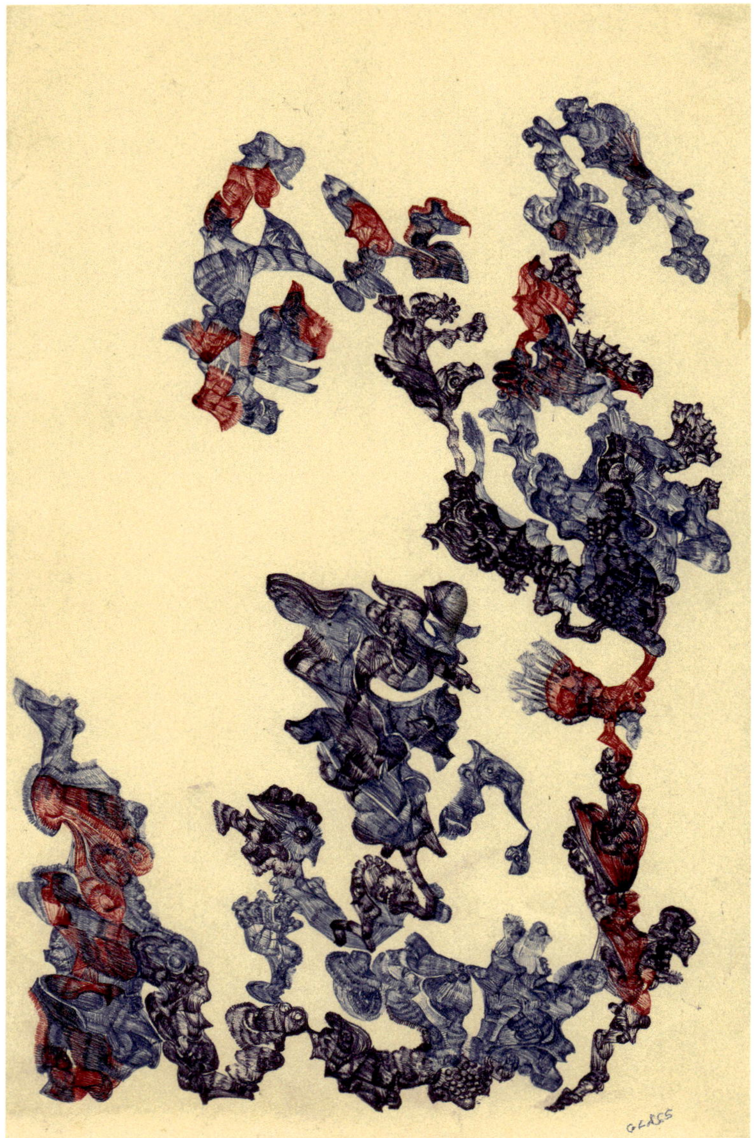

Untitled
(Galerie Le Terrain Vague period)
ca. 1954-1962
Drawing in blue, purple, and red tricolor pen with green and olive green pencil, on paper.
26 x 17 cm
Artist's collection

Untitled
(Galerie Le Terrain Vague period)
ca. 1954-1962
Blue, violet, and red tricolor ballpoint pen drawing, on paper.
26 x 17 cm
Artist's collection

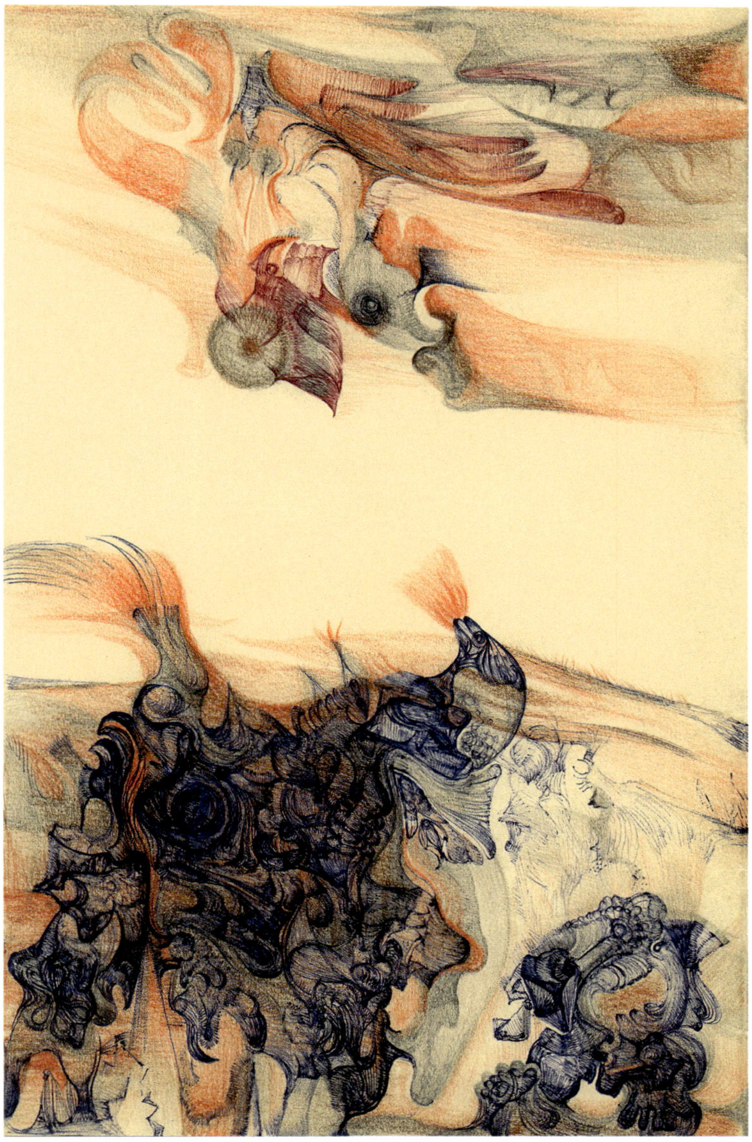

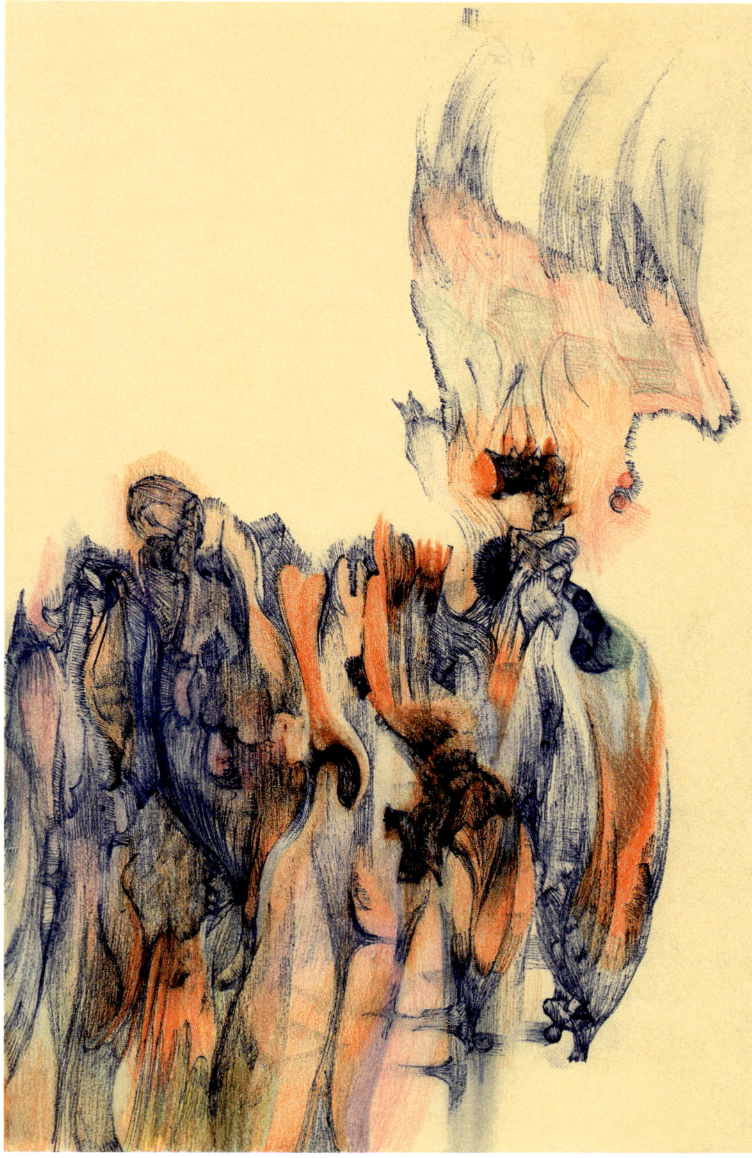

Untitled
(Galerie Le Terrain Vague period)
ca. 1954-1962
Drawing in blue and red bicolor pen with orange, brown, and gray pencil, on paper.
26 x 17 cm
Artist's collection

Untitled
(Galerie Le Terrain Vague period)
ca. 1954-1962
Drawing in blue monocolor ballpoint pen with turquoise, orange, sky blue, lilac, and pink pencil, on paper.
26 x 17 cm
Artist's collection

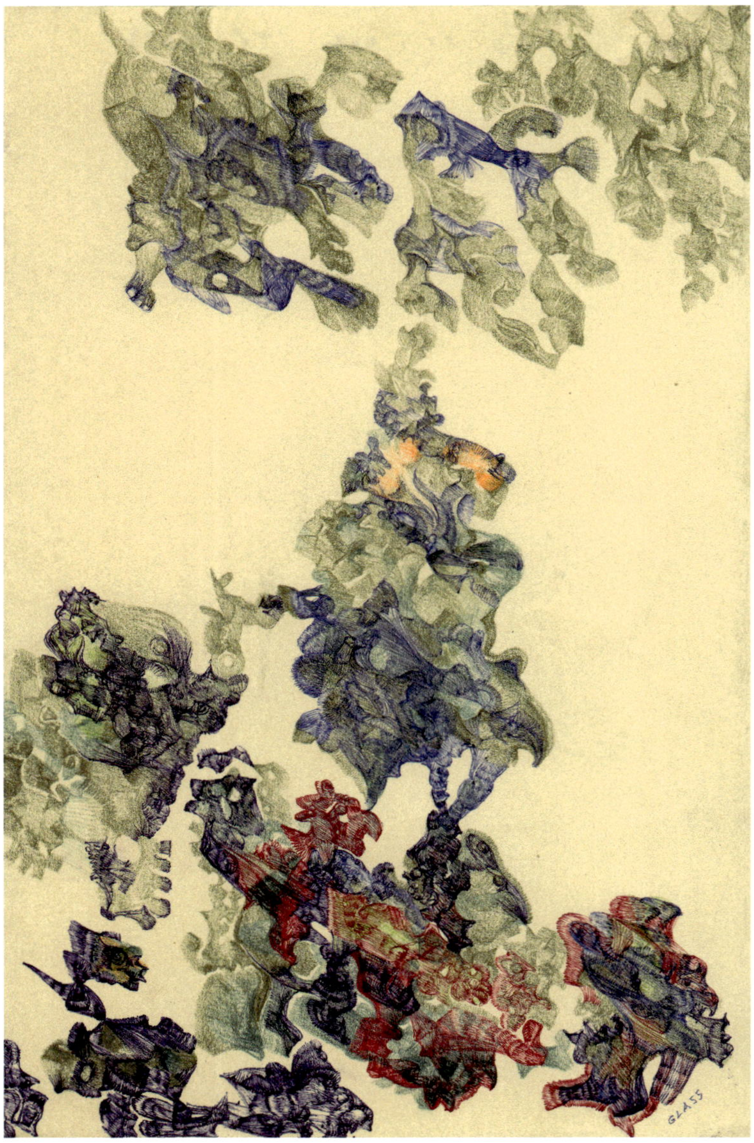

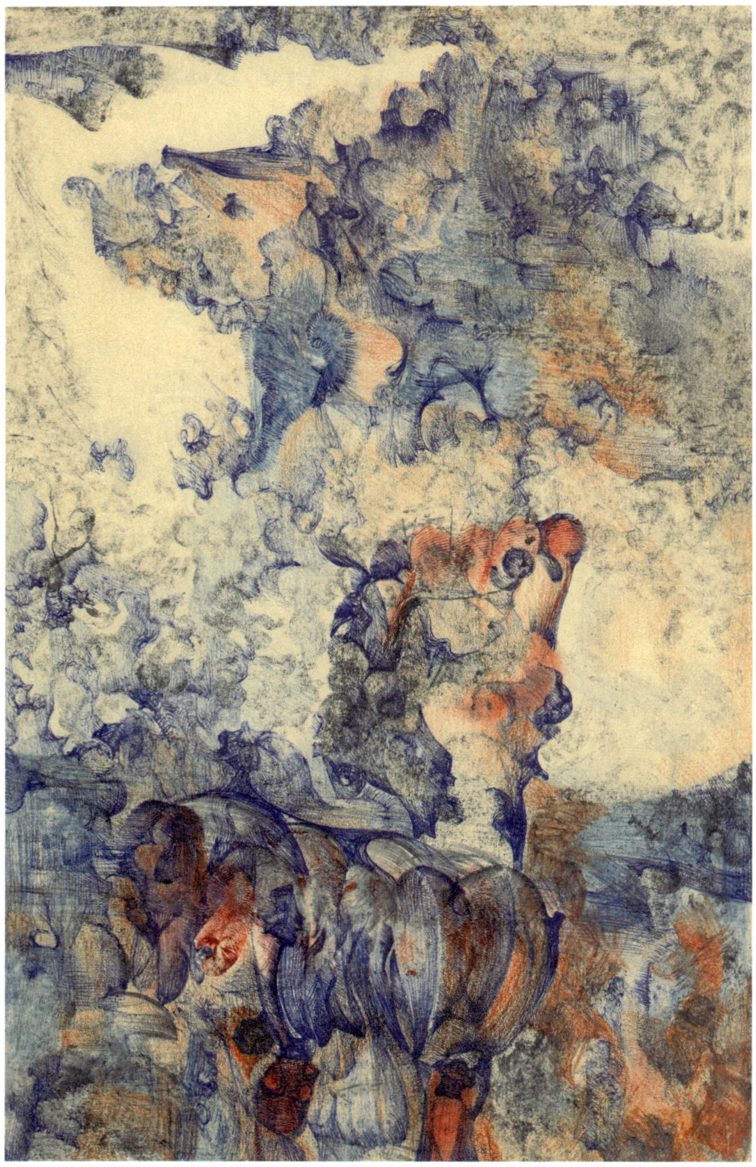

Untitled
(Galerie Le Terrain Vague period)
ca. 1954-1962
Four-color ballpoint pen drawing blue, purple, red, and black, with olive-grass green and orange pencils, on paper.
26 x 17 cm
Artist's collection

Untitled
(Galerie Le Terrain Vague period)
ca. 1954-1962
Blue, violet, and red tricolor pen drawing, with orange and sky blue pencil, on paper.
26 x 17 cm
Artist's collection

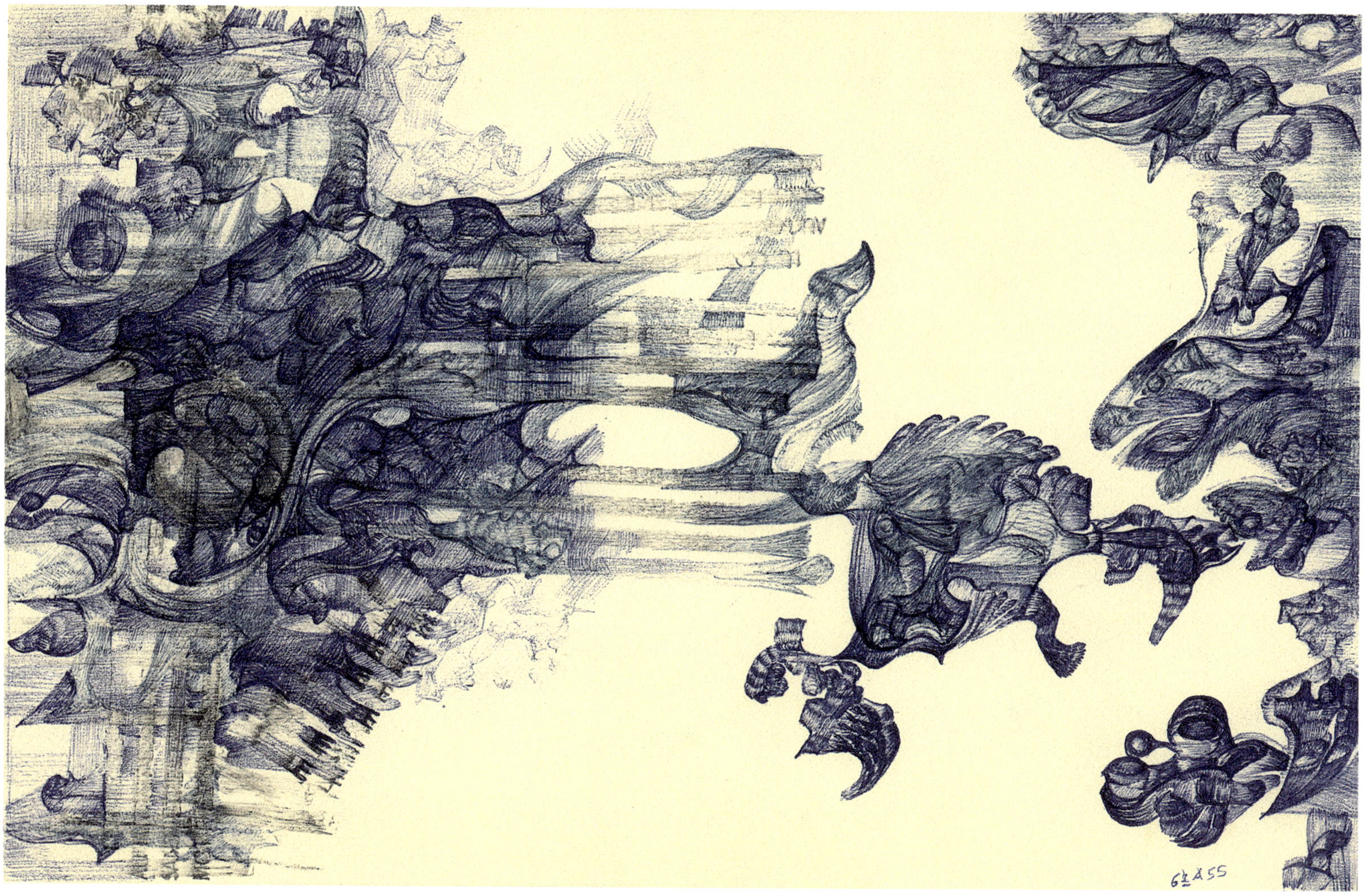

Untitled
(Galerie Le Terrain Vague period)
ca. 1954-1962
Drawing in blue and navy blue bicolor ballpoint pen with black seal ink, on paper.
24.2 x 15.5 cm
Artist's collection

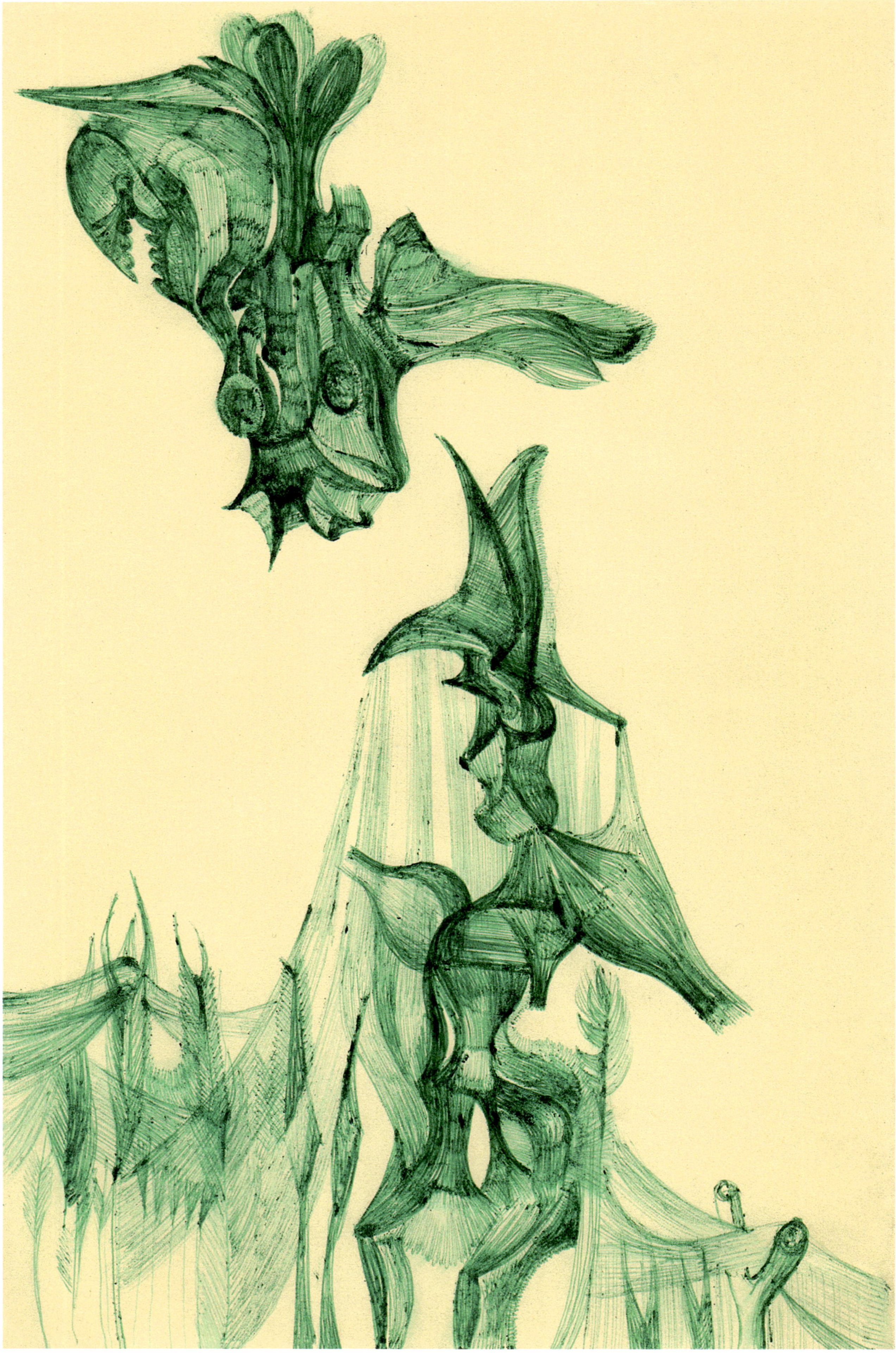

Untitled
(Galerie Le Terrain Vague period)
ca. 1954-1962
Drawing in green monocolor
pen, on paper.
26 x 17 cm
Artist's collection

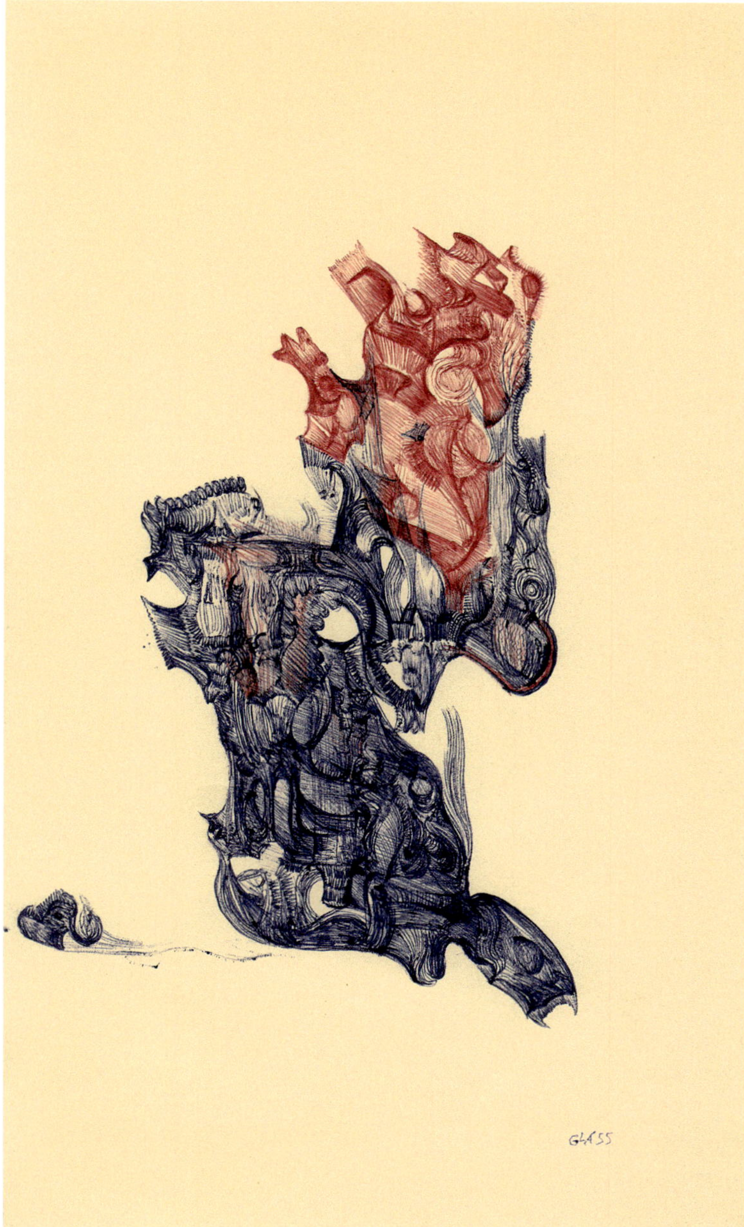

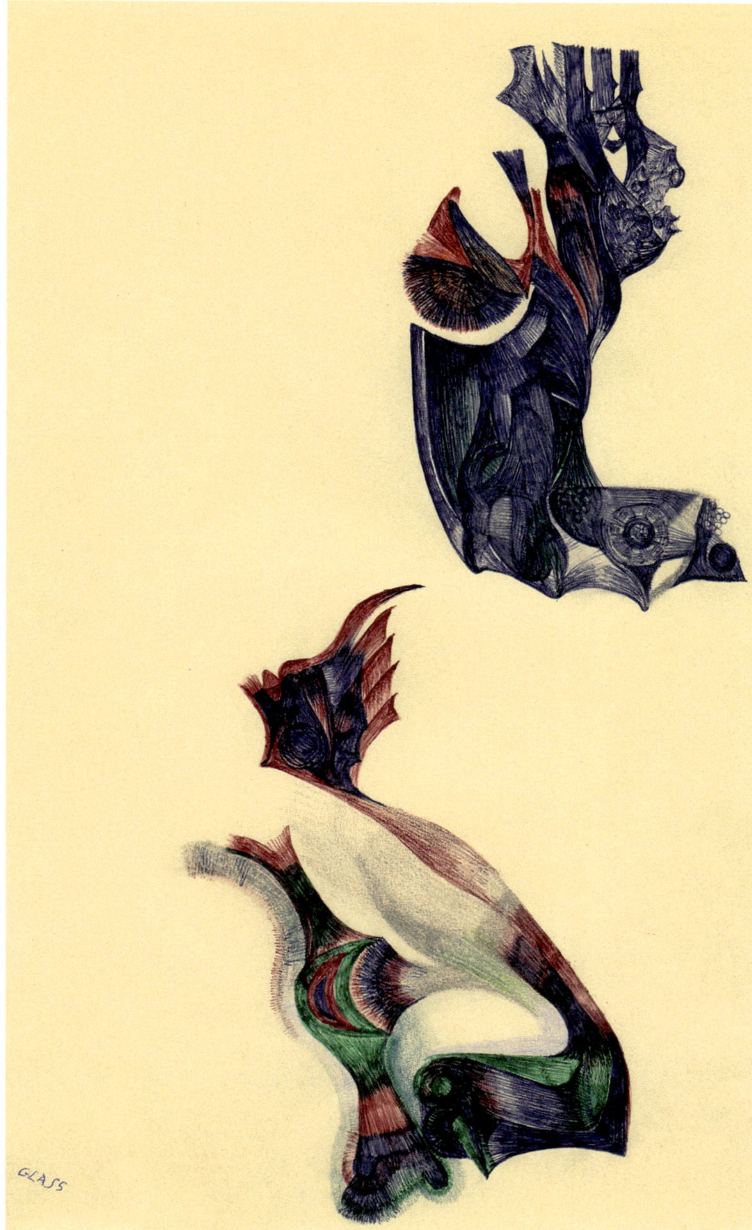

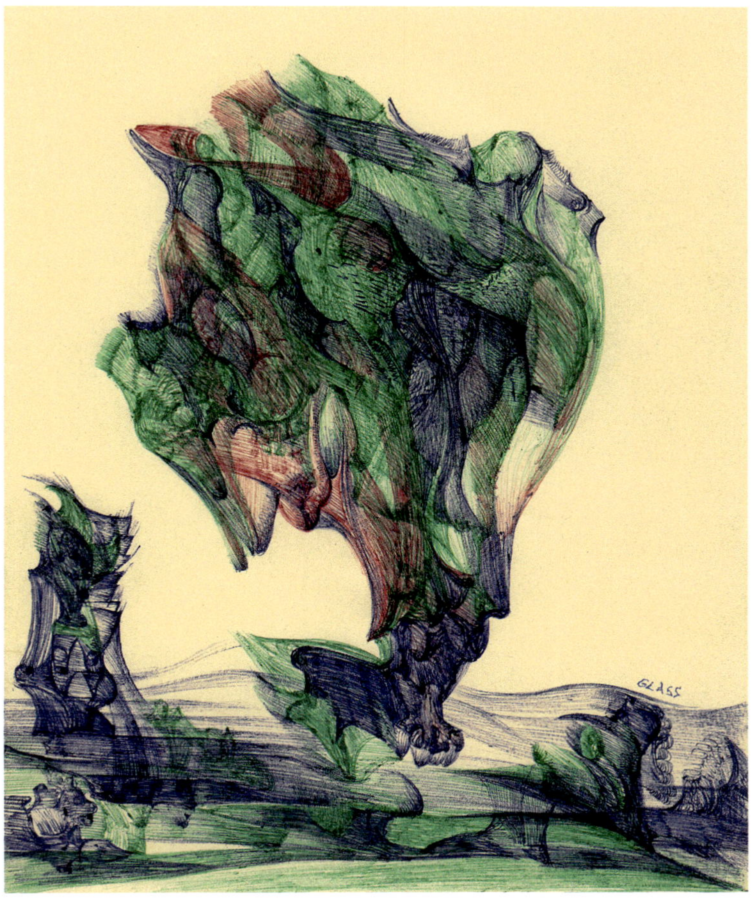

Untitled
(Galerie Le Terrain Vague period)
ca. 1954-1962
Drawing in blue and red bicolor pen, on paper.
26 x 17 cm
Artist's collection

Untitled
(Galerie Le Terrain Vague period)
ca. 1954-1962
Drawing in blue, green, and red tricolor pen, with sky blue, green, and gray pencil, on paper.
26 x 17 cm
Artist's collection

Untitled
(Galerie Le Terrain Vague period)
ca. 1954-1962
Drawing in blue, green, and red tricolor ballpoint pen, on paper.
26 x 17 cm
Artist's collection

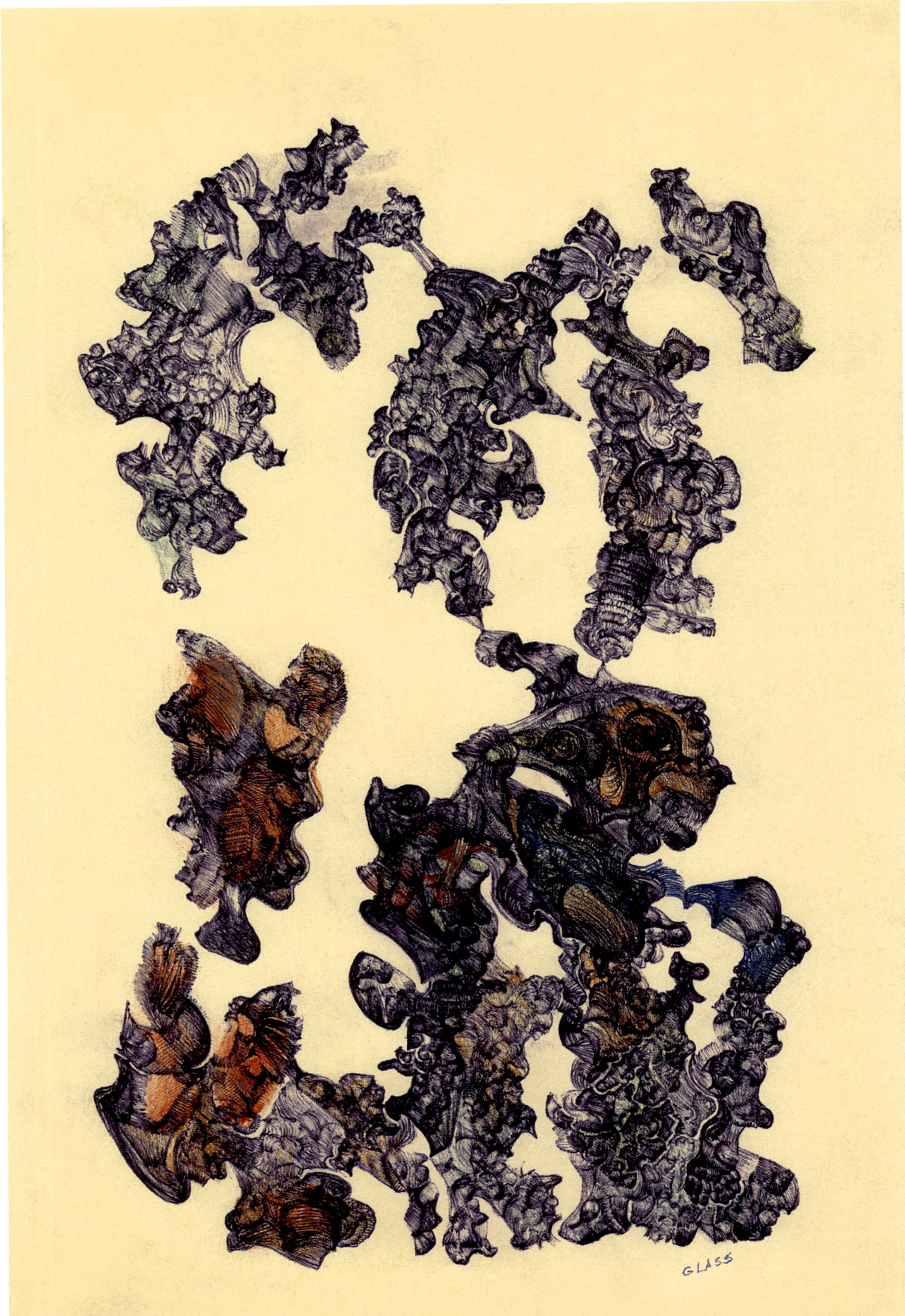

Untitled
(Galerie Le Terrain Vague period)
ca. 1954-1962
Drawing in purple, red, and
blue tricolor pen with orange,
turquoise, olive green,
and red ink, on paper.
26 x 17 cm
Artist's collection

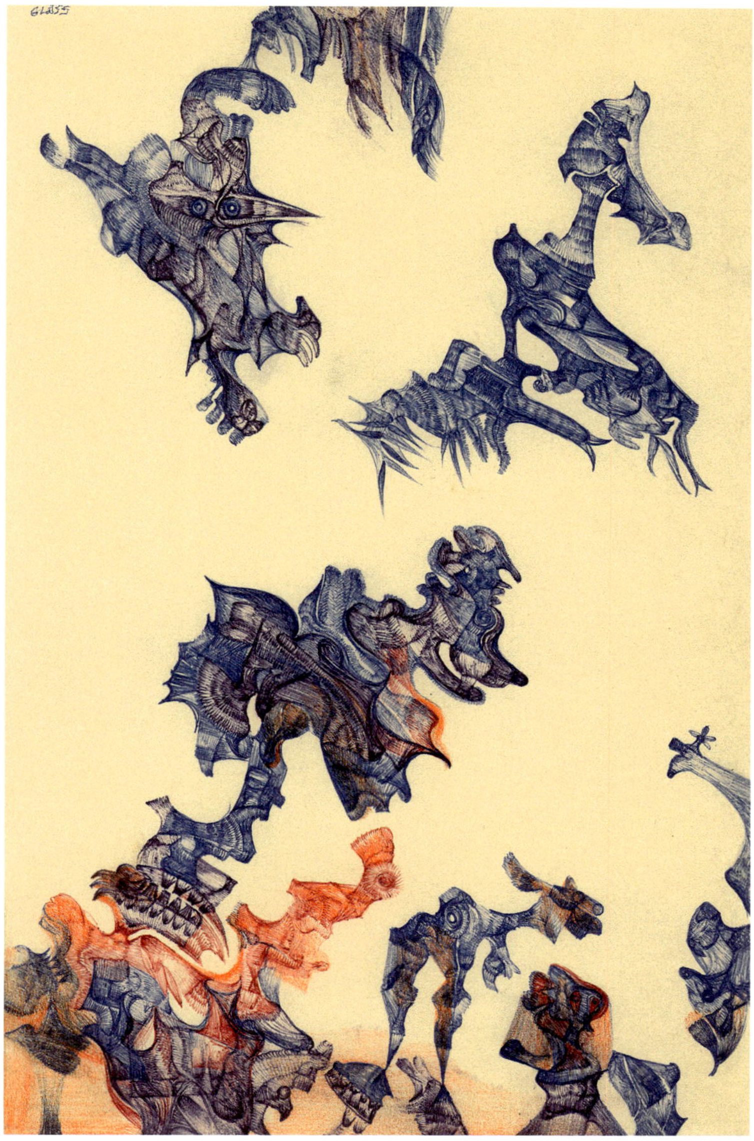

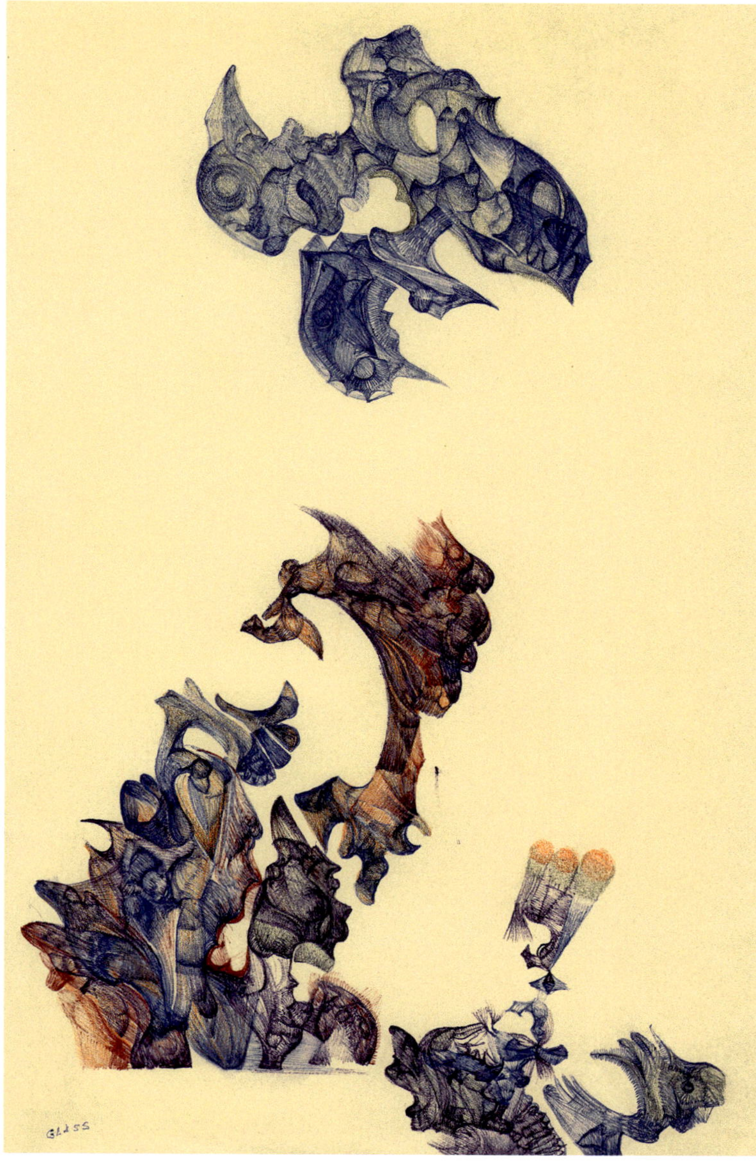

Untitled
(Galerie Le Terrain Vague period)
ca. 1954-1962
Drawing in blue, purple, and red tricolor ballpoint pen, with orange colored pencil, on paper.
26 x 17 cm
Artist's collection

Untitled
(Galerie Le Terrain Vague period)
ca. 1954-1962
Drawing in blue, red, and purple tricolor pen with orange and gray pencil, on paper.
26 x 17 cm
Artist's collection

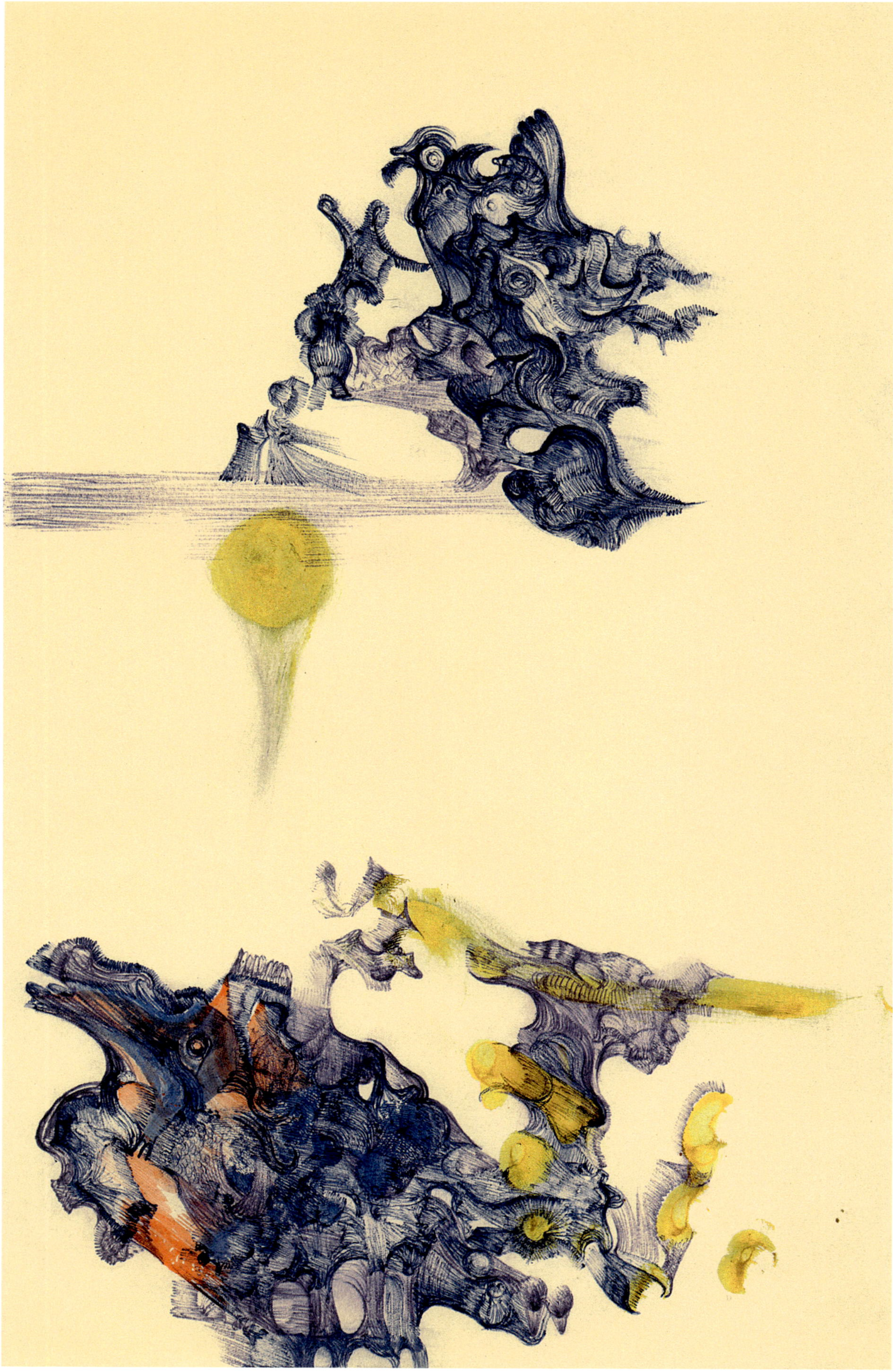

Untitled
(Galerie Le Terrain Vague period)
ca. 1954-1962
Drawing in blue and purple bicolor pen with orange, yellow, and blue watercolor, on paper.
26 x 17 cm
Artist's collection

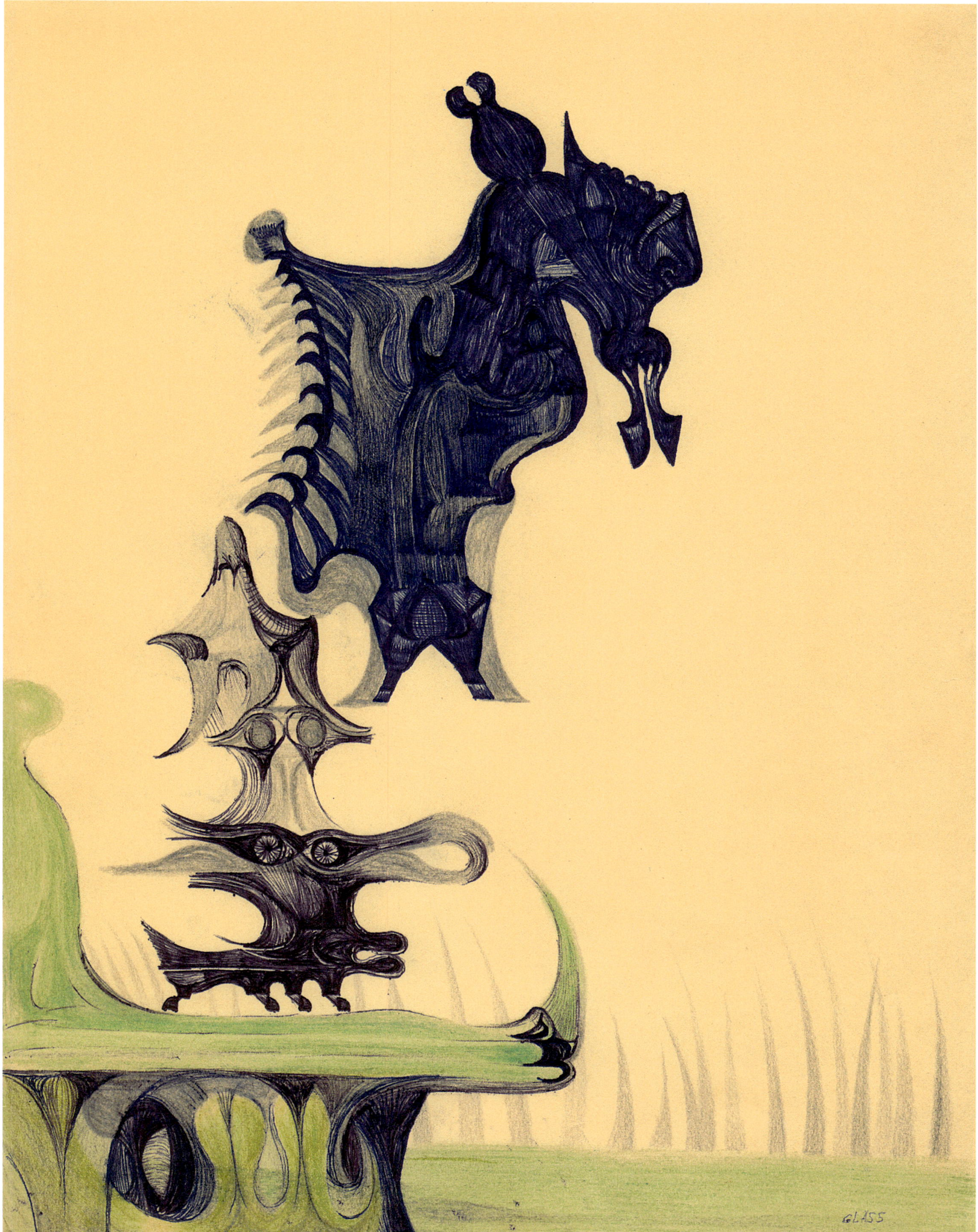

Untitled
(Galerie Le Terrain Vague period)
ca. 1954-1962
Drawing in blue and navy blue bicolor pen with lemon green and gray pencil, on paper.
27 x 21.2 cm
Artist's collection

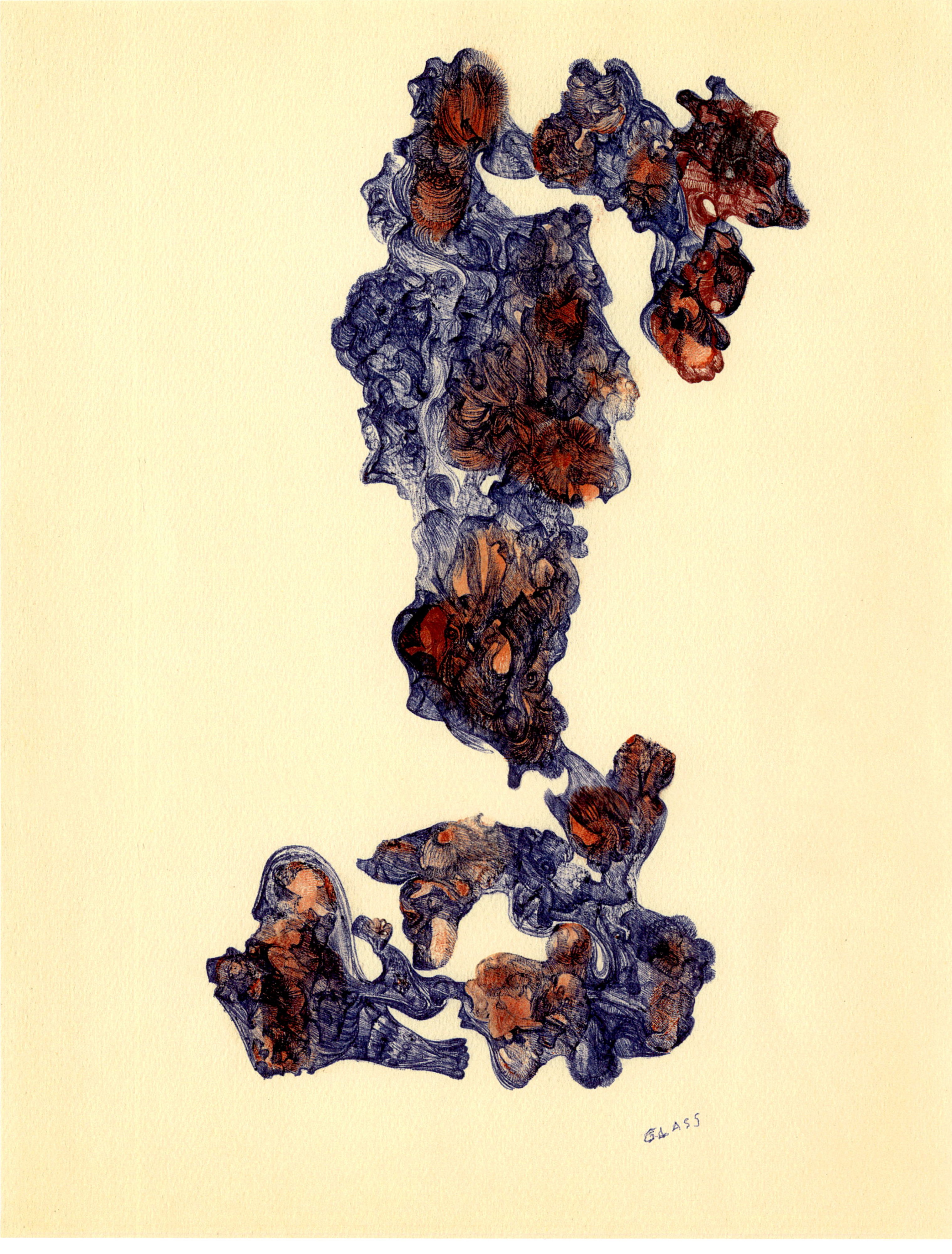
GLASS

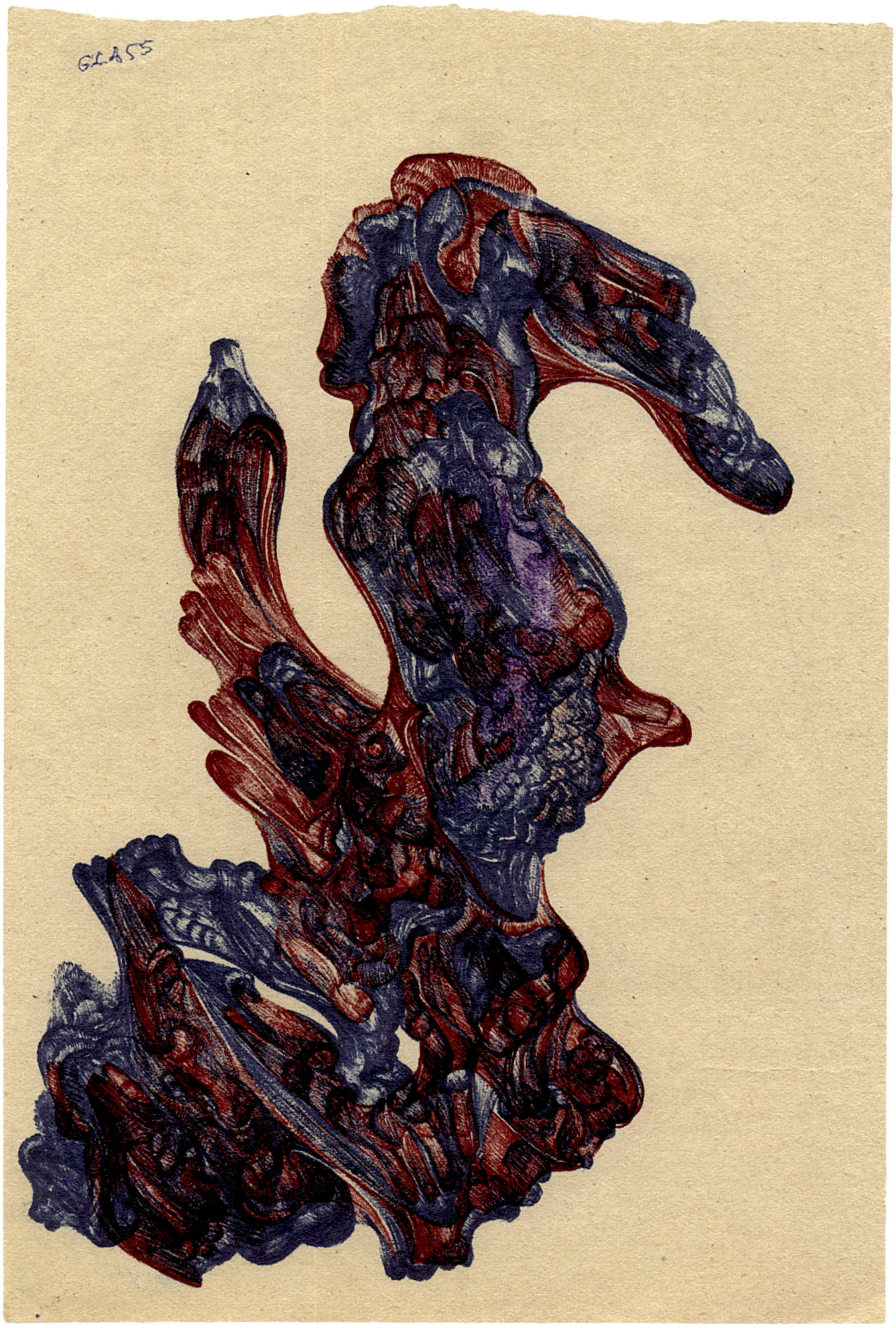

Untitled
(Galerie Le Terrain Vague period)
ca. 1954-1962
Drawing in blue and red
bicolor pen with red watercolor
and orange pencil,
on corrugated paper.
31.4 x 23.8 cm
Artist's collection
Previous page

Untitled
(Galerie Le Terrain Vague period)
ca. 1954-1962
Drawing in blue, red, and
purple tricolor ballpoint pen,
on paper.
12.9 x 7 cm
Artist's collection

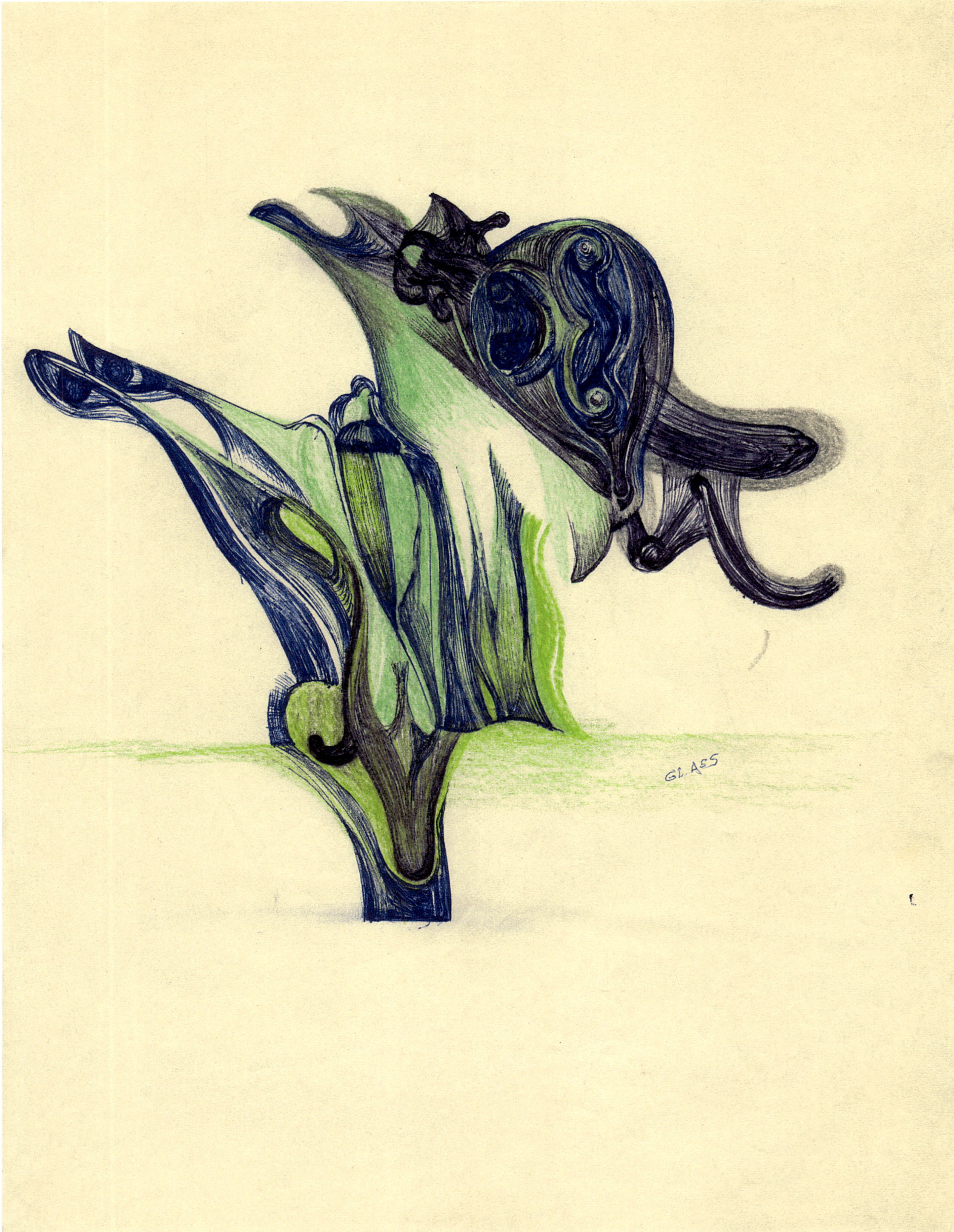

Untitled
(Galerie Le Terrain Vague period)
ca. 1954-1962
Drawing in blue and navy blue bicolor pen with lemon green and gray pencil, on paper.
27 x 21.2 cm
Artist's collection

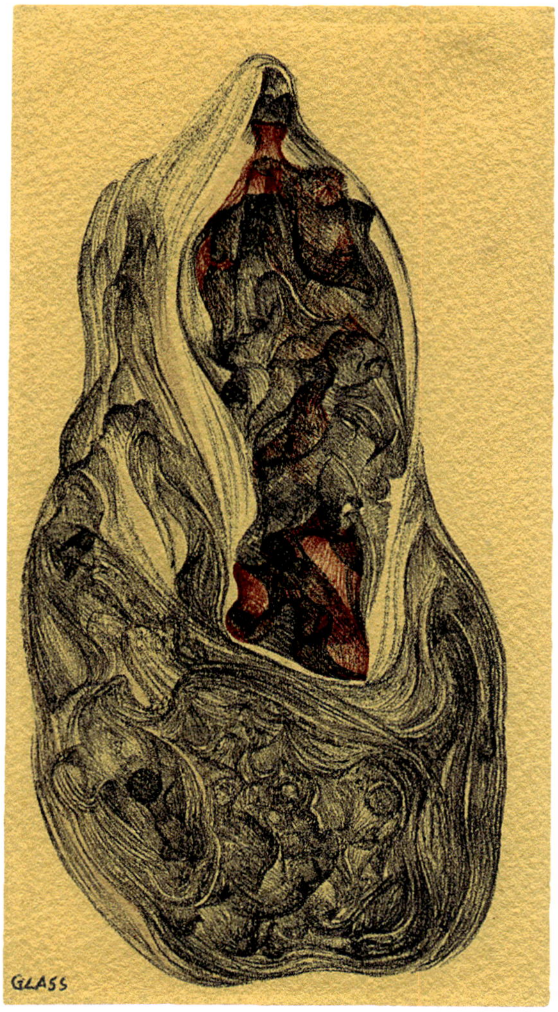

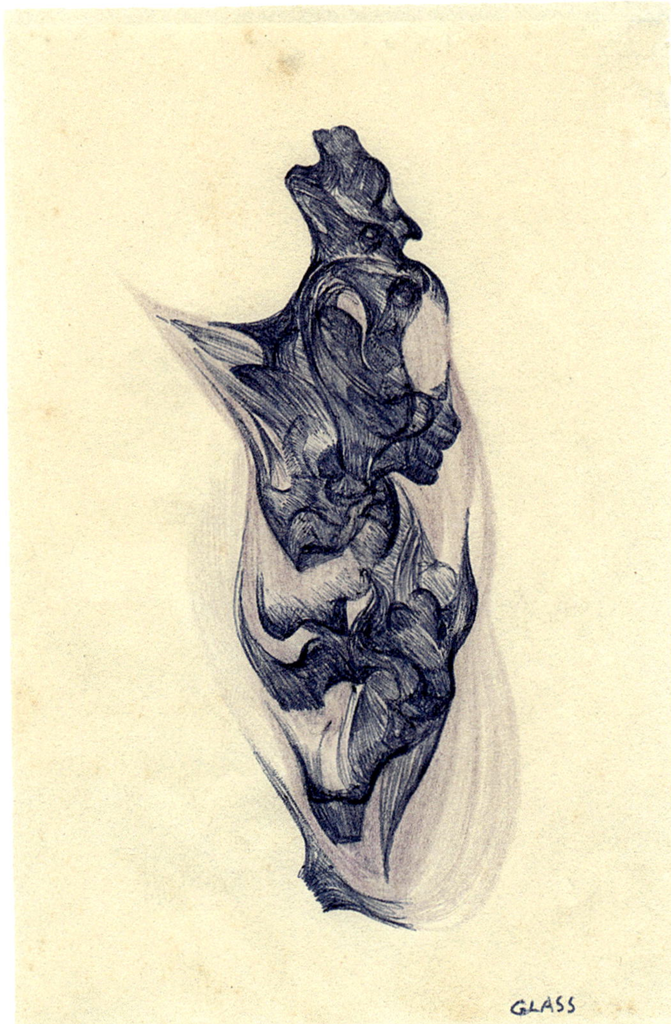

Untitled
(Galerie Le Terrain Vague period)
ca. 1954-1962
Drawing in blue and red bicolor ballpoint pen, on invitation to Mimi de Saint-Tropp restaurant on yellow corrugated paper.
12.9 x 7 cm
Artist's collection

Untitled
(Galerie Le Terrain Vague period)
ca. 1954-1962
Drawing in blue monocolor pen with lilac pencil, on paper.
13.2 x 8.6 cm
Artist's collection

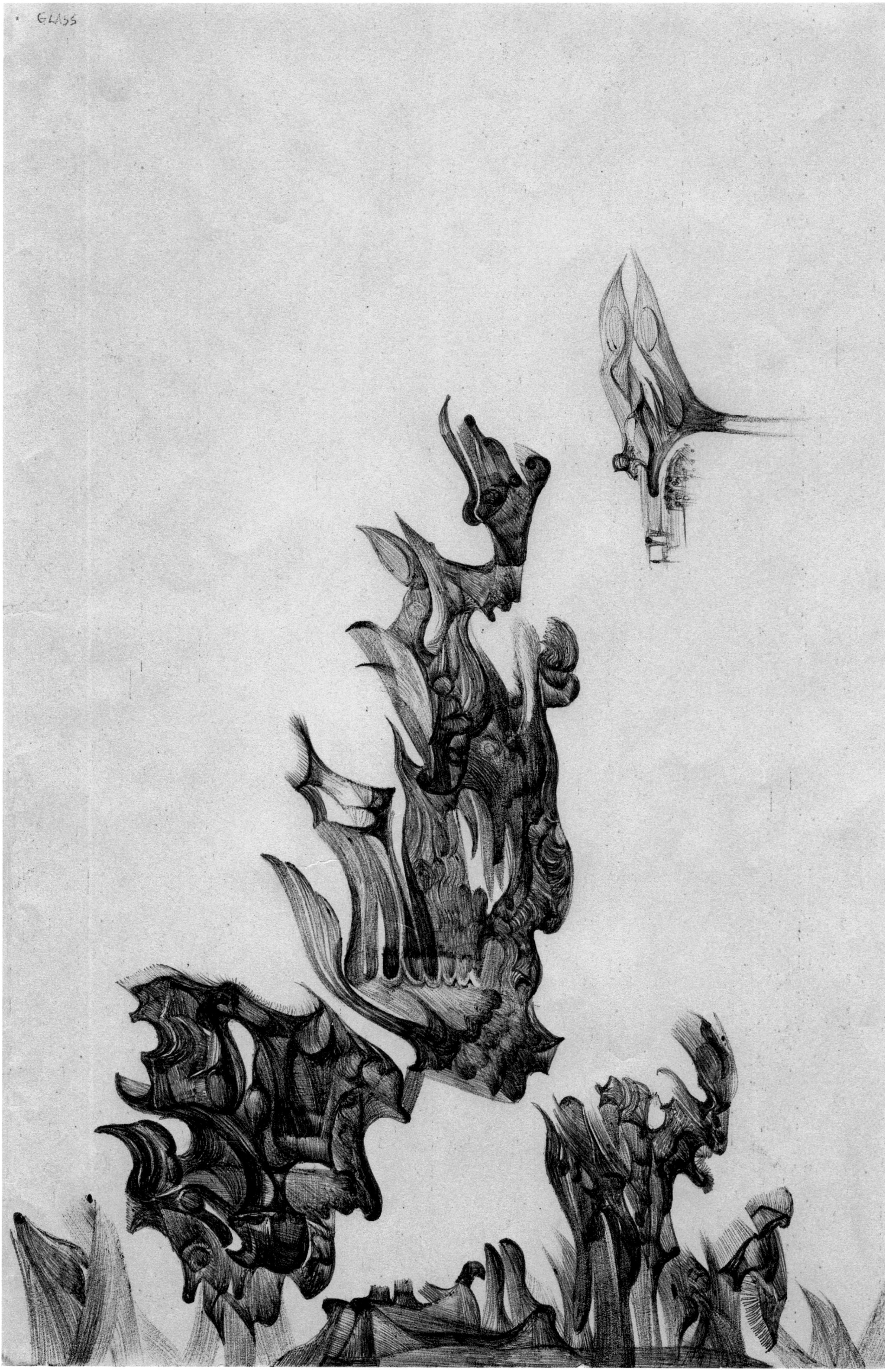
GLASS

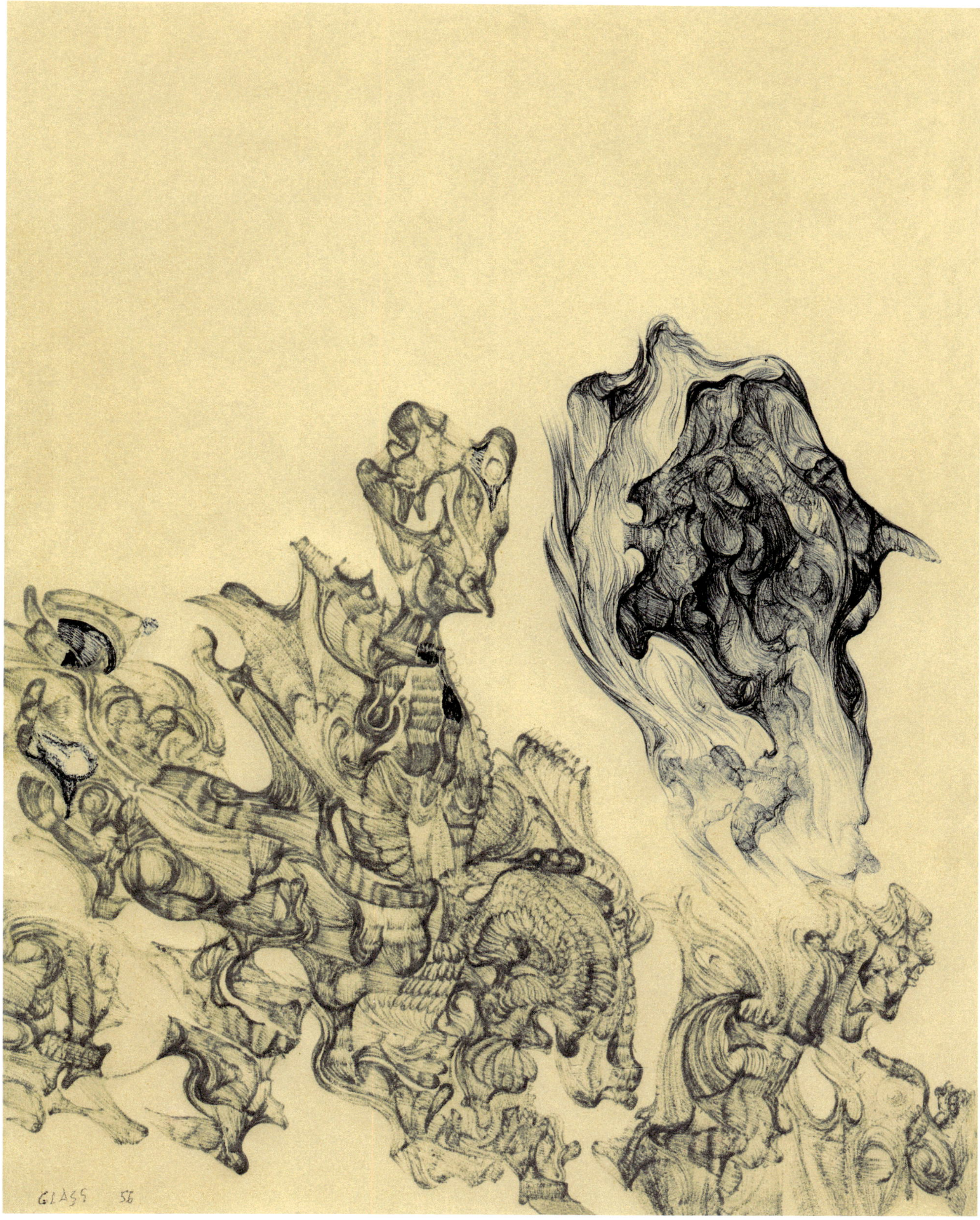

Untitled
(Galerie Le Terrain Vague period)
ca. 1954-1962
Monochrome blue ballpoint pen drawing, on paper.
26 x 17 cm
Artist's collection
Previous page

Untitled
(Galerie Le Terrain Vague period)
1956
Black and navy blue two-tone ballpoint pen drawing, on paper.
21.3 x 17 cm
Private collection

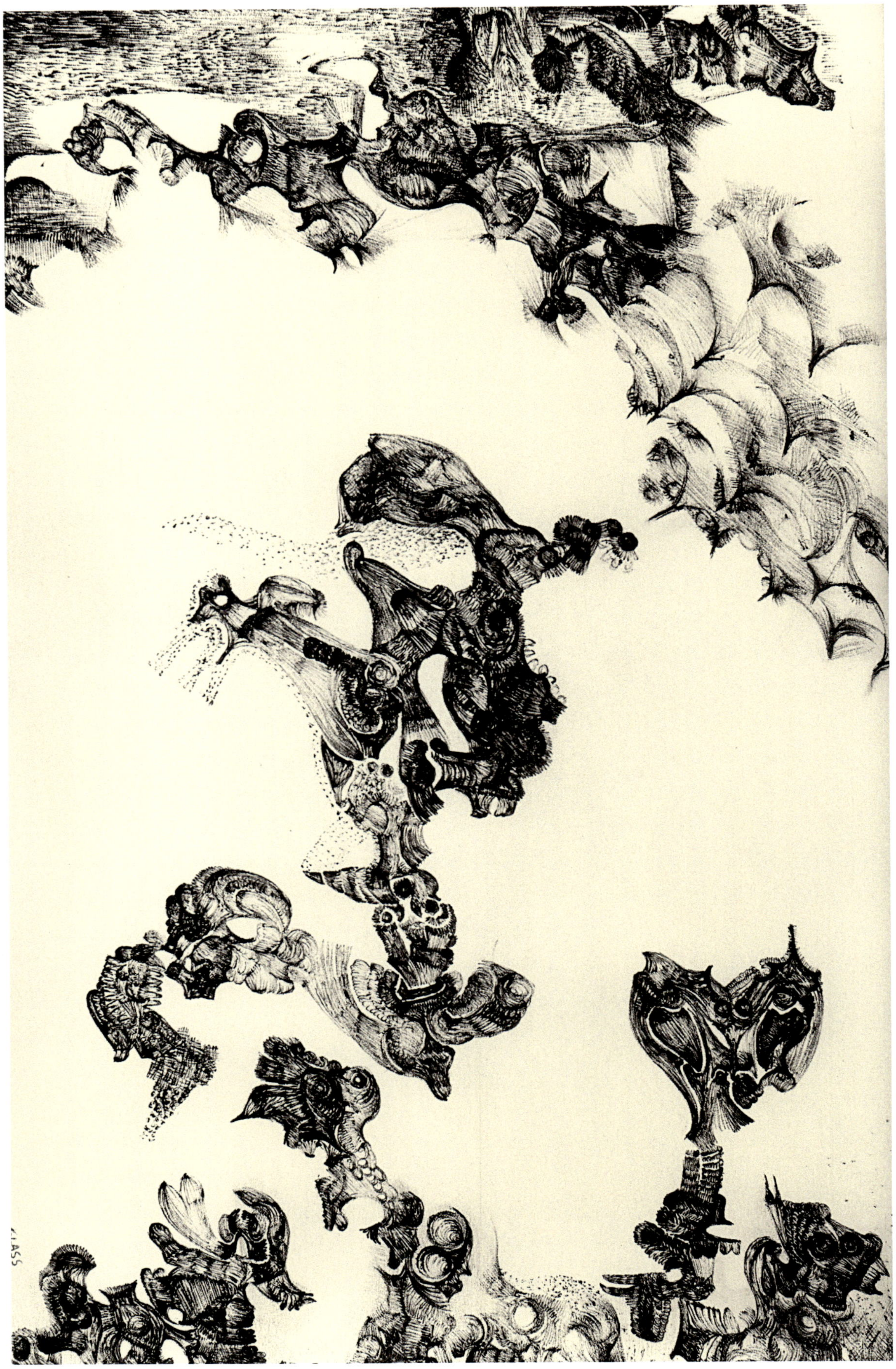

Untitled
(Galerie Le Terrain Vague period)
1957
Drawing in blue monocolor ballpoint pen, on paper.
B/W photograph of drawing,
Bicen Collection, Paris; Photo Marc Vaux archives, Centre Pompidou, Bibliothèque Kandinsky, Paris, France.
11.4 x 17 cm
Artist's collection

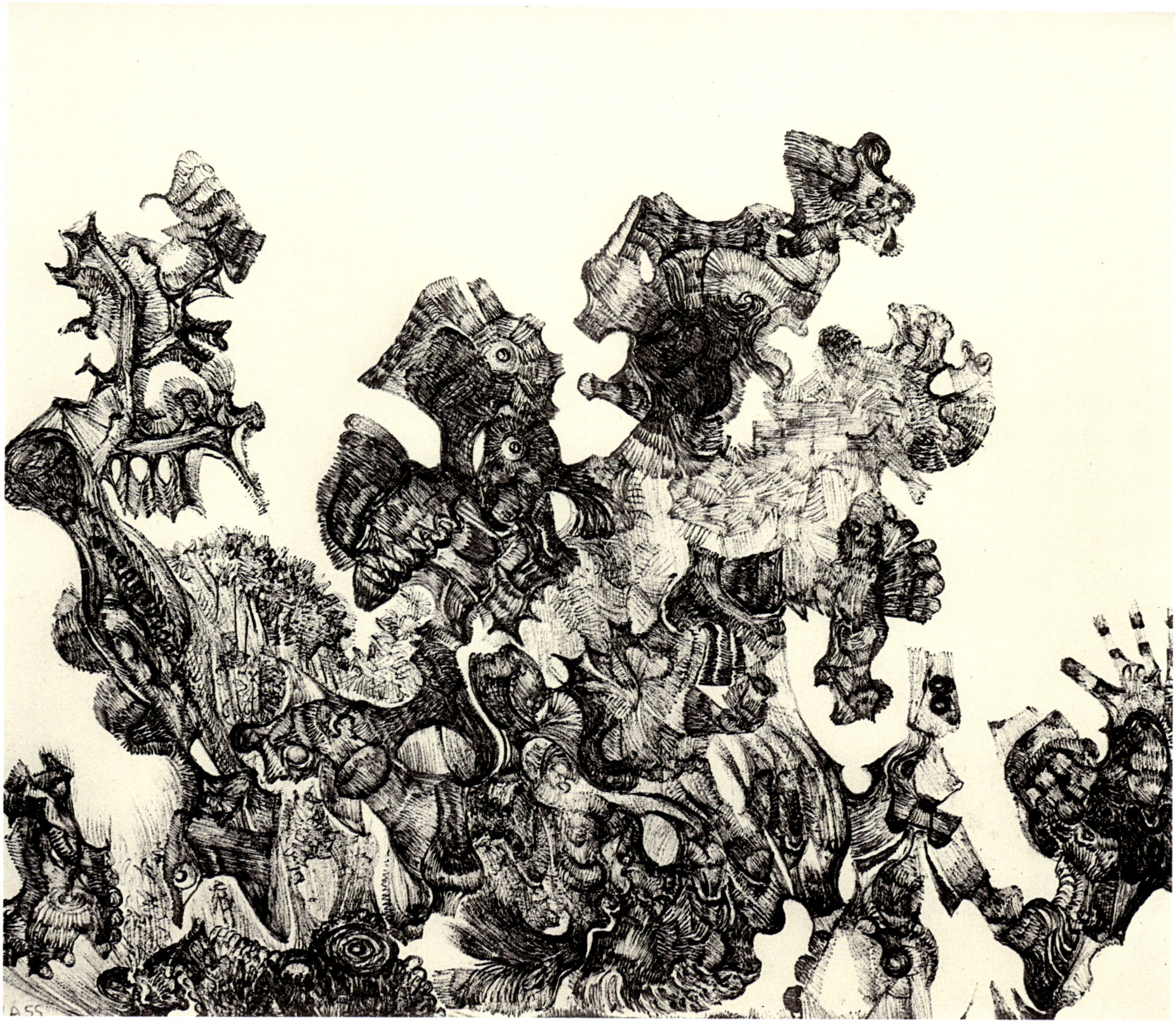

Untitled
(Galerie Le Terrain Vague period)
ca. 1950
Drawing in blue monocolor
ballpoint pen, on paper.
B/W photograph of drawing,
Gigere Collection, Canada;
Photo Marc Vaux archives,
Centre Pompidou, Bibliothèque
Kandinsky, Paris, France.
12.2 x 14.2 cm
Artist's collection

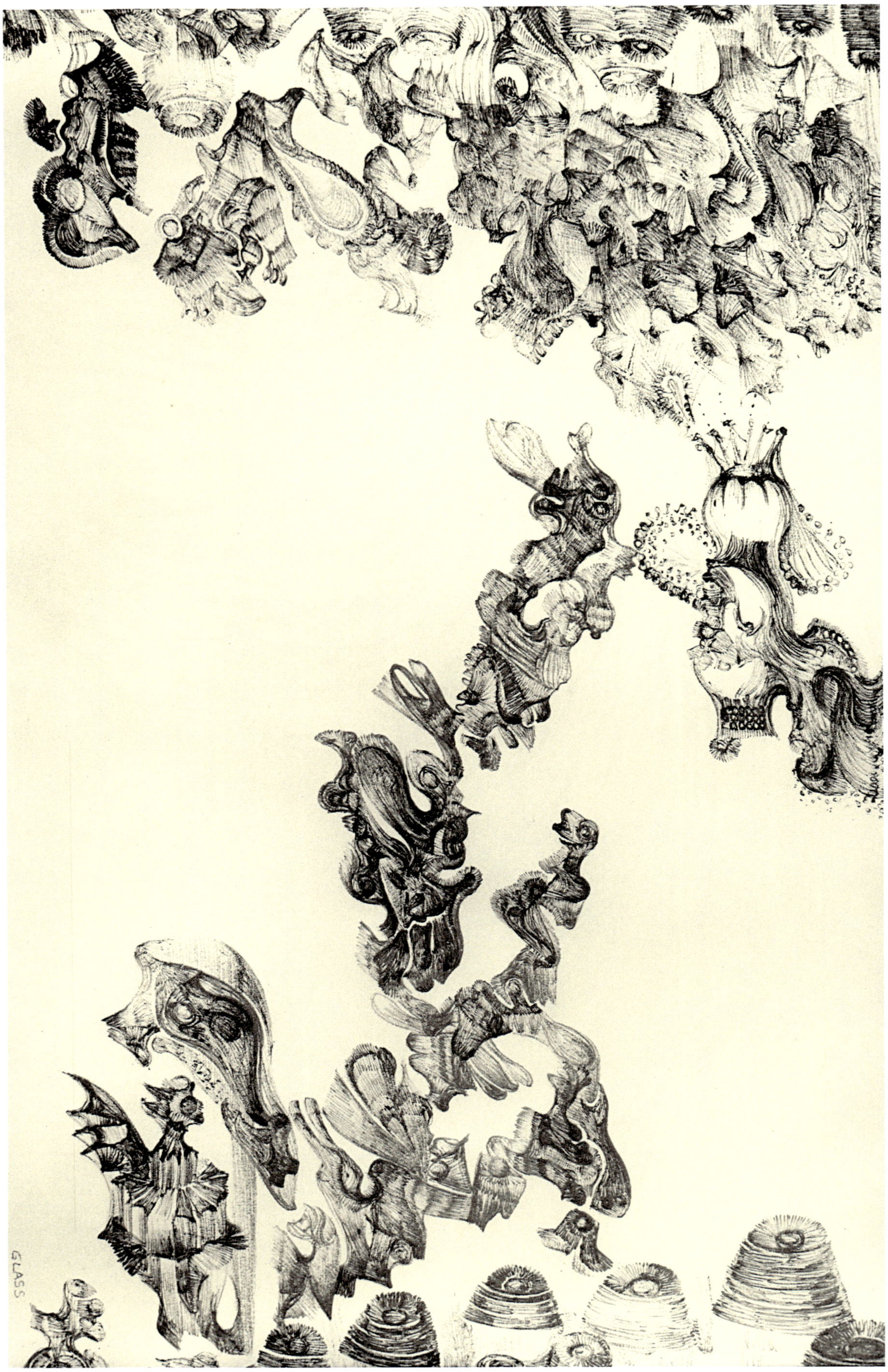

Untitled
(Galerie Le Terrain Vague period)
ca. 1954-1962
Drawing in blue and purple bicolor pen, on paper.
B/W photograph of drawing,
Unknown Collection; Photo
Marc Vaux archives, Centre
Pompidou, Bibliothèque
Kandinsky, Paris, France.
15.4 x 13.4 cm
Artist's collection

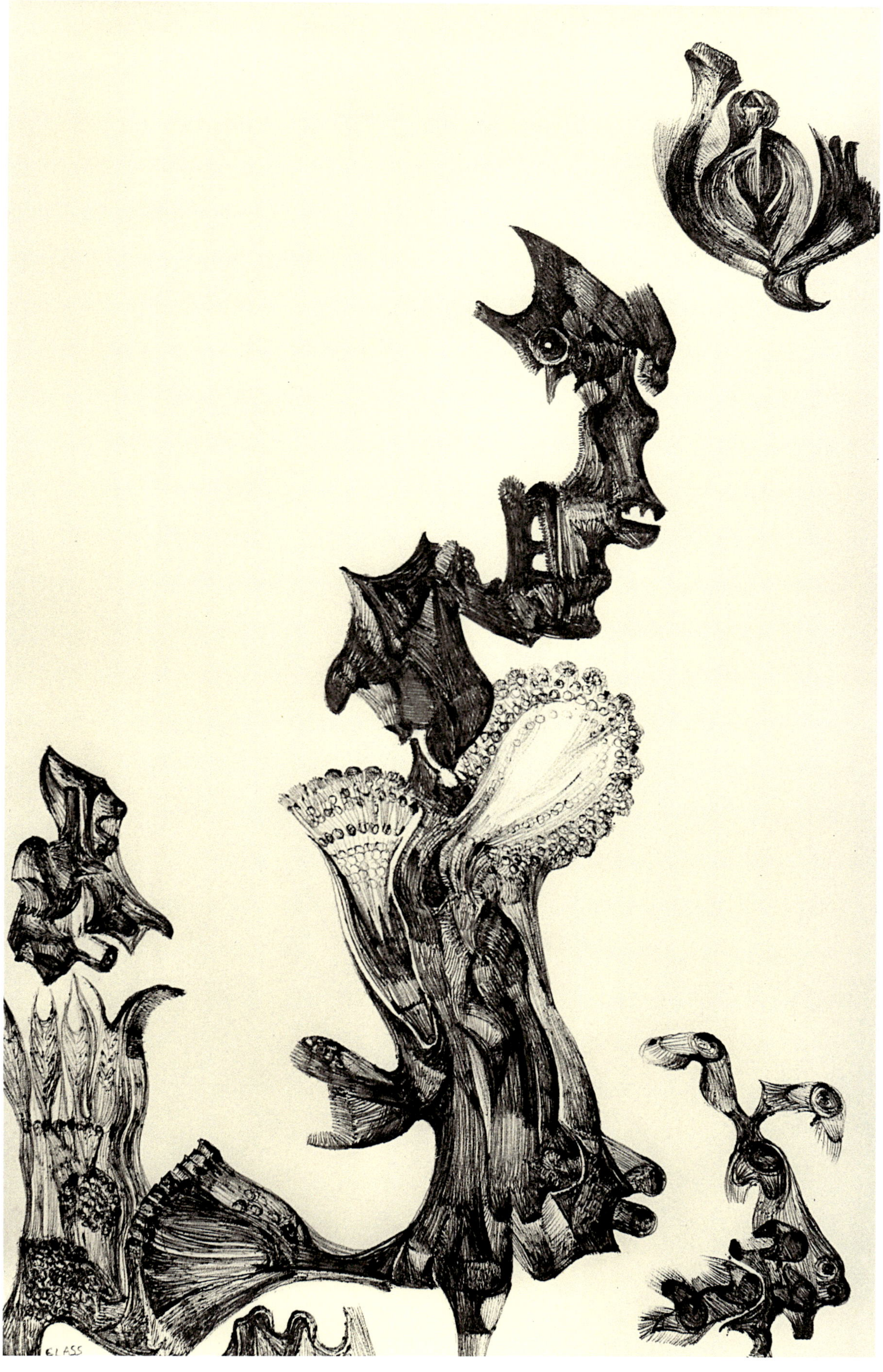

Untitled
(Galerie Le Terrain Vague period)
1957
Drawing in blue monocolor
ballpoint pen, on paper.
B/W photograph of drawing,
Private Collection, Canada;
Photo Marc Vaux archives,
Centre Pompidou, Bibliothèque
Kandinsky, Paris, France.
17.4 x 11.5 cm
Artist's collection

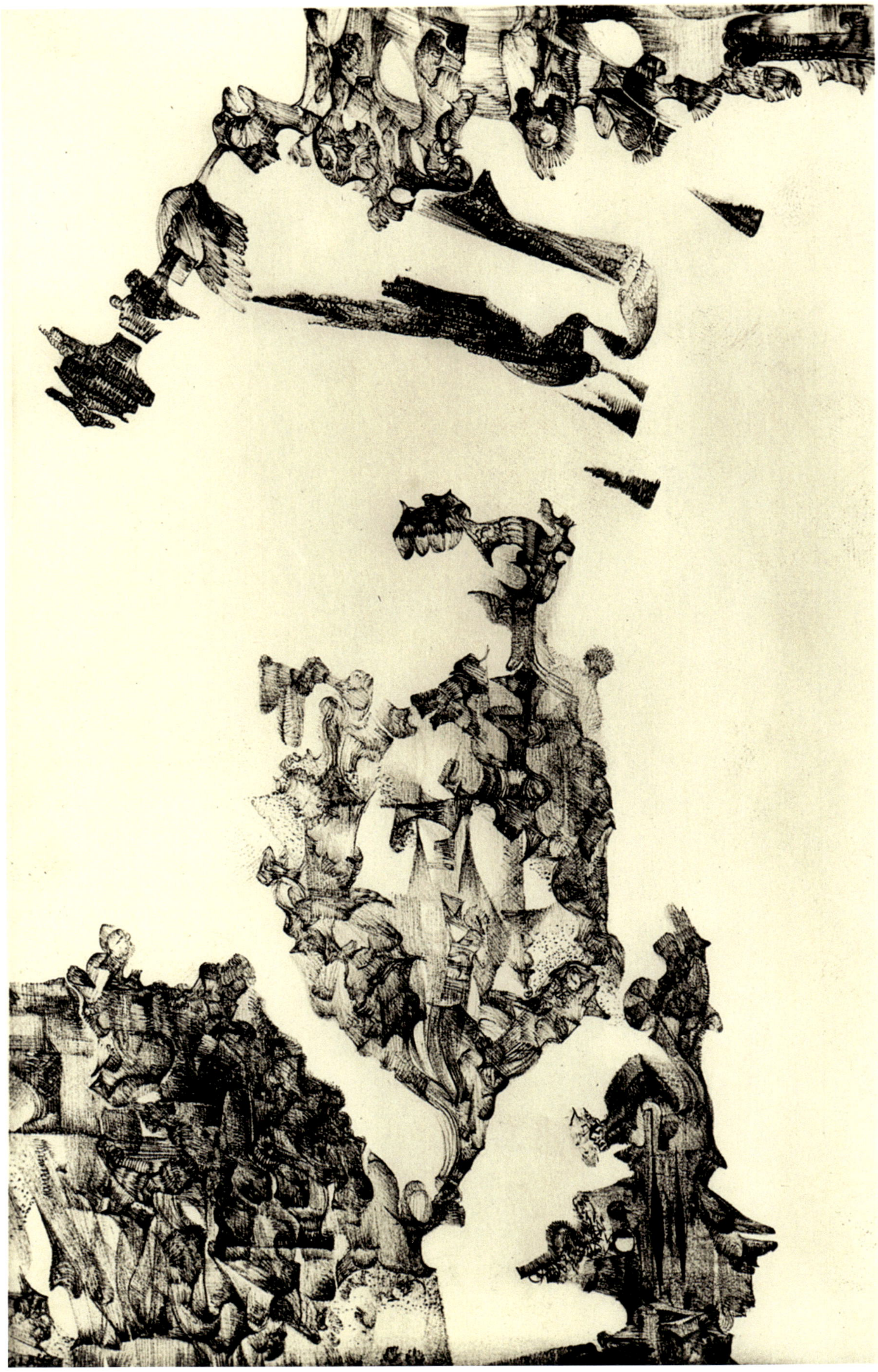

Untitled
(Galerie Le Terrain Vague period)
ca. 1950
Drawing in blue monocolor
ballpoint pen, on paper.
B/W photograph of drawing,
Lotbiniére Collection, The
Hague, Netherlands; Photo
Marc Vaux archives, Centre
Pompidou, Bibliothèque
Kandinsky, Paris, France.
17.4 x 11.5 cm
Artist's collection

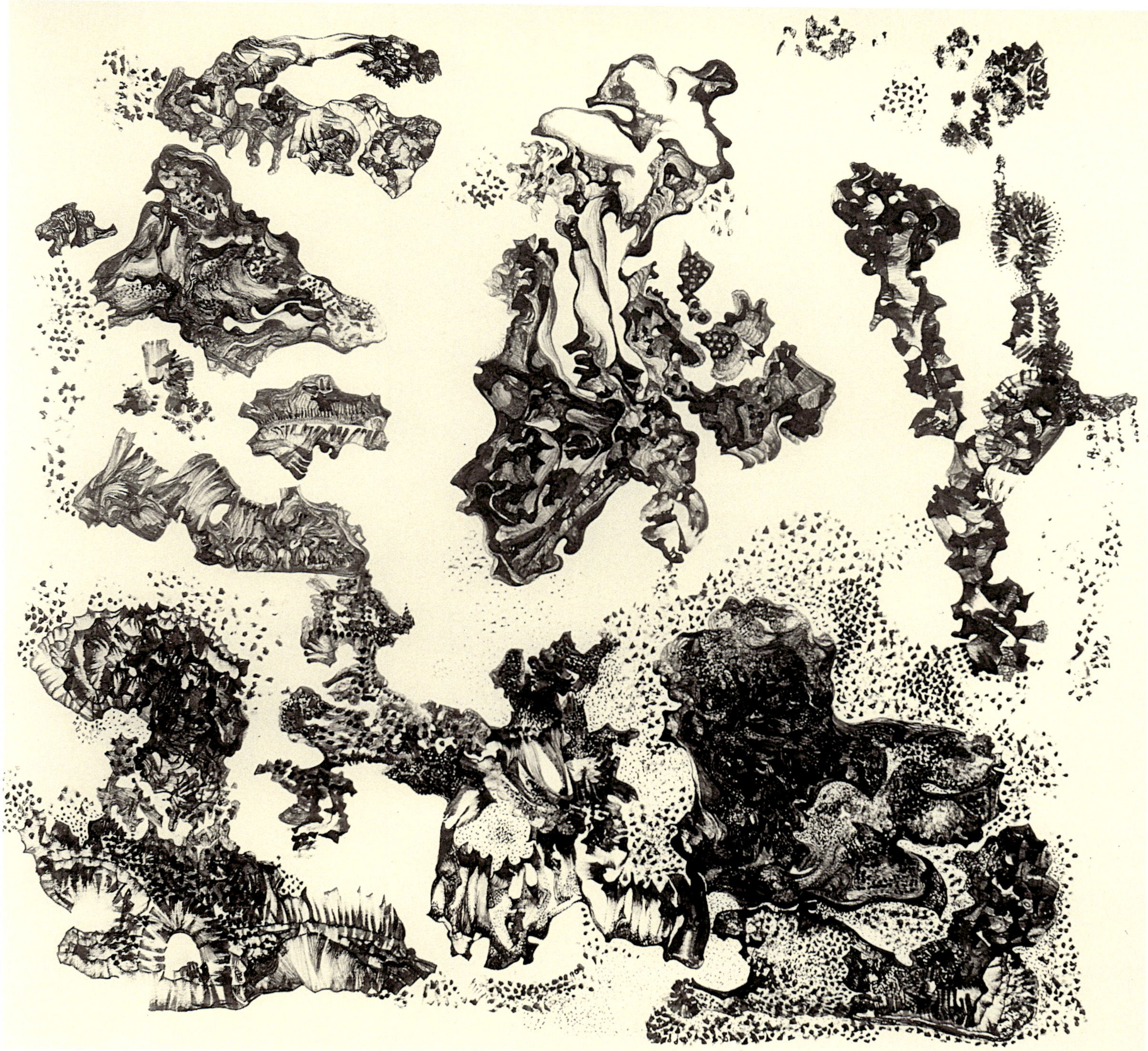

Untitled
(Galerie Le Terrain Vague period)
1957
Drawing in blue monocolor ballpoint pen, on paper.
B/W photograph of drawing,
Private Collection, Canada;
Photo Marc Vaux archives,
Centre Pompidou, Bibliothèque
Kandinsky, Paris, France.
12.3 x 13.8 cm
Artist's collection

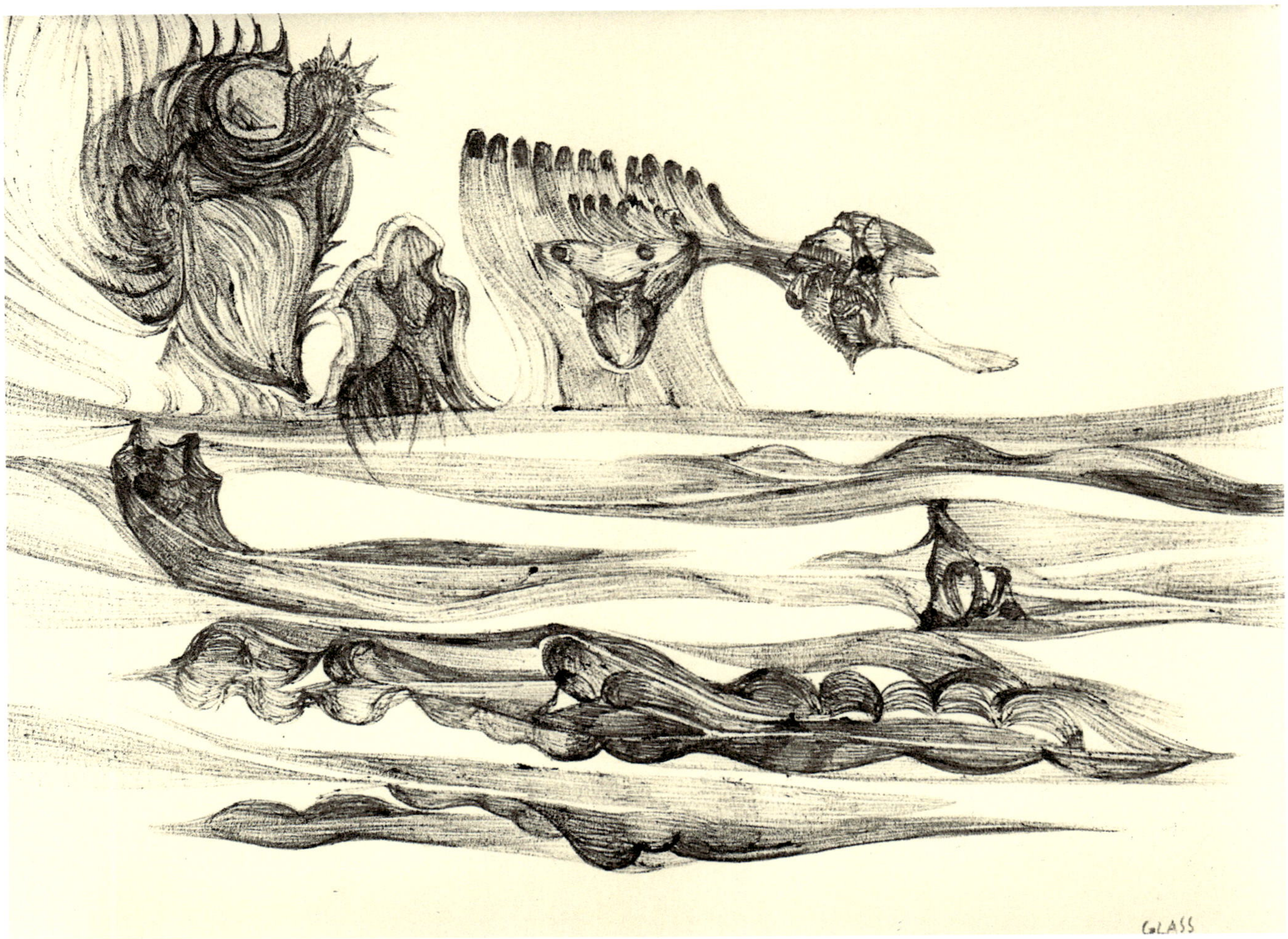

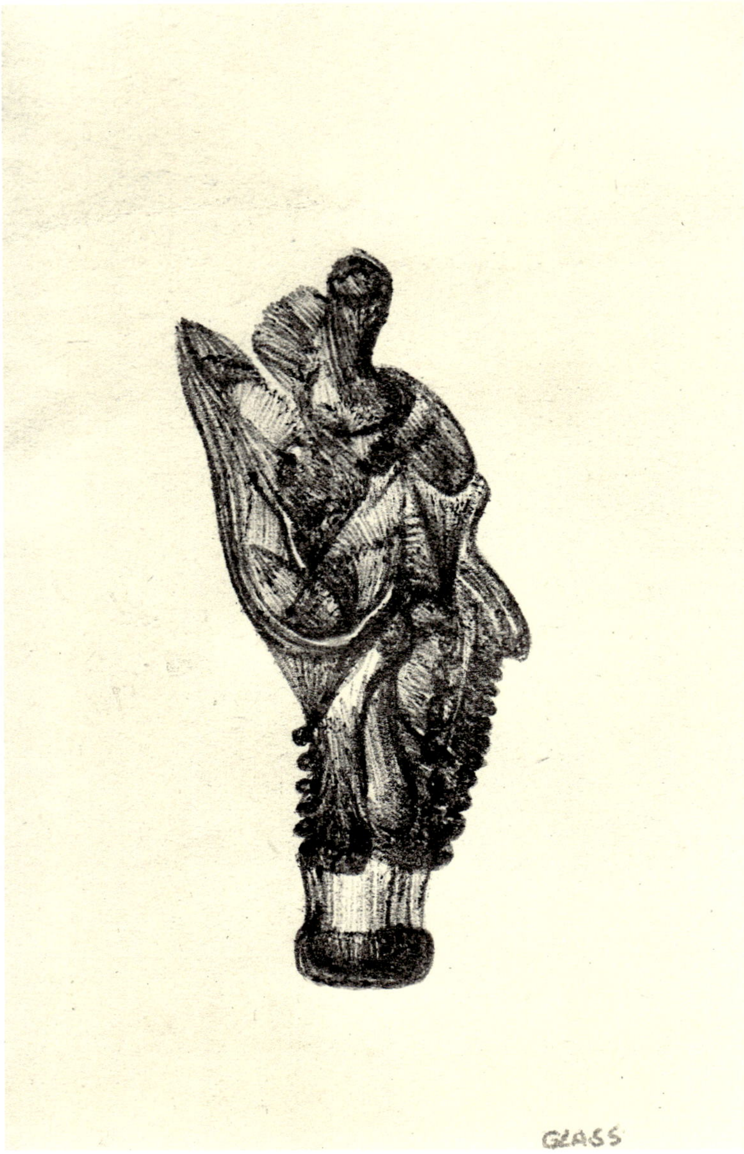

Untitled
(Galerie Le Terrain Vague period)
1956
Drawing in blue monocolor ballpoint pen, on paper.
B/W photograph of drawing.
Roberto Matta Collection, Paris;
Photo Marc Vaux archives,
Centre Pompidou, Bibliothèque Kandinsky, Paris, France.
12.2 x 16.6 cm
Artist's collection

Untitled
(Galerie Le Terrain Vague period)
1956
Drawing in blue monocolor ballpoint pen, on paper.
B/W photograph of prawing,
Jacques Stern Collection (heirs), Paris; Photo Marc Vaux archives, Centre Pompidou, Bibliothèque Kandinsky, Paris, France.
12 x 7.7 cm
Artist's collection

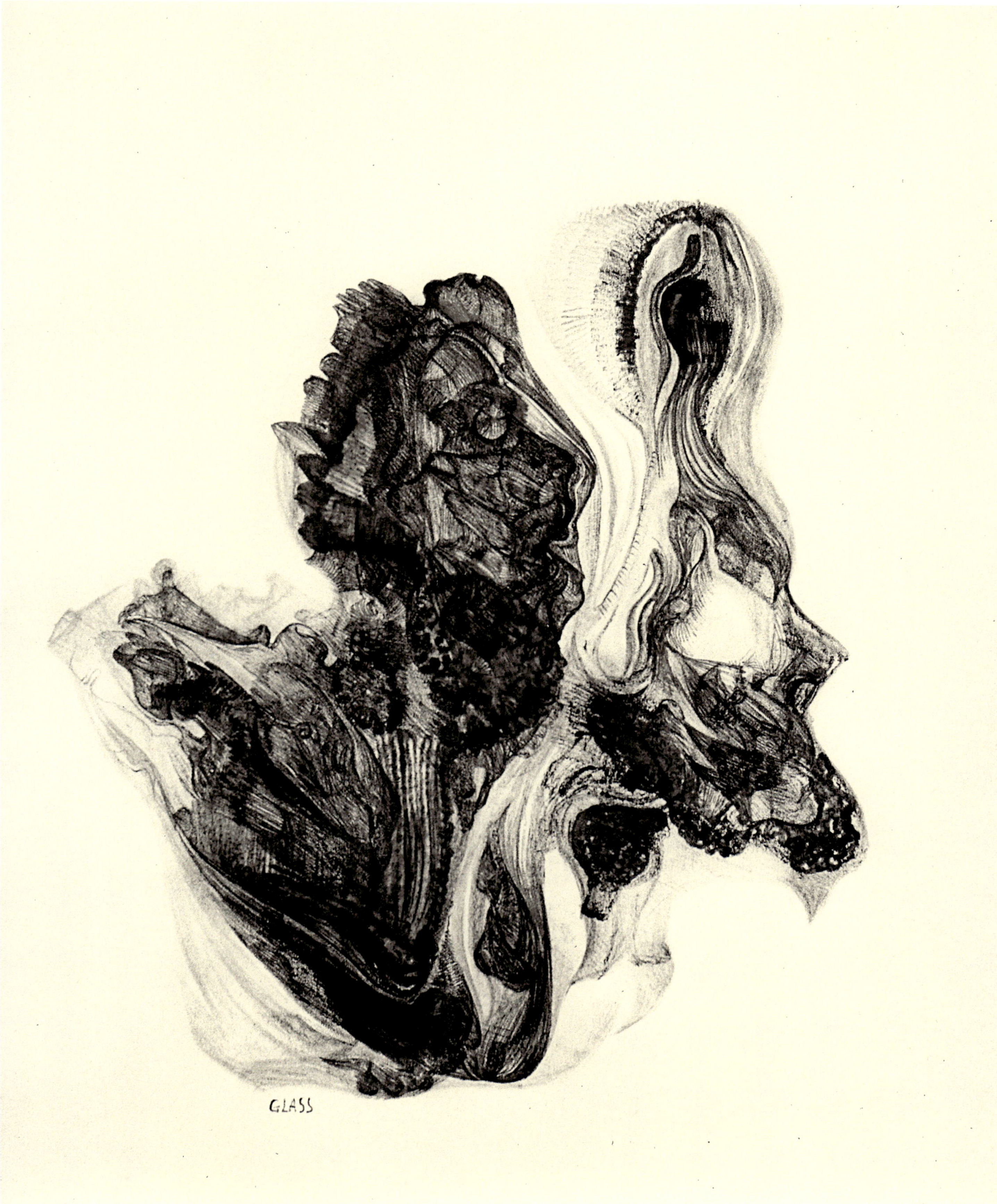

Untitled
(Galerie Le Terrain Vague period)
ca. 1950
Drawing in blue and purple bicolor pen, on paper.
B/W photograph of drawing (*ca.* 1950), Unknown Collection; Photo Marc Vaux archives, Centre Pompidou, Bibliothèque Kandinsky, Paris, France.
15.4 x 13.4 cm
Artist's collection

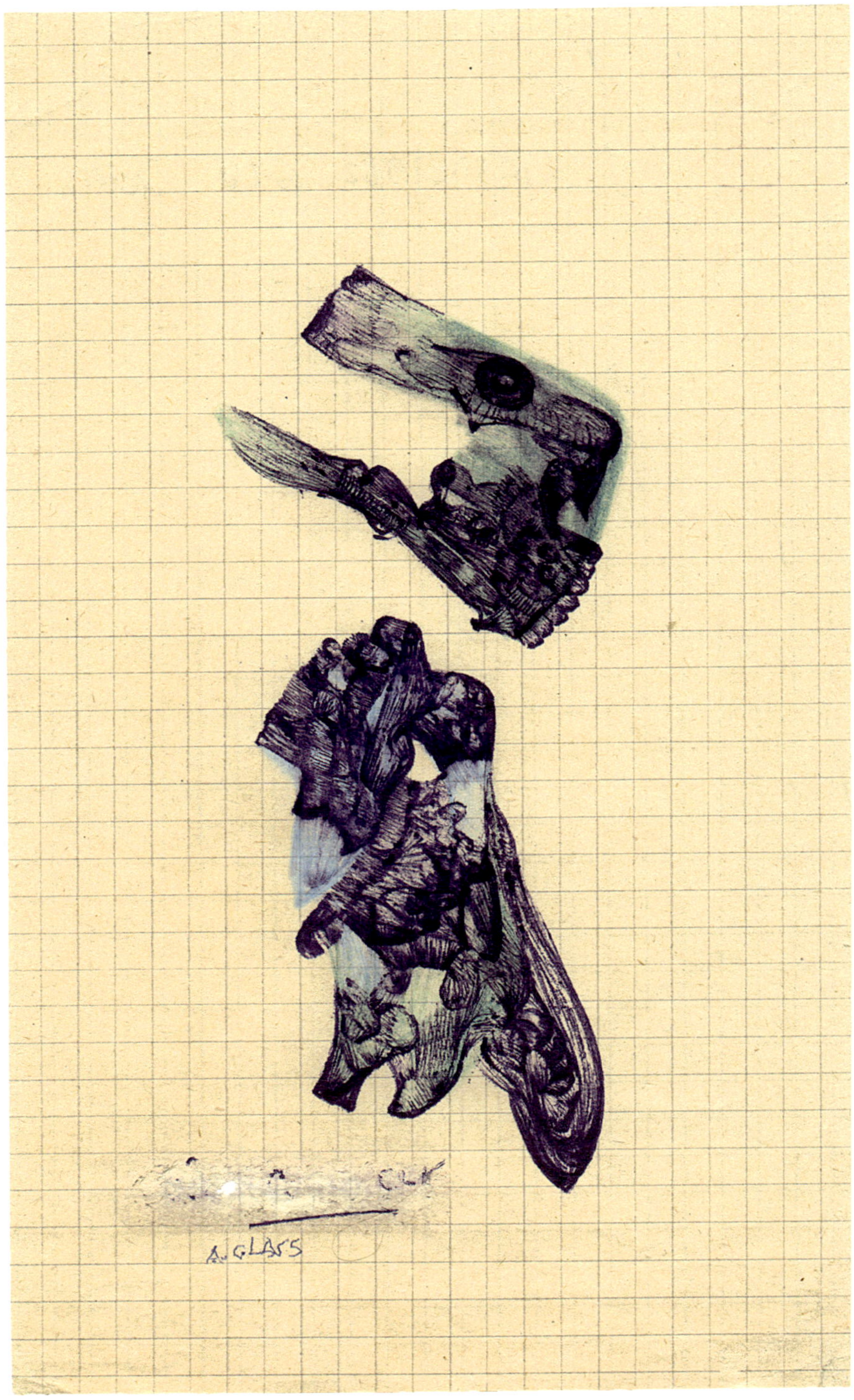
A. GLASS

CURRICULUM VITAE

Member of the *Sistema Nacional de Creadores de Arte* 1999.
Mexico City, 2023

CONTENTS:

BIOGRAPHICAL INFORMATION:

1932 Born in Montreal, Canada.

1949-1952 École des beaux-arts de Montréal (EBAM), Montreal (Alfred Pellan Studio).

1952 Scholarship awarded by the French Government.

1953 École nationale supérieure des beaux-arts (ENSBA), Paris (Maurice Jaudon Lithography Studio).

1953-1954 École du Musée de l'Homme, Paris.

1955-1962 Travels in Europe and the Middle East.

1962 First trip to Mexico.

1963 Second trip to Mexico.

1963-1964 Partners with Manuel Felguérez putting together an important collection of Mexican popular art for the *Popular Art – From Alaska to Tierra del Fuego* exhibit organized by Luis González Robles for Casa de las Américas at the Parque de las Américas in Madrid, Spain.

1967 Receives a grant from the Canada Council for the Arts.

1968-1969 Travels to India.

1999 Admitted to Mexico's Sistema Nacional de Creadores de Arte del Fondo Nacional para la Cultura y las Artes [National System of Art Creators under the National Endowment for Culture and the Arts]

2017 Awarded the 2017 Bellas Artes Medal for his exceptional artistic output, Mexico.

2022 Currently lives and works in Mexico City.

2023 Dies on January 16 at his home, surrounded by his friends, Mexico City.

SOLO EXHIBITIONS:

1958 Galerie Le Terrain Vague, Paris, organized by André Breton and Bejamin Péret.

1965 Galerie du Siècle, Montreal, Canada.

1967 Galería Antonio Souza, Mexico City, "Los relicarios".

1972 Galería Pecanins, Mexico City.

1972 Galerie de Montréal, Montreal, Canada.

1976 Museo de Arte Moderno, Mexico City.

1977 Galerie Gilles Corbeil, Montreal, Canada.

1982 Galería Pecanins, Mexico City.

1985 Galerie du Grand Théâtre, Quebec, Canada.

1991 Claude Bernard Gallery, New York City, U.S.

1997 Claude Bernard Gallery, International Art Fair, Chicago, U.S.

2001 Galerie 1900-2000, Paris, France, September 12 – October 17

2002 Art Brussels, Belgium.

2002 Galerie Claude Bernard, Paris, France, May.

Untitled
(Galerie Le Terrain Vague period)
ca. 1954-1962
Drawing in blue monocolor pen, with sky blue and green pencil, on squared paper.
18.8 x 11.3 cm
Artist's collection
Previous page

2003 Galería López Quiroga, Mexico City, May and June.

2003 Museo de Arte Contemporáneo de Oaxaca (MACO), Oaxaca, Mexico. October 18 – November 28.

2005 *La unidad del múltiple*, 20 parchment-lined binders containing 20 prints, drypoint on copper, a poem by Leonora Carrington, and presentation of the book *La unidad del múltiple* plus a series of boxes. Galería López Quiroga, Mexico City. August 20 – September 17.

2007 *Gabinete surrealista,* Galería Michel Soskine Inc., Madrid, Spain. May 31 – July 14.

2008 *Zurcidos invisibles. Construcciones y pinturas de Alan Glass* (1960 – 2008), Museo de Arte Moderno, Mexico City, November 27, 2008 – April 12, 2009.

2013 Galería López Quiroga, Mexico City. May 16 – July 6.

2022 *Estampillas para viajar,* Museo de Filatelia de Oaxaca, April – June.

2022 *Dessins automatiques, Paris 1954/1962*, Centre du Vieux Presbytère, Saint Bruno de Montarville, Canada, September 4 – October 9.

GROUP EXHIBITIONS:

1964 *The Box Show,* Byron Gallery, New York City, U.S.

1967 *Arte fantástico y surrealismo,* Galería Aristos, Mexico City.

1967 *Arte fantástico y surrealismo,* Museo de Arte Moderno, Mexico City.

1970 *Homenaje a los pintores que venidos de otras latitudes se arraigaron en México,* Museo de Arte Moderno, Mexico City.

1972 *Watercolors and Graphics*, Museum of Fine Arts, Saint Petersburg, Florida, Miami, U.S.

1974 *En presencia viva de Wolfgang Paalen*, Museo Carrillo Gil, Mexico City.

1975 *15 Cajas*, Galería Pecanins, Mexico City.

1976 *Juegos,* Galería Pecanins, Mexico City.

1977 *Micro Bienal,* Galería Mer Kup, Mexico City.

1978 *Alcoholismo y Tabaquismo*, Galería La Chinche. Mexico City.

1979 *Sculpture contemporaire canadienne,* Centre Saidye Bronfman, Montreal, Canada.

1979 Musée d'Art de St-Laurent, Montreal, Canada.

1979 *Le Dessin Surréealiste au Québec*, Musée d'Art Contemporain, Montreal, Canada.

1979 *La Corbata Catrina*, Galería La Chinche. Mexico City.

1979 *Violines y Zeppelines*, Galería La Chinche. Mexico City.

1985 *Imágenes en Cajas*, Museo Rufino Tamayo, Mexico City, July 18 – September 8.

1985 *El árbol,* Galería Pecanins, Mexico City, September 12.

1986 *Los surrealistas en México,* Museo Nacional de Arte, Mexico City.

1987 *La Caja,* Galería Sloane Racotta, Mexico City.

1988 *Utensilios,* Galería Juan Martín, Mexico City

1990 *Micro Bienal,* Galería Mer Kup, Mexico City.

1993 *Lateinamerika und der Surrealimus,* Kunstmuseum Bochum, Germany.

1993 *Objeto-Sujeto*, Museo Regional Alóndiga de Granaditas, Guanajuato, Mexico.

1994 Museo de Arte Contemporáneo de Monterrey, MARCO, Monterrey, Mexico.

1997 *Diálogos insólitos,* Museo de Arte Moderno, Mexico City.

1999 *Alegría de vivir,* Museo José Luis Cuevas, Mexico City.

1999 *Gatos,* Museo Galería Pedro Friedeberg, San Miguel de Allende, Mexico.

2000 *De mi colección – 100 artistas pertenecientes al Sistema Nacional de Creadores de Arte*. Consejo Nacional para la Cultura y las Artes, Mexico City.

2000 *De la academia al objeto,* Palacio de Bellas Artes, Mexico City.

2000 *Homenaje al Maestro Fernando Gamboa,* Fondo Cultural Carmen, San Ángel, Mexico City.

2001 Y a cada quien con su caja de miel, XVII Festival del Centro Histórico, Casa de la primera imprenta de América, Mexico City, March – April.

2001 *Bitácora y obra,* Travelling exhibition throughout Mexico. May 2001 – July 2002.

2001 *Tramas y ensamblaje*, Museo de Arte Contemporáneo de Oaxaca, MACO, Oaxaca, Mexico. October 5 – December 3.

2003 *Cicatrizada de arte la hoja*, Consejo Nacional para la Cultura y las Artes, Travelling exhibition, Mexico. May 9, 2003 – June 11, 2004.

2004 *Collage, des années 50 à nos jours*. Galerie 1900-2000, Paris, France. October 12 – 30.

2004 *Archipiélagos gráficos*. Graphic binder commemorating the 30th anniversary of the Universidad Autónoma Metropolitana, Mexico City. November.

2004-2006 *Papalotes: Ojos del cielo y ojos de papel volando,* Consejo Nacional para la Cultura y las Artes, Travelling exhibition, Mexico.

2005 ARCO Madrid, Spain, Galerie 1900-2000.

2005 *Wonderboxland; cornelliana*, Galería Utopía Parkway, Madrid. June 10 – July 22.

2006 ARCO Madrid, Spain, Galerie 1900-2000.

2006 Cow Parade, Mexico City.

2007 *El ojo del tiempo a través del surrealismo*, Galería Oscar Román, Mexico City. May 16 – June 8.

2007 *La era de la discrepancia*. Arte y cultura visual en México 1968 – 1997, Museo Universitario de Ciencias y Arte, Universidad Nacional Autónoma de México, MUCA Campus, Mexico City. March – August.

2007 Taller de Gráfica Bordes, *Artistas en México,* Museo de Arte Moderno, Mexico City.

2009 *Paréntesis*, Museo de Arte Contemporáneo de Oaxaca, MACO, Oaxaca, Mexico. April.

2011 Galería Michel Soskine, Madrid. January – April.

2011 *Caras y máscaras: Identidad primitiva y contemporánea*, Galería Michel Soskine, Madrid, Spain. December 2011 – January 2012.

2012 Galería Michel Soskine, Madrid. June – July.

2013 *El objeto contenido y reivindicado*. Museo de Arte de la Secretaría de Hacienda y Crédito Público, Mexico City. Dirección General de Promoción Cultural y Acervo Patrimonial, Ciudad de México, April 11 – June 9.

KEY:
(α) *Article*
(β) *Catalog*
(λ) *Book*
(ω) *Film, video, interview*

2013 *Artistas en México*, Museo de Arte Moderno, Mexico City, November 23.

2016 *Variaciones sobre tema mexicano*, Torre Iberdrola, Bilbao, Spain. April to July.

2016 FIAC Grand Palais-Paris, Galerie 1900-2000, France. October.

2017 *Horizontes*, a tribute and celebration of the career of seven important artists, eMe Espacio de Arte, Mexico City. May 11 – July 11.

2017 *Imagerie surréaliste des Amériques*, Galerie 1900-2000, Paris, France. September 13 – October 27.

2022 *Only the wonderful is beautiful. Surrealism in dialogue*, Masterpieces from Museum Boijmans Van Beuningen, Museo del Palacio de Bellas Artes, Mexico City. May 31 – September 19.

BIBLIOGRAPHY:

LE TERRAIN VAGUE – EXHIBITION CATALOG β
Paris, France. Text by Alejandro Jodorowsky, January 8 to 24, 1958.

UN JEUNE ARTISTE CANADIEN À PARIS α
Jean-V. Dufresne, La Presse Montréal, January 1958.

ALAIN GLASS, PORTIER POUR VIVRE α
Expose des desseins Surrealistes Jean Gachon, *La Presse* (Paris) 1958.

PANDERMA REVUE DE LA FIN DU MONDE α
Basel, Switzerland, 1958.

GLASS: DE FOLICHONNES ET INQUIETANTES BOÎTES α
Claude Jasmin, *La Presse Montréal*, May 1965.

ALAN GLASS, À LA GALERIE DU SIÈCLE. α
Laurent Lamy, *Le Devoir* (Montreal), May 1965.

L'ART EN BOÎTE α
Guy Fournier
Perspectives (Montreal), No. 19, May 8, 1965.

THE BOX SHOW α – Press Release
Brian O'Doherty, Byron Gallery, Inc. New York, February 2, 1965.

ART NOTES α
Grace Glueck
The New York Times,
Sunday, February 2, 1965.

LA DE ALAN GLASS α
"Exposiciones", Margarita Nelken, Diorama de la Cultura (supplement), *Excélsior* (Mexico), Saturday, February 11, 1967.

PROPÓSITOS Y RELICARIOS α
Enrique F. Gual. De la cultura *Excélsior* (Mexico), Sunday, February 12, 1967.

ALAN GLASS, CREADOR DE LO INSÓLITO α
Alfonso de Neuvillatte, México en la Cultura (supplement), *Novedades* (Mexico), April 16, 1967.

EL ROMANTICISMO DE ALAN GLASS α
Juan García Ponce, *Siempre*! (Mexico), February 1967.

ALAN GLASS: UNE ŒUVRE INSOLITE α
Michelle Lasnier, Vie des arts (Montreal), No. 40, 1965, pp. 40-45.

http://www.erudit.org/culture/va1081917/va1201508/58416ac.pdf.

ALEJANDRO JODOROWSKY HABLA DE ALAN GLASS α
Ovaciones (Mexico City), Sunday, April 9, 1967.

INCURSION AU PAYS DES MINIATURES PERSANES, AVEC ALAN GLASS, QUI EXPOSE À LA GALERIE D'ANTONIO SOUZA α
Stefane Corbett, *Le Journal français* (Mexico), Tuesday, January 31, 1967

GLASS, EL ORDEN POÉTICO, α
Moisés de Guevara, El Heraldo Cultural (supplement), No. 74, *El Heraldo de México* (Mexico), Sunday, April 9, 1967.

ALAN GLASS, LA POESÍA DE LOS OBJETOS α
Moisés Ladrón de Guevara 1967.

EXPOSICIÓN DE ALAN GLASS α
Esperanza Z. de Brault, Arte y Cultura, *El Sol de México* (Mexico), January 31, 1967.

SURREALISMO Y ARTE FANTÁSTICO EN MÉXICO λ
Ida Rodríguez Prampolini, UNAM Instituto de Investigaciones Estéticas (Mexico), Alan Glass pp. 108-109 III 132 –133 – 133 – 134 – 135 XXII 1967.

"ALAN GLASS" LA APARICIÓN DE LO INVISIBLE λ
Juan García Ponce.
Alan Glass, pp. 175-178
Mexico City: Siglo Veintiuno Editores, S.A., 1968,

GALERÍA PECANINS Exhibition catalog β
Text by Leonora Carrington, Mexico, 1972.

AT THE GALLERIES – ALAN GLASS α
Michael White, *The Gazette* (Montreal), 1972.

ALAN GLASS: SOUS LE SIGNE DE L'ALLIANCE α
Gaetan Ouellet. *Vie des arts* (Montreal), No. 68, Fall 1972, pp. 70-71.

LOS MITOS Y EL MUNDO MÍTICO DE ALAN GLASS α
Alfonso de Neuvillate. *El Heraldo de México* (Mexico), Thursday, February 24, 1972.

LA PRÉSENCE DU MALIN α
Christian Allègre.
Le Devoir (Montreal), Saturday, May 6,1972.

LES BOÎTES À SURPRISE D'ALAN GLASS α
Jacques de Roussan. *Perspectives* (Montreal), May 6, 1972.

40 OBRAS RECIENTES ALAN GLASS ARTISTA CANADIENSE – Exhibition catalog β
Texts by Gloria F. Orenstein and Fernando Gamboa
Museo de Arte Moderno, Mexico City, November – December 1976.

PORTRAIT BAROQUE α
Pierre de Ligny Boudreau. *Vie des arts* (Montreal), Vol. 21, No. 84, Fall 1976, pp. 32-37.

ESTUVE AUSENTE, ESTOY DE REGRESO DÓNDE? – ABRIR β
Galería Pecanins exhibition, Wednesday, June 30, 1982.

LAS CAJAS PARADÓJICAS DE ALAN GLASS α
Leila Driben. "En los ochenta todo entró en el museo," *Uno Más Uno* (Mexico), Saturday, July 3, 1982.

IMÁGENES EN CAJAS – Exhibition catalog β
Museo Rufino Tamayo, Mexico City, July 18 – September 8, 1985.

EL ARTE DE HACER LO INVISIBLE, PATENTE LO SOÑADO Y RITUAL LO COTIDIANO α
Graciela Kartofel. *Vogue* (Mexico), No. 29, October 1982.

DICTIONNAIRE INTERNACIONAL DE SURREALISME α
Presses Universitaires de France 1982.
https://www.amazon.fr/DICTIONNAIRE-GENERAL-SURREALISME-ENVIRONS-1982/dp/B00GHQZMS6

ALAN GLASS OBJETS – VITRINE ET AQUARELLES – Exposition β ?
Galerie du Grand Théâtre de Québec, Quebec. March 31, 1985.

MEXICAN MONUMENTS, STRANGE ENCOUNTERS α
Paolo Gori.
New York: Abbeville Press, 1989, p. 34.

STUDIO VOICE
Masayo Nonaka, No. 178, Tokyo, 1990.

KEY:
(α) *Article*
(β) *Catalog*
(λ) *Book*
(ω) *Film, video, interview*

ALAN GLASS – Exhibition catalog β
Texts by Roland Giguère and Leonora Carrington. Claude Bernard Gallery, New York, Fall 1991.

FIELD NOTES ON A MIGRATORY CANADIAN α
Linda Genereaux. *Canadian Art*, Fall 1992.

LAS MIGAJAS Y LOS PÁJAROS. λ
Jorge Lobillo. Poem: "Informe de la casa," dedicated to Alan Glass. Mexico: Editorial Tierra Adentro, 1992, p. 55.

KATI HORNA: RECUERDO DE UNA OBRA β
Emma Cecilia García Krinsky. Mexico: CENIDIAP-INBA, 1995.

PARTICIPARÁ YOKO ONO EN LA COLECTIVA DE ARTE OBJETO DEL MAM λ
Merry MacMasters. Cultura, *La Jornada* (Mexico), May 13, 1997.

ALAN GLASS Y EL GUANTE DE BRONCE, β
Gloria F. Orenstein. Translated by Annunziata Rossi. *La Jornada Semanal* (Mexico), Sunday, October 14, 2001.

LETTRES ET IDEES α
Le Calepin de Pierre de Boisdeffre
Iris Espace No. 63, Alan Glass, Galerie 1900-2000, Paris, October 2001

LA GAZETTE DROUOT α
Lydia Harambourg. "De musées en galeries," Alan Glass – Galerie 1900-2000, Paris, October 5, 2001.

BALAD DANS LE VIÉME – FABIENNE FULCHERI α
Le journal des arts
Alan Glass at the Galerie 1900-2000, FIAC 2001.
Le quotidien No. 6, 15, Paris, October 2001.

LOS VISITANTES FUGACES α
"México en el surrealismo," *Artes de México* (Mexico), No. 63, 2003, p. 78.

LA TRANSFUSIÓN CREATIVA α
"México en el surrealismo," Artes de México (Mexico), No. 74, 2003, pp. 1 and 3.
Supplement pp. 6, 7, 8, 9, 10, 11, 12, 13.

LAS JAULAS DEL TIEMPO, LAS CAJAS DE ALAN GLASS, POR ALBERTO BLANCO β
Alberto Blanco. Galería López Quiroga catalog, Mexico, May 2003.

POEM DEDICATED TO ALAN GLASS BY ALBERTO BLANCO α
Letras Libres (Mexico), year V, No. 56, August 2003.

POEM DEDICATED TO ALAN GLASS BY ALEJANDRA PIZARNIK, PARÍS 1962 λ
"El árbol de Diana" in *Poesía completa* 1955 a 1972, Poem 36.
Barcelona: Editorial Lumen, 2003, p. 138.

LABERINTO INFINITO Y ALUCINADO α
Juan José Gurrola. *Reforma* (Mexico), September 14, 2003.

ALAN GLASS EN LA GALERÍA LÓPEZ QUIROGA α
Macario Matus.
Suplemento Cultural, *Excélsior* (Mexico), June 15, 2003.

CONVERSANDO CON CRISTINA PACHECO ω
"Las Jaulas del Tiempo de Alan Glass", Canal Once TV, July 2003.

CARD RECEIVED FROM THE PLAYWRIGHT FERNANDO ARRABAL α
Paris, July 21, 2003.

ALAN GLASS, MASTER OF MAGIC SURREALISM α
John Maxim. *Miami Herald*, Arts and Leisure section, June 8, 2003.

ALAN GLASS, LO TRANSPARENTE DE LO INESPERADO α
Marcela Quiroz Luna. *Casas & Gente* (Mexico), Vol. 18, No. 180, November 2003, pp. 82, 83, 84, 85.

EXPOSITION ALAN GLASS AU MEXIQUE α
Alain Joubert. *La Quinzaine littéraire* (Paris), No. 857, July 15, 2003.

EL ARCOÍRIS NOCTURNO β
Exhibition catalog and compilation of various authors articles.
Galería López Quiroga
Mexico, May 2003.

FOR ALAN FROM LEONORA, HELLO, POEM BY LEONORA CARRINGTON α
La Jornada Semanal, No. 471, March 14, 2004.

A TRAVÉS DE ALAN GLASS / THROUGH A (LAN) GLASS ω
Documentary film directed by Tufic Makhlouf Akl, 54 minutes. With Bridget Bate Tichenor, Alberto Blanco, Leonora Carrington, Manuel Felguérez, Pedro Friedeberg, Alejandro Jodorowsky, Ramón López Quiroga, Masayo Nonaka, Ana María and Teresa Pecanins, Vicente Rojo, Roger Von Gunten. 2006.
Mexico. DVD; audio Spanish, English, French; subtitles English, Spanish.

A TRAVÉS DE ALAN GLASS / THROUGH A (LAN) GLASS ω
Morelia Film Festival 2006, Guanajuato and San Miguel de Allende Film Festival, 2006.
Casa Universitaria del Libro, Cineteca Nacional, Casa Lam, Mexico 2007.
Bogotá Film Festival, Colombia, Documentaries section, Enrique Grau, October 2007.

"EN PANTALLA EL UNIVERSO ONÍRICO DE ALAN GLASS" α
Alberto Solís. Milenio (Mexico), Thursday, 2 July 2007.

"REGISTRAN LA MAGIA DE GLASS" α
Oscar Cid de León. *Reforma* (Mexico City), June 9, 2007.

"DIFUNDEN LA OBRA DE ALAN GLASS ARTISTA ALEJADO DE LOS REFLECTORES" α
Merry MacMasters. *La Jornada* (Mexico), Thursday, June 7, 2007.
https://www.jornada.com.mx/2007/06/07/index.php?section=cultura&article=a04n1cul.

DOCUMENTAL "A TRAVÉS A TRAVÉS DE ALAN GLASS / THROUGH A (LAN) GLASS ω
Documentary film directed by Tufic Makhlouf Akl. Winner in Documentary Category: Best Director and Best Editing at the Pantalla de Cristal film festival (Mexico), October 2007.

"RECREA EL ARTE SURREAL" α
Óscar Cid de León, Reforma (Mexico), January 21, 2008.

"INDIGNATION DEVANT LA SÉLECTION DU FIFA" α
Brigitte Morissette, Le Devoir (Montreal), April 1, 2008, https://www.ledevoir.com/opinion/idees/182993/indignation-devant-la-selection-du-fifa.

ALAN GLASS EL AZAR OBJETIVO α
Donatella Lockhart. *Casas & Gente* (Mexico), No. 251, Dec-Jan 2010-2011.

ALAN AU PAYS DES MERVEILLES α
Alain Joubert. *La Quinzaine littéraire* (Paris), May 16-31, 2010.

LE MIROIR DU MERVEILLEUX α
Alan Glass le Dernier des surréalistes.
Jean Paul Perret.
Arts – up 2010.

VERRE MAGNIFIANT α
Benoît Chaput. *Le Bathyscaphe* (Quebec), No. 5, Spring 2010.

INVISIBLE SEAMS α
Marci Denesiuk. *Le Bathyscaphe* (Quebec), No. 5, Spring 2010.

EL SURREALISMO VIVE. —GLASS α
Oscar Cid de León. *Reforma* (Mexico City), July 2, 2011.

PRIMERA MONOGRAFÍA DE LA VIDA Y OBRA DE ALAN GLASS α
Merry Mac Masters. *La Jornada*.
Diciembre 10, 2012.

GLASS EMPIRE, SCRAP BOOK λ
Book with artwork and images of Alan Glass
TEOPAN, Mexico, February 2012.

ALAN GLASS λ
Masayo Nonaka,
Turner
Spain, July 2012.

LA COSECHA PRECEDE A LA SIEMBRA, ALAN GLASS EN SUS 80 AÑOS β
Exhibition catalog and compilation of articles by various authors.
Galería López Quiroga, Mexico, May 2013.

MÉXICO SIGUE SIENDO SURREALISTA Y SIEMPRE LO SERÁ: ALAN GLASS α
Merry MacMasters.
La Jornada (Mexico),
December 10, 2012.
https://www.jornada.com.mx/2012/12/10/cultura/a07n3cul.

KEY:
(α) *Article*
(β) *Catalog*
(λ) *Book*
(ω) *Film, video, interview*

EL ÚLTIMO DE LOS SURREALISTAS: ALAN GLASS α
Sagrario Saraid. Smash7 (Mexico), May 28, 2013. https://sagrariosaraid.wordpress.com/2013/05/28/el-ultimo-de-los-surrealistas-alan-glass/.

DIE DINGE REDEN MIT MIR [THINGS TALK TO ME] α
Corinna Koch. Der Freitag (Germany), No. 27, July 18, 2013. https://www.freitag.de/autoren/corinna-koch/die-dinge-reden-mit-mir.

L'OR AUX ILES, α
Paris publication,
2014, front cover and pp. 8 – 63.

CENTRE D'EXPOSITION DU VIEUX PRESBYTÉRE – INAUGURATION DE LA SALLE ALAN GLASS α
Saint-Bruno-de-Montarville, Canada. Opening of the Alan Glass Hall, January 15, 2016. https://stbruno.ca/nouvelles/centre-dexposition-du-vieux-presbytere-inauguration-de-la-salle-alan-glass/.

THROUGH A(LAN) GLASS α
Tufic Makhlouf Akl. ArTheorica (Mexico), Year 1, No. 2, print date February 1, 2018, pp. 33 – 43. https://www.artheorica.com/magazine.

RECONOCERÁN A SURREALISTA ALAN GLASS CON LA MEDALLA BELLAS ARTES α
Notimex Especial (Mexico),
November 11, 2017.

ALAN GLASS, UN LABERINTO TRANSPARENTE α
Alberto Blanco. Este país (Mexico), December 1, 2017. https://anterior.estepais.com/articulo.php?id=1285&t=alan-glass-un-laberinto-transparente.

SORPRENDENTE HALLAZGO (CHANCE FIND): α
Alan Glass and Contemporary Surrealism in Mexico
Abigail Susik and Kristoffer Noheden
Magazine Burlington Contemporary, no. 4 (2021).

DET HIMMELSKA ÅKERBRUKET: α
Alan Glass och assemblagekonstens alkeim
Kristoffer Noheden
Magazine Hjärnstorm, no. 150-151
Stockholm, Sweden (2022).

CREVER LE TAMBOUR DE LA RAISON RAISONNANTE λ
Alan Glass and Kristoffer Noheden
Book with works by Alan Glass and poems by Kristoffer Noheden,
Published by TEOPAN
Mexico, June 2022.

PRINCIPAL PUBLIC COLLECTIONS AND MUSEUMS:

Musée National des Beaux-Arts du Québec, Canada.
Canada Council Art Bank, Ottawa, Canada.
Manuel Alvarez Bravo Collection, Mexico City.
Leonard and Bina Ellen Art Gallery, formerly the Concordia Art Gallery, formerly the Sir George Williams Art Galleries, Montreal, Canada.
Musée d'Art Contemporain de Montréal, Canada.
Museo de Arte Moderno, Mexico City.
Wendel, Art Gallery, Saskatoon, Saskatchewan, Canadá.
Musée d'Art Moderne de Paris, France.
Bibliothèque nationale de France, Paris.
Metropolitan Museum of Art, New York.
Galería López Quiroga, Mexico City.
The Museum of Fine Arts, Houston, Texas.
MUFI – Museo de Filatelia de Oaxaca, Oaxaca, Mexico.
Musée Cantini, Marseille, France.

PRINCIPAL PRIVATE COLLECTIONS:

Bicen Collection, Paris, France.
Gigere Collection, Quebec, Canada.
Roberto Matta Collection, Paris, France.
Jacques Stern Collection, Paris, France.
Lotbiniere Collection, The Hague, The Netherlands.
Carlos de Laborde Collection, Mexico City and Paris, France.
Alejandro González Iñárritu Collection, Mexico City and Los Angeles, USA.
Aube Elléouët Breton Collection, Paris, France.

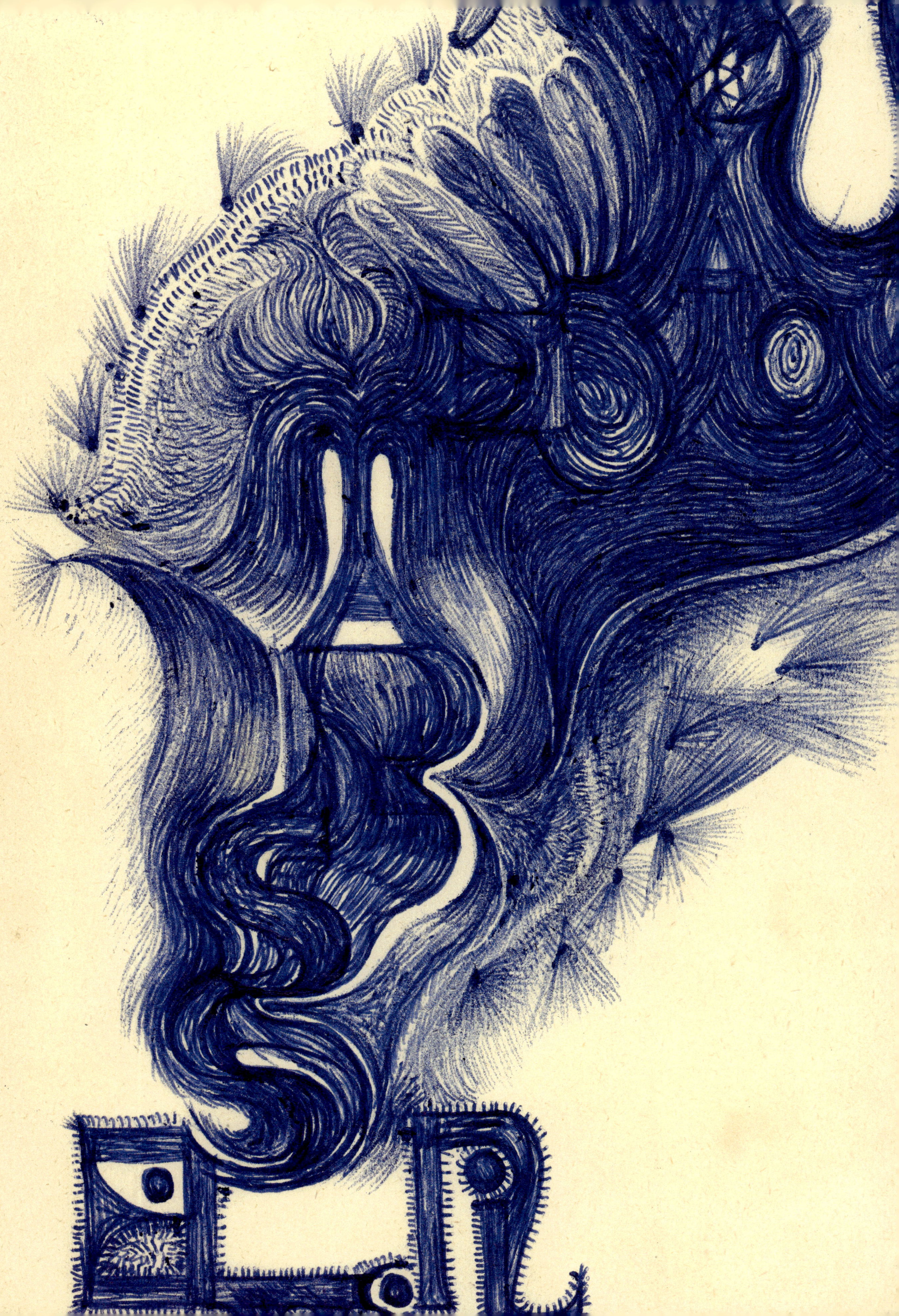

ARTWORK INDEX

INTRODUCTION

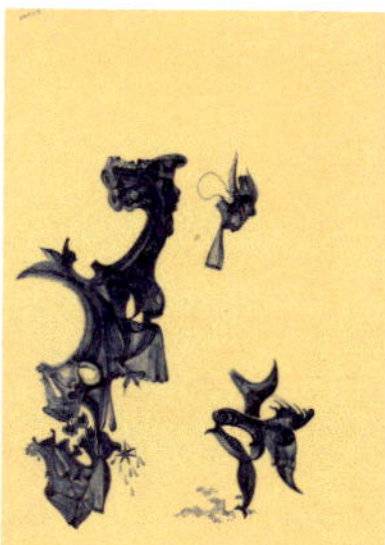

Untitled
(Rue Manuel period)
ca. 1954-1962
Monochrome blue ballpoint pen drawing, on paper.
30 x 21 cm
Artist's collection
AG1954_1962_RM_D0044
p. 8

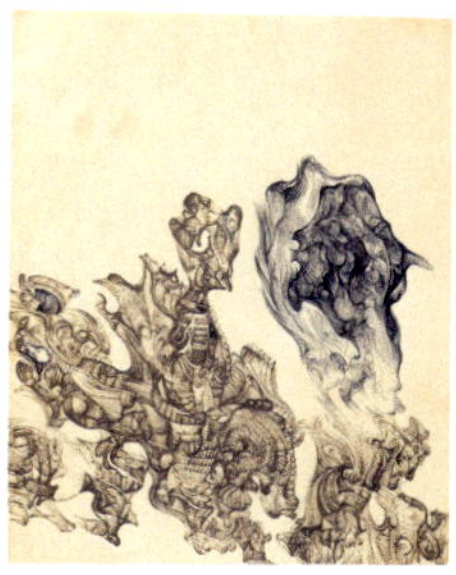

Untitled
(Galerie Le Terrain Vague period)
1956
Black and navy blue two-tone ballpoint pen drawing, on paper.
21.3 x 17 cm
Private collection
AG1954_1962_GTV_D0099
p. 10

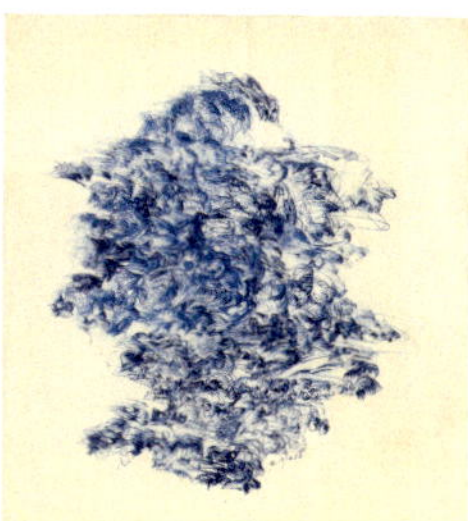

Untitled
(Club Saint-Germain period)
ca. 1954-1962
Blue and navy blue two-tone ballpoint pen drawing, on paper.
27.5 x 25 cm
Artist's collection
AG1954_1962_CSG_D0120
p. 15

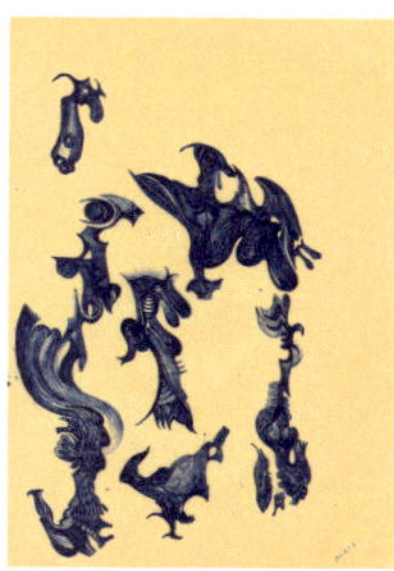

Untitled
(Club Saint-Germain period)
ca. 1954-1962
Monochrome blue ballpoint pen drawing, on paper.
13.5 x 10.5 cm
Artist's collection
AG1954_1962_CSG_D0036
p. 16

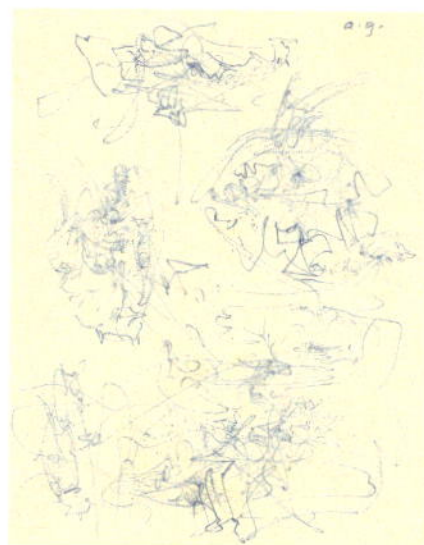

Untitled
(Rue Manuel period)
ca. 1954-1962
Monochrome blue ballpoint pen drawing, on paper.
30 x 21 cm
Artist's collection
AG1954_1962_RM_D0036
p. 17

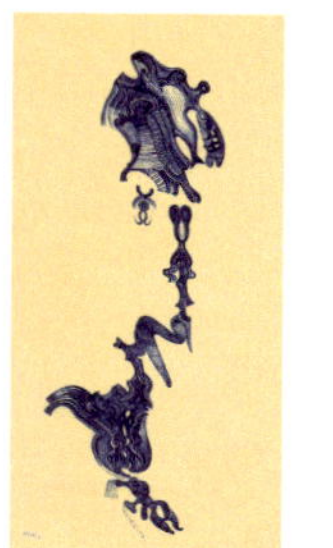

Untitled
(Rue Manuel period)
ca. 1954-1962
Monochrome blue ballpoint pen drawing, on paper.
30 x 15 cm
Artist's collection
AG1954_1962_RM_D0003
p. 18

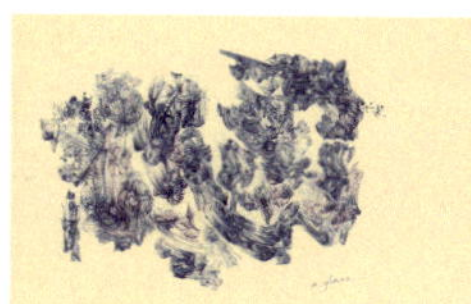

Untitled
(Club Saint-Germain period)
ca. 1954-1962
Monochrome blue ballpoint pen drawing with touch of violet pencil, on paper.
16 x 24 cm
Artist's collection
AG1954_1962_RM_D0018
p. 19

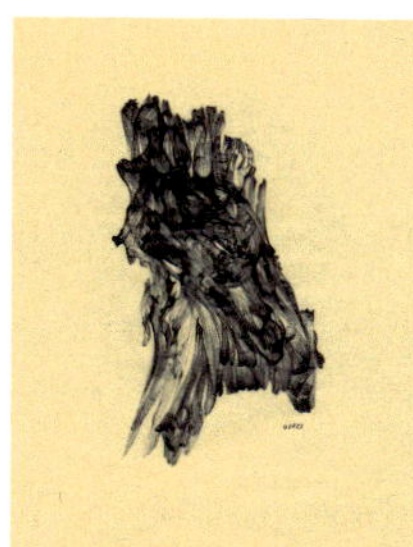

Untitled
(Club Saint-Germain period)
ca. 1954-1962
Monochrome black ballpoint pen drawing, on paper.
28 x 22.5 cm
Artist's collection
AG1954_1962_CSG_D0070
p. 19

Untitled
(Rue Manuel period)
1955
Drawing in blue monocolor ballpoint pen, on paper.
21.9 x 17 cm
Artist's collection
Detail
Previous page

CHAPTER I

5 RUE MANUEL PARIS IXE

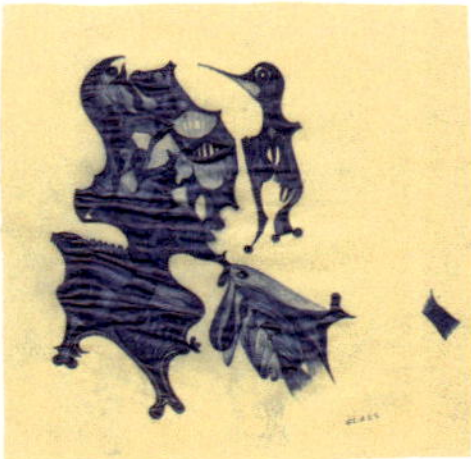

Untitled
(Rue Manuel period)
ca. 1954-1962
Monochrome blue ballpoint pen drawing, on paper.
18.6 x 18.4 cm
Artist's collection
AG1954_1962_RM_D0001
p. 23

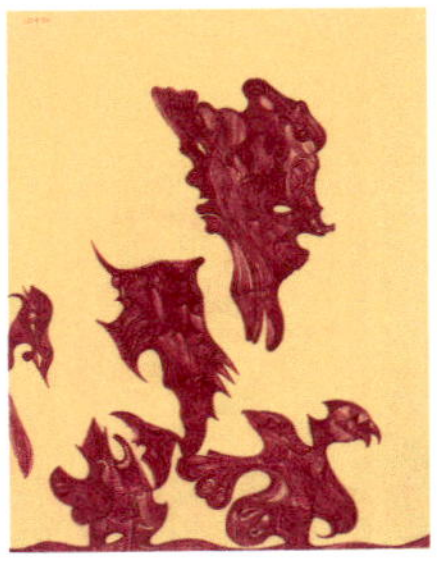

Untitled
(Rue Manuel period)
ca. 1954-1962
Monochrome red ballpoint pen drawing, on paper.
27 x 21 cm
Artist's collection
AG1954_1962_RM_D0025
p. 24

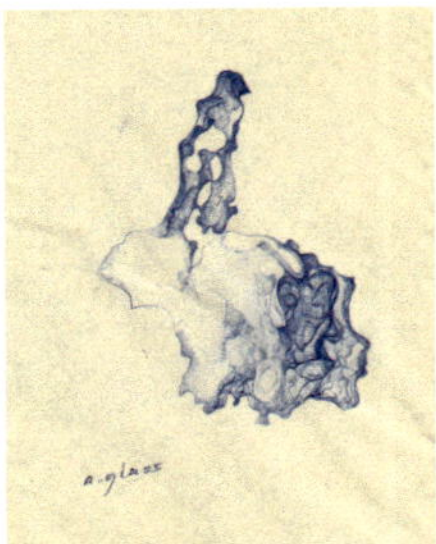

Untitled
(Rue Manuel period)
ca. 1954-1962
Monochrome blue pen drawing, on a paper envelope.
14.5 x 11.5 cm
Artist's collection
AG1954_1962_RM_D0055
p. 25

Untitled
(Rue Manuel period)
ca. 1954-1962
Monochrome blue ballpoint pen drawing, on paper.
28 x 22.5 cm
Artist's collection
AG1954_1962_RM_D0060
p. 26

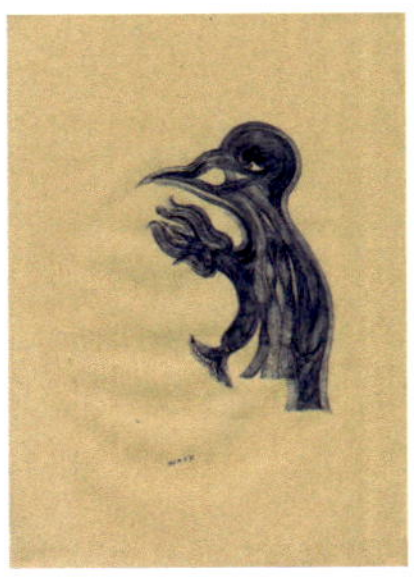

Untitled
(Rue Manuel period)
ca. 1954-1962
Monochrome blue ballpoint pen drawing, on paper.
29.5 x 21 cm
Artist's collection
AG1954_1962_RM_D0011
p. 27

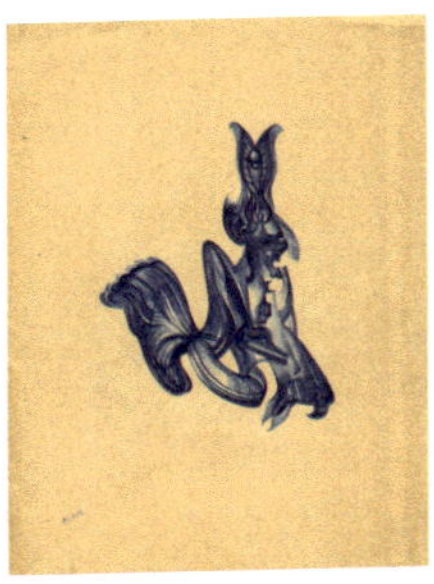

Untitled
(Rue Manuel period)
ca. 1954-1962
Monochrome blue ballpoint pen drawing, on paper.
28 x 22 cm
Artist's collection
AG1954_1962_RM_D0002
p. 28

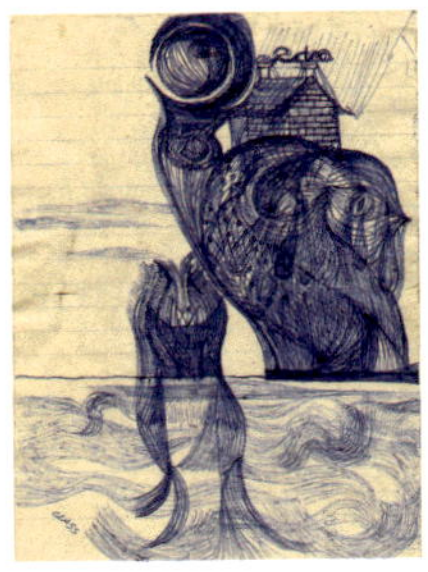

Untitled
(Rue Manuel period)
ca. 1954-1962
Monochrome blue ballpoint pen drawing, on paper.
18.5 x 13.5 cm
Artist's collection
AG1954_1962_RM_D0005
p. 29

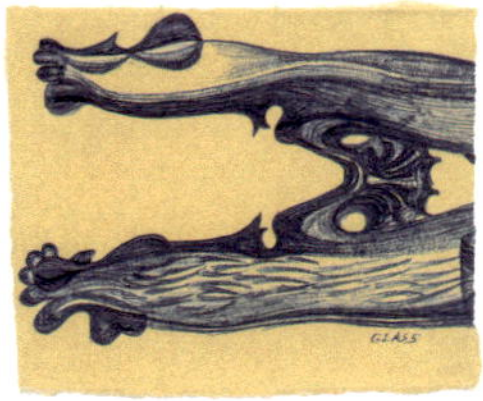

Untitled
(Rue Manuel period)
ca. 1954-1962
Monochrome blue ballpoint pen drawing, on paper.
10.5 x 8.5 cm
Artist's collection
AG1954_1962_RM_D0004
p. 29

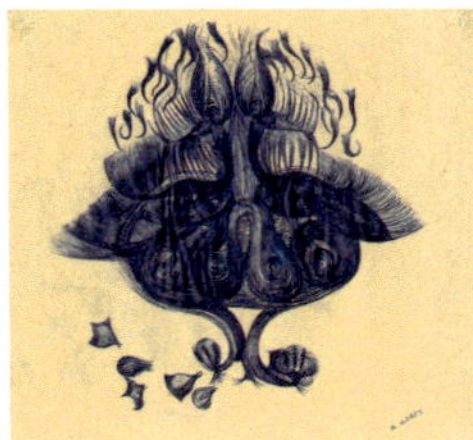

Untitled
(Rue Manuel period)
ca. 1954-1962
Monochrome blue ballpoint pen drawing, on paper.
19.5 x 21 cm
Artist's collection
AG1954_1962_RM_D0009
p. 30

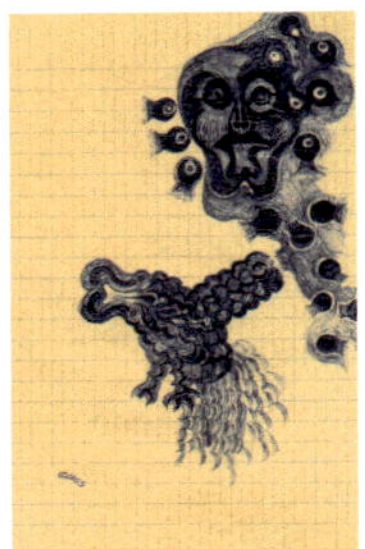

Untitled
(Rue Manuel period)
ca. 1954-1962
Monochrome blue ballpoint pen drawing, on paper.
21 x 13.5 cm
Artist's collection
AG1954_1962_RM_D0010
p. 31

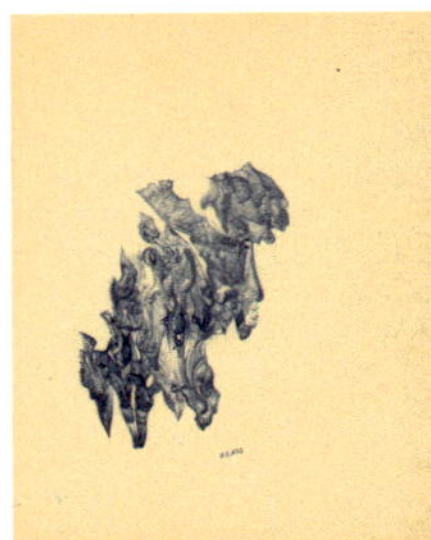

Untitled
(Rue Manuel period)
ca. 1954-1962
Monochrome blue ballpoint pen drawing, on paper.
27 x 21 cm
Artist's collection
AG1954_1962_RM_D0006
p. 32

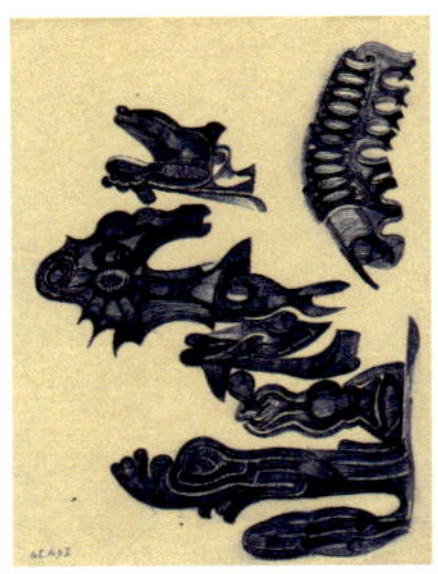

Untitled
(Rue Manuel period)
ca. 1954-1962
Monochrome blue ballpoint pen drawing, on paper.
13 x 17 cm
Artist's collection
AG1954_1962_RM_D0007
p. 32

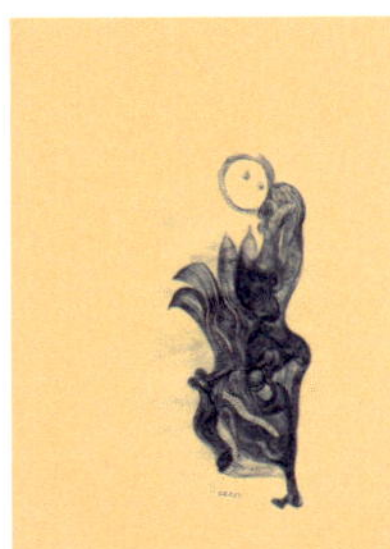

Untitled
(Rue Manuel period)
ca. 1954-1962
Monochrome blue ballpoint pen drawing, on paper.
29.5 x 21 cm
Artist's collection
AG1954_1962_RM_D0012
p. 33

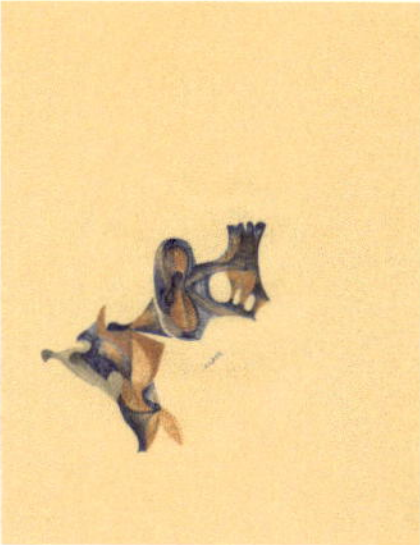

Untitled
(Rue Manuel period)
ca. 1954-1962
Blue pen drawing, with graphite and brown color, on paper.
27 x 21 cm
Artist's collection
AG1954_1962_RM_D0019
p. 34

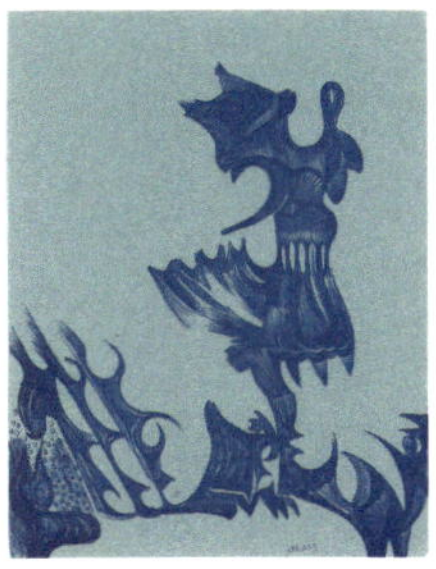

Untitled
(Rue Manuel period)
ca. 1954-1962
Monochrome blue ballpoint pen drawing, on blue paper.
21 x 16 cm
Artist's collection
AG1954_1962_RM_D0032
p. 35

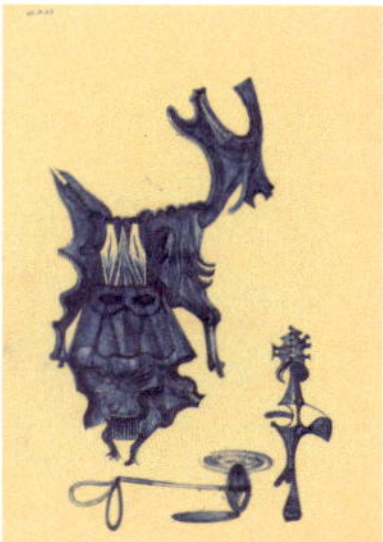

Untitled
(Rue Manuel period)
ca. 1954-1962
Monochrome blue ballpoint pen drawing, on paper.
30 x 21 cm
Artist's collection
AG1954_1962_RM_D0042
p. 36

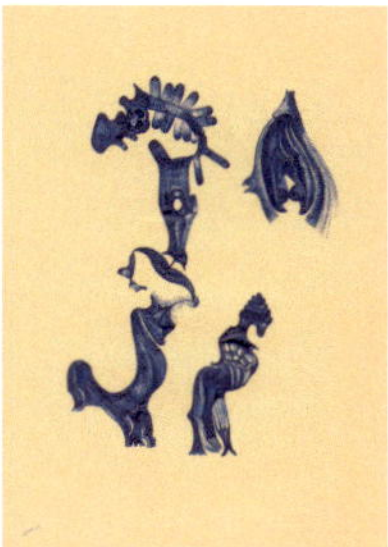

Untitled
(Rue Manuel period)
ca. 1954-1962
Monochrome blue ballpoint pen drawing, on paper.
30 x 21 cm
Artist's collection
AG1954_1962_RM_D0041
p. 36

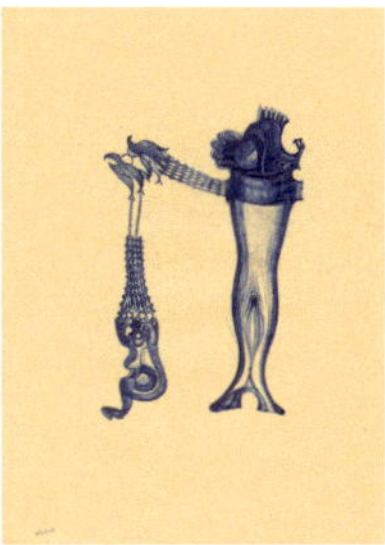

Untitled
(Rue Manuel period)
ca. 1954-1962
Monochrome blue ballpoint pen drawing, on paper.
30 x 21 cm
Artist's collection
AG1954_1962_RM_D0039
p. 37

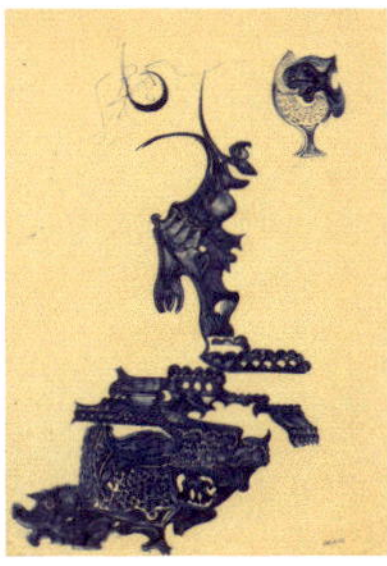

Untitled
(Rue Manuel period)
ca. 1954-1962
Monochrome blue ballpoint pen drawing, on paper.
30 x 21 cm
Artist's collection
AG1954_1962_RM_D0034
p. 38

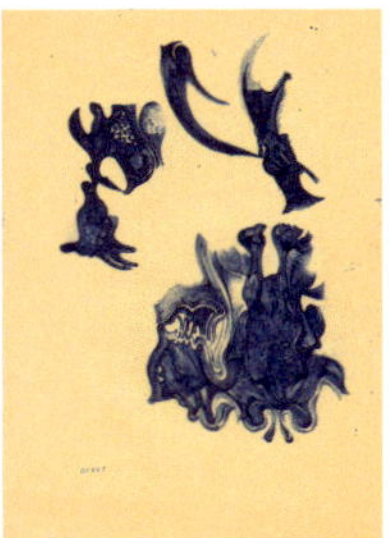

Untitled
(Rue Manuel period)
ca. 1954-1962
Monochrome blue ballpoint pen drawing, on paper.
30 x 21 cm
Artist's collection
AG1954_1962_RM_D0037
p. 39

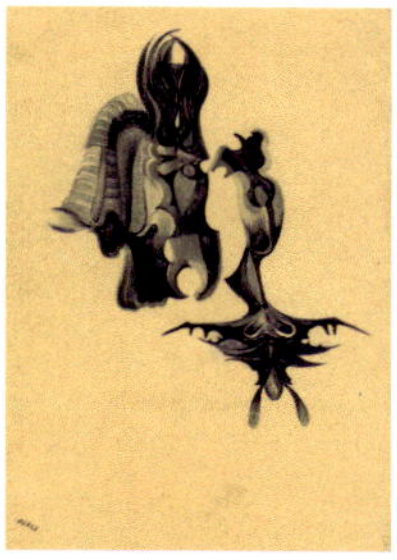

Untitled
(Rue Manuel period)
ca. 1954-1962
Bicolor blue and black ballpoint pen drawing, on paper.
27 x 19 cm
Artist's collection
AG1954_1962_RM_D0008
p. 40

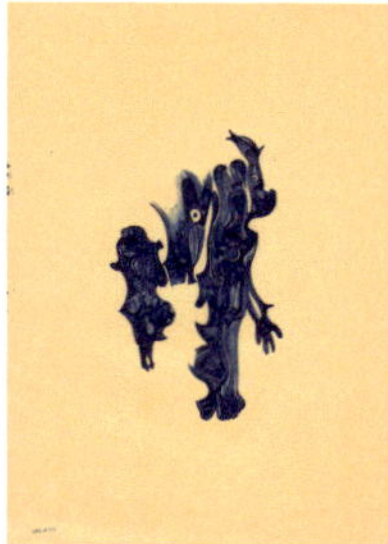

Untitled
(Rue Manuel period)
ca. 1954-1962
Monochrome blue ballpoint pen drawing, on paper.
30 x 21 cm
Artist's collection
AG1954_1962_RM_D0035
p. 40

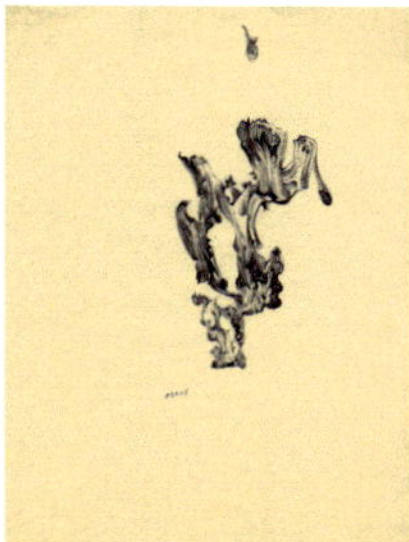

Untitled
(Rue Manuel period)
ca. 1954-1962
Monochrome black ballpoint pen drawing, on paper.
28 x 22.5 cm
Artist's collection
AG1954_1962_RM_D0059
p. 40

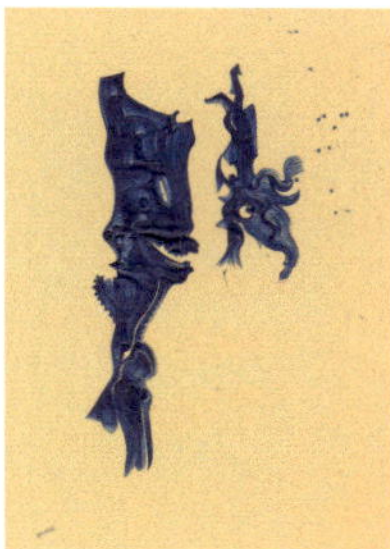

Untitled
(Rue Manuel period)
ca. 1954-1962
Monochrome blue ballpoint pen drawing, on paper.
30 x 21 cm
Artist's collection
AG1954_1962_RM_D0040
p. 41

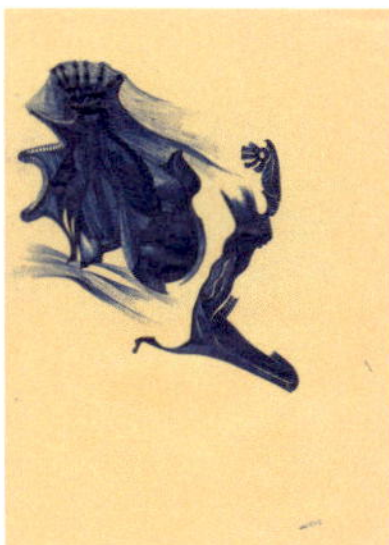

Untitled
(Rue Manuel period)
ca. 1954-1962
Monochrome blue ballpoint pen drawing, on paper.
30 x 21 cm
Artist's collectionn
AG1954_1962_RM_D0038
p.41

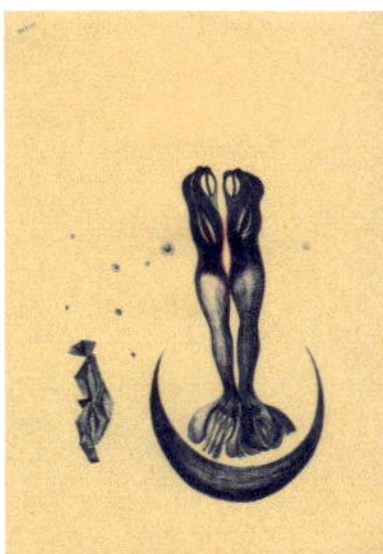

Untitled
(Rue Manuel period)
ca. 1954-1962
Bicolor blue and red ballpoint pen drawing, on paper.
30 x 21 cm
Artist's collection
AG1954_1962_RM_D0033
p. 42

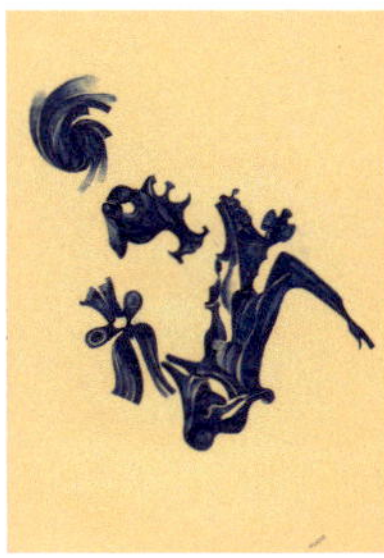

Untitled
(Rue Manuel period)
ca. 1954-1962
Monochrome blue ballpoint pen drawing, on paper.
30 x 21 cm
Artist's collection
AG1954_1962_RM_D0043
p. 43

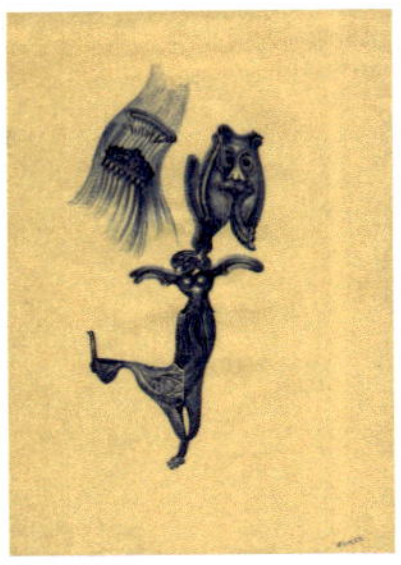

Untitled
(Rue Manuel period)
ca. 1954-1962
Monochrome blue ballpoint pen drawing
on paper.
30 x 21 cm
Artist's collection
AG1954_1962_RM_D0045
p. 44

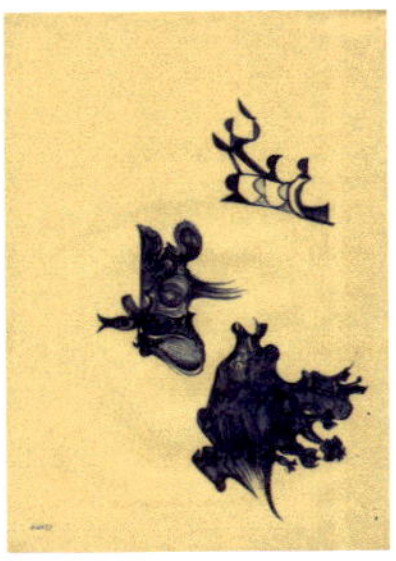

Untitled
(Rue Manuel period)
ca. 1954-1962
Monochrome blue ballpoint pen drawing,
on paper.
30 x 21 cm
Artist's collection
AG1954_1962_RM_D0046
p. 45

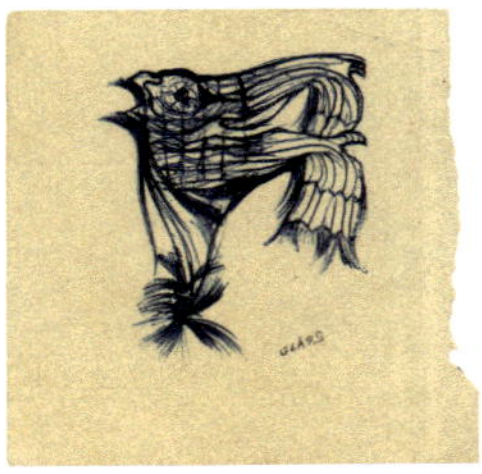

Untitled
(Rue Manuel period)
ca. 1954-1962
Monochrome blue ballpoint pen drawing,
on advertising paper.
12.5 x 12 cm
Artist's collection
AG1954_1962_RM_D0052
p. 46

Untitled
(Rue Manuel period)
ca. 1954-1962
Monochrome black ballpoint pen drawing
on paper.
28 x 22.5 cm
Artist's collection
AG1954_1962_RM_D0058
p. 47

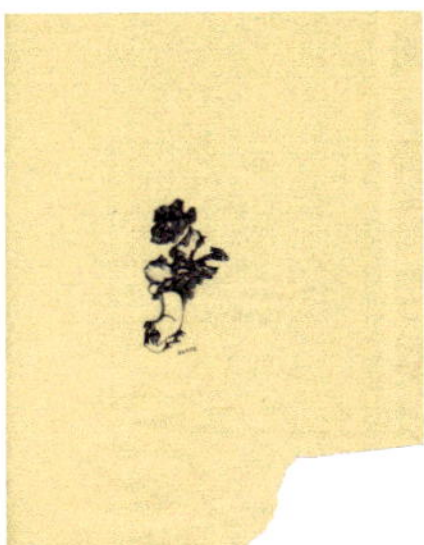

Untitled
(Rue Manuel period)
ca. 1954-1962
Monochrome black ballpoint pen drawing,
on paper.
28 x 22.5 cm
Artist's collection
AG1954_1962_RM_D0057
p. 48

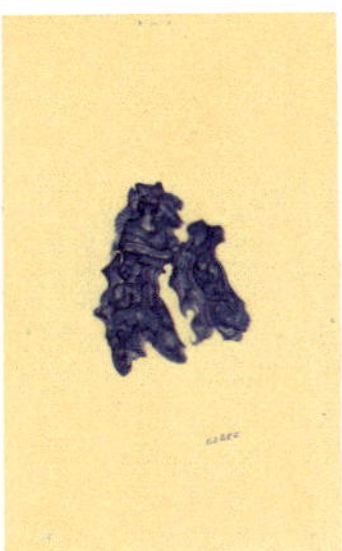

Untitled
(Rue Manuel period)
ca. 1954-1962
Monochrome blue ballpoint pen drawing,
on paper.
22 x 13.5 cm
Artist's collection
AG1954_1962_RM_D0053
p. 48

Untitled
(Rue Manuel period)
ca. 1954-1962
Monochrome blue ballpoint pen drawing,
on paper.
32 x 25 cm
Artist's collection
AG1954_1962_RM_D0063
p. 49

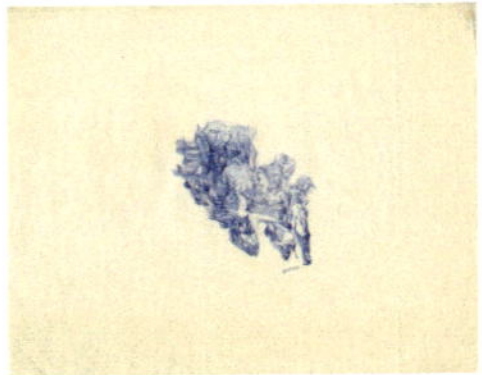

Untitled
(Rue Manuel period)
ca. 1954-1962
Monochrome blue ballpoint pen drawing,
on paper.
21 x 27 cm
Artist's collection
AG1954_1962_RM_D0013
p.49

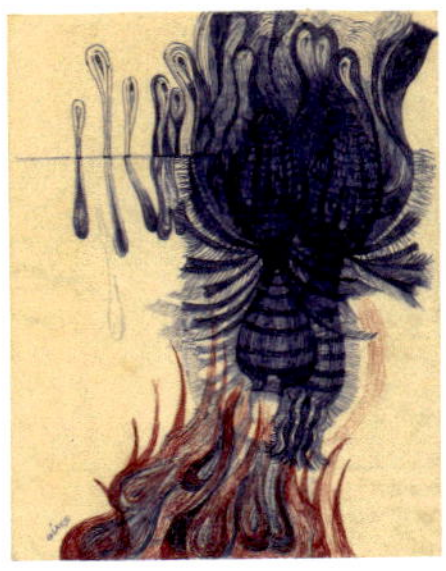

Untitled
(Rue Manuel period)
ca. 1954-1962
Bicolor blue and red ballpoint pen drawing
on paper.
21.5 x 17 cm
Artist's collection
AG1954_1962_RM_D0015
p. 50

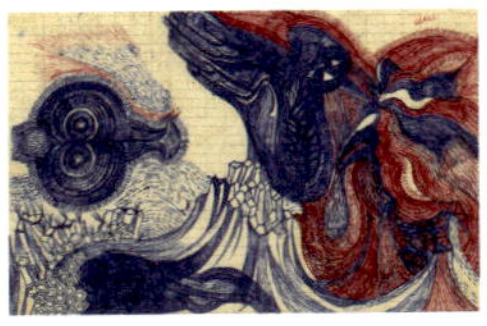

Untitled
(Rue Manuel period)
ca. 1954-1962
Bicolor blue and red ballpoint pen drawing
on paper.
13.5 x 20.5 cm
Artist's collection
AG1954_1962_RM_D0016
p. 51

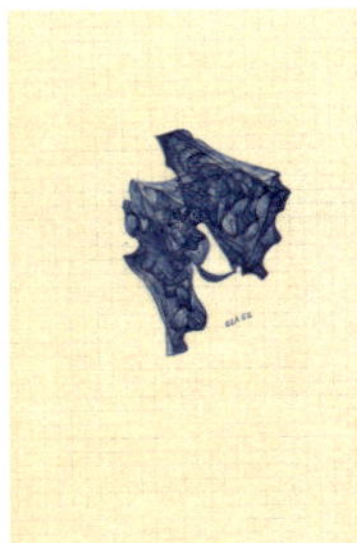

Untitled
(Rue Manuel period)
ca. 1954-1962
Monochrome blue ballpoint pen drawing,
on paper.
19 x 13 cm
Artist's collection
AG1954_1962_RM_D0014
p.51

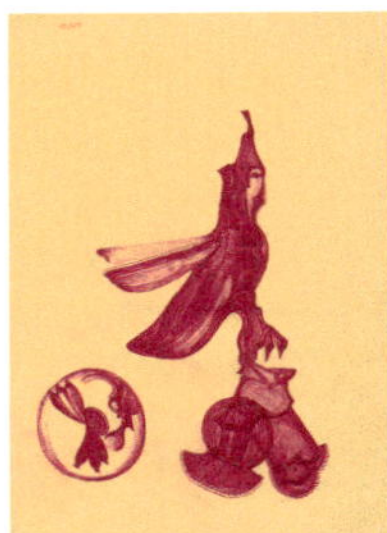

Untitled
(Rue Manuel period)
ca. 1954-1962
Monochrome red ballpoint pen drawing,
on paper.
30 x 21 cm
Artist's collection
AG1954_1962_RM_D0023
p. 52

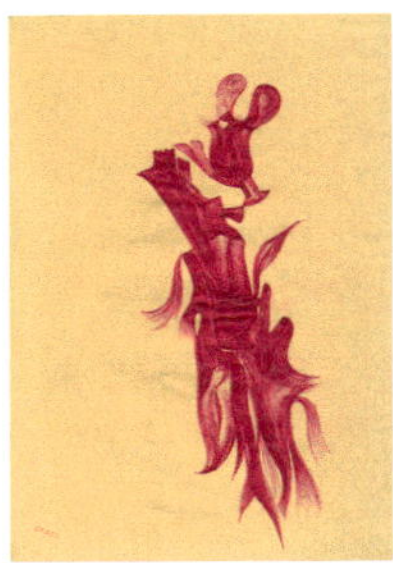

Untitled
(Rue Manuel period)
ca. 1954-1962
Monochrome red ballpoint pen drawing,
on paper.
30 x 21 cm
Artist's collection
AG1954_1962_RM_D0030
p. 53

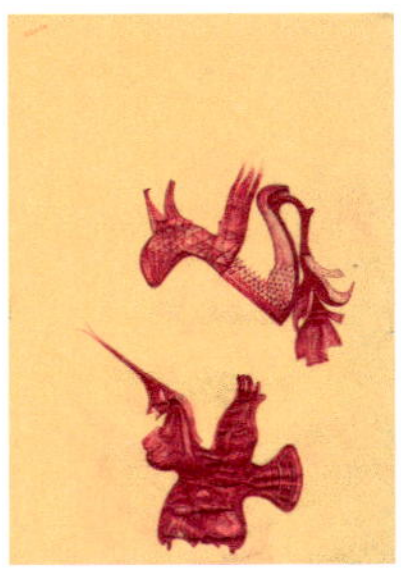

Untitled
(Rue Manuel period)
ca. 1954-1962
Monochrome red ballpoint pen drawing,
on paper.
30 x 21 cm
Artist's collection
AG1954_1962_RM_D0024
p. 54

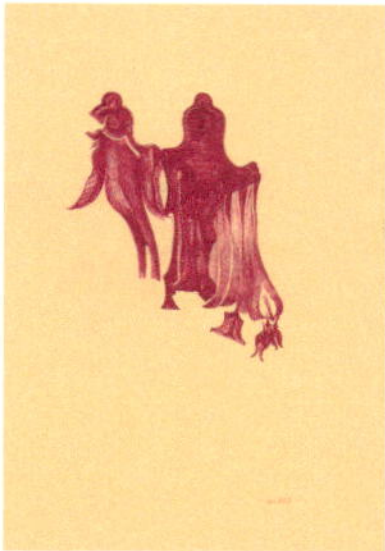

Untitled
(Rue Manuel period)
ca. 1954-1962
Monochrome red ballpoint pen drawing,
on paper.
30 x 21 cm
Artist's collection
AG1954_1962_RM_D0027
p. 54

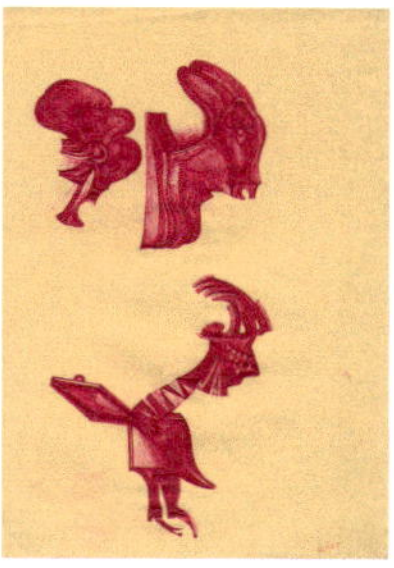

Untitled
(Rue Manuel period)
ca. 1954-1962
Monochrome red ballpoint pen drawing,
on paper.
30 x 21 cm
Artist's collection
AG1954_1962_RM_D0026
p. 55

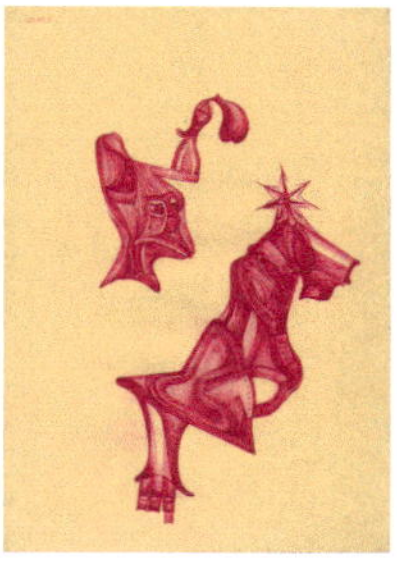

Untitled
(Rue Manuel period)
ca. 1954-1962
Monochrome red ballpoint pen drawing,
on paper.
30 x 21 cm
Artist's collection
AG1954_1962_RM_D0031
p. 55

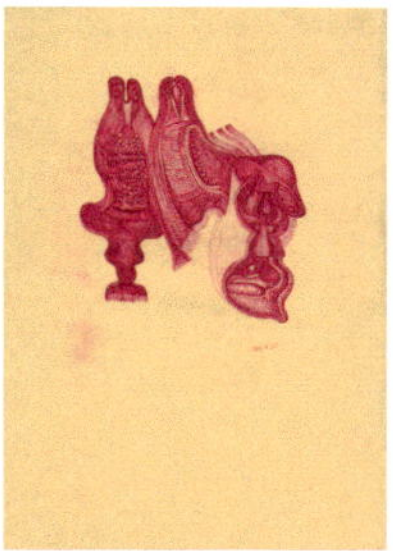

Untitled
(Rue Manuel period)
ca. 1954-1962
Monochrome red ballpoint pen drawing,
on paper.
30 x 21 cm
Artist's collection
AG1954_1962_RM_D0028
p. 56

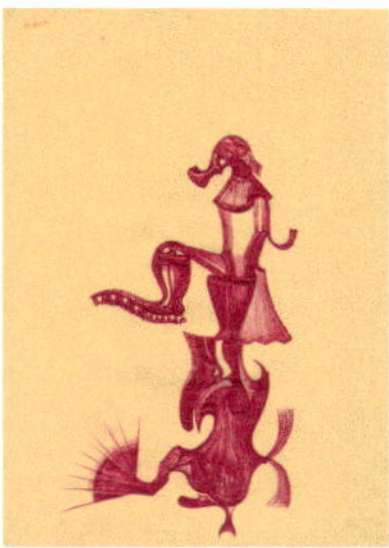

Untitled
(Rue Manuel period)
ca. 1954-1962
Monochrome red ballpoint pen drawing,
on paper.
30 x 21 cm
Artist's collection
AG1954_1962_RM_D0029
p. 57

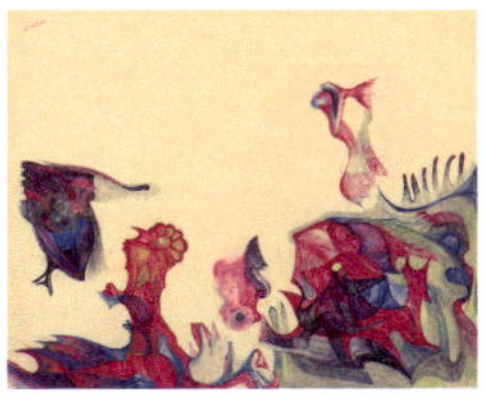

Untitled
(Rue Manuel period)
ca. 1954-1962
Blue pen drawing, graphite, green and brown
colors, on paper.
21 x 27 cm
Artist's collection
AG1954_1962_RM_D0021
p. 58

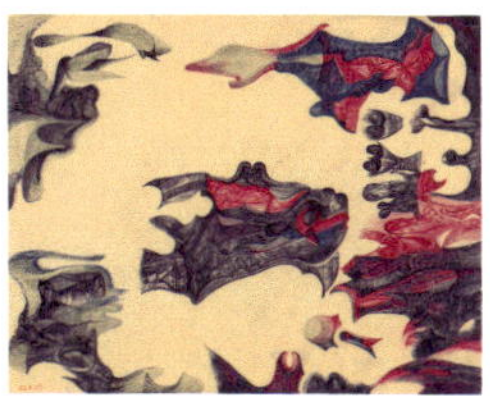

Untitled
(Rue Manuel period)
ca. 1954-1962
Blue, navy blue, and red pen drawing with
graphite, on paper.
21 x 27 cm
Artist's collection
AG1954_1962_RM_D0022
p. 59

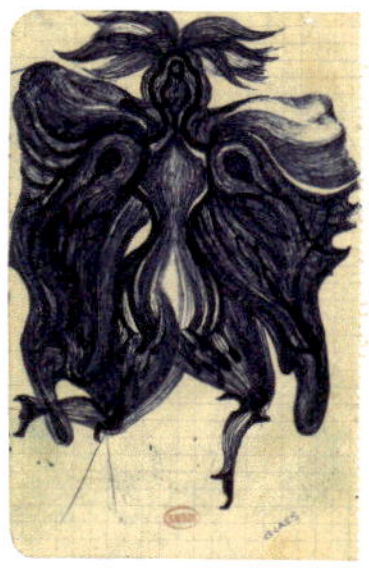

Untitled
(Rue Manuel period)
ca. 1954-1962
Monochrome blue ballpoint pen drawing,
on both sides, on squared paper.
17 x 10.5 cm
Artist's collection
AG1954_1962_RM_D0050/1
p. 60

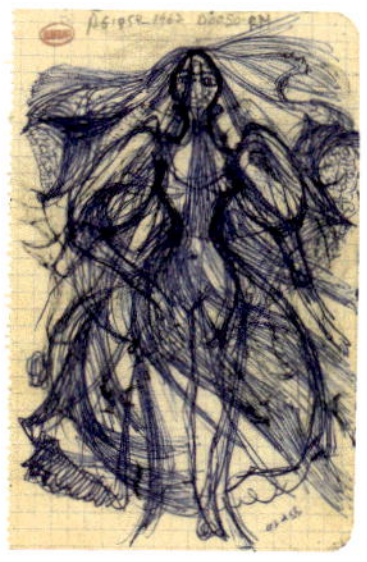

Untitled
(Rue Manuel period)
ca. 1954-1962
Monochrome blue ballpoint pen drawing,
on squared paper.
17 x 10.5 cm
Artist's collection
AG1954_1962_RM_D0049
p. 60

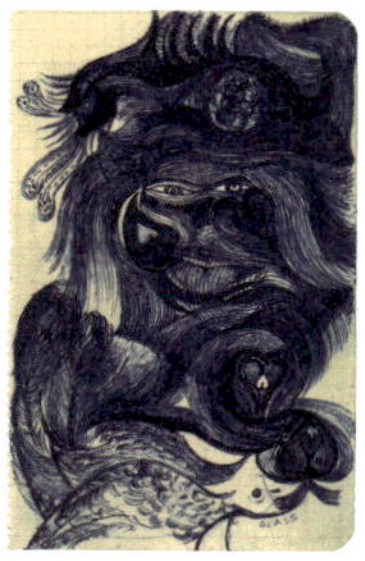

Untitled
(Rue Manuel period)
ca. 1954-1962
Monochrome blue ballpoint pen drawing,
on squared paper.
17 x 10.5 cm
Artist's collection
AG1954_1962_RM_D0048
p. 61

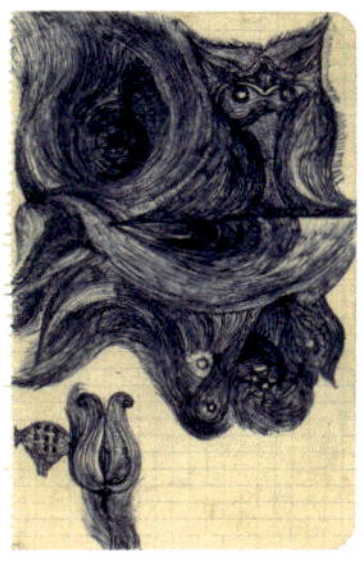

Untitled
(Rue Manuel period)
ca. 1954-1962
Monochrome blue ballpoint pen drawing,
on both sides, on squared paper.
17 x 10.5 cm
Artist's collection
AG1954_1962_RM_D0050
p. 61

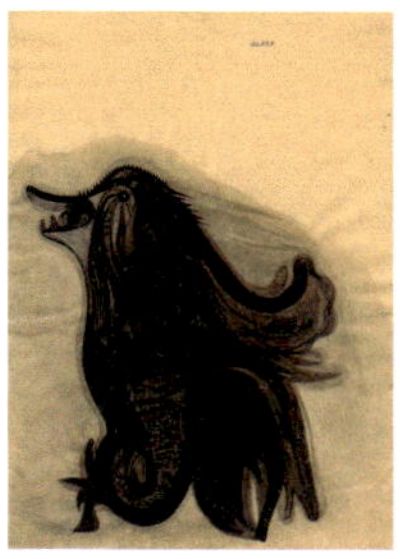

Untitled
(Rue Manuel period)
ca. 1954-1962
Monochrome black pen drawing
and India ink, on paper.
29.5 x 21 cm
Artist's collection
AG1954_1962_RM_D0061
p. 62

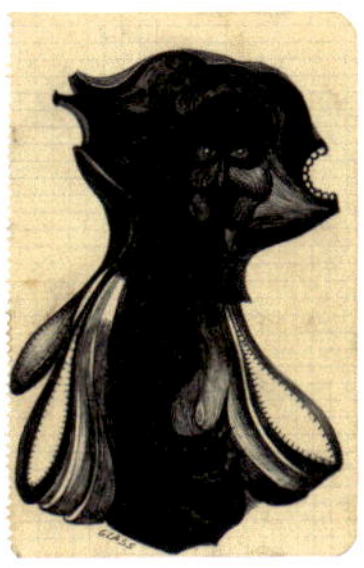

Untitled
(Rue Manuel period)
ca. 1954-1962
Monochrome black ballpoint pen drawing,
on squared paper.
17 x 10.5 cm
Artist's collection
AG1954_1962_RM_D0051
p. 62

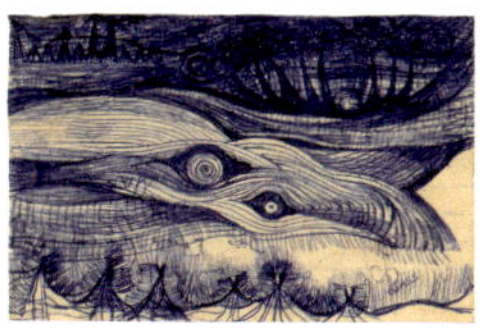

Untitled
(Rue Manuel period)
ca. 1954-1962
Monochrome blue ballpoint pen drawing,
on lined notebook paper.
9 x 14 cm
Artist's collection
AG1954_1962_RM_D0056
p. 63

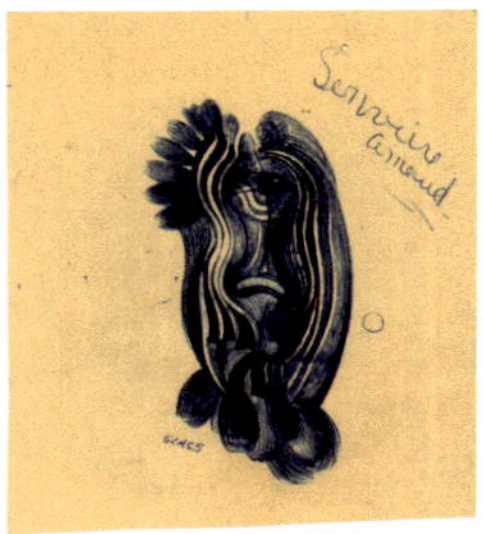

Untitled
(Rue Manuel period)
ca. 1954-1962
Monochrome blue ballpoint pen drawing, on paper.
14 x 12.5 cm
Artist's collection
AG1954_1962_RM_D0054
p. 63

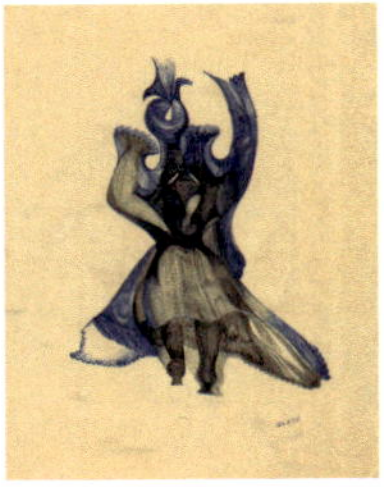

Untitled
(Rue Manuel period)
ca. 1954-1962
Drawing in blue pen and graphite, on paper.
27 x 21 cm
Artist's collection
AG1954_1962_RM_D0017
p. 64

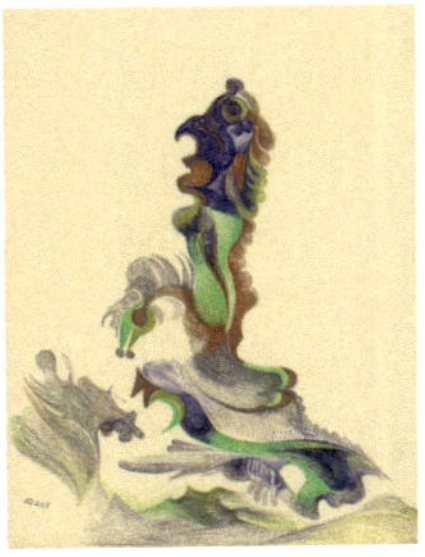

Untitled
(Rue Manuel period)
ca. 1954-1962
Drawing in blue pen, graphite, and green, brown and yellow colors, on paper.
27 x 20.5 cm
Artist's collection
AG1954_1962_RM_D0018
p. 65

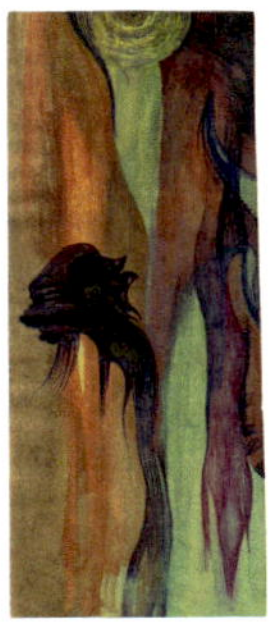

Untitled
(Rue Manuel period)
ca. 1954-1962
Blue, black, and red pen drawing with green, yellow, orange and violet colors, on paper.
23.5 x 10 cm
Artist's collection
AG1954_1962_RM_D0066
p. 66

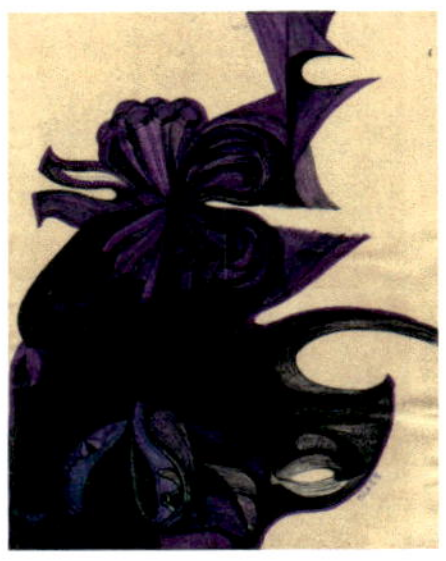

Untitled
(Rue Manuel period)
ca. 1954-1962
Drawing in blue, black, and purple ballpoint pen, with a touch of aquamarine, on paper.
21.5 x 17 cm
Artist's collection
AG1954_1962_RM_D0067
p. 67

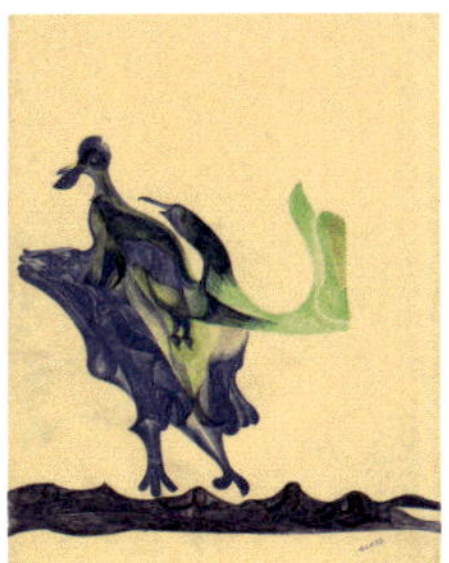

Untitled
(Rue Manuel period)
ca. 1954-1962
Blue pen drawing with green color, on paper.
27 x 21 cm
Artist's collection
AG1954_1962_RM_D0020
p. 67

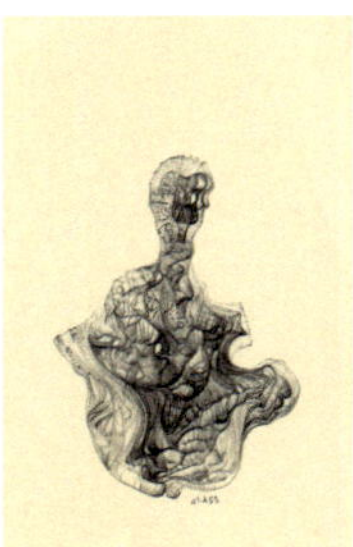

Untitled
(Rue Manuel period)
ca. 1954-1962
Monochrome black ballpoint pen drawing, on paper.
21 x 13.5 cm
Artist's collection
AG1954_1962_RM_D0062
p. 68

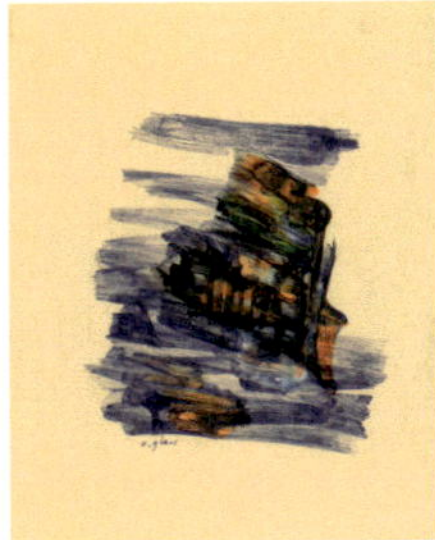

Untitled
(Rue Manuel period)
ca. 1954-1962
Drawing in blue and black pen, with blue, orange and green colors, on paper.
28 x 22.5 cm
Artist's collection
AG1954_1962_RM_D0064
p. 69

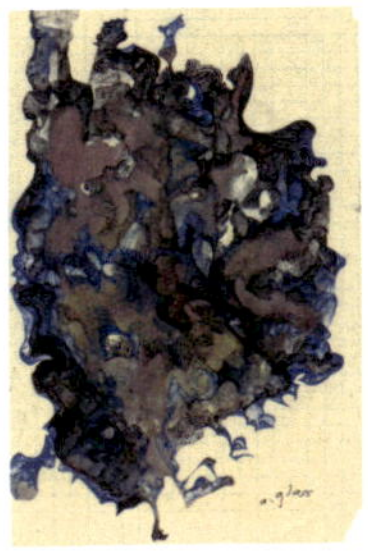

Untitled
(Rue Manuel period)
ca. 1954-1962
Drawing in bicolor blue and black ballpoint pen with wine color, on squared paper.
17 x 10.5 cm
Artist's collection
AG1954_1962_RM_D0047
p. 70

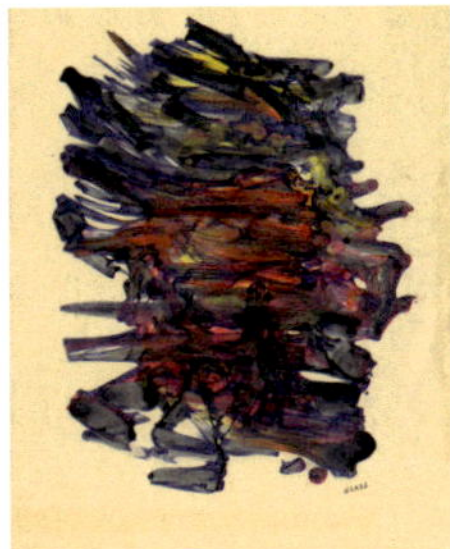

Untitled
(Rue Manuel period)
ca. 1954-1962
Blue pen drawing with red, yellow, and orange watercolor, on paper.
28 x 22.5 cm
Artist's collection
AG1954_1962_RM_D0065
p. 71

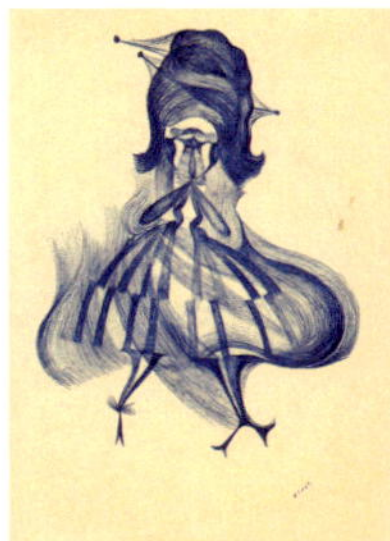

Untitled
(Rue Manuel period)
ca. 1954-1962
Drawing in blue monocolor ballpoint pen, on paper.
29.8 x 21.1 cm
Artist's collection
AG1954_1962_ RM_D0081
p. 72

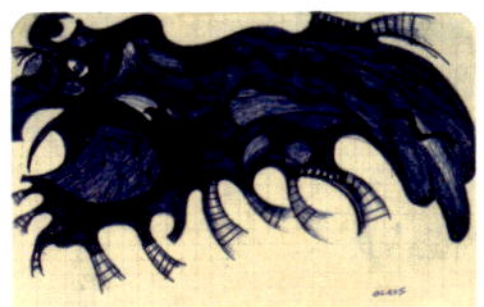

Untitled
(Rue Manuel period)
ca. 1954-1962
Drawing in blue monocolor ballpoint pen, on squared paper.
10.3 x 16 cm
Artist's collection
AG1954_1962_ RM_D0073
p. 73

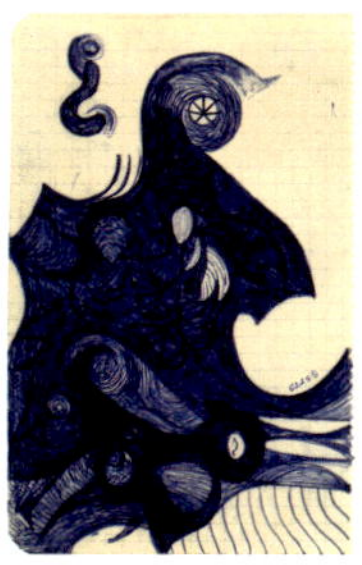

Untitled
(Rue Manuel period)
ca. 1954-1962
Drawing in blue monocolor ballpoint pen, on squared paper.
16 x 10.3 cm
Artist's collection
AG1954_1962_ RM_D0072
p. 73

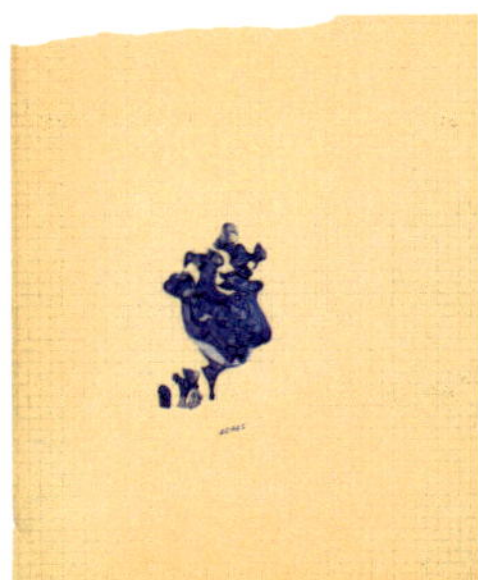

Untitled
(Rue Manuel period)
ca. 1954-1962
Monochrome blue ballpoint pen drawing, with a touch of sky blue pencil, on squared paper.
25.4 x 21.1 cm
Artist's collection
AG1954_1962_ RM_D0068
p. 74

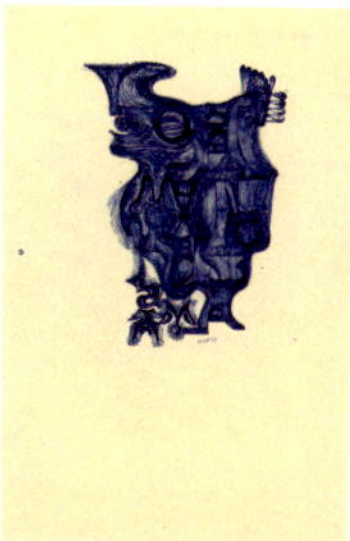

Untitled
(Rue Manuel period)
ca. 1954-1962
Monochrome blue ballpoint pen drawing, on paper.
27.2 x 17.9 cm
Artist's collection
AG1954_1962_ RM_D0069
p. 75

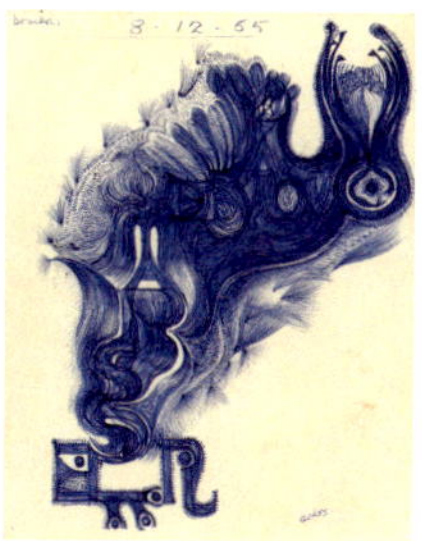

Untitled
(Rue Manuel period)
1955
Drawing in blue monocolor ballpoint pen, on paper.
21.9 x 17 cm
Artist's collection
AG1954_1962_ RM_D0075
p. 75

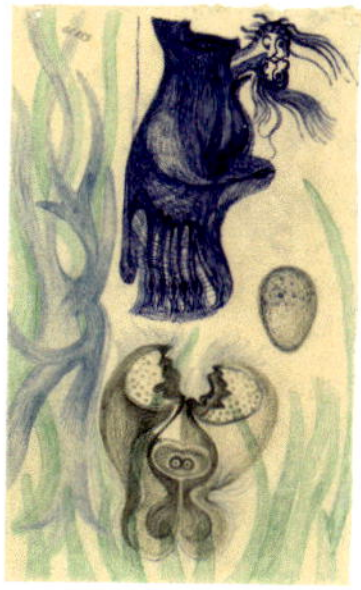

Untitled
(Rue Manuel period)
ca. 1954-1962
Drawing in blue monocolor ballpoint pen with graphite, green and blue pencil, on paper.
22.2 x 13.4 cm
Artist's collection
AG1954_1962_ RM_D0076
p. 76

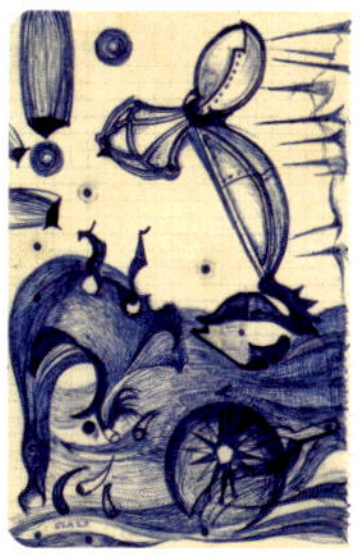

Untitled
(Rue Manuel period)
ca. 1954-1962
Drawing in blue monocolor ballpoint pen, on squared paper.
16 x 10.3 cm
Artist's collection
AG1954_1962_ RM_D0074
p. 77

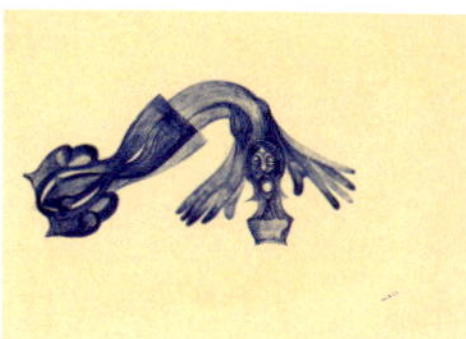

Untitled
(Rue Manuel period)
ca. 1954-1962
Drawing in blue monocolor ballpoint pen, on paper.
21 x 29.7 cm
Artist's collection
AG1954_1962_ RM_D0077
p. 78

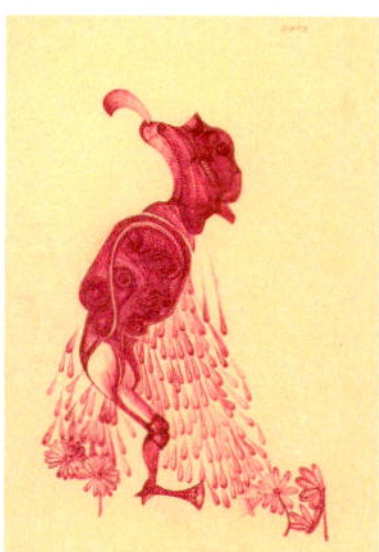

Untitled
(Rue Manuel period)
ca. 1954-1962
Drawing in red monocolor ballpoint pen, on paper.
29.8 x 21.1 cm
Artist's collection
AG1954_1962_ RM_D0079
p. 78

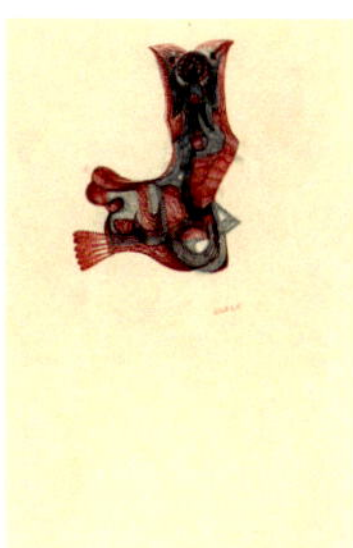

Untitled
(Rue Manuel period)
ca. 1954-1962
Drawing in red monocolor pen with graphite, on paper.
27.2 x 17.9 cm
Artist's collection
AG1954_1962_ RM_D0080
p. 79

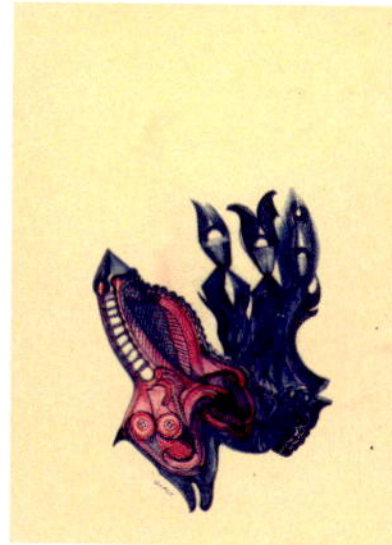

Untitled
(Rue Manuel period)
ca. 1954-1962
Drawing in blue and red bicolor ballpoint pen, on paper.
29.8 x 21.1 cm
Artist's collection
AG1954_1962_ RM_D0078
p. 79

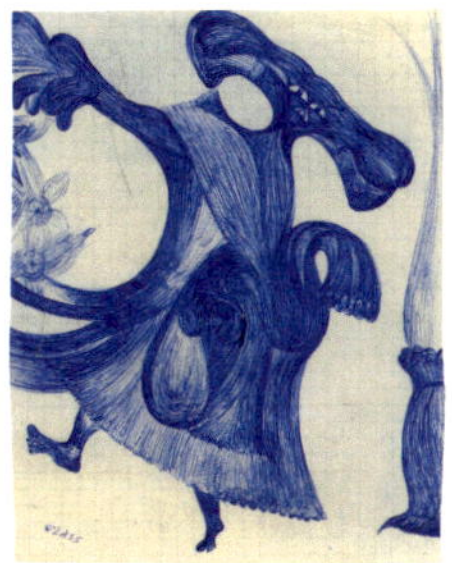

Untitled
(Rue Manuel period)
ca. 1954-1962
Monochrome blue ballpoint pen drawing, blurred with a sky blue pencil, on squared paper.
16.8 x 13.1 cm
Artist's collection
AG1954_1962_ RM_D0070
p. 80

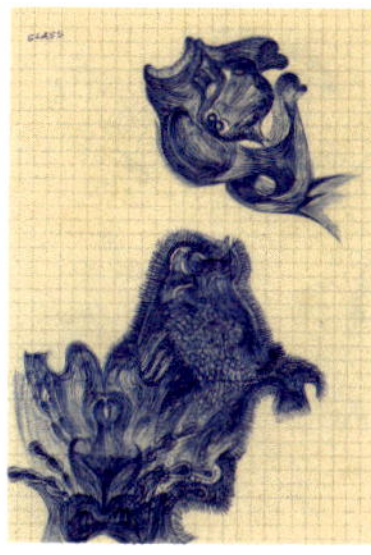

Untitled
(Rue Manuel period)
ca. 1954-1962
Drawing in blue monocolor ballpoint pen, on squared paper.
19.5 x 13.1 cm
Artist's collection
AG1954_1962_ RM_D0071
p. 81

CHAPTER II
CLUB S^{T} GERMAIN -DES-PRÉS PARIS VI^{E}

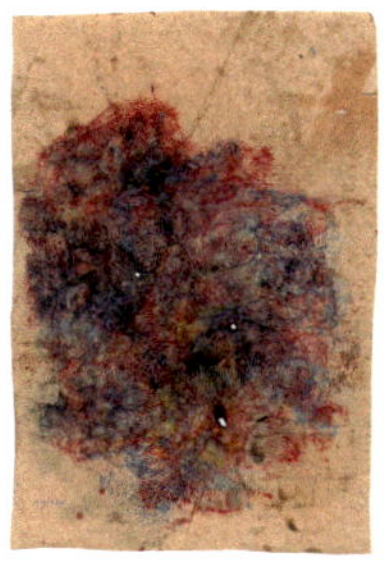

Untitled
(Club Saint-Germain period)
ca. 1954-1962
Bicolor blue and red ballpoint pen drawing, with touches of allumettage, on amate paper.
29.4 x 19.9 cm
Artist's collection
AG1954_1962_CSG_D0166
p. 88

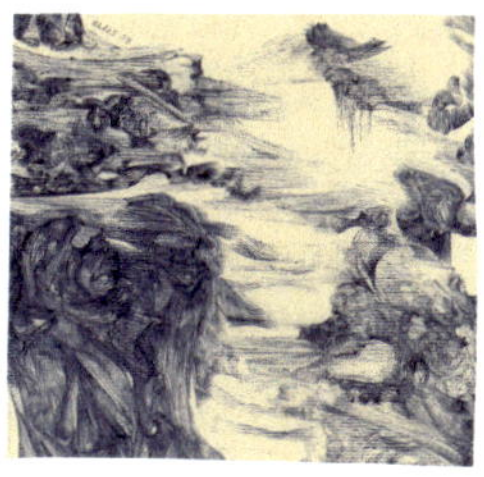

Untitled
(Club Saint-Germain period)
1958
Monochrome blue ballpoint pen drawing, on corrugated paper.
18 x 19.4 cm
Artist's collection
AG1954_1962_CSG_D0073
p. 100

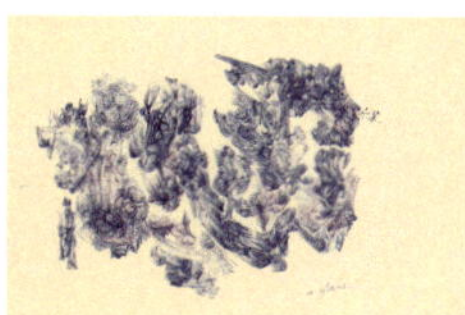

Untitled
(Club Saint-Germain period)
ca. 1954-1962
Monochrome blue ballpoint pen drawing, with hints of violet, on paper.
16 x 24 cm
Artist's collection
AG1954_1962_CSG_D0118
p. 101

Untitled
(Club Saint-Germain period)
ca. 1954-1962
Monochrome blue ballpoint pen drawing, on paper.
32 x 25 cm
Artist's collection
AG1954_1962_CSG_D0023
p. 102

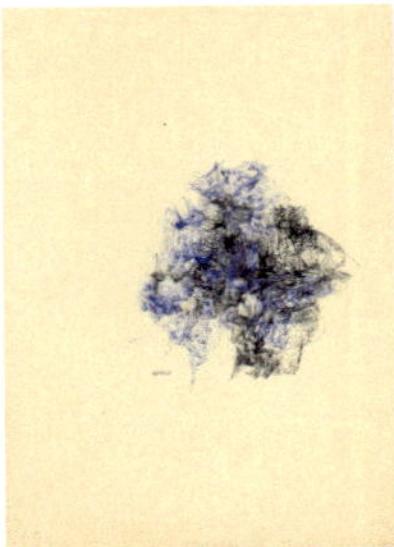

Untitled
(Club Saint-Germain period)
ca. 1954-1962
Blue and navy blue two-tone ballpoint pen drawing, on paper.
31 x 28 cm
Artist's collection
AG1954_1962_CSG_D0022
p. 102

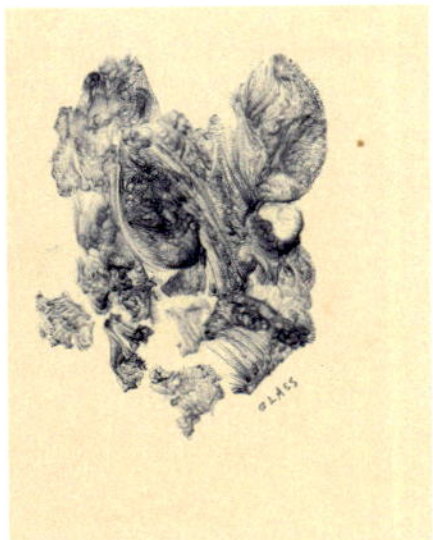

Untitled
(Club Saint-Germain period)
ca. 1954-1962
Monochrome blue ballpoint pen drawing, on paper.
13.5 x 10.5 cm
Artist's collection
AG1954_1962_CSG_D0025
p. 103

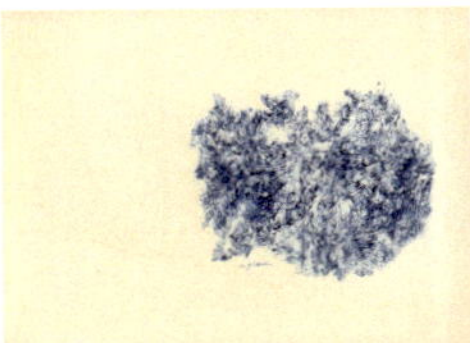

Untitled
(Club Saint-Germain period)
ca. 1954-1962
Monochrome blue ballpoint pen drawing, on paper.
25 x 32.5 cm
Artist's collection
AG1954_1962_CSG_D0024
p. 103

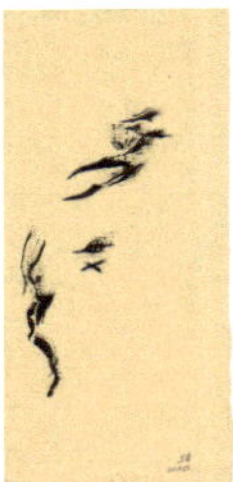

Untitled
(Club Saint-Germain period)
1958
India ink strokes, on paper.
21.2 x 14 cm
Artist's collection
AG1954_1962_CSG_D0006
p. 107

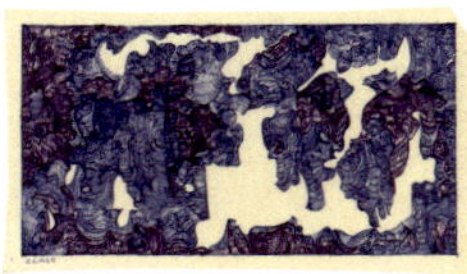

Untitled
(Club Saint-Germain period)
ca. 1954-1962
Blue and navy blue two-tone ballpoint pen drawing, on paper.
9.5 x 17.5 cm
Artist's collection
AG1954_1962_CSG_D0016
p. 108

Untitled
(Club Saint-Germain period)
ca. 1954-1962
Monochrome blue ballpoint pen drawing, on paper.
28 x 22.5 cm
Artist's collection
AG1954_1962_CSG_D0009
p. 109

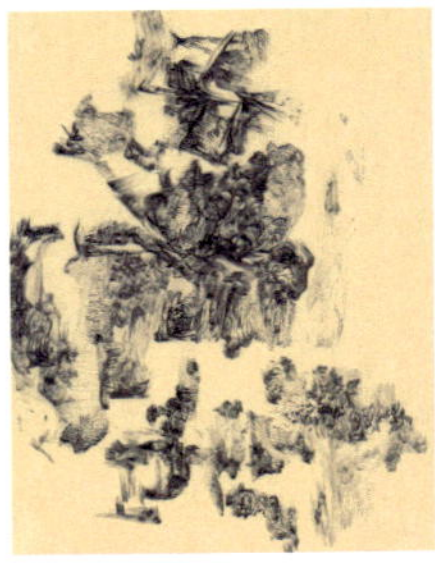

Untitled
(Club Saint-Germain period)
ca. 1954-1962
Monochrome black ballpoint pen drawing, on paper.
28 x 22 cm
Artist's collection
AG1954_1962_CSG_D0068
p. 110

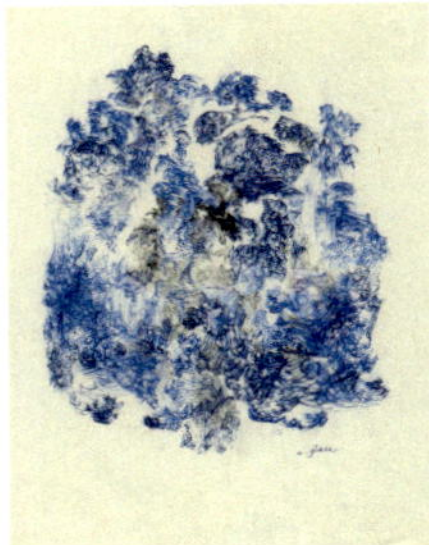

Untitled
(Club Saint-Germain period)
ca. 1954-1962
Blue, black and violet tricolor ballpoint pen drawing, on paper.
27 x 21 cm
Artist's collection
AG1954_1962_CSG_D0129
p. 111

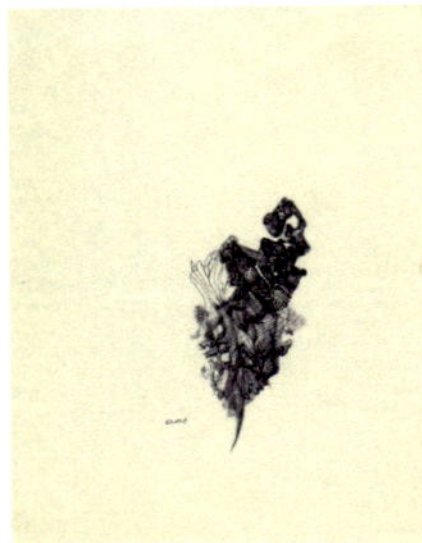

Untitled
(Club Saint-Germain period)
ca. 1954-1962
Monochrome black ballpoint pen drawing, on paper.
27.1 x 21.2 cm
Artist's collection
AG1954_1962_CSG_D0019
p. 112

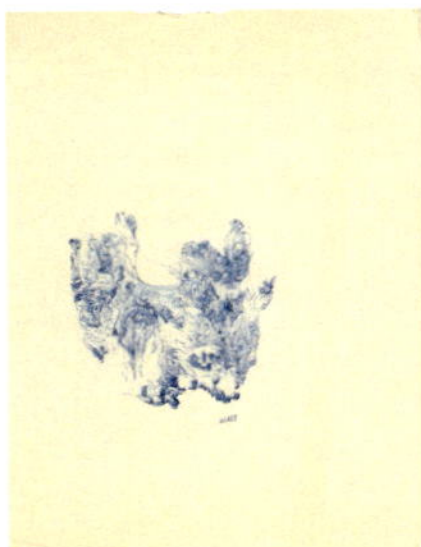

Untitled
(Club Saint-Germain period)
ca. 1954-1962
Monochrome blue ballpoint pen drawing, on paper.
27 x 21 cm
Artist's collection
AG1954_1962_CSG_D0013
p. 112

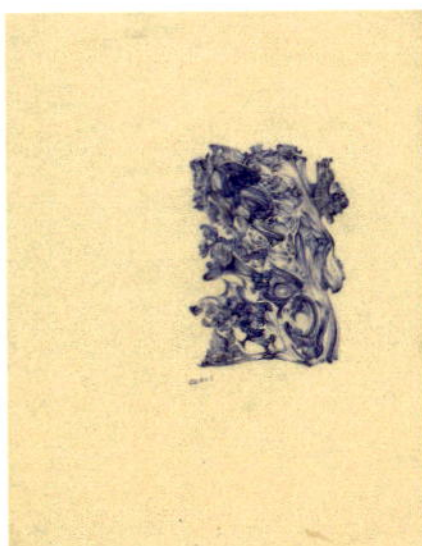

Untitled
(Club Saint-Germain period)
ca. 1954-1962
Monochrome blue ballpoint pen drawing, on paper.
28 x 22.5 cm
Artist's collection
AG1954_1962_CSG_D0012
p. 113

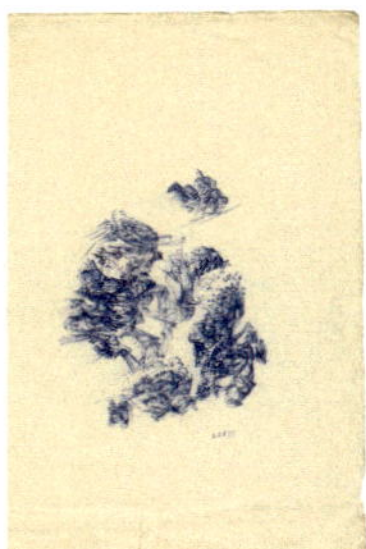

Untitled
(Club Saint-Germain period)
ca. 1954-1962
Monochrome blue ballpoint pen drawing, on paper.
24 x 16 cm
Artist's collection
AG1954_1962_CSG_D0010
p. 113

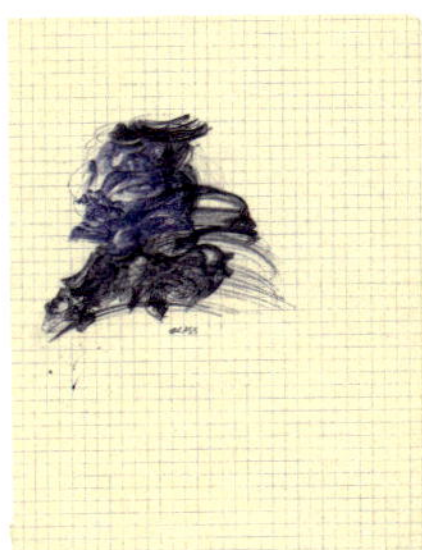

Untitled
(Club Saint-Germain period)
ca. 1954-1962
Bicolor blue and black ballpoint pen drawing, on squared paper.
21.5 x 16.5 cm
Artist's collection
AG1954_1962_CSG_D0014
p. 114

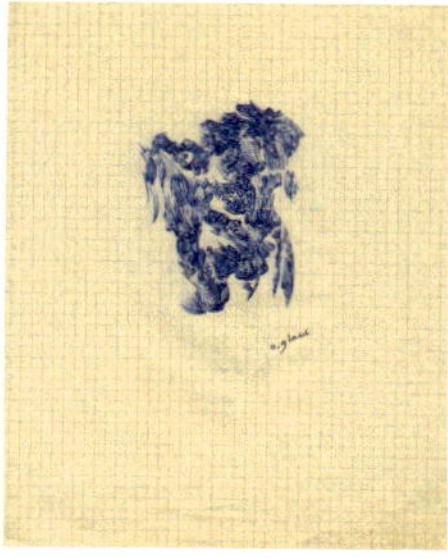

Untitled
(Club Saint-Germain period)
ca. 1954-1962
Monochrome blue ballpoint pen drawing,
on squared paper.
25.5 x 21 cm
Artist's collection
AG1954_1962_CSG_D0015
p. 114

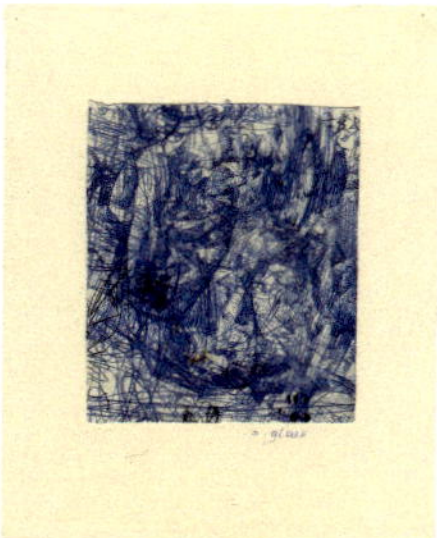

Untitled
(Club Saint-Germain period)
ca. 1954-1962
Monochrome blue ballpoint pen drawing with
alumettage detail, on paper.
16.5 x 13.2 cm
Artist's collection
AG1954_1962_CSG_D0020
p. 114

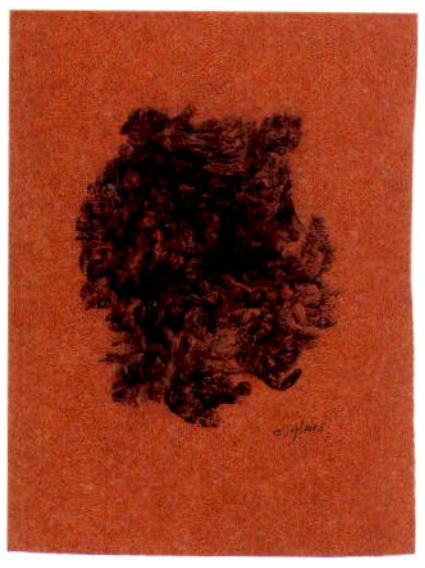

Untitled
(Club Saint-Germain period)
ca. 1954-1962
Monochrome black ballpoint pen drawing,
on red paper.
20.5 x 15.5 cm
Artist's collection
AG1954_1962_CSG_D0021
p. 115

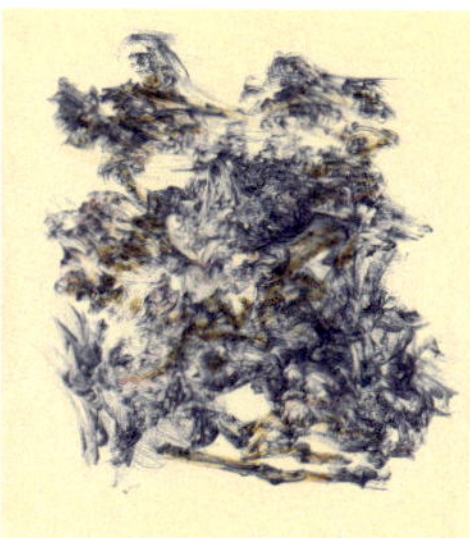

Untitled
(Club Saint Germain period)
ca. 1954-1962
Monochrome blue ballpoint pen drawing with
touches of allumettage, on paper.
28.2 x 25.2 cm
Artist's collection
AG1954_1962_CSG_D0161
p. 116

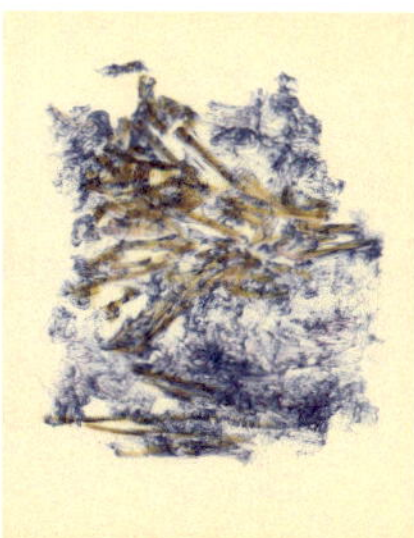

Untitled
(Club Saint Germain period)
ca. 1954-1962
Monochrome blue ballpoint pen drawing with
touches of allumettage, on paper.
31.4 x 24.4 cm
Artist's collection
AG1954_1962_CSG_D0171
p. 117

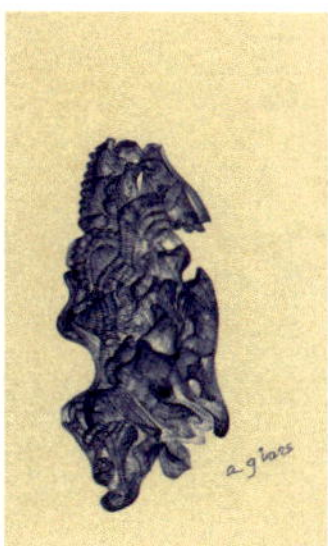

Untitled
(Club Saint-Germain period)
ca. 1954-1962
Monochrome blue ballpoint pen drawing,
on the order of Club Saint-Germain.
12.6 x 7.6 cm
Artist's collection
AG1954_1962_CSG_D0190
p. 118

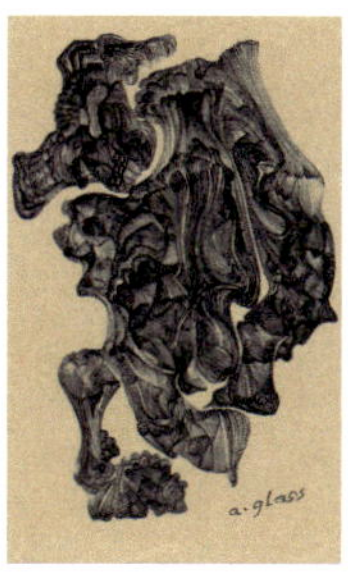

Untitled
(Club Saint-Germain period)
ca. 1954-1962
Monochrome black ballpoint pen drawing,
on the order of Club Saint-Germain.
13.2 x 8 cm
Artist's collection
AG1954_1962_CSG_D0193
p. 118

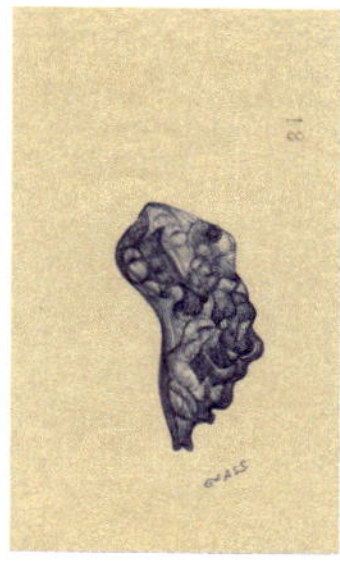

Untitled
(Club Saint-Germain period)
ca. 1954-1962
Monochrome blue ballpoint pen drawing,
on the order of Club Saint-Germain.
13.1 x 8 cm
Artist's collection
AG1954_1962_CSG_D0194
p. 119

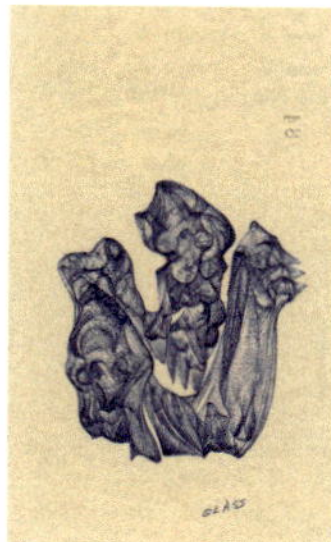

Untitled
(Club Saint-Germain period)
ca. 1954-1962
Monochrome blue ballpoint pen drawing,
on the order of Club Saint-Germain.
13.1 x 8 cm
Artist's collection
AG1954_1962_CSG_D0195
p. 119

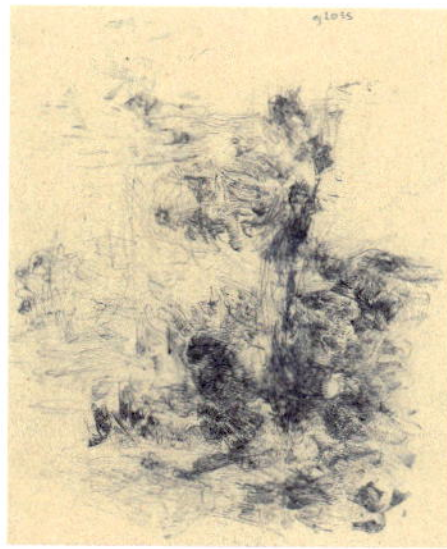

Untitled
(Club Saint-Germain period)
ca. 1954-1962
Monochrome navy blue ballpoint pen
drawing, on paper.
12 x 10 cm
Artist's collection
AG1954_1962_CSG_D0026
p. 120

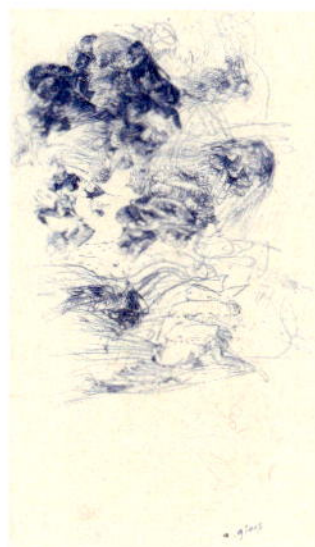

Untitled
(Club Saint-Germain period)
ca. 1954-1962
Monochrome blue ballpoint pen drawing,
on paper.
23.5 x 13.5 cm
Artist's collection
AG1954_1962_CSG_D0027
p. 120

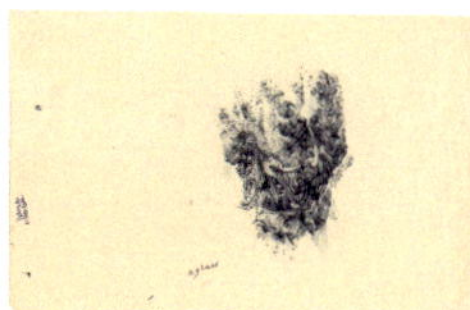

Untitled
(Club Saint-Germain period)
ca. 1954-1962
Monochrome navy blue ballpoint pen
drawing, on paper.
16.5 x 25.2 cm
Artist's collection
AG1954_1962_CSG_D0030
p. 120

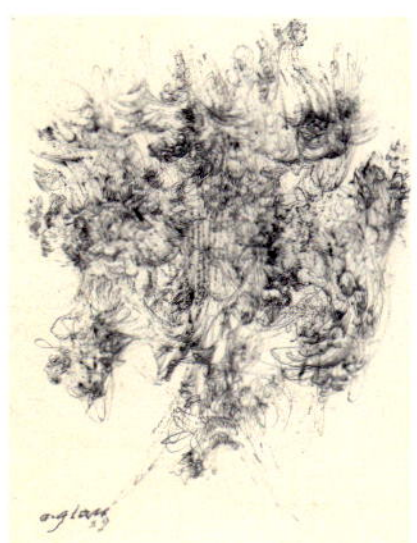

Untitled
(Club Saint-Germain period)
1959
Monochrome black ballpoint pen drawing,
on Club Saint-Germain invitation card.
14 x 10.5 cm
Artist's collection
AG1954_1962_CSG_D0029
p. 121

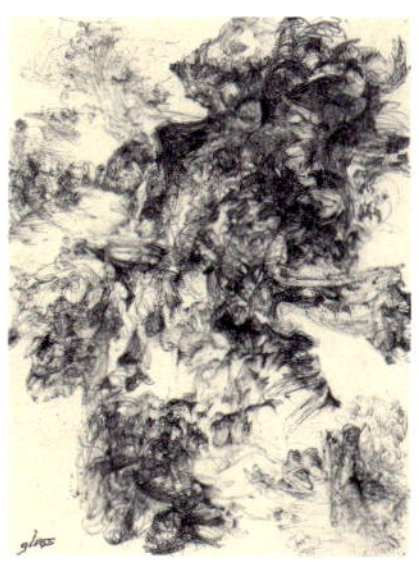

Untitled
(Club Saint-Germain period)
ca. 1954-1962
Monochrome black ballpoint pen drawing,
on Club Saint-Germain invitation card.
14 x 10.5 cm
Artist's collection
AG1954_1962_CSG_D0028
p. 121

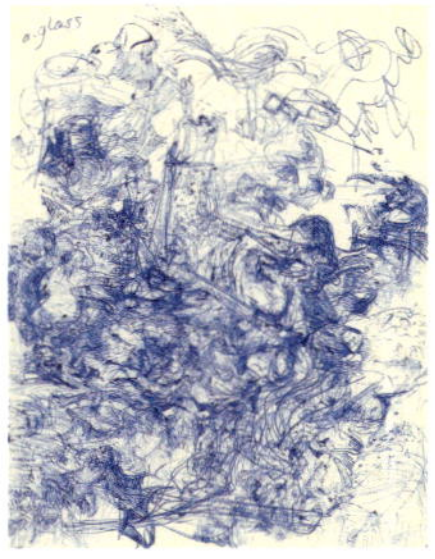

Untitled
(Club Saint-Germain period)
ca. 1954-1962
Monochrome blue ballpoint pen drawing, on Club Saint-Germain invitation card.
13.5 x 10.5 cm
Artist's collection
AG1954_1962_CSG_D0032
p. 122

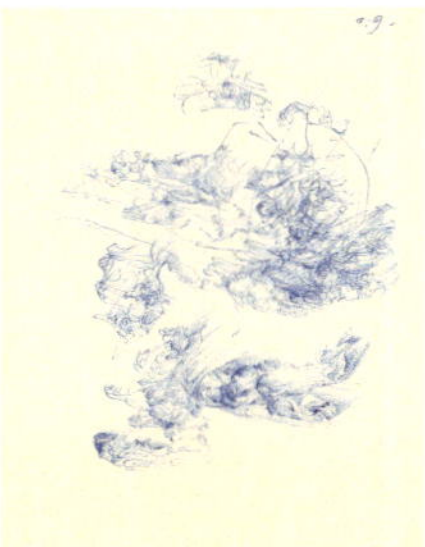

Untitled
(Club Saint-Germain period)
ca. 1954-1962
Monochrome blue ballpoint pen drawing, on Club Saint-Germain invitation card.
13.5 x 10.5 cm
Artist's collection
AG1954_1962_CSG_D0033
P. 123

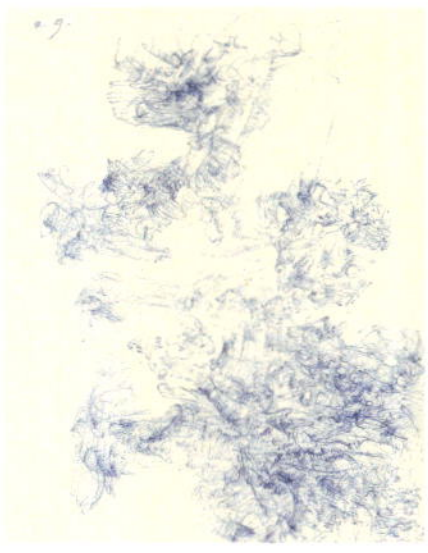

Untitled
(Club Saint-Germain period)
ca. 1954-1962
Monochrome blue ballpoint pen drawing, on Club Saint-Germain invitation card.
13.5 x 10.5 cm
Artist's collection
AG1954_1962_CSG_D0035
p. 123

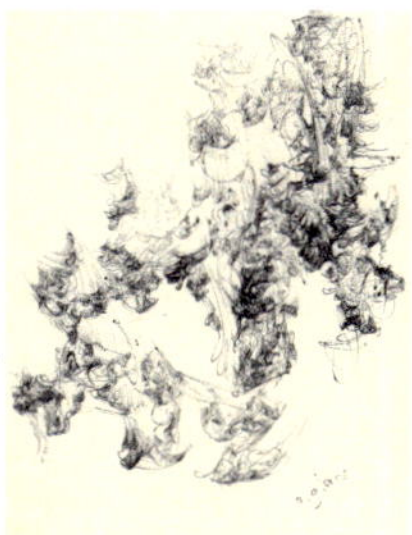

Untitled
(Club Saint-Germain period)
ca. 1954-1962
Monochrome black ballpoint pen drawing, on Club Saint-Germain invitation card.
14 x 10.5 cm
Artist's collection
AG1954_1962_CSG_D0034
p. 123

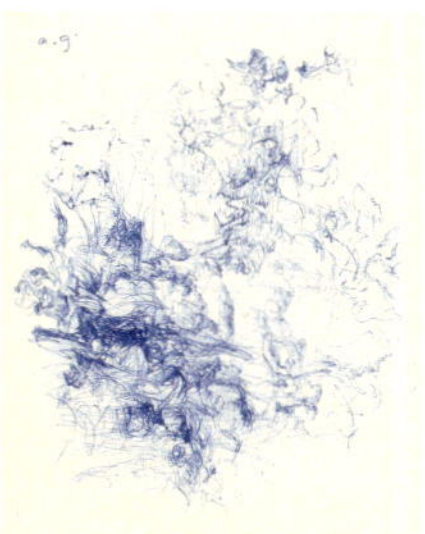

Untitled
(Club Saint-Germain period)
ca. 1954-1962
Monochrome blue ballpoint pen drawing, on Club Saint-Germain invitation card.
13.5 x 10.5 cm
Artist's collection
AG1954_1962_CSG_D0038
p. 124

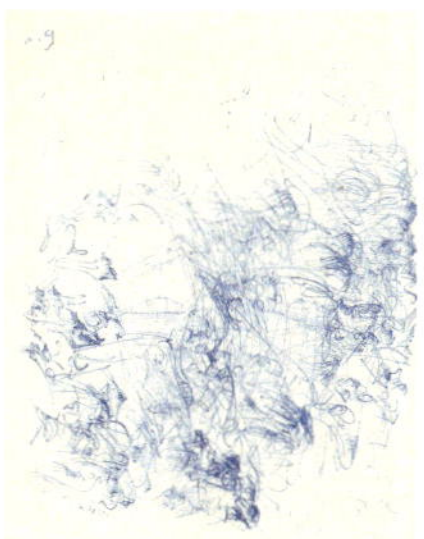

Untitled
(Club Saint-Germain period)
ca. 1954-1962
Monochrome blue ballpoint pen drawing, on Club Saint-Germain invitation card.
13.5 x 10.5 cm
Artist's collection
AG1954_1962_CSG_D0037
p. 124

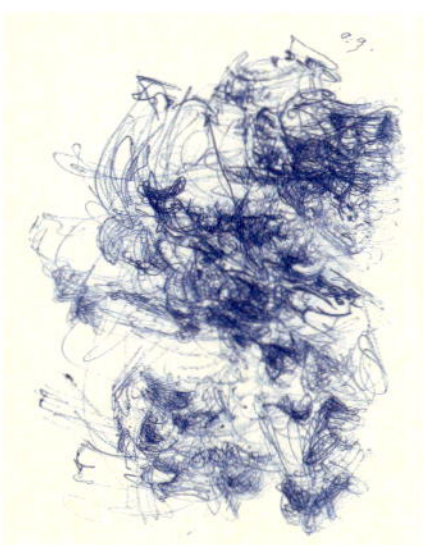

Untitled
(Club Saint-Germain period)
ca. 1954-1962
Monochrome blue ballpoint pen drawing, on Club Saint-Germain invitation card.
13.5 x 10.5 cm
Artist's collection
AG1954_1962_CSG_D0039
p. 125

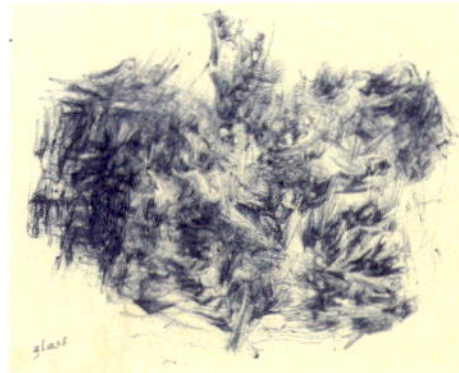

Untitled
(Club Saint-Germain period)
ca. 1954-1962
Monochrome navy blue ballpoint pen drawing, on paper.
14.5 x 18.5 cm
Artist's collection
AG1954_1962_CSG_D0040
p. 125

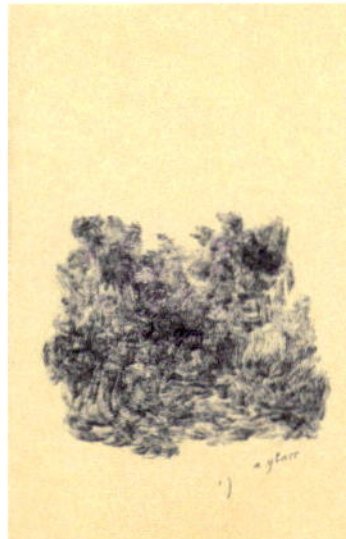

Untitled
(Club Saint-Germain period)
ca. 1954-1962
Bicolor blue and violet pen drawing, on paper.
22 x 13.7 cm
Artist's collection
AG1954_1962_CSG_D0041
p. 126

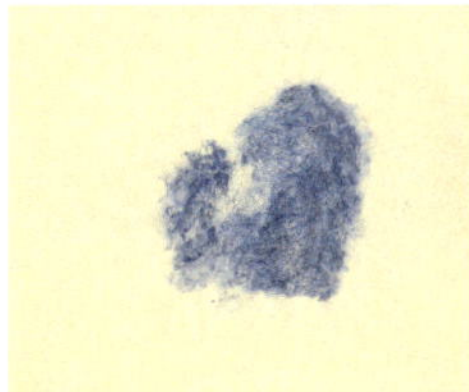

Untitled
(Club Saint-Germain period)
ca. 1954-1962
Monochrome blue ballpoint pen drawing with a touch of watercolor, on paper.
20.6 x 24.6 cm
Artist's collection
AG1954_1962_CSG_D0044
p. 126

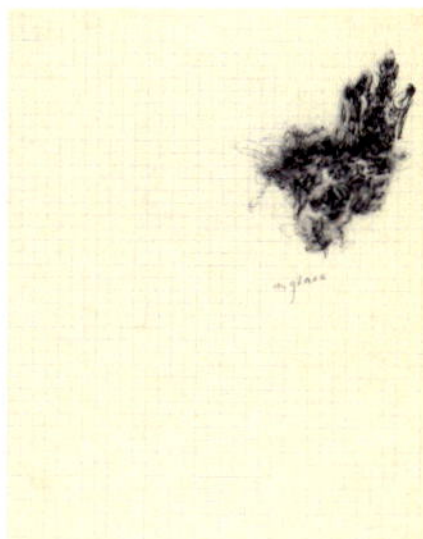

Untitled
(Club Saint-Germain period)
ca. 1954-1962
Monochrome black ballpoint pen drawing, on squared paper.
21.8 x 17 cm
Artist's collection
AG1954_1962_CSG_D0042
p. 127

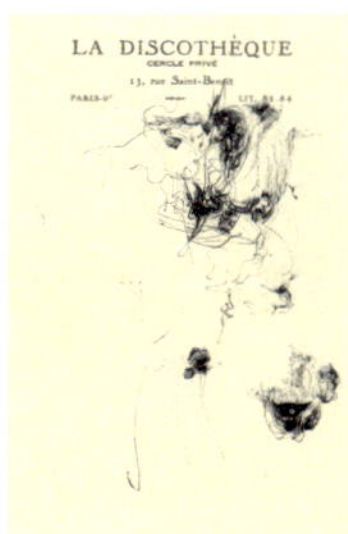

Untitled
(Club Saint-Germain period)
ca. 1954-1962
Monochrome black ballpoint pen drawing, on invitation from La Discothèque.
17.9 x 11.5 cm
Artist's collection
AG1954_1962_CSG_D0043
p. 127

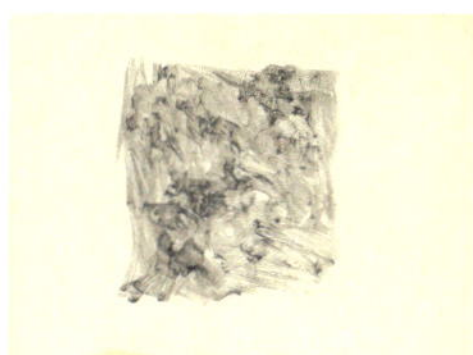

Untitled
(Club Saint-Germain period)
ca. 1954-1962
Graphite pencil drawing, on paper.
21 x 27 cm
Artist's collection
AG1954_1962_CSG_D0056
p. 128

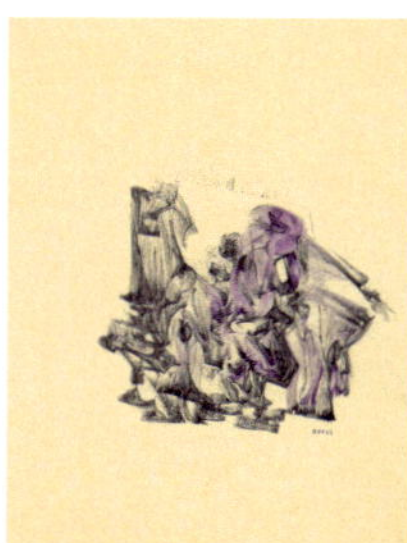

Untitled
(Club Saint-Germain period)
ca. 1954-1962
Monochrome pen drawing in navy blue and violet watercolor, on paper.
28 x 22.5 cm
Artist's collection
AG1954_1962_CSG_D0060
p. 129

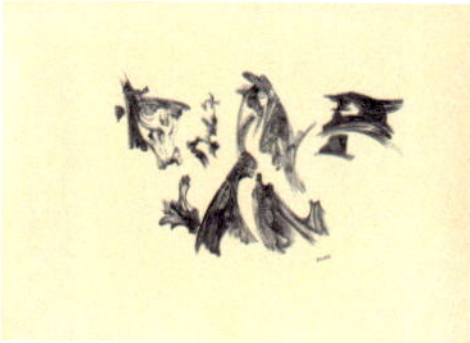

Untitled
(Club Saint-Germain period)
ca. 1954-1962
Monochrome navy blue ballpoint pen drawing, on paper.
25 x 32.5 cm
Artist's collection
AG1954_1962_CSG_D0057
p. 130

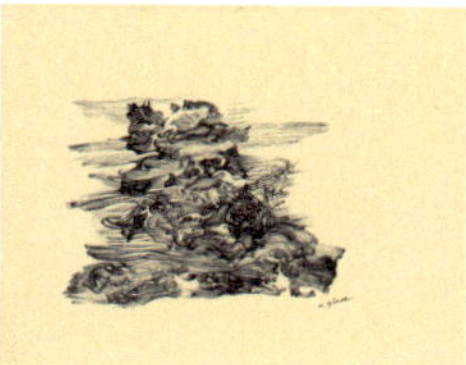

Untitled
(Club Saint-Germain period)
ca. 1954-1962
Monochrome navy blue ballpoint pen drawing, on paper.
22.5 x 28 cm
Artist's collection
AG1954_1962_CSG_D0058
p. 130

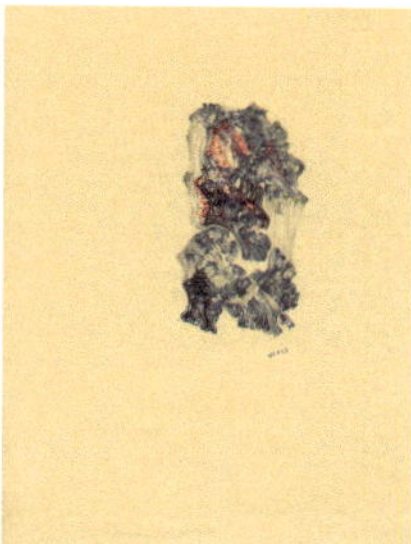

Untitled
(Club Saint-Germain period)
ca. 1954-1962
Monochrome blue ballpoint pen drawing, on paper.
28 x 22.5 cm
Artist's collection
AG1954_1962_CSG_D0055
p. 131

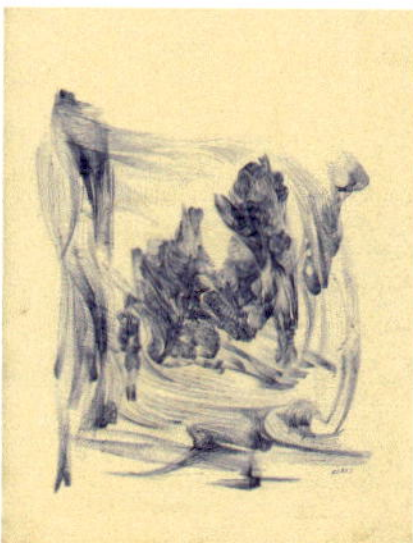

Untitled
(Club Saint-Germain period)
ca. 1954-1962
Monochrome pen drawing in navy blue and red, on paper.
28 x 22.5 cm
Artist's collection
AG1954_1962_CSG_D0059
p. 131

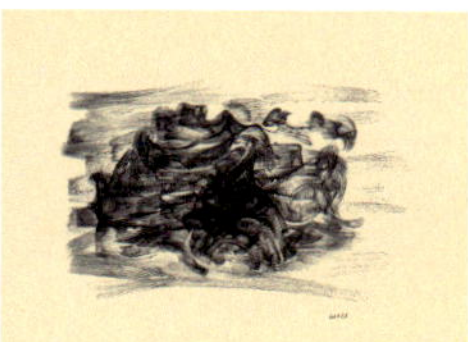

Untitled
(Club Saint-Germain period)
ca. 1954-1962
Navy blue monocolor ballpoint pen drawing, on cardboard paper.
18 x 26 cm
Artist's collection
AG1954_1962_CSG_D0061
p. 132

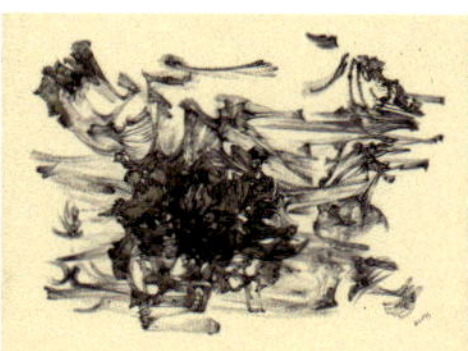

Untitled
(Club Saint-Germain period)
ca. 1954-1962
Monochrome black pen drawing and Indian ink, on cardboard paper.
18 x 26 cm
Artist's collection
AG1954_1962_CSG_D0062
p. 132

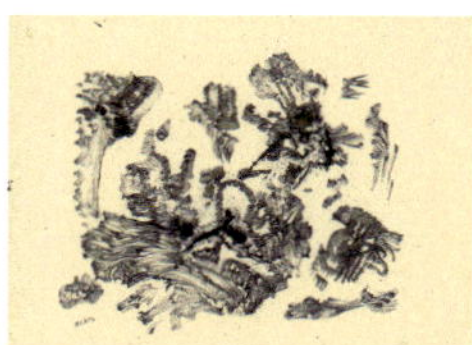

Untitled
(Club Saint-Germain period)
ca. 1954-1962
Monochrome black pen drawing and Indian ink, on cardboard paper.
18 x 26 cm
Artist's collection
AG1954_1962_CSG_D0063
p. 132

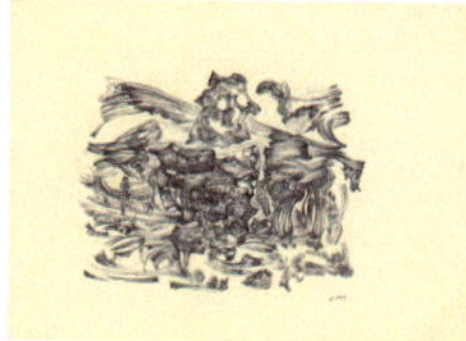

Untitled
(Club Saint-Germain period)
ca. 1954-1962
Monochrome black pen drawing and Indian ink, on cardboard paper.
18.5 x 25.7 cm
Artist's collection
AG1954_1962_CSG_D0064
p. 133

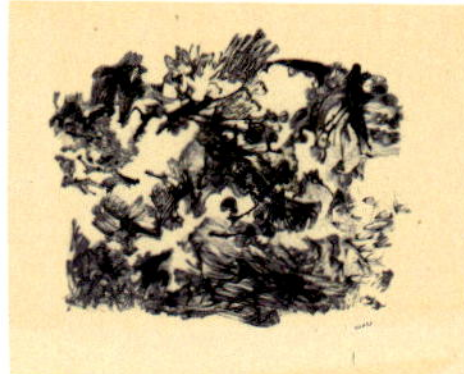

Untitled
(Club Saint-Germain period)
ca. 1954-1962
Monochrome black pen drawing and Indian ink, on paper.
21.5 x 26 cm
Artist's collection
AG1954_1962_CSG_D0066
p. 133

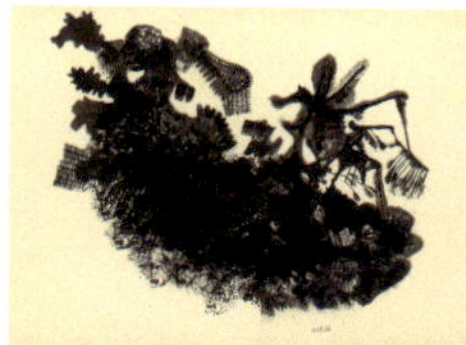

Untitled
(Club Saint-Germain period)
ca. 1954-1962
Monochrome black pen drawing and Indian ink, on cardboard paper.
26 x 37.5 cm
Artist's collection
AG1954_1962_CSG_D0065
p. 133

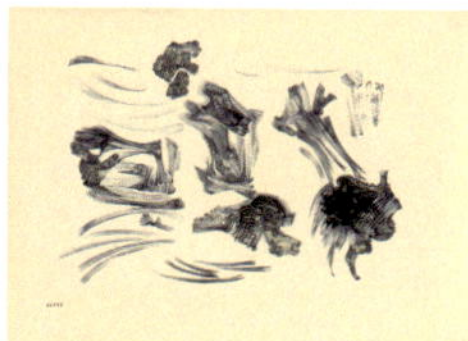

Untitled
(Club Saint-Germain period)
ca. 1954-1962
Monochrome black pen drawing, on paper.
25 x 32.5 cm
Artist's collection
AG1954_1962_CSG_D0067
p. 134

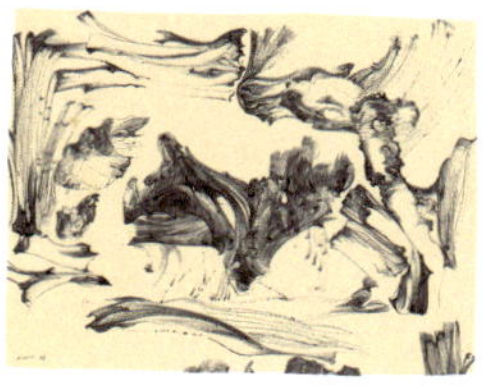

Untitled
(Club Saint-Germain period)
1958
Monochrome black pen drawing, on paper.
28.5 x 21.5 cm
Artist's collection
AG1954_1962_CSG_D0072
p. 134

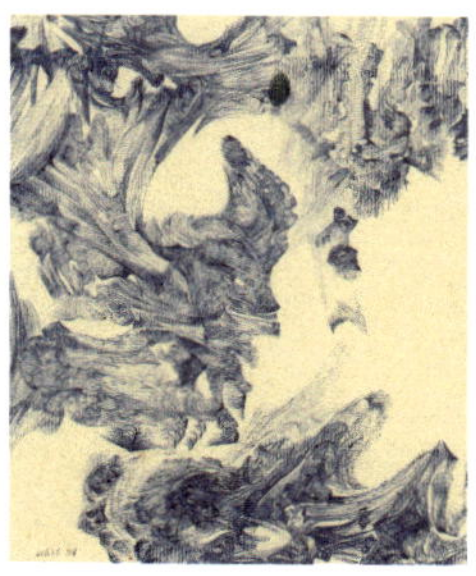

Untitled
(Club Saint-Germain period)
1958
Monochrome blue ballpoint pen drawing, on corrugated paper.
22.3 x 18.8 cm
Artist's collection
AG1954_1962_CSG_D0074
p. 135

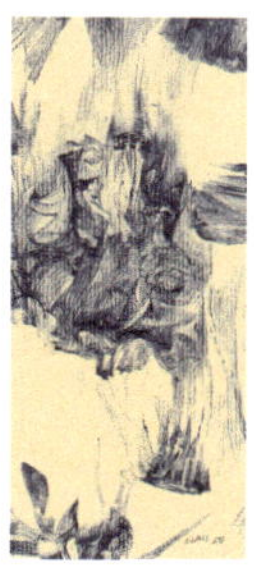

Untitled
(Club Saint-Germain period)
1958
Monochrome blue ballpoint pen drawing, on corrugated paper.
19.2 x 8.5 cm
Artist's collection
AG1954_1962_CSG_D0075
p. 135

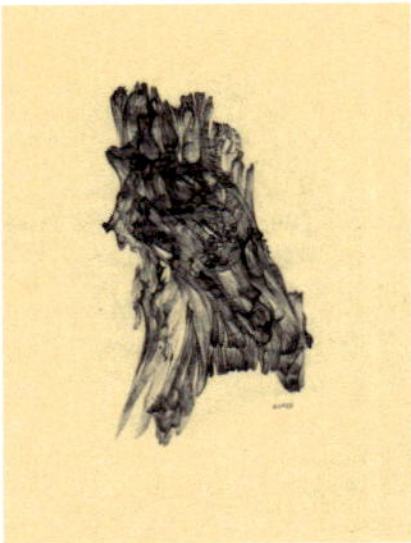

Untitled
(Club Saint-Germain period)
ca. 1954-1962
Monochrome black pen drawing,
on paper.
28 x 22.5 cm
Artist's collection
AG1954_1962_CSG_D0070
p. 136

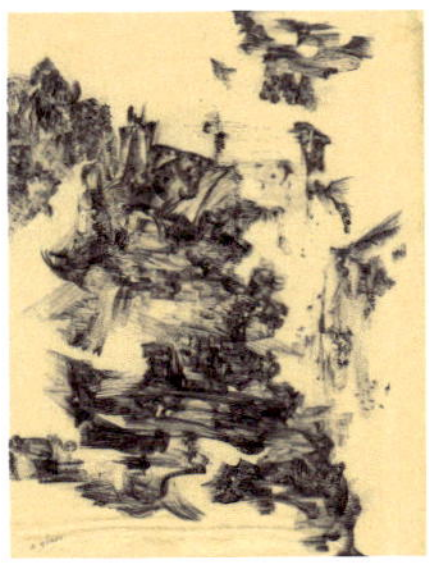

Untitled
(Club Saint-Germain period)
ca. 1954-1962
Monochrome black pen drawing,
on paper.
28 x 22 cm
Artist's collection
AG1954_1962_CSG_D0069
p. 137

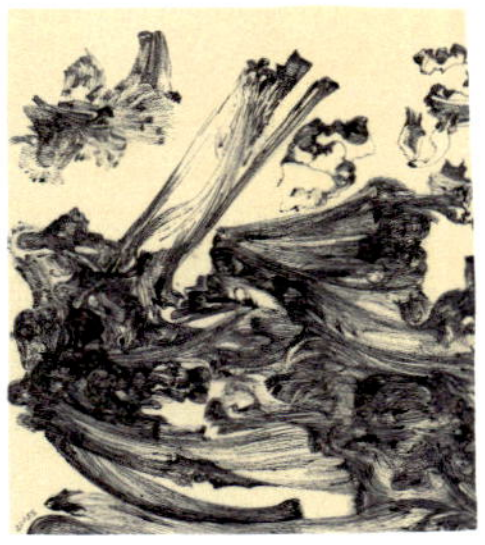

Untitled
(Club Saint-Germain period)
ca. 1954-1962
Monochrome black pen drawing,
on paper.
19.5 x 17 cm
Artist's collection
AG1954_1962_CSG_D0071
p. 138

Untitled
(Club Saint-Germain period)
ca. 1954-1962
Monochrome black ballpoint pen drawing,
on paper.
26 x 17 cm
Artist's collection
AG1954_1962_CSG_D0089
p. 139

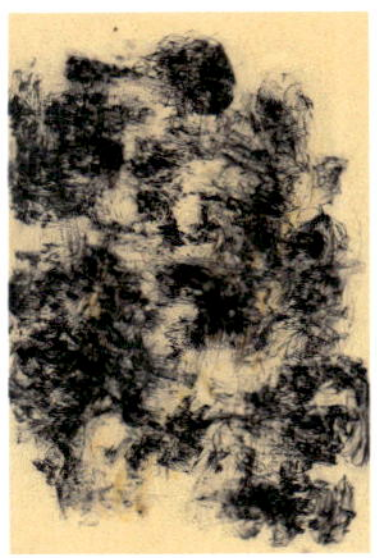

Untitled
(Club Saint-Germain period)
ca. 1954-1962
Monochrome black ballpoint pen drawing
with touch of alumettage, on paper.
26 x 17 cm
Artist's collection
AG1954_1962_CSG_D0088
p. 139

Untitled
(Club Saint-Germain period)
1959
Blue and navy blue two-tone ballpoint
pen drawing, on paper.
28 x 22.5 cm
Artist's collection
AG1954_1962_CSG_D0090
p. 139

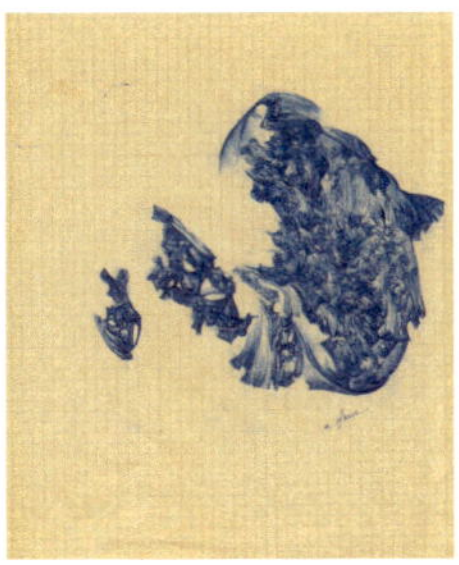

Untitled
(Club Saint-Germain period)
ca. 1954-1962
Monochrome blue ballpoint pen drawing,
on squared paper.
25.4 x 21 cm
Artist's collection
AG1954_1962_CSG_D0076
p. 140

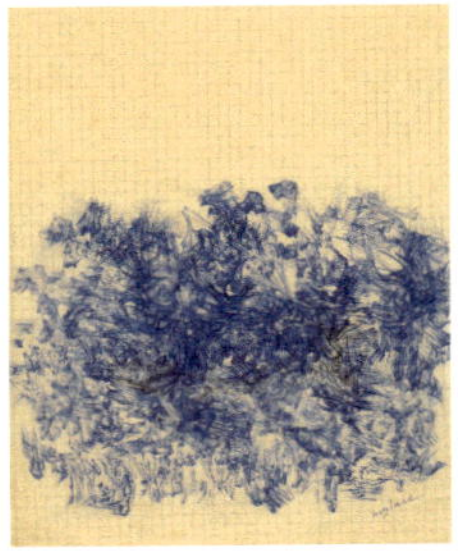

Untitled
(Club Saint-Germain period)
ca. 1954-1962
Monochrome blue ballpoint pen drawing,
on squared paper
25.4 x 21 cm
Artist's collection
AG1954_1962_CSG_D0077
p. 140

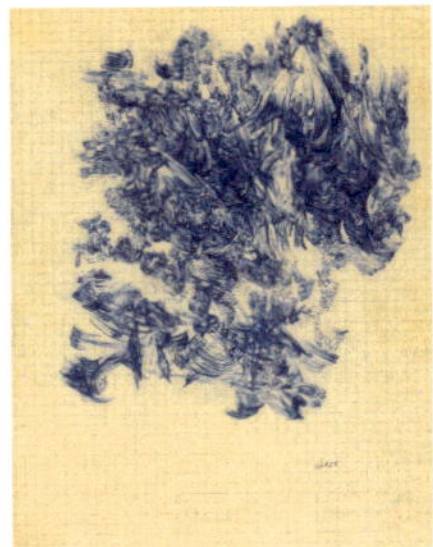

Untitled
(Club Saint-Germain period)
ca. 1954-1962
Monochrome blue ballpoint pen drawing
on squared paper.
27 x 21 cm
Artist's collection
AG1954_1962_CSG_D0078
p. 140

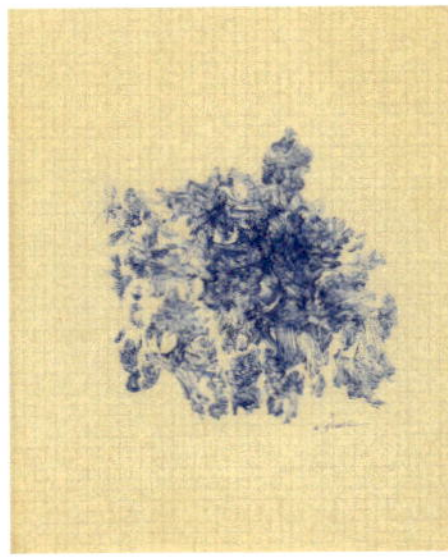

Untitled
(Club Saint-Germain period)
ca. 1954-1962
Monochrome blue ballpoint pen drawing
on squared paper.
25.5 x 21 cm
Artist's collection
AG1954_1962_CSG_D0080
p. 141

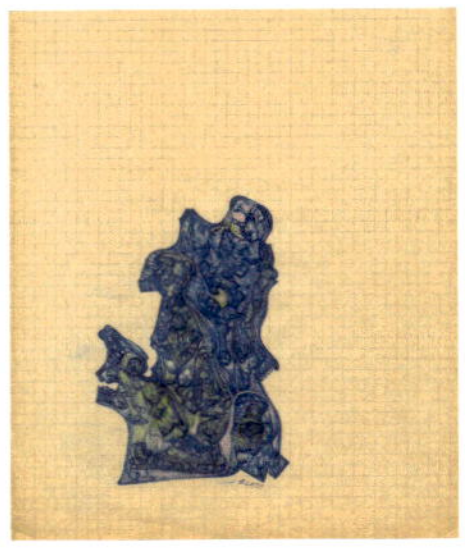

Untitled
(Club Saint-Germain period)
ca. 1954-1962
Bicolor blue and green ballpoint pen
drawing, on squared paper.
25.5 x 21 cm
Artist's collection
AG1954_1962_CSG_D0081
p. 141

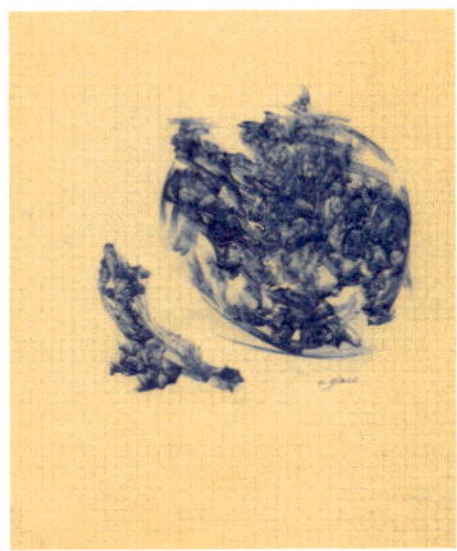

Untitled
(Club Saint-Germain period)
ca. 1954-1962
Monochrome blue ballpoint pen drawing
on squared paper.
25.5 x 21 cm
Artist's collection
AG1954_1962_CSG_D0082
p. 141

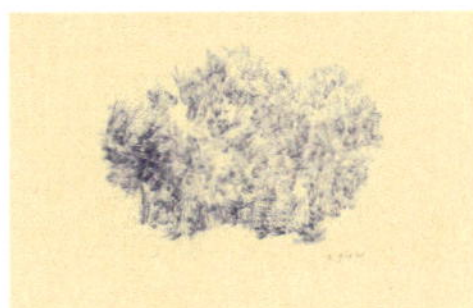

Untitled
(Club Saint-Germain period)
ca. 1954-1962
Bicolor blue and violet pen drawing
on paper.
15.5 x 24 cm
Artist's collection
AG1954_1962_CSG_D0045
p. 142

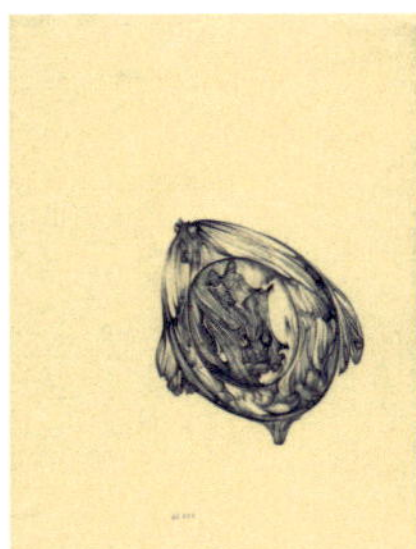

Untitled
(Club Saint-Germain period)
ca. 1954-1962
Monochrome navy blue ballpoint pen
drawing, on paper.
28 x 22.5 cm
Artist's collection
AG1954_1962_CSG_D0054
p. 143

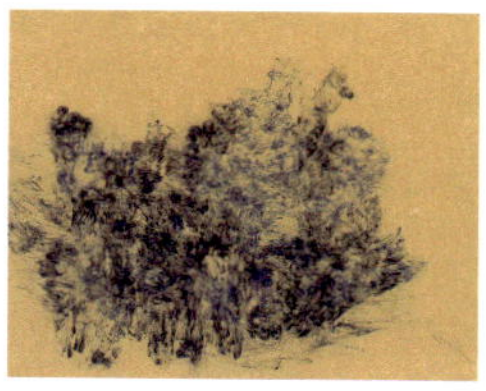

Untitled
(Club Saint-Germain period)
ca. 1954-1962
Monochrome black ballpoint pen drawing, on paper.
21.7 x 28 cm
Artist's collection
AG1954_1962_CSG_D0093
p. 144

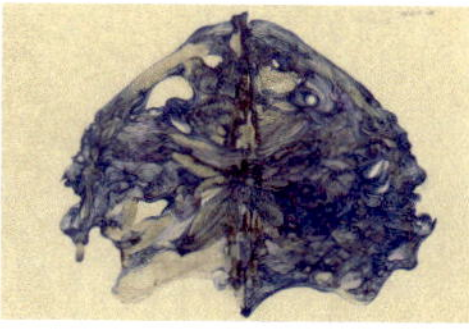

Untitled
(Club Saint-Germain period)
1958
Bicolor blue and black ballpoint pen drawing, with violet color and graphite, on paper.
18 x 26.5 cm
Artist's collection
AG1954_1962_CSG_D0086
p. 144

Untitled
(Club Saint-Germain period)
1959
Monochrome blue ballpoint pen drawing, on paper.
21.9 x 28 cm
Artist's collection
AG1954_1962_CSG_D0095
p. 145

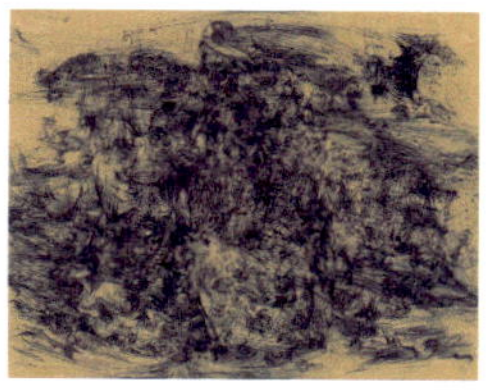

Untitled
(Club Saint-Germain period)
1959
Monochrome navy blue ballpoint pen drawing, on paper.
22 x 28 cm
Artist's collection
AG1954_1962_CSG_D0096
p. 145

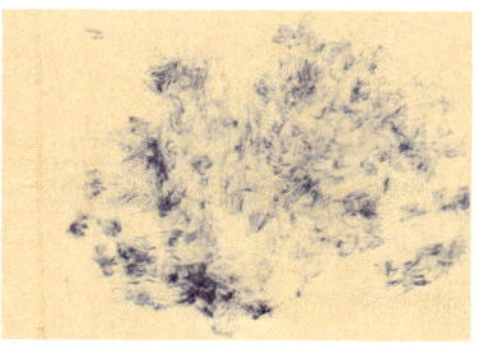

Untitled
(Club Saint-Germain period)
1959
Monochrome blue ballpoint pen drawing, on paper.
24.5 x 32.5 cm
Artist's collection
AG1954_1962_CSG_D0097
p. 145

Untitled
(Club Saint-Germain period)
ca. 1954-1962
Monochrome blue ballpoint pen drawing, on paper.
26 x 17 cm
Artist's collection
AG1954_1962_CSG_D0087
p. 146

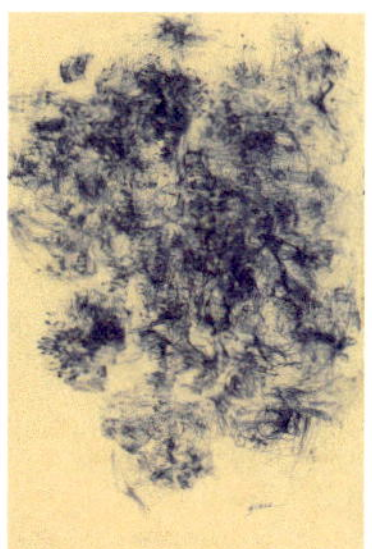

Untitled
(Club Saint-Germain period)
ca. 1954-1962
Monochrome blue ballpoint pen drawing, on paper.
28 x 24 cm
Artist's collection
AG1954_1962_CSG_D0091
p. 146

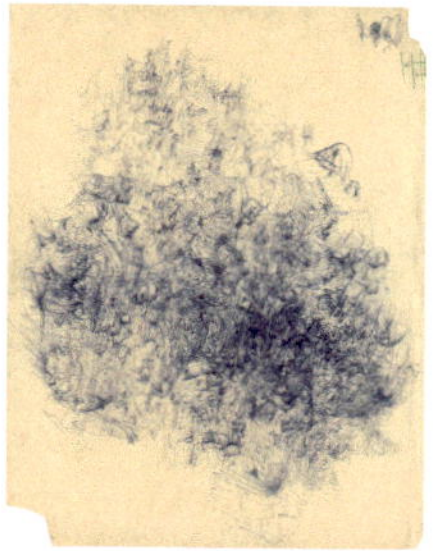

Untitled
(Club Saint-Germain period)
1959
Monochrome navy blue ballpoint pen drawing, on paper.
32 x 25.5 cm
Artist's collection
AG1954_1962_CSG_D0092
p. 146

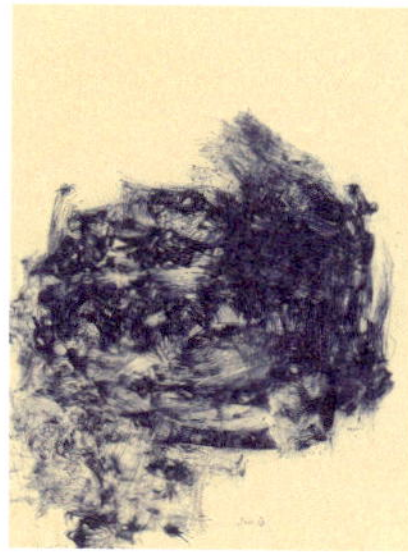

Untitled
(Club Saint-Germain period)
1959
Monochrome blue ballpoint pen drawing, on paper.
32 x 24.5 cm
Artist's collection
AG1954_1962_CSG_D0100
p. 147

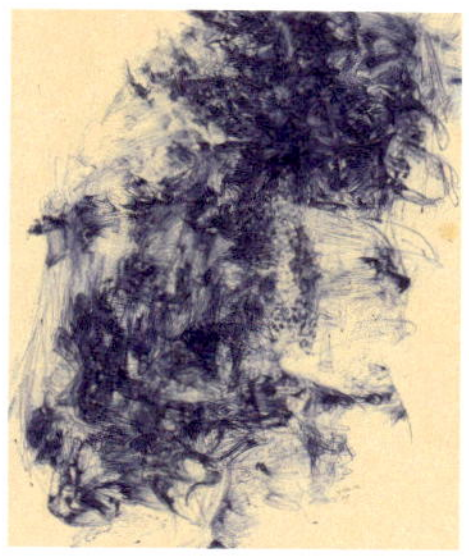

Untitled
(Club Saint-Germain period)
1959
Monochrome blue ballpoint pen drawing, on paper.
26.5 x 22.5 cm
Artist's collection
AG1954_1962_CSG_D0098
p. 147

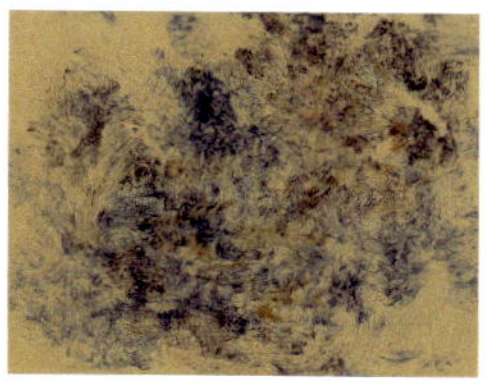

Untitled
(Club Saint-Germain period)
ca. 1954-1962
Monochrome navy blue ballpoint pen drawing with touches of allumettage.
21.5 x 28 cm
Artist's collection
AG1954_1962_CSG_D0099
p. 148

Untitled
(Club Saint-Germain period)
ca. 1954-1962
Monochrome blue ballpoint pen drawing on squared paper.
25.5 x 21 cm
Artist's collection
AG1954_1962_CSG_D0083
p. 149

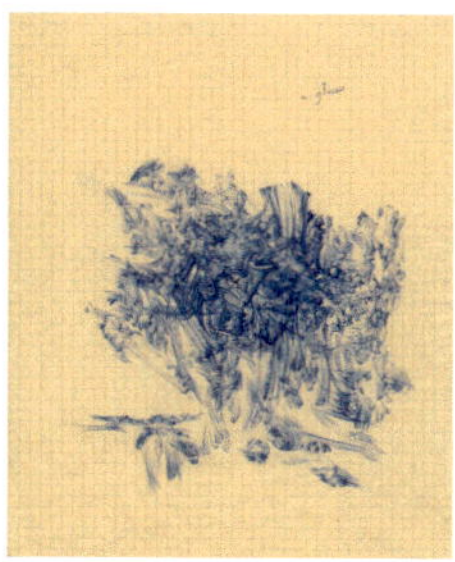

Untitled
(Club Saint-Germain period)
ca. 1954-1962
Monochrome blue ballpoint pen drawing on squared paper.
25.5 x 21 cm
Artist's collection
AG1954_1962_CSG_D0084
p. 149

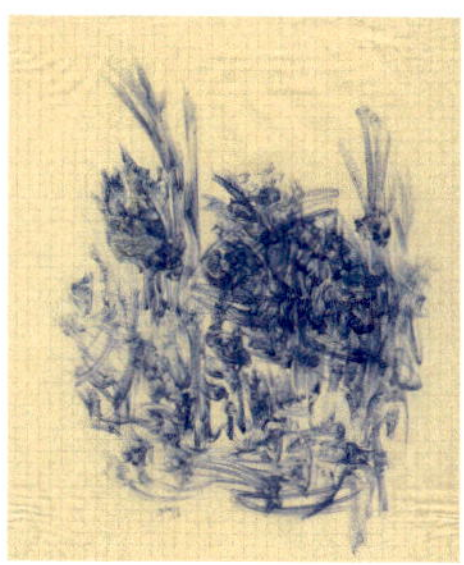

Untitled
(Club Saint-Germain period)
1958
Monochrome blue ballpoint pen drawing on squared paper.
27.9 x 23.9 cm
Artist's collection
AG1954_1962_CSG_D0085
p. 149

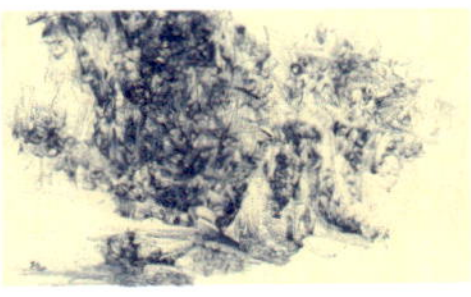

Untitled
(Club Saint-Germain period)
ca. 1954-1962
Monochrome navy blue ballpoint pen drawing, on Club Saint Germain invitation.
13.5 x 23.5 cm
Artist's collection
AG1954_1962_CSG_D0102
p. 150

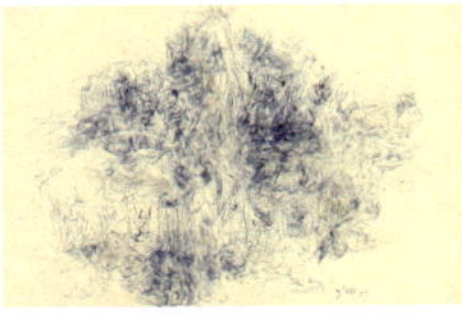

Untitled
(Club Saint-Germain period)
1959
Monochrome navy blue ballpoint pen drawing, on paper.
15.5 x 24 cm
Artist's collection
AG1954_1962_CSG_D0101
p. 150

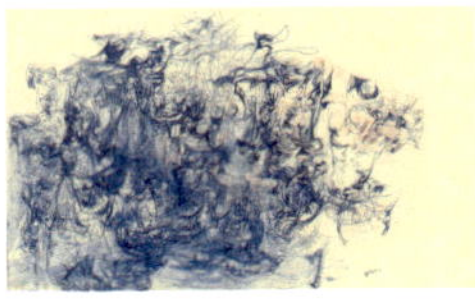

Untitled
(Club Saint-Germain period)
ca. 1954-1962
Monochrome blue ballpoint pen drawing with red markings, on Club Saint Germain invitation.
13.5 x 23.5 cm
Artist's collection
AG1954_1962_CSG_D0103
p. 150

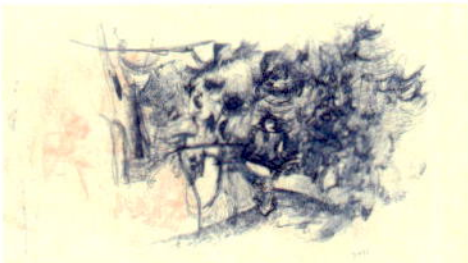

Untitled
(Club Saint-Germain period)
ca. 1954-1962
Monochrome blue ballpoint pen drawing with red markings, on Club Saint Germain invitation.
13.5 x 23.5 cm
Artist's collection
AG1954_1962_CSG_D0104
p. 151

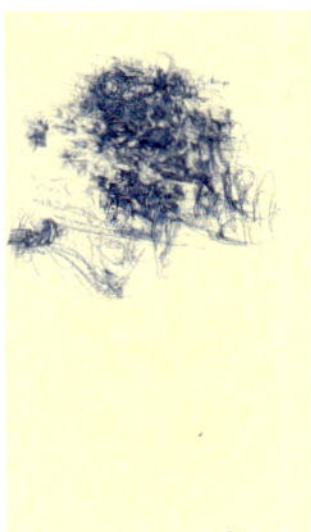

Untitled
(Club Saint-Germain period)
ca. 1954-1962
Monochrome blue ballpoint pen drawing, on Club Saint Germain invitation.
13.5 x 23.5 cm
Artist's collection
AG1954_1962_CSG_D0105
p. 151

Untitled
(Club Saint-Germain period)
ca. 1954-1962
Monochrome blue ballpoint pen drawing, on paper.
19 x 17.5 cm
Artist's collection
AG1954_1962_CSG_D0106
p. 151

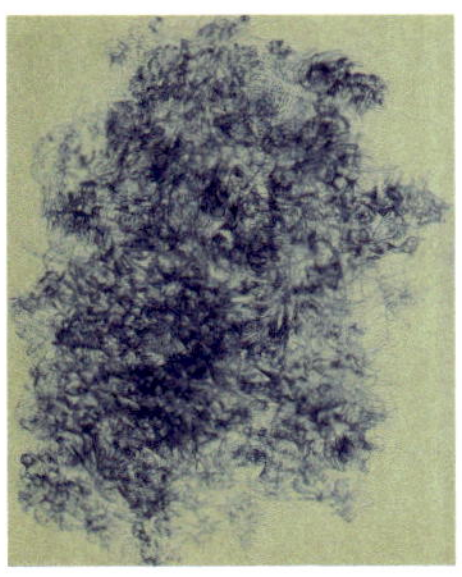

Untitled
(Club Saint-Germain period)
ca. 1954-1962
Monochrome blue ballpoint pen drawing, on green corrugated paper.
21 x 25.5 cm
Artist's collection
AG1954_1962_CSG_D0107
p. 152

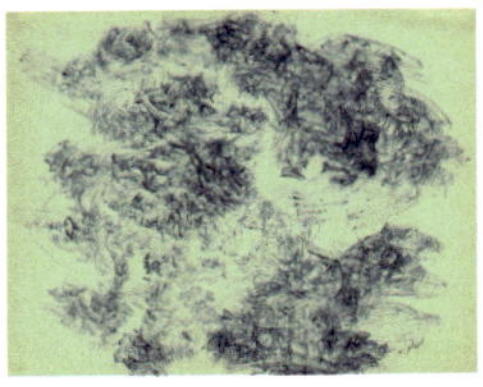

Untitled
(Club Saint-Germain period)
ca. 1954-1962
Monochrome blue ballpoint pen drawing, on green corrugated paper.
25.5 x 32.5 cm
Artist's collection
AG1954_1962_CSG_D0108
p. 153

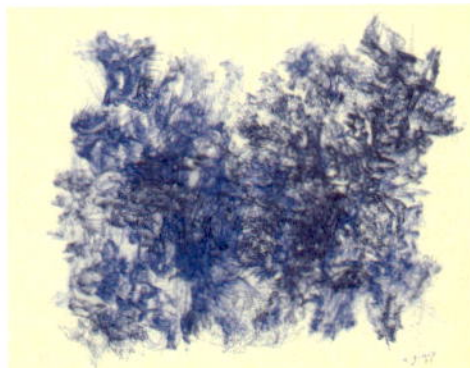

Untitled
(Club Saint-Germain period)
1959
Monochrome blue ballpoint pen drawing on paper.
21 x 27 cm
Artist's collection
AG1954_1962_CSG_D0109
p. 153

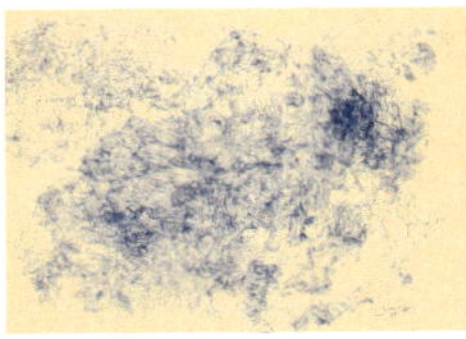

Untitled
(Club Saint-Germain period)
1959
Monochrome blue ballpoint pen drawing, on paper.
19 x 28 cm
Artist's collection
AG1954_1962_CSG_D0110
p. 154

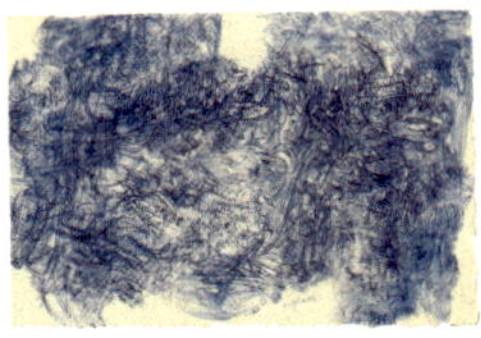

Untitled
(Club Saint-Germain period)
ca. 1954-1962
Monochrome blue ballpoint pen drawing, on corrugated paper.
19 x 28 cm
Artist's collection
AG1954_1962_CSG_D0111
p. 154

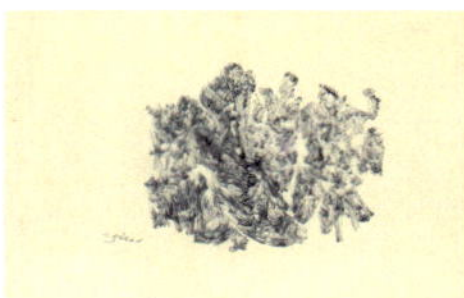

Untitled
(Club Saint-Germain period)
ca. 1954-1962
Monochrome navy blue ballpoint pen drawing, on paper.
16.5 x 25 cm
Artist's collection
AG1954_1962_CSG_D0119
p. 154

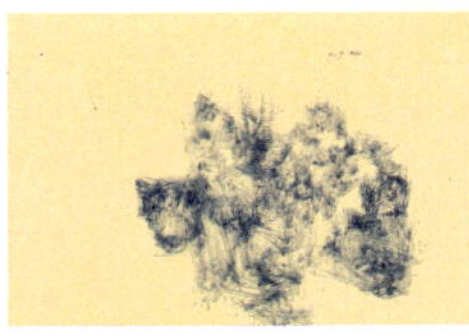

Untitled
(Club Saint-Germain period)
ca. 1954-1962
Monochrome navy blue ballpoint pen drawing, on paper.
17 x 26 cm
Artist's collection
AG1954_1962_CSG_D0115
p. 155

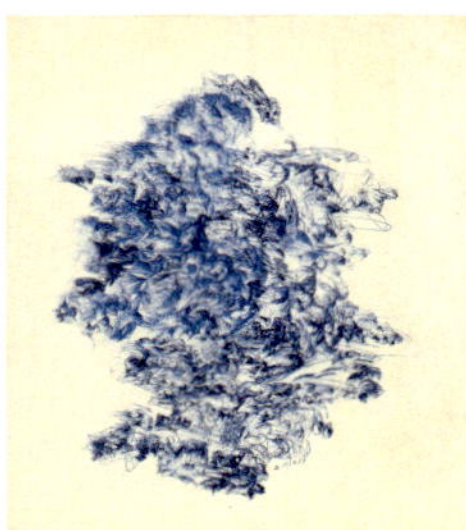

Untitled
(Club Saint-Germain period)
ca. 1954-1962
Blue and navy blue two-tone ballpoint pen drawing, on paper.
27.5 x 25 cm
Artist's collection
AG1954_1962_CSG_D0120
p. 155

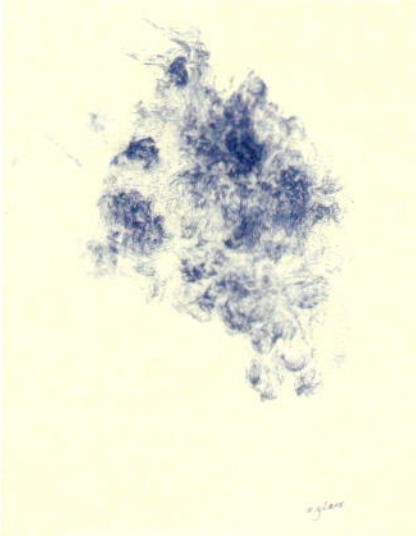

Untitled
(Club Saint-Germain period)
ca. 1954-1962
Monochrome blue ballpoint pen drawing, on paper.
27 x 21 cm
Artist's collection
AG1954_1962_CSG_D0124
p. 156

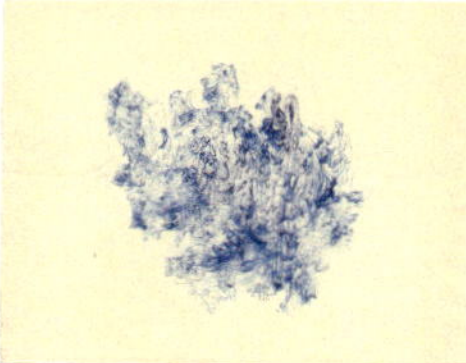

Untitled
(Club Saint-Germain period)
1959
Blue and navy blue two-tone ballpoint pen drawing, on paper.
32 x 25 cm
Artist's collection
AG1954_1962_CSG_D0125
p. 156

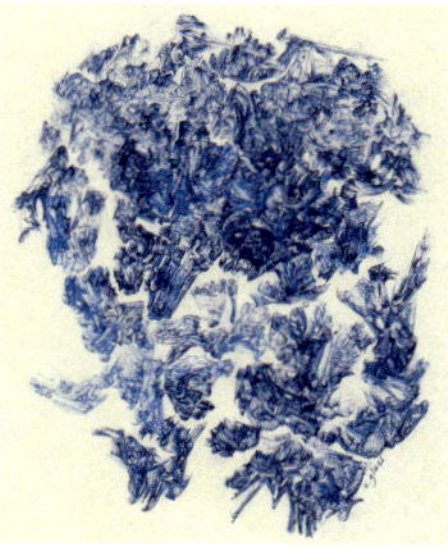

Untitled
(Club Saint-Germain period)
ca. 1954-1962
Monochrome blue ballpoint pen drawing, on paper.
27 x 21 cm
Artist's collection
AG1954_1962_CSG_D0127
p. 157

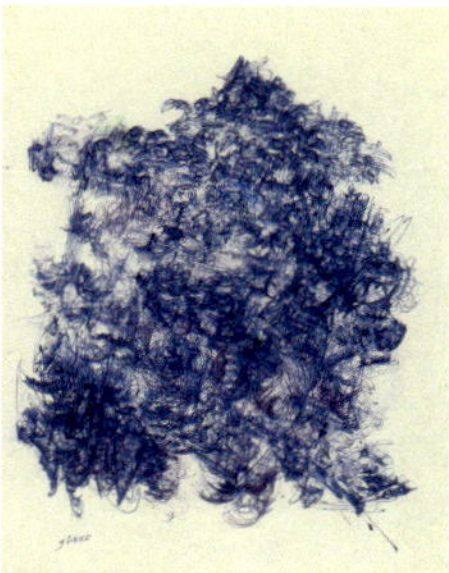

Untitled
(Club Saint-Germain period)
ca. 1954-1962
Bicolor blue and violet pen drawing, on paper.
27 x 21 cm
Artist's collection
AG1954_1962_CSG_D0128
p. 157

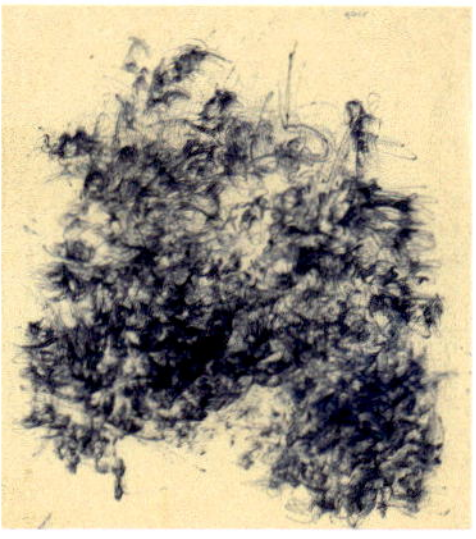

Untitled
(Club Saint-Germain period)
ca. 1954-1962
Monochrome navy blue ballpoint pen drawing, on paper.
30.5 x 28 cm
Artist's collection
AG1954_1962_CSG_D0130
p. 158

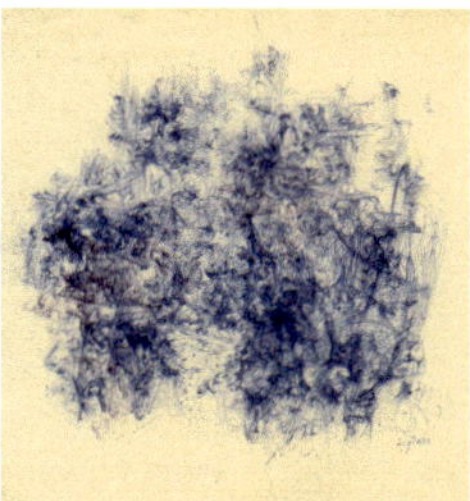

Untitled
(Club Saint Germain period)
ca. 1954-1962
Bicolor blue and violet ballpoint pen drawing, on paper.
28 x 32 cm
Artist's collection
AG1954_1962_CSG_D0131
p. 158

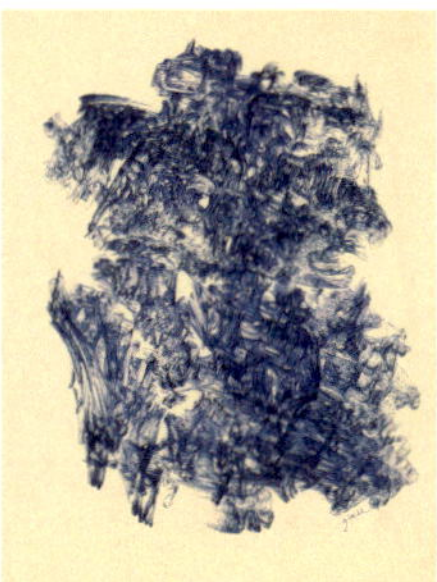

Untitled
(Club Saint-Germain period)
ca. 1954-1962
Blue and navy blue two-tone ballpoint pen drawing, on paper.
32 x 24 cm
Artist's collection
AG1954_1962_CSG_D0114
p. 158

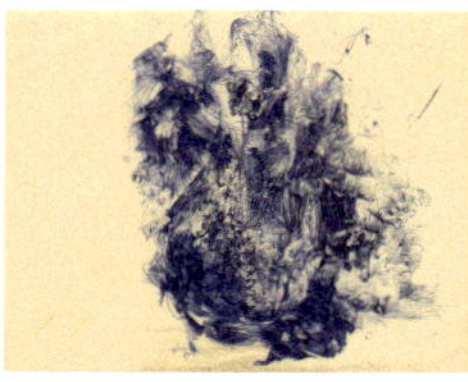

Untitled
(Club Saint-Germain period)
1959
Monochrome navy blue ballpoint pen drawing, on paper.
24 x 32 cm
Artist's collection
AG1954_1962_CSG_D0133
p. 159

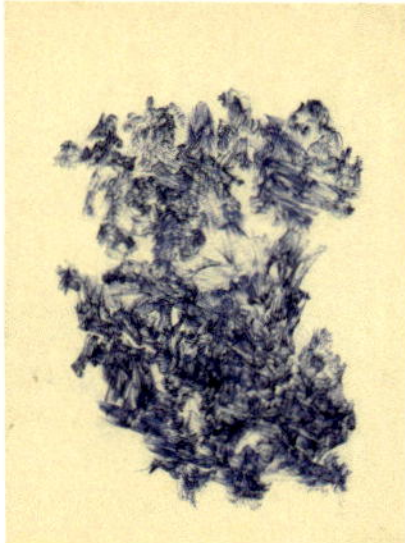

Untitled
(Club Saint-Germain period)
1959
Blue and navy blue two-tone ballpoint pen drawing on paper.
32 x 24 cm
Artist's collection
AG1954_1962_CSG_D0132
p. 159

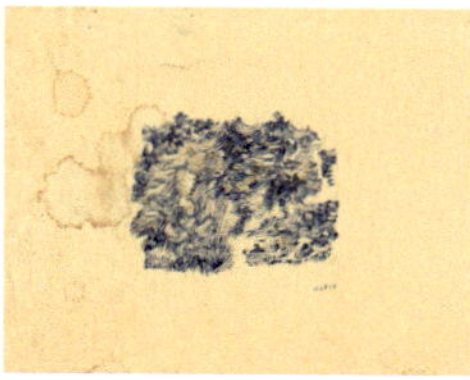

Untitled
(Club Saint Germain period)
ca. 1954-1962
Monochrome blue ballpoint pen and graphite drawing, on paper.
22.5 x 28 cm
Artist's collection
AG1954_1962_CSG_D0136
p. 160

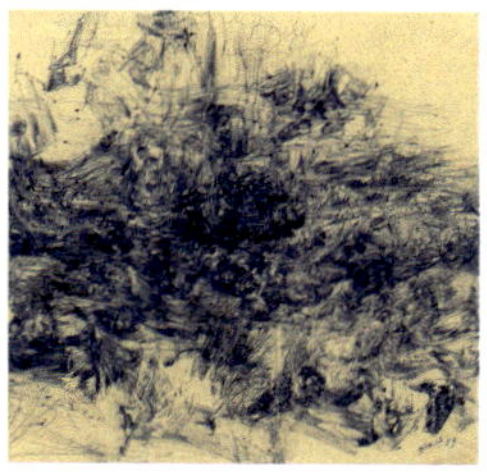

Untitled
(Club Saint-Germain period)
1959
Monochrome navy blue ballpoint pen drawing, on paper.
14.5 x 15 cm
Artist's collection
AG1954_1962_CSG_D0135
p. 160

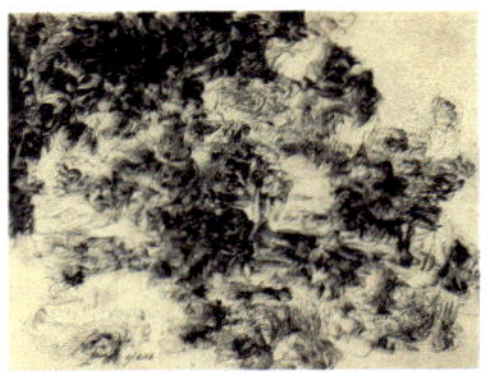

Untitled
(Club Saint-Germain period)
ca. 1954-1962
Monochrome black ballpoint pen drawing, on paper.
13.5 x 17.5 cm
Artist's collection
AG1954_1962_CSG_D0140
p. 161

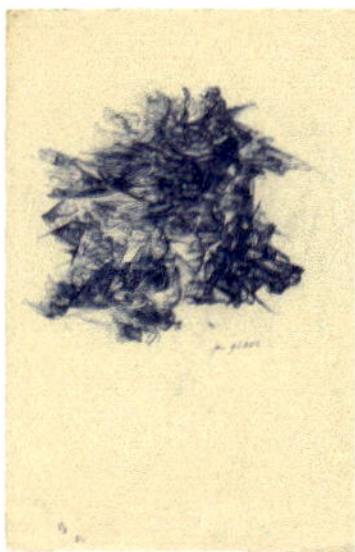

Untitled
(Club Saint-Germain period)
ca. 1954-1962
Monochrome blue ballpoint pen drawing, on paper.
24 x 16 cm
Artist's collection
AG1954_1962_CSG_D0139
p. 161

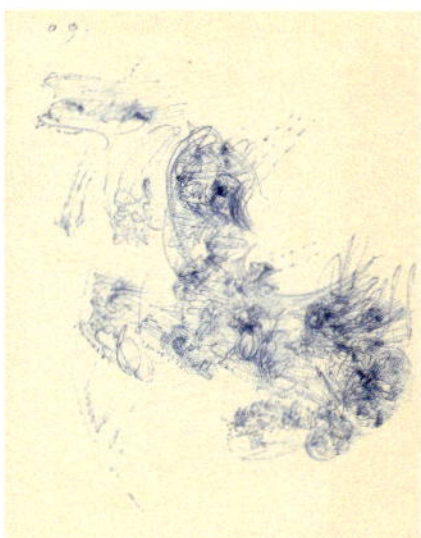

Untitled
(Club Saint-Germain period)
ca. 1954-1962
Monochrome blue ballpoint pen drawing, on Club Saint-Germain invitation card.
13.5 x 10.5 cm
Artist's collection
AG1954_1962_CSG_D0031
p. 162

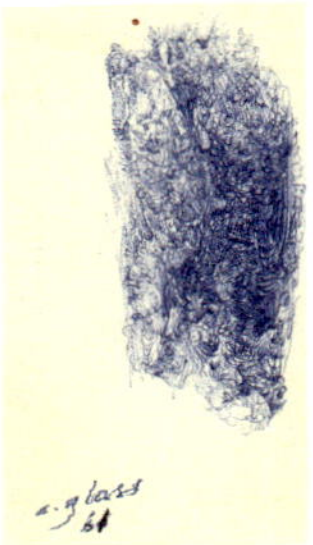

Untitled
(Club Saint-Germain period)
1961
Monochrome blue ballpoint pen drawing, on business card.
9 x 5 cm
Artist's collection
AG1954_1962_CSG_D0018
p. 162

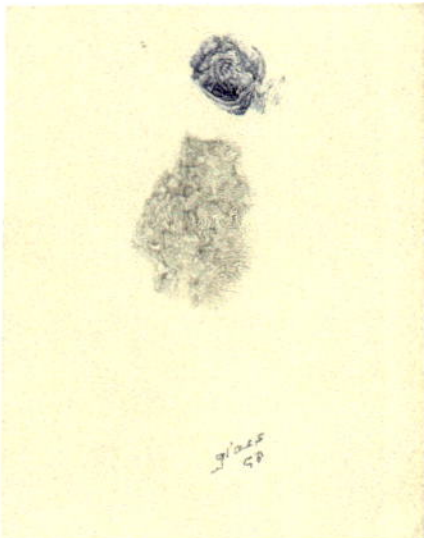

Untitled
(Club Saint-Germain period)
1958
Monochrome blue ballpoint pen drawing and graphite, on paper.
11.7 x 9.2 cm
Artist's collection
AG1954_1962_CSG_D0017
p. 162

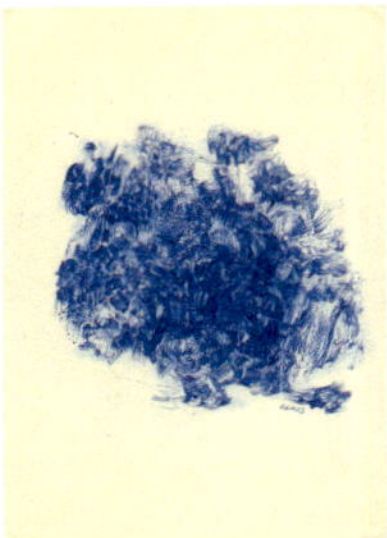

Untitled
(Club Saint-Germain period)
ca. 1954-1962
Monochrome blue ballpoint pen drawing, on paper.
22 x 16 cm
Artist's collection
AG1954_1962_CSG_D0116
p. 163

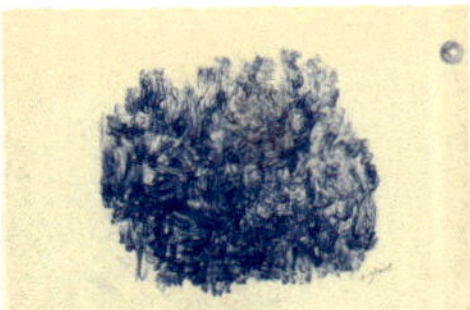

Untitled
(Club Saint-Germain period)
ca. 1954-1962
Blue and navy blue two-tone ballpoint pen drawing, on paper.
16 x 24 cm
Artist's collection
AG1954_1962_CSG_D0117
p. 163

Untitled
(Club Saint-Germain period)
ca. 1954-1962
Monochrome blue ballpoint pen drawing, on paper.
29 x 25 cm
Artist's collection
AG1954_1962_CSG_D0121
p. 164

Untitled
(Club Saint Germain period)
ca. 1954-1962
Bicolor blue and black ballpoint pen drawing, on paper.
19 x 28 cm
Artist's collection
AG1954_1962_CSG_D0112
p. 164

Untitled
(Club Saint-Germain period)
1959
Monochrome navy blue ballpoint pen drawing, on paper.
32 x 25 cm
Artist's collection
AG1954_1962_CSG_D0122
p. 165

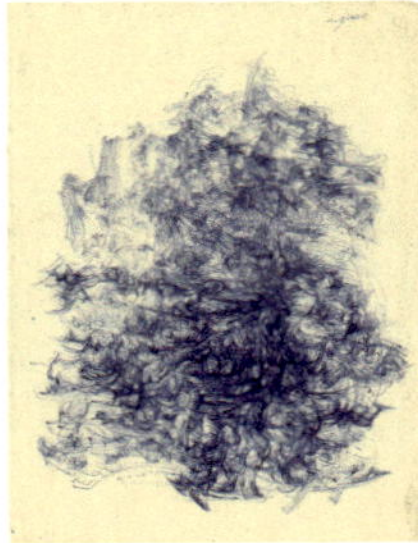

Untitled
(Club Saint-Germain period)
ca. 1954-1962
Monochrome blue ballpoint pen drawing, on paper.
32 x 25 cm
Artist's collection
AG1954_1962_CSG_D0134
p. 166

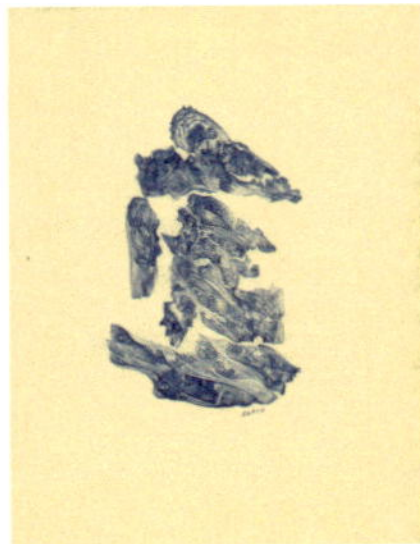

Untitled
(Club Saint-Germain period)
ca. 1954-1962
Monochrome blue ballpoint pen drawing, on paper.
28 x 22.5 cm
Artist's collection
AG1954_1962_CSG_D0113
p. 167

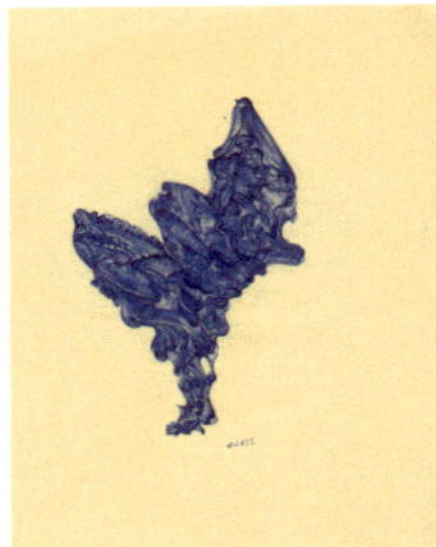

Untitled
(Club Saint-Germain period)
ca. 1954-1962
Monochrome blue ballpoint pen drawing, on paper.
27 x 22 cm
Artist's collection
AG1954_1962_CSG_D0184
p. 167

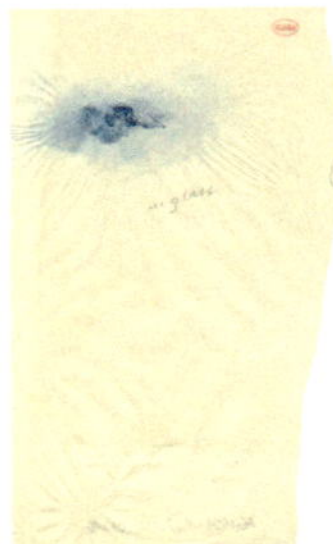

Untitled
(Club Saint-Germain period)
ca. 1954-1962
Monochrome blue ballpoint pen drawing with blue watercolor, on paper.
21 x 13 cm
Artist's collection
AG1954_1962_CSG_D0246
p. 168

Untitled
(Club Saint-Germain period)
ca. 1954-1962
Graphite drawing, on paper.
9.2 x 5 cm
Artist's collection
AG1954_1962_CSG_D0242
p. 168

Untitled
(Club Saint-Germain period)
ca. 1954-1962
Monochrome navy blue ballpoint pen drawing, on paper.
32 x 25 cm.
Artist's collection
AG1954_1962_CSG_D0123
p. 169

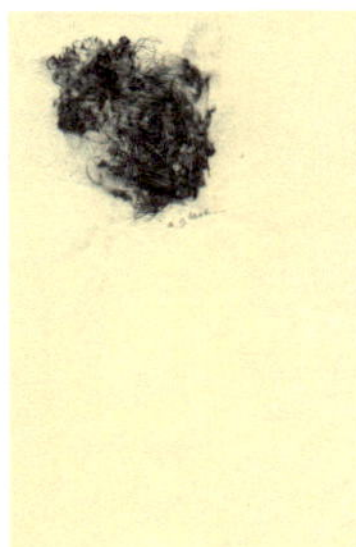

Untitled
(Club Saint-Germain period)
ca. 1954-1962
Monochrome black ballpoint pen drawing, on paper.
21 x 13.5cm
Artist's collection
AG1954_1962_CSG_D0245
p. 169

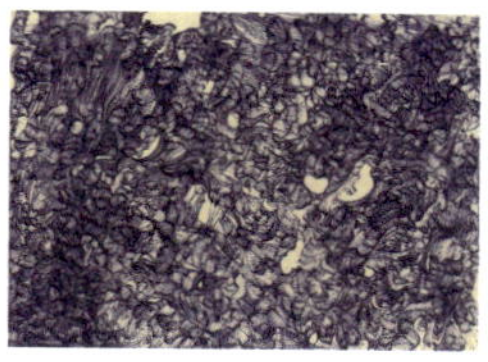

Untitled
(Club Saint-Germain period)
ca. 1954-1962
Drawing in violet monochrome ballpoint pen, on paper.
15 x 21 cm
Artist's collection
AG1954_1962_CSG_D0138
p. 170

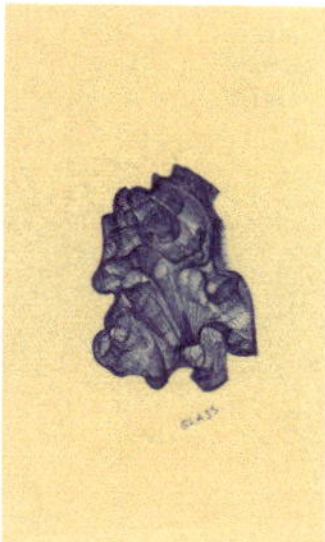

Untitled
(Club Saint-Germain period)
ca. 1954-1962
Monochrome blue ballpoint pen drawing, on the order slip of Club Saint-Germain.
12.6 x 7.6 cm
Artist's collection
AG1954_1962_CSG_D0191
p. 170

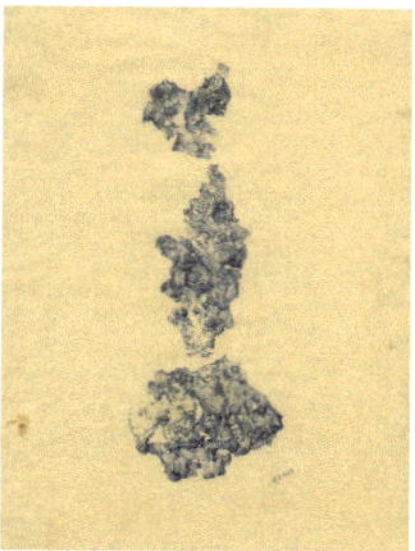

Untitled
(Club Saint-Germain period)
ca. 1954-1962
Monochrome blue ballpoint pen drawing, on paper.
28 x 22.5 cm
Artist's collection
AG1954_1962_CSG_D0011
p. 171

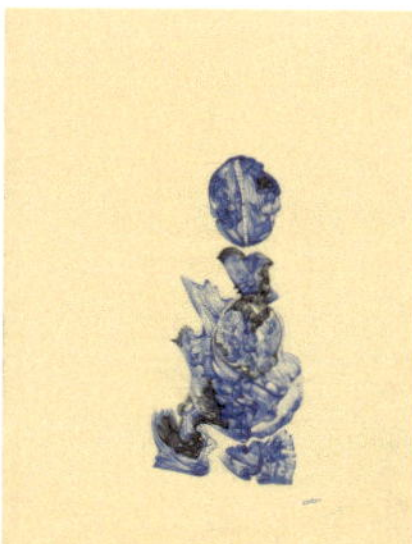

Untitled
(Club Saint-Germain period)
ca. 1954-1962
Bicolor blue and black ballpoint pen drawing on paper.
28 x 22.6 cm
Artist's collection
AG1954_1962_CSG_D0185
p. 172

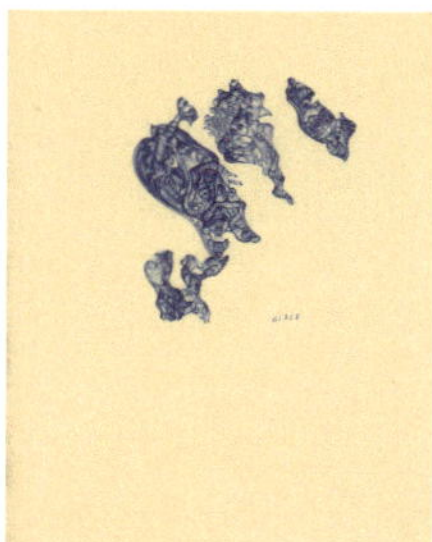

Untitled
(Club Saint-Germain period)
ca. 1954-1962
Monochrome blue ballpoint pen drawing, on paper.
27 x 22.3 cm
Artist's collection
AG1954_1962_CSG_D0186
p. 172

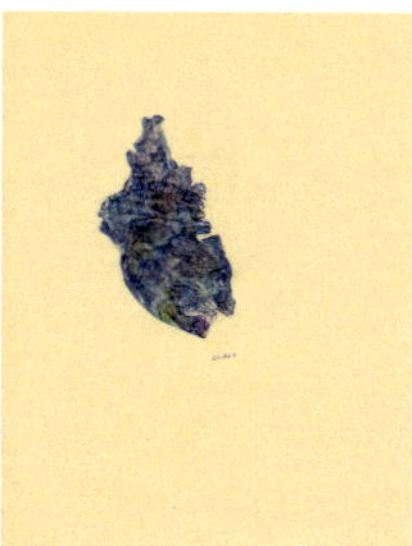

Untitled
(Club Saint-Germain period)
ca. 1954-1962
Blue, green and violet tricolor ballpoint pen drawing, on paper.
28 x 22.5 cm
Artist's collection
AG1954_1962_CSG_D0137
p. 172

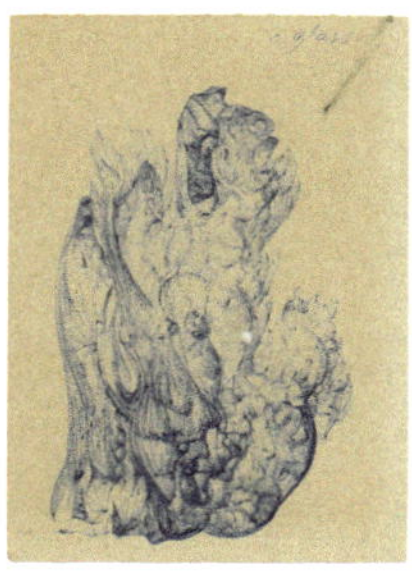

Untitled
(Club Saint-Germain period)
ca. 1954-1962
Monochrome blue ballpoint pen drawing, on olive paper.
10.7 x 7.9 cm
Artist's collection
AG1954_1962_CSG_D0240
p. 173

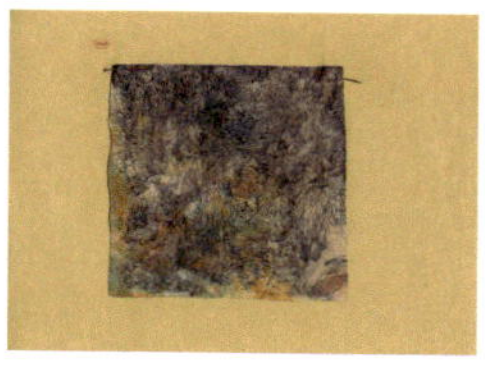

Untitled
(Club Saint-Germain period)
ca. 1954-1962
Monochrome black ballpoint pen drawing, with green and brown pencil, with a touch of allumettage, on paper.
14.7 x 15 cm.
Artist's collection
AG1954_1962_CSG_D0238
p. 173

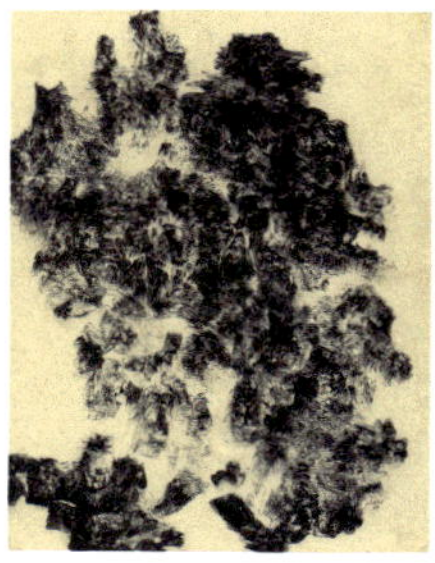

Untitled
(Club Saint-Germain period)
1959
Monochrome black pen drawing and India ink, on paper.
26.9 x 20.9 cm
Artist's collection
AG1954_1962_CSG_D0141
p. 174

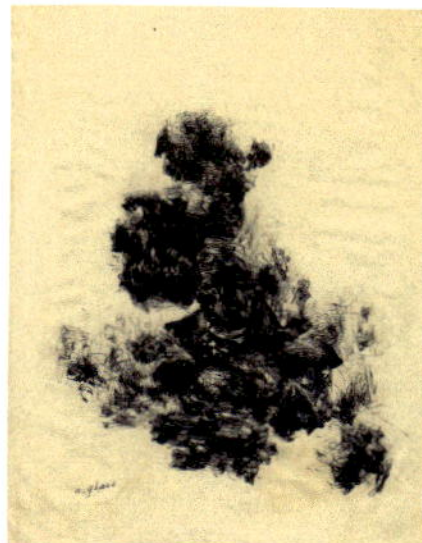

Untitled
(Club Saint-Germain period)
ca. 1954-1962
Monochrome black pen drawing and India ink, on paper.
27 x 20.5 cm
Artist's collection
AG1954_1962_CSG_D0143
p. 174

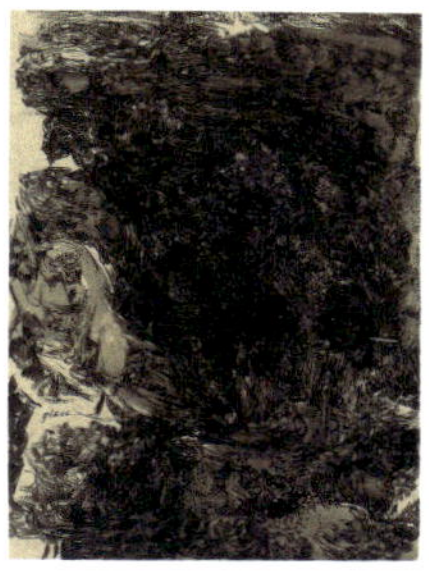

Untitled
(Club Saint-Germain period)
ca. 1954-1962
Monochrome black pen drawing and India ink, on paper.
19.5 x 14.5 cm
Artist's collection
AG1954_1962_CSG_D0145
p. 175

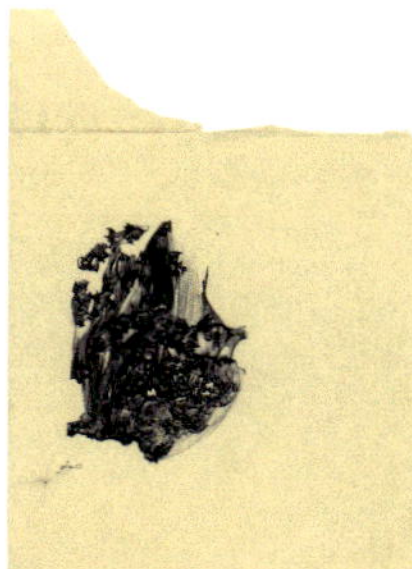

Untitled
(Club Saint-Germain period)
ca. 1954-1962
Monochrome black ballpoint pen drawing, on paper.
22.5 x 20.5 cm
Artist's collection
AG1954_1962_CSG_D0144
p. 175

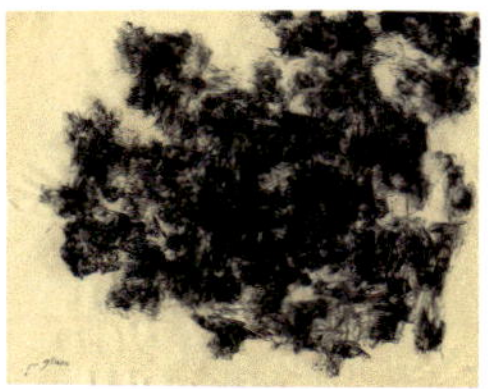

Untitled
(Club Saint-Germain period)
ca. 1954-1962
Black fountain pen drawing and Indian ink, on paper.
21 x 27 cm
Artist's collection
AG1954_1962_CSG_D0146
p. 176

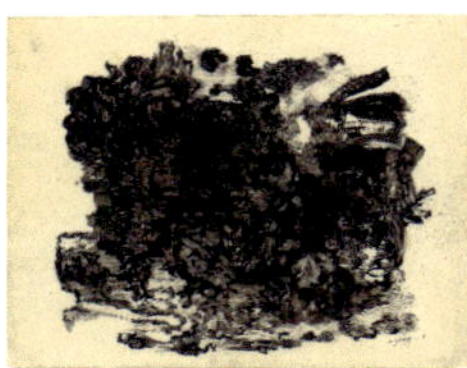

Untitled
(Club Saint-Germain period)
1959
Black fountain pen drawing and Indian ink, on paper.
28 x 37.5 cm
Artist's collection
AG1954_1962_CSG_D0147
p. 176

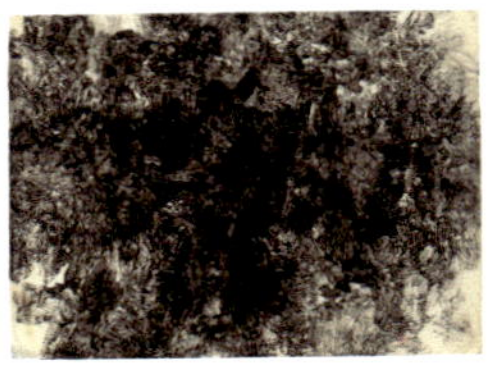

Untitled
(Club Saint-Germain period)
1959
Black fountain pen drawing and Indian ink, on Japanese paper.
27.5 x 38.5 cm
Artist's collection
AG1954_1962_CSG_D0148
p. 177

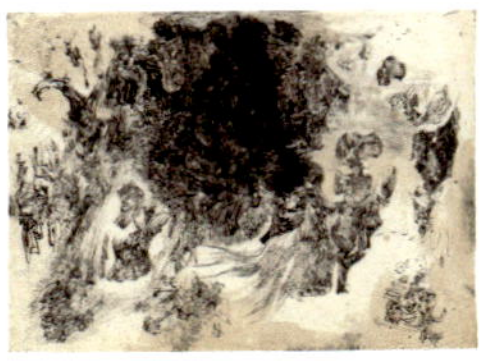

Untitled
(Club Saint-Germain period)
1959
Black fountain pen drawing and Indian ink, on Japanese paper.
27.5 x 38.5 cm
Artist's collection
AG1954_1962_CSG_D0149
p. 178

Untitled
(Club Saint-Germain period)
1959
Navy blue and violet two-tone ballpoint pen drawing, on paper.
32 x 28 cm
Artist's collection
AG1954_1962_CSG_D0152
p. 178

Untitled
(Club Saint-Germain period)
ca. 1954-1962
Blue and violet two-tone ballpoint pen drawing on composite paper.
20 x 34.5 cm
Artist's collection
AG1954_1962_CSG_D0150
p. 179

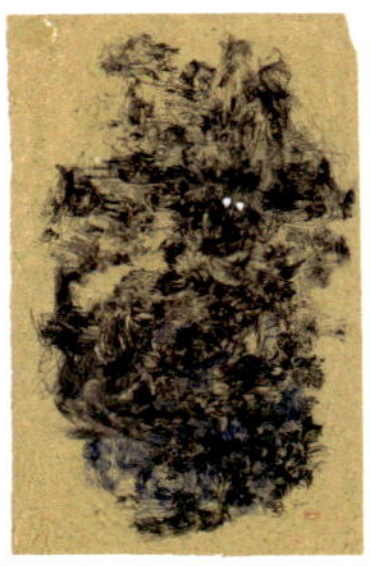

Untitled
(Club Saint-Germain period)
ca. 1954-1962
Blue and black two-tone ballpoint pen drawing on composite paper.
32.5 x 21 cm
Artist's collection
AG1954_1962_CSG_D0151
p. 179

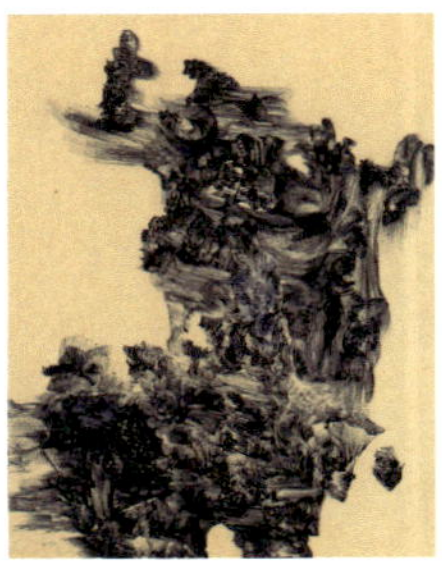

Untitled
(Club Saint-Germain period)
ca. 1954-1962
Monochrome black ballpoint pen drawing, on paper.
28 x 22 cm
Artist's collection
AG1954_1962_CSG_D0153
p. 180

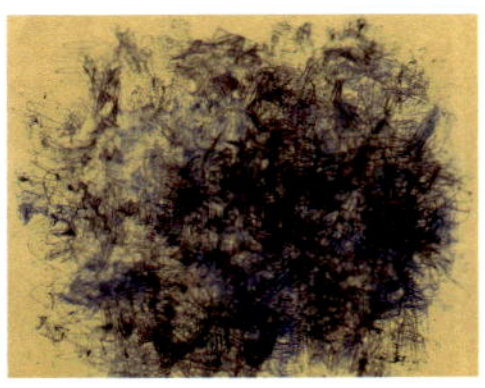

Untitled
(Club Saint-Germain period)
ca. 1954-1962
Bicolor blue and black ballpoint pen drawing, on paper.
22 x 28 cm
Artist's collection
AG1954_1962_CSG_D0155
p. 181

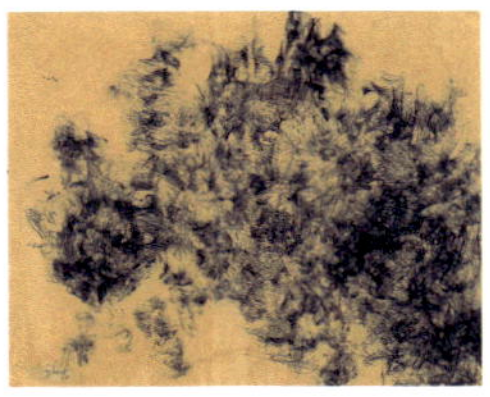

Untitled
(Club Saint-Germain period)
1959
Monochrome blue ballpoint pen drawing, on paper.
21.5 x 28 cm
Artist's collection
AG1954_1962_CSG_D0156
p. 181

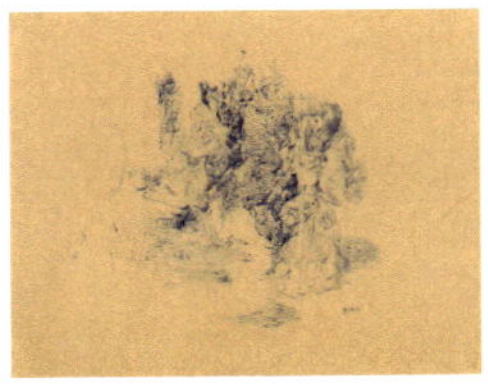

Untitled
(Club Saint-Germain period)
ca. 1954-1962
Monochrome blue ballpoint pen drawing, on paper.
21 x 28 cm
Artist's collection
AG1954_1962_CSG_D0154
p. 181

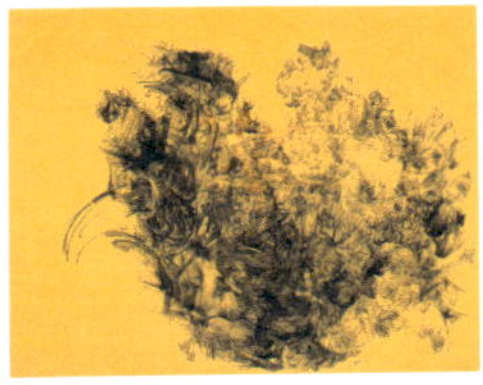

Untitled
(Club Saint-Germain period)
ca. 1954-1962
Monochrome blue ballpoint pen drawing with a touch of allumettage, on yellow paper.
22.8 x 28.8 cm
Artist's collection
AG1954_1962_CSG_D0198
p. 182

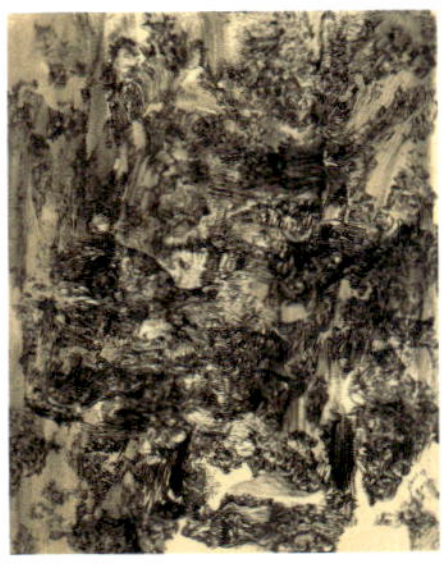

Untitled
(Club Saint-Germain period)
1959
Drawing with Indian ink and black watercolor, on paper.
28 x 22.6 cm
Artist's collection
AG1954_1962_CSG_D0199
p. 183

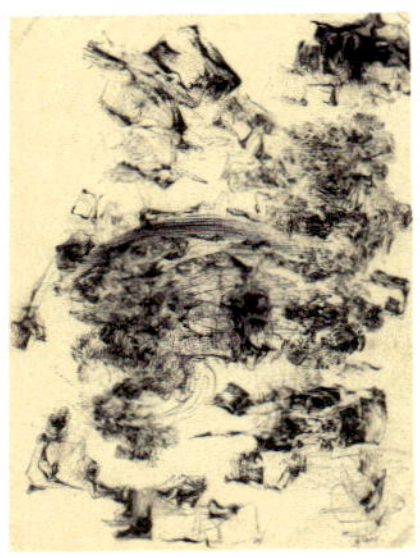

Untitled
(Club Saint-Germain period)
ca. 1954-1962
Monochrome black ballpoint pen drawing, on paper.
28 x 21 cm
Artist's collection
AG1954_1962_CSG_D0142
p. 183

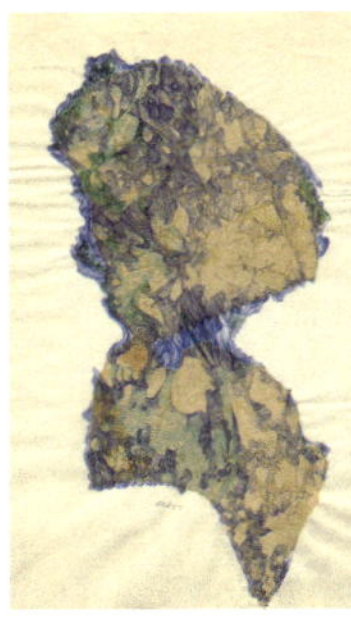

Untitled
(Club Saint-Germain period)
ca. 1954-1962
Blue, navy blue and green tricolor pen drawing, beige watercolor, collage applications, on paper.
35 x 21 cm
Artist's collection
AG1954_1962_CSG_D0047
p. 184

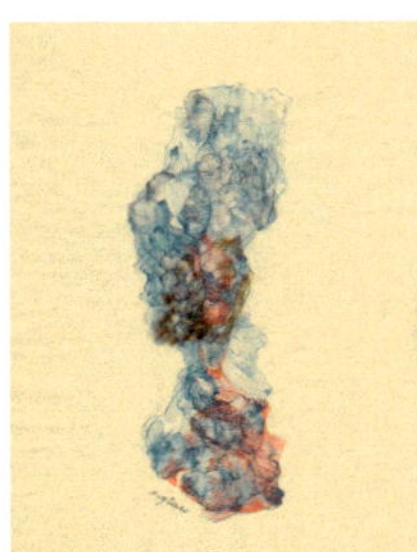

Untitled
(Club Saint-Germain period)
ca. 1954-1962
Red and blue colored pencil drawing, watercolored and with a touch of alumettage, on paper.
28 x 22.5 cm
Artist's collection
AG1954_1962_CSG_D0052
p. 184

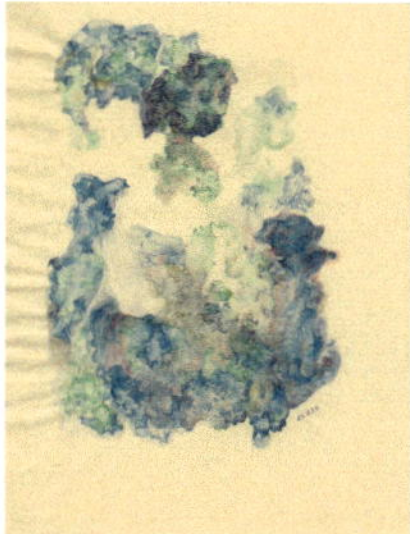

Untitled
(Club Saint-Germain period)
ca. 1954-1962
Bicolor blue and navy blue ballpoint pen drawing, with green, blue and red watercolor, with a touch of graphite, on paper.
28 x 22.5 cm
Artist's collection
AG1954_1962_CSG_D0053
p. 185

Untitled
(Club Saint-Germain period)
1959
Bicolor blue and violet ballpoint pen drawing, with touches of allumettage, on paper.
30 x 28.5 cm
Artist's collection
AG1954_1962_CSG_D0157
p. 186

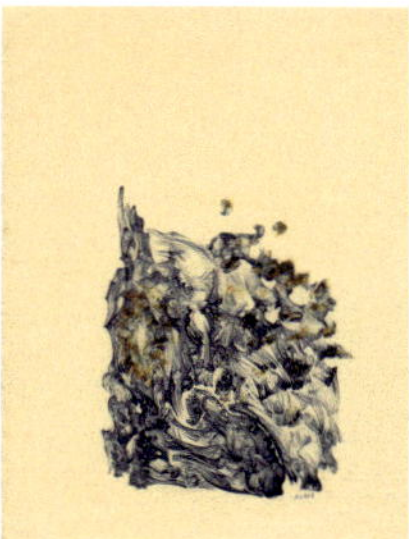

Untitled
(Club Saint-Germain period)
ca. 1954-1962
Monochrome blue ballpoint pen drawing with touches of allumettage, on paper.
28 x 22.5 cm
Artist's collection
AG1954_1962_CSG_D0159
p. 187

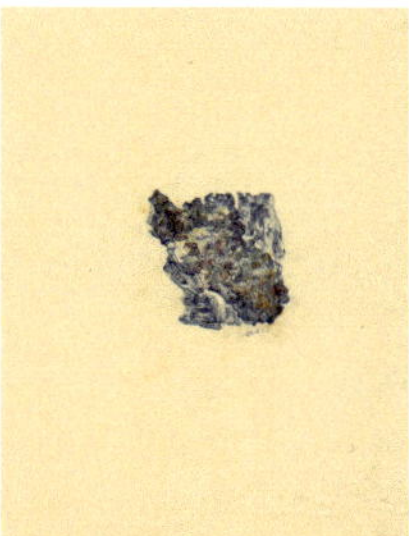

Untitled
(Club Saint-Germain period)
ca. 1954-1962
Monochrome blue ballpoint pen drawing with touches of allumettage, on paper.
28 x 22.5 cm
Artist's collection
AG1954_1962_CSG_D0160
p. 177

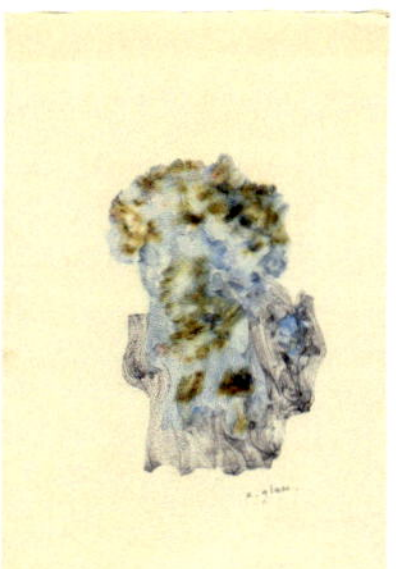

Untitled
(Club Saint-Germain period)
ca. 1954-1962
Monochrome navy blue ballpoint pen drawing and sky blue pencil, with touches of allumettage, on paper.
28 x 18.8 cm
Artist's collection
AG1954_1962_CSG_D0165
p. 188

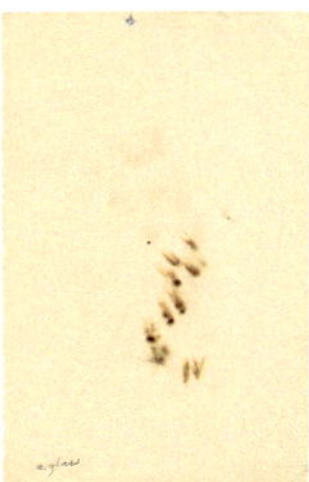

Untitled
(Club Saint-Germain period)
ca. 1954-1962
Touches of allumettage, on paper.
24.5 x 15.8 cm
Artist's collection
AG1954_1962_CSG_D0162
p. 189

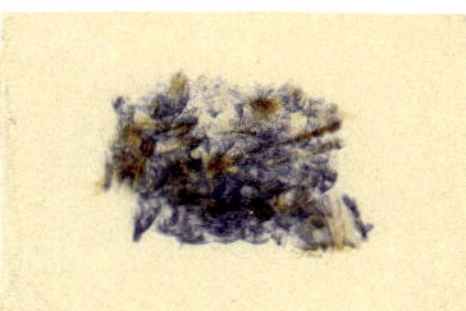

Untitled
(Club Saint-Germain period)
ca. 1954-1962
Monochrome blue ballpoint pen drawing with touches of allumettage, on paper.
15.9 x 24.4 cm
Artist's collection
AG1954_1962_CSG_D0164
p. 189

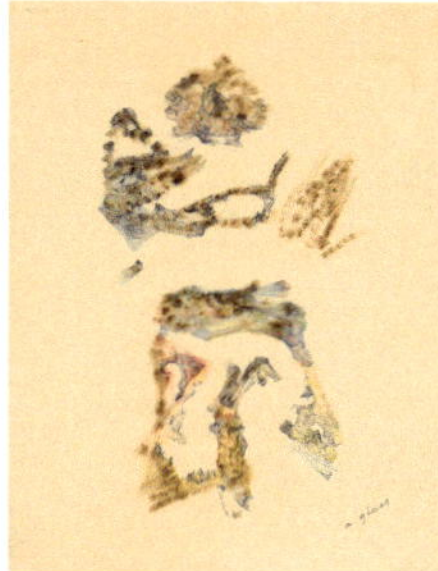

Untitled
(Club Saint-Germain period)
ca. 1954-1962
Drawing in blue monocolor ballpoint pen and blue and red colored pencil, with touches of allumettage, on paper.
28 x 22.5 cm
Artist's collection
AG1954_1962_CSG_D0158
p. 190

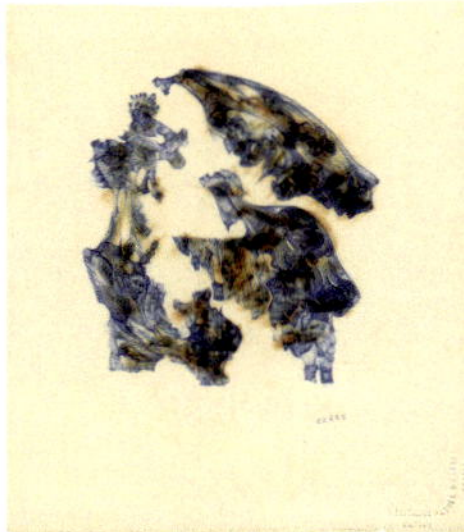

Untitled
(Club Saint-Germain period)
ca. 1954-1962
Monochrome blue ballpoint pen drawing with touches of allumettage, on paper.
21.7 x 19 cm
Artist's collection
AG1954_1962_CSG_D0163
p. 191

Untitled
(Club Saint-Germain period)
ca. 1954-1962
Monochrome blue ballpoint pen drawing, with red watercolor and a touch of alumettage, on squared paper.
25.5 x 21 cm
Artist's collection
AG1954_1962_CSG_D0079
p. 192

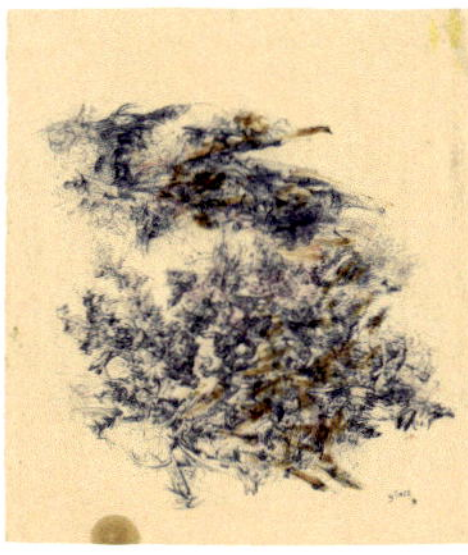

Untitled
(Club Saint-Germain period)
1958
Bicolor blue and purple ballpoint pen drawing with touches of allumettage, on paper.
31.6 x 28.3 cm
Artist's collection
AG1954_1962_CSG_D0168
p. 193

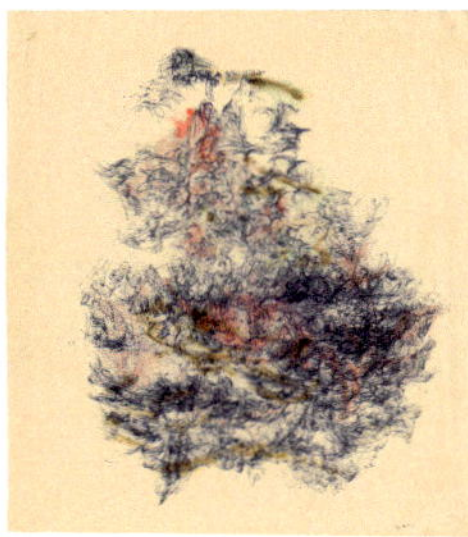

Untitled
(Club Saint-Germain period)
ca. 1954-1962
Monochrome blue ballpoint pen drawing and orange and aqua pencil, with touches of allumettage, on paper.
31 x 28.3 cm
Artist's collection
AG1954_1962_CSG_D0169
p. 193

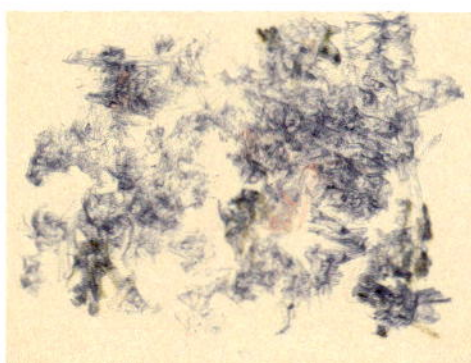

Untitled
(Club Saint-Germain period)
ca. 1954-1962
Monochrome blue ballpoint pen and orange pencil drawing, with touches of allumettage, on paper.
25 x 32.5 cm
Artist's collection
AG1954_1962_CSG_D0170
p. 194

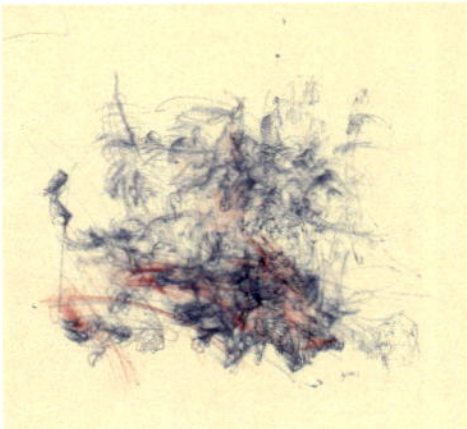

Untitled
(Club Saint-Germain period)
ca. 1954-1962
Monochrome blue ballpoint pen and red pencil drawing, on paper.
21 x 23.4 cm
Artist's collection
AG1954_1962_CSG_D0172
p. 194

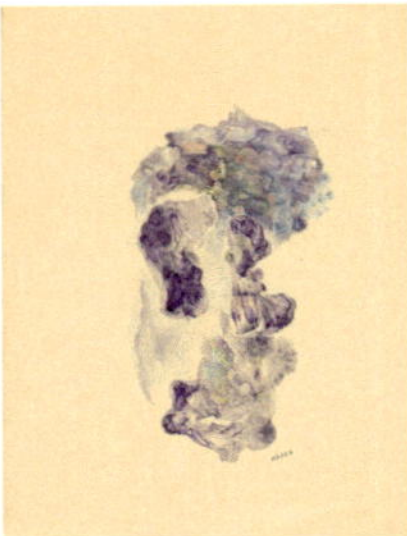

Untitled
(Club Saint-Germain period)
ca. 1954-1962
Monochrome purple ballpoint pen drawing with red, blue and green colored pencil, on paper.
28 x 22.6 cm
Artist's collection
AG1954_1962_CSG_D0173
p. 195

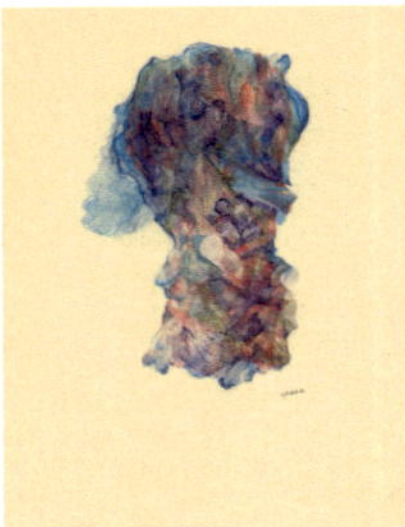

Untitled
(Club Saint-Germain period)
ca. 1954-1962
Monochrome purple ballpoint pen drawing with blue, green, red and purple colored pencil, on paper.
28 x 22.8 cm
Artist's collection
AG1954_1962_CSG_D0174
p. 195

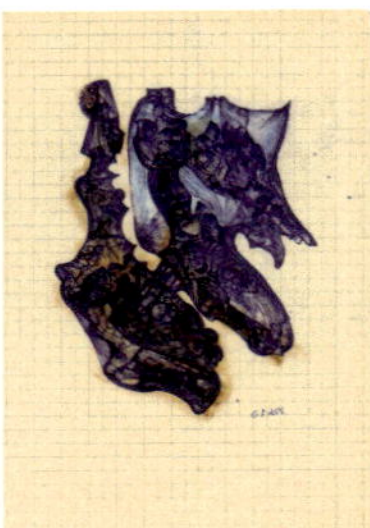

Untitled
(Club Saint-Germain period)
ca. 1954-1962
Bicolor blue and purple ballpoint pen drawing with touches of allumettage, on squared paper.
19.5 x 13.5 cm
Artist's collection
AG1954_1962_CSG_D0167
p. 196

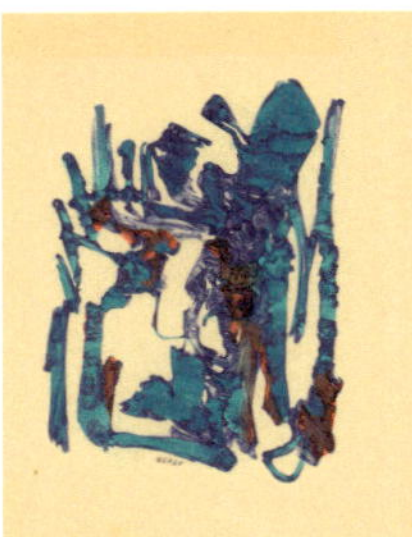

Untitled
(Club Saint Germain period)
ca. 1954-1962
Blue pen drawing with blue and orange watercolor, on paper.
28 x 22.5 cm
Artist's collection
AG1954_1962_CSG_D0048
p. 197

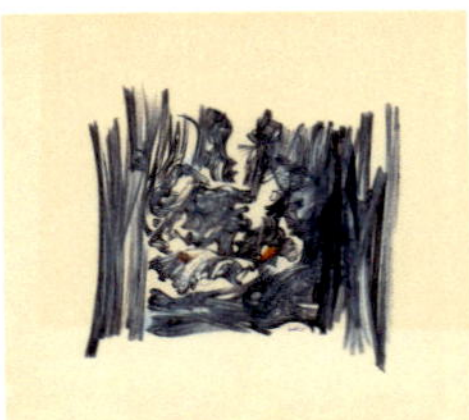

Untitled
(Club Saint-Germain period)
ca. 1954-1962
Monochrome black ballpoint pen drawing with orange and sky blue pencil, on paper.
25 x 27.6 cm
Artist's collection
AG1954_1962_CSG_D0178
p. 198

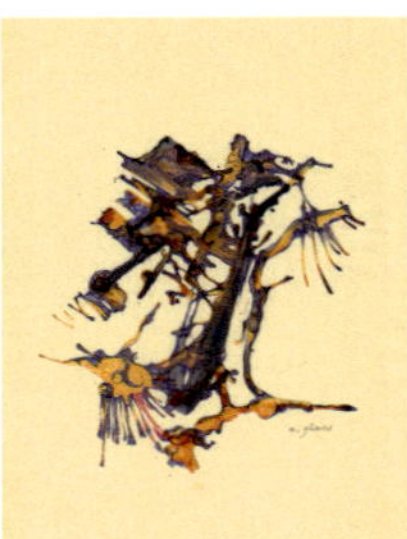

Untitled
(Club Saint-Germain period)
ca. 1954-1962
Bicolor blue and red ballpoint pen drawing, with black and brown watercolor, on paper.
28 x 22.5 cm
Artist's collection
AG1954_1962_CSG_D0049
p. 199

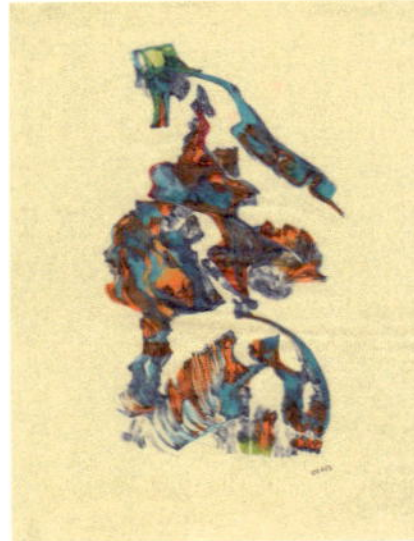

Untitled
(Club Saint-Germain period)
ca. 1954-1962
Drawing in blue pen, with red and green watercolor, on paper.
28 x 22.5 cm
Artist's collection
AG1954_1962_CSG_D0050
p. 200

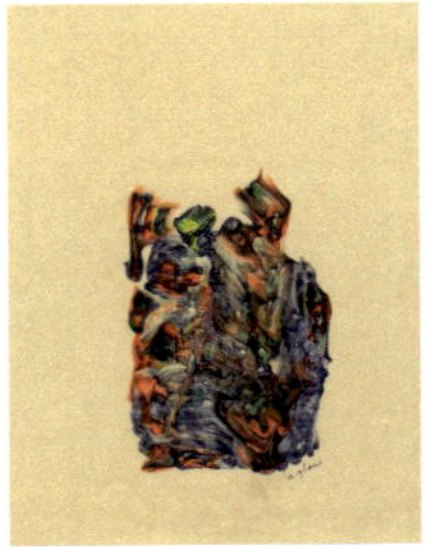

Untitled
(Club Saint-Germain period)
ca. 1954-1962
Drawing in ballpoint blue pen with green and red watercolor, on paper.
28 x 22.5 cm
Artist's collection
AG1954_1962_CSG_D0051
p. 201

Untitled
(Club Saint-Germain period)
1959
Monochrome blue ballpoint pen drawing with purple, green, and blue pencil, on paper.
28.6 x 25 cm
Artist's collection
AG1954_1962_CSG_D0176
p. 202

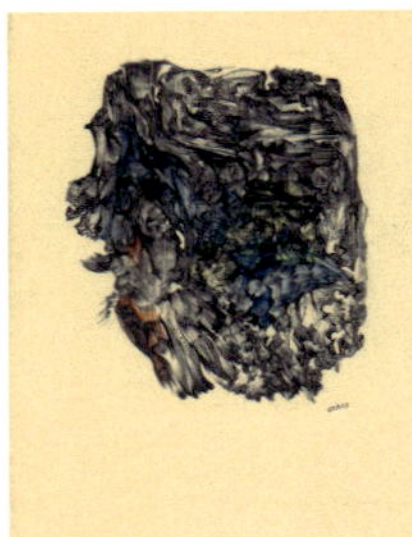

Untitled
(Club Saint-Germain period)
ca. 1954-1962
Monochrome black ballpoint pen drawing with orange, blue, and green pencil, on paper.
28 x 22.8 cm
Artist's collection
AG1954_1962_CSG_D0175
p. 202

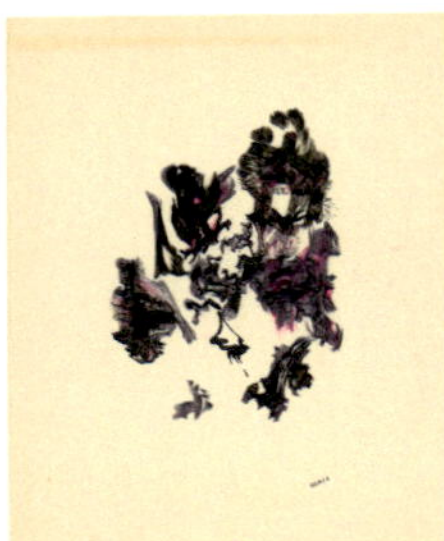

Untitled
(Club Saint-Germain period)
ca. 1954-1962
Bicolor black and pink ballpoint pen drawing with touches of Indian ink, on paper.
29.8 x 25 cm
Artist's collection
AG1954_1962_CSG_D0177
p. 203

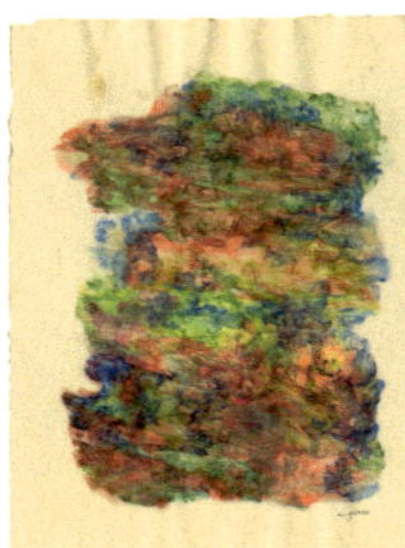

Untitled
(Club Saint-Germain period)
ca. 1954-1962
Blue, orange, green, and yellow watercolor drawing, on paper.
32.8 x 25 cm
Artist's collection
AG1954_1962_CSG_D0180
P. 204

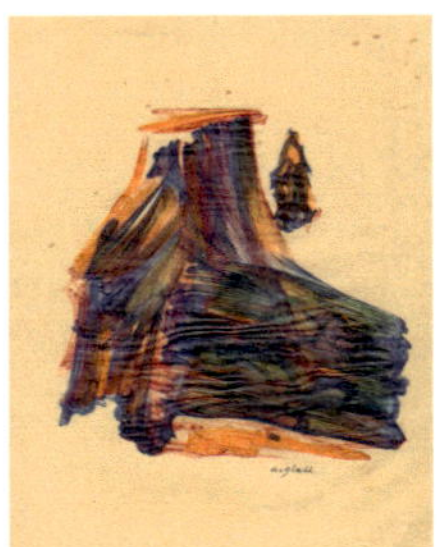

Untitled
(Club Saint-Germain period)
ca. 1954-1962
Bicolor blue and red ballpoint pen drawing, with orange, green and blue colored pencil, on paper.
28 x 22.6 cm
Artist's collection
AG1954_1962_CSG_D0182
p. 205

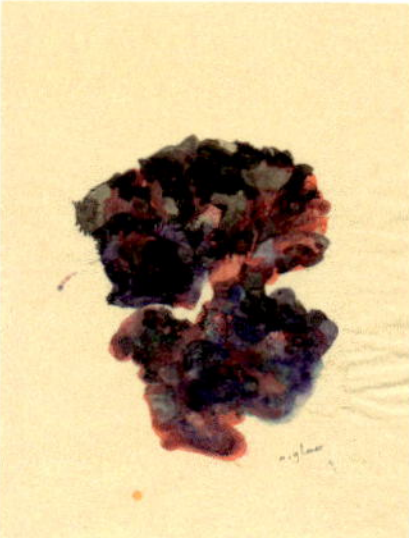

Untitled
(Club Saint-Germain period)
ca. 1954-1962
Black, orange, purple, and aqua watercolor drawing on paper.
28 x 25.6 cm
Artist's collection
AG1954_1962_CSG_D0181
p. 205

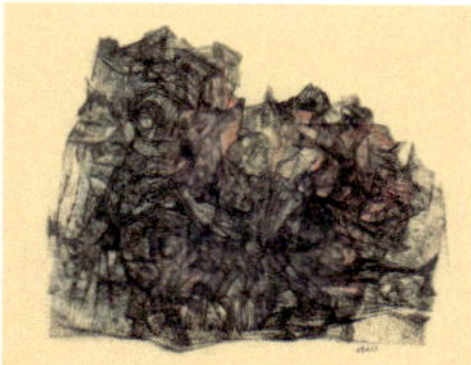

Untitled
(Club Saint-Germain period)
ca. 1954-1962
Monochrome black ballpoint pen drawing with red, blue, and black pencil, on paper.
22.5 x 28 cm
Artist's collection
AG1954_1962_CSG_D0183
p.206

Untitled
(Club Saint-Germain period)
ca. 1954-1962
Monochrome blue ballpoint pen drawing with olive green and grass green pencil, with a touch of allumettage, on paper.
28 x 25 cm
Artist's collection
AG1954_1962_CSG_D0187
p. 206

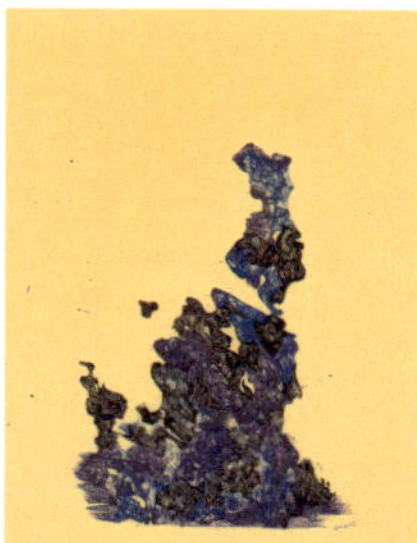

Untitled
(Club Saint-Germain period)
ca. 1954-1962
Blue, black, and purple tricolor ballpoint pen drawing, on paper.
27 x 21.1 cm
Artist's collection
AG1954_1962_CSG_D0188
p. 207

Untitled
(Club Saint-Germain period)
ca. 1954-1962
Monochrome blue ballpoint pen drawing, on paper.
32.8 x 25 cm
Artist's collection
AG1954_1962_CSG_D0189
p. 207

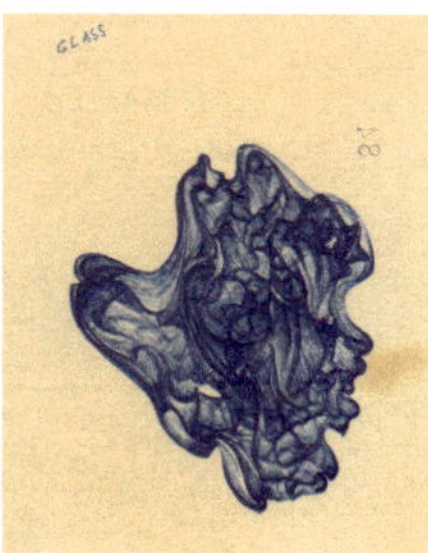

Untitled
(Club Saint Germain period)
ca. 1954-1962
Monochrome blue ballpoint pen drawing, on the order of Club Saint-Germain.
10.8 x 7.6 cm
Artist's collection
AG1954_1962_CSG_D0192
p. 207

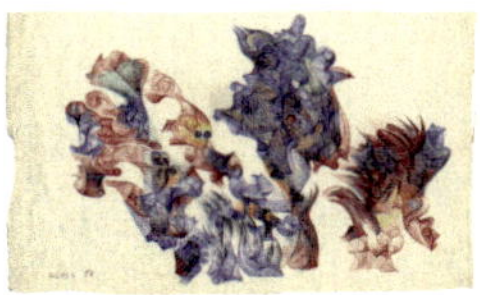

Untitled
(Club Saint-Germain period)
1958
Blue, red, and black tricolor pen drawing, with turquoise and brown pencil, on canvas.
13.3 x 22.5 cm
Artist's collection
AG1954_1962_CSG_D0219
p. 208

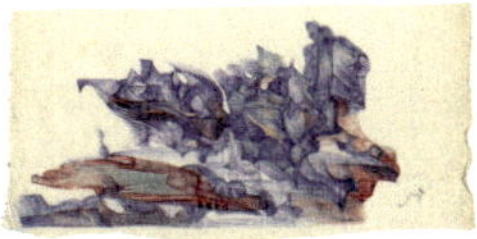

Untitled
(Club Saint-Germain period)
1958
Blue, red, and black tricolor pen drawing, with turquoise and brown pencil, on canvas.
11.5 x 23.3 cm
Artist's collection
AG1954_1962_CSG_D0218
p. 209

Untitled
(Club Saint-Germain period)
ca. 1954-1962
Monochrome black ballpoint pen drawing, on paper.
22 x 29 cm
Artist's collection
AG1954_1962_CSG_D0222
p. 210

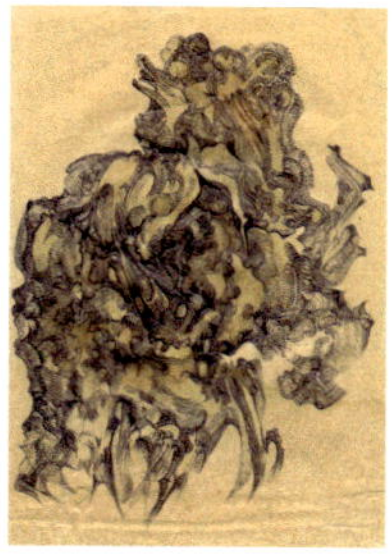

Untitled
(Club Saint-Germain period)
ca. 1954-1962
Monochrome black ballpoint pen drawing, with a touch of allumettage, on paper.
14.9 x 10.4 cm
Artist's collection
AG1954_1962_CSG_D0220
p. 211

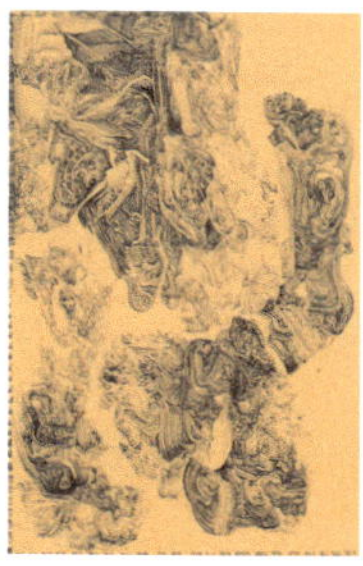

Untitled
(Club Saint-Germain period)
ca. 1954-1962
Monochrome black ballpoint pen drawing, on paper.
21.5 x 13.8 cm
Private collection
AG1954_1962_CSG_D0221
p. 211

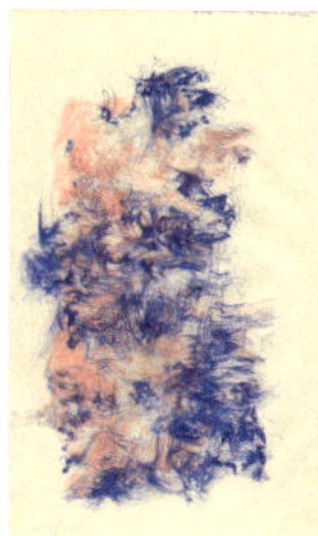

Untitled
(Club Saint-Germain period)
ca. 1954-1962
Bicolor blue and red ballpoint pen drawing, on Club Saint Germain invitation.
23.5 x 13.6 cm
Artist's collection
AG1954_1962_CSG_D0223
p. 212

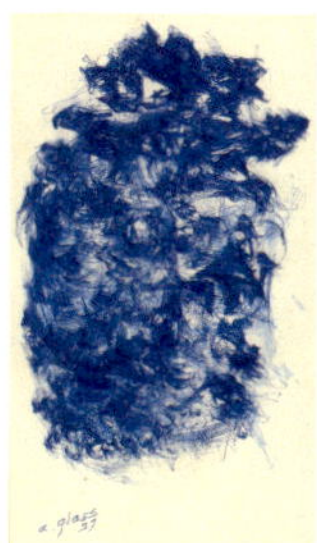

Untitled
(Club Saint Germain period)
1959
Bicolor blue and red ballpoint pen drawing, on Club Saint Germain invitation.
23.5 x 13.6 cm
Artist's collection
AG1954_1962_CSG_D0224
p. 212

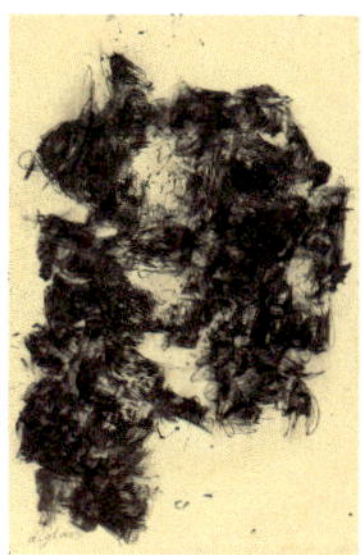

Untitled
(Club Saint-Germain period)
ca. 1954-1962
Monochrome black ballpoint pen drawing, on paper.
26 x 17 cm
Artist's collection
AG1954_1962_CSG_D0225
p. 213

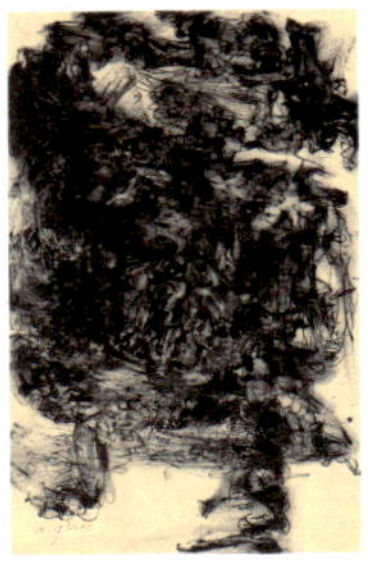

Untitled
(Club Saint-Germain period)
ca. 1954-1962
Monochrome black ballpoint pen drawing, on paper.
26 x 17 cm
Artist's collection
AG1954_1962_CSG_D0226
p. 203

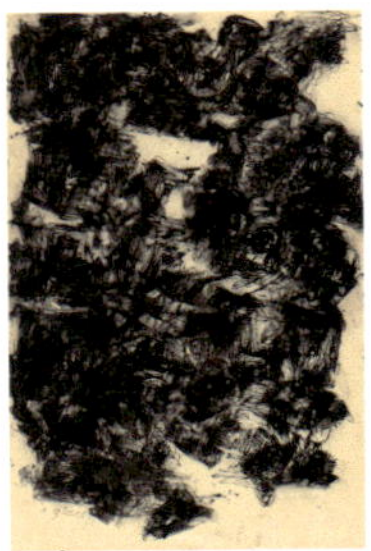

Untitled
(Club Saint-Germain period)
ca. 1954-1962
Monochrome black ballpoint pen drawing, on paper.
26 x 17.3 cm
Artist's collectionn
AG1954_1962_CSG_D0232
p. 204

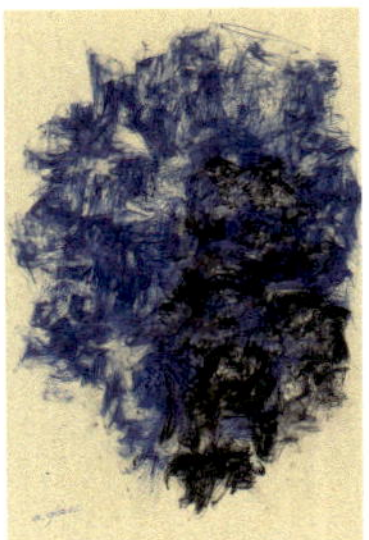

Untitled
(Club Saint-Germain period)
ca. 1954-1962
Bicolor blue and black ballpoint pen drawing on paper.
26 x 17 cm
Artist's collection
AG1954_1962_CSG_D0227
p. 204

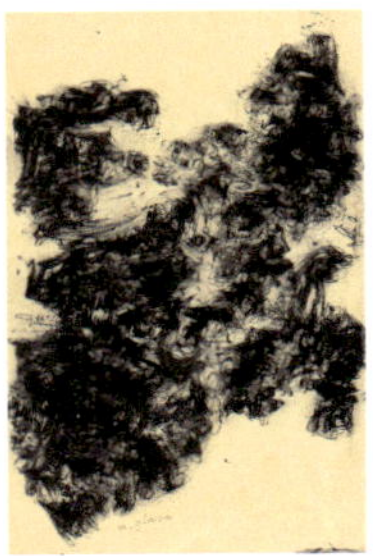

Untitled
(Club Saint-Germain period)
ca. 1954-1962
Monochrome black ballpoint pen drawing, on paper.
26 x 17 cm
Artist's collection
AG1954_1962_CSG_D0234
p. 205

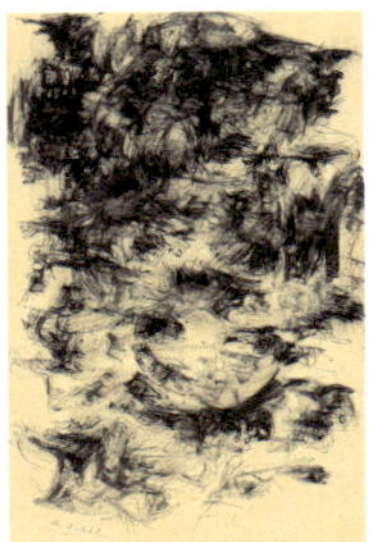

Untitled
(Club Saint-Germain period)
ca. 1954-1962
Monochrome black ballpoint pen drawing, on paper.
26 x 17 cm
Artist's collection
AG1954_1962_CSG_D0235
p. 205

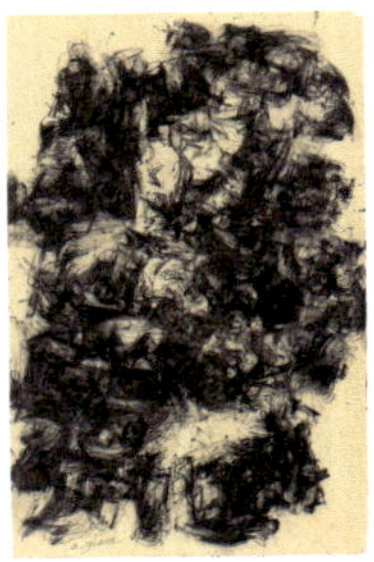

Untitled
(Club Saint-Germain period)
ca. 1954-1962
Monochrome black ballpoint pen drawing, on paper.
26 x 17.3 cm
Artist's collection
AG1954_1962_CSG_D0230
p. 206

Untitled
(Club Saint-Germain period)
ca. 1954-1962
Monochrome black ballpoint pen drawing, on paper.
26 x 17 cm
Artist's collection
AG1954_1962_CSG_D0228
p. 207

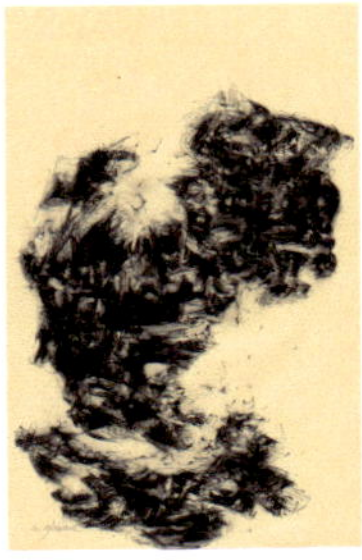

Untitled
(Club Saint-Germain period)
ca. 1954-1962
Monochrome black ballpoint pen drawing, on paper.
26 x 17 cm
Artist's collection
AG1954_1962_CSG_D0231
p. 207

Untitled
(Club Saint-Germain period)
ca. 1954-1962
Monochrome blue ballpoint pen drawing, on paper.
26 x 17.3 cm
Artist's collection
AG1954_1962_CSG_D0229
p. 208

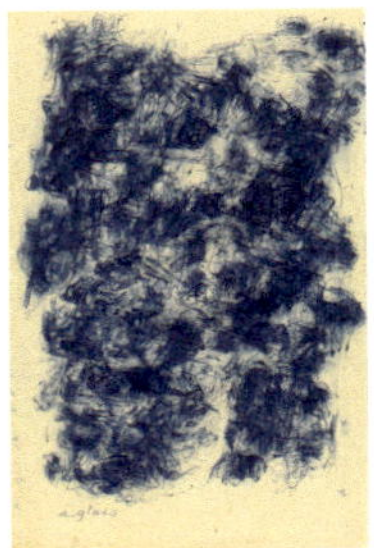

Untitled
(Club Saint-Germain period)
ca. 1954-1962
Monochrome blue ballpoint pen drawing, on paper.
26 x 17.1 cm
Artist's collection
AG1954_1962_CSG_D0236
p. 209

Untitled
(Club Saint-Germain period)
ca. 1954-1962
Monochrome blue ballpoint pen drawing, on paper.
26 x 17.3 cm
Artist's collection
AG1954_1962_CSG_D0237
p. 209

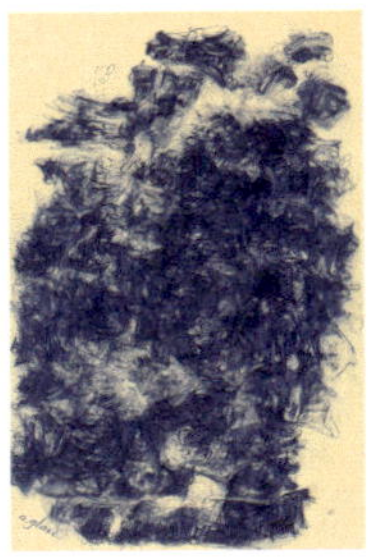

Untitled
(Club Saint-Germain period)
ca. 1954-1962
Monochrome blue ballpoint pen drawing, on paper.
26 x 17.1 cm
Artist's collection
AG1954_1962_CSG_D0233
p. 209

Untitled
(Club Saint-Germain period)
ca. 1954-1962
Monochrome black ballpoint pen drawing, with yellow, green, aqua, orange, pink and lilac watercolor, on paper.
20.9 x 26.8 cm
Artist's collection
AG1954_1962_CSG_D0251
p. 210

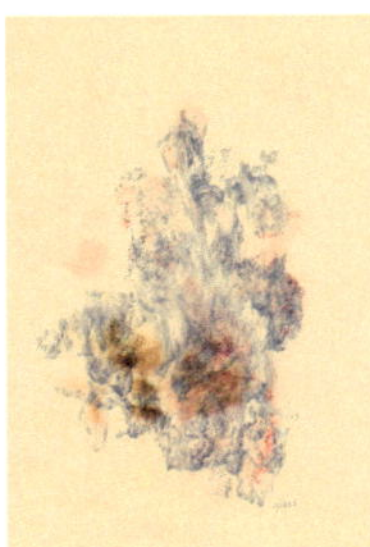

Untitled
(Club Saint-Germain period)
ca. 1954-1962
Bicolor blue and red ballpoint pen drawing, with a touch of allumettage, on paper.
17.7 x 12 cm
Artist's collection
AG1954_1962_CSG_D0241
p. 211

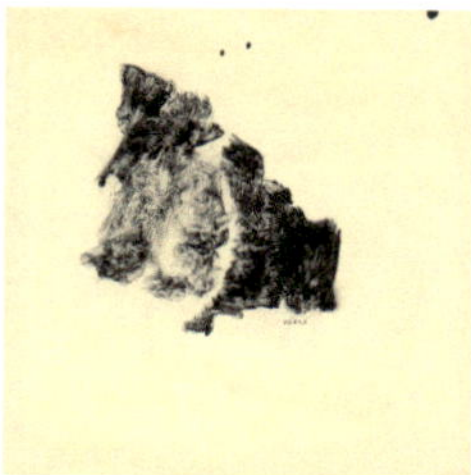

Untitled
(Club Saint-Germain period)
ca. 1954-1962
Monochrome black ballpoint pen drawing, on paper.
20 x 20 cm
Artist's collection
AG1954_1962_CSG_D0243
p. 211

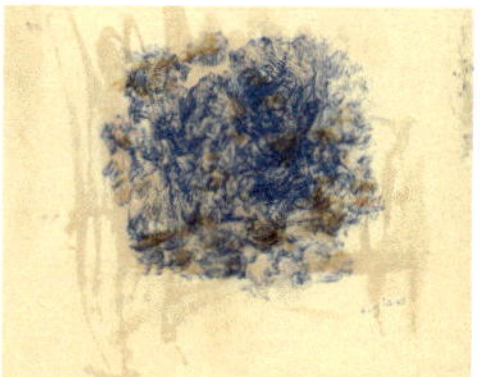

Untitled
(Club Saint-Germain period)
ca. 1954-1962
Monochrome blue ballpoint pen drawing with watercolor and touch of allumettage, on paper.
15.7 x 19.9 cm
Artist's collection
AG1954_1962_CSG_D0244, p. 211

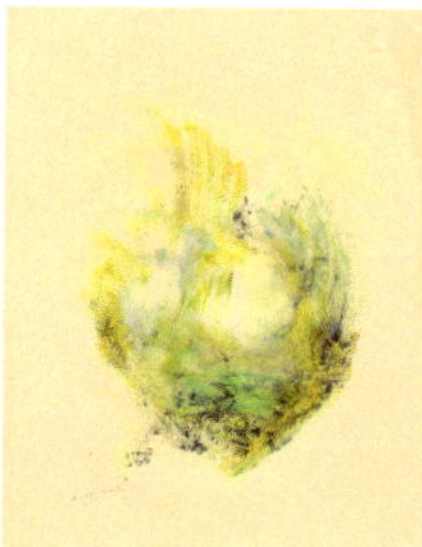

Untitled
(Club Saint-Germain period)
ca. 1954-1962
Monochrome black ballpoint pen drawing with yellow, green, and aqua watercolor, on paper.
27 x 21 cm
Artist's collection
AG1954_1962_CSG_D0248
p. 212

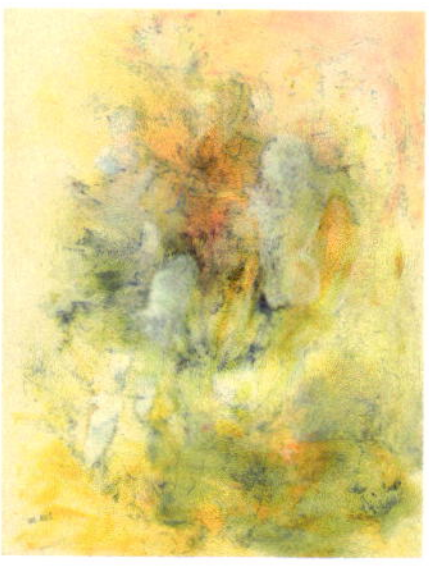

Untitled
(Club Saint-Germain period)
ca. 1954-1962
Monochrome blue ballpoint pen drawing with yellow, green, aqua, and orange watercolor, on paper.
27 x 21 cm
Artist's collection
AG1954_1962_CSG_D0249
p. 212

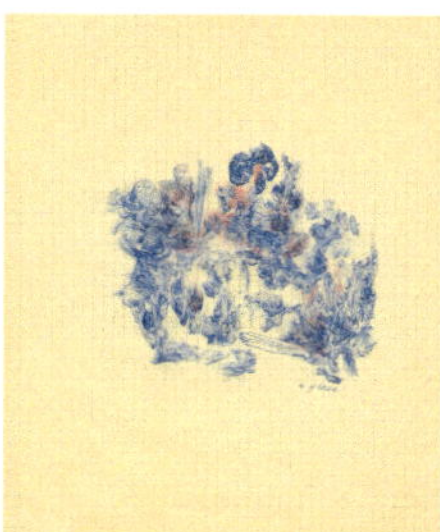

Untitled
(Club Saint-Germain period)
ca. 1954-1962
Monochrome blue ballpoint pen drawing with orange pencil, on squared paper.
25.5 x 21 cm
Artist's collection
AG1954_1962_CSG_D0247
p. 212

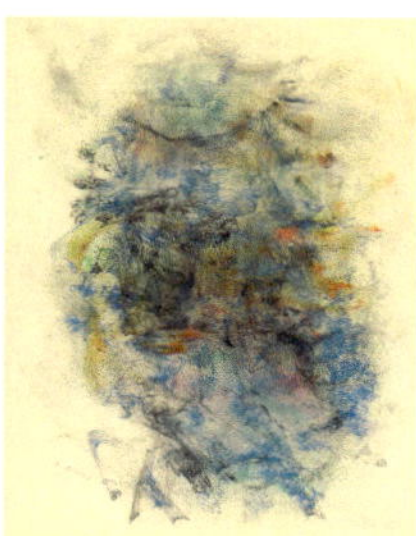

Untitled
(Club Saint-Germain period)
ca. 1954-1962
Bicolor blue and black ballpoint pen drawing, with yellow, green, aqua, orange, pink, and blue watercolor, on paper.
27 x 21 cm
Artist's collection
AG1954_1962_CSG_D0250
p. 213

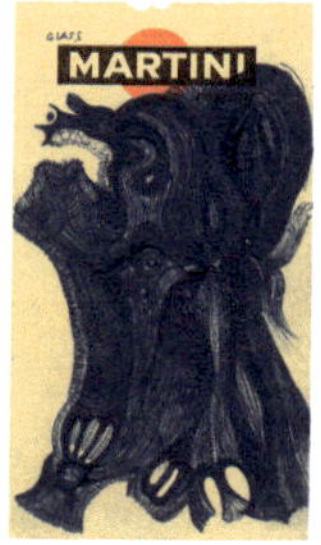

Untitled
(Club Saint-Germain period)
ca. 1954-1962
Monochrome blue ballpoint pen drawing, on the order slip of Club Saint-Germain.
15 x 8.4 cm
Artist's collection
AG1954_1962_CSG_D0196
p. 214

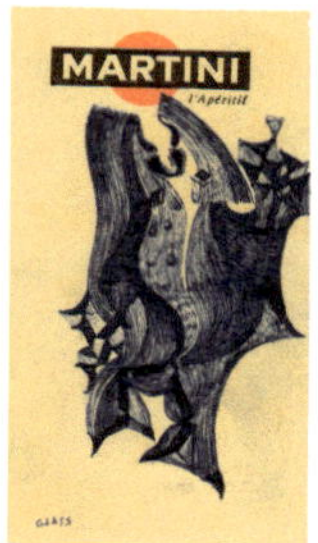

Untitled
(Club Saint-Germain period)
ca. 1954-1962
Monochrome blue ballpoint pen drawing, slip of Club Saint-Germain.
15 x 8.4 cm
Artist's collection
AG1954_1962_CSG_D0197
p. 214

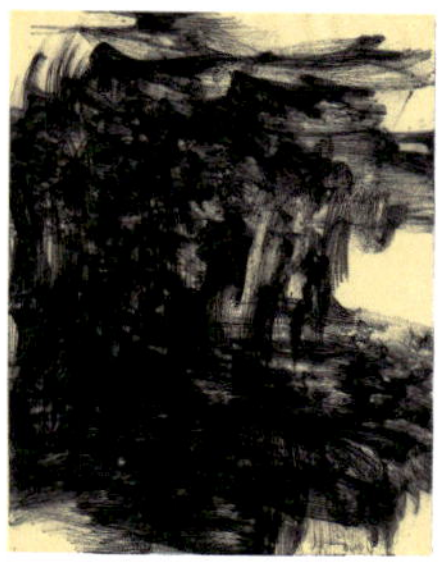

Untitled
(Club Saint-Germain period)
ca. 1954-1962
Monochrome black ballpoint pen drawing, on paper.
28.2 x 22.4 cm
Artist's collection
AG1954_1962_CSG_D0202
p. 215

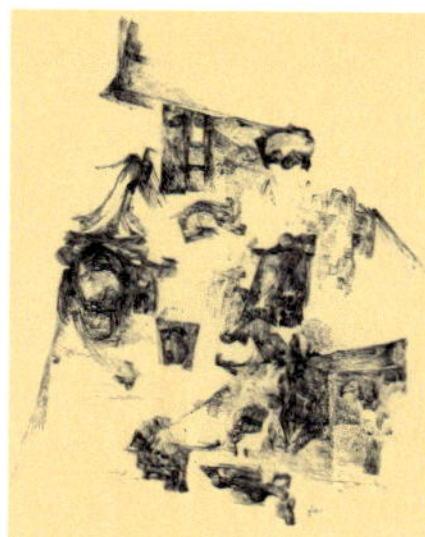

Untitled
(Club Saint Germain period)
ca. 1954-1962
Monochrome black ballpoint pen drawing, on paper.
28 x 22.3 cm
Artist's collection
AG1954_1962_CSG_D0201
p. 215

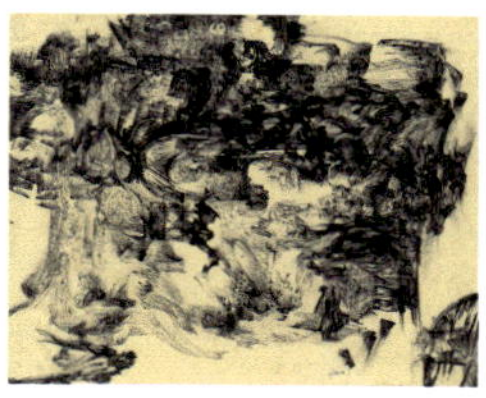

Untitled
(Club Saint-Germain period)
ca. 1954-1962
Monochrome black ballpoint pen drawing, on paper.
22.4 x 28.1 cm
Artist's collection
AG1954_1962_CSG_D0203
p. 216

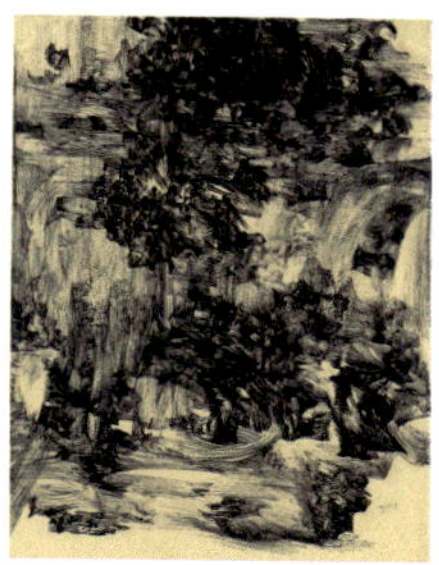

Untitled
(Club Saint-Germain period)
ca. 1954-1962
Monochrome black ballpoint pen drawing, on paper.
28.1 x 22.3 cm
Artist's collection
AG1954_1962_CSG_D0204
p. 216

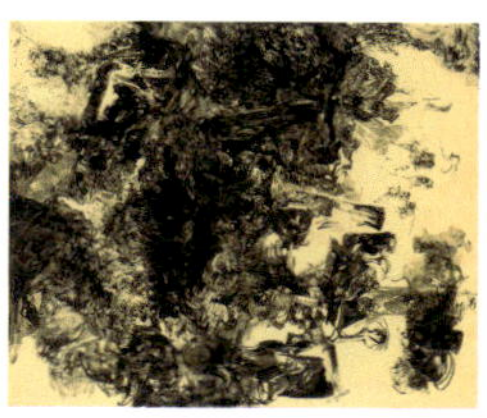

Untitled
(Club Saint-Germain period)
ca. 1954-1962
Drawing with Chinese ink and black watercolor, on paper.
22 x 27 cm
Artist's collection
AG1954_1962_CSG_D0200
p. 217

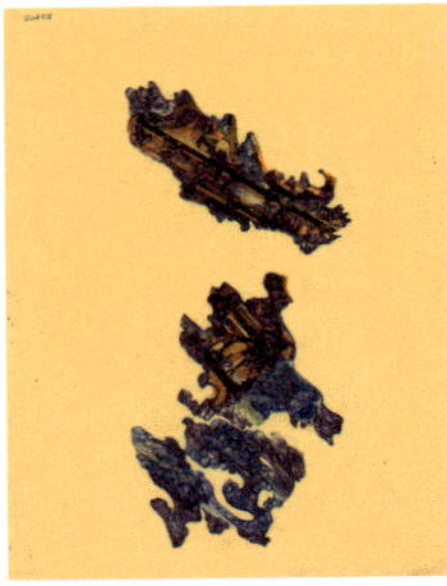

Untitled
(Club Saint-Germain period)
ca. 1954-1962
Bicolor blue and purple ballpoint pen drawing, with green and orange colored pencil, with collage application, on paper.
27 x 21 cm
Artist's collection
AG1954_1962_CSG_D0216
p. 228

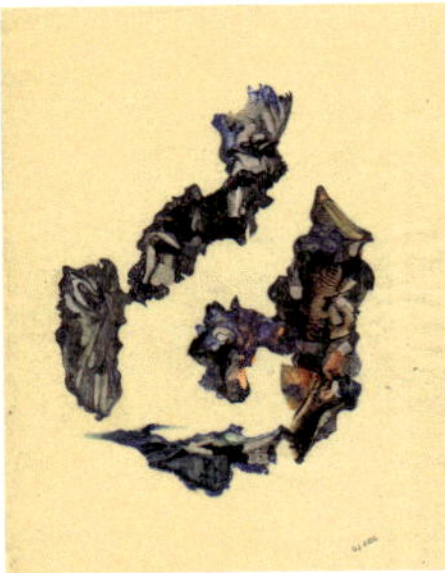

Untitled
(Club Saint-Germain period)
ca. 1954-1962
Drawing in blue, purple and black tricolor ballpoint pen, with orange and green colored pencil, with collage application, on paper.
27 x 21.7 cm
Artist's collection
AG1954_1962_CSG_D0214
p. 229

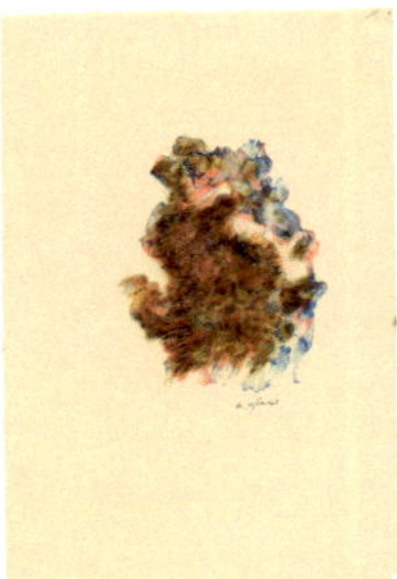

Untitled
(Club Saint-Germain period)
ca. 1954-1962
Monochrome blue ballpoint pen drawing with orange pencil and touches of allumettage, on paper.
28 x 19 cm
Artist's collection
AG1954_1962_CSG_D0179
p. 230

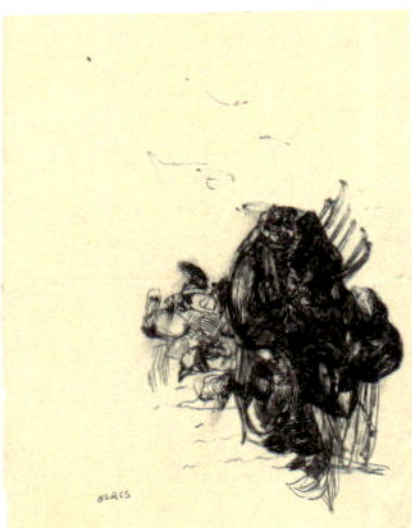

Untitled
(Club Saint-Germain period)
ca. 1954-1962
Monochrome black ballpoint pen drawing, on paper.
17.7 x 13.5 cm
Artist's collection
AG1954_1962_CSG_D0239
p. 230

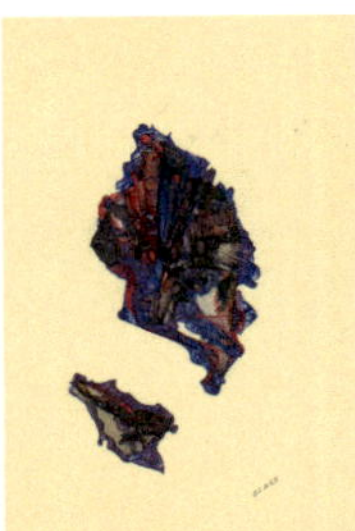

Untitled
(Club Saint-Germain period)
ca. 1954-1962
Blue, purple, and red tricolor pen drawing, with collage application, on paper.
26 x 17 cm
Artist's collection
AG1954_1962_CSG_D0210
p. 231

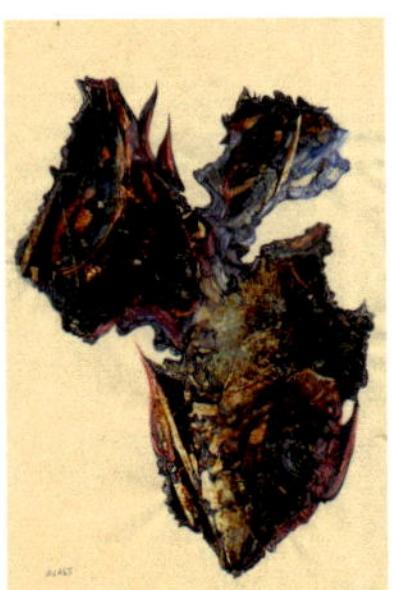

Untitled
(Club Saint-Germain period)
ca. 1954-1962
Drawing in black and blue bicolor ballpoint pen, with green, orange, and red colored pencil, with collage application, on paper.
27.1 x 17.9 cm
Artist's collection
AG1954_1962_CSG_D0209
p. 232

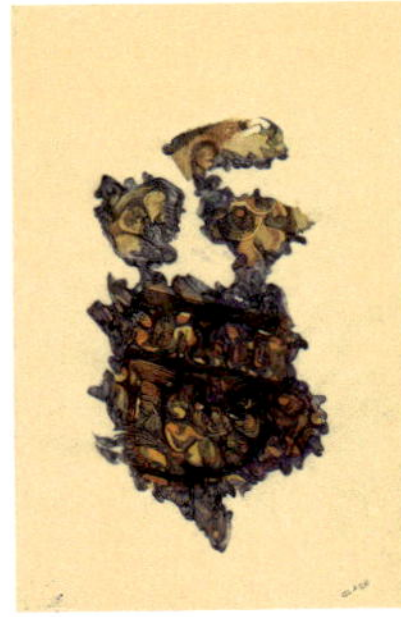

Untitled
(Club Saint-Germain period)
ca. 1954-1962
Drawing in black and purple bicolor ballpoint pen, with green and orange pencil, with collage application, on paper.
26 x 17 cm
Artist's collection
AG1954_1962_CSG_D0205
p. 233

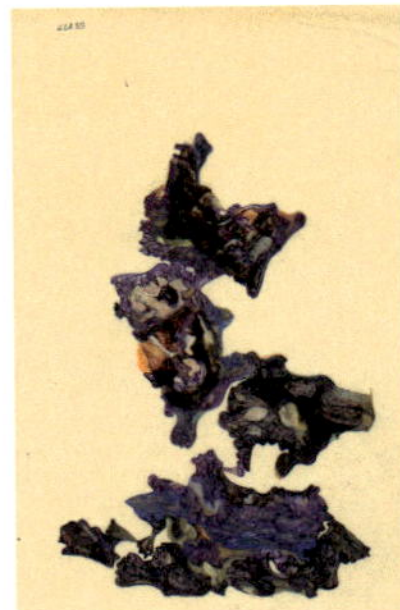

Untitled
(Club Saint-Germain period)
ca. 1954-1962
Bicolor black and purple ballpoint pen drawing, with green and orange colored pencil, with collage application, on paper.
26 x 17 cm
Artist's collection
AG1954_1962_CSG_D0206
p. 233

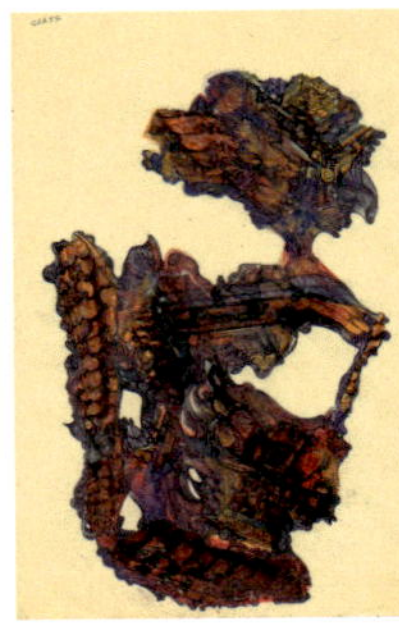

Untitled
(Club Saint-Germain period)
ca. 1954-1962
Drawing in black and purple bicolor ballpoint pen, with green, orange, and red colored pencil, with collage application, on paper.
26 x 17 cm
Artist's collection
AG1954_1962_CSG_D0207
p. 233

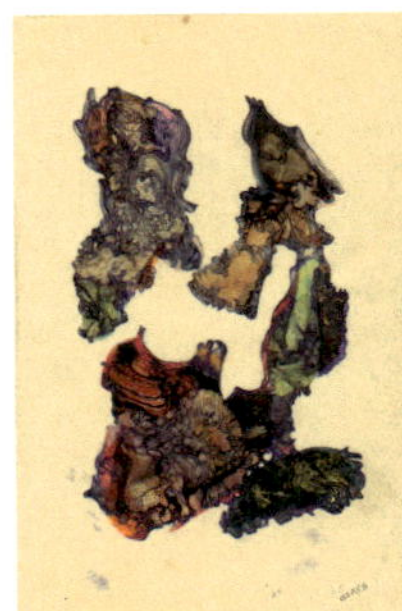

Untitled
(Club Saint-Germain period)
ca. 1954-1962
Drawing in black and blue bicolor ballpoint pen, with green, orange, and red colored pencil, with collage application, on paper.
26 x 17 cm
Artist's collection
AG1954_1962_CSG_D0208
p. 234

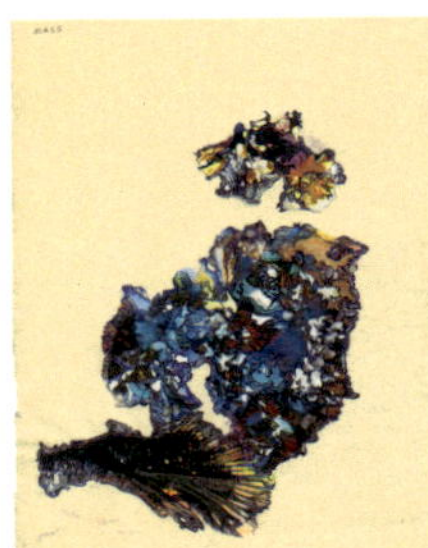

Untitled
(Club Saint-Germain period)
ca. 1954-1962
Drawing in blue, purple, and black tricolor ballpoint pen, with orange and yellow colored pencil, with collage application, on paper.
27 x 21.7 cm
Artist's collection
AG1954_1962_CSG_D0213
p. 235

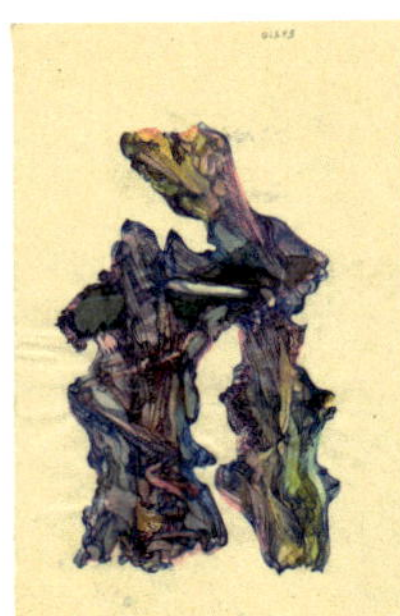

Untitled
(Club Saint-Germain period)
ca. 1954-1962
Bicolor blue and purple ballpoint pen drawing, with green, yellow, and pink colored pencil, with collage application, on paper.
26 x 17 cm
Artist's collection
AG1954_1962_CSG_D0211
p. 235

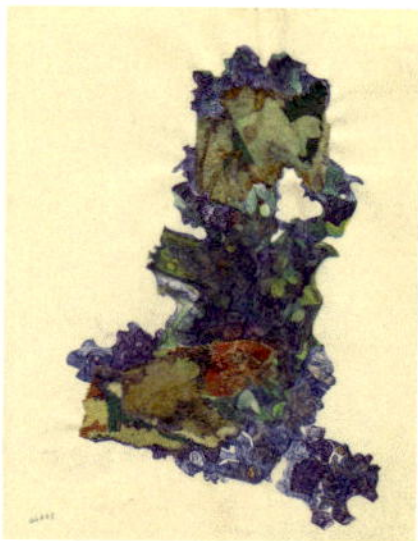

Untitled
(Club Saint-Germain period)
ca. 1954-1962
Bicolor blue and purple ballpoint pen drawing, with green and orange colored pencil, with collage application, on paper.
27 x 21 cm
Artist's collection
AG1954_1962_CSG_D0212
p. 235

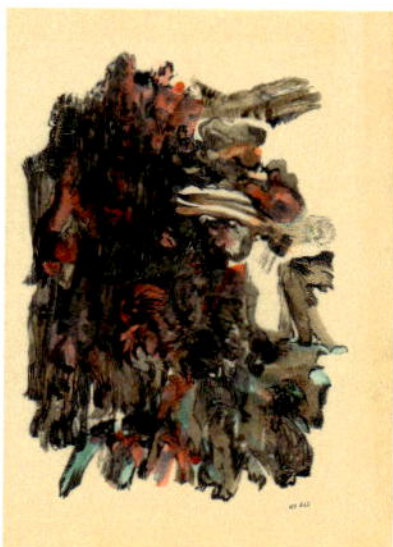

Untitled
(Club Saint-Germain period)
ca. 1954-1962
Indian ink drawing, blue and red watercolor, on paper.
30 x 24.5 cm
Artist's collection
AG1954_1962_CSG_D0046
p. 236

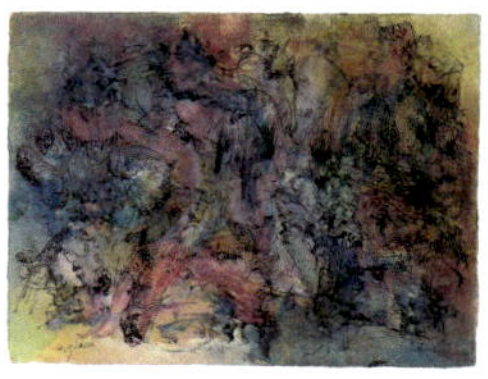

Untitled
(Club Saint-Germain period)
ca. 1954-1962
Black pen drawing, Indian ink, with brown, aqua blue, pink and yellow watercolor, on paper.
14 x 19.1 cm
Artist's collection
AG1954_1962_CSG_D0003
p. 237

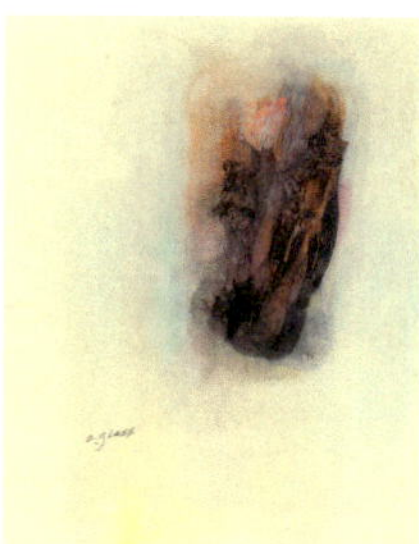

Untitled
(Club Saint-Germain period)
ca. 1954-1962
Black pen drawing, Indian ink, with brown, aqua blue, and pink watercolor, on paper.
19.8 x 12.2 cm
Artist's collection
AG1954_1962_CSG_D0002
p. 238

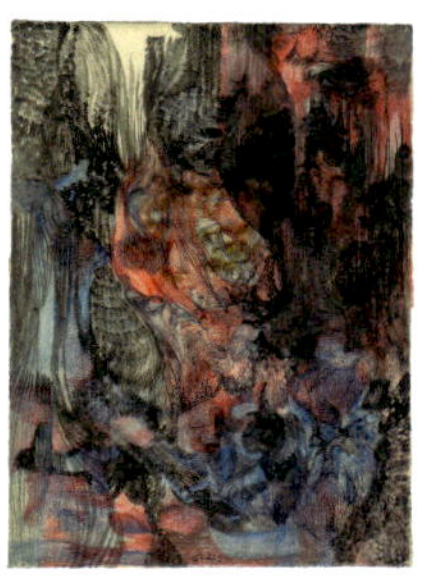

Untitled
(Club Saint-Germain period)
ca. 1954-1962
Blue pen drawing, India ink, blue and red color, on paper.
19 x 14 cm
Artist's collection
AG1954_1962_CSG_D0004
p. 239

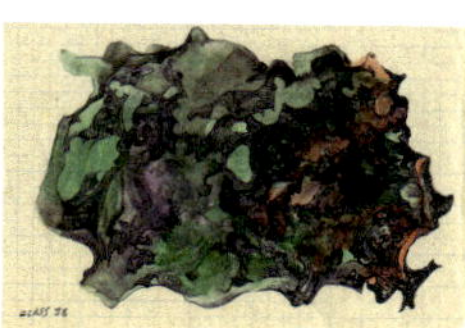

Untitled
(Club Saint-Germain period)
1958
Black pen drawing, India ink, with green, violet and orange watercolor, on squared paper.
9.5 x 15.1 cm
Artist's collection
AG1954_1962_CSG_D0005
p. 240

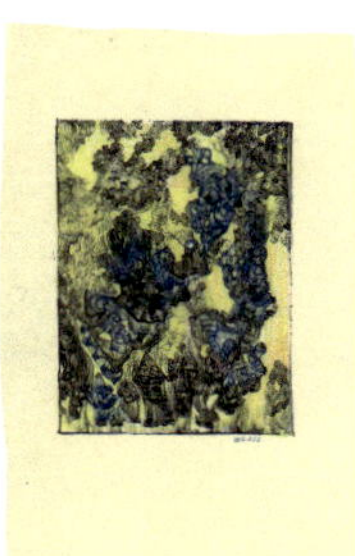

Untitled
(Club Saint-Germain period)
ca. 1954-1962
Blue, purple, orange, yellow, and black watercolor, on paper.
21.5 x 14 cm
Artist's collection
AG1954_1962_CSG_D0008
p. 240

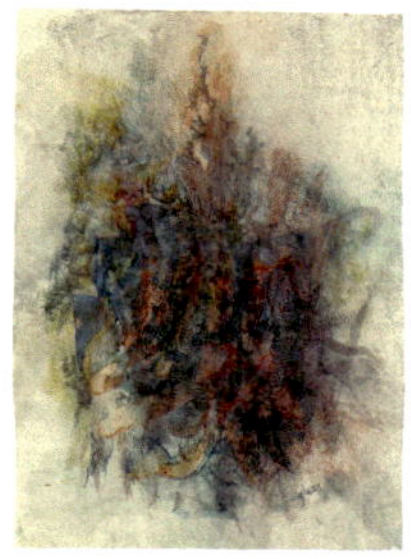

Untitled
(Club Saint-Germain period)
ca. 1954-1962
Blue, purple, orange, yellow, and black watercolor, on paper.
17.3 x 12.5 cm
Artist's collection
AG1954_1962_CSG_D0007
p. 241

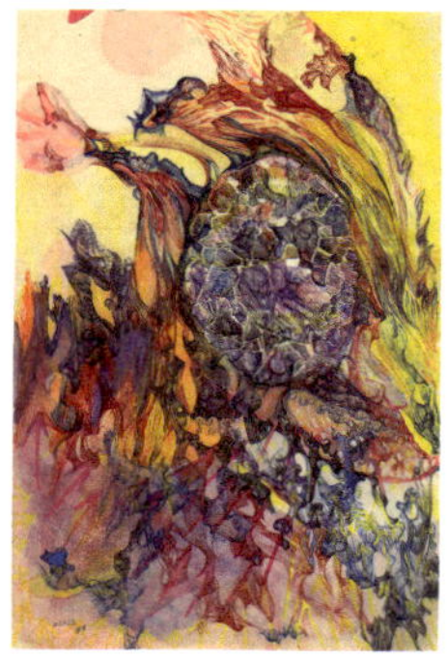

Untitled
(Club Saint-Germain period)
1958
Blue, purple, red, and black quadricolor pen drawing, with orange, yellow, and lilac watercolor pencil with eggshell application, on paper.
27 x 18 cm
Artist's collection
AG1954_1962_CSG_D0217
p. 242

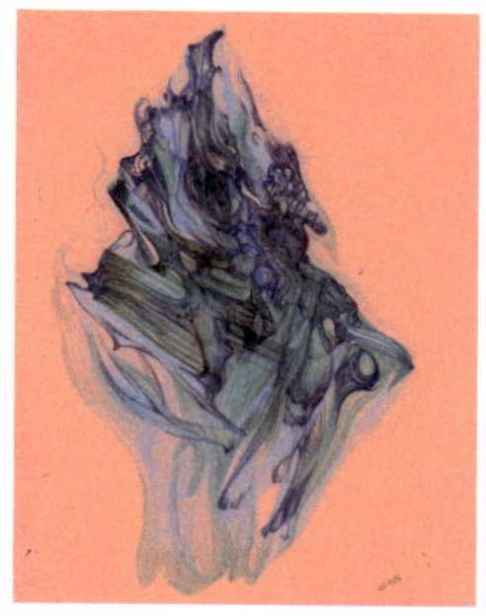

Untitled
(Club Saint Germain period)
ca. 1954-1962
Blue, purple, and black tricolor pen drawing, with sky blue, turquoise, and olive green pencil, on pink paper.
27 x 21.1 cm
Artist's collection
AG1954_1962_CSG_D0215
p. 243

CHAPTER III
LE TERRAIN VAGUE PARIS VI[E]

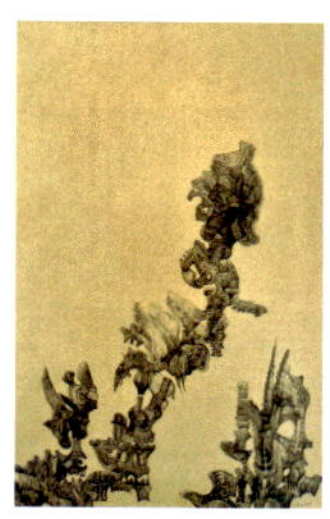

Untitled
(Galerie Le Terrain Vague period)
ca. 1950
Blue Bic pen, on paper.
21.5 x 14 cm
Philippe Scrive collection, France
p. 250

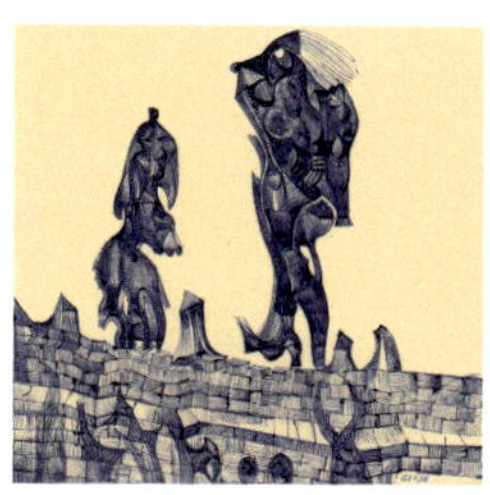

Untitled
(Galerie Le Terrain Vague period)
ca. 1954-1962
Monochrome blue ballpoint pen drawing, on paper.
15.2 x 15.8 cm. Artist's collection
AG1954_1962_GTV_D0018
p. 252

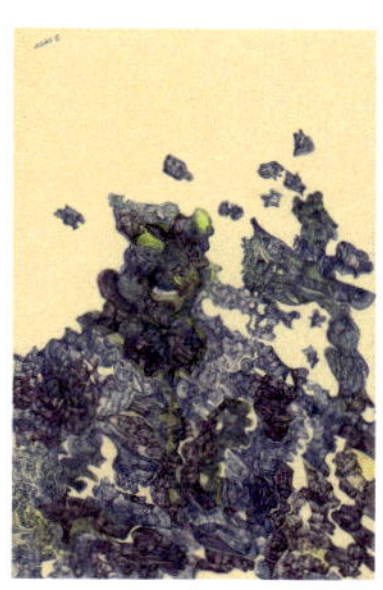

Untitled
(Galerie Le Terrain Vague period)
ca. 1954-1962
Drawing in blue and purple bicolor pen with yellow, olive green, and lemon green pencil, on paper.
26 x 17 cm
Artist's collection
AG1954_1962_GTV_D0080
p. 253

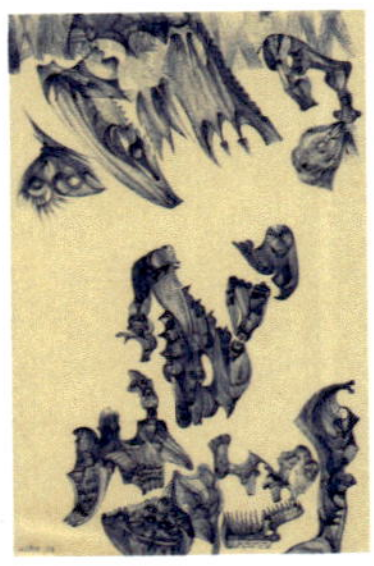

Untitled
(Galerie Le Terrain Vague period)
1958
Monochrome blue ballpoint pen drawing, on paper.
26 x 17 cm
Artist's collection
AG1954_1962_GTV_D0004
p. 254

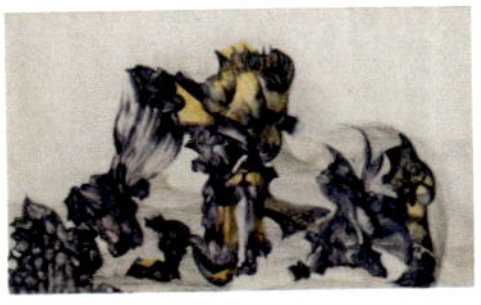

Untitled
(Galerie Le Terrain Vague period)
ca. 1950
Blue Bic pen, on paper.
14 x 25 cm
Louise Deschetelet collection, Canada
p. 255

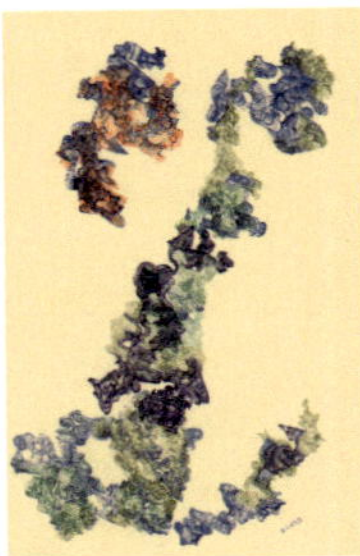

Untitled
(Galerie Le Terrain Vague period)
ca. 1954-1962
Drawing in blue and purple bicolor pen with orange, olive green, grass green and turquoise pencil, on paper.
26 x 17 cm
Artist's collection
AG1954_1962_GTV_D0085
p. 256

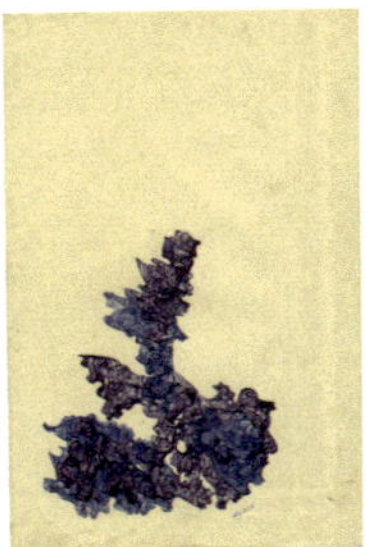

Untitled
(Galerie Le Terrain Vague period)
ca. 1954-1962
Drawing in blue and violet bicolor pen, on paper.
26 x 17 cm
Artist's collection
AG1954_1962_GTV_D0002
p. 260

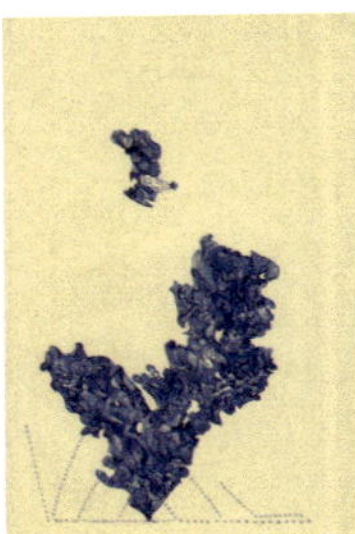

Untitled
(Galerie Le Terrain Vague period)
ca. 1954-1962
Monochrome blue ballpoint pen drawing, on paper.
26 x 17 cm
Artist's collection
AG1954_1962_GTV_D0003
p. 260

Untitled
(Galerie Le Terrain Vague period)
ca. 1954-1962
Monochrome blue ballpoint pen drawing, on paper.
26 x 17 cm
Artist's collection
AG1954_1962_GTV_D0005
p. 261

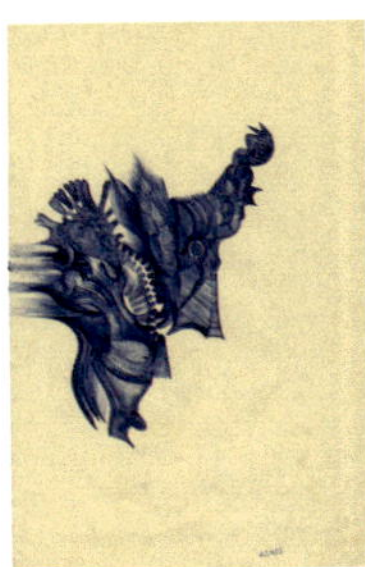

Untitled
(Galerie Le Terrain Vague period)
ca. 1954-1962
Monochrome blue ballpoint pen drawing, on paper.
26 x 17 cm
Artist's collection
AG1954_1962_GTV_D0006
p. 264

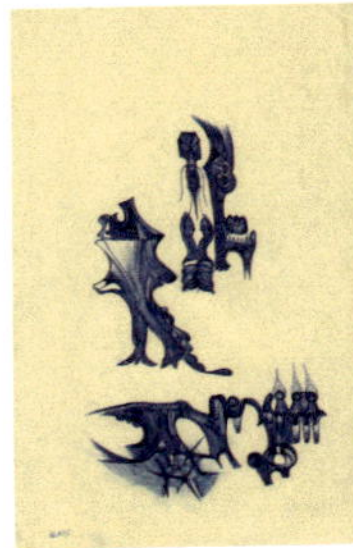

Untitled
(Galerie Le Terrain Vague period)
ca. 1954-1962
Monochrome blue ballpoint pen drawing, on paper.
26 x 17 cm
Artist's collection
AG1954_1962_GTV_D0007
p. 264

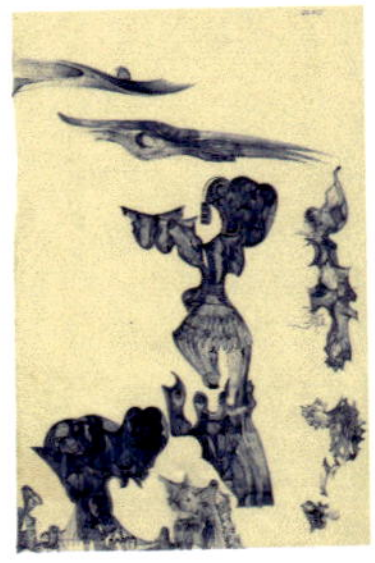

Untitled
(Galerie Le Terrain Vague period)
ca. 1954-1962
Monochrome blue ballpoint pen drawing, on paper.
26 x 17 cm
Artist's collection
AG1954_1962_GTV_D0008
p. 265

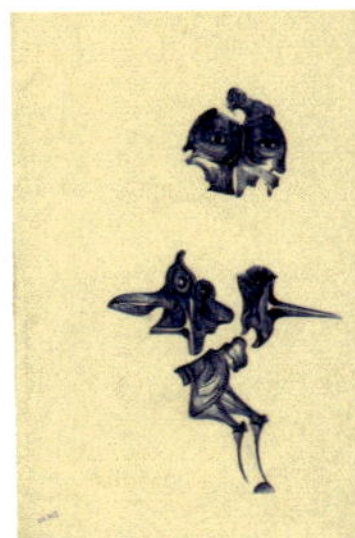

Untitled
(Galerie Le Terrain Vague period)
ca. 1954-1962
Monochrome blue ballpoint pen drawing, on paper.
26 x 17 cm
Artist's collection
AG1954_1962_GTV_D0009
p. 265

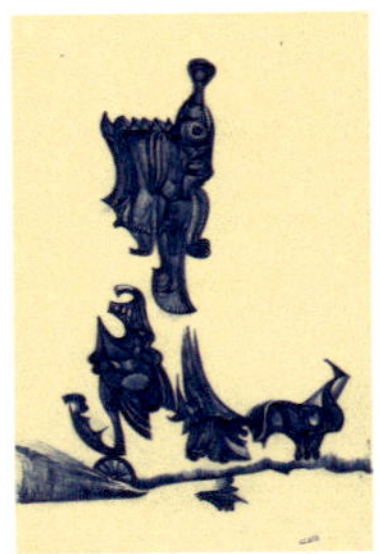

Untitled
(Galerie Le Terrain Vague period)
ca. 1954-1962
Monochrome blue ballpoint pen drawing, on paper.
26 x 17 cm
Artist's collection
AG1954_1962_GTV_D0010
p. 268

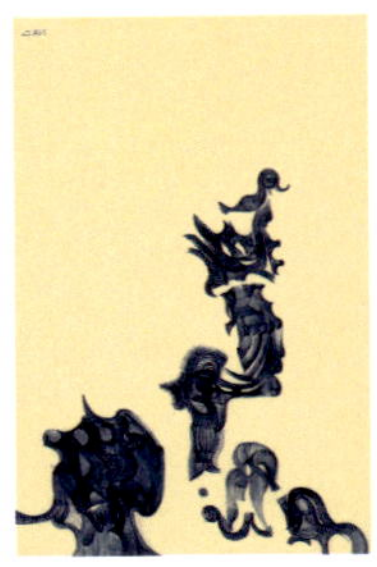

Untitled
(Galerie Le Terrain Vague period)
ca. 1954-1962
Monochrome blue ballpoint pen drawing, on paper.
26 x 17 cm
Artist's collection
AG1954_1962_GTV_D0011
p. 268

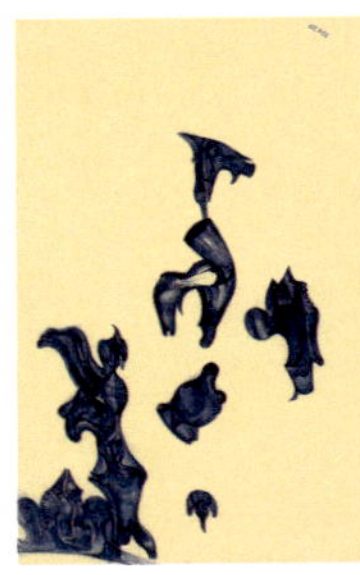

Untitled
(Galerie Le Terrain Vague period)
ca. 1954-1962
Monochrome blue ballpoint pen drawing, on paper.
26 x 17 cm
Artist's collection
AG1954_1962_GTV_D0012
p. 269

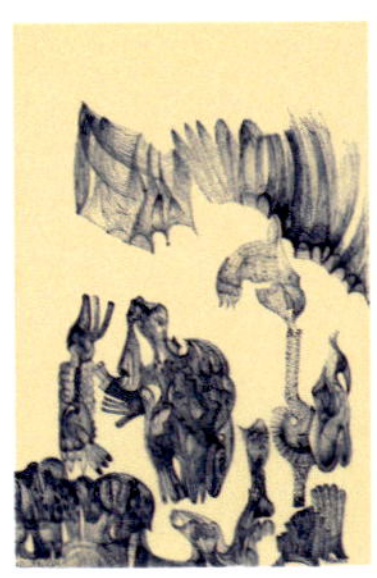

Untitled
(Galerie Le Terrain Vague period)
ca. 1954-1962
Monochrome blue ballpoint pen drawing, on paper.
26 x 17 cm
Artist's collection
AG1954_1962_GTV_D0013
p. 269

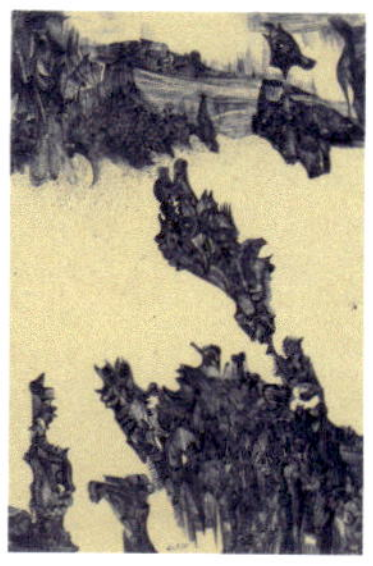

Untitled
(Galerie Le Terrain Vague period)
ca. 1954-1962
Monochrome blue ballpoint pen drawing, on paper.
26 x 17 cm
Artist's collection
AG1954_1962_GTV_D0014
p. 269

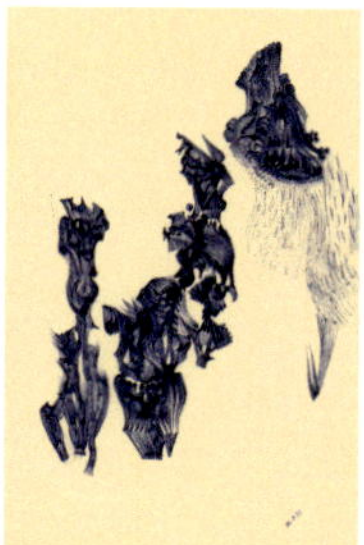

Untitled
(Galerie Le Terrain Vague period)
ca. 1954-1962
Monochrome blue ballpoint pen drawing, on paper.
26 x 17 cm
Artist's collection
AG1954_1962_GTV_D0015
p. 272

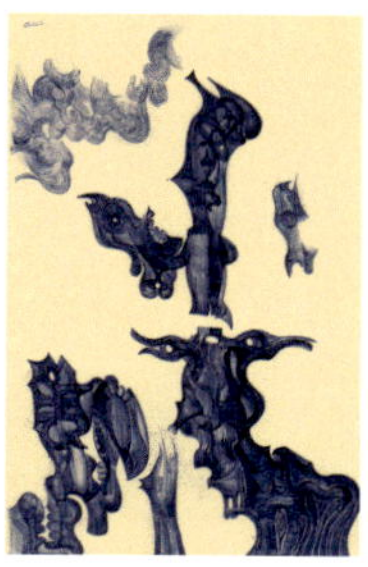

Untitled
(Galerie Le Terrain Vague period)
ca. 1954-1962
Monochrome blue ballpoint pen drawing, on paper.
26 x 17 cm
Artist's collection
AG1954_1962_GTV_D0016
p. 272

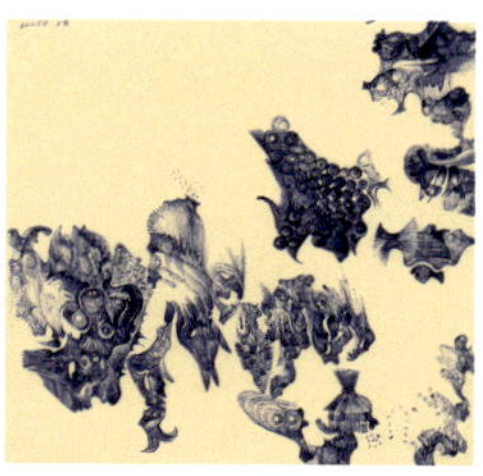

Untitled
(Galerie Le Terrain Vague period)
1958
Monochrome blue ballpoint pen drawing, on paper.
16.4 x 17.1 cm
Artist's collection
AG1954_1962_GTV_D0017
p. 273

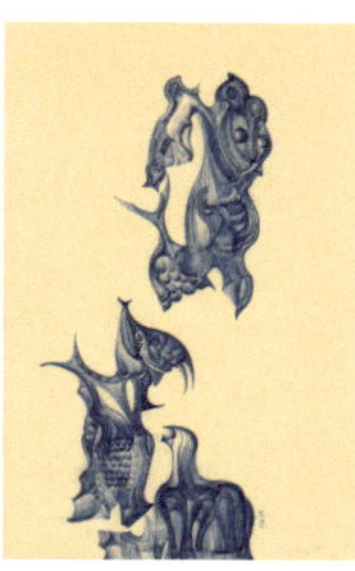

Untitled
(Galerie Le Terrain Vague period)
ca. 1954-1962
Monochrome blue ballpoint pen drawing, on paper.
26 x 17 cm
Artist's collection
AG1954_1962_GTV_D0038
p. 276

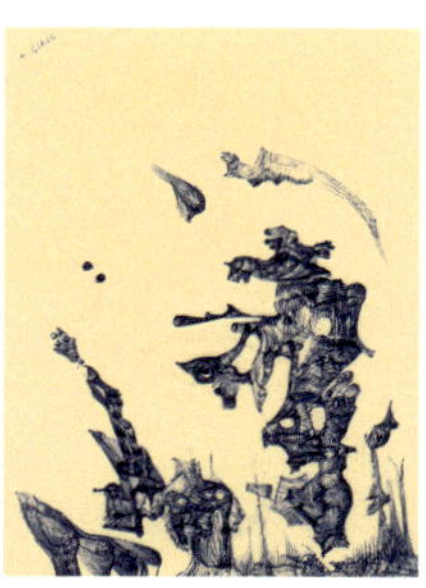

Untitled
(Galerie Le Terrain Vague period)
ca. 1954-1962
Monochrome blue ballpoint pen drawing, on paper.
17.1 x 13 cm
Artist's collection
AG1954_1962_GTV_D0019
p. 276

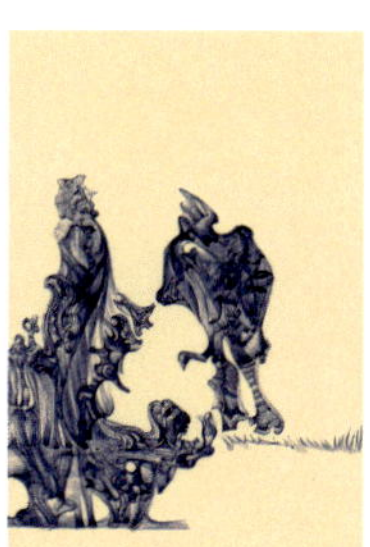

Untitled
(Galerie Le Terrain Vague period)
ca. 1954-1962
Monochrome blue ballpoint pen drawing, on paper.
26 x 17 cm
Artist's collection
AG1954_1962_GTV_D0021
p. 277

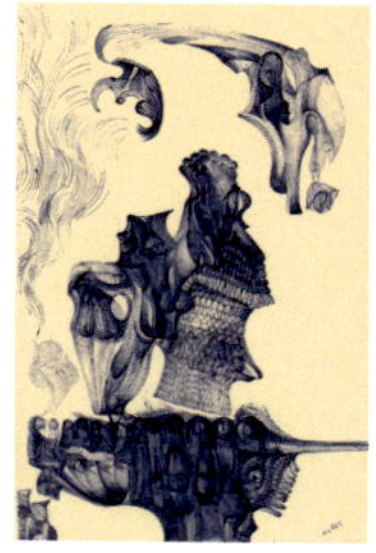

Untitled
(Galerie Le Terrain Vague period)
ca. 1954-1962
Monochrome blue ballpoint pen drawing, on paper.
26 x 17 cm
Artist's collection
AG1954_1962_GTV_D0020
p. 277

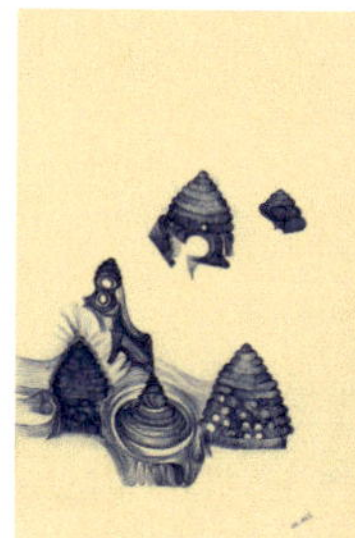

Untitled
(Galerie Le Terrain Vague period)
ca. 1954-1962
Monochrome blue ballpoint pen drawing, on paper.
26 x 17 cm
Artist's collection
AG1954_1962_GTV_D0022
p. 280

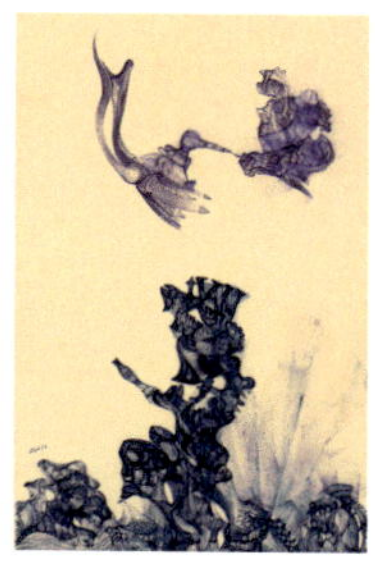

Untitled
(Galerie Le Terrain Vague period)
ca. 1954-1962
Drawing in blue and violet bicolor pen, on paper.
26 x 17 cm
Artist's collection
AG1954_1962_GTV_D0023
p. 280

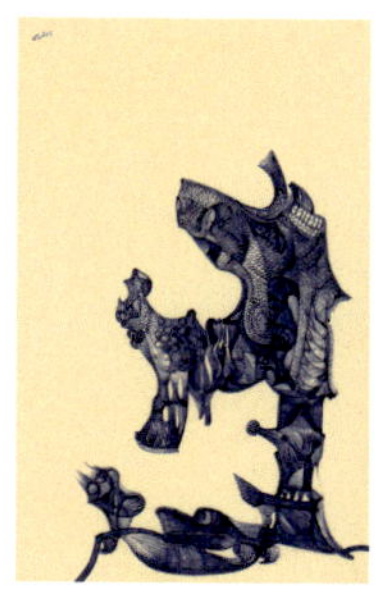

Untitled
(Galerie Le Terrain Vague period)
ca. 1954-1962
Monochrome blue ballpoint pen drawing, on paper.
26 x 17 cm
Artist's collection
AG1954_1962_GTV_D0024
p. 281

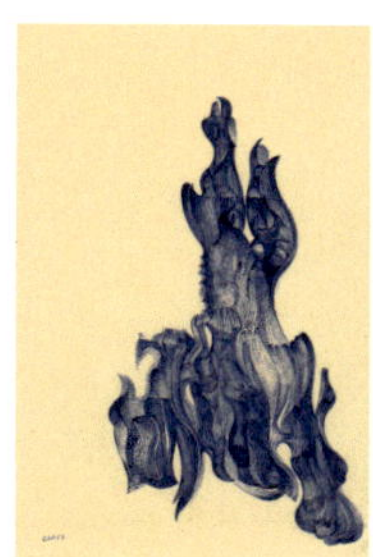

Untitled
(Galerie Le Terrain Vague period)
ca. 1954-1962
Monochrome blue ballpoint pen drawing, on paper.
26 x 17 cm
Artist's collection
AG1954_1962_GTV_D0025
p. 281

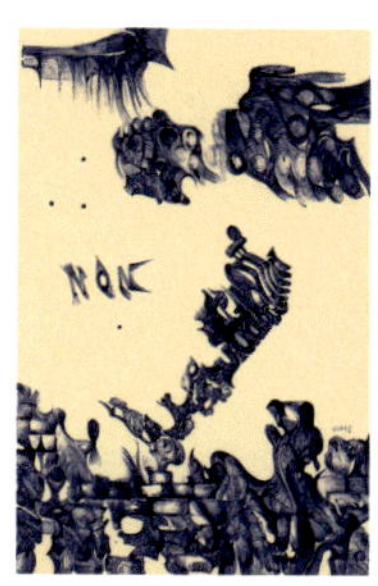

Untitled
(Galerie Le Terrain Vague period)
ca. 1954-1962
Monochrome blue ballpoint pen drawing, on paper.
26 x 17 cm
Artist's collection
AG1954_1962_GTV_D0026
p. 284

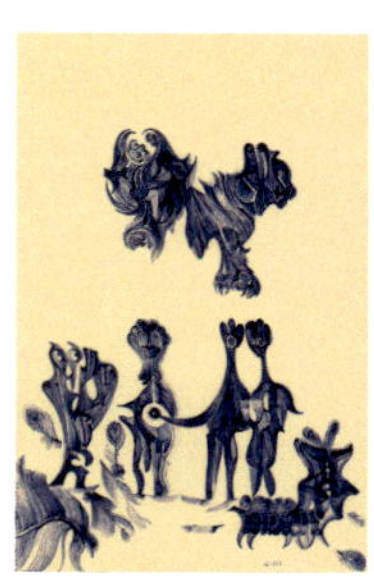

Untitled
(Galerie Le Terrain Vague period)
ca. 1954-1962
Monochrome blue ballpoint pen drawing, on paper.
25.8 x 17 cm
Artist's collectionn
AG1954_1962_GTV_D0028
p. 285

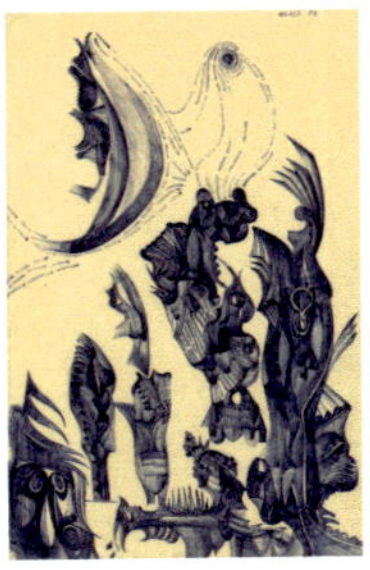

Untitled
(Galerie Le Terrain Vague period)
1958
Monochrome blue ballpoint pen drawing, on paper.
26 x 17 cm
Artist's collection
AG1954_1962_GTV_D0027
p. 286

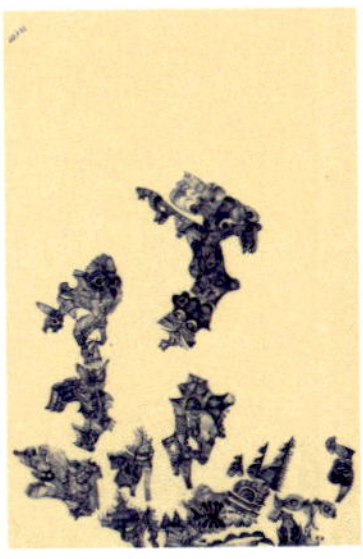

Untitled
(Galerie Le Terrain Vague period)
ca. 1954-1962
Monochrome blue ballpoint pen drawing, on paper.
25.6 x 17 cm
Artist's collection
AG1954_1962_GTV_D0029
p. 287

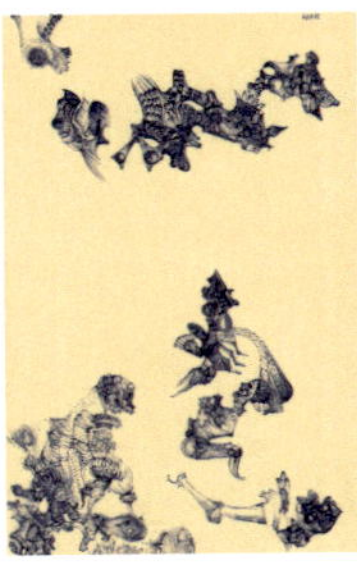

Untitled
(Galerie Le Terrain Vague period)
ca. 1954-1962
Monochrome blue ballpoint pen drawing, on paper.
26 x 17 cm
Artist's collection
AG1954_1962_GTV_D0030
p. 287

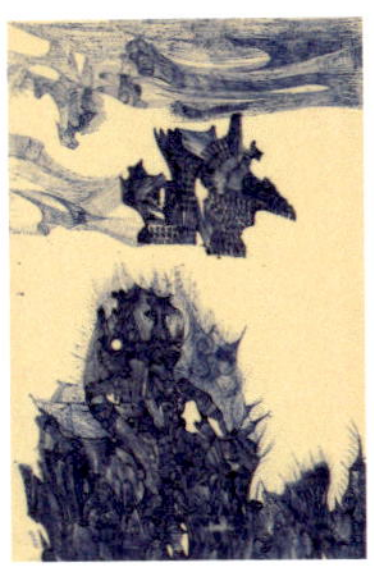

Untitled
(Galerie Le Terrain Vague period)
ca. 1954-1962
Monochrome blue ballpoint pen drawing, on paper.
26 x 17 cm
Artist's collection
AG1954_1962_GTV_D0033
p. 290

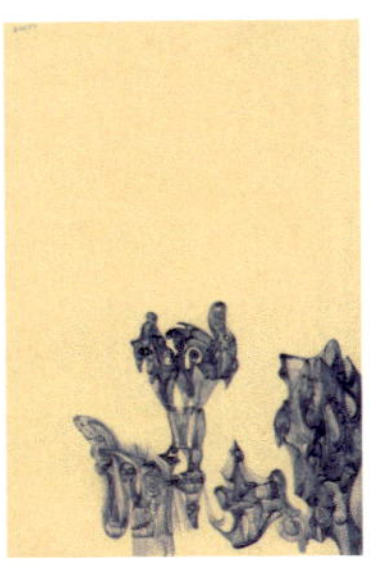

Untitled
(Galerie Le Terrain Vague period)
ca. 1954-1962
Monochrome blue ballpoint pen drawing, on paper.
26 x 17 cm
Artist's collection
AG1954_1962_GTV_D0036
p. 290

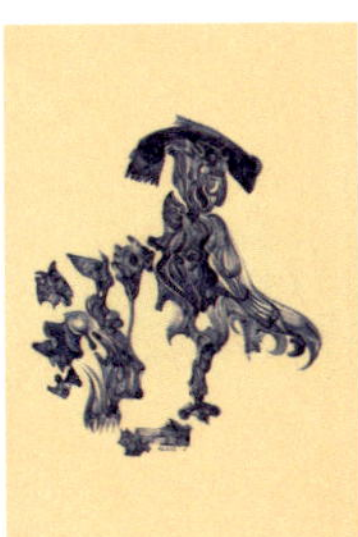

Untitled
(Galerie Le Terrain Vague period)
ca. 1954-1962
Monochrome blue ballpoint pen drawing, on paper.
26 x 17 cm
Artist's collection
AG1954_1962_GTV_D0035
p. 291

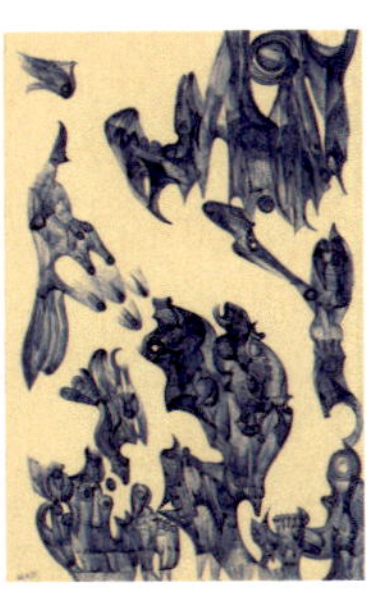

Untitled
(Galerie Le Terrain Vague period)
ca. 1954-1962
Monochrome blue ballpoint pen drawing, on paper.
26 x 17 cm
Artist's collection
AG1954_1962_GTV_D0034
p. 291

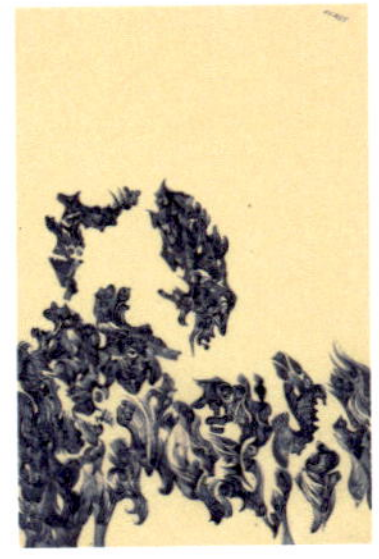

Untitled
(Galerie Le Terrain Vague period)
ca. 1954-1962
Monochrome blue ballpoint pen drawing, on paper.
26 x 17 cm
Artist's collection
AG1954_1962_GTV_D0040
p. 294

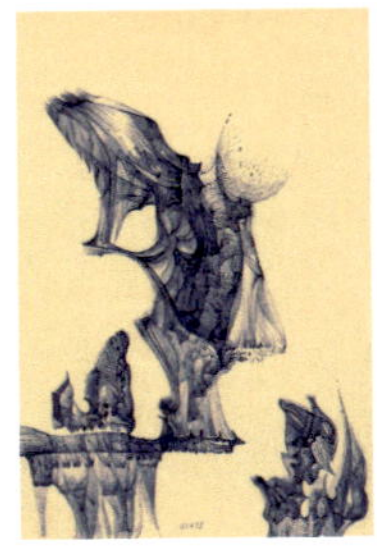

Untitled
(Galerie Le Terrain Vague period)
ca. 1954-1962
Monochrome blue ballpoint pen drawing, on paper.
26 x 17.2 cm
Artist's collection
AG1954_1962_GTV_D0039
p. 295

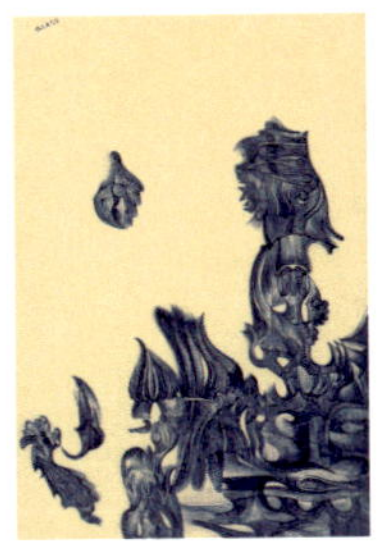

Untitled
(Galerie Le Terrain Vague period)
ca. 1954-1962
Monochrome blue ballpoint pen drawing, on paper.
26 x 17 cm
Artist's collection
AG1954_1962_GTV_D0037
p. 295

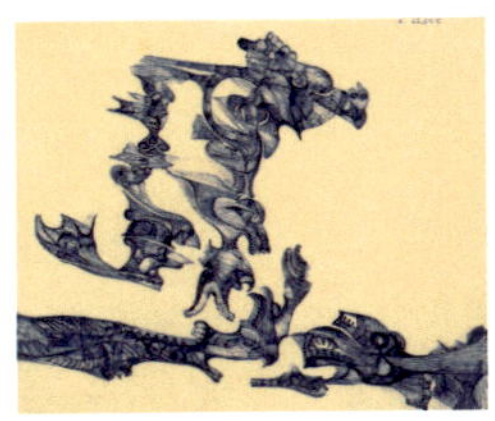

Untitled
(Galerie Le Terrain Vague period)
ca. 1954-1962
Monochrome blue ballpoint pen drawing, on paper.
14.3 x 17 cm
Artist's collection
AG1954_1962_GTV_D0042
p. 296

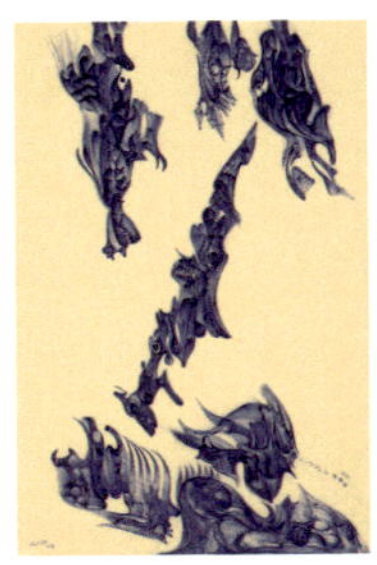

Untitled
(Galerie Le Terrain Vague period)
1958
Monochrome blue ballpoint pen drawing, on paper.
26 x 17 cm
Artist's collection
AG1954_1962_GTV_D0041
p. 296

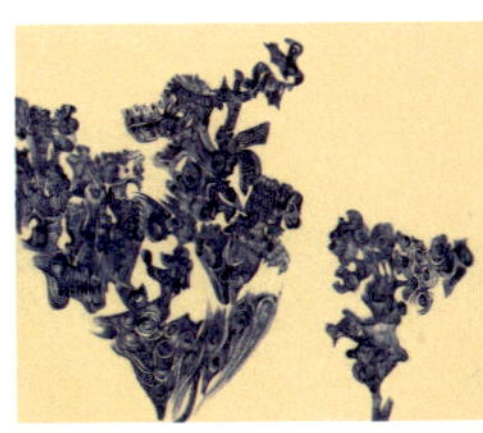

Untitled
(Galerie Le Terrain Vague period)
ca. 1954-1962
Monochrome blue ballpoint pen drawing, on paper.
14.5 x 17 cm
Artist's collection
AG1954_1962_GTV_D0043
p. 297

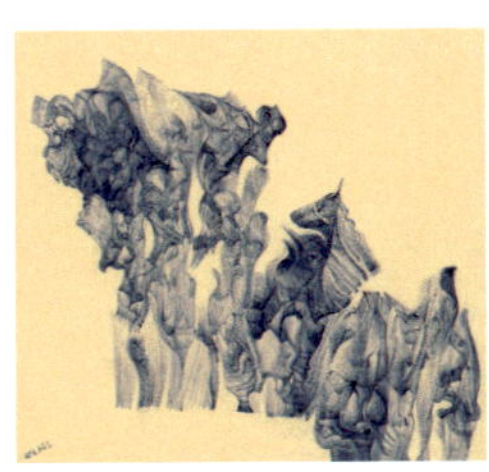

Untitled
(Galerie Le Terrain Vague period)
ca. 1954-1962
Monochrome blue ballpoint pen drawing, on paper.
15.5 x 17 cm
Artist's collection
AG1954_1962_GTV_D0044
p. 297

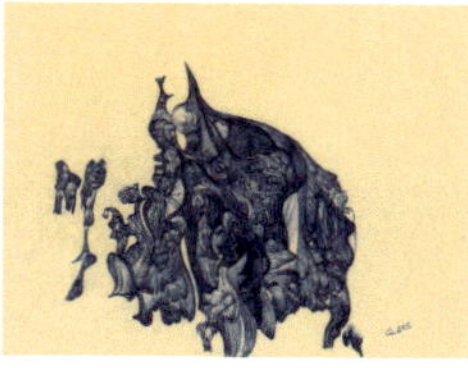

Untitled
(Galerie Le Terrain Vague period)
ca. 1954-1962
Monochrome blue ballpoint pen drawing, on paper.
13 x 17 cm
Artist's collection
AG1954_1962_GTV_D0045
p. 298

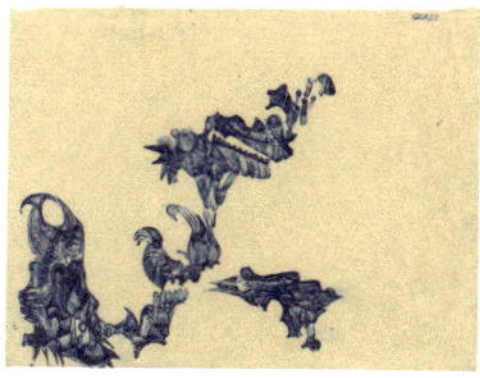

Untitled
(Galerie Le Terrain Vague period)
ca. 1954-1962
Monochrome blue ballpoint pen drawing, on paper.
13 x 17 cm
Artist's collection
AG1954_1962_GTV_D0046
p. 298

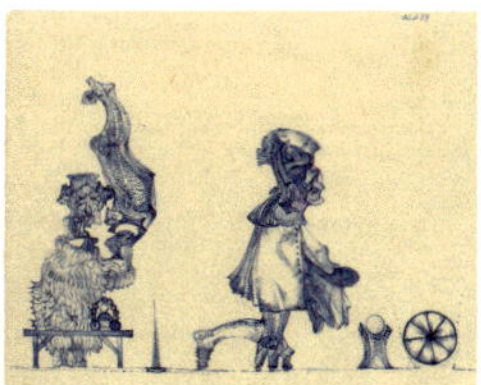

Untitled
(Galerie Le Terrain Vague period)
1959
Drawing in blue and purple bicolor pen, on paper.
13.6 x 17 cm
Artist's collection
AG1954_1962_GTV_D0047
p. 299

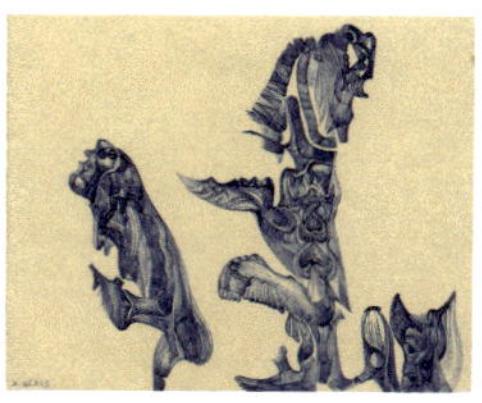

Untitled
(Galerie Le Terrain Vague period)
ca. 1954-1962
Monochrome blue ballpoint pen drawing, on paper.
13.7 x 17 cm
Artist's collection
AG1954_1962_GTV_D0048
p. 300

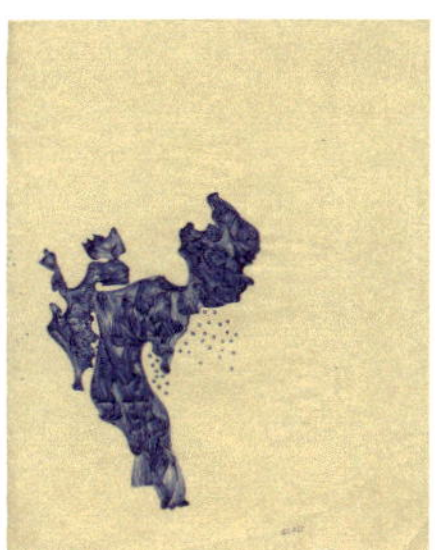

Untitled
(Galerie Le Terrain Vague period)
ca. 1954-1962
Monochrome blue ballpoint pen drawing, on paper.
27 x 21.5 cm
Artist's collection
AG1954_1962_GTV_D0050
p. 300

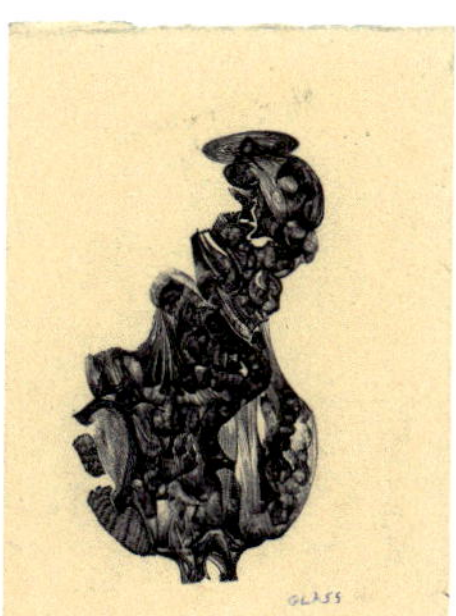

Untitled
(Galerie Le Terrain Vague period)
ca. 1954-1962
Drawing in black monocolor ballpoint pen, on invitation to the 6th anniversary of the Discothèque de Jean-Claude Merle.
14 x 10.4 cm
Artist's collection
AG1954_1962_GTV_D0049
p. 301

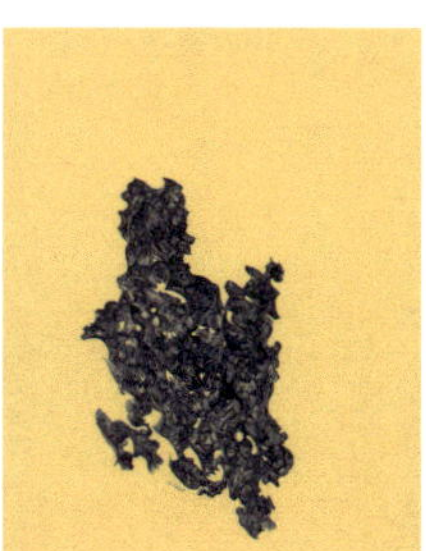

Untitled
(Galerie Le Terrain Vague period)
ca. 1954-1962
Monochrome blue ballpoint pen drawing, on paper.
27 x 21 cm
Artist's collection
AG1954_1962_GTV_D0051
p. 301

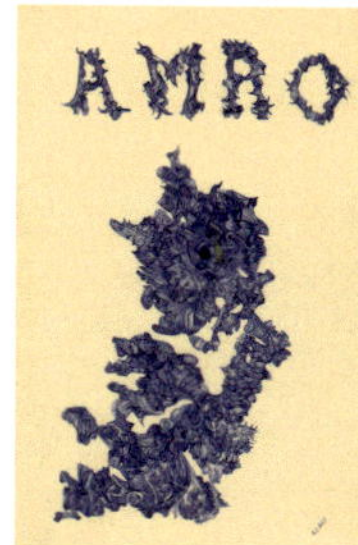

Untitled
(Galerie Le Terrain Vague period)
ca. 1954-1962
Drawing in blue monocolor ballpoint pen with a touch of olive green pencil, on paper.
26 x 17 cm
Artist's collection
AG1954_1962_GTV_D0031
p. 302

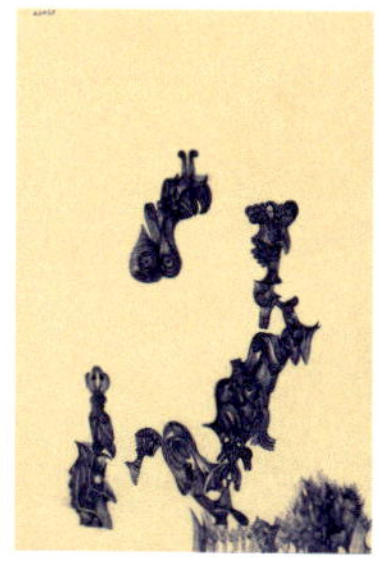

Untitled
(Galerie Le Terrain Vague period)
ca. 1954-1962
Monochrome blue ballpoint pen drawing, on paper.
26 x 17.1 cm
Artist's collection
AG1954_1962_GTV_D0032
p. 303

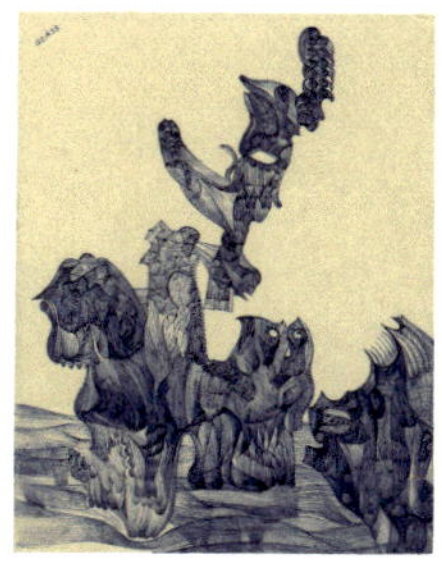

Untitled
(Galerie Le Terrain Vague period)
ca. 1954-1962
Monochrome blue ballpoint pen drawing, on paper.
22.1 x 17 cm
Artist's collection
AG1954_1962_GTV_D0001
p. 303

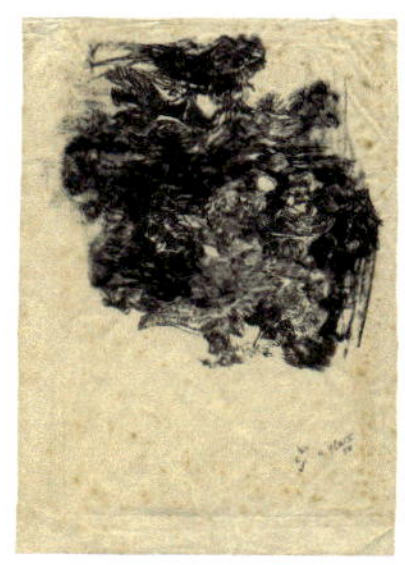

Untitled
(Galerie Le Terrain Vague period)
1958
Drawing in black monocolor ballpoint pen with Chinese ink, on butter paper.
27.8 x 19.5 cm
Artist's collection
AG1954_1962_GTV_D0053
p. 304

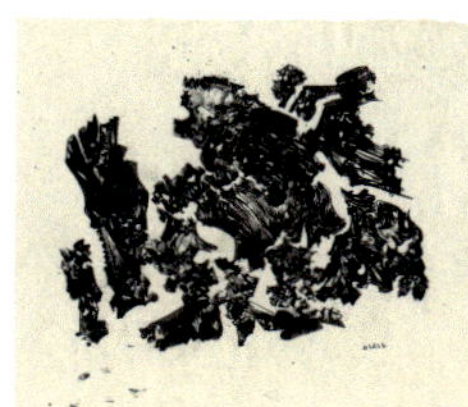

Untitled
(Galerie Le Terrain Vague period)
ca. 1954-1962
Drawing with fountain pen and Chinese ink, on paper.
18.3 x 21.1 cm
Artist's collection
AG1954_1962_GTV_D0054
p. 305

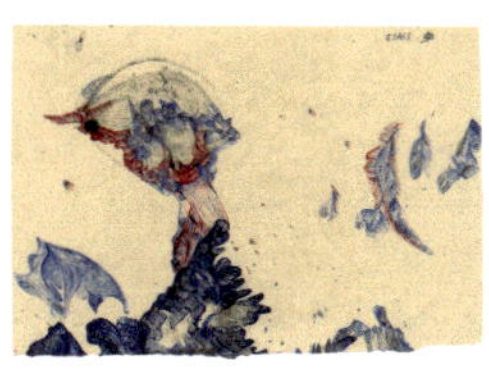

Untitled
(Galerie Le Terrain Vague period)
1958
Drawing in blue and red bicolor pen with graphite, on paper.
10.2 x 14.9 cm
Artist's collection
AG1954_1962_GTV_D0057
p. 306

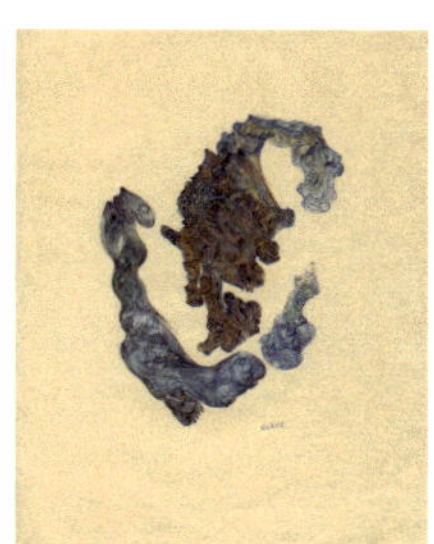

Untitled
(Galerie Le Terrain Vague period)
ca. 1954-1962
Drawing in blue and black bicolor pen with orange and green pencil, on paper.
28.1 x 21.5 cm
Artist's collection
AG1954_1962_GTV_D0058
p. 307

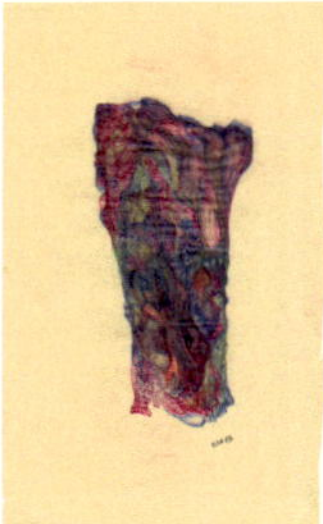

Untitled
(Galerie Le Terrain Vague period)
ca. 1954-1962
Drawing in blue and pink bicolor pen with orange, lemon green, olive green, and pink pencil, on paper.
28.1 x 17.3 cm
Artist's collection
AG1954_1962_GTV_D0059
p. 308

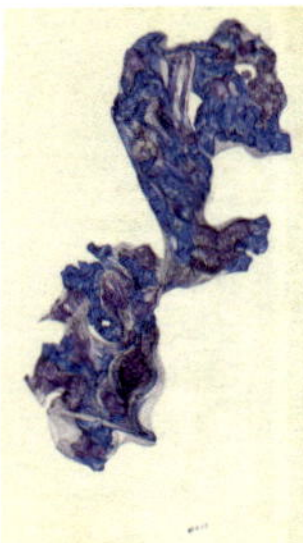

Untitled
(Galerie Terrain Vague period)
ca. 1954-1962
Drawing in blue and purple bicolor ballpoint pen, on paper.
27.1 x 15.5 cm
Artist's collection
AG1954_1962_GTV_D0060
p. 308

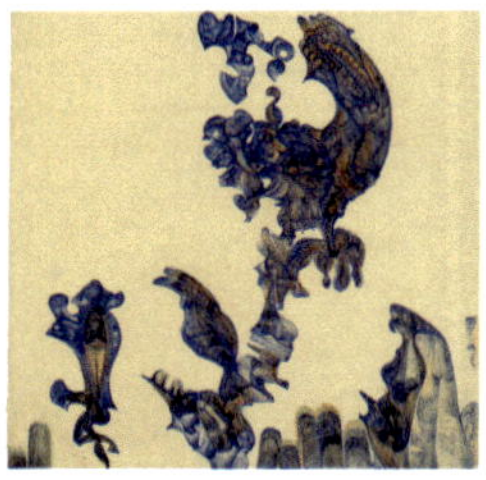

Untitled
(Galerie Le Terrain Vague period)
ca. 1954-1962
Drawing in blue monocolor pen with orange pencil, on paper.
16.7 x 17.1 cm
Artist's collection
AG1954_1962_GTV_D0061
p. 309

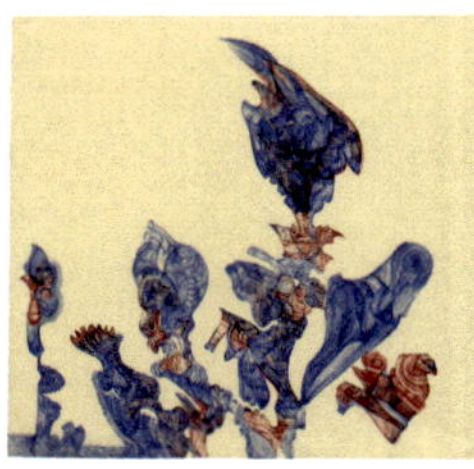

Untitled
(Galerie Le Terrain Vague period)
ca. 1954-1962
Drawing in blue and red bicolor ballpoint pen, on paper.
16.3 x 17.1 cm
Artist's collection
AG1954_1962_GTV_D0062
p. 310

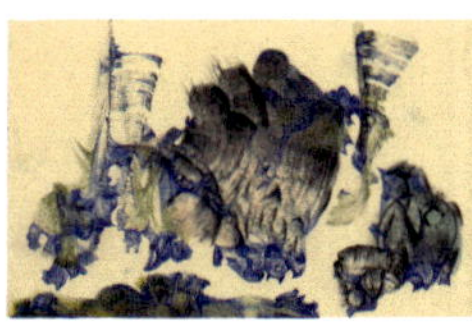

Untitled
(Galerie Le Terrain Vague period)
ca. 1954-1962
Drawing in a monocolor blue ballpoint pen with turquoise, olive green, and yellow pencils. Fingerprints with black seal ink, on paper.
10.9 x 17.1 cm
Artist's collection
AG1954_1962_GTV_D0064
p. 311

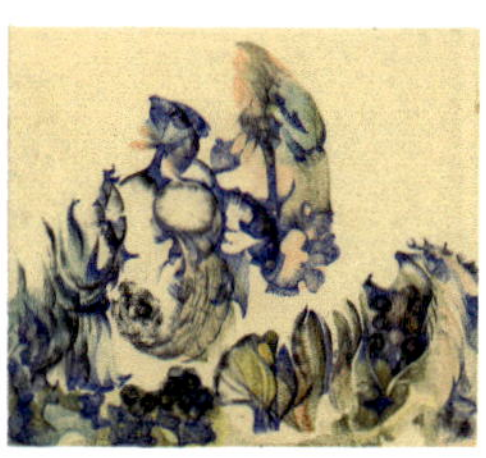

Untitled
(Galerie Le Terrain Vague period)
ca. 1954-1962
Drawing in blue monocolor ballpoint pen with beige, turquoise, olive green, and yellow pencil, on paper.
15.1 x 17 cm
Artist's collection
AG1954_1962_GTV_D0063
p. 311

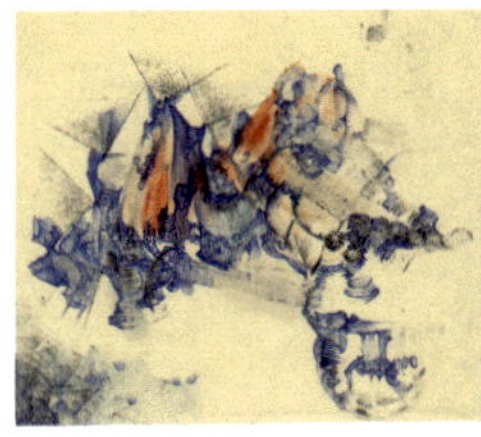

Untitled
(Galerie Le Terrain Vague period)
ca. 1954-1962
Drawing in blue monocolor ballpoint pen with orange, sky blue, and black stamp ink, on paper.
19.4 x 17.1 cm
Artist's collection
AG1954_1962_GTV_D0065
p. 312

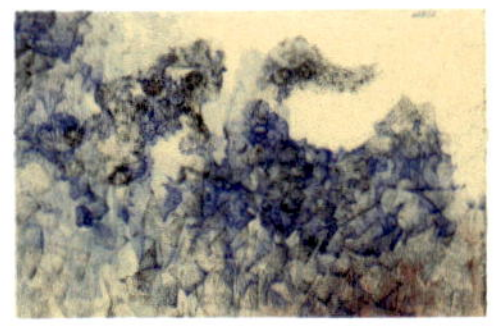

Untitled
(Galerie Le Terrain Vague period)
ca. 1954-1962
Drawing in monocolor blue pen with brown, sky blue, black pencil, and black seal ink, on paper.
11.1 x 17.1 cm
Artist's collection
AG1954_1962_GTV_D0068
p. 313

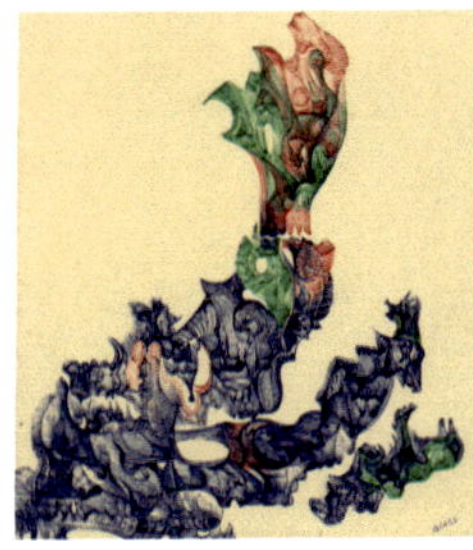

Untitled
(Galerie Le Terrain Vague period)
ca. 1954-1962
Drawing in blue, green, and red tricolor ballpoint pen, on paper.
19.4 x 17.1 cm
Artist's collection
AG1954_1962_GTV_D0067
p. 313

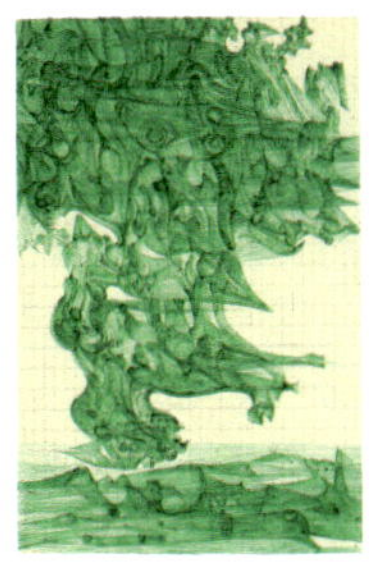

Untitled
(Galerie Le Terrain Vague period)
ca. 1954-1962
Drawing in green monocolor ballpoint pen, on squared paper.
21 x 13.4 cm
Artist's collection
AG1954_1962_GTV_D0055
p. 314

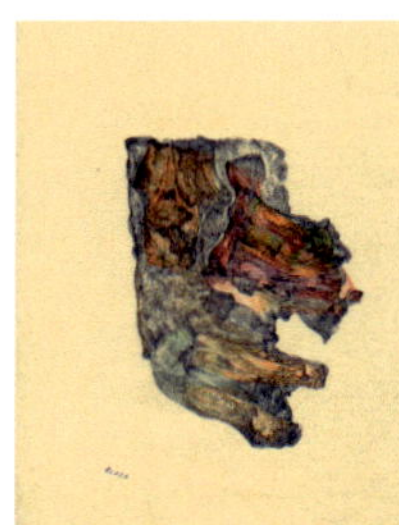

Untitled
(Galerie Le Terrain Vague period)
ca. 1954-1962
Drawing in blue monocolor ballpoint pen with turquoise, orange, grass green, and pink pencil, on paper.
28 x 21.7 cm
Artist's collection
AG1954_1962_GTV_D0069
p. 315

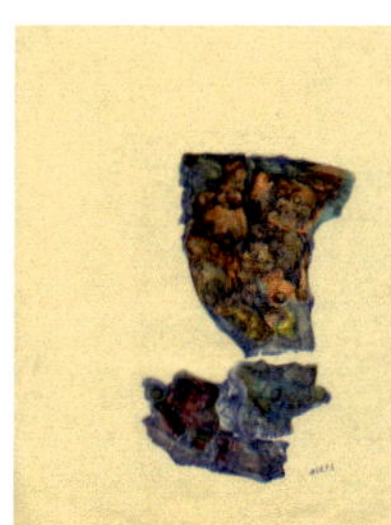

Untitled
(Galerie Le Terrain Vague period)
ca. 1954-1962
Drawing in blue monocolor ballpoint pen with turquoise, orange, olive green, yellow, and red pencil, on paper.
28 x 21.7 cm
Artist's collection
AG1954_1962_GTV_D0071
p. 315

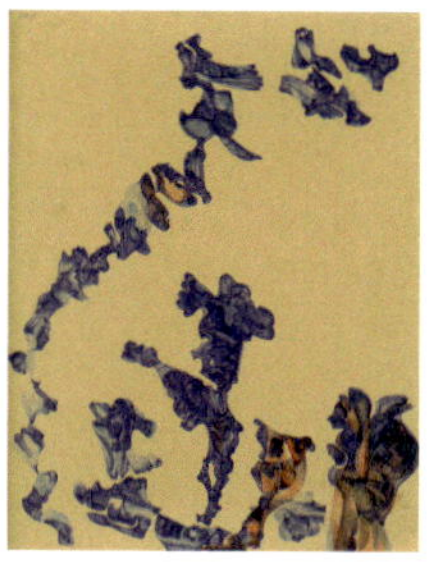

Untitled
(Galerie Le Terrain Vague period)
ca. 1954-1962
Drawing in blue monocolor pen ballpoint with orange and blue pencil, on paper.
28 x 22 cm
Artist's collection
AG1954_1962_GTV_D0070
p. 315

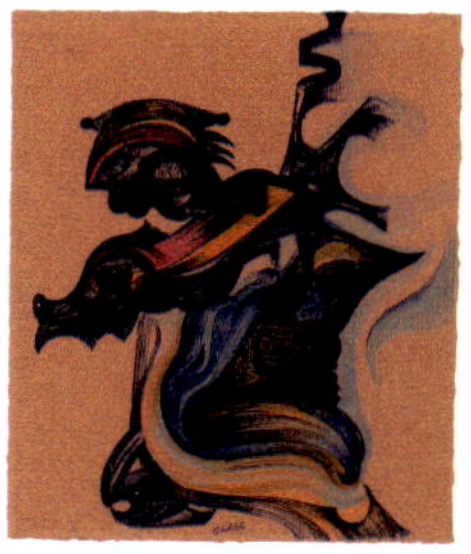

Untitled
(Galerie Le Terrain Vague period)
ca. 1954-1962
Drawing in blue monocolor ballpoint pen with orange, sky blue, olive green, and pink pencil, on red corrugated paper.
16.5 x 14 cm
Artist's collection
AG1954_1962_GTV_D0066
p. 316

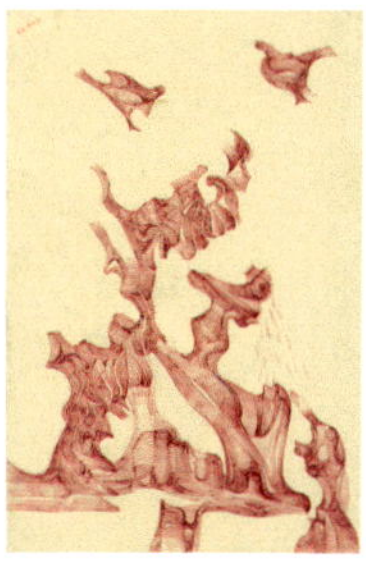

Untitled
(Galerie Le Terrain Vague period)
ca. 1954-1962
Drawing in red monocolor ballpoint pen, on paper.
26 x 17 cm
Artist's collection
AG1954_1962_GTV_D0074
p. 317

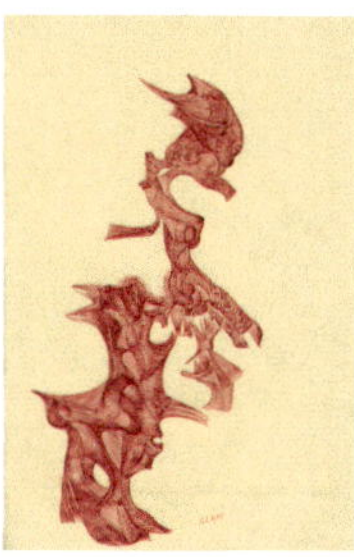

Untitled
(Galerie Le Terrain Vague period)
ca. 1954-1962
Drawing in red monocolor ballpoint pen, on paper.
26 x 17.1 cm
Artist's collection
AG1954_1962_GTV_D0073
p. 317

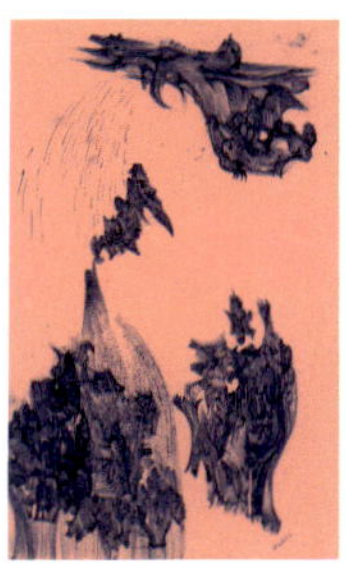

Untitled
(Galerie Le Terrain Vague period)
ca. 1954-1962
Drawing in blue monocolor ballpoint pen, on pink paper.
27 x 16.5 cm
Artist's collection
AG1954_1962_GTV_D0052
p. 318

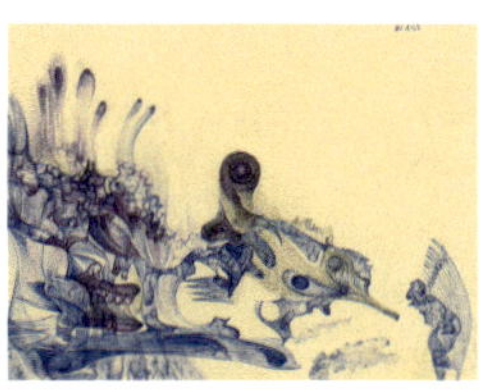

Untitled
(Galerie Terrain Vague period)
ca. 1954-1962
Drawing in blue and purple bicolor pen with black pencil, on paper.
12.8 x 17 cm
Artist's collection
AG1954_1962_GTV_D0075
p. 319

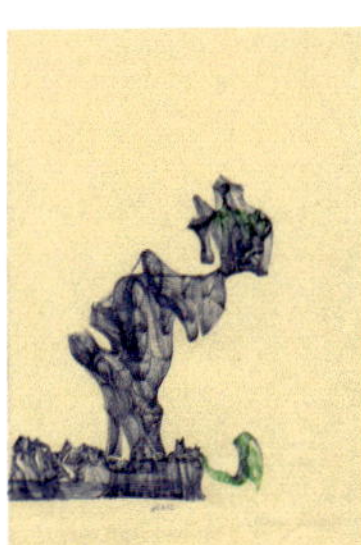

Untitled
(Galerie Le Terrain Vague period)
ca. 1954-1962
Drawing in blue and green bicolor pen, on paper.
26 x 17.1 cm
Artist's collection
AG1954_1962_GTV_D0072
p. 319

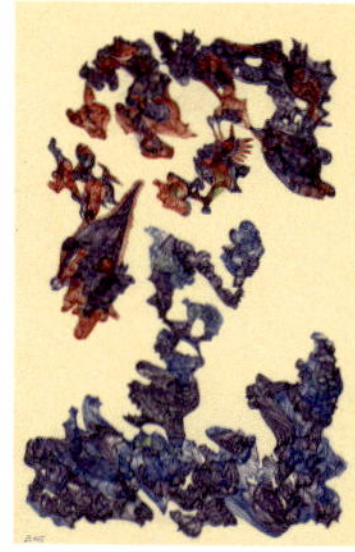

Untitled
(Galerie Le Terrain Vague period)
ca. 1954-1962
Drawing in blue, purple, and red tricolor pen with green and olive green pencil, on paper.
26 x 17 cm
Artist's collection
AG1954_1962_GTV_D0077
p. 320

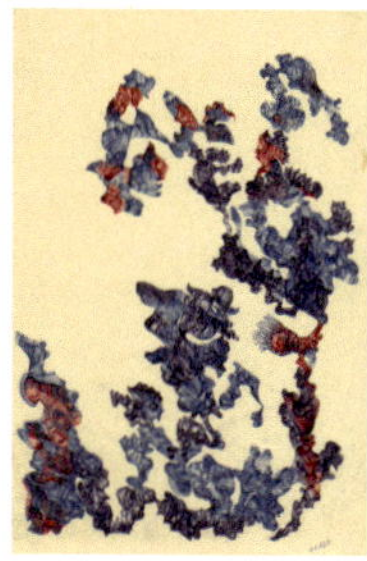

Untitled
(Galerie Le Terrain Vague period)
ca. 1954-1962
Blue, violet, and red tricolor ballpoint pen drawing on paper.
26 x 17 cm
Artist's collection
AG1954_1962_GTV_D0076
p. 320

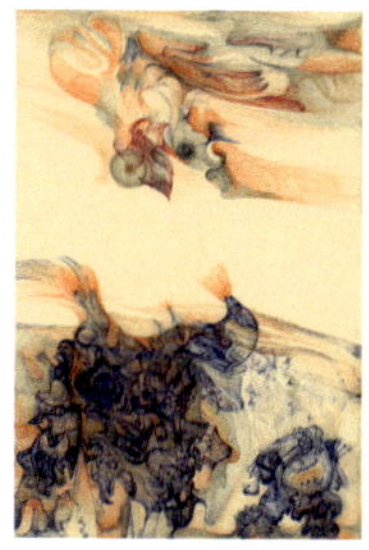

Untitled
(Galerie Le Terrain Vague period)
ca. 1954-1962
Drawing in blue and red bicolor pen with orange, brown, and gray pencil, on paper.
26 x 17 cm
Artist's collection
AG1954_1962_GTV_D0079
p. 321

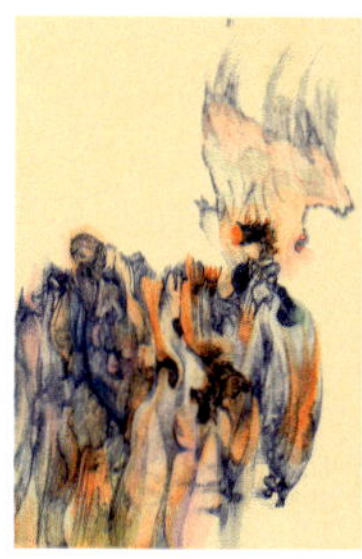

Untitled
(Galerie Le Terrain Vague period)
ca. 1954-1962
Drawing in blue monocolor ballpoint pen with turquoise, orange, sky blue, lilac, and pink pencil, on paper.
26 x 17 cm
Artist's collection
AG1954_1962_GTV_D0078
p. 321

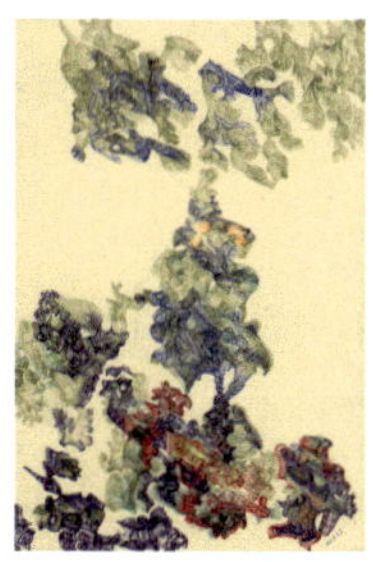

Untitled
(Galerie Le Terrain Vague period)
ca. 1954-1962
Four-color ballpoint pen drawing blue, purple, red, and black, with olive-grass green and orange pencils, on paper.
26 x 17 cm
Artist's collection
AG1954_1962_GTV_D0083
p. 322

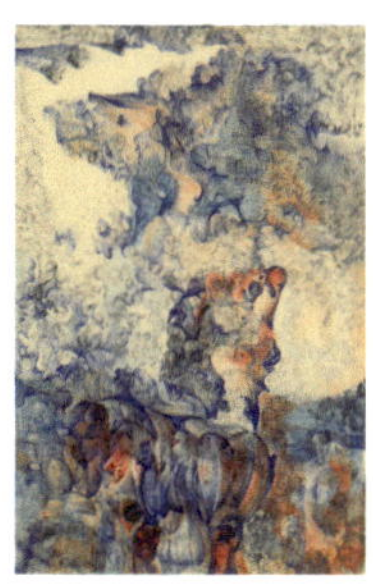

Untitled
(Galerie Le Terrain Vague period)
ca. 1954-1962
Blue, violet, and red tricolor pen drawing, with orange and sky blue pencil, on paper.
26 x 17 cm
Artist's collection
AG1954_1962_GTV_D0082
p. 322

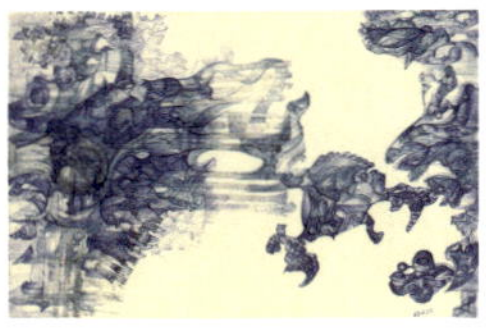

Untitled
(Galerie Le Terrain Vague period)
ca. 1954-1962
Drawing in blue and navy blue bicolor ballpoint pen with black seal ink, on paper.
24.2 x 15.5 cm
Artist's collection
AG1954_1962_GTV_D0081
p. 323

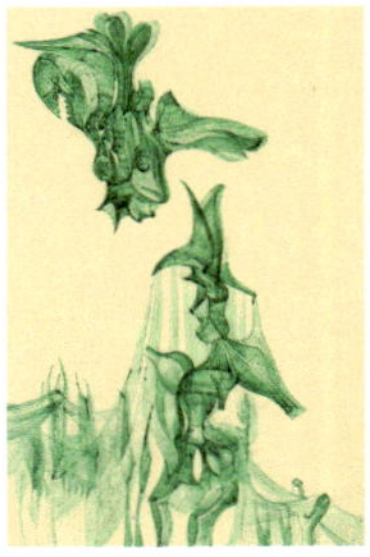

Untitled
(Galerie Le Terrain Vague period)
ca. 1954-1962
Drawing in green monocolor pen, on paper.
26 x 17 cm
Artist's collection
AG1954_1962_GTV_D0089
p. 324

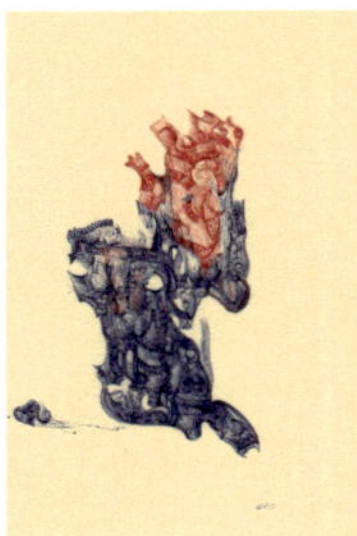

Untitled
(Galerie Le Terrain Vague period)
ca. 1954-1962
Drawing in blue and red bicolor pen, on paper.
26 x 17 cm
Artist's collection
AG1954_1962_GTV_D0086
p. 325

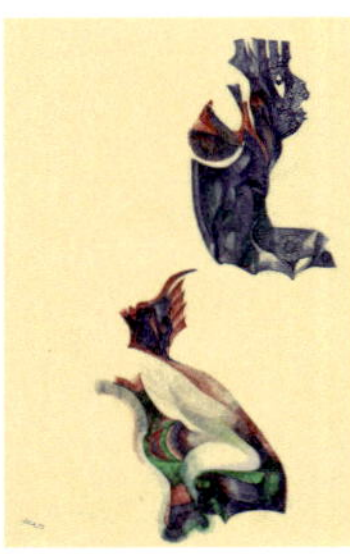

Untitled
(Galerie Le Terrain Vague period)
ca. 1954-1962
Drawing in blue, green, and red tricolor pen, with sky blue, green, and gray pencil, on paper.
26 x 17 cm
Artist's collection
AG1954_1962_GTV_D0087
p. 325

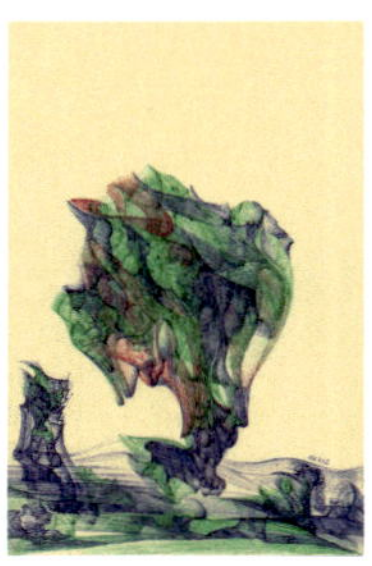

Untitled
(Galerie Le Terrain Vague period)
ca. 1954-1962
Drawing in blue, green, and red tricolor ballpoint pen, on paper.
26 x 17 cm
Artist's collection
AG1954_1962_GTV_D0088
p. 325

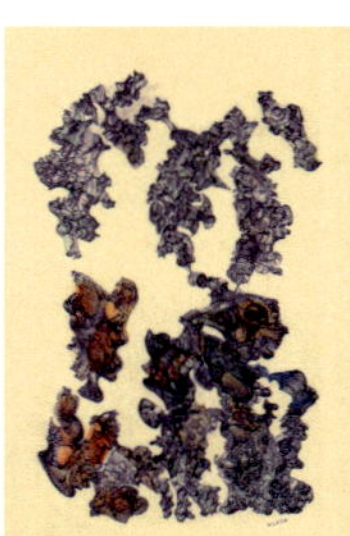

Untitled
(Galerie Le Terrain Vague period)
ca. 1954-1962
Drawing in purple, red, and blue tricolor pen with orange, turquoise, olive green, and red ink, on paper.
26 x 17 cm
Artist's collection n
AG1954_1962_GTV_D0084
p. 326

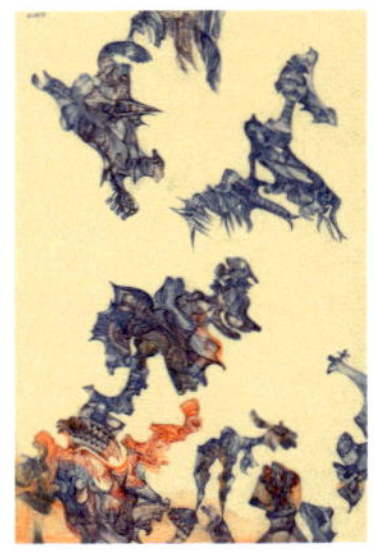

Untitled
(Galerie Le Terrain Vague period)
ca. 1954-1962
Drawing in blue, purple, and red tricolor ballpoint pen, with orange colored pencil, on paper.
26 x 17 cm
Artist's collection
AG1954_1962_GTV_D0090
p. 327

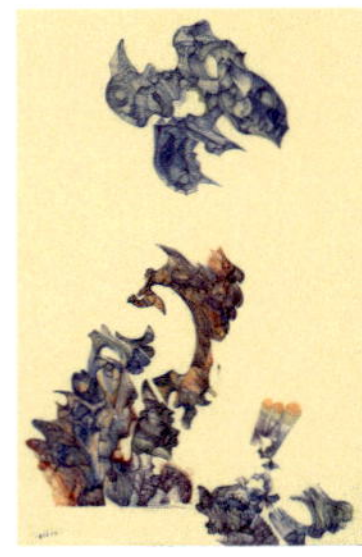

Untitled
(Galerie Le Terrain Vague period)
ca. 1954-1962
Drawing in blue, red, and purple tricolor pen with orange and gray pencil, on paper.
26 x 17 cm
Artist's collection
AG1954_1962_GTV_D0091
p. 327

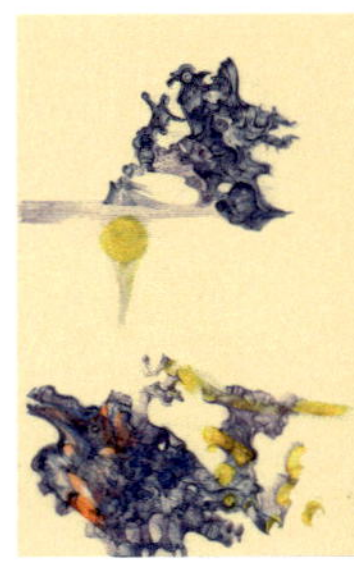

Untitled
(Galerie Le Terrain Vague period)
ca. 1954-1962
Drawing in blue and purple bicolor pen with orange, yellow, and blue watercolor, on paper.
26 x 17 cm
Artist's collection
AG1954_1962_GTV_D0092
p. 328

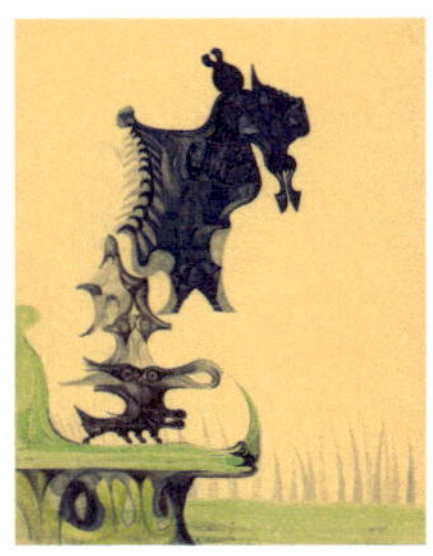

Untitled
(Galerie Le Terrain Vague period)
ca. 1954-1962
Drawing in blue and navy blue bicolor pen with lemon green and gray pencil, on paper.
27 x 21.2 cm
Artist's collection
AG1954_1962_GTV_D0094
p. 329

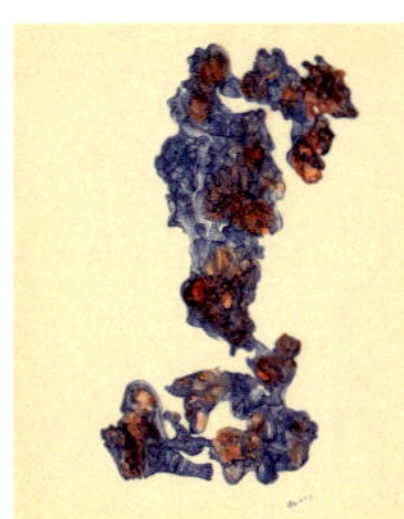

Untitled
(Galerie Le Terrain Vague period)
ca. 1954-1962
Drawing in blue and red bicolor pen with red watercolor and orange pencil, on corrugated paper.
31.4 x 23.8 cm
Artist's collection
AG1954_1962_GTV_D0093
p. 330

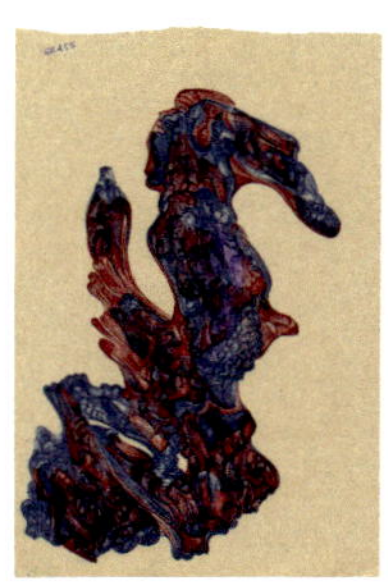

Untitled
(Galerie Le Terrain Vague period)
ca. 1954-1962
Drawing in blue, red, and purple tricolor ballpoint pen, on paper.
12.9 x 7 cm
Artist's collection
AG1954_1962_GTV_D0098
p. 331

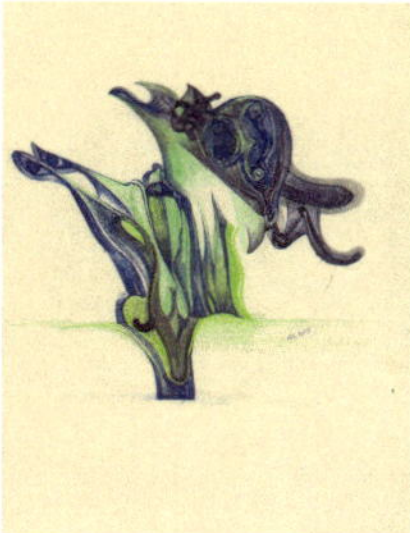

Untitled
(Galerie Le Terrain Vague period)
ca. 1954-1962
Drawing in blue and navy blue bicolor pen with lemon green and gray pencil, on paper.
27 x 21.2 cm
Artist's collection
AG1954_1962_GTV_D0095
p. 332

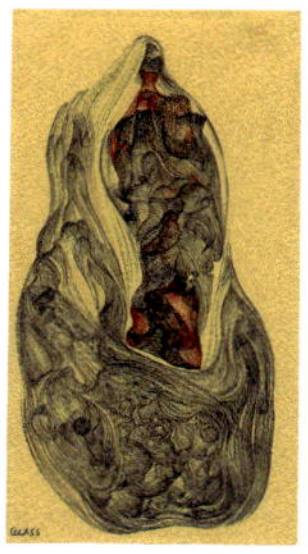

Untitled
(Galerie Le Terrain Vague period)
ca. 1954-1962
Drawing in blue and red bicolor ballpoint pen, on invitation to Mimi de Saint-Tropp restaurant on yellow corrugated paper.
12.9 x 7 cm
Artist's collection
AG1954_1962_GTV_D0097
p. 333

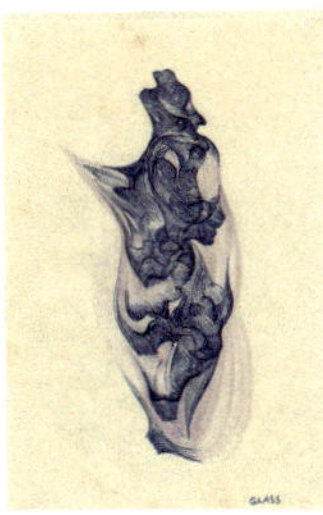

Untitled
(Galerie Le Terrain Vague period)
ca. 1954-1962
Drawing in blue monocolor pen with lilac pencil, on paper.
13.2 x 8.6 cm
Artist's collection
AG1954_1962_GTV_D0096
p. 333

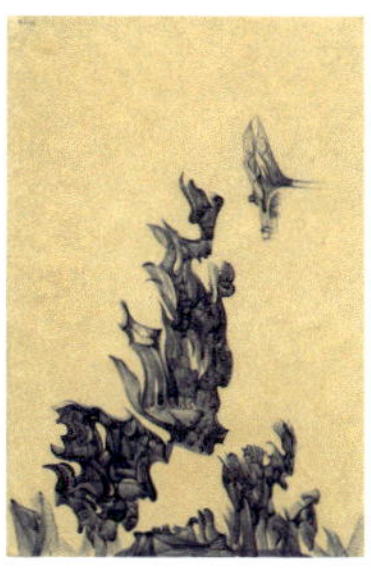

Untitled
(Galerie Le Terrain Vague period)
ca. 1954-1962
Monochrome blue ballpoint pen drawing, on paper.
26 x 17 cm
Artist's collection
AG1954_1962_GTV_D0100
p. 334

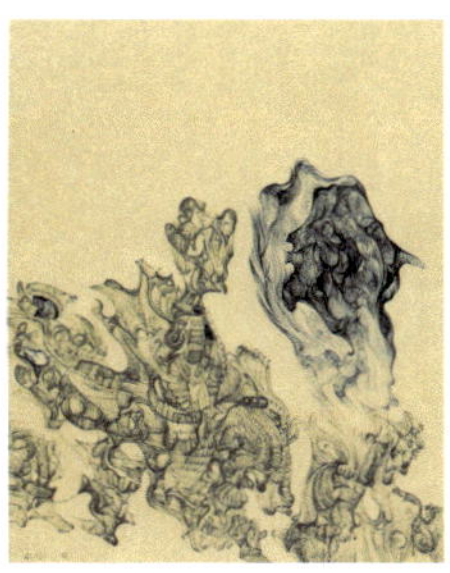

Untitled
(Galerie Le Terrain Vague period)
1956
Black and navy blue two-tone ballpoint pen drawing, on paper.
21.3 x 17 cm
Artist's collection
AG1954_1962_GTV_D0099
p. 335

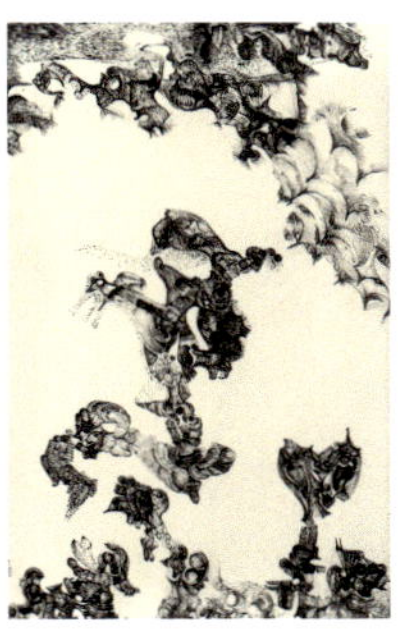

Untitled
(Galerie Le Terrain Vague period)
1957
Drawing in blue monocolor ballpoint pen, on paper.
B/W photograph of drawing, Bicen Collection, Paris; Photo Marc Vaux archives, Centre Pompidou, Bibliothèque Kandinsky, Paris, France.
11.4 x 17 cm
Artist's collection
AG1954_1962_GTV_D0107
p. 336

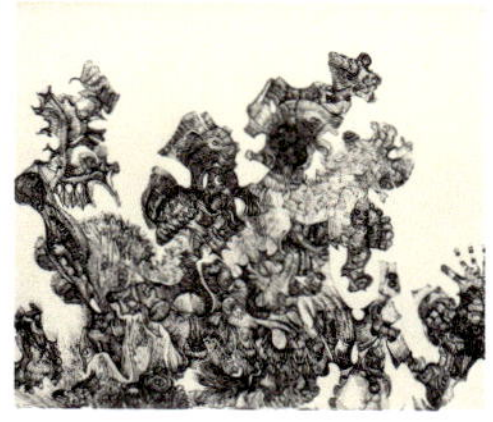

Untitled
(Galerie Le Terrain Vague period)
ca. 1950
Drawing in blue monocolor ballpoint pen, on paper. B/W photograph of drawing, Gigere Collection, Canada; Photo Marc Vaux archives, Centre Pompidou, Bibliothèque Kandinsky, Paris, France.
12.2 x 14.2 cm
Artist's collection
AG1954_1962_GTV_D0104
p. 337

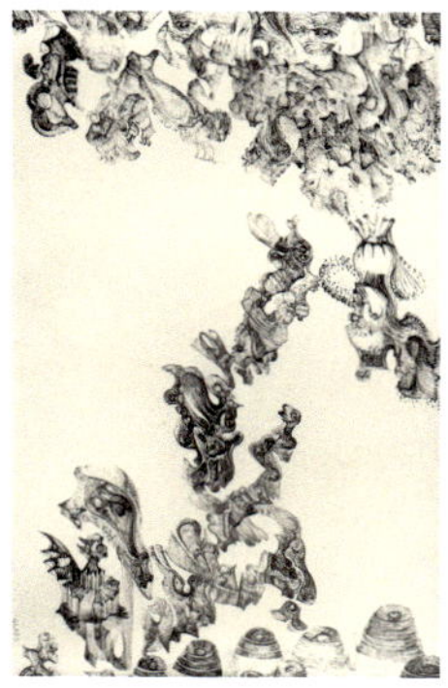

Untitled
(Galerie Le Terrain Vague period)
ca. 1954-1962
Drawing in blue and purple bicolor pen, on paper.
B/W photograph of drawing, Unknown Collection; Photo Marc Vaux archives, Centre Pompidou, Bibliothèque Kandinsky, Paris, France.
15.4 x 13.4 cm
Artist's collection
AG1954_1962_GTV_D0109
p. 338

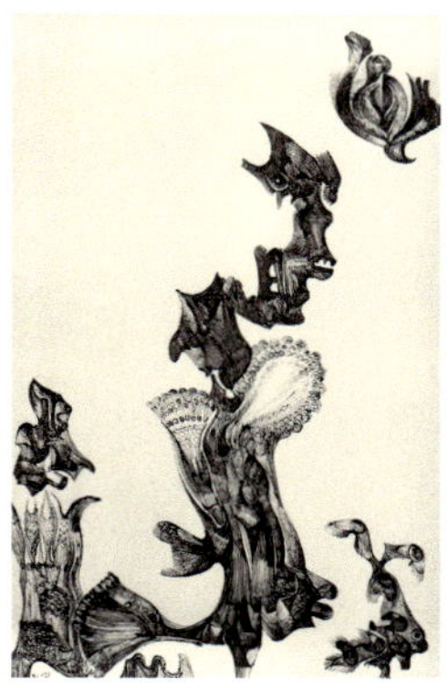

Untitled
(Galerie Le Terrain Vague period)
1957
Drawing in blue monocolor ballpoint pen, on paper.
B/W photograph of drawing, Private Collection, Canada; Photo Marc Vaux archives, Centre Pompidou, Bibliothèque Kandinsky, Paris, France.
17.4 x 11.5 cm. Artist's collection
AG1954_1962_GTV_D0102
p. 339

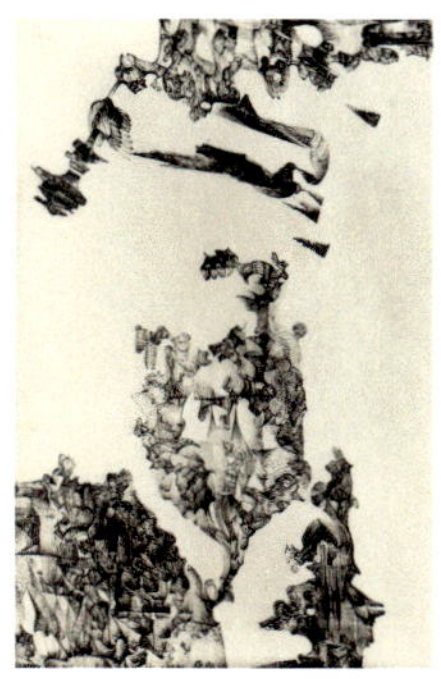

Untitled
(Galerie Le Terrain Vague period)
ca. 1950
Drawing in blue monocolor ballpoint pen, on paper.
B/W photograph of drawing, Lotbiniére Collection, The Hague, Netherlands; Photo Marc Vaux archives, Centre Pompidou, Bibliothèque Kandinsky, Paris, France.
17.4 x 11.5 cm
Artist's collection
AG1954_1962_GTV_D0108
p. 340

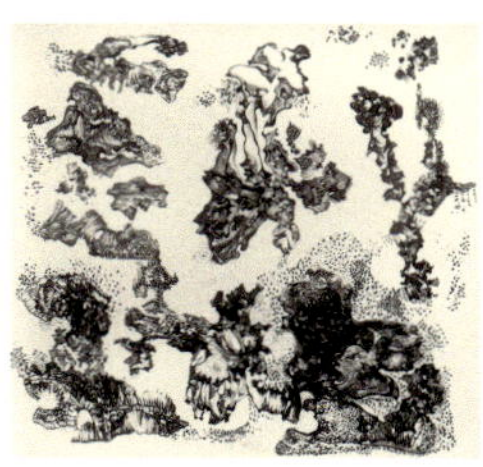

Untitled
(Galerie Le Terrain Vague period)
1957
Drawing in blue monocolor ballpoint pen, on paper.
B/W photograph of drawing, Private Collection, Canada; Photo Marc Vaux archives, Centre Pompidou, Bibliothèque Kandinsky, Paris, France.
12.3 x 13.8 cm
Artist's collection
AG1954_1962_GTV_D0105
p. 341

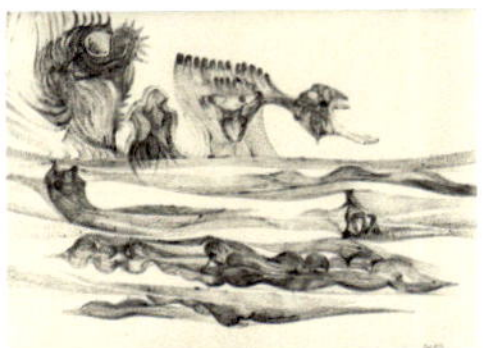

Untitled
(Galerie Le Terrain Vague period)
1956
Drawing in blue monocolor ballpoint pen, on paper.
B/W photograph of drawing.
Roberto Matta Collection, Paris;
Photo Marc Vaux archives, Centre Pompidou, Bibliothèque Kandinsky, Paris, France.
12.2 x 16.6 cm
Artist's collection
AG1954_1962_GTV_D0103
p. 342

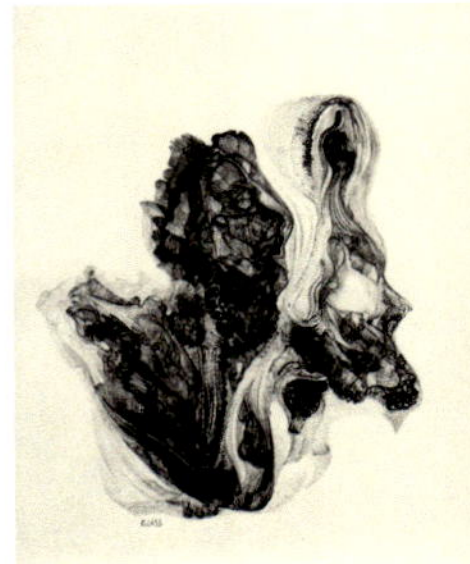

Untitled
(Galerie Le Terrain Vague period)
ca. 1950
Drawing in blue and purple bicolor pen, on paper.
B/W photograph of drawing (*ca.* 1950), Unknown Collection; Photo Marc Vaux archives, Centre Pompidou, Bibliothèque Kandinsky, Paris, France.
15.4 x 13.4 cm
Artist's collection
AG1954_1962_GTV_D0106
p. 343

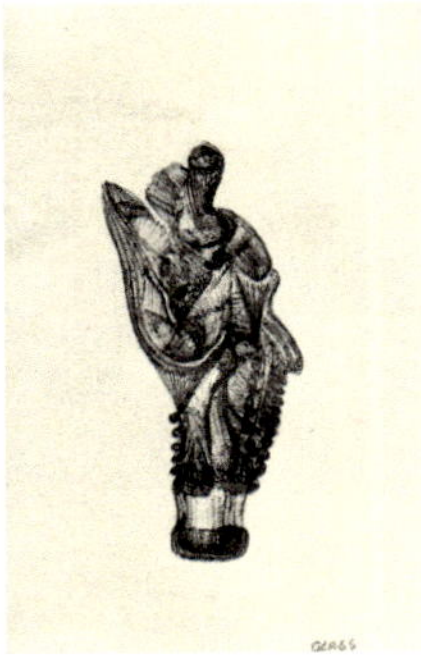

Untitled
(Galerie Le Terrain Vague period)
1956
Drawing in blue monocolor ballpoint pen, on paper.
B/W photograph of drawing (ca. 1956), Jacques Stern Collection (heirs), Paris;
Photo Marc Vaux archives, Centre Pompidou, Bibliothèque Kandinsky, Paris, France.
12 x 7.7 cm
Artist's collection
AG1954_1962_GTV_D0101
p. 342

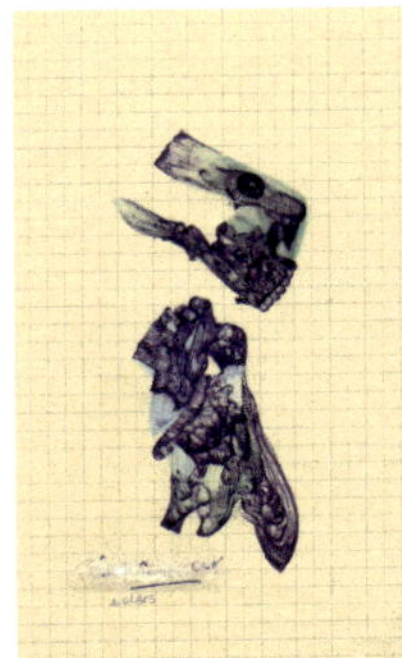

Untitled
(Galerie Le Terrain Vague period)
ca. 1954-1962
Drawing in blue monocolor pen, with sky blue and green pencil, on squared paper.
18.8 x 11.3 cm
Artist's collection
AG1954_1962_GTV_D0056
p. 344

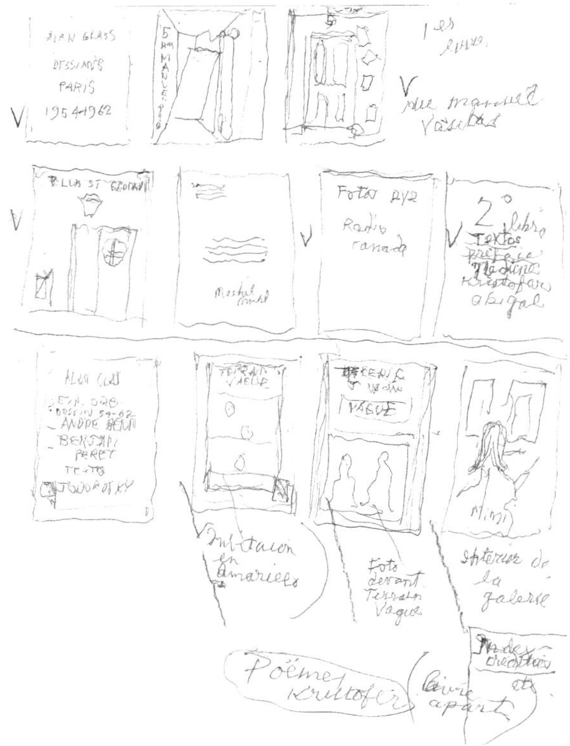

DRAWINGS
ALAN GLASS
PARIS

Printing was finished in March 2024 in Palermo's Graphic Arts in Madrid, Spain. In its composition, the Linotype Didot and Trajan Pro font families were used in 8.5, 9, 10.7, 22, and 24 points. It was printed on 130-gram Gardamatt Ultra couché paper. Bound in hardcover and Arena Natural Rough endpapers of 140 grams. Carlos de Laborde-Noguez, Carolina Escalante, Lilian Luna, Eleazar Cruz, and Ricardo Salas & Frontespizio & Ediciones El Viso were responsible for the printing concept, coordination, and production. Print run of 2500 copies, 1500 copies in Spanish, 600 copies in English and 400 copies in French.

Sketch by Alan Glass for this publication.